T5-DHV-455

THE LAW OF
LETTERS OF CREDIT

Commercial and Standby Credits

SECOND EDITION

THE LAW OF LETTERS OF CREDIT

Commercial and Standby Credits

SECOND EDITION

JOHN F. DOLAN

Professor of Law
Wayne State University Law School

WARREN, GORHAM & LAMONT
Boston • New York

Again, to Carole

Preface

THERE IS A POINT in the life of a book with semi-annual supplements when matters become unwieldy. Since the publication of the main volume in 1984, there have been 10 supplements discussing more than 460 new cases and innumerable regulations and rulings, with 38 additional paragraph and subparagraph headings, extensive revision of 8 others, and a new appendix. The text in the main volume was about 500 pages; the text in the last supplement was more than 300 pages. In short, the continued, sustained growth of letters of credit and litigation surrounding them made the main volume of this treatise and its supplement exceedingly complex. The time for a revised edition had arrived.

The first three chapters of this edition deal, respectively, with the transactions out of which the credit arises, the nature of the credit, and the credit's functions. Thus, the first three chapters explain the credit as a unique creature of commercial law and frame the inquiry that the balance of the work pursues. For the person unfamiliar with the credit or with its unique nature, these chapters are indispensable. They provide the benchmark against which the remaining chapters measure the success or failure of the cases and regulations governing credits.

The remaining chapters deal with the substantive issues of credit law. Chapter 4 discusses the sources of credit law and choice of law issues. Chapter 5 examines the unique rules for establishing, amending, and terminating obligations. Chapters 6 and 7 inquire into the grand controversies in credit law: the documentary compliance question and the fraud issue, and, in the latter case, with bankruptcy problems in credit practice. Chapter 8 discusses the relationship between the issuer and third parties—usually parties with an interest in the beneficiary's draft or documents of title. Chapter 9 explains the problems that arise when the credit transaction breaks down and includes discussion of the remedies for breach of the credit engagement and the defenses that arise in the credit context. Chapter 10 deals with the unique rules for conveying interests in credits, and Chapter 11 deals with procedural issues, including the notorious injunction problem of credit law. Chapter 12 discusses the regulatory questions that arise in credit law by virtue of the fact that issuers are usually commercial banks subject to state and federal regulation.

In this respect, the second edition follows the scope, organization, and purposes of the first, but every paragraph and subparagraph has been revised. I have deleted discussion of cases and rulings that are no longer germane, have integrated text on recent authority into the purged text of the main volume, and have added new paragraphs, new subparagraphs, and discussion of more than 100 new cases since the last supplement and more than 550 since the publication of the first edition. I also have made a serious effort here to bring into the text greater consideration of foreign cases from England and Canada. The text remains a treatise on American law, but the international nature of the credit and of the law that governs it requires American courts and lawyers to know the law of credits in other jurisdictions.

The guiding premise of this work from the beginning has been that letters of credit are creatures of the law merchant. That law, by definition, is part of the jus gentium. It is at once reassuring and enlightening to see that the trends in U.S. law generally have paralleled those in other common-law jurisdictions. The success of the credit as a mercantile device depends as much on our learning from others as on their learning from us. As this second edition reveals, there is a healthy symbiosis at work in letter of credit law. This comparative exercise, moreover, confirms the wisdom of U.S. credit law that such law must have constant regard for the needs and practices of merchants and bankers.

That is not to suggest that the law of letters of credit has reached a stage of repose or equilibrium. Each year, courts decide more cases than they did in the last. At this writing, the agencies that sponsor the Uniform Commercial Code are preparing to initiate a revision of Article 5, and the Commission on Banking Technique and Practice of the International Chamber of Commerce has commenced meetings, with a view to revision of the Uniform Customs and Practice for Documentary Credits. Within the next two or three years, we probably will have a new Article 5 for the states to consider and a new Uniform Customs for the banking committees of the trading nations to adopt. In the meantime, this treatise, with its periodic supplements, will continue to provide comprehensive treatment of the subject and reports on the latest developments.

Acknowledgments

It is not possible to list here all of the people who have accorded me favors and granted help in the preparation of this edition. A few, however, merit special mention. First, this time, must be the bankers. Many of the same people who gave of their time and advice for the first edition assisted me over the years in the preparation of this one. In addition to those mentioned in the acknowledgments to the first edition, Egon David, Bank of America; Vincent Maullela, Manufacturers Hanover Trust Co.; and Johan Wendt and David Barnett, Comerica Bank, have been patient and more than generous. Similarly, C. Thorne Corse merits thanks.

I wrote and researched much of the first edition during a stint in 1982 as a visiting professor at the Molengraff Institute of the State University of Utrecht in the Netherlands. During the fall of 1989, I did much of the revision and research into some of the foreign materials incorporated into the second edition while I was a visiting scholar at University College Dublin. I recognized my Utrecht colleagues in the acknowledgments to the first edition. Now I recognize my Irish colleagues. My time at the Belfield campus of University College was busy, but the warmth of the welcome accorded me by the staff and students at the Law Faculty made the experience a pleasant one. My thanks to all of my Dublin hosts, and especially to Dean James P. Casey, associate Dean Paul A. O'Connor, Mr. Finbar McAuley, and Mr. Arnaud Cras.

Again, my own colleagues at Wayne State University have provided support, though not without a dollop of humor here and there. The letter of credit remains a mystery to most of them, writers and teachers as they are in different fields. I take their cheerful encouragement as a sign of their affection and their regard for this effort. Special thanks to my dean, John W. Reed, who provided financial grants, as did his predecessor, John Roberts, so that I could spend time on this project. Also, many thanks to Ms. June Frierson for secretarial assistance.

JOHN F. DOLAN

Detroit
October 1, 1990

Summary of Contents

Table of Contents

1 Credits in the Credit Transaction—An Introduction

2 The Nature of Credits: What They Are and Are Not

3 The Function of Credits

4   Sources of Credit Law

5 Establishing, Amending, and Terminating the Credit

8 The Issuer and Third Parties

9 Breach: Remedies and Defenses

10 Transfer and Assignment

11   Questions of Procedure and Practice

12 Credits and Bank Regulation

CHAPTER 1

Credits in the Credit Transaction—An Introduction

¶ 1.01 STANDARD COMMERCIAL CREDIT TRANSACTIONS

Letters of credit have played a role in commercial transactions for a long time.[1] Their current form and the rules that generally govern them come to us, as so many commercial devices do,[2] out of practices in the international sale of goods. Merchants and bankers have gradually expanded the scope of credit activity, however, to areas that formerly were the domain of secondary guaranties—a domain that is neither international nor sales-related. The merchants and bankers that use the credit distinguish those that serve the sale of commodities and those that guarantee the performance of an obligation, calling the former a "commercial" credit and the latter a "standby" credit.[3] There is nothing in the commercial credit that limits its use to the international setting, although it does entail transaction costs that are unnecessary in the many open account sales that characterize the domestic sales transaction. The credit involves a modicum of expertise and learning, furthermore, that international sellers and bankers already have acquired and that domestic sellers and bankers are fast acquiring.

[1] Open Account Selling

The commercial credit grows out of a contract for the sale of goods between a buyer and a seller. In that contract, the commercial parties (buy-

---

[1]For a discussion of the history of credits, see ¶¶ 3.02–3.06.

[2]Bills of exchange (drafts) and bills of lading, which, like credits, are inventions of merchants, not lawyers or legislators, are also derived from international trade. They have been in use since the great fairs of the Middle Ages or earlier. See generally F. Sanborn, Origins of the Early English Maritime and Commercial Law (1930); W. Bewes, The Romance of the Law Merchant (1923); Trimble, "The Law Merchant and the Letter of Credit," 61 Harv. L. Rev. 981 (1948).

[3]Some of the more common terms in the letter of credit lexicon are defined in this chapter. These terms also appear in the Glossary.

er and seller) must decide on credit and payment terms. They have a number of options. In domestic sales, the seller most often ships on open account. In an open account sale, the seller initiates delivery of the goods through his shipping department and initiates collection of the purchase price by having his credit department send an invoice to the buyer. The open account seller usually gives the buyer credit terms (e.g., thirty or sixty days) and may grant discounts to a buyer who pays early.

The practice of open account selling has a number of strengths and a few corresponding weaknesses. Open account selling obviously reduces transaction costs, since it involves a relatively small number of documents and facilitates high volume and efficient shipping and billing practices. The open account sale, however, yields some costs. Credit managers must maintain credit histories or pay independent credit agencies to do so, and there are losses when buyers are unable or unwilling to pay. The open account seller has no security interest in the goods after they have been shipped and generally loses his seller's lien upon shipment.[4] The seller also runs the risk that the buyer will refuse to accept delivery of the goods. Finally, and most important to the open account seller, the open account seller must deliver the goods and wait for his money unless he insists on prepayment, a highly unusual occurrence in commercial sales of goods.

[2] Documentary Sales

Sellers can avoid some of the risks that attend the open account sale by resorting to a commercial practice that predates open account selling. That practice is the documentary draft transaction. Under this arrangement, the seller uses a carrier to withhold delivery of the goods until the buyer either pays for them or signs a negotiable instrument promising to pay for them. While there are many variations, in the classic documentary draft transaction the seller ships the goods by common carrier and forwards two pieces of paper through the banking chain to the buyer's city. One of the papers is a draft, that is, an order directing the buyer to pay the purchase price to the seller or to the seller's nominee. The second paper is a negotiable bill of lading that the carrier issues to the seller and that the seller has endorsed. The seller has an agent in the buyer's city, usually a correspondent of the seller's bank. When the agent receives the draft and the bill of lading, he notifies the buyer. The buyer then pays the draft, if it is a sight draft; or he accepts it, if it is a time

---

[4] There are two narrow exceptions to the general rule that a seller loses his lien upon shipment of the goods. See U.C.C. §§ 2-502(1), 2-702(2). The seller may also reserve a security interest by shipping the goods under reservation. See U.C.C. § 2-505.

draft. The agent then delivers the bill of lading to the buyer. At that point, the buyer is able to take delivery of the goods from the carrier, who will deliver only when the buyer surrenders the bill. The following example illustrates the documentary sale.

B, a broker in New York, enters into a contract to sell specialty steel to F, a fabricator in Kansas City. F is unwilling to make payment until he is assured of delivery, and B is unwilling to ship on open account. B and F agree in their sales contract that F will pay "against documents."[5] B, who is an importer, obtains the steel from a Dutch seller and delivers the steel to a railroad that issues a negotiable bill of lading made out to the order of B. Under transport law, the carrier must deliver the goods to the holder of that negotiable document of title.[6] B also draws a draft on F, ordering F to pay at sight to B's order a sum equal to the contract price. After endorsing both of them, B takes the draft and the document of title to his bank, which takes them, usually with recourse in the event of default by F, and forwards them for collection to a correspondent bank in Kansas City. The Kansas City correspondent usually receives the "documentary draft" (i.e., the draft accompanied by the document of title) before the steel arrives. If all goes well, as it usually does, the correspondent bank notifies F, who must then pay the sight draft promptly,[7] even though the goods are still en route. Upon that payment, but not until then, the correspondent bank will deliver the bill of lading to F, thereby giving F control of the goods.[8]

Sometimes, of course, F will insist that B grant F favorable credit terms in the sales contract. In that event, the draft is payable not at sight but at some later date that the sales contract stipulates. Upon notice from the correspondent bank in Kansas City, F will honor this draft not by paying it but by accepting it,[9] usually by signing and dating the face of the draft. Such a draft then becomes a negotiable trade acceptance, under which F, the acceptor, must pay any holder when the draft ma-

---

[5] Cf. U.C.C. § 2-513(3) (providing, in general, that buyer who agrees to pay against documents of title has no right to inspect goods); U.C.C. §§ 2-319(4), 2-320(4) (rules for common transactions that involve payment against documents).

[6] See Federal Bills of Lading (Pomerene) Act, 49 U.S.C. app. §§ 88, 89 (Supp. V 1987); U.C.C. §§ 7-403(1), 7-403(4).

[7] See U.C.C. § 3-506; cf. U.C.C. § 5-112 (stipulating time allowed for honor of drafts drawn under letter of credit).

[8] If the collecting bank surrenders the bill before the drawee's payment or acceptance, the bank is liable for damages caused by that surrender. See Bar-Ram Irrigation Prods. v. Phenix-Girard Bank, 779 F.2d 1501 (11th Cir. 1986).

[9] For the definition and operation of "acceptance," see U.C.C. § 3-410.

tures.[10] By its nature, the trade acceptance tends to vary in value with the financial reputation of *F*, who has made the contract of acceptance. Because of its negotiable feature and its concomitant independence from any defenses *F* may have under the sales contract with *B*, the acceptance is often an investment attractive to *B*'s bank.

The documentary draft transaction provides some advantages to *B* that are not available in the open account sale. First, the transaction gives *B* a security interest in the goods until the correspondent bank delivers the bill of lading to *F*,[11] thereby protecting *B* in the sight draft case against the possibility that *F* will take the goods without paying for them. Second, the transaction achieves prompt payment to *B* even when the sales contract grants *F* credit terms. If *F* defaults, *B* may have to return that payment to his bank, but not always. If *F*'s credit reputation is strong enough, the bank may take the negotiable draft without recourse to *B*. *B* must pay the bank a fee for this early payment. In time draft cases, the fee is determined by "discounting" the face amount of the draft by a percentage that reflects interest during the period from the time of discount until the time the bank expects to receive its money, the acceptance's maturity date. *B* pays that discount if it is less than the cost of waiting for *F*'s payment. When *B* endorses with recourse, *B* pays the cost of bearing the risk of *F*'s nonpayment. *B* also incurs some additional costs in the documentary draft transaction by virtue of the fact that it generates more paper than does the open account sale.[12]

[3] Commercial Credit Sales

B, the New York broker in the preceding section's illustration, has contracted to sell specialty steel to *F*, a fabricator in Kansas City. *B* can reduce his risk with a documentary sale but still must bear the significant risk that *F* will dishonor the draft either by refusing to pay a sight draft or by refusing to accept a time draft. In either event, *B* would have a large shipment of steel headed for Kansas City and no customer to take it. *B* then would face the difficulty of looking for another customer,

---

[10] See U.C.C. § 4-413(1).

[11] See U.C.C. § 2-505.

[12] The documentary sale may involve insurance or inspection certificates on which the buyer insists in order to protect himself in those cases where he pays for goods before he has a chance to inspect them. Inspection certificates come in all varieties. Careful buyers insist that the credit specify their nature and the identity of the signer. Document 11 in Appendix C is an illustration of an inspection certificate. Insurance certificates are products of the insurance industry. Document 7 in Appendix C is an illustration of a certificate of insurance.

shipping the goods elsewhere, or perhaps selling at a reduced price. In many cases, *B* would not have acquired the steel in the first place had he not been relying on *F*'s contractual duty to take it. *B* would have a good claim against *F* for breach of contract, but the expenses and delays of litigation and the uncertainty of collecting a judgment after trial render any cause of action a poor substitute for a paying customer. Given these deficiencies of the documentary sale transaction, merchants and bankers developed the commercial credit.

When *F* approaches *B* about obtaining the steel, *B* may be concerned about *F*'s creditworthiness. *B* may not know *F* and may be reluctant to look for a source for the steel or to order the steel. *B*, therefore, negotiates a sales contract with *F* that requires *F* to obtain from *F*'s bank (in Missouri) a letter of credit running to the benefit of *B* and engaging the Missouri bank to honor the very drafts *B* fears *F* will not honor. By substituting the Missouri bank's promise in the credit transaction for *F*'s promise in the documentary sale transaction, *B* has reduced risks significantly. *B*'s success, however, rests upon two assumptions. The first assumption is that the creditworthiness of the Missouri bank exceeds that of *F*, which is a virtual certainty in light of the Uniform Commercial Code (UCC or the Code) rules favoring beneficiaries of credits[13] and in light of experience in U.S. bank insolvencies.[14] The second assumption is that the law of credits leads to a vigorous enforcement of the bank's obligation, an assumption less certain than the first but still valid.[15]

In the commercial credit, *B* is called the "beneficiary,"[16] and *F* is called the "customer"[17] (of the Missouri bank) or the "account party."[18] The Missouri bank is the "issuer," or the "opening bank" or "issuing bank."[19]

---

[13] See U.C.C. § 5-117.

[14] For a discussion of the effect of bank insolvency on credits, see ¶ 12.01.

[15] See ¶¶ 6.04–6.05, 7.03–7.04.

[16] See U.C.C. § 5-103(1)(d); U.C.P. art. 2 (1983).

[17] See U.C.C. § 5-103(1)(g). The Uniform Customs refer to the customer as the "applicant." See U.C.P. art. 2 (1983).

[18] Traditionally, bank letter of credit forms refer to the customer ("Ace Corporation") in the following way: "We hereby engage to honor your drafts at sight for the account of Ace Corporation." Hence, the use of the term "account party." See App. C, Doc. 1.

[19] See U.C.C. § 5-103(1)(c); U.C.P. art. 2 (1983). For a case explaining the commercial letter of credit and the beneficiary's use of it to facilitate the financing of an international sale, see Ng Chee Chong v. Austin Taylor & Co., [1975] 1 Lloyd's Rep. 156 (Q.B.).

¶ 1.02 "PAY, ACCEPT, OR NEGOTIATE"

Traditionally, issuers have made credits available in one of three ways: by payment, by acceptance, or by negotiation.

[1] Payment Credit

A payment credit, sometimes called a "sight" credit, provides simply that the payor bank[20] will honor the beneficiary's drafts at sight. The only way to honor a sight draft is to pay it within the short time allowed by the Code.[21] The payment credit designates a payor, which may be the issuing bank or some other nominated bank. Frequently, this bank is the correspondent of the issuer and is located in the seller's city, thereby affording the seller a convenient means of effecting collection of his drafts.[22] In the event the credit provides for honor at the issuing bank, the seller deposits the draft for collection at a bank in his city. That bank (the collecting bank) then acts as the seller's agent for collection or acts in its own right as holder of the draft. It is significant, however, that the beneficiary of a payment credit must present the draft to the payor on or before the credit's expiration date. Thus, a credit available by payment in Missouri that runs to the benefit of a beneficiary in New York may be a little awkward. If the credit were about to expire, for example, a New York beneficiary would find it much easier to present documents or to make corrections on defective documents at a local bank than it would at a distant bank. A bank may issue a payment credit that directs the beneficiary to present drafts at the issuer's correspondent. In another variation, the credit allows the beneficiary to negotiate his draft at any bank or at a designated bank near the seller. Such a credit is a negotiation credit.[23] If the correspondent bank refuses to honor by payment or negotiation,[24] the issuer must pay the beneficiary.[25]

---

[20] See U.C.C. § 4-105(b) (defining "payor bank" as bank by which item is payable as drawn or accepted).

[21] For the UCC time rule, see U.C.C. § 5-112. For the Uniform Customs rule, see U.C.P. art. 16(c) (1983). For discussion of the bank's duties with respect to the documents, see ¶¶ 6.03–6.06.

[22] In the international setting, the use of a correspondent also facilitates payment in local currency.

[23] For discussion of the negotiation credit, see infra ¶¶ 1.02[3], 1.02[4].

[24] A bank designated by the issuer as a payor or negotiating bank has not undertaken to negotiate the beneficiary's drafts unless it confirms the credit. See U.C.C. § 5-103(1)(f).

[25] See U.C.P. art. 10(a)(iv) (1983).

[2] Acceptance Credit

If the issuer engages to honor a time draft, such as a draft drawn at sixty days' date, the method of honor is acceptance.[26] When the issuer accepts the draft, it becomes a banker's acceptance and entails the bank's primary obligation to pay it at maturity.[27] A banker's acceptance, especially that of a bank well recognized in the commercial credit industry, is a prime medium of investment. The beneficiary whose sixty-day draft is accepted by a well-recognized bank can convert it to cash easily and at favorable discount rates with his own bank, with the issuing bank (which frequently invests in its own acceptances), or in the discount market.

Sometimes, as in the case of a sight credit, the issuer designates a correspondent in the city of the seller to honor a time draft. In that case, the credit designates the correspondent as the drawee by stipulating that the draft is to be drawn on that correspondent. Such a correspondent then honors the draft on behalf of the issuer, although the correspondent, unless it is a confirming bank,[28] has no obligation of its own to do so.

[3] Negotiation Credit

Frequently, especially when the credit serves the international sale of goods, the opening bank designates another bank or group of banks at which the beneficiary negotiates his draft. The designated bank or banks have no obligation to negotiate but generally will do so in order to earn a fee. The negotiating bank usually acts in reliance on the strength of the opening bank's obligation under the credit to reimburse the negotiating bank—a transfer of funds achieved easily through the banking system.[29]

---

[26] In fact, under the Uniform Customs and Practice for Documentary Credits, not only must the acceptance credit issuer accept, it is also responsible for the payment of the acceptance at maturity. See U.C.P. art. 10(a)(iii) (1983); cf. U.C.C. § 1-201(21) (defining "to honor" as "to accept and pay"). There is a measure of redundancy in these rules if the issuer is the acceptor, since it is also liable to pay as an acceptor. See U.C.C. § 3-413(1). For discussion of the confusion in some opinions on the distinction between issuer liability and acceptor liability, see ¶ 2.09[1].

[27] See U.C.C. § 3-413(1).

[28] See U.C.C. § 5-103(1)(f) as well as the Glossary herein for the definition of "confirming bank."

[29] For a case involving a typical negotiation credit in a commercial credit setting, see Supreme Merchandise Co. v. Chemical Bank, 70 N.Y.2d 344, 514 N.E.2d 1358, 520 N.Y.S.2d 734 (1987). For a case involving a standby credit that was a negotiation credit, see Apex Oil Co. v. Archem Co., 770 F.2d 1353 (5th Cir. 1985).

[4] Circular Negotiation Credit

A buyer may insist that the sales price be expressed in the currency of his own country and that the credit be payable in that currency. The buyer, in this instance, is imposing an exchange risk on the seller. In such cases, the seller may want the option of negotiating his drafts at whichever bank in his area is offering the best rate of exchange, or he may want to be in a position to take his draft to a bank that offers him other inducements. In these cases, the sales contract provides that the credit permit free negotiation by the seller of his drafts. Such "freely negotiable credits" or "circular negotiation credits" contain language whereby (1) the issuer engages with the drawer (i.e., the seller) and with endorsers and bona fide holders that the drafts will be honored, or (2) the issuer specifically states that the drafts are available by negotiation at any bank. Note that the credit itself is not negotiable. The freely negotiable credit is misnamed. It is the drafts drawn under it that are freely negotiable.[30]

As a matter of negotiable instruments law, the taking of a draft by negotiation does not constitute honor of that draft. Sight drafts are honored by payment; time drafts are honored by acceptance and payment.[31] Both drafts, however, may be negotiated. Negotiation occurs when the drawer endorses the draft and transfers it to a holder. Thus, when the seller endorses the draft to a bank for deposit or collection, the draft has been negotiated.

Negotiation, however, can occur in any credit situation. Drafts drawn under a payment credit or under an acceptance credit may be negotiated by the seller who wants his bank to initiate collection for him. Significantly, however, such negotiation by the seller does not satisfy the presentation requirements of those credits. It does not trigger the issuer's engagement to honor the draft. The seller who negotiates his draft[32] prior to expiry of a negotiation credit has acted within the cred-

---

[30] For a case in which the court referred to a negotiation credit as having been "negotiated" to the negotiating bank, see Westpac Banking Corp. v. South Carolina Nat'l Bank, [1986] 1 Lloyd's Rep. 311, 313 (P.C.). See also First Nat'l Bank v. Carmouche, 504 So. 2d 1153 (La. Ct. App.), rev'd, 515 So. 2d 785 (La. 1987) (assuming incorrectly that draft submitted to issuer under negotiation credit is not "negotiated" until issuer honors); Supreme Merchandise Co. v. Chemical Bank, 70 N.Y.2d 344, 514 N.E.2d 1358, 520 N.Y.S.2d 734 (1987) (opinion referring to negotiation credit as "negotiable" credit).

[31] See U.C.C. § 1-201(21).

[32] Throughout, this discussion assumes that the seller has presented, along with his draft, whatever other documents the credit requires.

it's time limit. The negotiation credit customarily designates the expiry in terms of negotiation.[33]

The seller who negotiates his draft under a payment or acceptance credit, however, does not make presentment until the collecting bank delivers the draft to the bank designated in the credit as the payor or accepting bank. Under payment and acceptance credits, the seller must hope that he has negotiated sufficiently in advance of expiry to permit the collecting bank to present in time. It is also significant that under a negotiation credit that calls for drafts drawn on the account party,[34] the beneficiary has the right against the issuer to negotiate without recourse[35]; that is, it has the right to avoid customary drawer and endorser liability vis-à-vis the issuer.[36] The same is true when the beneficiary negotiates his draft on the issuer with the confirming bank.[37]

[5] Differences Among Payment, Acceptance, and Negotiation Credits

The preceding discussion illustrates the advantages and disadvantages to the beneficiary in the three types of credits. Under the payment credit, the issuer's performance gives the beneficiary cash without risk of chargeback. The seller-beneficiary must watch the payment credit carefully, however, to be certain that he presents the draft at the proper place and within the prescribed time limit. There are risks if payment is to occur at a place distant from the beneficiary. The beneficiary must allow for interbank transfers, and he risks difficulties if the distant payor properly rejects his presentment because of some minor but correctable defect in the presentation. If a necessary signature is missing, a European seller-beneficiary will not find it easy to correct documents that he forwards to New York.

The acceptance credit does not give the beneficiary payment but does provide him with a negotiable acceptance that he can usually discount without difficulty or great cost. Again, the beneficiary prefers that

---

[33] The credit will provide, for example, that "drafts must be negotiated on or before [date]." See App. C, Doc. 1.

[34] For examples of transactions in which the credit calls for drafts drawn on the bank's customer, rather than the bank issuer itself, see European Asian Bank A.G. v. Punjab & Sind Bank, [1983] 2 All E.R. 508 (C.A.); Kydon Compania Naviera S.A. v. National Westminster Bank Ltd., [1981] 1 Lloyd's Rep. 68 (Q.B.).

[35] See U.C.P. art. 10(a)(iv) (1983).

[36] See U.C.C. §§ 3-413(2), 3-414(1).

[37] See U.C.P. art. 10(b)(iv) (1983); Ng Chee Chong v. Austin Taylor & Co., [1975] 1 Lloyd's Rep. 156 (Q.B.).

the credit designate a local bank as the accepting bank. In circular negotiation credits, the beneficiary may choose his bank and has more time to assemble documents for presentation. In addition, he is in a better position to correct any defect in his presentation.

The nature of the credit, then, affects the extent of the seller-beneficiary's protection as well as the buyer account party's duty to pay. The issuer has the right of prompt reimbursement by the buyer.[38] The amount and timing of that reimbursement are determined in part by whether the credit is available by payment, by acceptance, or by negotiation.

Finally, the nature of the credit may affect the attractiveness of the seller's drafts. In a circular negotiation credit transaction, the negotiating bank knows that it benefits from the direct promise of the issuer that complying presentations will be paid or accepted. Such a negotiating bank may be in a better position to enforce the issuer's promise than is the seller-beneficiary. The negotiating bank that takes in a regular transaction will probably rise to the level of a holder in due course of the draft[39] or to a "person" to whom a negotiable document of title has been duly negotiated.[40] Such good faith purchase qualities of a negotiating bank permit it to cut off certain defenses to payment and claims to the goods that are available against the beneficiary.[41]

[6] Deferred Payment Credit

Because some jurisdictions tax or otherwise regulate drafts or banker's acceptances, parties that prefer a time credit sometimes avoid the use of a time draft and its acceptance altogether. Such parties have created the deferred payment credit, which is strikingly similar to the acceptance credit in that both of them call for payment on a date that is a fixed period of time after a specified date. The deferred payment credit differs from the acceptance credit in that it generates no draft and no acceptance. The issuer signals its obligation by letter, by advice, or by some other nonnegotiable undertaking.[42]

---

[38] See U.C.C. § 5-114(3); U.C.P. art. 16(a) (1983).

[39] See U.C.C. § 3-302.

[40] See U.C.C. § 7-501.

[41] See U.C.C. § 5-114(2)(a). For discussion of these defenses and the negotiating bank's ability to avoid them, see ¶ 8.01.

[42] For further discussion of the similarities between acceptance credits and deferred payment credits, see Eberth & Ellinger, "Deferred Payment Credits: A Comparative Analysis of Their Special Problems," 14 J. Mar. L. & Com. 387 (1983).

¶ 1.03　ROLE OF THE CORRESPONDENT BANK

In nearly all credits arising out of the international sale and in many domestic credit cases, the seller insists that the sales contract with the buyer stipulate that a bank local to the seller be involved. The local bank may be the issuer[43] but is usually a correspondent of the issuer. Its first function is to advise the beneficiary that the credit is indeed open.[44] By performing that function, the correspondent becomes an advising bank.[45] Sometimes the seller is not satisfied with the credit standing of a bank in a foreign country or in a distant city. In that event, the seller bargains in the sales contract with the buyer for a contract term stipulating that a bank in the seller's community not only will advise that the credit is open but also will add its engagement to that of the issuing bank. Such added engagement is a confirmation,[46] and the bank that makes it is a confirming bank.[47]

The duties of the advising bank, then, are much lighter than those of the confirming bank. Section 5-107(1) of the Code stipulates that an advising bank does not assume any obligation to honor the beneficiary's drafts but that it does assume the obligation to be accurate in its advice.

In *Sound of Market Street, Inc. v. Continental Bank International,*[48] an advising bank that received the opening bank's credit and reviewed it on August 9 failed to send its advice until August 18. The beneficiary did not receive the advice until August 25. By then, the beneficiary claimed, it was too late to meet the latest shipping date of the credit and avoid a consequent loss. When the beneficiary sued the advising bank, the bank moved for summary judgment. The trial court denied the motion, but the Court of Appeals for the Third Circuit reversed. The Third Circuit held that as a matter of common law and under the Code and the Uniform Customs and Practice for Documentary Credits (Uniform Customs or the UCP), there was no privity between the advising bank

---

[43] Sometimes the buyer asks his bank to cause the credit to be issued by a bank in the seller's country. Thus, in the hypothetical example supra ¶ 1.01, instead of issuing the credit and having it confirmed, the Kansas City bank of a Missouri buyer may ask an Amsterdam bank to issue the credit to a Dutch seller.

[44] See App. C, Doc. 2, for an example of an advice.

[45] See U.C.C. § 5-103(1)(e) for the definition of "advising bank."

[46] See App. C, Doc. 3, for an example of such a confirmation. See also U.C.C. § 5-103(1)(f) for the definition of "confirming bank."

[47] Cf. U.C.C. § 5-107 (distinguishing obligations of advising and confirming banks). In Banco De Vizcaya, S.A. v. First Nat'l Bank, 514 F. Supp. 1280 (N.D. Ill. 1981), opinion vacated, id., the court held that whether a bank is a confirming bank is a question to be determined by the intent of the parties.

[48] 623 F. Supp. 93 (E.D. Pa. 1985), rev'd, 819 F.2d 384 (3d Cir. 1987).

and the beneficiary.[49] The Third Circuit concluded that the beneficiary should recover its damages from the account party, not from the advising bank.

The *Sound of Market Street* court also held that an advising bank is the agent of the issuer and that the account party, not the beneficiary, is the third-party beneficiary of that agency contract. Those holdings are at once significant and persuasive. They are significant because they impose liability on the commercial parties for commercial losses and relieve the banking system from commercial loss burdens. They are also persuasive. In all probability, the beneficiary has a cause of action against an account party when the advising bank or, for that matter, the issuer fails to establish the credit in time. The underlying sales contract, to which the beneficiary is a party, is the source of the beneficiary's right to have a letter of credit. It is upon the beneficiary's commercial counterpart, the account party buyer, that the beneficiary relies in the transaction. To permit the beneficiary to recover from a bank about which it had no knowledge whatsoever and upon whom it placed no reliance is to give the beneficiary a fortuitous recovery. Law that encourages commercial parties to choose the parties on which they rely carefully is superior to law that supplies fortuitous defendants. The *Sound of Market Street* holding effects an efficient result.

The Code, in defining "confirming bank" in Section 5-103(1)(f), speaks in terms of confirmation of a credit "already issued by another bank." In *Barclays Bank D.C.O. v. Mercantile National Bank*,[50] a bank that had expressly confirmed a nonbank credit argued that it was not a confirming bank under Article 5. It is not clear from the court's opinion why the defendant thought a holding that Article 5 did not apply to its confirmation might support the view that its confirmation was not enforceable. It does not follow that because the bank does not meet the Code definition of "confirming bank," such a bank cannot be liable on its express promise confirming a credit. In any event, the *Barclays* court did not agree with the defendant that Article 5 applies only to confirmations and credits issued by banks. By giving weight to the Code's express policy of permitting the continued expansion of commercial practices[51] and to the implications of Section 5-102(3) that Article 5 does not codify all of letter of credit law, the court properly extended the Code definition to banks that confirm nonbank credits.[52]

---

[49] Sound of Mkt. St., Inc. v. Continental Bank Int'l, 819 F.2d 384 (3d Cir. 1987).

[50] 481 F.2d 1224 (5th Cir. 1973), cert. dismissed, 414 U.S. 1139 (1974).

[51] See U.C.C. § 1-102(2)(b).

[52] For further discussion of the liability of the correspondent bank, see ¶¶ 9.03[3], 9.04.

The Section 2-325 requirement that the buyer of goods obtain a confirmed credit pursuant to the underlying sales agreement was the subject of dispute in *Texas Trading & Milling Corp. v. H.I.T. Corp.*[53] The buyer argued that the Code provision is meaningless when the opening bank is in the seller's market and that the seller cannot complain that the irrevocable credit was not confirmed.[54] The court ruled, by way of dictum,[55] that the absence of the confirmation deprived the seller-beneficiary of the primary liability of two banks, a condition that the parties had agreed upon in the sales agreement. The court hinted that a beneficiary may want two banks to be liable on the credit in order to guard against the possibility that the issuer, the buyer's bank, might favor the buyer in any dispute over whether the documents were in compliance. That concern is well founded, and the *Texas Trading* holding makes good commercial sense.

Letter of credit law must observe a rather fine distinction between correspondents of the issuer who act as the issuer's agents in advising the credit, collecting banks that act as agents of the beneficiary in collecting the beneficiary's draft, and the negotiating bank under a negotiation credit that acts for itself. In *European Asian Bank A.G. v. Punjab & Sind Bank*,[56] a bank that took the beneficiary's draft under a negotiation credit could not rely, the court held, on agency law in acting on an ambiguous credit. Had the bank been an agent of the issuer, it could have acted as a reasonable person in the circumstances and could have bound the issuer thereby. The court held that the bank was not an agent, however, and that therefore the bank could not rely on that agency doctrine. The bank acted at its peril and should have sought instructions from the issuer concerning the meaning of the credit.

The *European Asian Bank* case is consistent with the traditional distinction between a collecting bank under a straight credit and a negotiating bank under a negotiation credit. The former is an agent of the beneficiary; the latter acts in its own right. Similarly, the negotiating bank is distinct from the nominated bank, that is, a bank nominated by

---

[53] No. 84 Civ. 3776 (LLS) (S.D.N.Y. Sept. 3, 1986).

[54] The confusion may have resulted from the fact that formerly to a significant extent and today in some markets the term "confirmed credit" means "irrevocable credit." See Mentschikoff, "Letters of Credit: The Need for Uniform Legislation," 23 U. Chi. L. Rev. 571, 589 n.72 (1956).

[55] The court held that the seller's cancelation of the contract for the buyer's failure to provide the confirmation was improper because the seller did not provide sufficient advance notice for the buyer to cure.

[56] [1983] 2 All E.R. 508 (C.A.).

the issuer to pay the beneficiary.[57] A nominated bank acts as the agent of the issuer.[58]

¶ 1.04 STANDBY CREDIT

Since the adoption of the Code in the 1950s, commercial law has witnessed a significant extension in the use of credits from the commercial sale, where they serve to reduce risk of nonpayment of the purchase price under a contract for the sale of goods, to nonsale settings, where they serve to reduce risk of nonperformance under a contract that calls for performance. Generally, credits in the nonsale setting have come to be known as standby credits.

There are three significant differences between commercial and standby credits. First, commercial credits involve the payment of money under a contract of sale. Such credits become payable upon the presentation by the seller-beneficiary of documents that show he has taken affirmative steps to comply with the sales agreement. In the standby case, the credit is payable upon certification of a party's nonperformance of the agreement. The documents that accompany the beneficiary's draft tend to show that the account party has not performed. The beneficiary of a commercial credit must demonstrate by documents that he has performed his contract. The beneficiary of the standby must certify that his obligor has not performed the contract.

This first difference in the two credit types is critical. It demonstrates the relative ease of drafting a commercial credit in a way that no payment will be made without performance. It also demonstrates the difficulty of drafting a standby credit in a way that no payment will be made when there has been performance. It is far easier to show by foolproof documents, whose existence is in the exclusive control of the beneficiary, that goods have been shipped than it is to show by fool-proof documents in the beneficiary's control that, for example, a building has not been constructed in accordance with design specifications.

This first distinction between commercial credits and standby credits illustrates the reason that the accompanying documents in a standby credit transaction differ in nature from those arising in the commercial credit. It is unusual to find a commercial credit that is payable on the presentation of the seller's draft, accompanied by his conclusory certificate that he has shipped conforming goods. It is not unusual, however,

---

[57] See U.C.P. art. 11 (1983).

[58] For further discussion of the differences between straight and negotiation credits, see ¶¶ 10.02[3], 10.02[4].

nor is it evidence of overreaching, to find a standby credit payable upon presentation of the beneficiary's draft accompanied by a conclusory certificate that the customer has not performed. The conclusory nature of the standby certificate is consistent with the nature of the standby credit.[59]

Second, commercial and standby credits differ in that the commercial credit issuer expects to pay the seller's drafts. Payment is consistent with normal performance of the underlying sales agreement in a commercial credit situation. The issuer of the standby credit, however, usually does not expect to pay; the presentation of drafts or demands under a standby credit is an indication that something has gone awry. Because the standby credit operates when the parties to the underlying contract are not in harmony, the standby credit issuer can be virtually certain that its customer does not want to see the beneficiary paid, whereas the customer of a commercial credit nearly always wants the seller to be paid. The nonperformance that triggers payment under the standby credit often signals the financial weakness of the account party, whereas payment of the commercial credit suggests that the account party is conducting his business as usual. The contingencies against which the issuer must protect itself are inherently different: In the one case, the issuer seeks reimbursement from a failing customer; in the other, from an account party that is healthy. In addition, the chances that the customer wants the issuer to dishonor the draft are much greater in standby cases than they are in commercial cases. In standby cases, the account party almost always contests the conclusion that it did not perform. In commercial cases, the account party almost always wants the issuer to pay.[60]

Third, the standby and commercial credit settings differ in that the commercial sale tends to follow a pattern, with the same documents accompanying the draft in case after case. The standby credit transaction,

---

[59] The account party under a standby credit may try to negotiate with the beneficiary for provisions in the credit that will render the credit payable not against the beneficiary's certificate of noncompliance but upon a certificate to that effect from an independent third party. In most cases, the beneficiary resists that provision, which alters an important feature of the standby credit and transforms it from the near equivalent of a cash bond into a surety contract. The purpose of the certificate is not to determine whether the recited facts indeed have occurred but to give the bank and the account party the beneficiary's warranty that they have occurred and therefore give the bank and the account party a clear cause of action against the beneficiary if they have not occurred. See U.C.C. § 5-111(1); see generally Dolan, "Letters of Credit, Article 5 Warranties, and the Beneficiary's Certificate," 41 Bus. Law. 347 (1986).

[60] The account party in the commercial credit usually wants to protect his reputation with the industry and often wants to continue doing business with the beneficiary.

however, can arise out of any number of industries, and frequently the documents are unique.[61] That is not to suggest that letter of credit law charges issuers with knowledge of industry practices and customs. It does not, and it specifically insulates the issuer from liability for not knowing such practices and customs.[62] Any party issuing a standby credit, however, must evaluate its risks and must understand the nature of the customer's undertaking. A bank that issues a standby credit is making a loan to its customer,[63] for all practical purposes, and it may not be able to determine whether that loan is bankable without understanding the performance called for by the customer's contract with the beneficiary.

Standby credits have introduced many bankers into the credit transaction who have had little to do with commercial credits. For a long time, a relatively small number of banks with large international banking departments issued most American commercial credits. International trade traditionally has been centered in a few cities, and the large banks in those cities formerly dominated the letter of credit industry. That picture has changed even in the area of commercial credits, and more banks are now involved in that business than before. In the standby credit area, there is much less concentration. The clientele of a small country bank seldom needs a commercial credit but almost certainly calls for standby credits from time to time.

Whether a credit is a commercial or a standby is a question of nature, not of nomenclature. In *Apex Oil Co. v. Archem Co.*,[64] the contract called for a standby, but the credit was denominated a documentary letter of credit. The court held that a documentary credit can be a standby, the term "documentary" describing the feature of the credit that calls for documents as a condition of payment.

¶ 1.05 DISTINGUISHING THE STANDBY CREDIT FROM PERFORMANCE AND PAYMENT BONDS

[1] The Distinction

The standby credit is an attractive commercial device for many of the same reasons that commercial credits are attractive. Essentially, these

---

[61] See infra ¶ 1.06.

[62] See U.C.C. § 5-109(1)(c) and comment 1 (4th para.); cf. U.C.P. art. 4 (1983) (similar rule).

[63] Thus, for example, federal bank regulators require banks to treat most standby credits as extensions of credit, that is, as loans. See 12 C.F.R. §§ 32.2(d) (1990), 337.2(b) (1989).

[64] 770 F.2d 1353 (5th Cir. 1985).

credits are inexpensive and efficient. Often they replace surety contracts, which tend to generate higher costs than credits do and which are usually triggered by a factual determination rather than by the examination of documents.

Because parties and courts should not confuse the different functions of the surety contract on the one hand and the standby credit on the other, the distinction between surety contracts and credits merits some reflection. The two commercial devices share a common purpose. Both ensure against the obligor's nonperformance. They function, however, in distinctly different ways.

Traditionally, upon the obligor's default, the surety company undertakes to complete the obligor's performance, usually by hiring someone to complete that performance. Surety contracts, then, often involve costs of determining whether the obligor has defaulted (a matter over which the surety and the beneficiary often litigate) plus the cost of performance. The benefit of the surety contract to the beneficiary is obvious. He knows that the surety company is a strong financial institution that will perform if the obligor does not. The beneficiary also should understand that such performance must await the sometimes lengthy and costly determination that the obligor has defaulted. In addition, the surety's performance takes time.

The standby credit beneficiary has different expectations. He reasonably expects that he will receive cash in the event of nonperformance, that he will receive it promptly, and that he will receive it before any litigation with the obligor (the account party) over the nature of the account party's performance takes place. The standby credit has this opposite effect of the surety contract: It reverses the financial burden of the parties during litigation.

In the surety contract situation, there is no duty to indemnify the beneficiary until the beneficiary establishes the fact of the obligor's nonperformance. The beneficiary may have to establish that fact in litigation. During the litigation, the surety holds the money and the beneficiary bears most of the cost of delay in performance.[65]

In the standby credit case, however, the beneficiary avoids that litigation burden and receives his money promptly upon presentation of the required documents. It may be that the account party has in fact performed and that the beneficiary's presentation of those documents is not rightful. In that case, the account party may sue the beneficiary in

---

[65] There may be rules giving a successful plaintiff interest and sometimes attorney fees when a surety company resists payment, but such relief is limited. See, e.g., Ill. Ann. Stat. ch. 73, § 767 (Smith-Hurd Supp. 1989).

tort, in contract, or in breach of warranty[66]; but during the litigation to determine whether the account party has in fact breached his obligation to perform, the beneficiary, not the account party, holds the money.[67] Parties that use a standby credit and courts construing such a credit should understand this allocation of burdens. There is a tendency in some courts to overlook this distinction between surety contracts and standby credits and to reallocate burdens by permitting the obligor or the issuer to litigate the performance question before payment to the beneficiary.[68]

Account parties who select standby credits over surety contracts presumably do so primarily because they assume that they will perform to the beneficiary's satisfaction and therefore that the risk of a draft under the standby credit is small. The account party also appreciates the standby credit because it usually costs less than the surety contract. The beneficiary of a standby credit often and properly insists that the credit be clean or nearly so, that is, that the credit be payable against a draft alone or against a draft accompanied by a simple certificate by the beneficiary to the effect that the account party has defaulted.[69] The account party must know that under a clean credit, there is a risk of fraud[70] or at least a risk that the beneficiary will draw when there is a bona fide dispute between the account party and the beneficiary over the account party's performance of the underlying agreement. Courts, however, should understand that the account party has agreed to the standby credit instead of the more expensive surety contract. These courts should not let the account party transform the quick, efficient payment mechanism of the standby credit into the protracted surety contract inquiry.

It would be misleading to leave the impression that courts have vigorously observed this distinction between surety contracts and standby credits. Sometimes they have not.[71] It is not clear whether those decisions that reallocate the burden do so because they find the parties' allocation offensive to legal principles or whether they do so unwittingly.

Credits and performance bonds also differ in the scope of their benefits. Traditionally, performance bonds benefit third parties who perform work on the project covered by the bond. Letters of credit specify

---

[66] See U.C.C. § 5-111(1).

[67] For further discussion of this important function of credits, see ¶ 3.07.

[68] See ¶¶ 7.03, 7.04.

[69] For the definition of "clean" credit, see the Glossary.

[70] If the customer is aware of it, such fraud may justify a temporary restraining order stopping payment. See U.C.C. § 5- 114(2). See generally Chapter 7.

[71] See generally ¶ 7.04.

the beneficiary and have strict rules on transfer.[72] In *Arbest Construction Co. v. First National Bank & Trust Co.*,[73] under the terms of a federally insured construction mortgage, the developer obtained a standby credit in favor of the mortgagee to protect the mortgagee in the event the prime contractor failed to perform. When the prime contractor failed to pay two subcontractors for work they performed on the job, the subcontractors sued the credit issuer, asking the court to reform the credit in order to provide them protection.[74] The court rejected the request and affirmed summary judgment for the issuer. The court held squarely that the subcontractors had no rights under the credit. In short, the third-party beneficiary principles of bonds do not find application in standby cases under the *Arbest* rule.

In *Kerr Construction Co. v. Plains National Bank*,[75] on the other hand, the court permitted a subcontractor to sue for dishonor of a credit issued in favor of a municipality. The *Kerr* credit was similar to that in *Arbest*, but the *Kerr* opinion does not address the distinctions that the *Arbest* opinion takes pains to make. Of the two cases, *Arbest* is the more persuasive.

In *Midstates Excavating, Inc. v. Farmers & Merchants Bank & Trust Co.*,[76] the court assumed that the issuing bank's undertaking was a letter of credit, as the bank had designated it. In fact, the bank's letter was not a letter of credit. It did not meet two critical features of the letter of credit definition, there being no undertaking to honor drafts or demands for payment and no express conditions upon which the issuer's obligation to pay turned.[77] After considering the circumstances surrounding the issuance of the letter, and in light of the fact that it was issued as a substitute for a payment bond, the court gave third parties (suppliers of the addressee of the letter) rights against the bank.

The holding of *Midstates* is a significant departure from letter of credit principles. The court did not consider the nature of credits and did not refer to any letter of credit authority to support its holding. *Midstates* is not a well-considered letter of credit decision and should not be taken as authority contrary to that of the well-reasoned *Arbest*

---

[72] For discussion of the transfer rules, see ¶ 10.03.

[73] 777 F.2d 581 (10th Cir. 1985).

[74] The court noted that the credit in the *Arbest* case had expired. That fact in and of itself may have justified a ruling against the subcontractors. Given the fact that the plaintiffs were seeking, in effect, to reform the credit, the court wisely did not rest its decision on that ground. For discussion of the expiry rules, see ¶ 5.03[3].

[75] 753 S.W.2d 181 (Tex. Ct. App. 1987).

[76] 410 N.W.2d 190 (S.D. 1987).

[77] For discussion of the requisites of a letter of credit, see ¶ 2.03.

case. That is not to say that standby credits cannot serve as payment bonds. In those situations in which the owner of a project and the contractor use the standby to secure payment to third parties, they make the letter of credit payable in favor of the owner, who, in the event of third-party claims, demands payment under the credit and holds the funds pending resolution of the claims brought by suppliers or subcontractors.[78]

City of Philadelphia v. American Coastal Industries, Inc.[79] may reflect another significant difference between performance and payment bonds and standby letters of credit. In that case, a contractor argued that a municipality that had accepted the contractor's bid acted arbitrarily and capriciously when it refused to accept a standby letter of credit in lieu of the performance and payment bonds called for in the municipality's contract specifications. The *American Coastal* court disagreed, however, holding that in that case there was a significant difference between the two products. Under a bond, the court held, the surety may be required to complete the project even if the cost of that completion exceeds the penal sum of the bond. Under a standby, on the other hand, the issuer's obligation is no greater than the amount of the credit. Thus, the municipality's refusal to accept the credit was reasonable, in the court's view.

Whether the *American Coastal* court's statement of suretyship law is correct is not material to this inquiry, but it is material that the court correctly determined that the law that applies to letters of credit is different from that which applies to performance bonds. Although the two products may serve similar purposes, their legal consequences arise from disparate sources in the law.

[2] The Primary "Guaranty"

The distinctions posited in the foregoing paragraph are distinctions of function and nature, not of nomenclature. If the banking industry were to begin marketing a primary obligation tomorrow that was payable against the presentation of documents and that was independent of the underlying transaction, it would not matter to letter of credit law if the banks were to call that product a "guaranty." Letter of credit law would be applicable to it.

---

[78] See, e.g., United States v. Challinor, 620 F. Supp. 78 (D. Mont. 1985) (beneficiary enforcing credit for third parties).

[79] 704 F. Supp. 587 (E.D. Pa. 1988).

In fact, foreign banks and foreign branches of domestic banks have introduced a product that they call a guaranty and to which letter of credit law is quite congenial. "First-demand guaranties,"[80] "performance guaranties,"[81] and "simple-demand guaranties" are the foreign bank equivalents of the standby. They are payable against drafts or requests for payment accompanied by documentation or with no documentation at all, and the parties that use them and the courts that handle litigation involving them think of them as being independent of the transactions that they serve.[82] American courts,[83] foreign courts,[84] and commentators[85] are in general agreement that this "guaranty" is subject to letter of credit rules.[86] In all events, of course, the critical distinction is the nature of the device, not its name.[87]

¶ 1.06 FREQUENT USES OF THE STANDBY CREDIT

There are virtually no limits to the variety of transactions that the standby credit can serve. In principle, standby credits can be used in any

---

[80] See R.D. Harbottle (Mercantile) Ltd. v. National Westminster Bank Ltd., [1977] 2 All E.R. 862 (Q.B.).

[81] See Bolivinter Oil S.A. v. Chase Manhattan Bank, [1984] 1 Lloyd's Rep. 251 (C.A.); Edward Owen Eng'g Ltd. v. Barclays Bank Int'l Ltd., [1978] 1 All E.R. 976 (C.A.).

[82] See, e.g., Howe Richardson Scale Co. v. Polimex-Cekop, [1978] 1 Lloyd's Rep. 161 (C.A.).

[83] See Egyptian Am. Bank, S.A.E. v. United States, No. 88-1220 (Fed. Cir. Sept. 21, 1988) (limited precedent op.); American Nat'l Bank & Trust Co. v. Hamilton Indus. Int'l, Inc., 583 F. Supp. 164 (N.D. Ill. 1984), rev'd on other grounds sub nom. Banque Paribas v. Hamilton Indus. Int'l, Inc., 767 F.2d 380 (7th Cir. 1985).

[84] See United Trading Corp. v. Allied Arab Bank Ltd., [1985] 2 Lloyd's Rep. 554 (C.A.); R.D. Harbottle (Mercantile) Ltd. v. National Westminster Bank Ltd., [1977] 2 All E.R. 862 (Q.B.).

[85] See, e.g., R. Goode, Commercial Law 697–698 (1985); Ellinger, "Performance Bonds, First-Demand Guarantees and Standby Letters of Credit — A Comparison," Letters of Credit Rep. 1 (May/June 1987); Giger, "Problems of Bank Guarantee Abuse in Swiss Law," 2 Ariz. J. Int'l & Comp. L. 38 (1987); Stoufflet, "Recent Developments in the Law of International Bank Guarantees in France and Belgium," 2 Ariz. J. Int'l & Comp. L. 48 (1987).

[86] For a case in which the issuer rendered a "guaranty" subject to the Uniform Customs, see Esal (Commodities) Ltd. v. Oriental Credit Ltd., [1985] 2 Lloyd's Rep. 546 (C.A.). It may be unfortunate that there are efforts at the international level to fashion rules for bank guarantees that may ultimately differ in some respects from those for letters of credit. For criticism of those efforts, see Dolan, "Efforts at International Standardization of Bank Guarantees," 4 Banking & Fin. L. Rev. 237 (1990).

[87] Accord J.H. Rayner (Mincing Lane) Ltd. v. Bank Fur Gemeinwirtschaft A.G., [1983] 1 Lloyd's Rep. 462 (C.A.).

contract where the performance of one party is executory. There are some industries and transactions, however, where standby credits arise with frequency. The following discussion reveals the extent of the standby's adaptability.

1. *Real Estate Development.* The real estate industry was one of the first to utilize standby credits in significant numbers and in imaginative ways. In real estate development, a mortgagee frequently conditions its loan commitment upon some contribution to the project by the developers; that is, the lender insists that the developers have some equity in the project. That equity comes under various guises: equity requirements,[88] loan imbalance,[89] working capital deposit,[90] or developer's gap.[91] All of them have been secured by standby letters of credit. In other real estate development transactions, the long-term lender insists on liquidated damages for the following reasons:

1. To protect it in the event the project fails during construction or in the event the developers do not draw on the commitment[92];
2. To cover costs in connection with the closing of the long-term take-out loan[93];
3. To cover working capital for the completed project[94];
4. To serve in lieu of a lender's loan commitment fee[95]; or

---

[88] See Edgewater Constr. Co. v. Percy Wilson Mortgage & Fin. Corp., 44 Ill. App. 3d 220, 222, 357 N.E.2d 1307, 1310 (1976).

[89] See Dovenmuehle, Inc. v. East Bank, 38 Colo. App. 507, 509, 563 P.2d 24, 26 (1977), aff'd, 196 Colo. 422, 589 P.2d 1361 (1978).

[90] See Lewis State Bank v. Advance Mortgage Corp., 362 So. 2d 406, 407 (Fla. Dist. Ct. App. 1978).

[91] See Lumbermans Acceptance Co. v. Security Pac. Nat'l Bank, 86 Cal. App. 3d 175, 177, 150 Cal. Rptr. 69, 70 (1978).

[92] See Sussex Leasing Corp. v. US W. Fin. Servs., Inc., 877 F.2d 200 (2d Cir. 1989); Chase Manhattan Bank v. Equibank, 550 F.2d 882 (3d Cir. 1977); Fidelity Bank v. Lutheran Mut. Life Ins. Co., 465 F.2d 211 (10th Cir. 1972); Harvey Estes Constr. Co. v. Dry Dock Sav. Bank, 381 F. Supp. 271 (W.D. Okla. 1974); New York Life Ins. Co. v. Hartford Nat'l Bank & Trust Co., 173 Conn. 492, 378 A.2d 562 (1977); CNA Mortgage Investors, Ltd. v. Hamilton Nat'l Bank, 540 S.W.2d 238 (Tenn. Ct. App. 1975).

[93] See Mid-States Mortgage Corp. v. National Bank, 77 Mich. App. 651, 259 N.W.2d 175 (1977).

[94] See West Virginia Hous. Dev. Fund v. Sroka, 415 F. Supp. 1107 (W.D. Pa. 1976).

[95] See Brummer v. Bankers Trust, 268 S.C. 21, 231 S.E.2d 298 (1977); cf. Connecticut Gen. Life Ins. Co. v. Chicago Title & Trust Co., 714 F.2d 48 (7th Cir. 1983) (referring to letter of credit that covered part of refundable commitment fee).

5. Simply to secure payment of sums due at the time of closing.[96]

In each of these transactions, parties have used standby credits in lieu of cash, bonds, or other security.[97]

2. *Obligations Under Municipal Regulation.* A developer frequently faces requirements from municipalities to furnish security for obligations that he owes the municipality. Municipalities demand security when, for example, the developer seeks approval of a project to provide improvements such as roads, utility services, and other additions. To secure these obligations, municipalities customarily require surety company bonds or bonds supported by cash or by government securities. Most municipalities also take the frequently less expensive standby credit as sufficient security.[98] In fact, municipalities seem more and more com-

---

[96] Imperial Devs. (Can.) Ltd. v. Ford Motor Co. of Can. Ltd., 42 Man. R. 2d 156 (Q.B. 1986).

[97] Cf. Brown v. Crown Life Ins. Co., No. 87-0456-CV-W-1 (W.D. Mo. June 9, 1988) (use of standby as liquidated damages for failure to borrow after beneficiary issued loan commitment); Mermaid Neptune Dev. Corp. v. Home Owners Warranty Corp., 85 Civ. 6318 (MGC) (S.D.N.Y. May 3, 1988) (use of standby to secure warranty obligations of new-home builder); Devco Dev. Corp. v. Hooker Homes, Inc., 518 So. 2d 922 (Fla. Dist. Ct. App. 1987) (use of standby letter of credit as seller's sole source of liquidated damages for buyer's failure to purchase lots); McKinley v. Francis (In re Francis), 75 Bankr. 27 (Bankr. S.D. Fla. 1987) (use of standby to secure obligation to purchase residential real estate); Dade Nat'l Dev. Corp. v. Southeast Invs. of Palm Beach County, Inc., 471 So. 2d 113 (Fla. Dist. Ct. App. 1985) (involving standby credit that was used in lieu of deposit by purchaser of real estate); FSLIC v. Sandor, 684 F. Supp. 403 (D.V.I. 1988) (use of standby as down payment on condominium); Swerdlow v. Mallin, 131 Ill. App. 3d 900, 476 N.E.2d 464 (1985) (same); Siegel v. Levy Org. Dev. Co., 182 Ill. App. 3d 859, 538 N.E.2d 715 (1989) (earnest money deposit); Yiakas v. Savoy, 26 Mass. App. Ct. 310, 526 N.E.2d 1305 (1988) (credit securing deposit on real estate purchase agreement); Griffin Cos. v. First Nat'l Bank, 374 N.W.2d 768 (Minn. Ct. App. 1985) (same); Carr v. Austin Forty, 744 S.W.2d 267 (Tex. Ct. App. 1988) (same); King v. Texacally Joint Venture, 690 S.W.2d 618 (Tex. Ct. App. 1985) (same).

[98] See, e.g., Board of County Comm'rs v. Colorado Nat'l Bank, 43 Colo. App. 186, 607 P.2d 1010 (1979), modified, 634 P.2d 32 (Colo. 1981); Zale Constr. Co. v. Hoffman, 145 Ill. App. 3d 235, 494 N.E.2d 830 (1986); Hickory Point Partnership v. Anne Arundal County, 316 Md. 118, 557 A.2d 626 (1989); cf. Tenpas v. Department of Natural Resources, 148 Wis. 2d 579, 436 N.W.2d 297 (1989) (use of letter of credit to secure dam owner's obligation to maintain dam); McCord Contract Floors, Inc. v. City of Dothan, 492 So. 2d 996 (Ala. 1986) (holding that letter of credit as substitute for statutorily required bond was permissible under instructions to bidders that permitted city to waive technical defects in bids). For discussion of the use of standby credits in lieu of bonds in connection with subdivision improvements, see Kelley & Shultz, " '. . . : Or Other Adequate Security': Using, Structuring, and Managing the Standby Letter of Credit to Ensure the Completion of Subdivision Improvements," 19 Urb. Law. 39 (1987).

fortable with the standby credit, which some accept as security for leases or as indemnity against other losses.[99]

3. *Obligations Evidenced by Notes.* A lender or credit seller often asks its obligor to secure the balance on promissory notes with a standby credit. In one case, purchasers of a corporation's stock questioned the value of a note the corporation owned.[100] The sellers allayed the buyers' concerns by securing the note with a standby letter of credit.[101] In other cases, limited partnerships use a standby credit to secure obligations under a note to the partnership itself.[102] Any partnership may ensure its obligations[103] or that of a corporate subsidiary[104] with a standby credit.

In each of these cases, the standby credit enhances the value of the note in the hands of the holder. Holders may not value the promise of a stranger to pay a note, but they do value it when a commercial bank engages under a standby credit to pay the note if the maker does not. Thus, for example, when syndicators market interests in speculative ventures, they often resort to the standby. In a model case,[105] syndicators of a cattle embryo venture seek capital from individual investors through brokers. The brokers find that they can attract investors and can satisfy the capital needs of the venture by obtaining only a portion of the investor's share in cash and the balance in the form of a promissory note. The syndicators use the note as collateral for loans that finance the venture. Although the investors, who are spread out all over the country, are financially sound, the syndicate's lender, an Oklahoma City bank, for example, is unfamiliar with them. The investors' own banks are quite

---

[99] See Hyland Hills Metro. Park & Recreational Dist. v. McCoy Enters., Inc., 38 Colo. App. 23, 554 P.2d 708 (1976); cf. Dixon Venture v. Joseph Dixon Crucible Co., 235 N.J. Super. 105, 561 A.2d 663 (App. Div. 1989) (letter of credit securing environmental cleanup obligation); Ohio Indus. Comm'n v. First Nat'l Bank, No. C-840840 (Ohio Ct. App. Aug. 28, 1985) (use of standby credit to satisfy self-insured employer's statutory obligation to indemnify against losses).

[100] See Republic Nat'l Bank v. Northwest Nat'l Bank, 578 S.W.2d 109 (Tex. 1978).

[101] See also Steinmeyer v. Warner Consol. Corp., 42 Cal. App. 3d 515, 116 Cal. Rptr. 57 (1974) (similar use of credit to secure notes).

[102] See, e.g., Shaffer v. Brooklyn Park Garden Apartments, 311 Minn. 452, 250 N.W.2d 172 (1977); cf. Marine Midland Bank, N.A. v. Goyak, No. 84 Civ. 1204 (S.D.N.Y. July 12, 1984) (letter of credit used to secure liability of endorser of limited partnership note).

[103] See Postal v. Smith (In re Marine Distribs., Inc.), 522 F.2d 791 (9th Cir. 1975).

[104] See Foreign Venture Ltd. Partnership v. Chemical Bank, 59 A.D.2d 352, 399 N.Y.S.2d 114 (1977).

[105] See Tanenbaum v. Agri-Capital, Inc., 885 F.2d 464 (8th Cir. 1989).

familiar with them, however, and are willing to lend their credit reputation to the investors' notes. By issuing a standby credit in favor of the venture or of the lending bank in Oklahoma City, the investors' banks give value to the investors' notes and make them good collateral for the Oklahoma City bank's loan to the venture.

Note that there is no sleight of hand here. The standby cannot give credit to an investor who is not creditworthy. It would be an unsound banking practice for a bank to issue a credit for the account of an investor who could not reimburse the bank in the event the bank were called upon to honor the lending bank's draft under the credit. Banks issue standby credits on the account of customers whom they know to be financially responsible and only to the extent of that financial responsibility. In effect, the standby obviates the need for the lending bank to investigate the credit standing of each investor. In view of the fact that the investors are many and geographically dispersed, that task is formidable for the lending bank. It is not formidable for the investors' banks, which already know the investors in many cases and usually are located in a community where the investor has an established credit reputation.

4. *Performance and Other Kinds of Bonds.* Sometimes the standby credit occurs in a reciprocal credit transaction. In such cases, the seller of goods benefits from a commercial credit guaranteeing the buyer's payment, and the buyer benefits from a standby credit guaranteeing the seller's performance.[106] In this situation, the standby credit serves in the nature of a performance bond. In other cases, the standby credit may stand alone as a guarantee of performance or payment,[107] serve as a supersedeas,[108] secure the surety on an appeal bond,[109] function as a bid

[106] See, e.g., KMW Int'l v. Chase Manhattan Bank, N.A., 606 F.2d 10 (2d Cir. 1979); American Bell Int'l, Inc. v. Islamic Republic of Iran, 474 F. Supp. 420 (S.D.N.Y. 1979).

[107] See, e.g., United Technologies Corp. v. Citibank, N.A., 469 F. Supp. 473 (S.D.N.Y. 1979); Dynamics Corp. of Am. v. Citizens & S. Nat'l Bank, 356 F. Supp. 991 (N.D. Ga. 1973); Alaska Nat'l Bank v. Gwitchyaa Zhee Corp., 639 P.2d 94 (Alaska 1981); cf. Pittston Warehouse Corp. v. American Motorist Ins. Co., 715 F. Supp. 1221 (S.D.N.Y. 1989) (use of letter of credit as security for bond issued on behalf of warehouse to U.S. Customs Service); Balboa Ins. Co. v. Coastal Bank, 42 U.C.C. Rep. Serv. (Callaghan) 1716 (S.D. Ga. 1986) (use of letter of credit as security for performance bond); United States v. Challinor, 620 F. Supp. 78 (D. Mont. 1985) (standby in lieu of Miller Act bond); Cornish v. Superior Court, 209 Cal. App. 3d 467, 257 Cal. Rptr. 383 (1989) (letter of credit used as security for performance and payment bond); Richards & Conover Steel Co. v. Nielsons, Inc., 755 P.2d 644 (Okla. 1988) (use of standby in lieu of payment and material bond in state contract).

[108] See Landau & Cleary, Ltd. v. Hribar Trucking, Inc., 867 F.2d 996 (7th Cir. 1989); Bose Corp. v. Consumers Union, 806 F.2d 304 (1st Cir. 1986); State Indus., Inc. v. Mor-Flo Indus., Inc., 124 F.R.D. 613 (E.D. Tenn. 1988); Cabot, Cabot & Forbes Co. v. Brian, Simon, Peragine, Smith & Redfearn, No. 80-2060 (E.D. La.

bond,[110] or serve in lieu of possession of attached goods or funds.[111] In short, standby credits serve many functions that formerly were the exclusive domain of bonds, and generally they do so at lower cost.[112]

Nov. 17, 1986); United Bank v. Quadrangle, Ltd., 42 Colo. App. 486, 596 P.2d 408 (1979); cf. Potter-Roemer, Inc. v. United States, 702 F. Supp. 911 (Ct. Int'l Trade 1988) (credit securing liability for additional tariffs pending appeal); Gallery House, Inc. v. Yi, 582 F. Supp. 1294 (N.D. Ill. 1984) (ordering bond or letter of credit as security for issuance of preliminary injunction); Realco Equities, Inc. v. John Hancock Mut. Life Ins. Co., 130 N.H. 345, 540 A.2d 1220 (1988) (standby used to protect owner of property during appeal of specific performance action). But cf. Dunlavey v. Arizona Title Ins. & Trust Co. (In re Charlton), 708 F.2d 1449 (9th Cir. 1983) (refusing, on ground that it was not supported by adequate security, to accept letter of credit in lieu of security bond for extension of stay of order approving sale of real estate in bankruptcy proceeding); City of Philadelphia v. American Coastal Indus., Inc., 704 F. Supp. 587 (E.D. Pa. 1988) (holding that municipality did not act arbitrarily in refusing letter of credit in lieu of performance and payment bond); Long Grove Country Club Estates, Inc. v. Village of Long Grove, No. 82 C 6868 (N.D. Ill. July 1, 1988) (distinguishing letter of credit from bond required under local improvements ordinance); Heritage Hous. Corp. v. Ferguson, 651 S.W.2d 272 (Tex. Ct. App. 1983) (rejecting letter of credit in lieu of supersedeas bond on ground that Texas rule of procedure did not authorize such substitution); State v. Morganstein, 703 S.W.2d 894 (Mo. 1986) (holding that letter of credit is not supersedeas bond and is subject to letter of credit law for enforcement, not to law of surety bonds).

[109] See Hanover Ins. Co. v. Smith, 182 Ill. App. 3d 793, 538 N.E.2d 710 (1989); INA v. Heritage Bank, N.A., 595 F.2d 171 (3d Cir. 1979); In re M.J. Sales & Distrib. Co., 25 Bankr. 608 (Bankr. S.D.N.Y. 1982); Citronelle Unit Operators Comm. v. AmSouth Bank, N.A., 536 So. 2d 1387 (Ala. 1988); cf. Bose Corp. v. Consumers Union, 806 F.2d 304 (1st Cir. 1986) (allowing expenses for letter of credit used in lieu of supersedeas bond to be taxed as costs); Hunt v. BP Exploration Co., 580 F. Supp. 304 (N.D. Tex. 1984) (involving letter of credit required by Appeal Committee of House of Lords in lieu of appeal bond); United States v. Bowler, 537 F. Supp. 933 (N.D. Ill. 1982) (letter of credit serving as security for a fine pending appeal); In re Prichard, 169 Mich. App. 140, 425 N.W.2d 744 (1988) (use of standby pending appeal as security for damages for wrongful issuance of injunction); Elegant v. Uchitel, 537 So. 2d 585 (Fla. Dist. Ct. App. 1988) (use of credit to secure judgment debt); Sayers v. Shell Can. Resources Ltd., 64 A.L.R. 319 (Ct. App. 1984) (use of credit in lieu of cash deposit as condition of jury trial). But cf. Johnson v. Pacific Lighting Land Co., 878 F.2d 297 (9th Cir. 1989) (holding that while premium for appeal bond could properly be taxed as costs, bank fees for issuance of letters of credit securing that bond could not be taxed); Lamborn v. Dittmer, 726 F. Supp. 510 (S.D.N.Y. 1989) (same); Golf W. of Ky., Inc. v. Life Investors, Inc., 178 Cal. App. 3d 313, 223 Cal. Rptr. 539 (1986) (same). Contra Whittle v. Seehusen, 113 Idaho 852, 748 P.2d 1382 (1987).

[110] See Comptroller of the Currency, Interpretive Letter No. 156, [1981–1982 Transfer Binder] Fed. Banking L. Rep. (CCH) ¶ 85,237 (June 23, 1980); see also Briggs v. Briggs, 432 So. 2d 1265 (Ala. 1983) (describing use of letter of credit to satisfy bid in partition sale). In Ensco Envtl. Servs., Inc. v. United States, 650 F. Supp. 583 (W.D. Mo. 1986), the U.S. Army Corps of Engineers, relying on an opinion of the Comptroller General of the United States, held that an irrevocable standby letter

In *CJL Co. v. Bank of Wallowa County (In re CJL Co.)*,[113] a logging company had been using cash bonds to guarantee performance under contracts with the U.S. Forest Service. The logging company decided that it was less expensive to deposit the cash in an interest-earning account and pay the charge for having a standby credit issue to the Forest Service than to leave the funds in the hands of the Service, where it would earn no interest. In other cases, parties have used standby credits as security for bonds of one kind or another.[114]

---

of credit was not sufficient as a bid bond. The *Ensco* court held that the Comptroller General's opinion was erroneous but upheld the decision of the U.S. Army Corps of Engineers on the ground that the decision was not arbitrary or capricious.

[111] See Armada Coal Export, Inc. v. Interbulk, Ltd., 726 F.2d 1566 (11th Cir. 1984); South Shore Bank v. International Jet Interiors, Inc., 721 F. Supp. 29 (E.D.N.Y. 1989); Wijsmuller RV v. Tug Benasque, 528 F. Supp. 1081 (D. Del. 1981); Schiavone Constr. Co. v. Elgood Mayo Corp., 105 Misc. 2d 431, 432 N.Y.S.2d 316 (Sup. Ct. 1980); Murray v. Eisenberg, 29 Wash. App. 42, 627 P.2d 146 (1981); Vijan Holdings Ltd. v. Newbery Energy Ltd., 18 S.R. 239 (Q.B. 1982).

[112] United States v. Goodman, 850 F.2d 1473 (11th Cir. 1988) (credit securing payment of fine); Dalkon Shield Claimants' Comm. v. Aetna Casualty & Sur. Co. (In re A.H. Robins Co.), 88 Bankr. 755 (E.D. Va. 1988) (credit securing $1.75 billion settlement); Wyle v. Bank Melli, 577 F. Supp. 1148 (N.D. Cal. 1983) (credit securing guaranty against losses or damage to cargo); Falk v. Hecker (In re Falk), 88 Bankr. 957 (Bankr. D. Minn. 1988) (credit securing cash settlement under divorce decree); see also In re Kem Solv, Inc., No. 84-5495 (E.D. Pa. Mar. 18, 1985) (involving credit used in lieu of bond under Section 303(e) of Bankruptcy Code); In re Brenton's Cove Dev. Co., No. 8400470 (Bankr. D.R.I. June 18, 1986) (use of credit as condition for granting creditor relief from Bankruptcy Code automatic stay); Reynolds v. Commodity Credit Corp., 300 Ark. 441, 780 S.W.2d 15 (1989) (letter of credit running to state agency that used proceeds to satsify claims against insolvent grain warehouse); Schumacher v. Tidswell, 138 Mich. App. 708, 360 N.W.2d 915 (1984) (standby used as bond to purge attorney cited with contempt); Rosenblum v. Jacks or Better of Am. W., Inc., 745 S.W.2d 754 (Mo. Ct. App. 1988) (use of standby to secure settlement agreement); Travelers Indem. Co. v. Flushing Nat'l Bank, 90 Misc. 2d 964, 396 N.Y.S.2d 754 (Sup. Ct. 1977) (credit securing lis pendens bond). But cf. Harsh Inv. Corp. v. State, 88 Or. App. 151, 744 P.2d 588 (1987), review denied, 305 Or. 273, 752 P.2d 1219 (1988) (rejecting letter of credit as unsatisfactory substitute for administrative agency rule requiring mortgage insurance).

[113] 71 Bankr. 261 (Bankr. D. Or. 1987).

[114] See, e.g., Guy C. Long, Inc. v. Dependable Ins. Co. (In re Guy C. Long, Inc.), 74 Bankr. 939 (Bankr. E.D. Pa. 1987) (standby securing performance bond issued by insurance company); McLean Trucking Co. v. Department of Indus. Relations (In re McLean Trucking Co.), 74 Bankr. 820 (Bankr. W.D.N.C. 1987) (involving standby that secured surety company's bond that satisfied self-insurance requirements under state labor code); Johnson Drilling Co. v. Bank of the S., N.A., 186 Ga. App. 162, 367 S.E.2d 559 (1988) (standby securing bonding company's obligations under reclamation bond); Sayyah v. Doumani, 521 So. 2d 715 (La. Ct. App. 1988) (standby securing appeal bond); Karp v. Redevelopment Auth., 566 A.2d 649 (Pa. Comm. Ct. 1989) (standby credit as bid bond).

5. *Leases.* Standby credits may secure the balance due on real estate or on equipment leases and may secure the requirement that the lessee of goods return the goods upon the lease's expiration.[115] In one of these cases,[116] the lessor of a hotel was concerned that the lessee might default on lease payments. In order to protect the lessor against that potential default and the losses that she would sustain in the course of securing a new tenant, the lease called for a standby credit covering what were, in effect, liquidated damages.

6. *Securities.* The standby credit has had significant impact in the securities industry, where it serves, for example, to guarantee obligations in connection with the private placement of securities[117]; the payment of revenue and development bonds[118] and mortgage-backed pass-through securities[119]; and in connection with the lending and borrowing of securities by brokers.[120] The use of credits in this industry has been especially critical for the success of some companies in marketing their short-term notes (commercial paper).[121] Industry ratings of such paper

---

[115] See Goodwin Bros. Leasing, Inc. v. Citizens Bank, 587 F.2d 730 (5th Cir. 1979); American Airlines, Inc. v. FDIC, 610 F. Supp. 199 (D. Kan. 1985); Intraworld Indus., Inc. v. Girard Trust Bank, 461 Pa. 343, 336 A.2d 316 (1975); Chiat/Day, Inc. v. Kalimian, 105 A.D.2d 94, 483 N.Y.S.2d 235 (1984); Tranarg, C.A. v. Banca Commerciale Italiana, 90 Misc. 829, 396 N.Y.S.2d 761 (Sup. Ct. 1977).

[116] Intraworld Indus., Inc. v. Girard Trust Bank, 461 Pa. 343, 336 A.2d 316 (1975).

[117] See Comptroller of the Currency, Interpretive Letter No. 212, [1981–1982 Transfer Binder] Fed. Banking L. Rep. (CCH) ¶ 85,293 (July 2, 1981).

[118] See Lindell Square Ltd. Partnership v. Savers Fed. Sav. & Loan Ass'n, 27 Ark. App. 66, 766 S.W.2d 41 (1989); Comptroller of the Currency, Interpretive Letter No. 144, [1981–1982 Transfer Binder] Fed. Banking L. Rep. (CCH) ¶ 85,225 (June 10, 1980); Comptroller of the Currency, Interpretive Letter No. 173, [1981–1982 Transfer Binder] Fed. Banking L. Rep. (CCH) ¶ 85,254 (Nov. 4, 1980); Comptroller of the Currency, Interpretive Letter No. 232, [1981–1982 Transfer Binder] Fed. Banking L. Rep. (CCH) ¶ 85,313 (Nov. 19, 1981); cf. Purvis v. City of Little Rock, 282 Ark. 102, 667 S.W.2d 936 (1984) (describing letter of credit that secured "tourism bonds"); State ex rel. Department of Employment Sec. v. Manchin, 361 S.E.2d 474 (W. Va. 1987) (holding payment of fee for use of letter of credit to enhance value of state bonds to be constitutionally permissible).

[119] See Comptroller of the Currency, Interpretive Letter No. 132, [1981–1982 Transfer Binder] Fed. Banking L. Rep. (CCH) ¶ 85,213 (Feb. 1, 1980).

[120] See Regulation T, 12 C.F.R. § 220.16 (1989); cf. United States v. Serrano, 870 F.2d 1 (7th Cir. 1989) (credit securing repurchase agreement obligation); Lombard-Wall, Inc. v. New York City Hous. Dev. Corp., 48 Bankr. 986 (S.D.N.Y. 1985) (same).

[121] See generally Joseph, "Letters of Credit: The Developing Concepts and Financing Functions," 94 Banking L.J. 816 (1977); Ryan, "Letters of Credit Supporting Debt for Borrowed Money: The Standby as Backup," 100 Banking L.J. 404

are higher, with a concomitantly lower interest rate, if a commercial bank's standby credit secures them against default.[122] It is worth mentioning that some underwriters have complained that banks, by virtue of their ability to issue standby credits to support securities, have taken away business that formerly belonged to the securities industry.[123]

7. *Sale of Goods.* In a process that brings the standby credit close to the function of a commercial credit, some sellers and buyers, in order to avoid the paper problems of commercial credits, are now using a standby arrangement to support sales. Under this plan, the seller invoices the buyer directly and draws under the standby credit only if the buyer fails to honor the invoice. This "invoice credit" may be clean; that is, it may be payable against a draft alone, or it may require the beneficiary to submit the invoices and a certificate reciting that they are unpaid. Unless the buyer fails to pay the invoice, the seller-beneficiary will not draw on the credit. The credit is standby in nature. If all goes well, the issuer will never honor drafts, and there will be no document examination charges. Often those charges vary directly with the amount of the drafts, and parties dealing with large volumes of high-priced commodities are resorting to this standby credit rather than to its commercial cousin. Under the commercial credit, the seller draws on each shipment rather than in the infrequent case where the buyer fails to pay an invoice.[124] The invoice credit, a standby, can save considerable bank charges for the parties.[125]

(1983); Note, "Recent Extensions in the Use of Commercial Letters of Credit," 66 Yale L.J. 902 (1957).

[122] See Ryan, supra note 121.

[123] See "Banks Luring Underwriters From Brokers," Wall St. J., Feb. 11, 1982, at 31, col. 2.

[124] For cases involving such credits, see, e.g., Tosco Corp. v. FDIC, 723 F.2d 1242 (6th Cir. 1983); J.H. Westerbeke Corp. v. Onan Corp., 580 F. Supp. 1173 (D. Mass. 1984); Consolidated Aluminum Corp. v. Bank of Va., 544 F. Supp. 386 (D. Md. 1982), aff'd, 704 F.2d 136 (4th Cir. 1983); Roman Ceramics Corp. v. Peoples Nat'l Bank, 517 F. Supp. 526 (M.D. Pa. 1981), aff'd, 714 F.2d 1207 (3d Cir. 1983); Peoples State Bank v. Gulf Oil Corp., 446 N.E.2d 1358 (Ind. Ct. App. 1983); Easton Tire Co. v. Farmers & Merchants Bank, 642 S.W.2d 396 (Mo. Ct. App. 1982); Temple-Eastex Inc. v. Addison Bank, 672 S.W.2d 793 (Tex. 1984); see also Challenger Sales & Supply v. Haltenberger, 730 S.W.2d 453 (Tex. Ct. App. 1987) (standby securing obligations under agreement to purchase oil rigs); cf. Buckeye Cellulose Corp. v. Atlantic Mut. Ins. Co., 643 F. Supp. 1030 (S.D.N.Y. 1986) (standby credit used in connection with international sale of goods). For an example of an invoice credit, see App. C, Doc. 18. In Dubuque Packing Co. v. Fitzgibbon, 599 P.2d 440 (Okla. Ct. App. 1979), the court held, incorrectly it seems, that because an invoice credit served as a guaranty, the liability of the issuer was secondary and that the engagement was not a letter of credit.

[125] See Maulella, "Uncorking the Letter of Credit for Quicker Export Collections," Corporate Cashflow (Feb. 1989), reprinted in Letter of Credit Update 42 (Oct. 1989).

The invoice standby also can serve as a device for enhancing the value of a seller's accounts. The seller who sells on open account may ask his customers to have their banks issue invoice standby letters of credit to secure payment of the account. Because those accounts then become secured, the seller's lender usually values them more than it values unsecured accounts and is more inclined to lend at favorable rates.[126]

8. *Some Additional Imaginative Uses.* Standby credits crop up in unique situations. A standby has secured future income under an installment sale without offending the Internal Revenue Code's favorable rules on such sales.[127] One standby secured deficits under an insurance agency's retrospective profit commission contract with an insurance company.[128] Standby credits also have secured bookings made by a travel agency,[129] salary payments promised to a football player,[130] and the return of hostages.[131]

---

[126] For an example of such financing, see Emery-Waterhouse Co. v. Rhode Island Hosp. Trust Nat'l Bank, 757 F.2d 399 (1st Cir. 1985).

[127] See Sprague v. United States, 627 F.2d 1044 (10th Cir. 1980). But cf. Watson v. Comm'r, 613 F.2d 594 (5th Cir. 1980) (holding that deferred payment "package" involving standby credit did not permit farmers to defer income); J.K. Griffith v. Comm'r, 73 T.C. 933 (1980) (similar case). See generally Ledlie, "Letters of Credit or Escrow Accounts Used as Security in Installment Sale Transactions," 60 Taxes 130 (1982).

[128] See Pastor v. National Republic Bank, 76 Ill. 2d 139, 390 N.E.2d 894 (1979); cf. National Union Fire Ins. Co. v. Walton Ins. Ltd., No. 86 Civ. 8571 (SWK) (S.D.N.Y. Sept. 14, 1988) (standby securing payments under reinsurance commutation agreement); Universal Marine Ins. Co. v. Beacon Ins. Co., 581 F. Supp. 1131 (W.D.N.C. 1984) (letter of credit used to secure retrocession and reinsurance agreements); Universal Marine Ins. Co. v. Beacon Ins. Co., 577 F. Supp. 829 (W.D.N.C. 1984) (letter of credit used to secure retrocession agreement); Wisconsin Barge Line, Inc. v. INA (In re Wisconsin Barge Line, Inc.), No. 86-00016 (SE) (Bankr. E.D. Mo. May 28, 1986) (credit that secured payment of retrospective premium under marine insurance policy); Summit Ins. Co. v. Central Nat'l Bank, 624 S.W.2d 222 (Tex. Civ. App. 1981) (letter of credit used as security fund against insurance agency's obligations to insurance company under agency agreement).

[129] See Airline Reporting Corp. v. First Nat'l Bank, 832 F.2d 823 (4th Cir. 1987); Flagship Cruises, Ltd. v. New England Merchants Nat'l Bank, 569 F.2d 699 (1st Cir. 1978); Travel Comm., Inc. v. Lehane, No. 82-2543-MA (D. Mass. Feb. 28, 1984).

[130] In Beathard v. Chicago Football Club, Inc., 419 F. Supp. 1133 (N.D. Ill. 1976), the attempt failed because the credit was revocable.

[131] See Wiley, "How to Use Letters of Credit in Financing the Sale of Goods," 20 Bus. Law. 495, 496 (1965); cf. In re Tischendorf, 321 N.W.2d 405 (1982), cert. denied, 460 U.S. 1037 (1983) (use of standby to secure return of child to jurisdiction pursuant to divorced parent's visitation rights).

In the 1980s, standby credits played a significant role in tax shelter arrangements that included oil and gas exploration,[132] coal mining,[133] computer software marketing,[134] equipment acquisition,[135] and similar ventures.[136] Parties used standby credits in at least one bankruptcy reorganization to effect payments to creditors of the debtor[137] and, in another, to secure the settlement of an antitrust class-action suit.[138] Standby letters of credit are routinely used by the federal government to transfer grant funds to state entities as they need them.[139] In at least one case, a speculator used a standby to secure obligations under silver futures contracts.[140] One commentator[141] reported that letters of credit secure interest payments in interest rate swaps; another case[142] revealed the use of a standby letter of credit in lieu of the tender of cash to toll the running of interest on an obligation. An opinion of the Comptroller of the Currency[143] describes a letter of credit that secured the performance of partici-

---

[132] E.g., Warner v. Central Trust Co., 715 F.2d 1121 (6th Cir. 1983); Brown v. United States Nat'l Bank, 220 Neb. 684, 371 N.W.2d 692 (1985); GATX Leasing Corp. v. DBM Drilling Corp., 657 S.W.2d 178 (Tex. Ct. App. 1983).

[133] Kennedy v. Josepthal & Co., [1983–1984 Transfer Binder] Fed. Sec. L. Rep. (CCH) ¶ 99,653 (D. Mass. 1984).

[134] Computer Corp. of Am. v. Zarecor, 16 Mass. App. Ct. 456, 452 N.E.2d 267 (1983); Perkins v. Feit, 117 Wis. 2d 784, 345 N.W.2d 79 (Ct. App. 1984) (unpublished limited precedent op.).

[135] Berry v. Bank of La., 439 So. 2d 1166 (La. Ct. App. 1983).

[136] In Cromwell v. Commerce & Energy Bank, 450 So. 2d 1 (La. Ct. App. 1984), aff'd in part, rev'd in part, 464 So. 2d 721 (La. 1985), the limited partnership set up a "blind pool" arrangement under which the general partner could invest the partnership funds as he chose. Id. at 4.

[137] In re AOV Indus., 31 Bankr. 1005 (Bankr. D.D.C. 1983).

[138] In re Shopping Carts Antitrust Litig., 1984-1 Trade Cas. (CCH) ¶ 65,823 (S.D.N.Y. 1983); cf. Dribeck Importers, Inc. v. G. Heileman Brewing Co., No. 86 C 4901 (N.D. Ill. July 19, 1988) (similar use of standby to secure settlement agreement obligations).

[139] Lowell Consortium v. United States Dep't of Labor, 893 F.2d 432 (1st Cir. 1990); City of Kan. City v. United States Dep't of Hous. & Urban Dev., 861 F.2d 739 (D.C. Cir. 1988); see generally "Responsibilities and Liabilities Under Letter of Credit—Treasury Financial Communications System (LOC–TFCS)," 31 C.F.R. § 204.1–204.6 (1989).

[140] See Fustok v. ContiCommodity Servs., Inc., 610 F. Supp. 986 (S.D.N.Y. 1985).

[141] See Arnold, "How to Do Interest Rate Swaps," 62 Harv. Bus. Rev. 96 (1984).

[142] Geupel Constr. Co. v. Manufacturers Hanover Leasing Corp., No. C-2-83-0945 (S.D. Ohio Aug. 22, 1986).

[143] See Comptroller of the Currency, No-Objection Letter No. 86-19, [1988–1989 Transfer Binder] Fed. Banking L. Rep. (CCH) ¶ 84,025 (Oct. 30, 1986).

pants in an over-the-counter options trading arrangement. In another case, sports promoters used a letter of credit to secure their obligations under a contract with a state university to broadcast basketball games,[144] and in yet another they used a standby to secure payments to a prizefighter.[145] At least one corporation used standby credits to fund golden parachutes for its officers.[146] A standby letter of credit permitted parties to proceed with the sale of an aircraft free and clear of liens. By virtue of the standby's benefit, the lienor released its lien and permitted the sale to proceed.[147] In *Broadcasting Co. v. Flair Broadcasting Corp.*,[148] the credit amount served as liquidated damages in the event of the buyers' failure to acquire a radio station.

¶ 1.07 ACCOMPANYING DOCUMENTS

[1] Commercial Credit Documents

[a] Draft or Demand for Payment

Traditionally, the commercial credit is payable against the beneficiary's draft, which may be payable either at sight or at a given time, usually a specified number of days after "sight" or after "date." Generally, drafts are negotiable in form[149] in order to make them more attractive to the banks that deal with them. In effect, the draft (sometimes called the bill of exchange) is simply an order to pay and therefore is a specific kind of demand for payment. Some credits permit "demands for payment" — a term that is broader than "draft" and that permits a written request for payment not in the form of a negotiable draft. If the credit calls for a demand or draft, a presentation without such a document is incomplete. One court held that a credit calling for a sight draft was not satisfied by a mere request for collection.[150]

---

[144] See University of Kan. Athletic Corp. v. Security Nat'l Bank, No. 87-2116 (D. Kan. July 17, 1987); cf. Mellon Bank, N.A. v. Metro Communications, Inc. (In re Metro Communications, Inc.), 95 Bankr. 921 (Bankr. W.D. Pa. 1989) (standby used to finance debtor's purchase of broadcasting rights for college football games).

[145] Alzado v. Blinder, Robinson Co., 752 P.2d 544 (Colo. 1988).

[146] Ocilla Indus., Inc. v. Katz, 677 F. Supp. 1291 (E.D.N.Y. 1987); cf. Robert M. Bass Group v. Evans, 552 A.2d 1227 (Del. Ch. 1988) (similar use of credit).

[147] South Shore Bank v. International Jet Interiors, Inc., 721 F. Supp. 29 (E.D.N.Y. 1989).

[148] 892 F.2d 372 (4th Cir. 1989).

[149] For an example of a negotiable draft, see App. C, Doc. 4.

[150] See Bounty Trading Corp. v. S.E.K. Sportswear, Ltd., 48 A.D.2d 811, 370 N.Y.S.2d 4 (1975).

[b] Commercial Invoice

The commercial invoice is a document prepared by the seller that describes the goods. It sets forth the product charges and usually the insurance and shipping costs.[151] It is a well-established principle of letter of credit law that the description of the goods in the commercial invoice must mirror the description in the credit itself.[152] The careful seller tracks the credit language in his invoice. The purpose of the invoice and that requirement is to give the bank an express warranty from the seller that it has complied with the credit[153] but is not so much to ensure that, in fact, the seller shipped conforming goods. The seller is in complete control of the invoice and may falsify it. Such falsification gives rise, of course, to a breach of warranty on which the bank and any other interested party[154] may sue the seller, and it may constitute fraud. If the bank or the account party is concerned about the conformity of the goods shipped, and if either is willing to pay the associated costs of ensuring that compliance, or if the seller is willing to pay that cost, then the credit can stipulate that the seller must obtain an inspection certificate from an independent third party.

The description of the goods in the invoice assists in the identification of the specific credit and is a further representation by the seller that the amount of the draft is justified and that the amount of insurance coverage is adequate.

Finally, the description of the goods in the invoice serves as a benchmark for the more general descriptions of the goods in other documents. The description in these documents may be general and need not track the language of the credit. The general description in these documents, however, must not conflict with the specific description set forth in the credit.[155]

[c] Bill of Lading

The bill of lading appears often in commercial credit transactions. When it is negotiable in form,[156] as it often is, the bill stands for the

---

[151] See App. C, Doc. 5, for an example of a commercial invoice.

[152] See U.C.P. art. 41(c) (1983).

[153] See U.C.C. § 5-111. In fact, the warranty extends to the customer as well, who is clearly an "interested party."

[154] Id.

[155] See U.C.P. art. 41(c) (1983); cf. S.B. Int'l, Inc. v. Union Bank of India, 783 S.W.2d 225 (Tex. Ct. App. 1989) (applying rule).

[156] For an example of such a negotiable bill, see App. C, Doc. 6. For discussion of the diminishing role of the negotiable bill in one industry, see de May, "Bills of Lading Problems in the Oil Trade: Documentary Credit Aspects," 2 J. Energy & Nat. Resources L. 197 (1984).

goods themselves and permits those to whom the bill is duly negotiated to treat it as the equivalent of the goods. The bill gives the issuer an interest in the goods in the event of default by the issuer's customer.[157] A negotiating bank that confronts dishonor by the issuer is usually a holder to whom the bill of lading has been duly negotiated, and it can look to the goods for compensation. Finally, if all goes well, the issuer pays the beneficiary and transfers the bill to the customer. The customer then uses the bill to obtain delivery from the carrier that is obliged to deliver the goods to the holder of the bill.[158]

It is important to distinguish the proper functions of the bill of lading as described here from the notion that it serves as the carrier's guaranty that the seller has shipped conforming goods. Under efficient transport practices, carriers are not inspectors of goods shipped. They nearly always disclaim this type of warranty by using such language as "shipper's load and count."[159] These disclaimers are entirely proper and do not render the bill defective under the credit.[160]

As part of the general effort of commercial parties to reduce the amount of paper in a commercial transaction, the transport and banking industries have experimented with "paperless" bills of lading. Under one procedure, a New York bank would take a negotiable bill covering a shipment and hold it. The original and successive holders could effect transfers by notifying the custodian bank. While the object of the program (to avoid having to transfer a piece of paper that is valuable and that can be lost or destroyed rather easily) seems worthwhile, the experi-

---

[157] See U.C.C. §§ 2-506, 4-208, 7-502. For general discussion of the issuer's interest in the goods, see ¶ 8.03.

[158] See Pomerene Act, 49 U.S.C. app. § 88 (Supp. V 1987); U.C.C. §§ 7-403(1), 7-403(4).

[159] For the effect of such disclaimers, see Pomerene Act, 49 U.S.C. § 101 (1976); U.C.C. § 7-301. Because of the frequent presence of the disclaimer, one authority has suggested that payment against the bill is not payment against the goods but payment against the beneficiary's representation that he shipped the goods. See McGowan, "Assignability of Documentary Credits," 13 Law & Contemp. Probs. 666, 681 (1948); see also Murray, "History and Development of the Bill of Lading," 37 Miami L. Rev. 689 (1983) (discussing rules of federal statutes and international conventions on carrier liability for misdescription of quality or quantity of goods shipped); cf. Austracan (USA) Inc. v. Neptune Orient Lines, Ltd., 612 F. Supp. 578 (S.D.N.Y. 1985) (applying Carriage of Goods by Sea Act, 46 U.S.C. § 1303(3) (1976), which limits power of carrier to disclaim in some instances).

[160] See U.C.P. art. 32 (1983). It is also significant, of course, that carriers frequently limit their liability for damage to cargo and that those limitations are usually enforced. See, e.g., Carman Tool & Abrasives, Inc. v. Evergreen Lines, 871 F.2d 897 (9th Cir. 1989).

ment failed when the sponsoring bank abandoned it for lack of sufficient interest among commercial parties.[161]

Efforts at computerization of documents of title continue nonetheless.[162] Clearly, there are good reasons to pursue those efforts. Bills of lading are a frequent source of error in the documents that a beneficiary presents under the credit. Under the Uniform Customs[163] and under cases decided under the Code,[164] issuers must give prompt notice to beneficiaries of defects in documents. Unfortunately, many beneficiaries cannot correct a curable defect in a bill of lading (such as a missing "on board" stamp or a missing date or signature) in time to resubmit the bill prior to the credit's expiry. Amended bills of lading are difficult to obtain when the container ship is in the North Atlantic. To the extent electronic innovation facilitates quick correction of those errors, payment under credits becomes more predictable and all parties benefit.

[d] Insurance Certificate

The purpose of the insurance certificate is to provide evidence that the seller has procured insurance. In addition, the certificate usually gives the holder of the certificate rights to the insurance proceeds in the event that the goods are lost or destroyed.[165] As a rule, the insurance documents must evidence coverage from the date that the seller delivered the goods to the carrier or the date that the goods are loaded on board and must be in an amount at least as great as that of the invoice value. Matters of franchise (deductibility) and risks to be covered can be specified in the credit. In the absence of these specifications, the Uniform Customs[166] set minimum standards for such insurance documents.[167]

---

[161] For an account of that effort, see Green, "Letters of Credit and the Computerization of Maritime Trade," 3 Fla. Int'l L.J. 221 (1988).

[162] See generally Byrne, An Examination of U.C.C. Article 5 (Letters of Credit) A Report of the Task Force on the Study of U.C.C. Article 5 (American Bar Association 1989); Green, supra note 161; Merges & Reynolds, "Toward a Computerized System for Negotiating Ocean Bills of Lading," 6 J.L. & Com. 23 (1986).

[163] See U.C.P. art. 16(d) (1983).

[164] For discussion of those cases, see ¶ 6.06[1].

[165] For an example of such a certificate, see App. C, Doc. 7.

[166] For the complete version of the Uniform Customs, see App. A.

[167] See U.C.P. arts. 35–40 (1983).

[e] Consular Documents

Some countries do not permit the importation of goods without a certificate by one of its consular officials residing in the seller's country. The certificate states that the shipment satisfies certain statutory or other regulations of the importing country. A consularized or visaed invoice[168] is a copy of the invoice stamped or countersigned by the consul for the importing country. A consular invoice[169] is an invoice issued and signed by such consul, usually on an official form.

[f] Certificates of Origin and Inspection

There is no limit to the number and function of certificates that a buyer and seller may agree in their sales contract should be incorporated into the requirements of the commercial credit. Certificates of origin[170] recite that the goods originated in a specified country. These documents traditionally have guarded against the substitution of second-quality merchandise and have been used by consular officials to satisfy themselves that the goods comply with the importing country's rules. Such certificates also have been known to serve politically inspired and unlawful boycotts.[171]

Inspection certificates come in many varieties,[172] so it is important to distinguish the roles of such certificates. When their issuance and content are in the control of an independent third party, the certificates provide documentary proof of the seller's compliance with the underlying contract. When the beneficiary controls their issuance or content, they serve to create warranties by the beneficiary.

[2] Standby Credit Documents

Generally, the documents showing the noncompliance that triggers the well-drafted standby credit are far simpler than the sometimes complex documents showing the compliance that triggers the commercial credit.

---

[168] For an example of a visaed invoice, see App. C, Doc. 8.

[169] For an example of a consular invoice, see App. C, Doc. 9.

[170] For an example of a certificate of origin, see App. C, Doc. 10.

[171] Such boycotts may contravene federal law. See Export Administration Act, 50 U.S.C. app. § 2407 (1982); 15 C.F.R. § 769.2(f) (1989); see generally W. Streng & F. Pedersen, "Letters of Credit," 418 Tax Manual A-25–A-29 (1980); Note, "The Trade Embargo and the Irrevocable Letter of Credit," 1 Ariz. J. Int'l & Comp. L. 213, 226–229 (1982); Comment, "United States Banks and the Arab Boycott of Israel," 17 Colum. J. Transnat'l L. 119 (1978).

[172] For an example of an inspection certificate, see App. C, Doc. 11.

The standby credit is often clean in that the beneficiary may draw upon it without any documents to support his draft or demand for payment.[173] At other times, standby credits call for the beneficiary's certificate containing the conclusory assertion that the account party has not performed according to the contract,[174] that the account party has defaulted on a promissory note,[175] or that the sum demanded is due.[176] The summary nature of these documents reflects the right of the beneficiary to effect payment under the credit without satisfying a third party that the account party has not in fact performed. To some extent, the certificate inhibits premature or rash drawings under the credit, since a false certificate may give rise to claims for breach of warranty or fraud and to criminal sanctions.[177] The summary nature of the document, however, should not invite courts to inquire beyond its face in order to determine its truth in light of the underlying contract. That line of inquiry violates the principle that the credit is independent of the underlying transaction. Some courts, however, rely on the language of Section 5-114(2) of the Code and pursue that inquiry, thereby weakening the standby credit, especially its function of shifting costs to the account party pending the outcome of litigation.[178]

---

[173] See, e.g., Baker v. National Boulevard Bank, 399 F. Supp. 1021 (N.D. Ill. 1975); CNA Mortgage Investors, Ltd. v. Hamilton Nat'l Bank, 540 S.W.2d 238 (Tenn. Ct. App. 1975).

[174] See, e.g., Chase Manhattan Bank v. Equibank, 550 F.2d 882 (3d Cir. 1977).

[175] See, e.g., Postal v. Smith (In re Marine Distribs., Inc.), 522 F.2d 791 (9th Cir. 1975); Steinmeyer v. Warner Consol. Corp., 42 Cal. App. 3d 515, 116 Cal. Rptr. 57 (1974).

[176] See, e.g., Intraworld Indus. Inc. v. Girard Trust Bank, 461 Pa. 343, 336 A.2d 316 (1975).

[177] See United States v. Sharder, 850 F.2d 1457 (11th Cir.), cert. denied, 109 S. Ct. 326 (1988) (conviction of beneficiary of wire fraud, uttering of false bills of lading, and interstate transportation of property taken by fraud); United States v. Soo Hoo, [1987–1988 Transfer Binder] Fed. Banking L. Rep. (CCH) ¶ 87,174 (3d Cir. 1987) (conviction of party that presented false documents under letter of credit); United States v. Tucker, 773 F.2d 136 (7th Cir. 1985), cert. denied, 478 U.S. 1022 (1986) (same).

[178] For further discussion of this tendency of the courts and its harmful effect on letters of credit, see ¶ 7.04.

¶ 1.08 BACK-TO-BACK CREDIT

Although letter of credit law sometimes restricts the transfer of credits,[179] credits are generally available as security.[180] Sometimes the beneficiary uses the credit to obtain funds to pay for the goods he needs to satisfy the credit. For example, if *B*, a New York broker, has agreed to supply *F*, a Kansas City fabricator, with specialty steel, and if in the sales agreement *B* has prevailed upon *F* to cause a bank to issue a credit to *B*, then *B* may be able to use that credit to pay his own supplier, *A*, a seller in Amsterdam.

B may use the credit by assigning its proceeds to his own bank in New York. Such an assignment gives the bank a security interest in the credit,[181] and, if the bank properly notifies the issuing bank in Kansas City, the New York bank is assured of payment (but only so long as the issuing bank receives documents that comply with the credit). The New York bank, to the extent it is relying on the credit as security for advances to *B*, will be vulnerable if *B* does not satisfy the terms of the Kansas City credit.

In order to reduce that vulnerability, *B* occasionally negotiates with *F* for a credit that *A*, *B*'s Dutch supplier, can help satisfy. *B* then asks his New York bank not to give *A* cash but to open a credit in *A*'s favor that calls for documents that are critical in satisfying the original credit from the Kansas City bank. The concept is attractive to the New York bank because it then knows that it will not disburse funds until it has documents it can use to satisfy the Kansas City credit and thereby recoup its outlay. This arrangement whereby the New York bank takes an assignment of the original credit and, on the strength of the assignment, issues a second credit is called a back-to-back credit transaction.[182] The transaction requires a good measure of care by the second bank, *B*'s New York bank. Even if *A*, the Dutch supplier, properly ships conforming goods and presents conforming documents, the New York bank will not have all the documents necessary to satisfy the Kansas City credit. It

---

[179] See U.C.C. § 5-116(1); U.C.P. art. 54 (1983). For general discussion of transfer rules for letters of credit, see Chapter 10.

[180] See U.C.C. § 5-116(2); U.C.P. art. 55 (1983).

[181] See U.C.C. § 5-116(2).

[182] Sometimes there are references to the second credit as the back-to-back credit. See, e.g., Delaware Valley Factors, Inc. v. Coma Export, Inc., 530 F. Supp. 180 (E.D. Pa. 1982); Kingdom of Swed. v. New York Trust Co., 197 Misc. 431, 96 N.Y.S.2d 779 (Sup. Ct. 1949); A. Watson, Finance of International Trade 176–177 (2d ed. 1981). For a case illustrating a buyer's and a seller's use of a back-to-back credit arrangement to facilitate the financing of the sales transaction, see California Overseas Bank v. French Am. Banking Corp., 154 Cal. App. 3d 179, 201 Cal. Rptr. 400 (1984).

will not have, for example, *B*'s invoices, nor will it have *B*'s drafts, documents that are traditionally required under a commercial credit such as the one that the Kansas City bank would issue. *A*'s drafts, of course, would not comply: first, because they are drawn by *A*, not by *B*, and, second, because they probably recite that they are drawn under the New York bank's credit, not under the Kansas City bank's credit. Similarly, *A*'s invoices would undoubtedly be for the wrong amount, since *B*'s price to *F* would exceed *A*'s price to *B* and would not satisfy the requirement of the Kansas City credit calling for *B*'s invoices.

There may also be bill of lading problems. The bill of lading that *A* presents will not comply with the Kansas City credit but will permit *B* (or the New York bank if *B* defaults) to take delivery of the goods, redeliver them to a U.S. carrier, and obtain the bill needed to satisfy the Kansas City credit.

During the whole transaction, the New York bank and *B* must be mindful of the expiration date of the Kansas City credit and must draw the second credit in a way to ensure that *B* or the New York bank receives the documents in time to comply with the Kansas City credit. The New York bank must also take care that there are no amendments to the original credit that will render it impracticable for the New York bank to comply with the credit's terms. Banks issuing the second credit in a back-to-back credit transaction sometimes insist that they be asked by the issuer to confirm the prime credit. By confirming, the issuer of the second credit becomes a party to, and enjoys the right to veto, any amendment of the prime credit.[183]

¶ 1.09 REVOLVING CREDIT

In commerce, and especially in the credit industry, there are many revolving loans. Working capital loans are frequently revolving accounts, as are many kinds of consumer loans. Similarly, letters of credit can revolve. Revolving credits anticipate a continuing credit line, with the beneficiary periodically drawing on that line and the account party periodically repaying the advances. Such a credit differs from the old notion that each loan is discrete and that each loan advance requires separate evaluation of creditworthiness and collateral.

---

[183] See U.C.P. art. 10(d) (1983). For a case illustrating the problems that can result when the timing of the back-to-back credit transaction is not planned carefully, see Mineralolhandelsgesellschaft MBH & Co. ("Mebro") v. Commonwealth Oil Ref. Co. (In re Commonwealth Oil Ref. Co.), 734 F.2d 1079 (5th Cir. 1984); cf. Pro-Fab, Inc. v. Vipa, Inc., 772 F.2d 847 (11th Cir. 1985) (similar case).

While many commercial credits and standby credits arise out of a discrete transaction, some of them revolve and permit the beneficiary to draw up to a given amount during a given period. An automobile dealer, for example, may ask his bank to issue a credit to his manufacturer that permits the manufacturer to draw a certain amount each month. The credit has no total maximum and no expiry, but the issuer retains the right to terminate the credit with short notice. Under this type of credit, the account party makes periodic payments. The borrower usually maintains an account with the issuer and authorizes the issuer to debit that account as the beneficiary's drafts are paid. Some banks permit their customers to use one application and one revolving line of credit for any number of separate credits running to any number of separate beneficiaries.[184]

¶ 1.10 REVOCABLE OR IRREVOCABLE CREDIT

By definition, a letter of credit substitutes the creditworthiness of a financially strong issuer for the unknown or questionable credit reputation of the account party or customer. A revocable credit may be terminated at any time, even after the beneficiary has presented his documents for payment.[185] It is something of an anomaly, then, to speak of such revocable credits as credits at all.

Chapters 4 and 5 deal with problems that arise under these credits. It suffices to say here that revocable credits arise in three situations. Under the first come those cases in which the drafter of the credit inadvertently neglects to denominate the credit irrevocable. Under the second come those instances when the drafter deliberately misleads the beneficiary into thinking that the revocable credit carries the benefit of an irrevocable credit. In neither of these cases is the beneficiary happy with its credit, and the lesson is plain: No beneficiary who seeks a credit should take one that is not denominated irrevocable.

---

[184] For an example of an application agreement, see App. C, Doc. 14. In Venizelos, S.A. v. Chase Manhattan Bank, N.A., 425 F.2d 461 (2d Cir. 1970), the parties used a revolving credit to cover five shipments of scrap metal. The credit ran to the benefit of the shipowner but was in an amount that covered only two of the shipments. The parties agreed that until the shipper reimbursed the issuer for the first two shipments, it could not load the vessel for later shipments. Cf. Philadelphia Gear Corp. v. Central Bank, 717 F.2d 230 (5th Cir. 1983) (similar case describing use of revolving credit).

[185] See U.C.C. § 5-106(3); U.C.P. art. 9(a) (1983). The issuer may not revoke if a third party, such as a negotiating bank, has given value before notice of revocation. See U.C.C. § 5-106, comment 2 (2d sentence); U.C.P. art. 9(b) (1983).

Article 7(c) of the Uniform Customs deems revocable all credits that are not designated irrevocable. The Code rule creates no presumption[186] and thus invites litigation. In these first two situations, the credit does not serve the beneficiary well.

The third case in which revocable credits arise is that in which the parties are seeking not to substitute the credit of the bank for that of the issuer but to use the issuer as the vehicle for collecting the beneficiary's drafts. In this case, the engagement of the issuer is not really a credit, although parties may refer to it as a revocable credit. The banking industry has traditionally avoided using the term "credit" in these engagements. When banks do issue revocable credits, they usually incorporate explicit language in the undertaking disclaiming any obligation on the part of the bank to honor drafts. Banks have further distinguished the engagement from the irrevocable credit by calling it an authority to purchase or an authority to pay.

There are some credits that are neither entirely revocable nor entirely irrevocable. These are credits that are revocable, but only on certain conditions. In one case, for example, the credit was revocable upon the account party's certification that the beneficiary had breached the underlying contract.[187]

¶ 1.11 SELLER'S PROTECTION UNDER SECTION 2-325(1) OF THE CODE

Section 2-325 of the Code governs a commercial party's duty to obtain a letter of credit under a contract for the sale of goods. The section provides, among other things, for the situation in which the buyer must cause a confirmed credit to be established and stipulates that, unless the parties otherwise agree, the confirmation must come from a bank in the beneficiary's market.

In *Texas Trading & Milling Corp. v. H.I.T. Corp.*,[188] the parties disputed the meaning of the term "confirmed credit" in U.C.C. § 2-325. Traditionally, in letter of credit law a confirmation consists of the undertaking of a bank other than the issuer to honor the beneficiary's

---

[186] See U.C.C. § 5-103, comment 1. But cf. Fla. Stat. Ann. § 675.5-103(1)(a) (West 1966) (nonuniform provision stipulating that when credit is silent on revocability, issuer's undertaking is irrevocable); La. Rev. Stat. Ann. § 10:5-103(1)(a) (West 1983) (same).

[187] See Fair Pavilions, Inc. v. First Nat'l City Bank, 19 N.Y.2d 512, 227 N.E.2d 839, 251 N.Y.S.2d 23 (1967). For discussion of similar cases, see ¶ 4.08[4].

[188] No. 84 Civ. 3776 (LLS) (S.D.N.Y. Sept. 3, 1986).

drafts or demands for payment.[189] The buyer in *Texas Trading* argued, however, that the traditional rule's purpose could be satisfied by causing the credit to issue in the locale of the beneficiary. The buyer contended that the definition and comment 3 suggest that confirmation is not necessary if the issuer is in the seller's market. The *Texas Trading* court rejected that reading.

While the court recognized the validity of the argument that the provision is designed to ensure that the seller has the primary obligation of a bank in its market, it reasoned that confirmation plays an additional important commercial role in the transaction between the buyer and the seller. A seller may desire the obligation of two banks precisely because it is concerned about the possibility that the issuing bank might not honor the credit. That concern is real in the frequent case in which the issuer is the buyer's bank.

Sellers who do not insist on a confirmed credit in the sales agreement lose the protection of Section 2-325 and the *Texas Trading* reasoning. Sellers should be aware, however, that nothing in Section 2-325 or in the *Texas Trading* case gives them veto power over the buyer's selection of the issuer and the confirming bank, so long as the confirming bank is in the seller's market. Sellers desiring such power must negotiate for it in the underlying sales negotiations.[190]

---

[189] See U.C.C. § 5-103(f).

[190] For discussion of cases construing U.C.C. § 2-325(2) and discussion of the implications of that subsection for contracts and relationships related to the letter of credit transaction, see ¶¶ 9.02[5][a], 12.01[2].

CHAPTER 2

The Nature of Credits: What They Are and Are Not

¶ 2.01   THE CREDIT IS UNIQUE

There is some confusion over the exact nature of credits. They resemble a number of similar commercial devices. First, there has been some confusion between letters of credit and negotiable instruments; second, between letters of credit and guaranties; and third, occasionally, between letters of credit and lines of credit.

In the broad credit transaction itself, that is, the relationships of all three parties (account party, issuer, and beneficiary), it is important to distinguish the credit from other contracts and from the acceptance. Generally, the broad credit transaction consists of three separate relationships:

1. The relationship between the issuer and the beneficiary;
2. The relationship between the beneficiary and the account party; and
3. The relationship between the account party and the issuer.

The first is the letter of credit engagement; the second is usually called the underlying contract; and the third is called the application agreement.[1] The acceptance arises out of an acceptance credit that calls for time drafts. When the beneficiary presents these drafts, the issuer accepts them and thereby becomes liable on the acceptance, a negotiable instrument.[2] Analysis of letter of credit transactions depends on proper differentiation of these related contracts[3] and the acceptance,[4] on the one hand, and the letter of credit on the other.

---

[1] For an example of an application agreement, see App. C, Doc. 14. See also the Glossary for definitions of various letter of credit terms.

[2] See U.C.C. §§ 3-104, 3-413(1).

[3] See infra ¶ 2.08 for discussion of some of the related contracts.

[4] See infra ¶ 2.08[4].

Letter of credit law assumes that the credit will not succeed unless the credit engagement is independent of these related contracts. This rule of credit law is the independence principle, which plays a central role in letter of credit analysis.[5] In that analysis, it is crucial to understand the definition of "letter of credit" and to distinguish the credit from similar and related devices.

This inquiry into the nature of the credit, the subject of this chapter, is of more than theoretical interest. Problems in letter of credit law often arise when courts construe the credit as just another contract, albeit one with a peculiar nature.[6] Courts that fashion rules on document compliance and the fraud exception cannot adequately treat these controversial subjects without careful regard for the proper commercial functions of the credit that merit judicial protection.

It is not an accident that the drafters of Article 5 of the Uniform Commercial Code (UCC or the Code) and the drafters of the Uniform Customs and Practice for Documentary Credits (UCP or the Uniform Customs) treat credits as unique devices. Article 5 may refer to letters of credit as a type of contract,[7] but generally the Code refers to the credit as an engagement.[8] That language is redolent of negotiable instruments law[9] — a creature not of contract but of the law merchant. The Code interdicts application of offer and acceptance theory in determining whether a credit is established,[10] has its own formal requirements for credits,[11] defines special damages rules,[12] restricts transfer of interests under credits,[13] attempts to fashion unusual rules for the parties in the event of issuer insolvency,[14] and generally renders credits independent

---

[5] The independence principle is codified in U.C.C. §§ 5-109 and 5-114(1) and U.C.P. arts. 3, 4 (1983).

[6] For an egregious example of this failing, see Kerr Constr. Co. v. Plains Nat'l Bank, 753 S.W.2d 181 (Tex. Ct. App. 1987). For criticism of that case and of cases construing the credit as just another contract, see ¶ 4.08[5]. See also Exxon Co. v. Banque De Paris Et Des Pays-Bas, 889 F.2d 674 (5th Cir. 1989) (opinion in diversity case that follows *Kerr* but implicitly criticizes it).

[7] "The letter of credit is essentially a contract between the issuer and the beneficiary." U.C.C. § 5-114, comment 1.

[8] See U.C.C. § 5-102(2); U.C.C. § 5-103(1)(a) and comment U.C.C. § 1; U.C.C. § 5-107, comment 2; U,C,C. § 5-114, comments 1 (2d sent.) and 2 (2d sent.).

[9] See, e.g., U.C.C. §§ 3-414, 3-414 (using term "engages" to describe obligations of parties to negotiable instruments).

[10] See U.C.C. § 5-106.

[11] See U.C.C. § 5-104.

[12] See U.C.C. § 5-115.

[13] See U.C.C. § 5-116.

[14] See U.C.C. § 5-117.

of related contracts.[15] Perhaps most significant of all is the fact that credits do not need consideration to be binding.[16]

Similarly, the Uniform Customs take pains to render credits independent from the transactions out of which they grow. Article 3 of the Uniform Customs stipulates that "[c]redits, by their nature, are separate transactions from the sales or other contract(s) on which they may be based and banks are in no way concerned with or bound by such contract(s), even if any reference whatsoever to such contract(s) is included in the credit." Article 4 cautions that "[i]n credit operations all parties concerned deal in documents and not in goods, services and/or other performances to which the documents relate."

These legislative decisions untether the credit from contract law and bring it firmly within the realm of the law merchant.[17] Throughout this treatise that conclusion serves as a benchmark for calculating the success of letter of credit law.

¶ 2.02　FUNCTIONAL DEFINITION

A credit is an original undertaking by one party (the issuer) to substitute his financial strength for that of another (the account party),[18] with that undertaking to be conditioned on the presentation of a draft or a demand for payment and, most often, other documents.[19] The credit arises in a number of situations, but generally the account party seeks the strength of the issuer's financial integrity or reputation so that a third party (the beneficiary of the credit) will give value to the account party. The beneficiary extends that value by selling goods or services to the account party on credit, by taking the account party's negotiable paper, or by extending credit to the account party.

In letter of credit jurisprudence, it is axiomatic that the undertaking of the credit issuer be original and not derivative and that the credit un-

---

[15] See U.C.C. §§ 5-109(1), 5-109(2), 5-114(1) (generally limiting rights in credit transaction by facial conformity of documents, without regard for actual conformity of documents and without regard for realities of underlying transaction).

[16] See U.C.C. § 5-105.

[17] For an expanded explanation of this view, see Dolan, "Documentary Credit Fundamentals: Comparative Aspects," 3 Banking & Fin. L. Rev. 121 (1989).

[18] See U.C.C. § 5-103(1)(a).

[19] Undertakings that do not contain any conditions should not be treated as letters of credit, even though they are so designated. But cf. Transparent Prods. v. Paysaver Credit Union, No. 85 C 1741 (N.D. Ill. Jan. 21, 1988), aff'd on other grounds, 864 F.2d 60 (7th Cir. 1988) (treating as letter of credit undertaking designated as such that did not contain conditions).

dertaking run directly from the issuer to the beneficiary. Surety contracts and the like are not credits,[20] and generally neither are promises of the issuer that run to the account party.

Most courts refer to the credit undertaking as a contract. That terminology is unfortunate because the credit is certainly a peculiar kind of contract, and it is a cold court indeed that attempts to weather the storm of credit analysis with nothing more than general contract principles for warmth. Credits need no consideration,[21] must be in writing,[22] are peculiarly independent of contracts directly related to them,[23] are transferable only in limited circumstances,[24] have unique provisions for damages in the event of breach,[25] and generally do not lend themselves to contract rules regarding performance.[26] In short, the law does not treat them in the way it treats most contracts. It is more accurate to say that credits are sui generis and that the law of contracts supplements the law of credits only to the extent that contract principles do not interfere with the unique nature of credits.[27]

There is in some commercial circles and often in some consumer-investor circles an aura of the esoteric surrounding letters of credit. Some entrepreneurs either have misunderstood them or perhaps have used them to mislead investors. In *American National Bank v. FDIC*,[28] the court recounted a money broker's use of the credit idea that may have seduced investors into thinking they had more protection than was

---

[20] But cf. Thomas v. Jones, No. CA87-249 (Ark. Ct. App. Feb. 3, 1988) (treating as letter of credit undertaking so denominated, but one unconditionally guaranteeing payment of debt and therefore constituting secondary, not primary, undertaking).

[21] See U.C.C. § 5-105.

[22] See U.C.C. § 5-104.

[23] See U.C.C. § 5-114(1); U.C.P. arts. 3, 4 (1983); see also U.C.C. § 5-109. See also infra ¶ 2.09[5].

[24] See U.C.C. § 5-116; U.C.P. art. 54 (1983).

[25] See U.C.C. § 5-115. See also ¶ 9.02[5].

[26] See ¶¶ 6.03–6.05.

[27] Accord Tradex Petroleum Am., Inc. v. Coral Petroleum, Inc. (In re Coral Petroleum, Inc.), 878 F.2d 830 (5th Cir. 1989). The opinion in Fiat Motors of N. Am., Inc. v. Mellon Bank, N.A., 649 F. Supp. 245 (W.D. Pa. 1986), aff'd, 827 F.2d 924 (3d Cir. 1987), illustrates the kind of problem that arises when the court confuses a letter of credit with a contract. The inartful credit in the *Fiat Motors* case carried the title "Wholesale Financing Commitment" and recited that the bank's undertaking was in consideration of the beneficiary's performance of obligations in a related contract. The court acknowledged that the commitment was a letter of credit but, swayed perhaps by the contractlike terminology of the document, construed it loosely, without regard for the strict compliance rule or for the rules on amendments of credits. For further discussion of the *Fiat Motors* case, see infra ¶¶ 2.10[2][a], 5.02.

[28] 710 F.2d 1528 (11th Cir. 1983).

available to any bank depositor. The money broker apparently talked the investors into depositing funds into the broker's account at Peoples State Savings Bank in Auburn, Michigan. The bank credited the broker's account and then issued letters of credit to the investors. The broker in turn disbursed most of the funds as loans to borrowers of the bank. The letters of credit, so called, were very much like certificates of deposit. They bore interest that was payable quarterly, and the *American National Bank* opinion recites that they provided for "a final repayment of the amount invested."[29] Such an arrangement is certainly unusual, and one wonders why the parties resorted to the letter of credit form in the first place. The Michigan court treated the amount as a deposit.[30]

In *United States v. Brown*,[31] loan brokers induced investors to advance funds to purchase ICC-290 letters of credit.[32] The *Brown* court concluded that the letters of credit were a sham and upheld the trial court's conviction of Mr. Brown and his codefendant. In *Bonavire v. Wampler*,[33] promoters defrauded investors with a scheme that involved a letter of credit and a $2 billion loan by a foreign source to an American bank.[34]

The letter of credit is a remarkable merchant device that can fit many commercial transactions, but its use in these cases is suspect, and the courts properly gave little attention to the law of credits in analyzing the transactions. The lesson of the cases may be that letters of credit mystify a few merchants and more than a few investors. Letters of credit are not mysterious, however. The Code and the Uniform Customs respect the letter of credit as an invention of merchants and as a proper subject of the law merchant. In short, letters of credit are not enigmatic

---

[29] Id. at 1531.

[30] In re Peoples State Bank, 51 Mich. App. 421, 215 N.W.2d 722 (1974). For discussion of the *Peoples State Bank* case, see ¶ 12.01[4][c].

[31] 739 F.2d 1136 (7th Cir.), cert. denied sub nom. Kenngott v. United States, 469 U.S. 933 (1984).

[32] The "ICC-290" language apparently referred to International Chamber of Commerce Publication 290, the 1974 revision of the Uniform Customs. See App. B. The *Brown* court saw this reference in the title as evidence of the brokers' bad faith.

[33] 779 F.2d 1011 (4th Cir. 1985).

[34] In February 1990, the Comptroller of the Currency issued a banking circular warning of prime bank discounted letters of credit and zero coupon letters of credit. The Comptroller cautioned that such instruments "are not known to be issued by the legitimate banking community" and that "the legality of such instruments is questionable." Comptroller of the Currency, Banking Circular 243 (Feb. 7, 1990); see also "Scam Alert: Another Phony '3039' L/C," Letter of Credit Update 27 (Mar. 1990); "L/C Scam Alert: Readers Urged to Use Caution," Letter of Credit Update 24 (June 1989).

contracts; they are commercial specialties subject to ancient and well-defined rules.[35]

¶ 2.03 UNIFORM COMMERCIAL CODE DEFINITION

The UCC provides a broad definition for "letters of credit" and brings within these special rules virtually all credit transactions arising in the commercial context. First, there must be a credit, that is, an undertaking or engagement by an issuer to honor drafts or other demands for payment. Absent such engagement, the inquiry must stop. Whatever similarities a document may have to a credit, it cannot satisfy the definition in the absence of this sine qua non.

Thus, in *Boise Cascade Corp. v. First Security Bank*,[36] the court held that there was no letter of credit, because there was no engagement of the defendant bank rendering it primarily liable to the beneficiary. In the *Boise Cascade* case, the bank had executed an assignment of funds whereby it undertook to pay those funds to the plaintiff. The notion is implicit in the *Boise Cascade* opinion that the undertaking was not a credit, because the bank had agreed to pay its customer's funds, not its own funds. The bank did not engage its own credit for that of its customer.[37]

---

[35] For further discussion of the credit's origins and its nature as a commercial specialty, see ¶¶ 3.02, 3.03.

[36] 183 Mont. 378, 600 P.2d 173 (1979).

[37] Similarly, in Dodge Motor Trucks, Inc. v. First Nat'l Bank, 519 F.2d 578 (8th Cir. 1975), the court held that a bank's promise to "take care" (id. at 580) of a customer's credit needs was not a letter of credit, because it did not constitute a promise to pay the plaintiff anything. A significant element of the letter of credit definition was missing. See also Transparent Prods. Corp. v. Paysaver Credit Union, 864 F.2d 60 (7th Cir. 1988) (holding that document denominated as letter of credit was not credit in absence of engagement to do anything); Johnston v. State Bank, 195 N.W.2d 126 (Iowa 1972) (same); Shogyo Int'l Corp. v. First Nat'l Bank, 475 So. 2d 425 (Miss. 1985) (holding that bank's letter to effect that its customer had made financial arrangements with it to purchase goods at quoted terms was not letter of credit); Western Petroleum Co. v. First Bank Aberdeen, N.A., 367 N.W.2d 773 (S.D. 1985) (holding that bank's letter to effect that it would guarantee addressee's invoices to bank's customer was not letter of credit, because undertaking was secondary); BA Commercial Corp. v. Hynutek, Inc., 705 S.W.2d 713 (Tex. Ct. App. 1986) (holding that guaranty of payment was not letter of credit and therefore was not subject to rule of strict compliance regarding beneficiary's documents and application of expiry); cf. Mead Corp. v. Farmers & Citizens Bank, 14 Ohio Misc. 163, 232 N.E.2d 431 (C.P. 1967) (pre-Code case holding that parties' intent plays role in determining whether bank's undertaking is letter of credit).

If there is such an engagement, Article 5 of the Code and its letter of credit rules, rather than the law of surety or general contract principles, apply only if the engagement also satisfies the further requirements of Section 5-102. That section divides credits into two classes: those that automatically fall within the letter of credit article and those that come within the article because the issuer conspicuously designates the undertaking as a letter of credit.

The Code's automatic provision stipulates that any credit issued by a bank comes within the scope of Article 5 if the credit calls for a documentary draft or a documentary demand for payment. Nonbank credits automatically fall under Article 5 only if they call for a draft or a demand accompanied by a document of title, such as a bill of lading. Article 5 leaves outside its provisions those nonbank credits that do not call for a document of title and do not conspicuously state that they are letters of credit. Also left out of its provisions are bank credits that do not call for any documents at all and that are not conspicuously designated as letters of credit.[38]

In *Midstates Excavating, Inc. v. Farmers & Merchants Bank & Trust Co.*,[39] the defendant bank executed a document denominated as a letter of credit that was supposed to operate in lieu of a payment bond on a tribal construction project. The letter did not engage to pay a draft or a demand for payment and did not state any conditions. It did indicate that it was contingent on the understanding that the issuer would receive the proceeds from the construction project and recited that the amount of the credit represented payment in full under the project. The court construed the issuer's undertaking in light of extrinsic evidence that it took to be proof of the parties' intent and concluded that suppliers should be able to recover from the bank, although they were not mentioned in the letter. That result may have been correct under the circumstances, but it is difficult to fashion any argument to support the view that the undertaking was a letter of credit, and the case should not stand as authority on questions of a letter of credit issuer's liability.[40] The critical first element of Article 5's credit definition, an engagement to pay, was missing from the undertaking in *Midstates Excavating*.

---

[38] In In re Kem Solv, Inc., No. 84-5495 (E.D. Pa. Mar. 18, 1985), the court held that a cablegram stating that a bank would issue a standby letter of credit in a certain amount for one year was not a letter of credit, because it did not so designate itself and did not call for the production of documents.

[39] 410 N.W.2d 190 (S.D. 1987).

[40] For discussion of the rights of nonbeneficiaries under letters of credit, see ¶ 1.05.

In *Security Finance Group, Inc. v. Northern Kentucky Bank & Trust Co.,*[41] the issuer argued that because the issuer did not have any consideration from or any contract with its customer, the nominal account party, the issuer's undertaking to honor demands for payment accompanied by documents was not a letter of credit. The court in *Security Finance Group* properly rejected that argument. There is nothing in the Code's definitional section to suggest a need for a contract of reimbursement or consideration from the account party to render the issuer's undertaking a letter of credit. Reasonable expectations and sound commercial policy support the Code definition on that point. If an undertaking meets the Code's definition, commercial parties should be able to rely on an issuer's engagement without investigating the relationship between the issuer and its customer, the account party.[42]

In a number of cases involving foreign buyers of American products, especially buyers in the Middle East, the buyer insists on a guaranty letter to secure, for example, the return of its down payment or the seller's performance.[43] For a number of reasons, the buyer insists that the guaranty letter be issued by a bank local to the buyer. That bank, a foreign bank, will not issue the guaranty letter without the security of a letter of credit issued to it by an American bank. International commercial parties usually distinguish the guaranty letter from the letter of credit, but the guaranty and the standby letter of credit are similar. Commentators have gone to some lengths to compare the two,[44] and, in *American National Bank & Trust Co. v. Hamilton Industries Interna-*

---

[41] 858 F.2d 304 (6th Cir.), clarified, 875 F.2d 529 (6th Cir. 1988).

[42] The bank issuer in the *Security Finance Group* case may have been relying on the general rule that it is an unsound banking practice for a bank to issue a credit when it does not have a right of reimbursement. See Comptroller of the Currency, Interpretive Ruling, 12 C.F.R. § 7.7016 (1989). That argument fails for two reasons. First, as the *Security Finance Group* court noted, U.C.C. § 5-114(3) gives the issuer a statutory right of reimbursement unless the parties agree otherwise. Second, in the event an issuer exceeds its authority, courts have held generally that such conduct does not give the issuer a ground to escape from liability on its undertaking. See generally ¶ 12.02[2].

[43] For discussion of some of these cases, see ¶ 7.04[4][e].

[44] See Kozolchyk, "Bank Guarantees and Letters of Credit: Time for a Return to the Fold," 11 U. Pa. Int'l J. Bus. L. 1 (1989); Wheble, "'Problem Children'—Stand-By Letters of Credit and Simple First Demand Guarantees," 24 Ariz. L. Rev. 301 (1982); cf. International Chamber of Commerce, Uniform Rules for Contract Guarantees, ICC Pub. No. 325 (1978); Ellinger, "Performance Bonds, First-Demand Guarantees and Standby Letters of Credit—A Comparison," Letters of Credit Report 1 (May/June 1987); Giger, "Problems of Bank Guarantee Abuse in Swiss Law," 2 Ariz. J. Int'l & Comp. L. 38 (1987); Stoufflet, "Recent Developments in the Law of International Bank Guarantees in France and Belgium," 2 Ariz. J. Int'l & Comp. L. 48 (1987).

tional, Inc.,[45] the court held that a guaranty letter was a letter of credit for the purposes of Article 5 of the Code.[46]

In *Wyle v. Bank Melli,*[47] however, an Iranian port authority rejected a letter of credit that called for documentation and insisted on a simple-demand guaranty.[48] The port authority's rejection of the credit may have rested on the credit's documentary conditions rather on than any notion that the credit per se was inferior to a guaranty. The port authority wanted a primary guaranty that was clean, that is, one that was payable against the authority's demand alone, without supporting documentation. This kind of primary guaranty, a simple-demand or first-demand guaranty, is in the nature of a clean credit.

To the extent that a first-demand guaranty or a letter of guaranty is the primary obligation of the issuer, independent of the underlying transaction and payable against the submission of documents, it may in fact be a standby credit. Application of Article 5 to such an undertaking is appropriate. To the extent that a guaranty is a secondary obligation that is payable not against documents but against factual determinations, application of Article 5 is not appropriate, the undertaking being a clear departure from the Code's definition as modified by the *Wichita* requirement discussed later in this chapter.[49]

---

[45] 583 F. Supp. 164 (N.D. Ill. 1984), rev'd on other grounds sub nom. Banque Paribas v. Hamilton Indus. Int'l, Inc., 767 F.2d 380 (7th Cir. 1985); cf. Egyptian Am. Bank, S.A.E. v. United States, No. 88-1220 (Fed. Cir. Sept. 21, 1988) (unpublished limited precedent opinion treating guaranty letter as standby letter of credit).

[46] For further authority that a performance guaranty is similar to a letter of credit and subject to letter of credit rules, see Esal (Commodities) Ltd. v. Oriental Credit Ltd., [1985] 2 Lloyd's Rep. 546 (C.A.); Edward Owen Eng'g Ltd. v. Barclays Bank Int'l Ltd., [1978] 1 All E.R. 976 (C.A.).

[47] 577 F. Supp. 1148 (N.D. Cal. 1983).

[48] In Spier v. Calzaturificio Tecnica S.p.A., No. 86 Civ. 3447 (CSH) (S.D.N.Y. Sept. 7, 1988), the court rejected a guaranty letter issued by an Italian bank but accepted a standby issued by a New York bank in determining which would be adequate security under an arbitration statute. The *Spier* court was unwilling to accept the guaranty letter because the letter would have been subject to Italian law, while the standby would have been subject to the law of New York.

[49] See infra ¶ 2.05. The International Chamber of Commerce (ICC) has adopted rules for contract guarantees. These guaranties are not first-demand guaranties but secondary obligations that are not akin to standby letters of credit. See International Chamber of Commerce, Uniform Rules for Contract Guarantees, ICC Pub. No. 325 (1978). Those rules do not cover the first-demand guaranty. Id. at 9. In 1988, the International Chamber of Commerce issued a draft of proposed rules for first-demand guaranties. See UNCITRAL, Report of the Secretary General, "Stand-By Letters of Credit and Guarantees," A/CN.9/301 (Mar. 21, 1988); Rowe, "Bank Guarantees: Rules Changes Proposed," 7 Int'l Fin. L. Rev. 36 (1988). The process of considering the ICC rules for first-demand guaranties continues. See generally UNCITRAL, Report of the Working Group on International Contract Practices on the Work of its

¶ 2.04   THE DOCUMENTARY DRAFT AND THE DOCUMENTARY DEMAND FOR PAYMENT

The drafters of the Code apparently intended to give the broadest meaning to the terms "documentary draft" and "documentary demand for payment" in order to bring automatically within Article 5 any bank credit conditioned on the presentation "of any piece of paper" with the draft or the demand for payment. Section 5-103(1)(b) states the requirement that the draft or demand be accompanied by a document and that such requirement is satisfied if the document consists of "any paper."[50]

Traditionally, in commercial law, a "documentary draft" is a draft accompanied by a document of title, usually a bill of lading or sometimes a warehouse receipt.[51] Article 4 of the Code refers to that traditional definition.[52] The classic commercial letter of credit transaction grew out of the traditional documentary draft transaction.[53] The use of the term "documentary draft" in the scope provision of Section 5-102(1) and in the definitional provision of Section 5-103(1) serves to bring this traditional credit automatically within the ambit of Article 5. The scope and definitional provisions taken together also extend the automatic rule to bank credits calling for drafts or demands that are accompanied by pieces of paper other than a document of title.

The draft referred to here, of course, is a negotiable instrument generally governed by Article 3.[54] Many credits do not call for such drafts. In order to make it clear that a negotiable order to pay is not an absolute prerequisite for an Article 5 letter of credit, the scope provision also refers to "demands for payment." Again, the automatic scope rules of Section 5-102(1) require that the demand for payment be documentary, that is, that it be accompanied by a piece of paper if a bank issues the

---

Twelfth Session, A/CN.9/316 (Dec. 12, 1988); Dolan, "Efforts at International Standardization of Bank Guarantees," 4 Banking & Fin. L. Rev. 237 (1990); Kozolchyk, "Bank Guarantees and Letters of Credit: Time for a Return to the Fold," 11 U. Pa. J. Int'l Bus. L. 1 (1989).

[50] See U.C.C. § 5-102, comment 1 (1st para., last sentence).

[51] For a discussion of the documentary draft transaction, see ¶ 1.01[2]. See also Farnsworth, "Documentary Drafts Under the Uniform Commercial Code," 84 Banking L.J. 189 (1967), reprinted in 22 Bus. Law. 479 (1967).

[52] Section 4-104(1)(f) provides: "'Documentary draft' means any negotiable or non-negotiable draft with accompanying documents, securities or other papers to be delivered against honor of the draft."

[53] See ¶ 1.01[2].

[54] See U.C.C. § 3-104.

credit and by a document of title if a nonbank issues it. There is nothing in the section, however, to suggest that the demand itself must be in writing. In fact, the comment to Section 5-102 suggests the contrary.[55]

While courts generally give full rein to this automatic scope provision of Section 5-102(1), they do not always differentiate between the traditional documentary draft and the piece of paper rule set out in the section. A bank credit calling for a draft accompanied by a bill of sale,[56] by a receipt and a signed statement of default,[57] by an invoice and a bill of sale,[58] or by a certificate[59] satisfies the documentary draft requirement of Section 5-102(1)(a).

In *First American National Bank v. Alcorn, Inc.*,[60] the court found that a demand for payment and an invoice constituted a documentary draft. In *O'Grady v. First Union National Bank*,[61] the court held that a credit vaguely calling for copies "of each instrument causing this establishment of credit to Thomas O'Grady to be called upon"[62] satisfied either the documentary draft definition or the documentary demand for payment definition. *O'Grady* suggests that the demand need not be in writing.

In *Housing Securities, Inc. v. Maine National Bank*,[63] the bank credit was payable "against a 'written notice' to the bank, accompanied by the original of the letter of credit,"[64] and the court held that the letter did not involve a documentary demand. The court reasoned that in order to satisfy the statutory definition of "documentary demand" in Section 5-103(1)(b), the demand must be accompanied by a document that

---

[55] "Paragraph (1)(a) is applicable to banks and states that whenever the promise to honor is conditioned on presentation of any piece of paper, the transaction is within this Article." U.C.C. § 5-102, comment 1 (1st para., 6th sentence). For the view that Section 5-102 calls for a demand for payment that is itself documentary, see J. Byrne, An Examination of U.C.C. Article 5 (Letters of Credit): A Report of the Task Force on the Study of U.C.C. Article 5 (American Bar Association 1989).

[56] Marfa Nat'l Bank v. Powell, 512 S.W.2d 356 (Tex. Civ. App. 1974).

[57] Intraworld Indus. Inc. v. Girard Trust Bank, 461 Pa. 343, 336 A.2d 316 (1975).

[58] Toyota Indus. Trucks U.S.A., Inc. v. Citizens Nat'l Bank, 611 F.2d 465 (3d Cir. 1979).

[59] American Coleman Co. v. Intrawest Bank, 887 F.2d 1382 (10th Cir. 1989); East Bank v. Dovenmuehle, Inc., 196 Colo. 422, 589 P.2d 1361 (1978).

[60] 361 So. 2d 481 (Miss. 1978).

[61] 296 N.C. 212, 250 S.E.2d 587 (1978).

[62] Id. at 229, 250 S.E.2d at 599.

[63] 391 A.2d 311 (Me. 1978).

[64] Id. at 319.

is evidentiary in nature, such as a "document of title, security, invoice, certificate, notice of default and the like."[65] Because the notice called for by the credit in *Housing Securities* did not have any evidentiary value, the court held that it was not a document of the kind Section 5-103(1)(b) requires.

Arguably, the *Housing Securities* court adopted a too narrow construction of the term "document," one that the opinion acknowledged is in conflict with the reference in Section 5-102, comment 1, to "any piece of paper." The holding probably would take out of the automatic scope provision many standby credits that the drafters would have preferred to include. *Housing Securities* is certainly a minority view, but the case appears to align itself with the trend of holding that the demand, as opposed to the documents that accompany it, need not be in writing. The significance of the court's holding is further diminished by the fact that the court ultimately applied Article 5 by invoking the "conspicuous" rule of Section 5-102(1)(c).[66] Similarly, in *Travis Bank & Trust v. State*,[67] the court held that a credit calling for a draft alone was not one that satisfied the documentary draft definition of Section 5-103(1)(b), although the credit did come under the "conspicuously entitled" rule of Section 5-102(1)(c).

In *Bank of North Carolina, N.A. v. Rock Island Bank*,[68] the court found a promissory note to be a documentary demand for payment. Significantly, the issuer's engagement in the *Rock Island Bank* case was to purchase the promissory note. The credit required the beneficiary's notice of intent to sell the note to the issuer but did not require a demand for payment. The bank's engagement used the word "credit" in the final paragraph, wherein the bank employed traditional letter of credit terminology.[69] However, the court did not consider whether the term "credit" in that traditional context satisfies the rule of Section 5-102(1)(c) that a credit which "conspicuously states that it is a letter of credit" comes within Article 5.

In general, the automatic rule of Section 5-102(1)(a) may snare unwary bankers. Courts do not seem reluctant to give the terms "documentary draft" and "documentary demand for payment" a liberal reading. The *Rock Island Bank* court did not overreach when it construed

---

[65] Id. at 318 n.9.

[66] For a discussion of the "conspicuous" requirement, see infra ¶ 2.07.

[67] 660 S.W.2d 851 (Tex. Ct. App. 1983).

[68] 570 F.2d 202 (7th Cir. 1978).

[69] The bank had used customary negotiation credit language. For the definition of a "negotiation credit," see the Glossary. For an example of a negotiation credit, see App. C, Doc. 16.

the presentation of the note as a documentary demand, especially since the written notice of intent to "sell" preceded it.

In *New Jersey Bank v. Palladino*,[70] however, the majority held, with little discussion, that a bank's commitment to assume the promissory note obligation of its customer upon notice that the note had not been paid was a letter of credit subject to the rules of Article 5. The court so held even though, as the dissenting opinion points out,[71] the commitment did not stipulate that the notice be in writing and even though there was no other "paper" involved. The majority held, without explanation, that the parties, "who were sophisticated businessmen and bankers,"[72] knew that a default notice must be in writing.

The *Palladino* case probably stretches the automatic rule of Section 5-102(1)(a) beyond its intended limit. That case, along with the *Rock Island Bank* case, reflects the unwillingness of courts to permit a commercial bank to escape the rule. It is significant that in both *Palladino* and *Rock Island Bank* the banks would have benefited from a holding that the letter was not a credit subject to Article 5. In both cases, the defendant banks argued that the undertaking was a guaranty contract subject to the ultra vires defense. Both courts sidestepped the ultra vires issue[73] by characterizing the bank obligation as a credit within the Article 5 definition and therefore as a proper exercise of the bank's corporate powers.

In *BA Commercial Corp. v. Hynutek, Inc.*,[74] the issuer of an engagement denominated "Guaranty of Payment" argued that the guaranty was a letter of credit subject to the rule of strict compliance on presentation of documents and strict enforcement of the expiry provision. The court held that the guaranty was not a letter of credit. It was not issued by a bank, was not designated a letter of credit, and did not call for a document of title. The guaranty did call for a written notice of demand, but the court held that such notice was not a document of title. The court concluded that because the undertaking fell outside the scope provision, neither Article 5 nor the law of letters of credit applied. The strict compliance rule, being peculiar to letter of credit law, the court ruled, was not available to the guarantor.

---

[70] 77 N.J. 33, 389 A.2d 454 (1978).
[71] Id. at 51, 389 A.2d at 463.
[72] Id. at 46, 389 A.2d at 461.
[73] See ¶ 12.02 for a discussion of the ultra vires question.
[74] 705 S.W.2d 713 (Tex. Ct. App. 1986).

¶ 2.05 THE *WICHITA* REQUIREMENT

A disposition to prevent a bank from avoiding liability similar to that evident in the *Palladino* and *Rock Island Bank* cases[75] may have prompted the Court of Appeals for the Ninth Circuit to add a requirement to the Code's "letter of credit" definition. In a remarkable decision in which it applied the Code prospectively,[76] the court held that a bank's undertaking expressly and conspicuously denominated as a letter of credit was not a credit and was not subject to the law of credits in Article 5.

[1] The *Wichita* Case

In *Wichita Eagle & Beacon Publishing Co. v. Pacific National Bank*,[77] the defendant bank issued an engagement denominated as a letter of credit to support the performance of a tenant's obligation to construct a parking garage. Among other things, the lease required the tenant to exercise diligence in obtaining a building permit and to construct the garage within certain time limits.[78] The engagement undertook to pay $250,000 to the lessors in the event that the tenant did not comply with the lease terms.

Significantly, the bank's undertaking did not rest on the presentation of documents, but rather on the occurrence or nonoccurrence of certain conditions.[79] These conditions included a showing that the tenant "has failed to perform the terms and conditions of paragraph IV(a) of the lease."[80] The bank's engagement also stipulated that it would expire if the city refused to issue a building permit and if the tenant accepted that refusal as final. The district court found that the permit did not issue for the reason that the tenant had not pursued it diligently.

---

[75] For discussion of those cases, see supra ¶ 2.04.

[76] The California legislature had adopted the Code, but it was not effective at the time the facts of the case developed.

[77] 493 F.2d 1285 (9th Cir. 1974).

[78] Most of the facts related in the text come from the opinion of the U.S. District Court, which the Ninth Circuit reversed but to which the Ninth Circuit referred on factual questions. See Wichita Eagle & Beacon Publishing Co. v. Pacific Nat'l Bank, 343 F. Supp. 332 (N.D. Cal. 1971), rev'd, 493 F.2d 1285 (9th Cir. 1974).

[79] Because of the fact that the credit was not payable on the presentation of documents, a national bank that issued a similar credit today would violate the sound-banking guidelines of the Office of the Comptroller of the Currency. See 12 C.F.R. § 7.7016 (1989).

[80] Wichita Eagle & Beacon Publishing Co. v. Pacific Nat'l Bank, 343 F. Supp. 332, 340 (N.D. Cal. 1971), rev'd, 493 F.2d 1255 (9th Cir. 1974).

The issuer apparently argued that the document was not a letter of credit but a guaranty subject to contract principles. The district court rejected the bank's characterization of the undertaking and held that the document was a letter of credit. Pre-Code California law governed. The court looked to Section 5-102(1) for guidance but refused to place great weight on the rule of subsection (c), which automatically brings within Article 5 a document that conspicuously states that it is a letter of credit. That rule, the court held, is designed to permit banks and other issuers of credits to bring within Article 5 clean credits,[81] or other credits that do not involve documents of title,[82] situations that the court felt did not describe the transaction in *Wichita.*

The trial court held, nonetheless, in part because of the parties' manifest intent and in part on the theory that the Article 5 definition is not meant to be restrictive, that the document was a credit. The court, however, refusing to apply the Article 5 damages rule, gave judgment not for the face amount of the dishonored draft as Section 5-115(1) suggests, but for that amount minus benefits the beneficiaries realized from the defendant's default.[83]

The Court of Appeals for the Ninth Circuit reversed on the damages question, not on the theory that the district court had misapplied Section 5-115(1) but on the theory that the document was a guaranty contract as the issuer had argued, not a letter of credit. The Ninth Circuit went on to hold, as the issuer surely did not argue, that the $250,000 designated in the letter was part of a liquidated damages clause that was reasonable under the circumstances and therefore fully enforceable.

The issuer had apparently contended, on appeal, that because the district court had found the document to be a letter of credit, the Ninth Circuit should hold that the credit was independent of the underlying lease and that the credit terminated upon the failure of the city to issue a building permit, the tenant's lack of diligence notwithstanding. The Ninth Circuit clearly did not accept that theory. By finding the document to be a guaranty, that court avoided the effect of the independence principle and was able to hold that the guaranty was subject to the terms of the underlying lease. The lease imposed the duty on the tenant to pur-

---

[81] See the Glossary for the definition of "clean credit." At least one writer suggests that the clean credit the Code drafters had in mind when they fashioned Section 5-102(1)(c) was the standby credit, which had just begun to develop. See Wiley, "How to Use Letters of Credit in Financing the Sale of Goods," 20 Bus. Law. 495, 503 (1965).

[82] See also U.C.C. § 5-102, comment 1 (2d para.) (supporting court's position).

[83] For discussion of the question of damages for wrongful dishonor of a draft drawn under a credit, see ¶ 9.02[5].

sue the permit diligently. The court held that duty to be a prerequisite to the provision in the bank's letter providing for expiration of the bank's engagement on the permit's nonissuance. Since the tenant did not pursue the permit diligently, the court held, the engagement did not expire and therefore the bank should pay the lessor.

[2] The *Wichita* Rationale and Nondocumentary Conditions

It is important to emphasize the *Wichita* court's stated reason for holding the document to be a guaranty contract and not a letter of credit. The bank's promise did not operate on the presentation of pieces of paper but on factual preconditions that were difficult to ascertain. The court reasoned that this undertaking strayed "too far from the basic purpose of letters of credit, namely, providing a means of assuring payment cheaply by eliminating the need for the issuer to police the underlying contract."[84] The court concluded that "it would hamper rather than advance the extension of the letter of credit concept to new situations if an instrument such as this were held to be a letter of credit."[85]

Generally, the expiration term of a credit should be construed independently of the underlying contract (in this case, a lease). By holding that the engagement was not a credit, the *Wichita* court was able to look at the lease. Significantly, the bank's undertaking in *Wichita* was described as a letter of credit, and the beneficiaries signed a copy of the document that stated, "Terms of the above Letter of Credit are accepted."[86]

Clearly, the document in *Wichita* contained provisions that should not appear in a credit. The *Wichita* court was correct in recognizing that a bank issuer's duty to pay should depend on the conformity of documents, not on the occurrence or nonoccurrence of conditions such as the issuance of a building permit, timely construction of a circular ramp garage, or the performance of a lease. Credits, especially standby credits, may secure such activity, but they operate on the issuer's examination of certificates or affidavits reciting such facts, not on the issuer's factual investigation. This poorly drafted credit prompted the court to add to

---

[84] Wichita Eagle & Beacon Publishing Co. v. Pacific Nat'l Bank, 493 F.2d 1285, 1286 (9th Cir. 1974).

[85] Id. Banks are wholly unfitted to perform the investigative function of determining whether the beneficiary has complied with the underlying transaction. Esal (Commodities) Ltd. v. Oriental Credit Ltd., [1985] 2 Lloyd's Rep. 546, 549 (C.A.).

[86] Wichita Eagle & Beacon Publishing Co. v. Pacific Nat'l Bank, 343 F. Supp. 332, 343 (app.) (N.D. Cal. 1971), rev'd, 493 F.2d 1285 (9th Cir. 1974).

the definition of Section 5-102(1)(c) a requirement that renders the scope rule imprecise.

Thus, the *Wichita* opinion imposes a requirement in addition to those of Section 5-102 for engagements to fall within the scope of Article 5. Under this requirement, the credit may not stray too far from the basic purpose of letters of credit. Taken together, the *Rock Island Bank*, *Palladino*, and *Wichita* cases suggest that courts are reluctant to apply the scope provision of Article 5 mechanically but look to the purpose of Section 5-102(1).

It is tempting to read the *Wichita* rule as one prohibiting nondocumentary conditions. That explanation may be too facile, however. Often credits contain references to factual conditions. A credit might recite that shipment must occur not later than May 1, 1990, for example. If the credit does not otherwise call for a document showing shipment on or before that date, the condition is factual and runs afoul of the notion that *Wichita* forbids nondocumentary conditions. In this case, however, the payor bank might transform the condition into a documentary condition by paying against a document showing shipment on or before the specified date, even though the credit did not call for that document.[87] In another common case, a credit might forbid transshipment of the goods subject to the underlying contract. That condition may well be factual, but as a matter of practice[88] that condition alone does not prevent payor banks from paying over documents indicating that transshipment was possible.

These examples illustrate actual practice of international bank letter of credit departments, and it probably is a disservice to the international banking industry to read *Wichita* as forbidding such practices, especially when, as in the latter example, the practice is codified in the industry's published standards.

A fair reading of *Wichita*, then, may prohibit only those nondocumentary conditions that cause the payor bank to stray too far from the essential purposes of the credit during the payment process. While the line which that reading of *Wichita* fashions is not always clear, it may serve the letter of credit industry better than a clear line such as one that

---

[87] For authority suggesting that foreign courts sometimes require issuers to obtain documentary evidence to show satisfaction of nondocumentary conditions, see Doise, "Recent Legal Developments in France Regarding Documentary Credits and Bank Guarantees," Letters of Credit Report 7 (Mar./Apr. 1989). For an example of such a case, see Banque De L'Indochine Et De Suez S.A. v. J.H. Rayner (Mincing Lane) Ltd., [1983] 1 Lloyd's Rep. 228 (C.A.). See also Universal Sav. Ass'n v. Killeen Sav. & Loan Ass'n, 757 S.W.2d 72 (Tex. Ct. App. 1988) (contending that payor banks should accept documentary proof of some nondocumentary conditions).

[88] See U.C.P. art. 29 (1983).

invalidates all credits that call for nondocumentary conditions. That reading does not conflict with case law refusing to apply letter of credit rules to credits that stray too far.[89] That reading is not consistent with other cases, however, which go too far in applying credit rules to engagements that do stray too far.[90]

[3] Documents Signed by the Account Party

In *Banco Nacional De Desarrollo v. Mellon Bank, N.A.*,[91] the credit called for a document to be signed by the account party. The beneficiary argued that under the *Wichita* rule such a requirement rendered the un-

---

[89] See, e.g., Calumet Nat'l Bank v. First Nat'l Bank, No. 83 C 2141 (N.D. Ill. Aug. 19, 1983) (holding that guaranties could not come within Section 5-103(1)(a) definition of "letter of credit," because they were subject to nondocumentary conditions (i.e., passage of time and nonsale of real estate parcels)); Mayhill Homes Corp. v. Family Fed. Sav. & Loan Ass'n, 324 S.E.2d 340 (S.C. Ct. App. 1984) (suggesting that contract law, not letter of credit law, should apply to thrift's engagement to pay against factual conditions); Western Petroleum Co. v. First Bank Aberdeen, N.A., 367 N.W.2d 773 (S.D. 1985) (refusing to treat secondary obligation as letter of credit); Gunn-Olson-Stordahl Joint Venture v. Early Bank, 748 S.W.2d 316 (Tex. Ct. App. 1988) (refusing to apply letter of credit law to undertaking to pay on condition that beneficiary was in "substantial compliance" with terms of underlying contract).

[90] See Transparent Prods. v. Paysaver Credit Union, No. 85 C 1741 (N.D. Ill. Jan. 21, 1988), aff'd on other grounds, 864 F.2d 60 (7th Cir. 1988) (granting letter of credit treatment to credit union engagement designated as letter of credit but containing no conditions and no expiry); Newvector Communications, Inc. v. Union Bank, 663 F. Supp. 252 (D. Utah 1987) (holding that credit rules apply to undertaking calling for "draft(s) as per Resellers Agreement"); Guilford Pattern Works, Inc. v. United Bank, 655 F. Supp. 378 (D. Colo. 1987) (credit payable against beneficiary's satisfaction of delivery terms in underlying contract); Offshore Trading Co. v. Citizens Nat'l Bank, 650 F. Supp. 1487 (D. Kan. 1987) (credit that became void upon failure of beneficiary to have another credit issue within five banking days of issuance of first credit); Bank of the Southeast v. Jackson, 413 So. 2d 1091 (Ala. 1982) (applying letter of credit rules to engagement calling for documentation of numerous facts, without specifying documents); Raiffeisen-Zentralkasse Tirol v. First Nat'l Bank, 36 U.C.C. Rep. Serv. (Callaghan) 254 (Colo. Ct. App. 1983) (applying letter of credit principles to engagement subject to conditions that were not documentary); Sherwood & Roberts, Inc. v. First Sec. Bank, 682 P.2d 149 (Mont. 1984) (applying Article 5 definition of "credit" to engagement so denominated but subject to factual, as opposed to documentary, conditions); CNA Mortgage Investors, Ltd. v. Hamilton Nat'l Bank, 540 S.W.2d 238 (Tenn. Ct. App. 1975) (containing dictum to effect that parties may incorporate underlying contract into letter of credit by reference). For a case holding that the *Raiffeisen-Zentralkasse* case was not persuasive authority, because it did not include the language of the credit in the opinion, and that a nondocumentary condition could be satisfied by documentary certification, see Universal Sav. Ass'n v. Killeen Sav. & Loan Ass'n, 757 S.W.2d 72 (Tex. Ct. App. 1988).

[91] 726 F.2d 87 (3d Cir. 1984).

dertaking a guaranty and that it violated the language of Section 5-114(1), which prohibits the issuer from rendering the credit subject to the issuer's own satisfaction with the documents.[92] The *Mellon Bank* court rejected that argument, which it saw as carrying the *Wichita* requirement too far. *Wichita* teaches that the "letter of credit" definition is not satisfied if the terms of the credit stray from the purpose of the credit by virtue of the fact that the credit's conditions are subject to complex factual determinations rather than the examination of documents. The beneficiary in the *Mellon Bank* case saw an issuer's engagement that was conditioned on a document completely in the hands of the account party to be a similar, and therefore fatal, departure from the purpose of a credit, rendering the engagement something other than a credit.

The *Mellon Bank* court's rejection of the beneficiary's appeal to *Wichita*, as well as its appeal to the language in Section 5-114(1), is persuasive. The *Wichita* court imposed a requirement that the credit's engagement to pay drafts turn on documentary conditions, reasoning that the credit does not work if the issuer must investigate facts instead of documents. Factual investigation interrupts the prompt payment feature that is unique to, and essential for, the credit. By the same token, the Section 5-114(1) rule nullifying any term in the credit that permits the issuer to reserve the right to reject documents that it finds unsatisfactory is designed to protect the beneficiary's expectation that if it complies with the credit's documentary requirements, the issuer will pay.

Wichita and Section 5-114(1) guard the certainty and prompt payment features of the credit. A provision in the credit calling for a document to be signed by the account party offends neither of those features. If the beneficiary supplies the document, the issuer can pay promptly. If the beneficiary does not supply it, he can assume that the issuer will dishonor. Although *Wichita* may introduce legal uncertainty into the scope provision, the requirement does not introduce factual uncertainties or delays into the document examination process.[93]

---

[92] "Attempts by the issuer to reserve a right to dishonor by including a clause that all documents must be satisfactory to itself are declared invalid as essentially repugnant to an irrevocable letter of credit." U.C.C. § 5-114, comment 1 (4th sent.).

[93] For additional cases in which the credit called for a document that the account party controlled, see Corporacion De Mercadeo Agricola v. Mellon Bank Int'l, 608 F.2d 43 (2d Cir. 1979); Scarsdale Nat'l Bank & Trust Co. v. Toronto-Dominion Bank, 533 F. Supp. 378 (S.D.N.Y. 1982); Bebco Distribs., Inc. v. Farmers & Merchants Bank, 485 So. 2d 330 (Ala. 1986); Carrera v. Bank of N.Y., 153 A.D.2d 918, 545 N.Y.S.2d 726 (1989); Key Appliance, Inc. v. First Nat'l City Bank, 46 A.D.2d 622, 359 N.Y.S.2d 886 (1974); Chilton Air Cooled Engines, Inc. v. First Citizens Bank, 726 S.W.2d 526 (Tenn. Ct. App. 1986); Astro Exito Navegacion S.A. v. Southland Enter. Co., [1983] 2 All E.R. 725 (H.L.). Cf. Texas Trading & Milling Corp. v. H.I.T. Corp., No. 84 Civ. 3776 (LLS) (S.D.N.Y. Sept. 3, 1986) (holding that account

[4] Drafting the Credit's Conditions

Even before the *Wichita* case, it was a wise and well-established precept of letter of credit practice that the credit should be payable against documentary conditions rather than factual conditions.[94] Although some courts have been lenient on that point, most of them and most commentators recognize the imperative of this manifestation of the *Wichita* rule and support it.[95]

It is not enough to say, however, that the conditions must be documentary; they must also be clear. The issuer's document examiners must be able to know from looking at the credit what documents the beneficiary must present. Vague references to "a copy of each instrument causing this establishment of credit . . . to be called upon,"[96] to "documentation" of various facts without specifying the documents,[97] or to "drafts per Resellers Agreement"[98] clearly are not satisfactory. The document examiner is not in a position to know whether the documents submitted satisfy the condition. In *Union County Bank v. FDIC*,[99] the court properly criticized as poorly drafted a credit that required the beneficiary to submit "all security documents executed in connection with

---

party's attempt to add similar documentary condition to credit constituted material change in sales agreement). For discussion of the effect of documents to be signed by the account party on the revocability of the credit, see ¶ 4.08[4]. In one English case, the account party's use of a condition in the credit requiring its countersignature on a document came to prevent the account party from obtaining an injunction against payment. In Tukan Timber Ltd. v. Barclays Bank PLC, [1987] 1 Lloyd's Rep. 171 (Q.B.), the court refused to enjoin the issuer from paying on the credit. In part because of the condition that the issuer countersign the beneficiary's receipt, the court held that the evidence of fraud by the beneficiary was so clear that any payment by the issuer would have given the account party a cause of action against a defendant that could respond in money damages. In that case, the court held, an injunction would not have been proper. For cases that illustrate the relief available to a beneficiary when the account party wrongfully refuses to provide the document in his control, see Weidner Communications, Inc. v. Faisal, 859 F.2d 1302 (7th Cir. 1988); Astro Exito Navegacion S.A. v. Southland Enter. Co., [1983] All E.R. 725 (H.L.). Cf. McLaughlin, "Structuring Commercial Letter-of-Credit Transactions to Safeguard the Interests of the Buyer," 21 U.C.C. L.J. 318 (1989) (contending that court may order account party to execute certificate or other document if refusal to execute is in bad faith).

[94] Comptroller of the Currency, Interpretive Ruling, 12 C.F.R. § 7.7016 (1989).

[95] See authority cited supra ¶¶ 2.05[1], 2.05[2].

[96] O'Grady v. First Union Nat'l Bank, 296 N.C. 212, 229, 250 S.E.2d 587, 599 (1978).

[97] Bank of the Southeast v. Jackson, 413 So. 2d 1091, 1098 (Ala. 1982).

[98] Newvector Communications, Inc. v. Union Bank, 663 F. Supp. 252, 253 (D. Utah 1987).

[99] No. 712 (Tenn. Ct. App. Sept. 18, 1987).

said loan." After a trial on the merits, the court was satisfied that all of the documents had been submitted. It is commercially unreasonable to ask a document examiner, however, to make that determination. Document examiners do not have the luxury of opening statements, testimony of sworn witnesses, the marshaling of evidence, and closing arguments. The determination *Union County Bank* requires is entirely inconsistent with the fast pace and low price of the letter of credit. That the conditions be clear is all the more critical in light of the strict compliance rule, which requires the beneficiary to observe the conditions punctiliously.[100] A number of cases illustrate the problems that arise when those conditions are unclear or when the parties attempt to stretch the credit to cover losses not anticipated by the credit's conditions.

In *Artoc Bank & Trust, Ltd. v. Sun Marine Terminals, Inc.*,[101] the commercial parties evidently intended the credit to secure sums due under a terminaling service agreement, including sums due under an acceleration clause in the agreement. The credit, however, did not anticipate acceleration and called for invoices covering services rendered and a letter reciting that the obligor had not paid for the services. The beneficiary elected to accelerate payments due on the underlying agreement and drew on the credit by presenting an invoice and a letter with the required recitation. At the time, charges against the account party for all services were current. The court in *Artoc Bank* held that the presentation, being untruthful, constituted a breach of the warranty provision of Article 5[102] and rendered the beneficiary liable to the account party for the full amount of the payment.

In *Atlas Mini Storage, Inc. v. First Interstate Bank*,[103] an invoice standby secured payments due for mini–storage buildings. When the buyer canceled the order, the beneficiary-seller sought to draw on the credit and presented an invoice in an amount equal to the benefit of the bargain it lost by virtue of the alleged contract breach. The *Atlas Mini Storage* court held that the beneficiary had not satisfied the conditions of the credit, and the court sustained injunctive relief against payment.

In *Auto-Owners Insurance Co. v. South Side Trust & Savings Bank*,[104] the opinion does not make it clear whether the credit expressly called for a copy of the performance bond that the credit secured or for certification from the beneficiary concerning the bond. The evidence

---

[100] For discussion of the strict compliance rule and its indispensable role in the letter of credit transaction, see ¶¶ 6.03, 6.04.

[101] 760 S.W.2d 311 (Tex. Ct. App. 1988).

[102] See U.C.C. § 5-111(1). For discussion of the warranty, see ¶¶ 6.07, 9.04.

[103] 426 N.W.2d 686 (Iowa Ct. App. 1988).

[104] 176 Ill. App. 3d 303, 531 N.E.2d 146 (1988).

showed that the issuer assumed that the bond would bear the name of an individual as principal, but the beneficiary assumed that a corporation would be the principal. When it became clear to the beneficiary that the issuer would resist payment under the credit on the ground that the bond secured the obligation of the wrong principal, the beneficiary sued for reformation. Although the court denied the requested relief, the opinion does not make it clear whether the fault in this transaction was that of the issuer or that of the beneficiary. If the credit did not require presentation of the bond or of certification concerning the bond and its principal, the beneficiary should have drawn on it; and the issuer would have been obligated to pay. If the credit did call for such documentation, and if the beneficiary was unable to comply, the issuer had ground to dishonor.

A beneficiary enjoys no cause of action against an issuer that issues a credit with terms that the beneficiary finds unacceptable. In that event, the beneficiary may have a cause of action against the account party for breach of the underlying contract, or it may have a defense giving it a right to suspend performance under that contract.[105] In addition, the account party may have a cause of action against an issuer that does not comply with the terms of the application agreement in issuing a credit.[106] In no event, however, should the beneficiary be able to complain when the issuer issues a poorly drafted credit. Above all, the law should encourage the beneficiary to examine the credit[107] promptly upon its receipt, at a time when the parties can still amend it.

¶ 2.06 DOCUMENTS REFERRED TO AS LETTERS OF CREDIT

The *Wichita* case is a pre-Code decision. Both the district court and the circuit court opinions, however, can be taken as authority that Section 5-102(1)(c) does not have full effect and may not always bring within the purview of Article 5 a credit that "conspicuously states that it is a letter of credit or is conspicuously so entitled."

---

[105] The beneficiary's cause of action or defense would arise as a matter of contract law if the underlying contract required the account party to establish a credit. Cf. U.C.C. § 2-325(1) ("Failure of the buyer seasonably to furnish an agreed letter of credit is a breach of the contract for sale.").

[106] For discussion of the account party's cause of action against the issuer for an improperly drafted credit, see ¶ 9.01.

[107] For additional cases in which drafting problems relating to the credit's expiry have forced courts to allocate losses between the issuer and the beneficiary, see ¶ 5.03[3][a].

Comment 1 to Section 5-102 explains the reason for this permissive scope rule of subsection (1)(c). The automatic rules of subsections (1)(a) and (1)(b) bring within Article 5 any bank letter of credit that calls for a draft or demand for payment or any other piece of paper,[108] as well as any nonbank letter of credit that calls for a draft or demand for payment and a document of title. Because some banks issue "clean" credits and because some nonbanks issue credits that call for drafts or demands and papers other than documents of title,[109] the Code permits banks and nonbanks in such settings to opt for Article 5 coverage by conspicuously designating or entitling the engagement a "letter of credit."[110]

This explanation in comment 1 leaves two scope questions unanswered. The first relates to nonbanks that issue clean letters of credit. The second relates to the question raised by the *Wichita* case concerning whether there is a test in addition to that posed by Section 5-102(1), namely, a test that the credit not be a poorly drafted one that imposes duties on the issuer beyond that of examining documents.

The official comment raises the doubt that Section 5-102(1)(c) covers clean, nonbank credits expressly denominated as credits. The plain language of Section 5-102(1)(c) contradicts the comment. The *Wichita* case raises the doubt that the subsection covers those documents that are denominated as letters of credit and that turn on factual determinations rather than on documentary examination. Again, the plain language of the subsection contradicts *Wichita*.

There is good reason to reject the implications of the first doubt and to accept the implications of the second. Nothing can be gained by denying the Code's coverage to clean, nonbank credits that the parties denominate as letters of credit, but the *Wichita* opinion makes a strong argument against applying letter of credit rules to credits that turn on factual determinations. Such credits, regardless of whether they are clearly denominated letters of credit, stray too far from the central purpose of credits. Credits whose payment depends on factual inquiry frustrate the inexpensive assurance that payment credits are designed to give. There is something to be gained, therefore, from the *Wichita* court's refusal to read Section 5-102(1)(c) literally, but there is little to be gained from reading the provision to exclude from Article 5 clean, nonbank credits.

---

[108] See supra ¶ 2.04.

[109] For a case dealing with such a nonbank credit, see Barclays Bank D.C.O. v. Mercantile Nat'l Bank, 481 F.2d 1224, 1228 n.5 (5th Cir. 1973), cert. dismissed, 414 U.S. 1139 (1974). For a case involving a clean credit issued by a bank, see Universal Marine Ins. Co. v. Beacon Ins. Co., 577 F. Supp. 829 (W.D.N.C. 1984).

[110] See U.C.C. § 5-102, comment 1 (2d para.); accord Baker v. National Boulevard Bank, 399 F. Supp. 1021 (N.D. Ill. 1975).

Courts are not always aware of these scope issues. In *Banque De Paris Et Des Pays-Bas v. Amoco Oil Co.*,[111] the plaintiff, a French bank, took an assignment of repurchase agreements on which the defendant was obligated. The bank asked that Amoco secure the repurchase obligations with a letter of credit or with documents that the bank called undertakings. It is clear from the facts in the opinion that the bank wanted the undertakings in order to insulate itself from the defenses available to Amoco on the repurchase agreements. The undertakings were telexes from Amoco to the bank, whereby Amoco undertook to pay the bank when it received oil under a given repurchase agreement; but Amoco had refused to include in the telex language reciting that the engagement was independent of the repurchase agreement. Ultimately, Amoco set off against its obligation on the undertakings sums due under a repurchase agreement.

The *Amoco* court did not explore the possibility that the undertakings might have been letters of credit, in which event Amoco might have lost its right of setoff.[112] The fact that Amoco did not intend its undertaking to be a letter of credit should not have been controlling. The opinion says little about the terms of the telexes; but, if the engagement called for a draft plus a document of title as the opinion suggests,[113] the undertakings may have constituted letters of credit subject to Article 5 and perhaps to the Uniform Customs.[114]

---

[111] 573 F. Supp. 1464 (S.D.N.Y. 1983).

[112] For discussion of the inability of the issuer to assert in the credit transaction a setoff arising out of the underlying transaction, see ¶ 9.06[3].

[113] "[T]he companies completed the Part I exchange of funds for bills of lading without problem." Banque De Paris Et Des Pays-Bas v. Amoco Oil Co., 573 F. Supp. 1464, 1467 (S.D.N.Y. 1983).

[114] This discussion assumes that an issuer may issue a letter of credit for its own account. The language of Section 5-103(1)(a) states the contrary when it defines a credit as being issued "at the request of a customer." It is difficult to see any reason to read that language in the definition as anything more than an attempt to describe the typical credit transaction. Absent any compelling justification for reading the language as a required element of the definition, courts arguably should extend the definition to the kind of undertaking described in the *Amoco* case. As a matter of banking law, there may be problems with a credit opened for the issuer's own account. The Comptroller of the Currency's interpretive ruling on letters of credit, 12 C.F.R. § 7.7016 (1989), warns that safe and sound banking practice requires a bank issuer to have a right of reimbursement—a right that does not exist if the issuer opens the credit for its own account.

¶ 2.07　MEANING OF "CONSPICUOUS"

Section 1-201(10) provides that a term is conspicuous when it is written so that a reasonable person ought to have noticed it. Certainly, a letter of credit so entitled would contain a conspicuous use of the term "letter of credit," but Sections 1-201(10) and 5-102(1)(c) imply that some engagements so entitled may not come within the provision unless the title is conspicuous.

Many letters of credit do not exceed one or two typewritten pages, and only a few credits involve lengthy provisions.[115] By their nature, if properly drawn, credits are brief, and surely any one- or two-page document entitled "letter of credit" or including such a term should satisfy the "conspicuous" rule.[116]

Section 1-201(10) provides that a printed heading is conspicuous if it is printed in capitals, and language in the body of a credit is conspicuous "if it is in larger or other contrasting type or color."[117] These examples are not mandatory. The term "letter of credit" is itself rather conspicuous and leaves little room for a merchant to deny that he reasonably ought to have noticed it.

A careful drafter always gives the engagement a title, if for no other reason than to give it a number and designate it as revocable or irrevocable.[118] Most credits also contain a requirement that drafts identify the credit by reciting, for example, that they are drawn under "First National Bank's irrevocable credit number _____ ." These and other similar references in a short document should satisfy the "conspicuous" requirement, as should the reference in any credit that begins, "Gentlemen: we hereby establish our irrevocable credit. . . ."

In addition, a credit that contains, as the document in *Wichita* did, a recital above a signature line stating "The terms of the above Letter of Credit are accepted" should satisfy the "conspicuous" rule. Even engagements that describe themselves simply as "credits" might satisfy the requirement of Section 5-102(1)(c), given the common interchanging of

---

[115] See, e.g., the credits in App. C, Docs. 15–18.

[116] See Bank of N.C. v. Rock Island Bank, 630 F.2d 1243 (7th Cir. 1980); Pringle-Associated Mortgage Corp. v. Southern Nat'l Bank, 571 F.2d 871 (5th Cir. 1978); Baker v. National Boulevard Bank, 399 F. Supp. 1021 (N.D. Ill. 1975), East Bank v. Dovenmuehle, Inc., 196 Colo. 422, 589 P.2d 1361 (1978); Housing Sec., Inc. v. Maine Nat'l Bank, 391 A.2d 311 (Me. 1978); O'Grady v. First Union Nat'l Bank, 296 N.C. 212, 250 S.E.2d 587 (1978).

[117] U.C.C. § 1-201(10); cf. Housing Sec., Inc. v. Maine Nat'l Bank, 391 A.2d 311 (Me. 1978) (to same effect).

[118] For discussion of the revocability problem and the need for designating credits as revocable or irrevocable, see ¶¶ 4.06[2][a], 4.08[4], 5.02[1].

the terms "letter of credit" and "credit" both in commercial transactions and in the Code.[119] The drafter who buries the term "credit" or "letter of credit" in a wordy and perhaps poorly drafted credit may run the risk of a holding that the reference does not satisfy the "conspicuous" requirement.

In *Sherwood & Roberts, Inc. v. First Security Bank,*[120] the court held that a clean credit that was entitled "Irrevocable Letter of Credit" in black letters and that referred to itself internally as a "letter of credit" had satisfied the "conspicuous" requirement of Section 5-102(1)(c). In *Travis Bank & Trust v. State,*[121] the court held that a document entitled "Irrevocable Letter of Credit No. 140" was conspicuously entitled. In *Transparent Products Corp. v. Paysaver Credit Union,*[122] the court held that a document that consisted of one sentence beginning "We hereby establish our letter of credit" was conspicuously designated a letter of credit for the purposes of Section 5-102(1)(c).

There is a clear implication in the permissive scope rule of Section 5-102(1)(c) and in the cases construing that section that the provision is designed to serve the intent of those issuers who wish to bring their credits within Article 5. It is a mistake, however, to substitute a subjective or extrinsic inquiry into the issuer's intent for the provision's objective rule requiring a conspicuous, intrinsic reference. Such a rule ignores the two purposes that the "conspicuous" requirement serves: judicial efficiency and a clear warning to the parties. The requirement of a conspicuous, intrinsic reference avoids the costly judicial inquiry of determining intent and avoids the risk that persons dealing with the credit (e.g., beneficiaries and transferees) will be unaware that the credit falls within the scope of Article 5.

¶ 2.08 DISTINGUISHING THE CREDIT FROM RELATED CONTRACTS

There are, in the broad scope of letter of credit transactions, any number of contracts and undertakings that are different from the credit engagement itself and of which the credit engagement is said so often to be independent. This section discusses those contracts and undertakings and distinguishes them from the credit engagement.

[119] See U.C.C. § 5-103(1)(a).
[120] 682 P.2d 149 (Mont. 1984).
[121] 660 S.W.2d 851 (Tex. Ct. App. 1983).
[122] No. 85 C 01741 (N.D. Ill. Dec. 24, 1985), aff'd, 864 F.2d 60 (7th Cir. 1988).

[1] Contracts Between Issuer and Account Party

When an account party asks its bank to issue the credit, the bank usually requires a signed application that contains the terms of the relationship between the account party and the issuing bank. The application also deals with matters relating to the method of the bank's reimbursement and any security interest the bank will hold pending reimbursement.[123] Even without a written agreement, the law imposes certain contractual duties on the account party.[124] This contractual or statutory relationship is not a letter of credit, and parties to it may have no rights under the credit engagement.

In *FDIC v. Borne*,[125] the account party sought to rely on the letter of credit as a modification of the application agreement, but the court held that the account party was not a party to the letter of credit and could not rely on its terms. *In re Munzenrieder*[126] held that an issuer that paid the beneficiary could not use subrogation or unjust enrichment to assert the rights of the beneficiary against the party that benefited from the payment. The court held that the issuer paid the beneficiary to satisfy its own obligation and not that of the party against which it was seeking reimbursement.[127]

Thus, *Borne* refuses to permit the account party to use the letter of credit relationship to modify the account party–issuer relationship; *Munzenrieder* refuses to permit the issuer to use the letter of credit relationship to modify the account party–issuer relationship.

[2] Contracts Between Account Party and Third Parties

In nearly all credit transactions, the account party enters into a contract with the beneficiary, and the purpose of the credit is to secure some aspect of performance of that contract that is the underlying contract. In the commercial credit setting, the underlying contract is one for the sale of goods. The beneficiary is the seller; the account party is the buyer; and the credit usually secures payment of the purchase price. In the

---

[123] See App. C, Doc. 14.

[124] See, e.g., U.C.C. § 5-114(3); U.C.P. art. 16(a) (1983). See generally ¶ 7.06. Because the commercial credit customarily calls for a negotiable document of title, the issuer, when it honors the beneficiary's draft and takes the document, is a holder to whom a negotiable document has been duly negotiated and therefore enjoys rights in the goods covered by the document. See U.C.C. §§ 7-501, 7-502, 9-102, 9-304(2); cf. U.C.C. § 4-208 (giving bank security interest as matter of law in some cases).

[125] 599 F. Supp. 891 (E.D.N.Y. 1984).

[126] 58 Bankr. 228 (Bankr. M.D. Fla. 1986).

[127] For further discussion of subrogation, see ¶ 7.05[2].

standby credit setting, the underlying contract entails some promise of the account party running to the beneficiary. The beneficiary draws on the standby if the beneficiary determines that the account party has not performed the underlying contract. These underlying contracts are not credits. They underlie the credit, and the credit facilitates them in some way. Parties to those underlying contracts are not necessarily parties to the credit engagement.

In *Jupiter Orrington Corp. v. Zweifel*,[128] the account party claimed that the beneficiary had breached the underlying contract by unreasonably refusing to accept a substitute letter of credit and by drawing on the original letter of credit. The account party sought to enjoin that draw and raised the breach of the underlying contract as justification for his injunction. The court held that breach of the underlying contract is not a ground to enjoin payment of the credit. Presumably, if the beneficiary's actions are in breach of the underlying contract, the account party can recover damages in a separate breach of contract action.

In *Union Engineering Co. v. Titan Industrial Corp.*,[129] the beneficiary of a credit sued the account party, claiming rights against the account party arising out of the credit. The court carefully explained that the credit was distinct from the underlying contract and that the beneficiary could not rely on the credit in its suit against the account party.

In *Trans-Global Alloy, Ltd. v. First National Bank*,[130] the court ruled that the beneficiary, by failing to make an installment shipment, caused the credit to expire under Article 36 of the 1974 version of the Uniform Customs. The court added, however, that the determination that the beneficiary did not have a cause of action for wrongful dishonor of the credit did not mean that it did not have a cause of action for breach of the underlying contract, because the contract was independent of the credit.[131]

[3] Contracts Between Banks

Many credits, especially those involving international transactions, involve banks other than the issuing bank. Often an advising bank or a confirming bank is designated in the credit as the party that will pay, ac-

---

[128] 127 Ill. App. 3d 559, 469 N.E.2d 590 (1984).

[129] No. 83 Civ. 6369 (CSH) (S.D.N.Y. June 27, 1985).

[130] 490 So. 2d 769 (La. Ct. App. 1986).

[131] Cf. Wing Hing (Tangs) Fabrics Mfg. Co. v. Rafaella Sportswear, Inc., No. 84 Civ. 9024 (JFK) (S.D.N.Y. Sept. 10, 1987) (holding that failure of seller to act in time to satisfy letter of credit conditions does not preclude it from recovering from buyer account party on underlying contract).

cept, or negotiate the beneficiary's drafts. The correspondent banks have an understanding, either written or customary, with the issuing bank governing the terms of the correspondent's reimbursement for funds disbursed in payment of drafts drawn under the issuer's credit. If, for example, an issuing bank in Hong Kong designates a New York bank as the payor bank, the beneficiary of the credit will present his draft and supporting documents at the New York bank, which will honor the draft if the presentation is conforming. The New York bank then seeks reimbursement from the opening bank by charging an account that the opening bank maintains with the New York bank, by drawing on the opening bank, or by some other arrangement to which the two banks have previously agreed or that is designated in the credit itself. These collection arrangements are contractual in nature and are distinct from the credit engagement that runs from the issuer to the beneficiary.

Frequently, an issuer engages to pay drawers, endorsers, and other bona fide holders of the named beneficiary's draft. That engagement runs to banks that purchase or negotiate the named beneficiary's draft. A claim against the issuer by one of these negotiating banks is a matter of credit law and is distinct from reimbursement arrangements, which are not.[132]

In *Worldwide Sugar Co. v. Royal Bank of Canada*,[133] the account party buyer attempted to avail itself of a performance guaranty that the advising bank had given to the issuer pursuant to the credit. The account party paid the beneficiary, which had agreed to the cancelation of the credit on the condition that the documents be delivered by the issuer to the account party. The account party then attempted to assert rights under the guaranty against the advising bank. The court construed the guaranty arrangement narrowly, however, and refused to bring the account party within its protection. The decision appears to turn on the intent of the parties at the time they canceled the credit. The court held that the arrangement for delivering the documents to the account party buyer was to permit it to take delivery of the merchandise shipped pursuant to the underlying contract and not to extend the advising bank's guaranty after the credit had been terminated.

[4] Acceptances

If the credit calls for time drafts, the payor bank honors the drafts by accepting them. Such an acceptance gives rise under negotiable instru-

---

[132] See generally ¶¶ 1.02[3], 10.02[3].

[133] 609 F. Supp. 19 (S.D.N.Y. 1984); cf. Braun v. Intercontinental Bank, 466 So. 2d 1130 (Fla. Dist. Ct. App. 1985) (holding that account party is not party to letter of credit and that issuer is not responsible for performance of underlying contract).

ments law to the well-defined contractual duty of paying the acceptance, as the draft is then called, when it matures. This obligation to pay an acceptance arises out of the negotiable instrument and is in addition to, and distinct from, the credit engagement.[134]

[5] Contracts Bewteen Issuer and Beneficiary

There are three relationships that may arise between the issuer and the beneficiary. The first is the relationship in the credit transaction itself, in which the issuer undertakes to honor the beneficiary's draft or demand for payment. That relationship is specifically a matter of letter of credit law. The second relationship is the one that arises when the issuer accepts the beneficiary's draft, and the beneficiary holds the draft, which is then an acceptance. That relationship is one of negotiable instruments law.

There may be times when the issuer and the beneficiary enter into an agreement of some kind that is neither a letter of credit nor an acceptance, and in that event the relationship is governed by contract law. In *State Bank v. South Mill Mushroom Sales, Inc.*,[135] for example, when the beneficiary drew on the credit, the issuer inveigled the beneficiary into a compromise under which he withdrew his draft and accepted a cashier's check and a new credit in place of payment under the credit. When the issuer breached that compromise agreement, the beneficiary sought to draw on the original, but now expired, credit. The *State Bank* court ruled, however, that the beneficiary's cause of action was on the compromise agreement, not on the expired credit.

¶ 2.09 CLARIFYING DISTINCTIONS BETWEEN CREDITS AND RELATED CONTRACTS

The credit engagement is distinct from and independent of all of the related contracts described in the preceding section. Sometimes there is confusion over whether to apply letter of credit principles to some of these contracts, even though they are not letters of credit.

---

[134] See U.C.C. §§ 3-410, 3-413(1); Voest-Alpine Int'l Corp. v. Chase Manhattan Bank, N.A., 707 F.2d 680 (2d Cir. 1983). The issuer's promise on an acceptance credit also entails the obligation to pay the acceptance at maturity. The holder who takes the acceptance under the credit may sue either on the credit or on the acceptance, or on both. See infra ¶ 2.09[1].

[135] 875 F.2d 158 (8th Cir. 1989).

[1] Suits on Acceptances

In *Ando International, Ltd. v. Woolmaster Corp.*,[136] for example, a non-bank issuer accepted a seller's time drafts under a credit. The buyer (the account party) objected to the quality of the seller's merchandise and sought to enjoin payment of the accepted drafts upon maturity. The court properly refused the injunction request. It justified the result exclusively by reasoning that a letter of credit is independent of the underlying contract. The court cited cases and a provision in Article 5 to that effect. Indeed, the cited authority supports the proposition, but letter of credit authority is not the sole source of law in a suit to enjoin payment of an acceptance under a credit. Article 5 governs letters of credit and certainly would determine the rights of the parties under that letter of credit, including the rights of a beneficiary who holds an acceptance. Articles 3 and 4, however, govern acceptances; any rights the parties have under the acceptance are subject to the rules of those articles.

The holder of the acceptance has rights under the credit[137] only if the terms of the credit are satisfied. Presumably they were satisfied, or the bank would not have accepted the draft. A holder of an acceptance also has rights on the acceptance, a negotiable instrument containing the acceptor's promise to pay at maturity.[138] Rights arising out of the credit are governed by Article 5, but rights on the acceptance are governed in part by Article 3. Article 3 lays down different prerequisites for recovery on a negotiable instrument from those Article 5 lays down for recovery on a letter of credit.[139]

It is a mistake to look solely to Article 5 in resolving disputes arising out of acceptances. It may have been a mistake in the *Ando* case to assume that Article 5 governed entirely, since there may have been rights arising under Article 3 (negotiable instruments) or Article 4 (bank collections).[140]

In *Banco De Viscaya, S.A. v. First National Bank*,[141] a foreign branch of the defendant accepted drafts that were later negotiated to third-party holders. In a suit by the holders, the court assumed that the holders had a claim under the credit and that the liability of the defend-

---

[136] 3 U.C.C. Rep. Serv. (Callaghan) 1071 (N.Y. Sup. Ct. 1966).

[137] See U.C.P. art. 10(b)(iii) (1983). See also authority cited infra note 143 (to same effect).

[138] Cf. See U.C.C. § 3-413(1).

[139] Compare U.C.C. § 3-307 with U.C.C. § 5-114.

[140] Cf. Michael Doyle & Assocs. v. Bank of Montreal, 140 D.L.R.3d 596 (B.C. 1982) (similar action involving liability on credit and on acceptances).

[141] 514 F. Supp. 1280 (N.D. Ill. 1981), vacated, id. (counsel for defendant advises that court vacated opinion after matter was settled).

ant was a matter of credit law. It is correct to say that such holders have rights under the credit. It is a mistake, however, to look only to credit law to determine what those rights are, for if holders of the acceptance do not have rights under the credit, it is wrong to conclude that they have no right to recover. The holder of a banker's acceptance, whether the acceptance arises out of a letter of credit or out of a transaction that does not involve a credit, may enforce the contract of acceptance. Such a contract arises when the bank executes the draft by signing its face.[142]

At this point, this much is clear: It is not indispensable for the holder of an acceptance to establish compliance with the credit in order to obtain payment from the acceptor. Such a holder may recover from the acceptor as a matter of negotiable instruments law or of bank collection law. Moreover, as a general rule, under Section 3-307(2) the holder need prove only that the signature of the acceptor is genuine in order to recover on a negotiable acceptance. It is far easier to recover on an acceptance than it is to recover on a credit, where the plaintiff must show that the beneficiary satisfied the credit's terms.[143]

In *First Commercial Bank v. Gotham Originals, Inc.*,[144] the issuer accepted time drafts drawn under the credit. The account party obtained a judgment against the beneficiaries of the credit and an order restraining transfer of the account party's assets. It then attempted to attach the proceeds of the credit. The court held, however, that the attachment came too late. "In other words, once Bank Leumi accepted the drafts and agreed to pay them, the letter of credit was extinguished and the monies were thereafter held by Bank Leumi on account of [the holder of the acceptances]."[145] On appeal, the New York Court of Appeals affirmed,[146] holding squarely that Article 4,[147] not Article 5, determined the rights of the parties.

---

[142] See U.C.C. § 3-410.

[143] For a case similar to the *Ando International* and *Banco De Viscaya* cases in its treatment of a holder of acceptances as one having rights only under the credit, see New Tech Devs., Div. of San Diego Carleton Lewis Corp. v. Bank of N.S., 191 Cal. App. 3d 1065, 236 Cal. Rptr. 746 (1987). Some cases suggest that the issuer's act of accepting time drafts does not discharge its liability on the credit, while other courts hold that the credit is the sole source of liability. See Voest-Alpine Int'l Corp. v. Chase Manhattan Bank, N.A., 545 F. Supp. 301 (S.D.N.Y. 1982), aff'd in part, rev'd in part, 707 F.2d 680 (2d Cir. 1983); Greenough v. Munroe, 46 F.2d 537 (S.D.N.Y.), aff'd, 53 F.2d 362 (2d Cir.), cert. denied sub nom. Irving Trust Co. v. Oliver Straw Goods Corp., 284 U.S. 672 (1931); Bank of U.S. v. Seltzer, 233 A.D. 225, 251 N.Y.S. 637 (Sup. Ct. 1931).

[144] 101 A.D.2d 790, 476 N.Y.S.2d 835 (1984), aff'd, 64 N.Y.2d 287, 475 N.E.2d 1255, 486 N.Y.S.2d 715 (1985).

[145] Id. at 791, 476 N.Y.S.2d at 837 (1984).

[146] See First Commercial Bank v. Gotham Originals, Inc., 64 N.Y.2d 287, 475 N.E.2d 1255, 486 N.Y.S.2d 715 (1985).

[147] The *First Commercial Bank* court applied Section 4-303 of the Code.

[2] Suits on Promissory Notes

Promissory notes arise in the letter of credit context often. Borrowers, the obligors on promissory notes, utilize the letter of credit to enhance the value of the notes, to make them more attractive in the markets, and to reduce the interest charges they must bear to attract investors. In disputes among the parties to transactions involving notes and letters of credit, it is crucial to distinguish the various parties and to differentiate obligations that arise under the note from obligations that arise under the credit.

The opinion in *Bank of North Carolina, N.A. v. Rock Island Bank*[148] reflects confusion between rights on the credit and rights on a promissory note. The *Rock Island Bank* court invoked negotiable instrument rules when letter of credit rules applied. In the *Rock Island Bank* case, the credit was open. It did not specify a beneficiary but ran to the holder in due course of a certain promissory note made by the issuer's customer, whoever that holder might be at maturity. Under the credit, the issuer agreed to purchase the note from the holder. When the holder ultimately sought to enforce the credit, the issuer refused to take the note, and the holder sued.

Clearly, the plaintiff's action was on the credit, yet the opinion refers to rules governing recovery "under the instrument"[149] and refers in that context to two provisions of Article 3. In fact, the court held that under Section 3-307 of the negotiable instruments article of the Code, it is not necessary for the plaintiff to show that it was a holder in due course in order to recover from an obligor on the note. That statement of negotiable instruments law is correct, but it is not correct to apply negotiable instruments rules to a claim on a letter of credit.

In the *Rock Island Bank* case, the plaintiff was not suing on the promissory note. The issuing bank was not a party to that note. The issuing bank's signature did not appear on the note, and it is the first rule of negotiable instruments law that no party is liable on an instrument unless his signature appears thereon.[150] The only rights the holder had against the issuing bank were rights arising under the letter of credit. The letter of credit expressly stipulated that the issuer would pay a "holder in due course." Certainly, that language was not a happy choice for a credit, because, in order to determine whether the holder complied with the terms of the credit, there were a number of facts that the holder

---

[148] 630 F.2d 1243 (7th Cir. 1980).
[149] Id. at 1246.
[150] See U.C.C. § 3-401(1).

had to establish, none of which could be ascertained easily from documents and none of which therefore were appropriate for the triggering mechanism of a letter of credit. Nevertheless, the plaintiff in the *Rock Island Bank* case took the note with knowledge of the credit's terms and therefore should not be heard to complain that those terms were burdensome or inoperative. If the holder could not satisfy the terms of the credit, it could sue the maker or prior endorsers of the note.[151]

In *First State Bank & Trust Co. v. McIver*,[152] the credit secured a promissory note given by the account party to the beneficiary. When the issuer refused to honor the beneficiary's demand for payment of the note, the beneficiary sued. The issuer and the beneficiary settled the action under an arrangement that called for the beneficiary to assign the note to the issuer. When the issuer's subsequent assignee[153] attempted to enforce the note, the account party claimed that the issuer had breached the application agreement by failing to pay the note and to secure the account party's release as maker. The court held that any such breach does not give the account party a defense on the note.

The *McIver* court justified its holding in part on the assertion that the credit and the note are independent of each other. That assertion is certainly correct; but it does not support the holding, because the account party was raising a breach of the application agreement, not a breach of the letter of credit undertaking, as a defense on the note. The intriguing issue raised by the account party in the *McIver* case stems from the account party's assumption that the issuer's payment to the beneficiary would have constituted payment of the note, discharging the account party from his liability as maker. The trial court did not address that issue.

The Circuit Court of Appeals for the Eleventh Circuit addressed that issue directly, however, and the holding is disappointing. The court held that the issuer's payment under the settlement agreement did not discharge the account party's liability on the note as maker. The court justified its holding on the ground that all of the "transfers" of the note were subject to the settlement agreement, which provided that the pay-

---

[151] See U.C.C. §§ 3-413, 3-414. This discussion assumes that the condition in the credit rendering it necessary to show that the holder was a holder in due course does not offend the *Wichita* principle, which it surely might. For discussion of the *Wichita* rule, see supra ¶ 2.05.

[152] 681 F. Supp. 1562 (M.D. Ga. 1988), aff'd, 893 F.2d 301 (11th Cir. 1990).

[153] The issuer transferred the note to its bonding company, which in turn assigned the note to the original beneficiary, who then brought suit. The court's use of terms such as "assign" and "purchase" to describe the travels of the note render it difficult to discern whether the plaintiff sought to enforce the note as a holder, as a transferee of the issuer, or as a transferee of the beneficiary itself.

ment by the issuer was not an admission of liability under the credit. The plaintiff in *McIver* was the original beneficiary of the credit that had taken the note from the issuer's bonding company.[154] The court accepted the plaintiff's argument that payments under the settlement agreement were not payments under the letter of credit.

Certainly, the independence principle should not interfere with the maker's argument that payment under the credit is a payment of the note that normally should discharge the maker. The issuer's lawyers evidently understood that rule when they insisted that any payments to the beneficiary would be characterized in the settlement agreement as the issuer's buying peace, not as its admission of liability under the credit. The trouble with that argument is that it invites issuers to dishonor credits, settle with the beneficiary, and use the beneficiary's rights against the account party. The effect of that arrangement is to subrogate the issuer (or its transferee, as in *McIver*) to the beneficiary's rights against the account party. Generally, courts have not favored that subrogation, which is decidedly unfair to the account party.[155] If the issuer is not satisfied with its rights in the application agreement against the account party, it should provide for subrogation by contract ex ante, when the account party can object. Subrogation after the fact is an unfair reallocation of liabilities at a time when the account party is not in a position to use his bargaining strength to prevent it. The effect of the arrangement in *McIver* is to deprive the account party of defenses he might have against the issue—defenses that he is certain to assert in the issuer's suit on the application agreement but that he cannot raise in a suit by the beneficiary on the note. *McIver* illustrates the difficulty some courts have in differentiating the sources of liability in the various contracts and undertakings in the broad letter of credit transaction.

The facts in *Gatz v. Southwest Bank*[156] gave rise to a unique variation of this argument. There the account party argued that under Section 3-802 of the Code, the beneficiary lost its right to draw on the credit. That section provides that the obligor on a negotiable instrument is discharged on the underlying obligation until the instrument is dishonored. The provision has no application to a letter of credit that secures a promissory note, but the account party in *Gatz* argued that the note was given in satisfaction of the letter of credit obligation.

---

[154] The issuer contended that the account party and a dishonest employee of the issuer had conspired to issue the credit without authorization. When the fidelity company settled the claim of the beneficiary, the beneficiary transferred the note to the issuer, which transferred it to the fidelity company. Later the fidelity company transferred the note back to the beneficiary.

[155] For discussion of subrogation in this context, see ¶ 7.05[2][b].

[156] 836 F.2d 1089 (8th Cir. 1988).

The account party contended, therefore, that, under the *Gatz* facts, the underlying obligation to which the section refers is the letter of credit obligation. If that obligation is discharged under the rule of Section 3-802, it was error for the court to order payment on the letter of credit. The *Gatz* court did not respond well to the argument, however, ruling simply that the letter of credit was independent of the note.

[3] Tying the Credit to the Underlying Contract

At times, issuers, perhaps in response to the importuning of their customers, attempt to tie the credit engagement to the underlying contract. In standby credit cases, for example, a customer may insist that the issuer not pay the beneficiary unless there is evidence of the account party's breach of the underlying contract. As the discussion of the *Wichita Eagle & Beacon Publishing Co. v. Pacific National Bank*[157] case demonstrates, however, such a connection destroys the effectiveness of the credit by rendering impossible the quick and inexpensive payment feature that characterizes its commercial success. To force an issuer to look beyond the documents to the performance of a contract is to render the credit a surety contract—a device with purposes different from those of credits and one to which the law of credits is ill suited.

One of the first principles of credit law is that the credit is independent of the underlying contract.[158] It is a commercial anomaly to reverse that rule by incorporating the underlying contract into the credit. Unfortunately, sometimes through the poor drafting of the credit and sometimes through lack of discipline in the courts, underlying contract equities insinuate themselves into the letter of credit engagement.

In *East Bank v. Dovenmuehle, Inc.*,[159] the court recited the rule that a credit is independent of the underlying contract and then proceeded to ignore the rule. The *East Bank* credit stated that it was to cover the loan imbalance arising out of the beneficiary's loan commitment to the issuer's customer. The credit provided supplemental funds for a construction project in the event the loan commitment was insufficient. Unfortunately, the standby credit referred to the commitment. When the project failed and the beneficiary sought payment under the credit, the issuer argued that the credit was payable only if the beneficiary ad-

---

[157] For that discussion, see supra ¶ 2.05.

[158] See, e.g., Bank of Taiwan, Ltd. v. Union Nat'l Bank, 1 F.2d 65 (3d Cir. 1924); Laudisi v. American Exch. Nat'l Bank, 239 N.Y. 234, 146 N.E. 347 (1924); Intraworld Indus., Inc. v. Girard Trust Bank, 461 Pa. 343, 336 A.2d 316 (1975). See generally supra ¶ 2.08, infra ¶ 2.09[5].

[159] 196 Colo. 422, 589 F.2d 1361 (1978).

vanced all funds under the loan commitment. The issuer argued that the purpose of the credit, as evidenced by the setting in which it was issued, limited its operation. The court properly rejected the bank's position. In doing so, however, it relied on the underlying contract to construe the term "loan imbalance" as it appeared in the credit. The bank's position, the opinion held, "disregards the plain language of . . . paragraph 9 of [the beneficiary's] loan commitment letter."[160]

A similar disposition to delve into matters governed by the underlying contract is evident in *Fair Pavilions, Inc. v. First National City Bank*.[161] The credit in the *Fair Pavilions* case stipulated that it was revocable upon presentation by the account party of an affidavit to the effect that one or more of the events of default described in a clause of the underlying contract had occurred. The account party presented such an affidavit and requested the issuer to withhold payment under the credit.

The court found the affidavit insufficient because it did not specify the event of default. The *Fair Pavilions* opinion holds that the "intention of paragraph 6 of the letter of credit, read in conjunction with clause XV of the building contract"[162] was to give the beneficiary an opportunity to cure any such defect. The court's own language belies the idea, although the court expressed it elsewhere, that the credit in the *Fair Pavilions* case was independent of the underlying contract. The error of the case is one that appears to be common among courts—that of construing the credit by referring to the underlying agreement.

The better approach, and one that is more faithful to the general principle that the credit is independent of the underlying contract, holds that such general references (to the underlying contract in the credit)

---

[160] Id. at 426, 589 P.2d at 1364. Similarly, in American Employers Ins. Co. v. Pioneer Bank & Trust Co., 538 F. Supp. 1354 (N.D. Ill. 1981), the court complained that the parties did not explain the underlying transaction in order to "cast light on the meaning" of the terms of the credit. Id. at 1358. Clearly, the *American Employers* court did not understand the independence principle. In Sperry Int'l Trade, Inc. v. Government of Isr., 689 F.2d 301 (2d Cir. 1982), it appears that arbitrators of a dispute arising out of the underlying contract incorrectly ordered the issuer to pay the credit's proceeds into escrow. The arbitration grew out of the underlying agreement, and there was no apparent justification for the arbitrators' decision to deprive the beneficiary of the funds during that arbitration. The reason for the letter of credit was to permit the beneficiary to obtain payment, without resort to the underlying contract. If that payment is erroneous, the account party ultimately will recover it in the arbitration. For further discussion of the function of credits and the way in which the independence principle enhances these functions, see ¶ 3.07.

[161] 19 N.Y.2d 512, 227 N.E.2d 839, 281 N.Y.S.2d 23 (1967).

[162] Id. at 517, 227 N.E.2d at 841, 281 N.Y.S.2d at 26.

may be disregarded as surplusage unless they clearly impose some condition to the issuer's liability.[163]

[4] Claims for Damages

Article 5 of the Code defines a damages rule for cases involving the issuer's breach of the credit obligation, that is, for wrongful dishonor of the credit. Unfortunately, some parties and courts are inclined to apply the rule of that provision to settings that do not involve wrongful dishonor.

In re F&T Contractors, Inc.[164] involved an account party's claim for damages when the issuer's successor revoked a letter of credit and refused to release the account party's mortgage. The account party's claim appears to be one for breach of the application agreement or for the tort of conversion, yet the court considered Section 5-115, the letter of credit damages section for breach of the credit engagement. The *F&T Contractors* court arguably reached the correct result, but in doing so it wrestled with Article 5 and ultimately concluded that because the credit was standby in nature, Section 5-115 did not apply. The court confused rights under the credit, which Article 5 governs, with rights under the application agreement, which are outside the scope of Article 5.

In *Balboa Insurance Co. v. Coastal Bank*,[165] the beneficiary sued the issuer for wrongful dishonor of the credit. The issuer argued that the beneficiary should show its damages, but the court held that the damages equaled the face amount of the credit. The *Balboa* beneficiary had taken the credit as security for a performance bond. The issuer argued that the beneficiary should be able to recover only those losses it sustained under the bond.

The *Balboa* court correctly held that the issuer could not insist that the beneficiary supply evidence of loss before it could draw on the letter of credit. Since the credit did not call for such evidence, the issuer could

---

[163] Banco Continental v. First Nat'l Bank, No. 84-5378 (6th Cir. 1985) (limited precedent op.); Pringle-Associated Mortgage Corp. v. Southern Nat'l Bank, 571 F.2d 871 (5th Cir. 1978); West Virginia Hous. Dev. Fund v. Sroka, 415 F. Supp. 1107 (W.D. Pa. 1976); Republic Nat'l Bank v. Northwest Nat'l Bank, 578 S.W.2d 109 (Tex. 1978); CNA Mortgage Investors, Ltd. v. Hamilton Nat'l Bank, 540 S.W.2d 238 (Tenn. Ct. App. 1975). But cf. Sawyer v. E.A. Gralia Constr. Co. (In re Pine Tree Elec. Co.), 16 Bankr. 105 (Bankr. D. Me. 1981) (involving credit subject to all terms and provisions of underlying contract). For further discussion of cases involving credits that refer to the underlying contract, see ¶ 7.04[4][c].

[164] 17 Bankr. 966 (Bankr. E.D. Mich. 1982), rev'd, on other grounds, 718 F.2d 171 (6th Cir. 1983).

[165] 42 U.C.C. Rep. Serv. (Callaghan) 1716 (S.D. Ga. 1986).

not refuse payment in its absence. The account party urged the court to distinguish commercial credits from standby credits and to require a showing of loss. In rejecting that argument, the court made much of the fact that the same law applies to standby credits and to commercial credits.

Significantly, the *Balboa* court did not distinguish between suits for wrongful payment and suits for wrongful dishonor. It is beyond any doubt that an account party cannot complain when an issuer pays in good faith over conforming documents, even though the beneficiary is not entitled to the funds in the underlying transaction. The credit transaction is independent of the underlying transaction, and payment of the credit cannot await investigation of the equities of the parties in the underlying transaction.[166] When the issuer dishonors, however, this may be another matter. Section 5-115 of the Code suggests that in an action for wrongful dishonor, those equities are a matter for concern.[167]

[5] Applying the Independence Principle

The independence principle does not always yield happy results in the short term. Its application to some cases tests the limits of the courts' patience with letter of credit law. In the long run, the principle has survived. Courts generally recognize that the credit cannot exist without independence from the underlying transaction. There are a few decisions, nonetheless, that depart from the rule.

New York Life Insurance Co. v. Hartford National Bank & Trust Co.[168] is a case demonstrating fidelity to the independence principle. In the *New York Life* case, the credit served in lieu of a liquidated damages deposit under a loan commitment. The beneficiary, New York Life, had issued the commitment to developers (TVC), who caused the issuing bank to open the credit. The credit, being tightly drawn, called only for drafts and a signed statement by the beneficiary to the effect that the liquidated damages deposit was due under the provisions of the credit. When the developers failed to satisfy the conditions of the loan commitment, New York Life sought its liquidated damages. The issuer resisted payment on two grounds: that the parties had modified the loan commitment (i.e., the underlying contract), thereby rendering the terms of

---

[166] For discussion of this independence principle, see infra ¶ 2.09[5]; see also ¶ 9.02[5][b][ii].

[167] See ¶ 9.02[5][b][ii].

[168] 173 Conn. 492, 378 A.2d 562 (1977).

the credit ambiguous, and that the provisions for liquidated damages were unenforceable as a penalty.

The *New York Life* court summarily rejected both contentions, which, by their nature, would have forced the court to look behind the credit into the underlying contract. Such arguments were "claims relating to the mortgage loan commitment contract between TVC and New York Life which . . . was entirely separate and independent from the letter of credit arrangement involving (the issuer) and New York Life."[169]

It has become customary in many standby credit situations for the credit to refer to the underlying contract. In *West Virginia Housing Development Fund v. Sroka*,[170] for example, the credit recited, "Applicant informs us that this letter of credit relates to working capital funds for the captioned project."[171]

The *Sroka* credit, issued at the request of a federal agency, was clean. The credit called only for the beneficiary's sight draft. It is difficult to see what function the reference to the relationship between the credit and the underlying contract served. Indeed, this language in the credit prompted litigation when the beneficiary presented its draft under circumstances indicating that the funds would not be used for working capital. In a labored opinion, the *Sroka* court finally concluded that the reference to the underlying contract did not create an additional obligation for the beneficiary.

The approach in *Sroka* is different from that of the *Fair Pavilions* case and is more consistent with that of *New York Life. Sroka* and *New*

---

[169] Id. at 502, 378 A.2d at 567; cf. Phoenix Mut. Life Ins. Co. v. Seafarers Officers & Employees Pension Plan, 128 F.R.D. 25 (E.D.N.Y. 1989) (ruling it irrelevant whether beneficiary's failure to make installment payment constitutes breach of underlying transaction, it being clear from credit that failure to make payment causes credit to terminate); Sabolyk v. Morgan Guar. Trust Co., No. 84 Civ. 3179 (MJL) (S.D.N.Y. Nov. 27, 1984) (holding that beneficiary of credit securing note could not draw on credit for later installment due on note, because acceleration clause was provision of note only and not of credit, which was independent of note); Berman v. LeBeau Inter-Am., Inc., 509 F. Supp. 156 (S.D.N.Y. 1981) (holding that even if funding of credit by account party is fraudulent, that fraud does not infect credit itself). In New York Life Ins. Co. v. Hartford Nat'l Bank & Trust Co., 2 Conn. App. 279, 477 A.2d 1033 (1984), the trustee in bankruptcy of one of the account parties finally succeeded in having the penalty argument litigated, but the trustee lost, the court holding that the liquidated damages provision was reasonable under the circumstances. In Hubbard Business Plaza v. Lincoln Liberty Life Ins. Co., 649 F. Supp. 1310 (D. Nev. 1986), aff'd, 844 F.2d 792 (9th Cir. 1988) (mem.), the court violated the independence principle and accepted the penalty argument that the *New York Life* court rejected. Significantly, the *Hubbard Business Plaza* opinion does not cite the *New York Life* case and does not appear to be aware of the independence principle.

[170] 415 F. Supp. 1107 (W.D. Pa. 1976).

[171] Id. at 1111.

York Life are the better-reasoned decisions. They recognize that to the extent courts begin delving into the underlying contract, they are impeding the swift completion of the credit transaction. The careful drafter altogether avoids any reference to the underlying contract or to the circumstances out of which the credit arises.[172]

In *Brown v. United States National Bank*,[173] the account parties complained that the amount of the draw under the credit exceeded the balance due on the underlying notes. The court, reflecting strong regard for the independence principle, refused to uphold the lower court's order reducing the payment by the amount of the excess. In response to the account parties' argument that the draw constituted fraud, the court countered that the beneficiary clearly would be under an obligation to return any excess to the account party.

In *CKB & Associates, Inc. v. Moore McCormack Petroleum*,[174] the credit served to secure quantity and quality obligations of the account party under an agreement to refine oil. When the parties fell into dispute over the quality and quantity of the account party's performance, the beneficiary drew on the credit. Before payment litigation ensued, the parties settled the matter with an agreement that permitted the beneficiary to draw and to receive payment. Later, when the account party sued the beneficiary on the oil refinement agreement, the beneficiary argued that the settlement in the letter of credit litigation was a bar to the plaintiff's claim. The *CKB* court disagreed. The settlement of the letter of credit litigation was a settlement of the letter of credit dispute over the identity of the party that would hold the funds while the commercial parties resolved the underlying contract dispute. It was not a resolution of that dispute. The *CKB* decision dramatizes the important cost-shifting function of the standby credit[175] and illustrates healthy regard for the independence of the credit from the underlying transaction.

Careful drafting does not overcome the predisposition of some courts, however, to litigate in the credit controversy questions that arise out of related contracts. In *Paccar International, Inc. v. Commercial Bank of Kuwait*,[176] the beneficiary of the credit was the issuer of a performance guaranty. The beneficiary of that guaranty, a middleman, had

---

[172] See also U.C.P. art. 3 (1983) (providing that no reference whatsoever in credit to other contracts destroys credit's independence from such contracts). For a discussion of cases involving certificates that refer to related contracts, see ¶ 7.04[4][c].

[173] 220 Neb. 684, 371 N.W.2d 692 (1985).

[174] 734 S.W.2d 653 (Tex. 1987).

[175] For discussion of that function, see ¶ 3.07[4].

[176] 587 F. Supp. 783 (C.D. Cal. 1984), vacated, 757 F.2d 1058 (9th Cir. 1985).

entered into a side agreement[177] with the account party. The arrangement was designed to prohibit the middleman from drawing on the guaranty—a draw that inevitably would have prompted the issuer of the guaranty to draw on the credit. When the account party sought to enjoin a draw on the credit, the court, in clear violation of the independence principle, construed the side agreement.[178] The *Paccar* case was reversed on appeal on a jurisdictional point.[179]

If the court is unaware of the importance of the independence principle, it may overlook critical distinctions in the case. In *Banque Paribas v. Hamilton Industries, International, Inc.*,[180] the court held that it was of no moment whether the defendant bank was a confirming bank or the beneficiary of a credit. In fact, the role of the defendant determines the content of its rights and duties. If the defendant is a confirming bank, its claim against the issuer is one for reimbursement. The claim will fail if the bank does not follow the instructions of the opening bank. If, on the other hand, the defendant is a beneficiary, it can recover from the issuer only by satisfying the documentary conditions of the credit; and payment can be stopped only if the beneficiary is practicing fraud on the issuer.

The language of the credit quoted in the *Banque Paribas* case indicates clearly that the defendant was indeed the beneficiary. The court remanded the case for determination of whether satisfaction of a provision in a related guaranty was a condition of the defendant's right to be paid by the opening bank. The independence principle teaches that the credit is unaffected by the related guaranty. The guaranty would have been relevant in *Banque Paribas* only if the defendant had been a confirming bank. Thus, it was important in *Paribas* to determine whether the defendant was making the claim either as a beneficiary on the credit or as a confirming bank seeking reimbursement as a matter of agency law.

It is also important in these cases to fashion some limits to the independence principle. Those limits should rest on the principle's purpose, which is to serve the commercial functions of the credit. If it does not

---

[177] Id. at 784.

[178] For an additional case that illustrates the quagmire of contract issues that courts must resolve when they violate the independence principle, see Itek Corp. v. First Nat'l Bank, 730 F.2d 19 (1st Cir. 1984). The *Paccar* and *Itek* courts were faced with the account party's claim that the beneficiary was practicing fraud. The *Paccar* opinion ignores the independence principle. The *Itek* opinion pays it lip service. For a discussion of the independence principle in the fraud cases, see ¶ 7.04[4].

[179] Paccar Int'l, Inc. v. Commercial Bank of Kuwait, 757 F.2d 1058 (9th Cir. 1985).

[180] 767 F.2d 380 (7th Cir. 1985).

serve those functions, application of the principle is not warranted and the common law principles of contract should apply.

In *State Bank v. South Mill Mushroom Sales, Inc.*,[181] the beneficiary and the issuer entered into a compromise agreement when the beneficiary drew on the credit. Later, in a dispute over the issuer's performance of the compromise agreement, the court invoked the independence principle. That approach carries the independence principle to its logical extreme but beyond the reason for the principle. The compromise agreement was a contract, not a letter of credit; it was a substitute for the issuer's obligation on the credit. Apparently, though the opinion is silent on the point, the court assumed that a contract obligation substituted for a letter of credit obligation was entitled to the protection of the independence principle. That approach ignores the fact that the compromise agreement, being a contract and not the letter of credit specialty, was not subject to the exigencies that make the independence principle necessary for letters of credit.

[6] Suits Between Parties to the Underlying Contract

It is not only in cases involving disputes between the beneficiary and the issuer that the question of the credit's independence arises. Sometimes the conflation of credits with other contracts in the broad credit transaction appears in suits by the beneficiary against the issuer and leads courts to apply contract or negotiable instrument rules to a letter of credit relationship.

The confusion can also operate the other way in that courts may incorrectly apply letter of credit rules to a relationship that is independent of the credit arrangement. In *Steinmeyer v. Warner Consolidated Corp.*,[182] the court thought that it was confronted with such a situation. The account party in the *Steinmeyer* case asked his bank to issue a credit to the holders of his promissory notes. The account party had promised to pay the beneficiaries in several installments for stock he had acquired from the beneficiaries. One of the installments, as evidenced by one of the promissory notes, was to be reduced if certain warranties made by the beneficiaries turned out to be untrue. The account party claimed this right of offset against the amount due on the note.

The credit did not speak of any offset and was payable against the holders' presentation of the note and a statement that the customer had failed to pay. The situation was ripe for application of the principle that

---

[181] 875 F.2d 158 (8th Cir. 1989).
[182] 42 Cal. App. 3d 515, 116 Cal. Rptr. 57 (1974).

a credit is independent of the underlying agreement (in this case, the note). Any argument by the issuer that the account party's offset rights excused the issuer from honoring the demand for payment should have failed.

Steinmeyer did not involve dishonor by the issuer. It arose when the account party sued both the issuer and the holders of the note seeking to enjoin the issuer from paying and the holders from presenting the documents. The trial court entered an injunction against the holders, who appealed. The appellate court saw the issue as one involving the rights of the holders against the account party. Apparently, the court recognized that the holders had rights under the credit. The court concluded, however, that in a suit by the account party against the holders, "the letter of credit cannot be construed in isolation from the underlying agreement and the promissory note."[183] The holders had argued that California's nonuniform version of Section 5-114 codified the independence principle, but, by its holding, the court firmly rejected the argument that Section 5-114 applied in this setting.

The error in *Steinmeyer* is one of misperceiving the source of the holders' rights. The holders had credit rights emanating from the credit and holder rights emanating from the notes. The account party may successfully challenge the credit rights or the holder rights or both, but each set of rights is subject to the law that governs the documentary source of those rights. It may well be that under credit law—namely, under Section 5-114—the account party did have the right to enjoin the bank and the beneficiary holders.[184] Inquiry into the issue, however, begins with the independence principle, not with the assertion that the *Steinmeyer* court makes: that Section 5-114 does not apply and that all of the documents, including the contract out of which the note arose, therefore must be construed together.

The *Steinmeyer* court considered, in a claim on a letter of credit, issues relating to the underlying contract. The account party's right of setoff against the holders arose out of the underlying contract and was not mentioned in the credit. The credit referred to the note. The note referred to the stock purchase agreement. The court construed the language of the credit by referring to the note and to the stock purchase agreement. Such inquiry hardly serves the low-cost and prompt pay-

---

[183] Id. at 518, 116 Cal. Rptr. at 59.

[184] The California version of U.C.C. § 5-114, however, does not authorize injunctions against the issuer. See Cal. Com. Code § 5-114 and comment 6 (West Supp. 1990); cf. Nev. Rev. Stat. § 104.5114 (1986) (same rule).

ment objectives of credits and conflicts with the independence principle.[185]

In *Wyle v. Bank Melli*,[186] the court acknowledged that *Steinmeyer* offends the independence principle, but it approved the rule of *Steinmeyer*. In *Wyle*, the court considered California's nonuniform version of Section 5-114(2)[187] and concluded that the California legislature had prohibited injunctions because it assumed that (1) in the account party's suit against the issuer, the beneficiary's interest might not be protected; and (2) the account party could obtain relief in an action against the beneficiary in the beneficiary's forum.

The *Wyle* court would not enforce the California provision when the beneficiary was subject to jurisdiction in California or when the courts in the beneficiary's forum appeared to be predisposed against the account party, as when Iranian courts were disposed against the American account party in *Wyle*. The *Wyle* holding leaves the California rule with little room to operate. Since many credits are entirely domestic or involve beneficiaries that are present in California under traditional standards, the *Wyle* court would apply the California rule in the rare case only.[188]

The *Wyle* court overlooked the main purposes of the independence principle: to permit the credit to shift costs and to effect prompt payment.[189] The court's jurisdiction over the beneficiary notwithstanding, an injunction against payment thwarts the functions of the credit. The *Wyle* and *Steinmeyer* courts did not understand the independence principle.[190] No policy of the independence principle is served by ignoring the effect in the underlying transaction of payment under the credit. Significantly, the Court of Appeals for the First Circuit declined to follow

---

[185] For a case similar to *Steinmeyer* in which the court refused to permit the account party to assert in the credit transaction defenses arising out of the underlying transaction, see Aspen Planners Ltd. v. Commerce Masonry & Forming Ltd., 100 D.L.R.3d 546 (Ont. H. Ct. 1979).

[186] 577 F. Supp. 1148 (N.D. Cal. 1983).

[187] See supra note 184.

[188] Cf. Trans Meridian Trading, Inc. v. Empresa Nacional De Comercializacion De Insumos, 829 F.2d 949 (9th Cir. 1987) (exposing narrowness of *Wyle* rule by denying injunction in favor of plaintiff account party that would have to sue beneficiary for wrongful draw under credit in Peru); see also Paccar Int'l, Inc. v. Commercial Bank of Kuwait, 587 F. Supp. 783 (C.D. Cal. 1984) (holding that foreign beneficiary was subject to jurisdiction by virtue of having drawn on credit issued by California bank), rev'd, 757 F.2d 1058 (9th Cir. 1985). For a general discussion of the jurisdiction rules, see ¶ 11.01.

[189] For discussion of the credit's functions, see ¶ 3.07.

[190] Cf. Mitsui Mfrs. Bank v. Texas Commerce Bank, 159 Cal. App. 3d 1051, 206 Cal. Rptr. 218 (1984) (following the *Steinmeyer* rule).

Steinmeyer in an action by the account party to enjoin the beneficiary. In *Ground Air Transfer, Inc. v. Westates Airlines, Inc.*,[191] the court viewed *Steinmeyer* as a departure from the policy of most cases, particularly from the policy of California law as reflected in California's non-uniform version of Section 5-114(2). The *Ground Air Transfer* court concluded that the California Supreme Court would not adhere to the rule of *Steinmeyer*.

In re Coleman Pipe, Inc.[192] involved the effect of payment under the credit on a beneficiary's security interest in the underlying transaction. Two secured parties were claiming an interest in a shipment of pipe on which one of the secured parties apparently had obtained payment under a letter of credit. The second secured party argued that the payment caused the first secured party's interest in the shipment to expire.

The *Coleman Pipe* court rejected the argument on the ground that it offended the independence principle. The purpose of the independence principle is to prevent disputes in the underlying transaction from interfering with the smooth functioning of the credit transaction. In *Coleman Pipe*, the credit transaction proceeded smoothly to its conclusion: payment of the beneficiary's draft. It would not have interfered with the credit transaction to take account of that payment in deciding whether the beneficiary had a valid security interest in pipe shipped pursuant to the underlying transaction.

Similarly, in *Universal Security Co. v. Ring*,[193] the court applied the independence principle to the account party's suit against the beneficiary for wrongful draw on the letter of credit. In language that may be dictum, the court held that the independence principle applied. That language is unfortunate. In the account party's lawsuit against the beneficiary for wrongful draw,[194] the facts of the underlying transaction are surely pertinent. If the beneficiary has practiced fraud, for example, or has breached the underlying contract, the account party might have recovery on a breach of warranty theory. Fraud gives rise to a narrow exception to the independence principle even in actions by the account party against the *issuer*.[195]

In the account party's action against the beneficiary, a suit that arises after payment under the credit, the exigencies of the credit pay-

[191] 899 F.2d 1269 (1st Cir. 1990).

[192] 40 Bankr. 338 (Bankr. N.D. Tex. 1984).

[193] 298 Ark. 582, 769 S.W.2d 750 (1989).

[194] Presumably, the action is one for breach of warranty. For discussion of the breach of warranty cause of action, see ¶ 6.07.

[195] For discussion of that narrow exception to the independence principle in actions against the issuer, see ¶ 7.04.

ment situation do not arise. In *Universal Security*, the court should have been able to delve into the underlying transaction and into related transactions to determine whether fraud had indeed occurred. By the same token, in the event the account party's action is one for breach of the letter of credit warranty, the court should be able to look to the underlying transaction to determine whether the beneficiary has performed the terms of the credit. That performance may well rest on facts arising in the underlying transaction. By the same reasoning, it is not impermissible or a violation of the independence principle for a court to look to the credit transaction to construe the underlying contract. In *Fertilizer Corp. of America v. P.S. International, Inc.*,[196] the commercial parties failed to incorporate a delivery term in their sales contract, and the court used the terms of the credit and an amendment to it to supply the delivery term.

In *Novus Equities Corp. v. EM-TY Partnership*,[197] the court used a broad inquiry into the underlying transaction to construe the credit. In the *Novus Equities* case, the buyer of real estate gave the seller cash and a note secured by a letter of credit and agreed to make further payments. When the buyer defaulted, the seller took back the real estate and drew on the letter of credit, arguing that the note was part of the down payment that served as liquidated damages. The buyer argued that the letter of credit secured a deferred payment and was not part of the down payment. The court held that because the letter of credit rendered the note the equivalent of cash, the note was part of the down payment; therefore, the seller was entitled to draw.

The holding rests on the court's inquiry into the underlying transaction and necessitated an order restraining payment of the credit until the court could complete the inquiry. Fidelity to the independence principle would have resulted in a denial of the restraining order and a refusal to inquire into the purpose of the credit. That inquiry is proper in a separate action by the account party against the beneficiary for breach of the underlying transaction. That separate action, of course, would have proceeded after payment, and the beneficiary would have held the funds during that litigation—the result that the cost-shifting functions of the credit are designed to achieve.

In *Banque Paribas v. Hamilton Industries International, Inc.*,[198] the court may have permitted the account party to render the credit subject to a related agreement. The credit in the *Banque Paribas* case appeared

[196] 729 F. Supp. 837 (S.D. Fla. 1989).

[197] 366 N.W.2d 732 (Minn. Ct. App. 1985), rev'd en banc, 381 N.W.2d 426 (Minn. 1986).

[198] 767 F.2d 380 (7th Cir. 1985).

to involve a beneficiary of a credit that issued in turn a guaranty letter to a third party.[199] The issuer brought an interpleader action. The court, seeing the issue as one of determining whether the beneficiary had paid properly on the guaranty, concluded that if the payment on the guaranty was improper, the payment on the credit was improper. Thus, the *Banque Paribas* court rendered the credit undertaking dependent on the ancillary guaranty, all in violation of the independence principle.[200]

To the extent inquiry into the underlying transaction does not interfere with payment under the credit, that inquiry is not offensive to the independence principle. In *Wood v. R.R. Donnelley & Sons Co.*,[201] after failing to obtain an injunction against payment, the account party sued the beneficiary for breaching the underlying transaction or an understanding related to it. The court properly noted that this suit does not violate the independence principle. In fact, one might argue that the proceedings in *Wood* are a necessary concomitant of the independence principle. In part, it is concern for the independence of the credit that prompts courts to deny equitable relief to account parties seeking to enjoin payment of the credit. Whatever the courts' concerns,[202] it is doubtful that they will refuse to interfere in the credit transaction if the account party has no remedy at law. The *Wood* holding is not inconsistent with the independence principle; it serves the independence principle.

Warner v. Central Trust[203] involved the account party's attempt to raise defenses to the underlying transaction in his action to recover payment made to the successor of the beneficiary under the credit. Warner

---

[199] The opinion describes the credit transaction in a manner that supports this conclusion, but it is a confusing opinion in which the court suggests that the beneficiary may in fact have been a confirming bank. See supra ¶ 2.09[5].

[200] For discussion of cases that involve documents that refer to the underlying transaction and that have the effect of elevating good faith disputes in the underlying transaction to fraud in the letter of credit transaction, see ¶ 7.04[4][c]. For discussion suggesting that interpleader is not proper in letter of credit cases, see American Bank v. Leasing Serv. Co. (In re Air Conditioning, Inc. of Stuart), 845 F.2d 293 (11th Cir. 1988), cert. denied sub nom. First Interstate Credit Alliance, Inc. v. American Bank, 109 S. Ct. 557 (1988); Lafayette Corp. v. Bank of Boston Int'l S., 723 F. Supp. 1461 (S.D. Fla. 1989); Sea Management Servs., Ltd. v. Club Sea, Inc., 512 So. 2d 1025 (Fla. Dist. Ct. App. 1987); Dallas Bank & Trust v. Commonwealth Dev. Corp., 686 S.W.2d 226 (Tex. Ct. App. 1984). See generally ¶ 11.06.

[201] 888 F.2d 313 (3d Cir. 1989).

[202] In part, of course, courts are concerned that account parties not enjoy the extraordinary remedies of equity when they have an adequate remedy at law — a concern that apparently prompted the lower state court, before removal, to deny the injunction in *Wood*. For general discussion of the rules of equity as they apply to the account party's efforts to stop payment of the credit, see ¶¶ 7.04[1], 11.04.

[203] 798 F.2d 167 (6th Cir. 1986).

was a limited partner who agreed to provide security for the partnership's loan from Penn Square Bank. Pursuant to his agreement with the partnership, Warner caused Central Trust Co. to issue its standby credit to the partnership, which transferred the credit to Penn Square. Warner claimed that, unbeknownst to him, Penn Square and the partnership had altered the terms of the loan agreement and that the change released him.

Warner relied on two theories. First, he argued that his obligation was that of a guarantor of the loan agreement and that a change in the terms of that agreement released him as a matter of guaranty law. Second, he argued that the partnership was his agent, that it exceeded its authority by agreeing to the alterations, that Penn Square knew that the agent was acting beyond the scope of its authority, and that as a matter of agency law he was not bound under the altered loan agreement.

The trial court rejected Warner's arguments on the ground that the letter of credit obligation is primary and is not subject to these defenses. The Court of Appeals for the Sixth Circuit reversed, holding that, in this suit by the account party against the beneficiary after payment of the credit, the nature of the account party's obligation is dispositive. The *Warner* court correctly held that the obligation of the issuer of the credit is primary and that the obligation of the account party on the underlying obligation may well be secondary, as Warner argued. The court remanded the case, however, to determine whether Warner knew of the alterations in the loan agreement and whether by his silence he had agreed to them, thereby making him liable under agency law or guaranty law.

The *Warner* opinion holds that the account party may recover the payment made to the beneficiary if his obligation on the underlying contract has been discharged or if he has some other defense in the underlying transaction. The independence principle does not conflict with that holding. In *Warner*, both courts properly protected the credit transaction and permitted it to proceed to payment. The dispute between the account party and the beneficiary in the underlying transaction did not harm the credit device.[204]

Significantly, in response to the claim of the FDIC as successor to Penn Square for interest over the eleven months that it had to litigate payment under the credit, the *Warner* court implicitly approved of the award of interest at the statutory rate. That item of damages would not have been recoverable, of course, if the trial court had found on remand that Warner had a defense on the underlying contract.

---

[204] Warner failed to enjoin payment of the credit precisely because he had an adequate remedy at law: this action against the beneficiary. See generally ¶ 7.04[1].

Gatz v. Southwest Bank[205] involved a similar credit securing a note to a limited partnership. When the beneficiary, Penn Square Bank, drew on the credit, the account party obtained a state court restraining order. Upon Penn Square Bank's insolvency, the FDIC, its receiver, removed to the federal court. Thereafter the account party and the FDIC entered into a settlement agreement. When the FDIC drew on the credit, the account party argued that the draw was in violation of the agreement. The *Gatz* court rejected the account party's reading of the settlement agreement and also held that the issuer's obligation under the credit was independent of the settlement agreement.

In *Procyon Corp. v. Components Direct, Inc.*,[206] the defendant seller and the plaintiff buyer agreed orally to the sale of computer components. The oral agreement included the understanding that the buyer would obtain a letter of credit to secure the purchase price. When the seller failed to deliver the components, the buyer sued on the oral agreement and the seller invoked the statute of frauds in Section 2-201 of the Code.

Under Section 2-201(2) the statute does not apply, and the seller has no defense if there is a written memorandum of the agreement "sufficient against" the buyer. The plaintiff buyer in *Procyon* argued that the letter of credit was such a memorandum, and the court agreed. Holding that the signature of the issuer on the credit was a signature in an agency capacity that constituted the signature of the buyer, the court found the memorandum "sufficient against" the buyer, rendering the transaction one within the subsection's exception.

The *Procyon* court made much of the fact that the purpose of the letter of credit was to bind the buyer to the sale and to give the seller recourse in the event the buyer failed to live up to its obligation under the oral agreement. Under that premise, there is some appeal in the court's conclusion that the exception to the statute of frauds should apply, since the obvious purpose of the exception is to permit both parties to enforce an agreement to which one of them is bound by the memorandum.

The court went too far, however, in support of its position. The *Procyon* opinion argues that the letter of credit itself binds the buyer. In fact, it does not, the credit being the primary obligation of the issuer independent of the sales agreement. The language in the opinion suggesting that the issuer signed the credit as an agent is contrary to the independence principle and to the notion that the credit is the primary undertaking of the issuer.

[205] 836 F.2d 1089 (8th Cir. 1988).
[206] 203 Cal. App. 3d 409, 249 Cal. Rptr. 813 (1988).

In short, the result in *Procyon* may be correct. A seller whose buyer causes a credit to issue in order to provide the seller with recourse in the event of the buyer's breach may well fall into the spirit of the subsection (2) exception to the statute of frauds. That result is consistent with the purpose of the exception and with the legislative command in the Code that its provisions be construed in accordance with the purpose of the provisions.[207] It is not correct to suggest that the *Procyon* facts come within the letter of the subsection. The issuer's undertaking to pay the seller is not the obligation of the buyer account party, and the signature of the issuer on the credit is not a signature of the account party's agent.

These cases illustrate the tension between the independence principle, on the one hand, and, on the other, the desire of courts to put the broad transaction together in order to achieve fair and efficient results. In dealing with the tension of those policies, courts must understand the purpose of the independence principle.

[7] Claims on the Reimbursement Agreement

The exigencies that give rise to the independence principle exist in the letter of credit context but do not appear in the issuer–account party relationship.

When the account party disputes the issuer's conduct, that dispute generally involves the respective rights and duties of the two parties under the reimbursement agreement, an ordinary contract. In that context, the independence principle and Code rules fashioned for the letter of credit do not apply.

In *Pioneer Bank & Trust Co. v. Seiko Sporting Goods, U.S.A. Co.*,[208] however, the court resorted to both the independence principle and Article 5 letter of credit rules. In *Pioneer Bank*, the account party, arguing that the beneficiary's documents were nonconforming,[209] sued the issuer for debiting its account after improper honor. The plaintiff in *Pioneer Bank* apparently had permitted the goods subject to the underlying contract to pass to its customer. The opinion indicates that the issuer had argued that, because the plaintiff permitted the third party to obtain the goods, the plaintiff should not be able to recover. In an opinion invoking the independence principle, the court rejected that argument. The

---

[207] See U.C.C. § 1-102 and comment 1.

[208] 184 Ill. App. 3d 783, 540 N.E.2d 808 (1989).

[209] For discussion of the standard of documentary compliance in the *Pioneer Bank* case, see ¶ 9.03[1][a].

court also cited cases decided under Section 5-115 that hold that a beneficiary of a credit does not have to mitigate damages.

Arguably, the *Pioneer Bank* court is wrong on both points. The exigencies of the letter of credit transaction, in which issuers must pay promptly, are not evident in the reimbursement context. The independence principle teaches that the *credit* is independent of conduct under related contracts; it does not teach that the *reimbursement agreement* is independent of that conduct. Section 5-115 and cases decided under it, moreover, are wholly inapposite in the *Pioneer Bank* litigation. Section 5-115 deals with beneficiary damages for wrongful dishonor. The claim in *Pioneer Bank* was by the account party for wrongful honor.

The *Pioneer Bank* opinion indicates that the account party obtained the goods and passed them on to its customer. If the issuer's payment over defective documents did not cause any loss to the account party, it is difficult to justify a rule that permits the account party to avoid reimbursement. The effect of the *Pioneer Bank* ruling may be reversed by subrogating the issuer to the rights of the beneficiary in the underlying contract in order to avoid unjust enrichment,[210] but that is a circuitous route without policy justification.

¶ 2.10 DISTINGUISHING CREDITS FROM SURETY CONTRACTS AND LOAN COMMITMENTS

There are two kinds of commercial undertakings, which themselves are sufficiently akin to letters of credit for them to be mistaken as credits. These undertakings are surety contracts and loan commitments. The credit is neither of these.

[1] Surety Contracts

Traditionally, a guaranty or surety contract is an undertaking by one party to assure a second party of payment or performance by a third party. The liability of the guarantor is secondary and arises upon nonperformance by the third party, the "principal obligor." The liability of an issuer under a credit is primary, not secondary, and it arises upon the presentation of documents, not on the nonperformance of a principal obligor.

---

[210] For discussion of subrogation in the issuer and account party setting, see ¶ 7.05[2][b].

Admittedly, a credit engagement often serves to guarantee payment or performance, and courts have long recognized that, in a sense, issuers of credits "must be regarded as sureties."[211] A seller of goods often insists on a commercial letter of credit because he is unsure of the buyer's ability to pay. The standby credit arises out of situations in which the beneficiary wants to guard against the account party's nonperformance. In both instances, the credit serves in the nature of a guaranty.

It is a misapplication of surety law, however, to apply it to credits, even though they serve to guarantee performance. Credits are primary obligations; surety law is the law of secondary obligations. Courts generally have accepted the distinction between the primary obligation of the credit issuer and the secondary obligation of a surety.[212] The courts recognize that surety rules regarding consideration,[213] damages,[214] construction,[215] security,[216] release,[217] and subrogation[218] do not apply to

---

[211] Birckhead v. George, 5 Hill 634, 640 (N.Y. 1843); accord Chase Manhattan Bank v. Equibank, 394 F. Supp, 352, 355 (W.D. Pa. 1975); Republic Nat'l Bank v. Northwest Nat'l Bank, 578 S.W.2d 109, 114 (Tex. 1978). It is not proper to conclude, then, as the court did in Dubuque Packing Co. v. Fitzgibbon, 599 P.2d 440 (Okla. Ct. App. 1979), that because a document serves as a guaranty, it cannot be a letter of credit. In International Multifoods Corp. v. Mardian, 379 N.W.2d 840 (S.D. 1985), the beneficiary of a document entitled "guaranty" argued that the obligors could not raise certain defenses, because the guaranty was really a letter of credit. The court held that the obligation was secondary and that, therefore, it was a guaranty, not a letter of credit. But cf. Thomas v. Jones, No. CA87-249 (Ark. Ct. App. Feb. 3, 1988) (improperly treating as letter of credit undertaking that, by its terms, was secondary obligation).

[212] See, e.g., Townsley v. Sumrall, 27 U.S. (2 Pet.) 170, 182 (1829); New York Life Ins. Co. v. Hartford Nat'l Bank & Trust Co., 173 Conn. 492, 378 A.2d 562 (1977).

[213] Cf. Bridge v. Welda State Bank, 222 Mo. App. 586, 292 S.W. 1079 (1927) (consideration may be necessary to support guaranty, but not to support letter of credit).

[214] Damages under a letter of credit are those arising from dishonor, not those arising from the default of the customer on the underlying agreement. New York Life Ins. Co. v. Hartford Nat'l Bank & Trust Co., 173 Conn. 492, 378 A.2d 562 (1977).

[215] Rules for construing a guaranty differ from those for construing a letter of credit. Dubuque Packing Co. v. Fitzgibbon, 599 P.2d 440 (Okla. Ct. App. 1979).

[216] State laws dealing with the rights of a surety's creditor in security held by the surety do not apply to the beneficiary of a credit. Royal Bank of Can. v. Trone (In re Westgate-Cal. Corp.), 634 F.2d 459 (9th Cir. 1980).

[217] Asociacion De Azucareros De Guat. v. United States Nat'l Bank, 423 F.2d 638, 641 (9th Cir. 1970) (beneficiary's release of account party on underlying contract does not release issuer on letter of credit).

[218] Merchants Bank & Trust Co. v. Economic Enters., Inc., 44 Bankr. 230 (Bankr. D. Conn. 1984) (holding that issuer may not subrogate itself to beneficiary's rights arising out of underlying contract); Overseas Trading Corp. v. Irving Trust

letters of credit, for which the law has developed special rules in these areas.[219]

In *Republic National Bank v. Northwest National Bank*,[220] the Texas Court of Civil Appeals construed a letter of credit, which served to guarantee payment of a promissory note, as a guaranty contract forbidden by laws regulating banks. The Texas Supreme Court, in a forceful opinion, overturned that holding.[221] The issue raised in the *Republic National Bank* case refuses to go away, however.[222] In *Wichita Eagle & Beacon Publishing Co. v. Pacific National Bank*,[223] the court held that a bank engagement, dubbed a letter of credit, was subject to the law of guaranty contracts because the credit operated against the occurrence or nonoccurrence of facts, rather than against the presentation of documents.

The *Wichita* case[224] serves to remind us of a second, and important, distinction between surety contracts and letters of credit. A surety or guaranty contract, because it is secondary in nature, depends on the nonperformance of the principal obligor, whose performance the surety contract guarantees. The determination of guaranty liability requires an examination of the principal obligor's conduct. That examination is often lengthy, complicated, and costly. It differs inherently from the letter of credit's prompt payment feature, which rests on the practice of examining documents at a desk in a bank. Factual determination is the business of surety company investigators and claims analysts and is probably not a proper function for commercial banks.[225]

Co., 82 N.Y.S. 2d 72, 76 (Sup. Ct. 1948) (issuer may not subrogate itself to account party's right against beneficiary). But cf. FDIC v. Liberty Nat'l Bank & Trust Co., 806 F.2d 961 (10th Cir. 1986) (confirming bank may subrogate itself to rights of beneficiary against issuer in FDIC liquidation proceedings); American Ins. Ass'n v. Clarke, 656 F. Supp. 404 (D.D.C. 1987), aff'd, 865 F.2d 278 (D.C. Cir. 1989) (assuming that issuer of functional equivalent of standby letter of credit will be subrogated to rights of beneficiary against account party).

[219] For the letter of credit rule on consideration, see U.C.C. § 5-105. For the letter of credit rule on damages, see U.C.C. § 5-115. For discussion of the rules for construing letters of credit, see ¶ 4.08. For discussion of the letter of credit rule on security, see ¶¶ 8.03, 10.04. For discussion of subrogation in letter of credit law, see ¶ 7.05[2].

[220] 566 S.W.2d 358 (Tex. Civ. App.), rev'd, 578 S.W.2d 109 (Tex. 1978).

[221] Republic Nat'l Bank v. Northwest Nat'l Bank, 578 S.W.2d 109 (Tex. 1978).

[222] For a full discussion of that issue in the context of government regulation of banks, see ¶ 12.02.

[223] 493 F.2d 1285 (9th Cir. 1974).

[224] For a discussion of the *Wichita* case, see supra ¶ 2.05.

[225] Cf. Arbest Constr. Co. v. First Nat'l Bank & Trust Co., 777 F.2d 581 (10th Cir. 1985) (holding that standby letter of credit securing prime contractor's performance did not benefit subcontractors under third-party beneficiary law); American Ins. Ass'n v. Clarke, 865 F.2d 278 (D.C. Cir. 1989) (holding that national bank oper-

In *Ensco Environmental Services, Inc. v. United States*,[226] the Comptroller General of the United States had opined that a standby letter of credit was insufficient as a bid bond because the account party on the credit and the bidding party, though cognate companies, were not identical. The Comptroller based the ruling on authority that surety bonds issued on behalf of one party to secure bids of another party are not enforceable against the surety when the bidding party defaults. The *Ensco* court rejected the Comptroller's analysis, which the court viewed as rooted in the notion that a surety is secondarily liable—a notion that is inapplicable to letters of credit, which are primary obligations.

In *City of Philadelphia v. American Coastal Industries, Inc.*,[227] on the other hand, the court held that a municipality properly rejected a letter of credit as a substitute for performance and payment bonds. Such bonds, the court held, differ materially from letters of credit. Under the former, a surety will complete a project even if it costs more than the penal sum stipulated in the bond, the court held. Under the latter, the issuer's obligation is limited to the amount stated in the letter of credit.

For a variety of reasons, foreign banks have tended to call their primary obligations "guaranties," while U.S. banks call theirs "standby letters of credit."[228] "First-demand guaranties," "performance guaranties," and "simple-demand guaranties" are generally terms that refer to primary guaranties, which are virtually the same as letters of credit, rather than surety arrangements, which are quite different.[229]

---

ating subsidiary may issue insurance because subsidiary makes credit, not actuarial judgments, and because subsidiary's obligation under insurance is primary, not secondary, rendering insurance functional equivalent of standby letter of credit—an instrument that national banks have traditionally issued); see also State v. Morganstein, 703 S.W.2d 894 (Mo. 1986) (holding that beneficiary of credit serving in lieu of supersedeas bond could not recover from issuer by showing that principal had defaulted, liability on credit being determined by documentary compliance, not by default of principal). For a practical discussion of the differences between letters of credit and bonds used in the construction industry, see Jones, "Letters of Credit in the United States Construction Industry," 14 Int'l Bus. Law. 17 (1986).

[226] 650 F. Supp. 583 (W.D. Mo. 1986).

[227] 704 F. Supp. 587 (E.D. Pa. 1988).

[228] For discussion of the reasons for U.S. banks' reluctance to use the term "guaranty," see ¶ 12.02[1].

[229] For further discussion of the growth in use of the primary "guaranty" and the adaptation of letter of credit law to them, see ¶ 1.05. In Eakin v. Continental Ill. Nat'l Bank & Trust Co., 875 F.2d 114 (7th Cir. 1989), the issuer of a credit securing a construction bond argued that the beneficiary's otherwise complying draw was premature in view of the fact that the beneficiary had yet to incur losses under the bond and that in any event the beneficiary had not suffered losses by virtue of the issuer's dishonor. The *Eakin* court rejected both arguments and ordered the issuer to pay. Standby letters of credit, the court held, serve to avoid "complex disputes about how much the [parties] 'really' owe. The promise and premise are 'pay now, argue later.'" Id. at 116.

[2] Loan Commitments

[a] Distinguishing Credits From Loan Commitments

The credit is not the same as a line of credit or a commitment to lend.[230] Borrowers sometimes ask their banks to open a commitment that is in the nature of an account available for future borrowing. A dealer who is about to enter into a significant contract with a supplier, for example, may want to secure a bank's assurances that financing will be available during the course of the supply contract. The borrower does not want the bank to disburse loan proceeds immediately but wants the bank to make a commitment that it will disburse funds later, when the dealer needs cash.

Sometimes the bank's commitment is one to honor the dealer's drafts or overdrafts. The bank often evidences its commitment in a letter. Carefully drawn commitment letters contain significant conditions to the bank's obligation to lend, not the least of which is often a provision that permits the bank to terminate its commitment in the event it deems itself insecure.[231]

Commitments also frequently contain a provision that extinguishes the bank's obligation in the event the borrower has failed in any respect to observe its obligations to the bank. The borrower's obligations include paying the unpaid principal, providing security, or furnishing financial information. Most commitment letters run to a specific borrower only and contain strict prohibition against transfer or assignment. That is not to say that a bank's commitment to lend is an illusory promise. It is not. It serves not to guarantee the honor of the borrower's checks or drafts, however, but to guarantee the borrower a source of credit, usually at specified rates and on specified conditions.

---

[230] See, e.g., Regulation H, 12 C.F.R. pt. 208, app. A (1990) (distinguishing letters of credit from loan commitments). But cf. 12 C.F.R. § 32.2(d) (1989) (Comptroller of the Currency regulation defining for loan limit purposes "contractual commitment to advance funds" to include a standby letter of credit but not loan commitments that are not drawn on). For a general discussion of bank lending limits, see ¶ 12.03. For discussion of a bank's authority to issue standby credits, see ¶ 12.02[1][c].

[231] Cf. Runnemede Owners, Inc. v. Crest Mortgage Corp., 861 F.2d 1053 (7th Cir. 1988) (distinguishing loan commitment with condition that bank's loan committee approve commitment from unconditional nature of letter of credit); Transparent Prods. Corp. v. Paysaver Credit Union, 864 F.2d 60 (7th Cir. 1988) (holding that document denominated as letter of credit evidenced line of credit but was not letter of credit).

In some respects, the bank's loan commitment resembles a revocable two-party credit.[232] Its function, however, if not its appearance, is significantly different from that of the credit. The letter of credit, even in two-party cases where the credit promise runs to the account party, is designed to give value to drafts drawn by the customer or by third parties. By virtue of a credit issuer's promise to pay, to accept, or to negotiate drafts that otherwise would be suspect become marketable.[233] The draft or demand for payment, which is so essential to the letter of credit transaction (so essential that Article 5 renders such draft or demand the central requisite of a letter of credit), is incidental to the loan commitment transaction in which the borrower's primary purpose is to obtain a promise of funds in the event certain conditions relating to the financial responsibility of the borrower are satisfied.

Banks treat a loan commitment in a manner far different from the way that they treat letters of credit. Under a loan commitment, a bank allocates a portion of its future lendable funds at an agreed-upon rate. A commitment generally emanates from the bank's commercial loan department, and the bank charges a considerable fee for the commitment.[234] Letters of credit, on the other hand, often do not involve payments on credit. Usually, the issuer requires the customer to put the bank in funds before it must make payment under the credit. The credit, furthermore, emanates from the international department or from the letter of credit department and usually generates only modest charges.[235]

It is not uncommon for banks that contemplate loans to a borrower to take from the borrower in advance of any loan disbursement a promissory note in the face amount of the maximum loan anticipated, with the understanding set forth in a written loan agreement approved by the loan committee and kept permanently in the bank's records that the

---

[232] In a two-party credit, the account party and the issuer are the same. For an example of such a credit, see Ufitec, S.A. v. Trade Bank & Trust Co., 21 A.D.2d 187, 249 N.Y.S.2d 557 (1964), aff'd, 16 N.Y.2d 698, 209 N.E.2d 551, 261 N.Y.S.2d 893 (1965).

[233] Cf. Coolidge v. Payson, 15 U.S. (2 Wheat.) 66, 72 (1817) (noting that purpose of acceptance is to give credit to draft).

[234] In New York Life Ins. Co. v. Hartford Nat'l Bank & Trust Co., 173 Conn. 492, 378 A.2d 562 (1977), the insurance company that issued a commitment for a take-out loan on a real estate development project charged $90,000 for its commitment.

[235] In a case in which the matter became public, a bank charged $626 for a $250,000 credit. See Kozolchyk, "The Letter of Credit in Court: An Expert Testifies," 99 Banking L.J. 340, 350 (1982). The charge for opening a commercial credit may be as low as 0.125 percent of the credit amount. See Maulella, "Uncorking the Letter of Credit for Quicker Export Collections," Corporate Cashflow (Feb. 1989), reprinted in Letter of Credit Update 42 (Oct. 1989).

amount due on the note will be the sum of all advances plus interest and other charges. In one case,[236] the trustee in bankruptcy of such a borrower argued that the maker of this kind of note was in a position analogous to that of the beneficiary of a letter of credit and that the bank did not have the right to refuse to make advances under the note any more than an issuer has the right to refuse to honor the conforming demands of a credit beneficiary. Finding the argument "implausible and unpersuasive,"[237] the court rejected the analogy.

In *Calumet National Bank v. First National Bank*,[238] a bank executed an engagement to make loans after a certain date so long as certain parcels of real estate were not sold. The engagement resembled a commitment to lend. The court held that it was not a letter of credit. In *Fiat Motors of North America, Inc. v. Mellon Bank N.A.*,[239] a bank issued a "wholesale financing commitment" to the dealer's supplier on behalf of its dealer customer. The commitment required the bank to honor invoices of the supplier provided that they were submitted with other documents, had a maximum daily amount, and contained a termination provision. Despite the title of the document, the trial court held that it was a letter of credit. Given that characterization of the floor planner's engagement, the court had little difficulty in deciding that an incentive program between the dealer and the supplier that had the effect of altering the payment arrangements between the commercial parties did not excuse the floor planner's liability under the commitment, the commitment being independent of the dealer-supplier contract.

In *Ford Motor Co. v. St. James Bank & Trust Co.*,[240] an automobile manufacturer asked the dealer's bank floor planner to execute the manufacturer's standard letter of credit form for floor planners. The bank's officer changed the term "letter of credit" wherever it appeared in the document to "verification of credit." The document contained a number of ambiguous terms, and the court heard testimony concerning the intent of the officer in executing the "verification." The court concluded, in part on the basis of that testimony, that the document was a verification of the dealer's line of credit and was not a letter of credit.

A document is a letter of credit subject to the rules of Article 5 of the Code if the document satisfies the Code's scope and definition provisions in Sections 5-102 and 5-103. The *Ford* opinion does not explain

---

[236] Whinnery v. Bank of Onalaska (In re Taggatz), 106 Bankr. 983 (Bankr. W.D. Wis. 1989).

[237] Id. at 990.

[238] No. 83 C 2141 (N.D. Ill. Aug. 19, 1983).

[239] 827 F.2d 924 (3d Cir. 1987).

[240] 731 F.2d 284 (5th Cir. 1984).

the reason why it was important to determine the nature of the document. Presumably, the revocability of the credit, if it was a credit, was at issue. The court does not indicate whether the form described the undertaking as irrevocable, but one suspects that it was revocable only with notice. In that event, the Code does not permit the bank to revoke without the requisite notice.[241] The Code scope and definition provisions imply strongly that the intent of the issuer should not govern,[242] and it is regrettable that the *Ford* court relied on intent and the document's label instead of on the nature of the document.

[b] Confusion in the Cases

In *Johnston v. State Bank*,[243] the defendant issued a loan commitment to its customers. Then, perhaps inadvisedly, it notified a contractor, whom the customers had employed for the construction of a home, that the loan commitment had issued. The contractor argued that the notice to him was a letter of credit independent of his underlying obligation to the bank's customer.

The court properly rejected the argument, noting that nothing the bank had done constituted a direct promise by it to the contractor. The court also could have pointed out that the bank's notice, which failed to call for drafts or demands for payment and which failed to use conspicuously the term "letter of credit," did not meet the Article 5 letter of credit definition.[244] Given those critical failures, courts should not invoke credit law.[245] Article 5 does not apply to an engagement to make advances.[246]

In *Toyota Industrial Trucks U.S.A., Inc. v. Citizens National Bank*,[247] the court distinguished a loan commitment from a letter of

---

[241] For a discussion of the revocation question, see ¶¶ 1.10, 4.08[4].

[242] See First Am. Nat'l Bank v. Alcorn, Inc., 361 So. 2d 481 (Miss. 1981).

[243] 195 N.W.2d 126 (Iowa 1972).

[244] For a discussion of the "letter of credit" definition, see supra ¶¶ 2.03–2.07.

[245] Thus, the *Johnston* case does not suffer the same criticism from which the *Wichita* case suffers. The document in *Wichita* refers to itself conspicuously as a letter of credit, and a holding that Article 5 applies would not justify a complaint of surprise. In *Johnston*, however, one gets the idea that the letter of credit argument was one that arose out of litigating exigency.

[246] U.C.C. § 5-102(2); see also Robert Mallory Lumber Corp. v. B&F Assocs. Inc., 294 Pa. Super. 503, 440 A.2d 579 (1982) (distinguishing line of credit from letter of credit). But cf. Chase Manhattan Bank, N.A. v. Banco Del Atlantico, F.A., 343 So. 2d 936 (Fla. Dist. Ct. App. 1977) (describing letter of credit as line of credit and applying credit law).

[247] 611 F.2d 465 (3d Cir. 1979).

credit, although the parties had not made the same distinction. The question in *Toyota* related to the measure of the plaintiff's damages. The law of damages arising under credits is specialized and does not follow general contract damages rules.[248] The plaintiff's predecessor, a supplier of lift trucks to Promat Corporation, had requested the defendant (Promat's bank) to establish a line of credit in order to secure payment of drafts covering trucks shipped to Promat. The bank negotiated the terms of the line of credit with Toyota and ultimately executed Toyota's standard revolving credit agreement used by Toyota's dealers.[249] The agreement required the bank to honor drafts accompanied by invoices and bills of sale. The court held that the engagement was a letter of credit and that the damages rules of Article 5 did not require the plaintiff to mitigate.

The holding appears to be correct and is significant for banks involved in that kind of inventory financing known as "floor planning." In the *Toyota* case, it was clear that the bank knew that Toyota would not grant a dealership to Promat unless Promat obtained the bank's assurances that Toyota would be paid. Thus, the title of the document notwithstanding, the arrangement appears to be more like a letter of credit than a line of credit or loan commitment. Although the *Toyota* opinion does not reproduce the bank's letter, it appears that the credit imposed requirements on Toyota and thus refers to Toyota. It is unlikely that a true loan commitment letter will impose duties on a third party who is not the borrower.

The *Toyota* case is significant to floor planners because such inventory lenders frequently enter into agreements with their customers' suppliers. Frequently these agreements, as in the *Toyota* case, are drafted by the supplier, are not designated as letters of credit, and are reviewed at the offices of the lender by a bank loan officer skilled in inventory financing but unfamiliar with letters of credit. Nevertheless, the *Toyota* holding properly suggests that such agreements between floor planners and their customers' suppliers are indeed letters of credit subject to the rules of Article 5.[250]

---

[248] See U.C.C. § 5-115. See generally ¶ 9.02[5].

[249] The bank had negotiated with a Toyota corporation that subsequently assigned its rights under the bank's letter. The opinion does not discuss the assignability issue, which U.C.C. § 5-116 appears to raise. For a discussion of the transfer rules of credit law, see ¶ 10.03.

[250] See Comptroller of the Currency, Interpretive Letter No. 214, Fed. Banking L. Rep. (CCH) ¶ 85,295 (July 23, 1981). For another case holding that Toyota's line of credit agreement is a letter of credit, see Dennis Chapman Toyota, Inc. v. Belle State Bank, 759 S.W.2d 330 (Mo. Ct. App. 1988).

In *Native Alaskan Reclamation & Pest Control, Inc. v. United Bank Alaska*,[251] the opinion recites that the defendant bank breached its loan commitment by refusing to disburse funds under a letter of credit. The court analyzed the damages issue as a matter of contract law, and it is not clear from the opinion whether the damages were for breach of the loan commitment or for dishonor of the credit. Also, it is not clear whether there was a loan commitment other than the credit.[252]

---

[251] 685 P.2d 1211 (Alaska 1984).

[252] Cf. Fallston Finishing, Inc. v. First Union Nat'l Bank, 76 N.C. App. 347, 333 S.E.2d 321, cert. denied, 314 N.C. 664, 336 S.E.2d 621 (1985) (involving loan commitment that banker referred to as letter of credit).

CHAPTER 3

The Function of Credits

¶ 3.01 A BASIC MISUNDERSTANDING—LETTERS OF CREDIT vs. CONTRACT AND NEGOTIABLE INSTRUMENT PRINCIPLES

Many of the legal problems confronting credits stem from a basic misunderstanding of the credit's nature and function. When courts attempt to resolve these matters without a clear understanding of the unique credit device involved, they do not contend well with the recurring issues of letter of credit law, especially with questions concerning the authority of banks to issue standby credits,[1] the conflict in the strict compliance rule,[2] and the confusion over the fraud-in-the-transaction rule.[3]

The preceding chapter considers the nature of the credit as a unique commercial specialty that is different from a number of related and similar contracts or instruments. This chapter considers the history, nature, and purpose of the credit in the broad commercial transaction.

The history of credits illustrates many of the functions that credits serve and demonstrates their development as a unique commercial device that is neither pure contract nor pure negotiable instrument but rather a little bit of each. Some decisions, perhaps out of a misperception of the credit's commercial functions, have constrained those functions, while other decisions, perhaps out of an analogous misunderstanding of the credit's nature, have applied, on the one hand, contract principles or, on the other hand, negotiable instrument principles that are inappropriate. This chapter covers the function and nature of credits in order to establish a benchmark against which decisions discussed throughout this treatise may be measured.

At the outset, it is important to dispel confusion that often arises over the nature of the credit itself and to make it clear that the credit is not a contract, though that notion appears to be rife. There is language in the commentary of the Uniform Commercial Code (UCC or the Code) suggesting that a letter of credit is akin to a contract: "The letter of credit is essentially a contract between the issuer and the beneficiary."[4]

Generally, however, the text of the statute itself as well as the commentary refer to the letter of credit as an "engagement."[5] The Code drafters' choice of the term "engagement" is significant. The term comes from the law merchant, not from contract law. It is the same terminology the Code drafters used to describe the obligation of parties to negotiable instruments, which are also creatures of the law merchant.[6] The law merchant implications of this statutory locution find support in the rules the Code fashions for credits themselves. Those rules are pecu-

---

[1] See ¶ 12.02.

[2] See ¶¶ 6.03–6.05.

[3] See ¶ 7.04.

[4] U.C.C. § 5-114, comment 1 (1st sentence).

[5] See U.C.C. § 5-102(2); U.C.C. § 5-103(1)(a) & comment 1; U.C.C. § 5-107, comment 2; U.C.C. § 5-114, comments 1 (2d sentence) and 2 (2d sentence).

[6] See U.C.C. §§ 3-413(1), 3-413(2), 3-414(1) (using term "engages").

liarly noncontractual in nature. For example, the Code (1) does not require consideration for the issuer's engagement to be enforceable[7] and (2) rejects offer and acceptance theory for the formation of a letter of credit in favor of a new concept, that of "establishment."[8]

These statutory choices were no accident. Prior to the adoption of Article 5, there was considerable controversy in American jurisprudence concerning the nature of the credit.[9] It is clear that the drafters thought they were putting that controversy to rest with the adoption of the statute: "This Article is intended within its limited scope . . . to set an *independent* theoretical frame for the further development of letters of credit."[10] The pre-Code controversy supports the conclusion that the drafters sought to free the credit from the fetters of contract theory.

Amoco Oil Co. v. First Bank & Trust Co.[11] illustrates the operation of this independent theoretical frame. In the *Amoco* case, the issuer established a credit in favor of Amoco but failed to make the credit subject to the Uniform Customs and Practice for Documentary Credits (UCP or the Uniform Customs) as Amoco had requested. The credit was in the nature of an invoice standby credit[12]; that is, it secured payment for shipments of product to the issuer's customer, the account party, in the event the account party did not pay. When Amoco officials received the credit, they objected to its form and wrote to the issuer, requesting that it be reissued subject to the Uniform Customs. The issuer ignored the request. When the account party defaulted on its obligation to pay the purchase price, Amoco drew on the credit as issued. The issuer dishonored, arguing that the oil company's letter requesting reissuance of the credit operated as a rejection of the initial credit and as a counteroffer that the issuer never accepted.

The *Amoco* court took the issuer's argument to be symptomatic of the erroneous view that the credit is a contract or an obligation subject to contract principles. Holding that a letter of credit is a commercial specialty, the court refused to accept an argument that essentially "sounds in basic contract law."[13] The court relied instead on Article 5 and characterized the Amoco request for reissuance as a request for a

[7] See U.C.C. § 5-105.

[8] See U.C.C. § 5-106.

[9] For discussion of the history of letters of credit, see ¶¶ 3.02, 3.03.

[10] U.C.C. § 5-101, comment (2d para., last sentence) (emphasis added).

[11] 759 S.W.2d 877 (Mo. Ct. App. 1988).

[12] For an example of an invoice standby credit, see App. C, Doc. 18.

[13] Amoco Oil Co. v. First Bank & Trust Co., 759 S.W.2d 877, 878 (Mo. Ct. App. 1988).

minor amendment, not a rejection of the original credit altogether, and held that the credit remained in force and effect.

¶ 3.02　EARLY USE OF BILLS OF EXCHANGE AND LETTERS OF CREDIT

The earliest function of the credit was to serve bills of exchange (drafts). It is clear that as early as the twelfth century,[14] commerce was confronted with two major problems: First, it was dangerous for merchants to travel with gold; second, commerce generated wealth but generated insufficient currency to satisfy the needs of trade. The bill of exchange addressed the problems of collection and payment that travel made difficult and also addressed the problem of liquidity. The bill, originally a "letter" of exchange,[15] was a request, or order, by a creditor to his debtor that directed the debtor to pay a third party.

A Florentine merchant who bought wool from an Amsterdam merchant might have used a bill of exchange to pay the Dutch seller. The Florentine buyer would have dealt v ith the seller's agent in Florence, probably a relative of the Dutch merchant. The buyer could issue a bill of exchange to the agent in Florence, directing a third party (the drawee) to pay the sum due for the wool. The drawee would have been a creditor of the Italian merchant, someone who owed him money. The agent, having taken the bill in payment for the wool, could travel across Europe or by sea to a commercial center, where he would meet the drawee and ask the drawee for payment. The drawee would pay the draft (1) in gold (though such payment would be rare); (2) by "clearing," that is, by setting the draft off against sums due from the Dutch merchant on other drafts; or (3) by accepting the draft and returning it to the agent. In the third case, if the drawee was a person of substance — a well-known merchant or a banker, as he probably would have been — the holder then

---

[14] "It is quite clear that so soon as commerce begins in any degree to develop, methods will be found of avoiding the risks attendant upon the physical transport of money." Holdsworth, "The Origins and Early History of Negotiable Instruments (II)," 31 L.Q. Rev. 173, 174 (1915). There is strong evidence that bills of exchange predate the late Middle Ages, when one first sees traces of them in the law merchant. That earlier history seemingly has little impact on the modern credit. See generally W. Bewes, The Romance of the Law Merchant 44–51 (1923); 8 W. Holdsworth, A History of English Law ch. iv (2d ed. 1937).

[15] See J. Story, Commentaries on the Law of Bills of Exchange, Foreign and Inland, as Administered in England and America 2 (1843). The word "exchange" reflects the fact that such bills originally served long-distance travel and therefore the exchange of one currency for another. F. Sanborn, Origins of the Early English Maritime and Commercial Law 218 (1930).

had a readily marketable instrument, one on which the banker or promi-
nent merchant was personally liable, having signed it. The agent could
use this "acceptance" to trade, or he could take it with him to other
commercial centers. He could do so armed with the knowledge that such
"currency," while valuable to merchants, was of little value to the brig-
ands who stalked the highways and the pirates who sailed the seas.

In fact, the unaccepted bill itself often was used as currency, because the signatures of the drawer and endorsers signaled the promise of
those signers to pay the instrument in the event the drawee merchant or
banker did not. It was important for merchant houses to maintain their
reputation and integrity, lest their paper not be valued, for the value of
bills was clearly a matter of concern to the merchants and bankers who
dealt in them. Thus, the bill of exchange solved two problems for the
merchants. It provided them with valuable currency, and it reduced the
risk of loss by theft.

It undoubtedly did not take long for some enterprising merchant
whose paper was suspect and therefore subject to heavy discount or to
outright rejection in the trade to strengthen his bills by obtaining the
drawee's announcement in advance of acceptance that he, the drawee,
would pay or accept the bills. That announcement was a "letter of credit" as the term is defined today.[16]

Sometimes merchants or other buyers themselves made such a
promise to pay or accept drafts. When the English King John sent his
"buyers" to Italy in the thirteenth century, he sent with them a letter in
which he engaged to honor the bills that merchants who sold goods to
his emissaries would draw on him. The sellers could use their own
drafts, along with the princely letter, to obtain credit for their own
bills.[17] Similarly, when Thomas Jefferson sent Lewis and Clark off to

---

[16] The evidence supports the assumption. Clearly, letters of credit were known
in England by the time of the seventeenth century, when the bill of exchange had ma-
tured into a negotiable instrument much like the drafts used today. See Malynes, The
Ancient Law Merchant ch. 14 (1629); Holdsworth, "The Origins and Early History
of Negotiable Instruments (IV)," 32 L.Q. Rev. 20 (1916). Professor Kozolchyk, while
he differentiates markedly the early forms of credits from the commercial credit,
traces letter of credit practices from the twelfth century in both English and continental commerce. See Kozolchyk, "The Legal Nature of the Irrevocable Commercial
Letter of Credit," 14 Am. J. Comp. L. 395 (1965).

[17] For accounts of these royal letters of credit, see J. Holden, The History of Negotiable Instruments in English Law 21 n.2 (1955); F. Sanborn, supra note 15, at 217.
For cases involving buyer's letters of credit issued by banks, see, e.g., Omaha Nat'l
Bank v. First Nat'l Bank, 59 Ill. 428 (1871); Nelson v. First Nat'l Bank, 48 Ill. 36
(1868); Bank of Seneca v. First Nat'l Bank, 105 Mo. App. 722, 78 S.W. 1092 (Kansas
City Ct. App. 1904). Banks also issued traveler's letters of credit, which were not
commercial letters of credit and were in the nature of traveler's checks. See, e.g., Ufitec, S.A. v. Trade Bank & Trust Co., 21 A.D.2d 187, 249 N.Y.S.2d 557 (1964), aff'd,
16 N.Y.2d 698, 209 N.E.2d 551, 261 N.Y.S.2d 893 (1965); Taussig v. Carnegie Trust

survey the newly acquired Louisiana Territory, he sent with them his letter of credit promising to honor Lewis's drafts on the U.S. government.[18] Note that in the first instance the king promised to honor the drafts of the sellers, while Jefferson promised to honor the drafts of Lewis. Both types of credit fit the Code's definition of "credit,"[19] but the type that Jefferson issued is closer to the kind of credit that is common today.

¶ 3.03   THE CREDIT CONFRONTS THE LAW OF CONTRACT AND THE LAW OF NEGOTIABLE INSTRUMENTS

Courts generally have sought to treat credits, which are promises, after all, as a kind of contract.[20] Occasionally, opinions analogize credits to guaranties,[21] sometimes to third-party beneficiary contracts,[22] and sometimes to a particular kind of negotiable promise, which the law now calls a negotiable instrument.[23] Court treatment of credits and the rules established by the Code make it clear, however, that it is best to think of the credit as a unique kind of device and not as a negotiable instrument or contract.[24]

Co., 156 A.D. 519, 141 N.Y.S. 347 (1913), aff'd, 213 N.Y. 672, 107 N.E. 1086 (1914). For examples of buyer's credits issued by merchants, see Schimmelpennich v. Bayard, 26 U.S. (1 Pet.) 264 (1828); Duval v. Trask, 12 Mass. 153 (1815); Regis v. Hebert, 16 La. Ann. 224 (1861). For additional cases, see infra note 91.

[18] For that early letter of credit and Jefferson's explanation of its use, see App. C, Doc. 22.

[19] For discussion of the Code's "credit" definition, see ¶ 2.03.

[20] See, e.g., Bossier Bank & Trust Co. v. Union Planters Nat'l Bank, 550 F.2d 1077 (6th Cir. 1977); Bank of Montreal v. Recknagel, 109 N.Y. 482, 17 N.E. 217 (1888); Intraworld Indus., Inc. v. Girard Trust Bank, 461 Pa. 343, 336 A.2d 316 (1975). In Century Fire & Marine Ins. Corp. v. Bank of New England, 405 Mass. 420, 540 N.E.2d 1334 (1989), for example, the court applied to a beneficiary's claim for wrongful dishonor against a bank issuer a contract statute of limitations rather than a statute of limitations covering bills, notes, and other bank-issued evidences of indebtedness.

[21] See, e.g., Evansville Nat'l Bank v. Kaufmann, 93 N.Y. 273 (1883); Walsh v. Bailie, 10 Johns. 180 (N.Y. 1813).

[22] See, e.g., Carnegie v. Morrison, 43 Mass. (2 Met.) 381 (1841).

[23] See, e.g., Russell v. Wiggin, 21 F. Cas. 68, 74 (No. 12,165) (C.C.D. Mass. 1842). Story suggested that credits are a form of draft to the world. See J. Story, supra note 15, at 540.

[24] "Letters of credit sit uneasily between two bodies of established legal doctrine: the law of contract and the law of negotiable instruments." Smith, "Irrevocable Letters of Credit and Third Party Fraud: The American Accord," 24 Va. J. Int'l L. 55, 71 (1983); cf. Arbest Constr. Co. v. First Nat'l Bank & Trust Co., 777 F.2d 581

[1] The Role of Consideration

In general, in order to be enforceable, a promise at common law must be supported by consideration. Consideration is not necessary to support the credit promise, but the law followed a tortuous route in achieving that rule. In *Pillans v. Van Mierop*,[25] Lord Mansfield attempted to establish the rule that no consideration was necessary to bind the issuer of a credit. *Pillans*, a 1765 case, involved Dutch merchants, the beneficiaries of the credit, who had asked White, whose creditworthiness they apparently considered suspect, to obtain a "confirmed credit upon a house of rank in London."[26] They gave value to White first and later asked the London merchants whether they would honor drafts for White's account. The London merchants responded affirmatively, but, when White failed, the London house sent its revocation to Amsterdam. To the beneficiaries' suit, the issuers argued that there was no consideration to support their promise, which they viewed as a contract to pay the debt of another.

The English judges decided the case on various grounds. Most of them seem to infer consideration on the theory that, by virtue of the defendant's promise, the beneficiaries did not pursue White. Lord Mansfield took a distinctly different tack. He held that a letter of credit "may be given as well for money already advanced, as for money to be advanced in future."[27] He saw the question as one of "great consequence to trade and commerce in every light"[28] and held that want of consideration, or the doctrine of nudum pactum, is no defense in the law merchant.

In short, Lord Mansfield was attempting to do for credits what the common law had done for bills of exchange: make them actionable

---

(10th Cir. 1985) (holding that issuer's obligation under credit is statutory rather than contractual); Philadelphia Gear Corp. v. FDIC, 587 F. Supp. 294 (W.D. Okla. 1984), aff'd in part, rev'd in part, 751 F.2d 1131 (10th Cir. 1984), rev'd, 476 U.S. 426 (1986) (holding that letter of credit is engagement to pay and not contract or negotiable instrument); Heritage Hous. Corp. v. Ferguson, 651 S.W.2d 272 (Tex. Ct. App. 1983) (holding that letter of credit is not negotiable obligation); City Nat'l Bank v. First Nat'l Bank, 22 Ark. App. 5, 732 S.W.2d 489 (1987) (dictum to effect that credit is not negotiable instrument). But cf. Supreme Merchandise Co. v. Chemical Bank, 70 N.Y.2d 344, 514 N.E.2d 1358, 520 N.Y.S.2d 734 (1987) (referring to negotiation credit as "negotiable" credit). For the view that letters of credit under English law are not negotiable instruments but "an institution sui generis," see Schmitthoff, "The Transferable Credit," J. Bus. L. 49, 51 (Jan. 1988).

[25] 97 Eng. Rep. 1035 (K.B. 1765).

[26] Id.

[27] Id. at 1037.

[28] Id. at 1038.

without a showing of consideration.[29] Such a rule rests on the view, later accepted by Chief Justice Marshall, that "there is an essential difference between common contracts and a letter of credit. The latter is like a mercantile instrument, bottomed upon the principles of good faith."[30] Mansfield and Marshall saw the letter of credit as a product of the law merchant, subject to suit secundum usum mercatorum.

Pillans is a landmark case in the view of some,[31] but Mansfield's view did not survive. Later English opinions rejected it, and in 1843 the Court of Exchequer announced that the position Mansfield had taken was "entirely exploded."[32] Some decisions rationalized that indeed there was consideration in *Pillans*. They saw the consideration moving not to the issuer, who complained that there was no consideration, but to a third party when that third party sold goods to the account party.[33] Under this view, the credit did not become complete until the third-party beneficiary acted upon it.[34] Some courts also argued that the views by Lord Mansfield in decisions subsequent to *Pillans*[35] restricted the rule and required a showing that the beneficiary gave value in reliance on the issuer's credit.[36] Most authorities agree that Mansfield's attempt failed

---

[29] They are still actionable without a showing of consideration, but want of consideration is now a defense. See U.C.C. § 3-307(2); McCurdy, "Commercial Letters of Credit," 35 Harv. L. Rev. 539, 564–565 (1922).

[30] Lawrason v. Mason, 7 U.S. (3 Cranch) 492, 493 (1806). The statement is that of one of the parties to the suit.

[31] Some commentators see the *Pillans* case as an attempt to import civil-law notions into the English law of contract and are critical of it. See G. Gilmore, The Ages of American Law 7, 114 n.6 (1977); M. Horwitz, The Transformation of American Law 178 (1977); G. Gilmore, The Death of Contract 18 (1974); 1 S. Williston & G. Thompson, A Treatise on the Law of Contracts 368 & n.1 (rev. ed. 1936); McCurdy, supra note 29, at 565. Other observers saw the *Pillans* case as an attempt to differentiate letters of credit, a mercantile specialty, from contract law in general. See Campbell, "Guaranties and the Suretyship Phases of Letters of Credit," 85 U. Pa. L. Rev. 175, 261 (1936–1937); Trimble, "The Law Merchant and the Letter of Credit," 61 Harv. L. Rev. 981 (1948); Hershey, "Letters of Credit," 32 Harv. L. Rev. 1 (1918).

[32] Bank of Ir. v. Archer, 152 Eng. Rep. 852, 855 (Ex. 1843).

[33] See, e.g., Lawrason v. Mason, 7 U.S. (3 Cranch) 492, 493 (1806); see also McCurdy, supra note 29.

[34] See, e.g., Evansville Nat'l Bank v. Kaufmann, 93 N.Y. 273 (1883), and authority cited infra note 91. See generally Davis, "The Relationship Between Banker and Seller Under a Confirmed Credit," 52 L.Q. Rev. 225 (1936); McCurdy, "The Right of the Beneficiary Under a Commercial Letter of Credit," 37 Harv. L. Rev. 323 (1924).

[35] See his comments in Pierson v. Dunlop, 98 Eng. Rep. 1246, 1248 (K.B. 1777), to the effect that a virtual acceptance does not arise unless the circumstances are such that a third party relies on the promise.

[36] See, e.g., Clarke v. Cock, 102 Eng. Rep. 751 (K.B. 1803).

and that subsequent decisions in England and in the United States reject the notion that no consideration is necessary in order to render a merchant's written promise binding.[37] There lingers, however, pre-Code authority that letters of credit need no consideration. In *Coolidge v. Payson*,[38] Chief Justice Marshall seems to accept the rule of *Pillans* in holding that a virtual acceptance[39] binds the issuer, even though the beneficiary takes it for a preexisting debt. Pre-Code law distinguished between such virtual acceptances and letters of credit,[40] but a clean acceptance credit,[41] which clearly would fall within the Code's definition of a credit,[42] is the same as a virtual acceptance. By holding that assumpsit would lie, Chief Justice Marshall in *Lawrason v. Mason*,[43] suggests, moreover, that he would enforce a letter of credit by inferring consideration, even though it passed to a third party. The defendants "are bound by every principle of moral rectitude and good faith to fulfill

---

[37] See authorities cited supra note 31. Professor McCurdy's prose reflects the ardor of the debate. He refers to Mansfield's rule in Pillans as "this conspicuous failure of a great judge." McCurdy, "Commercial Letters of Credit," 35 Harv. L. Rev. 539, 565 (1922).

[38] 15 U.S. (2 Wheat.) 66 (1817).

[39] A virtual acceptance was a promise to accept, which the law promoted to an acceptance. An acceptance itself is a mercantile specialty, an engagement to pay the accepted instrument at maturity according to its tenor. See U.C.C. § 3-413(1). The virtual acceptance (made before the bill was drawn) and its cousin, the extrinsic acceptance (made after the bill was drawn), did not appear on the face of the negotiable instrument. That separation of the engagement to accept from the instrument was the feature that rendered the acceptance virtual or extrinsic. A letter of credit may involve an engagement to accept drafts. See ¶ 1.02[2]. Such a credit, if it is clean, appears to be a virtual acceptance, and much of the authority does not distinguish the two. See, e.g., Johnson v. Collings, 102 Eng. Rep. 40 (K.B. 1800); Boyce v. Edwards, 29 U.S. (4 Pet.) 111 (1830). Lord Mansfield, however, clearly did distinguish them. When the holder of a draft argued in one case that a promise to accept the draft was a virtual acceptance, the reporter noted, "But Lord Mansfield said, he rather thought it a letter of credit, and that, to make it an acceptance, it should have been sent to the holder of the [draft]." Pierson v. Dunlop, 98 Eng. Rep. 1246, 1247 (K.B. 1777). This distinction between engagements made to the drawer of a draft and engagements made to the holder (the former being a letter of credit, the latter being a virtual acceptance) survives not to distinguish letters of credit from virtual acceptances but to distinguish the reach of the credit engagement. That is, the distinction between straight credits and negotiation credits. See ¶ 10.02. For a discussion of the virtual acceptance, see infra ¶ 3.03[5]. See generally Finkelstein, "Acceptances and Promises to Accept," 26 Colum. L. Rev. 684 (1926).

[40] See Carnegie v. Morrison, 43 Mass. (2 Met.) 381, 406 (1841).

[41] The acceptance credit involves the engagement of the credit issuer to accept drafts. See ¶ 1.02[2].

[42] See U.C.C. §§ 5-102, 5-103. See generally ¶ 2.03.

[43] 7 U.S. (3 Cranch) 492 (1806).

those expectations which they thus raised, and which induced the plaintiff to part with his property."[44]

Chief Justice Marshall's dictum and Lord Mansfield's holding were attempts to bring into the Anglo-American system of law a foreign notion: the civil-law idea that merchant promises did not need new consideration to be enforceable. Later American authority emphasized the view that there was consideration that consisted of the beneficiary's act in reliance on the issuer's engagement.[45]

This account illustrates a problem with credits that does not go away. For many reasons, the doctrine of consideration did not fit letters of credit.[46] Yet courts insisted on applying their common-law principles to the credit, a mercantile device,[47] until the legislature commanded them to stop.[48] Unfortunately, the question of consideration is not the only issue. There are other instances in which the law of contracts ill suits letters of credit, and there remains resistance among some courts to the idea that the credit is not a typical common-law promise.

The rule of Section 5-105 of the Code lays the immediate question to rest. The Code has rendered the letter of credit a commercial specialty. No consideration is necessary to support a letter of credit. According to the comments to Section 5-105, it is asking too much to require a beneficiary to inquire about or, indeed, to prove that there was consideration for the issuance or amendment of the credit. In short, as the court said in *East Girard Savings Association v. Citizens National Bank & Trust Co.*,[49] "a letter of credit simply is not an ordinary contract."[50]

---

[44] Id. at 495. The beneficiary of the credit in the *Lawrason* case argued in part that a letter of credit is "a mercantile instrument, bottomed upon the principles of *good faith*." Id. (emphasis in original). Both the beneficiary's argument and Chief Justice Marshall's opinion make a case for estoppel by virtue of the act of the beneficiary in reliance on the credit promise.

[45] See 4 S. Williston & G. Thompson, A Treatise on the Law of Contracts § 1195A (rev. ed. 1936); McCurdy, "Commercial Letters of Credit," 35 Harv. L. Rev. 539 (1922).

[46] See U.C.C. § 5-105 & comment; Trimble, supra note 31.

[47] See authority cited supra note 34 and infra note 91.

[48] It is revealing that legislatures have had to correct judicial unwillingness in the case of two other important commercial devices. By the Statute of Anne, Parliament overturned Buller v. Crips, 87 Eng. Rep. 793 (Q.B. 1704), and similar cases that had attacked the law merchant's negotiable promissory note. See 1704, 3 & 4 Anne, c.9. By adopting the Federal Bills of Lading Act, Congress overturned Shaw v. Railroad, 101 U.S. 557 (1879), a court decision that had refused to grant full negotiability to bills of lading. See Pomerene Act, 49 U.S.C. app. §§ 81–124 (Supp. V 1987); Pere Marquette Ry. v. J.F. French & Co., 254 U.S. 538 (1921).

[49] 593 F.2d 598 (5th Cir. 1979).

[50] Id. at 603. In at least one case, however, the disappointed beneficiary suing an issuer for breach of the credit obligation felt obliged to recite in the complaint that

[2] Effective Date of the Credit

The credit is unique in a number of ways. The consideration rule is one.[51] A second unique feature is the idea of revocation. In the *Pillans* case, the defendants had argued at trial that the credit given in prospect of a future advance might well be countermanded before the advance of any money. Lord Mansfield agreed that, subject to conditions not present in *Pillans*, a credit promise could be revoked prior to the time the beneficiary acted.[52] *Evansville National Bank v. Kaufmann*,[53] an early New York case, held that the letter of credit becomes irrevocable only when the beneficiary acts on it. Also, in *Union Bank v. Executors of John G. Coster*,[54] another early case, the court observed that the contract was closed, and the rights and liabilities of the parties were "fixed," when the beneficiary of a credit acted by accepting drafts. In 1838, the U.S. Supreme Court held that the beneficiary who acts on a letter of guaranty must notify the issuer so that the issuer knows the extent of his obligation.[55] Absent such notice, the issuer may revoke.

The Code and the Uniform Customs respond to these cases when they fashion rules regarding the revocability of credits. Article 9(a) of the Uniform Customs stipulates that an irrevocable credit may not be canceled without the agreement of all parties thereto, and Section 5-106(3) of the Code posits a similar rule. In addition, Section 5-106 lays down express rules for "establishing" a credit, that is, for determining the time when the credit becomes effective.[56] It is also clear that there is no duty on the part of the beneficiary, in order to establish his rights under the credit, to notify the issuer that he has acted, or that he intends to act, on the credit, except to the extent that the presentation of a draft or demand for payment might constitute such notice. The Uniform Customs provide that credits expire by their own terms.[57]

Chapter 5 explains in more detail the question of revocation, establishment, and expiry of credits. The point here is that the Uniform Customs and the Code recognize that special rules are necessary in order to

---

it had relied on the credit to its detriment — an allegation that would not appear to be necessary for the beneficiary to recover damages. See Sun Bank v. Pelican Homestead & Sav. Ass'n, 874 F.2d 274 (5th Cir. 1989).

[51] See supra ¶ 3.03[1].

[52] Pillans v. Van Mierop, 97 Eng. Rep. 1035, 1036 (K.B. 1765).

[53] 93 N.Y. 273, 279 (1883).

[54] 3 N.Y. 203, 210 (1850).

[55] Adams v. Jones, 37 U.S. (12 Pet.) 207, 213 (1838).

[56] See ¶ 5.01 for a discussion of the rules on "establishing" the credit engagement.

[57] See U.C.P. art. 46 (1983).

contend with the unique features of the credit contract, if indeed it is to be thought of as a contract.

[3] Oral Engagement as a Credit

Although the statute of frauds requires a promise made to satisfy the debt of another to be in writing, courts long ago recognized that a promise to accept or to pay the drafts of another need not be in writing.[58] The decisions distinguished at an early date between credits, which are primary obligations of the issuer, and guaranties, which are secondary obligations of the guarantor. The latter fall within the statute of frauds; the former do not. This distinction remains important, even though Section 5-104(1) of the Code reverses the common-law rule and expressly requires the credit to be in writing and signed by the issuer. Some courts have argued that the guaranty nature of a credit, especially in standby transactions, renders the credit beyond the proper scope of a commercial bank's business. Generally, banks may engage only in activities authorized by statute. These statutes usually limit bank activity to the business of banking and implicitly or explicitly forbid such banks to issue guaranties. Most cases preserve this long-recognized distinction between credits, which are primary obligations, and guaranties, which are secondary.[59] These decisions reject the idea that standby credits are beyond the powers of commercial banks.

[4] Transferability of a Credit

General contract notions of free assignability have not meshed well with letters of credit. There are two concerns here. The account party that causes a credit to issue reposes considerable trust in the beneficiary. By virtue of the credit's nature, that is, payment under it being conditioned on the presentation of documents, the beneficiary to whom the credit runs is in a position to effect payment easily. The record of credit litigation is replete with instances of beneficiaries that draw on credits when they are not authorized to do so. They implement these unauthorized draws with false documents. There is a risk, then, whenever an account party causes a credit to issue; and account parties exercise caution in selecting their beneficiaries. They select people whom they can trust.

---

[58] See, e.g., Townsley v. Sumrall, 27 U.S. (2 Pet.) 170 (1829); Nelson v. First Nat'l Bank, 48 Ill. 36 (1868).

[59] For a discussion of that important distinction, see ¶¶ 1.05, 12.02[1][c].

Easy rules for transferring credits permits the original beneficiary to lodge in a stranger, one who might not have earned the trust of the account party, the power to draw under the credit by the mere presentation of documents. Credit law properly reflects concern for the account party by generally restricting the transfer of the credit engagement, unless the credit expressly allows such transfer.

There is a second reason for restricting transfer of credits. Issuers that pay a stranger instead of the beneficiary arguably have not satisfied either the credit engagement, which runs to the beneficiary, or the application agreement with the account party. The issuer has a duty to pay the beneficiary, and the issuer that pays a stranger presumably is liable to the beneficiary and will not be able to obtain reimbursement from the account party. Issuers guard against liability in these cases. They might require a specimen signature of the beneficiary or they might refuse to issue a credit to parties whose identity they cannot verify. Free transferability of the credit destroys the benefit of these precautions.

Generally, credit law has taken account of these and similar concerns. In *Walsh v. Bailie*,[60] for example, the engagement of Sherman to honor Walsh's drafts on Bailie could not be availed by Dox. Walsh was a seller of farm supplies in Albany, New York; Dox was a supplier of farm goods in Geneva, New York. It was late in the season; since Walsh apparently was unable to supply Bailie, he sent Bailie to Dox. The New York court held that the benefit of Sherman's promise to Walsh could not be transferred to Dox. The court contended that Dox's terms of sale may have been different from those of Walsh.[61] This distinction was one to which the courts adhered in the absence of the issuer's willingness to extend the engagement "generally" to anyone who sold to the account party. The distinction gave rise to the notion that some credits were special and not assignable, while others were general and ran to the world at large.[62]

The courts also recognized that a special credit might be assigned after the beneficiary complied with its terms.[63] They distinguished, therefore, between the transferability of the right to draw under a general credit and the assignability of the right to proceeds under any credit,

---

[60] 10 Johns. 179 (N.Y. 1813).

[61] For criticism of this common-law rule, see McGowan, "Assignability of Documentary Credits," 13 Law & Contemp. Probs. 666 (1948). See generally ¶¶ 10.03–10.05.

[62] See, e.g., Fletcher Guano Co. v. Burnside, 142 Ga. 803, 83 S.E. 935 (1914); Birckhead v. George, 5 Hill 634 (N.Y. Sup. Ct. 1843); Robbins v. Bingham, 4 Johns. 476 (N.Y. 1809).

[63] See, e.g., Evansville Nat'l Bank v. Kaufmann, 93 N.Y. 273, 277–278 (1883). For a discussion of the pre-Code transfer and assignment rules, see ¶ 10.03.

as long as there is performance in accord with the credit's terms. This distinction is one that the Code preserves in Section 5-116 and one that the Uniform Customs preserve in Articles 54 and 55.[64]

[5] Virtual Acceptance

The virtual acceptance was a curious legal anomaly. Partly negotiable instrument fish and partly letter of credit fowl, it excited controversy among English judges, fostered conflicting treatment by English and American courts, and ultimately faced extinction by statute in both countries. It retains a glimmer of life, however, in the negotiation credit.

The virtual acceptance[65] was a promise to accept that, unlike the acceptance, was separate from the draft. A true acceptance must be written on the negotiable draft itself and operates to bind the acceptor to pay the draft at maturity.[66] The virtual acceptance carries the same promise, but it is extrinsic to the draft.

It was difficult to call the virtual acceptance a negotiable instrument, because the virtual acceptance did not appear on the instrument. English courts decided to enforce the virtual acceptance, but there arose something of a grand controversy over whether promises to accept non-existing bills were enforceable virtual acceptances. It is clear that merchants considered them as such. Lord Mansfield, in the *Pillans* case,[67] which involved an extrinsic acceptance of an existing bill, suggested that any rule to the contrary would discommode commerce. *Pillans*, however, presented English jurists with a conceptual morsel that they were unwilling to swallow, even though its rejection created commercial difficulties.

Subsequent to *Pillans*, the English courts held that a promise to accept a nonexisting bill was a promise that runs to the drawer of the draft but not to subsequent holders. In *Bank of Ireland v. Archer*,[68] Daly promised Scroder that Daly's house would honor Scroder's drafts. The court held that the Bank of Ireland, which discounted those drafts from Scroder, could not enforce the promise. There was no privity between

---

[64] For a discussion of the transfer rules, see ¶¶ 10.03–10.06.

[65] This discussion does not distinguish the virtual acceptance (made before the draft was drawn) from the extrinsic acceptance (made after the draft was drawn). See Uniform Negotiable Instruments Law §§ 134, 135 (1896). See discussion supra note 39.

[66] See U.C.C. §§ 3-104, 3-410, 3-413(1).

[67] See Pillans v. Van Mierop, 97 Eng. Rep. 1035 (K.B. 1765). For a discussion of *Pillans*, see supra ¶ 3.03[1].

[68] 152 Eng. Rep. 852 (Ex. 1843).

Daly and the Bank of Ireland, and the bank paid no consideration to Daly. The court rejected the suggestion that *Pillans* had done away with the necessity for consideration in commercial contracts.

English courts objected to the rule of *Pillans*, in part because they took exception to the idea that an endorser who relies on the extrinsic acceptance should be able to enforce it, while an endorser who does not rely on it may not enforce it.[69] Such a rule gives some endorsers (those who rely on the promise) rights against the promisor and gives other endorsers no such right.

The difficulty with the English objections was that they made too much of the confusion between the letter of credit (a type of virtual acceptance) and the acceptance. They allowed that confusion to obstruct the concern that should have been paramount: the convenience of commerce. It was that concern upon which Mansfield so emphatically bottomed his rule in *Pillans*.

Chief Justice Marshall, in *Coolidge v. Payson*,[70] and Justice Story, in *Russell v. Wiggin*,[71] firmly rejected the English view. They understood, as Lord Mansfield did, that most credits, in fact, were issued to give value to nonexisting bills. The practice at the end of the eighteenth century and at the beginning of the nineteenth century was to send agents off to distant places with instructions to buy goods.[72] Rather than send currency with the agent, the principal sent his promise to accept drafts drawn by the sellers of those goods. This promise later came to be known as a buyer's letter of credit. The English rule posed a serious obstacle for this valuable commercial device. American jurists did not dwell on the want of privity that such a device revealed. "The Law, operating upon the act of the parties, creates the duty, establishes the privity, and implies the promise and obligation, on which the action is founded," said Chief Justice Shaw in *Carnegie v. Morrison*.[73] In *Russell v. Wiggin*, Justice Story agreed with him.[74]

This history of the virtual acceptance controversy demonstrates the flawed analysis of those who conceptualize the letter of credit as some kind of acceptance. An acceptance is a negotiable instrument. A letter of credit is a different commercial creature, and there is nothing anoma-

---

[69] Id. at 855.

[70] 15 U.S. (2 Wheat.) 66 (1817).

[71] 21 F. Cas. 68 (No. 12,165) (C.C.D. Mass. 1842).

[72] See, e.g., Regis v. Hebert, 16 La. Ann. 224 (1861); Bank of Seneca v. First Nat'l Bank, 105 Mo. App. 722, 724 (Kansas City Ct. App. 1904); Union Bank v. Executors of John G. Coster, 3 N.Y. 203, 215 (1850).

[73] 43 Mass. (2 Met.) 381, 396 (1841).

[74] 21 F. Cas. 68, 74 (No. 12,165) (C.C.D. Mass. 1842).

lous in letting the beneficiary of a credit sue the issuer on the credit while other endorsers of the draft, having rights only on the unaccepted draft, are not permitted to sue on the credit.[75]

In the late nineteenth century, England abolished the virtual acceptance.[76] It is perhaps significant that American jurisdictions, which had fewer conceptual difficulties with the virtual acceptance, did not see the need to abolish it until the last half of the twentieth century, when they adopted the Code.[77]

At present, there should be no confusion on this point. Letters of credit are not negotiable instruments. They usually do not contain the language of negotiability[78]; they often contain a conditioned promise[79]; and negotiability is not necessary for, and perhaps would be harmful to, their effective operation.[80]

[6] Independence Principle

It is significant to note that in one important respect the credit does resemble a negotiable instrument. In both cases, the "holder" or "beneficiary" is not subject to defenses arising out of the underlying transaction. In *Coolidge v. Payson*,[81] Chief Justice Marshall recognized that a party acting upon the credit is not subject to equities between the draw-

---

[75] In Boyce v. Edwards, 29 U.S. (4 Pet.) 111 (1830), the court maintained the distinction between letters of credit and virtual acceptances. In *Boyce*, the court held that the beneficiary of a letter of credit could not sue on it as an acceptance, because the letter did not identify the drafts. The rule was that the virtual acceptance must identify the draft. This rule comes from Coolidge v. Payson, 15 U.S. 66 (1817), and is one reason credits traditionally require that the draft recite that it is "drawn under credit no. _____." See McCurdy, "Commercial Letters of Credit" (concluded), 35 Harv. L. Rev. 715, 721 (1922). The *Boyce* court suggested, however, that the plaintiff could sue the defendants for breach of promise to accept. 29 U.S. (4 Pet.) 111, 123 (1830).

[76] Bills of Exchange Act, 1882, 45 & 46 Vict., ch. 61, § 17.

[77] See U.C.C. § 3-410 & comment 3.

[78] Section 3-104(1)(d) of the Code requires a negotiable instrument to be payable to order or to bearer.

[79] The promise to pay in a negotiable instrument must be unconditional. U.C.C. §§ 3-104(1)(b), 3-105.

[80] For such a view, see Dolan, "The U.C.C. Framework: Conveyancing Principles and Property Interests," 59 B.U.L. Rev. 811, 828–832 (1979); cf. Philadelphia Gear Corp. v. FDIC, 587 F. Supp. 294 (W.D. Okla. 1984), aff'd in part, rev'd in part, 751 F.2d 1131 (10th Cir. 1984), rev'd, 476 U.S. 426 (1986) (holding that letter of credit is not negotiable instrument); Heritage Hous. Corp. v. Ferguson, 651 S.W.2d 272 (Tex. Ct. App. 1983) (holding that letter of credit is not negotiable obligation).

[81] 15 U.S. (2 Wheat.) 66, 72–73 (1817).

er and the issuer. In so doing, Marshall gave full effect to Lord Mans-field's earlier dictum in *Mason v. Hunt*.[82]

Thus, long before the advent of the commercial credit, courts recognized that the credit can give value to drafts only if it, like the negotiable draft, is independent of the underlying transaction. Sections 5-109 and 5-114 of the Code and Articles 3 and 4 of the Uniform Customs make it clear that modern credits benefit from the same principle. Courts generally give full effect to that principle, although some, perhaps unwittingly, have weakened it and, to some extent, have put credit transactions in peril.[83]

[7] Fraud in the Transaction

It is significant to observe in this review of the history of credits that the landmark cases establishing the independence of credits (not just from the underlying contract but also from the shackles of inappropriate rules, such as privity and consideration) observe in passing that fraud may undermine the credit construct. In the *Pillans* case, Lord Mansfield conditioned his rule (that consideration was not necessary) on the understanding that "there is no fraud,"[84] a condition to which he referred in *Mason v. Hunt* also.[85] Similarly, Chief Justice Marshall notes in *Coolidge* that "[a]ny ingredient of fraud would, unquestionably, affect the whole transaction."[86]

The impact of the law of fraud on credit rules is uneven and incomplete. Mansfield and Marshall may have been referring to the notion that the beneficiary of the credit would take his benefit subject to real defenses, just as the holder of a negotiable instrument takes the benefit subject to real defenses. Courts eventually fashioned rules permitting the issuer to escape its engagement under a commercial credit when the accompanying documents were forged or fraudulent,[87] and Section 5-114(2) of the Code extends the rule to cases involving fraud "in the transaction." The interpretation of that clause in Section 5-114(2), especially in standby credit situations, has left the scope of the exception unsettled, a subject that Chapter 7 explores.

---

[82] 99 Eng. Rep. 192, 193–194 (K.B. 1779).

[83] See generally ¶¶ 2.09, 7.03–7.04.

[84] Pillans v. Van Mierop, 97 Eng. Rep. 1035, 1036 (K.B. 1765).

[85] 99 Eng. Rep. 192, 194 (K.B. 1779).

[86] Coolidge v. Payson, 15 U.S. (2 Wheat.) 66, 73 (1817).

[87] See McCurdy, "Commercial Letters of Credit" (pt. 1), 35 Harv. L. Rev. 539, 579–581 (1922); Hershey, "Letters of Credit," 32 Harv. L. Rev. 1, 3–4 (1918).

[8] Lessons From the History of the Credit

A review of decisions dealing with credits as they have advanced from the early buyer's credit to the mature devices of today's commercial and standby credits illustrates three points.

First, it shows that credits, if they are contracts, are unique contracts and that any attempt to apply contract rules to them must abide careful examination of the effect such rules will have on the special commercial role that this unique contract plays. Second, a review of credit decisions indicates that there is a clear distinction between the credit law theory of an independent credit and the negotiable instruments law theory of a negotiable specialty. Credits are not negotiable instruments. Finally, and most importantly, this history reveals that the credit is indeed a unique commercial device. Credits are not contracts or negotiable instruments but probably are creatures of the law merchant.

In *Bank of Nova Scotia v. Angelica-Whitewear Ltd.*,[88] the Supreme Court of Canada considered the sources of letter of credit law for that country. The case arose in Quebec, and it would have been easy for the court to treat the matter as one governed by the law of that province. The *Bank of Nova Scotia* court, however, surveyed not just the law of Quebec but that of other Canadian provinces, that of England, and that of the United States. The decision stands as scholarly testimony that the credit is a creature of commerce which is subject not to the parochial concerns of local law but to the universal concerns of the law merchant.

It is useful at times to draw analogies from negotiable instruments law and to invoke contract rules for credits. Courts frequently may say, for example, that a credit is a contract and that contract rules of construction should apply to it.[89] In all events, however, the ultimate test of any analogy or any contract rule in the credit transaction must be one of determining whether the analogy or the rule serves the proper purpose of the credit, a unique commercial specialty.

¶ 3.04 COMMERCIAL CREDIT

Until the middle of the nineteenth century, letters of credit that appeared in English and American reports were similar to the two credit varieties that were evident in medieval times. More frequently, it seems,

---

[88] 36 D.L.R.4th 161 (Can. 1987).

[89] See authority cited supra note 20. For a case in which the court grudgingly follows state law to that effect but exposes the fallacy of that approach, see Exxon Co. v. Banque De Paris Et Des Pays-Bas, 889 F.2d 675 (5th Cir. 1989). See generally ¶ 4.08[3].

the credit followed the pattern whereby the issuer of the credit, usually a merchant but sometimes a bank,[90] sent the credit off with his agents, who used the credit to induce sellers to extend credit to the agents.[91] This was the buyer's credit. There is also evidence that sometimes the letter of credit's purpose was solely to enhance the marketability of the account party's drafts, as in *Mason v. Hunt*[92] and as in the Florentine merchant example discussed previously.

In the last half of the nineteenth century, there appeared in commerce a new kind of credit: the commercial credit.[93] This engagement, usually made by a bank, entailed the promise to honor the drafts (bills of exchange) of a merchant seller, who complied with certain conditions in the credit. The stipulated conditions usually required the seller to supply documents, such as his commercial invoice, bills of lading, and insurance documents. These documents evidenced the seller's compliance with an underlying contract of sale between himself and the buyer who had procured the credit. The English buyer of American cotton, for example, would have his bank engage to honor the drafts of his American seller, provided that the seller presented the drafts with his invoice, an ocean bill of lading, an insurance certificate, and any other documents that the contract for the sale of the cotton required and that the bank had incorporated into the terms of the credit.

It is not clear whether this new credit contributed to the demise of agent-buyers and factors (their agent-seller cognate) or whether it was itself caused by their demise. In fact, however, the end of the nineteenth century witnessed the end of these agents as important commercial personages and concurrently saw the virtual end of the buyer's credit that had served agents so well.

The history and maturation of the early form of the credit, from the Middle Ages to the nineteenth century, has been all but forgotten by some courts, which seem to assume that the law of letters of credit be-

---

[90] Story says that both banks and merchants issued such credits. See J. Story, supra note 15, at 540. See also cases cited supra note 17 (authority to same effect).

[91] See, e.g., Schimmelpennich v. Bayard, 26 U.S. (1 Pet.) 264 (1828); Russell v. Wiggin, 21 F. Cas. 68 (No. 12,165) (C.C.D. Mass. 1842); Duval v. Trask, 12 Mass. 153 (1815); Union Bank v. Executors of John G. Coster, 3 N.Y. 203, 215 (1850). The practice continued into the twentieth century but became much less prevalent. See Wilson & Co. v. Niffenegger, 211 Mich. 311, 178 N.W. 667 (1920).

[92] 99 Eng. Rep. 192 (K.B. 1779); see also Lawrason v. Mason, 7 U.S. (3 Cranch) 492 (1806).

[93] It is clear that by 1881 banks were experienced with commercial letters of credit. See, e.g., Bank of Montreal v. Recknagel, 109 N.Y. 482, 17 N.E. 217 (1888); see generally Kozolchyk, "The Legal Nature of the Irrevocable Commercial Letter of Credit," 14 Am. J. Comp. L. 395 (1965).

gins with the advent of the commercial credit. This view is incorrect and obscures the fact that some banks had long been issuing credits other than the commercial credit.

¶ 3.05 INCREASED USE OF THE COMMERCIAL CREDIT AND ADOPTION OF THE UNIFORM CUSTOMS

By the end of World War I, the advantage of commercial credits had become obvious, as had the need for establishing international rules for them. International trade grew in the latter part of the nineteenth century and in the early part of the twentieth, and, in general, that growth pattern has continued to the present.[94]

Today the commercial credit has become indispensable to international trade.[95] Trade credit is notoriously difficult to obtain. A manufacturer usually finds a ready market for his domestic receivables but scarcely any interest in foreign receivables. The commercial letter of credit under which the commercial bank in the foreign country supplies the credit provides the much needed credit that facilitates international trade. Any interruption in the use of these credits would have serious consequences for the economies of all trading countries. Commercial credits are also used in domestic sales,[96] but their use in domestic trade, although growing, is far less pervasive.

With the growth of commercial credit use, bank issuers confronted the acute problem of determining whether the seller's documents accompanying the draft were in proper order. There was insufficient stan-

---

[94] For an account of the growth in the case of commercial credits, see Kozolchyk, supra note 93.

[95] Credits are indispensable to international trade when sellers do not know buyers well enough to ship on open account. Once a seller knows his buyer, the value of the credit diminishes, just as the value to domestic commerce of the documentary sale diminished with the advent of reliable credit reporting and quick communication. See ¶ 1.01. At present, there is an effort to achieve better communication and credit reporting in the international setting. The Foreign Credit Insurance Association, for example, issues commercial risk insurance to American sellers of goods to foreign buyers whose credit standing satisfies the Association. Some American exporters are using this insurance in lieu of letters of credit. In addition, some commercial lenders finance foreign accounts receivable, though usually they insist on credit insurance. Foreign credit insurance is not nearly so widespread as the commercial letter of credit.

[96] See, e.g., Courtaulds N. Am., Inc. v. North Carolina Nat'l Bank, 387 F. Supp. 92 (M.D.N.C.), rev'd, 528 F.2d 802 (4th Cir. 1975); Weyerhaeuser Co. v. First Nat'l Bank, 27 U.C.C. Rep. Serv. (Callaghan) 777 (S.D. Iowa 1979); Doelger v. Battery Park Nat'l Bank, 201 A.D. 515, 194 N.Y.S. 582 (1922).

dardization of forms. Although bills of lading generally were standardized, the plethora of other documents were not. These documents might be issued by any number of persons, such as consular officials, industry inspectors, chamber of commerce officers, and local government functionaries. They might also appear in any number of languages. Banks were concerned about the integrity of the credit transaction. They wanted, on the one hand, to maintain their reputation as issuers of reliable credits; but, on the other hand, they did not want to offend their customers, who sometimes clamored that the documents were defective and that the bank should not honor the seller's draft.

American banks took the lead in promoting international rules for commercial credits, and, by stages,[97] the world banking community achieved consensus under the auspices of the International Chamber of Commerce (ICC), in the publication of the first version of the Uniform Customs. By 1962 banks in virtually all countries utilizing credits had signaled their adherence to the Uniform Customs, which the ICC Banking Commission revised in 1953,[98] 1974,[99] and 1983.[100]

The drafting of the 1983 Uniform Customs began in June 1980 at the urging of, among others, American representatives to the ICC. The ICC Commission on Banking Technique and Practice, which consists of members appointed by each ICC National Committee, charged a small "working party" to draft the new Uniform Customs. The Commission completed the 1983 revision on June 6, 1983, and the Council of the ICC adopted it on June 21 of the same year. The 1983 version of the Uniform Customs applies to credits issued on or after October 1, 1984. Credits issued prior to that date are subject to the 1974 Uniform Customs.

For a number of reasons, the growth of commercial credits did not witness a great deal of litigation. First, until the last half of the twentieth

---

[97] For an account of that effort, see Note, "Revised International Rules for Documentary Credits," 65 Harv. L. Rev. 1420 (1952).

[98] For a discussion of the force of the Uniform Customs as customs or law, see ¶¶ 4.04–4.06.

[99] The 1974 Revision of the Uniform Customs, effective in 1975, supplemented the widely adopted 1962 version. The changes were effected primarily to adapt the Uniform Customs to developments in the transportation industry. See International Chamber of Commerce, "Uniform Customs and Practice for Documentary Credits," Doc. No. 290, at 6–7 (1974); Wheble, "Uniform Customs and Practice for Documentary Credits (1974 rev.)," 1975 J. Bus. L. 281.

[100] For a discussion of the 1983 revision of the Uniform Customs, effective October 1, 1984, see authority cited in Appendix A. The 1983 version of the Uniform Customs is the version to which this treatise generally refers and is set out in full in Appendix A.

century, the number of banks issuing such credits was relatively small.[101] Second, the parties to the commercial credit transaction (unlike their analogues in the standby credit transaction) generally expected a credit to be honored. They wanted it to be honored, except in rather extraordinary circumstances, such as a market debacle. There was litigation over commercial credits from time to time, often with respect to the sufficiency of the accompanying documents. The widespread adherence to the UCP, however, has obviated many of the potential difficulties with commercial credits.

There remains evidence of two distinct approaches by American courts to documentary credits in general and especially to the problem of evaluating the accompanying documents. Indeed, questions concerning documentary compliance remain a frequent subject for litigation over documentary credits. One of these approaches, a clear majority view, is more consistent with the principles of the Uniform Customs and insists on rather strict compliance with the letter of credit's terms. The second approach, motivated by equity notions, sanctions judicial inquiry into such matters as (1) the intent of the parties as reflected in contracts other than the credit itself and (2) the fundamental fairness of the parties' conduct.[102] While the latter approach appeals to many American judges' sense of fair play, it may not adequately reckon the costs it imposes on the credit transaction and the concomitant reduction it effects in the credit's efficiency as a commercial device. For lawyers, the question of rules relating to the compliance of the accompanying documents remains a chief area of concern.

¶ 3.06 STANDBY CREDIT

Sometime after World War II, the standby credit became an important commercial device.[103] It is now used in a significant number of set-

---

[101] One commentator reported in 1954 that while there were more than 1,400 commercial banks in the country, only 100 did international business "of any consequence" and 25 did 75 percent of the letter of credit business. Chadsey, "Practical Effect of the Uniform Commercial Code on Documentary Letter of Credit Transactions," 102 U. Pa. L. Rev. 618, 620 (1954).

[102] See cases discussed in ¶¶ 6.05–6.06.

[103] Often, especially in the merchant context, a legal device, such as a bill of exchange or a letter of credit, develops for a significant period of time before the law takes note of it. It is not clear at what time bankers and merchants adapted the commercial letter of credit to the standby transaction. Professor Verkuil suggested in 1973 that it occurred "in the last decade or so." See Verkuil, "Bank Solvency and Guaranty Letters of Credit," 25 Stan. L. Rev. 716, 717 (1973). Wiley cites evidence of its common usage in the real estate development and shipbuilding industries of the mid-1960s. See Wiley, "How to Use Letters of Credit in Financing the Sale of

tings[104] and could well grow in use as more lawyers and more industries become familiar with it. The standby credit lends itself readily to domestic transactions where one party's performance extends over a period of time. It also arises in international transactions involving the sale of goods, in which the parties want to avoid the cost of examining documents.[105] In both cases, the party obligated to perform is the account party, who causes the standby credit to issue in order to assure the promisee. While the obligor is performing or is preparing to perform, the promisee, who awaits that performance, has the benefit of a separate promise (from the issuer) that if the account party defaults, the issuer will pay the beneficiary money. The standby credit closely resembles a performance bond, but it differs from such a bond in that it substitutes the quick payment of funds for the surety's promise of performance.[106]

The inevitability of prompt payment in the event of default is the standby credit's hallmark and is the feature that renders it most attractive. There has developed, however, a doctrine that justifies nonpayment of the credit (even against conforming documents) in certain cases of fraud. The codification of that rule in Section 5-114(2) has given rise to cases in which the courts enjoin payment under the credit until the court has inquired into the credit transaction sufficiently to satisfy itself that there is no fraud.[107] This challenge to prompt payment under the credit may be open to abuse by account parties who want to delay payment. By making unfounded charges of fraud, account parties can seriously weaken the promptness feature of the standby credit. Some account parties have gone further and have attempted to use claims of fraud in the underlying transaction to delay or prohibit payment of the credit. Most courts[108] have rejected these attempts, which, if widely suc-

---

Goods," 20 Bus. Law. 495, 496 (1965); see also Armstrong, "The Letter of Credit as a Lending Device in a Tight Money Market," 22 Bus. Law. 1105 (1967); Note, "Recent Extensions in the Use of Commercial Letters of Credit," 66 Yale L.J. 902 (1957).

[104] For examples of frequent uses, see ¶ 1.06.

[105] The invoice standby credit is payable against the seller's invoice and a certificate that the invoice is not paid. See discussion at ¶ 1.06. For an example of an invoice credit, see App. C, Doc. 18.

[106] For a discussion of the differences between performance bonds and standby credits, see ¶¶ 1.05, 2.10[1].

[107] See cases discussed in ¶ 7.04.

[108] There are a large number of cases that reflect the courts' reluctance to permit the account party to use fraud as a lever in opening the underlying transaction to inquiry. They inhibit that inquiry in several ways, some of which are procedural. See, e.g., KMW Int'l v. Chase Manhattan Bank, N.A., 606 F.2d 10 (2d Cir. 1979); Dynamics Corp. of Am. v. Citizens & S. Nat'l Bank, 356 F. Supp. 991 (N.D. Ga. 1973); Intraworld Indus., Inc. v. Girard Trust Bank, 461 Pa. 343, 336 A.2d 316 (1975). This reluctance does not always prevent the court from granting the account party relief, as the *Dynamics* case indicates. See generally ¶ 7.04.

cessful, would destroy the standby credit. A number of commentators[109] would alter the credit's nature, however, and inhibit the credit's function.

¶ 3.07 THE CREDIT'S FUNCTIONS

No evaluation of commercial or standby credits is complete without full consideration of the credit's functions. Those commentators and cases, for example, that would expand the fraud-in-the-transaction defense are often responding to short-term exigencies. They may not appreciate fully that the expansion of that defense changes the credit into a surety contract.

The functions of the credit are different from those of a surety contract, and parties that choose the credit over a surety arrangement do so in order to avail themselves of the benefit in those differences. Similarly, those courts that tamper with the strict compliance rule[110] do not appear to understand the significant impact their substantial compliance rule has on the liquidity, cost-effectiveness, and prompt payment features of credits. Analysis of the credit's several commercial objectives is critical to each of the controversies that has arisen in letter of credit law.

[1] Providing Liquidity

When the nineteenth century common-law judges spoke of the credit as giving value to bills or drafts drawn under them,[111] they identified the liquidity function of the credit. That function survives, even though drafts have lost their primary role as a medium of exchange, that is, their role as currency. Both types of medieval credit benefited the holder of drafts by rendering them valuable and by making it easier for the holder to "sell" them and to receive goods or services for them. In short,

---

[109] See, e.g., Kimball & Sanders, "Preventing Wrongful Payment of Guaranty Letters of Credit — Lessons From Iran," 39 Bus. Law. 417 (1984); Verner, "'Fraud in the Transaction': *Intraworld* Comes of Age in *Itek*," 14 Mem. St. U.L. Rev. 153 (1984); Ellinger, "Fraud in Documentary Letter of Credit Transactions," 1981 J. Bus. L. 258, 267; Weisz & Blackman, "Standby Letters of Credit After Iran: Remedies of the Account Party," 1982 U. Ill. L. Rev. 355; Comment, "'Fraud in the Transaction:' Enjoining Letters of Credit During the Iranian Revolution," 93 Harv. L. Rev. 992 (1980); Note, "Enjoining the International Standby Letter of Credit: The Iranian Letter of Credit Cases," 21 Harv. Int'l L.J. 189 (1980).

[110] See cases cited at ¶ 6.05.

[111] See, e.g., Coolidge v. Payson, 15 U.S. (2 Wheat.) 66, 72 (1817). See also supra ¶ 3.02.

the old types of credit, which were used until the advent of the commercial credit in the nineteenth century, overcame the payment delay that attended the collection and final payment of the draft.

Similarly, the new device, the commercial credit, serves that same purpose. Without the commercial credit, if a London importer agrees to purchase cotton from an American supplier, the supplier must insist on prepayment or wait for his money. By virtue of the credit, the seller is put in funds promptly upon shipment of the merchandise. The seller can sell his drafts under the credit at an American bank. The prompt payment will occur, even though the seller has sold on credit. If the sales contract gives the London buyer ninety days after sight to pay the supplier's drafts, the supplier may obtain funds upon shipment by paying a bank charge and discounting his time drafts at the American correspondent of the issuing bank or at some other bank.[112]

A supplier of $2 million worth of cotton who must wait ninety days for his money, for example, faces considerable cash costs. He might be able to borrow money, but his collateral is questionable. He can reserve a security interest in the cotton[113] and assign that interest to a lender, but many lenders are not interested in a security interest that attaches to cotton located at a distant port, where buyers may be scarce and prices may be low. If the supplier has the right to draw under a letter of credit, the lender's interest is heightened. Now the supplier can offer the lender not only a security interest in the cotton but also the right to the proceeds under the credit and, directly or indirectly, the benefit of the issuing bank's engagement.[114]

Similarly, the standby credit serves to put the beneficiary in funds upon the customer's nonperformance of the underlying contract. Since most well-drafted standby credits call for little documentation, upon the account party's default, the beneficiary draws on the credit and receive prompt payment, thereby rendering liquid a claim for damages, one of the least liquid of all assets.

The commercial parties may alter the functions of the credit themselves by, for example, lodging the credit in the hands of an escrow

---

[112] If the credit is a circular negotiation credit, the seller can choose his bank. If the credit designates a payor bank, the beneficiary must take his drafts to that bank. See App. C, Docs. 15, 16.

[113] See U.C.C. § 2-505.

[114] If the credit is a circular negotiation credit, the issuer's engagement to honor the drafts runs to the negotiating bank. If the credit is not a circular negotiation credit, the bank can obtain a security interest in the credit proceeds. See U.C.C. § 5-117. See generally ¶¶ 10.02–10.04. For a case in which a seller used a standby letter of credit to enhance the liquidity of its accounts, see Emery-Waterhouse Co. v. Rhode Island Hosp. Trust Nat'l Bank, 757 F.2d 399 (1st Cir. 1985).

agent, along with instructions that the agent draw on the credit and then hold the funds pending resolution of the underlying contract dispute. The law's deference to the commercial parties' freedom of contract and their voluntary, negotiated allocation of costs and losses in the underlying transaction is different from third-party reallocation of those costs and losses. In some cases, for example, issuers have resorted to interpleader and similar actions in order to avoid having to determine whether to pay a beneficiary demanding payment under the credit.[115] The mere filing of that action, contrary to the impression issuers would have the court draw, is a direct, serious reallocation of those costs and losses.

In *Wyzata Bank & Trust Co. v. A&B Farms*,[116] the credit secured claims due creditors of a trader on a grain exchange. Under the broad arrangement, upon the insolvency of the trader, the beneficiary of the credit would draw and hold the proceeds in trust for the creditors. In fact, when the trader defaulted, the issuer and the trustee deposited the funds in court and interpleaded the creditors. Such conduct by the trustee and the issuer is a palpable alteration of the original plan. Even more egregious are those cases in which the issuer, confronted with a facially complying presentation by the beneficiary and an account party that is claiming fraud, flinches from the duty implicit in the very issuance of the credit and interpleads the funds.

[2] Substituting Credit

By providing liquidity, the credit facilitates the efficient collection of the customer's obligation once the parties have established their underlying contract. The credit also serves the underlying contract at its inception by reducing the beneficiary's reluctance to do business with the account party. It also gives the account party entree to the beneficiary's custom and perhaps to the beneficiary's credit. The beneficiary's reluctance to accept the account party's promise or to extend the account party credit often stems from the fact that the beneficiary does not know enough about the account party's creditworthiness to take the risks. By substituting the issuer's credit for that of the customer, the letter of credit overcomes the beneficiary's reluctance.

A merchant in Bordeaux, for example, can sell wine to a New York account about whom the merchant knows very little, so long as the New York account buyer obtains a bank credit engaging to honor the French

---

[115] For discussion of those cases, see ¶ 11.06.

[116] 855 F.2d 590 (8th Cir. 1988).

seller's drafts. If the seller is reluctant to accept the credit of the account party's bank, he can insist in the sales agreement with the account party that the credit be confirmed by a French bank. That confirmation renders the French bank liable as if it were the issuer.[117]

The standby credit enhances the attractiveness of the account party's promise to perform. Municipalities, for example, are properly reluctant to issue construction permits to developers without some assurances that the developers will see to the construction of certain common roadways, sidewalks, sewers, and other improvements in conformity with the municipality's building ordinances and regulations. The municipality simply could take the promise of the developer that it will construct facilities in accordance with such laws. It would much prefer to take the promise of a bank that, if the developer does not perform, the bank will put the municipality in funds sufficient to see that someone else does. The credit allows the municipality to avoid having to evaluate the financial strength and good faith of the developer.

Credits, of course, cannot achieve miracles. They do not permit an insolvent buyer to obtain credit for shipments of wine, nor do they permit a weak developer to guarantee performance of his plans and specifications. Banks generally do not issue credits on behalf of customers who cannot perform. The credit, however, permits a bank that is familiar with the financial strength of the buyer or the developer to substitute its evaluation for that of the French seller or the municipality that cannot evaluate the buyer or contractor.

The evaluation of a party's fiscal condition is a function that banks are perhaps as well suited as any other enterprise to perform. Such is their business as financial intermediaries that borrow money from one party and lend it to others. Banks that issue credits know that they must make that evaluation. Thus, if they are not satisfied that the account party is able to reimburse the bank immediately upon the bank's honor of drafts under the credit, the bankers will insist on whatever collateral or guaranties are necessary in order to make the bank's "loan" of credit to its customer bankable. Such evaluation of an account party's financial integrity, or of collateral security or guaranties, has long been the proper business of banks. They perform such evaluations as a matter of routine.

---

[117] See U.C.C. § 5-103(1)(f); Barclays Bank D.C.O. v. Mercantile Nat'l Bank, 481 F.2d 1224 (5th Cir. 1973), cert. dismissed, 414 U.S. 1139 (1974); cf. U.C.C. § 2-325(3) (defining requirement in sales contract for "confirmed credit" to mean credit confirmed by bank in seller's financial market). See generally ¶ 1.03.

[3] Reducing Cost

It would be misleading to suggest that credits are the only way to achieve some of the commercial objectives described in the two preceding subsections.[118] A municipality and a seller can take a performance bond or a payment bond to protect against the account party's default of the underlying agreement. Alternatively, the municipality or seller can undertake the credit examination of the account party. Both alternatives, however, are usually more costly than the credit.

The issuer usually is the account party's bank. It is familiar with the account party and may have decided earlier to extend the account party a line of credit. In that case, the bank will have taken what it deems to be adequate security for its commitment. Because the customer-bank relationship precedes the credit transaction, the bank's cost of issuing a credit is minimal. The seller's cost of investigation would be much higher.

By the same token, a municipality that insists on performance bonds finds that bidders, who must include the cost of such bonds in their price, quote higher bids than do those who can use letters of credit in lieu of performance bonds. The premium for a performance bond is usually higher than banks charge for standby credits. While the standby credit does not always suffice to protect the obligee of a developer's promise,[119] the costs are usually less when it does.

[4] Shifting Litigation Costs

Parties often negotiate the terms of their relationship with the risks of litigation in mind. Every seller and buyer of goods knows that, after delivery, the buyer may raise questions about the seller's compliance with the contract specifications, especially those relating to the quality of the merchandise. When the buyer and seller agree on a sale against documents in which the buyer has no right to inspect the goods before pay-

---

[118] See ¶¶ 3.07[1], 3.07[2].

[119] The credit provides the beneficiary protection up to a fixed maximum upon which the account party and the beneficiary presumably have agreed. That maximum may be either more than or less than sufficient to protect the beneficiary. It is in the nature of a liquidated damages figure and therefore lacks the flexible protection a performance bond provides. Cf. City of Philadelphia v. American Coastal Indus., Inc., 704 F. Supp. 587 (E.D. Pa. 1988) (holding that municipality could properly refuse to accept standby letter of credit in lieu of performance and payment bonds in virtue of fact that bonds required performance of construction contract, while standby permitted municipality to obtain only money).

ment,[120] the parties have in fact agreed that, in the event the buyer raises such questions, he bears the cost of litigating them without the purchase money. The buyer will have paid for the goods before seeing the defects, and, during the months or years of litigation, the seller has the use of that money. Conversely, if the buyer and seller agree to a delivery on credit, the buyer refuses to pay for nonconforming goods; and, during any subsequent litigation, the seller bears the cost of litigating without the funds, the buyer having kept the purchase price.

It is a first principle of credit law that the credit itself is independent of the underlying transaction and that so long as the beneficiary complies with the credit, it is of no moment that he has not complied with the underlying contract. In any credit, the parties have implicitly made an agreement concerning this litigation cost. They have agreed upon a "payment against documents" sale.[121] They also have agreed that the buyer will pay even if the goods are nonconforming. One party or the other will face litigation without the purchase price. If the buyer prepays, he litigates without the price; if he does not prepay, the seller litigates without the price.

The sales contract designates the party that bears the litigation costs when it provides either for prepayment or for delivery on credit. The parties can allocate the burden one way or the other; or they can apportion it, as they often do, by some kind of down payment feature. They also can allocate the burden under a letter of credit. There is no way to escape the burden. The seller may bear it; the buyer may bear it; or both may bear it.[122] The point is that somebody must bear it. Under a system of party autonomy, the parties, not someone else, should make the determination.

To the extent of payment of the price under a credit, the parties shift the burden of litigating without the funds to the account party.[123] The credit invariably shifts the risk in that fashion, regardless of whether the sale is one for cash against documents, whether it is on credit, or whether the credit is commercial or standby.

---

[120] See U.C.C. § 2-513(3).

[121] Cf. id. (recognizing such agreements).

[122] The buyer and seller often allocate the burden between themselves. A 20 percent down payment, for example, allocates 20 percent of the burden to the buyer and 80 percent to the seller.

[123] The account party who bears this burden under the credit is not necessarily the buyer. In the classic commercial credit, the account party is a buyer. See supra ¶ 3.04. In many standby cases, the account party is a seller. See, e.g., KMW Int'l v. Chase Manhattan Bank, N.A., 606 F.2d 10 (2d Cir. 1979); American Bell Int'l Inc. v. Islamic Republic of Iran, 474 F. Supp. 420 (S.D.N.Y. 1979). See generally ¶ 7.04[4][e].

When courts delay payment under a credit and permit litigation before payment, they have upset the allocation of litigation costs to which the parties have agreed. Courts are not always as reluctant as they should be to effect that reallocation. In *Itek Corp. v. First National Bank*,[124] for example, the court recognized that "[p]arties to a contract may use a letter of credit to make certain that contractual disputes wend their way toward resolution with money in the beneficiary's pocket rather than in the pocket of the contracting party."[125] Moved, however, by what it saw as the futility of the account party's suit in Iran, the court enjoined the issuer from paying and thereby put the money in the pocket of the "contracting party."[126]

In *Foxboro Co. v. Arabian American Oil Co.*,[127] the same court that decided *Itek* carefully preserved the cost-shifting function of the credit. The *Foxboro Co.* case involved a credit payable to a Saudi party. The account party claimed that the beneficiary's draw was fraudulent and should be enjoined. The trial court viewed the draw as an attempt by the beneficiary to obtain an "unfair"[128] advantage over the account party, but the Court of Appeals for the First Circuit held that the purpose of the credit was to provide the beneficiary with that advantage. Accordingly, the First Circuit dissolved the preliminary injunction that the trial court had entered.

In *Ground Air Transfer, Inc. v. Westates Airlines, Inc.*,[129] in a thoughtful opinion by the author of *Itek*, the court vacated the lower court's injunction, holding that to restrain a beneficiary from drawing on a credit disturbs the parties' allocation of risks. Although the *Ground Air Transfer* opinion does not entirely eschew the prerogative of looking

---

[124] 730 F.2d 19 (1st Cir. 1984).

[125] Id. at 24.

[126] For additional cases that reallocate the litigation costs, see ¶¶ 7.04[4][c], 7.04[4][e][ii]. In Banco Continental v. First Nat'l Bank, 100 F.R.D. 426 (E.D. Tenn. 1983), the court apparently saw no harm to the credit transaction in letting the account party intervene in a suit by the beneficiary for the issuer's dishonor of the credit. By permitting intervention, the court virtually guaranteed that the beneficiary would have to litigate the issues arising out of the underlying transaction before the beneficiary was paid. The *Banco Continental* court indicated, however, that it would not entertain a full-blown trial of these issues but would adopt the *Intraworld* approach discussed in ¶ 11.04[3][b]. For a discussion of intervention in credit litigation, see ¶ 9.02[3].

[127] 805 F.2d 34 (1st Cir. 1986).

[128] Foxboro Co. v. Arabian Am. Oil Co., 634 F. Supp. 1226, 1232 (D. Mass. 1986), rev'd, 805 F.2d 34 (1st Cir. 1986).

[129] 899 F.2d 1269 (1st Cir. 1990).

to the underlying transaction for fraud,[130] one might conclude from *Foxboro Co.* and *Ground Air Transfer* that the First Circuit's intrusion into the underlying contract in *Itek* may be as much a consequence of the account party's questionable ability to obtain relief in Iranian tribunals at the time of the U.S.-Iran crisis than it is a considered position of that court to broaden the fraud exception.

In *Recon Optical, Inc. v. Israel*,[131] the buyer of an aerial reconnaissance system agreed to make advance payments to the seller on the condition that in the event of the seller's breach of the design and production agreement, the buyer would have the right to return of the payments. The agreement provided for the seller to have a standby credit issue in favor of the buyer and payable against the buyer's drafts and a certificate that the seller was in breach of the agreement. Disputes under the agreement were subject to arbitration. When a dispute arose, the buyer drew on the standby credit; and the seller sought to enjoin payment. It was the seller's position that it was not in default under the agreement, that the buyer's assertion to the contrary was false, and that an injunction should be issued.

The trial court denied a request for a preliminary restraining order, and the Court of Appeals for the Second Circuit affirmed. The court viewed the standby arrangement as a device for shifting the cost of litigating without the advance payments. Had the court granted the seller injunctive relief until it was certain that the beneficiary's assertions were correct, the court would have deprived the beneficiary of the very protection it had negotiated for itself in the underlying agreement.[132]

In *CKB & Associates, Inc. v. Moore McCormack Petroleum*,[133] the court denied a satisfaction-and-accord defense to a credit beneficiary that had settled its dispute with the account party in litigation over payments due under the credit. The credit secured a refiner's obligations under an oil refinement agreement. The *CKB* court ruled that the settlement in the credit litigation was a settlement of a dispute over the identity of the party that would hold the funds during resolution of the underlying contract dispute regarding the quality and quantity of the

---

[130] For discussion of that issue in *Ground Air Transfer*, see ¶ 7.04[4][f].

[131] 816 F.2d 854 (2d Cir. 1987).

[132] The *Recon Optical* court noted that the provisions in the agreement that the State of Israel had fashioned for defense contracts stemmed in part from the failure of a similar effort at risk shifting when a panel of arbitrators stopped the beneficiary from drawing on a credit. See the discussion of Sperry Int'l Trade, Inc. v. Government of Isr., 690 F.2d 8 (2d Cir. 1982), at ¶ 7.04[4][f] and in Dolan, "Standby Letters of Credit and Fraud (Is the Standby Only Another Invention of the Goldsmiths in Lombard Street?)," 7 Cardozo L. Rev. 1 (1985).

[133] 734 S.W.2d 653 (Tex. 1987).

refiner's performance. The decision reflects proper regard for the cost-shifting function of the credit, which was fully satisfied by settlement of the credit dispute. That settlement did not resolve the dispute in the underlying refinement contract.

[5] Shifting the Forum

Whenever the account party and the beneficiary are located at a distance from each other, as they usually are in the international sale setting, the use of a letter of credit effects a shift in the forum of most litigation arising out of performance of the underlying contract. If a buyer in Singapore causes a commercial credit to issue to a Houston seller, the buyer must understand that, in the event the merchandise is defective, he will have little chance of litigating in Singapore. Even though the buyer obtains credit terms, by the time he discovers defects in the goods, the seller will hold or will have discounted drafts accepted by the buyer's bank or by a confirming bank. In either case, the acceptances are payable, notwithstanding any defects in the goods,[134] and the buyer who suffers a breach of warranty will have to litigate in Texas.

The buyer may protect himself in a number of ways:

1. He can insist on a sales contract that requires a letter of credit payable against an inspection certificate executed by an independent inspector.
2. He can require the seller to cause its bank to establish a standby credit to secure all, or a portion, of the seller's performance.[135]
3. He can negotiate a reduced purchase price to reflect the forum cost he is assuming.
4. He can refuse to agree to a sales contract calling for a commercial credit.

These contract arrangements determine whether the seller or the buyer will bear the forum risk. One of them has to bear it. If the buyer agrees to a credit with no independent inspection certificate and no reciprocal standby, he has agreed to bear that risk. When courts interrupt operation of the credit, they are reallocating the risk.

Courts are not always conscious of this function of the credit. In *Wyle v. Bank Melli,*[136] for example, an Iranian port authority had suc-

---

[134] See U.C.C. § 5-114(1); U.C.P. arts. 3, 16(b) (1983).

[135] This practice of insisting on standby credits to secure the seller's compliance with the underlying contract is evident in the authority cited supra note 123.

[136] 577 F. Supp. 1148 (N.D. Cal. 1983).

cessfully negotiated for a simple-demand guaranty[137] to secure against damage to cargo. The issuer of the guaranty, an Iranian bank, had insisted in turn on a standby credit to secure itself in the event of a draw on the guaranty. When that draw occurred, the Iranian bank sought reimbursement under the standby; and the American account party's trustee in bankruptcy claimed that there were no cargo losses, that the draw on the guaranty was fraudulent, and that payment under the credit should be enjoined.

On the basis of rather meager evidence (i.e., that there had been no claim of cargo losses for two and one-half years), the court concluded that the claim made was in bad faith and that payment under the standby credit should be enjoined. Significantly, the court professed to be moved by the view that the trustee would not have a fair hearing in Iranian courts, but it ignored the fact that the Iranian bank was not faring well in a California court and had undoubtedly bargained for the credit in order to avoid having to litigate in California. The *Wyle* opinion does not mention the fact that its holding reallocates the forum costs from the U.S. party to the Iranian party.[138]

[6] Additional Functions

In addition to the functions mentioned in the preceding sections, letters of credit can be used to shift risks arising out of currency fluctuation or inconvertibility or out of trade embargoes. If, for example, a seller agrees to provide oil-drilling equipment to a Nigerian buyer, the seller may be concerned that the Nigerian government will block the export of dollars, or that payment in nairas, the Nigerian currency, will be valueless because of relative increases in the dollar's value. If the buyer is strong, the seller may have to shoulder these risks by accepting the credit of a Nigerian bank payable in nairas, for example. If the seller is strong, he can insist that the buyer obtain a dollar-denominated credit confirmed by an American bank. In either case, the credit reflects the market strengths and bargaining position of the parties. When a seller must accept payment in nairas, he may charge a higher price or enter the currency futures market to hedge against his risks. A Nigerian buyer who must pay in U.S. dollars may take the same kind of action. Reallo-

---

[137] For a discussion of the simple-demand guaranty and its similarity to, and perhaps differences from, standby letters of credit, see ¶ 2.03.

[138] For additional cases that reallocate the forum risk from an Iranian party to a U.S. party, see ¶ 7.04[4][e][ii]. For other forum reallocation cases, see ¶ 7.04[4][c].

cation of these risks will occur if the courts interfere with the swift operation of the credit.[139]

Strong international sellers also may use credits to avoid the risks of trade embargoes. An Argentine seller dealing with a Dutch buyer, for example, may fear a European Common Market embargo of shipments to Argentina or an Argentine embargo against export to Common Market ports. The seller can negotiate protection for himself by means of a letter of credit issued by a strong bank with an international reputation as a credit issuer and payable against documents he can secure, any embargo notwithstanding.[140]

[7]　Prompt Payment Feature

Each of the credit's functions depends on the prompt payment of the beneficiary's drafts or demands for payment. Any delay in that payment diminishes the benefit of the credit as a commercial device. Courts have long recognized the primary role that promptness plays in the commercial credit.[141]

It is abundantly clear that a court which enjoins payment of a credit and entertains a lawsuit growing out of the underlying transaction or out of any other transaction or instrument extraneous to the four corners of the letter of credit has reallocated risks and restructured the broad transaction. That restructuring upsets the assumptions on which the commercial parties have computed their price and on which they have negotiated their own contracts of supply, resale, and financing with third parties.

Courts should be aware also that delay in payment of a credit upsets the assumptions of the issuer. By delaying payment of the credit, the court may compel the issuer in effect to extend the commitment it made to a customer. If, for example, a bank agrees to issue a credit with a six-month expiry, it may conclude that the account party's financial posture is strong enough for the bank to issue the credit on an unsecured basis, with the understanding that the account party will put the bank in funds before payment under the credit is due. If the court enjoins the bank from paying and then permits the account party and the beneficiary to

---

[139] See Wiley, "How to Use Letters of Credit in Financing the Sale of Goods," 20 Bus. Law. 495, 498 (1965).

[140] Note, "The Trade Embargo and the Irrevocable Letter of Credit," 1 Ariz. J. Int'l & Comp. L. 213 (1982).

[141] See, e.g., Maurice O'Meara Co. v. National Park Bank, 239 N.Y. 386, 146 N.E. 636 (1925); Sztejn v. J. Henry Schroder Banking Corp., 177 Misc. 719, 31 N.Y.S.2d 631 (Sup. Ct. 1941).

litigate fraud questions and similar issues, the bank's commitment may be extended for months or years beyond the original six months' undertaking.[142]

In all events, the parties can assume the worst—that a court will reallocate their negotiated bargain, but they will have few ways to protect themselves. Sellers can charge higher prices or insist on prepayment. Buyers can refuse to buy. The net effect is less trade and higher costs, with the consumer ultimately paying the bill.

In recognition of the credit's functions and the important way in which promptness serves them, the Code[143] and the Uniform Customs[144] stress the first principle of letter of credit law, which is that the credit engagement is independent of the underlying contract. Any relaxation of that rule results in delay while courts inquire not into documents called for by the credit but into the underlying transaction itself. That extraneous inquiry involves questions of performance, contract interpretation, and parties' intent. It involves all of the questions that arise in contract disputes.

Courts have fashioned exceptions to the principle that the credit is independent of the underlying contract. There have been unfortunate occasions on which courts have construed the credit loosely, sometimes engrafting conditions to it[145] and at other times excusing conditions that the court deems immaterial.[146] These cases are in the minority; most courts recognize that the effectiveness of the credit itself suffers from any departure from the independence principle and the prompt payment feature.

---

[142] See Harfield, "Identity Crises in Letter of Credit Law," 24 Ariz. L. Rev. 239, 253 (1982). Some courts will impose on the petitioner in an injunction action the duty of obtaining an extension of the credit. See, e.g., Atwood Turnkey Drilling, Inc. v. Petroleo Brasileiro, S.A., 875 F.2d 1174 (5th Cir. 1989). Presumably, that duty entails the financial obligation of satisfying the issuer that an extension of the credit is justified.

[143] See U.C.C. §§ 5-109, 5-114.

[144] See U.C.P. arts. 3, 4 (1983).

[145] See, e.g., Fair Pavilions, Inc. v. First Nat'l City Bank, 19 N.Y.2d 512, 227 N.E.2d 839, 281 N.Y.S.2d 23 (1967). See also ¶ 2.09[3].

[146] See, e.g., Banco Espanol de Credito v. State St. Bank & Trust Co., 385 F.2d 230 (1st Cir. 1967), cert. denied, 390 U.S. 1013 (1968). See also ¶ 6.05[1][a].

CHAPTER **4**

Sources of Credit Law

¶ 4.01   BASIC SOURCES OF CREDIT LAW

Article 5 of the Uniform Commercial Code (UCC or the Code) goes to some length to fashion the credit as a unique type of undertaking. The article renders the credit enforceable without the showing of any consideration.[1] It establishes its own statute of frauds for credits[2] and a special rule for the time at which credits become effective.[3] Credits have special rules for damages in the event of dishonor[4] and transfer rules that are quite different from the general rule favoring free alienability of choses.[5] Article 5 even has a special rule for rights of beneficiaries and account parties in the event of issuer bank insolvency[6] and inhibits judicial interference with payment under credits.[7] The definition of "credit" itself turns in part on the status of the issuer, with one rule for banks and another for nonbanks.[8] In short, the statute not only fashions special rules for credits, it fashions them in a way markedly different from analogous rules for contracts.

Courts, moreover, in creating common law for credits have altered much of the law of general obligations to meet the unique nature of the credit. Thus, generally, although not always, courts construe credits

---

[1] See U.C.C. § 5-105.
[2] See U.C.C. § 5-104.
[3] See U.C.C. § 5-106.
[4] See U.C.C. § 5-115.
[5] See U.C.C. § 5-116.
[6] See U.C.C. § 5-117.
[7] See U.C.C. §§ 5-114(1), 5-114(2).
[8] See U.C.C. § 5-102(1).

strictly[9] and render them independent from related contracts and relationships.[10]

These statutory and common-law rules reflect, in part, the unique nature of credits and support the view that it is best to think of credits as sui generis and to apply general contract principles to them carefully and with proper regard for the credit's international and commercial purposes.[11]

In *Bank of Nova Scotia v. Angelica-Whitewear Ltd.*,[12] the Supreme Court of Canada captures this unique approach for enhancing the credit as a product with a domestic role and an international role. In that case, the court considered a credit dispute brought in the courts of Quebec, a civil-law jurisdiction. The court was careful in fashioning its broad rulings on letters of credit not to limit its consideration to the law of Quebec, however. Rather, the *Bank of Nova Scotia* court reviewed the law of Canada's common-law provinces, the Uniform Customs and Practice for Documentary Credits (UCP or the Uniform Customs), and the law of England and of the United States. The opinion reflects the thoughtful view that credits, by virtue of their international roots and role, are creatures of the law merchant, a part not of local law, but of the jus gentium.

This chapter deals first with choices for supplementing the statutory and party-selected rules for credits and with choice of law questions. It then reviews the roles played by the three basic sources of credit law and by contract law. In general, the basic sources do not conflict, because they treat different subject matter within the field. Occasionally, however, the Code, the Uniform Customs, and common-law rules do bump into one another; and the courts must work out a method for resolving the conflicts. Most supplemental letter of credit rules from the law of contract work well only if their application abides a determination that the contract rules are not incompatible with the nature of the credit device.

[1] Supplemental Sources

A significant body of case law, along with banking industry customs and practice, supplements the special statutory rules fashioned for letters of

---

[9] For a discussion of the strict rules for interpreting credits, see ¶¶ 6.03–6.04.

[10] For discussion of this independence principle, see ¶¶ 2.08–2.10.

[11] For a summary of the unique features of credits, see ¶ 3.07 and Chapter 3 generally.

[12] 36 D.L.R.4th 161 (Can. 1987).

credit in Article 5 of the Code. That article and the many customs set forth in the Uniform Customs do not treat credits comprehensively. Courts must supplement Code rules and Uniform Customs principles considerably, therefore. Even the rather well-developed body of letter of credit case law is incomplete and leaves room for courts to fashion additional principles as that case law grows with the credit device.

Generally, courts have looked to contract rules to provide that final supplement, but sometimes they fashion common law for letters of credit. In brief, there are three basic sources for letter of credit law outside the credit itself: the Code, the Uniform Customs, and the law of credits. In addition, the common law of contract provides a general, though sometimes unreliable, source of supplemental rules for the common law of credits.

[2] The Law Merchant

This description of the sources of credit law makes allowance for the fact that the credit is a device often used in international trade. That fact imposes a duty on courts to avoid application of strictly local rules to the device. Generally, the courts have responded well.

A few cases illustrate the problem. In *Power Curber International Ltd. v. National Bank of Kuwait S.A.K.*,[13] a North Carolina exporter sold equipment to its distributor, a Kuwaiti company. The distributor caused a Kuwaiti bank to issue a credit in favor of the exporter. A North Carolina bank advised the credit, which was payable at the advising bank's counters. Before the exporter could obtain payment under the credit, the buyer, invoking a counterclaim by way of setoff, caused an attachment order to issue against the Kuwaiti bank in Kuwait ordering the issuer not to pay. The seller sued in England, arguing that the Kuwaiti order was contrary to letter of credit principles, as indeed it was.[14]

In *Banco De Vizcaya, S.A. v. First National Bank*,[15] the credit was payable in Chicago; but an Abu Dhabi court, having jurisdiction of the branch that issued the credit, ordered the bank not to pay, despite the fact that the issuer had accepted drafts under the credit, which drafts, now acceptances, were in the hands of a holder. The holder argued quite correctly that its rights were not subject to the equities of the underlying transaction.[16]

---

[13] [1981] 3 All E.R. 607 (C.A.).

[14] See, e.g., U.C.P. art. 3 (1983). See generally ¶ 9.06[3].

[15] 514 F. Supp. 1280 (N.D. Ill. 1981), vacated, id.

[16] Although the *Banco De Vizcaya* case does not make anything of the fact, the holder held a negotiable instrument for which it had given value. In all probability, the holder was a holder in due course and could recover on the acceptances, without regard to commercial defenses in the underlying transaction. See U.C.C. § 3-305(2).

Finally, in *J.H. Rayner (Mincing Lane) Ltd. v. Bank Fur Gemein-wirtschaft A.G.*,[17] courts in the Federal Republic of Germany issued orders preventing a beneficiary of two guaranties from drawing on the guaranties. The beneficiary then commenced suit in England, where a branch of the issuer, a German bank, was situated. The beneficiary contended that its suit was not an abuse of process, because the German courts had violated the independence principle,[18] the indispensable feature of credit law, by looking to the underlying transaction to determine whether payment under the guaranties was proper.

In these cases, two facts are readily apparent: first, that bank issuers of international credits may face inconsistent orders from two jurisdictions; second, that the credit device may suffer if courts from one jurisdiction, in the interests of comity, blindly follow the courts of another jurisdiction. To their credit, the courts in all three of these cases ruled in favor of the device; that is, they invoked credit law to the detriment of the issuers in the instant cases but to the benefit of bank issuers in general. By ruling against the banks in these cases, and by putting them in the vise of inconsistent judgments, the courts strengthened the credit device and protected the banking industry's product.

In fashioning credit rules, moreover, courts have demonstrated their willingness to resort not to local law but to the law merchant. In the *Power Curber* case, for example, the court decided that because North Carolina was the place of performance, its law would apply; but the court invoked general letter of credit principles in interpreting the Uniform Customs and did not confine itself to North Carolina cases. The *Power Curber* approach is similar to that of the Supreme Court of Canada in the *Bank of Nova Scotia* case. In short, these cases make the argument for the invocation of the law merchant, an international body of law, rather than local common law as the law that supplements statutory law, the Uniform Customs, and the law in the credit itself.

¶ 4.02 CHOICE OF LAW

Because of the international setting in which credits originated and in which they often operate, it is natural for them to confront some choice of law questions. Originally, American courts resolved such issues in favor of the law of the jurisdiction where the parties entered into the con-

---

[17] [1983] 1 Lloyd's Rep. 462 (C.A.).

[18] For authority that primary guaranties are virtually the same as standby letters of credit and are subject to the law of letters of credit, see ¶ 1.05.

tract. Thus, in *Carnegie v. Morrison*[19] and in *Russell v. Wiggin*,[20] two leading cases, Chief Justice Shaw and Justice Story, respectively, took the position that, because the agent of a London issuer executed the engagement in Massachusetts, the law of that jurisdiction would govern, rather than the contrary law of England, where actual payment was to occur.

More recent cases reflect a different view. In *J. Zeevi & Sons Ltd. v. Grindlays Bank (Uganda) Ltd.*,[21] the account party and the issuer negotiated in Uganda, where the credit issued, but the court applied the law of New York, where it was payable. Similarly, in *Banco De Vizcaya, S.A. v. First National Bank*,[22] the credit issued in Abu Dhabi but was payable in Illinois. The court applied Illinois law.

The *Zeevi* court based its application of New York law on the view that New York had great interest in the litigation by dint of its position as a world financial center. The *Banco De Vizcaya* court justified the use of Illinois law on the theory that the parties had secured arrangements for payment in Illinois precisely because they were wary of having to pursue payment in Abu Dhabi.[23]

In *Instituto Nacional De Comercializacion Agricola (Indeca) v. Continental Illinois National Bank & Trust Co.*,[24] the beneficiary and the issuer were located in Guatemala. In a suit against the confirming bank, a national banking association located in Illinois, the court applied Illinois law.

To an extent, all of these cases are consistent. In each, the courts invoked the law of the forum. More important, however, is that they are consistent in that most of them use that law to uphold the credit. In the two early cases, *Carnegie* and *Russell*, the London issuer attempted to use English rules of privity and consideration that would have rendered

---

[19] 43 Mass. (2 Met.) 381 (1841).

[20] 21 F. Cas. 68 (No. 12,165) (C.C.D. Mass. 1842).

[21] 37 N.Y.2d 220, 333 N.E.2d 168, 371 N.Y.S.2d 892, cert. denied, 432 U.S. 866 (1975).

[22] 514 F. Supp. 1280 (N.D. Ill. 1981), vacated, id.

[23] The *Banco De Vizcaya* court treated the issue as one of letter of credit law. The drafts had been accepted. It is not clear from the opinion whether the plaintiff was making a claim on the acceptances, on the credit, or on both. For other cases holding that the law of the place of performance governs, see Consolidated Aluminum Corp. v. Bank of Va., 544 F. Supp. 386 (D. Md. 1982), aff'd, 704 F.2d 136 (4th Cir. 1983); Roman Ceramics Corp. v. Peoples Nat'l Bank, 517 F. Supp. 526 (M.D. Pa. 1981), aff'd, 714 F.2d 1207 (3d Cir. 1983); North Valley Bank v. National Bank, 437 F. Supp. 70 (N.D. Ill. 1977); cf. Agnew v. FDIC, 548 F. Supp. 1235 (N.D. Cal. 1982) (adopting law of state where issuer was located as federal law).

[24] 530 F. Supp. 279, 281 n.2 (N.D. Ill. 1982).

the credits unenforceable. In *Zeevi*, the issuer attempted to escape liability under Ugandan law aimed at Israeli nationals. In *Banco De Vizcaya*, the Abu Dhabi court had enjoined payment of the credit, and the American court had enforced payment.

These cases, then, may reflect concern that the value of credits as a commercial device not suffer from the vagaries of foreign law. The issue does not arise often, in part because so many international credits are subject to the Uniform Customs and in part because all American jurisdictions have adopted Article 5 of the Code.[25] On balance, it is probably fair to say that the law of the place of performance governs, but that rule may give way when the issuer uses it to avoid payment.[26]

---

[25] In North Valley Bank v. National Bank, 437 F. Supp. 70 (N.D. Ill. 1977), for example, the court notes that the parties did not address the question of choosing between Colorado law, where the beneficiary resided, and Illinois law, where the credit issued. In Atari, Inc. v. Harris Trust & Sav. Bank, 599 F. Supp. 592 (N.D. Ill. 1984), aff'd in part and rev'd in part mem., 785 F.2d 312 (7th Cir. 1986), the parties agreed that in a suit by a California beneficiary against an Illinois issuer, Illinois law would govern. In Pubali Bank v. City Nat'l Bank, 777 F.2d 1340 (9th Cir. 1985), the issuer was a New York bank, but the court decided that the law of the forum, California, should control. In First State Bank & Trust Co. v. McIver, 681 F. Supp. 1562 (M.D. Ga. 1988), aff'd, 893 F.2d 301 (11th Cir. 1990), the court applied the law of Florida when the issuer was a Florida bank and the credit recited that it was subject to Florida law.

[26] In addition to the cases cited, see Consolidated Aluminum Corp. v. Bank of Va., 704 F.2d 136 (4th Cir. 1983); Almatrood v. Sallee Int'l Inc., No. 83 Civ. 1800 (WCC) (S.D.N.Y. May 13, 1985); Power Curber Int'l Ltd. v. National Bank of Kuwait S.A.K., [1981] 3 All E.R. 607 (C.A.); Offshore Int'l S.A. v. Banco Central S.A., [1976] 2 Lloyd's Rep. 402 (Q.B.); Eberth & Ellinger, "Assignment and Presentation of Documents in Commercial Credit Transactions," 24 Ariz. L. Rev. 277, 283 (1982); cf. Trans Meridian Trading, Inc. v. Empresa Nacional De Comercializacion De Insumos, 829 F.2d 949 (9th Cir. 1987) (diversity case applying California law to dispute over credit issued by California bank in favor of Peruvian beneficiary); Sound of Mkt. St., Inc. v. Continental Bank, Int'l, 819 F.2d 384 (3d Cir. 1987) (dispute between New York advising bank and Pennsylvania beneficiary to which court declined to decide whether New York or Pennsylvania law governed, because same result obtained under law of both jurisdictions); Five Star Parking v. Philadelphia Parking Auth., 703 F. Supp. 20 (E.D. Pa. 1989) (decision not to choose law, because that of California, location of issuer, and that of Pennsylvania, location of beneficiary, were not different); Spier v. Calzaturificio Tecnica S.p.A., No. 86 Civ. 3447 (CSH) (S.D.N.Y. Sept. 7, 1988) (rejecting Italian bank's letter of guaranty as security for stay of arbitral award in New York court on ground that letter would be subject to Italian law); Arabian Fiberglass Insulation Co. v. Continental Ill. Nat'l Bank & Trust Co., No. 85 C 1268 (N.D. Ill. Dec. 12, 1986) (applying Illinois law to credit issued by Illinois bank in favor of Saudi beneficiary); Bank of Cochin Ltd. v. Manufacturers Hanover Trust Co., 612 F. Supp. 1533 (S.D.N.Y. 1985), aff'd, 808 F.2d 209 (2d Cir. 1986) (holding that New York law, not Indian law, would govern rights of Indian issuer against New York paying bank); Sabolyk v. Morgan Guar. Trust Co., No. 84 Civ. 3179 (MJL) (S.D.N.Y. Nov. 27, 1984) (holding that Swiss court's attach-

Courts have had no difficulty in distinguishing the parties' selection of law in the underlying contract from choice of law questions under the credit. The broad credit transaction consists of several relationships. One of the key relationships is the underlying contract between the account party and the beneficiary of the credit. The credit itself supports the underlying contract but is distinct from it.[27] Frequently, as in any contract, the parties to the underlying transaction choose the law of a specified jurisdiction. The Code explicitly sanctions that choice, so long as the underlying transaction bears a reasonable relationship to the jurisdiction selected.[28]

Often in disputes over the credit engagement, the real parties in interest are identical to the parties to the underlying transaction. When the account party seeks to stop payment on a credit, for example, the issuer often encourages its customer to sue for a restraining order. In the litigation that follows, the beneficiary will resist the account party's action; the issuer will not. That dispute, although it is actually between the account party and the beneficiary, arises out of the credit, not out of the underlying contract. The parties' choice of law in that contract has no bearing on choice of law questions in the credit dispute.

In *Dynamics Corp. of America v. Citizens & Southern National Bank*,[29] for example, an American seller of radio equipment and the Indian government buyer agreed to arbitrate their disputes under Indian law. The court invoked Georgia law, however, in a suit for injunction against payment under the credit. Similarly, the court in *Intraworld Industries, Inc. v. Girard Trust Bank*[30] used Pennsylvania law to unravel a dispute over a letter of credit; it did not use the Swiss law that the par-

---

ment order would protect New York bank whose Zurich branch complied with order, since credit was issued by branch and was to be performed in Switzerland); In re Glade Springs, Inc., 47 Bankr. 780 (Bankr. E.D. Tenn. 1985) (holding that rights of confirming bank to subrogate itself to rights of issuer in real estate collateral would be governed by law of state where collateral was situated); Amoco Oil Co. v. First Bank & Trust Co., 759 S.W.2d 877 (Mo. Ct. App. 1988) (holding that Illinois law applied to credit issued by Illinois bank in favor of Maryland beneficiary with office in Missouri); RSB Mfg. Corp. v. Bank of Boroda, 15 Bankr. 650 (S.D.N.Y. 1981) (holding that Indian court's injunction against Indian issuer provided issuer with defense in court sitting in New York); see also Griffin Cos. v. First Nat'l Bank, 374 N.W.2d 768 (Minn. Ct. App. 1985) (suggesting that law of state where real estate development was located might govern credit, even though parties to credit resided in another state).

[27] For discussion of the independence principle, see ¶¶ 2.08–2.09.

[28] See U.C.C. § 1-105.

[29] 356 F. Supp. 991 (N.D. Ga. 1973).

[30] 461 Pa. 343, 336 A.2d 316 (1975).

ties had agreed would govern the lease whose payments the credit secured.[31]

In *Wyle v. Bank Melli*,[32] the account party's trustee in bankruptcy sought to enjoin payment under a letter of credit issued in favor of an Iranian bank. The plaintiff argued that federal common law or the Uniform Customs should govern relief for fraud, rather than California's unique version of Section 5-114(2).[33] The court ruled, however, that the Uniform Customs, to which the credit was subject, did not address the fraud questions and that there was no reason to apply federal common law.

In *Philadelphia Gear Corp. v. FDIC*,[34] the beneficiary of a credit sued the FDIC in its corporate capacity and as receiver of a failed bank for wrongful dishonor of a letter of credit. The court noted that the suit was "deemed to arise under federal law"[35] but that the Code, state law, would determine federal common law.[36] Significantly, the court looked to the Code to determine the substantive rights of the beneficiary but looked to non-Code state law as a source for the federal rule to determine the beneficiary's remedies.

In *Arbest Construction Co. v. First National Bank & Trust Co.*,[37] the court declined to decide in a diversity suit whether Oklahoma law or federal law governed the parties' rights under a credit issued pursuant to the regulations of the Federal Housing Commission. The court reasoned that federal law probably would be the same as the law of Oklahoma, because it probably would select the Code as the source of federal law.[38]

---

[31] Cf. American Bell Int'l, Inc. v. Islamic Republic of Iran, 474 F. Supp. 420 (S.D.N.Y. 1979) (holding by implication that New York law governs credit dispute rather than Iranian law, which underlying contract specified).

[32] 577 F. Supp. 1148 (N.D. Cal. 1983).

[33] For general discussion of the California rule, see ¶ 2.09[6].

[34] 587 F. Supp. 294 (W.D. Okla. 1984), aff'd in part, rev'd in part, 751 F.2d 1131 (10th Cir. 1984), rev'd, 476 U.S. 426 (1986).

[35] Id. at 298 (citing 12 U.S.C. § 1819 (fourth) (1982)).

[36] Cf. United States v. Mercantile Nat'l Bank, 795 F.2d 492 (5th Cir. 1986) (using state law under *Clearfield Trust* doctrine as source of federal law in action by Department of Energy against issuer that dishonored draft drawn under letter of credit).

[37] 777 F.2d 581 (10th Cir. 1985).

[38] For further authority holding that state law may serve as federal law in suits involving federal agencies, see Warner v. FDIC, 605 F. Supp. 521 (S.D. Ohio 1984), rev'd and remanded on other grounds, 798 F.2d 167 (6th Cir. 1986); Agnew v. FDIC, 548 F. Supp. 1235 (N.D. Cal. 1982).

¶ 4.03　THE UNIFORM COMMERCIAL CODE

Sometimes statutory drafters succumb to the temptation to resolve all of the issues. Those attempts usually yield a skewed statutory product. Drafters with this bent emphasize the most recent litigation that they consider to be the latest outrage or instance of judicial wickedness. In all probability, the latest cases are part of a larger trend that will not be evident for some time.

A second failing of the legislative drafters is to fashion the statute to forestall problems that they see, or think they see, on the horizon. These efforts are usually futile for the reason that what one lawyer or a group of lawyers or law professors discerns as the next great issue rarely arises. It is not hyperbole to say that if the law professoriat makes any consistent blunder, it is that of predicting what the issues under a statute or line of cases will be in the future.

Fortunately, the drafters of Article 5 did not make either of these errors. Article 5 of the Code treats credits in rather summary fashion. The statute is skeletal. It resolves a few fundamental questions, leaves many major issues for the courts, and reserves much space for merchants and bankers to fashion the letter of credit product in new ways to serve commercial activity.

[1]　Definitions and Scope

Article 5 begins with a broad scope provision that brings within the article's coverage most mercantile letters of credit.[39] It also defines most of the common letter of credit terms and invents the term "customer," which it uses for the Uniform Customs' term "applicant"[40]; that is, the party the letter of credit industry traditionally has called the account party. The customer is the person who applies to the issuer for the credit and on whose account it is issued.[41]

[2]　Formal Requisites

By stipulating that a credit engagement must be in writing, the Code resolves a question that has bedeviled lawyers for over a century. The issue concerned the extrinsic and virtual acceptances—promises to ac-

---

[39] See ¶¶ 2.03–2.07. Cf. Arbest Constr. Co. v. First Nat'l Bank & Trust Co., 777 F.2d 581 (10th Cir. 1985) (holding that Article 5 governs standby credit issued pursuant to federal regulation).

[40] Compare U.C.C. § 5-103(1)(g) with U.C.P. art. 2 (1983).

[41] See U.C.C. § 5-103(1)(g).

cept drafts that were not written on the drafts themselves. Some courts indicated that oral promises to accept were enforceable as acceptances.[42] The oral promise to accept drafts is similar to a clean acceptance credit.[43] Section 5-104 of the Code makes it clear, however, that no oral promise to accept is enforceable as a credit engagement, just as Section 3-410 makes it clear that an oral promise cannot operate as an acceptance.

[3] Consideration

Prior to the adoption of the Code, there was considerable controversy over the nature of the credit undertaking. If it was a contractual promise, the credit needed consideration to support it. A number of cases worked out elaborate theories of consideration that usually turned on the notion that the credit was a promise that the negotiating bank or other beneficiary accepted by taking the account party's paper or by extending him credit.[44] On the other hand, some authorities argued that the credit was not a contract but a mercantile specialty—a creature of the law merchant where consideration should play no role.[45]

In retrospect, it is probably fair to say that the drafters of Article 5 resolved that issue once and for all, though not all courts or scholars have accepted that resolution.[46] By rejecting consideration doctrine as a basis for rendering a credit undertaking binding, the drafters removed the credit from the aegis of contract and recognized it as a commercial specialty. The rule of Section 5-105 makes it clear that on the consider-

---

[42] See, e.g., Nelson v. First Nat'l Bank, 48 Ill. 36 (1868); cf. Johnson v. Collings, 102 Eng. Rep. 40 (K.B. 1800) (oral promise enforceable only if made after draft is drawn).

[43] See Evansville Nat'l Bank v. Kaufmann, 93 N.Y. 273 (1883); 3 N.Y.L. Revision Comm'n, Study of the Uniform Commercial Code 1580 (1955) [hereinafter New York Study]; Mentschikoff, "Letters of Credit: The Need for Uniform Legislation," 23 U. Chi. L. Rev. 571, 619 (1956).

[44] See generally Thayer, "Irrevocable Credits in International Commerce: Their Legal Nature," 36 Colum. L. Rev. 1031 (1936); McCurdy, "Commercial Letters of Credit" (pts. 1 & 2), 35 Harv. L. Rev. 539, 715 (1922).

[45] See generally New York Study, supra note 43, at 1614; Hershey, "Letters of Credit," 32 Harv. L. Rev. 1, 38 (1918); Thayer, supra note 44, at 1059; Trimble, "The Law Merchant and the Letter of Credit," 61 Harv. L. Rev. 981, 995 (1948).

[46] See, U.C.C. § 5-114, comment 1; West Virginia Hous. Dev. Fund v. Sroka, 415 F. Supp. 1107 (W.D. Pa. 1976); Venizelos S.A. v. Chase Manhattan Bank, N.A., 425 F.2d 461 (2d Cir. 1970).

ation question, the law merchant and not the law of contract governs.[47] That drafting decision is heavy with historical implication. The controversy that attended Lord Mansfield's decision in *Pillans v. Van Mierop*[48] could not have been unknown to the Code drafters. By throwing their lot with Mansfield, the drafters accepted his reasoning in *Pillans* to the effect that certain merchant obligations cannot be subject to the rules of contract.[49] Section 5-105 makes it clear that a letter of credit is one of those merchant obligations.

[4] Establishment and Revocability

The controversy over the nature of the credit as a contract or as a mercantile specialty[50] bore directly on the question of revocability. If the credit was an offer, it could be revoked until it was accepted[51]; yet merchants and bankers treated the commercial credit engagement as irrevocable.[52]

Section 5-106 resolves that issue in favor of the mercantile specialty conclusion. The section provides precise rules for the establishment of the credit engagement and prefers the merchants' expectations over the vagaries of offer and acceptance law. The provision makes it clear that an irrevocable credit may not be revoked once it is established.

[5] Relationships With Account Party

[a] Account Party and Issuer

Article 5 takes some pains to delineate the duties owed by various parties to the customer or account party. The critical relationship is that between the account party and the issuer. Section 5-109 sets forth the obligations of the issuer toward the account party and introduces a significant element of credit law. The provision stipulates that the issuer must act in good faith and that, while the issuer must also observe usages of its industry, it is not required to observe usages of other industries. This rule reflects the concept that the credit, to which the issuer is

---

[47] See ¶ 3.03[1].

[48] 97 Eng. Rep. 1035 (K.B. 1765).

[49] For discussion of the *Pillans* case and the controversy that grew out of it, see ¶ 3.03[1].

[50] For a discussion of that controversy, see ¶ 3.03.

[51] See generally McCurdy, supra note 44.

[52] See 4 S. Williston & G. Thompson, A Treatise on the Law of Contracts § 1011D (rev. ed. 1936).

a party, is independent of the underlying transaction, to which the issuer is not a party.

The independence principle is evident elsewhere in Article 5.[53] This feature of it in Section 5-109 recognizes that an issuer that examines documents presented with a request for payment under the credit may deal with the documents on their face and is not charged with knowledge that familiarity with the underlying transaction would yield. This rule is critical in evaluating the issuer's performance when there are questions about document compliance.[54]

[b] Account Party and Others

Often in the credit transaction a party other than the issuer plays a role. A correspondent of the issuer may advise[55] or confirm[56] the credit. An unrelated party, acting at the request of the beneficiary, may present documents to the issuer for payment.[57]

Generally, the account party has few rights against these parties. The account party is not in privity with correspondents of the issuer, for example.[58] In addition, Section 5-111 constructs severely restricted warranties in favor of the account party from advising, confirming, negotiating, and collecting banks. The section imposes heavy warranties on the beneficiary who presents documents and requests payment under a credit. Those warranties include the representation that the necessary conditions of the credit are satisfied and that the warranties run to "all interested parties,"[59] a term that clearly includes the account party. By

---

[53] See U.C.C. § 5-114. See also ¶¶ 2.08–2.09, 3.03[6], 7.03–7.04.

[54] See ¶¶ 6.03–6.05.

[55] See U.C.C. §§ 5-103(1)(e), 5-107(1).

[56] See U.C.C. §§ 5-103(1)(f), 5-107(2).

[57] See U.C.C. § 5-112(3).

[58] See, e.g., Instituto Nacional De Comercializacion Agricola (Indeca) v. Continental Ill. Nat'l Bank & Trust Co., 858 F.2d 1264 (7th Cir. 1988); Auto Servicio San Ignacio, S.R.L. v. Compania Anonima Venezolana De Navegacion (Venezuelan Line), 765 F.2d 1306 (5th Cir. 1985); Bank of Cochin Ltd. v. Manufacturers Hanover Trust Co., 612 F. Supp. 1533 (S.D.N.Y. 1985), aff'd, 808 F.2d 209 (2d Cir. 1986); Instituto Nacional De Comercializacion Agricola (Indeca) v. Continental Ill. Nat'l Bank & Trust Co., 530 F. Supp. 279 (N.D. Ill. 1982); cf. Worldwide Sugar Co. v. Royal Bank of Can., No. 83 Civ. 1208 (ADS) (S.D.N.Y. July 9, 1984) (holding that account party of credit that was canceled could not benefit from guaranty letter from advising bank, even though credit was canceled with understanding that "documents" would be delivered to account party).

[59] See U.C.C. § 5-111(1). For authority in which the account party was able to recover the full amount of the credit from a beneficiary that breached that warranty, see Mellon Bank, N.A. v. General Elec. Credit Corp., 724 F. Supp. 360 (W.D. Pa. 1989); Artoc Bank & Trust, Ltd. v. Sun Marine Terminals, Inc., 760 S.W.2d 311 (Tex. Ct. App. 1988).

contrast, the warranties of the intermediary banks are light, entailing only the burden of good faith and authority.[60]

[6] The Credit Engagement

[a] Independence Principle

The central obligation in credit law is that of the issuer or confirming bank to honor the beneficiary's draft or demand for payment. Section 5-114 defines that obligation for the issuer; Section 5-107(2) establishes the same obligation for a confirming bank.

Section 5-114 begins by imposing on the issuer the duty to honor the beneficiary's presentation if it complies with the terms of the credit. The section immediately qualifies that obligation with a statement of the independence principle. The provision stipulates that the issuer must honor a presentation complying with the credit, "regardless of whether the goods or documents conform to the underlying contract for sale or other contract between the customer and the beneficiary."[61] This language is a codification of the independence of the issuer's duty toward the beneficiary from the underlying transaction, just as Section 5-109 codifies the independence of the issuer's duty toward the account party from that transaction.[62] In general, the effect of this language is to prevent the beneficiary and the account party from raising in the credit transaction matters that arise out of the underlying transaction. The issue appears most often when the account party attempts to stop payment under the credit.[63] It also appears when courts confuse the credit obligation with obligations arising out of related contracts.[64]

[b] The *Sztejn* Rule

There is an important exception to the independence principle. Courts and the Code recognize that in limited circumstances, it is necessary to go beyond the face of the beneficiary's documents to determine whether the documents are in some respect false or fraudulent. The contours of that exception are the subject of considerable litigation and controversy. Section 5-114(2) codifies the exception as it was fashioned

---

[60] See U.C.C. § 5-111, comment (penultimate sentence).

[61] U.C.C. § 5-114(1).

[62] See ¶¶ 6.02–6.05.

[63] See ¶ 7.04.

[64] See ¶¶ 2.08–2.09.

in *Sztejn v. J. Henry Schroder Banking Corp.*,[65] which recognized an exception when an "unscrupulous"[66] party attempts to defraud the account party and the issuer. The subsection also defines a class of persons who are good faith purchasers and who are protected even if the beneficiary has made a fraudulent presentation.[67]

[7] Additional Questions of Codification

Article 5 treats a few matters in addition to those discussed previously.[68] The drafters acknowledged, however, that they were not attempting to codify all of credit law. Section 5-102, the scope provision, stipulates:

> This Article deals with some but not all of the rules and concepts of letters of credit as such rules or concepts have developed prior to this act or may hereafter develop. The fact that this Article states a rule does not by itself require, imply or negate application of the same or a converse rule to a situation not provided for or to a person not specified by this Article.

The official comment notes that the article attempts to codify the fundamental theories underlying letters of credit.[69]

All American jurisdictions have adopted Article 5, and, although it was drafted before the standby credit became a common commercial device, courts have not hesitated to apply it to standby credits[70] as the scope provision of Section 5-102 suggests they should.[71] There is, therefore, a good measure of uniformity in American letter of credit law.

---

[65] 177 Misc. 719, 31 N.Y.S.2d 631 (Sup. Ct. 1941). U.C.C. § 5-114(2) is the most heavily litigated provision in Article 5. Chapter 7 discusses the cases.

[66] Id. at 722, 31 N.Y.S.2d at 634.

[67] For general discussion of the fraud exception to the independence principle, see ¶¶ 7.03, 7.04.

[68] Some of the provisions are important but others are housekeeping in nature. They relate to the availability of the credit in portions and to the presenter's lien (U.C.C. § 5-110); the important timing rule for honor or rejection (U.C.C. § 5-112), discussed infra ¶ 4.06[2][b]; indemnities for defects in documents (U.C.C. § 5-113); remedies, discussed in ¶ 9.02 (U.C.C. § 5-115); transfer and assignment, discussed in Chapter 10 (U.C.C. § 5-116); and insolvency, discussed at ¶ 12.01 (U.C.C. § 5-117).

[69] See U.C.C. § 5-102, comment 2 (4th sentence).

[70] See East Bank v. Dovenmuehle, Inc., 196 Colo. 422, 589 P.2d 1361 (1978); Board of County Comm'rs v. Colorado Nat'l Bank, 43 Colo. App. 186, 607 P.2d 1010 (1979), modified on other grounds, 634 P.2d 32 (Colo. 1981); O'Grady v. First Union Nat'l Bank, 296 N.C. 212, 250 S.E.2d 587 (1978).

[71] See discussion in ¶¶ 2.03–2.07. At least one commentator has suggested that Article 5 should be revised to remove standby credits or to fashion treatment for them that differs from that of commercial credits. See, e.g., Rapson, "Problems in Perspective: The Lure and Snare of 'Standby Letters of Credit,'" New Jersey L.J.,

In the international setting, and frequently in the domestic credit case, the Code confronts the Uniform Customs that issuers frequently incorporate into both commercial and standby credits. Article 5 itself states that it is not complete and that "no statute can effectively or wisely codify all the possible law of letters of credit without stultifying further development of this useful financing device."[72] The Code does not cover all matters of credit law and, in fact, leaves many questions to the parties themselves, to usage, or to resolution by the courts.

¶ 4.04 THE UNIFORM CUSTOMS AND PRACTICE FOR DOCUMENTARY CREDITS

The Uniform Customs stipulate rather circuitously in Article 1 that they apply to the extent they are applicable to all documentary credits[73] and that all parties are bound "unless otherwise expressly agreed."[74] The Article goes on to provide, however, that "[t]hey shall be incorporated into each documentary credit by wording in the credit indicating that such credit is issued subject to [them]."[75]

There are contradictory implications in this language of Article 1. On the one hand, the article suggests that the Uniform Customs apply to all documentary credits; on the other hand, it suggests that they apply only if the credit incorporates them expressly. Certainly, any careful

---

Feb. 24, 1983, at 8. Another commentator contends that the drafters had standby credits in mind when they drafted Section 5-102(1)(c). See Wiley, "How to Use Letters of Credit in Financing the Sale of Goods," 20 Bus. Law. 495, 503 (1965); see also U.C.C. § 5-102, comment 1 (3d & 4th sentences) (referring to "money credits" that call for certificates of performance or default). The 1983 Uniform Customs apply expressly to standby letters of credit. See U.C.P. art. 1 (1983).

[72] See U.C.C. § 5-102, comment 2.

[73] But cf. Raiffeisen-Zentralkasse Tirol v. First Nat'l Bank, 671 P.2d 1008 (Colo. Ct. App. 1983) (holding that Uniform Customs do not apply to credit subject to nondocumentary conditions). One of the conditions that the *Raiffeisen* court deemed nondocumentary was a term, not uncommon in commercial credits, prohibiting partial shipments. Such a term usually is satisfied by remitting a draft, an invoice, and a shipping document showing that the shipment was not partial. Thus, the court could have found the Uniform Customs to be applicable to that term, which was clearly documentary. For a case holding that the issuer or confirmer may insist on documentary evidence of compliance with a nondocumentary condition of a letter of credit subject to the Uniform Customs, see Banque De L'Indochine Et De Suez S.A. v. J.H. Rayner (Mincing Lane) Ltd., [1983] 1 Lloyd's Rep. 228 (C.A.). For further discussion of nondocumentary conditions, see ¶ 6.04[7].

[74] U.C.P. art. 1 (1983).

[75] Id.; cf. U.C.P. art. 12(c) (1983) (requiring credits issued by telex to state expressly that they are subject to the Uniform Customs).

drafter that intends to have the Uniform Customs apply will use the incorporating language, but the absence of such language is no fail-safe assurance that they do not apply. The Uniform Customs are a record of banking practice and arguably may supplement the terms of a credit that does not refer to them.[76]

Banks themselves are the moving force behind the Customs. If the scope of the Code is general, the scope of the Customs is specific. Arguably, the Customs do not apply to the clean credit, which, by definition, is not a "documentary" credit. To that extent, the Customs are narrower than the Code; but, in practice, issuers of clean credits often make them subject to the Uniform Customs, and there is no compelling reason not to satisfy the parties' reasonable expectations by applying the Uniform Customs to them.

Otherwise, Articles 15 through 21 of the UCP, dealing with liabilities and responsibilities, are sufficiently similar to such rules in the Code to prompt one court to observe that a prior version of the Uniform Customs "in substance [states] only what is contained in the Uni-

---

[76] For a discussion of the role of the Uniform Customs as evidence of industry custom, see infra ¶ 4.06[1][b]. In at least one case, the court held that the Uniform Customs had the force of law. See Oriental Pac. (U.S.A.), Inc. v. Toronto Dominion Bank, 78 Misc. 2d 819, 357 N.Y.S.2d 957 (Sup. Ct. 1974). In Instituto Nacional De Comercializacion Agricola (Indeca) v. Continental Ill. Nat'l Bank & Trust Co., 530 F. Supp. 279 (N.D. Ill. 1982) the court refused to apply the Uniform Customs to a dispute between the account party and the confirming bank, even though the credit was subject to the Uniform Customs. The court held that the Uniform Customs apply only if the parties so agree and that the fact that the account party and the issuer adopted the Uniform Customs does not mean that the confirming bank adopted them. The opinion does not explain why it is that the confirmation by a bank of a credit that is expressly subject to the Uniform Customs should not also be subject to them. But cf. Voest-Alpine Int'l Corp. v. Chase Manhattan Bank, N.A., 545 F. Supp. 301 (S.D.N.Y. 1982), aff'd in part, rev'd in part on other grounds, 707 F.2d 680 (2d Cir. 1983) (suggesting that confirmation is subject to Uniform Customs if credit is subject to them); Almatrood v. Sallee Int'l, Inc., No. 83 Civ. 1800 (WCC) (S.D.N.Y. May 13, 1985) (applying Uniform Customs to account party's claim against confirming bank); Bank of Cochin Ltd. v. Manufacturers Hanover Trust Co., 612 F. Supp. 1533 (S.D.N.Y. 1985), aff'd, 808 F.2d 209 (2d Cir. 1986) (holding squarely that if credit is subject to Uniform Customs, relationship between issuer and confirming bank is also so governed). See also Funk, "Letters of Credit: U.C.C. Article 5 and the Uniform Customs and Practice," 11 How. L.J. 88, 94 (1965) (contending that Uniform Customs do not apply if credit does not refer to them). The drafters of the Uniform Customs consistently have protested that the Uniform Customs are not law, but they cannot deny that the Customs may have the force of law. Jhirad, "Uniform Customs and Practice for Documentary Credits, 1974 Revision: The Principal Emendations of the 1962 Text," 9 U.C.C. L.J. 109, 119 (1976).

form Commercial Code."[77] There are, however, a number of exceptions to the general concord between these two sources of credit law.[78]

The Uniform Customs address with particularity such matters as communications among issuing, confirming, advising, and negotiating banks; the form of the credit; the conformity of the accompanying documents; and the issuing bank's duty in connection with those documents. The Customs also contain a number of miscellaneous provisions codifying date and amount rules and also deal with the question of transferring the credit or its proceeds. Finally, the Customs leave much unsaid and call for supplemental rules, just as the Code does.

¶ 4.05 LEGISLATIVE DEFERENCE TO THE UNIFORM CUSTOMS—SECTION 5-102(4)

Although the Code and the Uniform Customs are in general agreement, the New York legislature adopted a significant nonconforming amendment to Section 5-102, which also was adopted by Alabama, Missouri, and Arizona.[79] That amendment renders Article 5 inapplicable in the event the credit is subject, in whole or in part, to the Uniform Customs. The amendment is curious in a number of ways. First, it does not merely give the Uniform Customs preference but rejects the Code altogether, regardless of whether the Uniform Customs and the Code conflict. It rejects the Code, furthermore, even though the parties incorporate the Uniform Customs into the credit only in part. Second, the provision begs for litigation when it applies not only to credits expressly incorporating the Uniform Customs but also to credits subject to the Uniform Customs by course of dealing or usage of trade.

The New York nonconforming amendment is unfortunate for two reasons. First, it suggests that parties must choose between the Code and the Uniform Customs when, in general, both sources treat different questions. A party that prefers the Code's specific and clarifying rules on the time and effect of establishing a credit, its clear rule on the presenter's warranties, or its explicit rule on remedies for improper dishonor (all matters that the Uniform Customs leave to the courts), must

---

[77] Banco Espanol de Credito v. State St. Bank & Trust Co., 266 F. Supp. 106, 109 n.1 (D. Mass.), rev'd on other grounds, 385 F.2d 230 (1st Cir. 1967), cert. denied, 390 U.S. 1013 (1968).

[78] For discussion of those conflicts, see ¶ 4.06[2].

[79] See Ala. Code § 7-5-102(4) (1984); Ariz. Rev. Stat. Ann. § 47-5102[D] (1988); Mo. Rev. Stat. § 400.5-102(4) (Vernon Supp. 1990); N.Y. U.C.C. § 5-102(4) (McKinney 1964).

choose the Code and sacrifice the Uniform Customs' specific rules on quantity and amount, expiry date, combined transport documents, marine bills, and similar matters on which the Code is silent.

There are a few instances, of course, when the Code and the Uniform Customs conflict, but these conflicts can be resolved easily. Generally, in states that have not adopted the nonconforming amendment, courts apply freedom of contract principles and let the parties' choice of the Uniform Customs prevail over the Code.

That common-law rule is not surprising. The four states that insisted on the nonconforming amendment could have assured it would have been the law of those jurisdictions by adopting a less radical provision in their Code rendering Code rules subject to the Uniform Customs in those cases where the parties select the Uniform Customs. In fact, the frequent deference in Article 5 to freedom of contract suggests that, in most cases, the Code does defer to the parties' selection of any rule they prefer to that of the Code.[80] In short, in their concern for the Uniform Customs, the legislatures of New York, Missouri, Alabama, and Arizona actually may have diminished the role of the Customs by forcing some parties to opt for the Code and thereby exclude the Customs.

The second objection to the rule of Section 5-102(4) is that it has fostered an unfortunate and probably unintended reading. Some courts have held that Section 5-102(4) forbids them to use Code rules when the Uniform Customs apply. That notion, however, is not well founded.

A statute, such as the Code, is a command whereby the legislature exercises its prerogative of fashioning rules that, in this instance, relate to letters of credit. By its command, the legislature preempts courts from fashioning different rules. When the legislature adopts a provision such as Section 5-102(4), it may be promulgating (1) a radical rule that the courts may not use the statute when the parties elect the Uniform Customs or (2) a moderate rule that the legislative preemption does not operate when the parties elect to use the Uniform Customs. The radical reading forbids the courts to use Code rules. The moderate reading leaves the courts free to fashion rules that may be the same as, similar to, or different from those of the Code. It is difficult to understand why the legislature would have intended the first meaning, yet the reason for the second meaning is clear: The legislature simply wanted the courts to be free to fashion letter of credit law in cases governed by the Uniform Customs. In fashioning such law under this moderate view, courts may look to the Code and may invoke those rules of the Code that they like and eschew those that they do not like. Under this reading, when they

---

[80] See Comment, "'Unless Otherwise Agreed' and Article 5: An Exercise in Freedom of Contract," 11 St. Louis U.L.J. 416 (1967).

invoke a Code rule, New York courts are not violating Section 5-102(4). In such instances, they are defining a common-law rule and are free to look at nonapplicable legislation in New York, just as they are free to look at nonapplicable legislation in any other jurisdiction or nonapplicable case law from any other jurisdiction.

Unfortunately, some courts have resorted to the first, radical reading of Section 5-102(4). In *Capehart Corp. v. Shanghai Commercial Bank Ltd.*,[81] the court expressed the view that the holder in due course rule of Section 5-114(2) does not apply to cases governed by the Uniform Customs. It is true that Section 5-114(2) was not binding on the *Capehart* court in a New York case involving a credit governed by the Uniform Customs. Surely, however, the court could have adopted such a rule, which is a logical exception to the fraud defense defined in that section and which is consistent with the policy of negotiable instruments rules.[82] Ironically, the exception outlined in Section 5-114(2) originally was recognized by common-law courts prior to the time when the Code itself adopted it, and New York provided the leading cases.[83]

In *W. Pat Crow Forgings, Inc. v. Moorings Aero Industries, Inc.*,[84] the court held that Section 5-102(4) commanded the court to use pre-Code New York case law to resolve a letter of credit issue. It is difficult to understand the reason for forbidding courts to look to all non-Code law rather than just to pre-Code law.[85] It is equally difficult to see why

---

[81] 49 A.D.2d 521, 369 N.Y.S.2d 751 (1975) (dictum).

[82] The holder in due course exception in Section 5-114(2) is consistent, but not necessarily coterminous, with the rule in Section 3-305(2) that a holder in due course takes an instrument free from "all defenses of any party to the instrument with whom the holder has not dealt." The exception is supported by dicta in some pre-Code cases in New York. See, e.g., Sztejn v. J. Henry Schroder Banking Corp., 177 Misc. 719, 723, 31 N.Y.S.2d 631, 635 (Sup. Ct. 1941). See generally ¶ 8.02.

[83] See authority cited supra note 65. In Decor by Nikkei Int'l, Inc. v. Federal Republic of Nig., 497 F. Supp. 893 (S.D.N.Y. 1980), aff'd, 647 F.2d 300 (2d Cir. 1981), cert. denied, 454 U.S. 1148 (1982), the court adopted a similar rule. Accord Almatrood v. Sallee Int'l, Inc., No. 83 Civ. 1800 (WCC) (S.D.N.Y. May 13, 1985); Continental Time Corp. v. Merchants Bank, 117 Misc. 2d 907, 459 N.Y.S.2d 396 (Sup. Ct. 1983); see also Tuthill v. Union Sav. Bank, 141 Misc. 2d 88, 534 N.Y.S.2d 88 (1988); Hohenberg Co. v. Comitex Knitters, Ltd., 104 Misc. 2d 232, 428 N.Y.S.2d 156 (Sup. Ct. 1980) ("[U]nder UCC section 5-102(4), the Uniform Customs alone controls."). In Missouri, courts have followed the mandate of the subsection strictly. See State v. Morganstein, 703 S.W.2d 894 (Mo. 1986); Waidmann v. Mercantile Trust Co., 711 S.W.2d 907 (Mo. Ct. App. 1986).

[84] 93 Misc. 2d 65, 403 N.Y.S.2d 399 (App. Term. 1978).

[85] Cf. U.C.C. § 5-102(3) & comment 2 (inviting application of non-Code rules to areas not covered by Article 5).

courts may not select Code rules that do not conflict with the Uniform Customs.[86]

The New York Court of Appeals, in *United Bank, Ltd. v. Cambridge Sporting Goods Corp.*,[87] observed by way of dictum that the Uniform Customs do not displace Section 5-114(2). The two sources of credit law do not overlap on the point covered in Section 5-114. The *Cambridge Sporting Goods* court would limit the New York rule, however, to the pre-Code cases that Section 5-114(2) codifies.[88]

The *Cambridge Sporting Goods* dictum suggests that Section 5-102(4) may not prevent New York courts from adopting a rule codified by Article 5 but that the courts must find the source of such a rule in pre-Code authority. That dictum makes more sense than the notion advanced by the *Capehart* case. It has the unfortunate effect, however, of freezing letter of credit law—an effect the New York legislature arguably did not intend.

In short, the nonconforming amendment to Section 5-102(4) may create more problems than it solves. Now that courts have fashioned a body of case law construing the Code and can see clearly that conflicts between the Code and the Uniform Customs are relatively insignificant, it may be time to discard the provision. In the meantime, courts may be well advised to limit its application.[89]

---

[86] See, e.g., Habib Bank Ltd. v. Convermat Corp., 145 Misc. 2d 980, 554, N.Y.S.2d 757 (App. Term. 1990) (per curiam) (using U.C.C. § 5-102(4) as basis for refusing to apply warranty provision of Article 5 when reason for provision interdicted its application in any event). For discussion of the *Habib Bank* case, see ¶ 4.06[2][g].

[87] 41 N.Y.2d 254, 360 N.E.2d 943, 392 N.Y.S.2d 265 (1976).

[88] See also Prutscher v. Fidelity Int'l Bank, 502 F. Supp. 535 (S.D.N.Y. 1980) (following *Cambridge Sporting Goods* rule).

[89] In Eljay, Jrs., Inc. v. Rahda Exports, 99 A.D.2d 408, 470 N.Y.S.2d 12 (1984), the court elected to apply Section 5-114(2) of the Code to a dispute arising out of a credit that expressly incorporated the Uniform Customs. In the *Eljay* case, the account party, claiming fraud, attempted to enjoin the issuer from paying against facially conforming documents. The court held that because the Uniform Customs did not address the fraud question, the Code applied. In Bank of Cochin, Ltd. v. Manufacturers Hanover Trust Co., 612 F. Supp. 1533 (S.D.N.Y. 1985), aff'd, 808 F.2d 209 (2d Cir. 1986), the court held that if the Uniform Customs are silent or ambiguous, the Code may apply. See also Trans Meridian Trading, Inc. v. Empresa Nacional De Comercializacion De Insumos, 829 F.2d 949 (9th Cir. 1987) (applying California's nonuniform version of U.C.C. § 5-114, despite incorporation of Uniform Customs in credit); cf. First Commercial Bank v. Gotham Originals, Inc., 64 N.Y.2d 287, 475 N.E.2d 1255, 486 N.Y.S.2d 715 (1985) (indicating that incorporation of Uniform Customs did not bar relief of Section 5-114); Larson v. First Interstate Bank, 603 F. Supp. 467 (D. Ariz. 1983) (holding that Arizona's nonconforming version of Section 5-102(4) does not prevent court from entering injunction against payment of credit, even though Uniform Customs do not address fraud issue). But cf. Merchants Bank

¶ 4.06   THE CODE AND THE UNIFORM CUSTOMS

[1]   Nature of the Uniform Customs

The first article of the Uniform Customs stipulates that the Customs govern all credits that do not expressly provide the contrary. This assertion of jurisdiction bears analysis. The International Chamber of Commerce (ICC) has no authority to legislate.

In 1962, the ICC published Brochure No. 222, which was the first widely adopted version of the Uniform Customs. By that time banks in all of the world's major commercial nations had signaled their adherence to the Uniform Customs. In 1974, the ICC published a revised version of the brochure, Publication No. 290.[90] That version became effective on October 1, 1975. Banks in 156 countries formally adhered to that version,[91] and, in April 1975, the United Nations Commission on International Trade Law (UNCITRAL) unanimously commended the use of the Uniform Customs.[92] The ICC revised the Uniform Customs again in 1983, and that version, ICC Publication No. 400, was effective as of October 1, 1984.[93]

This display of international cooperation undoubtedly does, and should, give the Uniform Customs force, but thoughtful commentators have questioned the nature of that force.[94] The Uniform Customs are

---

v. Credit Suisse Bank, 585 F. Supp. 304 (S.D.N.Y. 1984) (reading rule of Section 5-102(4) as interdicting application of Code); Fertico Belg., S.A. v. Phosphate Chems. Export Ass'n, 100 A.D.2d 165, 473 N.Y.S.2d 403, appeal dismissed, 62 N.Y.2d 802 (1984) (same).

[90] For discussion of these 1974 revisions, see Axworthy, "The Revisions of the Uniform Customs on Documentary Credits," 1971 J. Bus. L. 38; Jhirad, supra note 76; B. Wheble, "Uniform Customs and Practice for Documentary Credits" (1974 Revision), 1975 J. Bus. L. 281. See generally App. B.

[91] The list of banks that signaled their adherence in one way or another includes those from eastern European countries. Banks in the People's Republic of China were the latest to signal formal adherence.

[92] See International Chamber of Commerce, Uniform Customs and Practice for Documentary Credits, ICC Pub. No. 290, at 5 (1975).

[93] For a complete discussion of the history of the Uniform Customs, see Ellinger, "The Uniform Customs — Their Nature and the 1983 Revision," 1984 Lloyd's Mar. & Com. L.Q. 578.

[94] The most vocal objections arose at the time that the New York Law Revision Commission was considering the adoption of the Code. At that time, proponents of the Code saw the Uniform Customs and the Code as competing bodies rather than complementary bodies of law. See New York Study, supra note 43, at 1586; Mentschikoff, "Letters of Credit: The Need for Uniform Legislation," 23 U. Chi. L. Rev. 571 (1956). Not all commentators accepted the view that the two were incompatible. See Chadsey, "Practical Effect of the Uniform Commercial Code on Documentary Letter of Credit Transactions," 102 U. Pa. L. Rev. 618 (1954); Funk, supra note 76; Harfield, "Article 5 — Trade Without Tears, or Around Letters of Credit in 17 Sections," 1952 Wis. L. Rev. 298.

not themselves law. To the extent that they describe banking practice, they may reflect trade usage.[95] It is not clear, however, that the mere assertion of Article 1 renders the Uniform Customs evidence of trade usage. Presumably, in any litigation, the parties may show that usage and the Uniform Customs differ. In that case, the Customs are prescriptive, not descriptive.[96]

The United States Council on International Banking participated in the drafting of the 1983 Uniform Customs by sending a representative to the working party.[97] That representative consulted with various international banking constituents.[98] It is perhaps significant that many community banks are not members of those councils, yet they usually issue credits, especially standby credits, and often expressly render them subject to the Uniform Customs.[99]

[a] Uniform Customs as a Contract Term

To the extent that a credit expressly incorporates the Uniform Customs, the Customs become a part of the undertaking and have binding force. That result is a direct consequence of the Code's strong commitment to party autonomy, set forth in the statute's first substantive provision, Section 1-102. That freedom is subject to limitation, however. Section 1-102(3) restricts the power of parties to vary the provisions of the Code if the Code itself prohibits such variation, or if the parties at-

---

[95] See AMF Head Sports Wear, Inc. v. Ray Scott's All-Am. Sports Club, Inc., 448 F. Supp. 222 (D. Ariz. 1978). See also infra ¶ 4.07.

[96] For a view supporting the notion that the Uniform Customs are evidence of trade usage, see Byrne, "The 1983 Revision of the Uniform Customs and Practice for Documentary Credits," 102 Banking L.J. 151 (1985). For the view that the credit must recite that it is subject to the Uniform Customs before the Uniform Customs will apply, see Chapman, "The 1983 Revisions to the Uniform Customs and Practice for Documentary Credits," 90 Com. L.J. 13 (1985).

[97] For discussion of the drafting of the 1983 Uniform Customs, see ¶ 3.05.

[98] Formerly, there were three regional councils in the United States: the Council on International Banking, the Mid-America Council on International Banking, and the Western Council on International Banking, and one umbrella organization: the National Association of Councils on International Banking. The regional councils merged into the Council on International Banking but still engage in regional activity. At the time of that merger, membership was approximately 650 banks.

[99] For discussion of the effect of the Uniform Customs on such bank credits that do not incorporate the Uniform Customs, see infra ¶¶ 4.06[1][b], 4.06[1][c]. For discussion of the 1983 Revision, see B. Wheble, "UCP 1974/1983 Revisions Compared and Explained (Documentary Credits)," ICC Pub. No. 411 (1984); Farrar, "UCC Survey, Letters of Credit," 39 Bus. Law. 1319 (1984). See also authority cited in Appendix A.

tempt to disclaim obligations of good faith, diligence, reasonableness, and care prescribed by the statute. Presumably, that exception applies to the Uniform Customs.

[b] Uniform Customs as a Descriptive Definition

To the extent that the Uniform Customs describe trade customs and usage, the Code gives them the force of law, even though the parties do not incorporate them. Section 1-102 codifies the legislative decision to give full vent to "the continued expansion of commercial practices through custom, usage and agreement of the parties."[100] Presumably, the effect of usage is limited by U.C.C. § 1-102(3), which does not permit the agreement of the parties to vary (1) provisions of the statute that prohibit it and (2) the obligations of good faith, diligence, reasonableness, and care prescribed by the statute.

Section 1-205(2) stipulates that trade usage is a fact that must be proved. The official comment indicates that there is "room . . . for proper recognition of usage agreed upon by merchants in trade codes."[101] Once proved, the usage has effect; but the section stipulates that the usage may not vary the contrary, express terms of an agreement and is subject to course of dealing.[102] Clearly, Section 1-205 permits a party to prove that a credit is subject to the Uniform Customs, even though the credit does not incorporate the provision. That proof includes the requirement that the Uniform Customs describe actual trade usage.[103]

[c] Uniform Customs as a Prescriptive Definition

If the proof discloses that the Uniform Customs do not reflect actual trade usage, they still may have impact on a credit that does not incorporate them. That effect results not from the force of the Uniform Customs as a source of law or as a contract term but as a body of rules reflecting the thoughtful judgment of the world's bankers. The Uniform Customs are promulgated by the world's leading commercial trade

---

[100] See U.C.C. § 1-102(2)(b).

[101] See U.C.C. § 1-205, comment 5 (last sentence).

[102] See U.C.C. § 1-205(4).

[103] Cf. Fertico Belg., S.A. v. Phosphate Chems. Export Ass'n, 100 A.D.2d 165, 473 N.Y.S.2d 403, appeal dismissed, 62 N.Y.2d 802 (1984) (characterizing Uniform Customs as record of practice); see also Banco Nacional De Desarrollo v. Mellon Bank, N.A., 726 F.2d 87, 93 n.5 (3d Cir. 1984) (holding that Uniform Customs are "recording of common practices").

group (the ICC) and endorsed by the trade arm (UNCITRAL) of the largest international organization (the United Nations). Certainly, courts may identify weaknesses in the Uniform Customs or policies that conflict with those of the Customs. Absent those weaknesses or conflicting policies, the Uniform Customs provide courts with a thoughtful body of rules that the courts may elect to use.

[d] Some Conclusions on the Role of the Uniform Customs

The Uniform Customs are not law, but the assertion of Article 1 that the Uniform Customs "apply to all documentary credits . . . and are binding on all parties thereto unless otherwise expressly agreed" is largely true. If the parties expressly incorporate the Uniform Customs, they become terms of the engagement and will apply, except to the extent that they vary Code provisions that do not permit variation.[104] If the parties expressly reject the Uniform Customs, under the terms of Article 1 the Customs do not apply. If the credit is silent, to the extent that a party proves that the Uniform Customs describe a regularly observed usage of trade,[105] the Uniform Customs "fill in points which the parties have not considered and in fact agreed upon."[106] If the credit is silent and if there is no proof that the Uniform Customs describe a regularly observed usage of trade, the Customs still serve as the latest, best, and most persuasive thinking on the practices in question.

[2] Conflicts Between the Code and the Uniform Customs

There are a few areas of conflict that have surfaced to date between Article 5 and U.S. common law on the one hand and the Uniform Customs on the other. These areas involve five rules:

1. Revocability
2. The issuer's time for examining documents
3. Estoppel against the issuer
4. Transfer
5. Warranties

There also has been some confusion over the use of fraud to stop payment in cases involving the Uniform Customs, but that conflict is not

---

[104] See U.C.C. § 1-102(3).

[105] See U.C.C. § 1-205, comment 5 (explaining meaning of "usage of trade").

[106] See U.C.C. § 1-205, comment 4 (4th sentence).

well established and probably does not exist at all. The other five have not caused serious problems, but parties should be aware of them. In addition, of course, parties must consider whether they want to be bound by all of the terms in the Uniform Customs. Nothing in credit law forbids the parties from incorporating some but not all of the UCP.[107]

[a] Revocability

Article 7 of the Uniform Customs provides, as does the Code's Section 5-103(1)(a), that credits may be either revocable or irrevocable. The Code expresses no preference between the two and leaves the matter to the courts.[108] Article 7 of the UCP stipulates, however, that if the credit is silent, it should be taken as a revocable engagement of the issuer. At this point, the Code and the Uniform Customs are only partially in conflict. The Code is silent. The Uniform Customs express a preference. The case law to which Section 5-103(1)(a) defers, however, has shown marked disposition to impose irrevocability on those credits that are silent.[109] These cases are part of the general trend toward applying contract construction rules to credits.[110] One such rule favors reading a contract in a fashion that avoids rendering the undertaking illusory. Since the courts view the revocable credit as an illusory promise, they invoke a rule of construction against that revocable characterization.

The cases are persuasive, and it is probably safe to say that the Code rule as fashioned by the courts generally opposes the Uniform

---

[107] Article 45 of the Uniform Customs, for example, contains something of a trap for the unwary. The Article stipulates that a beneficiary who fails to draw or ship within a period provided for in the credit for installment drawing or shipment loses the benefit of the credit not only for the missed installment but for subsequent installments, unless the credit provides otherwise. Under Article 36 of the 1974 version of the Uniform Customs, the credit expired if the beneficiary missed a shipment under a credit that called for shipment in installments.

Briefly, the difference between the Code or common-law rule and the Uniform Customs on missed installments is significant. It is difficult to fashion the Uniform Customs rule out of whole cloth. Clearly the rule rests on the express language of Article 45. Parties wanting to avoid it must reject the Uniform Customs altogether or must adopt the Uniform Customs with an express exception for Article 45.

[108] See U.C.C. § 5-103, comment 1 (last two sentences). But cf. Fla. Stat. Ann. § 675.5-103(1)(a) (West 1966) (nonconforming Code provision stipulating that if credit does not indicate whether it is irrevocable or revocable, it is irrevocable); La. Rev. Stat. Ann. § 10:5-103(1)(a) (West 1983) (same).

[109] See, e.g., West Virginia Hous. Dev. Fund v. Sroka, 415 F. Supp. 1107 (W.D. Pa. 1976); Housing Sec., Inc. v. Maine Nat'l Bank, 391 A.2d 311 (Me. 1978). See also cases cited infra ¶¶ 4.08[4], 5.03[1].

[110] See generally infra ¶ 4.08.

Customs rule. This conflict should not give rise to serious concern, however. The careful drafter always designates the credit as revocable or irrevocable, and the careless beneficiary finds protection under the Code and difficulty under the Uniform Customs. Such disappointment stems not from any conflict between Article 5 and the UCP but from the rule of the Uniform Customs. In addition, the policy of the cases probably overrides the prescriptive role of the Uniform Customs. An issuer may attempt to prove that trade usage is contrary to the rule of the cases. Any banker would be hard put, however, to defend the good faith of one intentionally drafting a revocable credit without so designating it.

In *Beathard v. Chicago Football Club, Inc.,*[111] the issuer made the credit subject to the Uniform Customs and did not designate it as either revocable or irrevocable. The court applied the UCP rule without much inquiry into the reasons for the bank's conduct and held that the credit was revocable.[112] In *Beathard,* the beneficiaries were professional athletes, not international traders who the bank might expect would appreciate the significance of the reference to the UCP. In the future, a disappointed, nonmerchant beneficiary, such as Beathard, may be well advised to question the good faith of an issuer and an account party who devise a credit similar to that in the *Beathard* case.[113]

---

[111] 419 F. Supp. 1133 (N.D. Ill. 1976).

[112] In so holding, it proved once again the risk of predicting what courts will do. "I am prepared to prophesy that the courts will perceive [the Uniform Customs rule presuming revocable credits] as constituting a trap and will never enforce it." Mentschikoff, supra note 94, at 589.

[113] Section 1-203 imposes an obligation of good faith in the performance and enforcement of a contract "within this Act." A letter of credit, even when subject to the Uniform Customs, is surely within the Code, except, perhaps, in states that have enacted Section 5-102(4). The bad faith in the *Beathard*-type situation may not stem from performance or from enforcement of the credit so much as from the drafting of it—an area where the Code does not tread with its good faith principle. Perhaps a court confronted with such a case could invoke Section 2-103(1)(b) by analogy and hold that a merchant issuer, which a bank surely is, must not only behave honestly in fact but must observe standards of fairness in the trade. Bankers would testify that customarily banks do not issue revocable credits and that they take care to make it explicit in documents that resemble credits that they do not carry the bank's irrevocable engagement to pay. The court might also hold by analogy that the reference to the Uniform Customs in a credit, such as the one in *Beathard,* has an unconscionable effect and that the court will not enforce it. Of course, if the beneficiary of such a credit were a real estate developer, a mortgage broker, or other merchant or trader, all of these arguments would lose some of their appeal. In at least one case, the court held that Section 2-325(3) supported a ruling that a credit should be read as irrevocable. See Weyerhaeuser Co. v. First Nat'l Bank, 27 U.C.C. Rep. Serv. (Callaghan) 777 (S.D. Iowa 1979).

In *Conoco, Inc. v. Norwest Bank Mason City, N.A.,*[114] the credit was subject to the Uniform Customs and did not contain any mention of revocability. The issuer argued that the credit was revocable under Article 1(c) of the 1974 Uniform Customs. The *Conoco* court noted that the credit recited that it was to "remain in force for a period of six (6) months" and also that it would "be available to Conoco."[115] The rule of Article 1(c) rendered credits revocable unless the credits clearly indicated that they were irrevocable. The *Conoco* court ruled that the language of the credit, taken together, clearly indicated the credit was irrevocable. "In a revocable letter of credit, such language would be meaningless."[116] The *Conoco* decision may leave the *Beathard* ruling little room for application.

The revocable credit usually arises out of inadvertence. The conflict between the Uniform Customs and Article 5 should be resolved in accordance with the cases[117] that favor irrevocability, if the credit is silent.

[b] Time for Honor

Article 16(c) of the Uniform Customs gives the issuing bank a "reasonable time in which to examine the documents" and to determine whether to honor the beneficiary's draft or demand for payment. This rule is different from the one the Code generally applies in Article 3 to documentary drafts.[118] It is also different from the three banking days rule in Section 5-112 that applies to drafts drawn on a bank issuer.[119] In short, there is a possible discrepancy between the provisions of the Code and those of the Uniform Customs. Unless the courts are inclined to hold that three days, and three days only, constitute a reasonable period

---

[114] 767 F.2d 470 (8th Cir. 1985).

[115] Id.

[116] Id. at 471.

[117] See cases cited supra note 109.

[118] Article 4 of the Code exempts documentary drafts drawn on a bank from the traditional midnight deadline rule. See U.C.C. § 4-301(1). Thus, the general Code rule of Section 3-506 applies, unless Section 5-112 defines an exception.

[119] The rule of Section 5-112 may be varied with the presenter's agreement. Id.; see also Summit Ins. Co. v. Central Nat'l Bank, 624 S.W.2d 222 (Tex. Civ. App. 1981) (credit gave issuer thirty days to honor drafts). For application of the three-day rule of Section 5-112(1), see Philadelphia Gear Corp. v. FDIC, 587 F. Supp. 294 (W.D. Okla.), aff'd in part, rev'd in part, 751 F.2d 1131 (10th Cir. 1984), rev'd, 476 U.S. 426 (1986).

for a bank under Article 16(c), the duties of banks will differ under the Code from their duties under the Uniform Customs.[120]

In *Marine Midland Grace Trust Co. v. Banco Del Pais, S.A.*,[121] one party introduced an affidavit in support of a motion for summary judgment, asserting that ten working days to two calendar weeks was a reasonable period for examining documents and for giving notice of their deficiency. The opposing party's affidavit asserted that a reasonable period was three days at the most. In *Peoples State Bank v. Gulf Oil Corp.*,[122] the court held that the issuer of a credit subject to the Uniform Customs had three days to decide whether to honor the beneficiary's drafts.[123]

In *Pro-Fab, Inc. v. Vipa, Inc.*,[124] the issuer failed to act within the three days provided by Section 5-112. Instead of holding that the issuer had dishonored the credit by that failure, as Section 5-112 provides, the *Pro-Fab* court held that the issuer was estopped from raising defects in the beneficiary's documents. That holding had the effect of making the issuer liable for the full amount of the credit. In other words, the court held that the issuer had honored the credit, and it erased the difference between the Code and the Uniform Customs.

---

[120] The working party that drafted the 1983 Uniform Customs considered answers to a questionnaire that solicited bankers' opinions on the "reasonable time" question. Those answers suggested periods ranging from thirty-six hours to thirty days. See B. Wheble, "UCP 1974/1983 Revisions Compared and Explained (Documentary Credits)," ICC Pub. No. 411, at 33 (1984).

[121] 261 F. Supp. 884 (S.D.N.Y. 1966).

[122] 446 N.E.2d 1358 (Ind. Ct. App. 1983).

[123] Cf. Auto Servicio San Ignacio, S.R.L. v. Compania Anonima Venezolana De Navegacion (Venezuelan Line), 765 F.2d 1306 (5th Cir. 1985) (because account party and issuer did not make any claim against paying bank within reasonable time, court refused to decide whether paying bank had more than three days to pay); see also Philadelphia Gear Corp. v. Central Bank, 717 F.2d 230 (5th Cir. 1983) (several days is reasonable); Occidental Fire & Casualty Co. v. Continental Ill. Nat'l Bank & Trust Co., 725 F. Supp. 383 (N.D. Ill. 1989) (holding that three days is not unreasonable time for issuer to take in examining documents and giving notice of defects); Bank of Cochin Ltd. v. Manufacturers Hanover Trust Co., 612 F. Supp. 1533 (S.D.N.Y. 1985), aff'd on other grounds, 808 F.2d 209 (2d Cir. 1986) (in New York, because three days are allowed by Code, three-day period is reasonable time allowed by Uniform Customs); First Nat'l Bank v. Carmouche, 504 So. 2d 1153 (La. Ct. App.), rev'd on other grounds, 515 So. 2d 785 (La. 1987) (payment within three banking days is timely); Price & Pierce Int'l, Inc. v. Cimex U.S.A., Inc., Letter of Credit Update 35 (July 1987) (N.Y. Sup. Ct. 1987), aff'd without op. sub nom. Price & Pierce Int'l, Inc. v. Hanil Bank Ltd., 136 A.D.2d 977, 523 N.Y.S.2d 333, appeal denied, 72 N.Y.2d 803, 528 N.E.2d 521, 532 N.Y.S.2d 369 (App. Div. 1988) (seven days is too long, and three days is reasonable time).

[124] 772 F.2d 847 (11th Cir. 1985).

[c] Estoppel Against the Issuer

Article 16(e) of the Uniform Customs provides that failure of the issuer to examine the documents within a reasonable time or to give prompt notice of defects in the documents raises an estoppel. The issuer that fails to meet the requirements of Article 16(c) and the prompt notice requirement in Article 16(d) may not raise documentary defects. That estoppel, of course, renders the issuer liable for the amount of the beneficiary's draft or demand.

There is considerable common law that fashions a similar rule, with an important difference. Under the cases, generally, courts estop a dilatory issuer only if the beneficiary can prove reliance and detriment.[125] Thus, the common-law rule differs from that of the Uniform Customs. The Uniform Customs appear to fashion a strict estoppel rule, while the common-law cases require the beneficiary to establish the traditional elements of common-law estoppel.

In *Datapoint Corp. v. M&I Bank*, the beneficiary presented its nonconforming draft on June 19. The credit, which was subject to the Uniform Customs, was to expire on June 20. The court held that because the issuer decided on June 19 that it would dishonor, the issuer lost any further time to consider the matter and was obliged under Article 16(d) of the Uniform Customs to give notice immediately by telephone to the beneficiary of the decision and the nonconformity.

The *Datapoint* decision imposes something of a penalty on issuers that make decisions promptly. Had the issuer delayed deciding until June 21—a delay that would be authorized under the Code's three-day rule and as it may have been authorized under the UCP reasonable time rule—the issuer would not have been estopped to assert the defect against the beneficiary in an action for wrongful dishonor.[126] In *Lennox Industries, Inc. v. Mid-American National Bank*,[127] the court held that expiration of the credit during the three-day period that the Code gives the issuer to examine documents excuses any requirement to give notice of defects, since there is no way that the beneficiary can cure.

Datapoint and *Lennox Industries* are in direct conflict. One would have to say that, of the two, *Datapoint* fashions the superior rule by advancing efficient practices and high standards in the letter of credit transaction. Under *Datapoint*, the issuer is under pressure to examine

---

[125] For discussion of those cases, see ¶ 6.06[1].

[126] Cf. Crist v. J. Henry Schroder Bank & Trust Co., 693 F. Supp. 1429 (S.D.N.Y. 1988) (holding that since beneficiary suffered no prejudice, delay of one day in giving notice of dishonor after deciding to dishonor was reasonable, even though issuer chose slow method of communication).

[127] 49 Ohio App. 3d 117, 550 N.E.2d 971 (1988).

documents promptly and to give notice of defects with equal promptness. Under the rule of the case, issuers cannot hope to show that there was no reliance or detriment to the beneficiary, and the rule relieves beneficiaries of the need to marshal evidence of such detriment and reliance.

To an extent, however, *Datapoint* may leave the issuer too little time to operate. It is a common and efficient practice for issuers that receive nonconforming documents to seek waivers of the nonconformities from the account party. It would be unfortunate to apply the *Datapoint* rule to an issuer that acted in good faith and took a reasonable time to seek such waivers, which benefit all parties.[128]

[d] Transfer

Both Article 5 and the Uniform Customs accept the distinction between the "transfer" of a credit, which is a conveyance of the right to draw drafts under the credit, and "assignment" of the credit proceeds, which is the transfer only of the right to payment, without altering the requirement that the assignor, not the assignee, comply with the terms of the credit.[129] Article 54(b) stipulates that a credit is transferable only if it expressly so provides and only if it uses the term "transferable." The word "assignable" does not connote "transfer" under the Uniform Customs. Article 55 suggests that the term "assign" refers to an assignment of the proceeds of the credit, that is, an assignment not of the right to draw but of the right to receive payment under the credit.

While Section 5-116 of the Code accepts the distinction between the right to draw and the right to proceeds, it does not accept the Uniform Customs' distinction between the terms "transferable" and "assignable" and their cognates. Under Section 5-116(1), a credit designated "assignable" permits the beneficiary to convey to a third party the right to draw under the credit. Such language is not sufficient to permit that conveyance under the Uniform Customs. The careful drafter uses the term "transfer" to designate a conveyance of the right to draw.[130]

---

[128] For further discussion of the *Datapoint* and similar cases on the waiver issue, see ¶ 6.06[1][b].

[129] See U.C.C. § 5-116; U.C.P. arts. 54, 55. The Uniform Customs reject, however, the term "assignable," which, under Article 54, "adds nothing to the meaning of the term 'transferable' and shall not be used." U.C.P. art. 54(b) (1983).

[130] This discussion of conflicts between the Code and the Uniform Customs in the transfer rules may be incomplete. Henry Harfield contends implicitly that there is more to the Uniform Customs distinction between "transfer" and "assignment" than the former's right to draw and the latter's right to proceeds. He argues that "transfer" involves the right to satisfy the conditions of the credit. See Harfield, "Identity Crises in Letter of Credit Law," 24 Ariz. L. Rev. 239 (1982). See generally ¶ 10.02.

After treating the matter in much more detail than the Code does, the Customs also stipulate in Article 54(e) that there may be only one transfer of a credit. The Code contains no such limitation. The customary method of transferring a credit may be such, however, that the rule of Article 54(e) has little application. Generally, issuers treat a transfer as a novation: They issue a new credit to the transferee. In that case, presumably, the beneficiary of the new credit would have one chance to transfer it, and his transferee of a second new credit would have one chance as well. Thus, the effect of Article 54(e) would be limited to those cases in which the issuer notes the transfer on the original credit or uses that original and an amendment to effect the transfer. Even in that case, the issuer may waive the limitation of Article 54(e) and permit a second transfer.

[e] Fraud Rule on Stopping Payment

There had developed at the time the Code was drafted a significant body of cases providing that an issuer might dishonor drafts (1) when the documents accompanying them appeared on their face to conform to the credit but in fact were forged or fraudulent, or (2) if there was other fraud in the credit transaction. Article 5 codifies the rule of these cases in Section 5-114(2). That section implicitly gives the issuer the right to dishonor in such instances. It also recognizes the right of an interested party to enjoin such honor if the standards of local practice for such an injunction are satisfied.

The cases that developed this fraud rule arose primarily in the United States.[131] The Uniform Customs do not refer to the American case law but do contain explicit rules that arguably support the view that fraud is no ground for dishonoring the beneficiary's draft. First, Article 15 charges bank issuers with the duty to examine all documents in order to determine that, "on their face," they appear to be in accordance with the terms and conditions of the credit.[132] Article 4 stipulates, furthermore, that all parties "deal in documents, and not in goods." Article 3 expresses the same principle. These references have led some to believe that the Uniform Customs eschew American case law that permits dis-

---

[131] For cases from other jurisdictions, see Kozolchyk, "Letters of Credit," in IX International Encyclopedia of Comparative Law ch. 5 (1979); Stoufflet, "Payment and Transfer in Documentary Letters of Credit: Interaction Between the French General Law of Obligations and the Uniform Customs and Practice," 24 Ariz. L. Rev. 267 (1982); Wheble, "'Problem Children'—Standby Letters of Credit and Simple First Demand Guaranties," 24 Ariz. L. Rev. 301 (1982).

[132] Cf. U.C.C. § 5-109(2) (similar rule).

honor on the ground of fraud when the documents conform "on their face."

Two New York appellate decisions have accepted that view.[133] A New York trial court,[134] and at least three federal cases[135] assert the contrary. The New York Court of Appeals also has endorsed that contrary view, but by way of dictum only.[136] In *Eljay, Jrs., Inc. v. Rahda Exports*,[137] the account party, claiming fraud, sought to enjoin the issuer from paying a credit that was expressly subject to the Uniform Customs. Holding that the Uniform Customs do not contain any provisions governing the fraud issue, the *Eljay* court ruled that Article 5 of the Code governed. *Eljay* appears to be a sensible rule,[138] holding in effect that the Uniform Customs' silence on the point is not an implicit rejection of the American cases.

Some New York lawyers regretted the advent of the Code,[139] and it might be fair to say that a hope of avoiding the fraud rule of Section 5-114 played a role in the movement to have New York adopt the nonuniform rule of Section 5-102(4).[140] It cannot be denied that the fraud rule creates problems for letters of credit and that it could cripple credits if courts were to carry it too far.[141] Yet the New York Court of Appeals's dictum probably spells defeat for those who would resort to the Uniform Customs as a safe harbor from the fraud rule.

---

[133] See Shanghai Commercial Bank, Ltd. v. Bank of Boston Int'l, 53 A.D.2d 830, 385 N.Y.S.2d 548 (1976); Capehart Corp. v. Shanghai Commercial Bank, Ltd., 49 A.D.2d 521, 369 N.Y.S.2d 751 (1975).

[134] See Banco Tornquist, S.A. v. American Bank & Trust Co., 71 Misc. 2d 874, 337 N.Y.S.2d 489 (Sup. Ct. 1972).

[135] Rockwell Int'l Sys., Inc. v. Citibank, N.A., 719 F.2d 583 (2d Cir. 1983); Cappaert Enters. v. Citizens & S. Int'l Bank, 486 F. Supp. 819 (E.D. La. 1980); Prutscher v. Fidelity Int'l Bank, 502 F. Supp. 535 (S.D.N.Y. 1980).

[136] See United Bank Ltd. v. Cambridge Sporting Goods Corp., 41 N.Y.2d 254, 360 N.E.2d 943, 392 N.Y.S.2d 265 (1976) (court's dictum indicating, however, that New York must apply pre-Code law on question).

[137] 99 A.D.2d 408, 470 N.Y.S.2d 12 (1984).

[138] See also B. Wheble, "UCP 1974/1983 Revisions Compared and Explained (Documentary Credits)," ICC Pub. No. 411, at 34 (1984) (suggesting that Uniform Customs do not attempt to resolve fraud question); cf. Wyle v. Bank Melli, 577 F. Supp. 1148 (N.D. Cal. 1983) (rejecting account party's argument that Uniform Customs prevent application of Code to fraud issue); Larson v. First Interstate Bank, 603 F. Supp. 467 (D. Ariz. 1983) (same).

[139] See generally Funk, supra note 76, at 117.

[140] See supra ¶ 4.05 for a discussion of that nonuniform provision.

[141] "[C]ourts are aware of the fact that indiscriminate issuance of injunctions upon the application of dissatisfied buyers would destroy the efficiency of the letter of credit device." See New York Study, supra note 43, at 1655–1656.

There is some support in Article 3 of the Uniform Customs for overturning a line of authority that has grown out of fraud situations. Some cases cabin the fraud exception to the duty of the issuer to pay against facially conforming documents by restricting the rule to cases in which the fraud occurs in the documents themselves. Other cases reject that reading of Section 5-114 by reasoning that references in the credit itself to the underlying transaction permit them to investigate that transaction for fraud.[142]

Article 3 of the Uniform Customs provides that the credit is separate from the underlying contract or contracts "even if any reference whatsoever to such contract(s) is included in the credit." Arguably, that language inhibits the reasoning of the line of cases that would resort to the language of the credit as an excuse to violate the independence principle by delving into the underlying transaction to look for fraud. That argument probably will not convince many courts, however. The urge to look into the underlying transaction is strong, probably too strong for the language of Article 3 to overcome it.

In short, there may not be any conflict between the Code and the Uniform Customs on the fraud question, because the courts are tending to read the Uniform Customs as consistent with a fraud defense. The rule of Article 3 may deprive account parties and issuers of only one excuse for delving into the underlying transaction.

[f] Warranties

In *Habib Bank Ltd. v. Convermat Corp.*,[143] the court refused to entertain an issuer's breach of warranty claim against a beneficiary that had received payment over defective documents. The *Habib Bank* court reasoned that Section 5-102(4) prevented application of warranty rules. The court also concluded that recovery under the *Habib Bank* facts would have conflicted with Article 16(e) of the Uniform Customs because that article estops an issuer from objecting to documents unless it notifies the beneficiary of the defects promptly after the beneficiary presents them.

The *Habib Bank* case illustrates well the argument that those legislatures which reject the Code in UCP cases are overreacting. First, breach of warranty, though it is an idea new to the Code, has its origins in pre-Code law of restitution.[144] At least one English commentator

---

[142] For a discussion of these cases, see ¶ 7.04[4][c].

[143] 145 Misc. 2d 980, 554 N.Y.S.2d 757 (App. Term. 1990) (per curiam).

[144] See Harfield, New York Practice Commentary, N.Y. U.C.C. § 5-111(1) (McKinney 1964).

would apply it as a matter of common law.[145] Thus, it does not follow that the presence of a warranty rule in Article 5 prevents New York courts from allowing the issuer to recover from an issuer that presents defective documents.

More convincing is the *Habib Bank* court's conclusion that the warranty provision should not apply when the issuer pays over defective documents, for the reason that it conflicts with the issuer's duties in the UCP. That argument also applies, however, to cases in which the credit is not subject to the UCP. Sections 5-109(2) and 5-114(2) require an issuer to review documents to see that they are facially conforming. That duty convinces some that the warranty provision should not apply if the defects are patent.[146]

[g] Resolving the Conflicts

In the years since the Code and the Uniform Customs were adopted, the differences have been minimal.[147] When the parties select the Uniform Customs, the dictates of contract freedom, a policy enshrined in the Code,[148] require courts to give the Uniform Customs precedence over the Code, absent some compelling policy reason to the contrary. The choice of the Uniform Customs may not avoid the Code's position on the fraud defense, however. The cases indicate that courts are not willing to read the Uniform Customs in a way that destroys the fraud rule.

A contrary Code policy also may be evident in the conflict over the presumption of irrevocability, which the Code cases favor and Article 7 of the Uniform Customs disfavors. Courts may not be willing to enforce the Uniform Customs rule unless the credit explicitly incorporates the Uniform Customs. Even then, they may view application of the rule against a nonmerchant beneficiary as unconscionable.

When the credit is silent and a party proves that the Uniform Customs describe trade usage, Sections 1-102 and 1-205 support application of the Uniform Customs unless they vary a Code provision that may not be varied. If the credit is silent and there is no proof that the Uniform Customs reflect trade usage, the prescriptive force of the Uniform Cus-

---

[145] See R. Goode, Commercial Law 679 (1982).

[146] See generally ¶¶ 6.07, 9.04.

[147] The key to resolving these "differences" may be to avoid viewing the Uniform Customs and the Code as competing sources of law. By accepting them as complementary sources, courts may be able to construe them together, as the Code suggests they should. See U.C.C. § 1-205(4). See also authorities cited supra note 94.

[148] See U.C.C. § 1-102(2)(b).

toms should not prevail over a conflicting public policy validated by the legislature in the Code.

¶ 4.07   ROLE OF CUSTOM AND USAGE

There are strong indications in letter of credit law that trade usage, course of dealing, and course of performance will supplement a credit's terms. It is the general view that credits are contracts subject to contract rules of construction, including the rules on custom.[149] In Section 5-102(3), the Code drafters acknowledged their attempt to frame in Article 5 only fundamental rules of credit law, while leaving some rules to case law and custom as they have developed and will develop in the future. The specific mention in the Section's comments of the "important" question of determining whether documents comply with the credit appears to be a reference to the Uniform Customs' carefully fashioned document rules.[150] The cases support these implications.

Board of Trade v. Swiss Credit Bank[151] expressed the view that the trial court must consider evidence in order to determine whether, under banking custom, the phrase "full set on board bills of lading" in a credit contemplated an air waybill. *AMF Head Sports Wear, Inc. v. Ray Scott's All-American Sports Club, Inc.*[152] implies that the Uniform Customs themselves are evidence of bank custom and usage.

The Code generally does not permit usage or course of dealing to alter express terms.[153] In *Titanium Metals Corp. of America v. Space Metals, Inc.*,[154] however, the court used course of dealing to read out of a credit what appears to be an express requirement that the beneficiary present a draft to the issuer. In this respect, the *Titanium Metals* case departs from the strict compliance principle of letter of credit law. The strict compliance principle, which both the Code[155] and the cases[156] acknowledge, recognizes that nonlawyer bank clerks must decide (often with little time to think about it or to seek counsel) whether drafts or documents submitted under a credit comply with that credit. Such con-

---

[149] See cases discussed infra ¶ 4.08.
[150] See U.C.C. § 5-102, comment 2 (2d sentence).
[151] 597 F.2d 146 (9th Cir. 1979).
[152] 448 F. Supp. 222 (D. Ariz. 1978).
[153] See U.C.C. § 1-205(4).
[154] 529 P.2d 431 (Utah 1974).
[155] See U.C.C. § 5-109(2).
[156] See authority cited in ¶ 6.04.

struction rules should be applied carefully, with these realities of letter of credit practice in mind.

The *Titanium Metals* court's position that course of dealing changes the explicit terms of a credit is not convincing, then, for two reasons. First, in all likelihood the document examiner that handles the first presentation by a beneficiary under a credit or series of credits will not be the same examiner that examines subsequent presentations. It is unfair to attribute knowledge of past course of dealing to an examiner and probably not something that a beneficiary should reasonably expect. In *Titanium Metals*, a document examiner had accepted earlier presentations without any draft, and the court bound the issuer to that course of dealing.

There is a second reason for rejecting the *Titanium Metals* holding. Section 1-205(3) acknowledges that course of dealing may give "particular meaning to and supplement or qualify terms of an agreement." It adds, however, that express terms govern course of dealing if the two are not consistent. There is some suggestion in the *Titanium Metals* opinion that the course of dealing differed from the express terms of the credit. While course of dealing may not overcome an express term in an agreement,[157] it may support waiver.[158] The *Titanium Metals* court, however, explicitly disclaimed any holding on the basis of waiver.[159]

In *East Bank v. Dovenmuhle, Inc.*,[160] the issuer attempted to introduce evidence that, under bank practices concerning standby credits, it was necessary for the beneficiary of the credit to show that it had disbursed a loan to the issuer's customer. The court rejected that attempt, holding that there was no such condition in the credit and that bank practices could not supply it. *East Bank* is more faithful to the role the Code fashions for industry custom than is the opinion in *Titanium Metals* to the role for course of dealing.

---

[157] See U.C.C. § 2-208(2).

[158] See U.C.C. § 2-208(3). For a case in which the court held that a beneficiary had waived rights under a credit by accepting nonconforming payments by the issuer, see W.J. Alan & Co. v. El Nasr Export & Import Co., [1972] 2 All E.R. 127 (C.A.).

[159] Cf. Texpor Traders, Inc. v. Trust Co. Bank, 720 F. Supp. 1100 (S.D.N.Y. 1989) (rejecting argument that acceptance of defective documents in connection with first shipment operated as waiver of defects in documents presented in connection with second shipment); Pro-Fab, Inc. v. Vipa, Inc., 772 F.2d 847 (11th Cir. 1985) (rejecting argument similar to that made in *Titanium Metals* on ground that, in prior instances, issuer notified beneficiary that account party had waived defects); Security State Bank v. Basin Petroleum Servs., Inc., 713 P.2d 1170 (Wyo. 1986) (rejecting argument similar to that of *Titanium Metals* on ground that beneficiary knew that earlier presentations were nonconforming). For further discussion of waiver in the document examination process, see ¶ 6.06[2].

[160] 196 Colo. 422, 589 P.2d 1361 (1978).

In *Bank of Canton, Ltd. v. Republic National Bank*,[161] the credit, which supported the purchase by the account party of electronic equipment from the beneficiary, called for numerous documents, including Federal Communications Commission (FCC) certificates. The bank dishonored, claiming that, under banking practice, the FCC certificates should have been issued to the beneficiary's seller and not to its supplier, the manufacturer. The court rejected the contention, noting that even if such were the practice of New York banks, a view the court doubted, a Hong Kong bank would not be bound by such local practice.[162]

In *Addison Bank v. Temple-Eastex, Inc.*,[163] the beneficiary attempted to introduce evidence concerning the custom of banks in connection with credits calling for sight drafts. The beneficiary apparently argued that the term "sight draft" was ambiguous and offered evidence that the banking industry accepted nonnegotiable demands for payment as sight drafts. That evidence, the beneficiary concluded, rendered its failure to submit a negotiable draft unimportant. The *Addison Bank* court ruled that it was not proper for the trial court to consider that evidence, but the Texas Supreme Court reversed the *Addison Bank* decision,[164] holding that such evidence was sufficient to excuse the beneficiary's failure to present a negotiable draft.[165] Arguably, the Texas Supreme Court misread the Code provisions as the *Titanium Metals* court misread them.

Similarly, the assertion of *Mead Corp. v. Farmers & Citizens Bank*,[166] a pre-Code case, that courts should construe credits with a view toward the "usages of the particular trade or business contemplated"[167] is too broad. In Section 5-109, the Code charges banks with a duty of good faith in observing "any general banking usage." However, unless the bank agrees otherwise, the section absolves the bank from liability or responsibility growing out of "knowledge or lack of knowledge of any usage of any particular trade." The section charges the bank with knowl-

---

[161] 509 F. Supp. 1310 (S.D.N.Y.), aff'd, 636 F.2d 30 (2d Cir. 1980).

[162] When the issuer appealed from summary judgment in favor of the Hong Kong Bank, the Court of Appeals for the Second Circuit termed the appeal "completely frivolous" and awarded double costs and damages to the appellee. See Bank of Canton, Ltd. v. Republic Nat'l Bank, 636 F.2d 30, 31 (2d Cir. 1980).

[163] 665 S.W.2d 550 (Tex. Ct. App.), rev'd, 672 S.W.2d 793 (Tex. 1984).

[164] Temple-Eastex, Inc. v. Addison Bank, 672 S.W.2d 793 (Tex. 1984).

[165] The Texas Supreme Court's ruling also rested on the notion that an ambiguous term in the credit should be construed most strictly against the drafter, which, in this case, was the issuing bank. See infra ¶ 4.08[3].

[166] 14 Ohio Misc. 163, 232 N.E.2d 431 (C.P. 1967).

[167] Id. at 165, 232 N.E.2d at 433.

edge of bank customs and usage, but not with those growing out of other industries.

This distinction correctly assumes that those bank employees who examine documents and decide whether to honor or dishonor a draft submitted under a credit must know banking practice. It also assumes that they cannot possibly know the usage and customs of those thousands of trades and industries that employ letters of credit.

[1] The *Dixon* Case

In a well-known and controversial opinion, *Dixon, Irmaos & CIA v. Chase National Bank*,[168] the Court of Appeals for the Second Circuit held that a bank must observe bank custom, even though the custom effects a change in the apparent meaning of the credit. In *Dixon*, the credit called for a "[f]ull set bills of lading,"[169] even though it was customary for banks to accept less than a full set, provided that the beneficiary obtained a sufficient guaranty indemnifying the issuer against losses resulting from the missing bill or bills.

The practice of issuing negotiable bills in sets responds to the vagaries of international mail and travel. If a carrier issues only one copy of a negotiable bill, for instance, and the negotiable bill becomes lost or delayed in the mail, there is no bill available when the goods arrive. In such a case, someone has to indemnify the carrier before it delivers the goods. Generally, carriers face liability if they deliver without surrender of the negotiable bill.[170] International traders found it easier to indemnify banks than to indemnify carriers and adopted the practice of having the carrier issue the bill in a set of multiple copies, with the provision that the carrier would honor any one of the copies, whichever was presented first. The seller of goods to be carried by oceangoing vessel sometimes sends one copy of the bill in the ship's safe for delivery to the buyer at the time the goods arrive. The seller mails the other copies to the buyer, to the issuer, or to an agent.

There is a risk in this arrangement that one of the copies will fall into the hands of an unscrupulous party who will use it to obtain the goods from the carrier. Buyers know, however, that the chances of misuse are remote. They assume that if a bill does not arrive by mail, it is probably lost. Similarly, bank issuers know that a missing bill usually is

---

[168] 144 F.2d 759 (2d Cir.), cert. denied, 324 U.S. 850 (1944).

[169] Id. at 760.

[170] See Federal Bills of Lading Act, 49 U.S.C. app. §§ 89–92 (Supp. V 1987); U.C.C. § 7-403.

not a matter of great concern. Issuers have routinely protected themselves by taking the indemnity of a responsible bank against any loss.[171] The indemnity is part and parcel of the arrangement for issuing bills in a set. If banks are not willing to accept the indemnity, the argument goes,[172] the practice is futile.

In *Dixon*, the seller shipped cotton to a Belgian buyer and presented his documents and time drafts to a New York bank, which had issued the credit at the buyer's bequest. That presentation occurred on May 15, 1940, a day when German forces were overrunning Belgium. The bank knew that if it accepted the drafts, it would have little chance of obtaining reimbursement from its customer. Accordingly, the bank took the position that because the seller had not submitted a full set of bills, the presentment did not comply with the credit. The bank professed not to be satisfied with the indemnity the seller offered.

The *Dixon* court obviously was not impressed with the issuer's self-concern. The court saw the dishonor as an effort by the bank to use an insubstantial defect in the documents to avoid the very kind of situation that the seller was attempting to protect itself against when it insisted that the buyer procure the credit in the first place. The court ruled that the bank was bound by banking custom and had to accept the indemnity. The *Dixon* court was fully aware that evidence of custom should not contradict the plain meaning of a credit. However, it contended, somewhat disingenuously, that "full set of bills of lading" was a "technical phrase"[173] and that the meaning of the phrase included a partial set supplemented by an indemnity. Significantly, the evidence in the *Dixon* case did not show that beneficiaries generally took the language "full set" to mean "partial set." It did show that when a seller presented a partial set, banks excused the less than full performance so long as the seller provided indemnity.

It is not true that this banking custom is indispensable to the efficiency of issuing bills in sets. So long as the seller insists that the credit recite that indemnities are acceptable in lieu of a full set of bills, the practice can continue without any banking custom.

The serious trouble with the *Dixon* case is that it expects bankers, in the fast-paced commerce of bank credits, to make judgments that are more properly the kind of judgments courts make after full briefing and oral argument. Banks frequently accept nonconforming documents and

---

[171] For an example of an indemnity agreement given to a carrier, see App. C, Doc. 19.

[172] See generally Honnold, "Letters of Credit, Custom, Missing Documents and the Dixon case. A Reply to Backus and Harfield," 53 Colum. L. Rev. 504 (1953).

[173] 144 F.2d 759, 762 (2d Cir.), cert. denied, 324 U.S. 850 (1944).

honor the drafts that such documents accompany. It is a common and perhaps universal banking practice, upon receipt of such documents, for the issuer to call its customer and ask whether the customer will waive the nonconformity. So long as the bank receives its customer's authorization, the bank will honor the drafts. In the vast majority of cases, customers will give that authorization; but when something goes awry, such as the invasion of Belgium, they do not. Such custom, and even such course of dealing or performance, should not alter the express language of the credit. Rather than encouraging beneficiaries to insist that the credit contain terms that the beneficiary can satisfy, the *Dixon* case excuses noncompliance and encourages a beneficiary to rely on facts extrinsic to the credit.

In *Courtaulds North America, Inc. v. North Carolina National Bank*,[174] the issuer had received a number of drafts with nonconforming invoices, but it always sought and received its customer's approval of payment, notwithstanding the nonconformity. It also never advised the beneficiary of the practice. The trial court found that it was not customary for banks to notify beneficiaries of such waiver by their customers. When the customer filed in bankruptcy, there was no one to waive the nonconformity; and the bank rejected a noncomplying invoice. The Court of Appeals for the Fourth Circuit refused to estop the bank, whose duties were "graven in the credit,"[175] and who therefore might face liability to the customer's trustee by departing from the credit's terms.[176]

The *Dixon* case fails to reckon the cost of its effect. Sellers should know that they cannot rely on payment unless they comply punctiliously with all of the credit's terms. *Dixon* sends sellers a different signal. The *Courtaulds* view, by insisting on strict compliance, forces the parties to draft the credit carefully and avoids the kind of ad hoc rule that *Dixon* fosters.

---

[174] 528 F.2d 802 (4th Cir. 1975).

[175] Id. at 806.

[176] There are grounds to distinguish the *Dixon* rule where, under Section 2-323(2), a customer may not complain if the bank accepts less than a full set of bills, while under *Courtaulds* a customer may well complain of a bank's accepting nonconforming invoices. For a case that takes a view different from *Courtaulds*, see Schweibish v. Pontchartrain State Bank, 389 So. 2d 731 (La. Ct. App. 1980). There the court estopped an issuer from insisting on strict compliance when the issuer had not required strict compliance in two or three prior transactions. For cases consistent with *Courtaulds*, see Dulien Steel Prods., Inc. v. Bankers Trust Co., 298 F.2d 836 (2d Cir. 1962); Far E. Textile, Ltd. v. City Nat'l Bank & Trust Co., 430 F. Supp. 193 (S.D. Ohio 1977). For a general discussion of the estoppel and waiver rules, see ¶ 6.06.

[2] Status of the *Dixon* Rule Under the Code

In the debate that followed the *Dixon* case,[177] the question arose whether adoption of the Code diminished the case's value as precedent. Some argued that the practice of accepting indemnities in lieu of a full set of bills of lading was no longer common among New York banks.[178] The question remains, however, whether the rule of *Dixon*, which has implications far broader than those relating to indemnities, survives adoption of the Code.

Article 5 does not address the question,[179] but Section 2-323(2) stipulates that a *buyer* who contracts for a full set of bills must accept a partial set accompanied by an indemnity. Section 2-323(2) prevents the *buyer* from upsetting the banking practice, if indeed the practice of accepting indemnities is still in effect.[180] The buyer cannot complain when his bank accepts the partial set with an appropriate indemnity. The section does not address the question of the *bank's* duty to accept the partial set; and the comment to the section observes that "neither this subsection nor Article 5 decides whether a bank which has issued a letter of credit is similarly bound. The issuing bank's obligation under a letter of credit is independent and depends on its own terms."[181]

There is perhaps a hint in the comment's language that courts should look to the credit's "own terms" rather than to banking practices. Those who support the *Dixon* rule would respond that the court looked to banking practices in *Dixon* in order to decipher the meaning of the credit's "own terms."

In short, the adoption of the Code does not affect the rule of the *Dixon* case. *Dixon*, however, may well not withstand the criticism that it (1) expects too much of bankers in requiring them to decide whether banking custom gives "new" meaning to language in a credit and (2) expects too little of beneficiaries by excusing them from strict compliance

---

[177] See Backus & Harfield, "Custom and Letters of Credit: The Dixon, Irmaos Case," 52 Colum. L. Rev. 589 (1952); Honnold, "Footnote to the Controversy Over the Dixon Case, Custom and Letters of Credit: The Position of the Uniform Commercial Code," 53 Colum. L. Rev. 973 (1953); Honnold, supra note 172; Note, "Letters of Credit Under the Proposed Uniform Commercial Code: An Opportunity Missed," 62 Yale L.J. 227 (1953).

[178] See Backus & Harfield, supra note 177.

[179] See U.C.C. § 5-113, comment 4.

[180] It appears that American banks continue to issue and accept such indemnities. The law clearly sanctions their use. See Comptroller of the Currency, Interpretive Letter No. 218, [1981–1982 Transfer Binder] Fed. Banking L. Rep. (CCH) ¶ 85,299 (Sept. 16, 1981); U.C.C. § 5-113.

[181] U.C.C. § 2-323, comment 2 (last two sentences).

with the credit and from insisting that credits contain terms with which they can comply.

¶ 4.08 RULES OF CONSTRUCTION

Because most courts think of credits as contracts, they often apply contract rules to them.[182] If, for example, there appears to be a mutual or unilateral mistake in a credit, courts are inclined to look to the contract law of mistake.[183] Similarly, courts use contract rules of construction in connection with credits, although most courts recognize that if a credit is a contract, it is not, as one court put it, "an ordinary contract."[184] If courts apply contract rules of construction, they should do so only with proper regard for the unique features of credits. Not all courts have done so.

Sometimes the credit drafter invites courts to make the mistake of plunging into contract law without regard for the credit's unique nature. In *Fiat Motors of North America, Inc. v. Mellon Bank, N.A.*,[185] the credit document was replete with contract terminology. The parties had designated the document as a "wholesale financing commitment" and included in it a recitation that the bank issuer's undertaking was "in consideration of" the beneficiary's performance of the underlying contract. Although the court properly held that the document was a letter of cred-

---

[182] Texas courts are particularly fond of saying that normal contract rules of construction apply to letters of credit. See, e.g., Kerr Constr. Co. v. Plains Nat'l Bank, 753 S.W.2d 181 (Tex. Ct. App. 1987); Universal Sav. Ass'n v. Killeen Sav. & Loan Ass'n, 757 S.W.2d 72 (Tex. Ct. App. 1988); Willow Bend Nat'l Bank v. Commonwealth Mortgage Corp., 722 S.W.2d 12 (Tex. Ct. App. 1986) (construing credit in fashion to avoid condition); Temple-Eastex, Inc. v. Addison Bank, 672 S.W.2d 793 (Tex. 1984) (favoring reading that renders performance of credit possible); INA v. Cypress Bank, 663 S.W.2d 122 (Tex. Ct. App. 1983) (holding that credit should be construed according to its plain meaning).

[183] See Tradex Petroleum Am., Inc. v. Coral Petroleum, Inc. (In re Coral Petroleum, Inc.), 878 F.2d 830 (5th Cir. 1989); Fidelity Bank v. Lutheran Mut. Life Ins. Co., 465 F.2d 211 (10th Cir. 1972); Asociacion De Azucareos De Guatemala v. United States Nat'l Bank, 423 F.2d 638 (9th Cir. 1970); Auto-Owners Ins. Co. v. South Side Trust & Sav. Bank, 176 Ill. App. 3d 303, 531 N.E.2d 146 (1988); Abilene Nat'l Bank v. Fina Supply, Inc., 706 S.W.2d 737 (Tex. Ct. App. 1986), aff'd, 726 S.W.2d 537 (Tex. 1987); cf. Barclay Knitwear Co. v. King'swear Enters., Ltd., 141 A.D.2d 241, 533 N.Y.S.2d 724 (1988), appeal denied, 74 N.Y.2d 605, 541 N.E.2d 427, 543 N.Y.S.2d 398 (1989) (construing letter of credit according to its plain meaning).

[184] East Girard Sav. Ass'n v. Citizens Nat'l Bank & Trust Co., 593 F.2d 598, 603 (5th Cir. 1979).

[185] 827 F.2d 924 (3d Cir. 1987).

it, it construed the document in a fashion that permitted the beneficiary to obtain payment without complying strictly with the terms of the credit. The court either was ignorant of the strict compliance rule or failed to appreciate the significance of the deviations that it ruled insignificant. The flavor of the *Fiat Motors* opinion and the court's language suggest that the court did not recognize the difference between letters of credit and contracts. Had it accepted that distinction, the court may have ruled differently.

The general rule for performance by the beneficiary of a credit is the rule recited in *Corporacion De Mercadeo Agricola v. Mellon Bank International*: "[I]t is black letter law that the terms and conditions of a letter of credit must be strictly adhered to."[186] This is the strict compliance rule. It prevents a beneficiary from claiming, as he might under some contract principles, that he is entitled to payment in the event that he substantially complies.[187]

The strict compliance rule cuts against the issuer as well as against the beneficiary. It forbids the issuer from adding conditions to the credit after it is established. In *Maurice O'Meara Co. v. National Park Bank*,[188] the issuer complained that although the documents complied with the credit, the bank suspected that the goods did not conform to the underlying contract. The issuer wanted to test the goods. The court denied the issuer that right in advance of payment, ruling that to hold otherwise would read into the credit a condition of payment that was not there. Similarly, in *Laudisi v. American Exchange National Bank*,[189] the court held that the issuer of a credit that did not require the bill of lading to describe the goods in any specific detail could not complain when the goods were, in fact, inferior but the description, being general, satisfied the credit.

Although the opinion makes no mention of it, the *Laudisi* case probably took into account the fact that, in the banking industry, issuers accepted documents attached to the draft, so long as at least one of them — in *Laudisi*, the invoice — described the goods as the credit described them.[190] The Uniform Customs have modified that practice.

[186] 608 F.2d 43, 47 (2d Cir. 1979).

[187] See, e.g., G. Gilmore, The Death of Contract 73, 74 (1974); 3 S. Williston & G. Thompson, A Treatise on the Law of Contracts § 842 (rev. ed. 1936); Note, "Letters of Credit: A Solution to the Problem of Documentary Compliance," 50 Fordham L. Rev. 848, 863 (1982).

[188] 239 N.Y. 386, 146 N.E. 636 (1925).

[189] 239 N.Y. 234, 146 N.E. 347 (1924).

[190] See Maurice O'Meara Co. v. National Park Bank, 239 N.Y. 386, 146 N.E. 636 (1925).

They require only that the invoice so describe the goods. The accompanying documents are satisfactory so long as they do not conflict with that description and, in many instances, so long as they describe the goods sufficiently to relate the document to the credit.[191] The *Laudisi* case, although professing to adhere to a rule of strict compliance with the credit, evidences the disposition of some courts to look beyond the credit (in this case, to banking custom) in order to determine whether there is such compliance.

The *Mellon Bank*, *Laudisi*, and *O'Meara* cases acknowledge that an account party who desires more description or additional conditions must ask for them. The cases suggest that the strict compliance rule may be used against any party (issuer, account party, or beneficiary) who wishes to alter the credit terms after establishment by adding or, by implication, by subtracting terms.[192]

[1] Questions of Intent

Some courts have expressed a willingness to construe credits by looking to the intent of the parties and the circumstances surrounding the issuance of the credit. It certainly is not problematic for a court to look at the terms of the credit itself in order to determine the intent of the parties. Reference to surrounding circumstances may prove troublesome, however.

In *Mead Corp. v. Farmers & Citizens Bank*,[193] the court considered a document that appeared to comply with the Article 5 definition of a "credit." The court declined to treat it as such because, it reasoned, the parties did not intend it to be a credit. Then, being unconstrained by letter of credit law, the court held that it was necessary for the beneficiary of the letter to present a bill of lading, even though the letter did not call for one—a result that clearly conflicts with the strict compliance rule. Under that rule, an issuer that wants to condition its credit promise on

---

[191] See U.C.P. arts. 15, 23 (1983). Article 23 of the Uniform Customs provides that "other documents" (i.e., other than transport documents, insurance documents, and commercial invoices) are satisfactory if their "data content" permits the issuer to "relate" the documents to the invoice or the credit. The Uniform Customs indicate, then, that "other" documents not only must not conflict but also must relate to the invoice or, in the absence of an invoice, to the credit. The "no-conflict" rule of Article 15 applies to all documents. See generally ¶ 6.04[5][a].

[192] Cf. Auto-Owners Ins. Co. v. South Side Trust & Sav. Bank, 176 Ill. App. 3d 303, 531 N.E.2d 146 (1988) (holding that issuer could not complain that beneficiary did not present bond, when credit did not call for bond). For further cases requiring strict compliance with a credit's terms, see ¶ 6.04.

[193] 14 Ohio Misc. 163, 232 N.E.2d 431 (C.P. 1967).

the presentation of a bill of lading must state that condition in the credit. *East Girard Savings Association v. Citizens National Bank & Trust Co.*[194] takes a different view of intent, holding that the intent of the party drafting a letter of credit is irrelevant and that the credit should be construed against such a party.

In *Venizelos, S.A. v. Chase Manhattan Bank, N.A.*,[195] a leading case, the court looked to the terms of a charter party (the underlying contract) in order to determine whether the beneficiary had complied with the credit's prohibition against partial shipments. Because the charter party contemplated the use of a liberty ship, whose capacity approximated the amount of scrap steel covered by the beneficiary's drafts and accompanying documents, the court held that the beneficiary had not violated the credit's ban on partial shipments.[196]

Venizelos is a departure from the independence principle, which generally dominates credit law. It may be significant that in *Venizelos*, the issue related to partial shipments. Credits often speak to that issue and do so without requiring any documents. Thus, a credit may recite that partial shipments are prohibited, but it will not expressly refer to a document to prove that the shipment is not partial.[197] Document examiners glean the answer to the partial shipment question by reviewing the documents together. If, for example, the credit calls for an invoice covering twenty cases of Châteauneuf-du-Pape, and the beneficiary presents a draft and invoice covering only ten cases, the examiner will dishonor the presentation if the credit forbids partial shipments.

In *Venizelos*, the documents indicated that the shipment might be partial, since the credit covered twice as many tons of scrap as the invoice and the bill of lading indicated were shipped. The discrepancy became quite benign, however, in light of the charter party and the fact that shipment was on a vessel whose capacity was approximately that indicated in the documents, all of which suggested that the credit was to cover two shipments. Thus, one shipment would entail a draft for about one half of the total volume of scrap covered by the credit.

Unfortunately, the *Venizelos* court failed to observe that the charter party and the information on the vessel's capacity were not, in all proba-

---

[194] 593 F.2d 598 (5th Cir. 1979).

[195] 425 F.2d 461 (2d Cir. 1970).

[196] Cf. Pubali Bank v. City Nat'l Bank, 676 F.2d 1326 (9th Cir. 1982) (court may look to charters in order to determine meaning of credit).

[197] To this extent, then, the credit varies a customary requirement that payment under the credit should be conditioned only on documentary matters, not on factual determinations. See generally ¶ 2.05[2]. The fact, however, that in most cases the examiner can determine from the documents whether the shipment is partial renders the partial shipment term documentary.

bility, before the document examiner and therefore normally could not justify a holding that the issuer had dishonored wrongfully.[198]

In *Wyle v. Bank Melli*,[199] the credit secured a simple-demand guaranty letter and was payable against the guaranty issuer's assertion that the guaranty had been called on. The account party's trustee in bankruptcy argued that the draw on the guaranty was fraudulent and that the draw on the credit therefore was fraudulent. The *Wyle* court analyzed the relationship between the credit and the guaranty to determine the intent of the commercial parties regarding the scope of the account party's liability. After concluding that payment under the circumstances would be in conflict with that intent, the court held the draw on the credit to be fraudulent.[200]

In *Ford Motor Co. v. St. James Bank & Trust Co.*,[201] the court considered parol evidence of the parties' intent in determining that the document under consideration was not a letter of credit. In *American National Bank & Trust Co. v. Hamilton Industries International, Inc.*,[202] the court considered the intent of the parties and the judicial admission of one of them in deciding that the advising bank, not the named beneficiary, was the actual beneficiary of the credit. In *Homestate Savings Association v. Westwind Exploration, Inc.*,[203] the court construed the documentary requirements of a credit according to the "objective intent of the parties . . . ascertained from the terms of the letter of credit itself."[204]

In *Bank of Montreal v. Federal National Bank & Trust Co.*,[205] a drafting error caused the credit to call for certification referring to loans to "Blow Out *Products*, Ltd." The loan was in fact made to "Blow Out

---

[198] The dishonor in *Venizelos* occurred not on the first draw by the beneficiary for the shipment, however, but on a supplemental draw for shipping charges. It was not until that point that the issuer raised the partial shipment objection, and the court held that at that point the objection was too late. That part of the *Venizelos* holding does not violate the independence principle.

[199] 577 F. Supp. 1148 (N.D. Cal. 1983).

[200] For criticism of cases that delve into the underlying transaction to determine whether there is fraud in the credit transaction, see ¶¶ 7.04[4][b], 7.04[4][c].

[201] 731 F.2d 284 (5th Cir. 1984).

[202] 583 F. Supp. 164 (N.D. Ill. 1984), rev'd on other grounds sub nom. Banque Paribas v. Hamilton Indus. Int'l, Inc., 767 F.2d 380 (7th Cir. 1985).

[203] 684 S.W.2d 788 (Tex. Ct. App.), aff'd, 696 S.W.2d 378 (Tex. 1985).

[204] Id. at 790; cf. International Multifoods Corp. v. Mardian, 379 N.W.2d 840 (S.D. 1985) (holding that in part because parties intended obligation to be guaranty, court would treat it as such and not as letter of credit, as beneficiary contended it should be treated).

[205] 622 F. Supp. 6 (W.D. Okla. 1984).

Preventions, Ltd." When the beneficiary drew, it supplied certificates referring to the latter; and the issuer dishonored. Concluding that the credit was ambiguous, the court invoked rules of construction to the end that ambiguous credits must be construed to make sense and to conform to the intent of the parties and that they must be construed against the issuer. The court then determined that the certificates were conforming.

These cases are not faithful to the strict compliance rule, and they create problems for the document examiner. The credit in the *Bank of Montreal* case, for example, was not ambiguous. It called quite clearly for certificates referring to "Blow Out Products, Ltd." There were two errors in the case: the drafting error and the failure of the beneficiary to note the error as soon as the credit was established. The court did not show that the issuer was to blame for the drafting error, nor did it show why liability should have turned on that error, rather than on the beneficiary's error. Unfortunately, the *Bank of Montreal* case burdens the document examination process with extrinsic fact determinations.

Not all cases are unmindful of the process, however. In *Tradex Petroleum American, Inc. v. Coral Petroleum, Inc. (In re Coral Petroleum, Inc.)*,[206] the court refused to reform the credit. The credit in *Tradex* called for inconsistent documents. When the beneficiary could not supply them, it sued for reformation. The *Tradex* court ruled, however, that it was incumbent on the beneficiary to examine the credit carefully to determine that it could comply with its terms. Negligence in that examination should impose costs on the beneficiary, not on the issuer, the court reasoned. The *Tradex* court made much of the fact that the terms involved were trade terms whose inconsistency would be much more apparent to the beneficiary, an oil trader, than to the issuer, a bank. The court did not restrict its rationale to the trade term facts, however.[207]

In *Bebco Distributors, Inc. v. Farmers & Merchants Bank*,[208] the credit recited that the issuer would honor checks drawn by the account party. When the beneficiary sought to recover under the credit and complained that the account party would not draw the checks, the court held that parol evidence was not admissible to vary the terms of a clear credit.

In *Abilene National Bank v. Fina Supply, Inc.*,[209] the beneficiary asked the court to reform the letter of credit so that it would cover shipments of products that were not covered by the express terms of the

---

[206] 878 F.2d 830 (5th Cir. 1989).

[207] For discussion of authority dealing with inconsistent provisions in a credit relating to its expiry, see ¶ 5.03[3][a].

[208] 485 So. 2d 330 (Ala. 1986).

[209] 706 S.W.2d 737 (Tex. Ct. App. 1986), aff'd, 726 S.W.2d 537 (Tex. 1987).

credit. The *Abilene National Bank* court refused to reform the credit, holding that reformation is available only where there is evidence of mutual mistake or of unilateral mistake and fraud, evidence that the court felt was lacking. The Supreme Court of Texas affirmed.[210]

Similarly, in *Artoc Bank & Trust, Ltd. v. Sun Marine Terminals, Inc.,*[211] the court expressed a willingness to consider the intent of the parties when they caused the credit to issue but refused to reform the credit in any way to protect the beneficiary. In *Artoc Bank*, the parties intended the credit to cover sums due under a terminaling service agreement, including sums due in the event the beneficiary accelerated obligations by virtue of the obligor's failure to secure an extension of the credit. When the credit was about to expire, the beneficiary drew and asserted, as the poorly drafted credit required, that the demand for payment was for services rendered as reflected in an unpaid invoice. The court held that the demand for payment was not in compliance with the terms of the credit, constituted a breach of the Code warranty,[212] and rendered the beneficiary liable to the account party for the amount of the payment.

In *Willow Bend National Bank v. Commonwealth Mortgage Corp.,*[213] the credit required the beneficiary to obtain on the reverse side of the credit an endorsement of the negotiating bank. The court concluded that the parties had intended to require the endorsement only in the event the beneficiary negotiated drafts drawn under the credit. Since the beneficiary presented its draft directly at the counters of the issuer, the court held that the endorsement was not necessary. This use of intent is far less intrusive than that of some cases. Bank document examiners are expected to know the purpose of an endorsement, which is a familiar part of banking practice.

The cases, then, do not lend themselves to easy reconciliation. It may be that intent plays a role only when the drafter of the credit is attempting to enforce what appears to be an ambiguous term. If so, these cases follow the general rule that holds that courts should construe credits strictly but should also construe them against the drafter or issuer.[214] There are a number of reported cases in which the credit is drafted in a way that incorporates the underlying contract into the credit. In most of

---

[210] Fina Supply, Inc. v. Abilene Nat'l Bank, 726 S.W.2d 537 (Tex. 1987). For discussion of the Texas Supreme Court's holding, see ¶ 5.02[1].

[211] 760 S.W.2d 311 (Tex. Ct. App. 1988).

[212] U.C.C. § 5-111(1).

[213] 722 S.W.2d 12 (Tex. Ct. App. 1986).

[214] See discussion infra ¶ 4.08[3].

these cases, the courts hold against the issuer.[215] Intent rules may be similar to scope rules[216] and construction rules[217] in that they may simply provide the courts with a rationale for the result they want to reach.

[2] Substantial Compliance Rule

There are a number of cases that reflect disfavor with the strict compliance rule. In *Banco Espanol de Credito v. State Street Bank & Trust Co.*,[218] the trial court held that a certificate of inspection called for by a letter of credit should comply strictly with the language of the credit. Unfortunately, the credit was ambiguous; but the court was unwilling to speculate on what the credit meant and whether the certificate supplied by the beneficiary met the credit's requirements. By implication, the trial court excused the issuer from making the same judgments. If the certificate did not comply strictly, the issuer could dishonor. The Court of Appeals for the First Circuit reversed holding that it would construe the credit "as strongly against the issuer as a reasonable reading will justify,"[219] and concluded that there must be "some leaven in the loaf of strict construction."[220] In reviewing the evidence, the court appeared to be moved by what it saw as the bad faith of the customer. He was trying to renege on his contract with the beneficiary, and the bank was attempting to shield him. The court held the certificate to be sufficient.

The *Banco Espanol* case has given rise to a troublesome view of the strict compliance rule. In *Flagship Cruises, Ltd. v. New England Merchants National Bank*,[221] the same circuit court noted with approval that the district court had read *Banco Espanol* as counseling "some relaxation in a strictissimi juris comparison of letters of credit requirements and documents submitted in compliance therewith."[222] Similarly, an

---

[215] See ¶ 7.04[4][c].

[216] See, e.g., Wichita Eagle & Beacon Publishing Co. v. Pacific Nat'l Bank, 493 F.2d 1285 (9th Cir. 1974).

[217] See, e.g., East Girard Sav. Ass'n v. Citizens Nat'l Bank & Trust Co., 593 F.2d 598 (5th Cir. 1979).

[218] 266 F. Supp. 106 (D. Mass.), rev'd, 385 F.2d 230 (1st Cir. 1967), cert. denied, 390 U.S. 1013 (1968).

[219] Banco Espanol de Credito v. State St. Bank & Trust Co., 385 F.2d 230, 237 (1st Cir. 1967), cert. denied, 390 U.S. 1013 (1968), quoting Fair Pavilions, Inc. v. First Nat'l City Bank, 24 A.D.2d 109, 112, 264, N.Y.S.2d 255, 256 (1965), rev'd, 19 N.Y.2d 512, 227 N.E.2d 839, 281 N.Y.S.2d 23 (1967).

[220] 385 F.2d at 234.

[221] 569 F.2d 699 (1st Cir. 1978).

[222] Id. at 702.

earlier case noted that it would not accept "mere technical defenses when in essence the contractual standing between the parties has been met."[223] A 1981 case went further. In colorful language that may betray the court's lack of appreciation for the rationale of the strict compliance rule, it viewed the strict compliance defenses as "hypertechnical"[224] and "pretextual"[225] and warned that the court would not permit the issuer "to palter with justice by its less than specious argument."[226]

This language has the ring of fairness to it, but it supports a rule more easily followed in judicial chambers than in bank letter of credit departments. The *Banco Espanol* rule, for example, deprives the document examiner of a simple rule: If the inspection certificate varies the credit, the certificate does not comply. The *Banco Espanol* case requires the banker to determine whether the inspection certificate satisfies the spirit, rather than the letter, of the credit. That inquiry often turns on an understanding of the industry or of the goods involved, and the *Banco Espanol* court expects too much of banks when it invokes such a requirement.[227]

[3] Construction Against Issuer or Drafter

The *Banco Espanol* view that courts should construe the credit "as strongly against the issuer as a reasonable reading will justify"[228] merits analysis. Generally, courts construe ambiguous contracts against the drafter, but the issuer of a credit may not draft all of the credit's terms. The customer and the beneficiary usually negotiate some of the credit's terms.

---

[223] Bank of Am. Nat'l Trust & Sav. Ass'n v. Liberty Nat'l Bank & Trust Co., 116 F. Supp. 233, 237 (W.D. Okla. 1953), aff'd, 218 F.2d 831 (10th Cir. 1955) (footnote omitted).

[224] Crocker Commercial Servs., Inc. v. Countryside Bank, 538 F. Supp. 1360, 1362 (N.D. Ill. 1981).

[225] Id.

[226] Id.

[227] The disposition of the *Banco Espanol* court to relate the credit transaction either directly to the underlying transaction or to facts extrinsic to the credit transaction, is evident in other cases. See, e.g., Exotic Traders Far E. Buying Office v. Exotic Trading U.S.A., Inc., 717 F. Supp. 14 (D. Mass. 1989); Instituto Nacional De Comercializacion Agricola (Indeca) v. Continental Ill. Nat'l Bank & Trust Co., 530 F. Supp. 279 (N.D. Ill. 1982); First Arlington Nat'l Bank v. Stathis, 90 Ill. App. 3d 802, 413 N.E.2d 1288 (1980). See generally ¶¶ 2.09, 6.05, 7.04.

[228] See authority cited supra note 219.

In *Board of Trade v. Swiss Credit Bank*,[229] the court declined to construe the credit against the issuer until after a trial, when the issuer's role in drafting the credit presumably would become apparent. *Bossier Bank & Trust Co. v. Union Planters National Bank*[230] states the rule as one favoring construction not against the issuer but against the party that drafted the credit. In the *Bossier* case, it appears that the bank issuer drafted the credit. In *Doelger v. Battery Park National Bank*,[231] the evidence indicated that the buyer had drafted the credit; and the court construed the credit against the buyer's interest. A general review of the cases indicates that some courts construe the ambiguous credit against the drafter and some construe it against the issuer.[232]

---

[229] 597 F.2d 146 (9th Cir. 1979).

[230] 550 F.2d 1077 (6th Cir. 1977).

[231] 201 A.D. 515, 194 N.Y.S. 582 (1922).

[232] In addition to the cases cited in the text, see, e.g., Kelley v. First Westroads Bank (In re Kelley), 840 F.2d 554 (8th Cir. 1988); Fiat Motors of N. Am., Inc. v. Mellon Bank, N.A., 827 F.2d 924 (3d Cir. 1987) (against issuer on credit drafted by beneficiary); Banque Paribas v. Hamilton Indus. Int'l, Inc., 767 F.2d 380 (7th Cir. 1985) (against drafter); Philadelphia Gear Corp. v. FDIC, 751 F.2d 1131 (10th Cir. 1984), rev'd, 106 S. Ct. 1931 (1986) (against drafter); Tosco Corp. v. FDIC, 723 F.2d 1242 (6th Cir. 1983) (against issuer); Marino Indus. Corp. v. Chase Manhattan Bank, N.A., 686 F.2d 112 (2d Cir. 1982) (against bank); East Girard Sav. Ass'n v. Citizens Nat'l Bank & Trust Co., 593 F.2d 598 (5th Cir. 1979) (against bank drafter); Venizelos, S.A. v. Chase Manhattan Bank, N.A., 425 F.2d 461 (2d Cir. 1970) (against issuer); North Beach Leather Int'l Inc. v. Morgan Guar. Trust Co., 687 F. Supp. 127 (S.D.N.Y. 1988) (against issuer); Banque Worms v. Banque Commerciale Privee, 679 F. Supp. 1173 (S.D.N.Y. 1988), aff'd per curiam, 849 F.2d 787 (2d Cir. 1988) (against beneficiary drafter); Transparent Prods. v. Paysaver Credit Union, No. 85 C 1741 (N.D. Ill. 1988), aff'd on other grounds, 864 F.2d 60 (7th Cir. 1988) (favorable [sic] to drafter); United Bank v. Citibank, N.A., No. 85 Civ. 5636 (CBM) (S.D.N.Y. Dec. 9, 1987) (against drafter); Ensco Envtl. Servs., Inc. v. United States, 650 F. Supp. 583 (W.D. Mo. 1986) (against issuer as drafter); Arabian Fiberglass Insulation Co. v. Continental Ill. Nat'l Bank & Trust Co., No. 85 C 1268 (N.D. Ill. Dec. 12, 1986) (same); Bank of Cochin Ltd. v. Manufacturers Hanover Trust Co., 612 F. Supp. 1533 (S.D.N.Y. 1985), aff'd, 808 F.2d 209 (2d Cir. 1986) (against party supplying language); United States Steel Corp. v. Chase Manhattan Bank, N.A., No. 83 Civ. 4966 (WCC) (S.D.N.Y. July 2, 1984) (against issuer); Interco, Inc. v. Schwartz, 20 U.C.C. Rep. Serv. (Callaghan) 716 (D. Mass. 1976), vacated on other grounds, 560 F.2d 480 (1st Cir. 1977) (strongly against issuer); West Virginia Hous. Dev. Fund v. Sroka, 415 F. Supp. 1107 (W.D. Pa. 1976) (against issuer); Utica Mut. Ins. Co. v. Walker, 725 S.W.2d 24 (Ky. Ct. App. 1987) (against beneficiary drafter); Bank of Montreal v. Federal Nat'l Bank & Trust Co., 622 F. Supp. 6 (W.D. Okla. 1984) (against issuer); Barclay Knitwear Co. v. King'swear Enters., Ltd., 141 A.D.2d 241, 533 N.Y.S.2d 724 (1988), appeal denied, 74 N.Y.2d 605, 541 N.E.2d 427, 543 N.Y.S.2d 398 (1989) (against drafter); Easton Tire Co. v. Farmers & Merchants Bank, 642 S.W.2d 396 (Mo. Ct. App. 1982) (against issuer); Western Petroleum Co. v. First Bank Aberdeen, N.A., 367 N.W.2d 773 (S.D. 1985) (against drafter); Borg-

There is merit in both rules. By construing the credit against the issuer, the courts favor the seller over the buyer in the commercial credit
and the obligor over the obligee in the standby credit.[233] It usually is not
the issuer but the issuer's customer who bears the cost if the issuer loses.
Often, especially in the standby credit situation, the *Banco Espanol* rule
of construing the credit strongly against the issuer may have the effect of
benefiting the drafter of the ambiguous language. In standby cases, it is
usually the beneficiary who dictates the terms of the credit, and it would
be fair in a dispute over the terms of such a credit to construe it against
the beneficiary (i.e., the "drafter"). The *Banco Espanol* rule construes it
against the issuer, and the account party, not the drafter, bears the cost
of an ambiguous term.

The *Banco Espanol* rule has the advantage of penalizing issuers,
usually bankers or merchants, who know more about credits than their
customers and the beneficiaries do. Thus, it encourages issuers to avoid
credits with ambiguous terms. Article 5 of the Uniform Customs warns
banks to "guard against confusion and misunderstanding" by discourag-
ing their customers from attempting to include in the credit "excessive
detail."[234] The *Banco Espanol* rule may serve that policy of keeping
credits simple and avoiding the ambiguities that give rise to this litigation.

Bankers argue that they have little or no control over the terms of
the credit and often are not in a position to know whether the language
is ambiguous. A rule that construes these ambiguous terms against the
issuer may expect them to know more about the underlying transaction
than the Code requires them to know.[235] When the bank's customer, the

---

Warner Acceptance Corp. v. Tascosa Nat'l Bank, 784 S.W.2d 129 (Tex. Ct. App.
1990) (against drafter); Willow Bend Nat'l Bank v. Commonwealth Mortgage Corp.,
722 S.W.2d 12 (Tex. Ct. App. 1986) (against drafter, but consistent with intent of
parties); First State Bank v. Shuford Mills, Inc., 716 S.W.2d 649 (Tex. Ct. App.
1986) (against issuer); Travis Bank & Trust v. State, 660 S.W.2d 851 (Tex. Ct. App.
1983) (against beneficiary drafter); cf. Egyptian Am. Bank, S.A.E. v. United States,
No. 88-1220 (Fed. Cir. Sept. 21, 1988) (unpublished limited precedent opinion construing first-demand guaranty against drafter).

[233] For a discussion of the uses of standby credits, see ¶ 1.06.

[234] See also U.C.P. art. 22(a) (urging issuers to describe documents precisely);
U.C.P. art. 38(a) (providing: "Credits should stipulate the type of insurance required
and, if any, the additional risks which are to be covered. Imprecise terms such as 'u-
sual risks' or 'customary risks' should not be used; if they are used, banks will accept
insurance documents as presented."). Thus, the Uniform Customs appear to favor
construction of a credit against the bank customer if the insurance term is vague. Accord Marino Indus. Corp. v. Chase Manhattan Bank, N.A., 686 F.2d 112 (2d Cir.
1982).

[235] See U.C.C. § 5-109; Marino Indus. Corp. v. Chase Manhattan Bank, N.A.,
686 F.2d 112 (2d Cir. 1982).

account party, is insolvent, the dispute is in fact one between the beneficiary and the issuer. Yet it may be good policy to construe the credit
against the issuer even if the beneficiary drafted the credit.

In *Toyota Industrial Trucks, U.S.A., Inc. v. Citizens National
Bank*,[236] the beneficiary required that the credit conform with its standard bank revolving credit agreement. Significantly, the credit was silent on the question of revocability, but the court notes in passing that
the credit was irrevocable. Such a construction is probably justified,
even though it goes against the nondrafting bank, which, incidentally,
was the real party in interest, its customer having failed.

In *Temple-Eastex, Inc. v. Addison Bank*,[237] the court thought the
word "draft" was an ambiguous term and decided that a credit should
be interpreted as any writing is interpreted. The court then went on to
say that if a writing is susceptible to two constructions, courts should reject the one "that renders its performance impossible or meaningless."[238] That choice of language is unfortunate if the court meant to
say that it favors a construction of ambiguous terms in favor of allowing
payment under the credit. To construe an ambiguous term in a way that
prevents payment is not to render "performance" of the credit "impossible or meaningless." If the court construes an ambiguous term against
a beneficiary, that court gives meaning to the credit and gives effect to
its commercial purpose. Credits protect beneficiaries by requiring
prompt payment in the event a presentation complies, and they protect
the account party and the issuer by requiring dishonor if the presentation does not comply. The quoted language from *Temple-Eastex* suggests that the credit is not working if the court construes an ambiguous
term against the beneficiary. That suggestion is incorrect.[239]

In *Atari, Inc. v. Harris Trust & Savings Bank*,[240] the court construed
an ambiguous term against the issuer and the account party for two reasons: (1) The issuer and the account party had the opportunity to insert
requirements in the credit and (2) a rule construing ambiguous terms
against the issuer is a necessary corollary to the strict compliance rule.
The first reason is less convincing than the second. In fact, beneficiaries

---

[236] 611 F.2d 465 (3d Cir. 1979).

[237] 672 S.W.2d 793 (Tex. 1984).

[238] Id. at 798.

[239] For additional authority to the effect that credits should be construed to render performance possible, see Barclay Knitwear Co. v. King'swear Enters., Ltd., 141
A.D.2d 241, 533 N.Y.S.2d 724 (1988), appeal denied, 74 N.Y.2d 605, 541 N.E.2d
427, 543 N.Y.S.2d 398 (1989); Universal Sav. Ass'n v. Killeen Sav. & Loan Ass'n,
757 S.W.2d 72 (Tex. Ct. App. 1988).

[240] 599 F. Supp. 592 (N.D. Ill. 1984), aff'd in part, rev'd in part mem., 785 F.2d
312 (7th Cir. 1986).

can, and often do, insist on language in the credit. In *Homestate Savings Association v. Westwind Exploration, Inc.*,[241] the court construed an ambiguous credit without reading it against any party, but rather according to what the court took to be the objective intent of the parties. In *Banque Worms v. Banque Commerciale Privee*,[242] the court agreed that credits should be construed against their drafters—in this case, the beneficiary—but refused to read a general condition in the credit that its proceeds be used to provide equity funds for a project as imposing a documentary condition certifying to the use of the funds. The rule of construction applies, the court held, only if the credit is ambiguous and cannot be used to read into the credit a term that is not there.

In *Tuthill v. Union Savings Bank*,[243] the issuer of a credit subject to the Uniform Customs failed to include an expiry. After observing by way of dictum that such a credit, which violated the 1974 version of Uniform Customs Article 37, having been drafted by the issuer, would be construed against the issuer, and that construction would prevent the issuer from terminating the credit more than one year after the event of default against which the credit was security. Applying the rule of Uniform Customs Article 41 in a somewhat tortured analogy,[244] the court avoided that result by holding that, twenty-one days after the event of default, the issuer was entitled to terminate the credit.

The law remains unsettled. Some courts prefer to invoke a rule construing the ambiguous credit against the drafter; some courts construe it against the issuer. The latter rule is simple and fosters simplicity in credit terms—a result that, in the long run, will protect issuers as well as beneficiaries and account parties.[245] Because it tends to construe ambig-

---

[241] 684 S.W.2d 788 (Tex. Ct. App.), aff'd, 696 S.W.2d 378 (Tex. 1985).

[242] 679 F. Supp. 1173 (S.D.N.Y. 1988).

[243] 141 Misc. 2d 88, 534 N.Y.S.2d 88 (1988).

[244] Article 41 of the 1974 version of the Uniform Customs, which applied in the *Tuthill* case, provided that when a letter of credit called for shipping documents and did not specify a date after which they may not be presented, the beneficiary was required to present them not more than twenty-one days after they issued. See U.C.P. art. 41 (1974 version); cf. U.C.P. art. 47(a) (1983) (same rule).

[245] For other examples of credits that banks never should have signed, see Wichita Eagle & Beacon Publishing Co. v. Pacific Nat'l Bank, 493 F.2d 1285 (9th Cir. 1974) (credit engagement being so complicated that court held it to be guaranty, not letter of credit); Newvector Communications, Inc. v. Union Bank, 663 F. Supp. 252, 253 (D. Utah 1987) (calling for "draft(s) as per Resellers Agreement"); Sawyer v. E.A. Gralia Constr. Co. (In re Pine Tree Elec. Co.), 16 Bankr. 105, 106 (Bankr. D. Me. 1981) (credit reciting that it was "subject to all of the terms and provisions" of underlying contract and to additional conditions, including account party's right to cure defaults in underlying contract and to submit disputes under contract to arbitration); Sherwood & Roberts, Inc. v. First Sec. Bank, 682 P.2d 149, 151 (Mont. 1984) (credit "exercisable . . . upon the unremedied default" of account party of certain

uous terms against the account party, who probably is not the source of those terms, the simpler rule may be unfair in the standby context. There is a strong dose of efficiency, moreover, especially when merchants are involved, in requiring the beneficiary to review the credit promptly in order to bring errors to the attention of all parties and to permit the beneficiary to suspend performance until the issuer and account party agree to an appropriate amendment. Courts can effect that efficiency by refusing to reform credits and by construing them strictly against the beneficiary.

[4] Questions of Revocability

Although the Uniform Customs cover the question explicitly in Article 7, the Code does not say whether a credit that is silent on the issue is revocable or irrevocable.[246] Comment 1 to Section 5-103 explains that Article 5 intentionally leaves the question to common law. Given this statutory deference, courts might have taken the Uniform Customs rule in favor of revocability as the common-law rule and might have concluded that silent credits were all revocable.[247] Instead, courts have followed the contract rule of construction, which favors an enforceable reading of a promise over one that renders the promise illusory.[248] Even though pre-Code cases were split,[249] more recent cases are virtually unanimous in finding the silent credit irrevocable.

"documents" arising out of underlying loan transaction); O'Grady v. First Union Bank, 296 N.C. 212, 229, 250 S.E.2d 587, 599 (1978) (credit requiring beneficiary to submit copy "of each instrument causing this establishment of credit to Thomas O'Grady to be called upon").

[246] See supra ¶ 4.06[2][a]. But cf. Fla. Stat. Ann. § 675.5-103(1)(a) (West 1966) (nonconforming Code provision stipulating that if credit does not indicate whether it is irrevocable or revocable, it is irrevocable); La. Rev. Stat. Ann. § 10:5-103(1)(a) (West 1983) (same).

[247] See authority cited in Kozolchyk, "Letters of Credit," at 16 n.64, in IX International Encyclopedia of Comparative Law ch. 5 (1979).

[248] See Weyerhaeuser Co. v. First Nat'l Bank, 27 U.C.C. Rep. Serv. (Callaghan) 777 (S.D. Iowa 1979); West Virginia Hous. Dev. Fund v. Sroka, 415 F. Supp. 1107 (W.D. Pa. 1976); Braun v. Intercontinental Bank, 466 So. 2d 1130 (Fla. Dist. Ct. App. 1985); Lewis State Bank v. Advance Mortgage Corp., 362 So. 2d 406 (Fla. Dist. Ct. App. 1978); cf. Venizelos, S.A. v. Chase Manhattan Bank, N.A., 425 F.2d 461 (2d Cir. 1970) (court preferring construction of credit that will "sustain" it over "one that will defeat it"); Ufitec, S.A. v. Trade Bank & Trust Co., 21 A.D.2d 187, 249 N.Y.S.2d 557 (1964), aff'd, 16 N.Y.2d 698, 209 N.E.2d 551, 261 N.Y.S.2d 893 (1965) (holding by way of dictum that it was difficult to see what purpose revocable traveler's letter of credit would serve).

[249] See First Wis. Nat'l Bank v. Forsyth Leather Co., 189 Wis. 9, 206 N.W. 843 (1926), and authority cited therein.

In the *Toyota* case, the court held the engagement, which the bank issuer thought was a commitment to make loans to its customer, to be a credit.[250] The letter recited that it could be revoked by the issuer upon notice to the beneficiary. The court held the credit irrevocable but suggested that the bank could have revoked had it given the proper notice. Section 5-106 of the Code assigns meanings to "revocable" and "irrevocable" that are different from those of the *Toyota* case. The section stipulates that the former type of credit may be revoked without notice and that the latter may never be revoked without the beneficiary's consent. The *Toyota* credit falls through a crack in the Code's definitions, and it is difficult to quarrel with the court's decision to give effect to the express terms of the credit.[251]

In *Beathard v. Chicago Football Club, Inc.*,[252] the court found letters silent on the revocability question to be revocable. The credits incorporated the Uniform Customs, which stipulate in the then Article 1(c) that such a credit must be taken as revocable. The *Beathard* credits contained termination dates, recited that they were to guarantee payment of the beneficiaries' salaries, and contained the traditional negotiation clause.[253] The beneficiaries argued that the language of the credits supported their position that the engagements were irrevocable. The court disagreed, holding as a matter of law that the credits were revocable.

The *Beathard* case puts the burden squarely on the beneficiary to show that a credit subject to the Uniform Customs is irrevocable and exposes the conflict between what appears to be the Code rule, as established by courts favoring irrevocability, and the Uniform Customs rule favoring revocability.[254] That conflict should be of little moment. The careful drafter always designates a credit as revocable or irrevocable. Any issuer that intentionally incorporates the Uniform Customs in order to benefit from Article 7 probably is acting in bad faith or is acting unconscionably,[255] although no cases thus far have so held.

---

[250] See supra ¶ 4.08[3].

[251] See also Dennis Chapman Toyota, Inc. v. Belle State Bank, 759 S.W.2d 330 (Mo. Ct. App. 1988) (involving similar Toyota line of credit agreement, which court treated as revocable letter of credit); Fair Pavilions, Inc. v. First Nat'l City Bank, 19 N.Y.2d 512, 227 N.E.2d 839, 281 N.Y.S.2d 23 (1967) (holding implicitly that credit may be revocable if customer satisfies conditions in credit for revocation).

[252] 419 F. Supp. 1133 (N.D. Ill. 1976).

[253] See App. C, Doc. 16, for a negotiation credit.

[254] For a discussion of this conflict and the *Beathard* case, see supra ¶ 4.06[2][a].

[255] In Weyerhaeuser Co. v. First Nat'l Bank, 27 U.C.C. Rep. Serv. (Callaghan) 777 (S.D. Iowa 1979), the court held the credit to be irrevocable because Section 2-325(3) required the buyer to provide an irrevocable credit. Cf. Harfield, "Code Treatment of Letters of Credit," 48 Cornell L.Q. 92, 98 (1962) (terming Uniform Customs rule "outrageous"); Mentschikoff, supra note 94, at 589 (predicting that courts would not enforce Uniform Customs rule).

In *Conoco, Inc. v. Norwest Bank Mason City, N.A.*,[256] the court decided that a credit not mentioning revocability but reciting that it would remain in force for a period of six months was irrevocable under the Uniform Customs. The court attempted to distinguish the *Beathard* decision, but the attempt is not altogether convincing. After *Conoco*, *Beathard* may be of questionable authority.

The strength of the traditional animus toward revocable credits is apparent in *Fair Pavilions, Inc. v. First National City Bank*,[257] where the credit provided that it was revocable upon the receipt by the issuer of its customer's affidavit to the effect that the beneficiary had breached the underlying contract. The credit stipulated that the certificate recite in conclusory form that one or more of the events described in a clause of the underlying contract had occurred. The customer served such an affidavit on the bank but did not specify the specific event of default. The court construed the credit's termination clause as calling for specification of the event of default. It concluded from an examination of the entire transaction, not from the language of the credit itself, that the purpose of the certificate was to give the beneficiary an opportunity to cure the alleged default. Because the certificate was not specific, the *Fair Pavilions* court held, the credit had not been revoked; and the bank had to pay. Although the *Fair Pavilions* animus against revocable credits is consistent with the general line of authority, its holding conflicts with the strict compliance rule.[258]

More true to the independence principle is *Phoenix Mutual Life Insurance Co. v. Seafarers Officers & Employees Pension Plan*.[259] In that case, the credit was to terminate in the event the beneficiary failed to pay an installment due under a lease.[260] The lease was part of a sale-and-leaseback arrangement under which the beneficiary would not owe the installment if the Internal Revenue Service (IRS) made certain determinations contrary to the interests of the beneficiary. The beneficiary argued that until the IRS made such determinations, it was unclear that the installment was due and therefore that the credit could not be terminated until the IRS had made its decision. The *Phoenix Mutual* court rejected that argument. Under the credit, it was necessary only to know whether the beneficiary had paid the installment. Whether the install-

---

[256] 767 F.2d 470 (8th Cir. 1985).

[257] 19 N.Y.2d 512, 227 N.E.2d 839, 281 N.Y.S.2d 23 (1967).

[258] See supra ¶¶ 4.08[2], 6.03–6.05.

[259] 128 F.R.D. 25 (E.D.N.Y. 1989).

[260] For discussion of the wisdom of making any condition in a credit factual as opposed to documentary, see ¶ 2.05[4].

ment was due was a question in the underlying sale-and-leaseback agreement, from which the credit was independent.

Two other cases demonstrate great reluctance to manipulate the credit in order to render it irrevocable. In *Key Appliance, Inc. v. First National City Bank*,[261] the credit called for invoices signed by the customer; that is, it called for invoices that the account party would have to approve. The credit was similar to that in *Fair Pavilions*. It appears to be irrevocable, but the account party retains the power to render it a nullity (as in *Fair Pavilions*) or to prevent the beneficiary from complying (as in *Key Appliances*). These credits do not provide much assurance for the seller-beneficiary. If any disputes arise over the quality of merchandise or over any other aspect of the seller's performance, the account party of a credit such as these can refuse to sign the invoices and can effectively deprive the beneficiary of the credit's benefit. Apparently, such a dispute arose in the *Key Appliances* case, and, when the beneficiary failed to provide the countersigned invoices, the bank dishonored. The court upheld that dishonor in the face of a dissent, which lamented that it was "unconscionable to deprive plaintiff of payment for merchandise concededly sold and delivered."[262]

Similarly, in *Corporacion De Mercadeo Agricola v. Mellon Bank International*,[263] the credit, according to the court's reading of it, required the beneficiary to present the *buyer's* signed statement of the *buyer's* default. Because the beneficiary failed to present that statement, the court held that the issuer properly dishonored the draft. The court noted that the beneficiary could have obtained a court order requiring the buyer to sign a statement of default. The holding prompted a vigorous dissent that was based, in part, on the facts[264] and that expressed dissatisfaction with a credit which left the beneficiary at the mercy of the account party.[265]

Key Appliances and *Mellon Bank* are probably better-reasoned decisions than the dissents suggest.[266] The cases that construe a silent credit

---

[261] 46 A.D.2d 622, 359 N.Y.S.2d 886 (1974).

[262] Id. at 622, 359 N.Y.S.2d at 887. The dissent apparently overlooked the fact that the plaintiff could sue the buyer on the underlying contract.

[263] 608 F.2d 43 (2d Cir. 1979).

[264] The credit was quite ambiguous, as the dissent points out. Under a rule construing the credit against the issuer, the court could have held that the credit's conditions were satisfied. See id. at 53 (Gurfein, J., dissenting).

[265] For a case similar to the *Mellon Bank* case, see Bebco Distribs., Inc. v. Farmers & Merchants Bank, 485 So. 2d 330 (Ala. 1986). For general discussion of documents to be signed by the account party, see ¶ 2.05[3].

[266] In Banco Nacional De Desarrolla v. Mellon Bank, N.A., 558 F. Supp. 1265 (W.D. Pa. 1983), the court refused to enforce a credit term that required the beneficiary to present the buyer's notice that the goods had arrived. The court viewed the

as irrevocable protect beneficiaries from a hidden trap. The onus of the credits in these two cases, however, was plain enough for all to see. It is of little benefit to commerce and the law to cloud the matter with rules altering the plain language of a credit in order to protect a merchant who apparently did not read his credit carefully. There was no trap in the *Key Appliances* and *Mellon Bank* credits, if the courts' characterization of the facts is accurate. It is also not fair to assume, as the *Fair Pavilions* court did, that the presentation of a conclusory affidavit by the customer leaves the beneficiary at the account party's mercy. Courts know how to deal with false assertions in an affidavit without cluttering up the law of credits. The beneficiary in *Fair Pavilions* was at the mercy only of an unscrupulous and fraudulent account party and had put itself in that position by not objecting to the credit at the outset.

In some credit transactions, the credit calls for a reciprocal draft from the beneficiary. Under this requirement, which appears from time to time in credits issued by banks in Far Eastern countries, the beneficiary must supply two drafts in the amount of the credit to the issuer. While the normal draft called for by the credit is a draft drawn by the beneficiary on the issuer, the reciprocal draft is drawn by the beneficiary on the account party.[267] When the issuer honors the beneficiary's draft under the credit, the issuer forwards the reciprocal draft to the account party as a method of obtaining reimbursement.

Unfortunately for beneficiaries of credits calling for a reciprocal draft, if the account party dishonors the reciprocal draft, the issuer holds a draft on which the beneficiary is now liable, the beneficiary having engaged as a matter of negotiable instruments law to honor the draft if the drawee (here, the account party) dishonors.[268] The issuer will then

---

term as "repugnant" to the notion of an irrevocable credit (id. at 1269) but refused to enforce it, not on that ground but because the term appeared in an amendment to which the beneficiary had not agreed. The *Banco De Desarrolla* case was reversed in an opinion that holds squarely that it does not violate letter of credit principles for a credit to call for a document to be executed by the account party. See Banco Nacional De Desarrollo v. Mellon Bank, N.A., 726 F.2d 87 (3d Cir. 1984). In Scarsdale Nat'l Bank & Trust Co. v. Toronto-Dominion Bank, 533 F. Supp. 378 (S.D.N.Y. 1982), the credit called for certificates of performance executed by the account party. The court enjoined honor of the credit under Section 5-114(2)(b) because the plaintiff had obtained the certificates fraudulently. For the suggestion that an account party may not refuse arbitrarily to execute a document called for in the credit, see McLaughlin, "Structuring Commercial Letter-of-Credit Transactions to Safeguard the Interests of the Buyer," 21 U.C.C. L.J. 318 (1989).

[267] For a case involving a reciprocal draft, see Interco, Inc. v. First Nat'l Bank, 560 F.2d 480 (1st Cir. 1977).

[268] The beneficiary usually must draw the draft payable to itself and then endorse it. By drawing, the beneficiary makes an engagement under U.C.C. § 3-413(2) to pay in the event of dishonor; by endorsing, it makes a similar engagement under U.C.C. § 3-414(1).

have a cause of action against the beneficiary for the amount the issuer paid the beneficiary under the credit.

Technically, the arrangement does not render the credit revocable, nor does it render the credit transaction entirely illusory. The issuer has paid the beneficiary, who will hold the funds in the event of any litigation and who may be able to avoid litigating in a distant forum.[269] The reciprocal draft arrangement does destroy the prime function of the credit, however, that of substituting the credit of the issuer for that of the account party.

Issuers of reciprocal draft credits claim that they need the reciprocal draft in order to satisfy currency exchange controls of the account party's domicile. If a draft drawn without recourse satisfies those control laws, the beneficiary should insist on that modification of the credit condition. The beneficiary that draws a draft without recourse is not liable in the event of dishonor.[270]

There are times when an issuer may denominate its engagement as irrevocable but may incorporate other conditions in the credit that may render the irrevocability illusory. The Code, in Section 5-114(1), interdicts the issuer practice of conditioning payment of the credit upon issuer satisfaction with the beneficiary's documents, though the section permits an issuer to specify the compliance of certain specified documents as being subject to its satisfaction. The section stipulates that a condition that all documents be satisfactory to the issuer does not operate to justify dishonor. By implication, a credit may not offend the section by identifying all documents except one and rendering them subject to a condition that they be satisfactory to the issuer. That is not to overlook the possibility, however, that a court might view any condition of satisfaction as being subject to a reasonableness requirement, which would prevent an issuer from rejecting documents arbitrarily.

Credits with a condition that documents be subject to issuer satisfaction have not appeared in the reports or in practice; and it is probably safe to say that beneficiaries recognize the illusory nature of such credits and refuse to accept them. There is no evidence, furthermore, of a practice of accepting credits that call for documents executed by the issuer. Such a credit probably would be subject to a reasonableness requirement or would not excuse dishonor if the issuer arbitrarily refused to execute the document. One can speculate on the question whether an issuer that refuses to execute a document under such a credit because the issuer's right of reimbursement is impaired would satisfy a requirement of commercial reasonableness. In all events, the well-advised ben-

---

[269] For discussion of these functions of the credit, see ¶ 3.07.
[270] See U.C.C. § 3-413(2).

eficiary examines its credit carefully and suspends performance if the credit contains such a condition.

[5] Credits With Inconsistent Terms

From time to time, parties draft credits that contain inconsistent terms, and the beneficiary cannot possibly comply. It is a wonder that a beneficiary does not examine his credit promptly upon receipt to determine that he can comply with it. The beneficiary is in the best position to make that determination. One assumes that a beneficiary is interested in the credit and reviews it to determine that it protects him in the fashion that he sought when he bargained for it in the underlying transaction. If the credit does not meet his satisfaction, either because it is in the wrong amount, contains a condition that he never agreed to satisfy, or contains inconsistent terms that nobody can satisfy, the beneficiary should object, seek an amendment, or refuse to perform the underlying contract. Unfortunately, not all beneficiaries exercise that care. Even more unfortunate is the fact that some courts are inclined to excuse them if they do not exercise it. The cases are a curious mix, with some indications that judges are willing to hold the beneficiary to a high standard.

Tradex Petroleum American, Inc. v. Coral Petroleum, Inc. (In re Coral Petroleum, Inc.)[271] represents the better approach. In *Tradex*, the court refused to construe against an issuer a credit whose terms were inconsistent. At one point, the credit called for a shipper's transfer listing referring to "sour" oil, but at another it required a document referring to "sweet" oil. Persons familiar with the industry know that sour oil and sweet oil are different products and that it is not possible for the beneficiary to satisfy these inconsistent provisions.

The inconsistency in *Tradex* was supplied to the issuer by the account party, was apparent on the face of the credit to anyone conversant with trade terminology, and was in the hands of the beneficiary in sufficient time for the beneficiary to ask for an amendment correcting it. Having failed to examine the credit carefully, the court held, the beneficiary should not succeed in having the credit construed against the issuer and should be required to comply with the impossible conditions.

On the surface, *Tradex* seems harsh; but it serves letter of credit policy, and there is much to commend it. Section 5-109(1)(c) excuses bank issuers from liability resting on knowledge of trade practices and usages. The ambiguity in *Tradex* was in trade terms whose meanings

---

[271] 878 F.2d 830 (5th Cir. 1989).

were apparent to the beneficiary, but not to the issuer. To rule against the issuer in such a case, as the court noted, is to ignore the purpose of Section 5-109(1)(c). The *Tradex* court went beyond that rationale, however, holding that whenever a credit contains ambiguities or inconsistent terms, the beneficiary, not the issuer, should bear the loss. That rule, the *Tradex* court intimates, is efficient. It puts the burden on the beneficiary to examine the credit early in the transaction to determine that compliance is possible.

The opposite view is apparent in *Kerr Construction Co. v. Plains National Bank.*[272] In that case, the credit secured the performance of a contractor under a city ordinance relating to local improvements. There was a recital early in the credit to the effect that the issuer would honor the beneficiary's draft and certificate to the effect that the contractor had not performed the work by July 17, 1985. The credit also contained a provision that the credit would expire on July 1, 1985.

The *Kerr* court read these inartful recitations in the credit to suggest that the expiry could be July 17 or July 1. The beneficiary drew on July 17. The issuer dishonored on the ground that the credit had expired by its terms on July 1.

In the face of these inconsistent credit terms, the *Kerr* court held that contract rules of construction applied and that, under those rules, a provision that appears early in the document (the reference to July 17), if that provision is clear and definite, controls over a later provision (the July 1 expiry). The court also justified its holding under the contract rule of construction to the effect that if two provisions of a contract are inconsistent, the one that contributes more essentially[273] to the agreement controls. The *Kerr* court saw the language creating the condition to payment as being more essential than the expiry.

The *Kerr* result is unfortunate. If any term in a letter of credit is "essential," it is the expiry term.[274] It is true that the language of this credit referred to a condition that had to occur before July 17—a period that might not permit a draw prior to the expiry. A reasonably cautious beneficiary, reading the expiry term in the *Kerr* credit, would be on notice that there was a problem. *Kerr* holds that the issuer is liable in the event of such inconsistent terms, and the *Kerr* rule relieves the beneficiary of the duty to examine its credit carefully. *Kerr*, moreover, applied contract rules of construction, without regard to the damage they might do to the commercial device involved.

---

[272] 753 S.W.2d 181 (Tex. Ct. App. 1987).

[273] Id. at 184.

[274] For discussion of the need for a firm expiry rule, see ¶ 5.03[3][e].

The *Kerr* case illustrates the uneasiness between the law of letters of credit and the law of contract. While the *Kerr* court may well have applied Texas contract law correctly, its misunderstanding of the critical role of the expiry term renders the opinion unconvincing as a matter of letter of credit law.

The court that decided *Tradex* under New York law confronted the rule of *Kerr* in a diversity action governed by Texas law. The result is an opinion that follows *Kerr* in language sufficiently disdainful of, and with analysis so obviously superior to, the *Kerr* approach that one might question the vitality of the *Kerr* rule even in the Texas Court of Appeals that issued it.

Exxon Co., U.S.A. v. Banque de Paris et des Pays-Bas[275] illustrates the inefficiencies that may result from construing a credit against the issuer. In the *Exxon* case, the credit secured a crude oil exchange obligation and called for certification by the beneficiary that the obligor had not delivered crude during the period from September through December 1981. The credit expired by its terms, as modified under Article 39 of the 1974 version of the Uniform Customs, on November 2, 1981.

Thus, the credit was inherently inconsistent. It expired in November but required the beneficiary to certify that the account party had not performed in December. The issuing banker brought the inconsistency to the attention of the account party, who told him to issue it anyway. The beneficiary, it seems, was less attentive to detail than the issuer was; and apparently it was not until the credit was about to expire that the beneficiary realized that it could not draw in time without making a false certification. Because the account party would not agree to an amendment, the beneficiary did not draw and make the truthful certification prior to the stated expiry.

In a suit against the issuer for wrongful dishonor of the postexpiry demand for payment, the beneficiary argued that the court should consider the credit ambiguous and should construe it against the issuer. In the face of a strong dissent and a lower-court opinion that accepted the beneficiary's position,[276] the court, in its original opinion (*Exxon* I) rejected the idea that the issuer owed a duty to the beneficiary to review the credit for sense. That obligation, the *Exxon* I court held, fell on the beneficiary itself. The court based its holding in part on the strong policy in favor of firm expiry rules. The court noted that, after the expiry, the issuer had released to the account party the collateral securing its right of reimbursement.

---

[275] 828 F.2d 1121 (5th Cir. 1987), vacated, 109 S. Ct. 299 (1988) (mem.).

[276] The opinion of the trial court is attached to the dissent as an appendix. See id. at 1127 (Garza, J., dissenting).

In the event, the judicial energy expended in *Exxon* I was for nought, for the Supreme Court vacated the ruling in *Exxon* I, a diversity case, and remanded for consideration in light of the *Kerr* case, which the Texas court had rendered about one month after the decision in *Exxon* I.

The second *Exxon* opinion[277] differs markedly from the first. Operating within the constraints of *Kerr*, the second opinion is devoid of the policy analysis and efficiency concerns for the credit that were evident in *Exxon* I. "We . . . must resist the view of sound commercial policy on which we relied in *Exxon* I."[278] Instead, the second *Exxon* case relied on "stock rules for the construction of contracts"[279] and "standard maxims of contractual construction."[280]

There were two compelling justifications for the result in *Exxon* I. First, it is more efficient for the beneficiary to review a credit to see that it complies with the underlying contract than it is for the issuer to undertake that review. By refusing to let the beneficiary force that duty on the issuer, *Exxon* I sent a message to all beneficiaries: Review the credit upon its establishment, at a time when an amendment or suspension of performance of the underlying contract can save everybody time and money. In *Exxon*, the beneficiary performed its part of the underlying transaction after it had the credit in hand, although, as the *Exxon* I court noted, the beneficiary could have refused to perform the underlying contract until it received a complying credit.

Second, the *Exxon* I result is particularly appropriate when the question deals with the expiry. All parties, especially issuers, need to know when the credit expires. If issuers are concerned that courts may reform a credit's expiry, they may be reluctant to release the account party's collateral, and bank issuers will not be able to apply their loan limits to borrowers.[281] Significantly, federal regulators require standby credits such as that in *Exxon* to contain an expiry term.[282] In short, there is much in the reality of letter of credit practice to commend the rule of *Exxon* I.

It is of little solace to the issuer in the *Exxon* case, but may be solace to those who decry *Kerr*, that the language of *Exxon* II exposes the

---

[277] 889 F.2d 674 (5th Cir. 1989).

[278] Id. at 678.

[279] Id.

[280] Id.

[281] See generally ¶ 12.03.

[282] See Comptroller of the Currency, Interpretive Ruling, 12 C.F.R. § 7.7016 (1989); Office of Thrift Supervision, Regulation, 12 C.F.R. § 545.48 (1990).

shortcomings of *Kerr* as a matter of letter of credit policy. *Exxon* II is a call for construction of credits, with a view to the role they play in commercial transactions. That view does not justify application of stock rules and maxims of contract construction in the fashion of *Kerr*.

CHAPTER 5

Establishing, Amending, and Terminating the Credit

¶ 5.01 ESTABLISHING THE CREDIT

[1] Historical Background

Prior to the adoption of the Uniform Commercial Code (UCC or the Code), there was considerable controversy over the precise time at which the credit became effective. Originally, courts viewed the credit as something akin to an offer that became binding upon the beneficiary's "acceptance." The beneficiary signaled that acceptance either by drawing on the issuer or by negotiating the account party's drafts.[1] That view satisfied the early buyer's credit, which was common in international trade during the nineteenth century[2] and which continued to be used into the twentieth century in some domestic markets.[3] It did not satisfy, however, the commercial credit, which grew to prominence after World War I.[4] Under the buyer's credit, the issuer, usually a merchant, undertook to honor drafts drawn by sellers of merchandise to the buyer.[5] There was no problem in construing the credit as an offer or in construing the seller's sale of goods and contemporaneous draft as an acceptance of that offer.

The commercial credit differs from the early credit in three ways that render the offer-acceptance analysis obsolete, or so many commentators have concluded.[6] First, the commercial credit usually runs to a specified seller. Unlike the old credit, it is special, not general. Second, the beneficiary of a commercial credit frequently is a broker or a manufacturer. The former must arrange with a supplier to obtain the merchandise; the latter must procure raw materials and parts to begin manufacture. Third, in the commercial credit, the beneficiary usually enters into the sales contract before the credit issues; in the old credit setting, the seller entered into the sales contract after the credit issued.

These differences create problems for the offer theory. Under that theory, the credit became firm when the seller acted upon it. Merchants and bankers, however, thought that a commercial credit was firm (i.e., could not be revoked) once it was issued. There were various attempts

---

[1] See, e.g., Schimmelpennich v. Bayard, 26 U.S. 264 (1828); Hall v. First Nat'l Bank, 133 Ill. 234, 24 N.E. 546 (1890); Russell v. Wiggin, 21 F. Cas. 68 (No. 12,165) (C.C.D. Mass. 1842); Duval v. Trask, 12 Mass. 153 (1815); Wilson & Co. v. Niffenegger, 211 Mich. 311, 178 N.W. 667 (1920); Union Bank v. Executors of John G. Coster, 3 N.Y. 203 (1850).

[2] For a discussion of those early uses of the credit, see ¶ 3.02.

[3] See, e.g., Wilson & Co. v. Niffenegger, 211 Mich. 311, 178 N.W. 667 (1920); Bridge v. Welda State Bank, 222 Mo. App. 586; 292 S.W. 1079 (1927).

[4] For a discussion of that growth, see ¶ 3.05.

[5] For an account of the earliest uses of the credit, see J. Holden, The History of Negotiable Instruments in English Law 21 n.2 (1955); F. Sanborn, Origins of the Early English Maritime and Commercial Law 218 (1930). See also ¶ 3.02.

[6] See, e.g., Davis, "The Relationship Between Banker and Seller Under a Confirmed Credit," 52 L.Q. Rev. 225 (1936); Hershey, "Letters of Credit," 32 Harv. L. Rev. 1 (1918); McCurdy, "Commercial Letters of Credit" (pts. 1 & 2), 35 Harv. L. Rev. 593, 715 (1922); Trimble, "The Law Merchant and the Letter of Credit," 61 Harv. L. Rev. 981 (1948).

to modify the thinking on credits in order to resolve these questions. In one view, the commercial credit was seen to be so different from the buyer's credit that it was considered a different instrument.[7] Some commentators took the position that a letter of credit was an authorization to draw, coupled with an interest (thereby rendering it irrevocable). Others said it was a guarantee or a promise rendered irrevocable by estoppel law or by some similar theory.[8] In yet another view, the commercial credit remained an offer, and any act in reliance by the beneficiary was sufficient to render it firm.[9] In the view accepted by most American commentators, the credit was a promise rendered firm by the implied promise of the account party to reimburse the issuer.[10] Ultimately, notwithstanding the controversy among the writers, the courts adopted a rule that fit the expectations of merchants and bankers by holding that an issuer was obligated from the moment it advised the beneficiary of the credit.[11]

[2] Section 5-106 of the Code

The Code affirms in Section 5-106 the rule that an issuer becomes obligated from the moment it advises the beneficiary of the credit. Specifically, Section 5-106 renders the issuer liable on the credit as to the customer when the credit is sent to him or when the credit or an advice of it is sent to the beneficiary. The section renders the issuer liable on the credit as to the beneficiary when the beneficiary *receives* the credit or an advice of it.

The effect of establishment of an irrevocable credit is twofold. After establishment, the issuer may not (1) revoke the credit or (2) amend it without the concurrence of the party as to whom it is established. There is no legal significance to the establishment of a revocable credit.[12] For such a credit, the critical event is not establishment but due honor or

---

[7] See Thayer, "Irrevocable Credits in International Commerce: Their Legal Nature," 36 Colum. L. Rev. 1031, 1032 (1936).

[8] For a summary of these theories, see Trimble, supra note 6.

[9] See Davis, supra note 6, at 229.

[10] See McCurdy, supra note 6; Thayer, supra note 7.

[11] See, e.g., Courteen Seed Co. v. Hong Kong & Shanghai Banking Corp., 216 A.D. 495, 215 N.Y.S. 525 (1926); Doelger v. Battery Park Nat'l Bank, 201 A.D. 515, 194 N.Y.S. 582 (1922); see generally McCurdy, "The Right of the Beneficiary Under a Commercial Letter of Credit," 37 Harv. L. Rev. 323 (1924).

[12] See U.C.C. § 5-106, comment 2.

negotiation under the credit by a third party authorized to honor or to negotiate.[13]

The rules on establishment are precise, and there have been only a few reported cases. In one case, *Amoco Oil Co. v. First Bank & Trust Co.*,[14] the beneficiary received the credit and objected that it was not subject to the Uniform Customs and Practice for Documentary Credits (UCP or the Uniform Customs). The issuer ignored the beneficiary's objection. When the account party defaulted on the underlying obligation, the beneficiary drew on the issuer. The issuer argued that the beneficiary's objection amounted to a rejection of the credit and a counteroffer, but the *Amoco* court would not accept the argument, holding that, once the credit was established, the beneficiary's objection did not amount to a release of the issuer's obligation under the credit. *Amoco* in one respect is a classic case, for the issuer in *Amoco* was making the arguments that parties made long ago, that is, that the issuance of a credit was the making of an offer. The Code rejects that theory of credits; the *Amoco* court rejected it as well.

Section 5-106 resolves the old problems, but it may not answer all of the new ones. The provision assumes an operational pattern for letter of credit transactions that parties do not always follow. With the advent of computer technology and wire transmissions, parties to the broad letter of credit transaction have adopted efficient modifications in the establishment procedure.

Traditionally, an issuer opened a credit after its customer prepared a written application agreement setting forth the terms to be incorporated into the credit.[15] Once the issuer had the application agreement, its clerks could prepare the credit instrument by lifting the terms from the agreement and incorporating them into the credit.

Today, however, some account parties may find the traditional procedures inefficient. High-volume importers, for example, have arranged with their issuers for direct contact, permitting the account party to generate the credit at its own office. Under this procedure, the customer's personnel enter the necessary information via computer terminals into the bank issuer's computer program, which is set up to permit the customer itself to fashion the credit within certain parameters. When the customer completes the process, the bank's personnel review the credit on the terminal and send the credit off, again by telecommunication, to the terminal of the advising bank or of the beneficiary itself.

---

[13] See infra ¶ 5.03[2].

[14] 759 S.W.2d 877 (Mo. Ct. App. 1988).

[15] For an illustration of a traditional application agreement, see App. C, Doc. 14.

Under these arrangements, the issuer may communicate the credit terms to a beneficiary or to a foreign advising bank without producing any hard copy and without sending anything to the account party. It would be unfortunate if, in this example, a court were to hold that the credit was not established with regard to the account party, when in fact the account party generated the credit.

Clearly, the Code did not anticipate microchips and the innovations that they make possible. Until there is legislative reform, courts will have to deal with the problem with a measure of imagination and with some disregard for the language of Section 5-106.[16]

Generally, there has been little litigation concerning the duties of the issuer toward the account party in the establishment process.[17] In at least one case, however, the court held that a potential issuer's negligence rendered it liable to a potential beneficiary. In *Champion International Corp. v. First National Bank*,[18] two bankers represented to the supplier of the bank's customer that a credit would issue. Although the facts are not clear from the opinion, it appears that the credit was in the nature of an invoice standby.[19] In fact, while the two bankers represented that the bank looked favorably on the request for the credit, other bank officers questioned whether to continue financing the customer. Ultimately, those officers decided against the customer; the credit did not issue; and bankruptcy ensued.

The *Champion International* court held that, because the supplier had relied on the bankers' representations, it was entitled to recover losses incurred on two of the customer's orders. Arguably, the liability in *Champion International* is a matter of promissory estoppel rather than liability on a credit engagement. As a matter of promissory estoppel, *Champion International* may well be correct; as a matter of credit law, it conflicts with the establishment rule of Section 5-106.

The time of establishment became a question in one transaction involving an "omnibus" letter of credit. The Office of the Comptroller of the Currency has approved an "omnibus" letter of credit that secured the obligations of participants in an over-the-counter arrangement for

---

[16] For discussion of the challenges that computer technology poses for Article 5, see Kozolchyk, "Is Present Letter of Credit Law Up to Its Task?" 8 Geo. Mason U.L. Rev. 285 (1986).

[17] There is some authority supporting the notion that the issuer has a duty to counsel the account party at the establishment phase, but that authority is meager and rather unpersuasive. See generally ¶ 7.06.

[18] 642 F. Supp. 237 (S.D. Miss. 1986).

[19] For an example of an invoice standby, see App. C, Doc. 18.

trading in treasury securities options.[20] Under the arrangement, the credit secured the obligation of unidentified participants. The program permitted parties to join the program (and thereby become account parties) after the bank issued the credit. The Comptroller's office raised the interesting question whether, in fact, the credit was established prior to the time any party had joined the arrangement. While the question may be academic, the Comptroller's opinion letter suggested that the credit engagement might be contingent upon participation by at least one party. The opinion makes it clear that, in the Comptroller's view, there is nothing amiss in a credit that issues prior to the time that there is an identified account party and that permits account parties to be added or deleted from the program.

Establishment was also an issue in *Devco Development Corp. v. Hooker Homes, Inc.*,[21] in which the parties to a contract for the sale of improved real estate lots agreed to stipulated damages. Under the arrangement, the aggrieved seller was to recover those damages by drawing on a standby letter of credit. The parties agreed further that the credit would be held in escrow by a title company. When the buyer defaulted on the purchase agreement, the seller failed to draw on the standby, claiming that the credit never was established. The court rejected the argument, holding that whether the credit was established related only to questions of modification or revocation. The court held that, because no party attempted modification or revocation without the beneficiary's consent, the question of establishment was irrelevant.

It might be that the *Devco Development* beneficiary could have prevailed in his argument that the credit had not been established and, therefore, that he was not bound by the stipulated damages provision. If the credit was not established, arguably, the stipulated damages provision was still executory. Whatever result the law of contracts would yield in that situation, it is significant that a beneficiary might indeed be correct that delivery of the credit to a third party is insufficient to establish the credit. In the event, however, that the third party is an agent of the beneficiary or that the beneficiary instructs the issuer to send the credit to the third party, it should be difficult for the beneficiary or anyone else to argue that the credit is not established as to the beneficiary.

The concept of establishment is the letter of credit law substitute for contract law rules of offer and acceptance. During the course of the grand dispute among courts and commentators over determination of

---

[20] Comptroller of the Currency, No-Objection Letter No. 86-19, reprinted in [1988–1989 Transfer Binder] Fed. Banking L. Rep. (CCH) ¶ 84,025 (Oct. 30, 1986).

[21] 518 So. 2d 922 (Fla. Dist. Ct. App. 1987), review denied, 525 So. 2d 877 (Fla. 1988).

the moment when the issuer became obligated to the beneficiary, most of the participants used contract formation theory to fasten liability on the issuer. The language of the *Devco Development Co.* opinion is superficially consistent with the Code's resolution of the controversy with its introduction of the concept of "establishment." The trouble with the opinion and with the holding is that the court also held that payment under the letter of credit was the seller's exclusive remedy. Thus, the buyer got away with a remedy that clearly was illusory, for even if the beneficiary had drawn on the credit prior to the expiry, under the *Devco Development Co.* reasoning, the credit was revocable; and a revocable credit may be revoked at any time, even after the beneficiary presents his documents.[22] The *Amoco* holding, on the other hand, is true to the Code's rejection of the offer and acceptance theory of credits.

[3] The Operative Credit Instrument

Just as modern technology has made the rules of establishment somewhat imprecise, so it has created problems in determining what document, computer printout, or even computer memory is the operative credit instrument.

In *Savarin Corp. v. National Bank of Pakistan*,[23] the court was confused by the manner in which the issuer communicated the credit. In *Savarin*, the seller's contract with the buyer called for credits in favor of the seller. The buyer's bank telexed its New York correspondent, which advised the seller with a written form incorporating the terms of the telex. The correspondent's advice form was ambiguous. It contained paragraphs presented in a checklist format. Presumably, a check alongside a paragraph meant that the paragraph applied; no check meant that the paragraph did not apply. The correspondent had not checked some paragraphs, which therefore appeared to be inoperative. Had the paragraphs been operative, they would have made it clear that the text of the telex constituted the credit. Although it was not critical to the case, the court questioned the assumption that the language in the advice served as the credit.

In the *Savarin* case, the credit expressly incorporated the 1962 version of the Uniform Customs. Article 4 of the 1962 version stipulated that the issuer of such a credit by telex should send the credit by mail following the telex if the issuer intended the letter, rather than the telex,

---

[22] See U.C.C. § 5-106(3); Beathard v. Chicago Football Club, Inc., 419 F. Supp. 1133 (N.D. Ill. 1976).

[23] 447 F.2d 727 (2d Cir. 1971).

to be the operative instrument. In *Savarin*, the confirming bank had violated the principle of Article 4. The writing that confirmed the telex contained terms not included in the telex. If the telex was the operative instrument, the writing confirming it should have contained no additional terms. If the telex was not the operative instrument, the telex should have said that a writing would follow.

The 1983 Uniform Customs, the current version adopted by the International Chamber of Commerce, provide that any "teletransmission" may serve as a credit or as an amendment, unless it stipulates "full details to follow" or that the mail confirmation is the operative credit instrument.[24] The Uniform Customs also provide that if the issuer does not intend the teletransmission to be the operative credit instrument, the issuer must forward the confirmation without delay.[25] Absent such a stipulation, the telex serves as the operative instrument. The additional terms in the writing would be an ineffective attempt by the issuer or by the confirming bank to amend the credit unilaterally after it was established.

Not all electronic or wire messages are credits, and sending such a message does not necessarily establish a credit. Frequently, the beneficiary wants to initiate shipping arrangements and asks the buyer to have the issuer notify a correspondent that the credit has issued. In such a situation, the issuer of a credit subject to the Uniform Customs must recite in the original advice that the advice is not the operative instrument and that the credit is effective only upon mailing the confirmation. An issuer of a credit not subject to the Uniform Customs may be well advised to follow the same practice. Beneficiaries acting on such conditional advices do so at their peril.

In *Lalaco v. Universal Housing Systems of America, Inc.,*[26] the advising bank acted on a telex that was not the operative instrument. The telex apparently contained sufficient information for the advising bank to make the determination that the beneficiary's documents were facially conforming. The bank paid the beneficiary and debited the issuer's account before the confirmation arrived. Because the beneficiary's documents, on their face, satisfied the confirmation, the court held that the advising bank had behaved properly.[27]

---

[24] U.C.P. art. 12(a) (1983).

[25] Id.

[26] No. 80 Civ. 178 (WCC) (S.D.N.Y. Oct. 25, 1983).

[27] The credit nominated the advising bank as the payor bank.

[4] Signed Writing Requirement

Modern telecommunications may also create a problem for the Code's statute of frauds rule in Article 5. Section 5-104 provides that a credit must be a signed writing of the issuer. Many letters of credit are transmitted by procedures under which the issuer's clerks transmit messages to advising banks or beneficiaries electronically. In these cases, there is no writing until the recipient's equipment prints out the issuer's message.

Surely, there are limits on the extent to which courts may ignore Section 5-104. An oral engagement cannot operate as a letter of credit under the section. In *M. Golodetz Export Corp. v. Credit Lyonnais*,[28] the court rejected the argument that course of dealing between a seller and his buyer's bank gave rise to a credit engagement. In the *Golodetz* case, the bank had collected the seller's drafts over a period of time, but the court held that it was under no obligation to continue to do so.

The Code contains a liberal definition, however, of the term "signed." That definition includes any symbol intended as a signature.[29] Banks generally use a "tested telex" system involving a code for verifying the identity of a telex sender. That system appears to satisfy the Code definition. The drafters of the Code wisely refrained from cataloging devices that might serve as signatures. The official comment indicates that initials, a thumbprint, or a letterhead suffices if used by a party "with present intention to authenticate the writing."[30]

Subsection 2 of Section 5-104(2) specifically recognizes as a signed writing a telegram that "identifies the sender by an authorized identification." The subsection stipulates that the authentication may be coded and goes on to say that when an advising bank is authorized to name the issuer in an advice, the advice is a sufficient signing by the issuer for purposes of the rule. The official comment acknowledges that subsection 2 may be superfluous but that it is useful in light of customary practices.[31] The definition of "telegram" in Section 1-201(41) includes messages "transmitted by radio, teletype, cable, any mechanical method of transmission, or the like" and surely includes a telex message.[32]

---

[28] 493 F. Supp. 480 (C.D. Cal. 1980).

[29] See U.C.C. § 1-201(39).

[30] See U.C.C. § 1-201, comment 39.

[31] See U.C.C. § 5-104, comment 2.

[32] But cf. Miller v. Wells Fargo Bank Int'l Corp., 406 F.Supp. 452, 482 n.33 (S.D.N.Y. 1975) (suggesting that tested telex might not be signed writing). Article 8 of the Uniform Customs stipulates that an advising bank must take "reasonable care" to determine the authenticity of a credit it advises. See U.C.P. art. 8 (1983). One commentator maintains that a tested telex is sufficient precaution. See B. Wheble, "UCP 1974/1983 Revisions Compared and Explained (Documentary Credits)," ICC Pub. No. 411, at 19 (1984).

Presumably, the signature, whatever form it takes, must be authorized, but corporate issuers will find it difficult to convince a court that a letter signed by an officer does not contain an authorized signature. One inadvertent issuer argued, without avail, that its president was not authorized to execute a credit.[33]

In *Tosco Corp. v. FDIC*,[34] the court held that a cashier and vice-president of the issuing bank had apparent authority to execute a credit and that the FDIC, as receiver of the bank, was bound by the terms of the credit. In *Interfirst Bank v. First Federal Savings & Loan Association*,[35] the court rejected an issuer's defense based on the argument that its officer had acted without authority in issuing two credits. The *Interfirst Bank* court held that the issuer had ratified its officer's acts (1) by subsequently promising to honor the credits and (2) by failing to alert the beneficiary to the ultra vires problem as soon as the issuer learned of it.

In *Northwestern Bank v. NCF Finance Corp.*,[36] the court held that uncontroverted testimony by an officer of the issuer that he was authorized to issue credits and had issued them over a period of time, coupled with evidence of the officer's apparent authority to issue credits, was sufficient evidence to let the issue of authority go to the jury.

[5] Confirmation

The Code does not address the matter of establishing a confirmation. Section 5-106 speaks only of "a credit" when it lays down the time rules on establishment.[37] There is no reason that the Section 5-106 establishment rules should not apply to a confirmation, but the parties to the confirmation are not the same as the parties to the credit of the opening bank.

When an opening bank issues a credit, Section 5-106 stipulates that the credit is established "as regards the customer" once it is sent to him. The customer of the opening bank is usually the account party.[38] Presumably, the confirming bank's obligation as an issuer is also establish-

---

[33] See Bank of N.C., N.A. v. Rock Island Bank, 630 F.2d 1243 (7th Cir. 1980).

[34] 723 F.2d 1242 (6th Cir. 1983).

[35] 242 Kan. 181, 747 P.2d 129 (Kan. 1987).

[36] 88 N.C. App. 614, 365 S.E.2d 14 (1988).

[37] For a discussion of the "establishment" rules, see supra ¶ 5.01[2].

[38] Sometimes the requester of the credit is a local bank with whom the account party does business. If the local bank does not issue credits, it will ask a correspondent bank to do so. In that case, the correspondent may look to the local bank for reimbursement. See U.C.C. § 5-103(1)(g).

ed "as regards the customer" when it sends the confirmation to its customer, the opening bank. In the confirmation setting, the account party does not deal with the confirming bank. Most courts hold that the account party is not in privity with the confirming bank and has no contractual rights against the confirming bank.[39] The critical relationship for the confirming bank is with the opening bank.[40]

With respect to the beneficiary, the credit is established only when the beneficiary receives it. Presumably, the advice of confirmation is the operative credit instrument. Accordingly, when the beneficiary receives that advice, the credit of the opening bank and the credit of the confirming bank are established simultaneously.

¶ 5.02 AMENDING THE CREDIT

[1] Irrevocable Credit

It follows from the notion of establishment[41] that once an irrevocable credit is established, the credit engagement may not be altered in any

---

[39] See Dulien Steel Prods. Inc. v. Bankers Trust Co., 298 F.2d 836 (2d Cir. 1962); United States v. Foster Wheeler Corp., 639 F. Supp. 1266 (S.D.N.Y. 1986); Samuel Kronman & Co. v. Public Nat'l Bank, 218 A.D. 624, 218 N.Y.S. 616 (1926); Courteen Seed Co. v. Hong Kong & Shanghai Banking Corp., 216 A.D. 495, 215 N.Y.S. 525 (1926). But cf. Instituto Nacional De Comercializacion Agricola (Indeca) v. Continental Ill. Nat'l Bank & Trust Co., 530 F. Supp. 279 (N.D. Ill. 1982) (using warranty theory to create liability of confirming bank to account party of opening bank). For criticism of the *Indeca* case, see ¶ 9.04. In a subsequent opinion, the *Indeca* trial court modified its position and held that under non-Code Illinois law, there was no duty on the confirmer to provide accurate information to the account party. See Instituto Nacional De Comercializacion Agricola (Indeca) v. Continental Ill. Nat'l Bank & Trust Co., 675 F. Supp. 1515 (N.D. Ill. 1987), aff'd, 858 F.2d 1264 (7th Cir. 1988). In Chemical Bank v. Broward (In re Glade Springs, Inc.), 826 F.2d 440 (6th Cir. 1987), the court subrogated the confirming bank to the rights of the failed issuer against the account party's collateral. The *Chemical Bank* court feared that any other result would have left the account party, whose debt had been paid by the confirming bank and against whom the confirming bank had no right of reimbursement, with a windfall at the confirming bank's expense. The court relied in part on the Restatement of Restitution § 162, comments b & e (1937), and noted that its holding did not violate the independence principle. For further discussion of subrogation, see ¶ 7.05[2].

[40] For cases discussing that relationship, see Investitions-Und Handels-Bank A.G. v. United Cal. Bank Int'l, 277 F. Supp. 1005 (S.D.N.Y. 1968); J. Zeevi & Sons, Ltd. v. Grindlays Bank (Uganda) Ltd., 37 N.Y.2d 220, 333 N.E.2d 168, 371 N.Y.S.2d 892 (1975), cert. denied, 432 U.S. 866 (1975); Kingdom of Swed. v. New York Trust Co., 197 Misc. 431, 96 N.Y.S.2d 779 (Sup. Ct. 1949).

[41] For a discussion of establishment, see supra ¶ 5.01.

way without the consent of all parties.[42] Section 5-106(2) specifies two of the concerned parties and indicates that there is a period of time (after a copy of the credit is sent to the customer but before the beneficiary receives it) during which the issuer may amend an "established" credit without the beneficiary's consent.[43] That conduct may be risky if the beneficiary receives the unamended credit before he receives the amended one. In that case, the issuer may have established an amended credit with respect to the customer and may have established the original credit with respect to the beneficiary.

Any attempt by an issuer to alter the terms of the credit unilaterally cannot relieve the issuer from its obligation.[44] Attempts to do so may constitute an anticipatory breach of the credit engagement[45] that relieves the beneficiary of the duty of performing the conditions of the credit. Similarly, the agreement between the account party and the beneficiary cannot alter the terms of the credit without the consent of the issuer,[46] and the agreement of the account party and the issuer cannot

[42]The Uniform Customs rule for amendments appears in Article 10(d). Note that the Article requires not the agreement of "all parties thereto" but the agreement of the issuing bank, the confirming bank (if any), and the beneficiary. The Article clearly does not require the consent of the account party. That is the construction courts have given the Article's predecessor. See Banque Worms v. Banque Commerciale Privee, 679 F. Supp. 1173 (S.D.N.Y. 1988), aff'd per curiam, 849 F.2d 787 (2d Cir. 1988); cf. Citronelle Unit Operators Comm. v. AmSouth Bank, N.A., 536 So. 2d 1387 (Ala. 1988) (holding that, under Article 10(d), account party cannot force issuer to cancel letter of credit without beneficiary's consent). That is not to suggest, however, that the issuing bank and the beneficiary can alter the account party's obligations to the issuer. See infra notes 56, 57. Note also that U.C.P. Article 12(d) requires the issuer to advise amendments through the same bank that advised the original credit.

[43]See Goodwin Bros. Leasing, Inc. v. Citizens Bank, 587 F.2d 730 (5th Cir. 1979).

[44]See, e.g., Barclays Bank D.C.O. v. Mercantile Nat'l Bank, 481 F.2d 1224 (5th Cir. 1973), cert. dismissed, 414 U.S. 1139 (1974); Weyerhaeuser Co. v. First Nat'l Bank, 27 U.C.C. Rep. Serv. (Callaghan) 777 (S.D. Iowa 1979).

[45]See Savarin Corp. v. National Bank of Pak., 447 F.2d 727 (2d Cir. 1971); Decor by Nikkei Int'l, Inc. v. Federal Republic of Nig., 497 F. Supp. 893 (S.D.N.Y. 1980), aff'd, 647 F.2d 300 (2d Cir. 1981), cert. denied, 454 U.S. 1148 (1982); National Bank & Trust Co. of N. Am. v. J.L.M. Int'l, Inc., 421 F. Supp. 1269 (S.D.N.Y. 1976); Atari, Inc. v. Harris Trust & Sav. Bank, 599 F. Supp 592 (N.D. Ill. 1984), aff'd in part, rev'd in part mem., 785 F.2d 312 (7th Cir. 1986). See generally ¶ 9.02[2].

[46]See Asociacion De Azucareros De Guat. v. United States Nat'l Bank, 423 F.2d 638 (9th Cir. 1970); AMF Head Sports Wear, Inc. v. Ray Scott's All-Am. Sports Club, Inc., 448 F. Supp. 222 (D. Ariz. 1978); Housing Sec., Inc. v. Maine Nat'l Bank, 391 A.2d 311 (Me. 1978); Dubose Steel, Inc. v. Branch Banking & Trust Co., 72 N.C. App. 598, 324 S.E.2d 859 (1985), review denied, 314 N.C. 115, 332 S.E.2d 480 (1985).

amend the credit without the consent of the beneficiary.[47]

In *American National Bank & Trust Co. v. Hamilton Industries International Inc.*,[48] the credit ran to a French bank as beneficiary.[49] That bank had issued its guaranty to a Saudi Arabian medical center to secure Hamilton's bid under a subcontract. The letter of credit in turn secured the French bank's guaranty. After the credit was established, the French bank and the Saudi beneficiary of the guaranty amended the guaranty. When the French bank later paid under the guaranty and sought repayment under the credit, the court held that, because the broad transaction involved "two linked letters of credit,"[50] the French bank and the Saudi beneficiary could not modify the guaranty without the agreement of the credit issuer.

The key to the *American National Bank* court's ruling is the fact that the original form of the guaranty was attached to the letter of credit. The court felt that modification of the guaranty by the French Bank and the Saudi beneficiary was an attempt to modify the original letter of credit without the consent of the credit issuer and the account party. The Court of Appeals for the Seventh Circuit reversed the holding in

---

[47] See Banco Nacional De Desarrolla v. Mellon Bank, N.A., 558 F. Supp. 1265 (W.D. Pa. 1983), rev'd, 726 F.2d 87 (3d Cir. 1984); Data Gen. Corp. v. Citizens Nat'l Bank, 502 F. Supp. 776 (D. Conn. 1980); West Virginia Hous. Dev. Fund v. Sroka, 415 F. Supp. 1107 (W.D. Pa. 1976); City Nat'l Bank v. Westland Towers Apartments, 152 Mich. App. 136, 393 N.W.2d 554 (1986) (per curiam); cf. Citronelle Unit Operators Comm. v. AmSouth Bank, N.A., 536 So. 2d 1387 (Ala. 1988) (holding that account party cannot force issuer to cancel letter of credit without beneficiary's consent); Guilford Pattern Works, Inc. v. United Bank, 655 F. Supp. 378 (D. Colo. 1987) (decision ignoring U.C.C. § 5-106(2) but holding that letter of credit is contract and that contracts may not be amended without consent of all parties); Muir v. Transportation Mut. Ins. Co., 107 Pa. Commw. Ct. 638, 529 A.2d 534 (1987) (holding that plan of rehabilitation of insolvent insurance company may not alter letter of credit terms of standby securing debtor's reinsurance obligations unless beneficiary reinsurer consents, but that reinsurer's failure to object to plan could have served as such consent).

[48] 583 F. Supp. 164 (N.D. Ill. 1984), rev'd sub nom. Banque Paribas v. Hamilton Indus. Int'l, Inc., 767 F.2d 380 (7th Cir. 1985).

[49] There was a drafting problem in the credit, which referred to the Saudi party as the beneficiary and to the French bank as the advising bank, but which in other respects indicated that the parties intended the French bank to be the beneficiary. The court treated the French bank as the beneficiary.

[50] American Nat'l Bank & Trust Co. v. Hamilton Indus. Int'l, Inc., 583 F. Supp. 164, 172 (N.D. Ill. 1984), rev'd sub nom. Banque Paribas v. Hamilton Indus. Int'l, Inc., 767 F.2d 380 (7th Cir. 1985). The court's ruling rested on other grounds as well, notably the view that the guaranty modifications rendered fraudulent the French bank's presentation to the issuer of a certificate that stated that the bank had paid under the guaranty. For a general discussion of that and similar fraud defenses, see ¶ 7.04[4][a].

American National Bank,[51] however, holding that summary judgment was improper because there was a factual dispute: whether the letter of credit and the guaranty were linked.

In *Fiat Motors of North America, Inc. v. Mellon Bank, N.A.*,[52] the credit required the issuer to honor invoices of the beneficiary. After the credit issued, the beneficiary and the account party entered into an incentive program that gave the account party delayed payment terms. When the beneficiary presented invoices under the incentive program, it instructed the issuer not to pay them until the account party had resold the goods or until 120 days had passed. The issuer argued that the beneficiary and the account party were attempting to alter the terms of the issuer's undertaking by imposing an additional condition, that is, that the issuer monitor the account party's sales. The *Fiat Motors* court brushed the argument aside, holding that there was no modification of the credit. The issuer's argument merited more consideration than the court gave it.

Letter of credit issuers deal in documents, not factual determinations extrinsic to documents; and issuers price their letter of credit product with regard to reimbursement risk and document examination costs, not off-premises monitoring expense. Federal regulators warn issuers against rendering credits payable on the kind of factual condition that the account party and the beneficiary forced on the issuer in the *Fiat Motors* case.[53]

In *First National Bank v. Carmouche*,[54] the account party and the beneficiary, after the beneficiary had negotiated its draft, asked the issuer to extend the term of the credit undertaking. The court held that since all parties have to agree in order to amend a credit, it was not bad faith for the issuer to refuse. It might have added that any change in the terms of the credit might affect the negotiating bank, whose consent presumably would be necessary also.[55]

There is judicial authority suggesting that an issuer and a beneficiary may agree to modify the terms of the credit between themselves.[56]

---

[51] Banque Paribas v. Hamilton Indus. Int'l, Inc., 767 F.2d 380 (7th Cir. 1985).

[52] 827 F.2d 924 (3d Cir. 1987).

[53] See Comptroller of the Currency, Interpretive Ruling, 12 C.F.R. § 7.7016(d) (1989); Office of Thrift Supervision, Regulation, 12 C.F.R. § 545.48 (1990).

[54] 515 So. 2d 785 (La. 1987).

[55] Cf. Centennial Indus., Inc. v. Union Trust Co., 75 Md. App. 202, 540 A.2d 1169 (Ct. Spec. App.), cert. denied, 313 Md. 505, 545 A.2d 1343 (1988) (holding that it is not bad faith for issuer to refuse to amend credit so that account party's suppliers can comply with its terms).

[56] See Chase Manhattan Bank v. Equibank, 394 F. Supp. 352 (W.D. Pa. 1975); cf. Continental Time Corp. v. Merchants Bank, 117 Misc. 2d 907, 459 N.Y.S.2d 396 (Sup. Ct. 1983) (suggesting that collecting bank as agent of beneficiary can waive is-

That modification cannot affect the rights of the account party without his consent and affects only the rights and duties of the issuer and the beneficiary with respect to each other.[57]

Section 5-104 requires not just that the credit be a signed writing but that the confirmation and amendments be signed writings as well.[58] The provision does not mean that the waiver of an account party or a beneficiary must be in writing. In *City National Bank v. Westland Towers Apartments*,[59] the court explicitly rejected that argument. It is common practice in the banking industry to obtain waivers by telephone. The *City National Bank* case is persuasive authority against the extension of the signed writing requirement to the practice of obtaining oral waivers.[60]

The practice of using a credit to cover numerous transactions that entail amendments can be problematic. Article 13 of the Uniform Customs stipulates that when an issuer is instructed to issue a credit similar to an earlier credit that has been amended, the issuer should not include the amendments in the new credit. The article discourages the practice of calling for "similar" credits.

Sometimes the parties use a long-term credit or a revolving credit to cover a number of transactions. In *Banco Nacional De Desarrollo v. Mel-*

---

suer's obligation to honor by presenting documents on a "collection basis"). But cf. Anchor Centre Partners, Ltd. v. Mercantile Bank, N.A., 783 S.W.2d 108 (Mo. Ct. App. 1989), aff'd on rehearing, id. (holding that account party and beneficiary were not bound by amendment issued unilaterally by issuer); Fina Supply, Inc. v. Abilene Nat'l Bank, 726 S.W.2d 537 (Tex. 1987) (holding that credit could not be reformed in accordance with understanding between issuer and beneficiary, because to do so would alter obligation of account party).

[57] See Lafayette Corp. v. Bank of Boston Int'l S., 723 F. Supp. 1461 (S.D. Fla. 1989); Eriksson v. Refiners Export Co., 264 A.D. 525, 35 N.Y.S.2d 829 (1942). For a discussion of the effect of such a modification on the issuer's right of reimbursement, see ¶ 9.03.

[58] It is the issuer, or the confirming bank in the case of a confirmation, that must sign the writing. U.C.C. § 5-104(1). The Code does not require the other interested parties to sign the amendment. Amoco Oil Co. v. First Bank & Trust Co., 759 S.W.2d 877 (Mo. Ct. App. 1988) (dictum). Article 12 of the Uniform Customs extends the requirements for the transmission of credits to the transmission of amendments.

[59] 107 Mich. App. 213, 309 N.W.2d 209 (1981), rev'd on other grounds, 413 Mich. 938, 320 N.W.2d 881 (1982).

[60] But cf. Banco Nacional De Desarrolla v. Mellon Bank, N.A., 558 F. Supp. 1265 (W.D. Pa. 1983), rev'd, 726 F.2d 87 (3d Cir. 1984) (holding that beneficiary's consent must be express and may not be inferred from course of dealing); Pioneer Bank & Trust Co. v. Seiko Sporting Goods, U.S.A. Co., 184 Ill. App. 3d 783, 540 N.E.2d 808 (1989) (requiring writing when evidence shows that bank's procedure requires it). Comment 1 to Section 5-104 makes it clear that the section itself does not require a waiver to be written.

lon Bank, N.A.,[61] an importer caused Mellon Bank to issue a credit in the initial amount of about $98,000 to cover a purchase of beef from a Nicaraguan seller. Subsequently, the importer and the seller entered into additional contracts for the importation of beef, and Mellon issued amendments to the initial credit to cover the later transactions. The advising bank paid the seller for all shipments, but Mellon refused to reimburse, on the ground that the seller's documents for one shipment were incomplete.

The trial court ruled that the beneficiary never had agreed to the amendment and that therefore, since the missing documents were called for by that amendment, Mellon was bound to reimburse.[62] The Court of Appeals for the Third Circuit reversed. Noting that the original credit would have expired but for the amendment, and that nothing in the original credit or in the first fourteen amendments had anticipated the shipment of beef in question, the court saw the "amendment" as a new credit to which the beneficiary's assent was not necessary.

[2] Revocable Credit

With one important exception, the revocable credit by its nature may be amended or revoked at any time, even after the beneficiary presents complying documents.[63] The exception to that general rule applies when the credit has been paid or otherwise honored by an authorized third party. Often an issuer designates a third party, usually a correspondent of the issuer, to make payment.

If a Detroit bank, for example, issues to a seller a credit payable in sterling, it will designate its London correspondent as the payor bank. At other times, the issuer does not designate a payor bank but invites banks to negotiate the beneficiary's drafts. If the underlying contract calls for payment to the English seller in U.S. dollars, the Detroit bank may issue a credit containing a negotiation clause whereby the bank engages to pay "drawers, endorsers, and bona fide holders" of drafts drawn under the credit. This language permits the beneficiary to shop among London banks for the most favorable terms.

In these two examples, the London bank is paying or negotiating "under the terms of the original credit." Section 5-106(4) stipulates that

---

[61] 726 F.2d 87 (3d Cir. 1984).

[62] Banco Nacional De Desarrolla v. Mellon Bank, N.A., 558 F. Supp. 1265 (W.D. Pa. 1983), rev'd, 726 F.2d 87 (3d Cir. 1984).

[63] See U.C.C. § 5-106(3); Beathard v. Chicago Football Club, Inc., 419 F. Supp. 1133 (N.D. Ill. 1976). For further discussion of revocable credits, see ¶¶ 1.10, 4.06[2][a], 5.03[1].

once a person who is authorized to pay or to negotiate does so, the issuer of a revocable credit loses the right to revoke and must reimburse.[64] The rule of Article 9 of the Uniform Customs is somewhat narrower than that of Section 5-106(4). The former protects only "a branch or bank with which a revocable credit has been made available" if the branch or bank has paid, negotiated, accepted, or incurred a deferred payment obligation before it receives notice of the credit's revocation.

The parties, by agreement, also may cancel a credit.[65] In *Offshore Trading Co. v. Citizens National Bank*,[66] the credit recited that it would expire if, within five banking days after its issuance, the beneficiary failed to cause a reciprocal credit to issue.[67] Prior to the termination of the five-day period, the beneficiary drew on the credit certifying that the account party was in default on the underlying contract. The issuer declined to pay and asserted as one defense the fact that the beneficiary had failed to have the reciprocal credit issue. The *Offshore Trading* court held that the requirement for the reciprocal credit was a condition subsequent, not a condition precedent, and that the credit was a binding obligation of the issuer on the day that the beneficiary drew.

¶ 5.03   TERMINATING THE CREDIT

A credit can be terminated in one of three ways:

1. It may be revoked, if it is revocable.
2. It can be satisfied by payment, by acceptance, or by negotiation.
3. It can expire by its terms when a beneficiary fails to satisfy the credit's conditions prior to the expiry date.

[1]   Revoking the Credit

It is unfortunate that the question of revocation has consumed so much judicial energy. Revocable credits have little commercial utility. The

---

[64] There may be some conflict of opinion on this view that only a party authorized to negotiate is protected by Section 5-106(4). The conflict has not arisen here but is evident in Section 5-114(2)(a). Compare Eberth & Ellinger, "Assignment and Presentation of Documents in Commercial Credit Transactions," 24 Ariz. L. Rev. 277, 293–294 (1982), with Harfield, "Article 5—Trade Without Tears, or Around Letters of Credit in 17 Sections," 1952 Wis. L. Rev. 298, 307–308. For a discussion of this problem under Section 5-114(2)(a), see ¶ 8.01.

[65] See Worldwide Sugar Co. v. Royal Bank of Can., 609 F. Supp. 19 (S.D.N.Y. 1984).

[66] 650 F. Supp. 1487 (D. Kan. 1987).

[67] For discussion of the general inadvisability of rendering credits subject to any factual conditions as opposed to documentary conditions, see ¶ 2.05[2].

Uniform Customs attempt to protect banks against a court's unanticipated holding that an undertaking is a credit. Article 7(c) provides that a credit is revocable unless it recites that it is irrevocable. The Code leaves the question to the courts, and the courts, preferring a binding promise to an illusory one, usually hold the credit to be irrevocable.[68] The question arises when the issuer acts inadvertently and does not appreciate the significance of his signed engagement, which, unbeknownst to him, falls within the "credit" definition.

In the event that such a revocable credit does rear its head, Section 5-106(4) provides that the issuer must revoke it before any person (usually, the issuer's correspondent) authorized to honor or to negotiate the beneficiary's drafts has done so.[69] In cases where no such protected third party enters the transaction, the issuer may revoke at any time and without notice.[70]

In *Beathard v. Chicago Football Club, Inc.*,[71] the issuer revoked after the beneficiaries presented their drafts and accompanying documents; and the court sustained the issuer's position.[72] There are some credits that are revocable only upon certain specified conditions.[73] In these cases, courts should require strict compliance with the credit's conditions for revocation, just as they generally require strict compliance by a beneficiary of the credit's conditions for payment.[74] In one such case, *Phoenix Mutual Life Insurance Co. v. Seafarers Officers & Employees Pension Plan*,[75] moreover, the court made it clear that the in-

---

[68] See, e.g., Data Gen. Corp. v. Citizens Nat'l Bank, 502 F. Supp. 776 (D. Conn. 1980); Weyerhaeuser Co. v. First Nat'l Bank, 27 U.C.C. Rep. Serv. (Callaghan) 777 (S.D. Iowa 1979); West Virginia Hous. Dev. Fund v. Sroka, 415 F. Supp. 1107 (W.D. Pa. 1976); Lewis State Bank v. Advance Mortgage Corp., 362 So. 2d 406 (Fla. Dist. Ct. App. 1978); see also Fla. Stat. Ann. § 675.5-103(1)(a) (West 1966) (nonconforming version of U.C.C. § 5-103 rendering irrevocable credit that is not designated revocable); La. Rev. Stat. Ann. § 10:5-103(1)(a) (West 1983) (same). But cf. Dennis Chapman Toyota, Inc. v. Belle State Bank, 759 S.W.2d 330 (Mo. Ct. App. 1988) (holding that credit that called for notice of termination by issuer was revocable). See generally ¶¶ 1.10, 4.06[2][a]. For general discussion of construction rules and the revocability issue, see ¶ 4.08[4].

[69] For a discussion of negotiation, see ¶¶ 1.02[3], 10.02[3].

[70] See U.C.C. § 5-106(3).

[71] 419 F. Supp. 1133 (N.D. Ill. 1976).

[72] But cf. Conoco, Inc. v. Norwest Bank Mason City, N.A., 767 F.2d 470 (8th Cir. 1985) (case with similar facts that reached contrary holding).

[73] See, e.g., Toyota Indus. Trucks U.S.A., Inc. v. Citizens Nat'l Bank, 611 F.2d 465 (3d Cir. 1979); Fair Pavilions, Inc. v. First Nat'l City Bank, 19 N.Y.2d 512, 227 N.E.2d 839, 281 N.Y.S.2d 23 (1967).

[74] For discussion of the strict compliance standard, see ¶ 6.03.

[75] 128 F.R.D. 25 (E.D.N.Y. 1989).

dependence principle applies to termination of a credit just as it applies to performance of the credit. In *Phoenix Mutual*, the credit terminated in the event the beneficiary failed to pay an installment under a sale-leaseback arrangement. The beneficiary argued that the installment was not due under the terms of the lease. The court held—correctly, it seems—that it mattered only that the beneficiary had failed to make the payment, not whether the failure was justified under the lease.

In *Merchants Bank v. Credit Suisse Bank*,[76] the presenting bank, which was also the advising bank and apparently was acting as agent for the beneficiary and not in its capacity as advising bank, presented the beneficiary's documents to the issuer. The issuer rejected them as non-conforming and asked the presenting bank to authorize the issuer "to present the documents on a collection basis."[77] The presenting bank agreed, and the *Merchants Bank* court opinion asserted that, once the presenting bank agreed to that authorization, "the irrevocability of the letter of credit [was] destroyed."[78]

It is not clear from the *Merchants Bank* opinion whether the parties had agreed with the court's assertion, which was not indispensable to any of the court's rulings on the liability questions at issue. The implication that the interested parties themselves can agree to terminate a credit is valid,[79] but the suggestion that the instruction to the issuer to present the documents to the account party for payment, by itself, constitutes such an agreement by the beneficiary deserves more explanation than the court provides.

The Uniform Rules for Collections[80] indicate that instructions to a bank to handle an item for collection is inconsistent with a presentation to an issuer for payment.[81] It is not clear from the *Merchants Bank* opinion, however, why, just as the presenting bank changed its instructions once, it could not change them again and reinstate the presentation as one for payment under the credit. If the presenting bank were to alter the nature of the presentation from one for collection to one for pay-

---

[76] 585 F. Supp. 304 (S.D.N.Y. 1984).

[77] Id. at 306.

[78] Id. at 306–307.

[79] See supra note 65.

[80] International Chamber of Commerce, Uniform Rules for Collections, ICC Pub. No. 322, general provision and definition B1(i) (1978).

[81] The credit in *Merchants Bank* was apparently a payment credit (i.e., one under which the issuer must pay the beneficiary's drafts). A presentation to the issuer on a collection basis constitutes a request that the issuer deliver the documents to the account party against payment. See International Chamber of Commerce, Uniform Rules for Collections, ICC Pub. No. 322, general provision and definition B1(i) (1978).

ment under the credit prior to the credit's expiry, the issuer would not seem to be harmed in any way, nor would any of the other parties. Absent more support than the *Merchants Bank* opinion provides, courts might be reluctant to rely heavily on this dictum.[82]

In *Bryant v. Kerr*,[83] the beneficiary of a credit claimed that the account party was in default on the underlying contract when the FDIC, as liquidator of the failed issuer, disaffirmed the credit obligation. The *Bryant* court held that the FDIC had no power to disaffirm[84] and that since the credit was in force, the beneficiary could not take advantage of the underlying contract's default provision.

[2] Honoring the Credit

Issuers may select one of four ways to honor the beneficiary's draft or demand for payment: payment, acceptance, negotiation, or incurring a deferred payment obligation.[85] The event, which must be specified in the credit (payment, acceptance, negotiation or incurring a deferred payment obligation) must occur before the expiration date. If it does, the credit engagement has been honored; and the issuer has satisfied the credit's terms. In the case of an acceptance or a deferred payment obligation, the beneficiary does not have his money. He holds an acceptance or a deferred payment obligation, and the acceptor or obligor may still dishonor at maturity. In that event, the holder of the acceptance may sue on the acceptance as a negotiable instrument,[86] or he may sue on the credit.[87] Similarly, the obligee of the deferred payment obligation should be able to sue on the obligation or on the credit.

---

[82] Cf. Michael Doyle & Assocs. Ltd. v. Bank of Montreal, 140 D.L.R.3d 596 (B.C. 1982) (holding that presentation of documents on collection basis does not prejudice rights of beneficiary). But cf. Forestal Mimosa Ltd. v. Oriental Credit Ltd., [1986] 1 W.L.R. 631 (C.A.) (suggesting that once bank presents documents "on clean collection basis not under L/C," it might be regarded as having admitted that documents do not comply with credit's conditions).

[83] 726 S.W.2d 373 (Mo. Ct. App. 1987).

[84] For discussion of the right of the FDIC, as receiver of a failed bank, to reject letter of credit obligations, see ¶ 12.01[1][a].

[85] For discussion of the payment, acceptance, negotiation, and deferred payment credits, see ¶ 1.02. The 1983 Uniform Customs differentiate these four methods of honoring a credit. See U.C.P. art. 10 (1983).

[86] See U.C.C. § 3-413(1).

[87] See Voest-Alpine Int'l Corp. v. Chase Manhattan Bank, N.A., 707 F.2d 680 (2d Cir. 1983). For a discussion of the two sources of liability, see ¶ 2.08[4].

If the credit authorizes negotiation, the beneficiary has the right to negotiate his draft without recourse by the issuer against him.[88] That is, if the draft is drawn on some party other than the issuer (e.g., the buyer account party), and if the third party dishonors the draft after the issuer honors it, the issuer has no rights against the drawer on his contract as a drawer under negotiable instruments law.[89] Sometimes, moreover, the drawer-beneficiary may be able to convince the negotiating bank to take a draft without recourse.[90] In that case, subsequent dishonor of the draft by the issuer is a matter of concern only to the negotiating bank.[91]

There are two ways to characterize the negotiating bank's position. First is the view that the negotiating bank is an agent that seeks reimbursement from its principal for making an authorized payment. If the drawer has drawn and endorsed without recourse, the negotiating bank holding the dishonored draft clearly has no action against the issuer on the draft.[92] Thus, its recovery of reimbursement from the issuer depends on its showing that the beneficiary complied with the credit and therefore that it complied with the instructions of its principal (the issuer). The act of the negotiating bank otherwise would be unauthorized, and consequently it would not be entitled to reimbursement.

Under a second view advanced by some commentators and by older and foreign authorities, the negotiating bank is a beneficiary of the negotiation credit.[93] That view makes good sense, and it gives the negotiating bank a right to payment under the credit itself rather than on any agency theory. Under this second theory, the negotiating bank still must show that the named beneficiary's documents comply. Under either theory, the negotiating bank does not obtain reimbursement unless the documents are in order.

Sometimes the negotiating bank questions the good order of the beneficiary's documents. In that case, it enters a provisional credit in fa-

---

[88] See U.C.P. art. 10(a)(iv) (1983).

[89] For that contract, see U.C.C. § 3-403(2).

[90] In fact, some beneficiaries insist that the credit be a "without recourse" credit, which means that the credit expressly permits the beneficiary to draw and endorse without recourse.

[91] If the negotiating bank has questions about the documents, it negotiates the draft but reserves its right to charge its customer if the opening bank dishonors. This practice is common. See Wheble, "Uniform Customs and Practice for Documentary Credits (1974 Revision)," 1975 J. Bus. L. 281, 284.

[92] No person is liable on a negotiable instrument unless he signs it. U.C.C. § 3-401.

[93] See, e.g., Harfield, supra note 64, at 307–308; McCurdy, supra note 11, at 322; accord Banco Nacional Ultramarino v. First Nat'l Bank, 289 F. 169 (D. Mass. 1923).

vor of the beneficiary or otherwise pays "under reserve."[94] If the issuer
does not honor the draft, the negotiating bank reverses the provisional
entry on its books or seeks repayment of the payment under reserve.
The beneficiary may then make a claim against the issuer on the credit
itself and succeeds if the presentation is conforming.

In theory, the issuer has initially satisfied the credit once the draft is
paid, accepted, or negotiated, or if the issuer incurs a deferred payment
obligation. In the latter three cases, there can be a subsequent dishonor.
In all four events, problems can arise in determining the time when the
events occur.

Clearly, completion of the underlying transaction out of which the
credit arises does not terminate the credit. The credit is independent of
that underlying transaction. In *C.A. Cavendes, Sociedad Financiera v.
John Alden Life Insurance Co.*,[95] the credit, a standby, secured payments under a stock purchase agreement. When the buyer paid for the
stock, it sought return of the letter of credit from the seller, but the court
held that the seller could hold the credit until it expired.

That is not to say that the parties to a credit may not cancel it. In
Worldwide Sugar Co. v. Royal Bank of Canada,[96] the account party, the
beneficiary, and the issuer agreed to the termination of the credit when
the beneficiary and the account party chose to effect payment outside
the credit transaction. The distinction between *Cavendes* and *Worldwide Sugar* lies in the critical fact that all parties agreed to the cancelation in the latter case, while, in the former case, the beneficiary did not
agree.[97]

The fourth method of honoring a credit is by incurring a deferred
payment obligation. On this question, there is little litigation—a consequence, no doubt, of the fact that such credits are comparatively rare.
The deferred payment credit is similar to the acceptance credit, the only
difference being that there is no negotiable instrument for the issuer to
accept. In the deferred payment credit transaction, the beneficiary presents a demand for payment that is not in negotiable form; and the issuer usually signals its willingness to pay by advice. Issues that arise in
the deferred payment setting may well find easy solution by analogy
with the acceptance credit, but there should be no confusing the two
credits.

---

[94]See, e.g., Banque De L'Indochine Et De Suez S.A. v. J.H. Rayner (Mincing
Lane) Ltd., [1983] 1 Lloyd's Rep. 228 (C.A.).

[95]591 F. Supp. 362 (app. A) (S.D. Fla. 1984).

[96]609 F. Supp. 19 (S.D.N.Y. 1984).

[97]The *Worldwide Sugar* cancelation is similar to the process of amending a
credit. That process also requires the assent of all parties. See generally supra ¶ 5.02.

The intriguing question is whether the holder of the deferred payment obligation is entitled to the same benefits that accrue to the holder of an acceptance. One surmises that the deferred payment obligation, not being a negotiable instrument, should not benefit from holder in due course principles. In that case, the deferred payment obligation holder would not be able to defeat an attaching creditor[98] and might not be able to benefit from the holder in due course protection that the common law fashioned in fraud cases.[99] The language of Article 5, however, suggests that persons who are transferees of nonnegotiable demands do have the benefit of holder in due course status if, but for the fact that they are not holders of a negotiable instrument, they otherwise qualify as holders in due course. In short, if the transferee takes the deferred payment obligation for value, in good faith, and without knowledge of any defenses or claims, the transferee of a nonnegotiable demand obtains the rights of a holder in due course of a negotiable instrument.[100] One cannot deny that the notion is a commercial anomaly, but the plain language of Section 5-114(2)(a) supports it.

[a] Time of Honor

The expiry date of a credit is the time by which the beneficiary must present the documents, not the time by which the issuer must pay. In *Morgan Guaranty Trust Co. v. Vend Technologies, Inc.,*[101] the court held that it was proper under the Uniform Customs for the issuer to honor on January 4, 1983 a credit whose expiry was January 1, 1983, so long as the issuer received the documents before the expiry as extended by Article 39(a) of the 1974 Uniform Customs.

In general, the time when honor occurs is a matter of negotiable instruments law, not letter of credit law. In *Tranarg, C.A. v. Banca Commerciale Italiana,*[102] the opening bank received the beneficiary's draft, decided to honor it, and issued a check or bank draft to the confirming bank. The account party sought to enjoin payment on the ground that the beneficiary's conduct had been fraudulent.[103] The *Tranarg* court held that there could be no injunction if the credit had been paid. The

---

[98] See ¶ 10.06[3][b].

[99] Under those cases, which are codified in U.C.C. § 5-114(2), a holder in due course of the beneficiary's draft could defeat the fraud defense recognized by the *Sztejn* rule. See generally ¶ 8.01[1].

[100] See U.C.C. § 5-114(2)(b). See also ¶ 8.01[3].

[101] 100 A.D.2d 782, 474 N.Y.S.2d 67 (1984).

[102] 90 Misc. 2d 829, 396 N.Y.S.2d 761 (Sup. Ct. 1977).

[103] For a discussion of the fraud question, see ¶ 7.04.

court then looked to the final payment rules of Article 4 of the Code[104] and concluded that, as a matter of negotiable instruments law, the credit had been paid. In *Pan-American Bank & Trust Co. v. National City Bank*,[105] the court held that a bank "negotiated" a draft when it took the draft in a fashion that rendered the bank a holder under negotiable instruments law. These two cases make sense, though the *Pan-American* rule may need a little refinement.[106]

In *Bazaar, Inc. v. Exchange National Bank*,[107] the account party obtained a preliminary injunction in the trial court against payment of the credit by the issuer after the issuer had accepted a time draft drawn under the credit. On appeal, the court dissolved the injunction on the ground that the injunction came too late. The court held that when the issuer accepted the time draft, it had honored the credit.

[b] Negotiation Credits

Flagship Cruises, Ltd. v. New England Merchants National Bank[108] raises a question that *Pan-American* did not anticipate and that confuses somewhat the rule for determining the time when negotiation occurs. In *Flagship*, the credit stipulated that drafts were to be negotiated no later than November 3, 1972. The issuer was a Boston bank. On October 31, 1972, the beneficiary, or a related company, which the court considered to be an authorized drawer under the credit, presented drafts and documents to a New York bank.

Unfortunately for the beneficiary, the New York bank routed the drafts not to its letter of credit department but to its international collections department. Apparently, the latter department, though the opinion is silent on the point, did not give value to the beneficiary and did not "present" the drafts and the documents to the issuer until nine business days later. The *Flagship* court remanded the case for trial to determine whether that delay, which brought the documents to the issuer on November 9, rendered the presentment timely.

The opinion recites that, had the documents been routed to the New York bank's letter of credit department, payment would have been made. Later the opinion asserted that if "negotiation took place on No-

---

[104] See U.C.C. § 4-213.

[105] 6 F.2d 762 (2d Cir.), cert. denied, 269 U.S. 554 (1925).

[106] See infra ¶ 5.03[2][b].

[107] 168 Ill. App. 3d 811, 523 N.E.2d 57 (1988), appeal denied, 122 Ill. 2d 595, 530 N.E.2d 239 (1988).

[108] 569 F.2d 699 (1st Cir. 1978).

vember 3,"[109] the trial court could not rule as a matter of law that delivery of the documents to the Boston bank nine business days later was timely "presentment."[110] The court concluded — incorrectly, it seems — that the question was one of fact, not one of law.

Although the opinion does not provide sufficient facts, it is clear from *Flagship* that the credit was available by negotiation. It was either freely negotiable or negotiable only at the New York bank. It makes sense to say that delivery of the drafts and documents to the New York bank by the beneficiary constituted timely presentment for negotiation. It is not clear why the New York bank misrouted these drafts to its international collections department rather than routing them to its letter of credit department. In many banks, the credit and international collection operations are adjacent or are part of the same international department. The mistake may well have been the fault of the bank, not that of the beneficiary. If the mistake was the bank's, the court should not hold that the beneficiary failed to negotiate on or before November 3 and should not penalize the beneficiary. When the beneficiary delivered the endorsed drafts to the New York bank on October 31, the bank became a holder of those drafts[111]; and, under the rule of the *Pan-American* case, at that point the beneficiary had negotiated the drafts before November 3. If the bank's delay in notifying the issuer of the negotiation is longer than banking custom permits, the loss should fall on the New York bank, not on the beneficiary.

If the facts show that the beneficiary's presentation of the documents to the New York bank was misleading, if testimony concerning banking usage sanctions the New York bank's failure to read the credit that accompanied the draft, and if the New York bank's rights against the issuer were prejudiced by the beneficiary's conduct, then the presentment was improper. In the case of improper presentment, the loss should fall on the beneficiary, who failed to negotiate the draft before November 3. It may be better to say that it is not enough to make the negotiating bank a holder, as *Pan-American* does, to satisfy the requirement of negotiation. Rather, it is better to say that the beneficiary must negotiate the documents in a way that permits the negotiating bank to protect itself against the issuing bank.[112]

---

[109] Id. at 702.

[110] Id.

[111] See U.C.C. § 1-201(20).

[112] For a case holding that the time of presentment of mailed documents is the time the documents are received by the issuer, see First State Bank v. Shuford Mills, Inc., 716 S.W.2d 649 (Tex. Ct. App. 1986).

In *First National Bank v. Carmouche*,[113] the court held that negotiation of a beneficiary's draft did not occur until the issuer honored it. In the *Carmouche* case, which involved a negotiation credit, the court was concerned with the fact that the "negotiation," as the court had defined that term, did not occur until after the expiry, though the beneficiary had submitted the draft prior to the expiry. The court held that payment is proper in that situation, but it apparently misconstrued the negotiation concept.

If the beneficiary of a credit presents his draft directly to the issuer, he has elected not to negotiate—negotiation being the act of transferring the draft for value and with proper endorsement at another bank.[114] The failure of the beneficiary to negotiate may not relieve the issuer of the obligation to honor the draft.[115] If a credit's expiry is expressed in terms of negotiation, as in credits that recite, "Drafts drawn under this credit must be negotiated on or before May 1, 1991," the beneficiary has satisfied the expiry by presenting the draft to the issuer prior to the specified date, as the *Carmouche* court held.

In the event the issuer of a negotiation credit nominates another bank to negotiate the draft, the beneficiary must present his draft at the counters of the nominated bank. If the nominated bank fails to honor the draft, the issuer is liable to pay.[116] Most bank issuers take the position that that duty is conditioned on the beneficiary's presentation of the documents at the counters of the issuer prior to the expiry—a position that has not been litigated to date. In short, for the beneficiary of a credit that calls for presentation of documents at a nominated bank that has not confirmed the credit and therefore has not added its own obligation, there is the risk that the nominated bank will refuse to negotiate and that there will be insufficient time after that refusal for the beneficiary to get the documents to the issuer prior to the expiry.[117]

---

[113] 504 So. 2d 1153 (La. Ct. App.), rev'd on other grounds, 515 So. 2d 785 (La. 1987).

[114] In the event the credit calls for drafts drawn on the account party, the issuer may in fact negotiate. In Kydon Compania Naviera S.A. v. National Westminster Bank Ltd., [1981] 1 Lloyd's Rep. 68 (Q.B.), the court held that "issuance" of the draft by the beneficiary to a bank as assignee of the credit did not constitute negotiation.

[115] See U.C.P. art. 10(a)(iv) (1983).

[116] Id.

[117] An analogous situation arises when a credit calls for the beneficiary to present his documents to the confirming bank. If the confirming bank dishonors, the question arises whether the beneficiary must present his documents to the issuer in advance of the expiry. That question also has not been litigated. A similar question has, however. The question arose in Northern Trust Co. v. Community Bank, 873 F.2d 227 (9th Cir. 1989), where the beneficiary presented the documents to the open-

[3] Expiration of the Credit
[a] Hints of a Relaxed Rule

There is an unsettling implication in the *Flagship* case—the idea that some additional, reasonable time for presentment is permissible after the expiration date. It is the general rule of credits that time is of the essence and that banks and courts will enforce the credit's expiry date strictly. Drafts under a negotiation credit must be negotiated before the expiry date.[118] The beneficiary need not always present the documents to the issuing bank by that date. Drafts under a payment credit must be presented to the designated payor bank on or before the expiry. A negotiation credit anticipates, however, that the beneficiary will present the documents at some bank other than the issuer; and, presumably, that presentation, not the presentation at the issuer's counters, is the critical one for purposes of the expiry.[119]

In *Courtaulds North America, Inc. v. North Carolina National Bank*,[120] the court held that negotiation of the draft on August 14 was timely when the credit expired on August 15, even though the documents arrived at the office of the issuer after August 15. In the *Flagship* case, however, if the presentation at the New York bank was not negotiation, any presentation to the issuer after November 3, the expiry, could not have been timely.[121]

---

ing bank, which dishonored. The beneficiary then sought payment from the confirming bank. The *Northern Trust Co.* court held that the confirmer was liable, even though no documents ever were presented to it. The court reasoned that since the confirmation did not require presentation at the confirmer's counters, presentation to the issuer prior to the expiry was sufficient to hold the confirmer. The court held, further, by way of dictum, that if the confirmation requires presentation at the counters of the confirmer, that presentation must occur prior to expiry. For discussion of the *Northern Trust Co.* case, see infra ¶ 5.03[3][a].

[118] See Courtaulds N. Am., Inc. v. North Carolina Nat'l Bank, 528 F.2d 802 (4th Cir. 1975); Easton Tire Co. v. Farmers & Merchants Bank, 642 S.W.2d 396 (Mo. Ct. App. 1982); Anglo-S. Am. Trust Co. v. Uhe, 261 N.Y. 150, 184 N.E. 741 (1933). Leary and Ippoliti argue that a negotiation credit requires that the beneficiary negotiate his drafts prior to the credit expiry and that the drafts be presented by the negotiating bank or its agent within a reasonable time. See Leary & Ippoliti, "Letters of Credit: Have We Fully Recovered from Three Insolvency Shocks?" U. Pa. J. Int'l Bus. L. 595, 599 (1987).

[119] See Pioneer Bank & Trust Co. v. Seiko Sporting Goods, U.S.A. Co., 184 Ill. App. 3d 783, 540 N.E.2d 808 (1989) (dictum).

[120] 387 F. Supp. 92 (M.D.N.C.), rev'd on other grounds, 528 F.2d 802 (4th Cir. 1975).

[121] See also Bank of Am. Nat'l Trust & Sav. Ass'n v. Liberty Nat'l Bank & Trust Co., 116 F. Supp. 233 (W.D. Okla. 1953), aff'd, 218 F.2d 831 (10th Cir. 1955) (rejecting strict compliance rule for documents in general, but insisting on strict enforcement of expiry date); Banco Tornquist, S.A. v. American Bank & Trust Co., 71

The issuer raised a novel argument in *United Technologies Corp. v. Citibank, N.A.*[122] that the designated expiry dates were not firm. In the *United Technologies* case, the account party agreed to sell telephone cable to an Iranian buyer. The buyer insisted on a performance guaranty from an Iranian bank, and Citibank issued two standby letters of credit to secure the Iranian bank.

The Iranian Imperial Government fell, and the account party, which claimed to have delivered all of the cable called for by the sales contract, was unable to secure the buyer's release of Citibank's standby credits as the sales contract provided. When the Iranian bank (the beneficiary) requested extension of the credits or payment, the account party brought an action against Citibank to enjoin any payment. Among the issues argued was the question whether the demands were timely. The account party argued that telexes received before the expiration dates were equivocal and therefore were not satisfactory demands. According to the opinion, the issuer apparently argued that the credits' expiration dates were not firm. It argued further that the beneficiary had a reasonable period of time (in this case, seven weeks) to determine whether its performance bond was outstanding. The issuer argued that the political turmoil in Iran at the time rendered the seven-week delay reasonable. The court ruled that it could not decide the matter on a motion for summary judgment but appeared disposed to reject the argument.[123]

In a case that arguably involved a letter of credit, although the court holds that the bank's engagement was a guaranty and not a letter of credit, the question arose whether the expiry date in the engagement referred to the date of obligations arising out of the underlying contract or to the date of presentation by the beneficiary. In *Dubuque Packing Co. v. Fitzgibbon*,[124] the issuer engaged to pay invoices of the beneficiary that the account party did not pay. The engagement was a typical invoice standby credit, but the court took it to be a guaranty and held that it applied to postexpiration requests for payment of preexpiration sales. As a matter of credit law, the holding appears to be incorrect. The

---

Misc. 2d 874, 337 N.Y.S.2d 489 (Sup. Ct. 1972) (holding that issuer may dishonor draft presented after expiry); Itek Corp. v. First Nat'l Bank, 511 F. Supp. 1341 (D. Mass. 1981) (same).

[122] 469 F. Supp. 473 (S.D.N.Y. 1979).

[123] Unfortunately, after citing strong authority to refute the position of the issuer that the beneficiary had a reasonable time after expiry to draw, the court equivocated and said that the matter was "a fair ground for litigation." Id. at 481. It is difficult to understand the reason why the court did not rule as a matter of law against the issuer on the expiry issue. The court ruled in favor of the issuer, but not on the expiry point.

[124] 599 P.2d 440 (Okla. Ct. App. 1979).

bank's undertaking expired one year from its date, and the court should not have permitted payment of demands made after that date.

There are cases in which court orders have interfered with the credit's expiry. Some of the orders reflect a rather cavalier attitude about the question; others reflect a cavalier attitude toward the rights of the beneficiary.

In *Brown v. United States National Bank*,[125] the beneficiary presented its demand for payment and the supporting documents prior to the expiry. Litigation ensued, and the final order of the Nebraska Supreme Court was not entered until after the expiry. The issuer argued that the credit had expired and that it was too late to order payment. Without discussing the issuer's expiry argument, the court entered an order in favor of the beneficiary.[126]

In *MBank Houston, N.A. v. Hendrix*,[127] the trial court entered a temporary restraining order prohibiting the beneficiary from drawing on the credit. The court then extended the order for a period beyond the credit's expiry. The beneficiary's appeal failed on a procedural point. The appellate court took the position that the beneficiary could not complain that it lost its rights under the credit and that, rather than appealing the order, the beneficiary should have sought mandamus.

In *Novus Equities Corp. v. Em-Ty Partnership*,[128] the account party obtained a temporary restraining order and caused the credit to be extended until the litigation was resolved. Although the opinion does not indicate whether the extension was a prerequisite for the extraordinary relief of a restraining order, it makes sense that the court insist that the party seeking to restrain payment be required to ensure that the credit is available at the time and in the event that the restraining order is dissolved.

Northern Trust Co. v. Community Bank[129] involved a suit on a confirmation. The confirming bank argued that the beneficiary could not recover for wrongful dishonor, because the beneficiary did not present the documents to the confirming bank prior to the expiry. The court ruled, however, that the expiry did not govern the beneficiary's rights against the confirmer. The beneficiary did present its documents to the opening bank in advance of the expiry, and the confirmation did not re-

---

[125] 220 Neb. 684, 371 N.W.2d 692 (1985).

[126] Cf. Enterprise Int'l, Inc. v. Corporacion Estatal Petrolera Ecuatoriana, 762 F.2d 464 (5th Cir. 1985) (court ignoring fact that letter of credit expired during litigation).

[127] No. 01-86-0609-CV (Tex. Ct. App. Aug. 12, 1986) (limited precedent op.).

[128] 381 N.W.2d 426 (Minn. 1986).

[129] 873 F.2d 227 (9th Cir. 1989).

quire the beneficiary to present documents to the issuer. *Northern Trust Co.* is rather lenient in enforcing the expiry and creates problems for confirming banks. Under the rule of the case, such banks cannot be assured that they are free of any obligations on the credit, even when the credit has expired.

There are two factors that mitigate the untoward effects of the *Northern Trust Co.* rule, however. First, the court gives the confirmer an escape from the rule by suggesting that a provision in the credit requiring presentation at the confirmer's counters would require presentation prior to the expiry. Second, confirmers are usually confirming credits issued by a bank. In *Northern Trust Co.*, the issuer was a failed bank. Confirmers should be able to determine the creditworthiness of their bank issuers. If they rely on an issuer that subsequently fails, they have misrelied and must bear the cost. Under the rule of *Northern Trust Co.*, the arrival of the expiry may not relieve a confirmer of its obligations.[130]

In *Atwood Turnkey Drilling, Inc. v. Petroleo Brasileiro, S.A.*,[131] a curious action by the beneficiary against the account party to extend the credit, the court entered the injunction after the credit had expired. The *Atwood* case is unusual in that the beneficiary apparently did not draw on the credit but preferred to seek an injunction extending it. Presumably, there were good reasons for the beneficiary's reluctance or inability to draw. Even though the credit had expired at the time the court entered the injunction extending it, the court held that it was restoring the parties to the status quo ante at the time the beneficiary filed its petition, when the credit was extant. Significantly, the order to extend was entered not against the issuer but against the account party. Presumably, *Atwood* involved an order requiring the account party to cause a credit to issue or requiring the account party to obtain an extension. The *Atwood* decision does not offend the strict expiry rule.

Sometimes courts must wrestle with ambiguous expiry terms; at other times, they fashion an argument that the credit is ambiguous and then construe it against the issuer. In both of those cases, of course, the expiry tends to be applied leniently.

In *Kerr Construction Co. v. Plains National Bank*,[132] the credit contained inconsistent expiry terms. In an early paragraph, the credit called for the beneficiary's certification that a third party had not performed

---

[130] For discussion of the need for a confirmation to distinguish between those confirmations that require the beneficiary to present documents at the counters of the issuer and those that permit the beneficiary to choose either the issuer or the confirmer, see del Busto, "Commentary," Letter of Credit Update 6 (Aug. 1989).

[131] 875 F.2d 1174 (5th Cir. 1989).

[132] 753 S.W.2d 181 (Tex. Ct. App. 1987).

certain work by July 17, 1985. The last sentence of the credit was an expiry provision that, under the facts of the case, required the beneficiary to draw before July 1, 1985. Thus, the credit appears to have been impossible for the beneficiary to satisfy, since it could not certify on July 1 that the account party had failed to perform by July 17. The beneficiary drew on July 17 and argued that the credit remained open until that date. The issuer argued that the credit expired on July 1. Under the beneficiary's reading of the credit, the presentation was timely; under the issuer's, it was late.

Invoking contract rules of construction, the court held that the beneficiary had the better part of the argument. In so holding, the *Kerr* opinion stands as authority for loose application of expiry rules. The court held, in effect, that an explicit expiry term may not apply if other provisions in the credit are at odds with it. Given the importance of fashioning rules that make the date of expiry clear, courts might be better advised to force beneficiaries to read their credits carefully and insist on amendments in the event of such inconsistencies. In an effort to follow contract construction rules, the *Kerr* case disserves the firm-expiry policy.[133]

[b] Strict Cases

Most courts enforce the expiration date strictly, even if the rule imposes hardships on the beneficiary. The credit, in *INA v. Heritage Bank, N.A.*,[134] for example, supported an appeal bond written by INA. The credit called for a draft and written evidence of one of three events:

1. Payment under the appeal bond;
2. Failure to pay the appeal bond premium; or
3. Failure of the principals to provide INA with satisfactory evidence that the principals had performed all of their obligations under the bond.

---

[133] Exxon Co., U.S.A. v. Banque de Paris et des Pays-Bas, 889 F.2d 674 (5th Cir. 1989), follows the *Kerr* rule in an opinion that implicitly criticizes the *Kerr* approach. The *Exxon* court had earlier ruled against the beneficiary of a credit with inconsistent terms, but it revised its ruling on the basis of *Kerr*. For a case explicitly rejecting the *Kerr* rule, on the ground that New York law, not Texas law, governed, and implicitly rejecting the rationale of *Kerr*, see the same court's opinion in Tradex Petroleum Am., Inc. v. Coral Petroleum, Inc. (In re Coral Petroleum, Inc.), 878 F.2d 830 (5th Cir. 1989). For criticism of *Kerr* and discussion of *Exxon*, see ¶ 4.08[3].

[134] 595 F.2d 171 (3d Cir. 1979).

The credit protected INA fully in the event that the principals lost their appeal. The credit failed to anticipate, however, that the appeal might not be resolved before the credit had expired. In fact, the appeal was still pending as that date approached; and INA drew on the credit and certified that it would use the funds only to satisfy demands under the bond and that it would return the balance. The court rejected the beneficiary's position, however, even though the expiration date effectively would deprive the beneficiary of its security.[135]

Similarly, in *Hyland Hills Metropolitan Park & Recreation District v. McCoy Enterprises, Inc.*,[136] the beneficiary of a standby credit had the right to draw in the event that the account party failed to construct a tennis court by June 5. The credit required the beneficiary to draw on or before that date, and the trial court held that the beneficiary must have a reasonable time after June 5 to draw, since the account party had until June 5 to perform. The appellate court reversed, however, holding that the credit and the underlying contract were independent of each other and that therefore the court should not have read the two together.[137]

Often a beneficiary presents documents that are defective. Banks call these defects in the documents to the beneficiary's attention, and frequently he cures them. Such a cure is too late, however, if it comes after the credit's expiry. In *Courtaulds North America, Inc. v. North Carolina National Bank*,[138] the court held squarely that the beneficiary cannot correct defects in his invoices after the credit's deadline.[139]

---

[135] Accord Cypress Bank v. Southwestern Bell Tel. Co., 610 S.W.2d 185 (Tex. Civ. App. 1980). For cases that set forth letters of credit with evergreen clauses drafted with the *INA* problem in mind, see Pittston Warehouse Corp. v. American Motorist Ins. Co., 715 F. Supp. 1221 (S.D.N.Y. 1989); Citronelle Unit Operators Comm. v. AmSouth Bank, N.A., 536 So. 2d 1387 (Ala. 1988); In Sports, Inc. v. Sportshop, Inc., 783 P.2d 1318 (Kan. Ct. App. 1989), the court read the evergreen clause as continuing the credit not for one additional year after the issuer failed to give notice of termination but for an additional year each year thereafter that the issuer failed to notify the beneficiary of its election to terminate the credit. That reading seems warranted, as does the holding in *Sports, Inc.* to the effect that such a credit is not one without an expiry in violation of the UCP. In a number of cases, parties draft a credit that expires before all of the events occur that would result in a draw. See, e.g., Exxon Co., U.S.A. v. Banque de Paris et des Pays-Bas, 889 F.2d 674 (5th Cir. 1989); Atlas Mini Storage, Inc. v. First Interstate Bank, 426 N.W.2d 686 (Iowa Ct. App. 1988); Audio Sys., Inc. v. First Nat'l Bank, 753 S.W.2d 553 (Ky. Ct. App. 1988); Artoc Bank & Trust, Ltd. v. Sun Marine Terminals, Inc., 760 S.W.2d 311 (Tex. Ct. App. 1988).

[136] 38 Colo. App. 23, 554 P.2d 708 (1976), modified, id.

[137] Cf. State Bank v. South Mill Mushroom Sales, Inc., 875 F.2d 158 (8th Cir. 1989) (holding that draw on credit was too late when it occurred after expiry, even though issuer breached promise to issue new credit).

[138] 528 F.2d 802 (4th Cir. 1975).

[139] Accord American Nat'l Bank & Trust Co. v. Hamilton Indus. Int'l, Inc., 583 F. Supp. 164 (N.D. Ill. 1984), rev'd on other grounds sub nom. Banque Paribas v.

In *General Cable CEAT, S.A. v. Futura Trading, Inc.*,[140] the court held that the advising bank was entitled to summary judgment on a claim by the beneficiary that presented a Treasury Department license under the Iranian Assets Control Regulations[141] after the expiry. The license was too late, the court held.

The Uniform Customs expressly provide that, if the expiry falls on a bank holiday, the beneficiary may present the documents on the first banking day that follows.[142] Article 5 of the Code does not address the question, but at least one court has construed Section 3-503(3) as calling for the same result as the Uniform Customs. In *Addison Bank v. Temple-Eastex, Inc.*,[143] the credit expired on December 7, 1980, a Sunday. The person seeking payment had mailed its presentment documents, and they arrived at the issuer's office on December 8, a business day. The *Addison Bank* court relied on Section 3-503(3) in holding that the presentation was timely. Section 3-503 sets forth the time of presentment rules for negotiable instruments. It plays an important role in determining the liability of an endorser or a drawer under a negotiable instrument.[144] A letter of credit is not a negotiable instrument, and courts should be reluctant to apply negotiable instrument provisions to letter of credit transactions.[145]

The rule of the *Addison Bank* case makes sense, however. If banks, in fashioning rules for themselves in the Uniform Customs, have opted for the rule extending the expiry, bank issuers should not complain that courts adopt a common-law rule to the same effect. Nonbank issuers might argue to the contrary that beneficiaries should not have the bene-

---

Hamilton Indus. Int'l, Inc., 767 F.2d 380 (7th Cir. 1985); Spencer v. First S. Sav. Ass'n, No. A14-87-00154-CV (Tex. Ct. App. Nov. 25, 1987) (limited precedent op.); Itek Corp. v. First Nat'l Bank, No. 80-58-MA (D. Mass. May 25, 1982), vacated on other grounds, 704 F.2d 1 (1st Cir. 1983). But cf. Dynamics Corp. of Am. v. Citizens & S. Nat'l Bank, 356 F. Supp. 991 (N.D. Ga. 1973) (permitting beneficiary to amend certificate after credit's expiry). Article 54(e) of the Uniform Customs specifically provides that a beneficiary transferring a credit may reduce the period of validity. See Goodsons & Co. v. Federal Republic of Nig., 558 F. Supp. 1204 (S.D.N.Y. 1983). For additional authority ignoring strict application of the expiry, see supra ¶ 5.03[3][a].

[140] No. 82 Civ. 1087 (RLC) (S.D.N.Y. Jan. 18, 1983).

[141] 31 C.F.R. §§ 535.101–535.905 (1989).

[142] U.C.P. art. 48(a) (1983).

[143] 665 S.W.2d 550 (Tex. Ct. App.), rev'd on other grounds, 672 S.W.2d 793 (Tex. 1984).

[144] See U.C.C. § 3-501.

[145] For discussion of a case that applied another negotiable instruments provision, U.C.C. § 3-511(1), to a letter of credit transaction, see infra ¶ 5.03[3][c].

fit of the extra time that the Uniform Customs and *Addison Bank* give them.

In *First State Bank v. Shuford Mills, Inc.*,[146] the beneficiary presented, prior to expiry, a draft payable after expiry. The court held that the liability of the issuer was fixed at the time of presentation and that the beneficiary had satisfied the credit.

In *Banco Nacional De Desarrollo v. Mellon Bank, N.A.*,[147] the credit expired on August 31, 1980; but the issuing bank, at the account party's request, issued fifteen amendments to the credit. The last amendment covered a shipment on February 10, 1981 and required greater documentation than the original credit did. The beneficiary apparently argued that it did not agree to the additional documentation and that the account party and the issuer were attempting to amend the credit without the beneficiary's approval, contrary to the Uniform Customs that governed the credit.[148] The *Mellon Bank* court rejected that argument, in part on the ground that the original credit had expired. The so-called amendments, then, were not amendments at all but new credits; and the beneficiary could not complain of the issuer when it declined to pay in the absence of the additional documentation.[149]

Under Article 36 of the 1974 version of the Uniform Customs, a credit that called for shipment in installments would expire if the beneficiary failed to make a shipment within the period provided. In *Trans-Global Alloy, Ltd. v. First Nat'l Bank*,[150] the credit required the beneficiary to present documents in connection with ten shipments over ten consecutive months. When the beneficiary failed to make a shipment during two months, the court held that the credit expired by its terms.[151]

Strict application of a credit's expiry may cut against the issuer. In *International Fidelity Insurance Co. v. State Bank of Commerce*,[152] the court held that the issuer had not shown by affidavit that it had termi-

---

[146] 716 S.W.2d 649 (Tex. Ct. App. 1986).

[147] 726 F.2d 87 (3d Cir. 1984).

[148] See U.C.P. art. 3(c) (1974).

[149] In Offshore Int'l S.A. v. Banco Central S.A., [1976] 2 Lloyd's Rep. 402 (Q.B.), the credit provided that it would be extended in the event the beneficiary submitted a dispute in the underlying transaction to arbitration. Because the beneficiary failed to make that submission under the applicable rules of arbitration until the credit had expired, the court refused to extend the credit beyond its stated expiry.

[150] 490 So. 2d 769 (La. Ct. App. 1986).

[151] For the rule under the 1983 version of the Uniform Customs, see ¶ 4.06[2][e].

[152] No. 87-3456 (E.D. La. June 6, 1988).

nated a credit as it had the right to do under an evergreen clause[153] and that the beneficiary was entitled to summary judgment against the issuer in an action for wrongful dishonor.

In *Christenson v. Broadway Bank & Trust Co.*,[154] the account party sued for an injunction against payment of a credit issued to Penn Square Bank as beneficiary. The credit had expired on February 28, 1983; on May 13, 1983, the FDIC, as receiver for the beneficiary, sought leave to intervene. The FDIC had drawn on the credit prior to the expiry, but the issuer had dishonored on the ground that the FDIC's documents were nonconforming. The *Christenson* court denied leave to intervene on the curious ground that the receiver had let the credit expire. If the *Christenson* court is suggesting that suits against an issuer for dishonor must be brought prior to expiry, the court has misconstrued the expiry rule.

[c] Section 3-511 of the Code: Excuse for Delay in Presentment

In one case, delay in the mails caused a beneficiary to lose its right to payment. In *Consolidated Aluminum Corp. v. Bank of Virginia*,[155] the beneficiary mailed its draft and accompanying certificate by certified mail, apparently from Missouri, on April 2, 1980. The credit expired on April 7. The draft arrived at the issuer's counters in Virginia on April 11.[156] The beneficiary argued that Section 3-511(1) applied and excused the delay. That section excuses delay "in presentment, protest or notice of dishonor." The court saw the question as a close one but held against the beneficiary. The *Consolidated Aluminum* court felt that the policy of enforcing letters of credit strictly outweighed the force of Section 3-511.

While the result in the *Consolidated Aluminum* case is reassuring, the court's concern with Section 3-511(1) is misplaced. That provision appears in Article 3 of the Code, the commercial paper article. Section 3-501 in that same article renders the liability of a party to a negotiable

---

[153] Under an evergreen clause, the credit provides that it is effective for a designated period, usually one year, and will be renewed automatically for an additional period, unless the issuer gives notice of its decision not to renew prior to an expiry. See National Sur. Corp. v. Midland Bank, 551 F.2d 21 (3d Cir. 1977); Comptroller of the Currency, Staff Interpretive Letter No. 239, reprinted in [1983–1984 Transfer Binder] Fed. Banking L. Rep. (CCH) ¶ 85,403 (Mar. 10, 1982).

[154] 129 Ill. App. 3d 928, 473 N.E.2d 431 (1984).

[155] 544 F. Supp. 386 (D. Md. 1982), aff'd, 704 F.2d 136 (4th Cir. 1983).

[156] For a case holding that presentment by mail occurs at the time when the documents are delivered to the issuer, see First State Bank v. Shuford Mills, Inc., 716 S.W.2d 649 (Tex. Ct. App. 1986).

instrument subject to the condition that the holder of the instrument present it in timely fashion.[157] The excuse provision of Article 3, Section 3-511, excuses delay in presentment for the purpose of establishing liability on a negotiable instrument. The beneficiary in the *Consolidated Aluminum* case was seeking to establish liability not on a negotiable instrument but on a letter of credit. Section 3-511 does not deal with presentment on a letter of credit, and it is unfortunate that the court suggests that it does. The timing question for negotiable instruments and that for letters of credit are subject to different industry exigencies and different commercial expectations.[158]

[d] Waiver of Right to Insist on Strict Compliance

An issuer may waive its right to insist on presentment on or before the expiration date. In *Beckman Cotton Co. v. First National Bank*,[159] for example, the ultimate beneficiary[160] of the credit obtained the necessary documents in New Orleans on October 27, 1977 and dispatched them by plane to the issuer in Atlanta. The credit expired on October 30. Bad weather forced the plane to return to New Orleans on October 27, and the beneficiary notified an officer of the issuer that there would be a delay. The officer agreed to accept the documents if they arrived by October 31. The court held that, since October 30 was a Sunday and since the bank officer had agreed to accept documents on October 31, the presentation was timely.

Both grounds for the extension appear to be correct. The *Beckman Cotton* credit was subject to the Uniform Customs. Article 39(a) of the Customs then in effect specifically covered the bank holiday problem and provided that an expiry that fell on a holiday should be extended to

---

[157] Section 3-501 provides: "Unless excused (Section 3-511) presentment is necessary to charge secondary parties as follows. . . ." U.C.C. § 3-501(1).

[158] See U.C.C. § 3-511, comments 1-7. On appeal, the Court of Appeals for the Fourth Circuit resolved the apparent conflict between letter of credit law and Section 3-511 by saying that the reference to the Uniform Customs in the credit overrides Section 3-511. It also asserted that the issue in the *Consolidated Aluminum* case was a letter of credit question, not a negotiable instruments question. The court did not make the point that Section 3-511 deals with excuse under the presentment rule of Section 3-501. Consolidated Aluminum Corp. v. Bank of Va., 704 F.2d 136 (4th Cir. 1983). Contra Second Nat'l Bank v. M. Samuel & Sons, Inc., 12 F.2d 963 (2d Cir.), cert. denied, 273 U.S. 720 (1926) (applying negotiable instruments rules to determination of timeliness of presentation of draft under letter of credit).

[159] 34 U.C.C. Rep. Serv. (Callaghan) 966 (N.D. Ga. 1982).

[160] The beneficiary of the credit in the *Beckman* case was the Commodity Credit Corporation, which, in turn, paid the seller. References in the text to the "beneficiary" are to the seller.

the next day. To the same effect is Article 48(a) of the 1983 version of the Uniform Customs.

The second ground for the *Beckman Cotton* ruling is similarly convincing. An issuer should have authority to extend the time for presentation, though that is not to say that it can bind the account party by its action. In *Consolidated Aluminum Corp. v. Bank of Virginia*,[161] the issuer argued that it could not honor, as a matter of law, a late presentation. The court dismissed that argument, noting that the issuer may waive the defect. The opinion points out, however, that any such waiver might imperil the issuer's right to reimbursement from its customer.[162]

In *Chase Manhattan Bank v. Equibank*,[163] the Court of Appeals for the Third Circuit addressed the question of reimbursement when the issuer unilaterally altered the expiry. The trial court had held that an attempt by the issuer and the beneficiary to amend a credit by extending the expiry was ineffective without the consent of the account party. The court did not disagree with the principle that the account party is not bound by an agreement to amend made by the beneficiary and the issuer but held that the issuer is bound by the agreement, which the court characterized as a waiver.[164]

[e] Need for a Firm Expiry

Under the majority rule, courts enforce the credit's expiry strictly.[165] That rule reflects, in part, the policy of strict compliance that most courts adopt in evaluating the beneficiary's compliance with the credit's conditions.[166] That policy alone supports strict enforcement of the expiry.

There is a second important reason for observing the expiry precisely. The nature of credits is such that issuers must know when their obligations expire. Often issuers take security from their customers, and they need to know exactly when they can release the security. A flexible expiry date that permits a seven-week delay, for which the issuer argued

[161] 544 F. Supp. 386 (D. Md. 1982), aff'd, 704 F.2d 136 (4th Cir. 1983).

[162] For a discussion of the issuer's right to reimbursement and the account party's defense based on improper honor of the credit, see ¶¶ 7.06, 9.03.

[163] 550 F.2d 882 (3d Cir. 1977).

[164] See also Marino Indus. Corp. v. Chase Manhattan Bank, N.A., 686 F.2d 112 (2d Cir. 1982) (suggesting that issuer's waiver of strict enforcement of expiry, without beneficiary's authorization, binds issuer).

[165] See generally authority cited supra ¶ 5.03[3][b].

[166] For a discussion of the strict compliance rule, see ¶¶ 6.03–6.04.

in *United Technologies Corp. v. Citibank, N.A.*,[167] makes it difficult for the account party to know when its collateral will be released.[168]

The Comptroller of the Currency's regulation on letters of credit[169] specifically requires that letters of credit include, as a matter of sound banking practice, an expiration date, or that they be effective only for a definite term. Article 46(a) of the Uniform Customs evinces the same policy in strong language.[170] Banking regulations[171] that require banks to aggregate standby letters of credit in applying statutory lending limits would become problematic if courts permitted beneficiaries to draw on a credit after it expired. Banks would not know when to delete a standby from a customer's list of loans. In short, there are a number of reasons for enforcing the expiry strictly.[172]

Drafters must take care that the expiration provision in the credit is clear. References to the underlying transaction or to nondocumentary facts serve poorly as termination provisions. In *Sea Management Services, Ltd. v. Club Sea, Inc.*,[173] the credit terminated upon the expiration of a charter party. An issuer's document examiners are not in a position to know whether a charter party has expired. In the *Sea Management Services* case, the court held that when the issuer had conflicting views

---

[167] 469 F. Supp. 473 (S.D.N.Y. 1979).

[168] Even more serious from the issuer's standpoint are injunctions or temporary restraining orders that disregard the expiry. For discussion of some of those cases, see supra ¶ 5.03[3][a].

[169] See 12 C.F.R. § 7.7016 (1989); cf. 12 C.F.R. § 545.48 (1990) (Office of Thrift Supervision regulation to same effect). The Comptroller has indicated that if the issuer has the power to terminate the credit by giving a short notice, no expiry is necessary. See Comptroller of the Currency, Interpretive Letter No. 239, reprinted in [1983–1984 Transfer Binder] Fed. Banking L. Rep. (CCH) ¶ 84,403 (Mar. 10, 1982). Banking regulators in Tennessee have taken a different approach, insisting on a firm expiry date. See Chilton Air Cooled Engines, Inc. v. First Citizens Bank, 726 S.W.2d 526 (Tenn. Ct. App. 1986). The Comptroller approves in principle of evergreen clauses in letters of credit but warns that such use may raise safety and soundness concerns and that banks issuing credits with evergreen clauses should do so with caution. See Comptroller of the Currency, Interpretive Letter No. 477, reprinted in Fed. Banking L. Rep. (CCH) ¶ 83,027 (Jan. 11, 1989).

[170] "All credits must stipulate an expiry date." U.C.P. art. 46(a) (1983).

[171] See 12 C.F.R. § 208.8(d)(2) (1989); cf. 12 C.F.R. § 208.8(d)(3) (1989) (requiring certain banks to report outstanding letters of credit to Federal Reserve Board).

[172] Because credits must have a firm expiry and because bank issuers are reluctant to issue credits with long terms, commercial parties have developed ways to use a number of consecutive credits to secure long-term obligations. In Bryant v. Kerr, 726 S.W.2d 373 (Mo. Ct. App. 1987), for example, the underlying contract required the obligors on a fifteen-year note to certify each year that the original credit had been renewed.

[173] 512 So. 2d 1025 (Fla. Dist. Ct. App. 1987).

from the beneficiary and the account party regarding the termination of the charter party, the issuer should have paid the beneficiary.[174]

In *Auto-Owners Insurance Co. v. South Side Trust & Savings Bank*,[175] the issuer took the unusual and highly inadvisable step of continuing the credit beyond its expiry "for a reasonable period of time."[176] In *Tuthill v. Union Savings Bank*,[177] the court held that a credit subject to the 1974 version of the Uniform Customs that contained no expiry provision should expire twenty-one days after the event described in the credit as the event that triggers payment. The *Tuthill* court fashioned the twenty-one-day rule by analogy out of the 1974 Uniform Customs Article 41. The analogy is not persuasive. In *Transparent Products Corp. v. Paysaver Credit Union*,[178] the court rejected the idea that the issuer of a letter of credit with no expiry can assert a laches defense against the beneficiary.

[4] Dishonoring the Credit

Sometimes it becomes important to know precisely at what time the issuer has dishonored the credit. If that dishonor is improper, the aggrieved beneficiary may have a claim for prejudgment interest.[179] In *Philadelphia Gear Corp. v. FDIC*,[180] for example, the beneficiary sought prejudgment interest from the FDIC as insurer of a failed bank. The beneficiary had presented its drafts under the credit on Wednesday, July 7, 1982. The court held that, under Section 5-112(1), the FDIC as receiver had until Monday, July 12 to honor the beneficiary's drafts and that prejudgment interest would begin to run from that date. The Court of Appeals for the Tenth Circuit reversed,[181] holding that the Federal Deposit Insurance Act's insurance provisions[182] contemplate reasonable

---

[174] For discussion of other cases involving inconsistent provisions that render the expiry problematic, see ¶ 5.03[3][a].

[175] 176 Ill. App. 3d 303, 531 N.E.2d 146 (1988).

[176] Id. at 176, 531 N.E.2d at 150.

[177] 141 Misc. 2d 88, 534 N.Y.S.2d 88 (1988).

[178] 864 F.2d 60 (7th Cir. 1988).

[179] For general discussion of incidental damages for dishonor of a credit, see ¶ 9.02[5][c].

[180] 587 F. Supp. 294 (W.D. Okla.), aff'd in part, rev'd in part, 751 F.2d 1131 (10th Cir. 1984), rev'd, 476 U.S. 426 (1986).

[181] Philadelphia Gear Corp. v. FDIC, 751 F.2d 1131 (10th Cir. 1984), rev'd, 476 U.S. 426 (1986).

[182] 12 U.S.C. § 1821(f) (1988).

delays for the FDIC, as insurer, to determine the validity of claims and that the FDIC is immune to claims for prejudgment interest.

In *Tosco Corp. v. FDIC*,[183] the beneficiary presented its draft to the soon-to-fail bank on Friday, May 8, 1981 after business hours. Bank officers decided to dishonor the draft that evening and returned the draft through banking channels. The trial court awarded interest from Friday, May 8, but the Court of Appeals for the Sixth Circuit held that interest would not begin to run until the following Monday, the next banking day.

In *Pro-Fab, Inc. v. Vipa, Inc.*,[184] the issuer failed to notify the beneficiary of its decision to dishonor the beneficiary's request for payment under the credit. The court held that unless the failure was excused by the beneficiary's breach of the Article 5 warranty,[185] the failure estopped the issuer from raising any defects in the beneficiary's documents. This ruling is at odds with the rule of Section 5-112(1) of the Code, which provides that failure by the issuer to notify the beneficiary within three banking days of presentation constitutes dishonor of the credit. The estoppel rule fashioned by the *Pro-Fab* court has the effect of holding that failure to give the notice constitutes honor of the credit. If the issuer cannot raise the defects, it is liable for the face amount of the credit. In the event of dishonor, however, the issuer is liable only for losses occasioned by the dishonor.[186]

---

[183] 723 F.2d 1242 (6th Cir. 1983).

[184] 772 F.2d 847 (11th Cir. 1985).

[185] See U.C.C. § 5-111(1). For discussion of the warranty section, see ¶¶ 6.07, 9.04.

[186] See U.C.C. § 5-115. See also ¶ 9.02[5].

CHAPTER **6**

The Issuer and the Beneficiary

¶ 6.01 DOCUMENTS AND THE DUTY TO DONOR

This chapter considers, first, the duty of the beneficiary toward the issuer and, second, the duty of the issuer toward the beneficiary.

The beneficiary must present conforming documents, and, if he does, the issuer must honor the beneficiary's draft. Section 5-109 of the Uniform Commercial Code (UCC or the Code), in defining the issuer's duty to its customer (i.e., the account party), stipulates that the issuer must examine the documents in order to determine that they comply on their face with the credit. The Code also stipulates that the issuer is not responsible for defects in any document that is regular on its face. Article 15 of the Uniform Customs and Practice for Documentary Credits (UCP or the Uniform Customs) imposes a similar duty.[1]

Section 5-114 commands the issuer to honor a draft or demand for payment when the presentment complies on its face with the credit. The Uniform Customs' Article 16 imposes a similar duty. Implicit in Section 5-114 and Article 16 is the doctrine, announced in *Maurice O'Meara Co. v. National Park Bank*,[2] that if the beneficiary's documents do comply, the bank, no matter what its suspicions, may not impose additional requirements. "To hold otherwise is to read into the letter of credit something which is not there."[3] If the documents satisfy the conditions of the credit, the issuer must honor, even though the account party claims that the merchandise is nonconforming.[4]

Also implicit in these rules is the notion that the issuer need not look outside the documents to the underlying transaction[5] or to industry practices.[6]

---

[1] Cf. See Gian Singh & Co. v. Banque de l'Indochine, [1974] 2 All E.R. 754 (P.C.) (applying prior version of UCP).

[2] 239 N.Y. 386, 146 N.E. 636 (1925).

[3] Id. at 397, 146 N.E. at 639.

[4] A significant exception to this rule arises in circumstances involving fraud. See ¶ 7.04.

[5] See, e.g., New York Life Ins. Co. v. Hartford Nat'l Bank & Trust Co., 173 Conn. 492, 378 A.2d 562 (1977); Shaffer v. Brooklyn Park Garden Apartments, 311 Minn. 452, 250 N.W.2d 172 (1977); Werner v. A.L. Grootemaat & Sons, 80 Wis. 2d 513, 259 N.W.2d 310 (1977). See also ¶¶ 2.08–2.09. Cf. Five Star Parking v. Philadelphia Parking Auth., 703 F. Supp. 20 (E.D. Pa. 1989) (holding that issuer had no duty to notify account party before paying beneficiary that presented conforming documents, notwithstanding fact that underlying transaction required beneficiary to notify account party of its draw); Esal (Commodities) Ltd. v. Oriental Credit Ltd., [1985] 2 Lloyd's Rep. 546 (C.A.) (no duty of issuer to notify account party of beneficiary's draw).

[6] See, e.g., First Nat'l Bank v. Rosebud Hous. Auth., 291 N.W.2d 41 (Iowa 1980); Schweibish v. Pontchartrain State Bank, 389 So. 2d 731 (La. Ct. App. 1980). See also infra ¶ 6.04[1]. That is not to say, however, that the issuer satisfies the credit obligation by paying the wrong party against facially conforming documents. In

¶ 6.02 TWO VIEWS ON DOCUMENT COMPLIANCE— STRICT COMPLIANCE vs. SUBSTANTIAL COMPLIANCE

It is far simpler to state the duties of an issuer under the Code and the Uniform Customs[7] than it is for the issuer and its document checkers to perform them. The nub of the problem is that of determining whether the documents do indeed conform to the conditions specified in the credit. That problem has two aspects. The first involves establishing credit industry standards for the documents. Thanks to the efforts of the international banking industry, the International Chamber of Commerce's Uniform Customs largely resolve that aspect of the problem. Since 1962, all significant banking centers, with few exceptions, have adopted the Uniform Customs formally or informally and thereby have removed a plethora of technical problems that could have sabotaged the smooth operation of documentary credits.

The great majority of documentary credits, including standby credits, incorporate the Uniform Customs. Even those that do not may benefit from them. Letter of credit law tends to be skeletal and presupposes a body of customary law to supplement it. The Uniform Customs are a good source of that customary law.[8] It would be a mistake to assume that because their roots lie in the international transaction, the Uniform Customs speak only to a credit arising out of the international sale of goods. Much of commercial law—for example, that of sales, negotiable instruments, and documents of title—grows out of the international setting. Commerce has domesticated these devices and has domesticated the credit. Growth in the use of the credit has arisen out of transactions that do not involve sales and that are not international.[9] Credits arising in those transactions may well benefit from the Uniform Customs nonetheless.

The second aspect of the problem of the issuer's duties with respect to documents involves the tendency, noted long ago, of common-law courts to give the death to contract. For a number of reasons, courts have nurtured a tradition of weakening the strict law of contract when

---

Cleveland Mfg. Co. v. Muslim Commercial Bank Ltd., [1981] 2 Lloyd's Rep. 646 (Q.B.), the documents were facially conforming, but the issuer paid a freight forwarder rather than the beneficiary. The court held that the beneficiary could recover the funds from the issuer. Although the rule of *Cleveland Manufacturing* forces the issuer to look beyond the face of the documents to determine the identity or authority of the party presenting them, the case is persuasive.

[7] See generally U.C.C. § 5-109; U.C.P. art. 15 (1983).

[8] For discussion of the Uniform Customs, see ¶¶ 4.04–4.06 and Apps. A, B.

[9] For discussion of those uses, see ¶ 1.06.

they perceive the operation of that law as yielding unfair results. A desire to protect consumers and an awareness of imbalance in the negotiating strength of contracting parties prompted that tradition. There are costs in the lack of precision introduced by the death of contract. By relaxing strict rules of performance and by introducing equitable notions of good faith and unconscionability, courts have blurred distinctions in contact law and have rendered problematic the effort of reducing to express terms the conditions of a contracting party's undertaking. There appears to be general agreement, however, that these departures from strict contract rules are worth the cost.

There is, however, a limit to the costs a transaction can bear efficiently. The letter of credit transaction is a mercantile, nonconsumer transaction. While it often entails some adhesion features, it is no secret that letters of credit involve a level of commercial sophistication that amateurs may not attain. Those who would render the device suitable for amateur issuers, account parties, and beneficiaries render it unsuitable for the professionals.

A majority of the cases accept this analysis in the context of the beneficiary's performance, hold that the beneficiary must comply strictly with the terms of the credit, and see any failure of the documents to conform as excusing the issuer from its duty to honor the beneficiary's draft or demand for payment.[10] A minority of courts, however, take a different approach, infusing into letter of credit law notions such as equity, "substantial compliance," and the other legal devices courts use to modify the terms of an arrangement that the parties originally accepted.[11] Analysis of the minority rule indicates that it lends itself well to the courtroom setting of legal briefs, oral arguments, and expert testimony on industry practices and to lengthy review of prior transactions. It does not lend itself well to the bank letter of credit department, where document examiners must review the documents against the credit and must decide promptly whether to honor the beneficiary's draft. The kind of inquiry that the minority rule commands takes more time and requires more legal analysis than document examiners can give, as well as more legal analysis than the credit transaction can afford.

The execution of a credit is much more akin to the collection of a negotiable instrument or to the negotiation of a document of title than to the performance of a bilateral contract. Most courts have properly re-

---

[10] See cases cited infra ¶¶ 6.03–6.04.

[11] See cases discussed infra ¶ 6.05. See also Heritage Hous. Corp. v. Ferguson, 651 S.W.2d 272 (Tex. Ct. App. 1983) (holding that contract law, not law of negotiable instruments, governs letters of credit and therefore that letter of credit does not satisfy Texas law requiring negotiable obligation in lieu of supersedeas bond).

fused to invoke the anticontract rules against the contract promises of negotiable instruments and negotiable documents, and courts should refuse to invoke them in the letter of credit setting. It is true that the credit resembles a contract, and contract rules often supplement letter of credit law.[12] There is a point, however, beyond which the analogy between letters of credit and contracts breaks down. The letter of credit collection process (i.e., the examination of the documents and the decision to honor or to dishonor) is that point.

The minority view is mistaken in adopting a rule that permits less than punctilious compliance by the beneficiary. The minority rule retards the prompt payment feature of the credit and weakens each of the credit's unique functions.[13] These effects reduce the efficiency of the credit device and result in higher costs for everyone who utilizes the credit. The minority rule protects the substantially complying beneficiary, but it does so by shifting the burden from that beneficiary to the credit itself. In the analysis of the majority and minority rules in the following paragraphs, it is apparent that the shift yields higher overall costs than leaving the loss on the noncomplying beneficiary yields. Thus, it is difficult to understand the reason why the minority rule appeals to so many courts. The strict view is better, even though it sometimes permits an issuer to seize upon a defect in order to protect its customer against the consequences of a falling market or in order to protect itself against the consequences of an insolvent customer.

Those who support the minority view may argue that most credit transactions involve defects of one kind or another and that the majority rule gives banks and their customers an unfair advantage over the beneficiaries. That argument rejects the majority rule for ignoring the experience of the credit transaction in favor of a theory that does not square with that experience. There are times, however, when the law must support high standards. If beneficiaries fail to comply with the conditions of a credit, that is their fault. They should insist that the credit contain only those conditions that they can satisfy. They should insist that the credit not include the "excessive detail" that the Uniform Customs warn against in Article 5. Far more important is the fact that the minority rule ignores the exigencies of document examination and

---

[12] For a discussion of those rules and the limits on the general principles, see ¶¶ 4.07–4.08. One commentator argues persuasively that, quite apart from letter of credit considerations, the substantial compliance rule of contract law does not apply to the beneficiary-issuer setting as a matter of contract law. See Note, "Letters of Credit: A Solution to the Problem of Documentary Compliance," 50 Fordham L. Rev. 848, 863 (1982).

[13] For a discussion of those functions, see ¶ 3.07.

could thrust the credit into a chaotic state that would render it virtually useless.

Whenever a court considers the compliance of documents, it must remember that the document examiner sits at a desk with the credit, the documents, and a copy of the Uniform Customs. The examiner does not have files of prior transactions, may not know the account party or beneficiary, probably knows nothing of their industry, and does not have a lawyer at his elbow.

The development of wire communications diminishes the efficacy of the argument that commercial parties cannot live with the strict compliance rule. Freight forwarders, trading company subsidiaries of bank holding companies, and importers themselves have begun the process of modernizing the production of documents called for by letters of credit.[14] Most document discrepancies arise in commercial credits, particularly in bills of lading. By permitting parties to generate bills and similar documents by wire, these efforts at modernization permit a beneficiary or his agent to correct defects promptly. It would be unfortunate if courts reject the strict compliance rule at a time when commercial practices are rendering it a simple rule for the commercial parties to observe.

Finally, it would be misleading to suggest that the strict compliance rule always benefits issuers and their customers. It does not. It operates against them often, for it prevents the issuer from dishonoring a conforming draft and from insisting that the beneficiaries supply more than the credit requires. It gives rise, moreover, to important corollaries in the rules of waiver and estoppel.[15] Those rules require the issuer to assert defects explicitly and without delay in order to give the beneficiary an opportunity to cure defects in the presentation. Careful beneficiaries avail themselves of these corollaries by presenting early and allowing time to cure. A most important aspect of the strict compliance standard is the rule requiring payment if the documents do conform. This rule, a strong pro-beneficiary rule, is under attack from the same people who would weaken the strict compliance rule. That attack centers on the

---

[14] See, e.g., Green, "Letters of Credit and the Computerization of Maritime Trade," 3 Fla. Int'l L.J. 221 (1988); "Automated Spotlight Turns to British SeaDocs Document Handling System," Letter of Credit Update 13 (Nov. 1986); "U.S. Banks Take the Lead in Electronic Documentation," Banking World 53 (June 1986). For a proposal that would permit bills of lading to be issued electronically, without paper, see Merges & Reynolds, "Toward a Computerized System for Negotiating Ocean Bills of Lading," 6 J.L. & Com. 23 (1986). Cf. Merchant, "New Developments in Transport Documents," 2 Letter of Credit Reports 8 (Mar./Apr. 1988) (discussing paperless systems); Rowe, "Automating International Trade Payments—Legal and Regulatory Issues," 4 J. Int'l Bus. L. 234 (1987) (same).

[15] See infra ¶ 6.06.

fraud in the transaction defense, and those who advocate the strict compliance standard must also advocate, as this treatise does, that the fraud defense be construed most narrowly.[16]

¶ 6.03 STRICT COMPLIANCE RULE

The majority of cases follow the strict compliance rule and enforce the conditions of the credit punctiliously. In doing so, they teach much about the nature of the credit device and the role it plays in the broad commercial transaction. A few cases illustrate those teachings.

In *Corporacion De Mercadeo Agricola v. Mellon Bank International*,[17] the court required the beneficiary to obtain the account party's signed statement of facts because the court concluded that the credit called for such a statement. In that case, the seller was the beneficiary of a standby credit issued to provide it with liquidated damages in the event the buyer account party defaulted on the purchase contract. The credit called for the account party's "statement of facts."[18] Arguably, the credit was of little value to the beneficiary, since in any dispute the account party, whose interests would be adverse to those of the beneficiary, might refuse to sign such a statement. It is difficult to see why the beneficiary agreed to such a credit. The Court of Appeals for the Second Circuit was satisfied, however, that the beneficiary had agreed and found it too late for the beneficiary to complain after the fact of issuance, that the credit imposed burdensome terms. "[I]t is black letter law," the court held, "that the terms and conditions of a letter of credit must be strictly adhered to."[19]

Similarly, in *AMF Head Sports Wear, Inc. v. Ray Scott's All-American Sports Club, Inc.*,[20] the court refused to alter the conditions of the credit. In the *AMF* case, the credit called for shipping documents show-

---

[16] For a discussion of the fraud defense, see ¶ 7.04.

[17] 608 F.2d 43 (2d Cir. 1979).

[18] Id. at 45. The credit was ambiguous, but the majority construed it as calling for a statement of facts signed by the account party.

[19] Corporacion De Mercadeo Agricola v. Mellon Bank Int'l, 608 F.2d 43, 47 (2d Cir. 1979); cf. Bebco Distribs., Inc. v. Farmers & Merchants Bank, 485 So. 2d 330 (Ala. 1986) (holding that beneficiary had to obtain checks drawn by account party in order to satisfy terms of credit); Chilton Air Cooled Engines, Inc. v. First Citizens Bank, 726 S.W.2d 526 (Tenn. Ct. App. 1986) (holding that because issuer was not authorized to pay beneficiary unless account party approved, beneficiary needed to obtain account party's signature on statement of sums due on underlying contract). For additional cases involving documents signed by the account party, see ¶ 2.05[3].

[20] 448 F. Supp. 222 (D. Ariz. 1978).

ing delivery of the goods in Scottsdale, Arizona, but the documents that the beneficiary presented showed delivery in Columbus, Indiana. The beneficiary argued that the bank elected to dishonor not because the documents were defective but because the bank's customer could not reimburse the bank. The beneficiary argued further that the bank's refusal to amend the credit to allow documents showing delivery at Columbus was an instance of bad faith. The court rejected both of these arguments and adhered to the strict compliance rule.[21]

In *North Woods Paper Mills, Ltd v. National City Bank*,[22] the beneficiary mistakenly presented drafts and invoices for amounts less than it was entitled to. The bank honored the drafts but dishonored the beneficiary's subsequent drafts submitted to recoup the loss that the beneficiary's oversight had occasioned. Because the second presentation did not include the documents accompanying the earlier drafts, the court held that the bank's dishonor was proper.

These three cases, *Mellon Bank*, *AMF*, and *North Woods*, demonstrate the operation of the strict compliance rule against the beneficiary. The *Mellon Bank* court rejected arguments that it redress what appeared to be the unbalanced bargain that the beneficiary had struck. The *AMF* court refused to require payment, despite the fact that the goods were shipped (albeit to a destination different from that required by the credit). It also found no bad faith in the bank's refusal to modify the credit's terms concerning delivery, even though the opinion suggests that the bank's customer was not displeased with that delivery. Finally, the *North Woods* case demonstrates the reluctance of the court to import notions of equity to reform a credit's conditions. The rule of these cases reflects the policy that prompted the famous dictum of Viscount Sumner in *Equitable Trust Co. v. Dawson Partners*,[23] when he characterized the strict compliance standard as one where "there is no room for documents which are almost the same, or which will do just as well."[24]

---

[21] Cf. Centennial Indus., Inc. v. Union Trust Co., 75 Md. App. 202, 540 A.2d 1169 (Ct. Spec. App.), cert. denied, 313 Md. 505, 545 A.2d 1343 (1988) (holding that it is not bad faith for issuer to refuse to amend credit so that account party's suppliers can comply with its terms).

[22] 121 N.Y.S.2d 543 (Sup. Ct. 1953), aff'd, 283 A.D. 731, 127 N.Y.S.2d 663 (1954).

[23] [1927] 27 Lloyd's List L.R. 49.

[24] Id. at 52; cf. Fidelity Nat'l Bank v. Dade County, 371 So. 2d 545, 546 (Fla. Dist. Ct. App. 1979) ("Compliance with the terms of a letter of credit is not like pitching horseshoes. No points are awarded for being close."). For additional cases that support the strict compliance rule explicitly, see Banco Nacional De Desarrollo v. Mellon Bank, N.A., 726 F.2d 87 (3d Cir. 1984); Philadelphia Gear Corp. v. Central Bank, 717 F.2d 230 (5th Cir. 1983); Voest-Alpine Int'l Corp. v. Chase Manhattan Bank, N.A., 707 F.2d 680 (2d Cir. 1983); Dulien Steel Prods., Inc. v. Bankers Trust Co., 298 F.2d 836 (2d Cir. 1962); Newvector Communications, Inc. v. Union

The strict compliance rule has the intended salutary effect of requiring the beneficiary to review the credit ex ante to be certain that he can comply with it. That inquiry, which permits the beneficiary to verify that the credit complies with the underlying contract,[25] also permits him to make timely requests for amendments and to withhold shipment or other performance if the credit does not comply with the underlying transaction or is impossible for him to satisfy. It is more efficient to require the beneficiary to conduct that review of the credit before the fact of performance than after it, and the beneficiary that performs without seeing or examining the credit should bear the costs.

The strict compliance rule rests on the conclusion that issuers should not be forced into the position of determining whether a documentary discrepancy is significant. The rule assumes that issuers are not in a position to know whether discrepancies matter to the commercial parties. Nothing in that assumption requires courts to absolve issuers from knowing the significance of discrepancies for their own business; while it is consistent with the strict compliance rule to say that an issuer should not be charged with knowledge of whether an airbill, rather than an ocean bill, covering computer components is a significant defect,[26] it is not consistent with the rule to say that a bank issuer is absolved from knowing whether the abbreviation of the word "number" to "No." in the legend on a draft is a significant defect.[27] Banks presumably know nothing about the shipment of computer components, but they know a

---

Bank, 663 F. Supp. 252 (D. Utah 1987); Consolidated Aluminum Corp. v. Bank of Va., 544 F. Supp. 386 (D. Md. 1982), aff'd, 704 F.2d 136 (4th Cir. 1983); Bank of the Southeast v. Jackson, 413 So. 2d 1091 (Ala. 1982); Armac Indus. Ltd. v. Citytrust, 203 Conn. 394, 525 A.2d 77 (1987); Mount Prospect State Bank v. Marine Midland Bank, 121 Ill. App. 3d 295, 459 N.E.2d 979 (1983); Mercantile-Safe Deposit & Trust Co. v. Baltimore County, 309 Md. 668, 526 A.2d 591 (1987); Waidmann v. Mercantile Trust Co., 711 S.W.2d 907 (Mo. Ct. App. 1986); Republic Nat'l Bank v. Northwest Nat'l Bank, 578 S.W.2d 109 (Tex. 1978); cf. Southern Marine Research, Inc. v. Nateman, 434 So. 2d 47 (Fla. Dist. Ct. App. 1983) (per curiam) (affirming directed verdict for beneficiary whose documents complied); Sherwood & Roberts, Inc. v. First Sec. Bank, 682 P.2d 149 (Mont. 1984) (refusing to inquire into claim that issuer prevented account party from performing underlying contract and affirming summary judgment for beneficiary). For cases involving facts to which the strict compliance rule is applied, see infra ¶ 6.04.

[25] See Massive Paper Mills v. Two-Ten Corp., 669 F. Supp. 94 (S.D.N.Y. 1987) (holding that beneficiary that failed to complain of terms in credit could not use his inability to satisfy those terms to justify nonperformance of underlying contract).

[26] See infra ¶ 6.04[4] for discussion of *Board of Trade*.

[27] See infra ¶ 6.04[3] for discussion of *Tosco Corp.*

great deal about legends on drafts—legends that credits require, usually because the banks insist on them.[28]

It may not always be easy to tell the difference between the commercial defect and the noncommercial one. In *Willow Bend National Bank v. Commonwealth Mortgage Corp.*,[29] for example, the court concluded that it confronted a noncommercial one. The credit in that case recited that it was payable against drafts drawn at sight on the issuer and stipulated that the negotiating bank must endorse the amount of the draft on the back of the credit instrument itself. The beneficiary did not use a negotiating bank but presented its draft directly at the office of the issuer, which dishonored on the ground that there was no negotiating bank's endorsement on the reverse side of the credit. In a suit for wrongful dishonor, the court rejected the issuer's defense, holding that the endorsement requirement was intended for cases in which the beneficiary used a negotiating bank.

The *Willow Bend* holding may not conflict with the strict compliance rule. If, as the court assumed, the issuer knew the purpose of the endorsement requirement, it does not offend the reason of the strict compliance rule to excuse noncompliance.

In *Washington Federal Savings & Loan Association v. Prince George's County*,[30] the court implicitly held that document examiners should know that extra statements in a certificate do not render the certificate defective. In the *Washington Federal* case, the credit served to secure payments to subcontractors and suppliers for certain public improvements. When the issuer received a presentation from the beneficiary reciting more than the credit required, the issuer sought a declaratory injunction. The court ruled that the additional recitals did not render the certificate noncomplying. If the court in *Washington Federal*

---

[28] In New Braunfels Nat'l Bank v. Odiorne, 780 S.W.2d 313 (Tex. Ct. App. 1989), the court explicitly adopted the banking-commercial distinction, which it saw as consistent with the reported decisions, if not with the language of reported opinions. In *New Braunfels*, the legend on the beneficiary's draft referred to the credit number as "86-122-*5*" instead of "86-122-*S*," id. at 316 (emphasis in original), as the credit had required. The court found that the legend was required by the bank issuer and that the number "86" in the legend referred to the year of issue, the number "122" to the number of credits issued thus far in that year, and the letter "S" to the fact that the credit was a standby. The issuer had dishonored, despite efforts by the presenter to change the "5" to "S" at the time of presentment, the day of expiry. Such a change, the issuer had contended, could not be effected without the written authorization of the beneficiary. The cases do not relieve the beneficiary altogether from the requirement of placing the legend on the draft, however. See, e.g., Datapoint Corp. v. M&I Bank, 665 F. Supp. 722 (W.D. Wis. 1987). See infra ¶ 6.04[3].

[29] 722 S.W.2d 12 (Tex. Ct. App. 1986).

[30] 80 Md. App. 142, 560 A.2d 582 (1989).

expects document examiners to know whether additional assertions in a certificate are relevant or extraneous, it expects too much; if it holds as a matter of law that additional assertions are always extraneous, it may render certificates of uncertain value. In theory, additions to a certificate may alter its nature. A certificate, for example, that asserts that a shipment is conforming is different from a certificate that asserts that, "based on a sample," the shipment is conforming. Letter of credit law should not thrust bank clerks into the position of making such determinations. The better rule is the simple one: Beneficiaries must comply strictly.[31]

It is a misapplication of the strict compliance rule to say, as the court did in *Breathless Associates v. First Savings & Loan Association*,[32] that only discrepancies that increase the risk of defective performance in the underlying transaction give the issuer grounds to dishonor. That application of the rule assumes that issuers know enough about the underlying transaction and the commercial parties' industry to make the judgment whether the defect increases the risk. In fact, most issuers are not in a position to make that judgment. It is significant, furthermore, that, in another context, the Code excuses issuers from being conversant with trade practices.[33]

¶ 6.04   STRICT COMPLIANCE CASES

[1]   Describing the Goods

Article 41 of the Uniform Customs provides that "[t]he description of the goods in the commercial invoice must correspond with the description in the credit." The article goes on to say that general descriptions of the goods in other documents is satisfactory as long as the descriptions are not inconsistent with those of the invoice. The careful beneficiary insists that the description in the credit accord with what he knows to be his invoice practices. He instructs his credit department to draw invoices with the credit in hand, lifting the description of the goods from the latter verbatim.[34]

---

[31] The Uniform Customs may anticipate this problem. Article 23 stipulates that issuers may accept documents (other than transport documents, insurance documents, and commercial invoices) as presented unless the credit specifies their "wording or data content." By implication, that article requires the issuer to reject a document if it varies the credit's specification by either omitting or adding terms.

[32] 654 F. Supp. 832 (N.D. Tex. 1986).

[33] See U.C.C. § 5-109(1)(c).

[34] The rule requiring the description of the goods in the invoice to be the same as that in the credit leaves some room for deviation. It is possible, for example, that words in the credit or in the invoice may not be descriptive. In Astro Exito Navegacion S.A. v. Chase Manhattan Bank N.A., [1986] 1 Lloyd's Rep. 455 (Q.B.), the lan-

As the court noted in *National City Bank v. Seattle National Bank*,[35] the issuer of a credit presumably knows "little or nothing about sugar"[36] or about the other industries that credits serve. Letter of credit law does not charge banks with such knowledge.[37] The leading case, *J.H. Rayner & Co. v. Hambros Bank, Ltd.*,[38] an English decision, holds that a bank is not charged with the custom of "gentlemen who deal [with groundnuts] on contracts in Mincing Lane,"[39] because the letter of credit, even though it supported the shipment of groundnuts, "does not concern any transaction in Mincing Lane."[40] The court insulated the credit transaction from the underlying transaction, in conformity with the general rule of credit law that the credit is independent of the underlying transaction. The *Rayner* case, however, has broader import.

The credit in *Rayner* called for three documents: an invoice, a marine and war insurance policy, and clean on-board bills of lading in full set covering the shipment of "about 1,400 tons Coromandel groundnuts."[41] The beneficiary supplied an invoice describing the merchandise in such terms, but the bill of lading described the goods as "machine shelled groundnut kernels," with reference in the margin to "OTC C.R.S. Aarhus." The court concluded that the credit called for a full description of the goods in both the invoice and the bill of lading and specifically rejected the beneficiary's argument that a full invoice description was sufficient. Unless the court concluded that the description in the bill conflicted with the invoice description, Article 41 of the Uniform Customs would yield a different result.

Independent witnesses in the *Rayner* case testified that a merchant buyer of Coromandel groundnuts would not expect more than the description in the bill of lading. In the trade, "C.R.S." stood for "Coro," an abbreviation for "Coromandels." Thus, the balance of the bill of lading description was quite consistent with the description in the credit. The court rejected the plaintiff's claim of improper dishonor, however,

---

guage in the credit referred to an oceangoing vessel and added that the vessel was "to arrive under own power . . . as is and always safely afloat and intact." Id. at 458. The court held that the quoted language was not part of the description of the goods and that its absence from the invoice did not render the invoice noncomplying.

[35] 121 Wash. 476, 209 P. 705 (1922).

[36] Id. at 482, 209 P. at 707.

[37] Cf. U.C.C. § 5-109(1)(c) (absolving issuers from any duty based on trade knowledge or use).

[38] [1942] 2 All E.R. 694 (C.A.).

[39] Id. at 701.

[40] Id.

[41] [1942] 2 All E.R. 699 (C.A.).

holding that the bank was excused because the bill of lading did not comply precisely with the terms of the letter of credit.[42] *Rayner* supports the general rule that banks are not charged with knowledge of industry practices and, even though the case involved a bill of lading, that bank issuers may dishonor an invoice that contains a nonconforming description.

In other cases, courts have held that invoices do not satisfy the credit when the credit (1) called for "California Whites Petaluma extras" and the invoice described "Petaluma Ranch extras"[43]; (2) referred to "ladies sweaters, dresses, pants and skirts" and the invoice referred to "woolen knitwears"[44]; or (3) called for "100% acrylic yarn" and the invoice gave "imported acrylic yarn" (even though the packing list corrected the invoice deficiency).[45] In *Davidcraft Corp. v. First National Bank*,[46] the credit described the goods as a "52" ceiling fan." The court held that the beneficiary's invoice describing the goods as a "52+ ceiling fan" was nonconforming.

Concern in the early cases over descriptions of the goods in documents other than the invoice is allayed by Article 41(c) of the Uniform Customs, but the early cases indicate the attitude that courts have taken in applying the strict compliance rule. In one instance, a credit description calling for "standard white granulated sugar" was not satisfied by a certificate that referred to "granulated white sugar, Java #24, direct 98.5."[47] In a second case, a credit describing "Java white granulated sugar" was not satisfied by a bill of lading referring to "Java white sugar."[48] In yet a third case, a credit calling for "dried grapes" was not satisfied by a bill of lading referring to "raisins."[49] On the other hand, in one of the sugar cases (prompted by a precipitous fall in sugar prices in the early part of the twentieth century), the court held that because the credit did not require any specific language in the permits, general refer-

---

[42] Id. at 701.

[43] Portuguese-Am. Bank v. Atlantic Nat'l Bank, 200 A.D. 575, 575–576, 193 N.Y.S. 423, 423–424 (1922).

[44] Oriental Pac. (U.S.A.), Inc. v. Toronto Dominion Bank, 78 Misc. 2d 819, 820, 357 N.Y.S.2d 957, 958 (Sup. Ct. 1974).

[45] Courtaulds N. Am., Inc. v. North Carolina Nat'l Bank, 528 F.2d 802, 803 (4th Cir. 1975).

[46] 675 F. Supp. 1515 (N.D. Ill. 1986).

[47] National City Bank v. Seattle Nat'l Bank, 121 Wash. 476, 481, 209 P. 705, 707 (1922).

[48] Lamborn v. Lakeshore Banking & Trust Co., 231 N.Y. 616, 616, 132 N.E. 911, 911 (1921).

[49] Bank of Italy v. Merchants Nat'l Bank, 236 N.Y. 106, 108, 140 N.E. 211, 211, cert. denied, 264 U.S. 581 (1923).

ences to "sugar" in customs house permits satisfied a credit referring to "Java white sugar."[50] The beneficiary in one case obviously used his own product description in preparing the invoice and then superimposed the credit description onto the invoice. The effect was somewhat misleading, but the court, in a rather lenient application of the strict compliance rule, held the invoice to be "regular on its face"[51] and therefore consistent with Section 5-109. The account party in that case argued unsuccessfully that reference in the superimposed description to "part 301" was inconsistent with another (apparently transposed) invoice reference to "Dialer NE 310." The court held that there was no irregularity apparent in the two references.

It does not affect the compliance of the documents that the account party claims that the merchandise does not conform to the descriptions. As the court held in *Maurice O'Meara Co. v. National Park Bank*,[52] such complaints by the account party are attempts to add conditions to the credit after the fact. Absent intentional fraud by the beneficiary, few courts listen to such account party complaints.[53]

These cases reflect the wisdom of incorporating the Uniform Customs into a credit. The Customs not only resolve many of the questions these cases raise but also provide a simple rule for the beneficiary: The invoice description of the merchandise should track the credit description verbatim, and descriptions in other documents should not be inconsistent with that in the invoice.

[2] Other Invoice Problems

Article 41(a) of the Uniform Customs provides that invoices submitted under the credit must be made out in the name of the account party and must be those of the beneficiary, not those of someone else.[54] Article 41(b) provides that the invoice amount must not exceed that specified in the credit. In *Oriental Pacific (U.S.A.), Inc. v. Toronto Dominion*

---

[50] Bank of Am. v. Whitney-Cent. Nat'l Bank, 291 F. 929, 933–934 (5th Cir. 1923), petition dismissed, 264 U.S. 598 (1924).

[51] Talbot v. Bank of Hendersonville, 495 S.W.2d 548, 553 (Tenn. Ct. App. 1972); cf. U.C.C. § 5-109(2) (requiring issuer to determine that documents are regular "on their face").

[52] 239 N.Y. 386, 146 N.E. 636 (1925).

[53] For a discussion of the fraud cases, see ¶ 7.04.

[54] There is an exception to this rule, however, in U.C.P. art. 54(f) (1983), the transfer article. See generally ¶ 10.03.

Bank,[55] the court held improper an invoice in the amount of $39,206.26 when the balance available under the credit was $37,919.41. The beneficiary in the *Oriental Pacific* case did not ask for payment in excess of the amount available. The draft was in an amount equal to the credit balance, but the invoice was for a greater amount and therefore offended the rule of the predecessor of Article 41(b), making the beneficiary's presentation defective.

The 1983 Uniform Customs change these rules somewhat. Under Article 41(b), a bank may refuse an invoice in excess of the maximum amount authorized in the credit. The provision permits the issuer to accept the invoice, however, as long as the issuer does not pay more than the credit authorizes. Under the *Oriental Pacific* facts, an issuer of a credit subject to the 1983 Uniform Customs has discretion to accept or to reject the invoice, provided that the issuer does not honor drafts that exceed the amount of the credit.[56]

Reported cases reveal a number of additional problems that arise in connection with commercial or other kinds of invoices. In *Key Appliance, Inc. v. First National City Bank*,[57] the credit required the buyer to countersign the seller's invoices. Thus, the credit was of questionable benefit to the seller-beneficiary because the buyer might refuse to countersign and thereby leave the seller with no way, short of obtaining an injunction,[58] to comply with the terms of the credit. The *Key Appliance* court held, nonetheless, that the beneficiary must meet the requirements and that invoices which did not contain the account party's signature gave the issuer reason to dishonor the beneficiary's draft.[59]

---

[55] 78 Misc. 2d 819, 357 N.Y.S.2d 957 (Sup. Ct. 1974).

[56] In State v. Morganstein, 703 S.W.2d 894 (Mo. 1986), the court held squarely that a draft in an amount exceeding the amount of the credit was nonconforming. In addition, Article 44 of the Uniform Customs makes it clear that an issuer may honor a draft for less than the amount of the credit, unless the credit prohibits partial drawings.

[57] 46 A.D.2d 622, 359 N.Y.S.2d 886 (1974).

[58] In Corporacion De Mercadeo Agricola v. Mellon Bank Int'l, 608 F.2d 43, 45 (2d Cir. 1979), the court suggested that a beneficiary should have obtained such an order. For a case in which the court entered such an order, see Astro Exito Navegacion S.A. v. Southland Enter. Co., [1983] 2 All E.R. 725 (H.L.).

[59] See also Dubose Steel, Inc. v. Branch Banking & Trust Co., 72 N.C. App. 598, 324 S.E.2d 859 (1985), review denied, 314 N.C. 115, 332 S.E.2d 480 (1985) (holding that it was necessary for beneficiary to present invoice, even though account party and beneficiary had agreed to cancel invoice and substitute two other invoices). But cf. Arabian Fiberglass Insulation Co. v. Continental Ill. Nat'l Bank & Trust Co., No. 85 C 1268 (N.D. Ill. Dec. 12, 1986) (holding that credit calling for invoices approved by Arnold H. Montgomery did not require Montgomery's signature on invoices presented by beneficiary); North Beach Leather Int'l, Inc. v. Morgan Guar. Trust Co., 687 F. Supp. 127 (S.D.N.Y. 1988) (holding that ambiguous credit would be con-

In *Kelly-Springfield Tire Co. v. Dakota Northwestern Bank, N.A.*,[60] the letter of credit called for invoices covering goods sold to Hoffman and Mosbrucker. The beneficiary submitted invoices addressed to "Mosbrucker/Dakota Tire Co." The court approved the issuer's refusal to pay the beneficiary, who had attempted to change the credit's terms.[61]

In *Fina Supply, Inc. v. Abilene National Bank*,[62] the court held that a credit calling for commercial invoices was not satisfied by the presentation of provisional invoices. In *Borg-Warner Acceptance Corp. v. Tascosa National Bank*,[63] however, the court held that it was not necessary to present invoices when the credit did not call for them. The credit did refer to invoices, but the court pointed out that it did not make presentation of them a condition of payment under the credit. The *Borg-Warner* court was unwilling to add to the credit's conditions. The holding squares with the strict compliance rule.

Similarly strict application of a credit's terms is evident in *Artoc Bank & Trust, Ltd. v. Sun Marine Terminals, Inc.*[64] There the credit called for an invoice for services rendered along with a letter stating that the services had been rendered and were unpaid for. The court's opinion

---

strued against issuer to permit multiple invoices showing combined single shipment under two letters of credit); United States Steel Corp. v. Chase Manhattan Bank, N.A., No. 83 Civ. 4966 (WCC) (S.D.N.Y. July 2, 1984) (excusing beneficiary, on questionable ground that credit was ambiguous, from supplying invoice with purchase order number when there was no purchase order, sales contract having been concluded orally).

[60] 321 N.W.2d 516 (N.D. 1982).

[61] Cf. Texpor Traders, Inc. v. Trust Co. Bank, 720 F. Supp. 1100 (S.D.N.Y. 1989) (rejecting invoice that omitted room number in beneficiary's address, used Lyons, Georgia address of account party instead of Atlanta address, and omitted one word in account party's name in referring to purchase order); Mount Prospect State Bank v. Marine Midland Bank, 121 Ill. App. 3d 295, 459 N.E.2d 979 (1983) (holding that invoices made out to Magic Auto Products of New York were not conforming under credit that was not subject to Uniform Customs and that required invoices issued to Magic Auto Products of Illinois). In Champion Int'l Corp. v. Continental Nat'l Bank, 715 S.W.2d 128 (Tex. Ct. App. 1986), the credit secured invoices made out in the name of Miracle Web, a trade name of the account party. When the beneficiary attempted to present invoices it had originally made out in the name of Alamo Web, another trade name, and later altered by substituting the name of Miracle Web, the court held that the invoices were facially nonconforming and that the issuer was authorized to dishonor the beneficiary's draft. But cf. Crocker Commercial Servs., Inc. v. Countryside Bank, 538 F. Supp. 1360 (N.D. Ill. 1981) (involving similar facts with holding against issuer).

[62] 726 S.W.2d 537 (Tex. 1987).

[63] 784 S.W.2d 129 (Tex. Ct. App. 1990).

[64] 760 S.W.2d 311 (Tex. Ct. App. 1988).

suggests that the parties had intended the credit to cover obligations other than those for services rendered, but the court held that the beneficiary's attempt to cover such obligations with an invoice and a recital that the services were not paid for constituted a breach of the warranty rule of Article 5.[65]

A similar drafting problem is apparent in *Atlas Mini Storage, Inc. v. First Interstate Bank*,[66] where the credit called for commercial invoices in connection with the sale of mini–storage buildings. When the buyer canceled the contract before delivery of any buildings, the seller beneficiary presented an invoice for the benefit of the bargain it had lost by virtue of the buyer's breach. The court held that the invoice was not a commercial invoice and that the trial court had properly enjoined payment of the credit. In *Audio Systems, Inc. v. First National Bank*,[67] on the other hand, the court held it was not improper for a beneficiary to present invoices arbitrarily, not knowing whether they had been paid. The credit secured payments due under the invoices; but the beneficiary was uncertain which invoices were unpaid, though it was certain that the amount claimed was due.[68]

[3] Drafts

Both Article 10 of the Uniform Customs and Section 5-114 anticipate that, in some cases, the credit will be made available against demands or requests for payment other than a draft; but if the credit calls for a draft, the beneficiary must present one. Failure to do so renders the presenta-

---

[65] See U.C.C. § 5-111(1).

[66] 426 N.W.2d 686 (Iowa Ct. App. 1988).

[67] 753 S.W.2d 553 (Ky. Ct. App. 1988).

[68] For a case involving an invoice in which the court failed to follow the strict compliance rule, see Barclay Knitwear Co. v. King'swear Enters., Ltd., 141 A.D.2d 241, 533 N.Y.S.2d 724 (1988). There the credit called for a special customs invoice bearing reference to "tariff quota category #645." At the time the beneficiary imported the goods, the U.S. Customs Service had combined two quota categories, so that the former category #645 fell into a new, combined category #645/646. When the negotiating bank presented the special customs invoice with reference to the new, combined category, the issuer rejected it as nonconforming under the credit. The *Barclay* court disagreed that the invoice was defective, holding that the issuer knew that the categories had been combined. The *Barclay* holding may not square with the strict compliance rule. If the court found, and it seems improbable that it would, that bank clerks would surely know of the combination when they examined the documents under the short time constraints allowed for such examination, the holding would be correct. If the court concluded that the bank knew at the time of the litigation or that it could have found out that the categories had been combined, the holding does not square with the rationale for strict compliance.

tion noncomplying.[69] *Bounty Trading Corp. v. S.E.K. Sportswear, Ltd.*[70] held, for example, that a collection letter is insufficient, since it is not a draft. On the other hand, *Chase Manhattan Bank v. Equibank*[71] held that a telex containing the words "please remit"[72] satisfied the credit's requirement for a sight draft. A draft is an order. "Please remit," although polite, is in the imperative mood; the absence of any usance rendered the order a draft at sight.[73] In *First State Bank v. Shuford Mills, Inc.*,[74] the court refused to require the beneficiary to present a negotiable draft where the credit did not specify that the draft be in negotiable form. But in *Kydon Compania Naviera S.A. v. National Westminster Bank Ltd.*,[75] the court rejected as improper drafts drawn on the bank issuer when the credit called for drafts on the account party.[76]

Credits frequently call for drafts to bear legends such as "Drafts must recite that they are drawn under First National Bank L/C No. 123." Difficulties arise when a beneficiary fails to insert the legend properly. In *Tosco Corp. v. FDIC*,[77] for example, the credit called for a draft containing the following legend: "[D]rawn under Bank of Clarks-

[69] International Leather Distribs., Inc. v. Chase Manhattan Bank, N.A., 464 F. Supp. 1197 (S.D.N.Y.), aff'd mem., 607 F.2d 996 (2d Cir. 1979); Astro Exito Navegacion S.A. v. Chase Manhattan Bank N.A., [1986] 1 Lloyd's Rep. 455 (Q.B.); Kydon Compania Naviera S.A. v. National Westminster Bank Ltd., [1981] 1 Lloyd's Rep. 68 (Q.B.); see also Farmer v. Crocker Nat'l Bank (In re Swift Aire Lines, Inc.), 21 Bankr. 12 (Bankr. 9th Cir. 1982) (defining term "sight draft"). But cf. Titanium Metals Corp. of Am. v. Space Metals, Inc., 529 P.2d 431 (Utah 1974) (holding that course of dealing excuses beneficiary from credit's requirement that draft be submitted). For criticism of that approach, see infra ¶ 6.05[2].

[70] 48 A.D.2d 811, 370 N.Y.S.2d 4 (1975).

[71] 394 F. Supp. 352 (W.D. Pa. 1975).

[72] Id. at 355 n.4.

[73] Cf. Colonial Cedar Co. v. Royal Wood Prods., Inc., 448 So. 2d 1218 (Fla. Dist. Ct. App. 1984) (remanding to determine whether letter requesting payment satisfied credit calling for formal draft or whether issuer waived requirement); Chilton Air Cooled Engines, Inc. v. First Citizens Bank, 726 S.W.2d 526 (Tenn. Ct. App. 1986) (dictum to effect that absence of signed draft may have been harmless defect in view of beneficiary's formal request for payment); Temple-Eastex, Inc. v. Addison Bank, 672 S.W.2d 793 (Tex. 1984) (holding that letter demanding payment satisfied credit requiring sight draft); Travis Bank & Trust v. State, 660 S.W.2d 851 (Tex. Ct. App. 1983) (holding that letter asking for payment satisfied credit requiring draft).

[74] 716 S.W.2d 649 (Tex. Ct. App. 1986).

[75] [1981] 1 Lloyd's Rep. 68 (Q.B.).

[76] The *Kydon* court also held that an invoice cannot substitute as a draft, even though the invoice contains the same information that a draft contains. The invoice does not constitute an order and therefore fails to satisfy an essential requirement for a draft.

[77] 723 F.2d 1242 (6th Cir. 1983).

ville Letter of Credit Number 105." The beneficiary presented a draft whose legend differed in three respects:

1. It added the word "Tennessee" after "Clarksville."
2. It used a lower case "l" rather than an upper case "L" in the term "Letter of Credit."
3. It abbreviated "Number" to "No."[78]

The *Tosco* court—in part, perhaps, because of the nature of these nonconformities—eschewed the strict compliance rule, opting for substantial compliance.[79] The court need not have rejected strict compliance on these points. Under the strict rule, this draft is clearly conforming. The reason for the strict rule is to protect the issuer from having to know the commercial impact of a discrepancy in the documents. Under the strict rule, a bank document examiner does not need to judge whether dried grapes are the same as raisins and does not need to know that "C.R.S." stands for Coromandel groundnuts.[80] The legend in question, and most such legends, are for the issuer's benefit. Such legends assist the banker in identifying the credit, and it would not offend the strict rule to require bankers to understand that minor discrepancies of this sort do not offend the reason of the strict compliance rule.

First Bank v. Paris Savings & Loan Association[81] reflects application of the rule in a manner consistent with its reason. In the *First Bank* case, the beneficiary added to the legend the date and amount of the letter of credit. The court held that the draft was complying. As long as the departure from the language of the credit does not confuse or harm the issuer or result in some kind of fraud, the court held, the beneficiary has not violated the strict compliance rule.[82]

In these cases, it is not asking too much of the document examiner to exercise discretion as a banker, even though it is too much to ask a

---

[78] Id. at 1247.

[79] For further discussion of the *Tosco* case, see infra ¶ 6.05[1].

[80] For a discussion of (1) the reason for the strict compliance standard, (2) the raisin and groundnut cases, and (3) other cases involving legends on drafts, see supra ¶ 6.03.

[81] 756 S.W.2d 329 (Tex. Ct. App. 1988).

[82] In Datapoint Corp. v. M&I Bank, 665 F. Supp. 722 (W.D. Wis. 1987), the court agreed with the issuer that failure to place the legend on the draft might have rendered it noncomplying but held that failure of the issuer to notify the beneficiary of the defect promptly by telephone so the beneficiary could submit a complying draft before the credit expired estopped the issuer from raising the defect. The *Datapoint Corp.* court relied on Article 16 of the Uniform Customs in reaching its conclusion that an estoppel was in order. For further discussion of the estoppel rule of Article 16, see ¶ 4.06[2][b].

document examiner to exercise discretion on a commercial matter. Any reasonably prudent document examiner would recognize immediately that the discrepancies in question were de minimis, and courts should not hesitate to hold that they do not violate the strict compliance standard.[83] That is not to suggest that courts should open the compliance issue by rendering the test one of reasonableness. It is one thing to say, as *First Bank* implies, that no one could possibly be misled by an obvious misspelling, by transposition of letters in a common word, or by additional terms in a legend that any bank clerk would recognize as consistent with the legend's banking purpose. It is quite another to say that the rule is one of reason, that is, one of determining whether, under all of the circumstances, a reasonable document examiner would know that the defects were de minimis. The latter approach, adopted by some courts, has yielded decisions that corrode the effectiveness of the credit.[84]

Drafts must be submitted in time[85]; they should refer to the appropriate transaction, as the credit usually requires; and they should bear the beneficiary's signature as drawer.[86] A credit issued to two insurance

---

[83] The requirement for the legend on the draft may stem from an opinion by Chief Justice Marshall during the height of the virtual acceptance controversy. See ¶ 3.03[5]. In any event, the legend in *Tosco* satisfies the bank's purposes without using a strict compliance measure. For further discussion of errors in the legends on drafts, see supra ¶ 6.03. See also New Braunfels Nat'l Bank v. Odiorne, 780 S.W.2d 313 (Tex. Ct. App. 1989) (excusing as de minimis minor deviation in legend on beneficiary's draft from legend called for by credit).

[84] See infra ¶ 6.05[1] for discussion of the *Banco Espanol*, *Flagship*, and *Exotic Traders* cases. See generally Harfield, "Operating Within Law: Harfield on Difficulties for International Bankers" (pt. 2), Letter of Credit Update 6 (Jan. 1990); David, "Rise and Fall of Strict Compliance Doctrine—A Banker's Thoughts," Letter of Credit Update 13 (Mar. 1988).

[85] See Banco Tornquist, S.A. v. American Bank & Trust Co., 71 Misc. 2d 874, 337 N.Y.S.2d 489 (Sup. Ct. 1972).

[86] See North Valley Bank v. Nat'l Bank, 437 F. Supp. 70 (N.D. Ill. 1977) (holding that endorsement on back of draft did not satisfy signature requirement, but estopping issuer by virtue of statement by bank officer that issuer would honor draft). In Bank of N.Y. & Trust Co. v. Atterbury Bros., 226 A.D. 117, 234 N.Y.S. 442 (1929), aff'd, 253 N.Y. 569, 171 N.E. 786 (1930), the court held that a draft signed by "A. James Brown" did not satisfy a credit calling for drafts drawn by "Arthur James Brown." It also held that since the issuer had paid the proper beneficiary, the account party could not complain of the error. In Flagship Cruises, Ltd. v. New England Merchants Nat'l Bank, 569 F.2d 699 (1st Cir. 1978), the court excused a draft drawn by an agent of the beneficiary when that agency was apparent in correspondence between the agent and the issuer. For criticism of the *Flagship* case, see infra ¶ 6.05[1][b].

companies as their interests appear is not satisfied if only one of the companies draws.[87]

Ufitec, S.A. v. Trade Bank & Trust Co.[88] involved a traveler's letter of credit that required the beneficiary to sign drafts in the presence of an employee of the issuer's correspondent. The employee then would be able to compare the drawer's signature with the beneficiary's specimen signature on a separate identification card. The court held that a draft presented by the beneficiary without following that procedure was defective, notwithstanding the fact that the signature was indeed that of the beneficiary.

Generally, if the credit is silent on the point, a draft need not specify the beneficiary's intended use of the funds even when the underlying contract between the beneficiary and the account party designates specific use for the funds and even when the letter of credit refers to the underlying contract.[89] Problems arise when the beneficiary of the credit is no longer in existence or when it lacks capacity at the time of presentation. In some cases, for example, the beneficiary may be dead or incompetent. Generally, bank issuers are willing to accept drafts drawn by the personal representative of such a beneficiary. It is not unusual for financial institutions to deal with such representatives, who can attach official evidence of their capacity (e.g., letters of administration) to their drafts.

A closer question arises in cases of corporate insolvency, liquidation, or dissolution.[90] In *Addison Bank v. Temple-Eastex, Inc.*,[91] the beneficiary of a credit, a wholly owned subsidiary of the plaintiff, was dissolved, and the parent, which had taken the assets of the dissolved company, attempted to draw on a standby letter of credit. The *Addison Bank* court held that the plaintiff was attempting to effect a transfer of the credit, contrary to the rules for transfer,[92] and upheld the issuer's dishonor. The Supreme Court of Texas reversed,[93] holding that the par-

---

[87] Occidental Fire & Casualty Co. v. Continental Ill. Nat'l Bank & Trust Co., 718 F. Supp. 1364 (1989).

[88] 12 A.D.2d 187, 249 N.Y.S 2d 557 (1964), aff'd, 16 N.Y.2d 698, 209 N.E.2d 551, 261 N.Y.S.2d 893 (1965).

[89] See United States v. Sun Bank, 609 F.2d 832 (5th Cir. 1980).

[90] These cases also raise serious questions under the transfer rules, as the *Addison Bank* case does. For a discussion of the transferability of a credit in the context of insolvency, liquidation, and dissolution, see ¶ 10.06.

[91] 665 S.W.2d 550 (Tex. Ct. App.), rev'd, 672 S.W.2d 793 (Tex. 1984).

[92] See supra note 90.

[93] Temple-Eastex, Inc. v. Addison Bank, 672 S.W.2d 793 (Tex. 1984).

ent was not a transferee but a "distributee"[94] of the beneficiary. The Texas court laid some store by the provision in Section 3-505 of the Code authorizing a party to whom presentment is made to require the presenter to identify himself. That section gives the payor rights. The court transformed it into a section imposing a duty. The *Addison Bank* rule, moreover, imposes a far greater burden on an issuer than does a rule requiring the issuer to honor the drafts of a personal representative; and the court's holding lends a hollow ring to its assertion that it is adhering to the strict compliance rule. A contrary holding in *Addison Bank* would put the burden on the parties planning a corporate dissolution to obtain the agreement of all parties to amend the credit.[95]

Critics may argue that, in any moderately complex corporate reorganization, the parties cannot possibly be aware of all standby credits and that it is inevitable that they will miss one and fail to have it amended. That may be true, but the costs of reorganizations should fall on the parties to it, not on the banking system. It is not fair to allocate the burden to the issuer, which has no knowledge of and no voice in the corporate reorganization.

In *American National Bank & Trust Co. v. Hamilton Industries International, Inc.*,[96] the credit named one party as beneficiary, but another party drew on the issuer. It appears from the opinion that no one objected to the fact that the second party drew and that, in fact, the parties had intended to make the second party the beneficiary. If the parties had been unwilling to agree to an amendment, the facts supported a claim for reformation of the instrument. In *American Airlines, Inc. v. FDIC*,[97] the court ignored the fact that the "draft" did not name a drawee. In *Armac Indus., Ltd. v. City Trust*,[98] however, the court did not ignore the fact that a draft must have a drawer. The beneficiary in that case presented a draft listing itself as payee and endorser and showing a signature line for the issuer's signature. The court held that the endorsement did not suffice as a drawer's signature and that the draft was not conforming.

---

[94] Id. at 796.

[95] For a discussion of the need to obtain the consent of all parties to amendments of a credit, see ¶ 5.02[1].

[96] 583 F. Supp. 164 (N.D. Ill. 1984), rev'd on other grounds sub nom. Banque Paribas v. Hamilton Indus. Int'l, Inc., 767 F.2d 380 (7th Cir. 1985).

[97] 610 F. Supp. 199 (D. Kan. 1985).

[98] 203 Conn. 394, 525 A.2d 77 (1987).

[4] Bills of Lading

Although courts are generally reluctant to consider evidence of practices relating to the industry of the beneficiary and the account party, the Court of Appeals for the Ninth Circuit, in *Board of Trade v. Swiss Credit Bank*,[99] remanded a case to consider evidence of banking industry custom in determining whether the term "full set clean on board bills of lading" included airbills.[100] On remand, the trial court upheld the issuer's dishonor, and, on a second appeal, the Ninth Circuit held squarely that it was not up to the issuer's document examiner to determine whether shipment of electronic integrated circuits by air rather than by sea was a substantial deviation that required dishonor.[101] That burden, the court held, should not fall on the issuer, who is entitled to enforce the credit strictly.

In *Marine Midland Grace Trust Co. v. Banco Del Pais, S.A.*,[102] the court refused to excuse a beneficiary's failure to present truck bills of lading with an "on-board" stamp. The credit called for the on-board stamp, but the evidence showed that the Mexican trucking industry did not issue bills in that form. The court refused to excuse the discrepancy.

The *Board of Trade* and *Marine Midland* cases illustrate application of the letter of credit rule with respect to industry practices. The issuer of a credit is charged with knowledge of banking industry practices, but not with practices of the industry out of which the underlying contract arises.[103]

In *Siderius, Inc. v. Wallace Co.*,[104] the court held that questions concerning the compliance of a bill of lading were questions of law and were not questions for a jury. The court also held that a "shipped bill" satisfied a credit calling for an on-board bill.

Laudisi v. American Exchange National Bank[105] anticipated the rule of Article 41(c) of the Uniform Customs in holding that the description of merchandise in the bill of lading need not follow that of the cred-

---

[99] 597 F.2d 146 (9th Cir. 1979).

[100] For authority defining the term "clean bill of lading," see British Imex Indus. Ltd. v. Midland Bank, Ltd., [1985] 1 All E.R. 264 (Q.B.); International Chamber of Commerce, The Problem of Clean Bills of Lading, ICC Doc. No. 283 (1963).

[101] See Board of Trade v. Swiss Credit Bank, 728 F.2d 1241 (9th Cir. 1984).

[102] 261 F. Supp 884 (S.D.N.Y. 1966).

[103] See U.C.C. § 5-109; Marino Indus. Corp. v. Chase Manhattan Bank, N.A., 686 F.2d 112 (2d Cir. 1982).

[104] 583 S.W.2d 852 (Tex. Civ. App. 1979).

[105] 239 N.Y. 234, 146 N.E. 347 (1924).

it, so long as it is not inconsistent with that of the credit.[106] *Camp v. Corn Exchange National Bank*[107] anticipated Section 5-109 of the Code by holding that a bank that examines a bill of lading must exercise good faith in determining whether to reject it.

In *Voest-Alpine International Corp v. Chase Manhattan Bank, N.A.,*[108] the court held that the issuer had properly dishonored a beneficiary's draft accompanied by on-board bills of lading dated January 31, 1981 and inspection certificates indicating that loading occurred in February. The credit called for bills dated no later than January 31.

In *Beyene v. Irving Trust Co.,*[109] the court held that a confirming bank properly refused to honor a presentation that included a bill of lading that misspelled the name of the party to be notified as So*r*an instead of So*f*an. In response to the plaintiff's argument that the discrepancy was trivial, the court noted that the "confirming bank need not ascertain the magnitude of each discrepancy before its obligation to pay is relieved."[110] On appeal, the court held that the error could be distinguished from an obvious typographical error and that the document examiner had no way of knowing whether the discrepancy was sufficient to prevent notice to Mr. Sofan.[111]

In *Austracan (USA) Inc. v. Neptune Orient Lines, Ltd.,*[112] furthermore, the court held that an issuer properly accepted a bill of lading with exculpatory language because the bank was not charged with industry knowledge that the language was inconsistent with other recitals in the bill.[113] In *Pro-Fab, Inc. v. Vipa, Inc.,*[114] the beneficiary failed to supply a bill of lading that was already in the issuer's possession in connection with the first credit in a back-to-back credit arrangement. The *Pro-*

---

[106] Cf. Atari, Inc. v. Harris Trust & Sav. Bank, 599 F. Supp. 592 (N.D. Ill. 1984), aff'd in part and rev'd in part mem., 785 F.2d 312 (7th Cir. 1986) (rejecting issuer's contention that description of goods and quantities in bills of lading must include detail of invoices).

[107] 285 Pa. 337, 132 A. 189 (1926); see also Cooper's Finer Foods, Inc. v. Pan Am. World Airways, Inc., 178 So. 2d 62 (Fla. Dist. Ct. App. 1965) (holding that issuer properly honored draft accompanied by nonnegotiable air waybill).

[108] 545 F. Supp. 301 (S.D.N.Y. 1982), aff'd in part and rev'd in part, 707 F.2d 680 (2d Cir. 1983).

[109] 596 F. Supp. 438 (S.D.N.Y. 1984), aff'd, 762 F.2d 4 (2d Cir. 1985).

[110] Id. at 442.

[111] 762 F.2d 4 (2d Cir. 1985).

[112] 612 F. Supp. 578 (S.D.N.Y. 1985).

[113] Cf. Larsen v. Carpenter, 620 F. Supp. 1084 (E.D.N.Y. 1985), aff'd mem., 800 F.2d 1128 (2d Cir. 1986) (holding that although bill of lading was subject to charter party and therefore was defective, parties were too late in raising objection).

[114] 772 F.2d 847 (11th Cir. 1985).

Fab court, noting that the document examiner was unaware that the issuer had the bill, held that the failure to supply the bill was a discrepancy that could justify dishonor.

In *Davidcraft Corp. v. First National Bank*,[115] the credit called for a
bill of lading "FOB vessel, Taiwan Port." The beneficiary presented a
bill with a shipment term of "FOB Baltimore." The court viewed the
discrepancy as one favoring the account party and held that the bill was
not defective. *Davidcraft* is consistent with the strict compliance rule
only if bank document examiners can be charged with knowledge of the
discrepancy's effects—a questionable conclusion. But in *Bank of Nova
Scotia v. Angelica-Whitewear Ltd.*,[116] the court held defective a bill specifying the port of discharge as Vancouver under a credit describing the
sale as CIF Montreal.

In *Bucci Imports, Ltd. v. Chase Bank International*,[117] a transport
document showed the destination of the goods as Scottsdale, Arizona.
The credit called for a document showing the destination as Houston,
Texas. The court granted summary judgment for the issuer on the beneficiary's claim for wrongful dishonor.

In *Westpac Banking Corp. v. South Carolina National Bank*,[118] the
credit called for an on-board bill of lading. The issuer complained that a
"received-for-shipment" bill that was modified to contain "on-board"
language did not comply, but the Judicial Committee of the Privy Council held that the bill satisfied the credit's requirements. Significantly, the
court also held that the presence of a "loaded-on-board" stamp on the
bill did not render it internally inconsistent and did not give the issuer
reason to dishonor. The court saw the issue as one of determining
whether a competent bank document examiner might reasonably regard
the bill of lading as not satisfying Article 20 of the 1974 Uniform Customs and concluded that the bill met the test.

In an arbitration opinion, *In re Standard Chartered Bank*,[119] written by the chairman of the ICC working party that drafted the 1983 version of the Uniform Customs, the arbitrators reached a conclusion arguably different from that of the Privy Council. In the *Standard Chartered*

---

[115]No. 83 Civ. 5481 (N.D. Ill. Jan. 6, 1986); see also U.C.P. art. 3 (1983) (to
same effect for "any reference whatsoever" in credit); cf. Banque Worms v. Banque
Commerciale Privee, 679 F. Supp. 1173 (S.D.N.Y. 1988), aff'd per curiam, 849 F.2d
787 (2d Cir. 1988) (holding that general reference to underlying transaction in credit
subject to Uniform Customs does not add to credit's documentary requirements).

[116]36 D.L.R.4th 161 (Can. 1987).

[117]132 A.D.2d 641, 518 N.Y.S.2d 15 (1987).

[118][1986] 1 Lloyd's Rep. 311 (P.C.).

[119]Letter of Credit Update 27 (Jan. 1988) (Wheble, arb.).

Bank arbitration, the arbitrators held that a bill of lading form that does not recite whether it is a received-for-shipment bill or an on-board bill is a received-for-shipment bill. The arbitrators went on to hold that language stamped on such a bill to the effect that the goods were "clean on board" does not satisfy the 1983 analogue of Article 20[120] unless it bears a signed and dated signature.[121]

[5] Certificates and Documents

[a] Documents in General

Article 23 of the Uniform Customs stipulates that when the credit calls for "other documents" (meaning documents other than transport documents, insurance documents, and commercial invoices) the "data content" of those other documents must make it possible for the document examiner to "relate the goods and/or services referred to therein to those referred to in the commercial invoice(s) presented, or to those referred to in the credit" if the credit does not call for a commercial invoice.

Article 41(c) of the UCP stipulates that the description of goods in documents other than the commercial invoice should not be inconsistent with the description in the invoice. In *S.B. International, Inc. v. Union Bank of India,*[122] the court rejected as nonconforming bills of lading containing language that appeared to a person unfamiliar with the stainless steel industry to be inconsistent. The beneficiary argued that in fact the descriptions were consistent, but the court ruled that it was not incumbent on the issuer's document checker to know the custom and lexicon of the commercial parties' industry.

When a credit calls for a certificate of some sort, failure to provide that certificate renders the presentation nonconforming and excuses the issuer from any duty to pay.[123] An issuer, however, may not add condi-

---

[120] That analogue is Article 27. See U.C.P. art. 27 (1983 version).

[121] In Kuntal, S.A. v. Bank of N.Y., 703 F. Supp. 312 (S.D.N.Y. 1989), the beneficiary acknowledged, and the court agreed, that an air waybill was not conforming when it (1) was consigned to the issuing bank instead of to the account party, (2) covered a short shipment, and (3) showed the wrong destination (Boston instead of New York).

[122] 783 S.W.2d 225 (Tex. Ct. App. 1989).

[123] Accord Banco Nacional De Desarrollo v. Mellon Bank, N.A., 726 F.2d 87 (3d Cir. 1984); Banco Nacional De Credito Ejidal S.A. v. Bank of Am., 118 F. Supp. 308 (N.D. Cal. 1954); Anglo-S. Am. Trust Co. v. Uhe, 261 N.Y. 150, 184 N.E. 741 (1933); see also Prudential-Bache Sec., Inc. v. Lisle Axis Assocs., No. 86 C 7634 (N.D. Ill. Oct. 22, 1986) (entering mandatory injunction against account party requiring it to execute certificate necessary for beneficiary to draw on credit or to provide substitute letter of credit with later expiry); Banque De L'Indochine Et De Suez

tions to the certificate that the credit does not require. In *Bank of Canton, Ltd. v. Republic National Bank*,[124] the issuer argued that a Federal Communications Commission certificate called for by the credit had to be issued to the shipper. The credit contained no such requirement, and the court rejected the issuer's argument that New York banking custom to the contrary could bind a Hong Kong bank that negotiated the beneficiary's drafts.[125]

In *Pringle-Associated Mortgage Corp. v. Southern National Bank*,[126] the credit referred to the underlying agreement, and the issuer argued that the beneficiary needed to show that the credit funds would be used to complete the construction project that was the subject of that underlying contract. The court rejected that position, holding that the credit's general reference to the underlying agreement was "surplusage."[127] The *Bank of Canton* and *Pringle* cases demonstrate the manner in which the strict compliance rule cuts one time against the beneficiary and another time against the issuer.[128]

S.A. v. J.H. Rayner (Mincing Lane) Ltd., [1983] 1 Lloyd's Rep. 228 (C.A.) (similar case); cf. President & Fellows of Harvard College v. United States Trust Co., 82 Civ. 7432 (WCC) (S.D.N.Y. Mar. 15, 1984) (indicating that failure to obtain, from recalcitrant party, certificate necessary to satisfy credit can be cured by court order to party, subject, in this case, to beneficiary's posting of indemnity bond). For further discussion of cases in which the beneficiary is required to present documents in the control of the account party, see ¶ 2.05[3].

[124] 509 F. Supp. 1310 (S.D.N.Y.), aff'd, 636 F.2d 30 (2d Cir. 1980).

[125] Cf. Marino Indus. Corp. v. Chase Manhattan Bank, N.A., 686 F.2d 112 (2d Cir. 1982) (holding that since credit did not limit signature on inspection certificate to those on facsimile card, issuer could not complain that it had no facsimile). Significantly, the *Marino Industries* court also held that a certificate of receipt was not conforming when the word "cash" was crossed out of it. The credit called for a recitation that freight charges were prepaid, and a witness testified that striking the word "cash" indicated prepayment of the charges. The court rejected the view that the issuer should have accepted the certificate. Id. at 119–120.

[126] 571 F.2d 871 (5th Cir. 1978).

[127] Id. at 874.

[128] Cf. Fertico Belg., S.A. v. Phosphate Chems. Export Ass'n, 100 A.D.2d 165, 473 N.Y.S.2d 403, appeal dismissed, 62 N.Y.2d 802 (1984) (holding that account party cannot complain of beneficiary that it did not present documents not required by credit). In Devco Dev. Corp. v. Hooker Homes, Inc., 518 So. 2d 922 (Fla. Dist. Ct. App. 1987), review denied, 525 So. 2d 877 (Fla. 1988), it was the beneficiary that insisted that it could not satisfy the credit's conditions prior to the expiry, because it did not have possession of the letter of credit and could not present it to the issuer. The court held that the credit did not contain any condition that the beneficiary present the credit and that the failure of the account party to see that the beneficiary obtained possession of the credit was no excuse for the beneficiary's failure to draw before the expiry. The court noted that none of the parties had the power to add a condition to the credit without the agreement of all other parties and argued that the

A negotiating bank may not obtain reimbursement from an issuer when a required certificate does not include a required signature and omits language called for by the credit. In *Eximetals Corp. v. Pinheiro Guimares, S.A.*,[129] the credit required that an inspection certificate be verified and countersigned by the president of the buyer. The credit also required that the inspection certificate recite that the "material shipped is 7124 units Ribbet Flange in accordance with sample and buyers [sic] drawing No. 17865."[130] The certificate did not use those terms but did recite that the material conformed to the shipper's "proforma invoice."[131] Eventually, the beneficiary supplied a pro forma invoice that included the omitted language. The court found the documents insufficient and explained that to require the issuer to judge whether the reference to the pro forma invoice was sufficient violated the principle that the issuer's duties are "ministerial."[132] The court also noted that the pro forma invoice was not countersigned by the buyer's president and held that a requirement that the certificate be countersigned calls not just for a countersignature but for a primary signature as well. The signature of the buyer's president on the certificate of inspection was insufficient without the signature of the inspector.[133]

In *Far Eastern Textile, Ltd. v. City Nat'l Bank & Trust Co.*,[134] the credit called for a purchase order signed by Larry Fannin. When the beneficiary submitted a purchase order signed "Larry Fannin by Paul Thomas," the issuer dishonored. In a suit by the beneficiary for wrongful dishonor, the court rendered summary judgment for the issuer, holding that to require the issuer to investigate the authority of Thomas "subverts the independent nature of the credit."[135]

In *Marino Industries Corp. v. Chase Manhattan Bank, N.A.*,[136] the court refused to excuse a beneficiary that failed to obtain a "legalized" packing list. The beneficiary complained that the importing country's

---

court itself did not have the power to add a condition. For discussion of the establishment issue in the *Devco Development* case, see ¶ 5.01[2].

[129] 73 A.D.2d 526, 422 N.Y.S.2d 684 (1979), aff'd, 51 N.Y.2d 865, 414 N.E.2d 399, 433 N.Y.S.2d 1019 (1980).

[130] Id., 422 N.Y.S.2d at 686.

[131] Id.

[132] Id. at 527, 422 N.Y.S.2d at 686.

[133] See also Occidental Fire & Casualty Co. v. Continental Ill. Nat'l Bank & Trust Co., 718 F. Supp. 1364 (1989) (holding that certificate signed by only one beneficiary of credit issued to two beneficiaries as their interests may appear does not conform).

[134] 430 F. Supp. 193 (S.D. Ohio 1977).

[135] Id. at 198.

[136] 686 F.2d 112 (2d Cir. 1982).

consulate did not legalize packing lists, but the court insisted on strict compliance.[137]

In *Bank of Cochin Ltd. v. Manufacturers Hanover Trust Co.,*[138] although a number of document discrepancies were held not sufficient to render the documents noncomplying, other discrepancies were. The following were among the discrepancies that the court considered trivial:

1. The failure of the beneficiary to submit proof that it had satisfied a factual condition of the credit;
2. Documents signed by an agent of the beneficiary without designating his relationship to the beneficiary;
3. A shipping company certificate that failed to specify the vessel registration number; and
4. Presentation of only five signed copies of the invoice instead of the six that for which the credit called.

Among the defects that the court held to be significant were a cable to an insurance company that referred to the cover note by the wrong number and presenter's omission of the term "Ltd." from the beneficiary's name. Unfortunately, the court did not explain its reasoning. One wonders why five copies of the invoice were as good as six and whether two or three would have been as good as six.

In *Davidcraft Corp. v. First National Bank,*[139] the credit called for an inspection certificate bearing the signature of "Joe Tung of Davidcraft's Taiwan office." The court held that the signature "Joe Tung," without any designation, was sufficient. In *Security State Bank v. Basin Petroleum Services, Inc.,*[140] the failure of a beneficiary to submit purchase orders in advance of manufacture of certain equipment and the failure to refer to the letter of credit in the purchase orders, as the credit required, rendered the documents noncomplying. In *Fina Supply, Inc. v. Abilene National Bank,*[141] the court held documents to be noncomplying in that they failed to specify the type of crude oil referred to in the credit and indicated delivery points other than those called for by the credit.

---

[137] The *Marino Industries* opinion hints that had the beneficiary informed the issuer of the problem with the consulate the result might have been different. Cf. Marine Midland Grace Trust Co. v. Banco Del Pais, S.A., 261 F. Supp. 884 (S.D.N.Y. 1966) (holding that failure to obtain Mexican on-board truck bill when industry did not issue such bills was not excused).

[138] 612 F. Supp. 1533 (S.D.N.Y. 1985), aff'd, 808 F.2d 209 (2d Cir. 1986).

[139] 675 F. Supp. 1515 (N.D. Ill. 1986).

[140] 713 P.2d 1170 (Wyo. 1986).

[141] 726 S.W.2d 537 (Tex. 1987).

[b] Documents With the Standby Credit

The standby credit is sometimes clean; that is, it calls for the beneficiary to present a draft and nothing more. Often, however, the standby credit also requires a certificate, and courts generally invoke the strict compliance rule against the beneficiary who fails to present such a document.

In *Chase Manhattan Bank v. Equibank*,[142] the credit called for a certificate reciting that the account party had defaulted on its loan transaction with the beneficiary. Although the beneficiary had sent a letter to the issuer referring to loan payment problems, and although the issuer knew that the account party was in default, the court held that the beneficiary was not excused from supplying the certificate.[143]

In *Lustrelon, Inc. v. Prutscher*,[144] the credit called for the beneficiary's certificate reciting that certain tools had not been returned to the beneficiary by the account party. When the beneficiary submitted such a certificate, the account party protested that it was not true. The court held that an issuer may accept a certificate as submitted and does not act in bad faith when it pays a draft over the account party's claim of fraud.[145]

In *Colorado National Bank v. Board of County Commissioners*,[146] the credit secured the account party's obligation to construct improvements in a planned development. When the account party became insolvent, the development was abandoned. The issuer argued that the bene-

---

[142] 394 F. Supp. 352 (W.D. Pa. 1975).

[143] Cf. Armac Indus., Ltd. v. Citytrust, 203 Conn. 394, 525 A.2d 77 (1987) (holding that requirement that beneficiary present certificate reciting that goods had been "picked up" was not satisfied by bill of lading showing that goods were shipped); Lennox Indus., Inc. v. Mid-Am. Nat'l Bank, 49 Ohio App. 3d 117, 550 N.E.2d 971 (1988) (rejecting beneficiary's claim for wrongful dishonor when beneficiary failed to present certificate required by credit); American Nat'l Bank v. Cashman Bros. Marine Contracting, 550 So. 2d 98 (Fla. Dist. Ct. App. 1989) (rejecting certificate reciting "hereby certifies that I have determined," when credit called for certificate to recite "hereby certifies"); Ronald A. & Caroline Olson, Inc. v. United States Nat'l Bank, 70 Or. App. 460, 689 P.2d 1021 (1984) (holding that demand that account party cure default was too late when it was delivered thirteen days after default and when credit called for certificate requiring delivery of demand within ten days of default).

[144] 178 N.J. Super. 128, 428 A.2d 518 (App. Div. 1981).

[145] Accord Brown v. United States Nat'l Bank, 220 Neb. 684, 371 N.W.2d 629 (1985). The *Brown* case also holds that a certificate need not contain the word "certify" in order to conform to a requirement that a certificate be presented. Accord Employers Mut. Casualty Co. v. Tascosa Nat'l Bank, 767 S.W.2d 279 (Tex. Ct. App. 1989). For further discussion of the fraud defense, see ¶ 7.04.

[146] 634 P.2d 32 (Colo. 1981).

ficiary (the county) did not plan to use the funds for any development but was attempting to garner a windfall. The court held that the county's lack of damages was irrelevant and that the bank should honor a draft accompanied by a conforming document. The court also approved the dishonor of sight drafts when the credit called for time drafts. The *Colorado National Bank* case demonstrates the manner in which the strict compliance rule may operate at one point in favor of the issuer and at another in favor of the beneficiary.[147]

In *Banco Nacional De Credito Ejidal S.A. v. Bank of America*,[148] the failure of the beneficiary to supply a cable advice from a customs broker to the effect that goods had passed Food and Drug Administration inspection justified the issuer's refusal to honor the beneficiary's draft.[149]

Courts generally do not look to the underlying transaction to determine the compliance of the beneficiary's documents. In *Utica Mutual Insurance Co. v. Walker*,[150] the court ordered the issuer not to pay the beneficiary. Although the opinion is unclear, it appears that the beneficiary argued that reference to the underlying transaction would support its position that it had complied with the terms of the credit. The *Utica Mutual* court held that the terms of the credit were unambiguous and that it would not refer to the underlying transaction to measure the compliance of the beneficiary's documents. Application of the independence principle would yield the same result.[151] In *Ensco Environmental Ser-*

---

[147] See generally the discussion of the *Pringle* and *Bank of Canton* cases in ¶ 4.08 and supra ¶ 6.04[5][a]. See also Chrysler Motors Corp. v. Florida Nat'l Bank, 382 So. 2d 32 (Fla. Dist. Ct. App. 1979), corrected, id. (1980) (holding that issuer could not require beneficiary to present certificates of origin when credit did not call for them); Travelers Indem. Co. v. Flushing Nat'l Bank, 90 Misc. 2d 964, 396 N.Y.S.2d 754 (Sup. Ct. 1977) (holding that credit calling for certification that beneficiary incurred liability does not justify issuer's insistence that beneficiary show it paid liability).

[148] 118 F. Supp. 308 (N.D. Cal. 1954).

[149] Cf. Seattle-First Nat'l Bank v. FDIC, 619 F. Supp. 1351 (W.D. Okla. 1985) (holding that if confirming bank failed to insist that beneficiary present original copies of letters of credit, as credits required, bank had not exacted strict compliance and would lose its right of reimbursement from issuer); Waidmann v. Mercantile Trust Co., 711 S.W.2d 907 (Mo. Ct. App. 1986) (holding that certificate reciting that account party defaulted on note did not satisfy credit calling for recital that account party defaulted on payment due under note).

[150] 725 S.W.2d 24 (Ky. Ct. App. 1987).

[151] For a similar result, see American Coleman Co. v. Intrawest Bank, 887 F.2d 1382 (10th Cir. 1989), in which the credit mistakenly referred to a note dated November 21, when in fact the note in the underlying transaction was dated November 16. When the beneficiary presented the issuer with a certificate referring to the note's correct date, the bank dishonored. The court held that the dishonor was proper. For general discussion of the independence principle, see ¶ 2.09[5].

vices, Inc. v. United States,[152] the court held that reference in a standby credit to the underlying transaction did not impart an obligation on the part of the beneficiary to present a certificate of default to the issuer.

In *Interfirst Bank v. First Federal Savings & Loan Association,*[153] the beneficiary certified that certain parties had not performed their contractual obligations satisfactorily. The issuer argued that it was not clear from the record that the parties had failed to perform. Since the lower court found no fraud on the part of the beneficiary in making the certification, the *Interfirst Bank* court refused to let the issuer add a condition to the credit by litigating the performance question and affirmed an award of summary judgment in favor of the beneficiary. Similarly, in *Northwestern Bank v. NCF Finance Corp.,*[154] the court refused to impose on the beneficiary of a standby securing an underlying obligation a requirement that the beneficiary seek payment from the underlying obligor before drawing on the credit.

An issuer of a standby credit may not require a certificate if the credit does not require it. In *United States v. Sun Bank,*[155] the credit recited that the beneficiary would use the funds supplied under the credit to complete a condominium project. In fact, the beneficiary used the funds to satisfy tax obligations, but the court refused to accept the view that such use justified dishonor. The court reasoned that the credit did not require documentation of the beneficiary's use of the funds. Similarly, in *Auto-Owners Insurance Co. v. South Side Trust & Savings Bank,*[156] the issuer complained that the beneficiary had used the credit's proceeds to satisfy a bond obligation on which the principal was a person other than the party the issuer thought was the principal. The court held, however, that since the issuer had not insisted that the beneficiary supply a copy of the bond when it presented its demand for payment, the issuer could not recover payments made under the credit.

In *Ohio Industrial Commission v. First National Bank,*[157] however, the credit recited that it was a condition of the credit that it cover all injuries and occupational disease claims payments incurred by the beneficiary. When the beneficiary drew, the parties and the court apparently

---

[152] 650 F. Supp. 583 (W.D. Mo. 1986).

[153] 242 Kan. 181, 747 P.2d 129 (1987).

[154] 88 N.C. App. 614, 365 S.E.2d 14 (1988).

[155] 609 F.2d 832 (5th Cir. 1980).

[156] 176 Ill. App. 3d 303, 531 N.E.2d 146 (1988).

[157] No. C-840840 (Ohio Ct. App. Aug. 28, 1985).

thought that such recital in the credit required the beneficiary to present a certificate to that effect.[158]

In *Pastor v. National Republic Bank*,[159] the court refused to let the issuer impose greater documentary burdens on the beneficiary than the credit itself imposed. In the *Pastor* case, the credit called for an "official statement setting forth the amount"[160] of the beneficiary's loss under its contract with the account party. The issuer wanted full accounting, but the court found the beneficiary's summary statement of its loss sufficient.

In *Bank of Montreal v. Federal National Bank & Trust Co.*,[161] the credit secured loans made to a subsidiary of the account party and called for the beneficiary to present an assignment of its rights against the debtor. The beneficiary presented the assignment, and the issuer complained that the beneficiary did not assign debentures it held from the debtor. The court held that because the credit did not call for the debentures, the issuer could not object to the beneficiary's failure to present them.

Customer account parties may not complain when an issuer honors a complying presentation. It is not the bank's duty to determine whether documents are fraudulent, whether signatures are genuine, or whether some signatures are missing.[162] As long as the documents comply on their face, the bank must honor the beneficiary's drafts. In *First Nation-*

---

[158] The beneficiary supplied the certificate but omitted the word "all" when referring to injuries. The court held that the omission did not constitute a defect in the certificate.

[159] 76 Ill. 2d 139, 390 N.E.2d 894 (1979).

[160] Id. at 145, 390 N.E.2d at 896.

[161] 622 F. Supp. 6 (W.D. Okla. 1984).

[162] Philip A. Feinberg, Inc. v. Varig, S.A., 80 Misc. 2d 305, 363 N.Y.S.2d 195 (Sup. Ct. 1974), aff'd mem., 47 A.D.2d 1005, 370 N.Y.S.2d 499 (1975). Contra Instituto Nacional De Comercializacion Agricola (Indeca) v. Continental Ill. Nat'l Bank & Trust Co., 530 F. Supp. 279 (N.D. Ill. 1982). In a subsequent opinion in the same case, the *Indeca* court limited the obligation of the confirming bank to detect fraud or forgeries to circumstances that constitute fraud or reckless disregard for the integrity of the documents. See Instituto Nacional De Comercializacion Agricola (Indeca) v. Continental Ill. Nat'l Bank & Trust Co., 675 F. Supp. 1515 (N.D. Ill. 1987), aff'd, 858 F.2d 1264 (7th Cir. 1988). On appeal, the Court of Appeals for the Seventh Circuit held squarely that the duties of a confirming bank are found in U.C.C. §§ 5-109 and 5-114 and that the confirming bank satisfies those sections when it examines the documents with care. Id. The court found no basis in the Code or under non-Code Illinois law to impose the tort of negligent misrepresentation on a confirmer. The Seventh Circuit emphasized that the policy of Article 5 was to promote the use of credits and that such policy is not served by fastening liability on confirmers in addition to that imposed by the Code. For further discussion of the confirmer's duties to the opening bank and the account party, see ¶¶ 9.03[3], 9.04.

al Bank v. Rosebud Housing Authority,[163] the credit required the beneficiary to submit a copy of an agreement. At the time of the presentation, the agreement had been superseded. The issuer dishonored, claiming that the beneficiary had submitted an agreement that was of no significance. The court rejected the issuer's argument and held that the strict compliance rule relates to the face of the documents, not to their underlying validity.

Amendments to credits can be problematic in determining whether documents comply. In *Westwind Exploration, Inc. v. Homestate Savings Association*,[164] the credit, which was scheduled to expire on September 27, originally called for evidence of oil shipments during August. In an apparent attempt to cover shipments during later months, the parties extended the credit by amendment, first to October 28 and then to November 29. Both amendments stipulated, however, that, except for the extension, all terms of the credit remained the same. When the beneficiary presented documents and requests for payment covering deliveries made in July, August, September, and October, the issuer dishonored. The court held that the dishonor was proper, the documents not being in strict compliance with the terms of the credit.[165]

The requirement that the beneficiary comply strictly in presenting documents under a standby credit does not extend to the point of absurdity. If departures from the exact language in the credit are such that any reasonably intelligent bank clerk would recognize that the departure is of no consequence, the issuer should pay the beneficiary. In *First Bank v. Paris Savings & Loan Association*,[166] for example, the credit required the beneficiary to present a letter referring to the note secured by the credit and to renewals and modifications of the note. The beneficiary submitted a letter referring to the note and adding that there had been no renewals or modifications. The issuer argued that the failure to follow the language of the credit in hæc verba constituted a violation of the strict compliance rule. The court in *First Bank* disagreed, holding that the departure from the language in the credit caused no harm, confusion, or fraud and did not give the issuer reason to dishonor.[167]

The strict compliance rule does apply, however, even though it may yield an impossible condition. In *Tradex Petroleum American, Inc. v.*

---

[163] 291 N.W.2d 41 (Iowa 1980).

[164] 696 S.W.2d 378 (Tex. 1985).

[165] See also Fina Supply, Inc. v. Abilene Nat'l Bank, 726 S.W.2d 537 (Tex. 1987) (following *Westwind* holding on similar facts).

[166] 756 S.W.2d 329 (Tex. Ct. App. 1988).

[167] For further discussion of defects that could not possibly mislead a clerk document examiner, see supra ¶ 6.04[3].

Coral Petroleum, Inc. (In re Coral Petroleum, Inc.),[168] the credit's terms required the beneficiary to submit a shipper's transfer listing that referred to "sour" oil and an invoice and a statement referring to "sweet" oil. The beneficiary argued that the inconsistency relieved it from the onus of the strict compliance rule, but the court held that it was incumbent on the beneficiary to examine the credit in advance of performance to ensure that it could comply with the credit's terms. The standby in the *Tradex* case secured payments due on an invoice. The beneficiary, the court held, should have delayed delivery of the oil or should have insisted on an amendment.

In *Bebco Distributors, Inc. v. Farmers & Merchants Bank*,[169] the court required the beneficiary to present checks drawn by the account party, even though the account party had refused to draw the checks. The *Bebco* credit required the issuer to honor checks drawn by the account party that had been dishonored by the drawee. The court held that the account party's refusal to draw the checks did not excuse the beneficiary from complying strictly with the conditions of the credit.[170]

[6] Bank Practices and the Uniform Customs

Banking industry publications and various provisions in the Uniform Customs deal at length with questions concerning the compliance or noncompliance of those documents that appear most frequently in the commercial credit transaction.[171] Article 34 of the Uniform Customs defines two "leeway" rules that relate to documentary compliance. The first, in Article 43(a), the 10 percent leeway rule, permits the parties to use such words as "about" or "circa" in connection with the amount of the credit, the quantity of goods, or the unit price. Under the 10 percent leeway rule, such terms render documents with an amount, quantity, or unit price 10 percent above or 10 percent below that stipulated in the credit as complying. A second leeway rule, the 5 percent leeway rule, is more complicated. It relates to the quantity term and does not apply if the credit stipulates that the quantity of the goods must not be exceeded or reduced. Absent such stipulation, the 5 percent leeway rule permits

---

[168] 878 F.2d 830 (5th Cir. 1989).

[169] 485 So. 2d 330 (Ala. 1986).

[170] For additional cases involving credits requiring the beneficiary to present documents in the control of the account party, see ¶ 2.05[3].

[171] The Uniform Customs contain general rules for documents (U.C.P. arts. 22–24 (1983)) and special rules for transport documents (U.C.P. arts. 25–34 (1983)), insurance documents (U.C.P. arts. 35–40 (1983)), commercial invoices (U.C.P. art. 41 (1983)), and other documents (U.C.P. art. 42 (1983)).

quantities of 5 percent above or 5 percent below if the quantity is expressed as a measurement, that is, if the quantity is expressed in tons, bushels, gallons, or similar measurements. The 5 percent leeway rule does not apply if the credit designates the quantity by packing units or individual items (e.g., "50 crates of tractor parts" or "100 woolen shirts").

Article 23 of the Uniform Customs obviates a host of problems and possible discrepancies when it distinguishes commercial invoices, transport documents, and insurance documents from other documents. Unless the credit specifies some feature of those other documents, the issuer may accept them as tendered.[172] Article 23 provides, however, that other documents must contain information sufficient to link them to the goods or services described in the commercial invoice or, in the absence of an invoice, to the goods or services described in the credit.

[7] Nondocumentary Conditions

There appears to be an increasing number of cases involving credits subject to nondocumentary conditions. Arguably, these undertakings violate the *Wichita* rule; that is, they stray so far from the purpose of a letter of credit that courts should not apply the law of letters of credit to them.[173] Some courts, however, reject the *Wichita* requirement and attempt to apply the strict compliance rule to undertakings to which the rule may be ill suited.

In *Sherwood & Roberts, Inc. v. First Security Bank*,[174] for example, the credit was payable on the "unremedied default by the [account party] in its performance"[175] of certain obligations evidenced by documents, including a note and a mortgage. The beneficiary sued the issuer; and the account party, a third-party defendant, sought to litigate the default issue. The court held, however, that the beneficiary was entitled to summary judgment as a matter of letter of credit law.

The apparent error of the *Sherwood & Roberts* case is in treating the engagement as a letter of credit. It is difficult to understand how the issuer could possibly know, without investigation, that a party is in unremedied default on a note or mortgage. The application of the strict compliance rule to the case is unfortunate. The issuer's undertaking ap-

---

[172] Cf. U.C.C. § 5-109, comment 2 (recognizing that parties might agree to such standard).

[173] For a discussion of the *Wichita* requirement and cases involving nondocumentary conditions, see ¶ 2.05.

[174] 682 P.2d 149 (Mont. 1984).

[175] Id. at 151.

pears to be secondary, and the account party should have the opportunity to litigate the default question.

In *Guilford Pattern Works, Inc. v. United Bank*,[176] the court observed what it took to be a distinction between documentary conditions and nondocumentary conditions. As to the former, the court would apply the strict compliance rule; as to the latter, the substantial compliance rule. The conditions in question arose out of a letter that was attached to the credit. The letter detailed the delivery terms of the underlying contract. The court held that in order to recover on the credit, the beneficiary would have to satisfy those terms. It also held that because the terms were incorporated in a document, the terms were documentary and called for strict compliance. In fact, documentary conditions are conditions that the beneficiary can satisfy by the submission of documents. The delivery terms were nondocumentary. In any event, issuers that incorporate nondocumentary terms may have violated the important *Wichita* principle. Many courts would refuse to apply letter of credit law to the credit in *Guilford.* The *Guilford* court ultimately remanded the case for determination of a factual question—whether the beneficiary had agreed to the amendment that incorporated the delivery terms.[177]

In *Newvector Communications, Inc. v. Union Bank*,[178] a poorly drafted credit called for "draft(s) as per Resellers Agreement."[179] Conscious of the *Wichita* rule that the issuer's undertaking not stray too far from the purpose of a letter of credit (prompt and certain payment)[180] but holding that credits can be subject to nondocumentary conditions, the court read the quoted language as requiring the presentation of the resellers agreement. Apparently, there was no resellers agreement. Although the court declined to enter judgment in favor of either party, it would have been better if the court had held that the credit was so vague that it failed to meet minimal requirements of a credit by leaving the documentary conditions unascertainable.

There is authority that in the event a letter of credit calls for a nondocumentary condition, the issuer should require the beneficiary to present documents evidencing satisfaction of the condition.[181] In *Banque*

---

[176] 655 F. Supp. 378 (D. Colo. 1987).

[177] For discussion of the court's handling of that issue, see ¶ 5.02[1].

[178] 663 F. Supp. 252 (D. Utah 1987).

[179] Id. at 253.

[180] For discussion of the *Wichita* requirement, see ¶ 2.05.

[181] For discussion of the practice in one foreign jurisdiction, see Doise, "Recent Legal Developments in France Regarding Documentary Credits and Bank Guarantees," Letters of Credit Report 7 (Mar./Apr. 1989).

De L'Indochine Et De Suez S.A. v. J.H. Rayner (Mincing Lane) Ltd.,[182] the credit called for shipment on a vessel belonging to an international shipping conference but did not require documentation of that fact. The court held that the issuer should have required documentary evidence of such fact.[183] In *Esal (Commodities) Ltd. v. Oriental Credit Ltd.,*[184] a performance guaranty called for payment of the guaranty "in the event that supplier fails to execute the contract in perfect performance."[185] The court read into the credit the requirement that the beneficiary present a certificate of noncompliance with its request for payment.

The nondocumentary condition in the *Banque De L'Indochine* case is easily satisfied by documents familiar to parties to international sales and to bank document examiners. That court's suggestion makes sense in that context but would not make sense in many standby situations, where the transactions are so often unique and where document examiners would be hard put to know which documents satisfy the nondocumentary condition. It is one thing to require a document examiner to look for documentation that a ship belongs to an international liner conference; it is quite another for the examiner to look for "draft(s) as per Resellers Agreement."[186] The court's reformation of the performance guaranty in the *Esal* case is not reassuring. Such guaranties are often in the nature of clean, "first-demand"[187] obligations, and it may have been quite contrary to the intention of the parties in *Esal* to require certification.

In short, it is no easy answer to the problem of nondocumentary conditions to say that courts should render those conditions documentary. In some cases, it is impossible to do so; in others, the reference to an underlying transaction may be surplusage that does not create a condition.

---

[182] [1983] 1 Lloyd's Rep. 228 (C.A.).

[183] In First Nat'l Bank v. Raiffeisen-Zentralkasse Tirol, 671 P.2d 1008 (Colo. Ct. App. 1983), the court considered a term nondocumentary that arguably was documentary and that easily could have been satisfied by the documents which the beneficiary presented. The credit in the *First National Bank* case prohibited partial shipments. That condition is not uncommon and is satisfied by the presentation of drafts, invoices, and transport documents indicating that the full quantity of goods has indeed been shipped.

[184] [1985] 2 Lloyd's Rep. 546 (C.A.).

[185] Id. at 549.

[186] The quoted language comes from a credit referred to in Newvector Communications, Inc. v. Union Bank, 663 F. Supp. 252 (D. Utah 1987).

[187] For further discussion of first-demand guaranties, see ¶ 2.03.

¶ 6.05 THE VIEW OPPOSING STRICT COMPLIANCE

Alongside the strong body of law that supports the rule requiring the beneficiary's strict compliance with the terms of the credit, there stands a line of cases—a distinct minority—that use time-honored notions of "substantiality" and "equity" to reject the strict compliance precept. These cases may fail to reckon the commercial costs that their ad hoc rules foster.[188] Some of the cases relax the strict compliance rule unwittingly, but others do so explicitly.

[1] Explicit Cases

The leading cases for the minority position come from the First Circuit. They are *Banco Espanol de Credito v. State Street Bank & Trust Co.*[189] and *Flagship Cruises, Ltd. v. New England Merchants National Bank.*[190] They state the rule explicitly but vaguely. In the latter respect, they have no choice. The substantial compliance rule they adopt is inherently vague.

[a] The *Banco Espanol* Case

In *Banco Espanol*, the dispute centered on the inspection certificate. The credit stipulated that the certificate state "that the goods are in conformity with the order."[191] The order documents, however, were garbled; it was not clear to either the court or the inspector which papers comprised the order. The court found that the order was not in the documents so entitled but was "supplanted" by documents entitled "stock sheets."[192] Before inspection, the buyer account party confused matters further by sending a flurry of cables that one might conclude were designed to intimidate or confuse the inspector. The net effect of the cables was further confusion. Ultimately, the beneficiary presented a certificate of inspection that did not recite that the goods were in conformity with the order, as the credit commanded, but did certify that, based on a 10 percent sample, the "whole . . . [was] found con-

---

[188] See generally supra ¶ 6.02.

[189] 385 F.2d 230 (1st Cir. 1967), cert. denied, 390 U.S. 1013 (1968).

[190] 569 F.2d 699 (1st Cir. 1978).

[191] Banco Espanol de Credito v. State St. Bank & Trust Co., 385 F.2d 230, 231 (1st Cir. 1967), cert. denied, 390 U.S. 1013 (1968).

[192] Id. at 232.

forming to the conditions estipulated [sic] on the Order-Stock-sheets."[193] The court held the certificate to be in compliance.

There are two reasons for objecting to the *Banco Espanol* certificate. The certificate failed both the strict compliance test and any fair substantial compliance test. It failed the strict compliance test because it did not recite that the goods conformed to the order. The strict compliance rule is clear and easy to apply. The certificate also flunked a fair application of the substantial compliance test. The analysis of that question is not clear or easy; invoking a substantial compliance test never is. The essential defect, from a substantial compliance standpoint, is the fact that the certificate attempted to limit the certification to samples.

The *Banco Espanol* court spent most of its time dealing with that objection. The court noted that a leading strict compliance case, *Maurice O'Meara Co. v. National Park Bank*,[194] involved an affidavit, with samples of merchandise attached, reciting that the samples were representative and that tests of them satisfied the description of the goods in the credit. The *Banco Espanol* court also seemed moved by the fact that any inspection, of necessity in most cases, must be limited to samples. These arguments do not justify the court's holding. The certificate in the *O'Meara* case was not called for by the credit. The fact that *O'Meara* finds the documents in conformity with the credit, therefore, does not support the idea that the certificate in *O'Meara* would have satisfied a credit calling for an inspection certificate reciting that the goods conformed.

A much more egregious error in *Banco Espanol* is the court's shifting to the account party a burden that should have been shouldered by the inspector. It may be that inspectors perforce select samples of the merchandise they examine and that they cannot, for example, examine each apple in a carload of apples or each bushel of grain in a twenty-ton shipment. This reality, however, does not alter the fact that a certificate reciting that samples conform differs from a certificate reciting that a shipment conforms. An inspector who must issue the latter certificate behaves far differently from one who need only issue the former. The number of samples that the inspector takes and the methods he uses in taking them are matters of industry expertise.[195] The inspector, for example, who tests salad oil at the top of a tank may be dismayed to learn

---

[193] Id. at 233.

[194] 239 N.Y. 386, 146 N.E. 636 (1925).

[195] For a case describing the central limit theorem for determining the number of samples necessary to guaranty the normality of the distribution of sample means, see Texpor Traders, Inc. v. Trust Co. Bank, 720 F. Supp. 1100, 1105 n.2 (S.D.N.Y. 1989).

that salad oil floats on water, and the grain inspector who takes samples from the perimeter of an elevator may be dismayed to learn that grain can rot from the inside out. Inspectors who certify with regard to the whole make two judgments: They decide whether the sample conforms, and they decide whether they have enough samples, properly selected, so that they can attest to a whole shipment. The inspector who certifies only to samples does not need to make the second judgment.

The *Banco Espanol* merchandise was garments. It might have been difficult to inspect all of the garments or to decide how much inspection was sufficient. It may be, and the *Banco Espanol* court would undoubtedly agree, that the buyer's request for a certificate that the goods conformed to the order was an unreasonable request. It may also be, as the court hinted, that the buyer, when he suggested that he would render the certificate himself, sent the flurry of cables to the inspector, indemnified the issuer, and instructed it not to honor the seller's drafts unless he approved the inspection certificate, was trying to escape from a bargain he no longer valued. The *Banco Espanol* opinion's frequent recital of such facts suggests as much, especially when it characterizes the risk of nonconformity as the buyer's risk and emphasizes its own view that the buyer caused the confusion. These last conclusions appear to carry weight with the court, but they do not withstand analysis.

The risk of nonconformity is the buyer's risk only if the seller does not agree to guarantee conformity by supplying an independent inspector's certificate stating that the goods do conform. By insisting that the risk was the buyer's, the *Banco Espanol* court predisposed itself to rule against the buyer on the ultimate issue. It is true that the papers in the *Banco Espanol* case were confusing, but it is difficult to see why the sellers, who had the right to negotiate the terms of the credit, should be blameless when those terms do not mesh well with the underlying contract. Contrary to the thrust of the *Banco Espanol* opinion, the credit was not established for the benefit of the buyer. It was established for the benefit of the sellers. True, the inspection certificate was for the buyer's benefit; but the sellers had the right to negotiate the terms of that certificate. Indeed, if they had wanted to limit the certificate to one by sample, they could have insisted on it. Apparently, they did not. They did not object to a credit that called for a certificate of full compliance, but they negotiated the drafts with a limited certificate and hoped that the negotiating bank would be able to collect the drafts for them with the help of either a lenient issuer or a lenient court.

The *Banco Espanol* opinion does not make the case for its holding. More important to an evaluation of *Banco Espanol* is the fact that the rule it announces ignores its effect on the document examination process. *Banco Espanol* acknowledges a "substantial body of case law" favoring strict compliance but then notes "some leaven in the loaf of strict construction."[196] The trouble with poetic rules is that they invite poetic license. The *Banco Espanol* recipe does not and cannot specify how much yeast to add. The opinion invites ad hoc jurisprudence. It is not clear from *Banco Espanol* that the State Street Bank should have accepted, for instance, a certificate reciting that representative samples were conforming, one reciting that one sample was conforming, or one reciting that random samples were conforming. The case may suggest that any certificate would comply but probably means that any "reasonable" certificate would comply. Banks, however, do not know what kind of sampling of garments, grain, steel, diodes, or cucumbers is reasonable, unless they know something about the industries that deal in such commodities. To require banks to have such knowledge is to insist on the impossible.[197]

The parties to the underlying contract presumably do know about the industry and do know what kind of inspection will pass in the trade. The commercial parties are the proper entities to designate in their sales contract and in the letter of credit what the nature of that inspection certificate should be. If the credit calls simply for an inspection certificate, Article 23 of the Uniform Customs requires the issuer to accept any inspection certificate.[198] When the credit issues, the seller must object if it calls for an inspection certificate more burdensome than the one to which the seller agreed in his sales contract with the buyer. If matters are confused, as they were in *Banco Espanol*, the seller and the buyer must resolve the ambiguities. Absent such a resolution, it only creates difficulties for letters of credit in general when a court burdens the issuer with the problems the *Banco Espanol* court expected the State Street Bank to shoulder.[199]

[b] The *Flagship* Case

The *Flagship* case represents the second attack on the strict compliance rule by the Court of Appeals for the First Circuit. The case is rele-

[196] Banco Espanol de Credito v. State St. Bank & Trust Co., 385 F.2d 230, 234 (1st Cir. 1967), cert. denied, 390 U.S. 1013 (1968).

[197] See U.C.C. § 5-109 & comment 1.

[198] For a case describing the minimum content necessary for a certificate to qualify as an inspection certificate, see Commonwealth Banking Co. v. Jalsard Pty. Ltd., [1972] 2 Lloyd's Rep. 529 (P.C.).

[199] The drafters of the Uniform Customs attempted in Article 23 to avoid the problem in *Banco Espanol*, but their attempt was not altogether successful. Article 23 provides that the credit "should" stipulate the wording of other documents and the identity of the party who is to issue them. The Article provides no guidance for the document examiner, who must deal after the fact with documents presented under a credit that does not comply with the suggestion of Article 23.

vant to this discussion because, in it, the author of *Banco Espanol* invokes the substantial compliance rule again to hold that documents need not follow verbatim the language of the credit. The *Flagship* credit called for the beneficiary's signed statement that the "draft" was "in conjunction with Letter of Agreement dated May 23, 1972 and Addendum dated June 15, 1972."[200] The document that the beneficiary presented recited that the "Letter of Credit" was "in conjunction with the Letter of Agreement dated May 23, 1972, and Addendum dated June 15, 1972."[201] In short, the document substituted the words "Letter of Credit" for the word "draft" that the credit used.

The court held that the document was in compliance and saw the matter "as a case of the greater including the smaller."[202] The court reasoned that "if a draft must reveal its nexus to a specific agreement, this requirement would be satisfied if the entire letter of credit, on which the draft depends, relates to the specific agreement."[203] Significantly, the court did not consider its holding to be a relaxation of the strict compliance rule. At the same time, the court refused to disapprove what it considered to be a functional, although not literal, compliance.

Document examiners may not conclude as readily as the *Flagship* court did that a reference to the letter of credit is a case of the greater including the smaller and that it operates as a reference to a draft drawn under the credit. *Flagship* requires them to do so. *Flagship* errs in the same way as *Banco Espanol*. It unrealistically expects document examiners to exercise something other than the ministerial function of comparing the documents with the credit.

Flagship may be significant in that it claims (though the claim does not appear to be justified) not to relax the strict compliance rule. The case may be something of a retreat from contrary language in the court's opinion in *Banco Espanol*. The district court adopted that view in *Exotic Traders Far East Buying Office v. Exotic Trading U.S.A., Inc.*[204] That court characterized *Banco Espanol* and *Flagship* as defining a rule that requires strict compliance in all cases except those in which the defect "could not have misled anyone."[205] The language of *Exotic Traders* is consistent with the majority rule, which also allows for deviations that

---

[200] Flagship Cruises, Ltd. v. New England Merchants Nat'l Bank, 569 F.2d 699, 701 (1st Cir. 1978).

[201] Id.

[202] See id. at 703.

[203] Id.

[204] 717 F. Supp. 14 (D. Mass. 1989).

[205] Id. at 17.

could not possibly be misleading to document examiners.[206] But the *Exotic Traders* holding reflects application of the rule in a manner redolent of *Banco Espanol*'s substantial compliance values.

The defects in *Exotic Traders* were several:

1. Telexes certifying that goods had been shipped were dated two days late in one case and one day late in another.
2. One telex did not include the price of the goods.
3. A commercial invoice recited the delivery term as F.O.B. Korea, while the credit called for delivery F.O.B. Seoul.

The court held that these defects would not mislead anyone. First, the telexes served their purpose, which, according to the court, was to obviate warehousing expense. The court did not indicate, however, that there was evidence that a document examiner would be aware of that purpose without investigating industry practices or inquiring of the account party. Second, the "F.O.B." recital was not misleading, in the court's view, because the invoice indicated elsewhere that the goods were loaded in Seoul, as did other documents (customs invoice, certificate of origin, and air waybill) presented with the invoice. Finally, the court held, other documents supplied the price that was missing from the telex.

Because *Exotic Traders* does not explain that a document examiner would have known the purpose of the telexes and would have known that the defects were commercially unimportant, the opinion is unconvincing. It may well be that the purpose of the telexes was to permit the buyer to make plans to receive the merchandise and avoid storage charges, but it is a great leap of faith from that conclusion to the conclusion that a bank clerk is aware of such industry practices when a buyer imports commodities by air.

The court's conclusion that information missing in one document may be gleaned from another document, though consistent with *Flagship*, is also unpersuasive. First, in many import transactions, the importer is acquiring not goods but documents, and he will "sell" the documents to his customer, a subpurchaser, before the goods arrive or shortly thereafter. While that does not appear to have been the case in *Exotic Traders*, the language of the opinion does not make allowance for that not uncommon situation and fashions a rule under which an account party will receive documents from the issuer that he may have difficulty selling to his subpurchaser. Second, under Article 23 of the Uniform Customs, an issuer generally does not have to review "other"

---

[206] See supra ¶ 6.03.

documents, except to determine that they are in fact what they purport to be. The *Exotic Trader* rule requires greater examination and requires a measure of judgment concerning the import of missing information in one document and the efficacy of abstracting the information from another document.[207] One can expect a federal judge to make those determinations, but one cannot reasonably expect a bank clerk to make them.

[c] Other Explicit Cases

Banco Espanol and *Flagship* have prompted other courts to relax the strict compliance rule considerably. *First National Bank v. Wynne*[208] involved a credit that required, as a credit often does, that the beneficiary submit a draft reciting that it was drawn under the credit and identifying the credit by number. The *Wynne* draft failed to include such recitation, but the court held that *Flagship* stood for the rule that no defect is significant if it does not mislead the issuer. The court held that since the beneficiary's cover letter did refer to the credit, the defect did not justify dishonor.[209] In *First Arlington National Bank v. Stathis*,[210] the credit called for far too much documentation:

1. The note that was the object of the underlying debt;
2. Any security agreements relating to the note's collateral;
3. An affidavit that the note was due;
4. A detailed statement of the nature of default;
5. An affidavit that the beneficiary demanded payment; and
6. Copies of the demand letters.

The parties who agreed to this credit failed to recognize that letters of credit do not serve well as performance bonds triggered by complex factual determinations. As one might expect, when the beneficiary presented his demand for payment, the issuer claimed a host of defects. The

---

[207] In fact, Maurice O'Meara Co. v. National Park Bank, 239 N.Y. 386, 146 N.E. 636 (1925), contains language to the same effect. The strict view is advanced by Courtaulds N. Am., Inc. v. North Carolina Nat'l Bank, 528 F.2d 802 (4th Cir. 1975), which holds, in a fashion consistent with the Uniform Customs, that defects in the invoice description may not be cured by information in packing lists.

[208] 149 Ga. App. 811, 256 S.E.2d 383 (1979).

[209] For similar cases that cast their eyes on more than one document, see Courtaulds N. Am., Inc. v. North Carolina Nat'l Bank, 387 F. Supp. 92 (M.D.N.C.), rev'd, 528 F.2d 802 (4th Cir. 1975); Bank of Am. Nat'l Trust & Sav. Ass'n v. Liberty Nat'l Bank & Trust Co., 116 F. Supp. 233 (W.D. Okla. 1953), aff'd, 218 F.2d 831 (10th Cir. 1955); Learner Co. v. Isbrandtsen, 140 N.Y.S.2d 316 (App. Term. 1955).

[210] 90 Ill. App. 3d 802, 413 N.E.2d 1288 (1980).

court disposed of most of the defects under the waiver rule, holding that by failing to list the defects in early correspondence with the beneficiary, the bank had waived them.[211] The court held that there was one defect, however, that the issuer did not waive. The credit required the beneficiary to make demand on the account parties at the note's accelerated maturity. The beneficiary made demand on the account parties for past-due installments and notified them of acceleration, but the beneficiary did not renew the demand, the court held, when the acceleration occurred.

The *Stathis* court unwittingly may have created a setting in which it had to deal with the strict compliance rule. The credit was ambiguous, and it was not at all clear that the credit required a demand for payment after acceleration. It required that demand be made according to the note's accelerated maturity. By construing the credit against the beneficiary, the court may have violated one of the general principles of credit construction—that ambiguous credits should be construed against the issuer or against the drafter.[212] The *Stathis* opinion failed to indicate which party was the source of the ambiguous language.

By construing the credit to require a demand at the time of acceleration, the court was forced to hold that, under the strict compliance rule, the demand was insufficient. Thus, the court opened the strict compliance standard to scrutiny. The *Stathis* court then aligned itself with the substantial compliance line of cases and held that the defect was insufficient to justify dishonor. *Stathis* is an unfortunate decision. The credit was so complicated that it begged the court to bend the law of credits out of shape.[213] The *Stathis* court obliged.[214]

---

[211] For a discussion of the waiver and estoppel limits on the strict construction rule, see infra ¶ 6.06.

[212] For discussion of that principle, see ¶ 4.08[3].

[213] In Mount Prospect State Bank v. Marine Midland Bank, 121 Ill. App. 3d 295, 459 N.E.2d 979 (1983), the court cited the *Stathis* case as authority for the strict compliance rule and then noted that one of the parties had argued that *Stathis* stood for substantial compliance. The court concluded that the presentation satisfied both rules. In Occidental Fire & Casualty Co. v. Continental Ill. Nat'l Bank & Trust Co., 718 F. Supp. 1364 (1989), the court read *Stathis* and *Mount Prospect*, among other authority, as fashioning a strict compliance rule for Illinois.

[214] There have been additional cases that eschew strict compliance for substantial compliance. See Itek Corp. v. First Nat'l Bank, No. 80-58-MA (D. Mass. May 25, 1982), vacated on other grounds, 704 F.2d 1 (1st Cir. 1983); Crocker Commercial Serv., Inc. v. Countryside Bank, 538 F. Supp. 1360 (N.D. Ill. 1981); American Employers Ins. Co. v. Pioneer Bank & Trust Co., 538 F. Supp. 1354 (N.D. Ill. 1981); Peoples State Bank v. Gulf Oil Corp., 446 N.E.2d 1358 (Ind. Ct. App. 1983); Schweibish v. Pontchartrain State Bank, 389 So. 2d 731 (La. Ct. App. 1980).

In *Tosco Corp. v. FDIC*,[215] the Court of Appeals for the Sixth Circuit, in a diversity case, applied Tennessee law to a claim against an issuer that dishonored the beneficiary's draft on the ground that it was not complying. Three of the defects were clearly de minimis: changing a letter from upper to lower case, adding the state's name after the city designation, and using a common abbreviation for the word "number."[216] In addition, the legend on the draft was endorsed by the beneficiary rather than by the negotiating bank, as the letter of credit required. The *Tosco* court appeared to be impatient with these objections and dismissed the strict compliance standard as the "New York" rule,[217] which, the court held, Tennessee courts had not adopted.

It is not clear why the issuer in *Tosco* required the beneficiary to obtain the negotiating bank's endorsement of the legend or why the negotiating bank's endorsement on the draft itself did not serve as the required endorsement. It is clear that the missing endorsement is a matter entirely different from the first three alleged discrepancies. The *Tosco* court may ask too much of document examiners. It forces them to decide whether the endorsement is important. It is precisely against that kind of burden that the strict compliance standard is designed to protect the document examiner. Absent the beneficiary's proof that any document examiner would know whether the missing endorsement is significant, the court should require the beneficiary to supply it.[218]

---

[215] 723 F.2d 1242 (6th Cir. 1983).

[216] For a discussion of these discrepancies, see supra ¶ 6.04[3].

[217] Tosco Corp. v. FDIC, 723 F.2d 1242, 1247 (6th Cir. 1983). The *Tosco* court may well have embraced the substantial compliance rule in reaction to the FDIC's litigating posture. By raising these de minimis arguments and by arguing that the failed bank's cashier did not have apparent authority to execute the letter of credit, the defendant may have provoked the panel. It may not always be easy for courts to know whether a defect is one that the document examiner should regard as de minimis. In the case of doubt, the better rule would hold the defects sufficient to refuse payment. In Mercantile-Safe Deposit & Trust Co. v. Baltimore County, 309 Md. 668, 526 A.2d 591 (1987), the court did not consider de minimis the following discrepancies in documents submitted against a letter of credit that secured a developer's obligations under a sediment-control grading permit:

1. The grading permit number omitted the letters "CGR" before the number "18868."
2. The certificate recited "I have been informed" instead of certifying on the basis of personal knowledge.
3. The certification did not identify the permittee.
4. The certification did not identify the real estate.

For a case acknowledging an exception in the strict compliance rule for de minimis defects, see Bank of N.S. v. Angelica-Whitewear Ltd., 36 D.L.R.4th 161 (Can. 1987).

[218] For discussion of a number of imaginative ways that courts have devised to avoid the strict compliance rule, some of them principled and some of them less so, see McLaughlin, "On the Periphery of Letter-of-Credit Law: Softening the Rigors of Strict Compliance," 106 Banking L.J. 4 (1989).

[2] Implicit Cases

The following decisions do not address the substantial compliance question so explicitly as the *Banco Espanol* line of cases,[219] but they have the effect of relaxing the strict compliance rule. In *Fair Pavilions, Inc. v. First National City Bank*,[220] for example, the credit provided that it could be revoked if the bank received from the account party an affidavit "to the effect that one or more of the events"[221] of default in the underlying contract had occurred. The account party supplied an affidavit reciting that "one or more of the events" had occurred. The court rejected the affidavit, holding that the parties had intended to give the beneficiary time to cure such default and that the affidavit should have recited the nature of the alleged default.[222]

In *U.S. Industries, Inc. v. Second New Haven Bank*,[223] the credit required a certificate reciting that goods had been shipped, that payment had been demanded, and that the account party had not paid within seven days of shipment. The certificate the beneficiary presented failed to recite that payment had been demanded. The court held that the presence of the invoices, as well as the recitals that the account party had not been paid, satisfied that requirement.

Both the *Fair Pavilions* and *U.S. Industries* cases depart from the strict compliance rule and create serious problems for the document examiner. Under the rule, he must engage in the kind of reasoning in which the courts engage. He must act without the benefit of oral arguments, briefs, and a lengthy period of time for that analysis, however.

Some courts are tempted to use course of dealing to justify a beneficiary's failure to satisfy a credit's conditions strictly. In *Titanium Metals Corp. of America v. Space Metals, Inc.*,[224] the court held that, because the issuer had not insisted on previous occasions that the beneficiary present a draft with his documents, it was not necessary that the beneficiary supply a draft, even though the credit called for one. The *Titanium* case does not stand alone, poses a serious problem for issuers, and is probably subject to the criticism that it imposes on the issuer burdens that are not consistent with those of credit operations.[225]

---

[219] See cases cited supra ¶ 6.05[1].

[220] 19 N.Y.2d 512, 227 N.E.2d 839, 281 N.Y.S.2d 23 (1967).

[221] Id. at 515, 227 N.E.2d at 840, 281 N.Y.S.2d at 24.

[222] For criticism of the *Fair Pavilions* case, see ¶ 2.09[3].

[223] 462 F. Supp. 662 (D. Conn. 1978).

[224] 529 P.2d 431 (Utah 1974).

[225] For additional authority and criticism of the rule that course of dealing or performance may modify the terms of a credit, see ¶ 4.07.

A number of cases from courts sitting in Texas illustrate the unwillingness of some courts to appreciate the significance of the strict compliance rule they profess to adopt. In *Temple-Eastex, Inc. v. Addison
Bank*,[226] the credit called for the beneficiary's sight draft and its affidavit of the account party's default. The beneficiary's parent company dissolved the beneficiary and proceeded to draw a letter demanding payment and to sign the affidavit. The court held that the documents
complied and thus would force a document examiner to make the judgment that a letter was a draft and that the corporate parent was the
proper party—judgments that the exigencies of the document examination process do not permit the examiner to make. Similarly, in *Travis
Bank & Trust v. State*,[227] the court held that a letter asking for payment
and referring to the letter of credit satisfied the credit's requirement for
a sight draft.[228]

These cases impose significant burdens on the document examination process. The strict rule puts the burden on the beneficiary to comply with the terms of the credit. If a corporate beneficiary is about to
dissolve or to merge, the parties should bear the burden of effecting a
proper transfer of, or an amendment to, the credit. Beneficiaries should
present their documents early, so that they have time to correct defects
such as those these cases paper over.[229]

In *Breathless Associates v. First Savings & Loan Association*,[230] a
credit called for presentation of a promissory note dated April 27, and
the beneficiary presented a note dated April 28. A second credit called
for a note in the face amount of $385,000, and the beneficiary presented

---

[226] 672 S.W.2d 793 (Tex. 1984).

[227] 660 S.W.2d 851 (Tex. Ct. App. 1983).

[228] Cf. American Airlines, Inc. v. FDIC, 610 F. Supp. 199 (D. Kan. 1985) (holding that draft, which was drawn by agent who neither identified himself as such nor
used name of beneficiary, was complying); Bank of Cochin Ltd. v. Manufacturers
Hanover Trust Co., 612 F. Supp. 1533 (S.D.N.Y. 1985), aff'd, 808 F.2d 209 (2d Cir.
1986) (asserting that strict compliance rule applies but rejecting a number of documentary discrepancies on ground that they would not mislead document examiner);
United States Steel Corp. v. Chase Manhattan Bank, N.A., No. 83 Civ. 4966 (WCC)
(S.D.N.Y. July 2, 1984) (paying lip service to strict compliance rule, yet approving
commercial invoice that did not contain purchase order number as credit required);
Colonial Cedar Co. v. Royal Wood Prods., Inc., 448 So. 2d 1218 (Fla. Dist. Ct. App.
1984) (remanding for trial court to determine whether letter from beneficiary satisfied credit's requirement for "formal draft and certificate").

[229] In both *Temple-Eastex* and *Travis*, the facts make an appealing case for estoppel against issuers that failed to specify defects properly. Regrettably, the courts
did not choose to rely on estoppel. For discussion of estoppel in this context, see infra ¶ 6.06[1].

[230] 654 F. Supp. 832 (N.D. Tex. 1986).

two notes whose face amounts aggregated that sum. The court held that the first presentation satisfied the strict compliance rule but that the second did not. In granting the beneficiary's motion for summary judgment regarding the first credit but denying it on the second, the court concluded that the issuer would have known that the April 28 date was an error but would not have known that the two-note discrepancy was immaterial. A bank document examiner who discovers a note bearing the wrong date might just as easily conclude that there was more than one note and that the beneficiary submitted the wrong one.[231]

Some of the impetus for relaxing the strict compliance rule undoubtedly stems from the notion that the beneficiary who fails to dot an "i" or to cross a "t" should not lose the entire benefit of his contract with the account party. In the event the account party is insolvent, the noncomplying beneficiary may lose the benefit of performance under that contract. It does not follow, however, that a ruling against the beneficiary under the credit forecloses all chances of recovery. In *Banco Espanol*, for example, the buyer was clearly solvent. If he breached his contract with the sellers, they could still bring an action against him, even though the court decided that they had not complied with the terms of the credit. It is true that the strict compliance rule deprives the noncomplying beneficiary of the credit's benefit, but it does not deprive him of everything.

It will not do to deny that the strict compliance rule often favors the account party; it does. The rule, however, is necessary for the proper working of credits. Any imbalance it creates in favor of account parties finds redress in two ways: first, in the estoppel and waiver rules that nar-

---

[231] There were allegations in the pleadings that the issuer in *Breathless Associates* had drafted the credit with the notes in hand and that any error in them was the consequence of the issuer's negligence. While the court did not rely on those allegations, it may have been moved by the notion that the issuer should not escape when its negligence causes the error. The trouble with that reasoning is that it encourages the beneficiary to rely on the issuer to draft the credit properly. It is more efficient to encourage the beneficiary to review the credit carefully. The law can assume that issuers draft credits to protect themselves; it also should assume that beneficiaries review credits to protect themselves and, in both cases, that the party that does not take steps to protect itself cannot look to the courts for relief. Cf. Exxon Co. U.S.A. v. Banque de Paris et des Pays-Bas, 889 F.2d 674 (5th Cir. 1989) (implying that under Texas law issuer owes duty to beneficiary in drafting credit, and rejecting view that beneficiary must review credit for errors). But cf. Tradex Petroleum Am., Inc. v. Coral Petroleum, Inc. (In re Coral Petroleum, Inc.), 878 F.2d 830 (5th Cir. 1989) (same court taking different view under New York law). That is not to say that a negligent issuer may not be liable; but its liability will be to the account party, its customer, with whom it has entered into a contract — the application agreement. For discussion of authority excusing the beneficiary when the expiry terms of the credit create an impossibility, see ¶ 5.03[3][a].

row the operation of the strict compliance rule; second, in the fact that the rule cuts two ways. It not only prevents the beneficiary from getting by with less than strict compliance, but it also prevents the issuer from adding conditions to the credit that require more than strict compliance.[232] The strict compliance rule stems not from any desire to favor account parties over beneficiaries or to favor buyers over sellers, but from the general, commercial nature of the credit itself. The rule satisfies a desire to fashion an efficient commercial device.

¶ 6.06 TEMPERING THE EFFECT OF THE STRICT COMPLIANCE RULE

The strict compliance rule would not be strict if courts riddled it with exceptions based on course of dealing, course of performance, estoppel, and waiver. There are roles, however, for estoppel and waiver in the strict compliance setting. These roles do not so much create exceptions to the rule as they impose outside limits on it. In addition, amendments to credits are quite common, and they may alter the credit's requirements.

[1] Estoppel

The most important limit on the strict compliance rule is estoppel. In this setting, estoppel generally prevents the issuer from asserting any complaints about the documents that it did not assert promptly.[233]

There is some confusion over terminology in estoppel cases, which sometimes use the term "waiver" in situations that are more akin to estoppel than to any intentional surrender of rights.[234] Generally, waiver

---

[232] See generally the discussion of the *Pringle* and *Bank of Canton* cases supra ¶ 6.04[5]. For a substantial compliance case that adds a condition to the credit and therefore favors the issuer over the beneficiary, see Easton Tire Co. v. Farmers & Merchants Bank, 642 S.W.2d 396 (Mo. Ct. App. 1982).

[233] Course of dealing or course of performance exceptions, and any waiver theories based on them, harm the certainty of documentary credit examination. The estoppel rule discussed in this paragraph may deprive the issuer of a defense. In so doing, it redresses what some may see as a pro–account party bias in the strict compliance rule. In any event, as the discussion in this paragraph reveals, this estoppel rule does not generate confusion for document examiners.

[234] See, e.g., Chase Manhattan Bank v. Equibank, 550 F.2d 882, 887 (3d Cir. 1977) (speaking almost entirely in terms of waiver until penultimate paragraph, where court refers to "possibility of an estoppel or waiver"); Apex Oil Co. v. Archem Co., 770 F.2d 1353 (5th Cir. 1985) (using waiver in situation that resembles estoppel); Bank of Cochin Ltd. v. Manufacturers Hanover Trust Co., 612 F. Supp. 1533 (S.D.N.Y. 1985), aff'd, 808 F.2d 209 (2d Cir. 1986) (positing distinction between es-

theory assumes an intentional act, while estoppel theory supplies the intent or prevents a party from alleging that no such intent existed. In this discussion, "waiver" of a condition arises when the issuer knowingly agrees to accept defective documents. Estoppel arises when the law considers it unfair or inefficient to permit the issuer to deny such agreement.

[a] The Classic Estoppel Case

Courts have fashioned two versions of estoppel in the credit setting. The first is the classic estoppel rule; the second is a tougher rule apparent in the Code, the Uniform Customs, and some of the cases.[235]

The majority, or classic estoppel, rule requires a beneficiary to show three elements:

1. Conduct on the part of the issuer that leads the beneficiary to believe that nonconforming documents do conform;
2. Reasonable reliance by the beneficiary; and
3. Detriment from that reliance.

In the classic case, the issuer rejects documents for one reason and thereafter, often when the credit has expired, raises additional objections. In *Board of County Commissioners v. Colorado National Bank*,[236] for example, the issuer dishonored the beneficiary's demands on grounds relating to the underlying transaction. Thereafter, the issuer asserted that the demands were defective. The court noted that if the issuer's conduct "misled"[237] the beneficiary, the issuer "waived"[238] any

---

toppel, which arises when issuer is silent, thus depriving beneficiary of opportunity to cure, and waiver, which arises when issuer states some objections and later attempts to rely on others); United Commodities-Greece v. Fidelity Int'l Bank, 99 A.D.2d 974, 473 N.Y.S.2d 10 (1984), modified, 64 N.Y.2d 449, 478 N.E.2d 172, 489 N.Y.S.2d 31 (1985) (waiver case); Addison Bank v. Temple-Eastex, Inc., 665 S.W.2d 550 (Tex. Ct. App.), rev'd, 672 S.W.2d 793 (Tex. 1984) (using term "waiver" but employing estoppel theory); W.J. Alan & Co. v. El Nasr Export & Import Co., [1972] 2 All E.R. 127 (C.A.) (defining "waiver" as failure to enforce strict rights with resulting reliance by other party, but not requiring detriment).

[235] See generally infra ¶¶ 6.06[1][b], 6.06[1][c]. See also Dorf Overseas, Inc. v. Chemical Bank, 91 A.D.2d 895, 457 N.Y.S.2d 513 (1983) (holding that by taking goods and thereby depriving issuer of ability to return them to beneficiary, account party waived defects in documents).

[236] 43 Colo. App. 186, 607 P.2d 1010 (1979), modified, 634 P.2d 32 (Colo. 1981).

[237] Id. at 190, 607 P.2d at 1013.

[238] Id. at 189, 607 P.2d at 1012.

such defects. Because there was no time for the beneficiary to cure, the lower court found no detriment in the failure to specify the defects earlier.[239]

In other cases, the issuers indicate that the documents are complying and thereafter claim that there are defects.[240] Such issuer conduct usually estops the issuer from making such claims, but even here a majority of the cases seem to require some kind of detrimental reliance by the beneficiary.[241] Indeed, other courts have indicated that a delay in re-

---

[239] For cases requiring detriment and reliance, see Apex Oil Co. v. Archem Co., 770 F.2d 1353 (5th Cir. 1985); Philadelphia Gear Corp. v. Central Bank, 717 F.2d 230 (5th Cir. 1983); General Cable CEAT, S.A. v. Futura Trading Inc., No. 82 Civ. 1087 (RLC) (S.D.N.Y. Jan. 18, 1983); Voest-Alpine Int'l Corp. v. Chase Manhattan Bank, N.A., 545 F. Supp. 301 (S.D.N.Y. 1982), aff'd in part, rev'd in part, 707 F.2d 680 (2d Cir. 1983); Addison Bank v. Temple-Eastex, Inc., 665 S.W.2d 550 (Tex. Ct. App.), rev'd on other grounds, 672 S.W.2d 793 (1984). But cf. Pro-Fab, Inc. v. Vipa, Inc., 772 F.2d 847 (11th Cir. 1985) (holding that issuer cannot excuse itself from giving notice of defects on ground that beneficiary could not cure); Northern Trust Co. v. Oxford Speaker Co., 109 Ill. App. 3d 433, 440 N.E.2d 968 (1982) (holding that it is not necessary for beneficiary to show that it could cure defect); European Asian Bank A.G. v. Punjab & Sind Bank, [1983] 2 All E.R. 508 (C.A.) (estopping issuer by virtue of its advice to negotiating bank that buyer had accepted documents, even though negotiating bank incorrectly notified issuer that it had given value to beneficiary).

[240] See U.S. Indus., Inc. v. Second New Haven Bank, 462 F. Supp. 662 (D. Conn. 1978); North Valley Bank v. Nat'l Bank, 437 F. Supp. 70 (N.D. Ill. 1977); Bank of Am. Nat'l Trust & Sav. Ass'n v. Liberty Nat'l Bank & Trust Co., 116 F. Supp. 233 (W.D. Okla. 1953), aff'd, 218 F.2d 831 (10th Cir. 1955); cf. City Nat'l Bank v. Westland Towers Apartments, 107 Mich. App. 213, 309 N.W.2d 209 (1981), rev'd on other grounds, 413 Mich. 938, 320 N.W.2d 881 (1982) (holding that U.C.C. § 5-106(2) does not require account party's consent to credit's modification to be in writing); Ohio Indus. Comm'n v. First Nat'l Bank, No. C-840840 (Ohio Ct. App. Aug. 28, 1985) (where issuer's silence regarding defects estopped it from raising them later).

[241] See American Coleman Co. v. Intrawest Bank, 887 F.2d 1382 (10th Cir. 1989); Flagship Cruises, Ltd. v. New England Merchants Nat'l Bank, 569 F.2d 699 (1st Cir. 1978); Barclays Bank D.C.O. v. Mercantile Nat'l Bank, 481 F.2d 1224 (5th Cir. 1973), cert. dismissed, 414 U.S. 1139 (1974); Wing On Bank Ltd. v. American Nat'l Bank & Trust Co., 457 F.2d 328 (5th Cir. 1972); Venizelos, S.A. v. Chase Manhattan Bank, N.A., 425 F.2d 461 (2d Cir. 1970); Continental Nat'l Bank v. National City Bank, 69 F.2d 312 (9th Cir.), cert. denied, 293 U.S. 557 (1934); U.S. Indus., Inc. v. Second New Haven Bank, 462 F. Supp. 662 (D. Conn. 1978); Beathard v. Chicago Football Club, Inc., 419 F. Supp. 1133 (N.D. Ill. 1976); Chase Manhattan Bank v. Equibank, 394 F. Supp. 352 (W.D. Pa. 1975); Bank of Am. Nat'l Trust & Sav. Ass'n v. Liberty Nat'l Bank & Trust Co., 116 F. Supp. 233 (W.D. Okla. 1953), aff'd, 218 F.2d 831 (10th Cir. 1955); Colorado Nat'l Bank v. Board of County Comm'rs, 634 P.2d 32 (Colo. 1981); East Bank v. Dovenmuehle, Inc. 196 Colo. 422, 589 P.2d 1361 (1978); Data Gen. Corp. v. Citizens Nat'l Bank, 502 F. Supp. 776 (D. Conn. 1980); First Arlington Nat'l Bank v. Stathis, 90 Ill. App. 3d 802, 413 N.E.2d 1288 (1980); Schweibish v. Ponchartrain State Bank, 389 So. 2d 731 (La. Ct. App. 1980); City

jecting documents that deprives the beneficiary of time to cure will estop the issuer.[242] Courts have used the same estoppel rule against account parties who approve documents and then, after the issuer has paid or accepted the beneficiary's drafts, try to avoid reimbursing the issuer on the ground that some of the documents were defective.[243] At least one court ruled against account party who was silent with regard to defects until the bank honored and who then attempted to raise them.[244]

It is not clear, in many of these cases, whether the court adds the reliance facts because such facts are indispensable to application of the estoppel rule or because such facts provide additional support for the holding.[245] In a few cases when such reliance has been absent, however, the courts have refused to estop the issuer.[246]

In *Lennox Industries, Inc. v. Mid-American National Bank*,[247] the court held that expiration of the credit prior to expiration of the three-day period that Section 5-112 gives the issuer to examine documents removes the requirement to give notice of defects. That rule conflicts with

---

Nat'l Bank v. Westland Towers Apartments, 107 Mich. App. 213, 309 N.W.2d 209 (1981), rev'd, 413 Mich. 938, 320 N.W.2d 881 (1982); Anglo-S. Am. Trust Co. v. Uhe, 261 N.Y. 150, 184 N.E. 741 (1933); Maurice O'Meara Co. v. National Park Bank, 239 N.Y. 386, 146 N.E. 636 (1925); Camp v. Corn Exch. Nat'l Bank, 285 Pa. 337, 132 A. 189 (1926); Siderius, Inc. v. Wallace Co., 583 S.W.2d 852 (Tex. Civ. App. 1979).

[242] See Marino Indus. Corp. v. Chase Manhattan Bank, N.A., 686 F.2d 112 (2d Cir. 1982); Crocker Commercial Serv., Inc. v. Countryside Bank, 538 F. Supp. 1360 (N.D. Ill. 1981); American Employers Ins. Co. v. Pioneer Bank & Trust Co., 538 F. Supp. 1354 (N.D. Ill. 1981); Exchange Mut. Ins. Co. v. Commerce Union Bank, 686 S.W.2d 913 (Tenn. Ct. App. 1984).

[243] See International Leather Distribs., Inc. v. Chase Manhattan Bank, N.A., 464 F. Supp. 1197 (S.D.N.Y.), aff'd mem., 607 F.2d 996 (2d Cir. 1979); Anglo-S. Am. Trust Co. v. Uhe, 261 N.Y. 150, 184 N.E. 741 (1933).

[244] See Bank of N.Y. & Trust Co. v. Atterbury Bros., 226 A.D. 117, 234 N.Y.S. 442 (1929), aff'd, 253 N.Y. 569, 171 N.E. 786 (1930).

[245] In Barclays Bank D.C.O. v. Mercantile Nat'l Bank, 339 F. Supp. 457 (N.D. Ga. 1972), aff'd, 481 F.2d 1221 (5th Cir. 1973), the lower court relied on both the rule of the *Bank of Taiwan* case (discussed infra ¶ 6.06[1][c]) and the fact of detrimental reliance. The circuit court appears to rest its affirmance of the estoppel holding on the detrimental reliance feature of classic estoppel.

[246] See Philadelphia Gear Corp. v. Central Bank, 717 F.2d 230 (5th Cir. 1983); Wing On Bank Ltd. v. American Nat'l Bank & Trust Co., 457 F.2d 328 (5th Cir. 1972); Breathless Assocs. v. First Sav. & Loan Ass'n, 654 F. Supp. 832 (N.D. Tex. 1986); United Commodities-Greece v. Fidelity Int'l Bank, 64 N.Y.2d 449, 478 N.E.2d 172, 489 N.Y.S.2d 31 (1985); Maurice O'Meara Co. v. National Park Bank, 239 N.Y. 386, 146 N.E. 636 (1925); Siderius, Inc. v. Wallace Co., 583 S.W.2d 852 (Tex. Civ. App. 1979).

[247] 49 Ohio App. 3d 117, 550 N.E.2d 971 (1988).

Datapoint Corp. v. M&I Bank,[248] which held that the three-day period is one only for examining the documents and that once the issuer determines that there are defects, the grace period stops. At that point, the issuer must give notice immediately and does not have until the end of the three-day period to give it. *Datapoint* reflects a closer reading of the language of the section and is consistent with efficient practices. All parties gain when the issuer notifies the beneficiary promptly that there are defects in the documents.[249]

[b] The Code and the Uniform Customs

Estoppel may arise if a party fails to object to defects within a short time after receiving the documents. Article 16(c) of the Uniform Customs provides that the issuer must examine the beneficiary's documents within a reasonable time. Article 16(d) adds that the issuer must notify the remitting bank, without delay, of any dishonor and must supply the reasons therefor. Finally, Article 16(e) stipulates that if the issuer violates Article 16(c) by failing to examine the documents within a reasonable time, or if it violates Article 16(d) by failing to advise, without delay, of any defects, the issuer is precluded from asserting the defects.

Article 16(e), then, creates an estoppel rule tougher than that of the cases and tougher than prior versions of the Uniform Customs. *Flagship Cruises, Ltd. v. New England Merchants National Bank*[250] considered an earlier version of the rule of Article 16. That provision, Article 8 of the 1962 Uniform Customs, required the issuer to give reasons for its dishonor,[251] but the 1962 Uniform Customs contained no preclusion rule. The beneficiary in *Flagship* argued that the notice requirement of 1962 Article 8 supported a rule estopping any issuer from raising reasons other than those it specified in the Article 8 notice. The *Flagship* court rejected that argument and held that the better rule requires the beneficiary to show that the notice was misleading and that the beneficiary could not have corrected any of the defects that were omitted.[252]

---

[248] 665 F. Supp. 722 (W.D. Wis. 1987).

[249] That is not to suggest, however, that issuers should be denied the chance to ask the account party to waive defects in the beneficiary's documents. For further discussion of that concern as well as *Datapoint* and similar cases, see infra ¶ 6.06[1][b].

[250] 569 F.2d 699 (1st Cir. 1978).

[251] See ICC, "Uniform Customs and Practice for Documentary Credits," ICC Brochure No. 222, art. 8 (1962).

[252] Accord Waidmann v. Mercantile Trust Co., 711 S.W.2d 907 (Mo. Ct. App. 1986). But cf. Exchange Mut. Ins. Co. v. Commerce Union Bank, 686 S.W.2d 913 (Tenn. Ct. App. 1984) (holding that failure to notify of defects estops issuer). In Newvector Communications, Inc. v. Union Bank, 663 F. Supp. 252 (D. Utah 1987), the court declined to grant summary judgment in favor of a beneficiary that present-

In *Price & Pierce International, Inc. v. Cimex U.S.A., Inc.*,[253] the court took a careful look at the estoppel rule of Article 8(f) of the 1974 version of the Uniform Customs. The issuer in the *Price* case had failed for seven days to notify of dishonor and that it was holding the documents at the disposal of the remitting bank. The *Price* court saw this failure as a serious breach of the issuer's duty and rejected the argument that it was incumbent on the beneficiary to show that the delay was detrimental. Expert testimony in the *Price* case by Henry Harfield[254] supported that holding. Harfield testified that prompt notice is essential in order to permit the beneficiary to resell its goods or to stop shipment. Damages caused by delays often are not easy to prove, and the strict preclusion rule of the *Price* case is an efficient rule. It costs issuers little to give notice promptly.

Article 16 also estops the issuer, as Article 8 of the 1974 Uniform Customs did, if the issuer fails to report that it is holding the documents for the beneficiary or that it is returning them. In *Bank of Cochin Ltd. v. Manufacturers Hanover Trust Co.*,[255] the court invoked the estoppel rule of Article 8(f) in the 1974 version of the Uniform Customs and added by way of dictum that the estoppel argument would be stronger under the 1983 revision.[256] More importantly, in affirming the decision of the lower court in the *Bank of Cochin* case,[257] the Court of Appeals for the Second Circuit held that an issuer's delay of twelve or thirteen days in

ed documents on January 21, 1986 to an issuer that failed to dishonor until March 11, 1986, the expiry date. The court held that there were issues of fact to be determined.

[253] Letter of Credit Update 35 (July 1987) (N.Y. Sup. Ct. 1987), aff'd without op. sub nom. Price & Pierce Int'l, Inc. v. Hanil Bank Ltd., 136 A.D.2d 977, 523 N.Y.S.2d 333, appeal denied, 72 N.Y.2d 803, 528 N.E.2d 521, 532 N.Y.S.2d 399 (1988).

[254] Harfield is the author of a leading letter of credit treatise. See H. Harfield, Bank Credits and Acceptances (5th ed. 1974). His testimony, which supports a strong penalty against banks that fail to give notice promptly, is doubly convincing. It makes sense as a fair and efficient rule, and it comes from an experienced lawyer who has represented a New York money center bank that issues a significant volume of credits.

[255] 612 F. Supp. 1533 (S.D.N.Y. 1985), aff'd, 808 F.2d 209 (2d Cir. 1986).

[256] Cf. Larsen v. Carpenter, 620 F. Supp. 1084 (E.D.N.Y. 1985), aff'd mem., 800 F.2d 1128 (2d Cir. 1986) (holding under 1974 UCP that when confirming bank, issuer, and account party accept bill of lading, they cannot complain subsequently that it is defective). But cf. Westpac Banking Corp. v. South Carolina Nat'l Bank, [1986] 1 Lloyd's Rep. 311 (P.C.) (holding that, under the 1974 Uniform Customs, issuer may rely on defects other than those raised in notice of dishonor, but it thereby loses "practical support which it could have derived from an actual rejection on the ground not relied upon by it.").

[257] 808 F.2d 209 (2d Cir. 1986).

giving notice of documentary discrepancies to the confirming bank constituted a waiver of the defects. Significantly, the appellate court's opinion does not consider the possibility of, or the need for, reliance and detriment.

The credit in *Bank of Cochin* was subject to the 1974 Uniform Customs, and the court invoked the rule of UCP Article 8(e), which it saw as instrumental in "effectuating the vital policy of promoting certainty in letter of credit transactions."[258] The issuer that fails to give timely notice of defects pays a "penalty."[259] It cannot raise the defects as a defense.

The *Bank of Cochin* result is consistent with the classic notion that a commercial party that fails to attend to commercial matters sedulously must bear the cost of losses that result. The duty in Article 8(e) to give notice without delay "connote[s] a sense of urgent action within the shortest interval of time possible."[260] The *Bank of Cochin* decision is a call to standards, a message to bank issuers that they are part of a profession and that at least one court, an important court for letter of credit law, will measure their conduct by the high standards of their own profession. In short, the *Bank of Cochin* court has paid the international banking community a compliment: It has taken the community's own expression of standards seriously.[261] In that respect, *Bank of Cochin* may not be alone.

In *Datapoint Corp. v. M&I Bank*,[262] the beneficiary presented documents the day before the credit expired. The credit required the draft to contain a recital that it was drawn under the designated credit, but the beneficiary's draft failed to contain the legend. On the day it received the draft, the issuer decided to dishonor and promptly mailed the documents and its notice of dishonor to the presenting bank. The *Datapoint* court held that the issuer should have given telephonic notice of the defect to the beneficiary to allow it to correct the problem with the draft, as it could have done by facsimile machine, and that the issuer's conduct ran afoul of Article 16. The court distinguished between the rule of Article 16(c) giving the issuer a reasonable time to examine the documents and the rule of Article 16(d) requiring the issuer to notify of defects without delay. Once the issuer had decided to dishonor, it had a

---

[258] Id. at 212.

[259] Id.

[260] Id. at 213.

[261] For discussion of the role of the international banking community in the drafting of the Uniform Customs, see ¶ 4.04 and authorities cited in the bibliographic notes in Appendix A.

[262] 665 F. Supp. 722 (W.D. Wis. 1987).

duty under the Uniform Customs, the court held, to make a reasonable effort to notify the beneficiary in time for the beneficiary to cure.[263]

In *Kuntal, S.A. v. Bank of New York*,[264] the court, relying on the *Bank of Cochin* case, went beyond *Datapoint's* requirement that the issuer give notice in time for the beneficiary to cure. The *Kuntal* court held that the requirement of Article 16 is not satisfied unless the issuer gives notice that is "immediate (*at once*), instant, instantaneous, instantly, prompt."[265] In *Kuntal*, the presenting bank had delivered defective documents to the issuer on February 19, 1987. The issuer claimed that it took two days for the bank clerks to examine the documents and to determine that there were discrepancies. At that point, the issuer requested of its customer, the account party buyer, whether the buyer wanted to accept the beneficiary's defective documents. Nine banking days later, the issuer notified the presenting bank of its dishonor and that it was holding the documents at the presenting bank's disposal. The court rejected the issuer's argument that its customer should have a reasonable time within which to determine whether it wanted to accept the beneficiary's documents and held that under Article 16(e) of the Uniform Customs the issuer was estopped from asserting that the beneficiary's documents were defective.[266]

While there is merit in the rule of these cases that the issuer must give prompt notice of dishonor, there is also merit in the suggestion that the issuer should be able to consult with its customer in commercial credit transactions. Often presentations under commercial letters of credit are not conforming. Most of the time, however, the issuer obtains a waiver of the defects from the account party and pays the beneficiary with notice that it is making payment despite nonconformities.[267] That procedure is efficient, and the law should encourage it. If the courts ap-

---

[263] For a different view of the duty of the issuer to give notice of defects, see Lennox Indus., Inc. v. Mid-Am. Nat'l Bank, 49 Ohio App. 3d 117, 550 N.E.2d 971 (1988). See supra ¶ 6.06[1][a].

[264] 703 F. Supp. 312 (S.D.N.Y. 1989).

[265] Id. at 313–314, citing Bank of Cochin Ltd. v. Manufacturers Hanover Trust Co., 808 F.2d 209, 213 (2d Cir. 1986).

[266] In Esso Petroleum Can., a Div. of Imperial Oil Ltd. v. Security Pac. Bank, 710 F. Supp. 275 (D. Or. 1989), the beneficiary presented its documents at 1:00 P.M. on a Friday; the credit expired on the following Monday; and, although it gave notice of dishonor at 5:15 P.M. on that Friday, the issuer did not give the reasons for dishonor until the following Monday. Without any discussion of reliance and detriment, the court held that, under Article 16(e), the beneficiary was entitled to summary judgment against the issuer.

[267] For discussion of documentary defects and the practice of obtaining waivers from the account party, see infra ¶ 6.06[2].

ply the rule of Article 16 so strictly that issuers begin giving notice of dishonor without seeking waivers of defects, the number of dishonors in the commercial credit context will increase significantly.[268]

These cases leave room, however, for an efficient rule. First, *Datapoint* holds that if a fast-approaching expiry may deprive the beneficiary of an opportunity to correct defects, the notice must be swift. *Kuntal* holds only that "[i]n the absence of any persuasive and reasonable justification for the . . . delay," the estoppel rule applies. The courts are saying that they will not permit the issuer to temporize but that they may be willing to entertain short, reasonable delays, that is, delays that are justified by some "reasonable and persuasive" set of facts. Delays of seven days (*Price & Pierce*), twelve or thirteen days (*Bank of Cochin*), and nine days (*Kuntal*), are too long. A short delay (one or two days, perhaps) solely for the purpose of obtaining the account party's waiver should not offend the concerns these cases evince.

Issuers, moreover, may use Section 5-112(1)(b) of the Code to gain time to obtain waivers. That provision permits an issuer to take more than the statutory three-day period if the presenter expressly or impliedly consents to an extension. Issuers that prefer not to dishonor but to seek waivers but that feel it may take more than the briefest time to obtain those waivers might seek consent from the presenter for additional time to obtain the account party's waiver of the documentary defect.

Omission of a defect in the notice of defects also invokes the rule of Article 16. In *Kerr-McGee Chemical Corp. v. FDIC*,[269] the issuer rejected a presentation on the ground that the draft was in the wrong amount. The beneficiary cured that defect, and, at trial, the issuer complained that the invoice was inconsistent with the credit. The court rejected the issuer's argument that notice of the defect in the draft constituted notice of the invoice defect. The court estopped the issuer under the rule of Article 16 from raising the invoice defect.

Not all courts are willing to accept the rather strict rule of these cases. In *Occidental Fire & Casualty Co. v. Continental Illinois National Bank & Trust Co.*,[270] the issuer decided to dishonor on a Wednesday but did not give notice, if at all, until the following Monday. The *Occidental* court declined to grant summary judgment for the beneficiary, holding that it was necessary to determine whether in fact the issuer gave notice

---

[268] For reports on the degree of documentary discrepancies in the first instance, that is, before notice of defects and cure, see Sinclair, "Commentary," Letter of Credit Update 24 (Feb. 1989).

[269] 872 F.2d 971 (11th Cir. 1989).

[270] 718 F. Supp. 1364 (1989) (The author of this treatise served as a consultant to the beneficiary insurance company in the *Occidental* case.).

of the defects on the Monday. Thus, *Occidental* is inconsistent with the *Datapoint* line of cases.[271]

The Code fashions a narrow estoppel rule in Section 5-113, which deals with the bank practice of providing issuers with indemnities against documentary defects. The drafters evidently were concerned that such bank indemnities not remain outstanding for long periods. Section 5-113(2)(b) provides that, unless the parties explicitly agree to a longer period, indemnities against documentary defects expire at the end of ten banking days following receipt of the documents by the account party, unless someone, presumably the account party, notifies the indemnitor of the documentary defects. If a bank, for example, indemnifies the issuer against losses arising from a set of documents containing three copies of the invoice instead of four copies as the credit requires, the account party who fails to object to that discrepancy within ten days after receipt of the documents is estopped from asserting it.

[c] Estoppel and Defects Asserted After the Fact

There is a strong line of authority that appears to do away with the reliance requirement of classic estoppel law. While estoppel is a creature of equity and generally responds to notions of fairness, there is also an element of efficiency in estoppel rules. A court properly concerned with equity may use estoppel in concluding that a beneficiary reasonably relied on the issuer's failure to object to defective documents within a short time and that it would be unfair to penalize that reliance.

Estoppel may serve a different end—to prevent issuers or account parties from complaining about defects after the fact when those defects did not really matter before the fact. This latter estoppel rule has two purposes: to force the issuer to make specific objections promptly and to save courts from having to litigate all of the afterthoughts that arise once lawyers get into the case. This second brand of estoppel is not new. In 1878, the U.S. Supreme Court decided *Ohio & Mississippi Railway v. McCarthy*,[272] a transport case. There the shipper sued the carrier for its gross negligence in causing damage to cattle because of delays in transshipment. Originally, the carrier argued that the delay stemmed from a

---

[271] In a subsequent opinion, the court found that the defendant bank did give notice of defects in timely fashion. The later opinion makes much of the fact that the court felt the beneficiary had reason to know that its documents did not conform when it presented them and of the fact that, in the court's opinion, the beneficiary had not acted promptly to correct the defects when the issuer did give notice. See Occidental Fire & Casualty Co. v. Continental Ill. Nat'l Bank & Trust Co., 725 F. Supp. 383 (N.D. Ill. 1989).

[272] 96 U.S. 258 (1878).

shortage of rolling stock, but, at trial, the carrier argued that West Virginia's sabbath law forced it to delay the transshipment. The Supreme Court rejected the latter argument, holding, "This point was an afterthought, suggested by the pressures and exigencies of the case,"[273] and, "He is not permitted thus to mend his hold. He is estopped from doing it by a settled principle of law."[274]

In *Bank of Taiwan, Ltd. v. Union National Bank*,[275] the issuer dishonored on the ground that the bill of lading was defective. At the trial, the issuer raised additional defenses. The court held that "[b]y formally placing its refusal to pay on one ground, the defendant must be held to have waived all others."[276] The opinion contains no suggestion that reliance is essential. Similarly, in *Weyerhaeuser Co. v. First National Bank*,[277] the issuer dishonored on the ground that the documents were defective. Later the issuer claimed that it had the right to refuse payment because the credit was revocable. Clearly, the beneficiary could not have been misled to his detriment by such a shift in the issuer's position. If the credit was revocable, there was nothing the beneficiary could have done about it. Indeed, there was no discussion in *Weyerhaeuser* of detriment. Nevertheless, the court used estoppel against the issuer's argument that the credit was revocable.

These cases may reflect the supposition that, by shifting its ground for dishonor, the beneficiary in fact often deprives the presenting party of opportunities to pursue other parties or to preserve evidence or otherwise to protect itself. It is often difficult to prove such detriment, and these cases are well advised in overlooking that feature of classic estoppel.

In *Banco Nacional De Desarrollo v. Mellon Bank, N.A.*,[278] the Court of Appeals for the Third Circuit, the same court that decided the *Bank of Taiwan* case, rejected the *Bank of Taiwan* rule that no detrimental reliance is necessary. The *Banco Nacional* holding is strengthened by the rule advocated by the court in *Philadelphia Gear Corp. v. Central Bank*,[279] to the effect that even under the 1974 Uniform Customs, with their estoppel implications,[280] a beneficiary that knows, or reasonably

---

[273] Id. at 267.
[274] Id. at 267–268.
[275] 1 F.2d 65 (3d Cir. 1924).
[276] Id. at 66.
[277] 27 U.C.C. Rep. Serv. (Callaghan) 777 (S.D. Iowa 1979).
[278] 726 F.2d 87 (3d Cir. 1984).
[279] 717 F.2d 230 (5th Cir. 1983).
[280] See supra ¶ 6.06[1][b].

should know, that its documents are defective cannot raise an estoppel against an issuer that fails or refuses to specify defects.[281]

In *Bank of Cochin Ltd. v. Manufacturers Hanover Trust Co.*,[282] the court held that there is no need for the beneficiary to show that the failure to give notice of defects resulted in detriment under the Uniform Customs. In *Pro-Fab, Inc. v. Vipa, Inc.*,[283] the court held by way of dictum that an issuer is "estopped" to assert a defect that it does not list in its notice of defects, because a refusal to pay on one ground "waives" all others.[284] Thus, the law remains unsettled. It appears that a majority of the courts enforce the strict estoppel rule under the UCP but that, outside the UCP setting, a majority require a showing of reliance and detriment.

In the letter of credit setting, the stricter estoppel rule is more efficient than the classic rule. Under the strict rule, beneficiaries may present documents early, and issuers have to notify them promptly of defects or else they lose the right to raise the defects. That rule cuts against the issuer's interest and is an efficient counterweight to the strict compliance rule, which usually cuts against the interest of the beneficiary. By insisting on a showing of detrimental reliance, the courts may be complicating matters unnecessarily.

In some cases, moreover, courts neglect estoppel analysis and resort to a substantial compliance test.[285] That rule has harmful consequences

---

[281] Accord Pro-Fab, Inc. v. Vipa, Inc., 772 F.2d 847 (11th Cir. 1985) (holding also that failure to give notice of dishonor is not excused by fact that beneficiary could not cure defects that would have been listed in that notice). For discussion of the effect of an issuer's failure to act within the statutory time limits, see ¶ 5.03[4]. Cf. American Nat'l Bank & Trust Co. v. Hamilton Indus. Int'l, Inc., 583 F. Supp. 164 (N.D. Ill. 1984), rev'd sub nom. Banque Paribas v. Hamilton Indus. Int'l, Inc., 767 F.2d 380 (7th Cir. 1985) (holding that beneficiary that knowingly submits fraudulent documents may not raise estoppel); S.B. Int'l, Inc. v. Union Bank of India, 783 S.W.2d 225 (Tex. Ct. App. 1989) (ruling that beneficiary that knew documents were inconsistent could not raise estoppel against issuer that failed to give notice of defects to presenter).

[282] 612 F. Supp. 1533 (S.D.N.Y. 1985), aff'd, 808 F.2d 209 (2d Cir. 1986). For discussion of the appellate court's strong affirmation of the *Bank of Cochin* decision on this point, see supra ¶ 6.06[1][b].

[283] 772 F.2d 847 (11th Cir. 1985).

[284] Id. at 852 n.9; cf. Crist v. J. Henry Schroder Bank & Trust Co., 693 F. Supp. 1429 (S.D.N.Y. 1988) (issuer cannot complain that beneficiary did not supply certified copy of appointment order, because notice of defects did not list that omission); Massive Paper Mills v. Two-Ten Corp., 669 F. Supp. 94 (S.D.N.Y. 1987) (holding that beneficiary that failed to object to terms of credit could not later complain that its failure to perform underlying contract stemmed from its inability to comply with credit terms).

[285] E.g., Tosco Corp. v. FDIC, 723 F.2d 1242 (6th Cir. 1983); American Airlines, Inc. v. FDIC, 610 F. Supp. 199 (D. Kan. 1985); Temple-Eastex, Inc. v. Addi-

for letters of credit in general. It is unfortunate that courts desiring to rule in favor of the beneficiary resort to it rather than to strict estoppel, which has the same effect but promotes, rather than harms, the letter of credit.[286]

[2] True Waiver

There are instances when a party knowingly waives a condition in the credit. Many presentations fail to comply in the first instance with the credit's terms. Often the beneficiary presents documents early so that it has time to cure any defects, and most of the time the account party waives the defects. It appears to be a practice in most cases for issuers that receive a nonconforming presentation to inquire of their account party whether the account party agrees to a waiver of the noted defect. In the great majority of cases, the account parties agree and waive the defects. Bank issuers obtain these waivers by telephone, and the law appears to support them by holding oral waivers binding.[287]

Waiver, unlike estoppel, requires a showing that the party making the waiver does so knowingly. In *Transamerica Delaval, Inc. v. Citibank, N.A.*, an attorney's "guess"[288] that the issuer would have to pay was not a waiver. He did not know the facts and did not intend to waive anything.[289] In *Overseas Trading Corp. v. Irving Trust Co.*,[290] the issuer alleged that the account party waived defects in documents when it accepted the documents and reimbursed the bank. The court held the

---

son Bank, 672 S.W.2d 793 (Tex. 1984); Travis Bank & Trust v. State, 660 S.W.2d 851 (Tex. Ct. App. 1983). It is significant that in the last two of these cases, the courts professed to abide by the strict compliance rule but arguably used a substantial compliance test. In both cases, the issuer failed to specify defects and, under the strict estoppel rule, would be precluded from raising any objection to the beneficiary's documents. See supra ¶ 6.05[2].

[286] For a further discussion of the desirability of using estoppel rather than substantial compliance to avoid issuer misconduct, see Dolan, "Strict Compliance With Letters of Credit: Striking a Fair Balance," 102 Banking L.J. 18 (1985).

[287] See U.C.C. § 5-104, comment 1 (last sentence); City Nat'l Bank v. Westland Towers Apartments, 107 Mich. App. 213, 309 N.W.2d 209 (1981), rev'd on other grounds, 413 Mich. 938, 320 N.W.2d 881 (1982). But cf. Pioneer Bank & Trust Co. v. Seiko Sporting Goods, U.S.A. Co., 184 Ill. App. 3d 783, 540 N.E.2d 808 (1989) (holding that because bank's practices required such waivers to be effected by signing a portion of a trust receipt form for that purpose, oral waivers would be ineffective).

[288] 545 F. Supp. 200, 202 n.3 (S.D.N.Y. 1982).

[289] Id.; accord Instituto Nacional De Comercializacion Agricola (Indeca) v. Continental Ill. Nat'l Bank & Trust Co., 530 F. Supp. 279 (N.D. Ill. 1982).

[290] 82 N.Y.S.2d 72 (Sup. Ct. 1948).

allegation insufficient to state a defense to the account party's suit against the issuer. Such a defense does not arise without a showing that the account party acted with knowledge of the defects.

In *United Commodities-Greece v. Fidelity International Bank*,[291] an officer of the confirming bank represented to the issuer that the beneficiary's documents conformed. The court held that the statement did not constitute waiver, because the officer was unaware of certain nonconformities. Similarly, in *North American Foreign Trading Corp. v. General Electronics, Ltd.*,[292] the court refused to infer waiver from the account party's conduct. In the *Foreign Trading Corp.* case, the account party prevailed upon the issuer, which was the consignee of a shipment, to release the merchandise to the account party before all of the documents called for by the credit had arrived. The account party agreed to indemnify the issuer for any losses it sustained as a consequence of the early release, but the court held that such indemnity did not waive documentary defects. Accordingly, when the documents arrived and were defective, it was improper for the bank to honor the beneficiary's request for payment.[293]

Because the doctrine of waiver requires the intentional relinquishment of a known right, course of dealing, though it may give rise to en estoppel, usually does not give rise to waiver. In *Texpor Traders, Inc. v. Trust Co. Bank*,[294] for example, the court held that the account party's waiver of defects on the beneficiary's first presentation of documents did not operate as a waiver of defects on a subsequent presentation.[295] Cautious bankers, in order to avoid any waiver or estoppel defenses, customarily advise beneficiaries that the issuer is paying over defects that have been waived by the account party.

Waiver is not the same as amendment and does not presuppose agreement by all parties, as amendment does. Thus, an issuer that waives strict compliance may be caught in the middle. Its waiver excuses the beneficiary's noncompliance, even though the account party

---

[291] 99 A.D.2d 974, 473 N.Y.S.2d 10 (1984), modified, 64 N.Y.2d 449, 478 N.E.2d 172, 489 N.Y.S.2d 31 (1985).

[292] 67 A.D.2d 890, 413 N.Y.S.2d 700 (1979).

[293] Cf. Lalaco v. Universal Hous. Sys. of Am., Inc., No. 80 Civ. 178 (WCC) (S.D.N.Y. Oct. 25, 1983) (holding that account party waived its claim against issuer by failing to request issuer to dishonor documents that account party knew were problematic).

[294] 720 F. Supp. 1100 (S.D.N.Y. 1989).

[295] But cf. Titanium Metals Corp. of Am. v. Space Metals, Inc., 529 P.2d 431 (Utah 1974) (using course of dealing to read out of credit requirement that beneficiary present drafts). For criticism of *Titanium Metals*, see ¶ 4.07.

has not agreed to it.[296] If the issuer waives strict compliance and must pay the noncomplying beneficiary, however, it will not be able to escape the duties it owes the account party and may not be able to claim reimbursement.[297]

[3] Amendment

Section 5-106(2) stipulates that once an irrevocable credit is established as to the customer, the issuer may modify the credit only with the customer's consent. Once it is established as to the beneficiary, it can be modified only with the beneficiary's consent. Article 10(d) of the Uniform Customs provides simply that an irrevocable credit may not be amended "without the agreement of the issuing bank, the confirming bank (if any), and the beneficiary." Certainly, courts should not infer from the narrower scope of Section 5-106(2) a rule permitting amendment of a credit without the approval of parties other than the beneficiary and the customer. If, for example, an advising bank confirms a credit, it becomes a party. No amendment agreed to by the beneficiary and the customer should bind the confirming bank. Similarly, the issuer should not be bound by any modification to which it has not agreed.

The courts have enforced the amendment rules with a degree of vigor. On that point, the court stated in *It's Divine Industries, Ltd. v. Bank Leumi Trust Co.*,[298] "The law in this state is crystal clear."[299] In *National Bank & Trust Co. of North America, Ltd. v. J.L.M. International, Inc.*,[300] the court held that the announcement by the account party that it would resist the issuer's payment of certain sums due under a credit

---

[296] Chase Manhattan Bank v. Equibank, 550 F.2d 882 (3d Cir. 1977). But cf. Chilton Air Cooled Engines, Inc. v. First Citizens Bank, 726 S.W.2d 526 (Tenn. Ct. App. 1986) (holding that even if issuer waived requirement that account party sign certification, beneficiary could not obtain payment on credit without account party's authorization).

[297] For discussion of the issuer's right to reimbursement in the event it honors a nonconforming presentation, see ¶ 9.03[1][a].

[298] 22 U.C.C. Rep. Serv. (Callaghan) 130 (N.Y. Sup. Ct. 1977).

[299] Id. at 131; accord Goodwin Bros. Leasing, Inc. v. Citizens Bank, 587 F.2d 730 (5th Cir. 1979); cf. Asociacion De Azucareros De Guat. v. United States Nat'l Bank, 423 F.2d 638 (9th Cir. 1970) (amendment of credit to which all agreed may be rescinded when issuer's request for amendment authority to beneficiary was misleading); Lewis State Bank v. Advance Mortgage Corp., 362 So. 2d 406 (Fla. Dist. Ct. App. 1978) (beneficiary that acquiesced in extension of credit's expiry date cannot claim that it did not agree to modification).

[300] 421 F. Supp. 1269 (S.D.N.Y. 1976).

was an attempt to amend the credit unilaterally. The court viewed the attempt as a reason to sue the account party for repudiation.

Issuers of back-to-back credits should consider carefully the effect of issuing a second credit on the strength of a first credit that the second issuer has not confirmed. In the back-to-back situation,[301] an importer may use a credit running to his benefit from his own buyer to induce his bank to issue a credit in favor of his supplier. The bank that issues the second credit should be mindful that it may not be a "party" to the first credit and may not be in a position to object to amendments to it. The cautious second issuer insists that the opening bank ask the second bank to confirm the first credit. Such a confirming bank is expressly protected by Article 10(d).

Designating an arrangement an "amendment" does not necessarily render it one. In *Banco Nacional De Desarrollo v. Mellon Bank, N.A.,*[302] the beneficiary and the account party used a letter of credit in connection with the beneficiary's sale of beef to the account party. When the same commercial parties entered into a subsequent contract, the account party asked the issuer to issue an amendment with a new expiry. The account party also asked the issuer to add a documentary requirement. When the beneficiary failed to satisfy that requirement, the issuer dishonored. The beneficiary argued that it was excused from satisfying the additional requirement, which was improper in an amendment, since the beneficiary did not agree to it. The court held that the "amendment" was, in reality, a new credit and that the beneficiary could not obtain payment without satisfying its terms.

¶6.07 WARRANTIES OF THE BENEFICIARY AND THE PRESENTING BANK

Letters of credit, although they are a kind of contract, are also different from contracts and, to some extent, manifest features of negotiable instruments. Support for the analogy between credits and negotiable instruments is apparent in the independence principle, which renders the letter of credit independent of the underlying transaction out of which it grows. This rule is similar to that for negotiable instruments, which are generally independent of the transaction that underlies them. Further support for the analogy is evident in the majority view that courts should construe credits strictly and thus enhance the rapid payment of

---

[301] For an explanation of the back-to-back transaction, see ¶ 1.08.
[302] 726 F.2d 87 (3d Cir. 1984).

them without extraneous inquiry, all in a fashion similar to the law's attitude on satisfaction of negotiable instruments.

A further indication of the legislature's treatment of credits in a fashion similar to its treatment of negotiable instruments is the fact that Section 5-111 defines a warranty given by a beneficiary on the transfer and presentment of his draft or payment demand. This warranty, which is an addition to those under Articles 3, 4, 7, and 8 of the Code, arises by operation of law and not out of any contractual promise. It consists of the representation that "the necessary conditions of the credit have been complied with."[303]

One purpose of Section 5-111 is to distinguish the warranty given by the beneficiary from warranties of intermediary parties. Those warranties are also described in the section, and they do not include the beneficiary's warranty of compliance. It is also clear that a purpose of the section is to give a cause of action to any party damaged by the beneficiary's breach of the warranty. An issuer, a negotiating bank, and an account party could all benefit from the warranty, which runs to "all interested parties."[304]

The warranty section has escaped much attention, sometimes when the facts appear to have justified its invocation.[305] There are implica-

---

[303] U.C.C. § 5-111(1).

[304] Id.

[305] In Sherkate Sahami Khass Rapol v. Henry R. Jahn & Son, 701 F.2d 1049 (2d Cir. 1983), for example, the court dismissed the account party's fraud claim because there was no evidence that the beneficiary knew that a shipping invoice misdescribed the goods. The court remanded for jury trial the account party's breach of contract claim. It appears from the facts that the buyer had a clear claim for breach of the Section 5-111 warranty but did not assert that claim, even though its breach of contract case had serious problems. In Fertico Belg., S.A. v. Phosphate Chems. Export Ass'n, 100 A.D.2d 165, 473 N.Y.S.2d 403, appeal dismissed, 62 N.Y.2d 802 (1984), a telex from the beneficiary to the issuer recited the carrier's date of embarkation erroneously. The account party claimed to suffer damages because of the late sailing, and it sued the beneficiary for fraud and conversion. The court held that the account party was not a party to the credit and could not base a claim on the defendant's receipt of payment under it. In fact, the credit called for the beneficiary's certificate advising the date of sailing. Arguably, the account party, as an interested party, did have a cause of action under the warranty section. Cf. Valet Parking Serv., Inc. v. Philadelphia Parking Auth., 662 F. Supp. 1053 (E.D. Pa. 1986) (case in which account party used breach of underlying contract as cause of action against beneficiary that allegedly presented false certificate); United City Merchants (Invs.) Ltd. v. Royal Bank of Can., [1983] A.C. 168 (H.L.) (case that yields unfortunate result, in part because English law may not recognize warranty described in U.C.C. § 5-111(1)); Dean Witter Reynolds, Inc. v. Fernandez, 741 F.2d 355 (11th Cir. 1984) (affirming judgment based on unjust enrichment claim against party that presented fraudulent documents under credit). But cf. Wood v. R.R. Donnelley & Sons Co., 888 F.2d 313 (3d Cir. 1989) (fraud action arising from facts that may not have constituted breach of Sec-

tions, especially for the issuing and the negotiating banks, in the warranty section that merit consideration. The implications bear on those parties' rights against a beneficiary of a standby credit who draws or demands payment when the underlying transaction does not authorize it.

Many standby credits require the beneficiary to present, along with his draft or demand, a certificate reciting that the sum is due or reciting that the account party has failed to perform the underlying contract. Given such a certificate or draft, the issuer will honor and seek reimbursement from the account party. If, however, the issuer cannot obtain reimbursement, and if the beneficiary was not entitled to draw, the warranty section may give the issuer a cause of action against the beneficiary. Certainly, a warranty that the conditions of the credit have been complied with should entail the truthfulness of any certificate. Thus, a beneficiary presenting a false certificate has breached the warranty.[306] Such a beneficiary also may be guilty of fraud,[307] but breach of warranty usually is easier to prove than fraud. Issuers may have good reason to suggest that the parties include such a certificate as a condition of payment under a standby credit. Courts should understand that such certificates have significance under the warranty section.[308] Unfortunately, courts do not give the warranty section full effect.

---

tion 5-111(1) warranty). For an English case suggesting that issuer does have a common-law cause of action against the beneficiary that submits fraudulent documents, see Etablissement Esefka Int'l Anstalt v. Central Bank of Nig., [1979] 1 Lloyd's Rep. 445 (C.A.).

[306] See U.C.C. § 5-114, comment 2 (2d para., last two sentences); accord Mellon Bank, N.A. v. General Elec. Credit Corp., 724 F. Supp. 360 (W.D. Pa. 1989); Artoc Bank & Trust, Ltd. v. Sun Marine Terminals, Inc., 760 S.W.2d 311 (Tex. Ct. App. 1988).

[307] Cf. United States v. Sharder, 850 F.2d 1457 (11th Cir.), cert. denied, 109 S. Ct. 326 (1988) (conviction of beneficiary of wire fraud, uttering false bills of lading, and interstate transportation of property taken by fraud); United States v. Soo Hoo, [1987–1988 Transfer Binder] Fed. Banking L. Rep. (CCH) ¶ 87,174 (3d Cir. 1987) (conviction of party that presented false documents to federally insured advising payor bank); United States v. Tucker, 773 F.2d 136 (7th Cir. 1985), cert. denied, 478 U.S. 1022 (1986) (involving conviction of parties that presented false documents to federally insured issuer).

[308] Cf. Wyle v. Bank Melli, 577 F. Supp. 1148, 1162 (N.D. Cal. 1983) (suggesting that demand for payment under clean letter of credit implicitly includes representation that some good faith claim underlies demand); GATX Leasing Corp. v. DBM Drilling Corp., 657 S.W.2d 178 (Tex. Ct. App. 1983) (denying account party's request for injunction on ground that account party had adequate remedy at law — claim for breach of warranty under Section 5-111).

In *First National City Bank v. Klatzer*,[309] the beneficiary submitted defective documents to a collecting bank, which forwarded them to the issuer. When the issuer dishonored, the collecting bank sought to recoup its loss against the beneficiary. The *Klatzer* court had difficulty framing a cause of action on which the collecting bank could recover. Although the facts of the *Klatzer* opinion are meager, it appears that the collecting bank was an interested party and could have made a breach of warranty claim against the beneficiary.

In *Shaffer v. Brooklyn Park Garden Apartments*,[310] the presenting party knowingly tendered documents to the issuer that the court held were fraudulent. The court enjoined payment of the credit, arguing that if it did not enter the injunction, the account parties would not be able to recover their money. The reasoning is not satisfactory. The account parties would have had a cause of action against the presenter (a bank) for breach of the Section 5-111(1) warranty if not for common-law fraud.

Although the warranty of Section 5-111(1) extends to all interested parties, nothing in the section should permit an issuing bank or an account party to recover payment for documents defective on their face. The waiver and estoppel rules[311] and Article 16 of the Uniform Customs render such a claim next to frivolous. The issuer must examine documents for defects on their face.[312] As to the issuer and the account party, only latent defects, such as forgery or fraudulent documents, constitute a breach of the Section 5-111(1) warranty.

In *Philadelphia Gear Corp. v. Central Bank*,[313] however, the court used the warranty notion in a curious way. When the beneficiary submitted documents, the issuer rejected them with a general assertion that they did not comply. Significantly, the issuer refused to specify defects when the beneficiary asked for specifics. Although the 1974 Uniform Customs, to which the credit was subject, required the issuer to specify defects, they did not expressly preclude the issuer from raising objections after failing to specify them.[314] The beneficiary argued, however, that because the defects were curable, the court should estop the issuer. The court held that since the plaintiff knew, or reasonably should have

---

[309] 28 U.C.C. Rep. Serv. (Callaghan) 497 (N.Y. Sup. Ct. 1979).

[310] 311 Minn. 452, 250 N.W.2d 172 (1977).

[311] For a discussion of waiver and estoppel as limits on the strict compliance rule, see supra ¶¶ 6.06[1], 6.06[2].

[312] See U.C.C. § 5-109; U.C.P. art. 125 (1983).

[313] 717 F.2d 230 (5th Cir. 1983).

[314] But cf. U.C.P. art. 16(c) (1983) (raising such estoppel).

known, of the defects, it could not expect the court to estop the issuer for failing to specify the defects.

In a way, the *Philadelphia Gear* court has extended the beneficiary's warranty so that it covers patent defects. That is an unfortunate rule. The legislature has imposed a duty on the issuer to examine documents for patent defects.[315] By relieving the issuer of that duty in some cases, the *Philadelphia Gear* court introduces uncertainty into the credit transaction. It is a far better rule that requires the issuer to specify defects promptly or risk losing them as a defense to nonpayment.[316]

Delta Brands, Inc. v. MBank Dallas, N.A.[317] follows the *Philadelphia Gear* reasoning. In *Delta Brands*, the credit called for a certificate approving the start-up at the account party's works. The beneficiary supplied the confirming bank with a work approval containing specific complaints, yet the confirming bank paid. When the opening bank declined to reimburse, the confirming bank sought to recoup the payment from the beneficiary. The court accepted the argument that the beneficiary had breached the Section 5-111(1) warranty.

Unfortunately, the *Delta Brands* opinion does not address the problem its holding creates for the general rule that payor banks must examine documents to see that they comply on their face with the terms of the credit[318] or for the Uniform Customs rule that issuing and confirming banks must give prompt notice of defects.[319] Given the rule of *Philadelphia Gear* and *Delta Brands*, one wonders why a bank that accepts documents from a financially strong beneficiary takes much time to examine them. Under the rule of these cases, the bank can recoup any loss

---

[315] See U.C.C. § 5-109(2).

[316] For further discussion of the use of estoppel in this situation, see supra ¶ 6.06[1][c]. For support of the *Philadelphia Gear* holding, see Pro-Fab, Inc. v. Vipa, Inc., 772 F.2d 847 (11th Cir. 1985). For further discussion and criticism of the *Philadelphia Gear* reasoning, see Dolan, "Letters of Credit, Article 5 Warranties, and the Beneficiary's Certificate," 41 Bus. Law. 347 (1986); R. Goode, Commercial Law (1982). In Habib Bank Ltd. v. Convermat Corp., 145 Misc. 2d 980, 554 N.Y.S.2d 757 (App. Term. 1990) (per curiam), the New York court refused, under New York's nonconforming provision, N.Y. U.C.C. § 5-102(4) (McKinney 1964), to permit the issuer to recover from the beneficiary for breach of warranty. The court refused to apply the warranty provision to an action under a credit subject to the Uniform Customs. The *Habib* court was concerned that the warranty provision might be inconsistent with the preclusion rule of Article 16(e), which estops an issuer to claim that documents are defective unless the issuer notifies the beneficiary of the defects promptly. The court might have reached the same result by restricting the application of the warranty provision to latent defects.

[317] 719 S.W.2d 355 (Tex. Ct. App. 1986).

[318] See U.C.C. § 5-109; U.C.P. art. 15 (1983).

[319] See U.C.P. art. 16(d) (1983).

under the warranty provision. *Philadelphia Gear* at least confronts the issue; *Delta Brands* ignores it.[320]

Paramount Export Co. v. Asia Trust Bank, Ltd.[321] rejects the rule of *Philadelphia Gear* and adopts a thoughtful rule that draws a parallel between the strict compliance rule for beneficiaries that present documents and a strict estoppel rule for issuers that examine those documents. In *Paramount Export*, the issuer failed to comply with Article 8(e) of the 1974 version of the Uniform Customs by not returning the defective documents or holding them at the disposal of the presenting bank. That failure, the *Paramount Export* court held, precluded the issuer from alleging the defects, any knowledge of the beneficiary of those defects notwithstanding. The rule of the *Paramount Export* case does not rest on a desire to excuse beneficiaries that knowingly present defective documents. Rather, it recognizes the efficiency of requiring the issuer to obtain the account party's waiver of the defects or to dishonor and give notice promptly, so that the beneficiary can cure or take other steps (such as stopping the transport of goods) in the underlying transaction to protect itself.

Section 5-111(2) also has significant bearing on the relationship between the confirming bank and the customer of the opening bank. By confirming the credit, the confirming bank undertakes the same obligation toward the beneficiary as that of the opening bank,[322] but it does not accept any obligations with respect to the opening bank's customer. That customer, the account party, is not in privity with the confirming bank.[323]

An account party of the opening bank might argue, as the plaintiff did in *Instituto Nacional De Comercializacion Agricola (Indeca) v. Continental Illinois National Bank & Trust Co.*,[324] that the confirming bank's tender of the documents to the opening bank amounted to a representation that it had acted with due care. The *Indeca* court accepted

---

[320] For another opinion (1) holding that a beneficiary knowingly failing to comply with the conditions of a credit may not recover for wrongful dishonor, but (2) failing to discuss the warranty provision or the issues raised in the text, see Newvector Communications, Inc. v. Union Bank, 663 F. Supp. 252 (D. Utah 1987).

[321] 193 Cal. App. 3d 1474, 238 Cal. Rptr. 920 (1987).

[322] See U.C.C. §§ 5-103(1)(f), 5-107(2); U.C.P. art. 10(b) (1983).

[323] See U.C.C. §§ 5-103(1)(g), 5-109. The confirming bank owes no duty toward the account party, who is not its customer, and the account party has no obligation to reimburse the confirming bank, which must look to the opening bank. See Dulien Steel Prods., Inc. v. Bankers Trust Co., 298 F.2d 836 (2d Cir. 1962); Instituto Nacional De Comercializacion Agricola (Indeca) v. Continental Ill. Nat'l Bank & Trust Co., 530 F. Supp. 279 (N.D. Ill. 1982).

[324] 530 F. Supp. 279 (N.D. Ill. 1982).

that argument, basing its rule on common-law principles. Such principles supplement the Code,[325] but only if they are not "displaced by the particular provisions"[326] of the Code.

Section 5-111(2) displaces any common-law rule that imposes warranties in addition to those set forth in the provision. The Comment to the section makes it clear that the warranty of the intermediary includes "primarily its own good faith and authority."[327] Good faith in Article 5 is honesty in fact[328] and does not include any notion of due care.[329] The *Indeca* holding is a significant departure from the rule of Section 5-111(2).[330]

In a subsequent opinion in the same litigation, the *Indeca* court retreated somewhat from its earlier position.[331] First, it concluded that recent changes in Illinois law, which was applicable in this diversity action, did not give the account party a cause of action against the confirming bank in negligence. Second, having heard testimony, the court concluded that the confirming bank had not been negligent, in any event. The change in Illinois common law left the account party with only two causes of action: fraud and negligent disregard for truth or falsity. The evidence supported neither of those theories of liability. The court's reading of Illinois common law, whose implications it preferred, is not far from the implications of the Illinois statute,[332] whose implications the court eschewed.

The rule of *Indeca* is still a departure from the rule advanced in the Section 5-111(2) comments, because a cause of action limited to bad faith—that is, dishonesty in fact—is narrower than a cause of action for reckless disregard of truth or falsity. Under either rule, the account party has a cause of action against the confirming bank in fraud.

---

[325] See U.C.C. § 1-103.

[326] Id.

[327] See U.C.C. § 5-111, comment.

[328] See U.C.C. § 1-201(19) & comment 19; U.C.C. § 5-103(4); Shaffer v. Brooklyn Park Garden Apartments, 311 Minn. 452, 50 N.W.2d 172 (1977); cf. Emery-Waterhouse Co. v. Rhode Island Hosp. Trust Nat'l Bank, 757 F.2d 399 (1st Cir. 1985) (holding assignee of credit proceeds liable for presenting documents in bad faith).

[329] Compare U.C.C. § 1-201(9) with U.C.C. § 2-103(1)(b).

[330] For criticism of the *Instituto* holding on the due care issue, see Farrar, "Uniform Commercial Code Annual Survey—Letters of Credit," 38 Bus. Law. 1169, 1175 (1983).

[331] Instituto Nacional De Comercializacion Agricola (Indeca) v. Continental Ill. Nat'l Bank & Trust Co., 675 F. Supp. 1515 (N.D. Ill. 1987), aff'd, 858 F.2d 1264 (7th Cir. 1988).

[332] See Ill. Ann. Stat. ch. 26, § 5-111(2) (Smith-Hurd 1963).

On appeal, the Court of Appeals for the Seventh Circuit affirmed the *Indeca* holding but fashioned a more restrictive view of the confirmer's liability.[333] The Seventh Circuit found that there was no duty under non-Code Illinois law that would impose liability on the confirmer for negligently misrepresenting that the documents of the beneficiary had complied with the terms of the credit. The court added that the duties of the confirmer are spelled out in Sections 5-109 and 5-114 of the Code and that those duties consist of examining the documents with care. The court also reasoned, in this significant and thoughtful opinion, that at the bottom of Article 5 is a policy of encouraging the use of the credit as a commercial facility and that the creation of duties in addition to those spelled out in the Code would discourage rather than encourage use of the device.

In short, the *Indeca* court held that even if a confirmer negligently misrepresents that the documents conform, the account party has no cause of action. The court holds squarely that there is no duty on the part of a confirmer not to make such misrepresentations. As long as the confirmer examines the documents with care, the *Indeca* court will leave it free of liability.

There are two additional aspects of the *Indeca* holding that merit comment. First, the court held that the duties imposed by the Code run to the opening bank, not to the account party. Second, the court made no mention of the implications in the Code's warranty provision that confirmers do not warrant that documents are complying.

A negotiating bank does breach its warranty under Section 5-111(2) if it violates a collecting bank's warranties under Sections 4-207, 7-507, or 8-306 of the Code. The comment to Section 5-111(2) characterizes these warranties as primarily relating to the bank's "own good faith and authority." While the language of the warranty sections may not entirely support that characterization, at least one case has permitted the account party to sue a negotiating bank that allegedly presented documents to the issuer when the terms of the credit were not satisfied.

In *Berry v. Bank of Louisiana*,[334] a negotiation credit called for the named beneficiary's draft and an affidavit of a loan officer certifying that the lending institution had made advances to the named beneficiary, a limited partnership. The account party complained that the defendant bank lent funds to the general partner for personal use, negotiated his draft, and then sought payment under the credit. The *Berry* court held that the complaint stated a cause of action under Section 5-111 but did not indicate what conduct constituted the breach of warranty. Since

---

[333] 858 F.2d 1264 (7th Cir. 1988).

[334] 439 So. 2d 1166 (La. Ct. App. 1983).

the credit called for the bank's affidavit that advances were made for partnership purposes, presumably the bank breached its good faith warranty.

In *Banque Paribas v. Hamilton Industries International, Inc.*,[335] the court appears to have confused the beneficiary of the credit with a confirming bank. The opinion holds that Paribas might have been a confirming bank and that it would have been liable if it had submitted to the issuer a certificate that was incorrect. If Paribas were the beneficiary, that holding would make sense, because such conduct by a beneficiary would constitute breach of the Section 5-111(1) warranty. If Paribas were a confirming bank, that holding would conflict with the plain language of Section 5-111(2). The *Banque Paribas* case was an action in interpleader. An unfortunate result of the holding and of the confusion over the role of Paribas is that the court appears to have given the account party a claim against the confirming bank for breach of warranty.[336]

Actions for breach of warranty are not actions on the credit itself, nor are they attempts to interfere with the credit undertaking. One might argue, in fact, that the breach of warranty cause of action is a legislative attempt to effect some balance in the strict rules that apply to the letter of credit, that is, the rule of strict compliance[337] and the independence principle.[338]

The account party and the issuer have little room to avoid paying if the documents comply strictly on their face with the terms of the credit. Under the strict compliance rule, if the documents comply, the issuer may not add conditions or look beyond the face of the documents, but must pay. Under the independence principle, the account party can rarely stop that payment and generally cannot resort to the underlying transaction to support efforts to do so. It would be a departure from the purpose of the breach of warranty cause of action, then, for the courts to interdict the account party's or the issuer's resort to the underlying transaction in pursuit of the breach of warranty remedy.

---

[335] 767 F.2d 380 (7th Cir. 1985).

[336] See also Kozolchyk, "Bank Guarantees and Letters of Credit: Time for a Return to the Fold," 11 U. Pa. Int'l J. Bus. L. 1 (1989) (criticizing *Paribas* on failure to distinguish confirming bank from beneficiary). For discussion of the problems with interpleader in letter of credit litigation, see ¶ 11.06.

[337] Under the strict compliance rule, the issuer cannot add terms to the credit, even though it appears the beneficiary's draw is in violation of the underlying transaction. See generally ¶ 6.02.

[338] For this argument, see Dolan, "Letters of Credit, Article 5 Warranties, and the Beneficiary's Certificate," 41 Bus. Law. 347 (1986).

In *Universal Security Insurance Co. v. Ring*,[339] however, the court suggests that an account party's action against the beneficiary after payment of the credit is so limited. In that case, the account party was apparently unaware of the breach of warranty cause of action and based its complaint on a "wrongful draw" theory. The court reversed a judgment in favor of the account party on the ground that the draw was not wrongful. In making that determination, the court referred to the independence principle and held that, under the principle, the account party could not use the underlying transaction facts to support its action.

The cause of action in *Universal Security Insurance Co.* appears to be one for breach of warranty. In such cases, the underlying transaction often sheds light on the meaning of the credit's terms, and there are no sound policy reasons for preventing the account party from using the underlying transaction to demonstrate that the beneficiary failed to comply with those terms. That is not to suggest that the cause of action under Section 5-111(1) extends to breach of the underlying transaction. It is clear from the language of the section that the warranty is not that broad. The argument is simply that the underlying transaction's facts may illuminate the credit's terms and that the independence principle's reason does not interdict that illumination.

There has been little discussion of the nature of latent defects necessary to sustain a claim made for breach of the Section 5-111(1) warranty. In effect, the purpose of the provision is to permit a payor to recover money paid by mistake. When an issuer honors the beneficiary's draft, and the draft is accompanied by documents containing defects that the issuer cannot discern, the beneficiary has received an unauthorized payment, and the law should require him to return it. The warranty provision reflects an understanding that payment under the credit is a significant event[340] and that the beneficiary who achieves the advantages of that payment without satisfying the credit's conditions ultimately must return the funds. The warranty provision is not simply a rule to avoid unjust enrichment; it is a rule to prevent beneficiaries from drawing on credits and benefitting from them when they are not entitled to do so.

In *Mellon Bank, N.A. v. General Electric Credit Corp.*,[341] the beneficiary obtained payment under a credit by certifying that it was entitled to $600,000 under an equipment lease. In fact, the beneficiary's certificate was false, though it appears that the erroneous certification was made in good faith. Because the beneficiary had failed to take steps un-

---

[339] 298 Ark. 582, 769 S.W.2d 750 (1989).

[340] Its significance is that it effects a shifting of costs and risks in the dispute over performance in the underlying transaction. See generally ¶ 3.07.

[341] 724 F.2d 360 (W.D. Pa. 1989).

der the lease to accelerate payment, the *Mellon Bank* court determined that the certification was incorrect and that the beneficiary had breached the warranty.

One commentator criticizes *Mellon Bank* on the theory that the breach in that case is not sufficient to allow recovery of damages.[342] Under that commentator's view, the only breach that justifies an action under Section 5-111(1) is a breach that justifies an injunction under Section 5-114(2). This theory conflicts, of course, with the plain language of the warranty section. If it is correct, moreover, only egregious fraud, the beneficiary's taking of the credit proceeds without any colorable claim to them, amounts to a breach of the warranty.[343]

If a beneficiary's certificate is technically defective, and if the account party is insolvent, use of the warranty will leave the beneficiary with a loss it cannot recoup. By the time the issuer commences the warranty action, in all probability the credit will have expired. *Mellon Bank* is not such a hard case, however, that it demands doing violence to the language of the section and crafting such a narrow definition of the warranty.

One cannot deny that there should be limits on the warranty. Under the view advanced in this treatise, the warranty relates only to latent defects. Thus, the issuer's payment over documents with improper dates, missing signatures, or other defects apparent on a document's face are not payments by mistake and do not give the issuer or the account party a cause of action against the beneficiary. By limiting the warranty to latent defects, credit law avoids recovery of payments against documents that are facially defective.

If the beneficiary procures payment by supplying documents that are erroneous or false, however, the issuer has paid under the mistaken notion that the certification was true. *Mellon Bank* raises two warnings for beneficiaries:

1. They should not make certifications without making certain that the certificates are true.
2. They should insist in the underlying transaction that the account party supply them with a credit whose conditions they can satisfy easily.

One suspects that the credit in *Mellon Bank* was drafted by the beneficiary, a sophisticated leasing company. Standby beneficiaries often sup-

---

[342] See Barnes, "Barnes Sees 'Mellon Bank' Case Stirring L/C Warranty Controversy," Letter of Credit Update 13 (Jan. 1990).

[343] For discussion of the level of fraud necessary for injunctive relief, see ¶ 11.04[3].

ply the terms of the credit. Whether they supply the terms or agree to them, *Mellon Bank* tells them not to lease or lend or sell in the underlying transaction if the credit's conditions are burdensome.

¶6.08 ISSUER'S DUTY TO COUNSEL BENEFICIARY

There are some cases in which courts have considered the duty of an issuer to counsel the beneficiary. In *Exxon Co. U.S.A. v. Banque de Paris et des Pays-Bas*,[344] the issuer, given the seeming impossibility of satisfying the conditions of a credit, sought assurances from its account party customer before it issued a credit that expired on October 31, 1981 and that was conditioned on presentation of a certificate that deliveries were not made during the months of September through December 1981. When the issuer dishonored a postexpiry demand for payment, the beneficiary sued, claiming that the issuer owed the beneficiary a duty to draft a credit that made sense and that the court should construe the credit to make it an enforceable undertaking.

The *Exxon* decision, which the court made clear was mandated by Texas law in this diversity case, implicitly imposed that duty on the issuer, holding, in effect, that the beneficiary does not need to read the credit to ensure itself that it can perform its conditions. The *Exxon* court would not relieve issuers of the duty to make sense out of credit engagements, which are often creatures of trade practices and exigencies of which the issuer has no knowledge. To the same effect is *Kerr Construction Co. v. Plains National Bank*,[345] the Texas law on which the *Exxon* court relied.[346]

In *Tradex Petroleum American, Inc. v. Coral Petroleum, Inc. (In re Coral Petroleum, Inc.)*,[347] the same circuit court of appeals that decided the *Exxon* case confronted a similar situation. In *Tradex*, it was not the expiry provisions that created problems but the credit's list of documents that the beneficiary was required to submit. The credit in *Tradex* was an invoice standby that required the beneficiary to submit evidence that oil was shipped to the account party. The credit called for a shipper's transfer listing that referred to the product as "WTNM SO or SR."[348] Two other documents called for by the credit required reference

---

[344] 889 F.2d 674 (5th Cir. 1989).

[345] 753 S.W.2d 181 (Tex. Ct. App. 1987).

[346] For further discussion of the *Exxon* and *Kerr* cases, see ¶¶ 4.08[3], 5.03[3][a], 9.07.

[347] 878 F.2d 830 (5th Cir. 1989).

[348] Tradex Petroleum Am., Inc. v. Coral Petroleum, Inc. (In re Coral Petroleum, Inc.), 878 F.2d 830, 831 (5th Cir. 1989).

to West Texas Intermediate crude oil. In point of fact, "WTNM SO or SR" refers to a "sour" oil, while West Texas Intermediate crude oil is "sweet." Thus, the terms of the credit created an impossibility. The beneficiary could not present a shipper's order for oil that, in fact, had not been transferred to the account party.

The *Tradex* court held, nonetheless, that the beneficiary could not recover from the issuer when it failed to honor the beneficiary's nonconforming presentation and could not have the credit reformed. The court applied New York law to the case and thereby avoided the holding in *Kerr*, but the reasoning of the *Tradex* opinion makes it clear that the *Tradex* court rejected the reasoning of *Kerr*. In the view of the *Tradex* court, the beneficiary should examine the credit to determine that it can comply with the credit's terms—a view directly contrary to the view of *Kerr* and one contrary to the notion that the issuer has an obligation to make sense out of the credit. It is significant, though the court did not expressly limit its holding to these facts, that the ambiguity in *Tradex* was in trade terminology, with which the beneficiary, but not the issuer, should have been familiar.

In *GATX Leasing Corp. v. Capital Bank & Trust Co.*,[349] the beneficiary argued that the issuance of the credit was fraudulent and that such fraud prevented the issuer from dishonoring a credit whose terms the beneficiary apparently could not satisfy. The court rejected that argument on the ground that the fraud would be relevant only if there were a special relationship between the beneficiary and the issuer—a relationship that was not evident in the *Gatx Leasing* case.

In *Abilene National Bank v. Fina Supply, Inc.*,[350] the beneficiary sued a bank issuer, alleging that an officer of the issuer had misrepresented the coverage of the credit. The credit in question was designed to secure payment for the shipment of crude oil from the beneficiary to the account party. The parties agreed to the extension of the credit's expiry on several occasions. Those amendments simply altered the expiry term but did not change the credit's description of the shipments that were covered. At and after the extensions, the beneficiary requested and received assurances from the bank officer that the credit covered additional deliveries. When the beneficiary subsequently drew and supplied documents relating to shipments later than those covered by the credit, the bank dishonored.

The trial court awarded $4.5 million in actual damages and $6.5 million in punitive damages in the beneficiary's action against the bank, but the Texas Court of Appeals reversed, holding that the misrepresen-

---

[349] 717 F. Supp. 1160 (M.D. La. 1988).
[350] 706 S.W.2d 737 (Tex. Ct. App. 1986), aff'd, 726 S.W.2d 537 (Tex. 1987).

tations did not support the beneficiary's fraud claim.[351] The Supreme Court of Texas affirmed, holding that, as a general rule, opinions on the legal effect of a document are not actionable and that none of the exceptions were applicable in the *Abilene National Bank* case.[352] Significantly, the court found that there was no fiduciary relationship under the facts of the case.[353]

---

[351] For discussion of the *Abilene National Bank* court's holding on the beneficiary's claim for reformation, see ¶ 4.08[1].

[352] Fina Supply, Inc. v. Abilene Nat'l Bank, 726 S.W.2d 537 (Tex. 1987).

[353] Cf. Kanetmatsu-Gosho (Can.) Inc. v. Sinclair Supplies Ltd., 16 B.L.R. 89 (Alta. Q.B. 1982) (similar holding).

CHAPTER 7

The Issuer and
the Account Party

¶ 7.01   PRELIMINARY OBSERVATIONS

The important aspects of the relationship between the issuer of the credit and its customer (the account party) are considered here. The inquiry begins with the issuer's duty to pay, a duty that runs not only to the beneficiary but also to the account party. Sometimes the account party does not want the issuer to honor the credit and attempts to prevent that honor. These attempts have prompted considerable litigation, and the cases are difficult to reconcile. The issuer's right to demand reimbursement from the account party is another important feature of the issuer–account party relationship.

There are a number of points to keep in mind throughout this discussion. It is important to recall first that the credit does not govern the relationship between the issuer and the account party. There is usually a written agreement between the issuer and the account party (the "application agreement"[1]) that should govern many of the questions that arise out of that relationship. The application agreement does not cover all of these questions, and the law must supplement the parties' contract. The critical feature of that supplemental law is that dealing with the account

---

[1] For an example of such an application agreement, see App. C, Doc. 14.

party's right to stop payment under the credit—an extraordinary right that the application agreement usually does not address but concerning which the Uniform Commercial Code (UCC or the Code) and the courts have had much to say.

The second important point to keep in mind during analysis of the issuer–account party relationship is that the independence principle plays a role here, just as it does in the analysis of the relationship between the issuer and the beneficiary, discussed in Chapter 6. Frequently, the beneficiary invites courts to probe the underlying transaction when strict enforcement of the credit poses difficulties for it. Similarly, the account party sometimes regrets the terms of the credit that it caused to issue and under which it must reimburse the issuer.[2] The account party then extends a similar invitation to the courts to delve into the underlying facts.

Chapter 6 illustrates the difficulties that such involvement of the underlying transaction with the credit creates[3] and notes a number of cases that have deviated from the independence rule.[4] The deviation is infrequent in the issuer–account party setting, where nearly all courts recognize that the commercial viability of credits suffers when the law relaxes the independence principle; but, again, there is some authority that has weakened the principle.

Finally, it is important to bear in mind from the outset that the rules relating to the issuer–account party relationship do not stand alone. They are part of a larger plan to balance the relative interests of all parties and to enhance the credit as a valuable commercial device.

The strict compliance rule, for example, which the courts generally follow, is often a pro-beneficiary rule. Strict compliance requires the issuer to honor conforming documents without regard to the underlying transaction and often works against the interests of the account party. When the market falls, an account party buyer is not pleased to see his bank honor the beneficiary's request for payment under the credit. Under the strict compliance rule, however, the issuer must pay if the beneficiary's documents conform. The strict rule may work against the issuer, for if the account party is insolvent, an issuer honoring a strictly complying presentation will have no one from whom it can obtain reimbursement.

Yet the strict compliance rule also requires the beneficiary to comply strictly with the terms of the credit. This facet of strict compliance tends to favor the account party, and, if the account party is insolvent, it

---

[2] For a discussion of reimbursement, see infra ¶ 7.05.
[3] See generally the discussion in ¶¶ 6.03–6.06.
[4] See ¶ 6.05.

favors the issuer against the beneficiary. In a given case, strict compliance may appear harsh; but, viewed from a wider perspective, its fairness is apparent.

The second grand principle of letter of credit law is the independence principle, which features prominently in this chapter. The injunction cases discussed here[5] often make the telling point that the account party who objects to the independence principle does not lose everything by the enforcement of that principle, which teaches that the courts will not interfere with the issuer-beneficiary relationship because of equities that arise in other transactions. The cases stress that the account party retains his rights arising out of the related transaction (the underlying contract) and that he often recoups his losses by suit on the underlying agreement, where the law of credits does not apply.

It is a mistake to view the strict compliance rule and the independence principle in the context of a single case. The law of letters of credit maintains a balance in the broad context of the credit. Ad hoc tinkering may appeal to courts in a given factual setting, but that tinkering disturbs the overall balance.

¶ 7.02 ISSUER'S DUTY TO PAY

It is well settled that a beneficiary may complain when the issuer fails to honor a draft or demand for payment if the beneficiary has satisfied the credit's conditions.[6] There is less authority, however, for the proposition that the account party also may complain about such improper dishonor.[7] The account party is not a party to the credit but is a party to the credit application agreement that governs the issuer–account party

---

[5] See infra ¶ 7.04.

[6] See authority cited in ¶ 6.03. For a case recognizing the beneficiary's cause of action when the issuer pays the wrong party, see Cleveland Mfg. Co. v. Muslim Commercial Bank Ltd., [1981] 2 Lloyd's Rep. 646 (Q.B.).

[7] But see Samuel Kronman & Co. v. Public Nat'l Bank, 218 A.D. 624, 218 N.Y.S. 616 (1926). In FDIC v. Kerr, 650 F. Supp. 1356 (W.D.N.C. 1986), the court dismissed a guarantor's claim against the issuer. The claimant had guaranteed the obligation of the account party, an obligation that the letter of credit secured. When the issuer's successor refused to honor the letter of credit, the guarantor argued that he had suffered damage. The Kerr court disagreed, resting its ruling on a number of theories. Among them were the arguments that the claimant (1) could not show that the issuer's successor, the FDIC, had ever made any undertaking on behalf of the claimant; and (2) did not obtain an interest in the account party corporation until after the FDIC had disaffirmed the credit.

relationship.[8] In addition, the application agreement usually contains explicit language requiring the issuer to honor conforming drafts. Even if the application agreement does not contain the issuer's explicit promise to the account party, in many commercial credit situations the account party clearly suffers from dishonor. Under the law of transport, a shipper of goods has the power to stop delivery of them until he negotiates the bill of lading.[9] If the issuer dishonors, the shipper or its agent will hold the bill and will be able to prevent the account party from obtaining the goods. In many cases, moreover, the issuer's dishonor may impair the credit of the account party.

Section 5-114(2)(b) of the Code permits the issuer to pay a beneficiary even if the account party alleges that the beneficiary is practicing fraud. The section limits the issuer's protection to situations in which it acts in good faith, and many issuers are reluctant to rely on the provision as a safe harbor.[10] Note that the provision protects payment. It absolves the bank that pays in the face of a fraud claim but does not protect the bank that dishonors in the face of a fraud claim.[11]

A bank issuer, especially a bank issuer with strong international business, often is concerned that its international reputation as a credit issuer be protected. Courts that order an issuer to refuse payment against conforming documents may well impose costs upon that issuer that are difficult to quantify but that are patent to those familiar with international letter of credit markets.

When the U.S.-recognized government of Panama sought to enjoin U.S. banks from honoring the withdrawal requests and drafts of the Noriega government, some of those banks sought and obtained exceptions for draws under outstanding letters of credit.[12] During the Iranian-U.S. diplomatic crisis of 1980, U.S. courts issued many injunctions against payment; and the President ultimately forbade payment under federal law.[13] That history has not removed the banks of the world's

---

[8] See U.C.C. § 5-109, comment 1, which says that the Code assumes that "[t]he extent of the issuer's obligation to its customer is based upon the agreement between the two."

[9] See U.C.C. § 7-303(1)(a).

[10] For discussion of issuer efforts to protect themselves by court action in cases of alleged fraud, see ¶ 11.06.

[11] See United States v. Mercantile Nat'l Bank, 795 F.2d 492 (5th Cir. 1986).

[12] See Republic of Pan. v. Republic Nat'l Bank, 681 F. Supp. 1066 (S.D.N.Y. 1988); Republic of Pan. v. Citizens & S. Int'l Bank, No. 88-410-Civ-Aronovitz (S.D. Fla. Mar. 22, 1988).

[13] For an account of that major crisis in international letter of credit transactions, see infra ¶ 7.04[4][e].

largest economic power from the market, but it arguably has had an effect.[14]

It is not enough to say, as one court did in a different context,[15] that surely it does not damage the international reputation of a bank to say that it is obeying a court order. Foreign commercial parties may decide simply that they will use banks from countries whose courts do not enter such orders. The commercial party in a foreign country whose language, state of commercial modernization, and legal tradition differ from those of the United States will not accept such an excuse as readily as someone with a U.S.-trained lawyer to explain the situation.

¶ 7.03 STOPPING PAYMENT

[1] Failure to Deliver Merchandise Under the Purchase Contract and Similar Defenses in the Underlying Transaction

It is the general rule accepted by virtually all courts that, absent some defect in the documents or fraud,[16] the account party has no right to stop the issuer from making payment under the credit. This general rule is the first corollary of the independence principle. The account party's rights arise out of the underlying contract with the beneficiary and the application contract with the issuer. The credit is independent of both, and any rights the account party may have under these contracts cannot affect the issuer's duty to pay under the credit.

A buyer of goods may agree to provide the seller with a letter of credit. The buyer asks his bank to issue the credit, knows that he must reimburse the bank, and expects to receive his merchandise in due course. If he does not receive the merchandise, he undoubtedly will take offense. He may have a claim on the underlying sales agreement with the seller, but he will not be able to stop payment on the credit or avoid having to reimburse his bank when it honors a conforming presentation.

In *Kingdom of Sweden v. New York Trust Co.*,[17] a buyer of toluene caused a credit to issue in favor of the seller. The issuer paid the seller; but, before delivery of the toluene, a government agency forbade its

---

[14] See generally Zimmett, "Standby Letters of Credit in the Iran Litigation: Two Hundred Problems in Search of a Solution," 16 Law & Pol'y Int'l Bus. 927 (1984).

[15] Jeri-Jo Knitwear, Inc. v. Gonul Besen Konfeksiyon Sanayii Ve Ticaret Ltd., No. 88 Civ. 2535 (E.D.N.Y. Sept. 9, 1988).

[16] The idea that fraud upsets the usual rules of credits is an old one. See, e.g., Mason v. Hunt, 99 Eng. Rep. 192, 194 (K.B. 1779); Pillans v. Van Mierop, 97 Eng. Rep. 1035 (K.B. 1765). For a discussion of the modern fraud rules, see infra ¶ 7.04.

[17] 197 Misc. 431, 96 N.Y.S.2d 779 (Sup. Ct. 1949).

shipment and later seized it. The buyer sued the issuer, claiming reimbursement of the funds the bank used to pay the beneficiary seller's draft. The court held that this attempt to reverse payment under the credit must founder on the independence principle and that the plaintiff should seek redress elsewhere.

In *Rosenfeld v. Banco Internacional*,[18] the issuer, presumably acting at the behest of its customer, dishonored drafts drawn under a credit. The beneficiary in *Rosenfeld* had presented conforming documents. The issuer alleged that, by virtue of some irregularity in the documents, the Argentine government had seized the merchandise that was the subject of the account party's contract with the beneficiary. The court ruled that the issuer's dishonor was improper, the failure of the seller to effect delivery of the merchandise notwithstanding.[19]

In *Public Loan Co. v. FDIC*,[20] the account party argued that, although the underlying debt had been paid, the beneficiary had not returned the standby that secured the debt. When the beneficiary became insolvent, its successor, the FDIC, attempted to draw under the credit. The court might have ruled that, as a matter of credit law, the defense of accord and satisfaction in the underlying transaction is no defense in the letter of credit transaction. Instead, the court rested its summary judgment in favor of the beneficiary on a provision of the Federal Deposit Insurance Act[21] that bars the use of oral understandings against the FDIC.[22]

In *Seguin Savings Association v. Vista Verde Plaza Joint Venture*,[23] the Texas Court of Appeals attempted to fashion a rule that departs significantly from the general rule that breach of contract in the underlying transaction does not justify an injunction. While the *Seguin Savings* opinion makes a thoughtful effort to justify this departure, the effort relies too heavily on the language of the Code and too little on the functions of letters of credit in general.

---

[18] 27 A.D.2d 826, 278 N.Y.S.2d 160 (1967).

[19] Cf. Lalaco v. Universal Hous. Sys. of Am., Inc., No. 80 Civ. 178 (WCC) (S.D.N.Y. Oct. 25, 1983) (holding, among other things, that payment is proper when documents conform, even though part of goods are not shipped).

[20] 803 F.2d 82 (3d Cir. 1986).

[21] 12 U.S.C. § 1823(e) (1988).

[22] For further discussion of the effects of the underlying contract on disputes in the letter of credit transaction, see ¶ 2.09[5]. For additional authority that breach of the underlying contract is an insufficient ground to stop payment on the credit, see PGA Mktg. Ltd. v. Windsor Plumbing Supply Co., 124 A.D.2d 577, 507 N.Y.S.2d 721 (1986).

[23] 7 U.C.C. Rep. Serv. 2d (Callaghan) 862 (Tex. Ct. App. 1988).

In *Seguin Savings*, the account party obtained an injunction on the ground that the beneficiary's draws on the credits in question were possible only because the beneficiary had breached the underlying transactions and had prevented the account party from performing. Assuming those assertions to be true, the trial court granted a temporary injunction and set the matter for trial. On accelerated appeal, the beneficiary argued that only forged or fraudulent documents or fraud in the transaction allows an injunction under Section 5-114 and that the court of appeals should lift the injunction. The Texas court agreed that the beneficiary's conduct did not amount to the kind of fraud that justifies an injunction; but, relying on the policy sections of the Code,[24] the court determined that, in this case, breach of the underlying contract, which breach operated to permit the beneficiary to draw, justified equitable relief.

Because it omits consideration of the effect of its ruling on the letter of credit as a commercial device, the *Seguin Savings* court's analysis is unpersuasive. The fraud exception to the general rule (that credits must be paid first with the parties talking about it later) is a response to the law's animus against fraud. It is well accepted that the rule of Section 5-114(2)(b) is a codification of the *Sztejn* rule, a rule authored by a judge who recognized the danger to credits in using breach of the underlying transaction as grounds for stopping payment.[25]

Injunctions, even when the law limits them to cases of egregious fraud that vitiates the purpose of the credit's independence from the underlying transaction, pose a serious threat to the letter of credit.[26] Promiscuous use of the injunction destroys the credit's functions.[27] Without adequate consideration of the costs it is imposing on the credit facility, the *Seguin Savings* case cannot be taken as well-considered authority and may be confined to the exigencies of the financial institution failures that plagued Texas and other states at the time of the *Seguin Savings* decision.[28]

---

[24] U.C.C. §§ 1-102, 1-106, 5-102 & comment 2.

[25] For discussion of the *Sztejn* rule, its codification, and its author's efforts to limit its effects on the independence principle, see infra ¶ 7.04[2].

[26] For discussion of the problems that the fraud exception poses for credits, see infra ¶ 7.04[3][c].

[27] For discussion of the functions of the credit, see ¶ 3.07.

[28] The *Seguin Savings* opinion makes much of the fact that the beneficiary, a savings and loan institution, was facing insolvency.

[2] Unlawfulness of the Underlying Agreement

Some account parties have argued that honor of the credit is unlawful, either because the credit itself is unlawful or because the underlying transaction is unlawful. Such attempts usually have failed.

In some cases, account parties have contended that a standby credit is, by its nature, a guaranty and that it is an ultra vires act of the issuer if the issuer is a commercial bank. Federal law governing commercial banks limits their activity to the business of banking,[29] and most authorities agree that guaranties are not the business of national banks.[30] A similar rule applies to most state banks.[31] A standby credit resembles a guaranty in an important functional way. The standby credit substitutes the bank's credit for that of the account party. It is paid, by virtue of its standby nature, usually when the account party does not pay or otherwise fails to perform an executory promise.

The guaranty and the standby credit differ, however, in a fundamental aspect that makes all the difference for this inquiry. Under the guaranty, the guarantor is secondarily liable; under the standby credit, the issuer is primarily liable. The guaranty is effective only after the account party defaults. The parties must determine that default in order to know whether payment is due under the guaranty. Under the standby credit, the bank issuer is primarily liable. Its liability rests not on an evaluation of the account party's performance but on the beneficiary's presentation of documents. Although it is not the business of banking to determine performance, it is the business of banking to examine documents.

Bank issuers do not evaluate their obligations under a credit by calculating the probability that the account party will default. It is traditional in the banking industry for a bank issuing a standby credit to assume that it will have to pay under the credit. Thus, each bank takes steps to secure itself in the same way that it secures a loan to the account party: It considers the standby an unfunded loan. The judgments that the bank makes on issuing the credit (e.g., the evaluation of the account party's financial strength or of the collateral pledged by the account party) are typical banking judgments. Courts have held generally that standby credits are not ultra vires and that the account party cannot en-

---

[29] 12 U.S.C. § 24 (seventh) (1988).

[30] Generally, a bank may issue a guaranty if it is interested in the transaction. See, e.g., U.C.C. § 5-113; 12 C.F.R. § 7.7010 (1989).

[31] See, e.g., United Bank v. Quadrangle, Ltd., 42 Colo. App. 486, 596 P.2d 408 (1979); Bridge v. Welda State Bank, 222 Mo. App. 586, 292 S.W. 1079 (1927); Republic Nat'l Bank v. Northwest Nat'l Bank, 566 S.W.2d 358 (Tex. Civ. App.), rev'd, 578 S.W.2d 109 (Tex. 1978).

join bank issuers from honoring them.[32] In many jurisdictions, the ultra vires doctrine is not a sufficient basis for an injunction against payment in any event.

This digression into the issue of whether issuing standby credits is a proper bank function cannot mask the fact that some courts hold, from time to time, that banks issuing such credits have exceeded their powers.[33] In most of these cases, however, courts have held that if a bank acts beyond the scope of its powers, the ultra vires defense will not be available to the account party seeking to stop payment under the credit. These courts will not enjoin payment of drafts drawn under the credit.[34]

Account parties have been more successful in stopping payment when they have argued that the underlying contract which the credit serves is unlawful or contrary to public policy. Such arguments run afoul of the independence principle and courts generally reject them.

In *New York Life Insurance Co. v. Hartford National Bank & Trust Co.*,[35] the credit served to provide the beneficiary, a long-term lender, with liquidated damages in the event the account party did not take the long-term loan that the beneficiary had committed to make. The account party argued that the amount of the credit rendered the arrangement not one for liquidated damages but one for a penalty and that therefore it was unenforceable. The court rejected the argument, noting that the penalty question was one arising out of the underlying contract, not out of the credit. The issue could not be litigated in the credit context.

In *Prudential Insurance Co. of America v. Marquette National Bank*,[36] the court rejected a similar penalty argument. Even if the payment amounts to an unenforceable penalty under the agreement between the account party and the beneficiary, the court held, the policy

---

[32] E.g., Prudential Ins. Co. of Am. v. Marquette Nat'l Bank, 419 F. Supp. 734 (D. Minn. 1976); Republic Nat'l Bank v. Northwest Nat'l Bank, 578 S.W.2d 109 (Tex. 1978).

[33] For discussion of those cases and the ultra vires issue in general, see ¶ 12.02.

[34] See Security Fin. Group, Inc. v. Northern Ky. Bank & Trust Co., 858 F.2d 304 (6th Cir.), clarified, 875 F.2d 529 (6th Cir. 1988); FDIC v. Freudenfeld, 492 F. Supp. 763 (E.D. Wis. 1980); First Am. Nat'l Bank v. Alcorn, Inc., 361 So. 2d 481 (Miss. 1978). But cf. International Dairy Queen, Inc. v. Bank of Wadley, 407 F. Supp. 1270 (M.D. Ala. 1976) (containing dictum to contrary). For other cases on the ultra vires question, see ¶ 9.06[5]. In Tosco Corp. v. FDIC, 723 F.2d 1242 (6th Cir. 1983), the FDIC apparently argued that the failed issuer's vice-president and cashier did not have authority to execute the credit, but the court held that such an officer has apparent authority to sign a letter of credit and can bind the bank.

[35] 173 Conn. 492, 378 A.2d 562 (1977).

[36] 419 F. Supp. 734 (D. Minn. 1976).

against penalties does not justify nonpayment of demands under the credit.[37]

Courts are not always willing to say that letter of credit policy overrides other concerns, however. In *United City Merchants (Investments) Ltd. v. Royal Bank of Canada*,[38] the account party, a Peruvian company, sought to use the credit as a device to move currency out of Peru in violation of Peruvian exchange control laws. The scheme involved asking the beneficiary to invoice the goods it was selling to the Peruvian buyer at double the contract price, with the understanding that the beneficiary would deposit the excess funds in a U.S. bank to the buyer's account. The *United City Merchants* court, bound by the International Monetary Fund Agreement,[39] held that, to the extent the credit was a device to move funds out of Peru in violation of the currency exchange rules, and to that extent only, the credit was unenforceable. Thus, the court cabined the effect of the International Monetary Fund Agreement to protect the credit to the extent that it did not violate the Agreement.[40]

---

[37] See also Shel-Al Corp. v. American Nat'l Ins. Co., 492 F.2d 87 (5th Cir. 1974) (holding that amount of credit was not unreasonable amount and was not penalty). But cf. Hubbard Business Plaza v. Lincoln Liberty Life Ins. Co., 649 F. Supp. 1310 (D. Nev. 1986), aff'd, 844 F.2d 792 (9th Cir. 1988) (mem.) (result contrary to *New York Life*). See generally McLaughlin, "Standby Letters of Credit and Penalty Clauses: An Unexpected Synergy," 43 Ohio St. L.J. 1 (1982).

[38] [1983] A.C. 168 (H.L.).

[39] See Articles of Agreement of the International Monetary Fund, art. VIII, § 2(b), 60 Stat. 1401, T.I.A.S. No. 1501, 2 U.N.T.S. 39.

[40] For additional cases holding that the illegality of the underlying agreement does not justify court interference with payment under the credit, see Berman v. LeBeau Inter-Am., Inc., 509 F. Supp. 156 (S.D.N.Y.), aff'd mem., 679 F.2d 872 (2d Cir. 1981) (holding that even if funding of credits was part of fraudulent scheme in violation of statute restricting corporate dividends and law of fraudulent conveyances, payment under credits was not fraudulent); Kupetz v. Wolf, 845 F.2d 842 (9th Cir. 1988) (payments under credit by bank issuer in connection with leveraged buyout may not be set aside by account party's trustee in bankruptcy, on ground that payments were arguably (1) in violation of California law limiting distribution of corporate assets, (2) in violation of Bankruptcy Code antifraud provisions, and (3) fraudulent conveyances); Panatlantic, Inc. v. Chester (In re Devaney), 99 Bankr. 533 (S.D.N.Y. 1989) (payment under primary bank obligation did not constitute fraudulent conveyance of account party's property, because issuer paid not with account party's funds but with its own); Originala Petroleum Corp. v. Beta Fin. & Inv. Corp. (In re Originala Petroleum Corp.), 39 Bankr. 1003 (Bankr. N.D. Tex. 1984) (holding that even if underlying promise of corporation violated Texas Business Corporation Act's prohibition against redemption of shares by insolvent corporation, violation is no defense, because statute is not absolute prohibition and because corporation had represented that its promise was lawful); Brown v. United States Nat'l Bank, 220 Neb. 684, 371 N.W.2d 692 (1985) (holding that alleged securities law violations in underlying contract did not prevent beneficiary from recovering under credit); Mount Carmel Energy Corp. v. Marine Midland Bank, 82 A.D.2d 729, 439 N.Y.S.2d

[3] Account Party Insolvency

There have been a number of attempts by account parties and their trustees in bankruptcy to use the Bankruptcy Code, a federal statute, to overcome the independence principle in Article 5 and in the common law of credits. *Postal v. Smith (In re Marine Distributors, Inc.)*,[41] a pre-Bankruptcy Code case, illustrates the problem. In the *Postal* case, the debtor (Marine) had entered into a contract to purchase the assets and assume the liabilities of a business. The contract required Marine to have its bank issue standby credits for the benefit of the sellers to secure notes Marine gave to the sellers. Before the sellers could draw on the credits, Marine filed in bankruptcy; and its trustee sought to enjoin the sellers from making any draw.

[a] Property of the Debtor

In *Postal*, as well as in most bankruptcy cases involving letters of credit, the crucial question is whether payment of the credit constitutes a transfer of the debtor's property. If no property of the debtor is involved, the bankruptcy law is not concerned. In *Postal*, the bankruptcy court assumed jurisdiction of the matter on the theory that payment of the credits would have an adverse impact on the debtor's assets. The notes in question gave Marine certain setoff rights, but the credits did not. The bankruptcy court enjoined the beneficiary, and the district court affirmed.

On appeal, the Court of Appeals for the Ninth Circuit reversed, concluding that no property of the debtor was involved. It is significant that the Ninth Circuit accepted the independence principle and saw the bank's credit engagement as independent of the dispute between Marine and the sellers. The Ninth Circuit, however, left open a question that has become significant. By noting that the credits in the *Postal* case were not secured by any property of the bankrupt, the court implied that, if they had been secured, its decision might have gone the other way.

In *Twist Cap, Inc. v. Southeast Bank (In re Twist Cap, Inc.)*,[42] the bankruptcy court tentatively explored that implication. The court con-

---

387 (1981) (holding that fact that account party's agent was not authorized to enter into underlying contract does not affect payments under credit). For a view favoring a rather expansive application of the argument that the impropriety of the underlying transaction can justify stopping payment in the letter of credit transaction, see McLaughlin, "Letters of Credit and Illegal Contracts: The Limits of the Independence Principle," 49 Ohio St. L.J. 1197 (1989).

[41] 522 F.2d 791 (9th Cir. 1975).

[42] 1 Bankr. 284 (Bankr. D. Fla. 1979).

cluded that when the credit is secured by the debtor's property, payment of the credit may operate indirectly to transfer property of the debtor to the beneficiary. The *Twist Cap* court refused to ignore the impact of the credit's payment on the debtor's estate and concluded that the beneficiaries were unsecured creditors who may have been benefiting from a preferential transfer that was voidable under the Bankruptcy Code.[43] Accordingly, the court entered a temporary restraining order to protect the status quo pending a hearing on the merits. Before that hearing, the case was settled.[44]

The apparent error in the *Twist Cap* analysis is the court's characterization of the beneficiaries as unsecured creditors. Far from it, the beneficiaries were well secured. They held the obligation of an issuer that itself was secured.

In *Page v. First National Bank (In re Page)*,[45] the district court reversed a decision of the bankruptcy court that had followed the *Twist Cap* reasoning. The *Page* court explicitly addressed the *Twist Cap* issue and held that no property of the debtor's estate had passed to the beneficiary. It held that the proceeds of the credit clearly were not an asset of the estate. The court recognized that, by virtue of its payment under the credit, the issuer would resort to the collateral and thereby would diminish the estate of the debtor. The court noted, however, that the Bankruptcy Code's automatic stay provision prevented the issuer from acting without the court's approval. *Page* was a clear rejection of *Twist Cap*.[46]

Because the creditors in the *Postal* and *Twist Cap* cases did not receive property of the debtor, the credits in those cases do not pose a threat to Bankruptcy Code policy. Even in *Twist Cap*, where the issuer's right of reimbursement is secured, stepping the transactions together does not yield a preferential transfer.

The facts of *American Bank v. Leasing Service Corp. (In re Air Conditioning, Inc. of Stuart)*,[47] may involve a situation in which creditors

---

[43] 11 U.S.C. § 547 (1988).

[44] See Chaitman & Sovern, "Enjoining Payment on a Letter of Credit in Bankruptcy: A Tempest in a Twist Cap," 38 Bus. Law. 21–23 (1982).

[45] 18 Bankr. 713 (D.D.C. 1982).

[46] It is also significant that Justice Paskay, who authored the *Twist Cap* opinion, held, in St. Petersburg Hotel Assocs., Ltd. v. Royal Trust Bank (In re St. Petersburg Hotel Assocs., Ltd.), 37 Bankr. 380 (Bankr. M.D. Fla. 1984), that a letter of credit was not an asset of the account party's estate. His opinion takes pains to limit the *Twist Cap* rule to the narrow facts of that case. Id. at 382–383; cf. Guy C. Long, Inc. v. Dependable Ins. Co. (In re Guy C. Long, Inc.), 74 Bankr. 939, 944 (Bankr. E.D. Pa. 1987) (referring to Justice Paskay's "retreat from his holding" in *Twist Cap*).

[47] 55 Bankr. 157 (Bankr. S.D. Fla. 1985), aff'd in part, rev'd in part sub nom. Leasing Serv. Corp. v. Wendel (In re Air Conditioning, Inc. of Stuart), No. 86-8006-CIV-Nesbitt (S.D. Fla. Jan. 12, 1987), aff'd in part, rev'd in part sub nom. American

can use letters of credit to thwart the Bankruptcy Code's antipreference rules. In the *Air Conditioning* case, a judgment creditor sought to replevin equipment of the debtor. In order to forestall the replevin, the debtor caused its bank to issue a letter of credit in favor of the creditor in the amount of $20,000. The debtor secured the issuer's right of reimbursement by pledging a $20,000 certificate of deposit with the bank. Sometime in the following month, the debtor filed a petition in bankruptcy. The bank, fearing it would be caught in the middle, sued the creditor and asked the court for instructions. The trustee intervened, and the court treated the matter as an action in interpleader.[48] Because the court saw the credit transaction as an avenue for effecting a preferential transfer, it held the assignment of the certificate of deposit to the bank to be a preference voidable under Section 547 of the Bankruptcy Code, and it nullified the credit.

On appeal,[49] the district court affirmed the bankruptcy court's holding that the transfer of the certificate of deposit to the issuer constituted a preferential transfer *to the beneficiary*, but it reversed the bankruptcy court's order nullifying the credit. The Court of Appeals for the Eleventh Circuit[50] affirmed that part of the district court's holding that related to the preference and reversed in part on a procedural question.[51] Both the court of appeals and the district court took pains to guard the integrity of the credit as a commercial device.

The *Air Conditioning* case poses severe problems for letters of credit. The fact situation is not rare: A debtor uses a letter of credit to induce a creditor to forgo a remedy. If bankruptcy ensues within ninety days, any security the debtor grants the issuer may be a preferential transfer to the beneficiary voidable by the trustee under the rule of the case. It is not enough to say, as the beneficiary did in *Air Conditioning*, that the ruling conflicts with letter of credit policy. Clearly, it does. The rule of

---

Bank v. Leasing Serv. Co. (In re Air Conditioning, Inc. of Stuart), 845 F.2d 293 (11th Cir.), cert. denied sub nom. First Interstate Credit Alliance, Inc. v. American Bank, 109 S. Ct. 557 (1988).

[48] For discussion of interpleader by the issuer, see ¶¶ 2.09[6], 7.04[4][g].

[49] Leasing Serv. Corp. v. Wendel (In re Air Conditioning, Inc. of Stuart), No. 86-8006-CIV-Nesbitt (S.D. Fla. Jan 12, 1987), aff'd in part, rev'd in part sub nom. American Bank v. Leasing Serv. Co. (In re Air Conditioning, Inc. of Stuart), 845 F.2d 293 (11th Cir.), cert. denied sub nom. First Interstate Credit Alliance, Inc. v. American Bank, 109 S. Ct. 557 (1988).

[50] American Bank v. Leasing Serv. Co. (In re Air Conditioning, Inc. of Stuart), 845 F.2d 293 (11th Cir.), cert. denied sub nom. First Interstate Credit Alliance, Inc. v. American Bank, 109 S. Ct. 557 (1988).

[51] The procedural question related to the propriety of the action in the nature of interpleader filed by the issuer. For discussion of that issue, see infra ¶ 7.04[4][g].

Air Conditioning flies in the face of the independence principle, but the independence principle in this case conflicts with bankruptcy policy. In the event of that conflict, the common-law principle of independence, even to the extent it is codified in state enactment of the Code, must give way.

The *Air Conditioning* opinion does not indicate whether the court would hold the issuer liable to the trustee for paying the beneficiary. Such a ruling might be attractive to bankruptcy courts. It is not the transaction between the issuer and the debtor that offends bankruptcy policy; it is the payment to the creditor that offends that policy. When the debtor grants the issuer a security interest in the certificate of deposit, there is no preference in favor of the issuer. The issuer has issued the credit simultaneously and thereby has undertaken a liability in the same amount as the certificate. The Bankruptcy Code protects that transaction.[52] If the *Air Conditioning* rule catches the creditor but leaves the bank alone, it will promote bankruptcy policy without wreaking havoc with letter of credit law.

The *Air Conditioning* opinions suggest that courts should let the credit transaction proceed and let the trustee look to the beneficiary in the preference action. Whether the district court's solution will obtain in all cases is unclear. The antipreference policy of the Bankruptcy Code may yet prompt a court to enjoin payment to a beneficiary over whom the court does not have jurisdiction.[53] Although any rule that permits suits to stop payment of credits harms the credit as a commercial device,[54] the Bankruptcy Code's antipreference policy may mandate such a result in a case where the trustee cannot recover the issuer's payment to the beneficiary.

On the other hand, the solicitude of the district court in *Air Conditioning* for commercial realities may support a principled exception to

---

[52] See 11 U.S.C. § 547(c)(1) (1988).

[53] In FSLIC v. Quinn, 711 F. Supp. 366 (N.D. Ohio 1989), the facts came close to satisfying the need to issue an injunction. *Quinn* is not a bankruptcy case but a case involving the insolvency of a thrift. The thrift had caused letters of credit to issue as golden parachutes in favor of two of the thrift's officers. The court found that there was risk of irreparable loss to the FSLIC if the officers received unrestricted use of the money. The court did not have to consider an injunction against payment of the credit, however, because the parties had agreed to pay the credit proceeds into a restricted account. Thus, the facts of *Quinn* and the court's holding suggest that an injunction against payment may have been in order. The opinion makes much of the point, with apparent relief, that the voluntary arrangement by the parties permitted the court to avoid any letter of credit ruling.

[54] See generally infra ¶¶ 7.04[2]–7.04[4]. See also Dolan, "Standby Letters of Credit and Fraud (Is the Standby Only Another Invention of the Goldsmiths in Lombard Street?)," 7 Cardozo L. Rev. 1 (1985).

the antipreference policy of the Bankruptcy Code. While that Bankruptcy Code policy is clear and strong, it is not clear that Congress intended to wreak havoc with honest commercial devices in order to promote the policy. If courts may enjoin payment of credits, beneficiaries and, importantly, agencies that rate municipal bonds or other securities secured by credits may decide that credits do not yield the certainty of payment that has been their hallmark and their chief virtue as a commercial device.[55]

In *Kellogg v. Blue Quail Energy, Inc. (In re Compton Corp.)*,[56] the court confronted a situation similar to that in *Air Conditioning* and reached a similar result. In an opinion rife with endorsement of applying bankruptcy rules so that they do not interfere unduly with the proper functioning of credits, the court held that the beneficiary had received a preference but that the credit transaction itself could proceed without offending bankruptcy law.

In *Compton*, the issuer opened a credit in favor of the beneficiary during the preference period and on account of an antecedent debt. At the time of the issuance, the issuer was fully protected under a security agreement that secured after advances and that was entered into outside the preference period. The beneficiary drew after the account party's bankruptcy filing, and the court held that the effect of the arrangement was to transfer property of the debtor (the issuer's collateral) to the beneficiary via the issuer's payment to the beneficiary. The court emphasized that the issuer did not receive any preference, because its security interest was perfected outside the preference period and because it gave contemporaneous consideration (issuance of the credit) when it received the benefit of the collateral.[57]

---

[55] Two commentators have argued that the rule of the *Air Conditioning* case is supported by Section 547(d) of the Bankruptcy Code. That section empowers the trustee to avoid a transfer of the debtor's property to a surety in order to secure reimbursement for a bond issued by the surety to dissolve a judicial lien that would have been avoidable by the trustee as a preference. One cannot deny that there are strong similarities between the facts of the *Air Conditioning* case and the scope of Section 547(d). Yet the nature of letters of credit is significantly different from that of surety bonds. See ¶ 2.10[1]. The decision of Congress to single out surety bonds for special treatment should not be taken as a signal that Congress would treat letters of credit in the same fashion. See generally Gross & Borowitz, "A New Twist on *Twist Cap*: Invalidating a Preferential Letter of Credit in *In re Air Conditioning*," 103 Banking L.J. 368 (1986).

[56] 831 F.2d 586 (5th Cir. 1987), modified, 835 F.2d 584 (5th Cir. 1988).

[57] The court also held that payment of the issuer's fee for the credit was not a preference. On rehearing, the *Compton* court ordered the trial court to measure the amount of the preference by the amount of the collateral that the issuer gained by paying the beneficiary. See Kellogg v. Blue Quail Energy, Inc. (In re Compton Corp.), 835 F.2d 584 (5th Cir. 1988).

The *Compton* court cited and approved the *Air Conditioning* rule and distinguished cases in which the beneficiary gave value at the time the credit issued.[58] In those cases, the court held, there is no preference, because the account party did not use the credit to secure an antecedent debt.

The antipreference policy dictated the results in other cases where the courts would not permit the letter of credit to insulate transfers to creditors. *Luring v. Miami Citizens National Bank (In re Val Decker Packing Co.)*[59] involved payments to the credit issuer of a letter of credit. The issuer, a bank, took a security agreement from the debtor outside the preference period; but the court held that the security agreement did not cover the debtor's duty to reimburse. Subsequently, the bank took a second security agreement and caused loan proceeds to be used to fund a certificate of deposit, which the bank took as security for the debtor's obligation to reimburse. Because these latter efforts occurred during the preference period and because their effect was to render the bank issuer perfected and able to resort to the collateral even before the beneficiary drew on the credit, the court held that the bank had benefited from a voidable transfer.[60]

Similarly, in *Erman v. Armco, Inc. (In re Formed Tubes, Inc.)*,[61] payments to a creditor were preferential, even though the creditor was the beneficiary of letters of credit. After the payments, the creditor drew on the credits up to their limits. The *Erman* court distinguished between payments made to a beneficiary of credits that are fully paid and payments made to a beneficiary of credits with amounts unpaid. The latter beneficiary, the court held, would not receive a preference.

In *Gulf Oil Corp. v. Fuel Oil Supply & Terminaling, Inc. (In re Fuel Oil Supply & Terminaling, Inc.)*,[62] the account party made payments to the beneficiary during the preference period, and the account party's trustee argued that they constituted preferences. The trial court agreed,[63] but the Court of Appeals for the Fifth Circuit reversed in an

---

[58] The cases are cited infra ¶ 7.03[3][d].

[59] 61 Bankr. 831 (Bankr. S.D. Ohio 1986).

[60] Cf. Mellon Bank, N.A. v. Metro Communications, Inc. (In re Metro Communications, Inc.), 95 Bankr. 921 (Bankr. W.D. Pa. 1989) (holding that payments to issuer are preferences); see also Boldt v. Alpha Beta Co. (In re Price Chopper Supermarkets, Inc.), 40 Bankr. 816 (Bankr. S.D. Cal. 1984) (holding that, in determining whether property of debtor has been transferred, payments to beneficiary should not be confused with payments to issuer).

[61] 12 Bankr. Ct. Dec. (CRR) 331 (Bankr. E.D. Mich. 1984).

[62] 837 F.2d 224 (5th Cir. 1988).

[63] Gulf Oil Corp. v. Fuel Oil Supply & Terminaling, Inc. (In re Fuel Oil Supply & Terminaling, Inc.), 72 Bankr. 752 (S.D. Tex. 1987), rev'd, 837 F.2d 224 (5th Cir. 1988).

opinion that stepped the credit transaction together with the underlying payments and found that there was no preference. Because the credit had secured the underlying debt, the court held, payments on that debt freed up portions of the credit, which itself was secured by the debtor's property. That freeing-up of the debtor's collateral by virtue of the payments protected them from the preference stigma. The effect of the payments—the releasing of the collateral—constituted the contemporaneous transfer of value by the beneficiary in a manner that qualified the transaction for the protection of Section 547(c)(1) of the Bankruptcy Code.[64]

The court in *Bakst v. A.M.I. Builders Corp. (In re Ameritech Homes, Inc.)*[65] held that there was no preference when a debtor transferred a certificate of deposit to a bank issuer within the preference period for two reasons: The certificate was the property of the debtor's parent corporation, not that of the debtor, and, at the time of the transfer, the debtor did not owe anything to the beneficiary. The trustee in the *Bakst* case had failed to satisfy two of the five elements of a preferential transfer: (1) transfer of the debtor's property and (2) on account of an antecedent debt.

Two commentators argue that literal application of Section 550 of the Bankruptcy Code gives the trustee in bankruptcy the power to recover transfers of the debtor's property to the issuer when the broad letter of credit transaction constitutes a preference.[66] Section 550 provides that the trustee may recover transfer of a preference from "the initial transferee of that transfer or the entity for whose benefit such transfer was made." To the extent that courts are inclined to step the broad letter of credit transactions together, that is, to the extent that they step the transfer from the account party to the issuer together with the transfer from the issuer to the beneficiary, Section 550, applied literally, stipulates that the trustee should be able to recover the property or its value from the issuer.

That view ignores the critical difference between most indirect transfers to a preferred creditor and the unique nature of the letter of credit. Significantly, the authorities, after explaining the literal theory for application of Section 550, conclude that proper regard for bankruptcy policy and letter of credit concerns dictates a rule that eschews

---

[64] Accord Gilchrist Mach. Co. v. Ross (In re Gilchrist Mach. Co.), 108 Bankr. 124 (Bankr. S.D. Miss. 1989).

[65] 88 Bankr. 432 (Bankr. S.D. Fla. 1988).

[66] McLaughlin & Cohen, "Scope of Bankruptcy Trustee's Avoidance Powers," 200 N.Y.L.J. 6 (Dec. 14, 1988).

the literal approach. They note, moreover, that other bankruptcy commentators and the cases generally approve of their position.[67]

In re San Jacinto Glass Industries, Inc.[68] raises the question of the debtor's interest in a letter of credit in the context of a subordinated creditor's efforts to have the bankruptcy court order a marshaling of the debtor's assets. The creditor holding a superior claim to collateral against which the subordinated creditor claimed an interest was also the beneficiary of a credit secured by property that did not belong to the debtor. The subordinated creditor sought an order requiring the beneficiary to draw on the credit, satisfy its claim with the proceeds, and leave the collateral for the subordinated creditor.

The *San Jacinto* court refused to order a marshaling of the assets, on the ground that such relief is available only if the two creditors have a common debtor. The court held that because the letter of credit was not property of the debtor, there was no common debtor and marshaling was inappropriate.[69]

Briefly, then, it appears that letter of credit policy and federal bankruptcy policy sometimes conflict. Under letter of credit law, courts generally refuse to step the underlying transaction and the letter of credit transaction together. Because the credit may be a device to effectuate a preference, that refusal becomes problematic when the account party is in bankruptcy. In the event the issuer establishes the credit during the

---

[67] In Levit v. Ingersoll Rand Fin. Corp. (In re V.N. Deprizio Constr. Co.), 874 F.2d 1186 (7th Cir. 1989), the court questioned, by way of dictum in a footnote, whether the *Air Conditioning* and *Compton* cases adequately considered the interplay of Sections 550 and 547 of the Bankruptcy Code in concluding that the issuer was immune from the trustee's avoidance power. For criticism of the *Deprizio* opinion on that point, see Katzen, "*Deprizio* and Bankruptcy Code Section 550: Extended Preference Exposure Via Insider Guarantees, and Other Perils of Initial Transfer Liability," 45 Bus. Law. 511 (1990). In re Liberty Constr. & Dev. Corp., 106 Bankr. 458 (Bankr. E.D. Va. 1989), involved advances by a mortgagee to improve the mortgaged property. The mortgagee was also the issuer of a letter of credit that secured the same improvements that the mortgagee had paid for with the advances. The trustee for the debtor (the mortgagor and account party on the letter of credit) argued that the mortgagee's advances had been for its own benefit in order to forestall draws on the letter of credit. The court was not compelled to reach the question whether the issuer's conduct violated bankruptcy policy, however, because the court concluded that the advances were not authorized by the mortgage and therefore were not secured by the mortgage.

[68] 93 Bankr. 934 (Bankr. S.D. Tex. 1988).

[69] The preference discussion in this paragraph deals with cases in which the account party becomes insolvent. For discussion of preference rules in the event the beneficiary becomes insolvent, see ¶ 10.05.

preference period and at a time when the account party is indebted to the beneficiary, payment under the credit may constitute a preference.[70]

[b] Automatic Stay

Section 362(a) of the Bankruptcy Code[71] automatically stays any act to obtain the property of the debtor's estate. The *Page* court refused to characterize a demand for payment under the credit as such an act, because it felt that no property of the debtor passed to the beneficiary. *Printing Department, Inc. v. Xerox Corp. (In re Printing Department, Inc.)*[72] reached the same conclusion. In the *Printing Department* case, the beneficiary drew on the credit after the account party had filed a petition for reorganization under the Bankruptcy Code. The account party, as debtor in possession, filed a motion for an order against the beneficiary to show cause why it should not be held in contempt for violating the automatic stay provision. The court denied the motion, holding that the letter of credit was not an asset of the estate and that the claim of the beneficiary was against the issuer, not against the debtor.[73]

In *Braucher v. Continental Illinois National Bank & Trust Co. (In re Illinois-California Express, Inc.)*,[74] the trustee of the account party and the banks that had issued letters of credit before the filing of the account party's petition agreed to deposit proceeds from the sale of collateral with the banks, on the understanding that all but a portion would be used by the banks to satisfy debts of the account party. When the banks used the proceeds to reimburse themselves for draws made after bankruptcy on the letters of credit, the trustee objected. The court held, however, that, for two reasons, the trustee could not complain: First, he had agreed to the arrangements, and, second, the transfers did not violate the automatic stay provision, because no property of the debtor was transferred.

---

[70] For an opinion that discusses the cases and makes these points with clarity in a state insolvency proceeding, see Pine Top Ins. Co. v. Century Indem. Co., 716 F. Supp. 311 (N.D. Ill. 1989).

[71] 11 U.S.C. § 362(a) (1988).

[72] 20 Bankr. 677 (Bankr. E.D. Va. 1981).

[73] Cf. Andy Marine, Inc. v. Zidell, Inc., 812 F.2d 534 (9th Cir. 1987) (holding that automatic stay does not affect beneficiary's appeal of claim against issuer, even though account party is in bankruptcy); L.B.G. Properties, Inc. v. Chisholm Realty Co. (In re L.B.G. Properties, Inc.), 33 Bankr. 196 (Bankr. S.D. Fla. 1983) (denying motion for order staying beneficiary from drawing on credit issued for account of debtor).

[74] 50 Bankr. 232 (Bankr. D. Colo. 1985).

In *Guy C. Long, Inc. v. Dependable Insurance Co. (In re Guy C. Long, Inc.)*,[75] the credit secured an insurance company's obligations under a performance bond. Under the credit, the beneficiary had the right to draw if, in its sole judgment, it concluded that a claim might be made under the bond. After holding that the beneficiary's acceptance of the credit in this situation constituted its agreement that any funds it obtained under the credit that were not needed to pay claims under the bond would be repaid to the debtor, the court concluded that a draw on the credit would not violate the automatic stay provision.

In two cases, however, courts have invoked the automatic stay to restrain beneficiaries from initiating claims under letters of credit. In *Joe DeLisi Fruit Co. v. State (In re Joe DeLisi Fruit Co.)*,[76] the court stayed an action of the beneficiary. The credit in that case served in lieu of a bond under a state license. The purpose of the credit was to secure payment of the licensee's suppliers. Thus, when the debtor filed a voluntary petition under Chapter 11 of the Bankruptcy Code, the state secretary of agriculture in Minnesota commenced an administrative proceeding to determine those claims. The debtor was a named party, and the court declared the proceedings void under the automatic stay provision.[77]

In *Arrow Air, Inc. v. United Airlines, Inc. (In re Arrow Air, Inc.)*,[78] the court ruled that a beneficiary that notified the debtor of its intention to draw on a letter of credit was in violation of the automatic stay provision. The court entered an order enjoining the beneficiary from drawing on the credit. Significantly, the *Arrow Air* opinion indicates that the beneficiary did not respond to the debtor's argument that the beneficiary had violated the automatic stay. The court may not have been briefed adequately on the issue.[79]

---

[75] 74 Bankr. 939 (Bankr. E.D. Pa. 1987).

[76] 11 Bankr. 694 (Bankr. D. Minn. 1981).

[77] 11 U.S.C. § 362(a)(1) (1988).

[78] 70 Bankr. 245 (Bankr. S.D. Fla. 1987).

[79] In In re Minoco Group of Cos., 799 F.2d 517 (9th Cir. 1986), the issuer of a prepaid insurance policy that covered the officers and directors of the debtor attempted to cancel the policy upon the debtor's bankruptcy. The court ruled that the automatic stay applied and prevented the cancelation. The court also noted, by way of dictum, that the automatic stay would not have prevented the issuer of a letter of credit from canceling a credit, which presumably is cancelable under credit law. The debtor has an interest in an insurance policy that it procures. The insurer's obligation runs to the debtor. The debtor account party has no interest in the letter of credit; the issuer's obligation runs only to the beneficiary. In Diamond Mach. Co. v. Casco N. Bank (In re Diamond Mach. Co.), 95 Bankr. 255 (Bankr. D. Me. 1988), the court refused to enjoin payment of a credit that secured development bonds. Although all principal and interest payments on the bonds were current, the account party's bankruptcy constituted an event of default under the note held by the credit beneficiary.

[c] Postpetition Transfer

In re M.J. Sales & Distributing Co.[80] holds that a successful suit by the beneficiary on the credit does not operate as a postpetition transfer of the debtor's property. Section 549 of the Bankruptcy Code empowers the trustee in bankruptcy to avoid postpetition transfers, but the *M.J. Sales* court rejected that characterization of the transaction. In this case, the issuer was secured, and the trustee, making the *Twist Cap* argument, claimed that the effect of a draw on the credit was to diminish the estate of the debtor. If the issuer were to pay the beneficiary, it then would resort to the debtor's collateral, and the debtor's estate would be diminished after the filing of the bankruptcy petition. The court held that the transfer of the debtor's interest in the collateral had occurred at the time the issuer established the credit, not at the time the bank resorted to the collateral.[81]

[d] The Need for a Theory

The *Twist Cap* case caused a considerable stir. Commentators are unanimous in their criticism of it,[82] and, when it intimates that the payment of a credit is a transfer of the debtor's assets, the case is clearly in the minority.[83] Some have taken pains to point out that the *Twist Cap*

The court reasoned that to allow the injunction would impair the marketability of revenue bonds unnecessarily. In Zenith Laboratories, Inc. v. Security Pac. Nat'l Bank (In re Zenith Laboratories, Inc.), 104 Bankr. 667 (Bankr. D.N.J. 1989), a similar case, the court held simply that payments under the credit were not transfers of the debtor's assets and therefore were not in violation of the automatic stay.

[80] 25 Bankr. 608 (Bankr. S.D.N.Y. 1982).

[81] Accord Braucher v. Continental Ill. Nat'l Bank & Trust Co. (In re Illinois-Cal. Express, Inc.), 50 Bankr. 232 (Bankr. D. Colo. 1985); Briggs Transp. Co. v. Norwest Bank Minneapolis, N.A. (In re Briggs Transp. Co.), 37 Bankr. 76 (Bankr. D. Minn. 1984); Armstrong v. FNB Fin. Co. (In re Clothes, Inc.), 35 Bankr. 487 (Bankr. D.N.D. 1983).

[82] McLaughlin & Cohen, Scope of the Bankruptcy Trustee's Avoidance Powers, 200 N.Y.L.J. 6 (Dec. 14, 1988); Weintraub & Resnick, "Enforceability of Letters of Credit When the Customer Is in Bankruptcy: From *Twist Cap* to *Air Conditioning*," 20 U.C.C. L.J. 96 (1987); see Hahn & Schwartz, "Letters of Credit Under the Bankruptcy Code," 16 U.C.C. L.J. 91 (1983); Baird, "Standby Letters of Credit in Bankruptcy," 49 U. Chi. L. Rev. 130 (1982); Chaitman & Sovern, supra note 44; McLaughlin, "Letters of Credit as Preferential Transfers in Bankruptcy," 50 Fordham L. Rev. 1033 (1982).

[83] See Kellogg v. Blue Quail Energy, Inc. (In re Compton Corp.), 831 F.2d 586 (5th Cir. 1987), modified, 835 F.2d 584 (5th Cir. 1988); Postal v. Smith (In re Marine Distribs., Inc.), 522 F.2d 791 (9th Cir. 1975); Wooten v. United States, 56 Bankr. 227 (W.D. La. 1985); Zenith Laboratories, Inc. v. Security Pac. Nat'l Bank (In re Zenith Laboratories, Inc.), 104 Bankr. 667 (Bankr. D.N.J. 1989); Guy C. Long,

result was not a decision after a hearing on the merits.[84]

Twist Cap nevertheless raises a serious question whether courts should look through the letter of credit transaction and step its parts together. Commercial lawyers respond to that question in several ways. They might say that:

1. *Twist Cap* violates the independence principle (which it surely does).

2. *Twist Cap* destroys credits as an effective commercial device (which is only moderately overstated).

3. The transfer of the debtor's property in *Twist Cap* occurred at the time the credit was established, not at the time the bank paid

---

Inc. v. Dependable Ins. Co. (In re Guy C. Long, Inc.), 74 Bankr. 939 (Bankr. E.D. Pa. 1987); Wisconsin Barge Line, Inc. v. INA (In re Wisconsin Barge Line, Inc.), 63 Bankr. 40 (Bankr. E.D. Mo. 1986); Braucher v. Continental Ill. Nat'l Bank & Trust Co. (In re Illinois-Cal. Express, Inc.), 50 Bankr. 232 (Bankr. D. Colo. 1985); Elegant Merchandising, Inc. v. Republic Nat'l Bank (In re Elegant Merchandising, Inc.), 41 Bankr. 398 (Bankr. S.D.N.Y. 1984); Boldt v. Alpha Beta Co. (In re Price Chopper Supermarkets, Inc.), 40 Bankr. 816 (Bankr. S.D. Cal. 1984); Originala Petroleum Corp. v. Beta Fin. & Inv. Corp. (In re Originala Petroleum Corp.), 39 Bankr. 1003 (Bankr. N.D. Tex. 1984); St. Petersburg Hotel Assocs., Ltd. v. Royal Trust Bank (In re St. Petersburg Hotel Assocs., Ltd.), 37 Bankr. 380 (Bankr. M.D. Fla. 1984); Briggs Transp. Co. v. Norwest Bank Minneapolis, N.A. (In re Briggs Transp. Co.), 37 Bankr. 76 (Bankr. D. Minn. 1984); L.B.G. Properties, Inc. v. Chisholm Realty Co. (In re L.B.G. Properties, Inc.), 33 Bankr. 196 (Bankr. S.D. Fla. 1983); North Shore & Cent. Ill. Freight Co. v. American Nat'l Bank & Trust Co. (In re North Shore & Cent. Ill. Freight Co.), 30 Bankr. 377 (Bankr. N.D. Ill. 1983); Planes, Inc. v. Fairchild Aircraft Corp. (In re Planes, Inc.), 29 Bankr. 370 (Bankr. N.D. Ga. 1983); In re Leisure Dynamics, Inc., Fed. Banking L. Rep. (CCH) ¶ 69,405 (Bankr. D. Minn. 1983); Page v. First Nat'l Bank (In re Page), 18 Bankr. 713 (D.D.C. 1982); American Employers Ins. Co. v. Pioneer Bank & Trust Co., 538 F. Supp. 354 (N.D. Ill. 1981); Printing Dep't, Inc. v. Xerox Corp. (In re Printing Dep't, Inc.), 20 Bankr. 677 (Bankr. E.D. Va. 1981); Aetna Business Credit, Inc. v. Hart Ski Mfg. Co. (In re Hart Ski Mfg. Co.), 6 Bankr. Ct. Dec. (CRR) 1430 (Bankr. D. Minn. 1980); FDIC v. Vogel, 437 F. Supp. 660 (E.D. Wis. 1977); Meridian Devs. Inc. v. Toronto-Dominion Bank, 53 Alta. Rep. 39 (Q.B. 1984); cf. Armstrong v. FNB Fin. Co. (In re Clothes, Inc.), 35 Bankr. 487 (Bankr. D.N.D. 1983) (implicitly rejecting trustee's claim that, by honoring outstanding letters of credit, issuer received voidable preference). But cf. Arrow Air, Inc. v. United Airlines, Inc., 70 Bankr. 245 (S.D. Fla. 1987) (holding that beneficiary's draw on letter of credit constituted attempted postpetition transfer of debtor's property in violation of automatic stay); Sawyer v. E.A. Gralia Constr. Co. (In re Pine Tree Elec. Co.), 16 Bankr. 105, 107 (Bankr. D. Me. 1981) (holding that beneficiary's attempt to enforce letter of credit was attempt to enforce a debt due from account party and to transform contingent claim to an "active" claim).

[84] In re M.J. Sales & Distrib. Co., 25 Bankr. 608 (Bankr. S.D.N.Y. 1982); Chaitman & Sovern, supra note 44.

the credit and decreased the debtor's equity in the collateral (which is true under bankruptcy law fiction).[85]

4. In *Twist Cap*, it was the issuer's funds, not the debtor's, that passed to the beneficiary.

5. *Twist Cap* forces the parties to utilize costly and complicated counter measures to avoid its rule.[86]

Also in need of a consistent theory reconciling bankruptcy and letter of credit policy is the question raised by *American Bank v. Leasing Service Corp. (In re Air Conditioning, Inc. of Stuart).*[87] That case poses a problem for beneficiaries that use credits within the preference period. The case prevents creditors from using credits to avoid the preference rule of Section 547 of the Bankruptcy Code. The case should not interfere, however, with credits established outside the preference period and does not render issuers liable under the preference provision.

[e] Standby Credit Securing Notes

Standby letters of credit often secure promissory notes, and bank counsel have warned beneficiaries of such credits that the bankruptcy antipreference rule may create problems. If the account party pays the note, there will be no draw on the credit, which may expire by its terms. If the account party later becomes bankrupt, and if the payment occurs during the preference period, the trustee may be able to set the payment aside. At that point, the beneficiary will have to surrender the payment it received and will not be able to draw on the expired credit. A beneficiary that doubts the account party's solvency will insist that the credit not expire for a sufficient period of time after payment and that it be payable against documents certifying the existence of bankruptcy proceedings.

---

[85] See 11 U.S.C. § 547(e) (1988).

[86] See the suggestions in the articles cited supra note 82. In addition to those suggestions, it appears that some banks have required account parties to grant the beneficiary a security interest in the same collateral it pledges to the bank under the application agreement. If both the issuer and the beneficiary are secured parties, the *Twist Cap* objections to the arrangement fall. Unfortunately, it is not always practicable to grant security interests to multiple beneficiaries or to transferees of the right to draw. There may be too many parties, and the paper work can disrupt the transaction. For a thorough review of the various devices bank counsel have fashioned to avoid the *Twist Cap* rule, see C. Mooney & R. Ryan, "Letters of Credit Supporting Debt Instruments," in Letters of Credit & Bankers' Acceptances 1986, at 484–498.

[87] 845 F.2d 293 (11th Cir.), cert. denied sub nom. First Interstate Credit Alliance, Inc. v. American Bank, 109 S. Ct. 557 (1988). For discussion of that theory, see supra ¶ 7.03[3][a].

Letters of credit often secure commercial paper offerings that may be "rolled over" from time to time as interest rates fluctuate. Payments to the holders of such paper should not be viewed as preferential transfers. As one commentator has taken pains to point out,[88] those payments either do not fit the preference definition or fall within one or more of the exceptions in Section 547 of the Bankruptcy Code.

[f] State Insolvency Proceedings

The policy considerations that are evident in bankruptcy cases are also relevant in state insolvency proceedings. In *Pine Top Insurance Co. v. Century Indemnity Co.*,[89] the liquidator of an insolvent insurance company that had caused a credit to issue as security for its obligations under certain reinsurance treaties sued to recover payments under the credit. The plaintiff alleged that the reinsurance obligations arose prior to the issuance of the credit; the credit issued during the preference period; the company collateralized its reimbursement obligation to the issuer after issuance of the credit; and the issuer made payments to the beneficiary. The *Pine Top* court denied the defendant beneficiary's motion to dismiss or for summary judgment in an opinion emphasizing that the critical dates are not the payment or collateralization dates but the date of the credit's issuance in relation to the date of the debts it secured. Because the plaintiff alleged that the credit issued during the preference period on account of an antecedent debt, the court held that the complaint stated a cause of action.

In *Muir v. Transportation Mutual Insurance Co.*,[90] an insurance company used a standby letter of credit to secure its obligations under a reinsurance agreement. When the insurer became insolvent, the state insurance commissioner fashioned a plan of rehabilitation under which claims against the insurer would be commuted. The *Muir* court held that because draws under the letter of credit would increase the claim of the bank issuer against the estate of the insolvent company, the court had jurisdiction to consider the state insurance commissioner's efforts, supported by the credit issuer, to enjoin draws under the credit. The court also held that a rehabilitation plan could not limit the beneficiary's draws unless the beneficiary agreed to the plan. The court noted that the reinsurer had not objected to the plan and therefore had con-

---

[88] Saunders, "Preference Avoidance and Letter of Credit Supported Debt: The Bank's Reimbursement Risk in Its Customer's Bankruptcy," 102 Banking L.J. 240 (1985).

[89] 716 F. Supp. 311 (N.D. Ill. 1989).

[90] 107 Pa. Commw. Ct. 638, 529 A.2d 534 (1987).

sented to it. Denying an injunction against the reinsurer, the court refused to take that consent as limiting the reinsurer's right to draw, because the plan limited only claims against the estate. The claim of the reinsurer was against the issuer, not against the estate.

In *Gillman v. Chase Manhattan Bank, N.A.*,[91] an assignee of the insolvent account party's claim against the issuer argued that when the issuer charged the account party's account after payment of the credit, the issuer enjoyed a preference under state insolvency law. The *Gillman* court disagreed, holding that the issuer held a perfected security interest in the account at the time of the assignment for the benefit of creditors.

[4] Government Intervention

As the *Kingdom of Sweden* case demonstrates,[92] government intervention into the underlying contract does not give the account party reason to complain about payment under the credit. In *J. Zeevi & Sons v. Grindlays Bank (Uganda) Ltd.*,[93] the Ugandan government attempted to cancel a credit. The credit in that case appeared to be an attempt by the account party to transfer funds out of Uganda to a partnership related to the account party. The defendant bank issued the credit in Uganda and promised to reimburse, out of its account with a New York bank, any bank that negotiated the beneficiary's drafts in compliance with the credit. The government of Uganda ordered the issuer to cancel the credit, which ran to the benefit of an Israeli beneficiary. The court held that the attempt to cancel the credit created a cause of action in New York, that the act of state doctrine did not sanction the conduct of the Ugandan government, and that, under the law of credits, the cancelation was an anticipatory breach. The account party was not seeking to stop payment of the credit in the *Zeevi* case, but the opinion stands as good authority for the position that an account party cannot complain when a U.S. issuer honors a credit in the face of efforts by a foreign government to render that payment unlawful.

In *Tribune-United Cable v. Montgomery County*,[94] the credit secured penalty provisions of a cable franchise agreement. Subsequent to the agreement, Congress enacted the Cable Communications Policy Act

---

[91] 135 A.D.2d 488, 521 N.Y.S.2d 729 (1987), aff'd, 73 N.Y.2d 1, 534 N.E.2d 824, 537 N.Y.S.2d 787 (1988).

[92] See supra ¶ 7.03[1] for discussion of the *Kingdom of Sweden* case.

[93] 37 N.Y.2d 220, 333 N.E.2d 168, 371 N.Y.S.2d 892, cert. denied, 432 U.S. 866 (1975).

[94] 784 F.2d 1227 (4th Cir. 1986).

of 1984,[95] permitting cable franchisees to request modification of commercially impracticable agreements. The Act permits the cable franchisee to request modification of the franchise agreement and to appeal an adverse decision. The *Tribune-United* court construed the Act as subordinating the right of a municipality to assert enforcement rights under the agreement until the franchisee's modification request is resolved. When the beneficiary of the credit in the *Tribune-United* case sought to draw on the credit, the account party franchisee sought an injunction, arguing that the draw would have the effect of depriving it of rights under the statute. The court agreed and reversed the district court's refusal to issue an injunction.

Kingdom of Sweden differs from *Tribune-United*. In the former case, payment under the credit did not thwart the government policy of forbidding exportation of goods. In the latter case, the court viewed payment under the credit as inimical to the purpose of the Cable Communications Policy Act. It may be that Congress intended the reach of its protection for cable franchisees to extend to this case and to have serious consequences for credits. Unfortunately, the court does not make that inquiry and fails to balance the competing policies.

[5] Attachment

In the *Zeevi*[96] case, the beneficiary successfully attached the proceeds of the credit. Sometimes the account party, as well, attempts to attach proceeds; but the account party, not being a party to the credit, should not succeed in doing so.

In *Hohenberg Co. v. Comitex Knitters, Ltd.*,[97] the account party, objecting to the quality of the merchandise that the beneficiary supplied under the purchase contract, brought suit to attach the proceeds of the credit. The court, however, denied a motion to confirm the order of attachment, holding that defects in the beneficiary's performance of the underlying agreement do not support an attachment by the account party. In *Capehart Corp. v. Shanghai Commercial Bank, Ltd.*,[98] the court rejected an attempt by the account party to attach "the letter of cred-

---

[95] 47 U.S.C. §§ 521–559 (Supp. V 1987).

[96] For discussion of the *Zeevi* case, see supra ¶ 7.03[4]. See also Sisalcords Do Brazil, Ltd. v. Fiacao Brasiliera De Sisal, S.A., 450 F.2d 419 (5th Cir. 1971), cert. denied, 406 U.S. 919 (1972) (case involving attachment by one claiming through beneficiary); United Bank Ltd. v. Cambridge Sporting Goods Corp., 41 N.Y.2d 254, 360 N.E.2d 943, 392 N.Y.S.2d 265 (1976) (same).

[97] 104 Misc. 2d 232, 428 N.Y.S.2d 156 (Sup. Ct. 1980).

[98] 49 A.D.2d 521, 369 N.Y.S.2d 751 (1975).

it."[99] The court held that the account party's complaint did not support attachment, because the account party was not seeking a money judgment and because the account party was not a party to the letter of credit. In *Key International Manufacturing, Inc. v. Stillman*,[100] the court held that it was improper for the lower court to grant the account party's petition to enjoin payment of cashier's checks that were given to the beneficiary by the issuer in payment of the credit.

In *Tueta v. Rodriguez*,[101] the account party had deposited funds to cover its obligation to reimburse the issuer of a credit and then sought to garnish the fund when the beneficiary's shipment of goods allegedly was not conforming to the underlying contract. The *Tueta* court saw the issue as jurisdictional[102] and refused to entertain the garnishment. The account party argued that the issuer was a debtor of the beneficiary and that the court could exercise in rem or quasi in rem jurisdiction over the debt. The court disagreed, holding that there was no debtor-creditor relationship between the issuer and the beneficiary.[103] The court also held that the account party's deposit was the property of neither the account party nor the beneficiary, but rather was the property of the issuer. The deposit was, the court said, "separate and apart from the letter of credit, which is the subject matter of this action."[104] Since the letter of credit was in Switzerland, the court would not exercise in rem jurisdiction.[105]

In *Lantz International Corp. v. Industria Termotecnica Campana, S.p.A.*,[106] the account party attempted to use attachment to stop payment under a credit after the issuer had accepted drafts presented by the beneficiary's banks. The court held that it was not necessary to determine whether the banks were holders in due course of the drafts. Once

---

[99] Id. at 522, 369 N.Y.S.2d at 752.

[100] 103 A.D.2d 475, 480 N.Y.S.2d 528 (1984), modified on other grounds, 66 N.Y.2d 924, 489 N.E.2d 764, 498 N.Y.S.2d 795 (1985).

[101] 176 So. 2d 550 (Fla. Dist. Ct. App. 1965).

[102] For discussion of the jurisdictional issues, see ¶ 11.01.

[103] The credit in the *Tueta* case was issued by a Florida bank but was made payable at a European bank. The opinion indicates that the beneficiary had been paid, but the decision does not turn on that point.

[104] Tueta v. Rodriguez, 176 So. 2d 550, 552 (Fla. Dist. Ct. App. 1965) (on rehearing).

[105] But cf. Sabolyk v. Morgan Guar. Trust Co., No. 84 Civ. 3179 (MJL) (S.D.N.Y. Nov. 27, 1984) (holding that Swiss court's attachment order preventing issuer from honoring credit did not violate law or public policy of New York or United States).

[106] 358 F. Supp. 510 (E.D. Pa. 1973).

the issuer had honored the credit by accepting drafts, there was no property of the account party or the beneficiary to attach.[107]

While these cases appear to resolve the attachment question on procedural issues, all of them reflect the fundamental point that the letter of credit is independent of the underlying contract. If the account party were able to attach the credit or its proceeds in furtherance of rights growing out of the underlying transaction, the independence of the credit would suffer. The issue here is no different from the question that arises when the account party resorts to equitable relief on the fraud ground.[108] Thus, the courts are correct in resisting these attempts to weaken the independence of the credit.[109]

¶ 7.04 FRAUD IN THE TRANSACTION

The most common procedural device to which account parties resort in their efforts to prevent payment under a credit is the injunction or restraining order. In support of their efforts, account parties argue that the beneficiary is guilty of fraud.[110] Sometimes these efforts succeed; but, in

---

[107] Accord First Commercial Bank v. Gotham Originals, Inc., 101 A.D.2d 790, 476 N.Y.S.2d 835 (1984), aff'd, 64 N.Y.2d 287, 475 N.E.2d 1255, 486 N.Y.S.2d 715 (1985).

[108] For discussion of the fraud issue, see infra ¶ 7.04.

[109] For further support of the view advanced in the text, see Boucher & Slack Contractors, Inc. v. McLean, 382 So. 2d 1030 (La. Ct. App. 1980). Contra Calcados Sandalo, S.A. v. Intershoe, Inc., 92 A.D.2d 529, 459 N.Y.S.2d 446 (1983); Lanificio Itlam v. Paris Sportswear Ltd., 7 C.A. 265 (1987). See generally Justice, "Letters of Credit: Expectations and Frustrations — Part 2," 94 Banking L.J. 493 (1977); Note, "The Application of Compulsory Joinder, Intervention, Impleader and Attachment to Letter of Credit Litigation," 52 Fordham L. Rev. 957 (1984). For discussion of attachment by creditors of the beneficiary, see ¶ 10.06[3][b]. For an English case that refused to issue a *Mareva* injunction forbidding the beneficiary to draw on a credit and thereby remove the credit proceeds from the court's jurisdiction, see Intraco Ltd. v. Notis Shipping Corp., [1981] 2 Lloyd's Rep. 256 (C.A.). Significantly, the *Intraco* judgment turns in part on procedural issues and in part on the law of primary bank guaranties, which are virtually the same as standby letters of credit. The *Intraco* court refused the injunction because the credit, though issued in England, was payable in Greece. Thus, there were no funds to be found in Britain. In addition, the court noted that an injunction to stop payment is contrary to bank primary guaranty law.

[110] Cf. Paris Sav. & Loan Ass'n v. Walden, 730 S.W.2d 355 (Tex. Ct. App. 1987) (holding that it is not enough for account party to satisfy equity prerequisites and that showing of fraud is also necessary for account party to have injunction). But cf. Originala Petroleum Corp. v. Beta Fin. & Inv. Corp. (In re Originala Petroleum Corp.), 39 Bankr. 1003 (Bankr. N.D. Tex. 1984) (holding that account party is entitled to injunction if it satisfies either equity prerequisites or fraud rule of Section 5-

general, the Code and the cases have fashioned the fraud exception carefully so that it does not interfere greatly with the smooth functioning of credits and so that it does not offend the independence principle. There are, however, a number of cases that appear to respond to hard facts and that apply the fraud exception less carefully. There is also an unsettling tendency among some in the letter of credit constituency that want to alter the rules.

[1] Prerequisites for Relief

There is nothing in letter of credit law to suggest that a plaintiff seeking an injunction should not have to satisfy the traditional rules for extraordinary relief. The courts that consider this point have held almost uniformly that general equity rules for obtaining an injunction apply in the letter of credit context. Usually, a plaintiff must show several facts before such relief is available. Those facts ordinarily include the following:

1. A reasonable probability of ultimate success;
2. A necessity to preserve the status quo; and
3. A showing of irreparable harm or that there is an inadequate remedy at law or similar requisite.[111]

114(2)); Spencer v. First S. Sav. Ass'n, No. A14-87-00154-CV (Tex. Ct. App. Nov. 25, 1987) (limited precedent op.) (same).

[111] See, e.g., Wood v. R.R. Donnelley & Sons Co., 888 F.2d 313 (3d Cir. 1989); Foxboro Co. v. Arabian Am. Oil Co., 805 F.2d 34 (1st Cir. 1986); Enterprise Int'l, Inc. v. Corporacion Estatal Petrolera Ecuatoriana, 762 F.2d 464 (5th Cir. 1985); Warner v. Central Trust Co., 715 F.2d 1121 (6th Cir. 1983); Harris Corp. v. National Iranian Radio & Television, 691 F.2d 1344 (11th Cir. 1982); KMW Int'l v. Chase Manhattan Bank, N.A., 606 F.2d 10 (2d Cir. 1979); Diamond Mach. Co. v. Casco N. Bank (In re Diamond Mach. Co.), 95 Bankr. 255 (D. Me. 1988); Reid v. Plantation Sea Farms, No. 86 C 6648 (N.D. Ill. Sept. 30, 1986); Itek Corp. v. First Nat'l Bank, 511 F. Supp. 1341 (D. Mass. 1981); Cappaert Enters. v. Citizens & S. Int'l Bank, 486 F. Supp. 819 (E.D. La. 1980); Werner Lehara Int'l, Inc. v. Harris Trust & Sav. Bank, 484 F. Supp. 65 (W.D. Mich. 1980); B.G.H. Ins. Syndicate, Inc. v. Prudential Fire & Casualty Co., 549 So. 2d 197 (Fla. Dist. Ct. App. 1989); Atlas Mini Storage, Inc. v. First Interstate Bank, 426 N.W.2d 686 (Iowa Ct. App. 1988); Ciambotti v. Decatur-St. Louis, Lupin, Properties Ventures, 533 So. 2d 1352 (La. Ct. App. 1988); Hamilton v. Central Nat'l Bank, 40 U.C.C. Rep. Serv. (Callaghan) 1008 (N.D. Ohio 1984); Wurttembergische Fire Ins. Co. v. Pan Atl. Underwriters, Ltd., 133 A.D.2d 268, 519 N.Y.S.2d 57 (1987); Werner v. A.L. Grootemaat & Sons, 80 Wis. 2d 513, 259 N.W.2d 310 (1977). But cf. Davidcraft Corp. v. First Nat'l Bank, 675 F. Supp. 1515 (N.D. Ill. 1986) (granting injunctive relief without discussing equity prerequisites); Cromwell v. Commerce & Energy Bank, 464 So. 2d 721 (La. 1985) (denying injunctive relief on merits without considering whether plaintiff had satisfied equity prerequisites); Brown v. United States Nat'l Bank, 220 Neb. 684, 371 N.W.2d 692 (1985) (same); Sawyer v. E.A. Gralia Constr. Co. (In re Pine Tree Elec. Co.), 16 Bankr. 105 (Bankr. D. Me. 1981) (applying different rule in bankruptcy setting). See

This last requirement of showing no adequate remedy at law or that irreparable harm would arise without the injunction is especially important in letter of credit cases and often serves to bar the account party's relief.[112] The account party usually stands in a contractual relationship with the beneficiary, who, the account party claims, is seeking payment under the credit without justification. In most of these cases, the account party is able to recover in the underlying transaction for the beneficiary's misconduct and therefore has an adequate remedy at law.[113]

Sometimes the account party complains that his remedy at law necessitates bringing suit in a foreign jurisdiction; but, as the court pointed out in *American Bell International, Inc. v. Islamic Republic of Iran*,[114] the account party chooses to do business with its foreign customer. One of the purposes of a credit is to shift the forum of litigation.[115] The account party should not be heard to complain when the distance or the risks of international collections create problems. Above all, the account party should not be able to weaken the commercial reliability of credits or the credit reputation of the issuer because the account party's bargain with the beneficiary has soured.

Account parties seeking an injunction also face the difficult task of convincing the courts that the remedy at law is inadequate. The Court of Appeals for the Second Circuit pointed out, in *KMW International v.*

Laycock, "The Death of the Irreparable Injury Rule," 103 Harv. L. Rev. 688 (1990) (arguing that courts never give irreparable injury rule more than lip service).

[112] See, e.g., Sperry Int'l Trade, Inc. v. Government of Isr., 670 F.2d 8 (2d Cir. 1982); KMW Int'l v. Chase Manhattan Bank, N.A., 606 F.2d 10 (2d Cir. 1979); Interco, Inc. v. Schwartz, 560 F.2d 480 (1st Cir. 1977); It's Devine Indus., Ltd. v. Bank Leumi Trust Co., 22 U.C.C. Rep. Serv. (Callaghan) 130 (N.Y. Sup. Ct. 1977); and cases cited supra note 111; see also Bush Dev. Corp. v. Harbour Place Assocs., 632 F. Supp. 1359 (E.D. Va. 1986); (balancing hardships and granting injunction); Universal Marine Ins. Co. v. Beacon Ins. Co., 577 F. Supp. 829 (W.D.N.C. 1984) (balancing hardships and denying injunction).

[113] See, e.g., Kennedy v. Josepthal & Co., Fed. Sec. L. Rep. (CCH) ¶ 99,653 (D. Mass. 1984) (suit against beneficiary for securities fraud); Berry v. Bank of La., 439 So. 2d 1166 (La. Ct. App. 1983) (suit against negotiating bank for breach of warranty); cf. GATX Leasing Corp. v. DBM Drilling Corp., 657 S.W.2d 178 (Tex. Ct. App. 1983) (denying injunction to party who had cause of action for breach of warranty).

[114] 474 F. Supp. 420 (S.D.N.Y. 1979).

[115] For a discussion of that purpose, see ¶ 3.07[5]. In Rockwell Int'l Sys., Inc. v. Citibank, N.A., 719 F.2d 583 (2d Cir. 1983), the court read KMW Int'l v. Chase Manhattan Bank, N.A., 606 F.2d 10 (2d Cir. 1979), discussed infra, quite restrictively. Significantly, the *Rockwell* court ignores this function of the credit. See also Itek Corp. v. First Nat'l Bank, 730 F.2d 19 (1st Cir. 1984) (same); Wyle v. Bank Melli, 577 F. Supp. 1148 (N.D. Cal. 1983) (same).

Chase Manhattan Bank, N.A.,[116] that the account party's loss in most letter of credit transactions is financial in nature and is not an appropriate basis for an injunction. A money judgment normally protects the account party.

Finally, the account party must admit that its attempt to enjoin payment under the credit is often an attempt to avoid losing the use of the funds during litigation between the account party and the beneficiary. In *State v. Lasky*,[117] the court pointed out that such a loss does not support a claim for injunctive relief. The court could have added that an injunction in such circumstances would amount to reallocation of the very risk the account party and the beneficiary have decided the account party should shoulder. One of the functions of the credit is to put the costs of that loss during litigation on the account party.[118]

Equity's prerequisites for injunctive relief provide a significant threshold for the account party to cross in order to obtain injunctive relief. The rules are justified, especially in the letter of credit setting. They reflect the unwillingness of the law to interfere with an arrangement that the parties themselves have made and an awareness that the account party had the opportunity at the outset to negotiate the terms of the credit.[119] If the account party fails to negotiate favorable terms, courts are reluctant to renegotiate them for him. By the same token, if the account party has selected a fraud with whom to do business, courts are willing to leave the account party with his action at law rather than destroy the credit with crippling rules.[120]

---

[116] 606 F.2d 10 (2d Cir. 1979).

[117] 581 S.W.2d 935 (Mo. Ct. App. 1979).

[118] See generally ¶ 3.07[4] for discussion of this credit function. See also Sperry Int'l Trade, Inc. v. Government of Isr., 670 F.2d 8 (2d Cir. 1982) (holding that when money damages can compensate plaintiff, there is no irreparable injury); American Export Group Int'l Servs., Inc. v. Salem M. AL-NISF Elec. Co., 661 F. Supp. 759 (D.D.C. 1987) (no injunction when account party had remedy under arbitration clause). But cf. Rockwell Int'l Sys., Inc. v. Citibank, N.A., 719 F.2d 583 (2d Cir. 1983) (holding that claim for money damages may not negate irreparable injury in some cases); Philadelphia Gear Corp. v. Central Bank, 717 F.2d 230 (5th Cir. 1983) (same); Warner v. Central Trust Co., 715 F.2d 1121 (6th Cir. 1983) (same).

[119] See Recon Optical, Inc. v. Israel, 816 F.2d 854 (2d Cir. 1987); Maurice O'Meara Co. v. National Park Bank, 239 N.Y. 386, 146 N.E. 636 (1925); Laudisi v. American Exch. Nat'l Bank, 239 N.Y. 234, 146 N.E. 347 (1924).

[120] "The way to avoid fraud is to avoid dealing with a rogue." B. Wheble, "UCP 1974/1983 Revisions Compared and Explained (Documentary Credits)," ICC Pub. No. 411, at 15 (1984). For authority that an account party that contributed to the possibility of losses by asking the issuer of guaranties to extend them and by entering into more contracts with the ultimate beneficiaries and causing more guaranties to issue, see United Trading Corp. v. Allied Arab Bank Ltd., [1985] 2 Lloyd's Rep. 554 (C.A.).

At least two courts have accepted the curious notion that a draw on a standby letter of credit causes irreparable harm to the account party's reputation.[121] That conclusion is at odds with commercial practices. Often beneficiaries draw on standby credits when the account party is not in default. Standby credits are sometimes "direct pay" credits under which the parties expect the beneficiary to draw; at other times, the credit serves a forum-shifting or litigation cost–shifting function. The better-reasoned cases have rejected the notion that a draw casts aspersions on the account party's integrity.[122]

Two commentators have analyzed the unique feature of Iranian credits in particular and Middle Eastern credits in general,[123] in that they usually run to the benefit of a foreign sovereign or an agency or bank that is its alter ego.[124] This feature has significant implications for questions of jurisdiction[125] and immunity,[126] and for the question whether the account party can satisfy the equity prerequisites for injunctive relief. Under one view,[127] if the sovereign beneficiary draws on the credit and deprives the account party of relief under its legal system, equitable relief is appropriate as a matter of fairness.

The second view[128] perceives the question as more complicated. First, there is a clear possibility that the foreign beneficiary is subject to the jurisdiction of American courts. That being true, the account party

---

[121] See Hubbard Business Plaza v. Lincoln Liberty Life Ins. Co., 649 F. Supp. 1310 (D. Nev. 1986), aff'd, 844 F.2d 792 (9th Cir. 1988) (mem.); Foxboro Co. v. Arabian Am. Oil Co., 634 F. Supp. 1226 (D. Mass.), rev'd, 805 F.2d 34 (1st Cir. 1986).

[122] See Foxboro Co. v. Arabian Am. Oil Co., 805 F.2d 34 (1st Cir. 1986); Enterprise Int'l, Inc. v. Corporacion Estatal Petrolera Ecuatoriana, 762 F.2d 464 (5th Cir. 1985).

[123] The credits involved are standby and usually secure the return of the buyer's down payment. They are the converse of the commercial credit that secures payment of the price to the seller. Some of the cases are discussed infra ¶ 7.04. The Iranian cases are collected in Weisz & Blackman, "Standby Letters of Credit After Iran: Remedies of the Account Party," 1982 U. Ill. L. Rev. 355; Note, "Enjoining the International Standby Letter of Credit: The Iranian Letter of Credit Cases," 21 Harv. Int'l L.J. 189 (1980) (hereinafter Harvard Note).

[124] See Note, "A Reconsideration of American Bell International v. Islamic Republic of Iran, 474 F. Supp. 420 (S.D.N.Y. 1979)," 19 Colum. J. Transnat'l L. 301 (1981) (hereinafter Columbia Note); Harvard Note, supra note 123.

[125] See generally ¶ 11.02.

[126] On the immunity question, see Columbia Note, supra note 124. See generally ¶ 9.06[4].

[127] Rockwell Int'l Sys., Inc. v. Citibank, N.A., 719 F.2d 583 (2d Cir. 1983); Harvard Note, supra note 123.

[128] Columbia Note, supra note 124.

cannot show that it will suffer irreparable harm. Second, the account party cannot demonstrate a likelihood of success on the merits if the purpose of the credit is to give the beneficiary the unqualified right to get its down payment back. If the credit serves this function, equitable relief will frustrate the intent of the parties and will force them into other arrangements that may be less desirable to buyers and sellers in general.[129]

[2] The *Sztejn* Rule

It is entirely consistent with the independence principle to say that a beneficiary who practices fraud on the account party by virtue of conduct in the credit transaction is not entitled to payment under the credit. Section 5-114(2) codifies that rule but insists that even if fraud is present, the issuer is not under an obligation to dishonor. Rather, the issuer may honor, as long as it does so in good faith. It is also consistent with the spirit of the strict compliance rule to say that a beneficiary who presents fraudulent or false documents has not complied with the credit.

The strict compliance rule, as defined in Section 5-109 of the Code and in Article 15 of the Uniform Customs and Practice for Documentary Credits (UCP or the Uniform Customs), applies only to the "face" of documents and does not require the issuer to engage in extrinsic inquiries. Section 5-114(2) insists, therefore, that even if fraud is present, the bank is under no obligation to dishonor a demand for payment. The rules reflect appropriate regard for banking and litigating realities. It is one thing to say that a beneficiary that practices fraud in the credit transaction should not receive payment; it is quite another to say that bank issuers should not pay and courts should prevent payment every time the account party alleges fraud. Given fraud, issuers should not pay and courts should enjoin payment. Rarely, however, is fraud a given in the real world.

Fraud has long been a source of major concern for commercial law; and if the law of credits can deal with fraud without seriously hampering the credit device, it should do so. The major line of cases does deal with the fraud question and appears to do so successfully. That line of cases, however, defines "fraud" narrowly, in order not to wreak havoc upon the credit as a commercial device.

---

[129] Columbia Note, supra note 124, makes this point. See also infra ¶ 7.04[3][d]. Cf. Enterprise Int'l, Inc. v. Corporacion Estatal Petrolera Ecuatoriana, 762 F.2d 464 (5th Cir. 1985) (supporting argument that injunction in these circumstances unfairly reallocates cost of international litigation).

The leading fraud case is *Sztejn v. J. Henry Schroder Banking Corp.*[130] In the *Sztejn* case, the beneficiary presented invoices and bills of lading describing the merchandise as "bristles," as the credit required. The account party, in a complaint for an injunction, alleged that the documents were fraudulent, in that the beneficiary had shipped cow hair and other worthless rubbish instead of bristles. The issue in *Sztejn* was whether the complaint stated a cause of action. The court assumed, as courts must in motions to dismiss a complaint, that the allegations were true. Fraud, therefore, was a given in the *Sztejn* case. Even with established fraud, however, the *Sztejn* court was careful to draw a narrow rule.

First, the opinion holds that letters of credit will not work unless they are independent of the underlying contract. The opinion also notes that if a buyer wants to examine merchandise before paying for it, he can so provide in the credit. Absent such a term in the credit, the court will not permit the account party to make that examination.

The *Sztejn* court found a situation different from that in which the seller-beneficiary merely breaches the underlying contract. The complaint did not allege contract breach. It alleged that the beneficiary was practicing fraud on the issuer by supplying the issuer with fraudulent documents. The documents, even though they complied on their face with the requirements of the credit, were not conforming—at least not insofar as the complaint alleged. The court denied the motion to dismiss.

It is clear from the *Sztejn* opinion that the court knew that the rule it fashioned departed from the independence principle. The fraud allegations required the court to take account of facts extrinsic to the documents themselves, but the court was unwilling to extend the independence principle "to protect the unscrupulous seller"[131] who practices "intentional fraud."[132]

Note, moreover, that the fraud in *Sztejn* was established by the pleadings. *Sztejn* is not a case in which the court granted an injunction on the basis of the account party's unsupported assertions that there was fraud. By virtue of the posture of the matter before the court, *Sztejn* holds only that when the fraud is established, an injunction is proper. Fraud was established there only for the purpose of testing the sufficiency of the complaint; it was not established for purposes of entering an injunction.

---

[130] 177 Misc. 719, 31 N.Y.S.2d 631 (Sup. Ct. 1941).

[131] Id. at 722, 31 N.Y.S.2d at 634.

[132] Id.

American courts appear to have forgotten this element of the *Sztejn* case. English courts, which regard *Sztejn* as the font of the fraud exception to the issuer's duty to pay against conforming documents and which rely on its holding, require established fraud before they will issue an injunction.[133] Not surprisingly, account parties in English courts have not been able to meet that burden.[134]

The reach of the *Sztejn* rule was tested about a year later in *Asbury Park & Ocean Grove Bank v. National City Bank*.[135] In that case, Justice Shientag, who authored *Sztejn*, confronted again the claim of an account party that payment of a credit constituted fraud. In *Asbury Park*, the plaintiff, a bank, secured the issuance of the credit in favor of a beneficiary selling merchandise to the plaintiff bank's customers. The plaintiff bank alleged that the parties had intended to use the credits in order to satisfy invoices for shipments to be made to the customers by the beneficiary. In fact, the beneficiary had billed the customers directly and had used the letters of credit only when the customers did not pay. The delays caused by the altered transaction prevented the plaintiff, it claimed, from resorting to the merchandise to reimburse itself for advances. During the delays, the plaintiff's customers had sold the merchandise. The plaintiff argued that the issuing bank had notice of the alleged fraud because of the dates on certain drafts and shipping tickets and because of certain corrections and erasures that the beneficiary had made on other documents.

---

[133] For discussion of the English rule, see ¶ 11.04[3][b][iv].

[134] One English court explained the rule for an injunction as requiring clear evidence of fraud and clear evidence that the bank knows there is fraud. There must, moreover, be "strong corroborative evidence of the allegation, usually in the form of contemporary documents," and fraud must be "the only realistic inference to draw." United Trading Corp. v. Allied Arab Bank Ltd., [1985] 2 Lloyd's Rep. 554, 561 (C.A.). For similar authority, see Bolivinter Oil S.A. v. Chase Manhattan Bank, [1984] 1 Lloyd's Rep. 251 (C.A.); Howe Richardson Scale Co. v. Polimex-Cekop, [1978] 1 Lloyd's Rep. 161 (C.A.); Edward Owen Eng'g Ltd. v. Barclays Bank Int'l Ltd., [1978] 1 All E.R. 976 (C.A.); R.D. Harbottle (Mercantile) Ltd. v. National Westminster Bank Ltd., [1977] 2 All E.R. 862 (Q.B.); Discount Records Ltd. v. Barclays Bank Ltd., [1975] 1 All E.R. 1071 (Ch.). For discussion of the English rule, see Goode, "Reflections on Letters of Credit—I," 1980 J. Bus. L. 291; Lawson, "Performance Bonds—Irrevocable Obligations," 1987 J. Bus. L. 259. The Canadian cases have fashioned a more lenient rule, but it is only slightly so. Generally, Canadian courts issue an injunction only if the account party can establish a strong prima facie case of fraud. See Bank of N.S. v. Angelica-Whitewear Ltd., 36 D.L.R.4th 161 (Can. 1987); C.D.N. Research & Dev. Ltd. v. Bank of N.S., 136 D.L.R.3d 656 (Ont. H. Ct. 1982); Rosen v. Pullen, 126 D.L.R.3d 62 (Ont. H. Ct. 1981); Canadian Pioneer Petroleums Inc. v. FDIC, 30 S.L.R. 315 (Q.B. 1984).

[135] 35 N.Y.S.2d 985 (Sup. Ct. 1942), aff'd mem., 268 A.D. 984, 52 N.Y.S.2d 583 (1944).

Justice Shientag rejected the fraud argument, pointing out that the law cannot impose a condition that the goods be shipped within a certain time, or that the drafts be presented within a certain time, because the credit did not contain such a provision. More importantly, the court's opinion goes to some length to endorse the independence principle. "The efficacy of the letter of credit as an instrument for financing trade is the primary consideration,"[136] the court stated. The opinion goes on to say:

> [A] notice given by the [plaintiff] to the issuing bank to the effect that the former was defrauded by either the buyer, the seller or both, is ineffective to void or suspend the operation of the letter of credit. Any other rule would destroy the effectiveness of this valuable commercial device. The common-law fraud action is one of the most difficult to prove, and the issuing bank cannot be expected to evaluate the soundness of the [plaintiff's] claim.[137]

Asbury Park was not a suit for injunction but a suit after payment for damages suffered by virtue of the issuer's honor of the beneficiary's drafts. Nonetheless, it is clear in an opinion handed down by the author of the *Sztejn* rule about one year after *Sztejn* that the fraud to which *Sztejn* objects is fraud in the letter of credit transaction, not fraud in any underlying transaction. The *Asbury Park* opinion reinforces the independence principle as one rendering letters of credit independent of the underlying contracts, "unless there was such a fraud on the part of the seller that there were no goods shipped even though shipping tickets were presented."[138]

Several points are clear from a comparison of the two opinions. First, credits are valuable commercial devices that the independence principle serves by assuring the effective functioning of the credit and any fraud exception to the independence principle must be limited. Second, fraud claims should not become surrogates for breach of warranty claims. Third, only the unscrupulous beneficiary who intentionally practices fraud should be enjoined. Fourth, the fraud should occur in the credit transaction as in *Sztejn*, where the documents were false.

---

[136] 35 N.Y.S.2d at 989.

[137] Id.

[138] Id. at 988–989 (citation omitted).

[3] Codification of the *Sztejn* Rule in Section 5-114(2) of the Code

Section 5-114(2) codifies the *Sztejn* rule.[139] The provision begins with
the supposition that when the documents comply on their face with the
credit, the issuer should honor the draft. It then poses four exceptions.
First, if a document does not conform to the warranties that the law in-
fers from its presentation, the issuer may dishonor. These warranties
arise out of Section 7-507 for documents of title and Section 8-306 for
securities. Warranties on presentation of documents of title, which arise
frequently in the letter of credit transaction, include a warranty to the issuer that the document is genuine, that the presenting party has no
knowledge of any fact that would impair its validity or worth, and that
negotiation or transfer is rightful and fully effective. Warranties on presentation of securities involve essentially the same representations plus
the warranty that the security has not been altered materially.[140]

The second exception to the presupposed rule that the issuer must
honor a draft accompanied by documents conforming on their face concerns documents that are forged. There is some overlap between the first
exception and the second. A bill of lading or a security that is forged is
not genuine and therefore violates the warranty provisions referred to in
the first exception. The forgery exception, however, extends to documents other than bills of lading and securities. It covers the commercial
invoice and the various certificates that credits frequently demand.

The third exception to the presupposed rule is for documents that
are fraudulent. Again, there is some overlap, since forged documents
probably would be fraudulent; yet since it also covers documents bear-

---

[139] For discussion of the *Sztejn* rule, see supra ¶ 7.04[2]. Section 5-114(2) provides:

> Unless otherwise agreed when documents appear on their face to comply with the
> terms of a credit but a required document does not in fact conform to the warranties
> made on negotiation or transfer of a document of title (Section 7-507) or of a certifi-
> cated security (Section 8-306) or is forged or fraudulent or there is fraud in the trans-
> action:
>
> (a) the issuer must honor the draft or demand for payment if honor is demanded by
>   a negotiating bank or other holder of the draft or demand which has taken the
>   draft or demand under the credit and under circumstances which would make it
>   a holder in due course (Section 3-302) and in an appropriate case would make it
>   a person to whom a document of title has been duly negotiated (Section 7-502)
>   or a bona fide purchaser of a certificated security (Section 8-302); and
>
> (b) in all other cases as against its customer, an issuer acting in good faith may hon-
>   or the draft or demand for payment despite notification from the customer of
>   fraud, forgery or other defect not apparent on the face of the documents but a
>   court of appropriate jurisdiction may enjoin such honor.

[140] For discussion of the use of breach of warranty as support for an injunction,
see Macintosh, "Letters of Credit: Dishonor When a Required Document Fails to
Conform to the Section 7-507(b) Warranty," 6 J.L. & Com. 1 (1986).

ing no forgery, the third exception is broader than the forgery exception. The documents in *Sztejn* were fraudulent documents. They described rubbish as bristles, and presumably the parties issuing the documents knew it. Otherwise, they would not have been fraudulent, but only erroneous.[141] Nonetheless, there was no allegation in *Sztejn* that the documents were forged.

The fourth exception to the presupposed rule, "fraud in the transaction," is the one that has fostered confusion and a measure of bad analysis. There are some who speculate that the word "transaction" refers to the underlying transaction, not to the credit transaction.[142] The argument supporting that view holds in part that the other exceptions cover all fraud in the credit transaction and that the fourth exception, in order to have some meaning, must refer to something other than fraud in the credit transaction. The argument finds superficial support in the drafting history of the provision itself, which did not always contain the "fraud in the transaction" language.

The argument, however, does not withstand close analysis, because the first three exceptions do not cover all fraud in the credit transaction; because such a reading would amount to a significant departure from the *Sztejn* rule—a departure that no one seems to have contemplated; and because such a rule seriously weakens the credit device. Finally, a closer look at the drafting history of the provision does not support the implications that some have drawn from it.

[a] Ambiguity in Section 5-114(2)

The first three exceptions in Section 5-114(2) do not cover the instance where a party breaches no Article 7 or Article 8 warranty and presents no document that is forged and no document that is fraudulent, but in which instance the presenter is practicing fraud on the issuer. A credit may call for an inspection certificate signed by an independent testing service. If the service issues the certificate erroneously, either because of the beneficiary's fraud or through negligence, the certificate would be neither forged nor fraudulent, nor would presentation of it breach any warranty in Article 7 or Article 8; but there would be fraud in the credit transaction when the beneficiary knowingly presented the erroneous certificate to the issuer. It could well be, then, that the "fraud in the transaction" language is intended to cover this situation or other

---

[141] See Sherkate Sahami Khass Rapol v. Henry R. Jahn & Son, 701 F.2d 1049 (2d Cir. 1983); It's Devine Indus., Ltd. v. Bank Leumi Trust Co., 22 U.C.C. Rep. Serv. (Callaghan) 130 (N.Y. Sup. Ct. 1977).

[142] For cases to that effect, see infra ¶ 7.04[4][b].

situations, not anticipated by the drafters, that do not involve a breach of warranty, a forged document, or a fraudulent document but do constitute fraud in the letter of credit transaction.

It is clear from this analysis that whatever the provision's language means, it is incorrect to conclude that it must be read broadly to avoid rendering the language redundant. "Fraud in the transaction" can be read narrowly without depriving it of meaning.

Scarsdale National Bank & Trust Co. v. Toronto-Dominion Bank[143] demonstrates fraud in the credit transaction with no breach of warranty, no forgery, and no fraudulent document. In *Scarsdale*, the credit grew out of a contract for the purchase and installation of equipment, and the credit called for certificates signed by the account party, verifying that the beneficiary had performed. The beneficiary apparently needed a loan to complete the preparation and installation of the equipment and asked its bank to take the credit as security for the loan. The bank was unwilling to make the loan until it held the documents that were necessary to draw under the credit, including the certificates that were to be signed by the account party. The seller went to the buyer, that is, the account party, and asked it to prepare and sign the certificates in advance and to deliver them to the account party's attorney. The seller explained that it was concerned that the buyer might refuse to sign the certificates after the seller had installed the equipment. The arrangement with the account party's attorney was in the nature of an escrow. Later the seller, who was situated in Scarsdale, New York, asked the account party's attorney, whose office was in Toronto, to send the certificates to Scarsdale as further assurance to the seller of the availability of the certificates.

The Toronto attorney's office agreed, on the condition that the seller's attorney hold the documents in trust pending the buyer's authorization that they be delivered. Apparently, the seller obtained the certificates from his attorney's office in the attorney's absence, took them to the lender, and obtained the loan. The lender then presented the documents to the issuer and demanded payment under the credit. The account party claimed fraud, and the issuer dishonored. The *Scarsdale* court upheld the issuer on the theory that the fraud here was fraud in the transaction and was a ground for dishonor under Section 5-114(2).

It is clear that the documents in *Scarsdale* did not fall into any of the first three categories in Section 5-114(2) permitting dishonor. The documents breached no warranty; they were not forged; and they were not fraudulent. It is equally clear that there was fraud in the credit transaction, and, arguably, it is that kind of fraud to which the section refers with the words "fraud in the transaction." Nothing in the language of

---

[143] 533 F. Supp. 378 (S.D.N.Y. 1982).

the section supports the inference that the quoted language must refer to the underlying transaction.

[b] Various Readings

While there is no question that Section 5-114(2) may be read as referring only to fraud intimately related to the credit transaction,[144] there is considerable controversy on that point. While some commentators have supported that narrow reading,[145] most of the writers read the "fraud in the transaction" language broadly to refer to fraud extrinsic to the credit and usually in the underlying transaction.[146] There are a number of cases[147] that explicitly adopt the broad view, though the holdings

---

[144] See supra ¶ 7.04[3][a].

[145] Henry Harfield, for example, argues that the account party seeking to enjoin payment of a credit asserts "defenses that would be available to the issuer," not defenses available to itself arising out of the underlying contract. Harfield, "Enjoining Letter of Credit Transactions," 95 Banking L.J. 596, 606 (1978); see also Thorup, "Injunctions Against Payment of Standby Letters of Credit: How Can Banks Best Protect Themselves?" 101 Banking L.J. 6 (1984); Geva, "Contractual Defenses as Claims to the Instrument: The Right to Block Payment on a Banker's Instrument," 58 Or. L. Rev. 283, 290 (1979); Justice, "Letters of Credit: Expectations and Frustrations" (pts. 1 & 2), 94 Banking L.J. 424, 493 (1977); McLaughlin, "The Letter of Credit Provisions of the Proposed Uniform Commercial Code," 63 Harv. L. Rev. 1373 (1950).

[146] See, e.g., Kimball & Sanders, "Preventing Wrongful Payment of Guaranty Letters of Credit—Lessons From Iran," 39 Bus. Law. 417 (1984); Becker, "Standby Letters of Credit and the Iranian Cases: Will the Independence of the Credit Survive?" 13 U.C.C. L.J. 335, 343 (1981); Ellinger, "Fraud in Documentary Letter of Credit Transactions," 1981 J. Bus. L. 258, 267; Harvard Note, supra note 123, at 208; Megrah, "Risk Aspects of the Irrevocable Documentary Credit," 24 Ariz. L. Rev. 255, 257 (1982); McLaughlin, "Standby Letters of Credit and Penalty Clauses: An Unexpected Synergy," 43 Ohio St. L.J. 1 (1982); Symons, "Letters of Credit: Fraud, Good Faith and the Basis for Injunctive Relief," 54 Tul. L. Rev. 338, 351 (1980); cf. Gable, "Standby Letters of Credit: Nomenclature Has Confounded Analysis," 12 Law & Pol'y Int'l Bus. 903 (1980) (arguing that U.C.C. § 5-114(2) should not apply to standby credits).

[147] See, e.g., Itek Corp. v. First Nat'l Bank, 730 F.2d 19 (1st Cir. 1984); Rockwell Int'l Sys., Inc. v. Citibank, N.A., 719 F.2d 583 (2d Cir. 1983); Harris Corp. v. National Iranian Radio & Television, 691 F.2d 1344 (11th Cir. 1982); Sabolyk v. Morgan Guar. Trust Co., No. 84 Civ. 3179 (MJL) (S.D.N.Y. Nov. 27, 1984); Hamilton v. Central Nat'l Bank, 40 U.C.C. Rep. Serv. (Callaghan) 1008 (N.D. Ohio 1984); Larson v. First Interstate Bank, 603 F. Supp. 467 (D. Ariz. 1983); Roman Ceramics Corp. v. Peoples Nat'l Bank, 517 F. Supp. 526 (M.D. Pa. 1981), aff'd, 714 F.2d 1207 (3d Cir. 1983); Baker v. National Boulevard Bank, 399 F. Supp. 1021 (N.D. Ill. 1975); Originala Petroleum Corp. v. Beta Fin. & Inv. Corp. (In re Originala Petroleum Corp.), 39 Bankr. 1003 (Bankr. N.D. Tex. 1984); Professional Modular Surface, Inc. v. Uniroyal, Inc., 108 Ill. App. 3d 1046, 440 N.E.2d 177 (1982); Stringer Constr. Co. v. American Ins. Co., 102 Ill. App. 3d 919, 430 N.E.2d 1 (1981); First Arlington

in those cases and in most others do not provide support for that view. The courts say that Section 5-114(2) covers fraud in the underlying transaction, but the facts reveal that there is fraud in the credit transaction[148]; the other assertions are dictum.[149] Thus, support in these cases for the broad reading is equivocal.[150]

Nat'l Bank v. Stathis, 90 Ill. App. 3d 802, 413 N.E.2d 1288 (1980) (claiming to be narrow approach, but clearly willing to look at underlying transaction); Morgan v. Depositors Trust Co., 33 U.C.C. Rep. Serv. (Callaghan) 1473, 1479 (Me. Super. Ct. Kennebec County 1982); Werner v. A.L. Grootemaat & Sons, 80 Wis. 2d 513, 259 N.W.2d 310 (1977); cf. CNA Mortgage Investors, Ltd. v. Hamilton Nat'l Bank, 540 S.W.2d 238 (Tenn. Ct. App. 1975) (holding that fraud in underlying transaction should be considered if credit incorporates underlying transaction). On the incorporation question, see infra ¶ 7.04[4][c].

[148] See Rockwell Int'l Sys., Inc. v. Citibank, N.A., 719 F.2d 583 (2d Cir. 1983); Roman Ceramics Corp. v. People's Nat'l Bank, 517 F. Supp. 526 (M.D. Pa. 1981), aff'd, 714 F.2d 1207 (3d Cir. 1983) (beneficiary certified that invoices were unpaid, when, in fact, account party had directed beneficiary to apply payments to them). In Harris Corp. v. National Iranian Radio & Television, 691 F.2d 1344 (11th Cir. 1982), the alleged fraud occurred when defendant made a false demand on the beneficiary, who, in turn, demanded payment under the credit. Although the court viewed this fraud as neither in the credit transaction, nor in the underlying transaction, the allegations showed clearly that the defendant caused the beneficiary to make a claim on the credit that was prompted by the defendant's own fraud.

[149] In these cases, the references to the rule on fraud are dicta. The cases hold that there was no fraud or that the plaintiff did not satisfy the equity prerequisites for an injunction. Airline Reporting Corp. v. First Nat'l Bank, 832 F.2d 823 (4th Cir. 1987); Baker v. National Boulevard Bank, 399 F. Supp. 1021 (N.D. Ill. 1975) (no fraud issue); Morgan v. Depositors Trust Co., 33 U.C.C. Rep. Serv. (Callaghan) 1473 (Me. Super. Ct. Kennebec County 1982) (no irreparable harm); Professional Modular Surface, Inc. v. Uniroyal, Inc., 108 Ill. App. 3d 1046, 440 N.E.2d 177 (1982) (no irreparable harm); Stringer Constr. Co. v. American Ins. Co., 102 Ill. App. 3d 919, 430 N.E.2d 1 (1981) (no fraud); First Arlington Nat'l Bank v. Stathis, 90 Ill. App. 3d 802, 413 N.E.2d 1288 (1980) (no fraud). For further discussion of these cases, see infra ¶ 7.04[4][b].

[150] In at least two cases, courts have defined the fraud necessary for an injunction as "fraud in the factum." See Bossier Bank & Trust Co. v. Union Planters Nat'l Bank, 550 F.2d 1077, 1082 (6th Cir. 1977) (app. A); Werner v. A.L. Grootemaat & Sons, 80 Wis. 2d 513, 523, 259 N.W.2d 310, 315 (1977). This description of fraud probably relates to its nature (i.e., to the degree of fraud, not to the locus of fraud). See infra ¶ 7.04[4][c]. Other cases use the term "fraud in the inducement" with respect to the underlying contract. These cases are not persuasive authority. See Baker v. National Boulevard Bank, 399 F. Supp. 1021 (N.D. Ill. 1975) (no fraud alleged); NMC Enters., Inc. v. CBS, Inc., 14 U.C.C. Rep. Serv. (Callaghan) 1427 (N.Y. Sup. Ct. 1974). For criticism of the *NMC* case, see Geva, supra note 145, at 290; Justice, supra note 145, at 502. See also infra ¶ 7.04[4][c]. The Court of Appeals for the Second Circuit has termed the *NMC* case "exceptional." Sperry Int'l Trade, Inc. v. Government of Isr., 670 F.2d 8, 12 (2d Cir. 1982). In Temtex Prods., Inc. v. Capital Bank & Trust Co., 623 F. Supp. 816 (M.D. La. 1985), aff'd mem., 788 F.2d 1563 (5th Cir.

Two often-cited articles[151] make much of the drafting history of the provision and argue that it supports the broad reading. Both articles misread the legislative history. The history discloses that indeed the drafters intended to add a "new gene"[152] to the *Sztejn* rule. Prior to 1957, the official version of the Code's fraud rule appeared in Section 5-111, which referred to "forgery or fraud in a required document."[153] That language defined a narrow fraud rule that would not cover the *Scarsdale* case, for example. The 1957 changes moved the fraud rule to Section 5-114(2) and added references to the Article 7 and Article 8 warranties, as well as the language "fraud in the transaction."[154]

The Code's editorial board noted, in connection with those changes, that they were designed to clarify the intent of the old Sections 5-111(1) and 5-111(2).[155] That authoritative comment does not suggest

---

1986), the court termed "fraud in the inducement," id. at 820, fraud by the beneficiary that induces the issuer to issue the credit. The *Temtex* court found that the facts of that case did not support a claim of such fraud. In Interfirst Bank v. First Fed. Sav. & Loan Ass'n, 242 Kan. 181, 747 P.2d 129 (1987), the court held that fraud by the account party on the issuer was not fraud in the transaction. Cf. Northwestern Bank v. NCF Fin. Corp., 88 N.C. App. 614, 365 S.E.2d 14 (1988) (similar rule so long as beneficiary is unaware of fraud). In Pickus Constr. & Equip. Co. v. Bank of Waukegan, 158 Ill. App. 3d 141, 511 N.E.2d 228, appeal denied, 158 Ill. App. 3d 141, 517 N.E.2d 1095 (1987), the credit secured the beneficiary's exposure from a mechanic's lien claim. The account party sought an injunction, arguing that the rights of the claimant had expired under the lien statute and that any draw on the credit would be fraudulent. The court sustained the injunction. The *Pickus* case obviously was tried on the underlying contract dispute. If the court's opinion is a fair indication, the beneficiary never raised the letter of credit fraud issue. In Oil Country Specialists, Ltd. v. Philipp Bros., Inc., 762 S.W.2d 170 (Tex. Ct. App. 1988), rev'd, 9 U.C.C. Rep. Serv. 2d 201 (Tex. 1989) (per curiam), the jury found no fraud but did find negligent misrepresentations in the underlying transaction. Given those findings, the Texas Court of Appeals reversed a lower court's dissolution of an injunction against draw on a standby. Since there were negligent misrepresentations, the court of appeals reasoned, the beneficiary's certification that sums were due on the underlying transaction was false, and payment should not have been made under the credit. The Supreme Court of Texas, however, reversed the Texas Court of Appeals in an opinion that flatly rejects the idea that an account party can promote breach of contract in the underlying transaction to fraud in the letter of credit transaction. See Philipp Bros., Inc. v. Oil Country Specialists, Ltd., 9 U.C.C. Rep. Serv. 2d (Callaghan) 201 (Tex. 1989) (per curiam).

[151] See Harvard Note, supra note 123; Comment, "'Fraud in the Transaction' Enjoining Letters of Credit During the Iranian Revolution," 93 Harv. L. Rev. 992 (1980).

[152] Harfield, supra note 145, at 605.

[153] U.C.C. §§ 5-111(1), 5-111(2) (1956 official version).

[154] See U.C.C. § 5-114(2) (1957 official version).

[155] 1956 Recommendations of the Editorial Board for the Uniform Commercial Code, § 5-114, reasons (4th sent.), reprinted in 18 E. Kelley, Uniform Commercial Code Drafts 205 (1984).

that the drafters intended by their "fraud in the transaction" language to expand the fraud defense beyond all prior limits. Rather, this drafting history suggests, at most, a modest extension from the prior limit— "forgery or fraud in a required document."

All of this discussion overlooks the fact, moreover, that those who argue that fraud in the underlying transaction may sustain an injunction are altering the nature of the credit and that, if their view would not destroy the credit, it certainly runs that risk. Ultimately, courts are not going to interpret the statute in a way that destroys the credit as an efficient commercial device. From time to time, there may be cases that go too far; but, in the long run, the courts recognize that indiscriminate interference with the credit operation will destroy the credit. There seems to be general agreement that Section 5-114(2) is a codification of the *Sztejn* rule.[156] Courts following the *Sztejn* case articulate well its concern for the independence principle. They argue that injunctions should be used only against the "unscrupulous" beneficiary[157] who is "mulcting"[158] the account party, or whose "egregious"[159] fraud vitiates or entirely thwarts the underlying transaction.[160] Courts have further limited the use of injunctions by enforcing the strict prerequisites for equitable relief.[161]

[c] Framework for Resolution

Unfortunately, the language of Section 5-114(2) referring to fraud in the transaction is vague, and the drafting history of the provision is itself equivocal. Ultimately, the question should be resolved in a way

---

[156] See, e.g., Harris Corp. v. National Iranian Radio & Television, 691 F.2d 1344 (11th Cir. 1982); Bank of Newport v. First Nat'l Bank & Trust Co., 687 F.2d 1257 (8th Cir. 1982); United Bank Ltd. v. Cambridge Sporting Goods Corp., 41 N.Y.2d 254, 360 N.E.2d 943, 392 N.Y.S.2d 265 (1976); Harfield, supra note 145.

[157] Sztejn v. J. Henry Schroder Banking Corp., 177 Misc. 719, 722, 31 N.Y.S.2d 631, 634 (1941); Roman Ceramics Corp. v. Peoples Nat'l Bank, 517 F. Supp. 526, 537 (M.D. Pa. 1981), aff'd, 714 F.2d 1207 (3d Cir. 1983).

[158] American Bell Int'l, Inc. v. Islamic Republic of Iran, 474 F. Supp. 420, 424 (S.D.N.Y. 1979).

[159] Roman Ceramics Corp. v. Peoples Nat'l Bank, 517 F. Supp. 526, 535 (M.D. Pa. 1981), aff'd, 714 F.2d 1207 (3d Cir. 1983); cf. Dynamics Corp. of Am. v. Citizens & S. Nat'l Bank, 356 F. Supp. 991, 999 (N.D. Ga. 1973) (beneficiary must not be allowed to take "unconscientious advantage" of situation).

[160] Bank of Newport v. First Nat'l Bank & Trust Co., 687 F.2d 1257, 1261 (8th Cir. 1982); Intraworld Indus., Inc. v. Girard Trust Bank, 461 Pa. 343, 359, 336 A.2d 316, 324 (1975). For criticism of these attempts to define a fraud rule narrower than intentional fraud, see Symons, supra note 146.

[161] See supra ¶ 7.04[1].

that serves commerce best. In the final analysis, the sharply divided opinions on the meaning of Section 5-114(2) reflect sharply divided views on the nature and functions of the credit.

The prevailing view among bankers and merchants is that the credit is their invention—a mercantile specialty different from any contract and any negotiable instrument.[162] Under this view, the credit has at least five functions:[163]

1. To provide liquidity to the beneficiary's paper;
2. To substitute the credit of the issuer for that of the beneficiary;
3. To reduce transaction costs;
4. To shift litigation costs; and
5. To shift the forum of litigation.

Each of these functions depends, in turn, on the prompt, inevitable payment feature of the credit. To the extent that promptness is missing or that inevitability is questioned, the credit fails in some respect to achieve the desired function.

In a letter of credit transaction, the parties can use the credit to shift litigation and forum costs. When a Detroit manufacturer sells merchandise on credit to a Los Angeles buyer, the parties have put the cost of litigating without the purchase price on the seller. If the buyer disputes the conformity of the goods, the seller will have to litigate in order to get his money. The parties also have put the forum risk on the seller. In all probability, he will have to litigate in California. The use of a typical invoice standby credit[164] reallocates these costs to the buyer. Under the invoice standby, the seller whose invoice is not paid when due will draw against the buyer's bank and receive immediate payment. During the months or years of litigation, the seller will have the purchase price, and, in all probability, the litigation will occur in Michigan instead of in California.[165] The parties may decide to prorate the litigation cost. If they do not use a credit, they may agree to a partial down payment. In the event of a 10 percent down payment, they will have shifted 10 percent of the litigation cost to the buyer. In the credit transaction, the parties may agree that the credit covers only 50 percent of the invoice price. In that case, they have allocated the costs evenly between themselves.

---

[162] For discussion of the development of credits as a mercantile device, see ¶¶ 3.02, 3.03, 5.01[1].

[163] See ¶ 3.07.

[164] See App. C, Doc. 18.

[165] Under the general view, unless the seller is doing business in California, the courts of that state may not exercise jurisdiction over him. See generally ¶ 11.01.

There are parties to transactions involving credits who do not understand the significance of their application agreement or of the issuer's credit engagement. At least two critics of the strict fraud view[166] appear to argue that the courts or the legislature should use the fraud rule of Section 5-114(2) to satisfy the expectations of the parties to the transaction. The crucial question is one of determining what expectations are reasonable. The law should not reward novice or unknowledgeable parties at the expense of a credit device fashioned by experienced merchants. Parties to credit transactions are nearly always merchants, and the few of them that do not understand what they are doing should not be able to destroy the credit for the majority who do. Neither should merchants who do know what they are doing, but then decide that they want out of the bargain, be able to damage the credit.

The idea that merchant parties to a credit transaction should be accorded equitable relief in order to refashion the transaction is akin to affording such relief to the endorser of a check or note because he did not appreciate the significance of his endorsement. Checks, notes, and letters of credit are mercantile specialties, and parties that deal with them are charged with knowledge of them. When the use of credits is expanding, as it did so dramatically in the 1970s and 1980s, the number of parties who misunderstand a complex commercial transaction like the letter of credit transaction will increase for a relatively brief period of time. During that period, there will be pressure to accommodate them at the expense of the credit device. Rather than accommodating those who misunderstand and thus destroying the credit, courts should enforce credits vigorously and hasten the learning process. The evidence suggests that, with a few exceptions, courts have followed that wise policy.[167]

[d] An Answer to the Critics

The weakness of the broad view of the "fraud in the transaction" language of Section 5-114(2) is that it undermines the credit device. By forcing courts to delve into the underlying transaction, the broad view inhibits the prompt, inevitable payment feature of credits and interferes with the functions of credits.

---

[166]See Harvard Note, supra note 123; Weisz & Blackman, "Standby Letters of Credit After Iran: Remedies of the Account Party," 1982 U. Ill. L. Rev. 355. Significantly, these critics ignore the impact of their arguments on the function of credits. The same is true of the courts, as a decision by the Court of Appeals for the Second Circuit demonstrates. See Rockwell Int'l Sys., Inc. v. Citibank, N.A., 719 F.2d 583 (2d Cir. 1983).

[167]See infra ¶¶ 7.04[4][d], 7.04[4][e].

When critics charge that courts should define "fraud" or invoke equitable remedies in a way that satisfies unreasonable expectations of the account party, they invite the account party to litigate these questions. Once that litigation begins, the prompt payment feature of the credit is destroyed. To the extent the account parties' litigation is successful, the inevitability feature of the credit is destroyed. The effect of the broad view is to reallocate the risks that the parties already have allocated.[168]

Similarly, those critics of the strict view, who argue for a special exception in the case of credits issued to foreign sovereigns,[169] may be ignoring the fact that foreign sovereigns who cannot obtain the litigation cost and forum risk protection they desire will refuse to accept American credits[170] and will resort to other commercial devices.[171] In fact, if the critics are successful in transforming the credit from the unique commercial device it currently is into something else, merchants will have to invent something new to take its place. They might resort to performance bonds or escrow arrangements. Unfortunately, both of these devices are bulkier, slower, and more costly than the credit is.

One cannot deny that courts are ever inclined to issue temporary restraining orders when petitioners allege that a beneficiary is seeking to spirit money out of the petitioner's bank account and, perhaps, out of the jurisdiction. The lawyer who argues for the court to stay its hand always has the more difficult task. On the hearing to determine whether to make the temporary restraining order a preliminary injunction, however, it ought to be apparent to the court that if fraud in the underlying

---

[168] For an egregious example of judicial interference with the credit transaction, see MBank Houston, N.A. v. Hendrix, No. 01-86-0609-CV (Tex. Ct. App. Aug. 12, 1986) (limited precedent op.), where the trial court issued a temporary restraining order against the beneficiary, prohibiting it from drawing on the credit, and then extended the order beyond the expiry date of the credit. For a case awarding significant damages, including attorney fees, in favor of a beneficiary and against an account party that caused an injunction to issue against payment of a credit, see Cromwell v. Commerce & Energy Bank, 528 So. 2d 759 (La. Ct. App. 1988).

[169] See Harvard Note, supra note 123; Weisz & Blackman, supra note 166.

[170] For a suggestion that Iranian buyers will not accept credits issued by American banks, see Weisz & Blackman, supra note 166, at 361 n.25.

[171] They might resort to first-demand guarantees, which are issued by European banks and foreign branches of American banks but not, to date, by domestic American banks. See Wheble, "'Problem Children': Stand-by Letters of Credit and Simple First Demand Guarantees," 24 Ariz. L. Rev. 301 (1982). For additional authority, see Dolan, "Standby Letters of Credit (Is the Standby Only Another Invention of the Goldsmiths in Lombard Street?)," 7 Cardozo L. Rev. 1 (1985); Comment, "The Independence Rule in Standby Letters of Credit," 52 U. Chi. L. Rev. 218 (1985). For the argument that the independence principle should apply somewhat less strictly in standby cases than in commercial credit cases, but vigorously nonetheless, see Graham & Geva, "Standby Credits in Canada," 9 Can. Bus. L.J. 180 (1984).

transaction is a proper defense to payment, the injunction litigation often will become a suit to determine the rights in the underlying transaction. By narrowing the fraud defense, as this treatise urges them to do, courts will limit the injunction inquiry and render it summary in nature.

It is probably too late to argue that *Sztejn*, the new gene in Section 5-114(2), applies only in cases of established fraud. That may be all that the drafters intended when they inserted new language in the section. It clearly is all that the court held in *Sztejn*. Whatever the intention of the drafters may have been, clearly they did not envision the destruction of the credit; nor does that purpose appear in *Sztejn*. To the contrary, the history of the fraud defense clearly supports efforts to restrict the defense, lest the credit lose its unique virtues as a commercial device.

[4] Fraud Cases

Generally, the cases follow the pattern of the *Sztejn* rule: They restrict the fraud defense to the credit transaction and define "fraud" narrowly, though there are exceptions.

[a] Fraud in the Documents

In *Sztejn*, the bill of lading and invoice were established as fraudulent in that they described rubbish as "bristles."[172] There are many cases in which that kind of fraud prompts courts to issue an injunction against payment or to justify the issuer's refusal to honor the beneficiary's demand for payment.[173]

---

[172] Sztejn v. J. Henry Schroder Banking Corp., 177 Misc. 719, 31 N.Y.S.2d 631 (Sup. Ct. 1941). It is important to bear in mind that in *Sztejn* the fraud was "established" by virtue of the unusual posture of the case. The issue in *Sztejn* was not whether the account party had marshaled sufficient evidence of fraud to justify the issuance of an injunction. The *Sztejn* opinion dealt with a motion to dismiss the account party's action. In that posture, the court had to take the allegations of fraud in the complaint as true, that is, as established.

[173] The U.S. cases generally have not considered the distinction between evidence of fraud in suits (1) by the account party before payment to enjoin that payment and (2) after payment between the account party and the issuer over the issuer's right to reimbursement. Some foreign common-law courts have considered that distinction, however. Under Canadian decisions, in the former actions, the account party must make a strong prima facie case of fraud; in the latter, the account party must establish knowledge of the issuer before payment of facts that would make the fraud clear or obvious. See Bank of N.S. v. Angelica-Whitewear Ltd., 36 D.L.R.4th 161 (Can. 1987).

In *United Bank Ltd. v. Cambridge Sporting Goods Corp.*,[174] holders of the beneficiary's drafts presented documents purporting to cover new boxing gloves, when, in fact, the gloves were old, ripped, and mildewed. The court held that fraud had been established and that an injunction was proper. In *Siderius, Inc. v. Wallace Co.*,[175] the jury found that the beneficiary obtained a bill of lading reciting that merchandise was loaded on board a vessel on or before January 15, 1975 when, in fact, it was loaded later. The jury also found that the beneficiary's conduct in obtaining the bill was with fraudulent intent. The court held that the issuer properly refused to honor the beneficiary's drafts.

Similarly, in *Merchants Corp. of America v. Chase Manhattan Bank, N.A.*,[176] the court granted a temporary injunction on the claim of the account party that the on-board bills of lading were dated January 31, 1968, when the specified vessel was not in port until February 13, 1968. In *Shaffer v. Brooklyn Park Garden Apartments*,[177] the Supreme Court of Minnesota posited the rule that the fraud of Section 5-114(2) must be fraud in the documents, not fraud in the underlying transaction. Then, finding such fraud in a false certificate, the court enjoined the issuer from honoring drafts under the credit.[178]

Other cases suggest that, absent fraud in the documents, no injunction should issue. In *First National Bank v. Rosebud Housing Authority*,[179] the issuer sought a declaratory judgment. The credit, a standby, called for a certificate reciting that the proceeds of the draft would be used solely for the purposes described in a certain underlying agreement between the account party and the beneficiary. It also required the beneficiary to attach the contract to the certificate. The parties amended the underlying agreement after the date of the letter of credit, but they did not amend the credit. The beneficiary submitted the certificate with the copy of the original underlying contract attached to it. The court held that dishonor would be proper only if there had been fraud in the documents, that the parties' amendment of the agreement was immaterial, and that there was no fraud in the documents and therefore no cause for an injunction to issue.

---

[174] 41 N.Y.2d 254, 360 N.E.2d 943, 392 N.Y.S.2d 265 (1976).

[175] 583 S.W.2d 852 (Tex. Civ. App. 1979).

[176] 5 U.C.C. Rep. Serv. (Callaghan) 196 (N.Y. Sup. Ct. 1968).

[177] 311 Minn. 452, 250 N.W.2d 172 (1977).

[178] See also Bank of N.S. v. Angelica-Whitewear Ltd., 36 D.L.R.4th 161 (Can. 1987) (finding invoice with inflated price fraudulent).

[179] 291 N.W.2d 41 (Iowa 1980).

In *It's Devine Industries, Ltd. v. Bank Leumi Trust Co.*,[180] the account party sought to enjoin the issuer from paying drafts accompanied by invoices that contained an obvious error. The court held, however, that only fraud justifies an injunction, and thus it implicitly held that "erroneous" documents are not "fraudulent" documents.

In *Bossier Bank & Trust Co. v. Union Planters National Bank*,[181] the issuer dishonored the beneficiary's draft on the ground of fraud. The issuer argued that the beneficiary was going to use the funds for a purpose not contemplated by the underlying agreement. The court vigorously rejected the suggestion that it look to the underlying contract.

In *Werner v. A.L. Grootemaat & Sons, Inc.*,[182] the account party argued that the beneficiary was guilty of "equitable fraud"[183] in seeking payment under a standby credit. The credit was established to cover the beneficiary's loan commitment fee, and the account party argued that the beneficiary had denied the loan in bad faith and was compounding its misconduct by demanding payment under the credit. The court rejected so "broad a definition of the word 'fraud'"[184] which, it held, would render fraud a synonym for "breach of the underlying agreement."

In *New York Life Insurance Co. v. Hartford National Bank & Trust Co.*,[185] the Supreme Court of Connecticut held that only egregious fraud justifies dishonor under Section 5-114. In that case, the account party argued that the payment of the credit would amount to enforcement of a penalty under the contract between the account party and the beneficiary. To consider such an argument, the court held, would require it to consider the underlying agreement, of which the credit must be independent.

In a remarkable English case, the House of Lords refused to justify dishonor even though a document was admittedly false. In *United City Merchants (Investments) Ltd. v. Royal Bank of Canada*,[186] a loading broker falsified bills of lading by backdating them. The evidence showed that when the beneficiary presented the bills, it did not know they were false. The law lords ruled that such fraud on the part of the broker could

---

[180] 22 U.C.C. Rep. Serv. (Callaghan) 130 (N.Y. Sup. Ct. 1977).

[181] 550 F.2d 1077 (6th Cir. 1977).

[182] 80 Wis. 2d 513, 259 N.W.2d 310 (1977).

[183] Id. at 523, 259 N.W.2d at 315.

[184] Id.

[185] 173 Conn. 492, 378 A.2d 562 (1977).

[186] [1983] A.C. 168 (H.L.).

not prevent the beneficiary from obtaining payment under the credit.[187] *United City Merchants* is not consistent with the language of Section 5-114(2) and is probably not good authority in the United States.[188]

In *Tandy Brands, Inc. v. Master Marketing Association*,[189] the trial court enjoined the issuer from paying a letter of credit when the account party claimed that the beneficiary had failed to market, package, ship, and warehouse products as agreed in the underlying contract. The appellate court reversed, holding that the account party's allegations did not support the kind of fraud that Section 5-114(2) envisions.

In *Temtex Products, Inc. v. Capital Bank & Trust Co.*,[190] the account party complained that the beneficiary's documents were false. The credit, an invoice standby,[191] called for invoices accompanied by certificates that the invoices were due. The account party argued that because of setoffs, the invoices were not due. The *Temtex* court held that disputes over setoffs were not to be resolved in the letter of credit transaction and that the credit should be paid.[192]

In *Offshore Trading Co. v. Citizens National Bank*,[193] the issuer supported its dishonor by arguing that the assertion in the beneficiary's certificate that the account party was in default was not true. The court held that it was insufficient for the issuer to show that the certificate was untrue; it also was necessary for the issuer to show that the beneficiary knew that it was untrue.

In *FDIC v. Bank of San Francisco*,[194] the court accepted the account parties' argument that, when the credit was issued, the note referred to in the certificate that the beneficiary was to present to the issuer was a

---

[187] In the United States, such a beneficiary would have breached the warranties of Section 5-111(1). For discussion of the beneficiary's liability under that section, see ¶¶ 4.03[5][b], 6.07. For a discussion of fraud by a third party in the underlying transaction, see infra ¶ 7.04[4][b].

[188] It may be good authority in Canada, however. See Bank of N.S. v. Angelica-Whitewear Ltd., 36 D.L.R.4th 161 (Can. 1987). For criticism of the *United City Merchants* case on this point, see Goode, "Reflections on Letters of Credit—I," 1980 J. Bus. L. 291; Smith, "Irrevocable Letters of Credit and Third Party Fraud: The American Accord," 24 Va. J. Int'l L. 55 (1983).

[189] 481 So. 2d 925 (Fla. Dist. Ct. App. 1985).

[190] 623 F. Supp. 816 (M.D. La. 1985), aff'd mem., 788 F.2d 1563 (5th Cir. 1986).

[191] For an example copy of an invoice standby, see App. C, Doc. 18.

[192] For a setting similar to *Temtex*, in which the court did consider the underlying transaction, see discussion of *Roman Ceramics* infra ¶ 7.04[4][c]. For additional cases similar to *Temtex*, see authority cited infra note 254.

[193] 650 F. Supp. 1487 (D. Kan. 1987).

[194] 817 F.2d 1395 (9th Cir. 1987).

$50,000 promissory note to be signed by the account parties. In fact, the account parties never signed such a note, but the receiver presented the affidavit that referred to a note and recited that it was not paid. The FDIC pointed out that there was an unpaid note—the note of a syndicator that had used the account parties' credit as security for its loan. That note was in default, and the court held that the certificate was not fraudulent and could not support the issuer's refusal to honor the credit.[195]

In *Airline Reporting Corp. v. First National Bank*,[196] the credit secured payments made by a company that administered travel agency ticket sales. The credit called for a certificate from the beneficiary that it had paid for tickets sold by the account party agency. The agreement between the agency and the company stipulated that the agency would remain liable for tickets issued by its transferees until they were approved by the company. In the *Airline Reporting Corp.* case, the account party transferred its business, and the transferee failed to pay for tickets on which the beneficiary had made payments. When the beneficiary drew and certified that the account party had sold the tickets, the issuer dishonored on the ground that the certification was fraudulent. The court rejected the defense, holding that the issue was not one of determining whether the beneficiary had a legally enforceable right to draw on the credit but whether the draw was fraudulent. Finding that the beneficiary had not intended to defraud anyone, the court reversed the lower court's holding in favor of the issuer. Significantly, the *Airline Reporting Corp.* court adopted the rule established in injunction cases[197] in holding that only egregious fraud excuses an issuer's dishonor.

In *City National Bank v. First National Bank*,[198] the issuer complained of the falsity of a certificate reciting that a loan to Shadyridge was due. After looking to the facts of the underlying loan, the court concluded that the loan proceeds, although not made to Shadyridge, had been deposited in the account of Shadyridge and that the issuer had no defense to the beneficiary's demand for payment under the credit.[199]

---

[195] The court also held that any fraud of the original beneficiary would not bar the FDIC as receiver of the bank from recovering on the credit. Under the doctrine of D'Oench, Duhme & Co. v. FDIC, 315 U.S. 447 (1942), the FDIC enjoys greater rights in an instrument than those of the failed bank from which it takes the instrument.

[196] 832 F.2d 823 (4th Cir. 1987).

[197] For discussion of the fraud standard in injunction cases, see infra ¶ 7.04[4][d].

[198] 22 Ark. App. 5, 732 S.W.2d 489 (1987).

[199] For further discussion of the relationship between the underlying transaction and the credit transaction, see infra ¶ 7.04[4][b].

This strong line of authority demonstrates a remarkable degree of loyalty to the independence principle. By defining fraud as that relating to the documents in the credit transaction, courts can successfully pretermit inquiry into the underlying transaction and thus can avoid the danger that the credit will become dependent on that transaction and thereby lose its unique commercial usefulness.

[b] The Underlying Transaction

In a number of additional cases, courts have refused to delve into the agreement between the account party and the beneficiary in the face of imaginative arguments that they do so. *Sztejn* itself warned against using breach of warranty as a basis for a fraud claim and distinguished breach of warranty claims from "active fraud on the part of the seller."[200] The fraud in *Sztejn* was discernible without looking to the underlying transaction because the credit itself described the invoice and the bill of lading that, on their face, complied with the credit. The account party in *Sztejn* complained that the discrepancy was apparent from the credit, without reference to the underlying contract of purchase. The posture of the proceedings in *Sztejn*, moreover, made it unnecessary for the court to look to any extrinsic evidence.

Unlike most fraud cases, in *Sztejn* the plaintiff's request for an injunction was not at issue. The issue in *Sztejn* was whether the defendant's motion to dismiss the complaint should be allowed. In that posture, the court was required to accept as true the allegations of the complaint, including the allegation that the documents were fraudulent and that rubbish, not bristles, had been shipped. Thus, *Sztejn*, as the English judges are fond of noting,[201] involved "established" fraud, and it was not necessary to look to the underlying transaction to make that determination.

Since *Sztejn*, courts have broadened the fraud inquiry; but they remain, for the most part, reluctant to let the beneficiary's breach of the underlying transaction justify an injunction against payment under the credit. This reluctance is evident and is well articulated in *Philipp Brothers, Inc. v. Oil Country Specialists, Ltd.*[202] In that case, a standby credit served to secure a buyer's obligation to pay a restocking fee to a seller of

---

[200] Sztejn v. J. Henry Schroder Banking Corp., 177 Misc. 719, 722, 31 N.Y.S.2d 631, 635 (Sup. Ct. 1941).

[201] See, e.g., Edward Owen Eng'g Ltd. v. Barclays Bank Int'l Ltd., [1978] 1 All E.R. 976 (C.A.); Discount Records Ltd. v. Barclays Bank Ltd., [1975] 1 All E.R. 1071 (Ch.).

[202] 9 U.C.C. Rep. Serv. 2d (Callaghan) 201 (Tex. 1989) (per curiam).

oil field casing pipe in the event the buyer did not accept the pipe. When the buyer rejected the goods, it claimed that they were nonconforming and that the seller-beneficiary had breached the contract of sale and had no right to the restocking fee. The buyer also argued that when the seller drew on the credit, the draw was fraudulent, and that an injunction was proper. The Supreme Court of Texas rejected that argument, realizing that the account party was promoting breach of the underlying contract to fraud in the transaction. A court cannot enjoin payment of a credit, the court held, "merely upon a showing that the letter of credit beneficiary's actions excused the credit account party from its underlying contractual liability."[203] "Fraud claims," the court warned, "should not become surrogates for breach of contract claims."[204]

In *Foreign Venture Ltd. Partnership v. Chemical Bank*,[205] the court refused to consider the account party's argument that was based on the underlying transaction. In the *Foreign Venture* case, the credit secured debts of the account party's Australian subsidiary. The account party claimed that, under Australian law, the beneficiary was not entitled to the amounts demanded under the credit. The court rejected the idea that there was any fraud in this "rather subtle dispute."[206]

Similarly, in *Mid-States Mortgage Corp. v. National Bank*,[207] the issuer dishonored the beneficiary's drafts, claiming that they "were not presented for the same reason that the letters of credit had originally been issued."[208] The underlying transaction revealed that the credit was to cover closing costs under a loan that never closed. The credit, being clean, was not so conditioned. It was payable against the beneficiary's drafts. The court held that the bank had not made a case of fraud in the transaction.[209]

---

[203] Id. at 203.

[204] Id. at 203–204.

[205] 59 A.D.2d 352, 399 N.Y.S.2d 114 (1977).

[206] Id. at 356, 399 N.Y.S.2d at 116.

[207] 77 Mich. App. 651, 259 N.W.2d 175 (1977).

[208] Id. at 653, 259 N.W.2d at 176.

[209] Cf. Benetton Servs. Corp. v. Benedot, Inc., 551 So. 2d 295 (Ala. 1989) (ordering payment to beneficiary, even though beneficiary had shipped nonconforming merchandise in underlying transaction). In Universal Marine Ins. Co. v. Beacon Ins. Co., 581 F. Supp. 1131 (W.D.N.C. 1984), the court enjoined payment of a credit on the basis of evidence that the beneficiary knew when it drew on the credit that the funds would not be used as the parties originally had intended. The rule of *Universal Marine* clearly conflicts with the rule of the *Mid-States* and *Benedot* cases.

Mid-States relies in part on *West Virginia Housing Development Fund v. Sroka.*[210] That case involved a similar credit that did refer to the underlying project and recited that the credit related to working capital funds for that project. The reference and the recital notwithstanding, the court rejected the issuer's argument that there was fraud in the transaction when the beneficiary drew on the credit with the intention of using the funds for purposes other than working capital. The project had failed, and the beneficiary was using the credit proceeds to compensate itself for losses it sustained as a consequence of the failure. The *Sroka* court clearly understood the issuer's argument but rejected it on two grounds: First, the argument did not show facts constituting "common-law fraud," and, second, the credit was independent of the underlying project. "The court fails to see how any fraud can be involved in regard to matters that are collateral to the bank's obligations under the letter of credit."[211] The *Sroka* case displays strong support for reading the *Sztejn* rule of Section 5-114(2) as limited to fraud in the credit transaction. The *Sroka* decision also supports the view that the party asserting fraud must satisfy the common law elements of fraud.[212]

Recon Optical, Inc. v. Israel[213] illustrates the use of the narrow fraud rule to protect the parties' allocation of costs and risks. In that case, the account party sought to enjoin payment of a letter of credit on the ground that the beneficiary had no right under the transaction between the account party and the beneficiary to make the draw. The credit secured the return of advance payments made by the beneficiary under a contract with the account party for the development and manufacture of an aerial reconnaissance system. The account party argued that it was not in breach of the underlying transaction and that the beneficiary's draw was fraudulent. In rejecting the argument, the court emphasized that one of the purposes of the credit was to permit the beneficiary to recover its advance payments and hold them during the course of arbitration of the underlying contract dispute. Given that pur-

---

[210] 415 F. Supp. 1107 (W.D. Pa. 1976).

[211] Id. at 1114 (citation omitted).

[212] At common law, a party alleging fraud must prove that the defendant made a material misstatement of fact with intent to mislead, that the plaintiff justifiably relied on the statement, and that the plaintiff suffered damages as a consequence of such reliance. See generally W. Prosser, Handbook of the Law of Torts 685–686 (4th ed. 1971); see also Symons, supra note 146. But cf. Emery-Waterhouse Co. v. Rhode Island Hosp. Trust Nat'l Bank, 757 F.2d 399 (1st Cir. 1985) (containing dictum to effect that fraud defined in Section 5-114(2) may not be equivalent of common-law fraud).

[213] 816 F.2d 854 (2d Cir. 1987).

pose of the credit,[214] the court reasoned that it could not be fraudulent for the beneficiary to draw, even if the beneficiary rather than the account party was in breach and even though the credit called for the beneficiary's certification that the account party was in material breach of the underlying transaction.[215]

In *FDIC v. Bank of San Francisco*,[216] the account parties of a four-party credit argued that the beneficiary bank was privy to the fraud of

---

[214] For discussion of the function of credits, see ¶ 3.07.

[215] In Ground Air Transfer, Inc. v. Westates Airlines, Inc., 899 F.2d 1269 (1st Cir. 1990), the court refused to litigate, in an injunction action, the account party's claim that the beneficiary was not authorized to declare a default in the underlying transaction. After a summary recital of the facts in the underlying transaction, the court concluded that the beneficiary had a colorable argument that it could declare a default and therefore that the beneficiary would not be acting fraudulently when it presented the notice of default to the issuer under the credit. In Airline Reporting Corp. v. First Nat'l Bank, 832 F.2d 823 (4th Cir. 1987), the court found no fraud in a certificate reciting that the account party had sold airline tickets, when in fact the account party's transferee had sold them. In United Bank v. Citibank, N.A., No. 85 Civ. 5636 (CBM) (S.D.N.Y. Dec. 9, 1987), the court found no fraud in a certification that a buyer had not made payments on a contract, even though an arbitrator had decided that the buyer did not owe anything under the contract. In Clement v. FDIC, 2 U.C.C. Rep. Serv. 2d (Callaghan) 1017 (W.D. Okla. 1986), the FDIC complained that the credit beneficiaries had filed a false proof of claim in the insolvency proceedings and that the false claim should prevent them from recovering as beneficiaries of the credit. The court held that the beneficiaries had asserted in the claim that the sums were due, when in fact the notes the credit secured were not due, because the beneficiaries believed in good faith that they had to file such claims. The court concluded that the FDIC did not rely on the assertions and was not misled by them. In First Nat'l Bank v. Carmouche, 504 So. 2d 1153 (La. Ct. App.), rev'd on other grounds, 515 So. 2d 785 (La. 1987), the credit called for the signature of David J. Porter, secretary treasurer of Pac Oil. At the time he executed the certificate, Porter was a vice-president of Pac Oil, yet he signed as secretary treasurer. The court held that his certificate was not fraudulent and that his misidentification was only an attempt to comply with the terms of the credit. In Andy Marine, Inc. v. Zidell, Inc., 812 F.2d 534 (9th Cir. 1987), the credit called for a certificate of sums actually due the beneficiary for damages sustained by an ocean vessel. The beneficiary supplied a certificate, which, on its face, indicated that the sums were due. Although the court accepted the account party's claim that the figure in the certificate was not the amount due but an estimate of the amount to become due when the repairs were complete, the court held that because the beneficiary had a colorable claim to the sums, the certificate was not fraudulent. Cf. Clayton v. DRG Fin. Corp., No. 87-2637-S (D. Kan. May 16, 1988) (alleged fraud in underlying transaction, consisting of recklessly underestimating cost of rehabilitating housing, is not kind of fraud that justifies injunction); Union Export Co. v. N.I.B. Intermarket, A.B., No. 88-67-II (Tenn. Ct. App. July 27, 1988) (lower court finding that short delivery and improper labeling constituted fraud in transaction). For further discussion of cases that promote breach of warranty claims to fraud in the transaction, see supra ¶ 7.04[3][b].

[216] 817 F.2d 1395 (9th Cir. 1987).

syndicators that had borrowed on the strength of the credit. The syndicators had sold limited partnership interests to the account parties, who had paid for the interests with notes secured by the credit, but the credit had issued directly to the beneficiary bank that had taken the notes as security for the syndicators' loan. In the course of an opinion that upholds summary judgment in favor of the failed beneficiary's receiver, the Court of Appeals for the Ninth Circuit made a point of the fact that the fraud defense to payment under a credit can harm the credit device. With that potential harm in mind, the court cautioned that the defense must be crafted carefully and concluded that only fraud in the credit transaction—that is, fraud in the required documents, not fraud in the underlying transaction—would support a refusal of the issuer to pay the beneficiary or its receiver.[217]

There are a number of cases that contain language suggesting that courts should look for fraud in the underlying transaction. The facts and holdings of these cases, however, often do not support that language. When the *Werner* court[218] rejected the account party's argument that equitable fraud satisfies Section 5-114(2), the court's holding is true to the strong line of authority that refuses to inquire into the underlying transaction. In fact, the account party's "equitable fraud" argument was an invitation to weigh the equities in the underlying transaction. Such an inquiry, the court held, would equate the term "fraud in the transaction" with the term "breach of contract," and the court firmly rejected that equation. The *Werner* opinion goes on to say, however, that the court in *Baker v. National Boulevard Bank*[219] held that Section 5-114 requires "fraud in the formation of the underlying contract."[220] Such a rule, of course, is a direct challenge to the independence principle and to the strict view of Section 5-114(2) that courts should not look to the underlying facts. Indeed, the *Baker* opinion does contain that language, but *Baker* did not hold anything of the kind. *Baker* was a hearing on a motion to remand to the state court an action that had been removed to the federal court. The issue was jurisdictional, that is, whether realigning the parties according to their real interests would show federal diversity. The court's assertion that the only defense the issuer could assert

---

[217] For discussion of the court's holding on the fraud issue as so defined, see supra ¶ 7.04[4][a]. For additional authority holding squarely that fraud must be in the letter of credit transaction, see Northwestern Bank v. NCF Fin. Corp., 88 N.C. App. 614, 365 S.E.2d 14 (1988). Cf. Leslie v. Minson, 679 F. Supp. 280 (S.D.N.Y. 1988) (involving similar allegations of fraud which court rejected as failing to state claim under federal securities laws).

[218] For a discussion of the *Werner* case, see supra ¶ 7.04[4][a].

[219] 399 F. Supp. 1021 (N.D. Ill. 1975).

[220] Id. at 1024.

was fraud in the formation of the underlying contract is pure dictum. Unfortunately, other courts citing *Werner* have picked up the *Baker* dictum.

First Arlington National Bank v. Stathis[221] is a strong holding whose facts support the idea that the court should not look to the underlying transaction, but the language of the opinion gives a different impression. In *First Arlington*, the credit secured a promissory note and required the beneficiary to present the note and other documents. When the beneficiary demanded payment under the credit, some of the account parties argued that they were not liable on the note and that the beneficiary's presentation of it was therefore fraudulent. The court did not accept the argument and referred to the *Werner* opinion as authority for a narrow definition of "fraud." That reference to *Werner* included reference to the language in *Werner* concerning "fraud in the formation of the underlying contract."[222] The court found no such fraud and then applied the strict fraud rule of *Intraworld Industries, Inc. v. Girard Trust Bank*,[223] a leading case.[224] After finding that the fraud alleged did not satisfy the *Intraworld* test, the court held that the account party had not shown fraud in the transaction.

Close on the heels of *First Arlington* came another Illinois case, *Stringer Construction Co. v. American Insurance Co.*[225] In *Stringer*, the account party claimed that the beneficiary's demand for payment under the credit was fraudulent in that the account party had not breached the contract that the credit secured. The court denied the injunction, citing *First Arlington*'s rule that there must be "[f]raud in the factum or fraud in the formation of the underlying contract"[226] in order to satisfy Section 5-114(2).[227] *Stringer*, of course, is true to the independence principle in its holding; but it fails in its rhetoric.

---

[221] 90 Ill. App. 3d 802, 413 N.E.2d 1288 (1980).

[222] Id. at 811, 413 N.E.2d at 1295.

[223] 461 Pa. 343 336 A.2d 316 (1975).

[224] See infra ¶ 7.04[4][d].

[225] 102 Ill. App. 3d 919, 430 N.E.2d 1 (1981).

[226] Id. at 924, 430 N.E.2d at 5.

[227] The "fraud in the factum" language appears to come from Bossier Bank & Trust Co. v. Union Planters Nat'l Bank, 550 F.2d 1077, 1082 (6th Cir. 1977) (app. A). For a discussion of *Bossier*, see supra ¶ 7.04[4][a]. The *Bossier* court refused to consider the underlying contract. In Jupiter Orrington Corp. v. Zweifel, 127 Ill. App. 3d 559, 469 N.E.2d 590 (1984), the Illinois court followed the "fraud in the formation" rule and held that even if a certificate presented by the beneficiary is false, the credit must be paid. It is only fraud in the issuance of the credit itself, it seems, that will satisfy the *Jupiter Orrington* court.

In *Reid v. Plantation Sea Farms*,[228] the beneficiary of the credit was a bank that had lent funds to a party that allegedly had defrauded the account party. The *Reid* court held that the *Stringer* opinion supports a narrow reading of the "fraud in the transaction" language and that only fraud in the loan transaction would support an injunction against payment of the credit.[229]

Similarly, in *Banque Worms v. Banque Commerciale Privee*,[230] the court refused to look to a collateral agreement that it found to be twice removed from the credit transaction. In the *Banque Worms* case, the beneficiary had lent funds to the account party. The credit secured repayment of those loans. In addition, the issuer alleged that the beneficiary had been party to the account party's fraud on the issuer in connection with a separate series of conveyances. Even if the issuer could establish such fraud, the court held, it would not have shown the kind of fraud that justifies a refusal to honor the credit obligation.

There is, then, a group of cases—*Werner, First Arlington, Baker, Stringer, Reid,* and *Banque Worms*—whose language is sometimes contrary to the independence principle but whose holdings, to the extent they reach the question, lend it at least grudging support. These cases are representative.[231] The danger is that courts will follow the language of these cases but not their holdings.

In *Cromwell v. Commerce & Energy Bank*,[232] the court attempted to posit a distinction between the normal three-party credit and a four-party credit. Generally, the credit transaction involves only three parties: the account party, the issuer, and the beneficiary. In standby cases, however, there are often four. The *Cromwell* case illustrates a typical four-party credit. There the beneficiary of the credit had made loans to a limited partnership that pledged promissory notes due from the limited partners as security for the loan. The partners obtained the standby credits to secure the notes but caused the credits to issue not to the payee, the partnership, but to the lender holding the notes as security for the loan. The partnership defaulted on the loan, and the lender resorted to the notes. When the partners did not pay the notes, the lender drew on the standby credits. The partners then argued that the general part-

---

[228] No. 86 C 6648 (N.D. Ill. Sept. 30, 1986).

[229] For discussion of the fraud issue in four-party letter of credit transactions similar to that in the *Reid* case, see infra ¶ 7.04[4][b].

[230] 679 F. Supp. 1173 (S.D.N.Y. 1988), aff'd per curiam, 849 F.2d 787 (2d Cir. 1988).

[231] For additional authority, see cases cited supra notes 147, 148.

[232] 450 So. 2d 1 (La. Ct. App. 1984), aff'd in part, rev'd in part, 464 So. 2d 721 (La. 1985).

ner had practiced fraud on them and that such fraud in the underlying transaction should support an injunction against payment of the credit.

The *Cromwell* court disagreed, holding, first, that the language "fraud in the transaction" refers to the credit transaction and, second, that the case is distinguishable from those cases that use underlying transaction fraud to enjoin payment. The *Cromwell* opinion's distinction makes sense. It fashions a clear and principled limit for those courts that prefer the broad reading of Section 5-114(2). Under *Cromwell*, even courts that consider "fraud in the transaction" to include fraud in the underlying transaction generally may not look to that transaction if the credit involves four parties.[233]

In another somewhat disappointing line of cases, courts have professed to follow the independence principle but then have examined conduct in related transactions to determine the validity of a certificate or other document. *Itek Corp. v. First National Bank*[234] is a rather striking example. In *Itek*, the credits secured the beneficiary's obligations under first-demand guaranties. Under the credit, the beneficiary could draw if it certified that it had been required to pay under the guaranties. When the beneficiary made that certification, the account party challenged it as fraudulent. The *Itek* court acknowledged that the purpose of the letters of credit was to shift risks and responsibilities, and the court recognized that letter of credit litigation can upset the credit's purposes.

---

[233] See Alamo Sav. Ass'n v. Forward Constr. Corp., 746 S.W.2d 897 (Tex. Ct. App. 1988); cf. Reid v. Plantation Sea Farms, No. 86 C 6648 (N.D. Ill. Sept. 30, 1986) (following *Cromwell* distinction); Larson v. First Interstate Bank, 603 F. Supp. 467 (D. Ariz. 1983) (holding similar to *Cromwell*); Sipe v. First Nat'l Bank, 41 U.C.C. Rep. Serv. (Callaghan) 938 (S.D. Iowa 1985) (same); Brown v. United States Nat'l Bank, 220 Neb. 684, 371 N.W.2d 692 (1985) (same). The *Cromwell* holding does not insulate the lending bank in the event it participates in the syndicator's fraud or is guilty of fraud by its own separate conduct. After the *Cromwell* plaintiffs lost their bid for an injunction, the Louisiana court allowed them to maintain an action against the lending bank for fraud. See Cromwell v. Commerce & Energy Bank, 514 So. 2d 198 (La. Ct. App. 1987); see also Northwestern Bank v. NCF Fin. Corp., 88 N.C. App. 614, 365 S.E.2d 14 (1988) (holding that issuer that is induced to issue at fraud of account party has no defense against beneficiary that was unaware of fraud). For detailed discussion of the role of the lending bank in the four-party credit transaction, including its role as drafter of the credit terms and evaluator of the issuers' credit standing, see Schlifke v. Seafirst Corp., 866 F.2d 935 (7th Cir. 1989). In the event, of course, that the beneficiary of a four-party credit is aware of the fraud, its conduct in the credit transaction may constitute fraud that will justify an injunction against payment. See the discussion infra of the *Paccar* and *American National Bank* cases.

[234] 730 F.2d 19 (1st Cir. 1984).

The court held, nonetheless, that the draw was fraudulent and in doing so engaged in a lengthy analysis of terms in the underlying contract.[235]

Itek may well be a response to the strained relations between the United States and Iran,[236] but those strains do not justify the results in two other cases involving first-demand guaranties. In *American National Bank & Trust Co. v. Hamilton Industries, Inc.*,[237] the court enjoined payment of a credit on the ground that the beneficiary's certificate was false. The beneficiary was Paribas, a French bank[238] that had issued a guaranty to a Saudi corporation. The credit was payable against Paribas's certification that it had been called upon to pay under the guaranty. When Paribas drew on the credit, the account party objected that the certification was fraudulent.

In an interpleader action, the court held that Paribas could not compel payment, because the certificate was false. The court reached that conclusion, however, only after analyzing the first-demand guaranty and the efforts of the Saudi party to obtain payment under it. Because the court saw the Saudi demand as defective or late, the court concluded that Paribas had not been required to pay under the guaranty and that its certificate was false. On appeal,[239] the Court of Appeals for the Seventh Circuit reversed the summary judgment in the *American National Bank* case, but the opinion of the Seventh Circuit does not reflect any dissatisfaction with the lower court's interest in the guaranty. The Seventh Circuit held only that the record did not support the judgment against the beneficiary and remanded the case for a determination whether the beneficiary had paid the guaranty properly.

---

[235] The opinion interpreted a number of provisions and terms in the underlying contract, including the force majeure provision and the meaning of "causal," "on his opinion," and "clearance." In Foxboro Co. v. Arabian Am. Oil Co., 634 F. Supp. 1226 (D. Mass. 1986), the trial court considered the propriety of a demand under a simple-demand guaranty and engaged in much the same kind of analysis that the *Itek* court used. The trial court's opinion in *Foxboro* was replete with frequent references to and lengthy excerpts from the underlying transaction. The court made several findings as to the meaning of that contract. The trial court's opinion in *Foxboro* did not cite *Itek* or any other letter of credit cases. Significantly, the Court of Appeals for the First Circuit reversed the trial court in an opinion that read *Itek* narrowly. See Foxboro Co. v. Arabian Am. Oil Co., 805 F.2d 34 (1st Cir. 1986).

[236] See also Wyle v. Bank Melli, 577 F. Supp. 1148 (C.D. Cal. 1983) (similar case involving Iranian beneficiary). For discussion of the Iranian cases, see infra ¶ 7.04[4][e].

[237] 583 F. Supp. 164 (N.D. Ill. 1984), rev'd sub nom. Banque Paribas v. Hamilton Indus. Int'l, Inc., 767 F.2d 380 (7th Cir. 1985).

[238] The court reformed the credit to render Paribas the beneficiary. The credit referred to Paribas as the advising bank.

[239] Banque Paribas v. Hamilton Indus. Int'l, Inc., 767 F.2d 380 (7th Cir. 1985).

Slender evidence prompted the court in *Paccar International, Inc. v. Commercial Bank of Kuwait*[240] to enjoin payment of a credit. In *Paccar*, the credit secured the Bank of Kuwait's obligations under a first-demand guaranty. There was a "side agreement" between the beneficiary of the guaranty (IHI) and the account party of the credit (Paccar) that IHI would not draw on the guaranty unless IHI paid funds to a third party. It appears that IHI breached that side agreement and drew on the guaranty. The issuer of the guaranty, in turn, drew on the letter of credit. The *Paccar* court granted a preliminary injunction pending the outcome of an arbitration proceeding in Geneva. The court rested its ruling on evidence supplied by the account party suggesting that IHI could not have made payment to the third party and on the equivocal assertion of the beneficiary's officer that he had no knowledge of the side agreement. As a consequence of the *Paccar* ruling, the beneficiary of the credit had to await, without the funds, the results of the arbitration between the commercial parties—a result it presumably had sought to guard against when it bargained for the letter of credit.[241]

These cases, *Itek*, *American National Bank*, and *Paccar*, illustrate the way in which an account party can successfully litigate in the credit transaction issues that arise out of related agreements. That success spells trouble for credits and may hamper their commercial effectiveness severely.

It may be significant that, in *Foxboro Co. v. Arabian American Oil Co.*,[242] the Court of Appeals for the First Circuit read *Itek* narrowly. In *Foxboro*, the trial court had enjoined the beneficiary from drawing on the credit. The trial court reasoned that to permit payment would give the beneficiary an "unfair" advantage over the account party in their settlement negotiations.[243] The First Circuit reversed, holding that the obvious purpose of this standby credit was to give the account party an advantage in those negotiations. Applying the rule that an account party may obtain an injunction against payment only if it has no adequate remedy at law,[244] the court held that the account party could recover from the beneficiary either on the underlying contract or on a fraud

---

[240] 587 F. Supp. 783 (C.D. Cal. 1984), rev'd, 757 F.2d 1058 (9th Cir. 1985).

[241] The *Paccar* case was reversed on appeal on a jurisdictional ground. Paccar Int'l, Inc. v. Commercial Bank of Kuwait, 757 F.2d 1058 (9th Cir. 1985). For discussion of the purposes of a credit, see ¶ 3.07.

[242] 805 F.2d 34 (1st Cir. 1986).

[243] Foxboro Co. v. Arabian Am. Oil Co., 634 F. Supp. 1226 (D. Mass. 1986), rev'd, 805 F.2d 34 (1st Cir. 1986).

[244] For discussion of the equity prerequisites in the fraud context, see supra ¶ 7.04[1].

theory if the draw was not proper. The court rejected the account party's appeal to *Itek* as authority for the injunction. The result in *Itek*, said the court, was dictated by the Iranian upheaval and the inability of the account party to obtain damages from an Iranian court during the throes of the revolution.

A similar result on similar reasoning is evident in *American Export Group International Services., Inc. v. Salem M. AL-NISF Electric Co.*[245] In that case, the court also noted that the account party was a sophisticated business enterprise and that it could have negotiated different letter of credit terms in the underlying transaction.

Thus, *Foxboro* and *American Export Group* may reflect a retreat from the inclination evident in the *Itek* and *Paccar* line of authority permitting fraud claims to open the credit transaction.

[c]　Credit That Incorporates the Underlying Contract Explicitly

There is persuasive authority that references in the credit to the underlying transaction are surplusage unless the credit makes partial or complete performance of the underlying contract a condition of payment.[246] In most events, a reading of the credit as containing such a condition invites trouble. Such a reading so varies the primary function of the credit (i.e., prompt payment against documents) that at least one court has refused to apply letter of credit law to such an engagement, even though the parties called it a letter of credit.[247] Courts should be loath to read a credit as one calling for the court to wade into the underlying transaction. Some courts have done so, and it was the language of the credits that invited these departures from the independence principle. Analysis of the cases suggests that the courts may not have appreciated the significance of the broadening of the fraud exception they effected. In fact, these courts have read the credits in a way that renders them the functional equivalent of the performance bond.[248]

---

[245] 661 F. Supp. 759 (D.D.C. 1987).

[246] See, e.g., Andy Marine, Inc. v. Zidell, Inc., 812 F.2d 534 (9th Cir. 1987); Pringle-Associated Mortgage Corp. v. Southern Nat'l Bank, 571 F.2d 871 (5th Cir. 1978); Bossier Bank & Trust Co. v. Union Planters Nat'l Bank, 550 F.2d 1077 (6th Cir. 1977); Data Gen. Corp. v. Citizens Nat'l Bank, 30 U.C.C. Rep. Serv. (Callaghan) 1378 (D. Conn. 1980); First Nat'l Bank v. Carmouche, 504 So. 2d 1153 (La. Ct. App. 1987).

[247] See Wichita Eagle & Beacon Publishing Co. v. Pacific Nat'l Bank, 493 F.2d 1285 (9th Cir. 1974).

[248] For a discussion of the critical distinction between credits and performance bonds, see ¶¶ 1.05, 2.10[1].

There are at least two cases that deal directly with the question of fraud in the inducement in the underlying transaction. Both of them suggest that such fraud may constitute fraud in the transaction for the purposes of Section 5-114(2), yet both involve credits that, by their express terms, require documents from the beneficiary asserting liability on the underlying contract. The courts did not read the credits as just referring to the underlying contracts. Instead, they virtually incorporated the contracts by making liability under the contracts conditions of the credits.

In *O'Grady v. First Union National Bank*,[249] the credit required the beneficiary to present a copy "of each instrument causing this establishment of credit . . . to be called upon."[250] At first, the court rejected the idea that fraud in the inducement can ever constitute Section 5-114 fraud in the transaction. That fraud, the court held, must arise out of the credit transaction. The *O'Grady* opinion goes on to hold that if the account party was fraudulently induced into executing the documents that the beneficiary presented, and if the beneficiary knew of the fraud at the time the account party executed those documents, then the documents themselves would be fraudulent in the Section 5-114(2) sense. Thus, there is a suggestion in the *O'Grady* opinion that fraud in the inducement is the kind of fraud that gives rise to fraud in the transaction.

NMC Enterprises, Inc. v. CBS, Inc.[251] reaches a similar conclusion. In the *NMC* case, the account party sought to restrain the issuer from honoring and the beneficiary from presenting drafts under the credit. According to the account party's complaint, the beneficiary's officers had fraudulently induced the account party to enter into the underlying contract of sale. The account party claimed that the beneficiary had knowingly misrepresented the quality of the merchandise that was the subject of the contract. The court noted the probability of the account party's bankruptcy if the temporary injunction did not issue, concluded that such an injunction would not seriously affect the beneficiary, and granted relief. The beneficiary argued that the Section 5-114 "fraud in the transaction" defense refers to fraud in the credit documents, but the court felt that the *NMC* facts showed such fraud. The *NMC* credit called for a certificate reciting that the amount of the draft was due the beneficiary under the contract of sale. Thus, the court reasoned, any certificate making such a recital would be tainted with the fraud of that underlying transaction.[252]

[249] 296 N.C. 212, 250 S.E.2d 587 (1978).

[250] Id. at 229, 250 S.E.2d at 599.

[251] 14 U.C.C. Rep. Serv. (Callaghan) 1427 (N.Y. Sup. Ct. 1974).

[252] In a case similar to *NMC*, the Court of Appeals for the Eighth Circuit held that a beneficiary had presented a fraudulent draft. The court upheld dishonor of the credit, which improvidently called for a draft reciting the reasons for the draw. After

O'Grady and *NMC* arguably are not departures from the *Sztejn* requirement that the fraud lie in the credit transaction, not in the underlying transaction. In fact, *O'Grady* characterizes Section 5-114(2) as a codification of the *Sztejn* rule. In both *O'Grady* and *NMC*, the drafters of the credit incorporated the underlying transaction not by mere reference to it but by requiring the beneficiary to assert implicitly in *O'Grady* and explicitly in *NMC* that the account party was liable under the contract between the account party and the beneficiary. The courts concluded that the credits themselves turned on that liability, and it is clear in retrospect that the drafting of those credits may well have seduced the courts into looking to the underlying agreement.

Courts more mindful of the underlying transaction inquiry's corrosive effect on the credit might have withstood that seduction. The trouble with the *O'Grady* and *NMC* opinions is that they treat the legal conclusions in certificates of compliance under standby credits in the same way that they treat the factual assertions in bills of lading and invoices under commercial credits. It is true that the language of Section 5-114(2) does not differentiate between the two kinds of assertions, but there are three important reasons for treating the two differently.

First, standby credits were not important commercial devices when the Code was drafted; their advent on the commercial scene in significant numbers occurred after the Code's widespread adoption. It may be presumptuous to apply Section 5-114(2) to standby credits without some regard for the differences between "fact" documents and "legal conclusion" documents.

Second, standby credits often call for the beneficiary's certificate. These certificates can play a significant role in preventing an unauthorized draw under a credit, because beneficiaries are well advised to use caution in making any certification. If the certificate is erroneous, the beneficiary has breached its Section 5-111(1) warranties and has given the account party a clear cause of action against the beneficiary. The beneficiary's certificate plays an important role in the standby credit. It is not necessary to use it as a device to open the underlying transaction to inquiry, as the *O'Grady* and *NMC* cases did.

Third, full inquiry into the underlying transaction destroys the efficacy of the credit. The credit sometimes calls for the beneficiary's certi-

---

considering the underlying transaction, the court concluded that the beneficiary knew that the reasons stated were not true. See Bank of Newport v. First Nat'l Bank & Trust Co., 687 F.2d 1257 (8th Cir. 1982). For criticism of the *NMC* case, see Geva, supra note 145, at 290; Justice, "Letters of Credit: Expectations and Frustrations" (pt. 2), 94 Banking L.J. 493, 502 (1977). The Court of Appeals for the Second Circuit has termed *NMC* one of the "exceptional cases." Sperry Int'l Trade, Inc. v. Government of Isr., 670 F.2d 8, 12 (2d Cir. 1982).

fication of ultimate facts or conclusions of law, for example, that the sum demanded is due or that the account party has defaulted. These certificates are the most troublesome, and courts should weigh carefully the charge that they are fraudulent. Full evaluation of that charge requires inquiry into the underlying transaction, and that inquiry destroys the credit. In the *NMC* case, it elevated a breach of warranty claim to a fraud claim. It might be best for courts to refuse the inquiry as inconsistent with the nature of the credit device and leave the account party to its rights on the underlying contract or on the Section 5-111(1) warranties.[253]

Absent a provision in the credit rendering liability of the underlying agreement a condition of the credit, fraud in the inducement or fraud in the underlying transaction should not constitute fraud in the transaction for Section 5-114 purposes.[254] To hold otherwise would open an even more serious breach in the independence principle. The authorities are unanimous that a breach of warranty in the underlying contract of sale does not constitute fraud in the transaction.[255] Fraud in the inducement

---

[253] Courts may also find some significance in the fact that Section 5-117 provides an incentive for beneficiaries of standby credits to insist that the credit not be clean. Under Section 5-117(1), certain advantage accrues to the beneficiary of a credit that falls within the automatic scope rules of Sections 5-102(1)(a) and 5-102(1)(b). That advantage does not accrue to beneficiaries of the credit that fall under Section 5-102(1)(c). By insisting on a credit that calls for a draft and a certificate, the beneficiary is assured of the full advantage of Section 5-117. If this rather curious distinction in Section 5-117(1) is a reason that standby credits often call for certificates with general conclusions, courts may hesitate to give them a great deal of independent significance.

[254] For cases holding, as the *NMC* court did, that a reference in the certificate to the underlying transaction created a condition that had to be true, see Mitsui Mfrs. Bank v. Texas Commerce Bank, 159 Cal. App. 3d 1051, 206 Cal. Rptr. 218 (1984); Oil Country Specialists, Ltd. v. Philipp Bros., Inc., 762 S.W.2d 170 (Tex. Ct. App. 1988), rev'd, 9 U.C.C. Rep. Serv. 2d (Callaghan) 201 (Tex. 1989) (per curiam). Cf. Larson v. First Interstate Bank, 603 F. Supp. 467 (D. Ariz. 1983) (holding that if FDIC breached promise of failed bank to make loan, its certificate that it was entitled to call letter of credit was false and gave ground for injunction). Contra Banque Worms v. Banque Commerciale Privee, 679 F. Supp. 1173 (S.D.N.Y. 1988), aff'd per curiam, 849 F.2d 787 (2d Cir. 1988) (holding that general reference in credit to underlying transaction does not create additional condition for payment); Griffin Cos. v. First Nat'l Bank, 374 N.W.2d 768 (Minn. Ct. App. 1985) (similar case).

[255] Justice Shientag states the rule in the *Sztejn* opinion:
It would be a most unfortunate interference with business transactions if a bank before honoring drafts drawn upon it was obliged or even allowed to go behind the documents, at the request of the buyer, and enter into controversies between the buyer and the seller regarding the quality of the merchandise shipped.
Sztejn v. J. Henry Schroder Banking Corp., 177 Misc. 719, 721, 31 N.Y.S.2d 631, 633 (Sup. Ct. 1941).

is only a step from breach of warranty. In the *NMC* case, for example, the account party's (buyer's) complaint was that the beneficiary seller had warranted radio equipment at a continuous power output rating higher than the actual rating the equipment delivered—a complaint that sounds very much like breach of warranty. In any event, courts should take care that account parties do not use the *O'Grady* and *NMC* cases as an invitation to turn any breach of warranty dispute into a fraud in the inducement claim.

In *Sawyer v. E.A. Gralia Construction Co. (In re Pine Tree Electric Co.)*,[256] the credit not only referred to the underlying agreement (a construction contract) but was replete with provisions incorporating both the terms of the contract and the performance under it into the credit. The credit recited that it was "subject to all of the terms and provisions"[257] of the underlying contract, specifically stipulated that the credit engagement was subject to the account party's right to cure any defaults in the performance of the contract, and gave the account party the right to arbitrate disputes over that performance. The credit expired, by its own terms, ninety days after the account party's substantial completion of the contract. The beneficiary made its request for payment in the full amount of the credit, as the credit apparently required; but the beneficiary admitted that the account party's alleged defaults entitled it to less than the face amount of the credit. The "actual amount" owed, the court held, was a question to be decided after looking to the underlying contract, and the beneficiary's claim for the full amount constituted fraud. The court also found other allegations by the account party to satisfy the fraud requirement and render the credit subject to injunction. It found that the beneficiary had not given the account party the chance to cure the alleged defaults or to arbitrate the disputes and that more than ninety days had elapsed since the account party's substantial compliance.

The *Sawyer* credit met the Section 5-103(1) definition of "credit," but the engagement strays so far from the credit paradigm that one cannot fault the court for issuing the injunction. Even though the independence principle forbids inquiry into the account party's substantial performance and the cure and default questions, as well as into the amount of the beneficiary's contract damages, it is probably best to accept the *Wichita* requirement,[258] to hold that this engagement was not a credit, and to dispense with credit rules altogether. As in the *Wichita* case, the

---

[256] 16 Bankr. 105 (Bankr. D. Me. 1981).

[257] Sawyer v. E.A. Gralia Constr. Co. (In re Pine Tree Elec. Co.), 16 Bankr. 105, 106 (Bankr. D. Me. 1981).

[258] For discussion of the *Wichita* requirement, see ¶ 2.05.

Sawyer credit was too enmeshed with the underlying contract for credit law to govern it.[259]

In *Roman Ceramics Corp. v. Peoples National Bank*,[260] the credit called for a certificate that invoices were unpaid. The account party disputed the beneficiary's certification, and the court held, "after it had reviewed facts developed at an extensive trial and had answered some difficult questions of law,"[261] that the certificate was untrue and that therefore there was fraud in the documents and that the issuer justifiably had dishonored. The dissenting opinion pointed out that the approach adopted by the majority meant that issuers would "constantly be drawn into litigation in which the primary dispute is between the bene-

---

[259] In Trans Meridian Trading, Inc. v. Empresa Nacional De Comercializacion De Insumos, 829 F.2d 949 (9th Cir. 1987), the court held that as long as there is a genuine dispute in the underlying transaction, there is no fraud in drawing on the credit. In Sea Management Servs., Ltd. v. Club Sea, Inc., 512 So. 2d 1025 (Fla. Dist. Ct. App. 1987), the court held that a credit that terminated upon termination of the underlying charter party was payable on the beneficiary's certification that the charter party had not terminated, despite account party's assertion that the charter party had terminated. In Chiat/Day, Inc., v. Kalimian, Inc., 105 A.D.2d 94, 483 N.Y.S.2d 235 (1984), the credit called for a certificate by the beneficiary that the account party had defaulted on a real estate lease. When the beneficiary presented the certificate, the account party argued that it was not in default. The court, however, dissolved the injunction holding that the lease dispute was not one for the credit transaction. Similarly, in Jupiter Orrington Corp. v. Zweifel, 127 Ill. App. 3d 559, 469 N.E.2d 590 (1984), the court held that even if a certificate is false, the issuer should pay. In the court's opinion the account party should bear the risk of a false certificate. A beneficiary that was unsure which invoices were unpaid was entitled to payment in Audio Sys., Inc. v. First Nat'l Bank, 753 S.W.2d 553 (Ky. Ct. App. 1988). The beneficiary in the *Audio Systems* case was certain that the sums were due, and the court held that there was no fraud in selecting invoices arbitrarily and presenting them to the issuer. In Artoc Bank & Trust, Ltd. v. Sun Marine Terminals, Inc., 760 S.W.2d 311 (Tex. Ct. App. 1988), however, a beneficiary that presented documents that the court found to be untrue was held liable under the warranty provision of Section 5-111(1). In Atlas Mini Storage, Inc. v. First Interstate Bank, 426 N.W.2d 686 (Iowa Ct. App. 1988), the court confronted a similar invoice problem and held that injunctive relief was proper. Cf. First Nat'l Bank v. Carmouche, 515 So. 2d 785 (La. 1987) (holding that issuer may pay beneficiary, even though beneficiary is uncertain that certification is accurate); Penn State Constr., Inc. v. Cambria Sav. & Loan Ass'n, 360 Pa. Super. 145, 519 A.2d 1034 (1987) (holding that claim of beneficiary's bad faith and fraud in procurement of letter of credit was not ground for enjoining beneficiary's draw under credit); see also Recon Optical, Inc. v. Israel, 816 F.2d 854 (2d Cir. 1987) (holding that even though beneficiary's certification that account party is in breach of underlying transaction is erroneous, there are no grounds for injunction); Clement v. FDIC, 2 U.C.C. Rep. Serv. 2d (Callaghan) 1017 (W.D. Okla. 1986) (same). For additional authority of a similar nature, see supra ¶ 7.04[4][a].

[260] 714 F.2d 1207 (3d Cir. 1983).

[261] Id. at 1218 (Adams, J., dissenting).

ficiary and the disappointed customer who already has an adequate remedy at law in a breach of warranty action."[262]

These cases reflect a line of authority that—unconsciously, perhaps—promotes breach of the underlying contract to fraud in the transaction, thereby weakening the credit considerably. In effect, these decisions imperil the credit as a commercial device. They have rendered "[f]raud claims . . . surrogates for breach of contract claims."[263]

[d] Plaintiff's Burden: A Limit on the Fraud Defense

In retrospect, one might say that beneficiaries should avoid a credit, such as that in *O'Grady*, conditioned on receipt of a copy of each document causing the credit "to be called upon."[264] That language does not supply the precision that a well-drafted credit should provide. The condition of the *NMC* credit, however, was quite precise: a certificate reciting that the amount of the draft was due the beneficiary under the sales agreement. Such a provision is common, but the careful drafter may want to forgo it in view of the rule of *O'Grady* and *NMC* and its effect of inviting the court to violate the independence principle and to delve into the underlying contract. Many credits similar to that in *NMC* provide instead that the beneficiary certify that it has invoiced the account party and that the invoice is unpaid, or to certify that the beneficiary has made demand on the account party who has not honored the demand. Conditions such as these do not invite the court to look to the underlying agreement; and they may preserve the independence of the credit.

It cannot be denied that in some cases, especially in standby credit cases, the account party's claim of fraud often opens the credit transaction to inquiry. The law cannot ignore a charge as serious as fraud. Section 5-114(2) properly permits courts to enjoin payment of credits when such fraud arises in the credit transaction. The trouble is that, by requesting the court to consider the issue, the account party's charge of fraud interrupts the credit transaction and destroys many of the credit's attractive commercial features. The credit is designed to achieve, above all, celerity and certainty. The fraud inquiry diminishes both.

---

[262] Id. For discussion of the warranty cause of action, see ¶¶ 6.07, 9.04.

[263] Philipp Bros., Inc. v. Oil Country Specialists, Ltd., 9 U.C.C. Rep. Serv. 2d (Callaghan) 201, 203–204 (Tex. 1989) (per curiam). For discussion of the *Philipp Brothers* case, see supra ¶ 7.04[4][b].

[264] O'Grady v. First Union Nat'l Bank, 296 N.C. 212, 229, 250 S.E.2d 587, 599 (1978).

Courts could deal with the issue of fraud by imposing severe sanctions against parties that raise the fraud question without good cause. There are grounds for such a response,[265] but it is remarkable that courts resort to such sanctions rarely. To some extent, court rules and statutes shorten the delay by establishing prompt procedural mechanisms for injunction matters. These efforts notwithstanding, there remains the danger that the account party's charge of fraud will result in a full-blown trial in the credit transaction of the ultimate dispute between the account party and the beneficiary—the very result that the independence principle is designed to avoid. In every case, there will be delay, and, because of the delay, the credit's efficiency will suffer.

Two leading cases confront the problem squarely and suggest that one way to deal with it is to impose a heavy burden of proof on the account party asserting fraud. That burden requires the account party to show that the beneficiary has no colorable claim to support his presentation. These courts refuse to engage in a full inquiry at the credit transaction level. They render the inquiry preliminary. Analysis of the cases also reveals that careful drafting may avoid the problem.

The first case is *Intraworld Industries, Inc. v. Girard Trust Bank*,[266] in which the credit was designed to secure payments under the lease of a hotel in Switzerland. The credit called for a draft, a receipt for the sum drawn, and a certificate to the effect that the drawer had not received the rent due under the lease within ten days after the rent was payable. By referring to lease payments that were due, the credit suggested that the court determine the truth of the assertion that the rent was due and payable—a determination that required the court to look at the lease transaction. When the account party claimed that the certificate was fraudulent, the court was faced with the possibility of having to make that inquiry. In fact, the account party did fail to make the rent payment, and, when the beneficiary presented the required documents, the account party asserted that there was fraud in the transaction. Significantly, the account party argued that the rent was not due, because the beneficiary had canceled the lease and because the beneficiary was not seeking rent but was trying to enforce the credit as a liquidated damages provision. The account party clearly was asserting that the certificate it-

---

[265] Cf. Bank of Canton, Ltd. v. Republic Nat'l Bank, 636 F.2d 30 (2d Cir. 1980) (awarding damages to appellee because of issuer's frivolous appeal); Les Mutuelles du Mans Vie v. Life Assurance Co., 128 F.R.D. 233, 241 (N.D. Ill. 1989) (allowing Fed. R. Civ. P. 11 sanctions against plaintiff, whose complaint for injunction against draws on letters of credit "ignored applicable law" and sought "to override the fundamental nature of letters of credit as an arm's-length allocation of risk distribution").

[266] 461 Pa. 343, 336 A.2d 316 (1975).

self was fraudulent and was claiming that the fraud arose not in the underlying transaction but in the credit transaction.

The Supreme Court of Pennsylvania, which decided the *Intraworld* case, was well aware of the independence principle and noted that "[t]he great utility of letters of credit flows from the independence of the issuer-bank's engagement from the underlying contract between beneficiary and customer."[267] The court felt, however, that it could not ignore the charge that there was fraud in the credit transaction. The account party was claiming that the allegations in the certificate were false. In short, the account party brought its claim within the scope of the *Sztejn* definition of "fraud in the transaction" as meaning fraud in the credit transaction.

The *Intraworld* court was reluctant to delay payment by a lengthy trial of the lease dispute. On May 21, 1974, when it received the beneficiary's draft and accompanying documents, the issuer had informed the account party that it intended to honor the draft. The account party sued for preliminary and permanent injunctions restraining the bank. The trial court issued the preliminary injunction and held a hearing on May 30 and May 31 of that same year. On July 11, it denied the permanent injunction. The account party appealed to the Supreme Court of Pennsylvania, which affirmed the trial court on April 17, 1975. No one can complain of a court system that responds as promptly as the Pennsylvania courts did here; but, even so, it took eleven months to achieve payment of a draft that should have been paid within a period of days.[268]

The *Intraworld* court was obviously conscious of the need to fashion a rule in such cases that would shorten the inquiry. In answer to the account party's fraud claims, the court noted that neither it nor the trial court could determine the beneficiary's actual entitlement to payment under the lease. Rather, the court engaged in a threshold inquiry of finding whether the beneficiary "has no bona fide claim to payment or that the documents presented to [the issuer] have absolutely no basis in fact."[269] Finding that the account party had failed to satisfy this heavy burden, the court denied the injunction.

---

[267] Id. at 357, 336 A.2d at 323.

[268] Section 5-112(1) imposes a three-day time limit, and the assertion in the text assumes that the Code's time provision is preempted by the Uniform Customs' "reasonable time" rule of Article 16(c). The *Intraworld* credit was subject to the Uniform Customs. For a general discussion of this conflict between the Code and the Uniform Customs, see ¶ 4.06[2][b].

[269] Intraworld Indus. Inc. v. Girard Trust Bank, 461 Pa. 343, 361, 336 A.2d 316, 325 (1975).

In part, the *Intraworld* decision relies on a trial court opinion in *Dynamics Corp. v. Citizens & Southern National Bank*.[270] In *Dynamics*, the court issued a preliminary injunction against the issuer. The credit called for drafts and a certificate to the effect that the account party had failed to fulfill certain obligations under the agreement between the account party and the beneficiary. Again, the problem arose because the credit referred to performance under the contract between the account party and the beneficiary. That underlying contract was for the supply of communications equipment and technical assistance. The credit was the reverse of the typical commercial credit. It ran to the benefit of the buyer, not the seller, and secured the return in the event of default of payments made to the seller. International events led the U.S. government to prohibit the shipment of such equipment at a time when the seller had shipped some of the equipment, but not all of it, and when one payment had been made on the buyer's account. The account party sought a temporary restraining order against the issuer, enjoining payment under the credit. The court entered the restraining order, even though, at that time, the beneficiary had not submitted any drafts under the credit. Thereafter the beneficiary did submit a draft and the required certificate.

The account party, arguing that the beneficiary's certificate was fraudulent in asserting that the account party had not performed, was asking the court for an opportunity to litigate the sales contract question. The court refused to take the bait and held that the only dispute properly before the court was that arising out of the letter of credit, not that arising out of the contract of sale. The court held that whether the certificate was fraudulent was a matter to be decided at trial, but that even then the trial court could not render an ultimate decision on the contract dispute. "Rather, the court views its task in this case as merely guaranteeing that [the beneficiary] not be allowed to take unconscientious advantage of the situation and run off with the plaintiff's money on a pro forma declaration which has absolutely no basis in fact."[271]

In *Intraworld* and *Dynamics*, the courts felt themselves forced by the unfortunate language of the credits to look at disputes arising out of the underlying transaction. They refused to adjudicate those disputed fully and required the account party to show that the beneficiary had no basis in fact to make the assertion called for by the credit.[272]

---

[270] 356 F. Supp. 991 (N.D. Ga. 1973).

[271] Id. at 999. Professor Ellinger paraphrases the rule as one permitting an injunction when "the beneficiary acts without any shred of honest belief in his rights." Ellinger, "Fraud in Documentary Credit Transactions," 1981 J. Bus. L. 258, 262.

[272] In GATX Leasing Corp. v. DBM Drilling Corp., 657 S.W.2d 178 (Tex. Ct. App. 1983), the credit called for the beneficiary's certificate that a partner had breached the terms of a security agreement. When the beneficiary presented that cer-

It is worth digressing momentarily to consider here the response of English courts to the same fraud issues that are plaguing the credit in U.S. courts. The English courts also have fashioned tough hurdles for the account party that seeks an injunction. In a series of cases, the courts have denied injunctions unless the evidence of fraud was "established"[273] or "obvious"[274] and even when the account party had made out a strong prima facie case of fraud.[275] One court held that the fraud exception arises only when fraud is the only realistic inference to be drawn from the beneficiary's conduct.[276]

Perhaps the most generous view of fraud in a reported English case is that adopted by the Court of Appeal in *Bolivinter Oil S.A. v. Chase Manhattan Bank*.[277] There the court held that payment may be enjoined when the bank issuer knows that the documents are forged or that the request for payment is made fraudulently. The fraud must be "clear,"[278] in the view of the *Bolivinter* court. Significantly, after reviewing the evidence, the *Bolivinter* court declined to enjoin payment. While the court accepted that the account party had demonstrated that the beneficiary's draw was in violation of the underlying contract, the account party had not demonstrated that the draw was fraudulent.[279] That holding is sig-

---

tification, the account party argued that the debt covered by the security agreement had been extinguished and that therefore the security agreement had expired. The *GATX Leasing* court saw the dispute as one involving something less than the fraud that the *Intraworld* case demands. Accordingly, the court dissolved the trial court's injunction. In United States v. Mercantile Nat'l Bank, 795 F.2d 492 (5th Cir. 1986), the court, applying Texas law, held that the only fraud that justifies dishonor by the issuer is fraud that "consists of nothing less than a conscious and egregious decision to deceive another." Id. at 495. The court reversed a holding that absolved a dishonoring issuer that rested its dishonor on a dispute in the meaning of the underlying transaction.

[273] R.D. Harbottle (Mercantile) Ltd. v. National Westminster Bank Ltd., [1977] 2 All E.R. 862, 870 (Q.B.); Discount Records Ltd. v. Barclays Bank Ltd., [1975] 1 All E.R. 1071, 1074 (Ch.).

[274] Edward Owen Eng'g Ltd. v. Barclays Bank Int'l Ltd., [1978] 1 All E.R. 976 (C.A.).

[275] Howe Richardson Scale Co. v. Polimex-Cekop, [1978] 1 Lloyd's Rep. 161 (C.A.).

[276] United Trading Corp. v. Allied Arab Bank Ltd., [1985] 2 Lloyd's Rep. 554 (C.A.). The same court acknowledged that the burden of proof under the English fraud rule is so difficult to satisfy that no one has been able to obtain an injunction.

[277] [1984] 1 Lloyd's Rep. 251 (C.A.).

[278] Id. at 255; accord United City Merchants (Invs.) Ltd. v. Royal Bank of Can., [1983] A.C. 168 (H.L.).

[279] The credit in *Bolivinter* was issued as a backup for a performance guaranty issued by the beneficiary of the credit. The references to the draw in this discussion telescopes the transaction. In fact, the alleged fraud occurred in the draw on the guar-

nificant in view of the fact that the account party was arguing that, because the beneficiary and the account party had agreed to a settlement under which the beneficiary had agreed to cancel the credit, any draw must perforce be fraudulent.[280]

The English record, then, appears to be similar to that of the U.S., but with a markedly higher hurdle for the account party that seeks injunctive relief.

[e] Iranian Cases

[i] **Strict cases.** The analysis of the *Intraworld* and *Dynamics* cases is helpful in explaining several decisions involving standby credit disputes that arose out of the U.S.-Iranian political problems of 1979. It is the practice of economically strong buyers, especially government buyers dealing with economically weaker sellers, to insist on performance guaranties when they enter into supply contracts. In the Iranian cases, the American sellers induced Iranian banks to issue those guaranties by having a domestic bank issue a standby credit in favor of the Iranian bank. Generally, the standby credit would call for the Iranian bank's draft and a certificate to the effect that it had been required to honor its guaranty. When the Iranian revolution interrupted commerce between the United States and Iran, sellers became anxious about these standby credits. Political and diplomatic turmoil prevented performance of the underlying agreements, and the Iranian political and financial structure appeared to be in the hands of persons who did not inspire the confidence that their counterparts in Amsterdam, London, and Tokyo inspired. The sellers resorted to the courts.

Some of the cases lent themselves to resolution on the ground that the account parties had not satisfied the equity prerequisites for injunctive relief. In *KMW International v. Chase Manhattan Bank, N.A.*,[281] for example, the account party sought an injunction, alleging that the Iranian buyer had breached the contract of sale and that any draw on the credit would be fraudulent. There had been no draw, however, and the court held that no injunction against payment should issue. The plain-

---

anty; and the account party was attempting to enjoin payment to the guaranty issuer. For further discussion of four-party credit transactions such as this one, see supra ¶ 7.04[4][b]. For the argument that performance guaranties are subject to letter of credit rules, see ¶ 2.03.

[280] For the argument that the English courts insist on established fraud or compelling fraud before they will enjoin payment, see Goode, "Reflections on Letters of Credit—I," 1980 J. Bus. L. 291. Cf. Lawson, "Performance Bonds—Irrevocable Obligations," 1987 J. Bus. L. 259 (lamenting strictness of English rule).

[281] 606 F.2d 10 (2d Cir. 1979).

tiff's claim for damages was too speculative and too conjectural to satisfy the rules of equity. The court did, however, order the issuer to give the account party three days' notice before honoring any demand.

In *United Technologies Corp. v. Citibank, N.A.*,[282] the account party alleged that it had performed the contract of sale and that any demand under the credit would be wrongful. The court denied the injunction, holding that the account party had an adequate remedy at law in the event a draft was fraudulent.

In *American Bell International Inc. v. Islamic Republic of Iran*,[283] the account party claimed that the Iranian buyer had breached the contract of sale and alleged further that the beneficiary's demand, which the issuer had received, was not timely. The court refused to grant the injunction. In response to the account party's argument that the demand was not timely, the court noted that if, in fact, the issuer honored a late demand, the account party would have an adequate remedy at law—a suit for money damages against the issuer.

In *Werner Lehara International, Inc. v. Harris Trust & Savings Bank*,[284] the court held that the plaintiff, who was seeking injunctive relief before the beneficiary made any demand, did not satisfy the equity prerequisites and had not made out a case of fraud.

It is also significant, perhaps, that, in the *Werner Lehara, KMW*, and *American Bell* cases, the courts weighed against the account party the fact that an injunction might affect the banking relationships of the issuer adversely. It is clear that the issuers in these cases were nervous about the effect the injunctions would have in general on the reputation of credits issued by American banks and by the implicit threat of retaliation from the Iranian government or from Iranian banks. In *United Technologies*, the court explicitly found such eventualities too speculative to be considered.

The *Werner Lehara, KMW*, and *American Bell* cases reject firmly the account party's argument that the demands of the Iranian beneficiaries were, or would be, fraudulent. Those courts viewed the contests as contract disputes, the risks of which the account parties should have foreseen when they entered into the sales contract. The courts refused to let the account parties shift to the banks or to the letter of credit industry in general a contract risk that inheres in international sales, a risk of political upheaval.

The conclusion of these cases that there was no fraud in the transaction sufficient to invoke the rule of Section 5-114(2) is consistent with

---

[282] 469 F. Supp. 473 (S.D.N.Y. 1979).
[283] 474 F. Supp. 420 (S.D.N.Y. 1979).
[284] 484 F. Supp. 65 (W.D. Mich. 1980).

the general rule. It may be that the beneficiaries of the guaranties issued by the Iranian banks were guilty of fraud when those beneficiaries required the Iranian banks to pay under the guaranties.[285] The plaintiff's allegations suggest as much. Fraud in that guaranty transaction is not fraud in the letter of credit transaction, as the *Sztejn* rule requires. The certificates required in the *KMW* and *American Bell* cases, moreover, did not invite the courts to look into that related contract, as the *NMC* and *O'Grady* cases did.[286] The Iranian certificates recited only that the beneficiary was called upon to pay under the letter of guaranty. These carefully drawn credits did not pierce the barrier that insulates the credit from the underlying transaction and did not force the court to look at that underlying transaction.

While a significant number of courts dealing with standby credits issued to Iranian beneficiaries granted notice injunctions requiring the issuer to delay honoring a credit for a short period of time,[287] the more significant cases are those such as *KMW, American Bell*, and *United Technologies*. The latter cases demonstrate the obstacles facing an account party once the demand arrives and show a marked willingness to enforce the equity prerequisites and a marked unwillingness to relax the strict fraud rule[288] of *Sztejn* or to reallocate the commercial and political

---

[285] The *Werner Lehara* credit ran directly to a government trading company, not to a bank as in the other cases.

[286] For discussion of these cases, see supra ¶ 7.04[4][c].

[287] The practice of issuing "notice" injunctions was a common response by courts that heard a petition by the account party prior to the time any demand for payment was made under the credit. In addition to the *KMW* case, see American Bell Int'l, Inc. v. Islamic Republic of Iran, 474 F. Supp. 420 (S.D.N.Y. 1979); Stromberg-Carlson Corp. v. Bank Melli Iran, 467 F. Supp. 530 (S.D.N.Y. 1979). For additional unreported cases, see Weisz & Blackman, supra note 166; Harvard Note, supra note 123; Comment, "'Fraud in the Transaction': Enjoining Letters of Credit During the Iranian Revolution," 93 Harv. L. Rev. 992 (1980).

[288] Thus, two practitioners who describe themselves as lawyers for account parties, having reviewed the Iranian cases, call for significant changes in the fraud rules. See Weisz & Blackman, supra note 166. To some extent, American political response to the Iranian revolution interrupted the operation of letter of credit law. In November 1979 and in February 1981, the president issued executive orders, first freezing Iranian assets and then directing all claims to these assets to the international arbitration tribunal established under the American-Iranian Hostage Agreement. See Exec. Order No. 12,170, 44 Fed. Reg. 65,729 (Nov. 14, 1979); Exec. Order No. 12,294, 46 Fed. Reg. 14,111 (Feb. 24, 1981). In Itek Corp. v. First Nat'l Bank, 730 F.2d 19 (1st Cir. 1984), the account party of a credit issued to an Iranian beneficiary sought to enjoin payment of the credit. The beneficiary argued that the account party had an adequate remedy under the U.S.-Iranian Hostage Agreement and could not have equitable relief. The court held that the Hostage Agreement was not an adequate remedy. The account party had not filed its claim under the agreement before the deadline and was correct in concluding that its claim was not covered by the

risks that these merchant sellers must now shoulder under letter of credit law.

[ii] Less-strict cases. Adherence to the strict *Sztejn* rule was not unanimous. In *Itek Corp. v. First National Bank*,[289] the defendant bank issued a standby credit to an Iranian bank, which, in turn, issued a guarantee to the Iranian Ministry of War. The account party had agreed to sell optical equipment to the Iranian government, and the sales contract contained a force majeure clause permitting either party to cancel the contract before performance under it was complete. The U.S. Department of State revoked the account party's export license, and the account party notified Iran of its election to terminate the contract under the force majeure clause. Subsequently, the account party obtained a temporary restraining order against the issuer, and, when the beneficiary presented a conforming demand under the credit, the court enjoined payment.

The *Itek* court held that, because the account party's suit against the Iranian government would be futile, irreparable injury was evident. With respect to the fraud question, the court held that Section 5-114(2) establishes an exception to the independence principle; but the court also held that it was not necessary to probe the question of whether the fraud would be in the credit transaction or in the underlying transaction. The *Itek* court found the fraud so "blatant" and "undisputed" that it issued the restraining order.[290] In a later appeal,[291] the Court of Appeals for the First Circuit affirmed the injunction in an opinion that goes to great lengths to interpret the underlying contract.[292]

Agreement. In Rockwell Int'l Sys., Inc. v. Citibank, N.A., 719 F.2d 583 (2d Cir. 1983), the court held that an action for a preliminary injunction is not barred by the Iranian Assets Control Regulations. See 31 C.F.R. §§ 535.101–535.905 (1989). For a general discussion of the Regulations and their effect on credit litigation, see Effros, "Current Legal Matters Affecting Central Banks," 123 Ga. J. Int'l & Comp. L. 621 (1983); Zimmett, "Standby Letters of Credit in the Iran Litigation: Two Hundred Problems in Search of a Solution," 16 Law & Pol'y Int'l Bus. 927 (1984).

[289] 611 F. Supp. 1341 (D. Mass. 1981).

[290] Id. at 1350 n.19. Later the district court made the injunction permanent. On appeal, the Court of Appeals for the First Circuit vacated the permanent injunction on the ground that it violated the Iranian Assets Control Regulations. Itek Corp. v. First Nat'l Bank, 704 F.2d 1 (1st Cir. 1983).

[291] Itek Corp. v. First Nat'l Bank, 730 F.2d 19 (1st Cir. 1984).

[292] For further discussion of the First Circuit's opinion in *Itek*, see supra ¶ 7.04[4][b]. See also Wyle v. Bank Melli, 577 F. Supp. 1148 (N.D. Cal. 1983) (granting injunction against payment of similar credit issued in favor of Iranian beneficiary).

A similar disposition to find fraud was evident in *Touche Ross & Co. v. Manufacturers Hanover Trust Co.*,[293] where the credit ran to the benefit of an Iranian bank that had issued a letter of guaranty to the Iranian Ministry of War. The underlying contract contained a force majeure clause and stipulated that, upon invocation of the clause, all letters of guaranty would terminate. The account party invoked the force majeure clause, and the court concluded, therefore, that there could be no legitimate call on the letter of credit. In short, the *Touche Ross* court resolved the underlying contract questions, concluded that the equities were with the account party, and issued the injunction.

The unlikelihood of recovery under the Iranian court system influenced the court in *Harris Corp. v. National Iranian Radio & Television*.[294] In that case, the court rejected the argument that the account party was attempting to reallocate the risks. The court acknowledged that the purpose of the credit was to permit the Iranian buyer to recover its down payment, but the court refused to accept the view that the account party should bear the risk of a fraudulent demand. To the issuer's argument that the account party could have protected itself by negotiating different terms, the court responded vaguely that such an argument ignores "the realities of the drafting of commercial documents."[295]

The *Harris Corp.* case rejects the view that the letter of credit used in Middle Eastern transactions reflects the bargaining strength of the Middle Eastern buyer and is a device with a purpose of permitting the buyer to recover its down payment.[296] If the *Harris Corp.* case were accepted as the majority rule, such buyers could avoid its effect in a number of ways. They could refuse to accept credits issued by American banks (as Iranian buyers have apparently done)[297]; they could refuse to make a down payment; or they could insist that the down payment be

---

[293] 107 Misc. 2d 438, 434 N.Y.S.2d 575 (Sup. Ct. 1980), modified, 185 N.Y.L.J. 11 (May 5, 1981).

[294] 691 F.2d 1344 (11th Cir. 1982); cf. Rockwell Int'l Sys., Inc. v. Citibank, N.A., 719 F.2d 583 (2d Cir. 1983) (holding that pattern of Iranian calls on standby letters of credit issued for account of American defense contractors and others amounted to attempt to reap benefit of guaranty after causing contract to terminate and that such conduct constituted fraud in transaction); Nadler v. Mei Loong Corp., 177 Misc. 263, 30 N.Y.S.2d 323 (Sup. Ct. 1941) (holding that, because of extraordinary times, i.e., war with Japan, account party could not obtain relief and injunction should issue).

[295] 691 F.2d 1344, 1358.

[296] See Note, "A Reconsideration of American Bell International v. Islamic Republic of Iran, 474 F. Supp. 420 (S.D.N.Y. 1979)," 19 Colum. J. Transnat'l L. 301, 329 (1981).

[297] See Weisz & Blackman, supra note 166, at 361 n.25.

held by the Middle Eastern bank that issues the guaranty letter. Although the account party in the *Harris Corp.* case might find solace in the result, it is doubtful that American sellers in general will be pleased by these attempts by strong buyers to avoid the *Harris Corp.* rule.[298]

[f] Suits Against the Beneficiary

It is necessary to digress here from consideration of the issuer-beneficiary relationship in order to consider suits for injunction brought by the account party against not the issuer but the beneficiary. This digression suggests that the independence principle and the strict fraud rule should apply to these suits as well as to those where the account party sues the issuer. The statutory support for that position is not clear. Section 5-114(2)(b) speaks of injunctions against issuers and does not address the case where the account party seeks not to enjoin the issuer from payment but to enjoin the beneficiary from presenting the documents with a demand for payment.

In *Steinmeyer v. Warner Consolidated Corp.*,[299] the court held that Section 5-114(2) does not apply to such suits. The *Steinmeyer* plaintiff was an account party who caused the credit to issue in favor of parties who held his promissory notes. Under one of these notes, the account party had certain rights of setoff, but the credit did not refer to these rights. The account party, in order to protect his setoff, sought to enjoin the beneficiaries from demanding payment under the credit. The court held that Section 5-114 does not apply to such a suit, refused to construe the credit in isolation from the promissory note, and enjoined the beneficiaries.

The trouble with *Steinmeyer* is that it ignores an important function of the credit, that of shifting the burden of litigating without the funds to the account party from the beneficiaries. The beneficiaries, in *Steinmeyer*, had rights against the account party on the promissory note. They presumably had asked for the credit so that they would not be without funds during any litigation with the account party over the bal-

---

[298] In Enterprise Int'l, Inc. v. Corporacion Estatal Petrolera Ecuatoriana, 762 F.2d 464 (5th Cir. 1985), the court attempts to distinguish the less-strict Iranian cases and makes the point that the costs of international litigation can be allocated by the commercial parties and should not be upset by a court of equity. See also Trans Meridian Trading, Inc. v. Empresa Nacional De Comercializacion De Insumos, 829 F.2d 949 (9th Cir. 1987) (distinguishing Iranian cases); Foxboro Co. v. Arabian Am. Oil Co., 805 F.2d 34 (1st Cir. 1986) (same).

[299] 42 Cal. App. 3d 515 116 Cal. Rptr. 57 (1974).

ance due on the note. Absent the credit, the account party would have had those funds during that litigation.[300]

The *Steinmeyer* case invites account parties to destroy the effect of the independence principle by substituting an injunction against the beneficiary for an injunction against the issuer. There is little to justify the *Steinmeyer* approach. Neither precedent[301] nor the policy of protecting the independence of the credit transaction supports the *Steinmeyer* rule.[302]

---

[300] For discussion of this feature of credits, see ¶ 3.07[4].

[301] Most courts assume, with little discussion, that Section 5-114(2) controls in suits in which the beneficiary is a party. See, e.g., Harris Corp. v. National Iranian Radio & Television, 691 F.2d 1344 (11th Cir. 1982); Jupiter Orrington Corp. v. Zweifel, 127 Ill. App. 3d 559, 469 N.E.2d 590 (1984); Professional Modular Surface, Inc. v. Uniroyal, Inc., 108 Ill. App. 3d 1046, 440 N.E.2d 177 (1982); Morgan v. Depositors Trust Co., 33 U.C.C. Rep. Serv. (Callaghan) 1473 (Me. Super. Ct. Kennebec County 1982); Shaffer v. Brooklyn Park Garden Apartments, 311 Minn. 452, 250 N.W.2d 172 (1977); Key Int'l Mfg., Inc. v. Stillman, 103 A.D.2d 475, 480 N.Y.S.2d 528 (1984), modified, 66 N.Y.2d 924, 489 N.E.2d 764, 498 N.Y.S.2d 795 (1985); Chiat/Day, Inc. v. Kaliman, 105 A.D.2d 94, 483 N.Y.S.2d 235 (1984); Siderius, Inc. v. Wallace Co., 583 S.W.2d 852 (Tex. Civ. App. 1979); Werner v. A.L. Grootemaat & Sons, 80 Wis. 2d 513, 259 N.W.2d 310 (1977). The *Steinmeyer* court, being governed by California law and evidently wanting to issue an injunction, was compelled to avoid California's nonuniform version of Section 5-114(2)(b), which has been taken to mean that California does not authorize courts to enjoin an issuer from paying. See Cal. Com. Code § 5114(2)(b) & comment 6 (West Supp. 1990); Agnew v. FDIC, 548 F. Supp. 1235 (N.D. Cal. 1982); see also Nev. Rev. Stat. § 104.5114(2)(b) (1986) (same nonuniform version). In Wyle v. Bank Melli, 577 F. Supp. 1148 (C.D. Cal. 1983), the court gave an eccentric construction to the California version of Section 5-114(2). The *Wyle* court concluded that the provision assumed that the beneficiary would not be subject to California jurisdiction. The rule, then, according to the *Wyle* court, is designed to prevent injunctions against the issuer when the beneficiary is not in court to litigate the issue. The court also felt that the absence of a convenient forum for suit in the underlying contract militated against an injunction. When the beneficiary is present, as it was in *Wyle*, the court would not feel constrained by the California rule of Section 5-114(2). There is not much to commend the *Wyle* reasoning. Nothing in the statute or the comments supports one rule when the beneficiary is present and another when he is absent. In fact, the California comments suggest the contrary. See Cal. Com. Code § 5114, comment 6 (West 1964). The Court of Appeals for the First Circuit, in a diversity case involving California law, refused to follow *Steinmeyer*, which it saw as such a significant departure from general letter of credit principles and from California's nonuniform version of U.C.C. § 5-114(2)(b), Cal. Com. Code § 5-114(2)(b) (West Supp. 1990), that the California Supreme Court would not adhere to it. See Ground Air Transfer, Inc. v. Westates Airlines, Inc., 899 F.2d 1269 (1st Cir. 1990). In New Tech Devs., Div. of San Diego Carleton Lewis Corp. v. Bynamics, Inc., 191 Cal. App. 1065, 236 Cal. Rptr. 746 (Cal. Ct. App. 1987), the California Court of Appeal found the *Wyle* reading of California's Section 5-114(2)(b) unpersuasive and declined to follow it.

[302] In a dispute between Sperry International Trade, Inc. and the Government of Israel, Sperry, a seller, used an arbitration clause to obtain an arbitrator's award

In *Trans Meridian Trading, Inc. v. Empresa Nacional De Comercializacion De Insumos*,[303] the court refused to enjoin the beneficiary. The *Trans Meridian* court, in a diversity suit to which California law applied, saw the injunction against the beneficiary as an impermissible attempt to avoid the clear purpose of the California legislature's proscription against injunctions that stop payment of credits. The court distinguished the *Steinmeyer* case on the facts but added implicit criticism of *Steinmeyer*, which the *Trans Meridian* court saw as an attempt to do indirectly what the California legislature had forbidden the courts to do directly.

[g] Good Faith

Section 5-114(2)(b) permits an issuer to honor the credit even when there is fraud, so long as the issuer acts in good faith.[304] Generally, if a bank issuer has reason to believe that its customer objects to payment under the credit, it notifies the customer when the beneficiary presents documents that are facially conforming.[305] The customer then must take whatever steps are reasonable to put the issuer on notice of any claimed

---

requiring the credit issuer to pay the proceeds into an escrow account. The escrow agreement was a part of the underlying contract, and the Court of Appeals for the Second Circuit had earlier found that the account party could not enjoin payment of the credit, because it could show no irreparable harm. Sperry Int'l Trade, Inc. v. Government of Isr., 670 F.2d 8 (2d Cir. 1982). The arbitrators apparently did not understand that, by ordering the payment of the credit proceeds into an escrow account, they were interfering with the independent credit transaction and were depriving the beneficiary of its right under the credit to have the funds during the arbitration. The beneficiary sought relief from the courts, but the Second Circuit held that it did not reach the merits during the injunction suit and left the arbitrators' escrow order undisturbed. Sperry Int'l Trade, Inc. v. Government of Isr., 689 F.2d 301 (2d Cir. 1982). The Court of Appeals for the Second Circuit did reach the stop payment issue in a similar case and rendered a ruling that implicitly criticizes the arbitrators' decision in the *Sperry International* case. In Recon Optical, Inc. v. Israel, 816 F.2d 854 (2d Cir. 1987), the court denied a preliminary injunction to a seller in much the same position that Sperry International had occupied. In *Recon Optical*, the court was able to do what it apparently wanted to do but could not do in *Sperry International*—protect the risk-shifting effects of the standby credit and permit the beneficiary to draw and to hold the funds during the arbitration.

[303] 829 F.2d 949 (9th Cir. 1987).

[304] It is not bad faith for a bank to insist on strict compliance, even though its customer asks it to accept nonconforming documents. AMF Head Sports Wear, Inc. v. Ray Scott's All-Am. Sports Club, Inc., 448 F. Supp. 222 (D. Ariz. 1978).

[305] It is not bad faith, however, for an issuer to reject a noncomplying presentation without consulting with the account party. See Philadelphia Gear Corp. v. Central Bank, 717 F.2d 230 (5th Cir. 1983).

fraud. A written notice bearing clear reference to the credit by number and directed to the issuer's letter of credit department far enough in advance to permit the issuer to act should be sufficient. The careful account party does no less. Frequently, when an issuer receives such a notice, it does not honor the beneficiary's draft without having the benefit of a court order. Issuers are understandably reluctant to pay and to risk a court's decision after the fact that the payment was in bad faith.[306]

Nothing in the good faith requirement of Section 5-114(2)(b) requires a bank to look beyond the documents. If no fraud is apparent on

---

[306] In some cases, the courts have avoided the risk of being found in bad faith by initiating interpleader or similar actions. See American Nat'l Bank & Trust Co. v. Hamilton Indus. Int'l, Inc., 583 F. Supp. 164 (N.D. Ill. 1984), rev'd on other grounds sub nom. Banque Paribas v. Hamilton Indus. Int'l, Inc., 767 F.2d 380 (7th Cir. 1985); GATX Leasing Corp. v. DBM Drilling Corp. 657 S.W.2d 178 (Tex. Ct. App. 1983); Edmonton Sav. & Credit Union Ltd. v. Koppe, 70 A.L.R. 373 (Q.B. 1986); cf. Wyle v. Bank Melli, 577 F. Supp. 1148, 1152 (N.D. Cal. 1983) (involving bank issuer in similar litigation that took "neutral position"); Wisconsin Barge Line, Inc. v. INA (In re Wisconsin Barge Line, Inc.), 63 Bankr. 40 (Bankr. E.D. Mo. 1986) (bank issuer failing to appear as defendant); Mercede Center, Inc. v. Equibank, 518 A.2d 1291 (Pa. Super. Ct. 1986), appeal denied, 518 Pa. 619, 541 A.2d 746 (1987) (interpleader filed by issuer after account party filed injunction petition); see also Johnson v. Levy Org. Dev. Co. 789 F.2d 601 (7th Cir. 1986) (involving motion for leave by issuer to intervene in litigation between account party and beneficiary and to permit issuer to interplead); Banque Worms v. Banque Commerciale Privee, 679 F. Supp. 1173 (S.D.N.Y. 1988), aff'd per curiam, 849 F.2d 787 (2d Cir. 1988) (interpleader by confirming bank); American Bank v. Leasing Serv. Corp. (In re Air Conditioning, Inc. of Stuart), 55 Bankr. 157 (Bankr. S.D. Fla. 1985), aff'd in part, rev'd in part sub nom. Leasing Serv. Corp. v. Wendel (In re Air Conditioning, Inc. of Stuart), No. 86-8006-CIV-Nesbitt (S.D. Fla. Jan. 12, 1987), aff'd in part, rev'd in part sub nom. American Bank v. Leasing Serv. Co. (In re Air Conditioning, Inc. of Stuart), 845 F.2d 293 (11th Cir. 1988), cert. denied sub nom. First Interstate Credit Alliance, Inc. v. American Bank, 109 S. Ct. 557 (1988) (involving suit by issuer against beneficiary in which account party's trustee joined and which court treated as federal interpleader); Mitsui Mfrs. Bank v. Texas Commerce Bank, 159 Cal. App. 3d 1051, 206 Cal. Rptr. 218 (1984) (involving issuer that sought declaratory relief and that supported account party's request for preliminary injunction); Sea Management Servs., Ltd. v. Club Sea, Inc., 512 So. 2d 1025 (Fla. Dist. Ct. App. 1987) (denying interpleader to issuer after beneficiary presented conforming documents); Washington Fed. Sav. & Loan Ass'n v. Prince George's County, 80 Md. App. 142, 560 A.2d 582 (1989) (issuer's suit for declaratory judgment); Aspen Planners Ltd. v. Commerce Masonry & Forming Ltd., 100 D.L.R.3d 546 (Ont. H. Ct. 1979) (permitting defendant issuer to leave funds in court and withdraw from litigation). In Dallas Bank & Trust v. Commonwealth Dev. Corp., 686 S.W.2d 226 (Tex. Ct. App. 1984), the court held that an issuer facing a dispute between the account party and the beneficiary could not file interpleader, because only one party, the beneficiary, would be claiming the funds. Accord Lafayette Corp. v. Bank of Boston Int'l S., 723 F. Supp. 1461 (S.D. Fla. 1989). For discussion of the *Dallas Bank* and *Lafayette Corp.* cases and the interpleader issue generally, see ¶ 11.06.

the face of the documents, it does not amount to bad faith for an issuer to pay the beneficiary, even when confronted by the account party's claim that there is fraud in the credit transaction.[307] In such cases, the law may not impose on the issuer the burden of deciding within a short time which of the two parties is telling the truth. Absent some collusion between the issuer and the beneficiary, or absent proof that the account party provided the issuer, prior to honor, with clear evidence of fraud, payment under the credit is not in bad faith.[308] Section 5-114(2), by recognizing the power of equity to enjoin payment when such fraud exists, puts the burden on the account party to litigate the fraud question before payment, not after it.

¶ 7.05 ISSUER'S RIGHT TO REIMBURSEMENT AND SUBROGATION

[1] Contract or Statute

By any number of legal theories, an issuer is entitled to reimbursement of payments properly made under a credit. The issuer is not a volunteer. It acts at the behest of its customer, the account party, and it pays under the credit, sometimes over the account party's objections. Article 16(a) of the Uniform Customs and Section 5-114(3) of the Code give the issuer a right of reimbursement.[309]

---

[307] See KMW Int'l v. Chase Manhattan Bank, N.A., 606 F.2d 10 (2d Cir. 1979); Shaffer v. Brooklyn Park Garden Apartments, 311 Minn. 452, 250 N.W.2d 172 (1977); Intraworld Indus., Inc. v. Girard Trust Bank, 461 Pa. 343, 336 A.2d 316 (1975); Roman Ceramics Corp. v. Peoples Nat'l Bank, 517 F. Supp. 526 (M.D. Pa. 1981), aff'd, 714 F.2d 1207 (3d Cir. 1983); Lalaco v. Universal Hous. Sys. of Am., Inc., 80 Civ. 178 (WCC) (S.D.N.Y. Oct. 25, 1983); cf. First Nat'l Bank v. Carmouche, 515 So. 2d 785 (La. 1987) (holding that it was not bad faith for issuer to pay over facially conforming certificate after person making certificate told issuer that he did not know whether assertions were true). But cf. Asbury Park & Ocean Grove Bank v. National City Bank, 35 N.Y.S.2d 985 (Sup. Ct. 1942), aff'd mem., 268 A.D. 984, 52 N.Y.S.2d 583 (1944) (suggesting that issuer may be liable to account party if documents are false).

[308] In Philadelphia Gear Corp. v. Central Bank, 717 F.2d 230 (5th Cir. 1983), and Lustrelon, Inc. v. Prutscher, 178 N.J. Super. 128, 428 A.2d 518 (App. Div. 1981), the courts held that the good faith required by Section 5-114(2)(b) is honesty in fact — a subjective rule defined in Section 1-201(19) — and suggest that there is no "reasonableness" or "negligence" feature to good faith as it is defined in that section. See also U.C.C. § 5-103(4) (referring to definitions of Article 1 that include the subjective good faith rule of Section 1-201(19)).

[309] Cf. Security Fin. Group, Inc. v. Northern Ky. Bank & Trust Co., 858 F.2d 304 (6th Cir.), clarified, 875 F.2d 529 (6th Cir. 1988) (dictum that issuer enjoys statutory right of reimbursement even when it has no contract with account party); Citibank, N.A. v. Singer Co., 684 F. Supp. 382 (S.D.N.Y. 1988) (granting issuer injunc-

Many bank letter of credit application agreements require the account party to put the bank in funds before payment under the credit is due.[310] If the credit is an acceptance credit, that date will be the day the acceptance matures.[311] It is of no moment that the account party does not realize any benefit from the underlying contract, so long as the issuer honors conforming documents.[312] Just as an account party may not use the underlying transaction's facts to enjoin the credit's payment, so he may not use them to avoid reimbursing the issuer.[313] Even if the documents are not conforming, the issuer may have a right to reimbursement under the misnamed bifurcated standard[314] or on the ground that

---

tion against account party requiring posting of additional collateral); Balzano v. United States, 761 P.2d 229 (Colo. Ct. App. 1988) (holding that issuer has right to freeze account party's bank account in anticipation of draws under letter of credit); Interfirst Bank v. First Fed. Sav. & Loan Ass'n, 242 Kan. 181, 747 P.2d 129 (1987) (per curiam) (not designated for publication) (holding that no signed reimbursement agreement is necessary, issuer's right being statutory); Richards Elec. Supply Co. v. First Nat'l Bank, 2 Ohio App. 3d 325, 441 N.E.2d 1130 (1981) (holding it to be of no moment whether issuer's undertaking is letter of credit or guaranty, because account party would be obliged to reimburse issuer in either case).

[310] For an example of such an application, see App. C, Doc. 14. For a case holding that it was not unconscionable for an application agreement to include, on the reverse side, a security agreement granting the issuer a security interest in the account party's deposit account, see Gillman v. Chase Manhattan Bank, N.A., 135 A.D.2d 488, 521 N.Y.S.2d 729 (1987), aff'd, 73 N.Y.2d 1, 534 N.E.2d 824, 537 N.Y.S.2d 787 (1988).

[311] See Anglo-S. Am. Trust Co. v. Uhe, 261 N.Y. 150, 184 N.E. 741 (1933).

[312] See Kingdom of Swed. v. New York Trust Co., 197 Misc. 431, 96 N.Y.S.2d 779 (Sup. Ct. 1949).

[313] See Lumbermans Acceptance Co. v. Security Pac. Nat'l Bank, 86 Cal. App. 3d 175, 150 Cal. Rptr. 69 (1978); Braun v. Intercontinental Bank, 466 So. 2d 1130 (Fla. Dist. Ct. App. 1985); First Nat'l Bank v. Carmouche, 515 So. 2d 785 (La. 1987); cf. FDIC v. Freudenfeld, 492 F. Supp. 763 (E.D. Wis. 1980) (issuer's alleged ultra vires act no defense to account party's liability under Section 5-114(3)); United States Trust Co. v. Revere Copper & Brass, Inc. (In re Revere Copper & Brass, Inc.), 60 Bankr. 887 (Bankr. S.D.N.Y. 1985) (holding that issuer's right of reimbursement was proper Class 6 claim, even though right was contingent at time of filing of petition, credit having been drawn on after filing); In re W.L. Mead, Inc., 42 Bankr. 57 (Bankr. N.D. Ohio 1984) (holding that Section 362(d)(2) of Bankruptcy Code does not prevent issuer from exercising its right of reimbursement). But cf. Brittain v. United States Lines, Inc. (In re McLean Indus., Inc.), 884 F.2d 1566 (2d Cir. 1989) (involving use of automatic stay to prevent issuer from obtaining reimbursement from account party debtor in bankruptcy).

[314] See National Bank of N. Am. v. Alizio, 103 A.D.2d 690, 477 N.Y.S.2d 356 (1984), aff'd mem., 65 N.Y.2d 788, 482 N.E.2d 907, 493 N.Y.S.2d 111 (1985). See generally ¶ 9.03[1][a].

the account party waived the defect.[315]

The issuer has no right of reimbursement, however, if the credit is not paid. In *Tomaso v. Plum Grove Bank*,[316] the issuer took security from the plaintiff, the party for whose account four credits were issued, though another party's name was listed as the account party. When two of the credits were not drawn upon, the issuer attempted to resort to the collateral to satisfy obligations of the named account party. The *Tomaso* court held that there was no right to take the collateral, because the issuer knew that the named account party was the agent of the plaintiff.

In *New Braunfels National Bank v. Odiorne*,[317] the account party argued that the issuer had lost its right of reimbursement when it dishonored the credit. Under the reimbursement agreement in *New Braunfels*, the account party had agreed to reimburse if the issuer honored. After the issuer dishonored, the court entered judgment against the issuer and in favor of the beneficiary. The court held that the issuer did not need to rely on the application agreement in its claim for reimbursement but that it could resort to Section 5-114(3), which creates a statutory right of reimbursement against the account party.[318]

Generally, issuers that seek reimbursement must show that they followed the account party's instructions. While there is some controversy over the right of the issuer to reimbursement in the event it pays over defective documents,[319] there should be no question that an issuer that knowingly pays against fraudulent documents loses its right of reimbursement. Such action probably amounts to bad faith and runs afoul of Section 5-114(2)(b). Such evidence must not be equivocal, however, because the section clearly is designed to avoid imposing a burden on the issuer to determine whether an account party's claim of fraud is truthful. In one case that has considered the matter, the court held that in order to avoid having to reimburse, the account party must show that the

---

[315] See Chemical Bank v. Daniel Laurent, Ltd., 100 A.D.2d 792, 474 N.Y.S.2d 955 (1984).

[316] 130 Ill. App. 3d 18, 473 N.E.2d 588 (1985).

[317] 780 S.W.2d 313 (Tex. Ct. App. 1989).

[318] The account party also argued in *New Braunfels* that its note was rendered unenforceable by virtue of the fact that it was conditioned on payment under the credit. It is common for bank issuers, at the time they enter into the application agreement, to take a note in the face amount of the maximum sum that may be drawn under the letter of credit, but to agree in the application agreement that the sum actually due on the note will be the amount paid by the issuer under the letter of credit. The *New Braunfels* court found nothing in that practice to render the note void.

[319] For discussion of that controversy, see ¶ 9.03[1][a].

issuer had clear or obvious notice of the fraud and that the issuer received the notice before it paid under the credit.[320]

[2] Subrogation

[a] Subrogating Issuer to Account Party's Rights Against Beneficiary

There is a hint in the comments to Section 5-109 that the issuer might be subrogated "in a proper case"[321] to the rights of the account party against the beneficiary.[322] An issuer that pays a beneficiary may want to use this kind of subrogation in the event the issuer cannot obtain reimbursement from the account party. In a commercial credit transaction, for example, if the account party becomes insolvent before the issuer pays the beneficiary, the issuer will look to the goods to recoup its payment.[323] If the goods are conforming and if the market has held, their value should be sufficient, or nearly so, to satisfy the issuer's advances. If the goods are nonconforming, the issuer may not be able to realize enough from the sale of the goods to make it whole. If that issuer can subrogate itself to the account party's breach of contract rights against the beneficiary in the underlying sales contract, it will be able to recoup its loss.

[b] Subrogating Issuer to Beneficiary's Rights Against Account Party

One commentator who advocates use of subrogation in letter of credit transactions properly warns that subrogation must be applied carefully so that it does not interfere with the functions of the credit.[324]

---

[320] See Bank of N.S. v. Angelica-Whitewear Ltd., 36 D.L.R.4th 161 (Can. 1987). For a case involving an unsuccessful attempt by an issuer to recover on its blanket bond for losses sustained when it accepted forged bills of lading from a beneficiary, see Republic Nat'l Bank v. Fidelity & Deposit Co., 894 F.2d 1255 (11th Cir. 1990).

[321] U.C.C. § 5-109, comment 1 (2d para., 3d sent.).

[322] Several commentators support that view, but no court appears to have invoked subrogation in those circumstances. See B. Clark, The Law of Bank Deposits, Collections, and Credit Cards ¶ 8.11[2] (rev. ed. 1981); Baird, "Standby Letters of Credit in Bankruptcy," 49 U. Chi. L. Rev. 130, 140 (1982); Jarvis, "Standby Letters of Credit—Issuers Subrogation and Assignment Rights" (pts. 1, 2), 9 U.C.C. L.J. 356, 10 U.C.C. L.J. 38 (1977); McLaughlin, "Letters of Credit as Preferential Transfers in Bankruptcy," 50 Fordham L. Rev. 1033, 1073 (1982).

[323] For discussion of the issuer's rights in the goods, see ¶ 8.03.

[324] He cautions, for example, that subrogation rights should not be used by the issuer prior to payment. Otherwise, the prompt and certain payment features of the credit will be hobbled. See Jarvis, supra note 322, at 368.

He would subrogate the issuer to the rights of the beneficiary against the account party. That kind of subrogation is beneficial to the issuer only in those infrequent cases where the beneficiary has a stronger claim to the account party's property than the issuer does. It is unlikely, however, that a beneficiary will have a stronger position than the issuer. In virtually all letter of credit transactions, the converse is true: The issuer's position is stronger. The beneficiary is relying on the issuer's credit, not on that of the account party. The issuer secures itself against the account party by taking a security interest in the account party's property.

Some courts, moreover, refuse to permit the issuer to subrogate itself to the beneficiary's rights against the party whose debt the credit secured. *In re Munzenrieder*[325] involved a credit issued for the account of the debtor's cognate. Because the cognate was in liquidation in a foreign jurisdiction with no prospects of a dividend to creditors, the issuer had no reimbursement and sought to make a claim in the bankruptcy of the debtor by subrogating itself to the claim of the beneficiary. The court held that a party seeking equitable subrogation must satisfy three requirements:

1. The party must pay the debt of another.
2. The party must demonstrate that it had a direct or indirect interest in discharging the debt.
3. There must be no injustice by virtue of the subrogation.

The *Munzenrieder* court held that the issuer had failed to satisfy the second requirement and suggested that it also had failed to satisfy the first. The court pointed out that the issuer received a fee for issuing the credit and emphasized that the issuer's payment under the credit had satisfied the issuer's own obligation. Finally, the court expressed little sympathy for the issuer, which had misjudged either the creditworthiness of its account party or the value of its collateral.

In *Merchants Bank & Trust Co. v. Economic Enterprises, Inc. (In re Economic Enterprises, Inc.)*,[326] the credit secured payments due under a mortgage held by the beneficiary. When the issuer paid under the credit, it argued that it should be subrogated to the beneficiary's interest under the mortgage. The court held that the issuer had satisfied its own obligation when it paid the beneficiary and that it was not entitled to any interest in the mortgage, which arose out of the underlying transaction.

---

[325] 58 Bankr. 228 (Bankr. M.D. Fla. 1986).
[326] 44 Bankr. 230 (Bankr. D. Conn. 1984).

Similar analysis prompted the court in *Bank of America National Trust & Savings Association v. Kaiser Steel Corp. (In re Kaiser Steel Corp.)*[327] to rule against an issuer that sought to subrogate itself to the beneficiary's rights against property of the account party. The *Bank of America* court held that there are five elements at common law that must be satisfied before a party may subrogate itself to the rights of a party it pays:

1. It must pay to protect its own interests.
2. It must not be a volunteer.
3. It must satisfy a debt for which it was not primarily liable.
4. The entire debt must be paid.
5. There must be no injustice by virtue of the subrogation.

Because the credit issuer was primarily liable, the court held, it could not have subrogation under the common-law test. In addition, the *Bank of America* court held that Section 509(a) of the Bankruptcy Code prevented the issuer from benefiting from subrogation. That provision allows subrogation by a codebtor of the debtor in bankruptcy. The issuer, in the view of the *Bank of America* court, must satisfy both the equity rule and the provisions of Section 509(a). Since the issuer was not a codebtor, its liability being primary and independent of that of the account party on the underlying contract, the issuer did not satisfy the provision, and there could be no subrogation.

Other cases provide slender support to the argument in favor of issuer subrogation to the interests of the beneficiary. In *American Insurance Association v. Clarke*,[328] the court upheld the right of a national bank's operating subsidiary to issue insurance to secure municipal obligations. The court viewed such activity as sufficiently analogous to traditional bank activity to be permissible under the National Bank Act. The court based its holding in part on the notion that such insurance is the functional equivalent of a financial standby letter of credit. In the course of its opinion, the court assumed that the issuer of the insurance would be subrogated to the rights of the insured against the municipality that issued the insured bonds. The assumption, implicit in the *American Insurance Association* opinion, that a credit issuer also would be subrogated conflicts with the rule of the *Munzenrieder, Economic Enterprises,* and *Bank of America* cases.

---

[327] 89 Bankr. 150 (Bankr. D. Colo. 1988).
[328] 865 F.2d 278 (D.C. Cir. 1989).

In *In re National Service Lines, Inc.*,[329] the bankruptcy court subrogated the issuer to the rights of the beneficiary against the debtor. The issuer's credit secured payment of services rendered and goods sold by the beneficiary to the debtor's employees. The beneficiary provided those services and sales to the debtor in possession. The beneficiary's claim was entitled to priority in bankruptcy as an administrative expense, and the issuer was attempting to avail itself of that priority. The *National Service Lines* court accepted the argument. Similarly, in *In re Sensor*,[330] the court permitted an issuer that had paid a beneficiary to assume the beneficiary's secured status in the bankruptcy.

The *American Insurance Association, National Service Lines,* and *Sensor* cases do not analyze the issues with letter of credit concerns in mind and offer no rebuttal to the more compelling analyses in *Munzenrieder, Economic Enterprises,* and *Bank of America.*

Subrogation of the issuer to the beneficiary's rights against the account party as a matter of law may have the unfortunate effect of cutting off the account party's defenses against the issuer in the application agreement relationship.[331] An issuer, for example, that violates the application agreement and loses its right to reimbursement under that agreement might seek reimbursement via subrogation. Subrogation by contract before the fact — that is, when the parties enter into the application agreement — would not offend the account party's rights or interfere with the account party's reasonable expectations. If the account party objects to contractual subrogation, it can find another issuer. Subrogation after the fact of payment under the credit, however, whether by the agreement of the issuer and the beneficiary or by operation of law, arguably is unfair to the account party.

[c] Subrogating Issuer to Account Party's Rights Against Third Parties

Issuers sometimes achieve the effects of subrogation by contract. In *Baii Banking Corp. v. Atlantic Richfield Co.*,[332] the application agreement between the issuer and the account party gave the issuer a secured position in all of the account party's interests in a contract between the account party and a sub-buyer of the goods. When the issuer paid the

---

[329] 80 Bankr. 144 (Bankr. E.D. Mo. 1987).

[330] 79 Bankr. 623 (Bankr. E.D. Pa. 1987).

[331] See ¶ 2.09[2] for discussion of First State Bank & Trust Co. v. McIver, 893 F.2d 301 (11th Cir. 1990).

[332] No. 86 Civ. 6651 (JFK) (S.D.N.Y. Sept. 15, 1987); cf. Torco Oil Co. v. LTV Steel Co., 709 F. Supp. 130 (N.D. Ill. 1989) (case involving similar arrangement).

seller-beneficiary, the account party was insolvent; but the issuer was able to resort to the sub-buyer, who had an obligation to purchase the goods that were the subject of the account party's contract with the beneficiary. By the same token, an issuer can take a security interest in the account party's rights against the beneficiary in the underlying contract.

The danger here is that the issuer may attempt to assert in the credit transaction rights it acquires by contract in the underlying transaction. That attempt contradicts the independence principle. The credit transaction should proceed to its conclusion: payment of the beneficiary. Then, and only then, should an issuer be able to assert rights arising by contract or subrogation against the beneficiary or anyone else.

[d] Subrogating Confirming Bank to Issuer's Rights

Section 5-107(2) of the Code stipulates that the confirming bank "acquires the rights of an issuer." In *In re Glade Springs, Inc.*,[333] the court used that provision to subrogate the confirming bank to the issuer's rights against the account party's collateral. In other words, the *Glade Springs* court, disregarding the distinction between the indefinite article "an" and the definite article "the," held not just that the confirming bank has the rights of *an* issuer but that it also has the rights of *the* issuer.

It is not clear that the section intends the confirming bank to have rights against the account party. Generally, courts have held that the confirming bank has no such rights.[334] One can read the word "an" in Section 5-107(2) to mean only that the confirming bank has the same rights against parties with whom it is in privity that *an* issuer would have.

After the district court reversed the *In re Glade Springs, Inc.* judgment in an unreported decision, the Court of Appeals for the Sixth Circuit reversed the district court and reinstated the judgment of the bankruptcy court.[335] The Sixth Circuit decision relied not on Section 5-107(2) but on notions of unjust enrichment. The confirming bank, the court held, had satisfied the debt of the account party and had a questionable claim for reimbursement from the failed issuer. Because the issuer's receiver had no claim against the account party, the court feared

---

[333] 47 Bankr. 780 (Bankr. E.D. Tenn. 1985), judgment reinstated sub nom. Chemical Bank v. Broward (In re Glade Springs, Inc.), 826 F.2d 440 (6th Cir. 1987).

[334] For discussion of the rights of the confirming bank against the account party, see ¶¶ 5.01[5], 9.03[3].

[335] Chemical Bank v. Broward (In re Glade Springs, Inc.), 826 F.2d 440 (6th Cir. 1987).

that the account party would retrieve its security and leave the confirming bank with a loss and the account party with a windfall. Resting its decision in part on the *Restatement of Restitution*,[336] the court viewed the case as one ripe for application of subrogation principles.

Although the opinion does not allude to the fact, any success the confirming bank might have in its claim for reimbursement against the issuer's receiver would give rise to a claim pro tanto by the receiver against the account party and its collateral. The Sixth Circuit apparently thought it the better part of judicial efficiency to invoke subrogation and avoid the difficulty of adjudicating the reimbursement claim in the receivership with, in all probability, the receiver's action over against the account party. There is, nonetheless, something disturbing about giving a confirming bank rights against parties with whom it has not dealt. In point of fact, confirming banks generally do not know or care anything about the account party. It is the opening bank on which they rely for reimbursement. If that reliance proves unwise, perhaps the confirmer should bear the loss. To give it rights against the account party is, in a subtle but real way, giving it a windfall.[337]

[3] Defenses

The first and most important defense to the issuer's right of reimbursement relates to the beneficiary's documents. If those documents do not conform with the terms of the credit, the issuer has not complied with the application agreement.

There is some authority to the effect that that breach is sufficient to give the account party a complete bar to the issuer's reimbursement claim.[338] Certainly, if the account party is a trader, as many importers who use credits are, purchasing documents that he plans to resell to his domestic customer, the issuer's payment to the beneficiary over defective documents has seriously damaged the account party's economic in-

---

[336] Restatement of Restitution § 162 & comments b & e (1937).

[337] In other settings, courts have looked favorably on subrogation arguments. In FDIC v. Liberty Nat'l Bank & Trust Co., 806 F.2d 961 (10th Cir. 1986), the court subrogated the confirming bank to the rights of the beneficiary against the issuer. In In re Minnesota Kicks, Inc., 48 Bankr. 93 (Bankr. D. Minn. 1985), the court subrogated the account party to the rights of the beneficiary against the debtor whose obligation was satisfied by payment of the credit. In In re St. Clair Supply Co., 100 Bankr. 263 (Bankr. W.D. Pa. 1989), the court refused, however, to subrogate a surety that had reimbursed the issuer. The issuer had paid the beneficiaries, and the surety sought to subrogate itself to the beneficiaries' rights against the account party debtor.

[338] See Anglo-S. Am. Trust Co. v. Uhe, 261 N.Y. 150, 184 N.E. 741 (1933); H. Harfield, Bank Credits and Acceptances 105–108 (5th ed. 1974).

terests. The authorities that would make that breach by the issuer a complete defense to its right of reimbursement evidently are concerned that such an account party be able to refuse to accept the documents and put the issuer into the position of having to dispose of the documents or the goods they represent.

The commercial letter of credit model that gives rise to the account party who purchases documents is less common today than it was during the first half of the twentieth century, when importing was a specialized branch of commerce situated in a few ports on the eastern seaboard. Today many importers act for their own account, not for that of a customer.

In the standby context, moreover, the concerns evidenced by these authorities have little application at all. The obligor on a note secured by a standby letter of credit may be anxious to have the note when the issuer pays it, but the account party that uses an invoice standby will not care a whit whether the issuer can give it the certified copy of the invoice which that kind of credit calls for.[339] In short, it may be that failure of the issuer to exact documentary compliance from the beneficiary is a less egregious error than it used to be, or it may be that it is an egregious error in some cases but not in others.

There is a second, though slightly different, question concerning documentary compliance that arises in the reimbursement context. The account party that resists reimbursing the issuer on the ground that the issuer has failed to obtain the necessary documents from the beneficiary is making a breach of contract argument. The account party is not a party to the letter of credit and has no rights under it. It is the application agreement in such a situation—an agreement between the issuer and the account party—that the account party claims that the issuer breached.[340] The general letter of credit principle that documents presented by the beneficiary must comply strictly with the terms of the credit is peculiar to commercial law and contrary to the general principles of contract law.[341] That strict rule obtains in the letter of credit transaction in order to satisfy the exigencies of the document examination process. Those exigencies generally do not arise in the reimbursement context, except when the account party is buying documents.

Arguably, therefore, the law should measure the efficacy of the account party's defense to the issuer's reimbursement claim against the template of contract law, not that of letter of credit law. Under general

---

[339] For an example of an invoice standby, see App. C, Doc. 18.

[340] For discussion of the distinction between the letter of credit and the application agreement, see ¶ 2.08[1].

[341] For discussion of the strict compliance rule of letter of credit law, see ¶ 6.03.

principles of contract law, however, a party can use another's breach only if that breach is material and can resist payment only if the breach causes loss.

Briefly, it may not be axiomatic that the issuer's failure to exact strict compliance from the beneficiary deprives the issuer of its reimbursement claim. It may be that substantial compliance in this context is enough. Unfortunately, the cases are not clear on these points.[342]

The account party attempted to use the Bankruptcy Code in *CJL Co. v. Bank of Wallowa County (In re CJL Co.)*[343] to avoid reimbursing the issuer. In that case, the debtor in possession sought to recover as an unlawful preferential transfer the issuing bank's transfer of sums from the debtor's account to the issuer's general ledger account. The court held that, because the transfer had occurred under common-law transfer rules more than nine months prior to the debtor's bankruptcy, the transfer was not a preferential transfer under Section 547 of the Bankruptcy Code.

In *First National Bank v. Carmouche*,[344] the account party urged the court to fashion a fraud defense to the issuer's right of reimbursement. The account party claimed that when the issuer paid the negotiating bank, the issuer knew that the certificate accompanying the draft might be in error. That knowledge notwithstanding, the court held, the issuer had a right to pay in good faith, and, having done so, the issuer had a right of reimbursement against the account party.

In *Gutierrez v. MBank*,[345] the court refused to enter summary judgment, however, against a guarantor of the account party's reimbursement obligation. The guarantor raised an affirmative defense of mutual mistake of fact, which the court held would be a proper defense on the reimbursement claim. The guarantor argued that the issuer had paid the beneficiary for purposes that were not proper under the application agreement.

[4] Restitution

In *City National Bank v. Westland Towers Apartments*,[346] an issuer that had extended the expiry of the credit and had paid the beneficiary, in

---

[342] See ¶ 9.03, which discusses them in some detail. See also Dolan, "Letter of Credit Disputes Between the Issuer and Its Customer: The Issuer's Rights Under the Misnamed 'Bifurcated Standard,'" 105 Banking L.J. 380 (1988).

[343] 71 Bankr. 261 (Bankr. D. Or. 1987).

[344] 515 So. 2d 785 (La. 1987).

[345] 761 S.W.2d 853 (Tex. Ct. App. 1988).

[346] 152 Mich. App. 136, 393 N.W.2d 554 (1986) (per curiam).

both cases without the account party's authority, sought to recover from the account party and its principals on a theory of unjust enrichment. The credit secured the account party, a limited partnership, on its obligation to pay a note secured by a mortgage. The issuer was a substantial participant in the mortgage loan, having acquired a 97 percent interest in the loan from the mortgage loan originator, and the court refused to grant the issuer restitutionary relief.

[5] Setoff

In re McLean Industries, Inc.[347] involved the attempt of an issuer to set off the account party's deposit account in satisfaction of the issuer's reimbursement claim. There are three possible sources for the issuer's right of setoff in these circumstances:

1. The reimbursement agreement (if there is one) between the account party and the issuer;
2. The common law; and
3. Section 5-114(3) of the Code.

Because the facts showed that the account party never had assented to the setoff provision in the reimbursement agreement but, in fact, had objected to it, the court rejected the issuer's claim of setoff rights by virtue of the reimbursement agreement. The court went on to hold that the evidence of the account party's objections to a right of setoff in the agreement was sufficient to defeat any common-law right. Finally, the court held that Section 5-114(3) by itself does not create any right of setoff.

¶ 7.06 ISSUER'S DUTY TO COUNSEL ACCOUNT PARTY

Some commentators have raised the question of the issuer's duty to advise the account party in structuring the letter of credit transaction. Two commentators[348] suggest that there may be a legal duty on the part of the bank to counsel the account party concerning, for example, the kinds of documents it needs to protect itself as a buyer in an international sale. One of these authorities is particularly concerned about

---

[347] 90 Bankr. 614 (Bankr. S.D.N.Y. 1988).

[348] See Kozolchyk, "The Letter of Credit in Court: An Expert Testifies," 99 Banking L.J. 340 (1982); Ellinger, "Fraud in Documentary Credit Transactions," 1981 J. Bus. L. 258, 267.

country banks that issue commercial letters of credit. He argues that the international sale needs to be planned carefully and that a banker experienced in international trade can play a planning role in the transaction. One cannot deny that the reports evidence commercial and standby letters of credit that never should have been written.[349]

The former chairman of the International Chamber of Commerce's Commission on Banking Technique and Practice takes a more cautious view.[350] He does not argue in favor of imposing liability on bank issuers that fail to advise their customers but urges issuers, in their own interests and as a guard against misunderstanding, to encourage simplicity in the credit.[351] Implicitly, this commentator is urging issuers not to promise too much to the account party. The issuer's role in the letter of credit transactions is usually no substitute for commercial expertise.

While the issuer that makes outlandish claims to an account party inexperienced in credit transactions may be liable for breach of an implied promise, courts may well be reluctant to impose a duty on issuers, especially bank issuers, that requires them to be familiar with commercial practices. The Code explicitly excuses banks from any duty to be learned in commercial matters.[352] The planning of a commercial transaction and the role of the credit in it are essentially commercial functions that require industry expertise—something most issuers do not have.

[349] See, e.g., Transparent Prods. v. Paysaver Credit Union, No. 85 C 1741 (N.D. Ill. Jan. 21, 1986), aff'd, 864 F.2d 60 (7th Cir. 1988) (credit containing no expiry and no conditions); Guilford Pattern Works, Inc. v. United Bank, 655 F. Supp. 378 (D. Colo. 1987) (credit payable against beneficiary's satisfaction of delivery terms in underlying contract); Newvector Communications, Inc. v. Union Bank, 663 F. Supp. 252 (D. Utah 1987) (suit on credit calling for "draft(s) as per Resellers Agreement"); Raiffeisen-Zentralkasse Tirol v. First Nat'l Bank, 671 P.2d 1008 (Colo. Ct. App. 1983) (credit that required delivery before specified date but no documentary certification of delivery); O'Grady v. First Union Bank, 296 N.C. 212, 250 S.E.2d 587 (1978) (credit that called for "copy of each instrument causing this establishment of credit to be called upon"); Sherwood & Roberts, Inc. v. First Sec. Bank, 682 P.2d 149 (Mont. 1984) (credit that was "exercisable upon the unremedied default" of specified documents); Union County Bank v. FDIC, No. 712 (Tenn. Ct. App. Sept. 18, 1987) (credit that required beneficiary to present note and "all security documents executed in connection with said loan").

[350] See B. Wheble, "UCP 1974/1983 Revisions Compared and Explained (Documentary Credits)," ICC Pub. No. 411, at 7, 54 (1983).

[351] Cf. U.C.P. art. 5 (1983) (urging banks to discourage "excessive" detail in credits).

[352] See U.C.C. § 5-109(1)(c).

In *Armstrong v. First National Bank*,[353] the purchaser of goods requested its bank to cause an invoice standby to issue,[354] and the purchaser's bank asked its correspondent to issue the credit. The credit called for an invoice and a certificate of nonpayment but did not call for any certificate of inspection. When the seller called for payment, the issuer paid. The purchaser argued that the goods were defective and that the banks should have advised it to obtain an inspection certificate or other protection against the seller's noncompliance with the underlying transaction.

The *Armstrong* court reasoned that Section 5-109 of the Code is the source of the issuer's duties toward its customer. The court emphasized that the provision requires "good faith," which it defined as honesty in fact and observance of general banking usage. The court concluded that there was no evidence of bad faith and no evidence that it was general banking usage to provide customers with advice on letter of credit conditions, especially when the customer did not ask for them. The *Armstrong* court did not distinguish between the two banks but held that neither was liable.

In *Hill v. Equitable Bank*,[355] the court found a duty on the part of a credit issuer that may have been breached by misleading statements made by the banker. The account parties alleged that an employee of the issuer had misrepresented the financial condition of the partnership venture to them as prospective limited partners. The *Hill* court noted that the duty to refrain from making misleading statements did not arise by the issuance of the credit itself but by virtue of the fact that the issuance of the credit was in conjunction with representations concerning the quality of an investment in return for deposits. Significantly, the *Hill* court differentiated the common-law duty, which it recognized, from fraud claims, which the plaintiffs also were asserting. The Court of Appeals for the Third Circuit affirmed the *Hill* decision in an opinion that observes that the issuance of the standby credit in question was akin to a loan to the account party and that the law has not reached the point at which a bank lender must ensure that its customer uses the proceeds of a loan soundly.[356]

In *Commercial Banking Co. v. Jalsard Pty. Ltd.*,[357] the account party argued that the issuer had failed to advise her concerning the nature of an inspection certificate that was required by the credit. Absent evidence that the issuer gave the account party advice on which she relied, the court would not consider the account party's claim.

---

[353] No. 3-85-1 (Ohio Ct. App. May 6, 1986).

[354] For an illustration of an invoice standby, see App. C, Doc. 18.

[355] 655 F. Supp. 631 (D. Del. 1987), aff'd, 851 F.2d 691 (3d Cir. 1988).

[356] Hill v. Equitable Trust Co., 851 F.2d 691 (3d Cir. 1988).

[357] [1972] 2 Lloyd's Rep. 529 (P.C.).

CHAPTER **8**

The Issuer and Third Parties

The credit issuer's rights and obligations arise most often out of its relationships with the account party and the beneficiary. There are occasions, however, when the issuer confronts third parties. These third parties usually fall into one of four categories:

1. Persons who have purchased the beneficiary's draft or documents;
2. Buyers or creditors of the account party;
3. Transferees; and
4. Creditors of the beneficiary or assignees of the beneficiary's credit proceeds.

This chapter deals with the first two categories; Chapter 10 deals with the last two.[1]

¶ 8.01 PURCHASERS OF BENEFICIARY'S DRAFT OR DEMAND

The earliest function of letters of credit was to give value to bills of exchange or drafts. The credit served the draft, which, until the twentieth century, was the principal commercial instrument.[2] It is now more accurate to say that the draft serves the credit, and, in fact, some modern credits do not involve drafts at all.[3] Nevertheless, the draft continues to play an important, although diminished, role in the credit transaction, as do other "negotiable" papers. This section considers those areas where negotiability law and credit law intersect.[4]

---

[1] For discussion of the issuer's rights against third parties under the doctrine of subrogation, see ¶ 7.05[2][c].

[2] For discussion of the history of credits and their relationship to the draft, see ¶ 3.02.

[3] Credits are often payable against the beneficiary's demand for payment. A deferred payment credit is a type of time credit designed to avoid the use of drafts in countries where drafts are subject to restrictive regulation or taxation. For an example of a deferred payment credit, see App. C, Doc. 20.

[4] A credit that contains a negotiation clause is a negotiation credit. See infra ¶ 8.01[6]. Often drafts drawn under a credit are negotiable in form, and documents of title presented with the drafts may be negotiable. A credit, however, is not negotiable in any sense, although it may be transferred in a proper case. See ¶¶ 10.03, 10.04. Clearly, a credit is not a negotiable instrument. See U.C.C. § 3-104; Philadelphia Gear Corp. v. FDIC, 587 F. Supp. 294 (W.D. Okla. 1984), aff'd in part, rev'd in part, 751 F.2d 1131 (10th Cir. 1984), rev'd on other grounds, 476 U.S. 426 (1986); Consolidated Aluminum Corp. v. Bank of Va., 544 F. Supp. 386 (D. Md. 1982), aff'd, 704 F.2d 136 (4th Cir. 1983); City Nat'l Bank v. First Nat'l Bank, 22 Ark. App. 5, 732 S.W.2d 489 (1987) (dictum); Shaffer v. Brooklyn Park Garden Apartments, 311 Minn. 452, 250 N.W.2d 172 (1977); Heritage Hous. Corp. v. Ferguson, 651 S.W.2d 272 (Tex. Ct. App. 1983); Comptroller of the Currency, Staff Interpretive Letter No. 322, [1985–1987 Transfer Binder] Fed. Banking L. Rep. (CCH) ¶ 85,492 (Dec. 31, 1984). But cf. Decker Steel Co. v. Exchange Nat'l Bank, 330 F.2d 82 (7th Cir. 1964) (suggesting that transferee of credit is holder in due course); Wyle v. Bank Melli, 577 F. Supp. 1148 (N.D. Cal. 1983) (same); Westpac Banking Corp. v. South Carolina

[1] Exceptions to Fraud Rule of Section 5-114

The discussion in Chapter 7 of Section 5-114 of the Uniform Commercial Code (UCC or the Code), the section litigated more frequently than any other in Article 5, explains the general rule that the issuer must honor the beneficiary's facially conforming presentations. The discussion then deals with four important exceptions to that rule. Generally, those exceptions arise when the documents appear to be conforming but in fact are intrinsically defective because of fraud, forgery, or the like. These four "intrinsic defect" exceptions permit the issuer to dishonor facially conforming presentations and permit a court to enjoin honor of such presentations. The discussion in Chapter 7 omits analysis of an important exception to the "intrinsic defect" rules, however. Under this exception, issuers may not dishonor some facially conforming but intrinsically defective presentations, and courts may not enjoin issuers from honoring those presentations.

Under Section 5-114 the intrinsic defects fall into four categories:

1. Some document does not conform to warranties that the law imposes on presentation of such document.
2. One of the documents is forged.
3. One of the documents is fraudulent.
4. There is "fraud in the transaction."[5]

Unfortunately, for the numbers here confuse the matter, the four "intrinsic defect" categories do not justify dishonor when the party seeking payment is one of a cast of four good faith purchasers.[6]

In short, Section 5-114 begins with the basic principle that the issuer must honor facially conforming presentations. The provision then proceeds to delimit four instances of intrinsic defect that prevent the application of the basic principle. Finally, the section completes the circle by recognizing four characters who prevent the application of the exception and who therefore can force payment even when they present facially conforming but intrinsically defective documents.

The first three good faith purchasers recognized in Section 5-114 are well-known personages: the holder in due course of a negotiable

---

Nat'l Bank, [1986] 1 Lloyd's Rep. 311, 313 (P.C.) (referring to beneficiary of negotiation credit as having "negotiated the credit" to negotiating bank).

[5] For discussion of these four events that give the issuer the right to dishonor and may give the court reason to enjoin honor, see ¶ 7.04.

[6] The good faith purchase exceptions apply only if the presenting party presents "under the credit." U.C.C. § 5-114(2)(a). For discussion of the significance of this language, see infra ¶ 8.01[6].

draft, the bona fide purchaser of a negotiable security, and a person to whom a negotiable document of title has been duly negotiated. The fourth appears to be a creature of Article 5: "a negotiating bank or other holder of the . . . demand which has taken the . . . demand under the credit and under circumstances which would make it a holder in due course." The benefit of achieving the level of a good faith purchaser under the section lies in the fact that such purchasers cut off the fraud defense that is so problematic in letter of credit law.

[2] Holder in Due Course

It is clear from the language of Section 5-114(2)(a), which refers to Section 3-302, a definitional provision, that Article 5 defers to Article 3 for determining whether a party is a holder in due course.[7] Under Section 3-302, a holder in due course first must be a holder of a negotiable instrument that has been negotiated to him.[8] Since letters of credit are not themselves negotiable instruments, not being negotiable in form,[9] beneficiaries[10] or transferees[11] of a credit may not, by virtue of being beneficiaries or transferees alone, qualify as holders in due course.

Holders in due course, for the purpose of Section 5-114(2)(a), must show, first, that they hold a negotiable instrument. They also must show that they took the instrument without notice of any defense against it. Account parties and issuers who discover fraud in the credit transaction may notify the beneficiary's bank (or banks in the beneficiary's city) of that fraud in order to prevent any such bank from becoming a holder in due course of the beneficiary's draft and thereby cut off the fraud defense.[12]

---

[7] Accord Banco Espanol de Credito v. State St. Bank & Trust Co., 409 F.2d 711 (1st Cir. 1969); United Bank Ltd. v. Cambridge Sporting Goods Corp., 41 N.Y.2d 254, 360 N.E.2d 943, 392 N.Y.S.2d 265 (1976).

[8] See U.C.C. § 3-302(1). The beneficiary of the credit might conceivably be a holder of a draft drawn to himself as payee, but he cannot benefit from the exception in Section 5-114(2)(a) if he is guilty of fraud. See U.C.C. § 3-305(2); Cronin v. Executive House Realty, [1982 Transfer Binder] Fed. Sec. L. Rep. (CCH) ¶ 98,670 (S.D.N.Y. 1982).

[9] See U.C.C. § 3-104(1). See also authority cited supra note 4.

[10] See United Technologies Corp. v. Citibank, N.A., 469 F. Supp. 473 (S.D.N.Y.1979).

[11] Shaffer v. Brooklyn Park Garden Apartments, 311 Minn. 452, 250 N.W.2d 172 (1977).

[12] See U.C.C. § 3-302(1)(c). Most of the time, the beneficiary takes his drafts to a bank in the community where he is located. Banks in other communities will be suspicious of drafts drawn by someone they do not know. When the account party can show fraud, it might be able to prevent the beneficiary from negotiating to a holder in due course by giving notice of the fraud to all banks in the beneficiary's community.

In *Shaffer v. Brooklyn Park Garden Apartments*,[13] the account parties notified the transferee of the credits that there had been no default on a loan obligation and that any assertion by the beneficiaries of that default would be fraudulent. The credits called for (1) a certificate to the effect that there was a default and (2) a negotiable draft. The *Shaffer* court held that, by virtue of the account parties' notice to the transferee of the beneficiaries' fraud, the transferee did not become a holder in due course of the drafts when the beneficiaries negotiated them to the transferee.

In *Scarsdale National Bank & Trust Co. v. Toronto-Dominion Bank*,[14] the plaintiff held the beneficiary's drafts and documents, all of which complied with the terms of the letter of credit that the defendant had issued. The beneficiary had obtained the documents by fraudulent conduct, however, and the court held that there was fraud in the transaction and that Section 5-114(2) authorized the defendant to dishonor the drafts.

The *Scarsdale* court would not apply the holder in due course exception in Section 5-114(2). The evidence indicated that the plaintiff holder knew that the terms of the underlying contract had not been performed. The court refused to see that knowledge as irrelevant, because such knowledge should have suggested to the plaintiff that the documents were fraudulent or procured by fraud. The plaintiff's evidence indicated that it did not have actual knowledge of the fraud, but the UCC's "notice" definition does not require actual knowledge. Under that definition, a person has notice of a fact when "from all the facts and circumstances known to him . . . he has reason to know that it exists."[15]

The *Scarsdale* court concluded that if the plaintiff did not know, its lack of knowledge resulted from its "willful ignorance."[16] *Scarsdale* is a unique case. The credit was a standby, and the evidence indicated that the plaintiff was involved intimately in financing the beneficiary's performance. The plaintiff was not simply a collecting bank that made advances against the drafts, as most presenting banks are under letters of credit.[17]

---

[13] 311 Minn. 452, 250 N.W.2d 172 (1977).

[14] 533 F. Supp. 378 (S.D.N.Y. 1982).

[15] U.C.C. § 1-201(25)(c).

[16] 533 F. Supp. 378, 387. For a case similar to *Scarsdale*, see Bank of Newport v. First Nat'l Bank & Trust Co., 687 F.2d 1257 (8th Cir. 1982). The *Bank of Newport* court did not address the holder in due course question.

[17] Cf. Emery-Waterhouse Co. v. Rhode Island Hosp. Trust Nat'l Bank, 757 F.2d 399 (1st Cir. 1985) (holding that because of its close connectedness with beneficiary and its knowledge of falsity in certificate, assignee of credit that took beneficiary's draft was not holder in due course).

In order to rise to the level of a holder in due course and avoid the fraud defense, then, a plaintiff must show that it took a negotiable instrument without notice. There are additional requirements. A party claiming holder in due course status also must show that it gave value,[18] a showing that may be difficult. Many negotiating banks, or other banks that undertake the collection of drafts under a credit, do so by giving their customers a provisional credit against which the customer may not draw. Provisional credit is not value. Such a bank would not have given value, and therefore it could not rise to the level of a holder in due course.[19]

In *Barclay Knitwear Co. v. King'swear Enterprises, Ltd.*,[20] the court concluded, perhaps erroneously, that the negotiating bank had given value for the full amount of the beneficiary's draft. The *Barclay* opinion recites that the negotiating bank allocated part of the value to satisfy preexisting indebtedness, part to satisfy bank charges, and part to the beneficiary's account. Under U.S. law, the negotiating bank clearly gave value to the extent of the first two allocations but may not have given value to the extent of the third. Under the Code, taking in satisfaction of a preexisting debt or for current charges is value.[21] The mere crediting of the beneficiary's account, however, is not value, unless the beneficiary draws against it or has the right to draw against it.[22]

A person who holds a negotiable draft and takes it under the credit in a fashion that does satisfy the requirements of Section 3-302 (i.e., for value, in good faith, and without notice of defenses or claims) is a holder in due course and will benefit from the exception of Section 5-114(2)(a).[23] The defense of fraud is no longer valid against him.[24]

---

[18] See U.C.C. § 3-302(1)(a).

[19] See U.C.C. §§ 3-303, 4-208, 4-209. A party may give value after it takes the drafts. In Union Export Co. v. N.I.B. Intermarket, A.B., No. 88-67-II (Tenn. Ct. App. July 27, 1988), the negotiating bank did not give value on time drafts until after they had been accepted; but the court recognized that once the bank gave value, it could become a holder in due course if it satisfied the other requirements for that status.

[20] 141 A.D.2d 241, 533 N.Y.S.2d 724 (1988), appeal denied, 74 N.Y.2d 605, 541 N.E.2d 427, 543 N.Y.S.2d 398 (1989).

[21] U.C.C. §§ 1-201(44)(a), 1-201(44)(d).

[22] U.C.C. §§ 4-208(1)(a), 4-208(1)(b), 4-209; Banque De L'Indochine Et De Suez S.A. v. J.H. Rayner (Mincing Lane) Ltd., [1983] 1 Lloyd's Rep. 228 (C.A.).

[23] There is a suggestion in Morgan v. Depositors Trust Co., 33 U.C.C. Rep. Serv. (Callaghan) 1473 (Me. Super. Ct. Kennebec County 1982), that the holder must also show that it did not deal with the fraudulent party. That notion comes from Section 3-305(2), but the *Morgan* court appears to have misapplied the provision. That particular rule in Section 3-305(2) applies to a party who takes an instrument from the maker or drawer, usually a buyer, and prohibits such a holder from cutting off defenses of the buyer that arise out of the transaction in which the holder and the

A simple example illustrates the operation of the rule. A fraudulent beneficiary delivers rubbish in twenty cartons to a freight forwarder and obtains a bill of lading reciting that the cartons contain computer peripherals. The beneficiary then draws a draft, obtains other documents (e.g., a certificate of origin, a customs invoice) and takes them with his letter of credit to the negotiating bank. The bank compares the documents with the terms of the credit and decides that the documents are in order. The bank then gives value to the beneficiary for his draft, taking the draft and the documents, including the fraudulent bill of lading. Though facially conforming, the bill of lading is intrinsically defective.

Before the negotiating bank presents the documents to the issuer, the account party learns of the fraud and warns the issuer not to pay. This fraud would give the issuer a defense to payment even if the documents were facially conforming. If the issuer raises the fraud, however, the negotiating bank will cut it off under Section 5-114(2)(a) because the negotiating bank is a holder in due course of the draft.[25]

The burden of establishing holder in due course status falls on the holder himself,[26] but there is no need to satisfy the burden unless the account party or issuer can first establish one of the four instances of in-

---

buyer dealt. A seller who delivers shoddy goods, for example, to a buyer cannot claim that he cuts off the breach of warranty defenses of the buyer, even though the seller may be a holder in due course of the buyer's note or check. See U.C.C. § 3-305(2). In the *Morgan* case, the holder had dealt with the account party, a bank that financed the transaction. The holder took the letter of credit as security. Such dealing with the account party does not fit the object of the prohibition in Section 3-305(2) and should not be used to prevent a holder from cutting off defenses if it otherwise satisfies the "holder in due course" definition.

[24] See, e.g., Marine Midland Grace Trust Co. v. Banco Del Pais, S.A., 261 F. Supp. 884 (S.D.N.Y. 1966); Balbo Oil Corp. v. Zigourakis, 40 Misc. 2d 710, 243 N.Y.S.2d 806 (Sup. Ct. 1963); Sztejn v. J. Henry Schroder Banking Corp., 177 Misc. 719, 31 N.Y.S.2d 631 (Sup. Ct. 1941).

[25] The negotiating bank is also a holder by due negotiation of the bill of lading. See U.C.C. § 7-501.

[26] U.C.C. § 3-307(3); Scarsdale Nat'l Bank & Trust Co. v. Toronto-Dominion Bank, 533 F. Supp. 378 (S.D.N.Y. 1982); Shaffer v. Brooklyn Park Garden Apartments, 311 Minn. 452, 250 N.W.2d 172 (1977); United Bank Ltd. v. Cambridge Sporting Goods Corp., 41 N.Y.2d 254, 360 N.E.2d 943, 392 N.Y.S.2d 265 (1976); Balbo Oil Corp. v. Zigourakis, 40 Misc. 2d 710, 243 N.Y.S.2d 806 (Sup. Ct. 1963). But cf. Eljay, Jrs., Inc. v. Rahda Exports, 99 A.D.2d 408, 470 N.Y.S.2d 12 (1984) (holding that burden is on account party in its suit for injunction against payment to show that negotiating bank is not holder in due course). But see Banco Espanol de Credito v. State St. Bank & Trust Co., 409 F.2d 711, 713 (1st Cir. 1969) (holding that beneficiary has burden of showing that it is holder in due course and of showing that it had no notice, but holding in next paragraph that on "notice" question, issuer has burden).

trinsic defect.[27] Once the account party or issuer does establish such defect, however, the party seeking payment must satisfy one of the good faith purchase exceptions. If he does not, the issuer may dishonor and a court may enjoin payment of the credit,[28] provided that the account party can show that such relief is appropriate under the rules of equity.[29]

[3] Holder of a Demand

There are credits that are payable not against drafts but against demands. Many standby credits call for simple demands (i.e., demands that are not accompanied by any other documents). The deferred payment credit also calls for a demand. It is clear from the language of Section 5-114(2)(a) that the Code drafters intended to include in the protected good faith purchase[30] category those persons who, in good faith, took such a "demand."

This concept is a new one in commercial law and in credit law,[31] and Section 5-114(2)(a) does not achieve this obvious purpose with the most artful language. The section refers to a "negotiating bank or other holder . . . which has taken the . . . demand . . . under circumstances which would make it a holder in due course." One of the circumstances that makes a holder a holder in due course is the fact that he holds a negotiable instrument, such as a draft. A demand for payment could be in draft form, but it does not seem likely that the drafters of Section 5-114(2)(a) used that awkward language in order to make it clear that a demand for payment may be in the form of a draft. It is much more likely

---

[27] See U.C.C. § 3-307; Bank of Canton, Ltd. v. Republic Nat'l Bank, 509 F. Supp. 1310 (S.D.N.Y.), aff'd, 636 F.2d 30 (2d Cir. 1980). In Bank of N.C., N.A. v. Rock Island Bank, 630 F.2d 1243 (7th Cir. 1980), the court held that a credit by which the issuer engaged to pay the holder in due course of a note did not require the party seeking payment to show that it was a holder in due course. For criticism of that holding, see ¶ 2.09[2].

[28] See United Bank Ltd. v. Cambridge Sporting Goods Corp., 41 N.Y.2d 254, 360 N.E.2d 943, 392 N.Y.S.2d 265 (1976).

[29] For discussion of the procedural rules for injunctions against honor of a letter of credit, see ¶ 11.05.

[30] For general discussion of the good faith purchase concept, see Dolan, "The U.C.C. Framework: Conveyancing Principles and Property Interests," 59 B.U.L. Rev. 811 (1979); Gilmore, "The Commercial Doctrine of Good Faith Purchase," 63 Yale L.J. 1057 (1954).

[31] But see Ellinger, "Discount of Letters of Credit," 1984 J. Bus. L. 379 (making the argument as matter of common law that holder of demand who is good faith purchaser for value should receive same protection that holder of negotiable draft receives).

that the purpose was to bring under the good faith purchase umbrella negotiating banks or other holders of requests for payment that are "demands" but not drafts.

Courts might construe Section 5-114(2)(a) in such a way that the terms "negotiating bank" and "other holder" would refer to parties that had taken some kind of negotiable demands for payment by due negotiation. Such a reading of the section, however, is not any more persuasive than is a reading that limits it to demands in the form of drafts. Issuers have been opening credits that call for demands rather than drafts precisely because they want to avoid negotiable instruments.[32] The issuers insist that the demands not satisfy the definition of "negotiable instrument" in Section 3-104. It is fair to conclude, especially in light of the Code's use of the term "demand," that the drafters were aware of this commercial practice and intended to protect persons who take nonnegotiable demands.

The reference, then, to Section 3-302 in Section 5-114(2)(a) should not be read to require the party to show that he holds a negotiable instrument, that is, to show that the negotiable instrument was duly negotiated to him by proper endorsement. The reference should be read only to require a showing that he has "taken" the demand in accordance with the three elements of a holder in due course set out in Section 3-302(1), namely, that he takes for value, in good faith, and without notice of any defense. The meaning of the subsection obviously is not free from doubt,[33] but there does not appear to be any reason to restrict the protection of the section to good faith purchasers for value of negotiable drafts and to deny it to good faith purchasers for value of nonnegotiable

---

[32] Some governments tax drafts and render them unattractive in credit settings when large sums are involved. Federal law permits banks to accept time drafts without incurring any reserve obligations if the drafts, among other conditions, have no more than six months' sight to run. Such acceptances are termed "eligible." See Federal Reserve Act, 12 U.S.C. § 372 (1988). A deferred payment credit, which does not call for acceptances, but for which a bank is committed, arguably overcomes that vagary of federal law and avoids the need to maintain reserves against a deferred payment obligation that matures more than 180 days after its creation. Ellinger observes that deferred payment letters of credit are more common in Southeast Asia and in Continental countries than in North America or in England. See Ellinger, supra note 31.

[33] In United Technologies Corp. v. Citibank, N.A., 469 F. Supp. 473 (S.D.N.Y. 1979), the issuer appears to have argued that the beneficiary of its credit calling for demands was entitled to good faith purchase protection. The court rejected the argument, ruling that only one who holds a negotiable draft can benefit from that protection. It is not clear from the opinion that the issuer made the argument that a holder of a nonnegotiable demand may benefit from good faith purchase protection. It also is not clear that the beneficiary, as opposed to a collecting bank, may ever use the good faith purchase protection of Section 5-114(2)(a).

demands. The policy in favor of including the latter good faith purchaser is manifest in the Code policy section itself, Section 1-102(2)(b), which expresses the command of the legislature that courts construe the Code liberally to promote the continued expansion of commercial practices.

Credits that call for demands instead of negotiable drafts are a new commercial practice and do not appear to be commercially harmful. This reading of Section 1-102(2)(b) suggests that courts construe Section 5-114 broadly to promote the new commercial practice of using demands and to lend the full protection of Section 5-114(2)(a) to it.[34]

[4] Bona Fide Purchaser

The drafters of Section 5-114(2)(a) concluded that purchasers of paper that is negotiable (i.e., negotiable instruments, negotiable securities, and negotiable documents) merit protection from the fraud defenses and included all three of such paper purchasers in Section 5-114(2)(a). The second of those purchasers is the bona fide purchaser of a security. In the event that a credit calls for a draft or a demand for payment accompanied by a negotiable security, the party seeking payment may qualify as a bona fide purchaser of that security under the good faith purchase provision of Article 8. If it does qualify, Section 5-114(2)(a) says that the party will defeat a claim of fraud in the credit transaction. In most cases, a person with bona fide purchaser status of a security also satisfies the definition either of a "holder in due course" or of the ill-defined "negotiating bank or other holder" who takes the nonnegotiable demand in good faith. In any event, the section protects the bona fide purchaser of a security.

Section 8-302 defines "bona fide purchaser" and makes it clear that such a purchaser must take for value, in good faith, and without notice of any adverse claim to the security. The bona fide purchaser may not avail himself of Section 5-114(2)(a) if he is in any way a party to the fraud. Such fraudulent conduct would amount to bad faith, would prevent the purchaser from satisfying the good faith element of the provision, and would prevent him from cutting off the fraud defenses.

---

[34] For commentary supporting the position that the party demanding payment should benefit from the holder in due course rule, see Ellinger, supra note 31; Eberth & Ellinger, "Deferred Payment Credits: A Comparative Analysis of Their Special Problems," 14 J. Mar. L. & Com. 387 (1983).

[5] Holder to Whom a Negotiable Document of Title Has Been Duly Negotiated

The last of the parties protected from the fraud exception in Section 5-114(2) is the good faith purchaser of a negotiable document of title. Because negotiable bills of lading and negotiable warehouse receipts often arise in credit transactions, such protection arises often, especially in commercial credit transactions.[35]

Section 7-501 sets out the requirements for due negotiation of a document of title, and, after including the traditional elements of good faith purchase (value, good faith, and no notice), it adds a fourth element unique to documents of title. That element of the definition requires that the document be taken in the ordinary course of business or finance and that it not be taken in settlement or payment of a monetary obligation.

It is not uncommon for banks other than the issuer to deal with drafts and documents called for by a letter of credit. If the credit calls for a negotiable bill of lading,[36] for example, as many commercial credits do, negotiating and collecting banks may qualify under Section 7-501 for good faith purchase protection. In order to qualify, the bank must take the negotiable bill of lading without notice of any defense or claim and in good faith, and the document must be in bearer form or properly indorsed.[37] Such a bank generally takes the bill in the regular course of its business because the collection of drafts accompanied by bills has long been a common banking activity.[38]

In order to gain the protection accorded one who takes a negotiable document by due negotiation, the collecting or negotiating banks must give value. If a bank takes a negotiable draft, it clearly benefits from the value rules of Articles 3 and 4. If the credit does not call for a draft, it seems that the bank must satisfy the value rule of Section 1-201. In either event, a bank that enters a provisional credit alone in favor of its customer, the beneficiary, has not given value. If the customer has the right to draw against the provisional entry or actually has drawn on it, the bank has given value and therefore can qualify as a person to whom a negotiable document of title has been duly negotiated.[39] Similarly, a

---

[35] For a general treatment of documents of title that deals with the "document" questions raised here in greater detail and cites many of the letter of credit cases, see R. Henson, Documents of Title Under the Uniform Commercial Code (1983).

[36] There are many kinds of documents of title. See U.C.C. § 1-201(15). Of them all, the bill of lading appears most frequently in the credit transaction.

[37] See U.C.C. § 7-501(1).

[38] See ¶ 3.04.

[39] See U.C.C. § 1-201, comment 44 (2d para.).

bank that takes the bill of lading as security for a contemporaneous or prior advance has a security interest in the bill and has given value.[40] In determining whether value has been given, it does not matter that the bank has a right of recourse against its depositor. So long as the customer has the right to draw against the deposit or does draw against it, the bank has given value, regardless of whether it has a right of recourse.[41] The giving of value is critical. Negotiating banks that take the beneficiary's documents under reserve, that is, under an arrangement whereby the beneficiary does not receive credit against which it may draw,[42] do not give value and may not qualify for good faith purchase protection.

Briefly, then, a negotiating bank that takes a beneficiary's documents may qualify for good faith purchase protection. In order to do so, however, it must rise to the status of one of four personages:

1. A holder in due course of a negotiable instrument;
2. A bona fide purchaser of a security;
3. A holder who takes a negotiable document of title by due negotiation; or
4. One who takes a demand for value, in good faith, and without notice of any claim or defense.

[6] Distinction Between a Straight Credit and a Negotiation Credit

Letter of credit law has long distinguished the straight credit from the negotiation credit. The engagement of the former runs to the beneficiary[43]; the engagement of the latter runs to negotiating banks or to "drawers, endorsers, and bona fide holders."[44] This quoted phrase is the traditional negotiation clause. The significance of it is that it obviously extends the credit engagement to parties other than the person with whom the account party is doing business.

If a Boston account party is purchasing garments from a New Orleans broker, the account party might agree to cause its Boston bank to issue a straight credit in favor of the broker payable, for example,

---

[40] See U.C.C. § 4-208, 4-209.

[41] See U.C.C. § 4-208(1)(b).

[42] See supra note 22.

[43] For an example of a straight credit, see App. C, Doc. 15.

[44] For an example of a negotiation credit, see App. C, Doc. 16. Sometimes courts and letter of credit bankers refer to negotiation credits as "negotiable credits." See, e.g., Supreme Merchandise Co. v. Chemical Bank, 70 N.Y.2d 344, 514 N.E.2d 1358, 520 N.Y.S.2d 734 (1987). For authority that the negotiation credit is not a negotiable instrument, see ¶ 3.03[5].

against time drafts. In that case, the broker can draw under the credit and can take his drafts to a New Orleans bank for discount. By discounting the drafts, the New Orleans bank probably will become a holder in due course of them, if it satisfies the elements of the "holder in due course" definition.[45] That bank may not benefit, however, from Section 5-114(2)(a), because it is not clear that the bank took the drafts "under the credit," as that section requires. The engagement of the Boston bank runs only to the broker, and, if the Boston bank or its account party establishes fraud in the credit transaction, it may not avail the New Orleans bank to prove that it is a holder in due course. It did not take "under the credit," is not a beneficiary of the Boston bank's engagement, and was not "authorized" by the issuer to negotiate the broker's drafts.[46]

On the other hand, if the Boston bank issues a negotiation credit, it implicitly authorizes the New Orleans bank to discount the drafts and explicitly engages to pay the New Orleans bank, which is a bona fide holder.[47] By discounting drafts drawn against a negotiation credit, the New Orleans bank takes "under the credit," as Section 5-114(2)(a) requires, and, if it satisfies the "holder in due course" definition, the bank will cut off the issuer's fraud defense.[48]

Some commentators disagree with this analysis.[49] Under their view, the New Orleans bank does not act solely for its own account when it

---

[45] See supra ¶ 8.01[2].

[46] Cf. U.C.C. § 5-106(4) & comment 2 (using notion that negotiating bank acts under authority of issuer in negotiating beneficiary's drafts); see also U.C.P. art. 10(a)(iv) (1983).

[47] That is not to say that the negotiating bank is an agent of the issuer. See Bank of N.S. v. Angelica-Whitewear Ltd., 36 D.L.R.4th 161 (Can. 1987). Under this analysis, the negotiating bank acts for itself, but it does so with the understanding that the issuer's undertaking runs to the negotiating bank and not just to the beneficiary.

[48] The ability to cut off the fraud defense depends, however, on the conformity of the documents. Throughout this discussion the text assumes that the documents conform. If they do not, the issuer has no duty to pay, notwithstanding the fact that the negotiating bank is a holder in due course. Regarding facial conformity, the negotiating bank acts "at its peril" when it takes the documents. Banco Nacional De Desarrollo v. Mellon Bank, N.A., 726 F.2d 87, 92 (3d Cir. 1984).

[49] See Eberth & Ellinger, "Assignment and Presentation of Documents in Commercial Credit Transactions," 24 Ariz. L. Rev. 277, 293 (1982). Professor Ellinger appears to take a contrary position, however, in a subsequently published piece. See Ellinger, "Discount of Letters of Credit," 1984 J. Bus. L. 379. Professors White and Summers do not approve of the distinction and take the further position — unwarranted, it seems — that the distinction has not been observed by U.S. courts. See J. White & R. Summers, 2 Handbook of the Uniform Commercial Code 74 (practitioner's ed. 1989). Other authority bears them out, however. See authority cited infra note 51 and in ¶ 10.02[4]. For other explanations of the distinction, see R.M. Goode,

presents the drafts and documents to the Boston issuer under a straight credit but also acts for the broker. Under this theory, by taking the drafts to the New Orleans bank, the broker beneficiary of a straight credit designates the bank as his agent for the purposes of collecting the draft, and the New Orleans bank has taken "under the credit."[50]

Many cases in the 1970s and 1980s did not take note of this distinction between straight and negotiation credits,[51] and the law is not clear. To hold that the distinction does not matter, however, is to ignore something issuers have thought has mattered for a long time[52] and de-

---

Commercial Law 674 (1985); Givray, "UCC Survey, Letters of Credit," 44 Bus. Law. 1567, 1633–1634 (1989). For further discussion of the question, see ¶ 10.02.

[50] While there is some inconsistency in the notion that the New Orleans bank is an agent when it collects an instrument it holds as owner, commercial law has accepted the notion in other contexts. See U.C.C. § 4-201(1).

[51] See Emery-Waterhouse Co. v. Rhode Island Hosp. Trust Nat'l Bank, 757 F.2d 399 (1st Cir. 1985); Scarsdale Nat'l Bank & Trust Co. v. Toronto-Dominion Bank, 533 F. Supp. 378 (S.D.N.Y. 1982); New Tech Devs., Div. of San Diego Carleton Lewis Corp. v. Bynamics, Inc., 191 Cal. App. 3d 1065, 236 Cal. Rptr. 746 (1987); Shaffer v. Brooklyn Park Garden Apartments, 311 Minn. 452, 250 N.W.2d 172 (1977); United Bank Ltd. v. Cambridge Sporting Goods Corp., 41 N.Y.2d 254, 360 N.E.2d 943, 392 N.Y.S.2d 265 (1976); Union Export Co. v. N.I.B. Intermarket, A.B., No. 88-67-II (Tenn. Ct. App. July 27, 1988); International Commercial Bank of China v. Hall-Fuston Corp., 767 S.W.2d 259 (Tex. Ct. App. 1989); cf. Barclay Knitwear Co. v. King'swear Enters., Ltd., 141 A.D.2d 241, 533 N.Y.S.2d 724 (1988), appeal denied, 74 N.Y.2d 605, 541 N.E.2d 427, 543 N.Y.S.2d 398 (1989) (unclear on point); Eljay, Jrs., Inc. v. Rahda Exports, 99 A.D.2d 408, 470 N.Y.S.2d 12 (1984) (same); First Commercial Bank v. Gotham Originals, Inc., 101 A.D.2d 790, 476 N.Y.S.2d 835 (Sup. Ct. 1984), aff'd, 64 N.Y.2d 287, 475 N.E.2d 1255, 486 N.Y.S.2d 715 (1985) (same).

[52] See Harfield, "Identity Crises in Letter of Credit Law," 24 Ariz. L. Rev. 239, 246–248 (1982); Ufford, "Transfer and Assignment of Letters of Credit Under the Uniform Commercial Code," 7 Wayne L. Rev. 263 (1960); McGowan, "Assignability of Documentary Credits," 13 Law & Contemp. Probs. 666, 679 n.28 (1948); U.C.C. § 2-506, comment 2 (6th sent.); U.C.C. § 5-116, comment 1 (2d para., 4th sent.). See generally ¶ 10.02. But cf. Colleran, "Negotiation Under L/Cs: Veteran Banker Colleran Looks at Possibilities," Letter of Credit Update 10 (April 1990). For a case that rules in favor of a holder in due course of drafts when there is fraud in the documents but that does not indicate whether the credit was a negotiation credit, see Banco Espanol de Credito v. State St. Bank & Trust Co., 409 F.2d 711 (1st Cir. 1969). Professor Ellinger questions the wisdom of the distinction as a common-law rule. See Ellinger, "Fraud in Documentary Credit Transactions," 1981 J. Bus. L. 258, 263–264. In his view, there is no reason to protect the negotiating bank under a negotiation credit and deny protection to a collecting bank under a straight credit. Since both may be holders in due course, he does not differentiate between them. The trouble with that view and the apparent view of Judge Coffin in the *Banco Espanol* case is that they may ignore reasonable expectations of both the issuer regarding its obligations and those of the presenting bank regarding its benefits under a credit,

prives commercial parties of the prerogative of fashioning credits as straight credits or negotiation credits in order to satisfy their commercial needs.

International Commercial Bank of China v. Hall-Fuston Corp.[53] illustrates the confusion. In that case, the account party sued in tort a bank that presented a forged document to the issuer. Clearly, if the defendant is a negotiating bank under a negotiation credit, the policy of Section 5-114(2)(a) is to protect the bank. Since the section gives the bank the right to payment, accepting the payment should not constitute a tort, as the complaint in *Hall-Fuston* alleged.

The court found, however, that the defendant bank was an agent of the beneficiary's bank; that is, it found that when the defendant bank presented the document to the issuer, the defendant acted not in its own behalf but in behalf of the beneficiary or its bank. In that event, the defendant was not a negotiating bank acting under a negotiation credit, because such a bank acts in its own right when it presents documents to the issuer. Nonetheless, it is clear from the opinion that the litigation centered on the holder in due course status of the defendant—an issue that is entirely irrelevant if the defendant is acting as agent for the beneficiary's bank.

International bankers take drafts drawn under negotiation credits in circumstances that make them holders in due course precisely because they know that under international letter of credit law, they are protected. Section 5-114(2)(a) codifies that protection. By negative implication, when a bank takes a draft, even under circumstances that make it a holder in due course, it has no protection if it acts as an agent for the beneficiary. It so acts if the credit is straight.

The inquiry into the holder in due course status of the bank in the *Fuston-Hall* case is inconsistent with the earlier holding that the bank had acted as agent of the beneficiary, which, in turn, is inconsistent with the fact, if it is a fact, that the credit was a negotiation credit.

---

a distinction that has antecedents in credit tradition. Cf. Diakan Love, S.A. v. Al-Haddad Bros. Enter., Inc. (In re Diakan Love, S.A.), 584 F. Supp. 782 (S.D.N.Y. 1984) (dismissing writ of attachment on ground that to permit attachment would impede effectiveness of negotiation credits); Supreme Merchandise Co. v. Chemical Bank, 117 A.D.2d 424, 503 N.Y.S.2d 9 (1986), aff'd, 70 N.Y.2d 344, 514 N.E.2d 1358, 520 N.Y.S.2d 734 (1987) (same). English authority generally accepts the distinctions advanced in the text. See European Asian Bank A.G. v. Punjab & Sind Bank, [1983] 2 All E.R. 508 (C.A.); R.M. Goode, Commercial Law 674 (1985).

[53] 767 S.W.2d 259 (Tex. Ct. App. 1989).

[7] Advising Banks and Confirming Banks

[a] Nature of Relationship

Although a significant number of credit transactions involve more than one bank, there are relatively few disputes that arise between the issuer and the advising or the confirming bank. As a general rule, the part of the transaction that involves the two banks goes off without any difficulty, and the paucity of litigation leaves undeveloped the nature of the issuer's relationship with the other bank. The rough contours of the relationships are evident, however.

In the event the issuer asks the confirming bank to confirm the credit, the role of the issuer (the opening bank) is then analogous to that of a customer, and the confirming bank's role is analogous to that of the issuer in the two-bank relationship. In the common event that the confirming bank honors the credit obligation, it has a right of reimbursement from the opening bank as a matter of letter of credit law,[54] rather than as a matter of contract or agency law. The confirming bank may be able to invoke the misnamed bifurcated standard[55] in seeking its reimbursement. If the beneficiary rather than the opening bank obtains the confirmation, the confirming bank has no right of reimbursement,[56] and the opening bank might be able to impose the standard of strict compliance that normally applies.[57]

If a bank, at the request of the opening bank, advises but does not confirm, the relationship between the banks is one of agency.[58] Sometimes the advising bank also is nominated in the credit as payor bank. If the advising bank pays, it can collect from its principal, the issuer to whom its duties regarding examination of the documents run. Those duties do not run to third parties.[59]

---

[54] See U.C.C. § 5-107(2) & comment 2 (3d sentence).

[55] But cf. Seattle First Nat'l Bank v. FDIC, 619 F. Supp. 1351 (W.D. Okla. 1985) (holding that opening bank can insist on strict compliance from confirming bank); Bank of Cochin Ltd. v. Manufacturers Hanover Trust Co., 612 F. Supp. 1533 (S.D.N.Y. 1985), aff'd on other grounds, 808 F.2d 209 (2d Cir. 1986) (same). For criticism of the *Bank of Cochin* and *Seattle First National Bank* cases, see ¶ 9.03[1][a].

[56] See Permanent Editorial Board for the Uniform Commercial Code, Rep. No. 2, at 101 (1964).

[57] See ¶ 6.03.

[58] See Sound of Mkt. St., Inc. v. Continental Bank, Int'l, 819 F.2d 384 (3d Cir. 1987); Bamberger Polymers Int'l Corp. v. Citibank, N.A., 124 Misc. 2d 653, 477 N.Y.S.2d 931 (Sup. Ct. 1983).

[59] See Auto Servicio San Ignacio, S.R.L. v. Compania Anonima Venezolana De Navegacion, 586 F. Supp. 259 (E.D. La. 1984), aff'd, 765 F.2d 1306 (5th Cir. 1985); cf. Worldwide Sugar Co. v. Royal Bank of Can., 609 F. Supp. 19 (S.D.N.Y. 1984) (holding that account party did not benefit from guaranty that advising bank gave to issuer).

[b] Warranties

Section 5-111(2) of the Code sets forth the warranties that advising, confirming, or negotiating banks make to the issuer. Significantly, Section 5-111 differentiates the warranties of the presenter in Section 5-111(1) from those of banks acting in one of the three mentioned capacities. While the presenter warrants under Section 5-111(1) that all of the conditions of the credit are complied with, the advising, confirming, and negotiating banks make the relatively light warranties under Section 5-111(2) that they act with authority and in good faith.[60] If a bank takes the beneficiary's draft and documents and obtains final payment from the issuer, and if the documents are defective because of fraud, for example, the issuer cannot recover from the bank on a breach of warranty theory, although it could recover from the beneficiary.

In *Merchants Bank v. Credit Suisse Bank*,[61] the advising bank submitted documents to the issuer. The issuer dishonored because the documents did not conform. The issuer then asked the advising bank for authority to present the documents to the account party "on a collection basis."[62] The advising bank extended that authority, but the account party refused to pay. When the beneficiary sued the advising bank, it settled and sought to recover the amount of its settlement from the issuer. On the issuing bank's motion to dismiss, the court held that the advising bank could proceed with a claim that the issuer, when it asked for authority to proceed on a collection basis, fraudulently had failed to disclose the account party's precarious financial condition. It was the beneficiary's theory that, by authorizing the collection, the advising bank had deprived the beneficiary of any rights against the issuer on the credit. Thus, the *Merchants Bank* case stands for the position that the issuer owes a duty to the advising bank when the advising bank is acting as a collecting agent for the beneficiary.

¶ 8.02   ISSUER AS GOOD FAITH PURCHASER

The law of negotiability bestows benefits on those who seek payment under the credit.[63] These same rules of negotiability often benefit the issuer. First, the issuer itself may qualify as a good faith purchaser of a negotiable instrument, document, or security presented by the beneficiary

---

[60] See U.C.C. § 5-111, comment (penultimate sentence).

[61] 585 F. Supp. 304 (S.D.N.Y. 1984).

[62] Id. at 306.

[63] See supra ¶ 8.01.

when it seeks payment under the credit. When the issuer pays a draft and takes a properly endorsed negotiable document or security, it is probably a good faith purchaser of that document or security. Similarly, if the issuer gives value for a draft drawn on the account party, as some credits provide, the issuer becomes a holder in due course of that negotiable draft.

In all events, an issuer claiming good faith purchase status must take the negotiable paper for value, in good faith, and without notice of claims or defenses.[64] In the case of negotiable documents, it must take in the regular course of business or finance and must not take in settlement or payment of a money obligation.[65] Virtually all issuers will satisfy the value requirement, because the credit invariably gives the beneficiary or negotiating bank the right to an unqualified payment, a negotiable obligation, or a deferred payment undertaking, all of which are value under the Code.[66] The issuer that takes documents of title accompanying a draft does so in the regular course of business or finance and does not take in settlement of or in payment of a money obligation.

In general, an issuer's right of reimbursement does not depend on its status as a holder of the beneficiary's drafts. In most cases, the draft is drawn on the issuer itself. The drawee of a draft is not a holder after payment, because payment extinguishes the instrument and discharges all parties from their contract liability.[67] The issuer's rights against the account party arise under the application agreement or under Section 5-114(3), not under the draft.[68] The importance to the issuer of good faith purchase status arises when it cannot obtain reimbursement and must look either to the merchandise covered by a document of title or to a negotiable security in the event that it holds a negotiable security under a credit.

Whether an issuer takes a negotiable document or security in good faith and without notice of claims or defenses is usually a question of fact. The Code defines two good faith rules: one in the general definition provision, Section 1-201, and one in Section 2-103(1)(b). The former is a subjective rule requiring honesty in fact; the latter is objective and requires "honesty in fact and the observance of reasonable commercial

---

[64] See supra ¶ 8.01[2].

[65] See U.C.C. § 7-501(4).

[66] See U.C.C. §§ 1-201(44), 3-303, 4-208, 4-209.

[67] For discussion of this concept that the obligor of negotiable paper who takes it up after satisfying the obligation is not a good faith purchaser, see E.F. Hutton & Co. v. Manufacturers Nat'l Bank, 259 F. Supp. 513 (E.D. Mich. 1966).

[68] Accord Talbot v. Bank of Hendersonville, 495 S.W.2d 548 (Tenn. Ct. App. 1972). See generally ¶ 7.05.

standards of fair dealing in the trade." The subjective rule, sometimes called the pure heart rule, permits an issuer to pay under the credit as long as the issuer is not acting dishonestly. The objective rule, which applies to merchants, requires honesty plus reasonable commercial conduct and thereby opens the inquiry considerably.

Credit issuers are probably within the Code definition of "merchant,"[69] but there are good reasons for not applying the merchant good faith rule to issuers for the purposes of determining the issuer's standing as a good faith purchaser of negotiable paper. First, the Code's drafters suggest in their definitional cross-references following the good faith purchase sections that the good faith requirement is that of the pure heart rule of Section 1-201. The references cite that section rather than the objective rule of Article 2. Second, cases construing the "holder in due course" definition of Article 3 support application of the pure heart definition rather than the objective definition.[70] These cases are persuasive and should control the good faith purchase question under Section 5-114(2). They serve the policy in favor of judicial efficiency in negotiability cases.

By preferring the honesty in fact rule—the subjective test—over the objective rule, courts are not trying to protect purchasers who fail to observe reasonable commercial practices; they are trying to avoid litigating questions of "reasonableness" in the negotiation setting. These questions often involve extended inquiry into trade practices, and the courts have concluded that such inquiry does not serve the fast pace of transactions in, and litigation over, negotiable paper. The Code drafters' selection of Article 1 for the definition of the objective rule, while not determinative,[71] supports this analysis. The definitions of Article 1 generally apply throughout the Code, while additional definitions "in the subsequent Articles of this Act . . . are applicable to specific Articles or Parts thereof."[72] Article 2, moreover, applies to transactions in goods, not to transactions in negotiable paper,[73] and Section 2-103, in defining the objective good faith rule, asserts that the definition applies in "this Article," that is, Article 2.

---

[69] For the Article 2 definition of "merchant," see U.C.C. § 2-104(1).

[70] E.g., Corporacion Venezolana de Fomento v. Vintero Sales Corp., 452 F. Supp. 1108 (S.D.N.Y. 1978); Shaffer v. Brooklyn Park Garden Apartments, 311 Minn. 452, 250 N.W.2d 172 (1977); cf. U.C.C. § 5-103(4) (indicating that Article 1 definitions apply in Article 5).

[71] See, e.g., Stowers v. Mahon (In re Samuels & Co.), 526 F.2d 1238 (5th Cir.), cert. denied, 429 U.S. 834 (1976). Contra Sherrock v. Commercial Credit Corp., 290 A.2d 648 (Del. 1972).

[72] U.C.C. § 1-201.

[73] U.C.C. § 2-102.

Intraworld Industries, Inc. v. Girard Trust Bank[74] involved a claim by the account party that the issuer's decision to make a payment under the credit was in bad faith because the issuer did not resolve a dispute between the account party and the beneficiary before deciding to honor the beneficiary's demand for payment. The court held that such a decision does not constitute bad faith and that any other holding would have put the issuer in an "intolerable position."[75] The *Intraworld* court appears to favor the subjective definition of "good faith" over the objective definition.

Lustrelon, Inc. v. Prutscher[76] explicitly adopts the subjective rule and holds that "good faith" for the purposes of Section 5-114(2)(b) means honesty in fact. *Philadelphia Gear Corp. v. Central Bank*[77] also adopts the pure heart test. In that case, the court held that it is not dishonest, and therefore not bad faith, for the issuer to reject a nonconforming presentation by the beneficiary without first soliciting the view of the account party. This authority construing an Article 5 provision supports the view that, outside of Article 2, the subjective test should apply. Issuers that take negotiable paper honestly, therefore, should satisfy the good faith requisite for good faith purchase status.

Sometimes a party may argue that the issuer fails the good faith purchase test because the issuer has notice of the account party's defenses against the beneficiary. Under negotiable instruments rules, that notice is sufficient to defeat good faith purchase status because the good faith purchaser must show that it took without notice of claims or defenses.[78] In some of these instances, however, the issuer, although not a good faith purchaser itself, may benefit from good faith purchase protection by virtue of the shelter principle. Under that rule,[79] a transferee of negotiable paper takes all of the rights of the transferor. If the transferor—a negotiating bank, for example—is a holder in due course of a draft drawn on the account party, the bank's transfer of the draft to the issuer will carry good faith purchase protection with it, even though the issuer has notice of the beneficiary's fraud. The rule is consistent with the command of Section 5-114(2)(a) that the issuer must honor the drafts when the negotiating bank is a good faith purchaser. The issuer would not be a holder in due course when it paid, but it would benefit from the shelter of the negotiating bank's holder in due course status.

[74] 461 Pa. 343, 336 A.2d 316 (1975).

[75] Id. at 364, 336 A.2d at 327.

[76] 178 N.J. Super. 128, 428 A.2d 518 (App. Div. 1981).

[77] 717 F.2d 230 (5th Cir. 1983).

[78] See U.C.C. §§ 3-302(1)(c), 7-501(4), 8-302(1).

[79] See U.C.C. §§ 3-201(1), 7-504(1), 8-301(1).

The same type of analysis holds for issuers that take negotiable bills of lading or negotiable securities from a good faith purchase negotiating bank, even though the issuer has notice of fraud. Once the issuer establishes its status as a good faith purchaser of negotiable paper, it is necessary to determine the nature of the issuer's interest in that paper and in the obligations it represents.[80]

¶ 8.03   ISSUER'S INTEREST IN THE DRAFT AND ACCOMPANYING DOCUMENTS

Issuers may assert a number of interests in the paper submitted by the beneficiary. They include the banker's lien, title, and the security interest. The last of these, the security interest, is the most important because it is a stronger right than the lien and because the Code relegates title to a minor role.

[1]   Banker's Lien

At common law, bankers enjoy a possessory lien in documents of a customer. The lien does not include a right of foreclosure or sale. It is simply the right of the bank to withhold documents from the customer until the customer satisfies the bank's charges.[81]

Documents subject to the banker's lien must come into the bank's possession in the course of the customer's banking business, not as part of an arrangement with the bank to secure the customer's obligations to the bank. This latter arrangement is a security interest. Article 9 of the Code governs security interests and generally requires a written security agreement signed by the debtor in order to create a security interest and certain filings or possession pursuant to an agreement to render the interest good against third parties. Any "lien" created by the agreement of the customer of the bank and intended as security comes within the scope of Article 9, must satisfy Article 9 rules, and does not constitute a banker's lien.[82]

Most letter of credit issuers are banks, and they can argue convincingly that documents coming into their possession upon payment of a draft or demand under a credit are subject to the common law banker's lien. In most instances, however, the bank also enjoys a security interest

---

[80] See infra ¶ 8.03.

[81] See Restatement of the Law of Security §§ 62, 72 (1941).

[82] See U.C.C. § 9-102(1)(a).

in these papers. That interest carries with it the right to foreclose and therefore is stronger than the lien.

[2] Title and the Security Interest

In some instances, the issuer may claim that it has title to the documents and even to the goods that the documents represent. Often a letter of credit calls for a negotiable bill of lading endorsed in blank or endorsed to the issuer.[83] Upon honoring the beneficiary's request for payment under such a credit, the issuer becomes a holder of the bill by due negotiation, that is, a good faith purchaser of a negotiable document of title.[84] Under Section 7-502, such a holder acquires title to the document and title to the goods.

This "title" rule of Section 7-502 effects an anomaly. Banks that issue credits often take a negotiable bill in such fashion and then become qualified holders of such bills, yet there are good reasons for banks not to want title to the goods. Banks are authorized to lend against paper, such as bills of lading; and they often take security interests in such paper; but they are not authorized to speculate in commodities for their own account.[85] When bankers speak of "purchasing" bills of lading, they mean "purchase" in the broad sense of taking a security interest.[86] It is probably fair to say that when banks take bills of lading, they have no intention of acquiring title to anything, but only of protecting themselves against advances they might have made. In short, their intention is to obtain a security interest, not to acquire merchandise.

Title plays a minor role in determining the interests of holders in negotiable documents of title.[87] If issuers cause the credit to call for a negotiable bill endorsed to the bank or in blank so that the bill secures the issuer, Article 9 governs the bank's interest in the documents. By its

---

[83] But cf. de May, "Bills of Lading Problems in the Oil Trade: Documentary Credit Aspects," 2 J. Energy & Nat. Resources L. 197 (1984) (suggesting that negotiable bills are no longer efficient in at least one industry); Merchant, "New Developments in Transport Documents," 2 Letter of Credit Reports 8 (Mar./Apr. 1988) (contending that paperless transport arrangements do not permit bills of lading to retain negotiable features); Murphy, "A Banker's View of Electronic Documents," Letters of Credit Report 12 (Sept./Oct. 1988) (cautioning against use of electronic documents).

[84] See U.C.C. §§ 7-501, 7-502. See generally supra ¶ 8.01[5].

[85] See 12 U.S.C. § 24 (1988).

[86] See U.C.C. §§ 1-201(32), 1-201(33).

[87] See generally Dolan, "Good Faith Purchase and Warehouse Receipts: Thoughts on the Interplay of Articles 2, 7, and 9 of the UCC," 30 Hastings L.J. 1 (1978).

terms, Section 9-102 preempts all other security law, and, under Article 9, the location of title to the collateral is not material.[88] For the purposes of determining the rights of the issuer in the negotiable document and in the goods[89] it represents, courts must look to Article 9. In short, courts must consider the issuer's interest a security interest.[90]

[a] Creating the Security Interest

Section 9-203 stipulates that a security interest does not attach to collateral until the secured party holds the collateral pursuant to agreement with the debtor or until the debtor has signed a security agreement granting a security interest to the secured party. Section 9-309 provides, however, that nothing in Article 9 limits the rights of a holder by due

---

[88] See U.C.C. § 9-202.

[89] Section 9-304(2) provides that while goods are in the possession of a bailee who has issued a negotiable document for them, a security interest in the goods should be perfected by perfecting a security interest in the negotiable document. This is an instance of the "simulacra" rule, whereby goods subject to a negotiable document of title become a mere shadow, with a document standing for the goods and under which parties who wish to deal with the goods must deal with the document.

[90] It may be misleading to suggest that bank issuers are always concerned about their security interest in the goods. It is probably fair to say that they do not mind having the security interest but are more concerned about the account party's ability to reimburse the issuer when it pays the beneficiary. See Smith, "Irrevocable Letters of Credit and Third Party Fraud: The American Accord," 24 Va. J. Int'l L. 55 (1983). In United City Merchants (Invs.) Ltd. v. Royal Bank of Can., [1983] A.C. 168 (H.L.), the court decided that a confirming bank could not dishonor a presentation that included a fraudulent bill of lading, so long as the beneficiary did not know of the fraud. That case suggests that English courts are not exceedingly concerned with the issuer's security. Although the fraud in *United City Merchants* related to a date, the rule of the case apparently would apply if the bills misrepresented the goods. For authority suggesting that commercial parties rely heavily on the goods that are the subject of a commercial letter of credit transaction, see INA v. S/S "Globe Nova," 638 F. Supp. 1413 (S.D.N.Y. 1986), rev'd, 820 F.2d 546 (2d Cir. 1987). Some authorities distinguish issuer reliance by the type of merchandise involved. Rowe suggests that sellers of "general merchandise" can obtain payment without resorting to a negotiable bill of lading but that other goods generally are covered by negotiable documents. See Rowe, "Automating International Trade Payments—Legal and Regulatory Issues," 4 J. Int'l Bus. L. 234, 239 (1987); cf. C. Schmitthoff, Schmitthoff's Export Trade 336–337 (8th ed. 1986) (suggesting that, in Britain, negotiable bill finances letter of credit transaction). Other authority distinguishes credits supporting the sale of goods that are readily marketable (when the issuer is relying on the goods) and sales of goods that are not readily marketable (when the issuer is not relying). See generally Murphy, "A Banker's View of Electronic Documents," Letters of Credit Report 12 (Sept./Oct. 1988) (contending that bankers look to goods in underlying transaction as secondary, but nonetheless important, source of protection against account party's failure to reimburse).

negotiation of a negotiable document of title. It appears, then, that the Article 9 requirement for a written security agreement or possession pursuant to agreement does not limit the rights of the issuer if the issuer qualifies as a good faith purchaser of a negotiable bill. The mere taking of the bill by due negotiation is sufficient to give the issuer a security interest. The careful issuer, nevertheless, usually provides in the credit application for security agreement language giving the issuer a security interest in both the document of title and the goods covered by it.[91]

[b] Extent of the Security Interest

Section 9-309 might be read to deny Article 9 limits to the issuer's security interest. The section stipulates that "[n]othing in this Article limits the rights of . . . a holder to whom a negotiable document of title has been duly negotiated."[92] It is not warranted, however, to conclude from that language that all limits in Article 9 are inapplicable.

In general, Article 9 provides that the secured party's interest shall extend only to the indebtedness secured. Section 9-504 requires the secured party to turn over to the debtor any excess over the debt that the secured party realizes on the sale of the collateral, and Section 9-505 permits the secured party to retain the collateral in satisfaction of the debt only if the debtor consents after default. These debtor protection rules are consistent with the reasonable expectations of the account party and of the issuer. Both of them would be surprised, indeed, if the court construed the title rule of Section 7-502 or the "nothing limits" rule of Section 9-309 to say that the bank is entitled to that value of the collateral that exceeds the debt.

It is difficult to deny the implication in the language of Section 9-309 that "nothing in Article 9" limits the rights of the holder and that the debtor protection rule of Article 9 should not limit the issuer's rights as a holder by due negotiation of a negotiable document of title. It is a cardinal precept of Code construction, however, that courts should not extend Code rules beyond their reason.[93] The obvious purpose of Section 9-309 is to protect the qualified holder from the claims of third parties that they have an interest in the goods that is superior to that of the holder by virtue of some priority rule in the Article.[94] It serves no apparent policy in the section to read it as depriving the debtor of his equity in the collateral. Courts should not extend the rule of Section 9-309 and

---

[91] For an example of an application agreement, see App. C, Doc. 14.
[92] U.C.C. § 9-309.
[93] See U.C.C. § 1-102, comment 1 (3d sent.).
[94] See Dolan, supra note 87, at 17–20.

the title language of Section 7-502 beyond what commercial parties reasonably anticipate.

In *Centola v. Italian Discount & Trust Co.*,[95] the credit covered a portion of the purchase price that the account party had agreed to pay the beneficiary. Payment under the credit provided the beneficiary with only partial protection, and, when the account party refused to accept the goods, the beneficiary's seller offered to return the issuer's payment and to take the goods back. The seller was attempting to realize the full value of the goods. The bank, however, claimed a security interest in the goods by virtue of the provision in the credit application giving the bank title to the goods as security. The credit also called for negotiable bills of lading, and it appears from the opinion that the bank was a holder to whom those negotiable bills had been duly negotiated. The issuer rejected the seller's offer to return the amount that the issuer had paid the beneficiary. The issuer's security interest under the application secured not only the amount paid under that credit but also other debts due from the account party to the issuer. The court held that the bank could enforce its security interest to the detriment of the seller.

Centola was a pre-Code case, but application of Code rules to the *Centola* facts yields the same result. Under Article 9, the issuer would have a security interest covering all debts due from the account party buyer, and the seller beneficiary would have no interest in the goods at all. Having shipped the goods under a bill of lading drawn to the order of the issuer, the beneficiary loses its seller's lien.[96] Section 5-110(2) stipulates that, unless otherwise agreed, a person presenting a document to the issuer relinquishes his interest in the document upon honor and that any explicit reservation of an interest in the document renders the presentation noncomplying. Even if the seller does retain an Article 9 security interest, that interest would be subordinate to the rights of the issuer under Section 9-309. That section prefers the issuer as a holder of a negotiable document of title by due negotiation over a prior perfected secured party.[97]

In *Hendries, Inc. v. American Express Co.*,[98] the credit called for negotiable warehouse receipts. When the bank issuer honored the benefi-

---

[95] 135 Misc. 697, 238 N.Y.S. 245 (N.Y. City Ct. 1929).

[96] Cf. U.C.C. § 2-505(1) (outlining procedure for reserving seller's security interest). For discussion of the issuer's interest when the seller does reserve a security interest, see U.C.C. § 2-506. See also infra ¶ 8.03[3].

[97] The secured party seller's rights arise under Article 9, and Section 9-309 stipulates that nothing in Article 9 will defeat the holder to whom a negotiable document has been duly negotiated.

[98] 35 A.D.2d 412, 316 N.Y.S.2d 554 (1970), appeal dismissed, 29 N.Y.2d 546, 272 N.E.2d 581, 324 N.Y.S.2d 92 (1971).

ciary's drafts, the bank held the receipts pending reimbursement by the account party. In the meantime, the account party entered into a contract to sell the merchandise to two buyers. The buyers then sued the bank, claiming that it held a security interest but that they were buyers in ordinary course who took the goods free of that security interest under the rule of Section 9-307(1). The court held that the bank, being a holder by due negotiation of the warehouse receipts, took title to the merchandise under Section 7-502 and was not a secured party but an owner. The court then concluded that Section 9-307(1) did not benefit the buyer plaintiffs, because the section provides that buyers in ordinary course take free only of a security interest, not of title.

The *Hendries* court was correct in concluding that the bank should prevail against the buyers, but its analysis may be flawed. The court relied on the title concept in concluding that Section 9-307(1) did not protect the plaintiffs. Section 9-202 states that the provisions of Article 9 apply, regardless of whether title is in the secured party or in the debtor. Section 9-102 commands that Article 9 applies "to any transaction (regardless of its form) which is intended to create a security interest."

The *Hendries* facts make it crystal clear that the bank's only interest in the merchandise was that of securing the advance that the bank had made for the account of its customer. Under Article 9 the issuing bank had a security interest, and, if the plaintiffs were indeed buyers in ordinary course, they should prevail under Section 9-307(1),[99] absent some other provision in Article 9 that interdicts application of that rule. There is another provision. Section 9-309 says that nothing in Article 9 limits the rights of a holder by due negotiation. Since the bank was a holder by due negotiation, the plaintiffs could not use Section 9-307(1), an Article 9 provision, to limit the bank's rights.[100]

[c] Perfection of the Security Interest

Clearly, the issuer's most important collateral is the document of title and the goods it covers, although there may be other negotiable in-

---

[99] It is not at all clear that buyers of goods stored in a warehouse, who pay for the goods without taking either the warehouse receipt or the goods, are buying in ordinary course. Industry experience suggests that such buying is not ordinary. But see Tanbro Fabrics Corp. v. Deering Milliken, Inc., 39 N.Y.2d 632, 350 N.E.2d 590, 385 N.Y.S.2d 260 (1976). For criticism of the *Tanbro* case, see Dolan, "The Uniform Commercial Code and the Concept of Possession in the Marketing and Financing of Goods," 56 Tex. L. Rev. 1147 (1978).

[100] Professor Skilton makes this point. See Skilton, "Buyer in Ordinary Course of Business Under Article 9 of the Uniform Commercial Code (and Related Matters)," 1974 Wis. L. Rev. 1, 49.

struments or securities that come into the hands of the issuer and that have independent value. As long as the document of title is negotiable and as long as it has been duly negotiated to the issuer, the issuer benefits from the provision of Section 9-309, to the effect that nothing in Article 9 shall limit the holder's rights. These rights, however, may be limited by Article 2 or Article 7 and, most importantly, by the Bankruptcy Code.

Sometimes issuers release the negotiable documents of title to the account party before the account party reimburses the issuer. In that event, Articles 2 and 7 and the Bankruptcy Code have serious impact on the issuer's rights, and the issuer must know that, by surrendering the document, it places its security interest in the document and in the goods at peril. There are many transactions in which an issuer delivers the bill of lading to the account party without being paid. The following is an example.

A San Francisco importer agrees to supply brass rods to a Peoria foundry. The importer has located a supply of the rods from a Canadian smelter and asks its bank to issue a credit in favor of the smelter that is payable against the smelter's drafts and accompanied by negotiable bills of lading and other documents. When the drafts arrive, the issuing bank pays them and holds the bills as security against the advance, which the importer cannot as yet pay.[101] The Peoria buyer, however, is in the wings, and, once it pays the importer, the importer will reimburse the bank.

Most of the time the Peoria foundry does not pay in advance. It may have agreed to obtain a credit in favor of the San Francisco importer to pay against documents,[102] or it may have agreed to accept time drafts upon delivery of documents. In both of these situations, the importer must present to the Peoria foundry or its agent railroad bills of lading covering transport of the brass from its port of entry—San Francisco, for example—to the Peoria plant. The importer will not be able to secure the rail bills unless it takes delivery of the rods from the ocean carrier and delivers them to the rail carrier for shipment to Peoria. There can be no delivery in San Francisco to the importer without surrender of the ocean bills that the bank is holding as security. The ocean carrier will not deliver the rods until the importer surrenders the bills.

The bank could supervise the reshipment itself and could then collect payment from the Peoria party, but transshipment of goods is an as-

---

[101] Importers are merchants, not banks. They cannot finance the transaction they facilitate. The letter of credit, in effect, permits the bank issuer to provide the financing.

[102] For discussion of the documentary sale transaction, see ¶ 1.01[2].

pect of the import business, not of banking. The bank knows that the importer can make all these arrangements much more efficiently than the bank can. Thus, the bank, having confidence in the integrity of the importer, releases the ocean bills to the importer when the ship arrives in San Francisco. The importer takes delivery of the brass rods, obtains railroad bills upon delivery of them to the railroad, and follows one of two courses. It can obtain payment from the buyer and reimburse the bank or it can deliver the bills to the bank and ask it to collect drafts on the Peoria buyer or its bank.

The critical point in the transaction is the bank's delivery of the ocean bills to the account party, the importer. That delivery clothes the importer with power to dispose of the bank's interest. First, the importer can sell the goods to the Peoria buyer or to someone else and then use the proceeds from the sale for some purpose other than reimbursing the bank. Because the importer is probably a merchant who deals in brass, Section 2-403(2) provides that his sale to a buyer in ordinary course gives that buyer all of the bank's rights in the rods. The importer may also negotiate the ocean bills to a buyer or lender, who then becomes a holder by due negotiation and defeats the bank under the rule of either Article 7[103] or Article 9.[104] Finally, the importer may take the bills from the bank and then have the poor grace to become bankrupt, in which event the trustee in bankruptcy will claim the bills and the rods as an asset of the importer's bankrupt estate.[105]

To some extent, Section 9-304 protects the bank against the last eventuality. That provision, along with Section 9-305, stipulates the method for perfecting a security interest in a negotiable document of title and the goods for which it stands. Perfection may be achieved either by filing a financing statement or by taking possession of the negotiable document. Most of the time credit issuers rely on possession as the method of perfection, or they rely on Section 9-309 and its implication that a holder by due negotiation need not comply with Article 9 rules for creating security interests and perfecting them.

Section 9-304(5) anticipates the practice of delivering the document to the account party for the purpose of reshipment. It provides that the security interest remains perfected without filing for a period of twenty-one days after such surrender of the document. That protection is good against the trustee in bankruptcy and deprives him of the argument that the bank is unperfected if the importer files a bankruptcy petition during those twenty-one days. The provision does not protect the bank,

---

[103] See U.C.C. § 7-502.

[104] See U.C.C. § 9-309.

[105] See 11 U.S.C. § 541 (1988).

however, against purchasers, who still may rely on the Article 2 rule protecting buyers in ordinary course of goods,[106] the Article 7 rule protecting good faith holders of negotiable documents,[107] or the Article 9 rule protecting good faith holders of negotiable documents.[108] Under each of these rules, the purchaser of the goods or documents will defeat the bank, even if the bank's security interest is perfected.

In many cases, the credit calls for nonnegotiable documents of title, and the issuing bank then must perfect its security interest under Section 9-304(3), which covers perfection of security interests in goods not subject to a negotiable document. That provision sets out three ways to perfect the security interest:

1. Causing the nonnegotiable document to be issued in the bank's name;
2. Notifying the bailee of the bank's security interest; or
3. Filing a financing statement describing the goods.

In no event can the holder of a nonnegotiable document of title look to Section 9-309 for protection. A holder of a nonnegotiable document cannot rise to the level of a holder by due negotiation, who, by definition, must hold a negotiable document.[109]

Perfection of the security interest generally defeats claims of the bankruptcy trustee and other creditors of the importer, but the bank faces some of the same problems here that it faces with the negotiable document. The bank still may want to release the goods to the importer for reshipment.[110]

Section 9-304(5) provides the same twenty-one-day grace period and therefore protects the bank against the trustee in the event of bankruptcy during that period. By surrendering the goods to the importer, however, the bank still runs the risk that the importer will resell them to a buyer in ordinary course. That buyer may use Section 2-403(2), or perhaps Section 9-307(1), to defeat the bank's interest. The latter provision, Section 9-307(1), may not be used against a bank that is a holder by due negotiation, but a bank with a security interest in goods covered by a nonnegotiable document is not a holder by due negotiation.

---

[106] U.C.C. § 2-403(2).

[107] U.C.C. § 7-502.

[108] U.C.C. § 9-309.

[109] See U.C.C. § 7-501(4).

[110] There are a number of valid commercial reasons for permitting the importer to obtain delivery from the ocean carrier. He may want to store the goods, transship them, or deliver them to a fabricator for processing. Section 9-304(5) anticipates all of that conduct.

[d]　Paperless Documents of Title

There has developed in international trade a call for electronically generated documents, including electronically generated bills of lading.[111] In 1988, the International Chamber of Commerce promulgated UNCID rules of conduct for the interchange of trade data by teletransmission.[112] Because of the Code's perfection requirements in Article 9, issuers that agree to issue credits in connection with documents that are generated electronically face problems. It is not altogether clear what "document" constitutes an electronically generated bill of lading. Under Article 9, many issuers want to take possession of a negotiable bill in order to secure an interest in the goods that bill represents. If a carrier causes a bill to issue electronically, there must be methods by which the issuer can determine that the copy of the bill presented is genuine. Such bills might be issued in duplicate. If the copy forwarded to the issuer is a duplicate, the issuer's possession of it does not satisfy Section 7-502 or Section 9-305 of the Code and leaves the issuer unprotected. By taking a copy, the issuer is neither a holder to whom a document is duly negotiated under Article 7 nor a perfected secured party under Article 9.[113]

[3]　Article 2 Security Interest

The Code permits a seller-beneficiary to reserve a security interest in goods without complying with the attachment and perfection rules of Article 9.[114] Under Section 2-505, the seller of goods may ship them under reservation, that is, by shipping under a negotiable bill of lading or under a nonnegotiable bill naming the seller or his agent, rather than the buyer, as consignee. When the issuer of a credit honors the seller-beneficiary's draft, the issuer, as a "financing agency" in the locution of Arti-

---

[111] For discussion of these developments, see Merchant, "New Developments in Transport Documents," Letter of Credit Reports 8 (Mar./Apr. 1988); Rowe, "Automating International Trade Payments — Legal and Regulatory Issues," 4 J. Int'l Bus. L. 234 (1987).

[112] See International Chamber of Commerce, UNCID, Uniform Rules of Conduct for Interchange of Trade Data by Teletransmission, ICC Pub. No. 452 (1988); cf. Chandler, "Electronic Transmission of Negotiable B/Ls: CMI Drafts Rules for a New Age," Letter of Credit Update 13 (Apr. 1990) (describing similar effort by Comite Maritime International, association of national maritime law associations).

[113] For complaints that these developments do not adequately take into account the problems that confront the bank document examination clerk, see Murphy, "A Banker's View of Electronic Documents," Letters of Credit Reports 12 (Sept./Oct. 1988).

[114] See U.C.C. §§ 9-113(a), 9-113(b).

cle 2,[115] succeeds to the rights of the seller.[116] The issuer enjoys, in addition to its own rights under the document (rights that may make it an Article 9 secured party),[117] "any rights of the shipper in the goods."[118]

Curiously, Section 2-506(1) limits itself to cases in which the issuer pays against a draft. The provision does not mention payments against demands. Some might infer that issuers of credits calling for demands do not benefit from the section. There do not appear to be any reasons for denying the benefit of the provision to such issuers. Extension of the section to credits calling for demands would be consistent with the Code's command of construing the Act liberally, of extending provisions in a manner consistent with their reasons, and of modernizing the law to permit the expansion of commercial practices.[119] The fact that the drafters of Article 5 were conscious of the use of credits calling for demands, and that the drafters of Article 2 were not, should not justify a refusal to apply Section 2-506 to issuers of credits that do not call for a draft.

[4] Extent of the Issuer's Interest

As earlier discussion illustrates,[120] the issuer of a credit that takes a negotiable document by due negotiation becomes a good faith purchaser of the document and benefits from Articles 7 and 9. Under the former, the issuer holds title to the document and to the goods it represents.[121] While Article 9 may limit that "title" interest to a security interest,[122] Article 7 gives the issuer, as a holder by due negotiation of a negotiable document, "all rights accruing under the law of agency or estoppel."[123] These rights are the rights of a good faith purchaser and cut off prior claims to the goods and the document,[124] with an important exception in Section 7-503(1).[125]

---

[115] Section 2-104(2) defines "financing agency."

[116] See U.C.C. § 2-506.

[117] For discussion of the issuer's rights under a negotiable document of title taken in connection with a letter of credit transaction, see supra ¶ 8.02.

[118] U.C.C. § 2-506(1).

[119] U.C.C. § 1-102(1) & comment 1.

[120] See supra ¶ 8.02.

[121] U.C.C. §§ 7-502(1)(a), 7-502(1)(b).

[122] See supra ¶ 8.03[2][b].

[123] U.C.C. § 7-502(1)(c).

[124] See generally Dolan, "Good Faith Purchase and Warehouse Receipts: Thoughts on the Interplay of Articles 2, 7, and 9 of the UCC," 30 Hastings L.J. 1 (1978).

[125] The exception appears in the cross reference to Section 7-503 in the first clause of Section 7-502.

Generally, the issuer's rights as a holder by due negotiation defeat any attempt by the beneficiary to assert an interest in the goods.[126] The issuer's interest as a secured party also generally defeats any claim of the account party buyer until the buyer satisfies the issuer's security interest. In short, the issuer that takes a negotiable document of title under a letter of credit defeats both the beneficiary and the account party to the extent of its advance.

If the credit calls for a nonnegotiable document of title, the issuer will have a perfected Article 9 security interest if it can satisfy the requirements of Section 9-304(3)[127] or if the application agreement creates a security interest in the goods. In the former event, the seller creates the security interest, and the account party buyer may be able to defeat it under the buyer in ordinary course rule of Article 9.[128] The careful issuer insists that the application agreement grant a security interest to the issuer in order to avoid that result. The buyer in ordinary course rule does not protect the account party buyer against security interests that the buyer creates.[129]

If the issuer fails to obtain an Article 9 security interest from the account party, it still may have the benefit of an Article 2 security interest.[130] The measure of the issuer's protection under the Article 2 security interest differs from that under the Article 9 security interest. Under the latter, the issuer is protected up to the amount of any advances it makes under the credit. Under the former, the issuer is protected only up to the amount of the unpaid purchase price specified in the contract of sale. A comment to Section 2-506 explains that the issuer, as a financing agency, stands in the shoes of the seller and has, against the buyer, only the seller's right to withhold the goods in order to secure payment on the underlying contract.[131]

---

[126] See U.C.C. §§ 7-502, 7-503. The exception of Section 7-503(1) generally does not apply against the issuer's rights. See also U.C.C. § 5-110(2) (providing that presenter relinquishes rights to document of title upon issuer's payment of credit).

[127] Any Article 9 security interest must attach and be perfected. Although Section 9-304(3) speaks only of perfection, it can be argued that the bailee holds the goods for the bailor and that such possession satisfies attachment as well as perfection. See U.C.C. §§ 9-203(1), 9-203(2).

[128] U.C.C. § 9-307(1).

[129] Section 9-307(1) protects the buyer only from security interests created by his seller.

[130] See supra ¶ 8.03[3].

[131] U.C.C. § 2-506, comment 4.

CHAPTER 9

Breach: Remedies and Defenses

¶ 9.01 BREAKDOWN IN THE TRANSACTION

This chapter attempts to rationalize the rules that apply when the letter of credit transaction breaks down. The most common breakdown occurs when the issuer dishonors, but the issuer's honor of the beneficiary's draft may also give cause for complaint. In the former case, the issuer confronts an angry beneficiary and possibly an angry account party.[1] In

---

[1] When the issuer dishonors the beneficiary's draft, the account party's interests may suffer. Frequently, an issuer dishonors at the request of an account party that has lost interest in the underlying transaction and wants to use a defect in the beneficiary's presentation to avoid payment. An issuer's dishonor also may serve its own interests, which can conflict with those of the account party. An issuer, fearing that the account party's promise to reimburse is shaky, may dishonor a draft even though the account party wants to have it honored. In Baker v. National Boulevard Bank, 399 F. Supp. 1021 (N.D. Ill. 1975), the beneficiary argued that, for purposes of federal diversity jurisdiction, the issuer's and the account party's interests should not be taken as adverse. The beneficiary reasoned that an issuer, nominally a defendant in the plaintiff's suit to enjoin payment, should be aligned with the plaintiff, thereby showing the complete diversity necessary for the beneficiary to remove the state action to a federal court. The Baker court would not probe the realities of the issuer's motivation. The court was satisfied that, under credit law, the issuer's duty to pay was independent of its agreement with the account party, and the court presumed that the interests were adverse. There are cases in which the issuer's efforts to protect its customer are evident. See, e.g., Bossier Bank & Trust Co. v. Union Planters Nat'l Bank, 550 F.2d 1077 (6th Cir. 1977); Banco Espanol de Credito v. State St. Bank & Trust Co., 385 F.2d 230 (1st Cir. 1967), cert. denied, 390 U.S. 1013 (1968). There are also cases that reflect the unwillingness of the issuer to take a position. See, e.g., American Nat'l Bank & Trust Co. v. Hamilton Indus. Int'l, Inc., 583 F. Supp. 164 (N.D. Ill. 1983), rev'd on other grounds sub nom. Banque Paribas v. Hamilton Indus. Int'l, Inc., 767 F.2d 380 (7th Cir. 1985) (issuer's interpleader action); Wyle v. Bank Melli, 577 F. Supp. 1148, 1152 (N.D. Cal. 1983) (issuer taking "neutral position"); GATX Leasing Corp. v. DBM Drilling Corp., 657 S.W.2d 178 (Tex. Ct. App. 1983) (issuer's interpleader). For discussion of cases that disagree with the reasoning of the Baker court, see ¶ 11.01[3].

the latter case, it is the account party alone who has cause for complaint. In both cases, it is important to identify the source of the complainant's rights. The beneficiary sues for default of the issuer's engagement to honor a draft or a demand for payment. Resorting to the analogy that the letter of credit resembles a contract more than anything else in the law, courts call that default a "breach" and generally invoke contract damage rules, but with significant limitations.[2]

The account party's more common complaint arises when the issuer wrongfully honors the beneficiary's draft. In that case and when the account party objects to the issuer's dishonor, the account party complains that the issuer has breached the application agreement between the account party and the issuer. The account party is not a party to the letter of credit and has no rights under it. Courts sometimes ignore this distinction and apply letter of credit rules to disputes that do not arise out of the credit.[3] The point bears repeating: The letter of credit, a unique commercial device, governs the issuer-beneficiary relationship. The application agreement, a traditional contract, governs the issuer–account party relationship.

This chapter also considers the warranty rule defined in Section 5-111(1) of the Uniform Commercial Code (UCC or the Code). The effect of that section is to balance other rules of credit law. The provision highlights the intrinsic fairness and efficiency of credit law and renders the strict compliance rule and the independence principle palatable. Litigators seem to overlook the warranty section, however. Few cases deal with it. Broader application of it might alleviate some of the problems that prompt courts to reject the strict compliance rule and to delve into the underlying transaction in violation of the independence principle.[4] This chapter concludes with discussion of some affirmative defense questions.

¶ 9.02 IMPROPER DISHONOR

[1] Nature of the Breach

The issuer's engagement to honor the beneficiary's draft is the critical feature of the credit, and its enforcement is a matter of concern not only to beneficiaries but to issuers themselves and to account parties. Bank issuers know that their reputation as a credit issuer may suffer from in-

---

[2] For discussion of the damage rules, see infra ¶ 9.02[5].

[3] See discussion and cases cited infra ¶ 9.03[5].

[4] For discussion of that problem, see ¶ 7.04[4][c].

stances of unprincipled dishonor, and courts have recognized that concern and acted on it in imposing strict requirements on those who attempt to restrain an issuer from honoring a beneficiary's draft.[5]

Account parties also may argue that they suffer from an issuer's failure to honor a credit engagement. A solvent account party whose issuer dishonors may find beneficiaries disinclined to contract with him in the future. The effectiveness of the credit as a commercial device depends on prompt and inevitable honor of the beneficiary's conforming presentation. The law supports that promptness and inevitability primarily in three ways: through the independence principle,[6] the strict compliance rule,[7] and the tough prerequisites for injunctions against honor.[8] Arguably, the remedy rules should serve the same policy of fostering promptness and inevitability. In doing so, however, they must observe some rather fine distinctions, the first of which relates to the nature of the issuer's misconduct.

In a manner consistent with the common perception that the issuer's engagement is more like a contract than anything else in the law,[9] most courts view the beneficiary's claim for wrongful dishonor as one akin to a claim for breach of contract. Indeed, the general damages rule of Section 5-115 treats the beneficiary as if it were an aggrieved seller of goods, who may claim the price[10] (i.e., the face amount of the draft) or resell the goods and sue for the difference.[11] In either of these events, the Code would permit the beneficiary to recover incidental damages but not consequential damages.[12]

The analogy holds well in the commercial credit setting, where the credit serves an underlying contract for the sale of goods and where the beneficiary is a seller. The analogy fails in the standby credit case, where the underlying contract may be one for payment of liquidated damages or for the repayment of an advance. Even in the standby case, however,

---

[5] See, e.g., KMW Int'l v. Chase Manhattan Bank, N.A., 606 F.2d 10 (2d Cir. 1979); American Bell Int'l, Inc. v. Islamic Republic of Iran, 474 F. Supp. 420 (S.D.N.Y. 1979). See generally ¶ 7.04[1].

[6] For general discussion of the independence principle, see ¶¶ 2.08, 2.09.

[7] See, e.g., Corporacion De Mercadeo Agricola v. Mellon Bank Int'l, 608 F.2d 43 (2d Cir. 1979); Courtaulds N. Am., Inc. v. North Carolina Nat'l Bank, 528 F.2d 802 (4th Cir. 1975). See generally ¶¶ 6.03, 6.04.

[8] For discussion of the prerequisites for injunctive relief in letter of credit cases, see ¶ 11.04.

[9] See ¶¶ 2.02, 4.08.

[10] Compare U.C.C. § 2-709(1) with U.C.C. § 5-115(1).

[11] Compare U.C.C. § 2-706(1) with U.C.C. § 5-115(1).

[12] Compare U.C.C. §§ 2-706(1), 2-708(1), 2-708(2), 2-709(1), 2-710 with U.C.C. § 5-115(1).

credit law is well advised to ignore the disappointed beneficiary's consequential damages or to assume simply that a party that expects payment and does not receive it is adequately compensated by damages in the amount of the payment plus interest.[13] In the standby cases, most courts award damages in the face amount of the draft.[14] The dishonor in these cases is more akin to dishonor by an acceptor of a negotiable instrument that is properly payable[15] than it is to breach of a contract for the sale of goods.

In the final analysis, remedies for dishonor of drafts drawn under a credit should depend on careful inquiry, not on superficial analogies of credits with contracts or negotiable instruments. Unfortunately, courts do not always avoid reliance on stereotypes. The following discussion demonstrates that the state of the law in this area is not always consistent or rational.

[2] Elements of Breach and Anticipatory Breach

At the outset, it is important to keep clear the distinctions among the kinds of promises that a party might breach. Clearly, an issuer that dishonors a conforming demand for payment breaches the credit engagement. That dishonor gives the beneficiary a cause of action on the credit; but any cause of action it gives the account party arises not out of the credit but out of the agreement between the issuer and the account party.[16] By the same reasoning, the failure of an issuer to comply with the application agreement does not give the beneficiary of the credit a claim against the issuer.

In *North American Manufacturers Export Associates v. Chase National Bank*,[17] the seller-beneficiary of the credit complained that the credit did not conform to the contract between the account party and the issuer. The court held, however, that, if the issuer failed to comply

---

[13] This rule is consistent with the general rule for liability on the part of banks that do not handle an item properly. Under Article 4 of the UCC, such a bank must respond in damages to the owner of an item for the item's face amount. See U.C.C. §§ 4-103(5), 4-213(1), 4-302. With respect to the bank's own customer, however, the damages rule is altogether different. See U.C.C. § 4-402 (permitting customer's recovery of consequential damages for bank's wrongful dishonor of customer's check). See also infra ¶ 9.03[5] for discussion of the account party's damages when the issuer wrongfully dishonors the beneficiary's draft or demand for payment.

[14] For discussion of these cases, see infra ¶ 9.02[5][b][ii].

[15] See U.C.C. § 3-413(1).

[16] See generally ¶ 2.08[1].

[17] 77 F. Supp. 55 (S.D.N.Y. 1948).

with the instructions of its customer (the account party), the beneficiary could not complain.

It is well settled that an issuer that dishonors a beneficiary's conforming presentation has breached the credit engagement and must respond in damages.[18] It is not always necessary, however, for the beneficiary to make a conforming presentation, for, if the issuer indicates in advance that it will not honor a conforming presentation, the law does not impose a useless duty upon the beneficiary.[19] Section 5-115 provides that the issuer's repudiation of the credit engagement gives the beneficiary the rights of a seller[20] under Section 2-610, which includes, among others, the right to suspend performance.[21] This language indicates that, in the event of the issuer's repudiation, the beneficiary need not procure the documents that the credit requires. The comment to Section 2-610 defines such repudiation as "an overt communication of intention or any action which renders performance impossible or demonstrates a clear determination not to continue with performance."[22]

An announcement by the issuer that it will not honor the credit promise constitutes such an anticipatory breach. In *Decor by Nikkei International, Inc. v. Federal Republic of Nigeria*,[23] the issuer unilaterally altered the documentary requirements of the credit by requiring additional certificates. The issuer also advised the beneficiaries that certain demurrage charges covered by the credit would not be paid. The court held that such conduct constituted an anticipatory repudiation.

---

[18] See U.C.C. § 5-115(1).

[19] See U.C.C. § 5-115(2); cf. U.C.C. § 5-112, comment 1 (dishonor of draft for portion of credit is anticipatory repudiation of whole credit).

[20] By giving the beneficiary the rights of an aggrieved seller against the issuer, Section 5-115(2) obviates the necessity for the beneficiary to resort to seller's remedies against the account party. Those remedies, however, may not avail the beneficiary at all. See Harfield, New York Practice Commentary, N.Y. U.C.C. § 5-115 (McKinney 1964). The courts have avoided problems by also giving the aggrieved beneficiary a remedy under Section 5-115(1) in the event of anticipatory repudiation. The remedies in the two subsections are cumulative, not mutually exclusive.

[21] The language of Section 5-115(2) suggests that the immediate right of action arises only if the beneficiary learns of the repudiation after he has obtained the documents. While the language supports that reading, good sense and the cases discussed in this paragraph (¶ 9.02[2]) do not support it. The aggrieved beneficiary should have both the immediate right of action for wrongful dishonor and the right of an aggrieved seller under Section 2-610. See also authority cited supra note 20. See generally U.C.C. § 2-610 (setting out options of an aggrieved party to a contract of sale when other party repudiates contract).

[22] U.C.C. § 2-610, comment 1 (1st para.).

[23] 497 F. Supp. 893 (S.D.N.Y. 1980), aff'd, 647 F.2d 300 (2d Cir. 1981), cert. denied, 454 U.S. 1148 (1982).

In *Savarin Corp. v. National Bank of Pakistan*,[24] the issuer's announced position that the credit called for shipment on three different ships constituted an anticipatory breach, the court held, when the credit itself permitted shipment in three lots on a single vessel. In *J. Zeevi & Sons v. Grindlays Bank (Uganda) Ltd.*,[25] the issuer attempted to "cancel" a credit pursuant to the law of Uganda. The court held that such conduct gave the beneficiary cause under New York law to attach the account of the issuer at a New York bank.

It is the general rule that a beneficiary faced with an issuer's anticipatory breach need not make a complying presentation. Section 5-115(2) codifies that rule by giving the beneficiary "an immediate right of action for wrongful dishonor" upon anticipatory breach. In *Pringle-Associated Mortgage Corp. v. Southern National Bank*,[26] the court noted that issuers traditionally ask the beneficiary to endorse a draft presented for payment and observed that the beneficiary's refusal to provide such an endorsement would justify the issuer's dishonor. When the issuer already had announced its intention to dishonor, however, it was not necessary for the beneficiary to endorse the draft before suing for dishonor. Similarly, in *Doelger v. Battery Park National Bank*,[27] the court excused the beneficiary from "going through the idle ceremony of making a tender of the remaining portion of the goods"[28] after the issuer's repudiation.[29]

The *Doelger* opinion stipulated, however, that a beneficiary must show that it is able to satisfy the terms of the credit. The failure of the beneficiary to establish that ability by credible evidence prompted the court to reverse a judgment in favor of the beneficiary. The evidence in *Doelger* was uncertain and speculative and did not demonstrate the ability of the beneficiary to supply bills of lading covering the merchandise described in the credit. In the *Decor by Nikkei* case, the plaintiffs went to great lengths to demonstrate their ability to fill contracts for cement and thereby satisfied the "ready, willing, and able" rule that the court adopted. The *Decor by Nikkei* defendant argued that one of the plaintiffs did not have the financial strength to fulfill its contract and to ob-

---

[24] 447 F.2d 727 (2d Cir. 1971).

[25] 37 N.Y.2d 220, 333 N.E.2d 168, 371 N.Y.S.2d 892, cert. denied, 432 U.S. 866 (1975).

[26] 571 F.2d 871 (5th Cir. 1978).

[27] 201 A.D. 515, 194 N.Y.S. 582 (1922).

[28] Id. at 521, 194 N.Y.S. at 587.

[29] See also Ernesto Foglino & Co. v. Webster, 217 A.D. 282, 216 N.Y.S. 225, modified, 244 N.Y. 516, 155 N.E. 878 (1926) (holding that issuer's repudiation of credit relieved beneficiary from need to supply documents and drafts).

tain the necessary documents to comply with the credit. The court held, however, that the plaintiff had proved the contrary.

In *Ufitec, S.A. v. Trade Banking Trust Co.*,[30] the defendant issued a credit payable at the office of its Swiss correspondent. The issuer, suspecting fraud by the beneficiary, wired its correspondent not to negotiate the beneficiary's draft. The credit required the beneficiary to sign the draft at the office of the correspondent, and the beneficiary argued that the issuer's repudiation excused that prerequisite for payment. The beneficiary was a fugitive from justice in Brazil and could not satisfy the prerequisite without risking extradition to the United States. The *Ufitec* court distinguished between a useless act, which the repudiation excuses, and a showing that the beneficiary is ready, willing, and able to perform, which it does not excuse. The court concluded that presence in Switzerland was not a useless act excused by repudiation and ruled for the issuer.

Doelger and *Ufitec* are pre-Code cases, and *Decor by Nikkei* applied pre-Code law under New York's nonuniform version of Section 5-102.[31] A fair reading of Section 5-115, however, supports the rule of these cases.[32]

[3] Standing: Determining the Proper Plaintiff

Breach of the credit promise may damage a number of parties. The designated beneficiary has an interest in the credit, and breach of the credit promise gives the beneficiary a cause of action. Most of the time the credit designates a beneficiary by name, but the credit may be "general," such as a credit that runs to the holder of negotiable paper.[33] The credit also may be a "negotiation" credit and may extend to all drawers,

---

[30] 21 A.D.2d 187, 249 N.Y.S.2d 557 (1964), aff'd, 16 N.Y.2d 698, 209 N.E.2d 551, 261 N.Y.S.2d 893 (1965).

[31] For discussion of that provision, see ¶ 4.05.

[32] Cf. Clement v. FDIC, 2 U.C.C. Rep. Serv. 2d (Callaghan) 1017 (W.D. Okla. 1986) (holding that FDIC disaffirmance of letter of credit issued by failed bank did not give beneficiaries claim for anticipatory breach, because, at time of disaffirmance, beneficiaries were not ready and able to satisfy credit's conditions); A.G. Edwards & Sons v. FDIC, No. 82 Civ. 2014-W (W.D. Okla. Feb. 18, 1986) (holding that FDIC's announced intention not to pay standby credit of failed bank did not give cause of action to beneficiary of standby credit that could not satisfy condition of credit).

[33] See, e.g., Bank of N.C., N.A. v. Rock Island Bank, 570 F.2d 202 (7th Cir. 1978).

endorsers, and bona fide holders of drafts drawn under, and in compliance with, the terms of the credit.[34]

In order to accelerate enjoyment of a credit's benefits, beneficiaries sometimes transfer the credit prior to the time payment is due according to the credit's terms. Such a transfer enables the original beneficiary to obtain immediate cash or credit.[35] The terms "right to draw" and "right to proceeds" are words of art in letter of credit law. Under a transfer of the former, the issuer issues a new credit advice to the transferee who becomes the beneficiary of the credit and is authorized to draw drafts under it. Credit law dubs the taker of the right to proceeds an assignee.[36] The assignee obtains only the right to the proceeds of the credit, the right to draw remaining in the beneficiary-assignor.

In the event of either transfer or assignment, courts have viewed the interest conveyed as sufficient to give the transferee or assignee standing to sue if the issuer breaches.[37] In *Offshore Trading Co. v. Citizens National Bank*,[38] the court refused to grant summary judgment against a beneficiary that had assigned irrevocably all of its interest in the proceeds of a credit. The *Offshore Trading* court construed the assignment document as one of proceeds only and held that, in such a case, the beneficiary has standing to sue for wrongful dishonor. The court also ruled, however, that if the beneficiary had agreed to act as the agent of the assignee in obtaining payment of the credit, the beneficiary would not be a party in interest. The court declined to grant summary judgment and remanded for determination of the actual facts.

Since the term "assignment" in letter of credit law generally refers to a conveyance of the proceeds, the *Offshore Trading* case supports the view that the beneficiary may sue for wrongful dishonor even if it has assigned all of the proceeds of the credit. In a later opinion in the same case, the court held that the assignee of the credit proceeds also has

---

[34] For an example of a negotiation credit, see App. C, Doc. 16.

[35] See generally ¶¶ 1.01[3], 10.02.

[36] The Code uses the terms "transfer" and "assign" less precisely than the letter of credit industry does, however. See U.C.C. § 5-116; see generally U.C.P. art. 54 (1983).

[37] See Continental Nat'l Bank v. National City Bank, 69 F.2d 312 (9th Cir.), cert. denied, 293 U.S. 557 (1934); Continental Time Corp. v. Swiss Credit Bank, 543 F. Supp. 408 (S.D.N.Y. 1982); City Nat'l Bank v. First Nat'l Bank, 22 Ark. App. 5, 732 S.W.2d 489 (1987); cf. National Bank & Trust Co. of N. Am., Ltd. v. J.L.M. Int'l, Inc., 421 F. Supp. 1269 (S.D.N.Y. 1976) (confusing opinion apparently holding that assignee of proceeds is proper plaintiff).

[38] 650 F. Supp. 1487 (D. Kan. 1987).

standing to sue for wrongful dishonor, provided that it has not reassigned the proceeds to the original beneficiary.[39]

In addition, there is authority that the beneficiary's successor in interest may maintain an action for breach of the credit promise. In *Banco Nacional De Cuba v. Chase Manhattan Bank*,[40] a New York bank issued a credit to Bancec, a bank established by the Cuban government in 1960. In 1961, by Cuban law, all of the assets of that bank "peculiar to the banking business"[41] passed to Banco National, and the court concluded that the successor was the proper plaintiff in a suit on a credit issued to Bancec. The court also noted that the successor had been the "agent for collection"[42] for Bancec and suggested that, in such capacity, Banco might be a proper party plaintiff.[43]

In *Board of Trade v. Swiss Credit Bank*,[44] the beneficiary of the credit had assigned its cause of action for wrongful dishonor of a credit to the plaintiff. The court held that the plaintiff could maintain the action but denied recovery on the ground that the dishonor was justified.

---

[39] Id. In AOV Indus., Inc. v. Lambert Coal Co., 64 Bankr. 933 (Bankr. D.D.C. 1986), the original beneficiary of a credit transferred the credit to a supplier. The disbursing agent under a plan of reorganization in the original beneficiary's bankruptcy argued that payments under the credit within ninety days of bankruptcy were preferential transfers under the Bankruptcy Code. The *AOV Industries* court held that, after the transfer, the original beneficiary had no interest in the letter of credit.

[40] 505 F. Supp. 412 (S.D.N.Y. 1980), rev'd sub nom. Banco Para El Comercio Exterior De Cuba v. First Nat'l City Bank, 658 F.2d 913 (2d Cir. 1981), rev'd, 462 U.S. 611 (1983).

[41] Id. at 424.

[42] Id. at 425.

[43] This suggestion departs significantly from letter of credit law's unique rules on transfer and assignment, and, being dictum, it should not be taken as a considered change in those rules. There is other authority dealing with successors of the beneficiary that covers the transfer question not in terms of deciding who is a proper plaintiff but in terms of deciding who may draw under the credit. That authority is in conflict, but most of it supports the holding in the *Banco National* case that the successor of the beneficiary has rights under the credit. See Allied Fidelity Ins. Co. v. Continental Ill. Nat'l Bank & Trust Co., 677 F. Supp. 562 (N.D. Ill. 1988). See generally ¶¶ 10.02–10.04. Sometimes an advising or other nominated bank pays the beneficiary and seeks reimbursement from the issuer. It is not clear whether such a bank seeks to recover as an agent suing its principal or as a beneficiary of the credit, though the former characterization accords with traditional distinctions between straight and negotiation credits. See Banco Nacional De Desarrolla v. Mellon Bank, N.A., 558 F. Supp. 1265 (W.D. Pa. 1983), rev'd, Banco Nacional De Desarrollo v. Mellon Bank, N.A., 726 F.2d 87 (3d Cir. 1984). See generally ¶ 10.02.

[44] 728 F.2d 1241 (9th Cir. 1984).

In *Beckman Cotton Co. v. First National Bank*,[45] the defendant issued a credit to the Commodity Credit Corporation, a federal agency that was financing the sale of cotton to a Philippine buyer in Manila. The buyer was the account party, and the credit called for payment over a three-year period. When the cotton arrived in Manila, the price had dropped considerably, and the buyer and the issuer took the position that the presentation of documents under the credit was late. The Commodity Credit Corporation declined to finance the sale, compliance with the credit being a condition precedent to the loan. The seller, by paying the buyer the difference between the contract and the market price, induced the buyer to waive the claims of delay. The issuer announced its intention to honor the credit engagement, and the Commodity Credit Corporation paid the seller the purchase price. The seller, arguing that the issuer's initial refusal to honor the presentation was unjustified, sued the issuer for the sum expended to induce the Philippine buyer to waive its objections. The Court of Appeals for the Fifth Circuit held that the seller was an "intended beneficiary"[46] of the credit with standing to sue for breach.[47]

---

[45] 666 F.2d 181 (5th Cir. 1982).

[46] Id. at 183.

[47] Cf. Arbest Constr. Co. v. First Nat'l Bank & Trust Co., 777 F.2d 581 (10th Cir. 1985) (holding that even though standby letter of credit was designed to protect subcontractors on construction contract, disappointed subcontractors who were not named as beneficiaries did not have any rights under credit, which had expired, in any event); Ahmed v. National Bank of Pak., 572 F. Supp. 550 (S.D.N.Y. 1983) (holding that beneficiary's agents were not intended third-party beneficiaries and could not maintain action for wrongful honor of credit); M. Golodetz Export Corp. v. Credit Lyonnais, 493 F. Supp. 480 (C.D. Cal. 1980) (holding that seller of goods to beneficiary could not maintain action on credit). But see Midstates Excavating, Inc. v. Farmers & Merchants Bank & Trust Co., 410 N.W.2d 190 (S.D. 1987) (holding that third parties may enforce document designated as letter of credit); Kerr Constr. Co. v. Plains Nat'l Bank, 753 S.W.2d 181 (Tex. Ct. App. 1987) (permitting subcontractor to maintain action against issuer of credit to municipality to secure payment for local improvements). For criticism of the *Midstates* case as letter of credit authority, see ¶ 1.05. For an example of a case in which the parties used a standby letter of credit to protect third parties by letting the beneficiary enforce the credit under federal statute, see United States v. Challinor, 620 F. Supp. 78 (D. Mont. 1985). In Schmidt-Tiago Constr. Co. v. City of Colorado Springs, 633 P.2d 533 (Colo. Ct. App. 1981), a standby ran to the benefit of the city to ensure construction of improvements in a subdivision. The plaintiff, a subcontractor, sued the city, claiming that the city was a trustee under the credit for unpaid subcontractors. The improvements were complete, but the subcontractor was not paid. The court found no intent to protect subcontractors in the ordinance requiring the letter of credit, held that the city could not make a proper demand under the credit, and denied the plaintiff's claim against the city. For discussion of the qualification of parties to enforce a credit, see ¶ 10.02[4].

In the second category of potential plaintiffs are those who take the beneficiary's draft, relying on the credit engagement that runs to drawers, endorsers, and bona fide holders of drafts drawn under the credit. That language appears in the typical negotiation credit, and the plaintiff in this category is usually a negotiating bank. These credits reflect one of the earliest functions of credits: to give value to the beneficiary's drafts.[48]

Generally, the holder under a negotiation credit must comply with the terms of the credit, and, if the credit calls for documents to accompany those drafts, the holder must present them.[49] Sometimes, however, the holder has more rights than the beneficiary enjoys. Under Section 5-114(2), holders in due course of the beneficiary's draft drawn under the credit and other specifically described good faith purchasers may enforce the credit promise, even though the beneficiary would not be able to enforce it.[50]

In some cases, the credit calls for time drafts, that is, drafts payable not at sight but at a later time. Such a credit usually requires the issuer to accept the drafts, thereby creating acceptances, and then to pay them at maturity. The beneficiary or his agent often discounts the acceptances with a third party that becomes a holder of them. The holder presents them to the issuer at maturity. Such holders have rights under the acceptances. The issuer's acceptance itself creates liability under negotiable instruments law. The holders also have rights under the credit.[51]

In *Banco De Vizcaya, S.A. v. First National Bank*,[52] the opinion asserts that the plaintiff advanced funds to the beneficiary in reliance on the credit. Later, after the issuer had accepted the beneficiary's drafts, the plaintiff held them and, when the accepted drafts came due, presented them for payment. When the issuer's agent failed to honor the acceptances, the plaintiff holder brought suit on the credit itself, and the court decided the case as a matter of credit law. The court assumed, with no discussion, that the holder of the acceptances had standing to sue on the credit.

In *Merchants Bank v. Credit Suisse Bank*,[53] the advising bank attempted to sue an issuer that had dishonored the beneficiary's presentation. The beneficiary had sued the advising bank, which settled and

---

[48] See generally ¶ 3.02.

[49] Eximetals Corp. v. Pinheiro Guimares, S.A., 73 A.D.2d 526, 422 N.Y.S.2d 684 (1979), aff'd, 51 N.Y.2d 865, 414 N.E.2d 399, 433 N.Y.S.2d 1019 (1980).

[50] For discussion of the good faith purchase rules, see ¶ 8.02.

[51] See generally ¶¶ 2.08[4], 2.09[1].

[52] 514 F. Supp. 1280 (N.D. Ill. 1981), vacated, id.

[53] 585 F. Supp. 304 (S.D.N.Y. 1984).

claimed, by way of subrogation, the right to sue for wrongful dishonor. The court rejected the argument, holding that the advising bank's settlement with the beneficiary arose out of the bank's liability as a collecting bank, not out of the issuer's dishonor.

In *Native Alaskan Reclamation & Pest Control, Inc. v. United Bank Alaska*,[54] the account party sued for breach of the defendant's loan commitment, which was in the form of a letter of credit. The court awarded significant damages to the account party, which had alleged that it had suffered the damages as a consequence of the issuer's dishonor of the credit. It is not altogether clear from the opinion whether the court viewed the plaintiff's cause of action as arising out of breach of the underlying loan commitment or out of the wrongful dishonor of the credit. It is the better view that the plaintiff's claim is one for contract damages for breach of the loan commitment, the credit being evidence of that collateral commitment.[55]

In *Rival 1981-IV Drilling Program, Ltd. v. Guaranty Bank & Trust*,[56] a limited partnership obtained standby letters of credit to secure obligations of the limited partners. The partnership caused the credits to issue directly to a lending bank to which the partnership had transferred the partners' notes as security for a loan. When the bank failed to draw on a letter of credit, the partnership complained that it had suffered the loss of an asset. The court held that the partnership had no interest in the credit.

[4] Liability: Determining the Proper Defendant

In most cases, the issuer is the proper defendant in an action for dishonor of the credit engagement. In *United Bank Ltd. v. Cambridge Sporting Goods Corp.*,[57] however, the account party had succeeded in having the issuer enjoined from honoring drafts under the credit and had attached the funds the issuer was holding to satisfy those drafts. The

---

[54] 685 P.2d 1211 (Alaska 1984).

[55] In FDIC v. Kerr, 650 F. Supp. 1356 (W.D.N.C. 1986), the court dismissed the claim of a guarantor of the account party because, among other reasons, the issuer's successor owed no obligation to the guarantor. The court did not articulate the reasons for its decision well, and it might have pointed out that the account party and persons claiming through the account party have no rights under the credit. If the account party suffers damages, as it well may by virtue of the issuer's dishonor of the credit, the account party's action is one for breach of the application agreement, not one for breach of the credit undertaking. For further discussion of the relationship between the issuer and the account party, see ¶ 7.02.

[56] 732 P.2d 1233 (Colo. Ct. App. 1986), cert. denied, 753 P.2d 770 (Colo. 1988).

[57] 41 N.Y.2d 254 360 N.E.2d 943, 392 N.Y.S.2d 265 (1976).

plaintiff, claiming to be a holder in due course of the beneficiary's drafts, brought an action against not the issuer but the account party. The *United Bank* opinion holds that, under the circumstances, the account party would have the same rights and duties as those of the issuer.

In *Chase Manhattan Bank v. Equibank*,[58] the court recited what seems to be a general principle: The beneficiary cannot complain of the account party if the issuer breaches the credit promise. The underlying agreement between the beneficiary and the account party causes the credit to issue. In that agreement, the beneficiary seeks to substitute the issuer's credit for that of the account party and insists that the account party cause the credit to issue. Section 2-325 provides that establishment of the credit suspends the account party's obligation to pay under the contract; but, if the issuer dishonors, the section lifts the suspension and permits the beneficiary to sue the account party on the underlying agreement. The *Chase Manhattan Bank* case says simply that the beneficiary may not sue the account party on the credit. If the issuer dishonors, the beneficiary may sue the issuer on the credit or the account party on the underlying contract.[59]

By virtue of its confirmation, a confirming bank is liable on a credit.[60] A beneficiary of a confirmed credit, therefore, has a choice. It may look to the opening bank, the original issuer of the credit, or to the confirmer. In the event one of the banks dishonors, the beneficiary may seek recovery from the other. In *Northern Trust Co. v. Community Bank*,[61] the beneficiary presented its documents to the opening bank's receiver, who dishonored. When the beneficiary sought payment from the confirmer, it refused, arguing that the beneficiary had not presented the documents at the counters of the confirmer prior to the credit's expiry. In fact, the opening bank's receiver was still holding the documents.[62]

In the beneficiary's suit against the confirming bank, the *Northern Trust* court affirmed a judgment against the bank. Because the confir-

---

[58] 394 F. Supp. 352 (W.D. Pa. 1975).

[59] Cf. Second Nat'l Bank v. M. Samuel & Sons, 12 F.2d 963 (2d Cir.), cert. denied, 273 U.S. 720 (1926) (holding that beneficiary may sue account party in tort for inducing issuer to dishonor); General Cable CEAT, S.A. v. Futura Trading, Inc., No. 82 Civ. 1087 (RLC) (S.D.N.Y. Jan. 18, 1983) (holding that beneficiary may sue advising and collecting bank that negligently handles documents).

[60] See U.C.C. § 5-107(2).

[61] 873 F.2d 227 (9th Cir. 1989).

[62] By failing to return the documents without delay or by failing to hold them at the disposal of the beneficiary, the receiver may have violated the Uniform Customs, to which the credit was subject. See U.C.P. art. 8(e) (1974 version); cf. U.C.P. art. 16(d) (1983) (current version).

mation did not require the beneficiary to present the documents at the confirmer's counters, the *Northern Trust* court held, the bank could not complain.

Northern Trust suggests that the parties using a confirmation draft its terms carefully. There may be times—in the back-to-back situation, for example[63]—when possession of the documents is crucial to the paying bank. In that case, the confirming bank must insist in its confirmation that the confirmation is conditioned on presentation of the documents at the office of the confirmer prior to expiry. If the confirming bank is acting in the nature of a surety, as the defendant bank appeared to be acting in the *Northern Trust* case, presentation of the documents at the confirmer's counters may be less important.

[5] Damages

[a] The Independence Principle and Section 5-115 of the Code

When the issuer dishonors, it would be consistent with the independence principle to regard the damages question as one independent of the underlying contract, that is, as independent of any proof that the beneficiary suffered a loss on the underlying agreement. When an issuer breaches the credit promise, the beneficiary's hands are empty; the only way to provide him with the full benefit of the credit promise is to require the issuer to pay damages in the face amount of the credit. There is strong evidence in the Code that such is not to be the rule in commercial credit cases (i.e., in cases where the credit supports an underlying contract for the sale of goods).

First, Article 2, Sales, suggests that a credit supporting a contract for the sale of goods should be treated in a fashion similar to that of a negotiable instrument given in payment of such a contract. Section 2-325(2) provides that delivery of the letter of credit "suspends the buyer's obligation to pay" and that, if the issuer dishonors, the seller-beneficiary may look to payment from the account party buyer.[64] Establishment of the credit has the same effect on the account party's under-

---

[63] For discussion of the back-to-back credit transaction, see ¶ 1.08.

[64] In at least one case, the court held that rightful dishonor by the issuer left the beneficiary with no recourse. In Shamsher Jute Mills Ltd. v. Sethia (London) Ltd., [1987] 1 Lloyd's Rep. 388 (Q.B.), the issuer dishonored when the beneficiary presented nonconforming documents. Because of the dishonor, the account party buyer never received the documents and was unable to obtain delivery of the goods from the carrier. Under the circumstances, the court held, the beneficiary was forced to sustain the loss when the carrier sold the goods in satisfaction of its carrier's lien.

lying obligation that the giving of a negotiable instrument would have.[65] The implication is that the beneficiary has an option in the event of dishonor. It can sue the issuer on the credit, or it can sue the account party on the sales contract.[66] Second, Section 5-115(1) permits the seller-beneficiary to claim damages in the face amount of the dishonored credit but, significantly, forces him to reduce that claim by the amount realized on resale of the goods.

Thus, the temporary discharge rule of Section 2-325(2) and the damages rule of Section 5-115 are consistent in their deviation from the independence principle. Both provisions evince concern that the seller not garner a windfall.[67] This exception to the independence principle is narrow. Some courts have not applied it to standby credit cases but have avoided questions of damages arising out of the underlying transaction and have awarded the disappointed beneficiary the full amount of the credit.[68]

In *Airline Reporting Corp. v. First National Bank*,[69] a standby credit that the beneficiary had drafted permitted the beneficiary to draw for the full amount of the credit without showing any loss. The credit also stipulated that, within six months of its draw, the beneficiary would have to return any sum by which the draw exceeded the sum actually due the beneficiary in the underlying transaction. In the beneficiary's suit against the issuer that dishonored a draft for the face amount of the credit, the court allowed damages for the full amount of the draft, even though the beneficiary's ad damnum was for actual losses.

Airline Reporting is persuasive. The function of a standby credit in some cases is to put the beneficiary in immediate funds upon certain events. Frequently, these credits require the beneficiary to disgorge all or some of those funds later, when losses in the underlying transaction become apparent. If courts are not careful, then, issuers may be able to use these rules to reduce their credit obligation. If the beneficiary of a

---

[65] See U.C.C. § 3-802(1)(b); Ng Chee Chong v. Austin Taylor & Co., [1975] 1 Lloyd's Rep. 156 (Q.B.); W.J. Alan & Co. v. El Nasr Export & Import Co., [1972] 2 All E.R. 127 (C.A.).

[66] Cf. AOV Indus. Inc. v. Lambert Coal Co., 64 Bankr. 933 (Bankr. D.D.C. 1986) (dictum to effect that transfer of credit by first beneficiary to supplier suspends supplier's claim against first beneficiary on supply contract); Dade Nat'l Dev. Corp. v. Southeast Invs. of Palm Beach County, Inc., 471 So. 2d 113 (Fla. Dist. Ct. App. 1985), review denied, 482 So. 2d 349 (Fla. 1986) (holding that when issuer of standby dishonored, beneficiary had cause of action on underlying contract).

[67] They are in accord with the Code's general damages policy. See U.C.C. § 1-106.

[68] For discussion of the standby cases, see infra ¶ 9.02[5][b][ii].

[69] 832 F.2d 823 (4th Cir. 1987).

credit must show damages before he can recover for dishonor, it will be efficient for an issuer to dishonor and put the beneficiary to his proof. In some cases, the beneficiary is not able to demonstrate damages. He may have insisted on the credit as a vehicle for collecting stipulated damages[70] or so that he would have funds while the damages accrue.[71] In these cases and in others, a rule that requires the beneficiary to demonstrate damages before recovering for dishonor will undermine the credit device.

[b] Mitigation

[i] Commercial credits. Whether a beneficiary must show that he attempted to mitigate damages is a question that turns on the independence principle as modified by the rule of Section 5-115. Since the provision reduces the damages of the beneficiary of a commercial credit to the extent of any sum received on resale, it might be argued that the provision hints that the normal damages rules for a disappointed seller apply. Generally, although not always, disappointed sellers must mitigate.[72] On the other hand, it might be argued that Section 5-115, being a unique departure from the independence principle, should be applied strictly.

In *Beckman Cotton Co. v. First National Bank*[73] and in *Toyota Industrial Trucks U.S.A., Inc. v. Citizens National Bank*,[74] the defendant issuers contended that a plaintiff beneficiary must show that it has taken steps to mitigate damages. In both cases, the beneficiary was a seller of goods. The policy of Section 5-115, evident in its concern that the beneficiary not enjoy a windfall, supported the issuer's argument that the beneficiary should mitigate. This result follows, even though consideration of the mitigation question forced the courts into the underlying transactions and thereby offended the principle that the credit is independent.

The *Beckman* court read Section 5-115 as neither requiring nor excusing proof of mitigation and held that the plaintiff had properly mitigated anyway. In *Toyota*, the court said at one point that it did not need

---

[70] For an example of a credit used to secure the payment of stipulated damages, see New York Life Ins. Co. v. Hartford Nat'l Bank & Trust Co., 173 Conn. 492, 378 A.2d 562 (1977).

[71] For an example of that use of a credit, see Eakin v. Continental Ill. Nat'l Bank & Trust Co., 875 F.2d 114 (7th Cir. 1989).

[72] See E. Farnsworth, Contracts 896–907 (2d ed. 1990).

[73] 34 U.C.C. Rep. Serv. (Callaghan) 966 (N.D. Ga. 1982).

[74] 611 F.2d 465 (3d Cir. 1979).

to decide whether Section 5-115 requires mitigation. It later said that even if there was a duty to reduce damages, the issuer could have reduced them as easily as the beneficiary.[75]

The *Toyota* case illustrates how complex the mitigation inquiry can become. In *Toyota*, the issuer was involved in the floor planning of the account party's inventory and issued the credit in favor of an inventory supplier of the account party. Under the terms of the credit, the issuer was obliged to honor the supplier's drafts. The drafts covered the price of lift trucks shipped by the beneficiary to the account party that were not paid for. The account party was apparently selling out of trust, that is, selling inventory without accounting to the floor planner for the proceeds. The issuer argued that the seller-beneficiary had failed to protect itself by repossessing inventory when the beneficiary had first learned of the sales out of trust.[76]

There is further authority for the view that credit law does not presume a beneficiary's damages. In *Wing On Bank Ltd. v. American National Bank & Trust Co.*,[77] the plaintiff, a negotiating bank, brought an action against the issuer. The plaintiff argued that the issuer had dishonored a credit subject to the Uniform Customs and Practice for Documentary Credits (UCP or the Uniform Customs) without complying with the provision of the UCP that requires the dishonoring issuer to specify promptly any defects in the documents. The *Wing On* court found that the documents were defective and that the issuer had failed to specify those defects promptly. The court held, however, that the negotiating bank could not recover because the liability arises not on the draft itself but as a consequence of actual loss. The court held that, in failing to show such loss, the negotiating bank had failed to satisfy a crucial part of its case.[78] Arguably, *Wing On* disserves the credit's proper functions.

These cases generally involve claims by the beneficiary of credits supporting sales of goods for wrongful dishonor. A different question arises when the beneficiary of a standby draws for the full amount of the

---

[75] Accord Fiat Motors of N. Am., Inc. v. Mellon Bank, N.A., 827 F.2d 924 (3d Cir. 1987).

[76] For a case similar to *Toyota*, in which the court held somewhat equivocally that the beneficiary who held a security interest in the property sold to the account party was not obliged to mitigate its damages by resorting to the collateral, see Chrysler Motors Corp. v. Florida Nat'l Bank, 382 So. 2d 32 (Fla. Dist. Ct. App. 1979), modified, id. (1980).

[77] 457 F.2d 328 (5th Cir. 1972).

[78] Cf. Philadelphia Gear Corp. v. FDIC, 751 F.2d 1131 (10th Cir. 1984), rev'd, 476 U.S. 426 (1986) (involving claim against receiver of failed bank for face amount of credit, minus $100,000, insured amount of obligation).

standby, even though the beneficiary's damages are less than that amount.

[ii] Standby credits.   It is not clear whether the mitigation implications in Section 5-115 should play a role in standby credit situations that do not involve the sale of commodities. In the long run, it may be a better rule that reads Section 5-115 strictly and permits inquiry into the underlying transaction only to the extent that the section explicitly authorizes it, that is, to cases in which the beneficiary is a seller of goods. In nonsale standby credit cases, courts generally have adopted a strict reading of the section and have refused to probe the underlying transaction on the damages issue.

In *Data General Corp. v. Citizens National Bank*,[79] the beneficiary sold computer equipment to the account party. The credit was standby in nature but supported a sale. It permitted the seller to draw after the equipment was delivered and had satisfied a standards test. The evidence indicated that the buyer had made payments directly to the seller. Although the documents in the case were equivocal, it appears that the parties intended to give the issuer the right to reduce the amount due the beneficiary under the credit by the amount of payments made by the account party in the underlying contract of sale. The court computed that reduction in fashioning its judgment, even though the beneficiary had drawn for the full amount of the credit. When the issuer dishonored the beneficiary's draft, the court gave the beneficiary damages in the face amount of the draft minus the total of payments the buyer account party had made in the underlying transaction. While Section 5-115 does not mandate such a result explicitly, *Data General* is consistent with the implication in the provision that, in sale of goods situations, courts should look to the underlying transaction to avoid a double-recovery by the beneficiary.

In *Datapoint Corp. v. M&I Bank*,[80] however, the standby secured defaults in a buyer's payments under open account sales. When the buyer did not make payment, the seller drew on the standby; and the issuer, the court held, dishonored wrongfully. In an action for damages, the court awarded the beneficiary the face amount of the draft plus incidental damages.

In *Kerr Construction Co. v. Plains National Bank*,[81] the court permitted a subcontractor on a subdivision improvements project to maintain a suit on a credit that had issued to the municipality in question.

---

[79] 502 F. Supp. 776 (D. Conn. 1980).
[80] 665 F. Supp. 722 (W.D. Wis. 1987).
[81] 753 S.W.2d 181 (Tex. Ct. App. 1987).

The purpose of the credit was to secure completion of the improvements. When the prime contractor defaulted on payments due the subcontractor, the city drew on the credit and the issuer dishonored. Both the city and the subcontractor sued, the subcontractor claiming damages in the amount due on its contract with the prime contractor and the city claiming damages for the balance of the credit's proceeds. The court granted judgment in favor of both in the absence of any showing in the opinion that the city had indeed suffered any loss. The *Kerr* court remanded the case to the trial court for determination of attorney fees for both parties.[82]

In *Balboa Insurance Co. v. Coastal Bank*,[83] the court invoked similar reasoning. In *Balboa*, the letter of credit secured a performance bond. When the beneficiary drew on the credit, the issuer dishonored, arguing that the beneficiary had not sustained losses under the bond equal to the amount of the credit. The court held that the losses under the bond were of no moment and that the independence principle applies to standby credits, just as it does to commercial credits. The *Balboa* court did not note the fact that, in an action for wrongful dishonor of a commercial credit, Section 5-115 interrupts application of the independence principle.

In *Colorado National Bank v. Board of County Commissioners*,[84] the credit secured the obligation of a developer to construct roads and other improvements. The developer abandoned the project, and the issuer argued that there was no need to construct the roads or improvements and that the county (the beneficiary) would realize a windfall if the court permitted it to recover on the credit. The court refused to concern itself with the question of the beneficiary's damages.[85]

In *New York Life Insurance Co. v. Hartford National Bank & Trust Co.*,[86] the beneficiary requested the credit in connection with a mortgage commitment. The credit served to provide a liquidated damages

---

[82] For discussion of the notion that the *Kerr* court disregarded the differences between a standby letter of credit and a performance bond, see ¶¶ 1.05, 2.10[1].

[83] 42 U.C.C. Rep. Serv. (Callaghan) 1716 (S.D. Ga. 1986).

[84] 634 P.2d 32 (Colo. 1981).

[85] Accord Temtex Prods., Inc. v. Capital Bank & Trust Co., 623 F. Supp. 816 (M.D. La. 1985), aff'd mem., 788 F.2d 1563 (5th Cir. 1986); West Virginia Hous. Dev. Fund v. Sroka., 415 F. Supp. 1107 (W.D. Pa. 1976); Mid-States Mortgage Corp. v. National Bank, 77 Mich. App. 651, 259 N.W.2d 175 (1977); INA v. Cypress Bank, 663 S.W.2d 122 (Tex. Ct. App. 1983). But cf. Sawyer v. E.A. Gralia Constr. Co. (In re Pine Tree Elec. Co.), 16 Bankr. 105 (Bankr. D. Me. 1981) (holding that, under circumstances, it was fraudulent for beneficiary to draw full amount of credit when lesser amount was due on underlying contract).

[86] 173 Conn. 492, 378 A.2d 562 (1977).

deposit that was payable to the beneficiary in the event the account parties breached the loan commitment agreement and did not borrow from the beneficiary. The account parties did breach, and, when the beneficiary sought payment under the credit, the issuer dishonored. The beneficiary sued, and the defendant argued that, because the current interest rate exceeded that of the loan commitment, the beneficiary had suffered no damages.

In fact, the trial court in *New York Life*[87] found it clear that higher interest rates gave the beneficiary a return on its investment that exceeded the return it would have received under the loan to the account parties. The beneficiary had gained, by the account party's default, more than the amount of the credit. Given these facts, the defendant argued that under the implications of Section 5-115 the beneficiary had suffered no damages.[88]

The court rejected the argument. First, the court acknowledged the importance of the independence principle and held that the beneficiary's suit was one for damages for breach of the credit engagement, not for breach of the loan commitment agreement. Second, the court ruled that Section 5-115 did not apply to this nonsale credit transaction. The section, the court held, "has generally been considered in the traditional context of the sale of goods."[89]

In *Eakin v. Continental Illinois National Bank & Trust Co.*,[90] the issuer was unsuccessful in its attempt to force the beneficiary to prove its losses under a bond secured by the issuer's standby. In *Eakin*, the credit secured a construction bond. The credit provided that, in the event of the contractor's insolvency, the beneficiary could draw on the credit. When the contractor became insolvent, the beneficiary's successor in interest[91] drew and the issuer dishonored. In the successor's suit for dam-

---

[87] New York Life Ins. Co. v. Hartford Nat'l Bank & Trust Co., 19 U.C.C. Rep. Serv. (Callaghan) 1377 (Conn. Super. Ct. Hartford County 1975), rev'd, 173 Conn. 492, 378 A.2d 562 (1977).

[88] The defendant also argued that payment under the credit would constitute payment of a penalty in violation of the common law's traditional abhorrence of penalties. The Connecticut Supreme Court held that the penalty issue was one arising out of the underlying contract and was not the proper subject matter of a suit on the credit engagement that is independent of that underlying contract. See infra ¶ 9.06[1].

[89] New York Life Ins. Co. v. Hartford Nat'l Bank & Trust Co., 173 Conn. 492, 504, 378 A.2d 562, 568 (1977) (citations omitted).

[90] 875 F.2d 114 (7th Cir. 1989).

[91] The plaintiff in *Eakin* was the liquidator of the failed beneficiary. Under the terms of the credit, the beneficiary was obliged to hold funds it did not need and to return them to the issuer after determination of losses under the construction bond. The issuer's major argument, it appears from the opinion, was that the insolvency of the beneficiary had altered the issuer's credit obligation sufficiently that it was enti-

ages, the issuer asked the court to require the plaintiff to show that it had suffered damage. The *Eakin* court, in an opinion that reflects a modicum of impatience with the issuer, rejected the argument and ordered the issuer to pay.

Eakin is strong authority for the proposition that an issuer may not use dishonor to reduce its credit obligation. In *Eakin*, the beneficiary had a clear right to draw but had yet to suffer damages. If the issuer's defense had succeeded, the issuer would not have had to pay any money to the plaintiff until it had settled or paid claims under the construction bond, and the issuer would have had the funds during that period. The *Eakin* court recognized that if the issuer had succeeded, the standby credit would have become the equivalent of the construction bond—a transmutation the court would not abide.

In *East Girard Savings Association v. Citizens National Bank & Trust Co.*,[92] the Court of Appeals for the Fifth Circuit adopted a similar rule. The credit in *East Girard* protected a mortgagee by providing a "Completion Assurance Fund."[93] When the issuer dishonored the beneficiary's request for payment, the beneficiary sued and the issuer argued that the claim had failed because the beneficiary had not shown damages, as Section 5-115 suggests it must. The court held that Section 5-115 applies not to standby credits but to commercial credits, where the goods are easily identified. In response to the issuer's argument that ordinary contract rules require a plaintiff to prove its damages, the *East Girard* court replied that "a letter of credit simply is not an ordinary contract."[94]

In *Bank of North Carolina, N.A. v. Rock Island Bank*,[95] the beneficiary of a credit held a note endorsed by a third party. The credit engaged the issuer to pay the face amount of the note to the holder in due course, but the issuer argued that the holder should first sue the endorser and mitigate its damages. The court disagreed, holding that any duty to mitigate would reduce the value of the letter of credit.[96]

---

tled to relief. Instead of having an insurance company's undertaking that it would return unused funds, the issuer was receiving such an undertaking from a liquidator. For discussion of that argument in *Eakin*, see ¶ 10.03[3].

[92] 593 F.2d 598 (5th Cir. 1979).

[93] Id. at 600.

[94] Id. at 603; cf. Key Int'l Mfg., Inc. v. Stillman, 66 N.Y.2d 924, 489 N.E.2d 764, 498 N.Y.S.2d 795 (1985) (denying damages over and above interest and face amount of cashier's checks drawn by credit issuer and dishonored in face of injunction forbidding honor).

[95] 630 F.2d 1243 (7th Cir. 1980).

[96] See also Housing Sec., Inc. v. Maine Nat'l Bank, 391 A.2d 311 (Me. 1978); Brummer v. Bankers Trust, 268 S.C. 21, 231 S.E.2d 298 (1977).

In *Clement v. FDIC*,[97] the beneficiaries of credits securing promissory notes recovered part of the sums due on the notes and then drew on the credits. The court held that the damages against the FDIC as successor to the failed issuer would be the balance unpaid on the notes plus interest at the statutory rate from the date of the first distribution in the liquidation.

[c] Incidental Damages

Section 5-115 gives the disappointed seller-beneficiary a claim for "incidental" damages and refers to Section 2-710, the provision captioned "seller's incidental damages." Courts generally do not limit recovery of incidental damages to the commercial credit setting, but they tend to give the term "incidental" the rather narrow scope that Section 2-710 gives it.

In *Bossier Bank & Trust Co. v. Union Planters National Bank*,[98] the court recognized the right of a standby credit beneficiary to claim incidental damages, although the credit secured a loan rather than a contract for the sale of goods. The court refused recovery of the claimed damages, however, because they were not incidental. The *Bossier* plaintiff was able to recover the face amount of the draft plus interest at the statutory rate from the date of dishonor.[99] The plaintiff also had claimed as incidental damages, attorney fees, litigation costs, and the difference between interest at the statutory rate and interest at the market rate, all of which claims the court denied.

The *Bossier* holding accords with the general rule on incidental damages. Litigation expenses, including attorney fees, traditionally are not recoverable, absent express statutory authority or an express provision in the credit itself.[100] Similarly, a recovery of interest greater than

---

[97] 2 U.C.C. Rep. Serv. 2d (Callaghan) 1017 (W.D. Okla. 1986).

[98] 550 F.2d 1077 (6th Cir. 1977).

[99] Cases generally hold that interest at the statutory rate begins to run from the date of the draft's dishonor. See, e.g., Data Gen. Corp. v. Citizens Nat'l Bank, 502 F. Supp. 776 (D. Conn. 1980); Decor by Nikkei Int'l, Inc. v. Federal Republic of Nig., 497 F. Supp. 893 (S.D.N.Y. 1980), aff'd, 647 F.2d 300 (2d Cir. 1981), cert. denied, 454 U.S. 1148 (1982); Board of County Comm'rs v. Colorado Nat'l Bank, 43 Colo. App. 186, 607 P.2d 1010 (1979), modified, 634 P.2d 32 (Colo. 1981); Employers Mut. Casualty Co. v. Tascosa Nat'l Bank, 767 S.W.2d 279 (Tex. Ct. App. 1989); cf. Clement v. FDIC, 2 U.C.C. Rep. Serv. 2d (Callaghan) 1017 (W.D. Okla. 1986) (awarding interest from date of first distribution in liquidation of failed issuer).

[100] See, e.g., Clement v. FDIC, 2 U.C.C. Rep. Serv. 2d (Callaghan) 1017 (W.D. Okla. 1986); Warner v. FDIC, 605 F. Supp. 521 (S.D. Ohio 1984); rev'd and remanded on other grounds, 798 F.2d 167 (6th Cir. 1986); Beckman Cotton Co. v. First Nat'l Bank, 34 U.C.C. Rep. Serv. (Callaghan) 966 (N.D. Ga. 1982); Data Gen. Corp. v. Citizens Nat'l Bank, 502 F. Supp. 776 (D. Conn. 1980); Florida Nat'l Bank v. Alfred & Ann Goldstein Found., Inc., 327 So. 2d 110 (Fla. Dist. Ct. App. 1976); First

that yielded by the statutory rate does not seem to be justified. There is nothing in the credit transaction itself to justify more favorable treatment of a disappointed beneficiary than the law provides to any disappointed obligee of a money obligation. Absent a provision in the credit for interest on default, the disappointed beneficiary should be satisfied with the statutory rate.[101] In *Board of County Commissioners v. Colorado National Bank*,[102] the court held expressly that the interest begins to run on the date of dishonor and not, as the issuer argued, on the date that the beneficiary incurs "actual" loss, it not being necessary to show that there was any such loss.[103]

In *Decor by Nikkei International, Inc. v. Federal Republic of Nigeria*,[104] the court, governed by New York's nonuniform version of Section 5-102(4), did not apply the Code to a credit whose terms rendered it subject to the Uniform Customs. The beneficiary in *Decor* sued the issuer after its anticipatory breach of the credit engagement and sought, among other damages, to recover profits it would have realized in the form of demurrage charges that the credit covered. The court rejected the claim as too speculative, because the beneficiary had not performed and the amount of the demurrage was not ascertainable. The *Decor* court did allow recovery of travel expenses, however, that were incurred by the beneficiary in an attempt to negotiate with the account party after it had prompted the issuer to announce its intention to breach the credit engagement.[105]

Nat'l Bank v. Wynne, 149 Ga. App. 811, 256 S.E.2d 383 (1979); Temple-Eastex, Inc. v. Addison Bank, 672 S.W.2d 793 (Tex. 1984).

[101] Accord Beckman Cotton Co. v. First Nat'l Bank, 34 U.C.C. Rep. Serv. (Callaghan) 966 (N.D. Ga. 1982); cf. Kelley v. First Westroads Bank (In re Kelley), 840 F.2d 554 (8th Cir. 1988) (allowing interest, but not specifying rate); Philadelphia Gear Corp. v. FDIC, 751 F.2d 1131 (10th Cir. 1984), rev'd, 476 U.S. 426 (1986) (denying prejudgment interest to party suing FDIC in its capacity as insurer of deposits); City Nat'l Bank v. First Nat'l Bank, 22 Ark. App. 5, 732 S.W.2d 489 (1987) (holding that interest on sums due under improperly dishonored letter of credit should run at Arkansas's constitutional rate, not at rate in note letter of credit secured).

[102] 43 Colo. App. 186, 607 P.2d 1010 (1979), modified, 634 P.2d 32 (Colo. 1981).

[103] In Decor by Nikkei Int'l, Inc. v. Federal Republic of Nig., 497 F. Supp. 893 (S.D.N.Y. 1980), aff'd, 647 F.2d 300 (2d Cir. 1981), cert. denied, 454 U.S. 1148 (1982), the issuer repudiated the credit, and the court held that interest should run from the midpoint of a twelve-month period, during which the beneficiaries would have been paid, absent the issuer's anticipatory breach.

[104] Id.

[105] Cf. Banco Continental v. First Nat'l Bank, No. 84-5378 (6th Cir. Apr. 30, 1985) (limited precedent op.) (allowing recovery of telephone, telex, travel, and banking expenses); Beckman Cotton Co. v. First Nat'l Bank, 34 U.C.C. Rep. Serv. (Callaghan) 966 (N.D. Ga. 1982) (permitting recovery of travel expenses incurred be-

In *Datapoint Corp. v. M&I Bank,*[106] the court held that the issuer's tardy notice of defects prevented the beneficiary from curing them. In a decision holding the issuer liable for the face amount of the beneficiary's draft, the court also allowed as incidental damages the costs incurred trying to cure: Federal Express and telegram charges as well as "labor" costs.[107]

[d] Punitive Damages

As a general rule, courts are reluctant to award punitive damages against an issuer that breaches the credit engagement. In the *Decor by Nikkei* case, the beneficiary argued that the issuer's cancelation of the credit was malicious. The facts indicated that the issuer, the Central Bank of Nigeria, had canceled a number of credits covering cement when it became clear that Nigerian ports could not handle the volume. The court denied recovery of punitive damages.

In *Savarin Corp. v. National Bank of Pakistan,*[108] the court suggested that it would allow exemplary damages in a tort count brought against an issuer guilty of anticipatory breach. For procedural reasons, however, the court denied the exemplary damages claim.

In *Hubbard Business Plaza v. Lincoln Liberty Life Insurance Co.,*[109] the beneficiary of a credit claimed punitive damages in three counts of a counterclaim for (1) wrongful dishonor of the credit, (2) conspiring to deprive the beneficiary of the benefit of the credit, and (3) inducing the issuer to dishonor. The court denied a motion for partial summary judg-

---

cause of issuer's breach). In Native Alaskan Reclamation & Pest Control, Inc. v. United Bank Alaska, 685 P.2d 1211 (Alaska 1984), the court permitted an account party to recover extensive consequential damages. The case may involve a claim for breach of a collateral agreement to make a loan rather than for breach of the letter of credit engagement.

[106] 665 F. Supp. 722 (W.D. Wis. 1987).

[107] In Ozalid Group (Export) Ltd. v. African Continental Bank Ltd., [1979] 2 Lloyd's Rep. 231 (Q.B.), the court permitted a beneficiary to whom the issuer had made late payments of amounts due under a credit to recover interest, fees paid to its bank in an effort to secure payment, and the exchange rate losses incurred by virtue of the late payment. One might question the court's grant of the last item of damages in *Ozalid Group.* In that case, however, the court pointed out that the issuer knew that the beneficiary would be required under exchange control laws to convert the dollars paid under the credit to sterling. Nonetheless, the holding on the exchange loss is questionable.

[108] 447 F.2d 727 (2d Cir. 1971).

[109] 596 F. Supp. 344 (D. Nev. 1984), aff'd, 844 F.2d 792 (9th Cir. 1988) (mem.).

ment on the punitive damages claim. Under Nevada law,[110] plaintiffs could recover punitive damages for fraudulent or malicious conduct arising from the "breach of an obligation not arising from contract."[111] The court, relying on the rule of Section 1-106,[112] rejected the issuer's argument that Section 5-115(1) deprived the beneficiary of punitive damages.

In *Bank of Canton, Ltd. v. Republic National Bank*,[113] the court went out of its way to award damages in the nature of exemplary damages, even though the plaintiff apparently did not ask for them. The *Bank of Canton* case involved the issuer's appeal from a ruling in favor of a negotiating bank. The Court of Appeals for the Second Circuit found the appeal frivolous and, under the rules of appellate procedure,[114] awarded the plaintiff double costs and "damages in the sum of five thousand dollars or its expenses other than costs of this appeal, including counsel fees, whichever sum is less."[115]

In *Eakin v. Continental Illinois National Bank & Trust Co.*,[116] the issuer hoisted itself with the petard of its own request that the court enter a money judgment rather than an order of specific performance. The credit in *Eakin* anticipated the potential situation in which the beneficiary would disgorge funds paid under the credit later if it became clear that the beneficiary had not suffered loss in the underlying transaction. The *Eakin* court held that its order granting judgment in the face amount of the credit deprived the issuer of its right to have any payment in excess of losses returned.[117]

---

[110] See Nev. Rev. Stat. Ann. § 42.05 (Michie Supp. 1981).

[111] Id. The Nevada law is patterned on a California statute. See Cal. Civ. Code § 3294(a) (West Supp. 1990).

[112] Section 1-106 denies recovery of punitive damages "except as specifically provided in the Act or by other rule of law." U.C.C. § 1-106.

[113] 636 F.2d 30 (2d Cir. 1980).

[114] See Fed. R. App. P. 38.

[115] Bank of Canton, Ltd. v. Republic Nat'l Bank, 636 F.2d 30, 31 (2d Cir. 1980); see also Les Mutuelles du Mans Vie v. Life Assurance Co., 128 F.R.D. 233 (N.D. Ill. 1989) (imposing sanctions under Fed. R. Civ. P. 11 against beneficiary that sought to enjoin payment of letter of credit); Eakin v. Continental Ill. Nat'l Bank & Trust Co., 121 F.R.D. 363 (N.D. Ill. 1988), aff'd, 875 F.2d 114 (7th Cir. 1989) (imposing sanctions against issuer under Fed. R. Civ. P. 11).

[116] 875 F.2d 114 (7th Cir. 1989).

[117] Thus, the issuer in *Eakin* suffered Rule 11 costs in the trial court, Fed. R. Civ. P. 11 (see supra note 115), and damages in the nature of a penalty in the Seventh Circuit.

¶ 9.03 IMPROPER PAYMENT AND DISPUTES AMONG ACCOUNT PARTY, ISSUER, AND OTHERS

[1] Nature of the Breach

In two situations, the interests of the account party and the issuer are adverse. Sometimes the account party seeks to enjoin payment or complains that payment is not proper.[118] At other times, the issuer must sue the account party in order to obtain reimbursement.[119] There are also instances in which the account party may litigate to recover damages from a presenting bank or from the beneficiary itself for breach of warranty.[120] In all of these cases, it is axiomatic that the credit cannot serve as the source of the account party's claim or defense.[121] The credit engagement runs from the issuer to the beneficiary. The account party is not a party to the credit and has no rights or duties under it.[122] Suits by or against the account party stand or fall on other contracts, warranties, or relationships.

[a] Another Substantial Compliance Rule

Section 5-109 of the Code and Article 15 of the Uniform Customs require the issuer to examine the documents to ensure that they comply on their face with the terms of the credit. It is an important precept of credit law that an issuer may insist that a beneficiary comply punctiliously with the terms of the credit.[123] Courts generally hold, however, that failure of the issuer to exact such strict compliance from the beneficiary does not give the account party cause to complain of the issuer. This state of affairs has prompted some to argue that courts have adopted a "bifurcated standard" on documentary compliance: The beneficiary cannot complain if he fails a strict compliance test, but the account party cannot complain if the issuer accepts less than strict compliance.

---

[118] For discussion of account party attempts to stop payment, see ¶ 7.03.

[119] See Transamerica Delaval, Inc. v. Citibank, N.A., 545 F. Supp. 200 (S.D.N.Y. 1982) (account party sued issuer for improper honor). For a general discussion of the wrongful honor question in the context of the issuer's right to reimbursement, see ¶ 7.05.

[120] For discussion of the warranty section, see infra ¶ 9.04.

[121] See ¶ 2.08[1].

[122] See, e.g., Shanghai Commercial Bank, Ltd. v. Bank of Boston Int'l, 53 A.D.2d 830, 385 N.Y.S.2d 548 (1976); Talbot v. Bank of Hendersonville, 495 S.W.2d 548 (Tenn. Ct. App. 1972).

[123] See generally ¶¶ 6.03, 6.04.

In fact, there may be only one standard of compliance; but, because the issuer-beneficiary relationship (governed by the letter of credit) is independent of the underlying transaction, while the issuer–account party relationship (governed by the application agreement) is dependent on that transaction, the consequences of a breach of the strict compliance rule are irrelevant in the former and quite relevant in the latter. Traditional breach of contract analysis commands inquiry in the issuer–account party relationship to determine whether the issuer's breach of the strict compliance rule has yielded damage to the account party. Damages are not the subject of inquiry in the issuer-beneficiary context, however. There the only issue is whether the beneficiary's documents comply. If they do not comply strictly, the issuer is justified in dishonoring, notwithstanding the presence or absence of damages. While the language of the cases is not always consistent, the holdings demonstrate marked fidelity to this distinction.

In an early and leading case,[124] the New York Court of Appeals viewed the issuer as the agent of the account party. Such an agent must not exceed the authority delegated by the account party. The court did not feel, however, that agency law imposed a strict rule on the issuer and defined the rule in terms of failure to comply with the delegated authority "in any material matter."[125] In other words, the court was unwilling to penalize an issuer that had failed to exact strict compliance from the beneficiary unless that failure was "material." A later New York case[126] allowed reimbursement from an account party when the issuer honored drafts drawn by A. James Brown, instead of by Arthur James Brown as the credit stipulated. Since the issuer paid the proper person, the court held, the account party could not complain.

In other cases, courts invoke similar rules, via dictum, to the effect that issuers need exact only substantial compliance from the beneficiary.[127] In *Transamerica Delaval, Inc. v. Citibank, N.A.*,[128] the court expressly applied a substantial compliance rule but fashioned a curious rationale for it. In *Transamerica*, the credit called for a statement by the beneficiary that it had paid under a guaranty. The beneficiary never

---

[124] Bank of Montreal v. Recknagel, 109 N.Y. 482, 17 N.E. 217 (1888).

[125] Id. at 488, 17 N.E. at 219.

[126] Bank of N.Y. & Trust Co. v. Atterbury Bros., 226 A.D. 117, 234 N.Y.S. 442 (1929), aff'd, 253 N.Y. 569, 171 N.E. 786 (1930).

[127] See Far E. Textile, Ltd. v. City Nat'l Bank & Trust Co., 430 F. Supp. 193 (S.D. Ohio 1977); Marine Midland Grace Trust Co. v. Banco Del Pais, S.A., 261 F. Supp. 884 (S.D.N.Y. 1966); Data Gen. Corp. v. Citizens Nat'l Bank, 502 F. Supp. 776 (D. Conn. 1980); Mount Prospect State Bank v. Marine Midland Bank, 121 Ill. App. 3d 295, 459 N.E.2d 979 (1983).

[128] 545 F. Supp. 200 (S.D.N.Y. 1982).

made that statement, but it did state that it was going to pay if the account party did not agree to extend the life of the credit. When the account party refused to agree to the extension, the issuer paid the beneficiary without obtaining any further statement. The court held that a substantial compliance rule was appropriate in a suit by the account party for wrongful honor. The court justified the rule, in part, on the ground that the account party had left to the issuer the choice of language in the credit and therefore could not complain if the beneficiary did not comply strictly with the issuer's language. The court added that, had the account party itself drafted the credit terms, it could have insisted on strict compliance.

One might rationalize the treatment in these cases by saying that the strict compliance rule applies in actions on the letter of credit because such a rule serves the ministerial role issuers play in the payment context. The substantial compliance test (the normal contract rule) is appropriate in suits on the contract between the issuer and the account party, where the exigencies of document examination (prompt payment without inquiry dehors the face of the documents) do not arise. The strict compliance standard recognizes the unique nature of credits; the substantial compliance standard recognizes that the credit application is just another contract. Unfortunately, the cases do not reflect any theory for differentiating these situations and are in a state of some disarray.

In *Morgan Guaranty Trust Co. v. Vend Technologies, Inc.*,[129] the account party complained that the issuer had failed to certify documents under the 1974 version of Article 37(d) of the Uniform Customs. The court, however, saw that error as an "informality" that did not affect the issuer's right of reimbursement from the account party. Similarly, in *First National Bank v. Carmouche*,[130] the court held that the account party could not complain when the party executing the certificate signed as secretary-treasurer rather than as vice-president, his actual title. The party executing the certificate had changed positions in the corporation, and the court rejected the argument that there was a documentary defect that deprived the issuer of its right of reimbursement.

These cases suggest that standards are more lenient in the issuer–account party setting. Not all courts appear willing, however, to recognize a rule of leniency. In *Bank of Nova Scotia v. Angelica-Whitewear Ltd.*,[131] for example, the Supreme Court of Canada, in a scholarly opinion that surveys much letter of credit law, recites the rule as one re-

---

[129] 100 A.D.2d 782, 474 N.Y.S.2d 67 (1984).

[130] 504 So. 2d 1153 (La. Ct. App.), rev'd on other grounds, 515 So. 2d 785 (La. 1987).

[131] 36 D.L.R.4th 161 (Can. 1987).

quiring the issuer to exact strict compliance before it can obtain reimbursement from the account party.

Some of the cases that reject the analysis offered here involve the right of a confirming bank to obtain reimbursement from the issuer. In *Voest-Alpine International Corp. v. Chase Manhattan Bank, N.A.*,[132] the beneficiary sued the confirming bank, which impleaded the opening bank. The opinion implies strongly that the strict standard applies not only to the beneficiary's claim on the credit, as this treatise suggests, but also to the confirming bank's right to reimbursement on the agreement with the opening bank, as it does not suggest. The discrepancy in *Voest-Alpine* may not have been substantial. The credit called for on-board bills of lading dated no later than January 31, 1981. The bills bore such a date, but accompanying inspection certificates recited that loading had occurred on February 2 and February 6 of that year. Under a substantial compliance rule, the account party would have to show that the delay was material.[133]

Voest-Alpine raises another unresolved question concerning the standard of documentary compliance. If there are two standards (or if damages are a proper inquiry in one context but not the other), it is not clear which rule applies when the confirming bank seeks reimbursement from the issuer. One might characterize the confirmer as a beneficiary

---

[132] 545 F. Supp. 301 (S.D.N.Y. 1982), aff'd in part, rev'd in part, 707 F.2d 680 (2d Cir. 1983).

[133] There are cases in addition to those cited in the text that reflect unwillingness to abide by a rule that treats the issuer-beneficiary relationship differently from the issuer–account party relationship. In International Leather Distribs., Inc. v. Chase Manhattan Bank, N.A., 464 F. Supp. 1197 (S.D.N.Y.), aff'd mem., 607 F.2d 996 (2d Cir. 1979), the court states in a footnote that the issuer is liable to the account party if the issuer fails to enforce the credit strictly. Id. at 1201 n.9. The court held, however, that the account party waived its right to insist on strict compliance. Similarly, in Philadelphia Gear Corp. v. Central Bank, 717 F.2d 230 (5th Cir. 1983), the court justified its requirement that the beneficiary comply strictly by asserting that the issuer cannot obtain reimbursement unless it exacts strict compliance. The assertion in *International Leather Distributors* is dictum; that in *Philadelphia Gear* is a bootstrap attempt to justify strict compliance in the issuer-beneficiary context. The justification for strict compliance in that context lies in the exigencies of the document examination process and the need to pay promptly and has nothing to do with the issuer's reimbursement rights. In Pioneer Bank & Trust Co. v. Seiko Sporting Goods, U.S.A. Co., 184 Ill. App. 3d 783, 540 N.E.2d 808 (1989), the court confronts the standard question squarely and rules that the issuer loses its right of reimbursement if it fails to exact strict compliance. The *Pioneer Bank* opinion is unconvincing, however. Seemingly unaware of the distinction between the issuer-beneficiary context and the issuer–account party context, it refers to Section 5-115 and cases decided under it—authority that bears on the issuer-beneficiary situation, not on the issuer–account party situation that arose in *Pioneer Bank*. For further criticism of the *Pioneer Bank* case, see ¶ 2.09[7].

seeking payment, in which case the confirmer would have to satisfy the strict standard and no inquiry into damages would be proper. On the other hand, one might view the confirmer as more akin to an issuer that has paid the beneficiary and is seeking reimbursement from its customer, the opening bank.[134]

In *Bank of Cochin Ltd. v. Manufacturers Hanover Trust Co.*,[135] the court held squarely that the opening bank can insist on strict compliance from the confirming paying bank. The *Bank of Cochin* court, however, had a rather narrow view of the purpose of the bifurcated approach, which it saw as a rule designed to protect the paying bank from the pressure of a falling market. In *Seattle-First National Bank v. FDIC*,[136] the court held that the confirming bank owed the opening bank a duty to examine the documents carefully. Because the confirming bank failed to show that it required the beneficiary to present the original copies of letters of credit, the court held that the bank could not have summary judgment on its claim for reimbursement. The *Seattle-First National* findings contain language favoring strict compliance but do not consider the bifurcated approach.

National Bank of North America v. Alizio[137] reflects values similar to those advanced here but does so in summary fashion. In that case, the credit designated the issuer as beneficiary and called for sight drafts.[138] The issuer paid itself without using drafts, and the account party resisted reimbursement on the ground that the issuer had not performed properly. In a memorandum opinion, the New York court affirmed summary judgment on the issuer's suit for reimbursement and noted that the account party had not disputed that the proper party had been paid or that any prejudice to the account party had resulted from the issuer's paying without using sight drafts. The *Alizio* case supports the ideas that strict compliance is inapposite in the issuer–account party context and illustrates the incomplete analysis of the *Bank of Cochin* case. The *Alizio* court required the account party to reimburse the issuer

---

[134] For discussion of the relationship between the issuer and other banks in the broad letter of credit transaction, see ¶¶ 1.03, 2.08[3]. For further discussion of the documentary compliance rule when the confirmer seeks reimbursement or payment from the opening bank, see Dolan, "Letter of Credit Disputes Between the Issuer and Its Customer: the Issuer's Rights under the Misnamed 'Bifurcated Standard,'" 105 Banking L.J. 380 (1988).

[135] 612 F. Supp. 1533 (S.D.N.Y. 1985), aff'd on other grounds, 808 F.2d 209 (2d Cir. 1986).

[136] 619 F. Supp. 1351 (W.D. Okla. 1985).

[137] 65 N.Y.2d 788, 482 N.E.2d 907, 493 N.Y.S.2d 111 (1985) (mem.).

[138] For discussion of the inadvisability of an issuer's issuing a credit to itself as beneficiary, see ¶ 12.04[1].

because the alleged defect did not contribute to the account party's loss, if any.

Account parties that suffer no loss from the issuer's failure to insist on strict compliance have no policy to support them. The issuer that insists on strict compliance from a beneficiary can rest its argument on the efficiencies that the strict compliance rule yields in the document examination process.[139] The account party that attempts to escape its reimbursement obligation because of the issuer's failure to exact strict compliance, however, is seeking a windfall. A typical commercial transaction resolves the apparent inconsistency.

Frequently, buyers cause commercial credits to issue in favor of their sellers. Those credits often call for on-board bills of lading. If the seller-beneficiary presents a bill without the on-board stamp, the issuer is justified in refusing to pay.[140] The defect may be insubstantial. If the goods are, in fact, on board, the missing stamp is only a technical error; but, in the document examination process, the issuer does not know and should not pause to find out whether the goods are on board.

If the issuer fails to detect the missing stamp and pays over the defect, and if, in fact, the goods are on board, it would be manifestly unfair in all but one setting to permit the account party buyer to refuse reimbursement. Under these facts, the on-board stamp has significance in the credit transaction but not in the underlying contract. If, on the ground that the stamp is missing, the issuer rightfully dishonors the beneficiary's draft, then the account party is still liable on the sales contract and will be required to pay for the goods, if, in fact, they are shipped.[141] If the issuer incorrectly pays over the defective bill, the seller has been paid, and the account party buyer is no longer liable on the underlying contract. The issuer's payment has satisfied its obligation in the sales contract. To deprive the issuer of reimbursement under these facts gives the buyer the option of playing the market at no cost to itself, but at the issuer's expense.

When the goods are worth less than the contract price, the account party buyer rejects the documents and argues that the issuer's failure to reject the defective bill left the buyer with the prospect of taking goods of diminished market value. Yet the buyer still has to pay the contract price for those goods if the issuer has dishonored, because the buyer is still liable under the sales agreement. The buyer should prevail only

---

[139] For discussion of the need for the strict compliance rule in the credit transaction, see ¶ 6.02.

[140] See U.C.P. arts. 27(b), 28(a) (1983); Marine Midland Grace Trust Co. v. Banco Del Pais, S.A., 261 F. Supp. 884 (S.D.N.Y. 1966).

[141] See U.C.C. § 2-325(2).

when the issuer's payment over a defective document causes the loss, or, as the *Alizio* court would have it, when the issuer's payment prejudices the account party. That prejudice arises when the goods are not on board and that fact causes a loss. In short, the reasoning in the *Alizio* opinion is more persuasive than that in *Bank of Cochin.*

The one exception to this analysis arises when the account party is an importer selling documents to his customer. In that case, he may have to satisfy a second letter of credit issuer and must satisfy the strict compliance rule. Such purchasers of documents deal with them swiftly, and it is virtually axiomatic that delay in determining the value of a bill with a missing stamp will damage the purchaser of documents. In this setting, therefore, the account party may be able to insist on strict compliance and avoid reimbursing the issuer if he does not get it.

In *City National Bank v. Westland Towers Apartments,*[142] the issuer extended the credit's expiry without obtaining the account party's prior consent.[143] When the issuer paid under the credit after the original expiry, it sought reimbursement from the guarantors of the account party. They asserted that the account party was not bound by the extension, because it had not been authorized. The *Westland Towers* court concluded that because the parties' factual stipulation at trial did not include a stipulation that the account party had benefited from the extension, the issuer's restitution and ratification arguments failed. The court might have added a fact reported in an earlier opinion in the same litigation,[144] to the effect that the issuer had taken 97 percent of the obligation to which the credit related and that, as a consequence, the issuer had benefited from the extension.

Westland Towers, a per curiam opinion, and *Alizio,* a memorandum opinion, do not explicitly address the bifurcated approach; but the holdings are consistent in their search for prejudice to the rights of the account party when it resists reimbursement of the issuer on the ground that the issuer failed to observe the terms of the credit.

In brief, there are justifications for treating differently the failure of a beneficiary to comply strictly, on the one hand, and the failure of the issuer to exact strict compliance, on the other. First, the strict compliance rule is consistent with the notion that the issuer's duties are ministerial. It would impose a heavy and perhaps intolerable burden on issuers if the law relaxed the strict compliance rule for beneficiaries

---

[142] 152 Mich. App. 136, 393 N.W.2d 554 (1986) (per curiam).

[143] For discussion of the effect of an amendment to a credit by the issuer and the beneficiary without the consent of the account party, see ¶ 5.02[1].

[144] See City Nat'l Bank v. Westland Towers Apartments, 107 Mich. App. 213, 309 N.W.2d 209 (1981), rev'd, 413 Mich. 938, 320 N.W.2d 881 (1982).

seeking payment under the credit.[145] In short, the credit device needs the strict compliance rule in order to work well.

Account parties, on the other hand, should be able to live with a rule that permits the courts to inquire whether the failure of the documents to comply strictly has damaged the account party. If the issuer's error substantially impairs the value of the account party's contract, the account party may complain; otherwise, he may not. This approach applies a strict rule to the letter of credit promise and a traditional substantial compliance rule to the ordinary contract promise of the issuer to the account party.

Under this analysis, the duty imposed by Section 5-109 and Article 15, requiring issuers to determine that the presented documents comply on their face with the terms of the credit is usually subject to general contract notions of compliance. The requirement does not apply to the peculiar letter of credit rule that governs the issuer's conduct with respect to the beneficiary, however. Ultimately, the issuer has the last word in determining whether the account party may sue for insubstantial discrepancies. The parties may strike their own agreement, and, if the issuer and the account party agree that the standard is one of substantial compliance, courts will enforce it.[146]

[b] Kinds of Breach

It is clear that the account party's contract to reimburse the issuer presupposes performance of the credit engagement, and the issuer's anticipatory breach of the credit promise is a breach of the agreement between the account party and the issuer.[147] Similarly, the issuer's attempt to alter the terms of the credit without obtaining the account party's consent violates the rule of Section 5-106(2).[148]

In *City National Bank v. Westland Towers Apartments*,[149] a Michigan appellate court found that the issuer had breached the application agreement by extending the expiration date of a credit without the account party's authority. The court concluded that the issuer could not

---

[145] See ¶ 6.03.

[146] See Overseas Trading Corp. v. Irving Trust Co., 82 N.Y.S.2d 72 (Sup. Ct. 1948).

[147] Accord In re F&T Contractors, Inc., 17 Bankr. 966 (Bankr. E.D. Mich. 1982), rev'd on other grounds sub nom. FDIC v. Cuvrell (In re F&T Contractors, Inc.), 718 F.2d 171 (6th Cir. 1983).

[148] See discussion and authority cited in ¶ 5.02.

[149] 107 Mich. App. 213, 309 N.W.2d 209 (1981), rev'd, 413 Mich. 938, 320 N.W.2d 881 (1982).

seek reimbursement from the account party. It is perhaps significant that the *City National* court did not pause to consider whether the issuer's breach was substantial or whether it damaged the account party. In fact, had the issuer failed to extend the credit, the court noted, personal liability of the account party and foreclosure of the mortgage that the credit secured would have resulted. The issuer argued persuasively that to deny reimbursement would unjustly enrich the account party, whose mortgage the issuer had paid. The court disagreed, because the issuer (the mortgagee of the project) also stood to lose by any foreclosure. At one point, the court questioned the good faith of the issuer; at another, it questioned the issuer's observance of reasonable commercial practices. Finally, the court decided that the equities of the case did not support the unjust enrichment claim.

City National is a harsh case. The Supreme Court of Michigan reversed and remanded for trial in a memorandum opinion that holds the appellate court's ruling "inappropriate"[150] on an unjust enrichment claim. On remand, the trial court again entered summary judgment against the issuer, and the Michigan Court of Appeals affirmed in a per curiam opinion that turns on the fact that the stipulation of fact entered into by the parties did not specify that the account party had benefited from the extension and therefore did not support the issuer's claim for ratification by affirmation or for unjust enrichment.[151]

[2] Standing: Determining the Proper Plaintiff

Section 5-109 defines the duty of the issuer to its "customer," the party that the credit industry traditionally calls the "account party." Section 5-103(1)(g) defines "customer" as the party who causes the credit to issue and expressly includes a bank that procures issuance or confirmation in its customer's behalf.[152] The Code's use of the term "bank" might be taken to mean that a nonbank that procures issuance of a credit for a third party is not a customer entitled to the benefit of the duties that the Code imposes on an issuer.[153] That reading has little to com-

---

[150] City Nat'l Bank v. Westland Towers Apartments, 413 Mich. 938, 320 N.W.2d 881 (1982).

[151] City Nat'l Bank v. Westland Towers Apartments, 152 Mich. App. 136, 393 N.W.2d 554 (1986) (per curiam).

[152] See also Talbot v. Bank of Hendersonville, 495 S.W.2d 548 (Tenn. Ct. App. 1972).

[153] Cf. Linden v. National City Bank, 12 A.D.2d 69, 208 N.Y.S.2d 182 (1960) (holding that buyers' agent, who caused credit to issue, could not recover commissions lost when buyers refused to accept goods under other contracts after issuer improperly had honored seller's drafts on first contract); Crocker Nat'l Bank v. Superior Court, 68 Cal. App. 3d 863, 136 Cal. Rptr. 481, cert. denied sub nom. Thomas J.

mend it, there being no reason to limit the protection of Section 5-109 to banks and to deny it to other agents of a buyer or other party in interest.[154] In another context, at least one court has refused to read the term "bank" restrictively when no reason for limiting the rule to banks is apparent.[155]

In *Edgewater Construction Co. v. Percy Wilson Mortgage & Finance Corp.*,[156] the plaintiff sought to enjoin the issuer from honoring a credit identifying a limited partnership as the account party. The sole shareholder of the plaintiff was the general partner in the partnership. The partnership, as owner, had contracted with the corporation to construct an apartment project. The opinion recites that the corporation entered into an assurance agreement with the mortgagee under which the corporation was required to obtain a letter of credit to secure the corporation's performance. In other words, the credit was to operate as the corporation's performance bond. The credit recited, however, that it was issued for the account of the partnership, and the defendant argued that the plaintiff corporation had no interest in the credit. Noting precedent to the effect that a party "cannot be permitted to adopt a legal entity and be blessed with both a sword and a shield depending upon varying facts and circumstances,"[157] the court held that the partnership was an indispensable party plaintiff.

In re *F&T Contractors, Inc.*[158] involved a similar situation. There the credit described the owner of a development as the account party; but a cognate of the owner, again a construction company, sought damages when the issuer's successor repudiated the credit engagement. The *F&T* court held that the contractor, being "in privity" with the issuer, was a customer under Section 5-103(1)(g) and was a proper claimant.

Palmer, Inc. v. Superior Court, 434 U.S. 984 (1977) (case in which nonbank procured credit for account party).

[154] Cf. Kingdom of Swed. v. New York Trust Co., 197 Misc. 431, 96 N.Y.S.2d 779 (1949) (holding that Swedish government, as alter ego of Swedish bank that procured credit, was proper party to question issuer's conduct).

[155] See Barclays Bank D.C.O. v. Mercantile Nat'l Bank, 481 F.2d 1224 (5th Cir. 1973), cert. dismissed, 414 U.S. 1139 (1974) (holding that bank that confirms credit issued by nonbank is confirming bank, even though Section 5-103(1)(f) defines "confirming bank" as one confirming credit issued by bank).

[156] 44 Ill. App. 3d 220, 357 N.E.2d 1307 (1976).

[157] Id. at 226, 357 N.E.2d at 1312, quoting In re Application of County Treasurer, 113 Ill. App. 2d 50, 57, 251 N.E.2d 757, 760–761 (1969).

[158] 17 Bankr. 966 (Bankr. E.D. Mich. 1982), rev'd sub nom. FDIC v. Cuvrell (In re F&T Contractors, Inc.), 718 F.2d 171 (6th Cir. 1983).

The court specifically rejected the implication in *Edgewater* that a party who is not named in the credit may not be a customer.[159]

In the *F&T* case, the evidence of the contractor's participation in the issuance of the credit was well developed. The contractor had executed a note to reimburse the issuer, had submitted financial records to the issuer, and had been the subject of the issuer's credit investigation. There was sufficient cause for the court to conclude that the contractor had participated in the credit's procurement. In *Edgewater*, the evidence also indicated that the corporation had provided security to the issuer. The *Edgewater* opinion, however, does not hold expressly that the contractor was not a customer; rather, it holds that the partnership was an indispensable party. The *F&T* case, furthermore, was an action for damages for anticipatory breach. *Edgewater* was a suit to enjoin the issuer from honoring the credit. In the former case, a broad reading of the term "customer" makes sense. Such a reading permits a party obliged to reimburse the issuer (a customer obligation)[160] to sue for damages (a customer benefit). In the latter case, a narrow reading of the term "customer" or a requirement that all interested parties be joined makes sense. It would be inconvenient to permit the account party's guarantor by itself to enjoin payment of the credit, but it would not be inconvenient to permit a guarantor to show damages in the event of wrongful dishonor.[161]

In *Bank of Cochin Ltd. v. Manufacturers Hanover Trust Co.*,[162] the court entertained a claim by the opening bank against the confirming payor bank and denied relief on the merits. In *Pubali Bank v. City National Bank*,[163] the court held that Pubali Bank had standing to sue the issuer and the beneficiary for drawing on credits when the draws were not authorized by the credit. In *Pubali*, the plaintiff had arranged for the issuance of the credits on behalf of its customer and had agreed to indemnify the issuer if the customer did not reimburse. The court held that Pubali stood in the shoes of an issuing bank. Under Section 5-103(1)(g) of the Code, Pubali is also a customer, that is, an account par-

---

[159] For a case in which the court held that an original beneficiary and the account party had standing to sue for an injunction against payment to a party claiming to be a transferee of the credit, see Anchor Centre Partners, Ltd. v. Mercantile Bank, N.A., 783 S.W.2d 108 (Mo. Ct. App. 1989), aff'd on rehearing, id.

[160] See U.C.C. §§ 5-106(4), 5-114(3) & comment 3.

[161] The damages in *F&T* resulted from the conduct of the FDIC, which was acting as the issuer's receiver. The FDIC repudiated the credit and refused to release collateral in which the plaintiff had granted the issuer a mortgage. For a discussion of the damages question in the *F&T* case, see infra ¶ 9.03[5].

[162] 612 F. Supp. 1533 (S.D.N.Y. 1985), aff'd, 808 F.2d 209 (2d Cir. 1986).

[163] 769 F.2d 605, superseded, 777 F.2d 1340 (9th Cir. 1985).

ty, and would have standing in that capacity to enforce the warranty of Section 5-111.[164]

[3] Liability: Determining the Proper Defendant

Most litigated disputes involving the account party are suits to enjoin payment of the credit, and the issuer is usually the defendant in those cases. Sometimes, however, the account party sues the beneficiary as well as the issuer or seeks to enjoin the beneficiary alone. In *Steinmeyer v. Warner Consolidated Corp.*,[165] for example, the court issued the injunction against the beneficiary and did not follow traditional letter of credit principles in doing so. While that failure to observe letter of credit rules may be questioned,[166] there is no reason to question the selection of the beneficiary as a defendant alone or with the issuer, provided that the plaintiff can establish justification for injunctive relief.[167]

Account parties sometimes attempt to recoup losses from confirming banks, but generally without success. In *United States v. Foster Wheeler Corp.*,[168] the court denied recovery to an account party in an action against the confirming bank, holding squarely that the confirming bank's duties run only to the beneficiary and the opening bank. The *Foster Wheeler* court also denied any action to the account party on a tort theory, holding that, because there was no duty running to the account party from the confirming bank, the account party could not complain if the confirming bank was negligent in performing its duties.

In *Samuel Kronman & Co. v. Public National Bank*,[169] the beneficiary sued both the issuing bank and the confirming bank for damages allegedly sustained as a consequence of the wrongful dishonor of the beneficiary's drafts. The court held that the account party had no rights against the confirming bank.

---

[164] See Pubali Bank v. City Nat'l Bank, 777 F.2d 1340 (9th Cir. 1985).

[165] 42 Cal. App. 3d 515, 116 Cal. Rptr. 57 (1974).

[166] For criticism of *Steinmeyer* on that holding, see Ground Air Transfer, Inc. v. Westates Airlines, Inc., 899 F.2d 1269 (1st Cir. 1990). See also ¶ 2.09[6].

[167] See, e.g., Paccar Int'l, Inc. v. Commercial Bank of Kuwait, 587 F. Supp. 783 (C.D. Cal. 1984), rev'd on other grounds, 757 F.2d 1058 (9th Cir. 1985); Morgan v. Depositors Trust Co., 33 U.C.C. Rep. Serv. (Callaghan) 1473 (Me. Super. Ct. Kennebec County 1982); Chiat/Day, Inc., v. Kalimian, 105 A.D.2d 94, 483 N.Y.S.2d 235 (1984). For additional authority, see ¶ 7.04[4][f].

[168] 639 F. Supp. 1266 (S.D.N.Y. 1986).

[169] 218 A.D. 624, 218 N.Y.S. 616 (1926).

In *Dulien Steel Products, Inc. v. Bankers Trust Co.*,[170] the account party sued the confirming bank for an allegedly wrongful honor of the beneficiary's draft. The court noted that there was no contract between the account party and the confirming bank and indicated that the account party recognized that it could not claim the benefits that privity with the confirming bank would yield. The account party made two arguments, however: (1) The confirming bank was negligent in not investigating the transaction before honoring the draft, a disputed assertion by the account party; and (2) the confirming bank's course of conduct estopped it from honoring the beneficiary's draft without the account party's approval.

The court rejected both arguments. It held that the negligence theory was an attempt by the account party to force the confirming bank to delve into the underlying transaction, contrary to the independence principle. The court rejected the estoppel argument because (1) the confirming bank's alleged assertions giving rise to the estoppel were made to the opening bank, not to the account party, and (2) the assertions did not give anyone reasonable ground on which to rely. The court pointed out that the opening bank was not the agent of the account party,[171] so that statements made to the issuer would not operate without more as statements to the account party.[172] The *Dulien* opinion denies liability but suggests that an account party might be able to make out a case against the confirming bank for wrongful honor—if not in contract, at least in tort or as a matter of estoppel.

The history of *Instituto Nacional De Comercializacion Agricola (Indeca) v. Continental Illinois National Bank & Trust Co.*[173] suggests a different rule. The first opinion of the trial court in *Indeca* made explicit the tort rule suggested in *Dulien*. The *Indeca* court dismissed a contract cause of action by the account party against the confirming bank but refused to dismiss the plaintiff's complaint to the extent it alleged fraud or negligence. The *Indeca* credit called for a certificate of origin to be "legalized" by the Guatemalan Consul whose office was in Miami. When the beneficiary presented the document to the confirming bank in Chi-

---

[170] 298 F.2d 836 (2d Cir. 1962).

[171] Accord Kingdom of Swed. v. New York Trust Co., 197 Misc. 431, 96 N.Y.S.2d 779 (Sup. Ct. 1949).

[172] For additional authority to the effect that the account party is not in privity with the confirming bank and therefore should not have an action against that bank for breach of contract, see Almatrood v. Sallee Int'l, Inc., No. 83 Civ. 1800 (WCC) (S.D.N.Y. May 13, 1985). But cf. In re Glade Springs, Inc., 47 Bankr. 780 (Bankr. E.D. Tenn. 1985) (holding that confirming bank is subrogated to rights of issuer against account party's collateral).

[173] 530 F. Supp. 279 (N.D. Ill. 1982).

cago, the document did not contain the consul's countersignature, and the issuer rejected it. The account party claimed, and the posture of the case at this point required the court to accept the claim, that three hours later, the beneficiary returned with the document signed and stamped with a Miami address. By accepting the document under such circumstances, the court held, the confirming bank might have been guilty of negligence or of knowingly[174] accepting a forged document. In either event, the court concluded, the confirming bank would be liable.

In a subsequent opinion in the same case, the court held that facts adduced at an evidentiary hearing and a change in applicable Illinois law provided grounds to reject the negligence cause of action.[175] In fact, the evidence showed that the beneficiary had returned with the corrected document three days later. That evidence, in the court's view, did not support either of the two remaining causes of action: (1) fraud (dishonesty) or reckless disregard for the truth or (2) falsity of the confirming bank's assertion to the opening bank that the documents were in order. On appeal, the Court of Appeals for the Seventh Circuit affirmed in an opinion that holds squarely that the obligations of the confirming bank run to the opening bank, not to the account party.[176] The Seventh Circuit also held that, under Illinois non-Code law and under the Code, there was no duty on the confirmer to provide accurate information to the account party.

Section 5-114(2) seems to govern here. If it does govern, the allegation that the defendant knowingly honored a draft accompanied by fraudulent documents supports a cause of action; but an allegation of negligently honoring a draft accompanied by fraudulent documents would not support a cause of action. Section 5-114(2)(b) provides that an issuer may honor a presentation accompanied by a fraudulent document, as long as the issuer acts in good faith. The allegation in *Indeca* that the confirming bank knowingly honored a fraudulent document is an allegation of dishonesty, an allegation of bad faith.[177] A charge that

---

[174] The *Indeca* court side-stepped what it saw as the difficult question whether the confirming bank might be liable to the opening bank's customer for "recklessness" in examining the documents. Id. at 281 n.3. Arguably, if the confirming bank acts honestly (i.e., in good faith), it should not be liable to a remote party for either recklessness or negligence, as discussion of *Indeca* below explains. See infra ¶ 9.04.

[175] Instituto Nacional De Comercializacion Agricola (Indeca) v. Continental Ill. Nat'l Bank & Trust Co., 675 F. Supp. 1515 (N.D. Ill. 1987), aff'd, 858 F.2d 1264 (7th Cir. 1988).

[176] Instituto Nacional De Comercializacion Agricola (Indeca) v. Continental Ill. Nat'l Bank & Trust Co., 858 F.2d 1264 (7th Cir. 1988).

[177] For the Code's general "good faith" definition, see U.C.C. § 1-201(19).

the issuer acted negligently (i.e., without due care) is not an allegation of bad faith. Due care or observance of reasonable commercial standards generally is not an ingredient of good faith in Article 5.[178] The *Indeca* holding on the fraud claim is well taken, but the negligence holding appears to be questionable.[179]

The Section 5-114(2) argument was ignored in *Lalaco v. Universal Housing Systems of America, Inc.*,[180] where the account party sued the advising payor bank for bad faith and negligence in paying the beneficiary. The *Lalaco* court found the presentation facially conforming and did not address the question whether the defendant owed any duty to the account party.

In *Auto Servicio San Ignacio, S.R.L. v. Compania Anonima Venezolana De Navegacion*,[181] the account party sued a confirming payor bank[182] for negligently failing to discover the forgery on a bill of lading. The court held squarely that the account party had no cause of action. The defendant bank's duty was to the issuer, not to anyone else.[183] In a strong opinion, the Court of Appeals for the Fifth Circuit affirmed the *Auto Servicio* holding. "The exchange function of the letter of credit rests upon objective predictable standards with defined expectations and risks. Injecting the uncertainty of the tort principles contended for is inconsistent with these necessities and is not supported by the Code, which implicitly rejects them."[184] The court added that it was not persuaded by the *Indeca* court's contrary holding.[185]

[178] See U.C.C. § 5-103(4); Philadelphia Gear Corp. v. Central Bank, 717 F.2d 230 (5th Cir. 1983); Shaffer v. Brooklyn Park Garden Apartments, 311 Minn. 452, 250 N.W.2d 172 (1977). Compare U.C.C. § 2-103(1)(b) with U.C.C. § 1-201(19).

[179] Lack of privity also hampers the account party's suit against the negotiating bank. In Courteen Seed Co. v. Hong Kong & Shanghai Banking Corp., 216 A.D. 495, 215 N.Y.S. 525 (1926), the court held that a negotiating bank that honors a defective presentation has not violated any duty to the account party. The warranty rules of Section 5-111(2) impose a measure of liability on the confirming and advising banks. For discussion of the warranty rules, see infra ¶ 9.04. For a suggestion that the account party should have a direct cause of action against the confirming bank, see Note, "Confirming Bank Liability in Letter of Credit Transactions: Whose Bank Is It Anyway?" 51 Fordham L. Rev. 1219 (1983).

[180] No. 80 Civ. 178 (WCC) (S.D.N.Y. Oct. 25, 1983).

[181] 586 F. Supp. 259 (E.D. La. 1984), aff'd, 765 F.2d 1306 (5th Cir. 1985).

[182] The court held that, despite its designation in the credit as the advising and payor bank, the defendant's undertaking rendered it a confirming bank.

[183] In addition to the beneficiary, a shipping company's agent and an insurer were plaintiffs in the *Auto Servicio* case.

[184] Auto Servicio San Ignacio, S.R.L. v. Compania Anonima Venezolana De Navegacion (Venezuelan Line), 765 F.2d 1306, 1308 (5th Cir. 1985).

[185] Cf. United States v. Foster Wheeler Corp., 639 F. Supp. 1266 (S.D.N.Y. 1986) (holding that account party does not have tort cause of action against confirming bank). For discussion of *Foster Wheeler*, see supra text at note 168.

In *Kingdom of Sweden v. New York Trust Co.*,[186] the account party sued the confirming bank when it issued a second credit to the beneficiary's supplier, thereby creating a classic back-to-back credit arrangement.[187] The original credit contained a prohibition against transfer, and the account party argued implicitly that it had benefited from that prohibition. The account party also argued that the issuer was liable for losses sustained when government intervention prevented shipment of the goods that the account party was buying. The court held, however, that issuance of the second credit did not constitute a breach of any duty that the issuer owed the account party.

In *Bank of Cochin Ltd. v. Manufacturers Hanover Trust Co.*,[188] the opening bank was unsuccessful in its suit against the confirming payor bank because the opening bank was estopped to claim that the documents were defective. In *Pubali Bank v. City National Bank*,[189] however, a plaintiff was successful in its suit against an advising bank that was assignee of the credit proceeds. The *Pubali* opinion was not precise in defining the claim as one for breach of warranty, but all of the warranty facts are evident in the opinion. The court did make it clear that the defendant bank's liability was predicated on its character as an assignee and not as an advising bank.[190]

In *Worldwide Sugar Co. v. Royal Bank of Canada*,[191] the advising bank undertook, on behalf of the beneficiary for whom it was acting as a collecting bank, to indemnify the issuer against defects in the beneficiary's performance. Before payment under the credit, all parties agreed to its cancelation and to the delivery to the account party of the "documents." The account party disputed the beneficiary's performance of the underlying contract and made a claim on the advising bank's indemnity. The court held that the advising bank's engagement ran only to the issuer.

FDIC v. Cuvrell (In re F&T Contractors, Inc.)[192] involved a claim against the FDIC in its capacity as receiver of a failed bank and in its capacity as insurer of the bank's deposits. The bank had issued three credits, and the FDIC-receiver had canceled them. The credits were issued

---

[186] 197 Misc. 431, 96 N.Y.S.2d 779 (Sup. Ct. 1949).
[187] For discussion of back-to-back credits, see ¶ 1.08.
[188] 612 F. Supp. 1533 (S.D.N.Y. 1985), aff'd, 808 F.2d 209 (2d Cir. 1986).
[189] 769 F.2d 605 (9th Cir. 1985).
[190] For general discussion of warranty claims, see infra ¶ 9.04.
[191] 609 F. Supp. 19 (S.D.N.Y. 1984).
[192] 612 F. Supp. 1533 (S.D.N.Y. 1985), aff'd, 808 F.2d 209 (2d Cir. 1986).

for the account of the debtor's affiliated partnership. The trial court[193] held that the FDIC-insurer, when it assumed certain liabilities of the failed bank, also assumed the liability of the FDIC-receiver for canceling the credits. The Court of Appeals for the Sixth Circuit reversed, holding that the FDIC-insurer had no interest in the credits and could not be liable for their cancelation or for failing to release collateral securing the account party's duty to reimburse.

[4] Injunctions

Injunctions are the common remedy for the account party who seeks to limit losses by preventing the issuer from honoring the beneficiary's draft or its demand for payment. In many such cases, the interests of the account party and the issuer coincide, because issuers often attempt to protect their customers. The law does not assume, however, that the interests coincide; and there have been clear instances in which the issuer and the account party were definitely at odds.[194]

In any event, an action to enjoin payment faces serious obstacles. First, the account party must satisfy certain equity prerequisites for the extraordinary relief it requests. Among the procedural barriers, the most serious are those that require the account party to show that it will suffer irreparable harm without injunctive relief or that it does not have an adequate remedy at law.[195]

The second obstacle to the account party's injunction is a matter of credit law. By virtue of the independence principle, Section 5-114(2) limits equitable relief to narrow situations involving breach of document or securities warranties, forged or fraudulent documents, or other fraud in the credit transaction.[196]

[5] Damages

While Section 5-115 defines letter of credit rules for the disappointed beneficiary's damages upon wrongful dishonor,[197] it is silent on the extent of the disappointed account party's damages for wrongful honor or

---

[193] 17 Bankr. 966 (Bankr. E.D. Mich. 1982), rev'd sub nom. FDIC v. Cuvrell (In re F&T Contractors, Inc.), 718 F.2d 171 (6th Cir. 1983).

[194] See supra note 1.

[195] See generally discussion and authorities cited in ¶ 7.04[1].

[196] See generally ¶¶ 7.04[2]–7.04[4].

[197] For discussion of Section 5-115, see supra ¶ 9.02[5].

dishonor. The matter appears to be one of non-Code law, and the cases are few.

In re F&T Contractors, Inc.[198] involved a claim against the FDIC for repudiating the credit engagement of a failed bank.[199] The credit was issued in connection with a construction contract, and the claimant had granted the failed bank a mortgage in real estate. Upon repudiation of the credit, the plaintiff asked the FDIC to release the mortgage. The FDIC refused, and the complainant argued that the refusal delayed the construction, caused lost profits, increased overhead costs and contract cost overruns, and resulted in expenses of the Chapter 11 bankruptcy that ensued.

The FDIC argued that Section 5-115 governed and that the plaintiffs could seek damages only in the face amount of the drafts that the issuer had engaged to pay. That argument, of course, is an egregious misconstruction of Section 5-115, which defines the rights of a beneficiary against the defaulting issuer for breach of the credit promise. The *F&T* case involved a suit by a person in the position of an account party against the issuer for breach of the application agreement.

The court rejected the FDIC's argument, but not on the ground that the provision did not govern the account party–issuer relationship. Rather, the court held that Section 5-115 is designed for commercial credits but not for standby credits. The court went on to permit recovery of lost profits, proportionate increases in overhead expenses, cost overruns, and bankruptcy expenses, including attorney fees. It is not altogether clear from the *F&T* opinion whether those damages resulted from the FDIC's repudiation of the credit or from its refusal to release the contractor's mortgage. On appeal, the *F&T* case was reversed on other grounds.[200]

In *Instituto Nacional De Comercializacion Agricola (Indeca) v. Continental Illinois National Bank & Trust Co.*,[201] a suit against the confirming bank, the account party sought recovery of damages that the opinion termed "economic"[202] but did not otherwise describe. The court noted by way of dictum that if the account party had been in privity with the confirming bank (the court previously had held there was no such privi-

---

[198] 17 Bankr. 966 (Bankr. E.D. Mich. 1982), rev'd sub nom. FDIC v. Cuvrell (In re F&T Contractors, Inc.), 718 F.2d 171 (6th Cir. 1983).

[199] For the facts of the *F&T* case, see supra ¶ 9.03[2].

[200] FDIC v. Cuvrell (In re F&T Contractors, Inc.), 718 F.2d 171 (6th Cir. 1983). For a position on the question of consequential damages different from that of the *F&T* case, see H. Harfield, Bank Credits and Acceptances 108 (5th ed. 1976).

[201] 530 F. Supp. 279 (N.D. Ill. 1982).

[202] Id. at 282 n.5.

ty),[203] there could be no recovery for economic losses. The court observed that Illinois law, which governed in that case, does not permit recovery of such economic losses when the plaintiff and defendant are in privity.

In *Linden v. National City Bank*,[204] a pre-Code case, a broker for the purchaser of tinplate arranged to have three credits issue for the benefit of the seller. The defendant confirmed two of the credits and honored a presentation under the first. The plaintiff alleged that the presentation was defective, that the honor was wrongful, and that, as a consequence, the purchaser had reneged on the second and third contracts covered by the credits. After noting that there was some question whether this plaintiff could sue the confirming bank, the court held that the plaintiff's attempt to recover the commissions it lost on sales under the contracts covered by the second and third credits should fail. The court held that the seller's failure to deliver conforming tinplate, not the confirming bank's conduct, prompted the buyer's repudiation. The bank's conduct could not be said to have caused the plaintiff's damages.

Damages, of course, may become a question when the issuing bank seeks to enforce its right of reimbursement from an account party. Section 5-114(3) gives the issuer a right of "immediate reimbursement of any payment made under the credit," unless the parties agree otherwise in the credit application. The careful issuer often insists that the account party put the issuer in funds at some time before payment is due. There are occasions when the issuer agrees to advance funds against the account party's promise to reimburse.

In *City National Bank v. Westland Towers Apartments*,[205] a Michigan appellate court denied the issuer any reimbursement.[206] The court held that the issuer had extended the expiration date[207] of the credit without authority[208] and had breached the terms of the agreement between the issuer and the account party, a partnership. The issuer argued that payment under the credit had unjustly enriched the account party, but the appellate court held that the extension had benefited the issuer, which desired to avoid foreclosure of its mortgage.

While the court appears to be correct in its view that the extension benefited the issuer, it is difficult to justify a $250,000 windfall for the

[203] For discussion of the account party's rights against the confirming bank, see supra ¶ 9.03[3].

[204] 12 A.D.2d 69, 208 N.Y.S.2d 182 (1960).

[205] 107 Mich. App. 213, 309 N.W.2d 209 (1981), rev'd, 413 Mich. 938, 320 N.W.2d 881 (1982).

[206] For general discussion of the issuer's right to reimbursement, see ¶ 7.05.

[207] For discussion of the important role of the credit's expiry, see ¶ 5.03[3].

[208] For the rules on amending letters of credit, see ¶ 5.02.

account party and for the guarantors of the account party's obligation to the issuer. The *City National* credit provided a portion of the partnership's equity in an apartment project that the Federal Housing Authority (FHA) was subsidizing. The issuer played two roles. It issued the credit to the mortgagee, and it participated in the mortgage loan. It benefited directly from its own credit that ran to the mortgagee. When the FHA sought final endorsement of the project, payment under the credit came due. Failure to extend it would have resulted in liability for the partners. It is true that the issuer derived benefit from the extension, but the partners did too. The opinion suggests, moreover, that the partners, because of differences among themselves that they could not or would not resolve, made the extension necessary.

It is difficult to see how the *City National* holding serves any reasonable notion of fairness. The decision's apparent effect was to provide the owners of the project with a significant windfall. In a brief memorandum opinion, the Supreme Court of Michigan reversed the summary judgment entered in favor of the account party and remanded the case to the lower court.[209]

In *Interco, Inc. v. First National Bank*,[210] the account party sought an injunction against honor of the credit. One of the prerequisites for that relief is a showing that the plaintiff has no adequate remedy at law.[211] The plaintiff argued that because Section 5-115 is silent on the question of damages for an account party aggrieved by an improper honor, a claim for damages would not provide adequate relief, if any. The *Interco* court disagreed and noted that Section 1-106 defines the Code's policy on damages by stipulating that Code remedies be administered liberally "to the end that the aggrieved party may be put in as good a position as if the other party had fully performed."[212]

The appellate court in *City National* and the court in *Interco* demonstrate a degree of confusion. *City National* suggests that the issuer's failure to insist on strict compliance with the terms of the credit justifies a windfall for the account party. The *Interco* case suggests that

---

[209] On remand, the trial court entered summary judgment against the issuer, and the court of appeals affirmed in an opinion that turns on the fact that the parties' factual stipulation did not indicate that the account party had benefited from the extension. See City Nat'l Bank v. Westland Towers Apartments, 152 Mich. App. 136, 393 N.W.2d 554 (1986) (per curiam).

[210] 560 F.2d 480 (1st Cir. 1977).

[211] See discussion and authorities cited in ¶ 7.04[1].

[212] U.C.C. § 1-106(1).

the silence of Article 5 on the question of the account party's damages is an oversight to be rectified by the policy provision, Section 1-106.

Both suggestions overlook the fact that the relationship between the account party and the issuer generally is not a matter of letter of credit law. That relationship is a contractual one, governed by the application agreement. The strict compliance rule is a principle of letter of credit law. Its sometimes harsh results are a consequence of letter of credit exigencies.[213] These exigencies arise in the issuer-beneficiary relationship, not in the issuer–account party relationship. By the same token, the omission of any mention of account party damages in Article 5 is no oversight. Article 5 deals primarily with letters of credit—engagements between issuers and beneficiaries. Issuer–account party disputes are only of secondary importance in Article 5 and need attention only to the extent that contract remedy rules are inadequate. In the issuer–account party context, they appear to be adequate enough, and there is no need to import letter of credit doctrines, such as strict compliance[214] or Article 5 damages[215] rules, into it.[216]

In *Emery-Waterhouse Co. v. Rhode Island Hospital Trust National Bank*,[217] the assignee of a credit knowingly and in bad faith participated in an unauthorized and fraudulent draw on a credit. The *Emery-Waterhouse* court affirmed an award of punitive damages in favor of the account party and against the assignee.

In *First Wyoming Bank v. Mudge*,[218] the account parties complained that the beneficiary had interfered with their contractual relations when it forced them to obtain the credit under threat of enforcing a security agreement. The court upheld an award of damages in the amount of the credit, the issuer's charges for the credit, and interest the account parties had paid after the beneficiary drew.

---

[213] See generally ¶¶ 6.02–6.03.

[214] Cf. supra ¶ 9.03[1][a] (discussing standards of document compliance that depend on same idea that issuer–account party relationship is matter for contract principles, not letter of credit principles).

[215] By the same reasoning, Article 1 provisions, such as Sections 1-103 and 1-106 of the Code, would have no application, except by analogy.

[216] For a case that does import those issuer-beneficiary rules into the issuer–account party setting, see Pioneer Bank & Trust Co. v. Seiko Sporting Goods, U.S.A. Co., 184 Ill. App. 3d 783, 540 N.E.2d 808 (1989). For criticism of *Pioneer Bank*, see ¶¶ 2.09[7], 9.03[1][a].

[217] 757 F.2d 399 (1st Cir. 1985).

[218] 748 P.2d 713 (Wyo. 1988).

¶ 9.04 BREACH OF WARRANTY, FRAUD, AND OTHER ACTIONS

Section 5-111(1) stipulates that "by transferring or presenting a documentary draft or demand for payment," a beneficiary "warrants to all interested parties that the necessary conditions of the credit have been complied with." The provision has not generated much interest, but it should, especially in standby cases where parties may be overlooking it. The object of this discussion is to outline the contours of the warranty and to suggest ways in which litigants might be able to exploit the warranty section.

First, it is consistent with the obvious purpose of the provision that the warranty survive the issuer's payment of the draft or demand, even though that payment may be "final" under the rules of negotiable instruments law. The ministerial function of the issuer does not permit it to go beyond the face of the documents that the beneficiary presents.[219] The provision would not avail the issuer unless the warranty survives payment of the draft or demand.[220]

In the event the documents comply on their face with the terms of the credit, the issuer should have a cause of action against the beneficiary if the issuer honors the conforming demand and then learns that, for some reason, the documents do not comply. If, for example, a beneficiary supplies a forged, fraudulent, or inaccurate document to the issuer, arguably the beneficiary has not complied with the conditions of the credit. Certainly, the law approves the issuer's good faith payment of a facially conforming presentation even when it later becomes apparent that the documents contained a latent defect.

The exigencies of credit law that require such a rule do not require that the rule permit a beneficiary to say, after payment, that his false, fraudulent, or inaccurate documents satisfied the conditions of the credit. The issuer must honor presentations that comply on their face and must not look beneath the documents. Any other rule would frustrate the credit's promptness feature, which is indispensable to the credit's success as a commercial device. After payment, however, the independence principle should not bar the issuer's claim against a beneficiary.[221]

---

[219] See generally ¶ 6.03.

[220] Cf. U.C.C. § 3-418 (providing that presentment warranties of Article 3 survive payment of negotiable instrument).

[221] Accord Werner v. A.L. Grootemaat & Sons, 80 Wis. 2d 513, 259 N.W.2d 310 (1977).

Mellon Bank, N.A. v. General Electric Credit Corp.[222] involved a claim by the issuer against the beneficiary after payment under the credit. The credit called for the beneficiary's certificate to the effect that the amount the beneficiary demanded was due on the equipment lease that comprised the underlying transaction. Because the beneficiary-lessor failed to take the necessary steps to accelerate the lease payments and render them due, the *Mellon Bank* court held that the certification was incorrect and, therefore, a breach of the Section 5-111(1) warranty. *Mellon Bank* is one of the few cases to enforce the warranty section. Its import is clear: The warranty survives payment under the credit.[223]

Nothing in Section 5-111 suggests that breach of the underlying agreement constitutes a breach of the Section 5-111 warranty. That warranty relates to the conditions of the credit, not to the conditions of the underlying agreement. Any notion that the warranty relates to the underlying contract would violate the independence principle. In *Imbrie v. D. Nagase & Co.*,[224] a pre-Code case, the court denied recovery to the issuer when the peanut oil the beneficiary supplied allegedly did not conform to the agreement.[225]

---

[222] 724 F. Supp. 360 (W.D. Pa. 1989).

[223] For discussion of the holding in *Mellon Bank* on the nature of the warranty in Section 5-111(1), see ¶ 6.07.

[224] 196 A.D. 380, 187 N.Y.S. 692 (1921).

[225] See also Bank of E. Asia, Ltd. v. Pang, 140 Wash. 603, 249 P. 1060 (1926) (similar holding). In Valet Parking Serv., Inc. v. Philadelphia Parking Auth., 662 F. Supp. 1053 (E.D. Pa. 1986), the account party claimed that the beneficiary's false certificate amounted to a breach of the underlying contract. The account party caused a letter of credit to issue pursuant to a license agreement. The credit secured the account party's performance under the agreement and called for the beneficiary's certificate to the effect that the account party had failed to perform. The beneficiary moved to dismiss the breach of contract claim, but the court sustained the cause of action. Thus, while breach of the underlying contract may not constitute breach of the credit warranty, breach of the warranty may constitute breach of the underlying contract. In Philadelphia Gear Corp. v. Central Bank, 717 F.2d 230 (5th Cir. 1983), the beneficiary sued when the issuer dishonored and failed to specify the defects in the documents on which it relied in dishonoring. The court held that the beneficiary knowingly had breached its Section 5-111(1) warranties and that therefore it could not recover for the issuer's failure to advise of the defects. This use of the warranty section is disturbing. The *Philadelphia Gear* court apparently overlooked the universal practice of waiving defects in documents. The court was not moved by a waiver argument. Cf. Pro-Fab, Inc. v. Vipa, Inc., 772 F.2d 847 (11th Cir. 1985) (supporting *Philadelphia Gear* analysis); Newvector Communications, Inc. v. Union Bank, 663 F. Supp. 252 (D. Utah 1987) (holding that beneficiary that knowingly does not perform terms and conditions of credit may not recover for wrongful dishonor); Delta Brands, Inc. v. MBank Dallas, N.A., 719 S.W.2d 355 (Tex. Ct. App. 1986) (holding similar to that of *Philadelphia Gear*). For a case that explicitly rejects *Philadelphia Gear*, see Paramount Export Co. v. Asia Trust Bank, 193 Cal. App. 3d 1474, 238 Cal. Rptr. 920 (1987). See also R.M. Goode, Commercial Law (1982) (suggesting that rule

If the documents themselves are facially conforming but there is forgery or fraud in them, the issuer should be able to maintain an action against the beneficiary.[226] In *First National City Bank v. Klatzer*,[227] a bank that may have been a negotiating bank[228] paid the beneficiary when the documents were defective. Without referring to Section 5-111, which may not have been controlling,[229] the court held that the bank could recoup the amount of its loss from the beneficiary.

Section 5-111 makes it clear that the issuer need not resort to subrogation or rely on non-Code causes of action, such as fraud or unjust enrichment.[230] The Code provides its own cause of action for breach of the Section 5-111 warranty. By its use of the term "interested parties" rather than the term "issuer," the provision makes it clear that a negotiating bank, a confirming bank,[231] and an account party[232] also benefit from the warranty.

---

permitting issuer to recover payments made over patent defects would violate requirement of Uniform Customs that issuer examine documents for such defects). For discussion of the importance of the waiver rules, see ¶ 6.06. In Habib Bank Ltd. v. Convermat Corp., 145 Misc. 2d 980, 554 N.Y.S.2d 757 (App. Term. 1990) (per curiam), the court, reading New York law as forbidding application of Article 5 to credits subject to the Uniform Customs (see generally ¶ 4.05), refused to apply the warranty provision. The issuer in the *Habib Bank* case was attempting to recover from the beneficiary payments made over defective documents. The court held that such recovery was inconsistent with Article 16(e) of the Uniform Customs, which estops the issuer from raising defects if it does not notify the beneficiary of them promptly. Restriction of the warranty claim to patent defects would overcome the *Habib* court's concern. See generally ¶ 4.06[2][g].

[226] See U.C.C. § 5-114, comment 2 (2d para., 3d sent.); accord Artoc Bank & Trust, Ltd. v. Sun Marine Terminals, Inc., 760 S.W.2d 311 (Tex. Ct. App. 1988).

[227] 28 U.C.C. Rep. Serv. (Callaghan) 497 (N.Y. Sup. Ct. 1979).

[228] The opinion recites that the plaintiff bank had "merely accepted a letter of credit for collection." Id. at 498. Presumably, the court meant to say that the plaintiff bank took the beneficiary's draft for collection.

[229] The case arose in New York, and, if the credit was subject to the Uniform Customs, Article 5 would not govern. See N.Y. U.C.C. § 5-102(4) (McKinney 1964). See generally ¶ 4.05.

[230] Cf. Giorgio Morandi, Inc. v. Textport Corp., 697 F. Supp. 777 (S.D.N.Y. 1988) (holding that beneficiary's fraudulent documents submitted to credit issuer gave account party ground for prejudgment attachment). But cf. Dean Witter Reynolds, Inc. v. Fernandez, 741 F.2d 355 (11th Cir. 1984) (affirming judgment based on unjust enrichment against party that presented fraudulent documents under credit).

[231] Accord Delta Brands, Inc. v. MBank Dallas, N.A., 719 S.W.2d 355 (Tex. Ct. App. 1986). The interest of the negotiating and the confirming banks is patent. The former may not be able to obtain payment and the latter reimbursement from the issuer if the beneficiary breached the warranty. See U.C.C. § 5-114, comment 2 (2d para., last sent.).

Some account parties appear to be unaware of the warranty rule. In *Fertico Belgium, S.A. v. Phosphate Chemicals Export Association*,[233] for example, the account party sued the beneficiary that it thought had obtained payment under the credit over defective documents. The account party styled its claim as one for fraud or conversion of the credit. The court rejected the conversion theory on the ground that the account party, not being a party to the letter of credit, had no standing to sue for its conversion. That ruling relegated the account party to the common-law fraud claim, with its burdensome scienter requirement. The account party would have been well advised to sue for breach of the Section 5-111(1) warranty, which covers unintentional and unknown defects in the documents.[234]

In *Banque Paribas v. Hamilton Industries International, Inc.*,[235] the court remanded an interpleader action in which the account party claimed that Paribas had presented a false certificate. The court concluded that Paribas was either the beneficiary of the credit or the confirming bank. If Paribas had been a beneficiary, the false certificate would have amounted to a breach of the Section 5-111(1) warranty. If Paribas had been a confirming bank, it would have made no warranty beyond that of its good faith and authority.[236] A confirming bank that unknowingly presented a false certificate would not be liable under the warranty section.

In *Emery-Waterhouse Co. v. Rhode Island Hospital Trust National Bank*,[237] the evidence indicated that the assignee of the proceeds of a credit had hired a former employee of the beneficiary to wind up the af-

---

[232] Werner v. A.L. Grootemaat & Sons, 80 Wis. 2d 513, 259 N.W.2d 310 (1977). For a case in which the account party apparently was unaware of its breach of warranty claim and had difficulty with breach of contract and common-law fraud claims, see Sherkate Sahami Kass Rapol v. Henry R. Jahn & Son, 701 F.2d 1049 (2d Cir. 1983). Cf. Atkinson & Mullen Travel, Inc. v. Suncoast Airlines, Inc. (In re Suncoast Airlines, Inc.), 101 Bankr. 350 (Bankr. S.D. Fla. 1989) (allowing account party's claim against debtor beneficiary for wrongful draw, without discussing theory of beneficiary's liability); Boucher & Slack Contractors, Inc. v. McLean, 397 So. 2d 45 (La. Ct. App. 1981) (suit involving breach of warranty claim that failed on proof).

[233] 100 A.D.2d 165, 473 N.Y.S.2d 403, appeal dismissed, 62 N.Y.2d 802 (1984).

[234] For a case similar to *Fertico Belgium*, see ¶ 6.07 and discussion of the *Sherkate Sahami* case. See also Kashi v. Gratsos, 790 F.2d 1050 (2d Cir. 1986) (involving activity that amounts to breach of warranty, but no breach of warranty claim); Valet Parking Serv., Inc. v. Philadelphia Parking Auth., 662 F. Supp. 1053 (E.D. Pa. 1986) (same).

[235] 767 F.2d 380 (7th Cir. 1985).

[236] See U.C.C. § 5-111, comment.

[237] 757 F.2d 399 (1st Cir. 1985).

fairs of the beneficiary. The effort failed. Despite the fact that the employee told the assignee that there were insufficient grounds to do so, the assignee ordered the employee to draw on the standby credit. The *Emery-Waterhouse* court held that the conduct amounted to fraud. The case is apt for a holding that the assignee breached the warranty of Section 5-111(1) or Section 5-111(2) by knowingly and in bad faith participating in an unauthorized draw under the credit.

In *Holmberg v. Morrisette*,[238] the account party sued the beneficiary and its president and major stockholder for presenting a false certificate, backdated invoices, and altered air waybills under a standby credit. The plaintiff sued in common-law fraud, conversion, and under the federal Racketeer Influenced and Corrupt Organizations Act (RICO) statute.[239] The plaintiff did not raise a breach of warranty claim. The *Holmberg* court denied recovery on the facts under RICO but allowed recovery for fraud and conversion. The court permitted recovery of punitive damages but denied the plaintiff attorney fees.

Holmberg illustrates the advantages and disadvantages of the common-law action for fraud. That action requires a showing that (1) the defendants knowingly submitted false documents to the issuer with the intent that the issuer rely on them; (2) the issuer did rely on them and paid on the credit; and (3) the account party suffered a loss. Those fraud requirements are clearly more burdensome than the requirements of the breach of warranty cause of action; but fraud permits punitive damages, while breach of warranty does not. Significantly, the *Holmberg* court did not permit the defendants to use the account party's liability on the underlying transaction to show that the account party did not suffer any loss.[240] It is difficult to accept the court's holding on the conversion cause of action. The court held that by taking the credit proceeds, the defendants converted the account party's funds. It is generally accepted teaching in letter of credit law that the issuer pays the beneficiary with its own funds, not those of the account party.[241]

In *Universal Security Insurance Co. v. Ring*,[242] the account party sued the beneficiary for "wrongful draw" on the letter of credit and obtained a substantial judgment for compensatory and punitive damages against the beneficiary. The Supreme Court of Arkansas reversed, bas-

[238] 800 F.2d 205 (8th Cir. 1986), cert. denied, 481 U.S. 1028 (1987).

[239] Organized Crime Control Act of 1970, tit. IX (Racketeer Influenced and Corrupt Organizations), 18 U.S.C. §§ 1961–1968 (1988).

[240] For discussion of the use of setoff as a defense in letter of credit disputes, see infra ¶ 9.06[3].

[241] See generally infra ¶ 9.05.

[242] 298 Ark. 582, 769 S.W.2d 750 (1989).

ing its decision in part on what appears to be a misunderstanding of the independence principle.[243] Significantly, there was no mention in the opinion of the fact that the plaintiff's allegations might have made out a case for breach of the Section 5-111(1) warranty.

A broad reading of the warranty section has significance in those frequent standby credit cases involving credits calling for the beneficiary's certificate reciting that certain conditions of the underlying contract are satisfied. Courts struggle with these credits when the account party claims that the certificate is false and that the beneficiary is guilty of fraud. These claims of fraud may give the court ground to enjoin payment of the credit under Section 5-114(2).[244] There is a hint in these cases that the courts do not see any purpose for the certificates, other than to give the account party a fraud argument if the certificate is false. The trouble with that view of the certificate's role is that it invites fraud claims, litigation of which seriously impedes the efficacy of the credit device.[245] Perhaps courts should be more willing to see the role of the certificate not as one to provide the account party with a fraud argument before payment of the credit but as one to provide any interested party with a breach of warranty claim after payment.[246]

Under Section 5-111(2), an intermediary does not make warranties beyond its warranty of good faith and authority. In *Kingdom of Sweden v. New York Trust Co.,*[247] the confirming bank paid the beneficiary and transferred the documents (including warehouse receipts) to the issuer. The account party then sued the confirming bank, claiming that, on transfer of the receipts, it warranted delivery of the goods. The court rejected that argument, noting that any contrary holding would force the confirming bank to go behind the documents. When the confirming bank honors conforming documents, the court held, it is entitled to reimbursement and to its commission. Section 5-111(2) codifies the rule of that case.

In *Pubali Bank v. City National Bank,*[248] the confirming bank was an "assignee" of the credit. The court held that when it forwarded the documents to the opening bank, the confirming bank made more than

---

[243] For discussion of that holding in the *Universal Security Insurance* case, see ¶¶ 2.09[5], 6.07.

[244] See generally ¶ 7.04[4][c].

[245] Id.

[246] For further discussion of the warranty section and the role of such certificates, see Dolan, "Letters of Credit, Article 5 Warranties, and the Beneficiary's Certificate," 41 Bus. Law. 347 (1986).

[247] 197 Misc. 431, 96 N.Y.S.2d 779 (Sup. Ct. 1949).

[248] 676 F.2d 1326 (9th Cir. 1982).

the traditional "good faith and authority" warranty of a confirming bank. By virtue of its interest in the credit, the confirming bank made the Section 5-111(1) warranties and was jointly liable with the beneficiary when the documents proved to contain an inaccurate statement. "CNB may not hide behind the cloak of a neutral advising bank in such circumstances."[249] The *Pubali* case imposes warranty liability on the confirming bank, but only in its role as a party interested in the credit, not in its role of confirming bank.

In *Nacional De Comercializacion Agricola (Indeca) v. Continental Illinois National Bank & Trust Co.*,[250] the court permitted the customer of the opening bank to maintain an action against the confirming bank for negligently honoring a demand for payment accompanied by an allegedly forged or fraudulent document. The bank originally had rejected the document because it was not countersigned by a consular official. The beneficiary resubmitted it with the required countersignature that the account party claimed was forged. The court held that, under non-Code negligence rules, "Continental represented to all who might foreseeably rely on such information that [the beneficiary] was honest in its revisions."[251]

That holding conflicts with Section 5-111(2), which says that the confirming bank only represents (i.e., only warrants) its good faith and authority. The *Indeca* opinion does not cite the warranty section, and it may be that the court's warranty holding took counsel by surprise. Non-Code law, such as that the *Indeca* opinion invoked, may supplement the Code, but not if that law is "displaced by the particular provisions" of the Code.[252] Clearly, the warranty rule of Section 5-111(2) does displace a rule such as that applied by the *Indeca* court.[253]

---

[249] Id. at 1330. The court emphasized that position in a later holding in the same litigation. See Pubali Bank v. City Nat'l Bank, 769 F.2d 605, superseded, 777 F.2d 1340 (9th Cir. 1985).

[250] 530 F. Supp. 279 (N.D. Ill. 1982).

[251] Id. at 284.

[252] U.C.C. § 1-103.

[253] The *Indeca* court's negligence holding is also contrary to the rule of Section 5-114(2)(b), which permits the issuer to honor a credit, even though it has notice of possible fraud or forgery, as long as it acts in good faith. The good faith concept in Article 5 does not include observance of due care. See U.C.C. § 1-201(9). See also authority cited supra note 178. In Auto Servicio San Ignacio, S.R.L. v. Compania Anonima Venezolana De Navegacion, 586 F. Supp. 259 (E.D. La. 1984), aff'd, 765 F.2d 1306 (5th Cir. 1985), the court held squarely that the negligence of a confirming bank is not a breach of the Section 5-111(2) warranty. Accord United States v. Foster Wheeler Corp., 639 F. Supp. 1266 (S.D.N.Y. 1986).

In a subsequent opinion in the same case, the *Indeca* court modified its position somewhat.[254] Based on changes in Illinois common law, the court ruled that an action in negligence against the confirming bank would not lie. The court acknowledged that counsel had not briefed the Section 5-111(2) issue in the earlier hearing but still declined to follow the implication of the section or the rule expressed in the comment. Instead, the court relied on Illinois non–letter of credit cases, which, it felt, supported a cause of action on theories of fraud (dishonesty) or reckless disregard for truth or falsity.

Under the facts of that case, it appeared that when the confirming bank forwarded the documents to the opening bank, the confirming bank had telexed the opening bank that the documents were in order. The *Indeca* court held in the second opinion that such a representation is actionable if it is dishonest or if it is made with reckless disregard for its truth or falsity.

On appeal, the Court of Appeals for the Seventh Circuit held that there was no duty on the confirming bank to provide accurate information to the account party.[255] The court held squarely that, under Illinois Code and non-Code law, the account party did not have a cause of action against the confirming bank for negligent misrepresentation. The duties of the confirming bank are spelled out in Sections 5-109 and 5-114 of the Code and do not include any duty that would give rise to that cause of action. The Seventh Circuit also held that the policy of Article 5 in promoting the use of letters of credit would not be advanced by fashioning duties for the confirming bank in addition to those created by the Code. In reaching its decision, the court did not discuss the negative implications of Section 5-111(1).

Nothing in Section 5-111(2) protects the confirming bank, however, in the event it is party to the beneficiary's fraud. In *Berry v. Bank of Louisiana*,[256] the trial court dismissed a complaint alleging that the confirming bank participated with the beneficiary in fraudulently obtaining payment under the credit. The state court of appeals reversed. Section 5-111(2) imposes on the confirming bank a warranty of good faith when it presents documents.[257] If the account party's allegations were true, the

---

[254] Instituto Nacional De Comercializacion Agricola (Indeca) v. Continental Ill. Nat'l Bank & Trust Co., 675 F. Supp. 1515 (N.D. Ill. 1987), aff'd, 858 F.2d 1264 (7th Cir. 1988).

[255] Instituto Nacional De Comercializacion Agricola (Indeca) v. Continental Ill. Nat'l Bank & Trust Co., 858 F.2d 1264 (7th Cir. 1988).

[256] 439 So. 2d 1166 (La. Ct. App. 1983).

[257] See U.C.C. § 5-111, comment (penultimate sentence).

confirming bank acted fraudulently—that is, dishonestly—and dishonest conduct is not good faith.[258]

In all of these cases, courts must distinguish factually inaccurate assertions in the documents that matter from those that do not. In *FDIC v. Bank of San Francisco*,[259] for instance, the court held that there was no fraud in a certificate that referred to a promissory note that had never been executed. In fact, another note was in default; and the court saw the factual discrepancy as insufficient to support a finding of fraud. Similarly, in *First National Bank v. Carmouche*,[260] the court refused to find fraud in a certificate executed by a corporate officer as secretary-treasurer of the company in order to comply with the terms of the credit, even though the officer was a vice-president of the company at the time he signed.[261] Such pro forma deviations from actual facts are not fraudulent and should not support causes of action for breach of warranty, just as they have not supported causes of action or defenses rooted in fraud.

¶ 9.05　ATTACHMENT

Attachment often plays a role in letter of credit disputes. Sometimes creditors of the account party or the beneficiary attempt to use attachment as a debt collection device. That use of attachment has serious implications for letter of credit transfer rules.[262] At other times, the account party or the beneficiary may resort to attachment in a dispute arising not out of unrelated transactions but out of the credit transaction itself.

In *National Bank & Trust Co. of North America, Ltd. v. J.L.M. International, Inc.*,[263] the assignee of the proceeds of a credit successfully maintained an action to attach those proceeds after the account party repudiated the credit and instructed the opening bank not to honor the beneficiary's drafts.[264] In *United Bank Ltd. v. Cambridge Sporting*

---

[258] See U.C.C. § 1-201(19).

[259] 817 F.2d 1395 (9th Cir. 1987).

[260] 504 So. 2d 1153 (La. Ct. App.), rev'd on other grounds, 515 So. 2d 785 (La. 1987).

[261] For other authority indicating that minor defects in documents do not constitute fraud, see ¶ 7.04[4][a].

[262] For general discussion of that remedy and the problems it creates for the independence principle and the transfer rules, see ¶¶ 7.03[5], 10.06.

[263] 421 F. Supp. 1269 (S.D.N.Y. 1976).

[264] It also appears that a beneficiary used attachment successfully in J. Zeevi & Sons v. Grindlay's Bank (Uganda) Ltd., 37 N.Y.2d 220, 333 N.E.2d 168, 371 N.Y.S.2d 892, cert. denied, 432 U.S. 866 (1975).

Goods Corp.,[265] negotiating banks sued the account party to recover on a credit after the account party had successfully enjoined the issuer from paying and had levied on the credit proceeds held by the issuer. Significantly, the *United Bank* court held that, by virtue of the injunction and the levy, the rights of the account party would be measured by those of the issuer.

These cases apply New York law, and it appears, as the *National Bank* court held, that the use of attachment among the parties to the credit arrangement is a matter of attachment law.[266] That view is undoubtedly correct, but courts must take care that the use of attachment does not conflict with letter of credit rules on assignment and transfer or with the independence principle.[267] By measuring the rights of the account party in the *United Bank* case by those of the issuer, the court was protecting the independence principle.

In *Furness Withy (Chartering), Inc., Panama v. World Energy Systems Associates, Inc.*,[268] the assignee of the proceeds of a credit sued a creditor of the beneficiary that had attached the proceeds. The court held that the attachment was wrongful, the rights to the proceeds of the assignee being greater than those of the creditor; but the court denied damages. The court held that admiralty law, under which the plaintiff was suing, required a showing of malice or other bad faith before allowing recovery for wrongful attachment.

In *Harvey Estes Construction Co. v. Dry Dock Savings Bank*,[269] a state court, at the behest of the account party, had ordered the issuer to pay into court funds held by the issuer to reimburse itself for honoring the credit. On removal, the federal district court held that the issuer's honor of the beneficiary's request for payment prior to the entry of the state court's order left the issuer without funds on which the state statute could operate. The account party argued that the beneficiary should pay the funds into court. The court held, however, that the statute involved authorized courts to enter such an order not against the beneficiary but only against a stakeholder such as the issuer. The court's characterization of the issuer as a stakeholder is contrary to traditional notions in letter of credit law, which holds generally that the issuer honors the beneficiary's drafts with its own funds, not with anyone else's.

---

[265] 41 N.Y.2d 254, 360 N.E.2d 943, 392 N.Y.S.2d 265 (1976).

[266] National Bank & Trust Co. of N. Am., Ltd. v. J.L.M. Int'l, Inc., 421 F. Supp. 1269 (S.D.N.Y. 1976).

[267] See ¶ 10.06; cf. ¶ 7.03[5] (discussing use of attachment by account party to stop payment of credit).

[268] 772 F.2d 802 (11th Cir. 1985).

[269] 381 F. Supp. 271 (W.D. Okla. 1974).

Other courts, truer to that traditional notion, have held that there was nothing for the complainant to attach. In *First Commercial Bank v. Gotham Originals, Inc.*,[270] the account party, having obtained a judgment against the beneficiary, sought to garnish the proceeds of the credit. At the time the sheriff served the attachment order, however, the issuer had accepted time drafts under the credit, and a negotiating bank held the acceptances. The court held that there were no assets of the beneficiary to satisfy the judgment debt.[271]

Similarly, in *Diakan Love, S.A. v. Al-Haddad Bros. Enterprises, Inc. (In re Diakan Love S.A.)*,[272] a third-party creditor had obtained an arbitrator's award against the beneficiary and sought to enforce it by attaching sums due under a letter of credit that the defendant bank had confirmed. The court held that there was nothing to attach, because the confirming bank's obligation under the credit was subject to conditions that had not been satisfied.[273] The creditor also sought to attach proceeds of a credit that the defendant had advised, and the court held that an advising bank never owes any duty to the beneficiary and that therefore there could not be any property or debt to garnish.

In *Union Planters National Bank v. World Energy Systems Associates, Inc.*,[274] the court held that a maritime attachment and writ of garnishment served on the advising bank could not defeat the assignees of the beneficiary, because:

1. The assignments were perfected security interests under the UCC;
2. There were no sums due under the credit at the time the writ was served; and
3. The advising bank served only as a conduit through which the funds passed and never possessed them in a way that would permit attachment.

---

[270] 101 A.D.2d 790, 476 N.Y.S.2d 835 (1984), aff'd, 64 N.Y.2d 287, 475 N.E.2d 1255, 486 N.Y.S.2d 715 (1985).

[271] Accord Supreme Merchandise Co. v. Chemical Bank, 117 A.D.2d 424, 503 N.Y.S.2d 9 (1986), aff'd, 70 N.Y.2d 344, 514 N.E.2d 1358, 520 N.Y.S.2d 734 (1987).

[272] 584 F. Supp. 782 (S.D.N.Y. 1984).

[273] The court also justified its holding as a matter of letter of credit law, reasoning that to permit the garnishment would seriously hamper the credit. Accord Ferrostaal Metals Corp. v. S.S. Lash Pacifico, 652 F. Supp. 420 (S.D.N.Y. 1987); Supreme Merchandise Co. v. Chemical Bank, 117 A.D.2d 424, 503 N.Y.S.2d 9 (1986). See generally ¶ 10.06[3][b].

[274] 816 F.2d 1092 (6th Cir. 1987).

The *Union Planters* court also held that the writ was not a continuing writ and that, if proceeds of the credit came into the hands of the advising bank after the writ was served and the interrogatories were answered, the previously served writ would not capture the proceeds.

The notion that an advising bank or other bank nominated to pay the credit is a conduit through which funds pass is not altogether contrary to letter of credit theory. While the issuer and the confirmer honor the beneficiary's drafts with their own funds, an advising or paying bank may hold an account against which it draws in order to satisfy the beneficiary's draft. Under another arrangement, a nominated bank pays the beneficiary and obtains reimbursement from the issuer or by drawing on an account maintained by the issuer at still another bank. Whether under any of these arrangements the paying bank holds funds of the issuer or confirmer is a question of banking law, not letter of credit law.[275]

In *United Trading Corp. v. Allied Arab Bank Ltd.*,[276] one bank issued a counterindemnity in favor of a second bank that had issued a guaranty to the account parties' buyer.[277] The account parties attempted to enjoin the second bank's use of the funds paid under the counterguaranty. Because the account parties were basing their claim on the conduct of the buyer, the court held, and because the funds in the hands of the second bank would be that bank's funds and not those of the buyer, the injunction should not issue.

¶ 9.06 SOME AFFIRMATIVE DEFENSES

The peculiar nature of credits and their independence from related transactions often affect the use of defenses. In this area, as in most others involving credit law, application of a traditional legal doctrine must abide consideration of its impact on the letter of credit device.

[1] Penalties

Commercial law generally disfavors penalties, and some account parties have argued that enforcement of the credit amounts to legal sanctioning

---

[275] In Intraco Ltd. v. Notis Shipping Corp., [1981] 2 Lloyd's Rep. 256 (C.A.), a London bank issued a credit payable in Greece. The account party sought a *Mareva* injunction to prevent the beneficiary from removing the credit proceeds from the jurisdiction. See Mareva Compania Naviera S.A. v. International Bulk Carriers S.A., [1975] 2 Lloyd's Rep. 509 (C.A.). The court held that there were no funds to be moved out of the jurisdiction, the credit being payable in Greece.

[276] [1985] 2 Lloyd's Rep. 554 (C.A.).

[277] For authority that performance guaranties of the kind in the *United Trading Corp.* case are subject to letter of credit law, see ¶ 1.05.

of a penalty. These account parties argue that courts should not enforce credits that effect payment of penalties. If account parties were to succeed in that argument, they would have done what letter of credit law forbids: They would have breached the independence principle. That breach destroys the credit as an effective commercial device.

Courts, then, before they accept the account party's penalty argument (or any other argument that payment under the credit violates public policy), must weigh the law's animus toward the penalty (or whatever other policy the account party raises) against the law's regard for the letter of credit. When courts strike this balance, they draw some comfort from the fact that payment under the credit does not always end the matter. Usually, the account party is able, after payment, to resort to policies that protect him in his action against the beneficiary. Generally, courts have struck the balance in favor of the credit.

In *New York Life Insurance Co. v. Hartford National Bank & Trust Co.*,[278] the credit served to provide the beneficiary with liquidated damages in the event of the account party's failure to perform the underlying agreement. The account party made the penalty argument; but the court refused to consider it, on the ground that to do so would violate the independence principle.[279]

In *Berman v. Le Beau Inter-America, Inc.*,[280] the trustee of a bankrupt account party alleged that the beneficiaries of a credit were using the letter of credit to convey assets of the bankrupt corporation to themselves in violation of state law governing payment of corporate dividends. The court rejected the plaintiff's request for return of funds paid under the credit, noting that, even if the funding of the credits had been fraudulent, payment under the credit would not be fraudulent. In *Jupi-*

---

[278] 173 Conn. 492, 378 A.2d 562 (1977).

[279] Cf. Prudential Ins. Co. of Am. v. Marquette Nat'l Bank, 419 F. Supp. 734 (D. Minn. 1976) (account party making similar penalty argument, but court deciding matter on procedural question); Harvey Estes Constr. Co. v. Dry Dock Sav. Bank, 381 F. Supp. 271 (W.D. Okla. 1974) (same). But cf. Shel-Al Corp. v. American Nat'l Ins. Co., 492 F.2d 87 (5th Cir. 1974) (suggesting that court should look to underlying transaction to determine whether credit that served as "stand-by deposit fee," id. at 88, was reasonable); Hubbard Business Plaza v. Lincoln Liberty Life Ins. Co., 649 F. Supp. 1310 (D. Nev. 1986), aff'd, 844 F.2d 792 (9th Cir. 1988) (mem.) (enjoining payment of credit on ground that it constituted penalty in underlying contract); Birdwell v. Farrell, 746 S.W.2d 338 (Tex. Ct. App. 1988) (ordering return of credit to buyer on grounds that arrangement constituted penalty). See also ¶ 12.02 (discussing issuer's ultra vires defense). See generally McLaughlin, "Letters of Credit and Illegal Contracts: the Limits of the Independence Principle," 49 Ohio St. L.J. 1197 (1989); McLaughlin, "Standby Letters of Credit and Penalty Clauses: An Unexpected Synergy," 43 Ohio State L.J. 1 (1982).

[280] 509 F. Supp. 156 (S.D.N.Y.), aff'd mem., 679 F.2d 872 (2d Cir. 1981).

ter Orrington Corp. v. Zweifel,[281] the account party argued that payment of the credit would amount to a forfeiture. The court, however, refused to enjoin payment, holding simply that the account party must bear the loss.

[2] Release

In *Asociacion De Azucareros De Guatemala v. United States National Bank,*[282] the issuer defended the beneficiary's suit on the credit on the ground that the beneficiary, a seller, had released the account party buyer and thereby had released the issuer. The court rejected the argument as an attempt to render the issuer's liability on the credit derivative of the account party's liability on the underlying contract of sale.[283]

In a confusing opinion, *Transparent Products v. Paysaver Credit Union,*[284] the court held that a beneficiary that had waited to draw on a credit until the account party had become insolvent would be barred from making a draw. While the opinion does not rationalize the holding, it implies that fairness demands that the beneficiary, who apparently sat on his rights, be estopped from using the credit after the issuer has lost its right of reimbursement. The result may be no more than the beneficiary deserved. The credit contained no expiry, and the well-advised beneficiary would have been suspicious of the credit union issuing it. The credit secured open account shipments to one of the account parties. It is frequently the case in such settings that the need for the credit will continue indefinitely. Renewing the credit periodically or utilizing an evergreen clause[285] are two efficient methods of dealing with that indefinite need.[286]

---

[281] 127 Ill. App. 3d 559, 469 N.E.2d 590 (1984).

[282] 423 F.2d 638 (9th Cir. 1970).

[283] Accord Housing Sec., Inc. v. Maine Nat'l Bank, 391 A.2d 311 (Me. 1978); Clement v. FDIC, 2 U.C.C. Rep. Serv. 2d (Callaghan) 1017 (W.D. Okla. 1986); CKB Assocs., Inc. v. Moore McCormack Petroleum, 734 S.W.2d 653 (Tex. 1987). For discussion of the account party's cause of action against the beneficiary after payment on the credit, see ¶ 2.09[6].

[284] No. 85 C 1741 (N.D. Ill. Jan. 21, 1988), aff'd on other grounds, 864 F.2d 60 (7th Cir. 1988).

[285] For discussion of evergreen clauses, see National Sur. Corp. v. Midland Bank, 551 F.2d 21 (3d Cir. 1977); Comptroller of the Currency, Staff Interpretive Letter No. 239, reprinted in [1983–1984 Transfer Binder] Fed. Banking L. Rep. (CCH) ¶ 85,403 (Mar. 10, 1982). For an illustration of a credit with an evergreen clause, see App. C, Doc. 24.

[286] For authority on the need for an expiry in any letter of credit, see ¶ 5.03[3]. Given the fact that the credit contained no expiry, the beneficiary should have been suspicious that the issuer did not appreciate the significance of its undertaking.

The *Transparent Products* result is disconcerting in other respects, however. Letters of credit, by their nature, secure the beneficiary against the financial failure of the account party. The first function of the credit is to substitute the creditworthiness of the issuer for that of the account party. It is incumbent on the issuer to evaluate that creditworthiness; the failure of the beneficiary to draw before the account party fails should not, in the normal course of letter of credit affairs, give the issuer a defense. Indeed, such a result is extraordinary and defeats the purpose of most credits.[287]

[3] Setoff

Setoff can create problems for the credit as an obligation of the issuer that is independent of related transactions. It is axiomatic as a matter of credit law, for example, that the letter of credit be independent of the underlying transaction, and it would destroy the credit if the account party that discovered defective goods were able to assign its claim in recoupment against the beneficiary to the issuer with the idea that the issuer would use the claim as a setoff in the credit transaction.[288] That is not to say, however, that setoff is never available to the issuer. In *Banco Nacional De Cuba v. Chase Manhattan Bank*,[289] the beneficiary drew a draft on the issuing bank and deposited it for collection with Banco Nacional De Cuba, which the court found to be the alter ego of the Cuban government. When that government expropriated property of the issuer, the issuer attempted to set its losses from the expropriation off against the amount of the draft that Banco Nacional De Cuba presented for payment. The court denied the setoff, to the extent that Banco Nacional was acting not in its own behalf but only as an agent of the beneficiary. The Code preserves the presumption that a collecting bank such as Banco Nacional is an agent,[290] but it provides that clear[291] evidence that the

---

[287] On appeal, the Court of Appeals for the Seventh Circuit affirmed the *Transparent Products* holding but rejected the idea that the undertaking was a letter of credit. For discussion of the case on appeal, see ¶ 2.10[2][a]. For discussion of the question whether payment by the issuer to the beneficiary discharges the account party on its underlying transaction obligations, see ¶ 2.09[2]. Cf. supra ¶ 9.06[2] (releases).

[288] Accord Hongkong & Shanghai Banking Corp. v. Kloeckner & Co., [1989] 2 Lloyd's Rep. 323 (Q.B.).

[289] 505 F. Supp. 412 (S.D.N.Y. 1980), rev'd on other grounds sub nom. Banco Para El Comercio Exterior De Cuba v. First Nat'l City Bank, 658 F.2d 913 (2d Cir. 1981), rev'd, 462 U.S. 611 (1983).

[290] See U.C.C. § 4-201(1).

[291] Id., comment 2 (2d para.).

bank has purchased the item and, therefore, is acting in its own right may overcome that "strong presumption."[292]

On appeal,[293] the issuer again attempted to assert by way of counterclaim its damages growing out of the Cuban government's expropriation. The Supreme Court held that, under all of the circumstances, the setoff was proper.[294]

Similarly, in *Hongkong & Shanghai Banking Corp. v. Kloeckner & Co.*,[295] the court permitted an issuer to exercise a setoff against the beneficiary's claim under a standby letter of credit. The *Kloeckner* court made much of the fact that the setoff in that case was not one assigned to the issuer from the account party. The court noted that the setoff arose in the "very banking transaction which gave rise to the letter of credit itself"[296] and that the bank's claim was liquidated.[297]

In *Bamberger Polymers International Corp. v. Citibank, N.A.*,[298] the advising payor bank held a claim against the beneficiary of a credit issued by the Bank of China. The beneficiary assigned the credit proceeds to the plaintiff and notified the payor bank, which acknowledged the assignment. When the plaintiff sought the proceeds, the payor asserted a setoff in the amount due it from the beneficiary. The court held that the payor bank did not have any right of setoff. In the court's view, the plaintiff had the rights of an assignee of an account under Section 9-318 of the Code. That provision, the court held, permits an account debtor to set off against an assignee only those amounts due the account debtor from the assignor. In this case, the account debtor was the Bank of China, and the assignor did not owe anything to that bank. The court also reasoned that because the payor bank had acknowledged the assignment, it should not be able to raise the setoff.

---

[292] Id., comment 2 (1st para., 1st sent.).

[293] Banco Para El Commercio Exterior De Cuba v. First Nat'l City Bank, 462 U.S. 611 (1983).

[294] Cf. Security Fin. Group, Inc. v. Northern Ky. Bank & Trust Co., 875 F.2d 529 (6th Cir. 1989) (indication that court was willing to permit issuer to use setoff against sums due beneficiary).

[295] [1989] 2 Lloyd's Rep. 323 (Q.B.).

[296] Id. at 331.

[297] In Etablissement Esefka Int'l Anstalt v. Central Bank of Nig., [1979] 1 Lloyd's Rep. 445 (C.A.), the court permitted the issuer of a credit that had a claim against the beneficiary for presenting forged documents to set that claim off against the beneficiary's claim for demurrage under the credit in connection with the same shipment for which it had submitted the forged documents.

[298] 124 Misc. 2d 653, 477 N.Y.S.2d 931 (Sup. Ct. 1983).

In *Board of Trade v. Swiss Credit Bank*,[299] the account party assigned its judgment against the beneficiary to the issuer. The beneficiary assigned its right to the credit proceeds and its cause of action for dishonor against the issuer to the plaintiff. The court ruled against the plaintiff in its claim against the issuer on the ground that the beneficiary's documents were not complying. In a comment that is probably obiter dictum, the court indicated that even if the issuer had been estopped to raise the defects as an excuse for dishonor, it would have been able to set off the account party's judgment under Section 9-318(1).

The court confronted a classic use of setoff in *Power Curber International Ltd. v. National Bank of Kuwait S.A.K.*[300] There the account party used setoffs in related transactions to obtain an order in Kuwait against payment of the credit by the Kuwaiti issuer. The *Power Curber* court, applying North Carolina law and the Uniform Customs, held that use of setoff was inappropriate and ordered the Kuwaiti issuer to honor the beneficiary's request for payment.

An issuer's attempt to use the doctrine of setoff poses serious questions and may violate the independence principle. Clearly, an account party may not successfully take amounts due from the beneficiary (whether on the underlying transaction or on some other agreement, whether in contract or in tort) and use them to reduce the sum due the beneficiary under the credit. The issuer's credit engagement is independent of those transactions, and such use of setoff would violate the independence principle.[301] The *Banco Nacional* case does not pose that clear conflict, because the issuer was not attempting to set off the account party's claim. It was attempting to set off its own claim against the Cuban government. The *Board of Trade* case is unpersuasive; the reasoning of *Power Curber* is compelling.

One cannot deny that there are aspects of judicial efficiency at work here. When the issuer holds a claim against the beneficiary and the beneficiary holds a claim against the issuer, courts are always anxious to litigate both matters at once. That inclination, however, upsets that allocation of risks that the credit effects.[302] When an account party buyer, for example, agrees to cause a credit to issue in favor of the seller-benefi-

---

[299] 728 F.2d 1241 (9th Cir. 1984).

[300] [1981] 3 All E.R. 607 (C.A.).

[301] See ¶ 2.09[6]. But cf. Cronin v. Executive House Realty, [1982 Transfer Binder] Fed. Sec. L. Rep. (CCH) ¶ 98,670 (S.D.N.Y. 1982) (permitting account parties to enjoin beneficiary from collecting on credit and requiring beneficiary to return account parties' promissory notes, because jury found that beneficiary, through its negligence, caused loss to account parties).

[302] For a description of those functions, see ¶ 3.07.

ciary, the buyer and seller are allocating litigation costs in a fashion that benefits the seller. Because the seller will obtain the purchase price before the buyer obtains the goods, the parties will have to litigate any dispute over the quality of the goods at a time when the seller holds the funds, and the litigation probably will arise in the seller's jurisdiction. If the issuer can take an assignment of claims and assert them or unrelated claims as setoffs against the beneficiary when it draws on the credit, the allocation of litigation costs agreed to by the buyer and seller are upset.

Thus, courts might be well advised to read the *Board of Trade* court's dictum narrowly. Otherwise, a beneficiary will lose the benefit of the credit's risk-shifting and forum-shifting functions. Under a broad reading of that dictum, an account party might assign its breach of warranty claim in the underlying contract to the issuer. If that assignment permits the issuer to dishonor the credit, the account party has succeeded in merging the letter of credit and underlying transactions. The facts and holding in the *Board of Trade* case do not effect that kind of merger, however. In *Board of Trade*, the account party had obtained a judgment; that is, it had litigated the underlying contract dispute outside of the credit context.[303]

Setoff has enjoyed mixed success in actions by beneficiaries for wrongful dishonor against the FDIC as liquidator of a failed issuer. In *FDIC v. Liberty National Bank & Trust Co.*,[304] bank beneficiaries set off letter of credit claims in the receivership against deposits due to the failed bank. The effect of the setoff was to give the beneficiaries security to the extent of the mutual debts while other claimants would presumably receive a dividend of less than 100 percent of their claim.

The *Liberty National Bank* court allowed the setoffs to the extent that they existed on the date of the failed bank's insolvency.[305] In *FDIC v. Miller*,[306] however, the court refused to permit the beneficiary of a credit by a failed state bank to set off sums due under the credit against sums due to the bank on a promissory note. Such setoff, the court held, would violate the state's statutory scheme for distributing

---

[303] If a beneficiary breaches its warranty under Section 5-111(1) or is liable in common-law fraud for presenting false documents, it may argue that given the fact that it is owed money in the underlying transaction, its misconduct in the credit transaction is harmless. The defendants in Holmberg v. Morrisette, 800 F.2d 205 (8th Cir. 1986), cert. denied, 481 U.S. 1028 (1987), made that argument, but the court rejected it. The trial court had found the facts against the defendants, however, and the holding may be dictum.

[304] 806 F.2d 961 (10th Cir. 1986).

[305] For further discussion of the Liberty National Bank setoffs, see ¶ 12.01[1][c].

[306] 659 F. Supp. 388 (D. Kan. 1987).

the assets of the failed bank by treating the beneficiary's unsecured claim more favorably than other unsecured claims.

[4] Act of State Doctrine and Similar Defenses

[a] Act of State Doctrine

Litigants sometimes attempt to use the act of state doctrine to affect the outcome of credit litigation.[307] That doctrine holds that courts should not frustrate efforts of a recognized foreign sovereign to give effect to its public interest within its own territory.[308] Generally, the attempts to use it in credit cases have not been successful.

In *Banco De Vizcaya, S.A. v. First National Bank*,[309] the plaintiff, a negotiating bank, advanced funds to the beneficiary and then sued in a federal district court sitting in Chicago to obtain payment from the Chicago payor bank. The opening bank, the payor bank's Abu Dhabi branch, had issued the credit with instructions to the beneficiary to seek payment through the Chicago bank. In addition the issuer had accepted the drafts. The payor bank sought to avoid liability on the grounds that an Abu Dhabi court, finding that the equipment delivered by the beneficiary was defective, had enjoined the opening bank from paying the acceptances. The defendant Chicago bank argued that any order to pay the acceptances would violate the sovereignty of Abu Dhabi.

The *Banco De Vizcaya* court saw the argument as an attempt to use the act of state doctrine by analogy and rejected the attempt. The court held that the doctrine usually does not apply to litigation instituted by a private party and that the purpose of the doctrine (to protect a foreign sovereign's acts to further a public interest) did not obtain. The court also noted that the American version of the doctrine stems from a desire by the courts not to interfere with the conduct of foreign policy by the

---

[307] In addition to the cases discussed here, there is a provision in the Foreign Assistance Act of 1965 relating to letters of credit and the act of state doctrine. See 22 U.S.C. § 2370(e)(2) (1988). Generally, this provision, the Hickenlooper or Sabbatino Amendment, forbids federal courts to invoke the act of state doctrine to protect a claim to goods that derives from their expropriation in violation of international law principles. In Banco Nacional De Cuba v. First Nat'l City Bank, 431 F.2d 394 (2d Cir. 1970), the court held that the amendment applies to the narrow case in which the property in dispute was expropriated and has been brought into the United States. The amendment contains a narrow exception stipulating that it does not operate if the person claiming through the expropriating government took under an irrevocable credit with a duration of not more than 180 days. The exception is a narrow one to a narrow rule.

[308] See Banco Nacional De Cuba v. Sabbatino, 376 U.S. 398 (1964).

[309] 514 F. Supp. 1280 (N.D. Ill. 1981), vacated, id.

legislative and executive branches. That consideration, the court held, was not present in the *Banco De Vizcaya* case.

In *J. Zeevi & Sons v. Grindlays Bank (Uganda) Ltd.*,[310] the opening bank in Kampala directed collecting banks to seek reimbursement from its New York correspondent. After issuance, the Government of Uganda forbade payment of the credit, and the opening bank wired the New York correspondent not to reimburse. The beneficiary and its assignee brought an action in a New York court, and the opening bank argued that the act of state doctrine prevented New York courts from interfering with Uganda's conduct. The *J. Zeevi* court held that the cause of action arose in New York, not in Uganda, and that the doctrine had no application.[311]

In *First National Bank v. Banco Nacional De Cuba*,[312] the defendant was party to a scheme to nationalize the plaintiff's branches in Cuba. The plaintiff argued that it had confirmed credits issued by the branches that held accounts securing the credit obligation and that, by virtue of the nationalization, it had lost its right of reimbursement. The defendant raised the act of state doctrine as a defense, and the court accepted it.

[b] Foreign Assets Control and Transactions Regulations

The Trading With the Enemy Act[313] permits the president, by executive order and by regulation, in the interest of national security, to limit commerce with foreign governments and nationals. As a consequence of the U.S.-Iranian diplomatic crisis of 1979, for example, the president blocked bank payments, including letter of credit payments to Iranian entities.[314] Similar executive branch action in the past has affected payments to Cuba,[315] the Noriega government in Panama,[316] and Libya.[317]

---

[310] 37 N.Y.2d 220, 333 N.E.2d 168, 371 N.Y.S.2d 892, cert denied, 432 U.S. 866 (1975).

[311] But cf. Verlinden, B.V. v. Central Bank of Nig., 488 F. Supp. 1284 (S.D.N.Y. 1980), rev'd, 647 F.2d 320 (2d Cir. 1981), rev'd, 461 U.S. 480 (1983) (holding that Foreign Sovereign Immunity Act bars jurisdiction in case with similar facts). See generally Comment, "Act of State Negated: J. Zeevi & Sons, Ltd. v. Grindlays Bank (Uganda) Ltd. (N.Y. Ct. App. 1975)," 15 Colum. J. Transnat'l L. 497 (1976).

[312] 658 F.2d 895 (2d Cir. 1981), cert. denied, 459 U.S. 1091 (1982).

[313] 50 U.S.C. app. 5(b) (1982).

[314] See Iranian Assets Control Regulations, 31 C.F.R. §§ 535.101–535.905 (1989).

[315] See Cuban Assets Control Regulations, 31 C.F.R. §§ 515.101–515.809 (1989).

[316] See Panamanian Transactions Regulations, 31 C.F.R. §§ 565.101–565.806 (1989).

[317] See Libyan Sanctions Regulations, 31 C.F.R. §§ 550.101–550.807 (1989).

These exercises of federal power undoubtedly affect the acceptability of credits issued by U.S. banks negatively. Any rule that weakens the inevitability of payment under a credit renders it a less attractive device as a commercial product. The credit is a strong, attractive device, and its growth suggests that assets control regulations and the like have not impaired it altogether.

Opportunity costs, however, are notoriously difficult to measure. No one can determine the number of international transactions that did not proceed as a result of fear that regulations such as these might interrupt them, and no one can compute the degree of increased costs incurred because of resort to the credit's more expensive alternatives and lost competition that these missed opportunities visit on the economy. It is axiomatic, however, that this kind of government interference is costly, and all must hope that no administration will invoke these measures unmindful of the costs they entail.

In *Itek Corp. v. First National Bank*,[318] the account party sought an injunction terminating its liability to reimburse the issuer of a standby credit running to an Iranian bank. The account party alleged fraud, and the beneficiary argued, among other things, that the Iranian Hostage Agreement, various executive orders, and Department of the Treasury regulations issued pursuant to the Hostage Agreement required the account party to arbitrate the matter with an international tribunal. *Itek* acknowledged that courts should give great weight to the executive branch's interpretation of international agreements, and it noted that the Treasury regulations in question expressly provided that the Iranian Assets Control Regulations did not apply to claims relating to the payment of standby letters of credit. The court concluded that the regulations did not bar the account party's action.

[c]　Foreign Sovereign Immunity

The act of state doctrine[319] and the Foreign Sovereign Immunity Act[320] are similar but distinct defenses. The former is a rule of judge-made law, the latter a question of legislatively fashioned limits on the exercise of jurisdiction.[321] Under the former, courts have fashioned a

---

[318] 511 F. Supp. 1341 (D. Mass. 1981).

[319] For discussion of that doctrine in the letter of credit context, see supra ¶ 9.06[4][a].

[320] Pub. L. No. 94-583, 90 Stat. 2891, 28 U.S.C. §§ 1330, 1332(a)(2)–1332(a)(4), 1391(f), 1441(d), 1602–1611 (1988).

[321] National Am. Corp. v. Federal Republic of Nig., 425 F. Supp. 1365 (S.D.N.Y. 1977).

doctrine whereby they choose to stay the application of commercial principles; under the latter, the legislature has deprived them of the power to apply those principles. The contours of the Foreign Sovereign Immunity Act are governed by the Act itself and by the due process clause of the Constitution.

In *Texas Trading & Milling Corp. v. Federal Republic of Nigeria*,[322] the court noted that the Act alone cannot set the parameters for jurisdiction over a foreign sovereign and that any assertion of jurisdiction must satisfy the due process standards laid down in such cases as *International Shoe Co. v. Washington*[323] and *Hanson v. Denckla*.[324] The letter of credit cases suggest, however, that the standards of the statute and the Constitution are pretty much the same.[325]

In *Decor by Nikkei International, Inc. v. Federal Republic of Nigeria*,[326] the sellers of cement sued the Government of Nigeria and its central bank for repudiation of the bank's letter of credit. The defendants argued that the Foreign Sovereign Immunity Act denied the court jurisdiction over them. The court noted that, under Section 1605(a)(2),[327] the statute provides that a foreign sovereign loses its immunity when the suit is for an act arising out of commercial activity that (1) occurs outside the United States but (2) "causes a direct effect in the United States."[328] The court held that unilateral revocation of the credit by the defendants satisfied both the "direct effect" requirement and the "minimum contacts" requirement that courts traditionally invoke before applying the statutory exception. The court weighed heavily the fact that the credits, being payable in New York, rendered the injury caused by their revocation an injury in New York. The court also found the New York situs of payment sufficient to satisfy the "minimum contacts" requisite. "[S]ince defendants chose New York as the place of payment, the burden of litigating in this forum should not be [too great]."[329]

---

[322] 647 F.2d 300 (2d Cir. 1981), cert. denied, 454 U.S. 1148 (1982).

[323] 326 U.S. 310 (1945).

[324] 357 U.S. 235 (1958).

[325] For discussion of jurisdiction and venue questions, see ¶ 11.01.

[326] 497 F. Supp. 893 (S.D.N.Y. 1980), aff'd, 647 F.2d 300 (2d Cir. 1981), cert. denied, 454 U.S. 1148 (1982).

[327] 28 U.S.C. § 1605(a)(2) (1988).

[328] Id.

[329] Decor by Nikkei Int'l, Inc. v. Federal Republic of Nig., 497 F. Supp. 893, 906 (S.D.N.Y. 1980), aff'd, 647 F.2d 300 (2d Cir. 1981), cert. denied, 454 U.S. 1148 (1982); see also Hester Int'l Corp. v. Federal Republic of Nig., 681 F. Supp. 371 (N.D. Miss. 1988), aff'd on other grounds, 879 F.2d 170 (5th Cir. 1089) (discussions in United States plus sending funds to United States via letters of credit in connection with agricultural development in Nigeria, is sufficient to satisfy 28 U.S.C. § 1605(a)(2)); Goodsons & Co. v. Federal Republic of Nig., 558 F. Supp. 1204

In *Verlinden B.V. v. Central Bank of Nigeria*,[330] the court took a contrary view. The beneficiary of a credit that was confirmed by and payable at a New York bank sued in the U.S. District Court for the Southern District of New York. Neither the beneficiary nor the defendant had contact with New York. The court saw it as decidedly disadvantageous for issuers of credits, such as the defendant, to believe that, because their credits were confirmed and payable by a New York bank, they might be hailed before a court sitting in New York. The court held that the plaintiff had not satisfied the statute.[331]

In *E-Systems, Inc. v. Islamic Republic of Iran*,[332] the court construed the 28 U.S.C. § 1609 requirement that a foreign sovereign must waive immunity before property can be attached. The account party was attempting to attach[333] a "blocked account" created by the issuer pursuant to the Iranian Assets Control Regulations. The court refused to permit attachment, finding that the U.S.-Iranian treaty did not constitute such a waiver. In *Sperry International Trade, Inc. v. Government of Israel*,[334] the account party was more successful because, the court found, the defendant had expressly waived its immunity in the underlying contract.

In *Harris Corp. v. National Iranian Radio & Television*,[335] the Court of Appeals for the Eleventh Circuit construed 28 U.S.C. § 1605(a)(2) and concluded that "the letter of credit arrangement . . . extends into

---

(S.D.N.Y. 1983) (similar case). But cf. S&S Mach. Co. v. Masinexportimport, 706 F.2d 411 (2d Cir. 1983) (applying Act and vacating prejudgment attachment and dissolving injunction against beneficiary of credit).

[330] 488 F. Supp. 1284 (S.D.N.Y. 1980), rev'd on other grounds, 647 F.2d 320 (2d Cir. 1981), rev'd, 461 U.S. 480 (1983).

[331] The Second Circuit dismissed the case for want of jurisdiction; but the Supreme Court reversed and remanded to determine whether one of the statute's exceptions applied, in which event, the Court held, federal jurisdiction would obtain. See Verlinden B.V. v. Central Bank of Nig., 647 F.2d 320 (2d Cir. 1981), rev'd, 461 U.S. 480 (1983). In International Hous. Ltd. v. Rafidain Bank Iraq, 712 F. Supp. 1112 (S.D.N.Y. 1989), the court ruled that a foreign sovereign that caused payments under bank guarantees issued by a foreign bank to be deposited with a New York correspondent satisfied the jurisdictional requisites of 28 U.S.C. § 1605(a)(2) but did not satisfy due process. For discussion of the due process feature of the *International Housing* case, see ¶ 11.01[1]. Cf. First Nat'l Bank v. Kaufman, 593 F. Supp. 1189 (N.D. Ala. 1984) (holding that only source of jurisdiction for declaratory judgment action by negotiating bank against sovereign issuer is Section 1330 of Foreign Sovereign Immunity Act).

[332] 491 F. Supp. 1294 (N.D. Tex. 1980).

[333] For discussion of attachment in various contexts, see ¶¶ 7.03[5], 9.05, 10.06.

[334] 532 F. Supp, 901 (S.D.N.Y. 1982).

[335] 691 F.2d 1344 (11th Cir. 1982).

this country."[336] The *Harris Corp.* credit was issued by a Chicago bank in favor of Bank Melli, which, in turn, issued a guaranty to the Iranian government television agency. During the Iranian troubles, Bank Melli demanded payment under the credit. That conduct had "significant, foreseeable financial consequences here,"[337] the court held.[338] On the other hand, in *Falcoal, Inc. v. Turkiye Komur Isletmeleri Kurumu,*[339] the court ruled under Section 1605 that a draw by a Turkish beneficiary on a guaranty issued in Ankara and a promise to open a letter of credit in New York did not constitute commercial activity in the United States. The court also held that although the draw on the guaranty did have a direct effect in the United States, by virtue of the guaranty issuer's draw on a Dallas issuer's standby credit that secured the guaranty, due process concerns prevented the court from asserting jurisdiction.[340]

[d] International Monetary Fund Agreement

To the extent that a letter of credit constitutes a currency exchange contract in violation of state currency laws, the International Monetary Fund (IMF) Agreement may bar payment. In *United City Merchants (Investments) Ltd. v. Royal Bank of Canada,*[341] the account party, a Peruvian company, sought to use its purchase of a glass-fiber-forming plant from a British seller to exchange Peruvian soles for U.S. dollars. The account party buyer caused the credit to issue in an amount double the seller's actual purchase price and obtained the seller's understanding that the excess over the price would be deposited in a U.S. bank to the account of the buyer. The arrangement, the court held, was in violation of Peruvian exchange control regulations; and the court refused to en-

---

[336] Id. at 1351.

[337] Id.

[338] Cf. Gemini Shipping, Inc. v. Foreign Trade Org. for Chems. & Foodstuffs, 647 F.2d 317 (2d Cir. 1981) (holding that solicitation of business in United States and arranging for payment and confirmation by American bank of letter of credit satisfied § 1605(a)(2) of Foreign Sovereign Immunity Act and permitted court to invoke jurisdiction); American Constr. Mach. & Equip. Corp. v. Mechanised Constr. of Pak., Ltd., No. 85 Civ. 3765 (JFK) (S.D.N.Y. Mar. 5, 1986) (holding that foreign sovereign that, among other things, caused letters of credit to be established by New York branches of foreign banks lost its immunity under Section 1605(a)(2) of the Act). But cf. Thos. P. Gonzalez Corp. v. Consejo Nacional De Producion De Costa Rica, 614 F.2d 1247 (9th Cir. 1980) (holding that recurring purchases of grain from American trader and contract involving letter of credit confirmed by California bank were not sufficient contacts to overcome foreign sovereign's immunity).

[339] 660 F. Supp. 1536 (S.D. Tex. 1987).

[340] For discussion of the due process question, see ¶ 11.01[1].

[341] [1983] A.C. 168 (H.L.).

force the credit for the excess, although it did enforce it for the amount of the price.

Article VIII(2)(b) of the IMF Agreement[342] renders unenforceable any exchange contract that violates exchange control regulations. The *United City Merchants* court saw the portion of the credit in excess of the purchase price as an exchange contract.[343] It is significant that the court refused to characterize all international letters of credit as exchange contracts under the IMF Agreement. Such an expansive definition of "exchange contract" would have serious consequences for international credits. The narrow definition the law lords adopted in *United City Merchants* strikes a sensible balance between the policy of credit law and that of the IMF Agreement. Only monetary transactions in disguise that violate exchange control regulations are unenforceable under the rule of *United City Merchants*. International credits that support the sale of goods and violate such regulations would not be unenforceable.

[e] Boycotts

A provision in the Export Administration Act[344] provides another defense to payment under a letter of credit. Under 50 U.S.C. § 2407(a)(1)(F) and regulations promulgated pursuant to it,[345] no issuer may be obligated to pay a letter of credit whose terms violate the Act's antiboycott provision. The provision stipulates that "[c]ompliance with this section shall provide an absolute defense in any action to compel payment of . . . a letter of credit, or for damages resulting from failure to pay . . . the letter of credit."[346]

[f] Comity

In at least one case, a court refused to enter judgment against an issuer whose foreign branch dishonored drafts under a letter of credit after a foreign court entered an order attaching the credit. In *Sabolyk v.*

---

[342] Articles of Agreement of the International Monetary Fund, art. VIII, § 2(b), 60 Stat. 1401, T.I.A.S. No. 1501, 2 U.N.T.S. 39.

[343] Cf. J. Zeevi & Sons v. Grindlays Bank (Uganda) Ltd., 37 N.Y.2d 220, 333 N.E.2d 168, 371 N.Y.S.2d 892, cert. denied, 432 U.S. 866 (1975) (holding on different facts that IMF Agreement did not bar enforcement of credit). For a discussion of the United City Merchants case, see Note, "The International Monetary Fund Agreement and Letters of Credit: A Balancing of Purposes," 44 U. Pitt. L. Rev. 1061 (1983).

[344] Export Administration Act, 50 U.S.C. app. § 2407(a)(1)(F) (1982).

[345] See 15 C.F.R. § 769.2(f)(1) (1989).

[346] 15 C.F.R. § 769.2(f)(5) (1989).

Morgan Guaranty Trust Co.,[347] the Zurich branch of a New York bank issued a credit to secure payments under an installment note. The account party sued in Texas to rescind the transaction, including the credit; and the Zurich court attached the credit pending the outcome of the Texas litigation. When the beneficiaries sued the New York bank for wrongful dishonor, the *Sabolyk* court held that principles of comity and a provision of the New York Banking Law[348] provided the New York bank with a defense.

In *Power Curber International Ltd. v. National Bank of Kuwait S.A.K.*,[349] on the other hand, the court refused to invoke the doctrine of comity. In *Power Curber*, the account party had obtained an order in Kuwait forbidding the issuer to pay the beneficiary. Because the *Power Curber* court saw that order as an attempt by the account party to assert a setoff in the credit transaction, contrary to general principles of letter of credit law and to the Uniform Customs, it rejected the comity argument and ordered the issuer to pay.[350]

[5] Ultra Vires Acts

Generally, courts have not excused credit issuers who attempt to avoid the burden of their engagement by arguing that it is ultra vires.[351] In at least two cases, however, bank issuers were successful. In *Western Petroleum Co. v. First Bank Aberdeen, N.A.*,[352] the court decided that the bank's undertaking was secondary in nature and therefore was not a letter of credit. The court then decided that the guaranty was beyond the power of the nationally chartered bank under the circumstances of the case. In *International Dairy Queen, Inc. v. Bank of Wadley*,[353] the court held that an engagement that violated a state lending-limit statute was void.

There is, however, authority contrary to *Bank of Wadley*. In *Security Finance Group, Inc. v. Northern Kentucky Bank & Trust Co.*,[354] the

---

[347] No. 84 Civ. 3179 (MJL) (S.D.N.Y. Nov. 27, 1984).

[348] See New York Banking Law § 138 (McKinney 1990).

[349] [1981] 3 All E.R. 607 (C.A.).

[350] Cf. Banco De Vizcaya, S.A. v. First Nat'l Bank, 514 F. Supp. 1280 (N.D. Ill. 1981), vacated, id. (similar holding when foreign court ordered issuer not to pay). For further discussion of comity questions, see ¶ 11.01[7].

[351] See generally ¶ 12.02.

[352] 367 N.W.2d 773 (S.D. 1985).

[353] 407 F. Supp. 1270 (M.D. Ala. 1976).

[354] 858 F.2d 304 (6th Cir.), clarified, 875 F.2d 529 (6th Cir. 1988).

court was unwilling to permit an issuer to rely on the ultra vires defense when the issuer's undertaking violated lending limits.

A similar result obtained in *City National Bank v. First National Bank*,[355] a suit for sums due under a credit. There the court denied an issuer a defense of ultra vires based on a lending-limit violation. The court reasoned that the defense was unavailable in light of the fact that the beneficiary did not have reason to know of the violation. In *Union County Bank v. FDIC*,[356] the lead bank in a letter of credit participation arrangement was aware of the participating bank's lending-limit violation; but the substitution of the FDIC as receiver for the lead bank gave the receiver, under federal common law, the power to enforce the participation agreement. The *Union County Bank* opinion indicates that, if the lead bank itself had attempted to enforce the participation agreement, the bank's knowledge of the lending-limit violation would have rendered the defense valid.

In *E. Huttenbauer & Sons, Inc. v. Dollar Dry Dock Savings Bank*,[357] the issuer raised the novel defense to the beneficiary's claim under the credit that the letter of credit was not authorized by law but was issued by the thrift only to satisfy the beneficiary's bank. The court did not hide its disdain for the defense, which the court saw as a possible admission of criminal activity, and ordered discovery to be completed and the matter to be given docket preference in view of the potential criminality involved.

[6] Fraud

Section 5-114(2)(b) of the Code permits an issuer to pay a beneficiary, notwithstanding the account party's claim that the beneficiary is practicing fraud. The statute limits the privilege by stipulating that the issuer exercising it must do so in good faith. It should be clear that the issuer's privilege to pay in good faith is not balanced by a privilege to dishonor in good faith when the account party alleges fraud. The issuer that decides not to pay the credit when the account party is alleging fraud may be guilty of wrongful dishonor and may not be able to use the fraud as a defense.

In *Airline Reporting Corp. v. First National Bank*,[358] the account party claimed that the beneficiary had presented false certificates in

---

[355] 22 Ark. App. 5, 732 S.W.2d 489 (1987).
[356] No. 712 (Tenn. Ct. App. Sept. 18, 1987).
[357] 116 F.R.D. 467 (S.D.N.Y. 1987).
[358] 832 F.2d 823 (4th Cir. 1987).

connection with its draw under the credit. While there was no evidence of bad faith on the part of the issuer in dishonoring the draft, the court found the dishonor wrongful. The *Airline Reporting Corp.* court held that the issuer bears the burden of proving fraud in such a case and that the fraud it must establish in order to prove a defense is fraud "so egregious as to vitiate the underlying transaction."[359] It is not enough, the court held, to show that the beneficiary intended to deceive. The court adopted the fraud rule that other courts[360] have used in injunction cases.[361]

In *First National Bank v. Carmouche*,[362] the account party argued that it had a fraud defense to the issuer's reimbursement claim. The account party asserted that the issuer knew, at the time it paid the negotiating bank, that the certificate accompanying the draft might have been in error. That knowledge notwithstanding, the court held, the issuer had a right to pay in good faith, and, having done so, the issuer had a right of reimbursement against the account party. The court added that the account party was attempting to use a fraud argument in the wrong setting. That argument should have been raised, the *Carmouche* court held, in an action to enjoin payment of the credit.[363]

In *Financial Trust Co. v. Caisse Populaire Ste. Anne D'Ottawa, Inc.*,[364] a Canadian court held that fraud is a matter for the issuer to raise if it dishonors on that ground. In the *Financial Trust Co.* case, the beneficiary moved for summary judgment in a suit for wrongful dishonor. The issuer resisted the motion by arguing that the beneficiary had failed to prove that the signature on a document presented by the beneficiary under the credit was authorized. The court rejected the argument. The *Financial Trust Co.* case reminds issuers that in a wrongful dishonor suit they must plead and prove fraud; it is not for the beneficiary to disprove it.

Briefly, fraud is a defense to payment under a credit only if it is egregious fraud of a kind that vitiates the transaction. There is convincing authority that the issuer itself may not raise the fraud defense after

---

[359] Id. at 828.

[360] For discussion of the test for fraud in injunction cases, see ¶¶ 7.04[4], 11.04[3].

[361] Cf. Banque Worms v. Banque Commerciale Privee, 679 F. Supp. 1173 (S.D.N.Y. 1988), aff'd per curiam, 849 F.2d 787 (2d Cir. 1988) (holding that fraud in collateral transaction would not justify issuer dishonor).

[362] 515 So. 2d 785 (La. 1987).

[363] Cf. Kupetz v. Wolf, 845 F.2d 842 (9th Cir. 1988) (holding that payments made under letter of credit may not be attacked by account party's trustee in bankruptcy on ground that they constituted fraudulent conveyance).

[364] 61 O.R.2d 538 (H. Ct. 1987).

dishonor, unless the fraud rises to that egregious level. There is also authority that the account party cannot raise the fraud issue after payment, so long as the issuer paid in good faith. In any event, fraud in these cases is a matter for the party raising it to plead and prove.

[7]　Election of Remedies

In *Interfirst Bank v. First Federal Savings & Loan Association*,[365] the issuer argued that the beneficiary, by suing borrowers on notes secured by the issuer's credits, had elected a remedy and could not pursue the issuer when it dishonored the beneficiary's draft. The court found nothing inconsistent with the two actions[366] and rejected the defense but allowed that the beneficiary could have only one recovery.[367] The case reflects the traditional idea that the credit is independent of the credit and that defenses that arise in the underlying transaction do not avail the issuer in the credit context.

¶ 9.07　REFORMING THE CREDIT

There is some confusion in the cases over the proper way to deal with a credit that has issued with terms that are not satisfactory to one or more of the parties. Usually, the issue arises when the beneficiary attempts to draw on a credit and finds that it cannot satisfy the credit's terms.

Some courts are inclined to entertain the beneficiary's complaint. In *Crocker Commercial Services, Inc. v. Countryside Bank*,[368] for example, the court relaxed the strict compliance rule in order to protect a beneficiary who could not satisfy the terms of the credit strictly. In *Kerr Construction Co. v. Plains National Bank*,[369] the court invoked liberal contract rules of construction to read a credit strongly in favor of the beneficiary, who would not have been able to comply with the credit under one quite reasonable reading of a patent inconsistency.[370]

---

[365] 242 Kan. 181, 747 P.2d 129 (1987).

[366] Accord Kelley v. First Westroads Bank (In re Kelley), 840 F.2d 554 (8th Cir. 1988).

[367] Cf. Gatz v. Southwest Bank, 836 F.2d 1089 (8th Cir. 1988) (similar result when account party made election of remedies argument).

[368] 538 F. Supp. 1360 (N.D. Ill. 1981).

[369] 753 S.W.2d 181 (Tex. Ct. App. 1987).

[370] Cf. Exxon Co., U.S.A. v. Banque de Paris et des Pays-Bas, 889 F.2d 674 (5th Cir. 1989) (grudging application of *Kerr* in diversity case).

On the other hand, in *Auto-Owners Insurance Co. v. South Side Trust & Savings Bank*,[371] the court, holding that there was no mutual mistake of fact, refused to reform a credit that issued with the bank assuming one set of facts and the beneficiary assuming another. Similarly, in other cases, courts have construed expiry terms strictly, even though, in retrospect, it was apparent that the beneficiary could not comply with the credit's terms.[372]

In *Barclay Knitwear Co. v. King'swear Enterprises, Ltd.*,[373] the credit called for a special customs invoice bearing a reference to tariff quota category #645. The negotiating bank presented a special customs invoice bearing reference to tariff quota category #645/646, the categories having been combined between the time the credit issued and the time of the bank's presentation. In a questionable holding, the *Barclay* court ruled that the issuer knew the categories had been combined and therefore should have honored the presentation. It is doubtful that a document clerk in a bank's letter of credit department would have known that the categories had been combined. If the *Barclay Knitwear* court expects bank document examiners to be familiar with changes in tariff quota classifications or to research questions concerning them, the court expects too much. In the latter event, the court has reformed the credit to give the negotiating bank and the beneficiary relief from the strict compliance rule.

In most of these cases, proper examination of the credit upon its issuance by the beneficiary would have avoided the problem. Such examination would not have protected the beneficiary in the *Barclay* case, but the holding in *Barclay* may be an unfortunate shifting of the risk of tariff category changes from the beneficiary to the issuer. While there is sentiment in some cases to read a credit strongly against an issuer,[374] the fact is that the issuer is unaware of the terms and exigencies of the underlying transactions. It may be inefficient for the law to impose on the issuer the burden of making sense out of the terms of the credit. If the law uniformly ruled against the beneficiary in these cases, the beneficiary would have an incentive to read the credit carefully to see that it can comply with the credit's terms, and the beneficiary would understand that it, not someone else, bears the risk that the beneficiary cannot

---

[371] 176 Ill. App. 3d 303, 531 N.E.2d 146 (1988).

[372] See INA v. Heritage Bank, N.A., 595 F.2d 171 (3d Cir. 1979); Hyland Hills Metro. Park & Recreation Dist. v. McCoy Enters., Inc. 38 Colo. App. 23, 554 P.2d 708 (1976).

[373] 141 A.D.2d 241, 533 N.Y.S.2d 724 (1988), appeal denied, 74 N.Y.2d 605, 541 N.E.2d 427, 543 N.Y.S.2d 398 (1989).

[374] For discussion of those cases, see ¶ 4.08[3].

perform. Absent that capability, the beneficiary should seek an amendment, suspend performance, or price his product or services in accordance with the risks. That kind of beneficiary response is more efficient than reforming the credit after the fact and is more efficient than imposing upon the issuer a duty to make sense out of the terms, thereby shifting these transaction risks to the banking industry.

CHAPTER **10**

Transfer and Assignment

¶ 10.01 INTRODUCTION

Letter of credit law distinguishes between the transfer of the right to draw under a credit and the assignment of the right to take the credit proceeds. Section 5-116 of the Uniform Commercial Code (UCC or the Code) makes it clear that a beneficiary may not transfer the right to draw unless the credit recites that it is transferable or assignable. Article 54(b) of the Uniform Customs and Practice for Documentary Credits (UCP or the Uniform Customs) provides in terminology more precise than that of the UCC that the right to draw may be transferred only if the credit is expressly designated as "transferable." Article 54(e) provides, furthermore, that the original beneficiary may transfer the credit only once. Thus, credit law reflects strong reservations on free alienation of the right to draw. This chapter explores the reasons for, and effects of, these reservations.

Credit law displays no reservations concerning the free alienability of the right to take the credit proceeds. UCP Article 55 provides that if the credit is silent on the transferability question, the beneficiary may assign the right to take the proceeds. Section 5-116 goes further. It stipulates that a beneficiary may assign the proceeds of a credit that is itself designated as "nontransferable" or "nonassignable."

In addition to these rules on transfer and assignment, there are other features of the credit and credit law that permit enjoyment of credit benefits by persons other than the beneficiary. These benefits arise without any conveyance of an interest in the credit, and the form of the transaction determines the extent of those benefits.

Traditionally, a buyer account party uses a commercial letter of credit to benefit a seller by causing the credit to issue in favor of the seller. Sometimes, however, a buyer causes a credit to issue before he knows who his seller is going to be or causes one credit to issue when he anticipates using it for the benefit of several sellers. In those cases, it is helpful if the account party can transfer the credit or assign its proceeds.

In *Bamberger Polymers International Corp. v. Citibank, N.A.*,[1] the account party buyer achieved such a result by causing the credit to be issued to itself and assigning the proceeds to the seller.[2] In *California Overseas Bank v. French American Banking Corp.*,[3] the buyer caused the

---

[1] 124 Misc. 2d 653, 477 N.Y.S.2d 931 (Sup. Ct. 1983).

[2] Cf. Rosenthal-Netter, Inc. v. United States, 679 F. Supp. 21 (Ct. Int'l Trade 1988), aff'd, 861 F.2d 261 (Fed. Cir. 1988) (similar arrangement for issuance of transferable credits to buyer for transfer to then-unascertained suppliers); Hawley Fuel Coalmart, Inc. v. Steag Handel GmBH, 796 F.2d 29 (2d Cir. 1986), cert. denied, 479 U.S. 1066 (1987) (similar arrangement); Barclay Knitwear Co. v. King'swear Enters., Ltd., 141 A.D.2d 241, 533 N.Y.S.2d 724 (1988), appeal denied, 74 N.Y.2d 605, 541 N.E.2d 427, 543 N.Y.S.2d 398 (1989) (issuance of transferable credit to Far Eastern agent of domestic account party for subsequent transfer to buyers).

[3] 154 Cal. App. 3d 179, 201 Cal. Rptr. 400 (1984).

credit to be issued to a financing party that, in turn, caused a second credit to be issued to the seller. In those cases, both sellers benefited from the original credit, yet the seller in *Bamberger* had to see that the buyer satisfied the requirements of the first credit, while the seller in *California Overseas Bank* had to satisfy the terms of the second credit. In short, the form of the transaction becomes important under credit law because it determines the rights and duties of the party relying on the credit.

As this chapter illustrates, commercial parties have devised various methods for using credits to benefit their commercial counterparties. In all events, courts must take care that application of letter of credit law to these arrangements is consistent with letter of credit theory and policy.

¶ 10.02 BENEFITS FROM THE CREDIT

[1] General Credit

A number of parties may benefit directly from the issuer's credit engagement. In some cases, the issuer opens the credit by permitting any person who complies with its terms to draw under it.[4] This "general" credit was common during the heyday of the factor and the buyer's agent. The earliest recorded credit in England was a general credit.[5] Similarly, the credit Thomas Jefferson issued on behalf of Meriwether Lewis was a general credit.[6]

The purpose of the general credit is to give value to the negotiable paper of the account party (e.g., "we will honor the account party's drafts") or to the paper of his suppliers (e.g., "we will honor drafts drawn on the account party"). While general credits are not common today, two modern credits are analogous to them. The first is the standby credit used in connection with commercial paper or municipal bonds.[7] This credit indirectly benefits a large group of people—the holders of securities that may be traded.[8] The second is the negotiation credit that

---

[4] See, e.g., Duval v. Trask, 12 Mass. 153 (1815); Bank of Seneca v. First Nat'l Bank 105, Mo. App. 722, 78 S.W. 1092 (Kansas City Ct. App. 1904).

[5] For a discussion of the early use of credits, see ¶ 3.02.

[6] A copy of that credit appears in App. C, Doc. 22.

[7] For discussion of the use of such a standby credit, see ¶ 1.06.

[8] For an example of a modern credit that ran to the benefit of holders in due course of a note, see Bank of N.C., N.A. v. Rock Island Bank, 630 F.2d 1243 (7th Cir. 1980).

runs to "drawers, endorsers and bona fide holders" of drafts drawn under the credit.[9]

[2] Straight Credit

Sometimes the issuer's undertaking does not run to holders of the beneficiary's draft. This credit is the "straight"[10] credit. It runs only to the beneficiary itself. Under letter of credit law, holders of the beneficiary's drafts are agents, even though under negotiable instruments law they might be holders in due course. That is to say that if the issuer limits its engagement by rendering it straight, holders of the beneficiary's drafts generally have no rights greater than those of the beneficiary. Generally, these holders stand in the shoes of the beneficiary.

Bankers and merchants have long distinguished the straight credit from the negotiation credit. The designation of a single, named beneficiary in a straight credit does not mean that other parties cannot derive benefit from the issuer's engagement. Straight credits may provide that they are transferable,[11] and the beneficiary may always assign their proceeds.[12] In addition, some commentators appear to take the view that the classic distinction between the straight credit and the negotiation credit no longer holds. Under that view, the issuer's obligation runs to those who collect the named beneficiary's drafts.[13]

[3] Negotiation Credit

The negotiation credit[14] is one that contains a negotiation clause to the effect that the issuer's engagement runs to "drawers, endorsers and bona fide holders of drafts drawn under and in compliance with the terms" of the credit or that otherwise indicates its availability by negotiation. The purpose of this language is to make it clear to third parties that if they

---

[9] For further discussion of the negotiation credit, see infra ¶ 10.02[3].

[10] For an example of a straight credit, see App. C, Doc. 15.

[11] See U.C.C. § 5-116(1); U.C.P. art. 54 (1983). For a case in which the court reformed a straight credit so that it ran to one other than the named beneficiary, see American Nat'l Bank & Trust Co. v. Hamilton Indus. Int'l, Inc., 583 F. Supp. 164 (N.D. Ill. 1984), rev'd on other grounds sub nom. Banque Paribas v. Hamilton Indus. Int'l, Inc., 767 F.2d 380 (7th Cir. 1985).

[12] U.C.C. § 5-116(2); U.C.P. art. 55 (1983).

[13] For further discussion of the right of the beneficiary's agent to enforce the credit promise, see infra ¶ 10.02[4].

[14] Drafts under negotiation credits may be freely negotiable or negotiable only with a named bank. See App. C, Docs. 16, 21.

take a draft with documents that comply with the terms of the credit, the third parties will then enjoy the direct obligation of the issuer to pay them.[15]

The issuer opens the negotiation credit in order to facilitate discount of the beneficiary's drafts. The third parties involved are almost always banks and are referred to as "negotiating banks." They negotiate the beneficiary's drafts per the authority in the credit itself. This feature of the transaction gives the negotiation credit its name and gives rise to the notion that some banks negotiate "under the credit."[16] Negotiating banks are favorites of credit law. Often they enjoy rights greater than those of the credit's beneficiary, whose drafts they hold.

[4] The Negotiation Credit Cases

Generally, the distinction between straight credits and negotiation credits has not been the subject of litigation,[17] and the rare case that deals with the issue prompts comment.[18] A lower court in Austria decided

---

[15] See, e.g., First Commercial Bank v. Gotham Originals, Inc., 101 A.D.2d 790, 476 N.Y.S.2d 835 (Sup. Ct. 1984), aff'd, 64 N.Y.2d 287, 475 N.E.2d 1255, 486 N.Y.S.2d 715 (1985). By negative implication, a negotiating bank that gives value for a nonconforming presentation does so at its peril and cannot force the issuer to pay under the credit. See, e.g., Banco Nacional De Desarrollo v. Mellon Bank, N.A., 726 F.2d 87 (3d Cir. 1984); European Asian Bank A.G. v. Punjab & Sind Bank, [1983] 2 All E.R. 508 (C.A.).

[16] For further discussion of the negotiation credit, see ¶ 1.02[3].

[17] Some cases in which the issue appears to be ripe do not discuss the question. See United States v. Sun Bank, 609 F.2d 832 (5th Cir. 1980); Scarsdale Nat'l Bank & Trust Co. v. Toronto-Dominion Bank, 533 F. Supp. 378 (S.D.N.Y. 1982); National Bank & Trust Co. of N. Am., Ltd. v. J.L.M. Int'l, Inc., 421 F. Supp. 1269 (S.D.N.Y. 1976); Barclay Knitwear Co. v. King'swear Enters., Ltd., 141 A.D.2d 241, 533 N.Y.S.2d 724 (1988), appeal denied, 74 N.Y.2d 605, 541 N.E.2d 427, 543 N.Y.S.2d 398 (1989); International Commercial Bank of China v. Hall-Fuston Corp., 767 S.W.2d 259 (Tex. Ct. App. 1989).

[18] The *Eriksson* case, discussed infra note 26, was, and still is, the subject of considerable criticism. See Eberth & Ellinger, "Assignment and Presentation of Documents in Commercial Credit Transactions," 24 Ariz. L. Rev. 277, 293 (1982); Mentschikoff, "Letters of Credit: The Need for Uniform Legislation," 23 U. Chi. L. Rev. 571, 607 (1956); McGowan, "Assignability of Documentary Credits," 13 Law & Contemp. Probs. 666, 677 (1948). *Eriksson* had at least one staunch defender. See Harfield, "Code Treatment of Letters of Credit," 48 Cornell L.Q. 92, 104 (1962). The *Creditanstalt* decision received similar criticism. See Megrah, "Risk Aspects of the Irrevocable Documentary Credit," 24 Ariz. L. Rev. 255, 261 (1982); Stoufflet, "Payment and Transfer in Documentary Letters of Credit: Interaction Between the French General Law of Obligation and the Uniform Customs and Practice," 24 Ariz. L. Rev. 267, 276 (1982). Again, Henry Harfield provided thoughtful defense of the case's rule restricting transfer of the right to claim the credit's benefits. See Harfield, "Identity Crises in Letter of Credit Law," 24 Ariz. L. Rev. 239, 247 (1982).

one of these noteworthy cases, and, while it is not controlling authority in the United States, the court's opinion illustrates the divergent views on the distinction between the straight credit and the negotiation credit.

In *Singer & Friedlander Ltd. v. Creditanstalt-Bankverein*,[19] the beneficiary assigned all of his "rights and benefit" under a straight[20] nontransferable credit to the plaintiff, a London bank. The credit, in the amount of $9.7 million, called for invoices and a delivery order covering pharmaceuticals. It did not require a draft or a written demand for payment.

When the plaintiff, the London bank, presented the credit and the documents to the issuer for payment, the account party (a subsidiary of the issuer) claimed that the beneficiary had practiced fraud. At the time of presentation, the issuer asked in whose interest the plaintiff was acting. The plaintiff's representative responded that he was presenting the documents in the plaintiff's own right.

The issuer dishonored, and the Austrian court upheld the dishonor on two grounds. First, it held that the presentation by the plaintiff in its own right was not complying. Because the credit was not transferable, the court reasoned that the only right the beneficiary had assigned was the right to proceeds[21] and that the "right to realize on his claim" remained in the beneficiary. The presentation on behalf of the plaintiff, who was not the designated beneficiary, was not in compliance. Second, the court held that the fraud defense[22] was valid against the plaintiff, who was not a holder in due course of negotiable paper taken "under a negotiation credit,"[23] the credit being a straight credit, not a negotiation credit.

---

[19] 17 Cg. 72/80 (Vienna Commercial Ct. 1980). The opinion is mostly in German. The facts and holding referred to throughout this discussion come from an English translation provided by the editors of the *Arizona Law Review*. The *Creditanstalt* case was the subject of a symposium in that journal. See Kozolchyk, "Preface (to Symposium)," 24 Ariz. L. Rev. 235 (1982).

[20] The court notes that the issuer used the International Chamber of Commerce (ICC) form for the credit and did not render the credit available by negotiation. This fact is significant. The ICC forms recommended at the time allowed for negotiation credits. See ICC, "Standard Forms for Issuing Documentary Credits," ICC Pub. No. 323 (1978). It appears that the issuer was careful not to check the "negotiation" box, but instead used the "payment" box of the standard form.

[21] The credit was subject to the 1962 version of the Uniform Customs, ICC Pub. No. 222 (1964). That version of the Customs did not explicitly recognize the right to assign proceeds as subsequent versions do. See U.C.P. art. 55 (1983); U.C.P. art. 47 (1974).

[22] For a discussion of the fraud defense, see ¶ 7.04.

[23] The court accepts the view that only a good faith purchaser who takes "under the credit" can qualify for the exceptions to the fraud defense. Cf. U.C.C. § 5-114(2)(a). See ¶ 8.02.

Significantly, the *Creditanstalt* case recognized that the beneficiary may designate an agent to present the documents for him. The failure of the plaintiff (its assertion that it was acting in its own behalf, not as the beneficiary's representative) related only to the compliance issue. Regardless of whether the plaintiff acted as the beneficiary's agent or in its own right, the presenter stood in the shoes of the beneficiary. The fraud defense was good against the plaintiff because the plaintiff enjoyed no good faith purchase benefits.[24]

The *Creditanstalt* case illustrates the difference between the straight credit and the negotiation credit. Under the latter type of credit, the plaintiff would have prevailed on both holdings. First, it would have had the right to present in its own behalf as a bona fide holder of drafts drawn "under the credit"; second, it would have benefited from the good faith purchase shield, which, under U.S. law is codified in Section 5-114(2)(a).[25]

Those who reject the distinction between straight credits and negotiation credits would let the holder of the beneficiary's draft, in its own right, enforce the credit promise, even though the credit is not transferable. They also would let the London bank cut off the fraud defense on the theory that the words "under the credit" in Section 5-114(2)(a) do not limit the subsection to negotiation credits.

The contrary view, that adopted by the *Creditanstalt* court, holds that the London bank could not enforce the credit, because it was not transferable. Also, it could not use the good faith purchase defense, because the credit did not run to bona fide holders, and, therefore, the bank did not take "under the credit."

The *Creditanstalt* case is similar to *Eriksson v. Refiners Export Co.*,[26] where the court held that an attempt to assign a special credit must fail. The assignee in *Eriksson* held a draft drawn by the original beneficiary, but the court ruled that the assignee's attempt to enforce the

---

[24] For a Canadian case recognizing the distinction between straight credits and negotiation credits, see Bank of N.S. v. Angelica-Whitewear Ltd., 36 D.L.R.4th 161 (Can. 1987). Curiously, the facts of that case strongly suggest that the negotiating bank was a holder in due course, in which case payment to it would have been justified, despite fraud in one of the documents. Because the account party had failed to notify the issuer of the fraud in time for the issuer to stop payment, the *Bank of Nova Scotia* court ruled that the payment to the negotiating bank was justified.

[25] Apparently, the delivery order in the *Creditanstalt* case was not negotiable, and, since there was no draft and no negotiable security, there was only one way the plaintiff could qualify as a good faith purchaser under Section 5-114(2)(a). It would have to fit itself into the special good faith purchase rule of Section 5-114(2)(a) for persons who take for value, in good faith, and without notice of claims or defenses. See generally ¶ 8.01[3].

[26] 264 A.D. 525, 35 N.Y.S.2d 829 (1942).

credit was an attempt to effect a transfer of a credit that was not transferable. The *Eriksson* case did not decide the fraud question, but it did consider the right of a party, not the beneficiary, to enforce the credit promise. On that point, the *Eriksson* holding squares with *Creditanstalt*.

Eriksson, however, may go beyond *Creditanstalt* in holding that even the assignment of the credit's proceeds is impermissible under credit law. If that is the holding in *Eriksson*,[27] the Code clearly overturns it in Section 5-116(2). The concerns *Eriksson* addressed remain, however, because, by permitting a beneficiary to assign the proceeds of a credit, the Code may create problems for negotiating, confirming, and paying banks.[28]

The law in this area is not clear.[29] Two policies are competing. On the one hand, the law favors free alienability of property rights; on the other, letter of credit law tries to protect the account party against presentation of sensitive documents by a person whom he may not trust. It is surprising that the issue has not arisen more often.[30] It may be that courts are not aware of the peculiar nature of the negotiation credit or of the reason that letter of credit law traditionally has restricted transfer of credit benefits.[31]

¶ 10.03　TRANSFERRING THE RIGHT TO CLAIM THE BENEFIT

[1]　Reasons for Restricting Transfer

In letter of credit law, "transfer" is a misleading term. In effect, when a beneficiary transfers the credit, he usually causes the issuer to issue a

---

[27] For authority that it is, see The American Law Institute and the National Conference of Commissioners on Uniform State Laws, Supplement No. 1 to the 1952 Official Draft of Text and Comments of the Uniform Commercial Code (Jan. 1955), reprinted in 17 E. Kelly, Uniform Commercial Code Drafts 476 (1984).

[28] For further discussion of these concerns, see infra ¶ 10.03[5].

[29] See authority cited supra note 18. See also Ufford, "Transfer and Assignment of Letters of Credit Under the Uniform Commercial Code," 7 Wayne L. Rev. 263 (1960).

[30] For some cases where the question might have arisen, see authority cited supra note 17.

[31] For a discussion of the rationale for restricting that transfer, see infra ¶ 10.03[1]. For further discussion of confusion in the cases over the distinction between straight credits and negotiation credits, see ¶ 8.01[6].

new credit to the transferee. In short, the transfer operates as a novation.[32]

The prohibition of the beneficiary's ability to transfer his right to draw grows out of the old agent credit[33] but retains vitality today because it serves the modern credit as well as it served the old forms of credit. When an English king sent his agents to Rome in the twelfth century, he did not know which Roman merchants would supply the goods he needed. The agents carried with them a general letter of credit, one that ran to the benefit of anyone who sold goods for the king's account. When the Italian merchant sold merchandise to the king's agent, the merchant would draw on the king, confident (or at least as confident as one could be of such things in those days) that the king would honor the draft as he said he would in the letter.

Similarly, when Thomas Jefferson sent Lewis and Clark off to explore the Louisiana Purchase, he knew that his explorers would need provisions. Jefferson issued a credit in favor of Lewis because he could not know in advance the identity of the parties who would supply Lewis. Under that credit, Lewis could draw on the federal government and use the drafts to pay his suppliers.[34]

The practice of using agents to purchase supplies continued into the beginning of the twentieth century. In many instances, the issuer undertook to honor the drafts of only certain suppliers. The courts were careful not to extend the undertaking to others. In *Walsh v. Bailie*,[35] for example, the issuer, a merchant, undertook to honor the drafts of Walsh for supplies sold to Shermans. When Shermans approached Walsh, he found that Walsh, the named beneficiary, did not have any supplies left. Walsh sent Shermans to Dox, who filled Shermans's order. Walsh then drew drafts to cover Shermans's purchases from Dox, but the court refused to let Walsh enforce the credit promise with respect to sales made by Dox. The terms of those sales, the court held, might differ from Walsh's customary terms. Thus, it would be improper to require the issuer to honor drafts covering sales by Dox. The import of Walsh's position was to make the credit transferable, that is, to make it benefit Dox. The credit being special, it could not be transferred directly or indirectly to Dox.[36]

---

[32] Accord Goode, "Reflections on Letters of Credit — V," 1981 J. Bus. L. 150.

[33] For a discussion of the early use of credits, see ¶ 3.02.

[34] For the language of the Jefferson credit, see App. C, Doc. 22.

[35] 10 Johns. 179 (N.Y. 1813).

[36] See also Fletcher Guano Co. v. Burnside, 142 Ga. 803, 83 S.E. 935 (1914) (mem.) (to same effect); Robbins v. Bingham, 4 Johns. 476 (N.Y. Sup. Ct. 1809) (same).

In *Lyon v. Van Raden*,[37] the court saw the parties' intent as the prime indicator of a credit's nature as special or general. In *Lyon*, the credit ran to a bank. The plaintiffs were the bank's successors in interest who advanced funds on the strength of the credit. Because the credit was special and not general, the court held, the plaintiffs could not enforce it against the issuers.

These cases reflect in part the common law's concern that the issuer not be compelled to rely on anyone other than the person to whom the issuer addresses the credit. The credit engagement usually is conditioned on the presentation of documents, and documents are easy to forge. Early cases assumed that an issuer that promised to pay against easily forged documents reposed confidence in the integrity of the named beneficiary. By restricting the transfer of the credit, these cases prevented a party in whom the issuer did not explicitly repose confidence from realizing on the credit engagement. Modern credit law continues these restrictions. Section 5-116 of the Code and Article 54 of the Uniform Customs limit transfers of the right to draw.

The full effect of the transfer rules is evident in *Cromwell v. Commerce & Energy Bank*,[38] where credits were transferred by the original beneficiary to a bank that had lent the original beneficiary money. When the bank drew on the credits, the account parties claimed that the original beneficiary had practiced fraud and that payment should not be made. The *Cromwell* court ruled that the fraud of the original beneficiary did not give the account parties ground to obtain an injunction for fraud in the transaction.[39] Had the credit in *Cromwell* not been transferable and absent any indication that the bank was acting "under" a negotiation credit,[40] the only interest the lending bank could have had in the credit would have been an interest in the proceeds, that is, a security interest. In that event, the rights of the lending bank should rise no higher than those of its assignor, the original beneficiary. If the original beneficiary practiced fraud in the letter of credit transaction, that fraud defense of the issuer would be good against the lending bank. If, on the other hand, the beneficiary's fraud is evident only in the underlying transaction, the lending bank's claim is not tainted with fraud.[41]

---

[37] 126 Mich. 259, 85 N.W. 727 (1910).

[38] 464 So. 2d 721 (La. 1985).

[39] For discussion of four-party credits and the fraud in the transaction defense, see ¶ 7.04[1].

[40] For discussion of the letter of credit meaning of "under the credit," see ¶¶ 8.01[6], 10.02[3], 10.02[4].

[41] See generally ¶¶ 7.04[3], 7.04[4]. As those paragraphs explain, many courts and commentators would let fraud in the underlying transaction be a defense against the beneficiary's claim under the letter of credit. That argument raises serious problems for lending banks, who are mere assignees and whose rights are no greater than

The independence principle,[42] its corollary of strict compliance,[43] and the tight rules against stopping payment[44] provide additional reasons for the rules against transfer of the right to draw and the right to assign the proceeds of the credit.[45] These unique rules of credit law effect dramatic shifts in the commercial risks of the underlying transaction. Of critical importance is the fact that the credit shifts the forum and litigation risks.[46] Account parties are willing to accept these risks because they trust the named beneficiary. They accept the risk of litigating in a distant jurisdiction without funds because they do not think the beneficiary will give them cause to sue.

When an American defense contractor, for example, agrees to the issuance of a standby credit in favor of a foreign customer — say, a Middle Eastern government — the contractor knows that he runs serious risks. The beneficiary may draw on the standby without justification. Under strict credit law, that draw will effect payment of the funds to the beneficiary. If the payment is wrongful under the contract between the defense contractor and the government buyer, the contractor will have to sue in a foreign country and will not have the money during the litigation. The contractor, then, agrees to the credit because he trusts the beneficiary or because he has factored into his price the cost of any mistrust. If credit law permits easy transfer of the right to draw, the account party faces the possibility that a party to whom it never would have entrusted such power, or for whom the level of mistrust might be greater than the account party's price justifies, can effect payment by the simple act of presenting pieces of paper.

[2] Notice of Transfer

Section 5-116(2) contains specific rules for notifying the issuer in the event the beneficiary assigns proceeds and generally treats the issuer as the Code treats any account debtor. Thus, under the section the issuer may pay the original beneficiary until it receives notice of the assign-

---

those of the beneficiary. The suggestion, however, that the lending bank, rather than the account party, should bear the cost of the beneficiary's fraud is an argument with serious flaws. Investors, not the banking system, should bear the loss of bad investments.

[42] For a discussion of the independence principle, see ¶¶ 2.08, 2.09.

[43] For a discussion of the strict compliance rule, see ¶¶ 6.03, 6.04.

[44] For a discussion of the rules on stopping payment, see ¶ 7.03.

[45] For a discussion of the idea that third parties may not claim the benefit of a letter of credit, see supra ¶ 10.02[4].

[46] For discussion of these effects of the credit, see ¶¶ 3.07[4], 3.07[5].

ment.[47] The section does not extend the treatment, however, to an issuer in the event the beneficiary transfers the right to draw. That omission reflects the letter of credit practice of transferring the right to draw under a credit in a two-step process. The first step is the notice of transfer, which the original beneficiary gives to the issuer. The second step is the issuer's sending of an advice to the second beneficiary (the transferee). The statute does not address the need to notify the issuer of a transfer, because it assumes that no transfer can occur without notice.

In fact, however, it is not clear that all issuers and beneficiaries, or, for that matter, all courts, understand or observe the practice the section assumes. It is not clear from the statute that a beneficiary *must* notify an issuer of a transfer. When a beneficiary takes a credit clearly denominated as transferable and delivers it to a third party with written evidence of an intent to transfer, the original beneficiary and the transferee may assume that the transfer is complete.

In the event courts are willing to accept such transfers as effective, they should extend the traditional account debtor protection to the issuer when the beneficiary transfers the right to draw.[48] Clearly, if the right to draw is transferable, the transferee's drafts should be paid.[49] The issuer, however, should be able to honor the original beneficiary's drafts absent notice of the transfer and should be able to insist on reasonable proof of the transfer when it receives a notice of purported transfer. Section 5-116 assumes that the parties transfer the right to draw by novation, as, in fact, most parties do. That assumption is silent, however, and issuers may not be able to avoid a transfer effected differently.[50]

The language of the Uniform Customs is rather ambiguous on the extent of the beneficiary's right to transfer. Under the Uniform Customs, the notice of transfer may not be sufficient in and of itself to effect a transfer. Article 54 speaks of the "request"[51] of the first beneficiary that the advising bank transfer the right to draw. That language implies that the advising bank may refuse to transfer the credit.[52] It also implies

---

[47] Compare U.C.C. § 9-318(3) with U.C.C. § 5-116(2).

[48] Note that Article 5 carries the account–debtor analogy to its extreme in Section 5-116(2) by designating the transferee's right to proceeds as an "account" under Article 9. Although a transferee's right to proceeds does not meet the Article 9 definition of an "account" (see U.C.C. § 9-106), it is a lot closer to the definition than the definition of "right to draw" is.

[49] Accord Marine Midland Grace Trust Co. v. Banco Del Pais, S.A., 261 F. Supp. 884 (S.D.N.Y. 1966).

[50] For various assignment and transfer documents, see App. C, Docs. 26–30.

[51] See U.C.P. arts. 54(a), 54(c), 54(g) (1983).

[52] Accord B. Wheble, "UCP 1974/1983 Revisions Compared and Explained (Documentary Credits)," ICC Pub. No. 411, at 84 (1984).

that the transfer is to be effected by novation, that is, by the issuer's issuance of a new advice to the transferee. Since bank issuers treat transfers of credits as novations and issue a new credit instrument to the transferee,[53] beneficiaries seeking to transfer the right to draw under a credit subject to the Uniform Customs should understand that the mere giving of the notice may be insufficient to effect the transfer and should request the advising bank to give the first beneficiary a copy of the advice that constitutes the new credit.[54]

In one case,[55] the court held that a third transferee could not draw on a credit, because the credit, being subject to the Uniform Customs, was transferable only once.[56] In an English case,[57] the issuer refused to permit a transfer requested by the beneficiary. The Privy Council interpreted Article 46(b) of the 1974 version of the Uniform Customs as permitting the issuer to decline a transfer request. In the court's view, Article 46(b) assumed that the extent and manner of the transfer must be agreed to by the issuer. The court held that that agreement cannot occur before the beneficiary requests the transfer.[58]

Article 54 of the 1983 version of the Uniform Customs corresponds to Article 46 of the 1974 version. Under Article 54(a), the beneficiary has the "right" to transfer the credit. Article 54(c), however, stipulates that the bank which is requested to make the transfer is under no obligation to effect the transfer, except to the extent and in the manner to which it expressly consents. These provisions correspond to Articles 46(a) and 46(b) of the 1974 version.

If courts read the provisions as the Privy Council did, Article 54(c) takes away what Article 54(a) grants. It may be that courts can apply both sections by restricting application of Article 54(c) to the issuer's correspondent, that is, the bank nominated to make payment. It makes sense to say that that bank should not be bound by a notice of transfer

---

[53] For examples of notices of transfer, see App. C, Docs. 27, 28. For examples of advices of transfers of the right to draw, see App. C, Docs. 29, 30.

[54] For a case in which the beneficiary argued that the issuer was estopped to assert that the credit was nontransferable, see Mount Prospect State Bank v. Marine Midland Bank, 121 Ill. App. 3d 295, 459 N.E.2d 979 (1983).

[55] Anchor Centre Partners, Ltd. v. Mercantile Bank, N.A., 783 S.W.2d 108 (Mo. Ct. App. 1989).

[56] The court could have reached the same result in *Anchor Centre* by noting that the first transfer, effected by an amendment of the original credit, was not assented to by the original beneficiary and therefore failed to bind the beneficiary.

[57] Bank Negara Indonesia 1946 v. Lariza (Singapore) Pte. Ltd., [1988] 1 W.L.R. 374 (P.C.).

[58] Accord Hongkong & Shanghai Banking Corp. v. Kloeckner & Co., [1989] 2 Lloyd's Rep. 323 (Q.B.) (dictum).

unless it agrees to be so bound. Such a reading does some violence to the language of the provision, but not nearly so much as the violence the Privy Council does to it. Note, moreover, that Article 54(c), when referring to the bank that may refuse a request for transfer, adds the language "whether it has confirmed the credit or not." That language is consistent with a reading that restricts application of Article 54(c) to correspondents of the issuer.[59]

[3] Consequences of the Restriction

The consequence of the rules restricting transfer of the right to draw is obvious. A draft drawn by one who is neither the beneficiary nor the transferee under a credit permitting transfer of the right to draw is not a conforming draft. An issuer that receives such a draft should dishonor it.

There are a number of cases, however, that relax the rule. In *Pastor v. National Republic Bank*,[60] the court permitted the liquidator of an insurance company beneficiary to draw drafts under a credit that was standby in nature. The *Pastor* court recognized that, under the controlling law of New York, the liquidator was "vested with title to all property, contracts and rights of action"[61] of the original beneficiary. Also, it recognized that the statute which effected that vesting constituted an assignment or transfer by operation of law. The court refused to defer to Section 5-116(1) and its transfer prohibition. That rule, the court held, rests on considerations growing out of concern that the beneficiary not be able to transfer to a third party the performance duties that the account party expects to receive from the original beneficiary. The *Pastor* court then looked to the underlying contract, concluded that the original beneficiary had performed its duties, and held that the liquidator could draw on the credit.

The problem with the *Pastor* approach, of course, is that it forces the issuer to inquire into the original beneficiary's performance. That inquiry destroys the independence of the credit and imposes on document examiners a duty that they cannot handle.[62]

---

[59] For commentary generally agreeing with the holding of the Privy Council in the *Bank of Negara* case but reading Article 54(c) as applying only to correspondent banks, see Godwin, "Transferable Letters of Credit — The Effect of Lariza," 1990 J. Bus. L. 48. For criticism of the *Bank of Negara* holding, see Schmittoff, "The Transferable Credit," 1988 J. Bus. L. 49.

[60] 76 Ill. 2d 139, 390 N.E.2d 894 (1979).

[61] Id. at 144, 390 N.E.2d at 895.

[62] In this respect, the *Pastor* holding violates the independence principle, which is so central to the efficacy of credits. See ¶¶ 2.08, 2.09. But cf. Eakin v. Continental Ill. Nat'l Bank & Trust Co., 687 F. Supp. 1259 (N.D. Ill. 1988), aff'd, 875 F.2d 114

In *Addison Bank v. Temple-Eastex, Inc.,*[63] the credit ran to Woodward, Inc., which was the wholly owned subsidiary of Temple-Eastex. The credit, a standby, secured an account assigned with recourse to a third party. When the account turned out to be bad, the third party reassigned it; but, in the meantime, Temple-Eastex had dissolved its subsidiary, the named beneficiary. Temple-Eastex then attempted to draw on the credit, but the issuer declined to pay. The *Addison Bank* court upheld the issuer's dishonor. On appeal, the Texas Supreme Court reversed,[64] holding that Temple-Eastex was not a transferee of a nontransferable credit but was a "'vertical' distributee."[65] The court reasoned that it was the issuer's burden to determine the relationship of the original beneficiary and the parent. Had it chosen a stricter rule, the court could have placed the burden on parties who effect corporate reorganizations to obtain amendments or to insist on credits that permit the parent to draw. The effect of the Texas Supreme Court's holding is to put the cost of the beneficiary's incomplete planning on issuers and all of their customers. Corporate counsel undoubtedly would respond that in a merger or reorganization of any magnitude, it is impossible for the parties to know how many standby credits may be outstanding in favor of one of the parties. In any event, the Texas court has put the cost on the issuers.[66]

In at least one case involving a credit running to the benefit of a foreign sovereign, the court was reluctant to enforce the transfer rules strictly. In *American Bell International, Inc. v. Islamic Republic of Iran,*[67] the court held that the Islamic Republic of Iran enjoys the same benefits under the credit as did the imperial government it replaced.[68]

The *American Bell* case and the *Pastor* case reflect deference to legal concerns outside of credit law. The rule in *Pastor* obviously defers to

---

(7th Cir. 1989) (following *Pastor* rule); Crist v. J. Henry Schroder Bank & Trust Co., 693 F. Supp. 1429 (S.D.N.Y. 1988) (same); Allied Fidelity Ins. Co. v. Continental Ill. Nat'l Bank & Trust Co., 677 F. Supp. 562 (N.D. Ill. 1988) (same).

[63] 665 S.W.2d 550 (Tex. Ct. App.), rev'd, 672 S.W.2d 793 (Tex. 1984).

[64] Temple-Eastex, Inc. v. Addison Bank, 672 S.W.2d 793 (Tex. 1984).

[65] Id. at 796.

[66] In that respect, the *Temple-Eastex* case conflicts with Lyon v. Van Raden, 126 Mich. 259, 85 N.W. 727 (1901). For discussion of *Lyon*, see supra ¶ 10.03[1].

[67] 474 F. Supp. 420 (S.D.N.Y. 1979). Generally, the Iranian cases did not deal with this issue. See Comment, "'Fraud in the Transaction' Enjoining Letters of Credit During the Iranian Revolution," 93 Harv. L. Rev. 992, 993 (1980).

[68] Cf. Banco Nacional De Cuba v. Chase Manhattan Bank, 505 F. Supp. 412 (S.D.N.Y. 1980), rev'd, 658 F.2d 913 (2d Cir. 1981), rev'd, 462 U.S. 611 (1983) (holding that Cuban government bank could enforce predecessor's interest in letter of credit).

legislative concern for orderly liquidation of a failed insurance company. In the *American Bell* case, the court deferred to foreign policy concerns that the law not deny credit benefits to a successor government recognized by the U.S. government.

In *Farmer v. Crocker National Bank (In re Swift Aire Lines, Inc.)*,[69] it was the policy of the Bankruptcy Code that conflicted with letter of credit rules. That case involved a letter of credit issued in favor of a corporation that filed for liquidation under the Bankruptcy Code. The beneficiary's trustee in bankruptcy drew on the credit, and the issuer objected that the trustee was not a beneficiary of the credit. The bankruptcy court ordered the issuer to pay; but the Bankruptcy Panel of the Court of Appeals for the Ninth Circuit granted a stay pending appeal, partly on the ground that the issuer's engagement did not run to the trustee. The panel distinguished the contrary rule of *American Bell* as a matter controlled by principles of international law that did not apply in *Swift Aire*.

In *FDIC v. Bank of Boulder*,[70] the district court accepted the distinction, implicit in many transfer cases, between transfers that arise by operation of law and transfers that are voluntary. In the *Bank of Boulder* case, the credit, which was not transferable, ran to the benefit of a bank that failed. Under state law, the state banking commissioner succeeded to all of the failed bank's assets, and, under federal law, the FDIC succeeded to the assets when the banking commissioner appointed the FDIC as receiver. The court recognized both of those transfers by operation of law; but, when the FDIC as receiver sought to transfer the credit to itself in its corporate capacity, the court objected that the transfer violated the rules of the Code and the Uniform Customs.[71]

---

[69] 20 Bankr. 286 (Bankr. C.D. Cal.), modified, 21 Bankr. 12 (Bankr. 9th Cir. 1982). Ultimately, the Ninth Circuit Bankruptcy Appellate Panel reversed the trial court's holding that the trustee could not draw on the credit. Farmer v. Crocker Nat'l Bank (In re Swift Aire Lines, Inc.), 30 Bankr. 490 (Bankr. 9th Cir. 1983).

[70] 622 F. Supp. 288 (D. Colo. 1985), rev'd, 865 F.2d 1134 (10th Cir. 1988).

[71] The *Bank of Boulder* holding may be partially dictum. The question was one of jurisdiction, and the court held that it had no jurisdiction to hear a claim against the issuer by the FDIC as receiver, such claims being subject to the jurisdiction of state courts. It refused to hear the claim of the FDIC in its corporate capacity, on the ground that the FDIC, acting in that capacity, could not take a transfer of the right to draw. In Public Loan Co. v. FDIC, 803 F.2d 82 (3d Cir. 1986), the court permitted the FDIC, in its corporate capacity, to draw on a letter of credit issued to the failed bank as beneficiary. It does not appear from the *Public Loan Co.* opinion that the parties raised the transfer issue. Cf. Kelley v. First Westroads Bank (In re Kelley), 840 F.2d 554 (8th Cir. 1988) (holding that draft drawn by FDIC liquidator is conforming, but not discussing transfer issue). In FDIC v. Bank of San Francisco, 817 F.2d 1395 (9th Cir. 1987), the court permitted the FDIC as receiver to draw on a credit, did not discuss the transfer issue, and under the *D'Oench, Duhme* doctrine

On appeal, the Court of Appeals for the Tenth Circuit reversed.[72] The Tenth Circuit concluded that the federal policy of supporting the FDIC in its use of purchase and assumption transactions was sufficiently strong to override state law. Relying on the doctrine of *United States v. Kimbell Foods, Inc.*,[73] the court held that federal common law should not follow state commercial law rules in this area, and it fashioned a rule of federal common law contrary to the Code's and contract law's antitransfer rule.[74] The majority opinion provoked a strong dissent.

In *Eakin v. Continental Illinois National Bank & Trust Co.*,[75] the credit ran to an insurance company that subsequently became insolvent. The credit required the beneficiary to certify that it would hold the credit proceeds and would return any portion that was not needed to satisfy claims under a construction bond that the credit secured. When the state insurance commissioner as liquidator of the beneficiary presented that certification, the issuer objected that such certification was not what it had bargained for. The court rejected the argument, however, holding that the risk of the beneficiary's insolvency was one that the issuer faced when it issued the credit.

Unfortunately, all of these cases demonstrate little regard for the strict compliance rule.[76] The issuer of a credit reasonably expects to receive a draft drawn by the beneficiary. These cases force the issuer to decide whether the concerns of international law, insurance liquidation law, or bankruptcy law excuse strict compliance with terms of the credit. The burden of that inquiry is far greater than the burden the strict compliance rule imposes on the issuer. Under the rule of these cases, issuers must invoke legal concepts and may have to litigate; under the strict compliance rule, the issuer need determine only whether the documents comply on their face with the terms of the credit.[77]

---

gave the FDIC greater rights than those of the original beneficiary. For discussion of that doctrine, see infra ¶ 10.05.

[72] FDIC v. Bank of Boulder, 858 F.2d 594 (10th Cir. 1988).

[73] 440 U.S. 715 (1979).

[74] The credit was subject to the 1974 version of the Uniform Customs, which provided in Article 46 that credits that do not expressly permit transfer are not transferable. See supra ¶ 10.01.

[75] 875 F.2d 114 (7th Cir. 1989).

[76] For a discussion of the strict compliance rule, see ¶ 6.03.

[77] Some issuers avoid the problem of determining whether courts will approve payments to trustees in bankruptcy, personal representatives, and successor corporations by providing in the application agreement that they may pay such successors in interest. For an example of such an application agreement provision, see App. C, Doc. 14, ¶ 6. The State of New York Insurance Department requires certain letters of credit issued in favor of insurance companies to contain express language in the clause designating the beneficiary to the end that the beneficiary includes any liquidator, rehabilitator, receiver, or conservator. See State of New York Insurance De-

Some commentators have objected, furthermore, that an issuer loses its right of setoff or other defenses by virtue of a transfer by operation of law.[78] While the issuer's defenses in the credit transaction are limited,[79] some defenses exist. An issuer may be willing to issue a credit to a beneficiary or to make advances on the assumption that it can exercise its defenses. Under a voluntary transfer of the credit, a novation between the issuer and the new beneficiary, defenses that would be good against the first beneficiary would not be good against the second. Unless courts restrict involuntary transfers in such a way that the transferee by operation of law takes subject to those defenses, these commentators' objections are well founded.

In a number of cases, it appears that the issuer failed to raise the transfer prohibitions and thus lost a possible defense. In *Toyota Industrial Trucks U.S.A., Inc. v. Citizens National Bank*,[80] the defendant executed and delivered to Toyota Motors Distributors, Inc. an agreement in the form of Toyota's standard revolving credit agreement as part of a floor plan financing arrangement. Subsequently, Toyota Motors assigned the product line covered by the agreement to Toyota Industrial Trucks, U.S.A., Inc. The court held that the revolving credit agreement was a letter of credit issued by the bank in favor of Toyota Motors. The opinion does not mention whether the bank's undertaking was designated as transferable. Toyota Industrial Trucks had drawn on the credit over a period of time, but eventually the bank dishonored two drafts. It may be that the bank never raised the transferability question, which appears to provide an appropriate ground for dishonor.

It could be argued that, by honoring over a period of time drafts drawn by Toyota Industrial, the issuer had waived the defect or had been estopped to assert it. There is a minority line of cases that accept this kind of analysis, although the better-reasoned cases reject it.[81] One case in the minority line is *Schweibish v. Pontchartrain State Bank*,[82] where the credit issued to the seller's bank. The seller itself presented

---

partment, Insurance News 9 (Dec. 10, 1987). For an illustration of such a letter of credit, see App. C, Doc. 24.

[78] See Kozolchyk, Letters of Credit in the Americas 498–500 (1966); Byrne, "L/C Transfer by Operation of Law — It Ought to Be Against the Law" (pt. 1), Letter of Credit Update 8 (July 1989); McGowan, "Assignability of Documentary Credits," 13 Law & Contemp. Probs. 666, 675 (1948); cf. Eriksson v. Refiners Export Co., 264 A.D. 525, 35 N.Y.S.2d 829 (1942) (making same point to justify rule against permitting assignee of credit and holder of beneficiary's draft to recover on straight credit).

[79] For discussion of those limits, see ¶ 9.06.

[80] 611 F.2d 465 (3d Cir. 1979).

[81] For a discussion of those cases, see ¶ 4.07.

[82] 389 So. 2d 731 (La. Ct. App. 1980).

the required supporting documents but neglected to provide the bank's sight draft called for by the credit. The *Schweibish* opinion contains language suggesting that the defect was not critical and notes that the issuer's conduct in evaluating documents must conform to a standard of reasonableness. The case held that the issuer's failure to notify the beneficiary's customer of the defects constituted a waiver of them under Article 8 of the 1974 Uniform Customs, to which the credit was subject. The opinion also notes that the issuer had not complained previously when the seller failed to present sight drafts.

The *Schweibish* case suggests that Article 16 of the Uniform Customs, the successor to Article 8 of the 1974 UCP, may operate to bar the issuer from justifying dishonor on the basis of the transfer rules if the issuer has not notified the presenting party of the defect promptly[83] or if the issuer has not objected to similar defects in the past. The import of *Schweibish* is to give rights under the credit to one who is a nonbeneficiary and is apparently a nontransferee.[84]

In *Agnew v. FDIC*,[85] the beneficiary of the credit was Penn Square Bank, N.A. The bank became insolvent, and an FDIC liquidator drew on the credit. The court disposed of the case on a fraud issue[86] and did not raise the transfer question.

In *Flagship Cruises, Ltd. v. New England Merchants National Bank*,[87] the issuer apparently did complain that the credit ran to Flagship Cruises, Ltd. and that Flagship Cruises, Inc., a cognate corporation, drew the draft. The court rejected the complaint, holding that the issuer could discern from the letterhead of certain correspondence that the latter corporation was acting for the former. The *Flagship* court did not lay much store by the strict compliance rule or by the rules limiting transfer.[88]

[4] Distinguishing Transferees From Holders of the Draft

There are some cases that seem to confuse the transferable credit with the negotiation credit. In the former case, the beneficiary may transfer

---

[83] The *Schweibish* opinion suggests that notice is not necessary if the beneficiary has no time within which it can cure the defect before the credit expires. For a different view of this "estoppel" rule, see ¶ 6.06[1][c].

[84] For general discussion of persons entitled to enforce the credit engagement, see ¶ 9.02[3], supra ¶ 10.02, infra ¶ 10.03[4].

[85] 548 F. Supp. 1235 (N.D. Cal. 1982).

[86] For discussion of the fraud question, see ¶ 7.04.

[87] 569 F.2d 699 (1st Cir. 1978).

[88] For further discussion of the *Flagship* case, see ¶ 6.05[1][b].

to a second beneficiary the right to draw drafts under the credit, and the issuer will issue a new advice of its undertaking to the transferee. In the latter case, unless the credit is also transferable, the beneficiary must draw the drafts himself but then may negotiate them with a bank other than the issuer. That "negotiating" bank then obtains payment from the issuer, which has not issued any new advice but has assumed all along that the beneficiary would negotiate the drafts. Briefly, transfer occurs before the beneficiary draws; negotiation occurs afterward; and a negotiation credit is not necessarily transferable.

In *Decker Steel Co. v. Exchange National Bank*,[89] the credit specifically provided for assignment, and the credit undertaking ran to "drawers, endorsers, and bona fide holders of drafts negotiable [sic] thereunder."[90] The original beneficiary, the opinion notes, assigned the credit to a second bank as security for a back-to-back[91] letter that the second bank issued to the original beneficiary's supplier. After payment of the original credit, the account party sued the opening bank and the transferee bank, raising issues based on the underlying transaction. The case appears to pose questions concerning the assignee's rights under the original credit, but the court treated the question as one determined in part by the holder in due course status of the assignee. The court held that the transferee prevailed at least in part because it was a holder in due course of drafts drawn under the original credit and because it was also a bona fide purchaser of bills of lading presented under the credit.

It is difficult of see how the holder in due course status of the second bank is determinative in *Decker*. It is true that Section 5-114(2)(a) permits the issuer to honor such a holder's presentation in the face of the account party's claims of fraud, but there was a distinct absence of fraud in the *Decker* facts. The account party had alleged that steel shipped pursuant to the underlying transaction was nonconforming, and the lower court found that the documents called for by the credit were in order.[92] Had the documents contained false information, they would have been fraudulent, and then the holder in due course issue would have been central to a proper decision. The *Decker* court put the cart before the horse and went to the holder in due course question before de-

---

[89] 330 F.2d 82 (7th Cir. 1964).

[90] Id. at 83.

[91] For discussion of the back-to-back letter of credit, see ¶ 1.08.

[92] The credit called for commercial invoices covering "36-inch" coils of hot rolled steel. Decker Steel Co. v. Exchange Nat'l Bank, 330 F.2d 82, 84 (7th Cir. 1964). The account party complained that the steel measured 37 inches. The trial court found, however, that in the industry the term "36-inch" as applied to this steel included steel that measured 37 inches, and the Seventh Circuit did not disturb that finding.

"ineffective" until the issuer receives the credit instrument, Section 5-116(2) of the Code protects issuers in these cases.

¶ 10.04 ASSIGNING THE RIGHT TO PROCEEDS

[1] Another Difference Between the Right to Draw and the Right to Proceeds

Both the Code and the Uniform Customs reflect attitudes toward assignments of the right to proceeds under a credit that are markedly different from that toward transfers of the right to draw. That difference reflects the fact that there are definite reasons to limit the latter type of conveyance, and there are definite reasons to encourage the former.

Restrictions on transfer of the right to draw protect the account party's expectations concerning performance and facilitate document examination. These concerns do not apply to assignments of the credit proceeds where there is no risk of substitute performance and no deviation from the strict compliance standard that permits document examiners to make payment decisions without looking beyond the face of the documents and the credit itself. It is true that the assignment of the credit proceeds imposes upon the issuer greater burdens than a nonassignment rule would impose; but issuers, usually banks, engage constantly in the process of collecting and paying obligations that pass from party to party, a process they find to be a modest burden.[102]

The ability of beneficiaries to alienate freely their "money interest,"[103] as one court termed the right to proceeds, is important to the value of the credit as a commercial device. Section 5-116(2) makes it clear that any prohibition in the credit against transfer does not limit the right to assign proceeds; and Article 55 of the Uniform Customs, while not going that far, suggests a disposition to support such assignments.[104]

---

[102] Thus, for example, Section 5-116(3) protects the right of the beneficiary to "transfer or negotiate drafts or demands drawn under the credit."

[103] Bank of Newport v. First Nat'l Bank & Trust Co., 32 U.C.C. Rep. Serv. (Callaghan) 1572, 1578 (D.N.D. 1981), aff'd, 687 F.2d 1257 (8th Cir. 1982).

[104] Accord Sipe v. First Nat'l Bank, 41 U.C.C. Rep. Serv. (Callaghan) 938 (S.D. Iowa 1985) (involving interbank participation agreement that court characterized as assignment of credit proceeds); City Nat'l Bank v. First Nat'l Bank, 22 Ark. App. 5, 732 S.W.2d 489 (1987) (holding that assignment of proceeds did not constitute transfer in violation of participating bank's rights under participation agreement). For a case in which the court sustained jury verdicts against the corporate assignor and its president for converting the proceeds of the assigned credit, including a verdict for punitive damages against the corporate defendant, see Intermarkets U.S.A., Inc. v. C-E Natco, a Div. of Combustion Eng'g, Inc., 749 S.W.2d 603 (Tex. Ct. App. 1988).

In *Furness Withy (Chartering), Inc., Panama v. World Energy Systems Associates, Inc.,*[105] the court expressed impatience with a party that it thought was quibbling over the distinction between the right to draw and the right to proceeds. In *Furness Withy,* there were a number of proceeds assignments, and the assignment notices included language to the effect that the assignments did not effect a transfer of the right to draw and did not interfere with the right of the beneficiary and the issuer to amend the credit. Creditors of the beneficiary, in an attempt to upset the assignments, argued that the language was inconsistent with the notion of an assignment. The court, in an opinion that emphasizes the difference between the right to draw and the right to proceeds, rejected the argument as an attempt "to obfuscate the issue."[106]

[2] Manner of Assigning Proceeds

Article 55 of the Uniform Customs leaves to "applicable law" the method of effecting an assignment of proceeds, thereby suggesting that credit law is not concerned with those assignments beyond the point of encouraging them. Section 5-116(2), however, perhaps out of an abundance of caution, specifies that no assignment of proceeds is effective until the credit document is delivered to the assignee. The section notes that such delivery constitutes perfection of an Article 9 security interest in the credit, and Section 9-305 stipulates that a security interest in a credit "may" be perfected by placing the secured party in possession of the credit document.

The Code uses the term "letter of credit or advice of credit" in both Article 5 and Article 9. The provisions raise two questions: one relating to the creation of the security interest as opposed to its perfection and one relating to the kind of paper that must be delivered to the assignee secured party.

[a] Creating the Security Interest

Arguably, some conveyances of credit proceeds do not create a security interest but are outright "sales" of the "money interest" under the credit. Some assignments of proceeds, one between related corporations, for example, might be made without consideration. Such conveyances would not be secured transactions. In the normal course of busi-

---

[105] 642 F. Supp. 50 (W.D. Tenn. 1985), aff'd sub nom. Union Planters Nat'l Bank v. World Energy Sys. Assocs., Inc., 816 F.2d 1092 (6th Cir. 1987).

[106] Id. at 54. For further discussion of the creditors' argument in the security interest context, see infra ¶ 10.04[2][b].

ness or finance, such "sales" are few and are difficult to distinguish from the more prevalent transaction: the assignment of proceeds as security for an advance or for a commitment to make an advance.

Parties often assign portions of the proceeds of a letter of credit to various parties in the broad commercial transaction. In *Furness Withy (Chartering), Inc., Panama v. World Energy Systems Associates, Inc.*,[107] for example, the beneficiary of a credit assigned part of the proceeds to its suppliers, its lender, a stevedore company, and a carrier. Apart from the lender, the assignees may not have considered themselves secured parties, yet the clear import of Section 5-116(2) is that such "payees" take the assignment as Article 9 secured parties.

In any event, it may not matter whether the assignment is one for security or whether it is a sale. Section 9-102(1)(b) provides that Article 9 applies to any sale of accounts. The issuer's engagement does not appear to satisfy the Article 9 definition of an "account" in Section 9-106. That article defines an account as "any right to payment for goods sold or leased or for services rendered which is not evidenced by an instrument or chattel paper, whether or not it has been earned by performance." Some credit engagements will meet the definition, provided that courts piece the credit transaction together with the underlying transaction; but many credits will not. Even if courts take the two transactions together, for example, it is difficult to characterize a beneficiary that takes municipal bonds and draws on the credit in the event of the municipality's default as a party enjoying a right to payment for goods sold or for services rendered. Section 5-116(2) stipulates, nonetheless, that an assignment of the proceeds of a credit is "an assignment of an account under Article 9."

Briefly, then, parties should assume that Article 9 governs an assignment of the right to proceeds, regardless of whether the assignment is one for security or is a form of payment. If the beneficiary transfers the right to draw, the distinction between a sale and a security interest should hold, with Article 9 governing the latter only. The cautious transferee of the right to draw assumes that Article 9 does apply, however, and therefore takes steps to ensure that he satisfies the article's rules for the proper creation of the security interest (i.e., attachment) and for the proper perfection of the security interest.

Section 9-203(1) stipulates that attachment occurs in one of two ways: when the debtor (the assignor) has signed a security agreement describing the credit and when the assignee takes possession of the credit pursuant to the agreement. Section 5-116(2)(a), however, preempts the

---

[107] 642 F. Supp. 50 (W.D. Tenn. 1985), aff'd sub nom. Union Planters Nat'l Bank v. World Energy Sys. Assocs., Inc., 816 F.2d 1092 (6th Cir. 1987).

first method of attachment. The provision stipulates that Article 9 governs but provides further that "the assignment is ineffective until the letter of credit or advice of credit is delivered to the assignee." The Code drafters appear to have been saying that no security interest attaches until that delivery. Such a reading negates any security interest that is not effected by delivering the credit document. Article 9 anticipates such rules when it provides in Section 9-201 that the effect of a security agreement may be limited by provisions elsewhere in the Code.

Assignees of the credit proceeds should insist, therefore, that the beneficiary deliver the credit document to the assignee. Delivery of the credit document effects attachment and enables the secured party to satisfy the issuer that, in fact, the assignment has been made. Section 5-116(2)(c) explicitly authorizes the issuer to withhold the credit proceeds until the assignee exhibits the credit document to the issuer.

[b] Perfecting the Security Interest

The Code provides in Section 5-116(2) and in Section 9-305 that the letter of credit must be delivered to the assignee of the credit proceeds in order to render that assignment "effective." The assignee of credit proceeds should insist that the beneficiary deliver the credit document to him. That requirement makes it important for the parties to know what papers comprise the document.

The Code addresses the paper question by stipulating that the beneficiary deliver the "letter of credit or advice of credit."[108] Thus, if a Dusseldorf bank issues a credit by telex in favor of a New York seller, and if a New York bank advises the credit, the New York bank's advice is the appropriate document for delivery to the assignee. If the New York bank confirms the credit, the confirmation is the appropriate document. If there is no advice or confirmation, presumably the telex itself must be delivered. Assignees should be careful, however, that the telex is the credit, not merely a preadvice. Article 12 of the Uniform Customs addresses that distinction and formulates rules for avoiding confusion.

Often there are multiple assignments of a credit. A beneficiary may, for example, assign part of the proceeds to pay some of his suppliers, part to pay the freight forwarder, and part to pay a lender that is financing part of the transaction. Because it is possible to deliver the letter of credit to only one of those parties, Article 9 of the Code permits the beneficiary to let one assignee hold the credit and to notify that party of the

---

[108] U.C.C. § 5-116(2)(a). For further discussion of perfecting the security interest in a letter of credit by possession, see R. Henson, Handbook on Secured Transactions Under the Uniform Commercial Code 102–107 (2d ed. 1979).

other assignments.[109] There should be no question that the party holding the credit is a bailee to whom notice may be given in order to effect perfection of the security interest of the subsequent assignees. In *Furness Withy (Chartering), Inc., Panama v. World Energy Systems Associates, Inc.,*[110] the court held squarely that Article 9 envisions this arrangement, that there is nothing improper in having the beneficiary's lender act as bailee for the other assignees, and that notice to the lender in this case rendered the other assignees perfected secured parties.[111]

¶ 10.05 CONSEQUENCES OF TRANSFER

The transferee of the right to draw is able to draw drafts or otherwise demand payment under the credit. He also may submit his invoices rather than those of the original beneficiary.[112] At least one court would permit both the transferee of the right to draw and the assignee of the proceeds to sue for breach of the credit promise.[113] In either case, the transferee or the assignee must bear the transferor's burden of showing that the credit conditions are satisfied.[114]

The rights of the assignee of the credit's proceeds are no greater than those of the original beneficiary. If the issuer has a defense of fraud

---

[109] See U.C.C. § 9-305.

[110] 642 F. Supp. 50 (W.D. Tenn. 1985), aff'd sub nom. Union Planters Nat'l Bank v. World Energy Sys. Assocs., Inc., 816 F.2d 1092 (6th Cir. 1987).

[111] Significantly, the *Furness Withy* court rejected an attaching creditor's argument that the assignments were ineffective because of language in the notices of assignment that the beneficiary reserved the right to amend the credit. The court saw that reservation as consistent with the distinction between the right to draw and the right to proceeds. See supra ¶ 10.04[1]. While not apparent from the opinion, it may be that the attaching creditor was arguing that the notion of an Article 9 security interest is inconsistent with the notion that the beneficiary can reserve the power to destroy the assignment by amending the document that is the subject of the pledge. That argument would have merit if the beneficiary could, for example, reduce the amount of a credit by amendment after assignment. The clear purpose of the delivery requirement in Section 5-116(2) is to prevent the beneficiary from exercising control over the credit. To the extent that he can reduce the value of the credit, the beneficiary may, in fact, have sufficient control to render the pledge fraudulent. Unfortunately, the courts have not addressed the problem.

[112] See U.C.P. art. 54(f) (1983).

[113] See Continental Time Corp. v. Swiss Credit Bank, 543 F. Supp. 408 (S.D.N.Y. 1982). See generally ¶ 9.02[3].

[114] See, e.g., Ufitec, S.A. v. Trade Bank & Trust Co., 21 A.D.2d 187, 249 N.Y.S.2d 557 (1964), aff'd, 16 N.Y.2d 698, 209 N.E.2d 551, 261 N.Y.S.2d 893 (1965); Bank of Newport v First Nat'l Bank & Trust Co. 32 U.C.C. Rep. Serv. (Callaghan) 1572 (D.N.D. 1981), aff'd, 687 F.2d 1257 (8th Cir. 1982).

that is good against the beneficiary, that defense should be good against the assignee.[115] The credit is not a negotiable instrument, and the assignee is not a holder in due course who cuts off defenses.[116]

Cromwell v. Commerce & Energy Bank[117] fashions a different rule for transferees of the right to draw. In that case, the account parties claimed that the first beneficiary had practiced fraud on them. The court held that that fraud was not relevant to the transferee's claim on the credit issuer.[118] The rule of the *Cromwell* case makes sense. By issuing the transferable credit, the issuer puts the original beneficiary in a position to transfer it in the normal course of business. Note that the law warns the issuer of the possibility of issuance by stipulating in both the Code and the Uniform Customs that the transferable credit be designated as such in some way. Thus, although it is true that the transferable credit is not a negotiable instrument, it is not necessarily true that the transferee cannot have greater rights than those which the first beneficiary has.

In *Bamberger Polymers International Corp. v. Citibank, N.A.*,[119] the court considered the rights of an assignee of a credit's proceeds. The advising bank attempted to set off against the credit proceeds an amount due from the original beneficiary. The court rejected the attempt, holding that the assignee of proceeds has the rights of an assignee of an account under Section 9-318 of the Code. Under that analysis, the issuer is the account debtor, and, while the *Bamberger* court implies that the issuer may use setoff if it satisfies the requirements of Section 9-318, the advising bank may not.[120]

In *FDIC v. Bank of San Francisco*,[121] the court invoked federal common law to give the successor in interest to the beneficiary greater rights than the beneficiary would have enjoyed. In the *Bank of San*

---

[115] See Pubali Bank v. City Nat'l Bank, 676 F.2d 1326 (9th Cir. 1982); cf. Ufford, "Transfer and Assignment of Letters of Credit Under the Uniform Commercial Code," 7 Wayne L. Rev. 263, 288 (1960) (positing rule that would render transferee subject to issuer's setoff rights against transferor).

[116] See Consolidated Aluminum Corp. v. Bank of Va., 704 F.2d 136 (4th Cir. 1983); Philadelphia Gear Corp. v. FDIC, 587 F. Supp. 194 (W.D. Okla.), aff'd in part, rev'd in part, 751 F.2d 1131 (10th Cir. 1984), rev'd, 476 U.S. 426 (1986); Shaffer v. Brooklyn Park Garden Apartments, 311 Minn. 452, 250 N.W.2d 172 (1977); Heritage Hous. Corp. v. Ferguson, 651 S.W.2d 272 (Tex. Ct. App. 1983).

[117] 464 So. 2d 721 (La. 1985).

[118] See also Brown v. United States Nat'l Bank, 220 Neb. 684, 371 N.W.2d 692 (1985) (similar to *Cromwell* case).

[119] 124 Misc. 2d 653, 477 N.Y.S.2d 931 (Sup. Ct. 1983).

[120] For discussion of the setoff point, see ¶ 9.06[3].

[121] 817 F.2d 1395 (9th Cir. 1987).

Francisco case, the account parties alleged that the beneficiary had participated in a fraud against them. That fraud, the court held, even if it justified dishonor of the credit, a question the court did not decide, did not hinder the FDIC as receiver of the failed beneficiary.

Under the doctrine of *D'Oench, Duhme & Co. v. FDIC*,[122] the FDIC does not take assets of the failed bank subject to such a claim. The *Bank of San Francisco* court rejected the idea that the *D'Oench, Duhme* doctrine rests on estoppel notions, that is, the idea that parties to a fraud should not be able to assert defenses against the FDIC. That view of *D'Oench, Duhme* would have protected the *Bank of San Francisco* issuer, which was not aware of the fraud. The policy basis of the *D'Oench, Duhme* rule, the court held, is one of protecting the FDIC and enhancing its position by permitting it to enforce obligations.

While the Uniform Customs expressly prohibit more than one transfer of the right to draw, Article 54 permits transfers of the credit in portions. In *Continental Time Corp. v. Swiss Credit Bank*,[123] the original beneficiary transferred the credit to two corporations, one of which reconveyed 75 percent of its interest to the original beneficiary. When the original beneficiary sued the issuer for dishonor, the court dismissed the action because the transferees had instituted suit in Switzerland. The court did not address the question whether the reconveyance to the original beneficiary had violated the Uniform Customs' prohibition against more than one transfer. It is not clear that the Uniform Customs governed in *Continental Time*, and the Code's transfer section does not expressly prohibit more than one transfer of the right to draw. Perhaps reconveyance does not constitute a second transfer, but merely cancelation of the first transfer.

In *AOV Industries, Inc. v. Lambert Coal Co.*,[124] a bankruptcy preference action, the court emphasized the distinction between an assignment of credit proceeds and a transfer of the right to draw. In the *AOV Industries* case, the beneficiary of several credits transferred them outside the preference period, but payments under the credits were made during the period.[125] The disbursing agent under the debtor's plan of reorganization sought to set the payments aside under Section 547 of the Bankruptcy Code.

---

[122] 315 U.S. 447 (1942).

[123] 543 F. Supp. 408 (S.D.N.Y. 1982).

[124] 64 Bankr. 933 (Bankr. D.D.C. 1986).

[125] In fact, some of the credits may have been transferred during the ninety-day period, but those transfers were protected by virtue of one or more of the exceptions set forth in 11 U.S.C. § 547(c). It is clear from the *AOV Industries* opinion that the court viewed the payments under the credits as the critical transfers for the purpose of applying the preference rules.

The effort failed. The court stressed that, under a transfer of the credit, the second beneficiary becomes obligated to perform the credit's conditions and that such performance renders the second beneficiary, not the original beneficiary, entitled to the proceeds of the credit. Thus, in the court's view, the payments were not transfers of the debtor's property. By way of dictum, the court pointed out that if the beneficiary had assigned the credits' proceeds outside the preference period but then had satisfied the credits' conditions during the period, there would have been transfers within the period under the rule of 11 U.S.C. § 547(e)(3).

¶ 10.06   ATTACHMENT AND OTHER INVOLUNTARY CONVEYANCES TO CREDITORS

It is consistent with the general policies served by the transfer rules to forbid involuntary transfers of the right to draw under nontransferable credits. These policies are a desire (1) to restrict the credit's benefit to the party in whom the account party reposes trust, so that parties whom he does not trust will not be permitted to present documents that are easily forged or that may be fraudulent, and (2) to maximize the cost and time efficiency of credits by making it easier for the issuer's document examiner to ascertain the conformity of drafts presented under a credit. In some contexts, courts have sacrificed these policies in favor of others; but generally, in the creditor context, courts have fashioned rules that support those underlying policies.

[1]   Involuntary Transfer of the Right to Draw

It seems inconsistent with the general policies of the transfer rules discussed previously to permit creditors of the beneficiary, through judicial proceedings or under statutory relief for creditors, to obtain the right to draw. In some cases, courts have permitted involuntary transfer by operation of law of the right to draw.[126] These cases may reflect a decision to subordinate letter of credit policy to overriding policies of federal insolvency laws, international law, or state liquidation regimes. Absent some similar compelling, explicit policy, it is difficult to justify the transfer of the right to draw when credit law under Section 5-116 or Article 54 of the Uniform Customs does not permit transfer.

---

[126] See supra ¶ 10.03[3] for discussion of the *Pastor*, *Temple-Eastex*, and *American Bell* cases. But cf. supra ¶ 10.03[3] for *Swift Aire* case (adopting strict rule).

[2] Involuntary Assignment of the Right to Proceeds

Frequently, a creditor of the beneficiary attempts to take the beneficiary's interest in the credit. Per se it does not offend letter of credit policies to permit that creditor to take by process or under statutory right the beneficiary's right to the proceeds of a credit. In such a case, the beneficiary itself, not the creditor, still must comply with the terms of the credit. The account party obtains the original beneficiary's performance, and the issuer that issues a nontransferable credit does not have to deal with documents drawn by a stranger to the transaction.

[3] Creditors

Both creditors of the beneficiary and creditors of the account party may attempt to use creditor remedies to claim an interest in the credit or in the account party's property pledged to secure the obligation to reimburse the issuer. Evaluation of these claims should consider the transfer rules, and courts should reject any attempt by a creditor to outflank these rules by resort to creditors' rights.

[a] The Beneficiary as Creditor

In *Venizelos, S.A. v. Chase Manhattan Bank, N.A.*,[127] the beneficiary of a credit obtained judgment against the account party and then sought to attach the credit's proceeds by initiating proceedings against the confirming bank. The confirming bank had been honoring drafts under the credit by debiting the opening bank's account. The beneficiary argued that the funds were assets of the account party subject to levy. The *Venizelos* court rejected that argument, holding that the beneficiary's suit was an attempt to turn the letter of credit into an asset of the beneficiary. The court also held that the credit was security for the beneficiary only to the extent that the conditions of the credit were satisfied.

In *J. Zeevi & Sons v. Grindlays Bank (Uganda) Ltd.*[128] and *National Bank & Trust Co. of North America, Ltd. v. J.L.M. International, Inc.*,[129] the courts treated attachment suits as strict matters of letter of credit law. A beneficiary in the former case and a party claiming through the beneficiary in the latter case were successful in attaching the proceeds of

---

[127] 425 F.2d 461 (2d Cir. 1970).

[128] 37 N.Y.2d 220, 333 N.E.2d 168, 371 N.Y.S.2d 892 (1975), cert. denied, 432 U.S. 866 (1975).

[129] 421 F. Supp. 1269 (S.D.N.Y. 1976).

a credit, but only after the issuer was found liable for breaching the credit engagement.[130]

In *Royal Bank of Canada v. Trone*,[131] the beneficiary of a credit argued that, by virtue of the credit, it was a secured creditor of the account party and therefore was entitled to object to a plan of reorganization in the account party's bankruptcy. The beneficiary, at the suggestion of the account party, had taken from the issuer an assignment of the account party's note to the issuer, along with the issuer's credit engagement to honor the beneficiary's draft if the account party defaulted on the note. The account party had given the issuer security for the note, and the beneficiary argued that the issuer was a guarantor of the note that the beneficiary held. The beneficiary reasoned that, under guaranty law, it had an interest in the collateral.

The *Royal Bank* court rejected the argument, noting that, under letter of credit principles, the issuer is not a guarantor of the note but a party primarily liable on the credit. The principle of guaranty law was inapplicable.[132]

Generally, attempts by the beneficiary to claim property in the hands of the issuer fail if the courts find that the beneficiary has not established that it complied with the credit's conditions. In the *J. Zeevi* case and in the *National Bank & Trust Co.* case, the plaintiffs succeeded. In the former, however, the plaintiff had complied with the terms of the credit. In the latter, an anticipatory breach case, the plaintiff had to show that it was ready and able to satisfy the credit's conditions.[133]

[b] Third-Party Creditor

Generally, persons who are not parties to the credit engagement may not assert an interest in the credit or in its proceeds. In *Capehart Corp. v. Shanghai Commercial Bank, Ltd.*,[134] the account party, apparently disputing the beneficiary's performance of the underlying transaction, sought to attach "the letter of credit."[135] The trial court denied the

---

[130] The *J.L.M. International* case does not discuss the question of the plaintiff's standing to bring the action in its own right. For a discussion of that issue, see supra ¶ 10.02[4].

[131] 634 F.2d 459 (9th Cir. 1980).

[132] For further discussion of subrogation in letter of credit law, see Neidle & Bishop, "Commercial Letters of Credit: Effect of Suspension of Issuing Bank," 32 Colum. L. Rev. 1 (1932). See also ¶ 7.05[2].

[133] For a discussion of the "ready and able" rule, see ¶ 9.02[2][a].

[134] 49 A.D.2d 521, 369 N.Y.S.2d 751 (1975).

[135] Id. at 522, 369 N.Y.S.2d at 752.

beneficiary's motion to vacate the attachment. The appellate division reversed on the ground, among others, that the account party was not a party to the credit and had no right to attach it and that the credit was independent of the underlying contract. Thus, the court used both attachment law and letter of credit law to defeat the attachment.

In *Lantz International Corp. v. Industrial Termotecnica, Campana, S.p.A.*,[136] the court held that there was no property of the beneficiary for the beneficiary's creditor to attach. In the *Lantz* case, the issuer had honored the credit by accepting the beneficiary's drafts. The beneficiary had negotiated the drafts (now acceptances) to two holders. The attempt by the beneficiary's creditor to attach the drafts was an attempt to attach the holders' property, and the court allowed the motion to vacate.

In *Furness Withy (Chartering), Inc., Panama v. World Energy Systems Associates, Inc.*,[137] the court held squarely that a creditor seeking to attach the proceeds of a credit under admiralty law may not succeed if the assignment occurs prior to the time the beneficiary satisfies the conditions of the credit. The court reasoned that there is nothing to attach prior to the time the beneficiary has performed because, at that point, the issuer owes nothing to the beneficiary. Because the assignee's security interest in the proceeds is perfected, the creditor may not attach the proceeds after the beneficiary satisfies the conditions. In short, under *Furness Withy*, the attaching creditor must satisfy three requirements: He must levy (1) after the conditions are satisfied, (2) before payment of the proceeds, and (3) before assignment of the proceeds.

By the same token, in *Supreme Merchandise Co. v. Chemical Bank*,[138] the court held that an attaching creditor of the beneficiary could not attach proceeds of the credit prior to the time that the beneficiary complied with the credit's terms. In *Supreme Merchandise*, the beneficiary's creditor caused attachment orders to be served on the issuer. The first was served before any drafts were submitted to the issuer and before the negotiating banks had taken the drafts for value. The second was served after the issuer had accepted time drafts negotiated by foreign banks under the credit but before the issuer had honored the acceptances.[139]

Regarding the second order of attachment, the court followed its earlier holding in *First Commercial Bank v. Gotham Originals, Inc.*[140]

---

[136] 358 F. Supp. 510 (E.D. Pa. 1973).

[137] 642 F. Supp. 50 (W.D. Tenn. 1985), aff'd sub nom. Union Planters Nat'l Bank v. World Energy Sys. Assocs., Inc., 816 F.2d 1092 (6th Cir. 1987).

[138] 70 N.Y.2d 344, 514 N.E.2d 1358, 520 N.Y.S.2d 734 (1987).

[139] For discussion of negotiation credits, see ¶¶ 1.02[3], 8.01[6].

[140] 64 N.Y.2d 287, 475 N.E.2d 1255, 486 N.Y.S.2d 715 (1985).

that, once the issuer accepts drafts submitted by a negotiating bank, there are no credit proceeds to be attached, the acceptances being the property of the holder of it (the negotiating bank or its transferee). Regarding the first order of attachment, the court was less sure of itself. In an opinion limited to the facts of the case, the court held that, prior to the time that the beneficiary performs the conditions of the credit, there is no "debt" due the beneficiary and no "property" of the beneficiary as the New York attachment law[141] defined those terms. Accordingly, the attachment effort failed.

The New York court's caution in *Supreme Merchandise Co.* stemmed from concern that, given the widespread use of letters of credit, there may be situations in which the beneficiary's interest under the credit may constitute "property" under the New York statute. The court did not give any examples of such instances, and it is probably safe to say that the *Supreme Merchandise Co.* rule is broad enough to encompass all commercial letter of credit transactions and most standby transactions. The *Supreme Merchandise Co.* court bottomed its decision in part on the commercial need to render negotiation letters of credit acceptable in the banking trade, but it also expressed respect for the need to encourage beneficiaries to perform the credit's conditions. If a creditor of the beneficiary can attach the credit's proceeds before the beneficiary performs, the beneficiary's incentive to perform is diminished. That loss of incentive has adverse consequences for the account party, who is innocent and whose rights in the underlying transaction could suffer. That concern for innocent parties, negotiating banks, and account parties, which prompted the *Supreme Merchandise Co.* court to rule as it did, is present in most letter of credit situations, both commercial and standby.

In *Sisalcords Do Brazil, Ltd. v. Fiacao Brasiliera De Sisal, S.A.,*[142] the beneficiary's creditor attempted to garnish the proceeds of a credit before the beneficiary had complied with the credit's terms. The court held that there was nothing for the creditor to garnish.[143]

---

[141] N.Y. Civ. Prac. L. & R. 5201(b) (McKinney 1978).

[142] 450 F.2d 419 (5th Cir. 1971), cert. denied, 406 U.S. 919 (1972).

[143] Accord Ferrostaal Metals Corp. v. S.S. Lash Pacifico, 652 F. Supp. 420 (S.D.N.Y. 1987); Diakan Love, S.A. v. Al-Haddad Bros. Enter., Inc. (In re Diakan Love, S.A.), 584 F. Supp. 782 (S.D.N.Y. 1984).

CHAPTER **11**

Questions of Procedure and Practice

Earlier chapters treat a number of issues that fall under the "procedure and practice" rubric. Chapter 9 covers questions of breach and remedies therefor and also deals with a number of defenses. In addition, other sections cover attachment (¶ 7.03[5]), injunctions (¶ 7.05), and some of the procedural questions that arise in the holder in due course cases (¶ 8.01). This chapter addresses specific procedural and practice rules that have arisen in letter of credit cases and analyzes the crucial questions that injunctions pose for letters of credit.

¶ 11.01 JURISDICTION AND VENUE

[1] Contacts and Fairness

No court may assert jurisdiction over a letter of credit dispute if the assertion violates the constitutional rule defined by the U.S. Supreme Court in the *International Shoe Co. v. Washington*[1] and *Hanson v. Denckla*[2] line of authority. The Court of Appeals for the Tenth Circuit held, in *Leney v. Plum Grove Bank*,[3] a letter of credit case, that that line of authority requires the plaintiff to show, first, that the defendant had

---

[1] 326 U.S. 310 (1945).
[2] 357 U.S. 235 (1958).
[3] 670 F.2d 878 (10th Cir. 1982).

"minimum contacts"[4] with the jurisdiction and, second, that requiring the defendant to litigate in the forum "does not offend traditional notions of fair play and substantial justice."[5]

In *Leney*, an Illinois account party caused the defendant, an Illinois bank, to open a credit in favor of a California resident. The issuer mailed the credit to the beneficiary's attorney at a Colorado address. The credit supported a contract for the purchase of property situated in Colorado, and the issuer probably knew about Colorado's connection with the transaction; but the credit required presentment of the credit and accompanying documents at the Illinois bank.

The beneficiary in *Leney* initiated collection of his draft through a California bank. The Illinois issuer dishonored, and the beneficiary sued in California. The trial court gave judgment for the defendant on the merits, and, on the beneficiary's appeal, the court pretermitted discussion of the merits and turned to the jurisdictional issue that the defendant had raised but lost in the trial court. The court concluded that the jurisdictional facts did not satisfy the *International Shoe* standard. It would not be fair, the *Leney* court concluded, "to burden an issuing bank with having to defend litigation over a letter of credit in any state in which the bank could reasonably expect the credit to be used."[6] Thus, *Leney* stands for the proposition that a beneficiary suing the issuer must show some contacts with the forum, other than the fact that the issuer could expect the beneficiary to initiate collection of the credit there. Any other rule, *Leney* holds, would violate due process.

In *H. Ray Baker, Inc. v. Associated Banking Corp.*,[7] a Philippine account party caused a Philippine bank to issue a credit that was advised by a New York bank and was payable in New York. The original beneficiary assigned the proceeds to Interquip, which had negotiated the underlying transaction in California with the Philippine account party. The opinion of the Court of Appeals for the Ninth Circuit in *H. Ray Baker* does not describe the nature of the credit. The transaction may have been a negotiation credit arrangement whereby the beneficiary could negotiate the draft with any bank, which then would reimburse itself from the New York advising bank. On the other hand, the credit may have been payable only in New York. In that case, the beneficiary could initiate collection elsewhere but could not negotiate drafts under

---

[4] Id. at 880.

[5] Id. (quoting International Shoe v. Washington, 326 U.S. 310, 316 (1945)).

[6] 670 F.2d at 881. The credit in *Leney* was not a negotiation credit. It was payable at the counter of the Illinois bank. The court did not rest its decision on that fact.

[7] 592 F.2d 550 (9th Cir.), cert. denied, 444 U.S. 832 (1979).

the credit. The opinion says, somewhat cryptically, that "Interquip presented the letter of credit for payment at a California bank."[8] In any event, the court concluded that a court sitting in California cannot exercise jurisdiction, there not being sufficient contacts to satisfy the due process standard of *International Shoe*.[9]

In *Stutsman v. Patterson*,[10] the issuer, a North Dakota bank, opened a credit in favor of California beneficiaries with whom it had negotiated. The bankers knew that the credit secured a transaction that was to be performed in California. The court held that the issuer's conduct did not satisfy the *International Shoe* test or that of *Hanson v. Denckla*[11] and that a court in California could not exercise jurisdiction.

In *Werner Lehara International, Inc. v. Harris Trust & Savings Bank*,[12] the court found that an Illinois issuer's contacts with Michigan were sufficient to hale the bank before a court sitting in Michigan. In the *Werner Lehara* case, the evidence showed that the issuer had been soliciting business from its Michigan correspondents for seventeen years and concluded that the activity came within the Michigan Long Arm Statute. In *Occidental Fire & Casualty Co. v. Continental Illinois National Bank & Trust Co.*,[13] the court held, however, that an Illinois issuer of a letter of credit in favor of two beneficiaries, one located in New York

---

[8] Id. at 551.

[9] Cf. Walpex Trading Co. v. Yacimientos Petroliferos Fiscales Bolivanos, 712 F. Supp. 383 (S.D.N.Y. 1989) (considering, among other factors, in determining that beneficiary was subject to jurisdiction in New York, (1) beneficiary's use of U.S. banks to facilitate payment under procurement contracts and (2) beneficiary's insistence that U.S. sellers provide performance standby credits); Hester Int'l Corp. v. Federal Republic of Nig., 681 F. Supp. 371 (N.D. Miss. 1988), aff'd on other grounds, 879 F.2d 170 (5th Cir. 1989) (holding that Nigerian account party that used letters of credit to transfer funds to United States and whose representative had held discussions in United States concerning agricultural project in Nigeria had sufficient contacts to be subject to in personam jurisdiction of court sitting in Mississippi).

[10] 457 F. Supp. 189 (C.D. Cal. 1978).

[11] For further authority to the effect that an issuer in one state does not subject itself to the jurisdiction of a second state by issuing a credit to a person in that second state, see Empire Abrasive Equip. Corp. v. H.H. Watson, Inc., 567 F.2d 554 (3d Cir. 1977); Delaware Valley Factors, Inc. v. Coma Export, Inc., 530 F. Supp. 180 (E.D. Pa 1982); E.I.C., Inc. v. Bank of Va., 108 Cal. App. 3d 148, 166 Cal. Rptr. 317 (1980); Chase Manhattan Bank v. Banco Del Atlantico, F.A., 343 So. 2d 936 (Fla. Dist. Ct. App. 1977); Ramsey Winch Co. v. Trust Co. Bank, 153 Ga. App. 500, 265 S.E.2d 848 (1980); cf. South Carolina Nat'l Bank v. Westpac Banking Corp., 678 F. Supp. 596 (D.S.C. 1987) (holding that Australian court would not have had jurisdiction over South Carolina issuer absent issuer's failure to preserve jurisdictional objection).

[12] 484 F. Supp. 65 (W.D. Mich. 1980).

[13] 689 F. Supp. 564 (E.D.N.C. 1988).

and one in North Carolina, even though it was subject to service under the North Carolina Long Arm Statute, could not be brought before a court sitting in that state without offending the rule of *International Shoe*.

In *Shenanigans Knits, Ltd. v. Ameritrust Co.*,[14] the court went far in holding that an Ohio bank that had issued a letter of credit in favor of a New York beneficiary was subject to jurisdiction in New York. The issuer corresponded with the beneficiary by telephone and by mail and had made payments on early drafts under the credit from its Ohio banking house. That activity, the court held, amounted to purposeful activity in New York that conferred jurisdiction. The *Shenanigans* opinion unfortunately does not review the letter of credit cases but relies on contract cases for authority to support its holding.[15]

Similarly, in *American National Bank & Trust Co. v. International Seafoods of Alaska, Inc.*,[16] the Supreme Court of Alaska found in personam jurisdiction over a Tennessee bank that appears to have been only an advising payor bank under a credit issued by a Florida bank in favor of an Alaskan beneficiary. The advising bank, to which the court's opinion refers at one point as a confirming bank, advised the beneficiary that it would review the beneficiary's documents and would pay the beneficiary upon receipt of the proceeds from the issuer. The court viewed that advice as the defendant's inducement of the beneficiary in a fashion that constituted purposeful avail of Alaska law.

In *Bank of Montreal v. Mitsui Manufacturers Bank*,[17] on the other hand, the court held that a California issuer of a credit in favor of a New York beneficiary was not subject to jurisdiction in New York. The issuer in *Bank of Montreal* used a New York bank to advise the credit. The court distinguished the *Shenanigans* case by pointing out that the issuer did not (1) make any payments in New York, (2) mail any letter of credit amendments to New York, or (3) contact the beneficiary. The mere existence of an advising bank in New York was not sufficient to confer jurisdiction.

Shenanigans and *American National Bank* are unconvincing opinions. A credit issuer's undertaking generally is governed by the law of the place where the credit issues.[18] An advising bank generally makes no undertaking, except to the extent of standing behind the accuracy of its

---

[14] No. 84 Civ. 8029 (RLC) (S.D.N.Y. July 30, 1985).

[15] For discussion of the nature of credits as commercial specialties that are distinct from contracts, see Chapter 3.

[16] 735 P.2d 747 (Alaska 1987).

[17] No. 85 Civ. 1519 (JFK) (S.D.N.Y. Jan. 21, 1987).

[18] See generally authority cited in ¶ 4.02.

advice.[19] It is stretching things to say, as these two opinions do, that the issuer or the advising bank is purposefully availing itself of the law of the jurisdiction where the beneficiary resides.[20]

Claims of jurisdiction over out-of-state beneficiaries have been more successful than have those over out-of-state issuers. In *Wyle v. Bank Melli*,[21] a California bank issued a credit in favor of an Iranian bank (Melli) as part of a four-party transaction in which Melli issued a first-demand guaranty. The California bank's credit secured the guaranty, and, when Melli called the credit, the trustee in bankruptcy of the California bank's customer, claiming fraud, sought to enjoin payment of the credit.

In the course of justifying its assertion of jurisdiction over Melli, the *Wyle* court noted that Melli maintained an office in San Francisco, and the court was "inclined toward the view that Bank Melli is 'present' here."[22] The court did not feel, however, that the evidence of Melli's presence was sufficiently developed, and it did not rely on that inclination in finding that Melli's contacts with California were sufficient to satisfy the *International Shoe* standard. The court relied instead on the fact that Melli was the beneficiary of the California bank's credit and thus, in the court's view, purposely had availed itself of the benefit of California law. The court characterized Melli's acceptance of a credit issued by a California bank as anchoring its indemnity in California and purposefully interjecting itself into California.[23] It is unfortunate that the *Wyle* court did not rest its holding on Melli's presence in California.

The district court in *Paccar International, Inc. v. Commercial Bank of Kuwait*[24] found the *Wyle* reasoning persuasive and held that a Kuwaiti bank was subject to personal jurisdiction in California by virtue of its draw on a letter of credit issued by a California bank. The beneficiary argued convincingly that it did not choose the issuer and therefore did not purposely avail itself of California law, but the court, relying on

---

[19] See U.C.P. art. 8 (1983).

[20] For discussion of decision invoking comity principles as a ground for refusing to exercise jurisdiction, see infra ¶ 11.01[7].

[21] 577 F. Supp. 1148 (N.D. Cal. 1983).

[22] Id. at 1160. The *Wyle* case also involved issues under the Foreign Sovereign Immunity Act, Pub. L. No. 94-583, 90 Stat. 2891 (codified in 28 U.S.C. §§ 1330, 1332(a)(2)–1332(a)(4), 1391(f), 1441(d), 1602–1611 (1988)). For a discussion of these questions, see ¶ 9.06[4][c].

[23] Wyle v. Bank Melli, 577 F. Supp. 1148, 1161 (N.D. Cal. 1983). The court also held that it had jurisdiction over the beneficiary of Bank Melli's guaranty. It justified that exercise of power by virtue of the failure of the beneficiary of the guaranty to comply with the plaintiff's discovery requests.

[24] 587 F. Supp. 783 (C.D. Cal. 1984), rev'd, 757 F.2d 1058 (9th Cir. 1985).

Wyle, held that the beneficiary implicitly relied on California law. The court conjectured that if the issuer had defaulted on the credit, the beneficiary would have sought to enforce the credit undertaking in a California court.

Wyle and *Paccar* may go too far in assuming that foreign banks purposely rely on American law when they take credits issued by American banks.[25] Foreign banks often rely on the reputation of the issuer and on their right of setoff.[26] Many credits are issued by a bank in one jurisdiction and are payable by a bank in a second jurisdiction. Under the reasoning of *Wyle* and *Paccar*, a beneficiary of that kind of credit has purposely availed itself of the law of both jurisdictions.[27]

The Court of Appeals for the Ninth Circuit reversed *Paccar* in an opinion that is critical of the *Wyle* holding.[28] In that opinion, the Ninth Circuit held that the existence of the letter of credit issued by a California-domiciled bank was not enough to establish jurisdiction. The court noted that the Kuwaiti bank did not participate in the selection of the California bank. The Ninth Circuit was not moved by the argument that California law governed the transaction. The draw by the Kuwaiti beneficiary did provide some contact with California. The court was not satisfied, however, that the contact was sufficient, especially in view of the court's position that (1) the draw was not a tort against the issuer and (2) the plaintiff, against whom it may have been a tort, was a Delaware corporation situated in the State of Washington.

In *Falcoal, Inc. v. Turkiye Komur Isletmeleri Kurumu*,[29] the court held that a Turkish beneficiary's draw on a guaranty issued by the Turkish branch of an American bank and secured by a credit issued by a Dallas issuer did not constitute sufficient activity in the United States to

---

[25] If the bank beneficiaries in the *Wyle* and *Paccar* cases relied on California law, they did so in vain, because the courts ultimately enjoined payment of the credits. In Arrow Trading Co. v. Sanyei Corp. (Hong Kong), Ltd., 576 F. Supp. 67 (S.D.N.Y. 1983), the court ruled that the Hong Kong beneficiary of two credits issued at the request of a New York account party had not "purposefully availed itself of the protection of New York's laws" (id. at 71) and was not subject to in personam jurisdiction in New York. The *Arrow Trading* opinion does not examine the letter of credit facts closely.

[26] For a discussion of setoff, see ¶ 9.06[3].

[27] Cf. Armada Supply, Inc. v. Wright, 858 F.2d 842 (2d Cir. 1988) (invoking in personam jurisdiction over Brazilian insurance company that issued certificate of insurance to company doing business in New York in connection with cargo whose destination, as reflected in certificate, was New York, all in connection with credit payable in New York).

[28] Paccar Int'l, Inc. v. Commercial Bank of Kuwait, 757 F.2d 1058 (9th Cir. 1985).

[29] 660 F. Supp. 1536 (S.D. Tex. 1987).

satisfy due process concerns. In *Falcoal*, the court applied the Foreign Sovereign Immunity Act[30] and concluded that, even though the allegedly fraudulent draw on the guaranty in Turkey had the effect of prompting the Turkish guaranty issuer to draw on the credit in Dallas, the impact of the conduct was not sufficient to satisfy due process safeguards.

Similarly, in *International Housing Ltd. v. Rafidain Bank Iraq*,[31] the court held it constitutionally impermissible to exercise jurisdiction over an Iraqi beneficiary that drew on bank guarantees issued by the Bahamian branch of a Canadian issuer. The beneficiary directed the paying bank to deposit the proceeds of the guarantees with the beneficiary's New York correspondent, but the court held that activity insufficient to satisfy due process.[32]

In *Weld Power Industries, Inc. v. C.S.I. Technologies, Inc.*,[33] the New Hampshire court refused to exercise jurisdiction over an out-of-state beneficiary that had drawn on a credit issued by a Massachusetts bank on behalf of a New Hampshire customer. Jurisdiction extended that far, the court held, would offend the due process rule of *International Shoe*.

In *C.E. Jamieson & Co. v. Willow Labs, Inc.*,[34] a federal court sitting in New York refused to exercise diversity jurisdiction over an account party. The plaintiff argued that the account party maintained an account with a New York bank, used a New York customs broker, and was doing business in New York under New York law. In fact, the defendant, a New Jersey company, maintained an account with a New Jersey bank that used a New York bank for its international banking ser-

---

[30] Foreign Sovereign Immunity Act, Pub. L. No. 94-583, 90 Stat. 2891 (codified in 28 U.S.C. §§ 1330, 1332(a)(2)–1332(a)(4), 1391(f), 1441(d), 1602–1611 (1988)). For further discussion of defenses under the Act, see ¶ 9.06[4][c]. For discussion of jurisdictional questions under the Foreign Sovereign Immunity Act, see ¶ 9.06[4][c].

[31] 712 F. Supp. 1112 (S.D.N.Y. 1989).

[32] Cf. California Overseas Bank v. French Am. Banking Corp., 154 Cal. App. 3d 179, 201 Cal. Rptr. 400 (1984) (Hanson, J., dissenting) (dissent claiming that majority would not have asserted jurisdiction over foreign beneficiary but for fact that its attorney made general appearance). But cf. Lister v. Morangorie Meccanica S.p.A., 728 F. Supp. 1524 (D. Utah 1990) (considering, among other important contacts with Utah, Italian beneficiary's draw on Minneapolis bank under credit apparently issued or confirmed at request of Utah bank in concluding that beneficiary was subject to in personam jurisdiction in Utah); Sorokwasz v. Kaiser, 549 So. 2d 1209 (Fla. Dist. Ct. App. 1989) (holding that solicitation of investment from Florida resident through telephone calls and correspondence to Florida and draw on letter of credit issued by Florida bank are sufficient contacts to render beneficiary subject to jurisdiction in Florida).

[33] 467 A.2d 568 (N.H. 1983).

[34] 585 F. Supp. 1410 (S.D.N.Y. 1984).

vices. Apparently, the New Jersey bank had transferred the defendant's funds to New York in connection with letters of credit issued by the New York bank. The *Jamieson* court held that the activity did not constitute doing business in New York.

[2] In Rem Jurisdiction

Some jurisdictional controversies turn on the notion that the credit obligation is a res over which the court may exercise jurisdiction. In *J. Zeevi & Sons v. Grindlays Bank (Uganda) Ltd.*,[35] the credit was issued by a Ugandan bank but was payable at a New York bank where the issuer maintained an account. When the issuer announced its intention to dishonor the credit engagement, the beneficiary sought attachment in New York; and the New York court held that it had jurisdiction because the cause of action arose in New York.

Similarly, in *Lustrelon, Inc. v. Prutscher*,[36] the plaintiff successfully invoked in rem jurisdiction. In *Lustrelon*, a New Jersey bank opened a credit in favor of the Austrian owner of certain tools. The credit was confirmed by an Austrian bank that honored the beneficiary's drafts. The court justified its jurisdiction on the ground that the opening bank from whom the confirming bank had yet to obtain reimbursement held funds of the confirming bank that the account party could attach.

In *Citibank, N.A. v. Klein*,[37] a Florida court evinced reluctance to assume jurisdiction when the account party sought to enjoin Citibank, the beneficiary, from collecting under the credit. The issuer was located in Florida, and the beneficiary, a New York bank, contested the Florida court's jurisdiction. Apparently, the account party argued that the court could reach the merits because the issuer was a debtor of the beneficiary. Under Florida law, the argument continued, courts may invoke in rem jurisdiction over such a dispute, the debt being a res located in Florida. The Florida court, noting that the letter itself was in New York, rejected the argument, relying on earlier Florida authority[38] to the effect that the issuer and the beneficiary do not stand in a debtor-creditor relationship. The *Citibank* court expressly held that Section 5-114(2)(b), by granting courts power to enjoin payment of letters of credit, does not alter Florida's jurisdictional rules. That latter holding is consistent with

---

[35] 37 N.Y.2d 220, 333 N.E.2d 168, 371 N.Y.S.2d 892 (1975), cert. denied, 432 U.S. 866 (1975).

[36] 178 N.J. Super. 128, 428 A.2d 518 (App. Div. 1981).

[37] 396 So. 2d 763 (Fla. Dist. Ct. App. 1981).

[38] See Tueta v. Rodriguez, 176 So. 2d 550 (Fla. Dist. Ct. App. 1965).

the section's explicit language that only a court of "appropriate jurisdiction may enjoin" payment of a credit. *Citibank* holds that the appropriateness of a court's jurisdiction is a matter not for credit law but for customary jurisdictional rules.

Thus, the jurisdictional rules of New Jersey, in the *Lustrelon* case, and of Florida, in the *Citibank* case, differ in theory and in result. The *Lustrelon* case did not consider the constitutional limitations on jurisdiction, although its facts seem to satisfy the rule of *International Shoe*.[39]

[3] Federal Diversity Jurisdiction

In *Baker v. National Boulevard Bank*,[40] the account parties, Illinois citizens, sued in an Illinois court to enjoin the issuer (an Illinois bank) from honoring the beneficiary's draft. The beneficiary, a Florida trust, sought removal to the federal district court, arguing that there was complete diversity and that the district court could invoke jurisdiction under the federal diversity statute.[41]

The beneficiary, claiming that the alignment of the account parties as plaintiffs and the issuer as defendant did not reflect the true interests of the parties, argued that the court should realign the parties to reflect the coinciding interests of the issuer and the account parties. Under that theory, the intervenor, the Florida trust, would be viewed as the defendant; the issuer and the account parties (of Illinois) would be viewed as the plaintiffs; and there would be complete diversity of citizenship necessary to satisfy federal diversity jurisdiction. In effect, the beneficiary argued that the issuer, fearing that the account parties would be unable to reimburse it, wanted the state court to enter the injunction in order to avoid the loss it would suffer if it were to honor the beneficiary's draft. The beneficiary argued that the issuer's failure to resist the state court's preliminary injunction supported realignment.

The *Baker* court cited a strict standard for realignment of parties when the petitioner is an intervenor, as the beneficiary was in *Baker*. "Only when it is shown that the plaintiff fraudulently misjoined the parties in an effort to deprive the federal courts of jurisdiction will a federal court realign the parties at the behest of an intervenor."[42] The benefi-

---

[39] For additional cases that dealt with the due process question in the context of foreign sovereign immunity, see ¶ 9.06[4][c].

[40] 399 F. Supp. 1021 (N.D. Ill. 1975).

[41] 28 U.S.C. § 1332 (1988).

[42] Baker v. National Boulevard Bank, 399 F. Supp. 1021, 1023 (N.D. Ill. 1975) (footnote omitted).

ciary sought to avoid the effect of that strict rule by referring to authority holding it permissible to remove when the only controversy in the litigation is that between the parties as realigned, the original cause being disregarded.

The *Baker* court proceeded to analyze the "true nature of the letter of credit transaction."[43] Noting that the issuer is under a legal duty to honor the beneficiary's draft, the issuer's fears of the account parties' ability to reimburse notwithstanding, the court held that the interests of the account parties and the issuer were diverse and granted the motion to remand the action to the state court.

Baker, with its emphasis on the issuer's legal obligation rather than on its fiscal concerns, apparently would refuse to align an issuer with the account party in any case, except, perhaps, one in which the plaintiff fraudulently attempts to deprive a federal court of its diversity jurisdiction. It is undeniable that the real interests of an account party and an issuer may conflict. More important, perhaps, than the legal duty on which *Baker* relies is the fact that issuers, especially bank issuers, are concerned about the reputation of their credits and about their standing as financial institutions.

At times, issuers obviously act out of concern for their own interests and, at other times, for the interests of their customers. In *KMW International v. Chase Manhattan Bank, N.A.*,[44] the issuer resisted vigorously the account party's efforts to enjoin payment under the issuer's credit and successfully convinced the court to recognize the threat to the issuer's "reputation"[45] and "commercial honor."[46] The court could have added that an injunction against the issuer might have invited retaliation of some kind by the beneficiary, an Iranian bank.[47] In *Banco Espanol de Credito v. State Street Bank & Trust Co.*,[48] on the other hand, the

---

[43] Id. at 1024.

[44] 606 F.2d 10 (2d Cir. 1979).

[45] Id. at 17.

[46] Id.

[47] Such fears are evident in the arguments of the issuers in other cases. See American Bell Int'l, Inc. v. Islamic Republic of Iran, 474 F. Supp. 420 (S.D.N.Y. 1979); United Technologies Corp. v. Citibank, N.A., 469 F. Supp. 473 (S.D.N.Y. 1979); Crocker Nat'l Bank v. Superior Court, 68 Cal. App. 3d 863, 136 Cal. Rptr. 481, cert. denied sub nom. Thomas J. Palmer, Inc. v. Superior Court, 434 U.S. 984 (1977).

[48] 266 F. Supp. 106 (D. Mass.), rev'd, 385 F.2d 230 (1st Cir. 1967), cert. denied, 390 U.S. 1013 (1968).

court detected a desire to protect its customer that had motivated the issuer to dishonor a beneficiary's drafts.[49]

The *Baker* rule forecloses any inquiry into intent or motivation, for an issuer is always under the duty on which the *Baker* court rested its refusal to accept diversity jurisdiction. Arguably, *Baker* seizes upon a technical point of credit law to avoid evaluation of the parties' real interests.

Hamilton v. Central National Bank[50] is in direct conflict with *Baker*. In *Hamilton*, the account party, an Ohio resident, sued the issuer, an Ohio bank, in state court to enjoin payment under the credit. The beneficiary, a non-Ohio resident, intervened and removed to federal court. The plaintiff sought to remand on the ground that diversity was incomplete, but the *Hamilton* court denied the remand on the ground that the issuer was a mere stakeholder whose Ohio residency did not destroy diversity jurisdiction.

In *Thomasson v. Amsouth Bank, N.A.*,[51] Alabama parties that had arranged for the issuance of a credit by an Alabama issuer in favor of a Texas beneficiary sued the issuer and the beneficiary. The court held that there was no diversity jurisdiction. *Thomasson*, then, is consistent with *Baker*.[52]

[4] Suits Against National Banks

There are two provisions in the federal statutes that bear on suits against bank issuers chartered by the federal government. The first lim-

---

[49] See also Bossier Bank & Trust Co. v. Union Planters Nat'l Bank, 550 F.2d 1077 (6th Cir. 1977); Fair Pavilions, Inc. v. First Nat'l City Bank, 19 N.Y.2d 512, 227 N.E.2d 839, 281 N.Y.S.2d 23 (1967) (cases evidencing similar concern).

[50] 40 U.C.C. Rep. Serv. (Callaghan) 1008 (N.D. Ohio 1984).

[51] 59 Bankr. 997 (N.D. Ala. 1986).

[52] In W.O.A., Inc. v. City Nat'l Bank, 640 F. Supp. 1157 (W.D. Ark. 1986), the account parties sued the beneficiaries and the issuers. One issuer and the account parties were citizens of the same state. The court held, without citing *Baker*, that because the issuer might pay the beneficiaries under Section 5-114(2), even though the account parties had alleged fraud, and because the issuer, to protect its right of reimbursement, had cross-claimed against the account parties, the interests of the account parties and the issuer were adverse; and complete diversity was lacking. In Tosco Corp. v. FDIC, 723 F.2d 1242 (6th Cir. 1983), a disappointed beneficiary sued the issuer for dishonoring the beneficiary's draft under the credit. The issuer then became insolvent, and the FDIC, as receiver, defended the plaintiff's claim. Because there was diversity jurisdiction at the time the plaintiff commenced the suit, the court held, the jurisdiction survived substitution of the FDIC as the defendant. For consideration of due process questions in diversity cases, see the discussion of the *Wyle* and *C.E. Jamieson* cases supra ¶ 11.01[1].

its the power of state courts to issue orders against national banks; the second limits, rather modestly, the venue in which parties may sue a national bank.

[a] The Anti-Attachment Section

Section 91 of the National Bank Act provides that "[N]o attachment, injunction or execution, shall be issued against [a national banking association] or its property before final judgment in any suit, action, or proceeding, in any State, county, or municipal court."[53] Taken literally, that language suggests that a state court may never allow a prejudgment attachment, a temporary restraining order, or a preliminary injunction against a national bank that issues a letter of credit. Cases construing the statute reflect a different view.

In *Third National Bank v. Impac Ltd.,*[54] the U.S. Supreme Court explicitly rejected the notion that the section absolutely prohibits state prejudgment writs. The Court held that the purpose of the statute is to protect the property of the national bank from suits by creditors and to avoid preferences and sanctioned the state court's preliminary injunction against the bank's private foreclosure sale of a debtor's property.[55]

The *Third National Bank* holding bears on credit cases. It suggests that a state court action is appropriate if the bank holds assets of a customer and if only those assets are affected by the writ.[56] Cases involving preliminary injunctions or restraining orders arguably are subject to the same kind of analysis. If they are, it is difficult to see how a state court's temporary restraining orders or preliminary injunctions against an issuer can jeopardize the bank's property in any way. A preliminary injunction that forbids a bank from honoring a beneficiary's draft does not deplete the bank's assets or prefer one creditor over another.

In *Interco, Inc. v. First National Bank,*[57] the account party first obtained a state court injunction against the beneficiary and then sued the issuing national bank in federal court. The *Interco* opinion does not address the question of the state court's power to enjoin a national bank,

---

[53] 12 U.S.C. § 91 (1988).

[54] 432 U.S. 312 (1977).

[55] It did so in the face of a strong dissent that argued for a literal reading of the statute and an absolute prohibition of state prejudgment writs against national banks. Id. at 324 (Blackmun, J., dissenting).

[56] Cf. Hohenberg Co. v. Comitex Knitters, Ltd., 104 Misc. 2d 232, 428 N.Y.S.2d 156 (Sup. Ct. 1980) (denying motion to confirm order of attachment without resort to 12 U.S.C. § 91). For discussion of additional attempts to attach a credit or its proceeds, see cases cited in ¶¶ 7.03[5], 9.05, 10.06[3].

[57] 560 F.2d 480 (1st Cir. 1977).

but it does observe that the complaint asserted that 12 U.S.C. § 91 prevents state courts from enjoining national banks.[58]

In an early case, *Drewes & Co. v. Ham & Seymour*,[59] the Louisiana court confronted the question squarely and held that 12 U.S.C. § 91 does not prohibit injunctions against national banks when the "final judgment" to which Section 91 refers is not one directed at the bank's assets. Banks may counter, of course, that the injunction affects the bank's reputation or even imperils assets unrelated to the credit transaction.[60] Section 91, however, does not address these perils. Its aim, as the *Third National Bank* case construes it, is to prevent creditors from obtaining prejudgment relief in state courts. Arguably, the *Drewes* case, a square holding on the question, is more persuasive than the observation in *Interco*.

In *Crocker National Bank v. Superior Court*,[61] the account party caused a national bank to issue a credit and later sought to enjoin payment of the credit in a California state court. The trial court issued a preliminary injunction, and the bank sued for a writ of prohibition on the ground that the injunction violated 12 U.S.C. § 91. The appellate court issued the writ after concluding (1) that the injunction exposed the issuer to the possibility that the beneficiary would set the unpaid credit obligation off against other obligations due from the beneficiary to the issuer and (2) that the issuer's reputation would be hurt by the injunction. The *Crocker* court distinguished *Drewes* on the ground that there was a special deposit to cover the credit in *Drewes* but that no such deposit existed in *Crocker*.

The *Crocker* case extends 12 U.S.C. § 91 well beyond the limits fashioned by the Supreme Court in the *Third National Bank* case. The injunction action in *Crocker* was not an attempt by a creditor to obtain assets of the bank in preference to other creditors. It is that attempt against which 12 U.S.C. § 91 guards, and the *Crocker* opinion does not satisfy the holding of *Third National Bank* that Section 91 be limited to those attempts.

---

[58] The *Third National Bank* opinion preceded that of *Interco* by less than two months.

[59] 157 La. 861, 103 So. 241 (1925).

[60] See, e.g., KMW Int'l v. Chase Manhattan Bank, N.A., 606 F.2d 10 (2d Cir. 1979); American Bell Int'l, Inc. v. Islamic Republic of Iran, 474 F. Supp. 420 (S.D.N.Y. 1979); United Technologies Corp. v. Citibank, N.A., 469 F. Supp. 473 (S.D.N.Y. 1979).

[61] 68 Cal. App. 3d 863, 136 Cal. Rptr. 481, cert. denied sub nom. Thomas J. Palmer, Inc. v. Superior Court, 434 U.S. 984 (1977).

[b] The Venue Section

Prior to 1982, federal law laid the venue for suits against national banks in the place where the bank was located.[62] As modified, the limited venue rule applies only to suits brought against national banks for which the FDIC is acting as receiver.[63]

[5] Bankruptcy Jurisdiction

Under federal law,[64] district courts have jurisdiction of:

1. All cases under the Bankruptcy Code;
2. Civil proceedings arising in or related to cases under the Bankruptcy Code; and
3. All of the property of the debtor as of the commencement of the case.

These provisions have raised a number of questions in letter of credit cases.

In *Thomasson v. Amsouth Bank, N.A.*,[65] the trustee in a Chapter 7 proceeding entered into an agreement with certain investors. Under that agreement, the investors caused a letter of credit to issue in the trustee's favor. When the trustee drew under the credit, the investors sued for an injunction and declaratory relief in an Alabama circuit court. The suit alleged fraud and sought, among other things, an injunction against the issuer and the beneficiary. The trustee removed to the district court, and the district court referred the matter to the bankruptcy court.[66] The bankruptcy court found that the suit was not a core proceeding under 28 U.S.C. § 1334(a) or 28 U.S.C. § 1334(b)[67] but that the district court had

---

[62] The Garn-St Germain Depository Institutions Act of 1982, § 406, Pub. L. No. 97-320, 96 Stat. 1469, 1512–1513 (1982), modified the rule, as explained in the text.

[63] See 12 U.S.C. § 94 (1988).

[64] 28 U.S.C. § 1334 (1988).

[65] 59 Bankr. 997 (N.D. Ala. 1986).

[66] Thomasson v. Amsouth Bank, N.A., No. CV-85-PT-2904S (Bankr. N.D. Ala. Jan. 7, 1986).

[67] The bankruptcy court devoted part of the opinion to explaining its view that the letter of credit was not property of the estate. In the course of that discussion, the court felt compelled to reject the rule of Twist Cap, Inc. v. Southeast Bank (In re Twist Cap, Inc.), 1 Bankr. 284 (Bankr. D. Fla. 1979). That case held that the trustee of an *account party* had an interest in a letter of credit. For discussion of the *Twist Cap* case and the line of authority that rejects it, see ¶ 7.03[3][a]. The *Thomasson* case involved a trustee of the *beneficiary*. The *Twist Cap* case was not at all apposite in *Thomasson*, although the court did not appear to appreciate the significance of the different roles the debtors played in the two credit transactions.

jurisdiction by virtue of the fact that the matter was a proceeding arising in or related to a case under the Bankruptcy Code. The court also found that the matter should be remanded to the state court under 28 U.S.C. § 1452(b). The district court adopted the findings of the bankruptcy court in an opinion that emphasized that the remand was warranted by three considerations: the state court's head start on the factual issues, comity, and the abstention doctrine of 28 U.S.C. § 1334(b).

In *Braucher v. Continental Illinois National Bank & Trust Co. (In re Illinois-California Express, Inc.)*,[68] the trustee of an account party that filed in bankruptcy after credits were issued entered into an agreement with the banks that had issued the credits for the allocation of proceeds from the sale of collateral that the banks held as security for the debtor's reimbursement obligation. When the banks honored drafts of the beneficiary after bankruptcy, the trustee, objecting that the banks had breached the agreement and that the credits had expired upon bankruptcy, sought damages and a declaratory judgment. The *Braucher* court held that the trustee's claims were not core proceedings but were related proceedings over which the bankruptcy court had no jurisdiction. The court acknowledged that the language of the federal statute[69] appeared to cover the claims in question but ruled that to extend the core proceeding section to these claims would violate the constitutional basis of *Northern Pipeline Construction Co. v. Marathon Pipe Line Co.*[70] The court acknowledged that it could adopt findings of fact and conclusions of law and refer them to the district court; but seeing the matter as one that should be a matter for abstention, the court declined to make findings and conclusions.

In a similar case, *Wisconsin Barge Line, Inc. v. INA (In re Wisconsin Barge Line, Inc.)*,[71] the court declined to make findings of fact and conclusions of law, in part, because a party that had guaranteed the debtor's obligation to reimburse the issuer had not filed in bankruptcy. The court held that the party had not sought protection under the Bankruptcy Code and should not have the benefit of litigation in the bankruptcy court. The *Wisconsin Barge Lines* court also made much of the fact that a suit to enjoin payment of a credit arises solely under state law. The suit therefore does not fall within the "arising under" jurisdiction conferred by 28 U.S.C. § 1334(b). The court agreed with *Braucher* that the matter was not a core proceeding but concluded that it did have "related to" jurisdiction under 28 U.S.C. § 1334(b), jurisdiction that the

---

[68] 50 Bankr. 232 (Bankr. D. Colo. 1985).

[69] 28 U.S.C. §§ 157(b)(2)(C), 157(b)(2)(O) (1988).

[70] 458 U.S. 50 (1982).

[71] 63 Bankr. 40 (Bankr. E.D. Mo. 1986).

court declined to exercise under the abstention doctrine of 28 U.S.C. § 1334(c)(1).[72]

In *Lombard-Wall, Inc. v. New York City Housing Development Corp.*,[73] the debtor sued the beneficiary of a credit issued for the debtor's account prior to bankruptcy. Once the beneficiary filed a claim in the bankruptcy, the claim against it by the debtor became a counter-claim, the court held, and therefore rendered the matter a core proceeding. The court concluded that there was a connection between the counterclaim filed by the debtor for wrongfully drawing on the letter of credit and the beneficiary's claim in bankruptcy, since both required the court to interpret the underlying contract. The court also noted that the beneficiary had consented to bankruptcy jurisdiction. *In re National Service Lines, Inc.*[74] involved a core proceeding, the court held, when the issuer of a credit sought to subrogate itself to the administrative expense claim of the beneficiary in the bankruptcy estate.

In *Beebe International, Inc. v. French American Banking Corp. (In re Wedtech Corp.)*,[75] the issuer of a credit on behalf of a party that later became bankrupt dishonored the beneficiary's request for payment. When the beneficiary sued for wrongful dishonor, the issuer removed the action from the district court to the bankruptcy court.[76] On the beneficiary's motion to remand, the bankruptcy court held that the case was one of "related jurisdiction" under 28 U.S.C. § 1334(b), for the following reasons:

1. The issuer was asserting a security interest in the debtor's property to the extent of payments made under the credit.
2. The outcome of the litigation would determine whether the issuer was a secured creditor or whether the beneficiary was an unsecured creditor.
3. The evidence on which the case turned involved the debtor.

The *Beebe* court emphatically rejected the beneficiary's argument that the commercial nature of credits makes litigation involving them a poor

---

[72] Cf. Weldpower Indus., Inc. v. C.S.I. Technologies, Inc. (In re Weldpower Indus., Inc.), 49 Bankr. 46 (Bankr. D.N.H. 1985) (refusing to decide jurisdictional question on ground that abstention doctrine permitted court to avoid substantial federal constitutional question: whether Fifth Amendment permits bankruptcy courts to exercise nationwide in personam jurisdiction).

[73] 48 Bankr. 986 (S.D.N.Y. 1985).

[74] 80 Bankr. 144 (Bankr. E.D. Mo. 1987).

[75] 72 Bankr. 313 (Bankr. S.D.N.Y. 1987).

[76] Under Section 157(a) of the Federal Code of Judicial Procedure, 28 U.S.C. § 157(a) (1988), the district courts, by standing order, may refer 28 U.S.C. § 1334(b) matters to the bankruptcy courts.

candidate for bankruptcy court jurisdiction. The court concluded that bankruptcy courts can deal with letter of credit matters with as much dispatch as the district courts can.

[6] Venue

In *Thomasson v. Amsouth Bank, N.A.*,[77] the trustee of a Texas corporation filed a bankruptcy petition in Houston. When certain Alabama investors sued an Alabama issuer and the trustee to enjoin payment on a letter of credit, the matter was removed to the federal court in Alabama. The trustee moved that the proceeding be transferred to Houston. The federal court sitting in Alabama remanded the matter to the Alabama state court and ruled that a change of venue to Houston was not warranted in view of the fact that many of the parties and much of the transaction originated in Alabama, whose law was applicable.[78]

In *American Construction Machinery & Equipment Corp. v. Mechanised Construction of Pakistan, Ltd.*,[79] the court considered the fact that a foreign corporation had caused letters of credit to issue in New York in deciding that New York was the proper venue for an action to confirm an arbitral award. In *Falcoal, Inc. v. Turkiye Komur Isletmeleri Kurumu*,[80] the court held, by way of dictum, that under Section 1391(f) of the Foreign Sovereign Immunity Act,[81] venue in Texas was improper for a suit by a Texas account party against a Turkish party that was beneficiary of a Turkish guaranty secured by a Texas issuer's standby credit.

[7] Comity

Given the close relationship in fact between the underlying transaction and the letter of credit transaction, and given the legal principle that the two transactions are independent, courts may have to decide whether the doctrine of comity applies when one suit arises out of the underlying transaction and the other arises out of the letter of credit transaction.

---

[77] 59 Bankr. 997 (N.D. Ala. 1986).

[78] In fact, Alabama law may not apply in the *Thomasson* case. The credit in that case was subject to the Uniform Customs, and Alabama has adopted the nonconforming version of Section 5-102(4) of the Code, stipulating that the Code does not apply if the credit is subject to the Uniform Customs. See Ala. Code § 7-5-102(4) (1984). For discussion of the nonconforming provision, see ¶ 4.05. The court observed that Alabama courts are as able as any to apply the Uniform Customs.

[79] No. 85 Civ. 3765 (JFK) (S.D.N.Y. Mar. 5, 1986).

[80] 660 F. Supp. 1536 (S.D. Tex. 1987).

[81] 28 U.S.C. § 1391(f) (1988).

In *Continental Time Corp. v. Swiss Credit Bank*,[82] the court invoked principles of comity to deny jurisdiction. In the *Continental Time* case, the beneficiary conveyed its interest in a Swiss bank's credit to two corporations. When the Swiss bank dishonored the transferees' request for payment, they sued the issuer in Switzerland. Thereafter one of the transferees reconveyed 75 percent of its interest to the original beneficiary, who instituted suit for damages against the issuer in the U.S. District Court for the Southern District of New York. The issuer asked the court to "exercise its discretionary power to dismiss suits involving the same parties where . . . the earlier initiated litigation will resolve the issues."[83] After considering the adequacy of the Swiss forum's relief, the identity of the parties and issues, the likelihood of prompt resolution in Switzerland, and the convenience of litigation there, the court concluded that the Swiss litigation, having been filed first, should proceed and that the New York suit should be dismissed.

In *University of Kansas Athletic Corp. v. Security National Bank*,[84] the account party sued the beneficiary in Missouri to enjoin draws on the credit. Later the beneficiary sued the issuer in Kansas for wrongful dishonor. Styling the Missouri suit as one on the underlying contract and the Kansas suit as one on the letter of credit, the issuer argued for a stay of the Kansas proceedings. The beneficiary resisted the stay, noting that it was contesting the Missouri court's jurisdiction over it personally and that the issuer had sought leave to intervene in the Missouri case. The Kansas tribunal, motivated by the doctrine of comity, entered the stay. The court reasoned that, the independence principle notwithstanding, comity dictated the result.

In another case invoking comity to refuse relief to a disappointed beneficiary, a New York court deferred to an attachment order entered by a Zurich court. The plaintiff in *Sabolyk v. Morgan Guaranty Trust Co.*[85] was a beneficiary of a credit issued by the defendant New York bank's Zurich branch. Before the beneficiary could draw, the Zurich court attached the credit under Swiss law that rendered it a crime for the Zurich branch to pay the beneficiary. When the beneficiary sued the issuer in New York, the issuer argued that the court should defer to the Zurich ruling. The *Sabolyk* court held that, since the Zurich court had jurisdiction over the parties and since the attachment order did not offend U.S. law or New York law, the doctrine of comity should apply and the issuer should have summary judgment.

---

[82] 543 F. Supp. 408 (S.D.N.Y. 1982).

[83] Id. at 409.

[84] No. 87-2116 (D. Kan. July 17, 1987).

[85] No. 84 Civ. 3179 (MJL) (S.D.N.Y. Nov. 27, 1984).

The *Sabolyk* court rejected the beneficiary's arguments that attachment of a letter of credit is indeed contrary to principles of New York law. In fact, attachment can seriously hamper the commercial effectiveness of credits,[86] and, since the rendering of *Sabolyk*, New York courts and federal courts have expressed their reservations about it in the letter of credit context.[87] That subsequent authority is persuasive, even though it sometimes presents issuers with problems. When a foreign court orders an issuer not to pay and a domestic court orders it to pay, one may say that the issuer faces a hard choice, especially if the laws of either one or both jurisdictions have fashioned criminal sanctions for recalcitrant litigants.

On the other hand, issuers with foreign branches assume the risk of doing business in two jurisdictions. It might be proper for the law to require them to price their product accordingly. If Switzerland entertains attachment actions that hamper credits, branches in Switzerland may be well advised to charge more for credits issued there or to refer their letter of credit customers to non-Swiss branches.

Unfortunately, the *Sabolyk* court insulated the issuer from the cost of the risk it assumed, passing it on to the beneficiary, who, unless he refused to accept credits issued by banks located in Switzerland, would be unable to prevent such losses. Issuers that pay their own funds to beneficiaries in the face of an attachment of their customers' funds are not violating the attachment but are protecting the integrity of the credit facility.[88]

¶ 11.02   JOINDER, INTERVENTION, AND CONSOLIDATION

This paragraph considers questions of joinder, intervention, and consolidation. Chapter 9 discusses standing issues.

---

[86] For discussion of those harmful effects, see ¶ 7.03[5].

[87] See authority cited in ¶ 7.03[5]. In Power Curber Int'l Ltd. v. National Bank of Kuwait SAK, [1981] 3 All E.R. 607 (C.A.), an English court applying North Carolina law declined to invoke the comity doctrine to defer to an attachment order entered by a Kuwaiti court.

[88] In Banco de Viscaya, S.A. v. First Nat'l Bank, 514 F. Supp. 1280 (N.D. Ill. 1981), vacated, id., a federal court ordered a Chicago bank to pay the holder of drafts drawn under a credit issued by the bank's Abu Dhabi branch. The branch had accepted the drafts, as the credit required. The court issued its order despite an earlier Abu Dhabi court order to the branch not to pay the holder, but to pay the funds into a suspense account. For further discussion of the effect of comity on jurisdiction, see supra ¶ 11.01[1].

[1] Joinder and Intervention

[a] Federal Rules

In *Banco De Vizcaya, S.A. v. First National Bank*,[89] the court confronted a joinder question under the federal rules. First National Bank's Abu Dhabi branch issued a negotiation credit, which instructed the negotiating bank to seek reimbursement from First National in Chicago. The credit called for time drafts payable after First National's acceptance. First National accepted the drafts, but, before payment, the account party obtained an injunction against the Abu Dhabi branch. The negotiating bank then instituted suit in Chicago,[90] and First National apparently argued that Rule 19(a)[91] of the Federal Rules of Civil Procedure required joinder of the account party. The court rejected the issuer's argument, holding that Rule 19(a) does not mandate joinder, because the credit engagement is independent of the underlying contract. The court also held that the account party could recoup any loss from the beneficiary and that it did not need to be a party to the beneficiary's claim on the credit. The court held further that joining the account party would not protect First National from inconsistent rulings, because "[t]he risk of double liability is plainly not the result of the absence of any party, but the result of the mistaken interpretation of letters of credit given by the Abu Dhabi court."[92]

The court added that even if the account party were an indispensable party under Rule 19(a), the court would have exercised its prerogative under Rule 19(b) to deny dismissal of the suit rather than forcing the beneficiary to litigate its claim in a forum whose courts, in its view, do not understand credit law. The court had noted earlier in its opinion that the beneficiary had obtained the protection of a credit reimbursable in U.S. dollars from a U.S. bank precisely because the beneficiary did not want to litigate in other jurisdictions.

Although there are often common questions in the three disputes (that between the beneficiary and the issuer, that between the issuer and the account party, and that between the beneficiary and the account party), courts are well advised to avoid litigating the last two controversies in a suit involving the first. The first dispute arises out of the credit en-

---

[89] 514 F. Supp. 1280 (N.D. Ill. 1981), vacated, id.

[90] It is not clear from the *Banco De Vizcaya* opinion whether the plaintiff sued on the credit or on the acceptances. For a discussion of that feature of the case, see ¶ 2.09[1].

[91] Fed. R. Civ. P. 19(a).

[92] Banco De Vizcaya, S.A. v. First Nat'l Bank, 514 F. Supp. 1280, 1288 (N.D. Ill. 1981).

gagement, which must be independent of the other two relationships in order for the credit to work as a commercial device.[93]

In *Johnson v. Levy Organization Development Co.*,[94] the account party sued the beneficiary for breach of the underlying contract. The beneficiary drew on the credit; and the issuer sought to intervene in two ways: first, to interplead the credit proceeds and, second, to obtain judgment against the account party on its reimbursement obligation if the court ordered payment of the credit proceeds to the beneficiary. The district court allowed the petition for the first purpose but denied it for the second.

[b] State Rules

Joinder questions may depend on variations in state law. *Housing Securities, Inc. v. Maine National Bank*[95] is a case similar to *Banco De Vizcaya*. In *Housing Securities*, the beneficiary of a credit sued the issuer, who objected that the account party should be joined. The issuer had dishonored the beneficiary's demand for payment and argued that the court might find the issuer liable to the beneficiary and that later a different court might find the payment improper and might deny the issuer reimbursement from the account party. The court rejected the argument, noting that the issuer's obligation to the beneficiary is independent of the application agreement between the issuer and the account party. The opinion observes further that if questions of revocability and compliance are close, it may be necessary to join the account party in the beneficiary's suit in order to avoid inconsistent rulings.

Neither the *Banco De Vizcaya* case nor the *Housing Securities* case considers the fact that the standard for issuer liability under the credit may differ from that under the application agreement.[96] If the standards

---

[93] For a discussion of the independence principle, see ¶¶ 2.08–2.10. But see Note, "The Application of Compulsory Joinder, Intervention, Impleader and Attachment to Letter of Credit Litigation," 52 Fordham L. Rev. 957 (1984) (generally advocating more liberal application of joinder rules than that advanced in text); Phoenix Mut. Life Ins. Co. v. Seafarers Officers & Employees Pension Plan, 128 F.R.D. 25 (E.D.N.Y. 1989) (allowing issuer to implead guarantor of account party's reimbursement obligation in issuer's declaratory judgment suit against beneficiary); Banco Continental v. First Nat'l Bank, 100 F.R.D. 426 (E.D. Tenn. 1983) (allowing account party to intervene in suit by beneficiary against issuer).

[94] 789 F.2d 601 (7th Cir. 1986).

[95] 391 A.2d 311 (Me. 1978).

[96] For discussion of the standards of liability in the two instances, see ¶ 9.03[1][a].

differ, there is no reason to join the account party in an action on the credit.

A Montana case suggests that the independence of the credit engagement should prevent the account party from joining his dispute with the beneficiary to a suit between the beneficiary and the issuer. In *Sherwood & Roberts, Inc. v. First Security Bank*,[97] the beneficiary sued the issuer for wrongful dishonor. The credit, inartfully drafted,[98] was "exercisable . . . upon the unremedied default"[99] of the account party under specified documents. The issuer claimed that the account party was in default because of the beneficiary's conduct, and the account party sought to intervene in the letter of credit litigation under Montana practice.[100] The court held that the credit undertaking was independent of the equities in the underlying dispute and that the account party did not have a right to intervene. The issuer had brought a third-party action against the account party, however, and the court held that, as a third-party defendant, the account party could assert its claims against the beneficiary.

In *National Bank & Trust Co. of North America, Ltd. v. J.L.M. International, Inc.*,[101] one of two joint venturers sued under a credit without joining its coventurer. The court held that the one joint venturer could maintain the action.[102]

[2] Consolidation

Concern for the independence of the credit should play a role in evaluating the efforts of parties to consolidate actions on the underlying transaction with actions on the credit. In *Bank of Montreal v. Eagle Associates*,[103] the beneficiary of a four-party credit[104] brought two actions:

---

[97] 682 P.2d 149 (Mont. 1984).

[98] For criticism of credits, such as that in the *Sherwood & Roberts* case, see ¶ 2.05.

[99] Sherwood & Roberts, Inc. v. First Sec. Bank, 682 P.2d 149, 151 (Mont. 1984).

[100] Mont. R. Civ. Proc. 24(a).

[101] 421 F. Supp. 1269 (S.D.N.Y. 1976).

[102] Cf. First Commercial Bank v. Gotham Originals, Inc., 101 A.D.2d 790, 476 N.Y.S.2d 835 (Sup. Ct. 1984), aff'd, 64 N.Y.2d 287, 475 N.E.2d 1255, 486 N.Y.S.2d 715 (1985) (holding that beneficiary was not necessary party in action to enforce acceptances created under letter of credit).

[103] 117 F.R.D. 530 (S.D.N.Y. 1987).

[104] For discussion of four-party credits similar to that in the *Bank of Montreal* case, see ¶ 7.04[4][b].

one against the borrowers who had pledged investor notes and a second against the investors and the issuer of a credit that secured the notes. The *Bank of Montreal* opinion, without mentioning the independence principle, held that the two actions presented common questions of law and fact and that consolidation was appropriate. The action on the credit in the second suit did not involve questions of fact and law in common with the first suit. The action on the letter of credit turned on the propriety of presenting the demand for payment at the issuer's counters in New York instead of in Los Angeles, as the credit required. That issue did not arise in any of the other claims and did not support consolidation.

The first and second suits may have had common questions of law and fact by virtue of the presence in both of them of defenses on the investors' notes. Although the *Bank of Montreal* court did not mention it, by bringing the action on the investors' notes with the action on the credit, the beneficiary weakened its argument that the defendants' motion to consolidate should have been denied.

¶ 11.03 QUESTIONS OF EVIDENCE AND PROOF

[1] Holders in Due Course

There are a few questions of evidence and proof that either arise frequently in the credit context or are somewhat peculiar to credit law. The burden of proof for those asserting holder in due course status is one of the questions that arises frequently, but the answer here is no different from the answer in other contexts. Generally, the question arises under Section 5-114(2), which renders various fraud defenses unavailable if the party seeking payment under the credit is a holder in due course. It is not necessary for a party seeking payment to show that he is such a holder, unless the issuer or account party establishes one of the defenses defined in the section.[105] Once the account party or issuer establishes fraud or one of the other defenses, however, the party seeking payment bears the burden of proving his holder in due course status.[106]

---

[105] See Bank of Canton, Ltd. v. Republic Nat'l Bank, 509 F. Supp. 1310 (S.D.N.Y.), aff'd, 636 F.2d 30 (2d Cir. 1980); United Bank Ltd. v. Cambridge Sporting Goods Corp., 41 N.Y.2d 254, 360 N.E.2d 943, 392 N.Y.S.2d 265 (1976); First Nat'l Bank v. Carmouche, 515 So. 2d 785 (La. 1987). For a discussion of these defenses, see ¶ 7.04[3].

[106] See, e.g., Banco Espanol de Credito v. State St. Bank & Trust Co., 409 F.2d 711 (1st Cir. 1969); Scarsdale Nat'l Bank & Trust Co. v. Toronto-Dominion Bank, 533 F. Supp. 378 (S.D.N.Y. 1982); Morgan v. Depositors Trust Co., 33 U.C.C. Rep. Serv. (Callaghan) 1473 (Me. Super. Ct. Kennebec County 1982); Balbo Oil Corp. v. Zigourakis, 40 Misc. 2d 710, 243 N.Y.S.2d 806 (Sup. Ct. 1963).

In one case, the court shifted that burden to the account party, requiring it to show that parties seeking payment under the credit were not holders in due course. In *Eljay, Jrs., Inc. v. Rahda Exports,*[107] the account party sought a preliminary injunction against payment of letters of credit to banks that had presented the beneficiary's drafts under the credits. The *Eljay, Jrs.* court held that no preliminary injunction could issue unless the account party demonstrated a likelihood of success on the merits. By failing to negate the possibility that the presenting banks were holders in due course, the court held, the account party had not demonstrated that likelihood. The rules of equity, with their concern that petitioners satisfy stringent requirements in order to have equitable relief, drive the result in *Eljay, Jrs.,* and the injunction setting limits the extent of the shift that the *Eljay, Jrs.* court would effect.

Eljay, Jrs. would not alter the traditional rule in the different case involving a beneficiary suing the issuer for wrongful dishonor. In that case, the issuer would make out a sufficient defense to payment by showing one of the Section 5-114(2) defenses and would not have to prove the negative: that the beneficiary is not a holder in due course. In this action against the issuer, the holder in due course issue would be part of the beneficiary's case in chief.

In *Bank of North Carolina, N.A. v. Rock Island Bank,*[108] the court misapplied these procedural rules for holders in due course. In the *Rock Island* case, the credit undertaking ran to the "holder in due course"[109] of a note made by the account party. The credit itself required the beneficiary to establish that it was a holder in due course. Curiously, however, the *Rock Island* court invoked the procedural rule that the beneficiary need not establish holder in due course status until the account party demonstrates fraud. The court relied on procedural rules in Article 3 and held that the beneficiary could recover "under the instrument"[110] without proving that it was a holder in due course. The claim, however, was not on the instrument (the note) but on the credit. Procedural rules on burden of proof for recovery on negotiable instruments should not govern the substantive requirement of credit law that the issuer pay only a beneficiary that has satisfied the credit's conditions. In this case, the condition was that the beneficiary be a holder in due course.

---

[107] 99 A.D.2d 408, 470 N.Y.S.2d 12 (1984).

[108] 630 F.2d 1243 (7th Cir. 1980).

[109] Id. at 1246 n.4.

[110] Id. at 1246. For criticism of credits that are subject to factual conditions such as those in the *Rock Island* case, see ¶ 2.05[2].

[2] Beneficiaries in General

The *Rock Island* opinion is also troubling in its assertion that Article 5 of the Uniform Commercial Code (UCC or the Code) "does not indicate whether the person seeking to recover under the letter of credit bears the burden of proof on the question whether he is 'the person entitled to honor.'"[111] Certainly, any party seeking recovery on a specialty should bear the burden of proving that he comes within the class of persons entitled to enforce the specialty. That burden is often light. A holder of a negotiable instrument can recover on the instrument by producing it and establishing the defendant's signature.[112] Presumably, under a negotiation credit, the negotiating bank would be required to show only that it holds the beneficiary's draft drawn under the credit.

Whether the beneficiary or the negotiating bank bears the burden of proving that documents comply with the terms of the credit, however, is a different question. Article 16(e) of the Uniform Customs and Practice for Documentary Credits (UCP or the Uniform Customs) and the estoppel rules fashioned by many courts[113] suggest that a presenter bears the burden of proving the conformity only of those documents to which the issuer makes timely objection.

[3] Evidentiary Issues

The unique nature of the credit sometimes bears on rules of evidence. In *Siderius, Inc. v. Wallace Co.*,[114] the court ruled that it was improper for the trial court to refer to a jury the question whether a bill of lading satisfied the terms of the credit. The trial court permitted the jury to decide whether it was the intent of the parties that time be of the essence in the issuance of the bill. The *Siderius* court held that question to be one of law.[115]

---

[111] Id. at 1247.

[112] See U.C.C. § 3-307.

[113] For a discussion of these estoppel rules, see ¶ 6.06[1].

[114] 583 S.W.2d 852 (Tex. Civ. App. 1979).

[115] The court also held that it was harmless error for the matter to be submitted to the jury. In Homestate Sav. Ass'n v. Westwind Exploration, Inc., 684 S.W.2d 788 (Tex. Ct. App.), aff'd, 696 S.W.2d 378 (Tex. 1985), the Texas Court of Appeals reversed a judgment on a verdict construing a credit against the issuer and rendered judgment for the issuer. In affirming the *Homestate* decision, the Texas Supreme Court held that compliance issues are questions of fact for the jury only if there is an ambiguity in the credit. Accord Employers Mut. Casualty Co. v. Tascosa Nat'l Bank, 767 S.W.2d 279 (Tex. Ct. App. 1989).

In *Far Eastern Textile, Ltd. v. City National Bank & Trust Co.*,[116] the credit called for a purchase order signed by Larry Fannin. The beneficiary presented a purchase order signed "Larry Fannin by Paul Thomas" and attempted to introduce evidence that Thomas was authorized to sign Fannin's name. The court held the purchase order to be noncomplying and ruled that the evidence was improper.

In *Board of County Commissioners v. Colorado National Bank*,[117] the issuer of a standby credit sought to introduce evidence to show the intent of the parties in causing the credit to issue and evidence to show that the beneficiary did not sustain any damages as a consequence of the account party's breach of the underlying transaction. The court held the evidence irrelevant.

The *Siderius*, *Far Eastern Textile*, and *Board of County Commissioners* cases demonstrate loyalty to the independence principle.[118] That principle asserts that the credit, in order to maintain its commercial effectiveness, must remain independent of the underlying transaction between the account party and the beneficiary. If the court in *Siderius*, for example, had permitted the jury to consider the buyer's and seller's intent concerning the bill of lading, it would have violated the independence principle. The engagement of the buyer's bank to honor the seller's draft, accompanied by a bill of lading bearing a certain date, should not depend on that intent. The issuer should be able to determine the seller's compliance with the credit by examining the face of the documents, not by delving into such time-consuming and often-contested evidentiary issues as the intent of parties to a contract of sale.

The *Far Eastern* court's refusal to admit evidence of the agent's authority rejects a rule requiring the issuer to make a similar inquiry. The *Far Eastern* court held that that inquiry is not consistent with the "ministerial"[119] role that the issuer plays. The implication is clear: time-consuming inquiries into matters beyond examination of the documents on their face is not consistent with efficient operation of credits. The *Far Eastern* and *Siderius* cases reflect adherence to the strict compliance rule[120] as well as to the independence principle.

Considerations of strict compliance were absent in the *Board of County Commissioners* case, but regard for the independence principle

---

[116] 430 F. Supp. 193 (S.D. Ohio 1977).

[117] 43 Colo. App. 186, 607 P.2d 1010 (1979), modified, 634 P.2d 32 (Colo. 1981).

[118] For a discussion of the independence principle, see ¶¶ 2.08, 2.09.

[119] Far E. Textile, Ltd. v. City Nat'l Bank & Trust Co., 430 F. Supp. 193, 196 (S.D. Ohio 1977).

[120] For a discussion of that strict compliance rule, see ¶¶ 6.03–6.05.

was evidently controlling. In that case, the credit issued to secure a developer's obligation to the municipality to build improvements in a real estate development. The developer went bankrupt before constructing the development. The issuer offered to show that the purpose of the credit was to protect the county from having to appropriate funds for the improvements. Since the development never came into being, the issuer argued, the county did not have to appropriate any funds; and enforcement of the credit would not have served its original purpose. The *Board of County Commissioners* court refused to violate the independence principle by inquiring into issues outside those evident from the face of the documents. Evidence of the parties' intent or of the absence of damages[121] was not admissible.

¶ 11.04　INJUNCTIONS

Frequent, indiscriminate use of injunctions against honor of a beneficiary's drafts or demands for payment under a credit destroys the effectiveness of the credit as a commercial device. The primary purpose of the credit is to render payment against conforming documents swift and inevitable. The purpose and effect of injunctions and restraining orders are to retard and question the payment of credits and render them the functional equivalent of performance bonds.

Courts generally have recognized the hazard injunctions pose to the credit device and have fashioned limitations on the injunction's use. These limitations include the standard prerequisites that equity requires for the injunction (a creature of equity) and additional prerequisites for the use of the injunction in the most common credit situation: when the account party claims that there is fraud in the transaction.[122]

[1]　Equity Standard

Although the various jurisdictions state the rule differently, most require the party seeking an injunction to show that he has a substantial probability of success on the merits and that he will suffer irreparable injury without an injunction or, stated differently, that he does not have an adequate remedy at law.[123]

---

[121] For more on the damages question in improper dishonor cases, see ¶ 9.02[5].

[122] For further discussion of the equity prerequisites, see ¶ 7.04[1].

[123] In a 1989 article, Professor Laycock argued that, in practice, courts do not observe this requirement. See Laycock, "The Death of Irreparable Injury," 103 Harv. L. Rev. 90 (1989). As the discussion in the text and the cases cited demonstrate, whatever validity Professor Laycock's thesis may have in other areas of the law, it is invalid in cases involving attempts by account parties to enjoin payment under letters of credit.

In *KMW International v. Chase Manhattan Bank, N.A.*,[124] the court set forth the Second Circuit's standard for preliminary injunctive relief: "a showing of (a) possible irreparable harm and (b) either (1) likelihood of success on the merits or (2) sufficiently serious questions going to the merits to make them a fair ground for litigation and a balance of hardships tipping decidedly toward the party requesting the preliminary relief."[125]

In *Itek Corp. v. First National Bank*,[126] the court stated the standard for the First Circuit somewhat differently:

> The Court must find: (1) that a plaintiff will suffer irreparable injury if the injunction is not granted; (2) that such injury outweighs any harm which granting injunctive relief would inflict on the defendant; (3) that plaintiff has exhibited a likelihood of success on the merits; and (4) that the public interest will not be adversely affected by the granting of the injunction.[127]

Other jurisdictions have adopted similar rules with similar language,[128] but the fact is that any statement of the rule is less important than the ways courts apply it. On its face, the rule of the First Circuit appears to impose greater burdens on the plaintiff than the Second Circuit does. The *Itek* case, however, on facts remarkably similar to those of *KMW*,[129] issued the injunction, while the *KMW* court did not. The cases usually turn on the court's view of the adequacy of remedies at law and

---

[124] 606 F.2d 10 (2d Cir. 1979).

[125] Id. at 14 (authority omitted).

[126] 511 F. Supp. 1341 (D. Mass. 1981). The *Itek* court entered a preliminary injunction and later made the injunction permanent. That permanent injunction was vacated on appeal. See Itek Corp. v. First Nat'l Bank, 704 F.2d 1 (1st Cir. 1983).

[127] Id. at 1348 (authority omitted).

[128] See, e.g., Bush Dev. Corp. v. Harbour Place Assocs., 632 F. Supp. 1359 (E.D. Va. 1986); Edgewater Constr. Co. v. Percy Wilson Mortgage & Fin. Corp., 44 Ill. App. 3d 220, 357 N.E.2d 1307 (1976); Atlas Mini Storage, Inc. v. First Interstate Bank, 426 N.W.2d 686 (Iowa Ct. App. 1988); Morgan v. Depositors Trust Co., 33 U.C.C. Rep. Serv. (Callaghan) 1473 (Me. Super. Ct. Kennebec County 1982); Werner v. A.L. Grootemaat & Sons, 80 Wis. 2d 513, 259 N.W.2d 310 (1977). For further discussion of the equity standard and cases invoking it, see ¶ 7.04[1].

[129] The *Itek* opinion attempts to distinguish the *KMW* case on the ground that the Iranian beneficiary in *KMW* had not demanded payment, while the Iranian beneficiary in *Itek* had demanded payment. See also Rockwell Int'l Sys., Inc. v. Citibank, N.A., 719 F.2d 583 (2d Cir. 1983) (making same distinction). It is clear from reading the opinions, however, that the *KMW* court felt that the account party, who had chosen to do business with the Iranian buyer, should bear the costs of the Iranian upheaval, while the *Itek* and *Rockwell* courts thought that account parties, which had made the same choice, should not bear those costs.

on its evaluation of the harm the plaintiff will suffer. These two considerations, although stated differently, usually turn on the same facts. In all cases, the judgment involves a balancing of interests by the courts.

Whatever variation in the language the courts adopt, it is always difficult for the account party to satisfy these threshold requirements because there are only two possible cases in which the account party will succeed on the merits:

1. When payment is improper because the documents are defective on their face; or
2. When payment is improper because of latent defects, such as fraud, forgery, and the like.

In the first case, there is usually no need for an injunction, because if the issuer honors documents that are patently defective, the issuer has violated Section 5-109 of the Code and Article 15 of the Uniform Customs. In that case, the account party has an adequate remedy at law—a claim for breach of contract against the issuer.

In the second case, when the documents carry latent defects, the beneficiary has breached its Section 5-111(1) warranty, may have practiced fraud, and probably is in breach of the underlying contract. In that case, the account party has a cause of action against the beneficiary for breach of warranty, fraud, or breach of contract. In short, it is not easy for the account party to satisfy the equity prerequisites.

[2] Absence of an Adequate Remedy at Law: Irreparable Injury

A review of some of the cases illustrates the meaning courts have given to the critical prerequisite for injunctive relief in the credit setting: absence of an adequate remedy at law or irreparable injury.

[a] Relief Requested

In *United Technologies Corp. v. Citibank, N.A.*,[130] the account party, the seller of goods to an Iranian buyer, alleged that it had fully performed its contract, that any demand for payment under the credit would be fraudulent, and that the domestic turmoil in Iran rendered its remedy in Iranian courts inadequate. The court rejected the account

---

[130] 469 F. Supp. 473 (S.D.N.Y. 1979).

party's argument, noting that the plaintiff chose to do business in Iran and took the risk of political turmoil in that country.[131]

In *Stromberg-Carlson Corp. v. Bank Melli Iran*,[132] however, the court, while implementing the same Second Circuit rule that the court used in *United Technologies*, viewed the Iranian turmoil differently. Because of the period of crisis and uncertainty in that country, and because the new Iranian government's interest in the plaintiff's contract might conflict with those of the former government, the court thought the balance of hardships tipped decidedly in favor of the plaintiff. The court laid great store by the fact that the plaintiff sought the "modest"[133] relief of an injunction ordering the issuer to give the plaintiff (the account party) ten days' notice of a demand from the beneficiary.[134]

[b] Monetary Damages

The ruling in *KMW* against the plaintiff account party stemmed in part from the fact that the potential harm to the account party was "financial in nature or, at best, of a speculative quality."[135] In *State v. Lasky*,[136] the issuer paid the credit, and the account party sought an injunction ordering the beneficiary to return the payment. The trial court entered the order, and the beneficiary obtained a writ of prohibition against the trial court on the ground that it had exceeded its jurisdiction. The loss of use of the funds during litigation, the *Lasky* court held, did not support the grant of injunctive relief.[137]

---

[131] Accord KMW Int'l v. Chase Manhattan Bank, N.A., 606 F.2d 10 (2d Cir. 1979). But cf. Itek Corp. v. First Nat'l Bank, 730 F.2d 19 (1st Cir. 1984) (holding that any attempt by account party to recover from beneficiary in Iran would be futile and that account party did not have adequate remedy at law); Wyle v. Bank Melli, 577 F. Supp. 1148 (N.D. Cal. 1984) (same).

[132] 467 F. Supp. 530 (S.D.N.Y. 1979).

[133] Id. at 532.

[134] Cf. Paccar Int'l, Inc. v. Commercial Bank of Kuwait, 587 F. Supp. 783 (C.D. Cal. 1984), rev'd on other grounds, 757 F.2d 1058 (9th Cir. 1985) (holding that possibility of irreparable harm is enough to justify preliminary injunction). But cf. Universal Marine Ins. Co. v. Beacon Ins. Co., 577 F. Supp. 829 (W.D.N.C. 1984) (holding that since issuer of credit was already enjoined from paying, it would do no harm to deny account party's effort to enjoin beneficiary from seeking payment under credit).

[135] KMW Int'l v. Chase Manhattan Bank, N.A., 606 F.2d 10, 15 (2d Cir. 1979).

[136] 581 S.W.2d 935 (Mo. Ct. App. 1979).

[137] Accord Cappaert Enters. v. Citizens & S. Int'l Bank, 486 F. Supp. 819 (E.D. La. 1980).

In *Morgan v. Depositors Trust Co.*,[138] the account party sought to enjoin payment of a standby credit. The court held that monetary loss is not enough to satisfy the requirement of showing irreparable harm and noted that the account party could resort to the remedy of attachment.[139]

---

[138] 33 U.C.C. Rep. Serv. (Callaghan) 1473 (Me. Super. Ct. Kennebec County 1982).

[139] In Sperry Int'l Trade, Inc. v. Government of Isr., 670 F.2d 8 (2d Cir. 1982), the court held that, by definition, "irreparable injury" is the kind of injury for which an award of money damages cannot provide compensation. The *Sperry* opinion termed "exceptional" (id. at 12) the rule of NMC Enters., Inc. v. CBS, 14 U.C.C. Rep. Serv. (Callaghan) 1427 (N.Y. Sup. Ct. 1974), to the effect that a buyer threatened by bankruptcy faced irreparable injury. In Philipp Bros. v. Oil Country Specialists, Ltd., 709 S.W.2d 262 (Tex. Ct. App. 1986), the court held that payment under a credit that would render the account party's net worth lower than the level required by its creditors and that would give the creditors the right to resort to the account party's property satisfied the equity requirement that the account party show irreparable harm; but, in Wurttembergische Fire Ins. Co. v. Pan Atl. Underwriters, Ltd., 133 A.D.2d 268, 519 N.Y.S.2d 57 (1987), the court held that the risk of the account party's insolvency was not sufficient to show irreparable harm, especially when the court had ordered that the proceeds of the credit be subject to a constructive trust pending action by the court. In Rockwell Int'l Sys., Inc. v. Citibank, N.A., 719 F.2d 583 (2d Cir. 1983), the same court that decided *KMW* and *Sperry* held that, in some instances, a claim for monetary damages is an inadequate remedy. The facts in *Rockwell* were markedly similar to those in *KMW*. The court distinguished the *KMW* case, in part, on the ground that *Rockwell* arrived at the court after repeated instances of Iranian banks' calling of standby credits had evidenced a pattern of unfair conduct by the Iranian beneficiaries. Philadelphia Gear Corp. v. Central Bank, 717 F.2d 230 (5th Cir. 1983), is another case that accepts the general principle that a claim for monetary damages at law is an adequate remedy that bars equitable relief. But cf. Bush Dev. Corp. v. Harbour Place Assocs., 632 F. Supp. 1359 (E.D. Va. 1986) (holding that beneficiary's precarious financial condition and probability of nominal harm to defendant account party satisfied balancing test and rendered injunction proper); Mitsui Mfrs. Bank v. Texas Commerce Bank, 159 Cal. App. 3d 1051, 206 Cal. Rptr. 218 (1984) (suggesting that cause of action against commercial bank still may leave account party with irreparable injury); Ciambotti v. Decatur-St. Louis, Lupin, Properties Ventures, 533 So. 2d 1352 (La. Ct. App. 1988) (holding that injunction against draw by beneficiary should issue when evidence showed that beneficiary was insolvent); Seguin Sav. Ass'n v. Vista Verde Plaza Joint Venture, 7 U.C.C. Rep. Serv. 2d (Callaghan) 862 (Tex. Ct. App. 1988) (holding that precarious financial condition of beneficiary rendered account party's remedy at law inadequate); Alamo Sav. Ass'n v. Forward Constr. Corp., 746 S.W.2d 897 (Tex. Ct. App. 1988) (holding it proper to enjoin draw under credit by beneficiary whose negative net worth exceeded $100 million).

[c] Suits at Law Against Solvent Defendants

In *Interco, Inc. v. First National Bank*,[140] a state court had restrained the beneficiary from drawing on credits, and the account party sought an injunction against the issuer. The *Interco* court denied the request, holding that if the bank issuer paid the credit improperly, the account party would have a cause of action against it at law. The account party had argued that the legal remedy for wrongful honor of a credit was speculative. Article 5 is silent on the damages question. The account party was arguing that uncertainty in the law of damages left it without an "adequate" remedy if the preliminary injunction did not issue and that it had demonstrated irreparable harm.

The *Interco* court pointed out that general damages provisions in the Code do indeed provide direction for the account party's damages. Section 1-106, a provision that Massachusetts courts (the case having arisen in Massachusetts) had embraced, instructs courts to administer remedies liberally in order to put the aggrieved party in as good a position as proper performance of the credit would yield. The court found that instruction sufficient to provide the account party with an adequate remedy at law.

In *Shaffer v. Brooklyn Park Garden Apartments*,[141] the court issued an injunction, even though the potential defendant in an action at law would have been a bank. In *Shaffer*, the account party sought to enjoin the beneficiary and a bank to which the beneficiary had transferred an interest in the credit from drawing on the credit. The plaintiffs argued that the bank, which had negotiated the beneficiary's drafts and had presented them to the issuer for payment, knew that the documents accompanying the drafts were false. The *Shaffer* court, holding that, if the injunction did not issue, the account parties would not have an action at law against the bank, upheld the trial court's injunction. The *Shaffer* court did not explain why the presenting bank would not be liable at common law for conduct that, if the account parties' allegations were true, smacked of fraud.[142]

---

[140] 560 F.2d 480 (1st Cir. 1977).

[141] 311 Minn. 452, 250 N.W.2d 172 (1977).

[142] The *Shaffer* court also fails to consider the effect of Section 5-111 on the bank's liability. That section narrows the warranties of the presenting bank in such a way that the account party would have had no warranty claim against the presenting bank. The bank in *Shaffer*, however, was a transferee of the proceeds of the credit. Had it been a transferee of the credit itself, it then would have become a "beneficiary" and would have made not only the warranties of a presenting bank but also the warranties of a beneficiary, which latter warranties would have sustained a breach of warranty claim. Arguably, a collecting bank that is also an assignee of the

In *Leslie v. Minson*,[143] the court denied a preliminary injunction because the record indicated that the plaintiff account parties, if their allegations were true, had a cause of action against a wealthy individual and a large brokerage house. The court was receptive to the argument that a draw under the credit would render two of the plaintiffs insolvent, but that argument failed for lack of proof. Similarly, in *Enterprise International, Inc. v. Corporacion Estatal Petrolera Ecuatoriana*,[144] the court denied an injunction, despite the account party's claim that (1) payment on the credit would have forced him to the inconvenience of suing an Ecuadorian state agency in the courts of Ecuador and (2) the draw on a standby would have hurt his reputation, an argument the court considered to be speculative.

In *Foxboro Co. v. Arabian American Oil Co.*,[145] the trial court ac-

---

credit's proceeds would make the warranty. See U.C.C. § 5-111(1); see also Wood v. R.R. Donnelley & Sons Co., 888 F.2d 313 (3d Cir. 1989) (action by account party against beneficiary after denial of injunction); GATX Leasing Corp. v. DBM Drilling Corp., 657 S.W.2d 178 (Tex. Ct. App. 1983) (holding that account party could not have payment of credit enjoined when, if facts were true, account party had breach of warranty claim against beneficiaries); Berry v. Bank of La., 439 So. 2d 1166 (La. Ct. App. 1983) (authority for holding liable negotiating bank that knowingly presents fraudulent documents to issuer); cf. Chiat/Day, Inc. v. Kalimian, 105 A.D.2d 94, 483 N.Y.S.2d 235 (1984) (holding that there was no need for injunction when beneficiary was solvent). But see Anchor Centre Partners, Ltd. v. Mercantile Bank, N.A., 783 S.W.2d 108 (Mo. Ct. App. 1989), aff'd on rehearing, id. (involving injunction against payment to beneficiary that was commercial bank). *Anchor Centre* is a curious case for an injunction. The original beneficiary and the account party sued to enjoin payment to a party they claimed had no rights under the credit. If those allegations were true, it is difficult to see how the plaintiffs could sustain a loss. The issuer's payment to the wrong party would give the account party a defense to any reimbursement claim, the issuer having violated the reimbursement agreement. That payment would not affect the rights of the beneficiary, who claimed not to have transferred any rights under the credit. If that fact is true, the issuer, a commercial bank, would be liable to the beneficiary if it failed to honor the beneficiary's demand for payment under the credit.

[143] Nos. 84 Civ. 8579 CSH, 84 Civ. 8674 CSH (S.D.N.Y. Dec. 12, 1984); accord Originala Petroleum Corp. v. Beta Fin. & Inv. Corp. (In re Originala Petroleum Corp.), 39 Bankr. 1003 (Bankr. N.D. Tex. 1984).

[144] 762 F.2d 464 (5th Cir. 1985); see also Trans Meridian Trading, Inc. v. Empresa Nacional De Comercializacion De Insumos, 829 F.2d 949 (9th Cir. 1987) (denying injunction when plaintiff had failed to show that it could not pursue cause of action against bank beneficiary in Peru); American Export Group Int'l Servs., Inc. v. Salem M. AL-NISF Elec. Co., 661 F. Supp. 759 (D.D.C. 1987) (denying injunction when petitioner had already initiated arbitration proceedings against Kuwaiti Party); B.G.H. Ins. Syndicate, Inc. v. Prudential Fire & Casualty Co., 549 So. 2d 197 (Fla. Dist. Ct. App. 1989) (denying injunction when account party reinsurer would have cause of action against ceding insurance syndicate in event draws were untimely).

[145] 634 F. Supp. 1226 (D. Mass. 1986), rev'd, 805 F.2d 34 (1st Cir. 1986).

cepted the account party's argument that drawing on a simple-demand guaranty and on a letter of credit would damage the account party's reputation and therefore sustained the account party's allegation of irreparable harm. *Foxboro* involved what the court took to be attempts of all or some of the defendants or their related entities to circumvent the court's temporary restraining order. The opinion is replete with harsh language, and the holding may be ill considered as a matter of credit law. Holding that if the account party's allegations were true, it would enjoy causes of action on the underlying contract and for fraud, the Court of Appeals for the First Circuit reversed the trial court and vacated the injunction.[146]

Significantly, the First Circuit, in *Foxboro*, rejected the account party's argument that a draw under a standby credit would damage the account party's reputation. The court held that because injunctions against payment of letters of credit are rare, the denial of the injunction would not have any adverse affect on the account party's reputation. The court added—wryly, perhaps—that the account party's attempt to enjoin payment might harm its reputation.[147]

In *Hubbard Business Plaza v. Lincoln Liberty Life Insurance Co.*,[148] the court entered a permanent injunction against payment of the credit. The court concluded that the reputations of the principals in the account party would suffer from a draw on the credit because they might be looked on as persons who had defaulted on their loans. In fact, the persons the *Hubbard Business Plaza* court sought to protect with the injunction were in default. According to the opinion, they had defaulted on their promise to take down a loan and had objected that the damages provision on the loan application, which was secured by the credit, was unreasonably high. It is difficult to accept as a matter of commercial policy or of equity that an injunction should protect petitioners from the consequences of their own default.

A proper understanding of the functions of standby credits[149] does not support the idea that a draw on a credit damages the account party's reputation. The credit often functions to shift costs during litigation or

---

[146] Foxboro Co. v. Arabian Am. Oil Co., 805 F.2d 34 (1st Cir. 1986).

[147] But cf. Seguin Sav. Ass'n v. Vista Verde Plaza Joint Venture, 7 U.C.C. Rep. Serv. 2d (Callaghan) 862 (Tex. Ct. App. 1988) (holding that damage to reputation, among other factors, constituted irreparable harm).

[148] 649 F. Supp. 1310 (D. Nev. 1986), aff'd, 844 F.2d 792 (9th Cir. 1988) (mem.).

[149] For discussion of the functions of credits, see ¶ 3.07.

to shift the forum of litigation. Draw on a standby simply may mean that the parties have entered a dispute phase and are allocating costs in anticipation of it. Standby credits, moreover, serve as a means for payment often enough that the industry has a name for them: "direct pay standby credits."[150] Draws on a standby do not always signal breach or improper conduct on the part of the account party; they sometimes signal that there is a contract dispute and sometimes that the parties are resorting to the standby credit for want of a better method of payment.

All of these cases arise in the common situation where the account party claims that the issuer is about to pay the beneficiary over facially conforming but latently defective documents. In these cases, the beneficiary is usually breaching the underlying transaction or the Section 5-111(1) warranty, or is practicing fraud, all of which situations justify an action by the account party against the beneficiary.[151]

The court in *North American Foreign Trading Corp. v. General Electronics, Ltd.*[152] considered a request for injunction in a different setting. In the *North American Foreign Trading* case, the beneficiary's documents were patently defective. There the account party sought to enjoin the beneficiaries from seeking payment and the issuer from paying under the credit. The beneficiaries countered that, because the account party would have an adequate remedy at law (a suit against the beneficiaries in Hong Kong), the injunction was not proper. The gravamen of the account party's charge was that the beneficiaries did not submit all of the documents for which the credit called; it was not, as is commonly the case, that the beneficiaries were guilty of fraud. Terming the defendant beneficiaries' argument "without merit"[153] but not otherwise explaining its ruling, the court held that injunctive relief is proper when documents required by the credit are defective or missing.[154] The *General Electronics* court failed to explain why the account party's common-law cause of action against the issuer for payment over a facially nonconforming presentation was an inadequate remedy at law.

---

[150] See the definition of "direct pay letter of credit" in the Glossary.

[151] For discussion distinguishing these actions from actions on the credit, see ¶ 2.09[6].

[152] 67 A.D. 2d 890, 413 N.Y.S.2d 700 (1979).

[153] Id. at 892, 413 N.Y.S.2d at 702.

[154] Accord Davidcraft Corp. v. First Nat'l Bank, 675 F. Supp. 1515 (N.D. Ill. 1986); Brown v. United States Nat'l Bank, 220 Neb. 684, 371 N.W.2d 692 (1985) (dictum); Home Sav. Ass'n v. Bevers, 745 S.W.2d 504 (Tex. Ct. App. 1988).

[3] Letter of Credit Standard

[a] Problems Created by Fraud Claims

In *United Technologies Corp. v. Citibank, N.A.*,[155] the state court entered a temporary restraining order against the issuer, and the issuer removed to the federal district court the following day. The amount of the credit exceeded $1 million. Eighteen days after removal, the district court dissolved the restraining order.[156] This dispatch undoubtedly reflects the district court's understanding that lengthy litigation delays corrode the commercial viability of credits that depend vitally on a tradition of prompt honor.

Most of the injunction cases arise when the account party claims that the beneficiary is practicing fraud. Section 5-114(2)(b) provides that courts "may" enjoin honor in such cases and, by using the permissive "may" rather than the imperative "shall," suggests that courts enjoy the prerogative of invoking the relief selectively, extending it in some cases and withholding it in others, as courts largely have done.

While many courts do not explicitly impose procedural or evidentiary requirements beyond those that equity rules normally impose, at least two courts have given lengthy attention to the anomalous nature of injunctive relief in the credit setting. These cases recognize that while *actual fraud* should be a proper ground for interrupting operation of the credit transaction, the mere *claim of fraud* should not. The courts confront squarely the problem that arises when a party to the credit transaction decides that he does not like the arrangement anymore and grasps at straws to fashion a fraud argument. The problem is particularly acute in the standby credit cases, where so many courts seem to be relaxing the independence principle to look at the underlying transaction.[157]

---

[155] 469 F. Supp. 473 (S.D.N.Y. 1979).

[156] Cf. Intraworld Indus., Inc. v. Girard Trust Bank, 461 Pa. 343, 336 A.2d 316 (1975) (case demonstrating dispatch with which courts have disposed of credit controversies). But cf. MBank Houston, N.A. v. Hendrix, No. 01-86-0609-CV (Tex. Ct. App. Aug. 12, 1986) (limited precedent op.) (involving temporary restraining order that (1) forbade beneficiary to draw, (2) extended beyond date of credit's expiry, and (3) was not dissolvable, matter being one for mandamus and not for direct appeal).

[157] See the discussion and cases in ¶¶ 7.04[4][c], 7.04[4][e]. For the suggestion that it should be more difficult in standby credit cases to obtain injunctive relief than it is in commercial credit cases, see Thorup, "Injunctions Against Payment of Standby Letters of Credit: How Can Banks Best Protect Themselves?" 101 Banking L.J. 6 (1984).

[b] *Dynamics* and *Intraworld* Responses

[i] **Absolutely no basis in fact.** In *Dynamics Corp. of America v. Citizens & Southern National Bank*,[158] the seller of equipment to the government of India sought to restrain payment under a credit in the nature of a performance bond. The seller, the account party under the credit, claimed in part that a certificate the beneficiary presented was fraudulent. The credit called for a certificate reciting that the seller had failed to perform the underlying contract, and the court recognized that to litigate that claim would open the credit to a trial over the underlying transaction.

The *Dynamics* court attempted to avoid that full-blown inquiry into the underlying contract by establishing an intermediate threshold. It concluded that a court hearing a request for a preliminary injunction "has no business making an ultimate adjudication regarding compliance with the provisions of the underlying sales Agreement."[159] The parties had agreed in their sales contract that that question was one for arbitration under Indian law. The court held that it was not necessary for the beneficiary to prove that the seller had breached. Rather, the question was one of determining whether the certificate entailed "a pro forma declaration which has absolutely no basis in fact."[160]

[ii] **Some basis in fact.** In *Intraworld Industries, Inc. v. Girard Trust Bank*,[161] the Supreme Court of Pennsylvania also recognized the dilemma posed by those standby credits that incorporate the terms of the underlying agreement. In *Intraworld*, the account party claimed that the beneficiary's certificate was fraudulent when it asserted that the account party owed rent under the lease between the account party and the beneficiary. It is clear from the *Intraworld* opinion that the court did not want to delve into the lease dispute. The court concluded that the "circumstances which will justify an injunction against honor must be narrowly limited to situations of fraud in which the wrongdoing of the beneficiary has so vitiated the entire transaction that the legitimate purposes of the independence of the issuer's obligation would no longer be served."[162] The court attempted to refine that rather vague rule further by concluding, "If the documents presented by the [beneficiary] are

---

[158] 356 F. Supp. 991 (N.D. Ga. 1973).
[159] Id. at 999.
[160] Id.
[161] 461 Pa. 343, 336 A.2d 316 (1975).
[162] Id. at 359, 336 A.2d at 324–325.

genuine in the sense of having some basis in fact, an injunction must be refused."[163]

Dynamics and *Intraworld* represent serious efforts to resolve what may be an intractable problem. Both chose to alleviate the problem by imposing an evidence threshold on the plaintiff or petitioner. To the extent that that threshold avoids the need to litigate some claims fully, the *Dynamics* and *Intraworld* standards succeed. The matter is far from resolved, however.[164]

---

[163] Id. at 361, 336 A.2d at 325; see also Universal Marine Ins. Co. v. Beacon Ins. Co., 577 F. Supp. 829 (W.D.N.C. 1984) (holding that there was no need to consider *Intraworld* rule if plaintiff failed to satisfy traditional equity prerequisites for injunctive relief); cf. Ground Air Transfer, Inc. v. Westates Airlines, Inc., 899 F.2d 1269 (1st Cir. 1990) (refusing injunction when dispute in underlying transaction arguably gave beneficiary right to declare default and present notice of default to issuer under credit); Guy C. Long, Inc. v. Dependable Ins. Co. (In re Guy C. Long, Inc.), 74 Bankr. 939 (Bankr. E.D. Pa. 1987) (holding that plaintiffs cannot succeed in injunction action, unless they prove, by clear and convincing evidence that is direct and precise, that beneficiary's draw is fraudulent); GATX Leasing Corp. v. DBM Drilling Corp., 657 S.W.2d 178 (Tex. Ct. App. 1983) (holding that dispute between the parties over whether lease was true lease or disguised security agreement could not support account party's claim that beneficiary was guilty of egregious fraud that *Intraworld* requires). But cf. Anchor Centre Partners, Ltd. v. Mercantile Bank, N.A., 783 S.W.2d 108 (Mo. Ct. App. 1989), aff'd on rehearing, id. (involving injunction at trial level, even though appellate court found that party drawing on credit was not practicing fraud and that its claim arose out of legitimate dispute); Seguin Sav. Ass'n v. Vista Verde Plaza Joint Venture, 7 U.C.C. Rep. Serv. 2d (Callaghan) 862 (Tex. Ct. App. 1988) (ruling that, although petitioner did not establish fraud of kind that vitiates purpose of independence principle, injunction should issue by virtue of breach of underlying contracts).

[164] In Roman Ceramics Corp. v. Peoples Nat'l Bank, 517 F. Supp. 526 (M.D. Pa. 1981), aff'd, 714 F.2d 1207 (3d Cir. 1983), the court adopted an "intentional fraud" test as defined in Symons, "Letters of Credit, Fraud, Good Faith and the Basis for Injunctive Relief," 54 Tul. L. Rev. 338 (1980). See also Bossier Bank & Trust Co. v. Union Planters Nat'l Bank, 550 F.2d 1077, 1082 app. A (6th Cir. 1977) (holding "fraud in the factum" to be sufficient ground for injunction); B.G.H. Ins. Syndicate, Inc. v. Prudential Fire & Casualty Co., 549 So. 2d 197 (Fla. Dist. Ct. App. 1989) (holding that untimely draws under letter of credit do not constitute fraud that justifies injunction); Stringer Constr. Co. v. American Ins. Co., 102 Ill. App. 3d 919, 430 N.E.2d 1 (1981) (same); O'Neill v. Poitras, 551 N.Y.S.2d 92, 93 (App. Div. 1990) (no injunction when allegations of fraud are "sharply in dispute"); Chiat/Day, Inc. v. Kalimian, 105 A.D.2d 94, 483 N.Y.S.2d 235 (1984) (holding that no injunction would issue absent evidence of active, intentional fraud); Paris Sav. & Loan Ass'n v. Walden, 730 S.W.2d 355 (Tex. Ct. App. 1987) (adopting egregious fraud test of *Intraworld*). Professor Ellinger, having reviewed the cases, concludes that the injunction will be denied if "the beneficiary acts with any shred of honest belief in his rights." Ellinger, "Fraud in Documentary Credit Transactions," 1981 J. Bus. L. 258, 262. For further discussion of the fraud rule, see ¶ 7.04.

[iii] **The California rule.** When they adopted the Code, California[165] and Nevada[166] deleted that portion of Section 5-114(2)(b) that permits courts to enjoin payment. Arguably, then, these legislatures decided that courts should not enjoin payment of a credit. In *Agnew v. FDIC*,[167] the account parties sought to enjoin the beneficiary's successor from drawing on the letter of credit. The account parties alleged that there was fraud in the transaction. Because the successor was a federal agency acting under a federal statute, the court held that federal law governed. It then adopted the California version of Section 5-114(2)(b) as the federal standard and denied the request for injunction.

In *Steinmeyer v. Warner Consolidated Corp.*,[168] however, the court thought it had found a way around the prohibition implicit in the California version of Section 5-114(2)(b). The *Steinmeyer* court held that Section 5-114(2)(b) does not apply to a suit for injunction against the beneficiary as opposed to one against the issuer. The *Steinmeyer* ruling is unconvincing. The opinion does not consider the fact that the policy against indiscriminate use of injunctions in the credit transaction applies as well to injunctions against the beneficiary as it does to injunctions against the issuer. The court betrayed its ignorance of that policy by its use of the underlying transaction, in complete disregard of the independence principle that requires the credit to be independent of the underlying transaction. *Steinmeyer* is not a well-considered opinion.[169]

In *Trans Meridian Trading, Inc. v. Empresa Nacional De Comercializacion De Insumos*,[170] a diversity case, the court distinguished the *Steinmeyer* rule on the facts and implicitly criticized *Steinmeyer* for stopping payment of the credit in the face of the California legislature's contrary command.

[iv] **The English and Canadian rules.** English courts, perhaps being more concerned than are their American brethren that the integrity of

---

[165] Cal. Com. Code § 5-114(2)(b) (West Supp. 1990).

[166] Nev. Rev. Stat. § 104.5114(2)(b) (1986).

[167] 548 F. Supp 1235 (N.D. Cal. 1982).

[168] 42 Cal. App. 3d 515, 116 Cal. Rptr. 57 (1974).

[169] See Ground Air Transfer, Inc. v. Westates Airlines, Inc., 899 F.2d 1269 (1st Cir. 1990) (diversity case in which court refuses to follow *Steinmeyer*, concluding that California Supreme Court would not follow it either). But cf. New Tech Devs., Div. of San Diego Carleton Lewis Corp. v. Bynamics, Inc., 191 Cal. App. 3d 1065, 236 Cal. Rptr. 746 (Cal. Ct. App. 1987) (containing dictum approving *Steinmeyer* distinction); Mitsui Mfrs. Bank v. Texas Commerce Bank, 159 Cal. App. 3d 1051, 206 Cal. Rptr. 218 (1984) (accepting *Steinmeyer* distinction between suits against beneficiary and suits against issuer).

[170] 829 F.2d 949 (9th Cir. 1987).

the credit not be compromised, also have fashioned a serious threshold for injunctions. Under the standard expression of the English rule, there are no grounds for an injunction unless the fraud is "established."[171] The English judges take that rule, curiously enough, from U.S. precedent. The English cases recognize *Sztejn v. J. Henry Schroder Banking Corp.*[172] as the source of the fraud exception to the issuer's duty to pay against facially conforming documents. In *Sztejn*, the court confronted a case of established fraud. The issue there was not one of deciding whether to grant an injunction, but one of deciding whether the complaint stated a cause of action. For purposes of the motion to dismiss in *Sztejn*, the court had to take the allegations of fraud as true, or "established."

The English courts, mindful of the havoc the injunction can wreak and unwilling to issue an injunction on the account party's allegation of fraud unsupported by findings to that effect, have fashioned a difficult rule for the account party. In one case,[173] the Court of Appeal denied that the account party had to negate every nonfraudulent possibility before obtaining an injunction but admitted that the English reports revealed no cases in which an account party had been successful. The court held, moreover, that there must not only be fraud, but the issuer must have clear knowledge of it. In another case,[174] the court held that an account party that shows clear fraud on the part of the beneficiary may have been too successful. Such a showing, the court ruled, gave the account party "a cast-iron claim against"[175] the issuer should it pay the beneficiary, rendering it needless for the court to issue an injunction.

Canadian courts are somewhat less rigorous in rejecting fraud defenses, but they generally require a strong prima facie case of fraud before entering an interlocutory injunction.[176]

---

[171] See R.D. Harbottle (Mercantile) Ltd. v. National Westminster Bank Ltd., [1977] 2 All E.R. 862 (Q.B.); Discount Records Ltd. v. Barclays Bank Ltd., [1975] 1 All E.R. 1071 (Ch.); cf. United Trading Corp. v. Allied Arab Bank Ltd., [1985] 2 Lloyd's Rep. 554 (C.A.) (denying injunction unless fraud is only realistic inference). Goode takes the position that the injunction will issue if the fraud is established or compelling. See Goode, "Reflections on Letters of Credit — I," 1980 J. Bus. l. 291.

[172] 177 Misc. 719, 31 N.Y.S.2d 631 (Sup. Ct. 1941).

[173] Bolivinter Oil S.A. v. Chase Manhattan Bank, [1984] 1 Lloyd's Rep. 251 (C.A.).

[174] Tukan Timber Ltd. v. Barclays Bank PLC, [1987] 1 Lloyd's Rep. 171 (Q.B.).

[175] Id. at 174.

[176] See Bank of N.S. v. Angelica White-Wear Ltd., 36 D.L.R.4th 161 (Can. 1987); C.D.N. Research & Dev. Ltd. v. Bank of N.S., 136 D.L.R.3d 656 (Ont. H. Ct. 1982); Rosen v. Pullen, 126 D.L.R.3d 62 (Ont. H. Ct. 1981); Canadian Pioneer Petroleums Inc. v. FDIC, 30 S.L.R. 315 (Q.B. 1984).

[4] Likelihood of Success on the Merits

Sometimes the requirement that the party seeking a preliminary injunction demonstrate a likelihood of success on the merits[177] works in favor of the petitioner, because it exposes the court to the facts of the fraud claim, facts that are often superficially appealing. In *Paccar International, Inc. v. Commercial Bank of Kuwait*,[178] for example, the court had to consider facts bearing on the fraud question in order to determine whether there was a likelihood that the plaintiff would prevail on the merits. If true, the plaintiff's allegations made out a clear case of fraud. One gets the feeling that the court's questionable ruling on a jurisdictional issue[179] and its failure to address the independence principle issue stemmed from an itch to see justice done for the allegedly aggrieved plaintiff. Thus, the likelihood of success requirement for a preliminary injunction gives the account party a chance to make its "hard case" argument and sometimes yields bad law, although not always.

In *Recon Optical, Inc. v. Israel*,[180] the court denied a preliminary injunction on the ground that the account party that was seeking the relief was not able to show a likelihood that it would succeed on the merits. The account party had entered into a contract with the beneficiary-buyer, under which the buyer had made advance payments. Under the contract, if the account party breached, the buyer had the right to the return of the payments; and that right was secured by the standby credit. When the beneficiary drew, the account party disputed the truth of the beneficiary's assertion in the presented documents that the account party was in breach.

The *Recon* court noted that the underlying transaction called for arbitration of contract disputes and concluded that the purpose of the letter of credit was to permit the beneficiary to have the use of the advance payments during that arbitration. The court concluded that the account party had not shown a likelihood of success on the merits in the proceeding to obtain a permanent injunction and that the petition for preliminary injunction was correctly denied. Significantly, the *Recon* court did not investigate the merits of the underlying dispute. It was enough that the purpose of the credit was to permit the beneficiary-buyer to recapture its advance payments. Given that finding, the court considered

---

[177] See generally supra ¶ 11.04[1].

[178] 587 F. Supp. 783 (C.D. Cal. 1984), rev'd, 757 F.2d 1058 (9th Cir. 1985).

[179] For discussion of the jurisdictional issue in the *Paccar* case, see supra ¶ 11.01[1]. The *Paccar* court was reversed on that issue. See supra note 178.

[180] 816 F.2d 854 (2d Cir. 1987).

neither the merits of the underlying contract dispute nor the accuracy of the beneficiary's certification that the account party was in default.

In *Eljay, Jrs., Inc. v. Rahda Exports*,[181] the court used the likelihood of success requirement to effect a significant reversal of normal evidentiary and pleading burdens. In that case, the account party failed in its bid for a preliminary injunction because it did not show that the banks seeking payment under the credit were not holders in due course of the beneficiary's drafts. Normally, of course, the party claiming to be a holder in due course must plead and prove that status in order to avail itself of the protection that status affords against fraud and other defenses.[182] The *Eljay, Jrs.* court ruled, however, that when the account party seeks an injunction, the account party must prove the negative. Otherwise, it will not have shown a likelihood of succeeding on the merits.[183]

In *American Export Group International Services, Inc. v. Salem M. AL-NISF Electrical Co.*,[184] the credit was a four-party credit, that is, the beneficiary of the credit was a bank that had issued a guaranty in favor of the account party's buyer. When the account party asserted that the buyer had drawn fraudulently on the guaranty, the court pointed out that even if the allegation were true, the account party would not be successful in a claim against the guaranty issuer that was the beneficiary of the credit. For that reason and for other reasons, not the least of which was the account party's adequate remedy under an arbitration clause,[185] the court denied equitable relief.

The *American Export Group* case is an encouraging example of the way in which courts can handle injunction claims with dispatch and protect the integrity and efficiency of the credit facility. The clear function of the credit in that case was to provide the buyer with a return of its payments in the event of a dispute with the seller. That return of payments was not the end of the matter. The parties had agreed to arbitrate disputes; but the return of the payments gave the buyer strength in negotiations with the seller, for, during the arbitration, the buyer held the funds. The seller's injunction action was an effort to reallocate the dispute risks in a fashion contrary to that which the parties had agreed

---

[181] 99 A.D.2d 408, 470 N.Y.S.2d 12 (1984).

[182] For discussion of that procedural rule in the letter of credit context, see supra ¶ 11.03[1].

[183] Accord Discount Records Ltd. v. Barclays Bank Ltd., [1975] 1 All E.R. 1071 (Ch.).

[184] 661 F. Supp. 759 (D.D.C. 1987).

[185] For further discussion of the need to show the absence of an adequate alternate remedy as a prerequisite for injunctive relief, see ¶ 7.04[1].

upon in the sales transaction. The *American Export Group* court entered a temporary restraining order on February 10, 1987, just four days after the guaranty issuer drew on the credit; and the court denied the preliminary injunction on February 24, 1987, at which time the issuer, having indicated its intention of so doing, undoubtedly paid the beneficiary bank.[186]

[5] Timing

Injunctions come too late if the credit already has been honored. In *Bazaar, Inc. v. Exchange National Bank*,[187] the account party learned of possible fraud in the shipment of worthless goods under a commercial credit but did not obtain an injunction until after the issuer had honored the credit engagement by accepting in good faith the beneficiary's time draft. Once the issuer had accepted, an injunction against honor was tardy, the action of acceptance being an act that constitutes honor.[188] In fact, the honor of a time credit is not complete until the issuer pays the acceptance,[189] but it would have been patently unfair and a serious obstacle to the negotiability of bankers' acceptances if the court had permitted the injunction to apply to payment of the acceptance.[190]

Expiration of a restraining order may present timing problems. In *Kelley v. First Westroads Bank (In re Kelley)*,[191] account parties obtained temporary restraining orders against issuers of credits that ran to the FDIC as receiver of a failed bank. The FDIC filed claims against the issuers and the account parties. Eventually, the account parties dismissed their request for injunctive relief. Upon termination of the restraining orders, the *Kelley* court held, the issuers had ten days plus that portion of the three-day period provided by Section 5-112(1)(a) remaining at the time the orders were entered to pay the FDIC. The issuers objected that they had returned the documents to the FDIC and that they should not

---

[186] See also Diamond Mach. Co. v. Casco N. Bank (In re Diamond Mach. Co.), 95 Bankr. 255 (D. Me. 1988) (restraining order entered on November 3; preliminary injunction hearing on November 10; injunction petition denied on December 12).

[187] 168 Ill. App. 3d 811, 523 N.E.2d 57 (1988), appeal denied, 122 Ill. 2d 595, 530 N.E.2d 239 (1988).

[188] For discussion of the time of honor of a letter of credit, see ¶ 5.03[2][a].

[189] See U.C.C. § 1-201(21) (defining "to honor" as "to pay or to accept *and* pay") (emphasis supplied).

[190] Cf. New Tech Devs., Div. of San Diego Carleton Lewis Corp. v. Bank of N.S., 191 Cal. App. 3d 1065, 236 Cal. Rptr. 746 (1987) (denying injunction on ground other than fact that draft under credit had been accepted).

[191] 840 F.2d 554 (8th Cir. 1988).

have to make payment until the FDIC resubmitted conforming documents. The court held that the parties' rights were frozen upon the entry of the restraining orders—a time when the issuers were holding the documents. It was not necessary for the FDIC to resubmit the documents.

Many of these cases, it seems, reflect awareness on the part of the courts that a restraining order has a serious impact on the risk allocation that the parties to the broad letter of credit transaction fashioned at the outset. The credit serves a number of functions, among them shifting the cost of litigating without the funds, shifting the forum, and substituting the financial strength of the issuer for that of the account party.[192] Issuance of an injunction alters those allocations in a manner adverse to the beneficiary ex post, that is, at a time when the account party has enjoyed their ex ante benefits. A temporary injunction that prevents draw until the trial on the merits concludes may have the additional untoward effect of extending beyond the credit's expiry and destroying the credit entirely, without any final determination that the allegations of the petitioner's pleadings are supported by the evidence.[193]

¶ 11.05   SUMMARY JUDGMENT

[1] In General

Courts often have held that disputes arising out of letters of credit present solely legal issues and are ripe for summary judgment.[194] In *Banco*

---

[192] For discussion of the credit's functions and the adverse effects of injunctions on them, see ¶ 3.07.

[193] Some courts that issue the injunction face the prospect of destroying all effects of the credit. In Seguin Sav. Ass'n v. Vista Verde Plaza Joint Venture, 7 U.C.C. Rep. Serv. 2d (Callaghan) 862 (Tex. Ct. App. 1988), the beneficiary argued that the trial court's temporary injunction was ill advised, in view of the fact that the credits might expire before the conclusion of the trial. The *Seguin Savings* court held that the beneficiary could request the trial court for relief by asking that the court require the account party to have the credits extended, as the court had previously done. In Ray v. Snow, 525 So. 2d 394 (Miss. 1988), the beneficiaries of a letter of credit lost the benefit of the credit, which expired by its terms during the life of an injunction that prevented payment. The party obtaining the injunction had posted a cash bond, but the beneficiaries failed to follow Mississippi procedure and were unable to recover on the bond.

[194] See, e.g., Arbest Constr. Co. v. First Nat'l Bank & Trust Co., 777 F.2d 581 (10th Cir. 1985); Dulien Steel Prods., Inc. v. Bankers Trust Co., 298 F.2d 836 (2d Cir. 1962); American Airlines, Inc. v. FDIC, 610 F. Supp. 199 (D. Kan. 1985); Bank of Montreal v. Federal Nat'l Bank & Trust Co., 622 F. Supp. 6 (W.D. Okla. 1984); Banco Nacional De Desarrolla v. Mellon Bank, N.A., 558 F. Supp. 1265 (W.D. Pa. 1983), rev'd on other grounds, 726 F.2d 87 (3d Cir. 1984); Data Gen. Corp. v. Citi-

De Vizcaya, S.A. v. First National Bank,[195] for example, the negotiating bank sought payment from the issuer's Chicago correspondent,[196] and the defendant moved for summary judgment. The court, relying on Rule 54(c) of the Federal Rules of Civil Procedure, held that the defendant's motion was without merit and should be denied. It held further that the plaintiff was entitled to summary judgment, even though it had not filed a motion. The court then entered judgment for the plaintiff. Similar impatience with litigation delay in the credit setting is evident in *Bank of Canton, Ltd. v. Republic National Bank*,[197] where the Court of Appeals for the Second Circuit awarded double costs and other damages against a party that appealed the trial court's award of summary judgment.[198]

---

zens Nat'l Bank, 502 F. Supp. 776 (D. Conn. 1980); Barclay Knitwear Co. v. King'swear Enters., Ltd., 141 A.D.2d 241, 533 N.Y.S.2d 724 (1988), appeal denied, 74 N.Y.2d 605, 541 N.E.2d 427, 543 N.Y.S.2d 398 (1989); North Woods Paper Mills, Ltd. v. National City Bank, 283 A.D. 731, 127 N.Y.S.2d 663 (1954); Dubose Steel, Inc. v. Branch Banking & Trust Co., 72 N.C. App. 598, 324 S.E.2d 859 (1985), review denied, 314 N.C. 115, 332 S.E.2d 480 (1985); Sunset Invs., Ltd. v. Sargent, 52 N.C. App. 284, 278 S.E.2d 558, review denied, 303 N.C. 550, 281 S.E.2d 401 (1981); Ronald A. & Caroline Olson, Inc. v. United States Nat'l Bank, 70 Or. App. 460, 689 P.2d 1021 (1984); First State Bank v. Shuford Mills, Inc., 716 S.W.2d 649 (Tex. Ct. App. 1986); see also Homestate Sav. Ass'n v. Westwind Exploration, Inc., 684 S.W.2d 788 (Tex. Ct. App.), aff'd, 696 S.W.2d 378 (Tex. 1985) (reversing judgment for beneficiary on document compliance issue and rendering judgment for issuer); cf. Southern Marine Research, Inc. v. Nateman, 434 So. 2d 47 (Fla. Dist. Ct. App. 1983) (holding that if documents presented by beneficiary comply with conditions of credit, beneficiary is entitled to directed verdict).

[195] 514 F. Supp. 1280 (N.D. Ill. 1981), vacated, id.

[196] It is not clear from the opinion whether the action was on the acceptances arising out of the credit or on the credit itself. For a discussion of that feature of the case, see ¶ 2.09[1].

[197] 636 F.2d 30 (2d Cir. 1980).

[198] See also Les Mutuelles du Mans Vie v. Life Assurance Co., 128 F.R.D. 233, 241 (N.D. Ill. 1989) (allowing Fed. R. Civ. P. 11 sanctions against plaintiff whose complaint for injunction against draws on letters of credit "ignored applicable law" and sought "to override the fundamental nature of letters of credit as an arm's-length allocation of risk distribution"). For cases granting accelerated judgment in disputes correlative to those under the letter of credit, see, e.g., Marine Midland Bank, N.A. v. Goyak, No. 84 Civ. 1204 (S.D.N.Y. July 12, 1984) (summary judgment for beneficiary against account party who imperfectly alleged securities fraud after issuer became insolvent); Worldwide Sugar Co. v. Royal Bank of Can., 609 F. Supp. 19 (S.D.N.Y. 1984) (summary judgment for advising bank in suit by account party on bank's guaranty to issuer); Fertico Belg., S.A. v. Phosphate Chems. Export Ass'n, 100 A.D.2d 165, 473 N.Y.S.2d 403, appeal dismissed, 62 N.Y.2d 802 (1984) (summary judgment for beneficiary in suit by account party for fraud and conversion in underlying contract).

[2] Independence Principle

The *Banco De Vizcaya* and *Bank of Canton* cases reflect strong commitment to the independence principle, which forbids consideration in the credit lawsuit of questions arising out of the underlying agreement. Prompt disposition of credit litigation is possible by virtue of the fact that the duties of an issuer are clear. These duties depend on the terms of the credit document alone, not on the terms of the underlying agreement.

In *Summit Insurance Co. v. Central National Bank*,[199] a credit issued to an insurance company to secure the obligations of one of its agencies. Apparently, through an inadvertent drafting error, the credit covered sums due at the time the credit issued (when the amount due was zero) rather than at the time the beneficiary demanded payment. When the beneficiary presented its drafts, the issuer dishonored them because they did not cover amounts due at the time of the credit's issuance. The beneficiary sued, and the issuer moved for summary judgment. The beneficiary filed affidavits showing that the credit was not consistent with company practices and was rendered meaningless by the drafting error. The court affirmed the summary holding that such an argument did not raise a question of fact and that the credit should be construed according to its plain meaning, not in light of the underlying contract.

Similarly, in *Sherwood & Roberts, Inc. v. First Security Bank*,[200] the court entered summary judgment for a beneficiary who satisfied the credit's requirement that the account party be in default of an obligation. The court would not entertain the account party's argument that the beneficiary's conduct caused the default. That issue was not one for the letter of credit suit, the court held.[201]

It is not surprising that courts that do not enforce the independence principle vigorously are less likely to grant motions for summary judgment. In *American Employers Insurance Co. v. Pioneer Bank & Trust Co.*,[202] standby credits called for the beneficiary's sight draft and a statement that (1) the beneficiary executed bonds for the account party; (2) a

---

[199] 624 S.W.2d 222 (Tex. Civ. App. 1981).

[200] 682 P.2d 149 (Mont. 1984).

[201] See also Interfirst Bank v. First Fed. Sav. & Loan Ass'n, 242 Kan. 181, 747 P.2d 129 (1987) (granting summary judgment against issuer, even though trial court had not found that beneficiary's certification was accurate). But cf. Sabolyk v. Morgan Guar. Trust Co., No. 84 Civ. 3179 (MJL) (S.D.N.Y. Nov. 27, 1984) (holding that acceleration provision in note secured by letter of credit could not support beneficiary's early draw and granting summary judgment against beneficiary).

[202] 538 F. Supp. 1354 (N.D. Ill. 1981).

claim or other situation existed that, in the beneficiary's sole judgment, might give rise to loss or expense under the bonds; and (3) funds would be required, in the discretion of the beneficiary, for its protection under the bond or for payment of premiums. The lawyer who drafted the credits took pains to protect the beneficiary by framing the judgment questions (whether loss or expense might arise and whether the company needed funds for its protection or to cover premiums) as matters within the beneficiary's discretion. When the issuer failed to honor the beneficiary's draft, the court denied the beneficiary's motion for summary judgment. The court held that the beneficiary had failed to explain the "circumstances of issuance" of the credits and had failed to offer "anything that would cast light on the meaning of their terms."[203]

The *American Employers* court implicitly rejects the independence principle. Similarly, in *Banque Paribas v. Hamilton Industries International, Inc.*,[204] the court, after holding that the credit might have incorporated a related guaranty, declined to enter summary judgment and remanded for a determination whether the credit did, in fact, incorporate the guaranty.

[3] Strict Compliance Rule

The *American Employers* case demonstrates the way in which the strict compliance rule can facilitate disposition of credit litigation through summary judgment. The credit in that case required the beneficiary to present an assertion that the beneficiary had executed one or more bonds on behalf of two entities. The statement the beneficiary presented described execution of bonds on behalf of only one of the two entities. Under the strict compliance standard that most courts follow,[205] the statement is defective; and summary judgment for the issuer would be in order. The *American Employers* court, however, chose the substantial compliance standard and therefore had to decide whether the variance between the credit and the statement was material—a decision that depended on the "circumstances of issuance" to which the court referred.

In *Bank of Montreal v. Federal National Bank & Trust Co.*,[206] the court reformed the letter of credit after concluding that it did not reflect the true intent of the parties and granted summary judgment against the

[203] Id. at 1358.
[204] 767 F.2d 380 (7th Cir. 1985).
[205] See ¶¶ 6.03, 6.04.
[206] 622 F. Supp. 6 (W.D. Okla. 1984).

issuer on the ground that the beneficiary had complied with the terms of the credit as reformed.[207]

Financial Trust Co. v. Caisse Populaire Ste. Anne D'Ottawa, Inc.[208] reflects the judicial economy that the strict compliance rule effects. In *Financial Trust Co.*, the credit secured a promissory note. When the beneficiary presented the note, the issuer dishonored. In the beneficiary's suit for improper dishonor, the issuer resisted the beneficiary's motion for summary judgment on the ground that the beneficiary had not shown that the note was executed by an authorized party. The court rejected the issuer's argument, however, on the ground that the credit did not require the beneficiary to provide any evidence of such authorization. It was sufficient to satisfy the credit and to have summary judgment, in the view of the *Financial Trust Co.* court, for the beneficiary to show that it had presented facially conforming documents. The court added that fraud is a defense to payment when documents comply but that failure to prove that the signature was authorized does not amount to fraud.[209]

[4] Questions of Fact

Summary judgment is appropriate only in the absence of factual disputes on matters that are relevant to the ultimate liability question. By reducing the arena of factual dispute, the independence principle reduces the number of factual questions. By the same token, a strict compliance standard avoids the plethora of factual disputes that arise in any inquiry into the substantiality of a defect in the documents.

There remain, however, even with vigorous application of these two letter of credit precepts (the independence principle and the strict com-

---

[207] Cf. United States Steel Corp. v. Chase Manhattan Bank, N.A., No. 83 Civ. 4966 (WCC) (S.D.N.Y. July 2, 1984) (denying summary judgment after excusing beneficiary's failure to comply strictly with credit). For authority that, absent ambiguity in the credit, documentary compliance is a question of law, see supra ¶ 11.03[3].

[208] 61 O.R.2d 538 (H. Ct. 1987).

[209] Of course, if the note was unauthorized, the beneficiary may have been practicing fraud. The *Financial Trust Co.* court implies — correctly, it seems — that fraud is an issue for the defendant to raise, not one for the plaintiff to negate. For discussion of fraud as an affirmative defense, see ¶ 9.06[6]. Cf. Carrera v. Bank of N.Y., 153 A.D.2d 918, 545 N.Y.S.2d 726 (1989) (estoppel raised by beneficiary presenting nonconforming documents preventing dismissal of beneficiary's action for wrongful dishonor). For further authority granting summary judgment on strict compliance issues, see New Braunfels Nat'l Bank v. Odiorne, 780 S.W.2d 313 (Tex. Ct. App. 1989).

pliance standard), areas in which some may argue that questions of fact arise. Courts generally have rendered these areas narrow.

[a] Good Faith

Frequently, an account party argues that the issuer's payment of a credit in the face of the account party's assertion that there is fraud in the credit transaction or in the underlying transaction constitutes bad faith. The account party contends that, in the event of such bad faith, the court should not permit the issuer to shield itself with strict compliance or with independence principles.

Section 5-114(2)(b) explicitly authorizes an issuer to honor a draft or demand for payment, "despite notification from the customer of fraud, forgery or other defect not apparent on the face of the documents," but it specifies that the issuer must act in good faith.

It is clear that the issuer's payment, despite notification, is not bad faith in and of itself. If it were, the section's authorization would become a nullity; no issuer could ever pay once it received the account party's allegations of a latent defect in the documents. It is also clear that the bad faith of which Section 5-114(2)(b) speaks is dishonesty in fact.[210] It is not dishonest for the issuer to honor the beneficiary's draft, even though the issuer harbors questions about the integrity of the beneficiary's presentation,[211] and it is not bad faith to rely on the account party's assertions and refuse payment of the credit.[212] The whole purpose of the option to pay is to avoid imposing upon the issuer the difficult and time-consuming inquiries that any other rule would require.[213] The account party may not avoid the thrust of that rule by forcing the issuer to litigate the reasonableness of its conduct. Absent facts indicating the issuer's dishonesty, courts should grant summary judgment for the issuer.[214]

---

[210] See U.C.C. § 5-103(4); Philadelphia Gear Corp. v. Central Bank, 717 F.2d 230 (5th Cir. 1983); Shaffer v. Brooklyn Park Garden Apartments, 311 Minn. 452, 250 N.W.2d 172 (1977).

[211] Intraworld Indus., Inc. v. Girard Trust Bank, 461 Pa. 343, 336 A.2d 316 (1975).

[212] Roman Ceramics Corp. v. Peoples Nat'l Bank, 517 F. Supp. 526 (M.D. Pa. 1981), aff'd, 714 F.2d 1207 (3d Cir. 1983). Note, however, that while honor of a fraudulent presentation in good faith excuses the issuer from liability to the account party, dishonor of a good presentation even when done in good faith does not excuse the issuer from liability to the beneficiary.

[213] See U.C.C. § 5-114, comment 2 (2d para.).

[214] Lalaco v. Universal Hous. Sys. of Am., Inc., No. 80 Civ. 178 (WCC) (S.D.N.Y. Oct. 25, 1983) (entering summary judgment for issuer after finding that there was no evidence of bad faith in its payment against facially conforming documents).

[b] Negligence

The account party may not avoid the purpose of Section 5-114(2)(b) by characterizing the issuer's payment of the beneficiary's draft as negligence for which the issuer is liable. As the Court of Appeals for the Second Circuit pointed out in *Dulien Steel Products, Inc. v. Bankers Trust Co.*,[215] it is not the function of an issuer to involve itself in the controversy between the account party and the beneficiary. The plaintiff in *Dulien* argued that the confirming bank had "failed to exercise that degree of care and prudence exercised by banks in comparable circumstances and to which plaintiff was entitled in conformity with established custom and usage in banks generally."[216] The *Dulien* court saw that allegation as an attempt to add to the issuer's ministerial function. "The duties [of the issuer] under a letter of credit are created by the document itself, the [issuer] being deprived of any discretion not granted therein."[217] The court held that the plaintiff would have the bank go beyond the terms of the credit to investigate the alleged fraud, but the court held that the bank was not obliged to conduct that investigation.[218]

[c] Waiver and Estoppel

Parties may be able to avoid summary judgment by raising a waiver question. In *Colonial Cedar Co. v. Royal Wood Products, Inc.*,[219] the beneficiary had failed to comply strictly with the terms of the credit but alleged that the issuer waived the requirement in question. The court reversed a summary judgment in the issuer's favor and remanded the case for determination of the waiver question.[220] Similarly, a party may raise

---

[215] 298 F.2d 836 (2d Cir. 1962).

[216] Id. at 840.

[217] Id.

[218] Cf. Almatrood v. Sallee Int'l, Inc., No. 83 Civ. 1800 (WCC) (S.D.N.Y. May 13, 1985) (summary judgment in favor of confirming bank and against account party's claim that bank paid over fraudulent documents); Lalaco v. Universal Hous. Sys. of Am., Inc., No. 80 Civ. 178 (WCC) (S.D.N.Y. Oct. 25, 1983) (holding (1) that there was no evidence that issuer was negligent in paying over facially conforming documents and (2) that summary judgment was proper).

[219] 448 So. 2d 1218 (Fla. Dist. Ct. App. 1984).

[220] Cf. Chemical Bank v. Daniel Laurent, Ltd., 100 A.D.2d 792, 474 N.Y.S.2d 955 (1984) (denying summary judgment on issuer's reimbursement claim against account party, there being factual issue on account party's alleged waiver of defects in documents).

estoppel facts in order to avoid summary judgment. As a general rule, estoppel and waiver questions must be pleaded.[221]

[d]　Documentary Compliance

In *Westwind Exploration, Inc. v. Homestate Savings Association*,[222] the court held that issues of documentary compliance under the strict compliance rule[223] are questions for the jury, but only when there is an ambiguity in the letter of credit.[224]

¶ 11.06　DECLARATORY JUDGMENT, INTERPLEADER, AND SIMILAR ACTIONS

Many, perhaps most, disputes concerning letters of credit arise out of actions by the account party to enjoin payment under the credit. These actions may lie directly against the issuer[225] or directly against the beneficiary.[226] Sometimes the issuer dishonors the demand for payment. The

---

[221] See, e.g., State v. Morganstein, 703 S.W.2d 894 (Mo. 1986). For general discussion of waiver and estoppel cases, see ¶ 6.06.

[222] 696 S.W.2d 378 (Tex. 1985).

[223] For discussion of the strict compliance rule, see ¶¶ 6.03–6.05.

[224] Accord Breathless Assocs. v. First Sav. & Loan Ass'n, 654 F. Supp. 832 (N.D. Tex. 1986); Delta Brands, Inc. v. MBank Dallas, N.A., 719 S.W.2d 355 (Tex. Ct. App. 1986); see also American Coleman Co. v. Intrawest Bank, 887 F.2d 1382 (10th Cir. 1989) (granting summary judgment without oral argument in favor of issuer when beneficiary presented certificate referring to documents dated November 21 under credit that required certificate referring to documents dated November 16); North Beach Leather Int'l, Inc. v. Morgan Guar. Trust Co., 687 F. Supp. 127 (S.D.N.Y. 1988) (denying summary judgment when credit is ambiguous); Bucci Imports, Ltd. v. Chase Bank Int'l, 132 A.D.2d 641, 518 N.Y.S.2d 15 (1987) (granting summary judgment in favor of issuer that refused to pay against transport document showing delivery in Arizona, when credit called for transport document showing delivery in Texas).

[225] See, e.g., Itek Corp. v. First Nat'l Bank, 511 F. Supp. 1341 (D. Mass. 1981), final judgment vacated on appeal, 704 F.2d 1 (1st Cir. 1983); Dynamics Corp. of Am. v. Citizens & S. Nat'l Bank, 356 F. Supp. 991 (N.D. Ga. 1973).

[226] See, e.g., American Bell Int'l, Inc. v. Islamic Republic of Iran, 474 F. Supp. 420 (S.D.N.Y. 1979); Steinmeyer v. Warner Consol. Corp., 42 Cal. App. 3d 515, 116 Cal. Rptr. 57 (1974); Edgewater Constr. Co. v. Percy Wilson Mortgage & Fin. Corp., 44 Ill. App. 3d 220, 357 N.E.2d 1307 (1976); Faravelli v. Bankers Trust Co., 85 A.D.2d 335, 447 N.Y.S.2d 962 (1982), aff'd, 59 N.Y.2d 615, 449 N.E.2d 1272, 463 N.Y.S.2d 194 (1983).

beneficiary's suit in such cases will be one for money damages[227] or for specific performance.[228]

In a few cases, however, it has been the issuer itself that initiated litigation through a declaratory judgment action,[229] and sometimes the ac-

---

[227] See, e.g., East Girard Sav. Ass'n v. Citizen Nat'l Bank & Trust Co., 593 F.2d 598 (5th Cir. 1979); New York Life Ins. Co. v. Hartford Nat'l Bank & Trust Co., 173 Conn. 492, 378 A.2d 562 (1977).

[228] See Eakin v. Continental Ill. Nat'l Bank & Trust Co., 875 F.2d 114 (7th Cir. 1989); American Employers Ins. Co. v. Pioneer Bank & Trust Co., 538 F. Supp. 354 (N.D. Ill. 1981).

[229] See, e.g., Lower Brule Constr. Co. v. Sheesley's Plumbing & Heating Co., 682 F. Supp. 1039 (D.S.D. 1988); Mount Prospect State Bank v. Marine Midland Bank, 121 Ill. App. 3d 295, 459 N.E.2d 979 (1983); Washington Fed. Sav. & Loan Ass'n v. Prince George's County, 80 Md. App. 142, 560 A.2d 582 (1989); Summit Ins. Co. v. Central Nat'l Bank, 624 S.W.2d 222 (Tex. Civ. App. 1981); cf. C.A. Cavendes, Sociedad Financiera v. John Alden Life Ins. Co., 591 F. Supp. 362 app. A (S.D. Fla. 1984) (declaratory relief sought by beneficiary and account party); Muir v. Transportation Mut. Ins. Co., 107 Pa. Commw. Ct. 638, 529 A.2d 534 (1987) (issuer supporting injunction action against beneficiary); Edmonton Sav. & Credit Union Ltd. v. Koppe, 70 A.L.R. 373 (Q.B. 1986) (interpleader by issuer); Aspen Planners Ltd. v. Commerce Masonry & Forming Ltd., 100 D.L.R.3d 546 (Ont. H. Ct. 1979) (treating issuer as stakeholder). But cf. Eakin v. Continental Ill. Nat'l Bank & Trust Co., 687 F. Supp. 1259 (N.D. Ill. 1988) (holding that declaratory judgment action comes too late when issuer has dishonored credit). See also Public Loan Co. v. FDIC, 803 F.2d 82 (3d Cir. 1986) (declaratory judgment action by account party and guarantors); Johnson v. Levy Org. Dev. Co., 789 F.2d 601 (7th Cir. 1986) (attempt by issuer to interplead); American Nat'l Bank & Trust Co. v. Hamilton Indus. Int'l, Inc., 583 F. Supp. 164 (N.D. Ill. 1984), rev'd on other grounds sub nom. Banque Paribas v. Hamilton Indus. Int'l, Inc., 767 F.2d 380 (7th Cir. 1985) (interpleader by issuer); American Bank v. Leasing Serv. Corp. (In re Air Conditioning, Inc. of Stuart), 55 Bankr. 157 (Bankr. S.D. Fla. 1985), aff'd in part, rev'd in part sub nom. Leasing Serv. Corp. v. Wendel (In re Air Conditioning, Inc. of Stuart), 72 Bankr. 657 (S.D. Fla. 1987), aff'd in part, rev'd in part sub nom. American Bank v. Leasing Serv. Co. (In re Air Conditioning, Inc. of Stuart), 845 F.2d 293 (11th Cir.), cert. denied sub nom. First Interstate Credit Alliance, Inc. v. American Bank, 109 S. Ct. 557 (1988) (action by issuer against beneficiary in which account party's trustee intervened and that court treated as federal interpleader); Braucher v. Continental Ill. Nat'l Bank & Trust Co. (In re Illinois-Cal. Express, Inc.), 50 Bankr. 323 (Bankr. D. Colo. 1985) (declaratory relief sought by trustee of account party); Sea Management Servs., Ltd. v. Club Sea, Inc., 512 So. 2d 1025 (Fla. Dist. Ct. App. 1987) (attempt by issuer to interplead); GATX Leasing Corp. v. DBM Drilling Corp., 657 S.W.2d 178 (Tex. Ct. App. 1983) (same). Braucher v. Continental Ill. Nat'l Bank & Trust Co. (In re Illinois-Cal. Express, Inc.), 50 Bankr. 232 (Bankr. D. Colo. 1985), featured declaratory judgment. In that case, the account party's trustee in bankruptcy brought a declaratory judgment action against the issuers of credits that had made payments under the credits after filing of the bankruptcy petition. The trustee argued that the filing caused the credits to terminate. The bankruptcy court declined to exercise jurisdiction, holding that the matter was not a core proceeding. See 28 U.S.C. § 1157(b)(2) (1988). Because the claims

count party fortifies his injunction efforts with attachment proceedings.[230]

In fact, one case, *Morgan v. Depositors Trust Co.*,[231] suggested that the aggrieved account party would be better off with a complaint in attachment, where it was not necessary to show the lack of a remedy at law, than with a complaint for an injunction where that showing was necessary.[232] In other cases, it may be the beneficiary itself that institutes attachment proceedings in order to recover sums due under a credit.[233]

When the issuer commences litigation in order to avoid deciding whether to pay the beneficiary or to dishonor, it also avoids the responsibility it assumed when it issued the credit. Section 5-114 stipulates that an issuer "must" honor a presentation that conforms to the terms of the credit. Beneficiaries bargain with account parties to obtain credits in order to shift costs and risks. The functions of the credit depend on prompt payment by the issuer against conforming documents.[234] Section 5-114 protects the issuer by stipulating further that it may pay the beneficiary even when there are allegations that the beneficiary's documents are fraudulent, so long as the issuer acts in good faith.

There is considerable evidence in the section, then, that the drafters supported a policy of prompt payment by the issuer. It is not surprising, therefore, to find that some courts view with hostility attempts by issuers to avoid the duty Section 5-114 imposes.

---

were the subject of a state court proceeding, the court exercised what it saw to be its prerogative to abstain from hearing the matter.

[230] See, e.g., Sperry Int'l Trade, Inc. v. Government of Isr., 670 F.2d 8 (2d Cir. 1982); Lustrelon, Inc. v. Prutscher, 178 N.J. Super. 128, 428 A.2d 518 (App. Div. 1981); United Bank Ltd. v. Cambridge Sporting Goods Corp., 41 N.Y.2d 254, 360 N.E.2d 943, 392 N.Y.S.2d 265 (1976); Hohenberg Co. v. Comitex Knitters Ltd., 104 Misc. 2d 232, 428 N.Y.S.2d 156 (Sup. Ct. 1980). See generally ¶ 7.03[5].

[231] 33 U.C.C. Rep. Serv. (Callaghan) 1473 (Me. Super. Ct. Kennebec County 1982).

[232] In Capehart Corp. v. Shanghai Commercial Bank, Ltd. 49 A.D.2d 521, 369 N.Y.S.2d 751 (1975), the court held that attachment would not lie if the plaintiff was seeking only an injunction and not money damages. For criticism of cases that allow attachment to interfere with the credit's independence from the underlying contract, see ¶ 7.03[5].

[233] See, e.g., National Bank & Trust Co. of N. Am., Ltd. v. J.L.M. Int'l, Inc., 421 Supp. 1269 (S.D.N.Y. 1976); J. Zeevi & Sons v. Grindlays Bank (Uganda) Ltd., 37 N.Y.2d 220, 333 N.E.2d 168, 371 N.Y.S.2d 892, cert. denied, 432 U.S. 866 (1975); Eriksson v. Refiners Export Co., 264 A.D. 525, 35 N.Y.S.2d 829 (1942).

[234] For discussion of the credit's functions and the critical role of the prompt payment feature, see ¶ 3.07.

In *Lafayette Corp. v. Bank of Boston International South*,[235] the issuer inadvertently extended a credit by an advice referring to the name of the original beneficiary rather than to the substitute beneficiary. When the second beneficiary drew after the original expiry, the account party claimed that the extension benefited the original beneficiary but not the second beneficiary. The issuer sought to interplead the account party's collateral and leave the matter for the parties and the court to resolve.

The *Lafayette Corp.* court was not impressed with the issuer's predicament. "[I]t would sound the death knell for letters of credit"[236] if courts were to decide whether beneficiaries should be paid, the court observed in ruling that interpleader was not proper. First, the court noted that there was not a single fund involved. The beneficiary had no claim to the account party's collateral. The beneficiary's claim was against the assets of the issuer, whose credit obligation was distinct from the account party's obligation to reimburse the issuer. Second, the court noted that the issuer faced no risk of multiple liability. The court recognized that the issuer might indeed be liable both to the account party on the application agreement and to the beneficiary on the credit. That liability was not the type of multiple liability, however, that interpleader is designed to avoid. Presumably, the issuer's liability on the application agreement was for its negligent advice; its liability on the credit was for failing to honor a proper presentation.

In *Dallas Bank & Trust v. Commonwealth Development Corp.*,[237] the issuer filed an interpleader action on the day after the beneficiary presented its demand for payment. The interpleader petition alleged that the issuer was unable to determine whether the beneficiary or the account party was entitled to the funds (which the issuer deposited in court). The court held that, because the issuer was never in any danger of facing inconsistent holdings, interpleader was not proper. Both of the account parties disclaimed any interest in the funds.

Because the beneficiary claimed the funds and the issuer disclaimed them in the interpleader petition, the court granted summary judgment for the beneficiary against the issuer. In addition, the court treated the petition as one for declaratory relief and proceeded to resolve the issuer's reimbursement rights against the account parties, after severing that matter from the dispute between the issuer and the beneficiary. With respect to the account parties, the court held that the issuer had no right to reimbursement, because its pleadings in that matter asserted

---

[235] 723 F. Supp. 1461 (S.D. Fla. 1989).

[236] Id. at 1464.

[237] 686 S.W.2d 226 (Tex. Ct. App. 1984).

that the beneficiary's documents were not complying. In short, inconsistent allegations in the pleadings trapped the issuer into a loss against the beneficiary on the credit and a loss against the account parties on the application agreement—the very result the bank had hoped to avoid when it filed the interpleader.

The key to understanding the *Lafayette Corp.* and *Dallas Bank* opinions lies in the independence of the credit undertaking from the right to reimbursement. Because those transactions are independent, there is no possibility that the issuer can face inconsistent judgments. The issuer's losses on both matters would not be inconsistent judgments.

In *American Bank v. Leasing Serv. Co. (In re Air Conditioning, Inc. of Stuart)*,[238] the court reversed that part of a lower court's decision awarding attorney fees to an issuer that had filed a suit for instructions when the account party's trustee in bankruptcy argued that payment under the credit would constitute an improper preference under the Bankruptcy Code. The lower court treated the action as one in interpleader and granted attorney fees to the issuer. The *American Bank* court reversed the award on the ground that interpleader was not the appropriate action.

Beaufort Navigation, Inc. v. Med Africa Line S.p.A.[239] illustrates a use of interpleader that should not offend the rule of these cases. In *Beaufort Navigation*, the issuer brought an interpleader action with respect to deposits made by the account party to secure its reimbursement obligation. Because there was a surplus left in the issuer's hands after the credit expired, this kind of interpleader did not offend the independence principle.

In all of these events, the form of the action should not restrict application of credit rules such as the independence principle and the strict compliance standard. Courts generally have not permitted procedural considerations to impair the commercial effectiveness of credits. To the contrary, as the discussion of the *Dynamics* and *Intraworld* cases[240] illustrates, courts have modified procedures and evidentiary burdens in order to accommodate the credit device.

An issuer that resorts to declaratory judgment, interpleader, or similar procedural devices in order to avoid honoring a credit or to reduce its own litigation costs may be sacrificing its reputation as a credit issuer. One commentator has cautioned that issuers sometimes act in con-

---

[238] 845 F.2d 293 (11th Cir. 1988).
[239] 624 F. Supp. 229 (S.D.N.Y. 1985).
[240] For a discussion of those cases, see supra ¶ 11.04[3][b].

cert with their customers to avoid the credit obligation.[241] Other issuers are jealous of their reputations and honor the beneficiary's demand for payment in the face of the customer's charge that the beneficiary is practicing fraud, as Section 5-114(2)(b) permits an issuer to do. The cautious beneficiary identifies such issuers and insists in the underlying agreement that it have the right to approve the account party's selection of the issuer. If that practice were to become widespread, beneficiaries could use their economic leverage to police issuer conduct.

---

[241] See Thorup, "Injunctions Against Payment of Standby Letters of Credit: How Can Banks Best Protect Themselves?" 101 Banking L.J. 6, 17 (1984). This assertion by a practitioner contradicts the assumption in at least one case that, for diversity purposes, the interests of the issuer and the account party do not coincide. See supra ¶ 11.01[3].

CHAPTER 12

Credits and Bank Regulation

Most of credit law applies to all issuers. There are, however, a number of important questions that stem from the unique nature of most issuers as commercial banks subject to complex government regulation. This chapter deals with questions that arise in connection with bank insolvency, the ultra vires controversy, loan-limit rules, and other bank regulations that apply to letters of credit.

¶ 12.01 ISSUER BANK INSOLVENCY

The dual nature of the U.S. banking system renders inquiry into this area of letter of credit law problematic. There are more than fifty jurisdictions with bank insolvency laws. The most important of those are the federal laws that deal with the failure of banks chartered by the federal government. The Federal Deposit Insurance Act[1] and regulations thereunder may play some role in state bank insolvencies, however, by virtue of the fact that the FDIC insures the deposits of state banks as well as national banks and acts as receiver of many failed state banks[2] and all failed national banks.[3]

Bank failures, furthermore, have given rise to a number of options. Among them, the straight liquidation of the failed institution and the purchase and assumption transaction have featured prominently in letter of credit controversies. The presence of depositor preference statutes in some states has also raised questions in state bank insolvencies.

Finally, Section 5-117 of the Uniform Commercial Code (UCC or the Code) contributes somewhat to the confusion. That section creates a general priority rule in favor of the credit beneficiary when a bank involved in the credit transaction becomes insolvent. This rule, which applies only if the letter of credit falls within Section 5-102(1)(a) or Section 5-102(1)(b) but not Section 5-102(1)(c),[4] gives the beneficiary priority to any deposits or collateral earmarked for the credit obligation.

This section of the text attempts to sort out the rules that apply in the various controversies, but the law is not settled in this area. As the following discussion indicates, the FDIC and some of the federal circuit

---

[1] 12 U.S.C. §§ 1811–1833(e) (1988).

[2] Under federal law, the FDIC must accept the receivership role of any failed state insured bank if the state authority that closes the bank tenders that responsibility to the FDIC. See Federal Deposit Insurance Corporation Act, 12 U.S.C. § 1821(e) (1988).

[3] See Federal Deposit Insurance Corporation Act, 12 U.S.C. § 1821(c) (1988).

[4] For a discussion of the exception to Section 5-117, see infra ¶ 12.01[4].

courts of appeals have failed to resolve a knotty problem over which they are in conflict.

[1] Beneficiary's Rights Against the Issuing Bank

[a] General Claimants

If the issuer becomes insolvent, the beneficiary of the credit faces the problem it seeks to avoid: It has a claim against an insolvent entity, and, unless there is collateral or a deposit earmarked for the credit transaction, the beneficiary will be only a general creditor of the insolvent issuer. The beneficiary's plight may be complicated further by a policy that the FDIC has taken on standby credits, to the effect that the beneficiary's claim under a standby credit is contingent and is not a provable claim in the failed issuer's insolvency proceedings. This development has serious, though not necessarily adverse, implications for the standby credit's success. It forces standby beneficiaries, however, to evaluate the strength of the issuer or to refuse to accept standby credits.

In *First Empire Bank-New York v. FDIC*,[5] the court found the FDIC's position in violation of federal law. Section 194[6] of the National Bank Act requires the receiver of an insolvent national bank to make ratable distribution of the bank's assets. In the *First Empire* case, the FDIC had subsidized the purchase of the insolvent bank's assets by Crocker National Bank, which also assumed certain liabilities, among them the insolvent bank's obligations under certain outstanding letters of credit. The FDIC argued, among other things, that its differentiation between beneficiaries of some credits and beneficiaries of other credits[7] was justified by the fact that standby beneficiaries' claims are "contingent" and not provable.

---

[5] 572 F.2d 1361 (9th Cir.), cert. denied, 439 U.S. 919 (1978); see also First Empire Bank-N.Y. v. FDIC, 634 F.2d 1222 (9th Cir. 1980), cert. denied, 452 U.S. 906 (1981) (connected case in which court clarifies its earlier holding somewhat); International Westminster Bank, Ltd. v. FDIC, 509 F.2d 641 (9th Cir. 1975) (per curiam holding that beneficiaries of letters of credit could state claim for relief under Section 194); cf. Bryant v. Kerr, 726 S.W.2d 373 (Mo. Ct. App. 1987) (holding that credit continued in full force and effect, despite FDIC's disaffirmance of any obligation on it as liquidator of failed issuer).

[6] 12 U.S.C. § 194 (1988).

[7] The standby credits in question were issued by the failed bank to secure loans made by the beneficiaries to the controlling stockholder of the failed bank and related entities and persons. Because these borrowers were all of doubtful credit standing, potential purchasing banks viewed their reimbursement obligations as doubtful as well and refused to assume the credit obligations.

The Court of Appeals for the Ninth Circuit rejected the argument, holding that contingent claims that will be certain at the time of presentation (even though they are uncertain at the time of insolvency) should be considered provable and available for pro rata distribution. The court, moved by equitable principles, held that because the beneficiaries' claims were due at the time of suit, even though they were not due at the time of insolvency, the beneficiaries were entitled to ratable treatment.[8]

In *FDIC v. Freudenfeld*,[9] the FDIC again took the position that the beneficiary of a standby credit held a contingent claim at the time of insolvency, and it repudiated the letter of credit. Although the reported decision does not deal with the matter, the court relates the facts of the beneficiary's claim against the FDIC and the court's judgment in favor of the beneficiary on the authority of the *First Empire* holding.

In *FDIC v. Liberty National Bank & Trust Co.*,[10] the Court of Appeals for the Tenth Circuit followed the *First Empire* rule, even though the *Liberty National Bank* case arose out of the liquidation of a failed bank without a purchase and assumption agreement. In *Liberty National Bank*, the beneficiaries of the credits convinced the court that the credits became due on the issuer's insolvency. Given that fact and the fact that the beneficiaries made their claims before there was any distribution in the liquidation proceedings, the court concluded that the beneficiaries satisfied the *First Empire* test as holders of provable claims. As long as the claims exist before insolvency and are not dependent on obligations arising after insolvency, total liability is certain at the time of suit, and the claim is made before assets are distributed, the *First Empire* and *Liberty National Bank* courts will allow the claims.[11]

One of the claims in *Liberty National Bank* arose out of a confirming bank's right of reimbursement against the failed issuer as the opening bank. The FDIC as receiver of the failed issuer argued that, because

---

[8] The *First Empire* court also based its holding on Section 91 of the National Bank Act, 12 U.S.C. § 91 (1988), which renders avoidable transfers that prefer one creditor over another.

[9] 492 F. Supp. 763 (E.D. Wis. 1980).

[10] 806 F.2d 961 (10th Cir. 1986); accord Clement v. FDIC, 2 U.C.C. Rep. Serv. 2d (Callaghan) 1017 (W.D. Okla. 1986).

[11] The difficulty in determining the amount of a claim under a standby securing against a default that has yet to occur is illustrated in Phenix Fed. Sav. & Loan Ass'n, F.A. v. Shearson Loeb Rhoades, Inc., 856 F.2d 1125 (8th Cir. 1988). In that case, the court charged a jury to determine the losses, if any, that a plaintiff would incur in the future under its obligation to reimburse the issuer of a credit that secured bonds that also were secured by a mortgage and two additional guarantors. The jury found that the plaintiff would suffer no damages.

the confirming bank did not pay the beneficiary until after the date of the issuer's insolvency, the reimbursement claim arose after insolvency and therefore did not satisfy the *First Empire* test. The *Liberty National Bank* court held that the confirming bank's claim for reimbursement was derivative, that it arose by nature of subrogation, and that the confirming bank stood in the shoes of the beneficiary of the credit, who held a provable claim at the time of insolvency. The court did not allow the confirming bank to set off the failed bank's deposits on the right of reimbursement, though it did allow similar setoff claims of other standby beneficiaries.[12]

The *First Empire* opinion does not limit itself to purchase and assumption cases, but the FDIC has taken the position that the rule does not apply to a case involving the liquidation of a failed bank. The agency has long contended that contingent claims are not provable in a bank receivership and that in no event can the beneficiary claim more than its actual damages, even when the amount of the credit exceeds those damages.[13] To the extent that other circuits follow *First Empire* and *Freudenfeld*, the FDIC will be unable to disallow as not provable claims by beneficiaries of standby credits against receivers of national banks.[14]

Nothing in the *First Empire* line of authority applies in state bank insolvencies. *First Empire* applies National Bank Act provisions. State bank insolvencies generally are governed by state insolvency statutes.[15]

Beneficiaries have argued that the Federal Deposit Insurance Act provides them with protection as depositors insured up to the $100,000 limit. The Act defines an insured deposit to include a deposit evidenced by a letter of credit,[16] and, in a few cases, beneficiaries have pursued the

[12] See discussion infra ¶ 12.01[1][c].

[13] For the rule that a beneficiary's rights under a standby are not determined by its losses in the transaction secured by the credit, see ¶ 9.02[5][b][ii]. For general discussion of the FDIC's position in circuits that have not followed *First Empire*, see Bates, "The FDIC Failed Bank Program and Letters of Credit" in American Bar Association, Letters of Credit and Financial Institution Insolvencies (1989).

[14] In A.G. Edwards & Sons v. FDIC, No. 82 Civ. 2014-W (W.D. Okla. Feb. 18, 1986), the court held that the beneficiary did not satisfy the second element of the *First Empire* test and could not maintain an action against the FDIC. In *A.G. Edwards*, the credit secured lease payments to the beneficiary by an equipment lessee that had filed for reorganization under the Bankruptcy Code. Because the credit called for the beneficiary's certificate to the effect that the lessee had defaulted and because, in fact, the lessee was not in default, the beneficiary could not satisfy *First Empire*.

[15] International Fidelity Ins. Co. v. State Bank of Commerce, No. 87-3456 (E.D. La. June 6, 1988).

[16] See 12 U.S.C. § 1813(l)(1)(1988).

argument vigorously.[17] The Supreme Court, however, has held specifically that standby letters of credit for which the account party has given the issuer a conditional[18] note are not insured deposits under the statute.[19] The Court held, in *Philadelphia Gear Corp. v. FDIC*, that it does not matter whether the note is negotiable or nonnegotiable.[20] The key consideration in the Court's view is whether the account party has given the issuer hard earnings. The fact that the note was conditioned upon payment to the beneficiary and that payment did not occur rendered the note something less than "hard earnings," which the *Philadelphia Gear* court felt Congress intended to protect when it enacted the Deposit Insurance Act.

The Court characterized the beneficiary's attempt to gain coverage for the standby as an effort to render the issuer's undertaking insured. There is little evidence in the statutory history, the Court held, to support that effort. In a dissenting opinion, three justices argued that the negotiability of the note in *Philadelphia Gear* rendered the credit one that came within the clear language of the statute. Significantly, the dissent opined that, in the event the account party gives the issuer a nonnegotiable note, the credit will not be an insured deposit.[21]

The Court's holding in *Philadelphia Gear* suggests that banks wanting to make it clear that their standby credits are not insured deposits may find it useful to incorporate the conditions of the note into the note itself. Such action is not required by the majority opinion and destroys the negotiability of the note, but the danger that a court may view a negotiable note as hard earnings may justify this caution.

---

[17] See Philadelphia Gear Corp. v. FDIC, 751 F.2d 1131 (10th Cir. 1984), rev'd, 476 U.S. 426 (1986); Allen v. FDIC, 599 F. Supp. 104 (E.D. Tenn. 1984), rev'd and remanded, 815 F.2d 75 (6th Cir. 1987); Seattle-First Nat'l Bank v. FDIC, 619 F. Supp. 1351 (W.D. Okla. 1985); Wilshire Bank v. FDIC (W.D. Okla. 1985), reported in Letter of Credit Update 24 (Nov. 1985).

[18] The note in *Philadelphia Gear* was conditional to the extent that the customer of the bank, the account party on the standby, would owe nothing to the bank unless it paid under the standby. As is often the case, however, the note did not indicate that it was conditional.

[19] Philadelphia Gear Corp. v. FDIC, 476 U.S. 426 (1986). For discussion of the issues in the *Philadelphia Gear* case, see Note, "Standby Letters of Credit: Are They Insured Deposits?" 32 Wayne L. Rev. 1165 (1986).

[20] The Court of Appeals for the Tenth Circuit, in *Philadelphia Gear*, ruled that the note in that case was negotiable; but the opinion contains language suggesting that, whether negotiable or not, the decision would have been the same. See Philadelphia Gear Corp. v. FDIC, 751 F.2d 1131, 1134–1135 (10th Cir. 1984), rev'd, 476 U.S. 426 (1986).

[21] FDIC v. Philadelphia Gear Corp., 476 U.S. 426 (1986) (Marshall, J., dissenting); cf. Allen v. FDIC, 599 F. Supp. 104 (E.D. Tenn. 1984), rev'd and remanded, 815 F.2d 75 (6th Cir. 1987) (involving a nonnegotiable promise to reimburse).

In *Tosco Corp. v. FDIC*,[22] the FDIC-receiver intervened in litigation on appeal. In *Tosco*, the beneficiary had obtained judgment against the bank issuer, and the bank had failed while the matter was on appeal. The *Tosco* court held that the FDIC-receiver's liabilities were measured under state law.[23] Significantly, the *Tosco* court found nothing in state law or federal law giving the FDIC "any special privileges as a receiver of a State bank as compared to any other receiver"[24] and held that the FDIC-receiver "stands in the shoes of the Bank."[25]

Generally, the FDIC takes the position that, in its capacity as receiver of a state bank or any bank, it stands on higher ground than the issuer does and that its rights are akin to those of a bona fide purchaser. That view rests on the decision of the U.S. Supreme Court in *D'Oench Duhme & Co. v. FDIC*.[26] In that case, the Court found that the claimant had conspired with the bank prior to its insolvency to give the bank a note, with the understanding that the bank would not call it. The Court held that the FDIC could enforce the note according to its terms.[27] The Court's rationale supports the FDIC's view that, to the extent the insolvent bank and the claimant have engaged in fraud, the rights of the FDIC-receiver are not constrained by the bank's misconduct.[28] There is strong and persuasive language in the concurring opinion of Justice Jackson in *D'Oench Duhme*, to the effect that, in a good faith transaction, the FDIC succeeds only to the rights of the issuer.[29]

---

[22] 723 F.2d 1242 (6th Cir. 1983).

[23] Cf. 12 U.S.C. § 1821(g) (1988) (subrogation rights of the FDIC-insurer determined by state law); FDIC v. Braemoor Assocs., 686 F.2d 550 (7th Cir. 1982) (looking to state law in FDIC-insurer suit).

[24] Tosco Corp. v. FDIC, 723 F.2d 1242, 1247 (6th Cir. 1983).

[25] Id.; see also 18 U.S.C. § 1819 (fourth) (1988) (providing that suits involving FDIC as receiver and rights of depositors and creditors shall not be deemed to arise under federal law). But cf. Warner v. Central Trust Co., 798 F.2d 167 (6th Cir. 1986) (holding that rights of FDIC as receiver of failed beneficiary, as opposed to failed issuer, are determined by federal law).

[26] 315 U.S. 447 (1942).

[27] The FDIC brought suit in the *D'Oench Duhme* case in its corporate capacity, but the language of the Court's opinion and the precedent on which it relies suggest that the policy served by the result is one of protecting the federal agency in both of its capacities. See id. at 457.

[28] See also FDIC v. Braemoor Assocs., 686 F.2d 550, 554 (7th Cir. 1982) ("*D'Oench* teaches that an asset can confer on its holder greater rights when it comes into the hands of the FDIC.").

[29] "The Corporation would succeed only to the rights which the bank itself acquired where ordinary and good faith commercial transactions are involved." D'Oench Duhme & Co. v. FDIC, 315 U.S. 447, 474 (Jackson, J., concurring); cf. In re Longhorn Sec. Litig., 573 F. Supp. 278 (J.P.M.D.L. W.D. Okla. 1983) (restricting *D'Oench Duhme* rule to situations where party participates in fraud on FDIC); Union County Bank v. FDIC, No. 712 (Tenn. Ct. App. Sept. 18, 1987) (same).

In *FDIC v. Kerr*,[30] the guarantor of the account party's obligation in the underlying contract complained when the FDIC, as liquidator of a failed state bank, disaffirmed the credit that secured the account party's undertaking. The *Kerr* court dismissed the claim because, among other reasons, the claimant had failed to file his proof of claim within the statutory period provided by state law[31] and the successor had not agreed to be bound by the failed bank's credit undertakings.

[b]　Claimants to a Specific Deposit

A brief review of the law that arose out of the wave of bank failures that occurred in the 1930s is essential to an understanding of the Code rule in Section 5-117 and especially of its distinctions based on the scope provisions of Article 5.[32] That review indicates that pre-Code letter of credit law gave priority to the beneficiary's claim if the account party had earmarked deposit funds or if it had granted the issuer a security interest in collateral to cover the issuer's undertaking. To the extent that the account party was subrogated to the rights of the beneficiary, he benefited from the priority also. Pre-Code law treated the deposit as trust funds, not as general deposits, and it treated the collateral as being impressed with a trust as well.

The leading case is *Bank of United States v. Seltzer*.[33] In that case, the account party took the unusual step of paying the holders of time drafts accepted by the bank issuer of a commercial credit. In other words, the account party purchased acceptances created by its bank in payment of the account party's own obligation to the beneficiary in an underlying transaction. Thus the account party was holding acceptances for which it would have had to reimburse the bank after the bank honored them. In light of the bank issuer's troubles, it was in the interest of the account party to buy the acceptances, thereby keeping the beneficiary happy and forestalling any suit on the underlying contract—a suit that would have eventuated if the issuer had failed to honor the acceptances.[34] Before the acceptances came due, the bank closed, and, by vir-

---

[30] 650 F. Supp. 1356 (W.D.N.C. 1986).

[31] Mo. Ann. Stat. § 361.570 (Vernon Supp. 1987).

[32] For general treatment of the many issues discussed in this subparagraph, see Schlesinger, Article 5—"Documentary Letters of Credit," in New York Law Revisions Commission, Study of Uniform Commercial Code 1707–1716 (1955); Berger, "The Effects of Issuing Bank Insolvency on Letters of Credit," 21 Harv. Int'l L.J. 161 (1980).

[33] 233 A.D. 225, 251 N.Y.S. 637 (1931).

[34] Cf. U.C.C. 2-325(2) (providing that establishment of credit suspends account party's obligation to beneficiary on underlying obligation and that dishonor of credit terminates that suspension).

tue of its payments to the acceptance holders, the account party stood in the shoes of the credit beneficiary.[35]

The bank's liquidator argued that the beneficiary would have been only a general creditor and, accordingly, that the account party's rights were no greater than those of a general creditor. The account party, however, had executed a trust receipt in the nature of a security agreement granting the issuer title to goods when the bank accepted the drafts, the arrangement serving to protect the bank's right of reimbursement. The liquidator argued that it could enforce the bank's title to the goods under the trust receipt and that the account party, clothed only with the rights of the credit beneficiary, would have to file a general claim in the liquidation.

The *Seltzer* court held that the bank's interest in the goods extended no further than the amount of the bank's payments under the acceptances. Since the account party had satisfied the acceptance obligations, the bank would not be called upon to make payments on the acceptances and therefore had no interest in the goods. *Seltzer* holds, in effect, that the issuer's interest in the goods was only that of a secured party and that, because the bank would not be making any advances (the account party having paid the acceptances), the bank had no interest in the goods.

Seltzer makes two points:

1. The interest of an issuer in the goods under a commercial credit is a security interest.
2. To the extent the account party makes provisions to pay the beneficiary, the bank realizes a benefit and cannot take action against the account party.

The first point presages the rule of the Code,[36] and the second is consistent with the rule. Less obvious is the implication in the second point that if the account party makes a deposit in order to satisfy the issuer's

---

[35] The *Seltzer* case, then, may have involved a strict question of acceptance law, not a question of letter of credit law. Good authority, however, supports the position that even after an issuer satisfies the credit undertaking by accepting a time draft, there remains the obligation under the credit to pay that draft when it matures. For a further discussion of this overlap between acceptance liability and credit liability, see ¶¶ 2.08[4], 2.09[1].

[36] See U.C.C. § 5-117 & comment. But cf. Hendries, Inc. v. American Express Co., 35 A.D.2d 412, 316 N.Y.S.2d 554 (1970), appeal dismissed, 29 N.Y.2d 546, 272 N.E.2d 581, 324 N.Y.S.2d 92 (1971) (holding that issuer was owner of goods subject to documents presented under letter of credit); U.C.C. § 7-502(1)(b) (same). See generally ¶ 8.03.

credit obligation, the beneficiary has a priority claim to that deposit. That implication follows, though the analysis is a bit complex.

In *Seltzer*, the account party, had it not given the bank issuer a security interest and had it not been subject to an obligation to reimburse the issuer for paying the acceptances, presumably would have presented the acceptances for payment. In that event, the issuer's liquidator would have treated the claim as any general claim and would have paid it with dividends on the same pro rata basis that it would pay other general claimants. In short, as a general claimant, the holder of the acceptances would receive, say, 10 percent of the face amount of the acceptances. Because the *Seltzer* account party had pledged assets to the issuer, however, it did not present the acceptances. Undoubtedly, its lawyers reasoned that to do so would be a useless act because any payment that the liquidator made on the acceptances would be charged against the account party's collateral. By presenting the acceptances, the account party would have been asking itself for payment. The *Seltzer* account party then completed the circle by asking the court to order the liquidator to return the collateral. By acceding to that request, the court, one may argue, gave the account party 100 percent of its claim.

The advantage the *Seltzer* account party achieved is evident by comparing the result in that case with the result advocated by the issuer's liquidator. The liquidator would have the account party present the acceptances for payment at the hypothetical 10 percent dividend. Then the liquidator would claim all of the collateral pledged by the account party. The account party would lose the collateral and get only 10 percent of the face value of the acceptances. The *Seltzer* court permitted the account party to sacrifice the 10 percent for the full value of its collateral.

On the other hand, since the account party never made any claim but only asked that its collateral be returned, one may view *Seltzer* as a case involving no claim at all. Under that view, of course, the account party is not a favored claimant but is simply an owner of collateral seeking its return when the issuer has no right to it.

Under the first view, however, under which the account party is receiving 100 percent of its claim, it is only a short step to the conclusion that the *beneficiary* should receive 100 percent of its claim as well. Had the account party in *Seltzer* not purchased the acceptances from the beneficiary, the beneficiary would have been able to make the same arguments that the account party had made, that is, that the issuer's rights in the collateral were measured by the amount it had paid on the acceptances and, therefore, that the beneficiary's position was directly related to the value of the collateral (or, by analogy, the deposit) pledged to the issuer by the account party. If the collateral was worth one-half of the face value of the acceptances, the beneficiary would get one-half of the value and would be a general claimant for the other half. If the collateral was worth 100 percent of the face amount of the acceptances, the beneficiary would get 100 percent of the face value. In any event, the account party would get any collateral that was not needed by the issuer to pay the beneficiary. All of those conclusions are implicit in the *Seltzer* holding.

In *Taussig v. Carnegie Trust Co.*,[37] the account party deposited funds to cover a traveler's letter of credit[38] issued to himself. Contrary to the implications of the *Seltzer* rule, the *Taussig* court held that the deposits were not trust funds and that the beneficiary had no claim to them prior to those of the insolvent bank's general creditors. *Taussig* may be a maverick case[39] that is impossible to reconcile with the *Seltzer* rule. On the other hand, *Taussig* may serve to illustrate the true rationale for *Seltzer* and for the exception in Section 5-117, discussed below.[40]

Seltzer was an appealing case. The bank liquidator was attempting to enforce its claim against the account party on the application agreement while reneging, in effect, on the bank's engagement under the credit to pay the beneficiary the face amount of the draft. The *Seltzer* court saw the bank's breach of the credit engagement as a failure of consideration that extinguished the account party's secured promise under the application agreement.

The same argument might have been appropriate in *Taussig*, where the bank also reneged on its credit engagement and sought to enforce the application agreement, in a sense, by charging the account party's special deposit account. The trouble with Taussig's argument was that it looked too much like an attempt by a depositor to escape the treatment the law accorded other depositors. Taussig wanted full reimbursement of his deposit, while other depositors would settle for dividends that would undoubtedly be less than 100 percent.

In fact, the *Seltzer* case is not different from *Taussig*; it only gives the appearance of being different. If Seltzer had deposited funds to cov-

---

[37] 156 A.D. 519, 141 N.Y.S. 347 (1913), aff'd, 213 N.Y. 627, 107 N.E. 1086 (1914).

[38] The traveler's letter of credit, now rare, resembled the agent credit described in ¶ 3.02. Prior to the advent of credit cards, a person embarking on foreign travel arranged for credit during his stay abroad by asking his bank to issue a traveler's letter of credit. Foreign banks then honored the traveler's drafts, confident that the credit issuer would reimburse them.

[39] See H. Harfield, Bank Credits and Acceptances 247–250 (5th ed. 1974).

[40] See infra ¶ 12.01[4].

er the credit, rather than pledging the goods as security, it would have been attempting to achieve the status of a preferred depositor.

Greenough v. Munroe,[41] a case that follows the rule of *Seltzer*, involved an account party's cash deposit, not collateral; yet the court held in favor of the depositor. *Greenough* differs from *Taussig* and resembles *Seltzer*, however, in the fact that the beneficiary was a third party. In *Taussig*, the beneficiary and the account party were the same.[42]

That the beneficiary was the account party does not justify different treatment. The effect of the *Seltzer* and *Greenough* holdings is to give the account party (a person who was a depositor in the second case and one analogous to a depositor in the first) rights superior to those of other depositors. The nature of the traveler's letter of credit in *Taussig* does not justify a different rule, and the case is either (1) bad law inconsistent with *Seltzer* and *Greenough* or (2) a reasoned decision that exposes the fallacy of *Seltzer* and *Greenough*. However one might characterize the cases, they explain away some of the confusion that arises out of Section 5-117.

The application of Section 5-117 in national bank failures must abide the determination that it does not conflict with federal law. The provision appears to be inconsistent with Sections 91[43] and 194[44] of the National Bank Act, which require ratable distribution and forbid preferential transfers of the failed bank's assets in insolvency proceedings. Pre-Code cases, however, generally validate the trust theory that Section 5-117 codifies.[45]

[c] Setoff

In *FDIC v. Liberty National Bank & Trust Co.*,[46] bank beneficiaries of a failed issuer's credits sought to set off deposit obligations due the issuer against sums due under the credits. The FDIC argued that the set-

---

[41] 46 F.2d 537 (S.D.N.Y.), aff'd, 53 F.2d 362 (2d Cir.), cert. denied sub nom. Irving Trust Co. v. Oliver Straw Goods Corp., 284 U.S. 672 (1931).

[42] See also Shawmut Corp. v. William H. Bobrick Sales Corp., 260 N.Y. 499, 184 N.E. 68 (1933); see generally Neidle & Bishop, "Commercial Letters of Credit: Effect of Suspension of Issuing Bank," 32 Colum. L. Rev. 1 (1932).

[43] 12 U.S.C. § 91 (1988).

[44] 12 U.S.C. § 194 (1988).

[45] The leading case is Jennings v. United States Fidelity & Guar. Co., 294 U.S. 216 (1935). Schlesinger argues that only to the extent depositors create the trust account by transferring funds from a general deposit account to the earmarked account does the rule of U.C.C. § 5-117 conflict with federal precedent. See, Schlesinger, supra note 32, at 1712–1713.

[46] 806 F.2d 961 (10th Cir. 1986).

offs violated the Act's policy of treating all claimants equally; but the court held that, under equitable principles, the beneficiaries should be able to exercise the setoff right. Significantly, the court denied the right to a confirming bank that paid the beneficiary after the date of the issuer's insolvency. The confirming bank's claim against the issuer for reimbursement and the deposit liability were not mutual at the time of insolvency, the court held.[47]

In *FDIC v. Miller*,[48] the court applied Kansas law[49] to a similar setoff claim. In the *Miller* case, the beneficiary of a credit issued by the failed bank was also the obligor on a promissory note held by the bank at the time it failed. The court reasoned that to permit the beneficiary to set off the balance on the note against the sums due on the credit would upset the Kansas legislature's scheme for distributing the assets of the bank.

There is something so basic in the setoff notion that courts are reluctant to deny setoff rights. When *A* owes *B* $100 and *B* owes *A* $100, there is a measure of Solomonic wisdom in saying that the parties do not owe each other anything.[50] That wisdom notwithstanding, setoff gives the party exercising the right 100 percent of his claim against the assets of an insolvent bank when other parties will receive less and when the legislature has decreed that other creditors should come first. The *Miller* case has something to commend it.

Generally, federal law recognizes setoff, however, in insolvency proceedings. Section 553 of the Bankruptcy Code[51] permits a bank, as a creditor, to set off a borrower's debt against the bank's deposit liability to the customer. Cases construing the National Bank Act's ratable distribution[52] and antipreference[53] sections have held that the converse is also true: the depositor may set off, against his debts due the failing bank, the bank's deposit obligation due him.[54]

---

[47] For discussion of the confirming bank's reimbursement claim as provable in the liquidation, see supra ¶ 12.01[1][a].

[48] 659 F. Supp. 388 (D. Kan. 1987).

[49] Kan. Stat. Ann. § 9-1906 (Supp. 1989).

[50] For discussion of setoff that is helpful in this context, see Lloyd, "The Development of Setoff," 64 U. Pa. L. Rev. 541 (1916); Comment, "Bank Insolvency and Depositor Setoff," 51 U. Chi. L. Rev. 188 (1984).

[51] 11 U.S.C. § 553 (1988).

[52] 12 U.S.C. § 91 (1988).

[53] 12 U.S.C. § 194 (1988).

[54] See, e.g., Scott v. Armstrong, 146 U.S. 499 (1892); FDIC v. Mademoiselle of Cal., 379 F.2d 660 (9th Cir. 1967); Davis v. McNair, 48 F.2d 494 (5th Cir. 1931); Chase Manhattan Bank, N.A. v. FDIC, 554 F. Supp. 251 (W.D. Okla. 1983).

The issue is one of balancing the appeal of setoff against the explicit policy of the National Bank Act and state depositor preference statutes to provide ratable distribution of the failed institution's assets, to avoid preferences, and to prefer depositors.[55] It is regrettable that the courts, with the exception of the *Miller* court, invoke setoff in the letter of credit cases without considering those competing policies.

[2] Beneficiary's Rights Against Account Party

The Section 5-117 rule giving the beneficiary a priority claim against deposits or collateral specifically designated for the credit codifies *Bank of United States v. Seltzer*[56] and *Greenough v. Monroe*.[57] Significantly, the opinions in both of these cases investigate the liability of the account party on the underlying agreement.[58] In *Greenough*, the trial court hesitated to impose a trust on the account party's deposit because it doubted that the account party was liable to the seller-beneficiaries. The appellate court, however, thought the liability was clear.[59] In *Seltzer*, the court expressed no reservations on the question, holding that issuance of a letter of credit does not extinguish the account party's liability on the underlying contract.

Section 2-325(2) of the Code stipulates that issuance of the credit discharges the account party only so long as the credit is not dishonored. In the event of dishonor, the beneficiary may sue the issuer on the credit[60] and may sue the account party on the underlying obligation.[61]

Arguably, the duty of the account party to pay the beneficiary on the issuer's default does not justify the rule of *Seltzer* and *Greenough*. If the account party is a general depositor, he loses his deposit and becomes a general creditor and must then pay the beneficiary; yet there is

---

[55] For discussion of those policies, see Comment, "Bank Insolvency and Depositor Setoff," 51 U. Chi. L. Rev. 188 (1984).

[56] 233 A.D. 225, 251 N.Y. 637 (1931).

[57] 46 F.2d 537 (S.D.N.Y.), aff'd, 53 F.2d 362 (2d Cir.), cert. denied sub nom. Irving Trust Co. v. Oliver Straw Goods Corp., 284 U.S. 672 (1931).

[58] For discussion of the *Seltzer* and *Greenough* cases, see supra ¶ 12.01[1][b].

[59] Greenough v. Monroe, 53 F.2d 362 (2d Cir.), cert. denied sub nom. Irving Trust Co. v. Oliver Straw Goods Corp., 284 U.S. 672 (1931).

[60] See discussion in ¶¶ 6.01–6.03.

[61] Cf. U.C.C. § 3-802(1) (similar rule for transactions involving negotiable instruments); see also FDIC v. Bachman, 894 F.2d 1233 (10th Cir. 1990) (holding that letters of credit were not equivalent of cash); AOV Indus. Inc. v. Lambert Coal Co., 64 Bankr. 933 (Bankr. D.D.C. 1986) (dictum to effect that transfer of credit to supplier suspends supplier's claim against first beneficiary under supply contract).

no double-loss. The account party, even though he must pay the beneficiary, faces only one loss—that of his deposit. The money he pays the beneficiary is in return for the benefit the account party receives out of the underlying contract. The account parties in *Seltzer* and *Greenough* would lose no more than the account party in *Taussig*, and the absence of account party liability in *Taussig* does not justify the different treatment.

[3] Nature of the Deposit

It is clear that the priority rule of Section 5-117 operates only if the account party turns over collateral to the bank, puts the bank in funds, or authorizes the bank to allocate previously deposited funds "to secure or meet obligations under the credit."[62] A general deposit account does not satisfy Section 5-117, and the beneficiary does not have priority in such an account.[63]

In *Suomen Pankki v. Bell*,[64] the account party attempted to assert a claim to payments it had made to a U.S. agency of a Japanese bank in order to cover credits that either never were issued or never were paid. Noting that the agency was not authorized to accept deposits in the United States, the court recognized the payments as creating a general debtor-creditor relationship, not a special account.

In re People's State Bank[65] involved a curious scheme whereby a money broker prompted a small bank to accept funds from individuals, issue "letters of credit" to the individuals, and allocate the funds (some $2.3 million) to the account of the broker, who withdrew most of the money. When the bank declared insolvency, the court held that the "letters of credit" were evidence of deposits and that the beneficiaries of the letters held valid claims as depositors in the receivership. Throughout the opinion, the court used the term "letters of credit" in quotation marks, and the case should not stand as authority for the proposition that such an arrangement between a bank and its depositors necessarily

---

[62] U.C.C. § 5-117(1).

[63] Note that the priority rule of Section 5-117(1) does not apply if the credit is clean, that is, if it does not come within Section 5-102(1)(a) or Section 5-102(1)(b). Parties may not assure themselves of priority simply by designating the bank's obligation as a letter of credit, thereby bringing the obligation within Section 5-102(1)(c). Beneficiaries of standby credits might avoid the problem by taking care that their credits call for some "piece of paper." See U.C.C. § 5-102, comment 1 (6th sentence). See also infra ¶ 12.01[4] (further discussion of the exception).

[64] 80 N.Y.S 2d 821 (Sup. Ct. 1948).

[65] 51 Mich. App. 421, 215 N.W.2d 722 (1974).

constitutes a letter of credit to which the priority rule of Section 5-117 applies. The *People's State Bank* holding turns on the fact that the beneficiaries provided the funds that were due under the "credits," not on the fact that the claimants were beneficiaries of a letter of credit. The facts suggest, moreover, that the "letters of credit" were in the nature of certificates of deposit.[66]

[4] Exception in Section 5-117 of the Code

Section 5-117(1) creates a preference in favor of the beneficiary or the account party if the account party has deposited funds for payment of the credit or if it has pledged collateral to secure its reimbursement obligation. The section applies only to credits that fall into Section 5-102(1)(a) or Section 5-102(1)(b) (the automatic scope provisions[67]) but not Section 5-102(1)(c) (the permissive scope provision). That exception for credits that do not fall within the automatic scope provisions merits discussion for two reasons:

1. It rests on a distinction that cases construing the scope provisions render invalid.
2. The exception exposes the weakness of the priority rule itself.

In short, the exception renders the rule irrational in operation and in theory.

[a] Distinction Between Automatic and Permissive Scope Provisions

It appears that the Code drafters originally fashioned the automatic scope provisions of Sections 5-102(1)(a) and 5-102(1)(b) to cover commercial credits. The permissive scope provision of Subsection 5-102(1)(c) apparently was fashioned to cover standby credits that were in their infancy and that were at that time called clean credits.[68] The drafters apparently thought that commercial credits always called for documents and therefore would fall into subsection (a) or (b) and thereby would be covered automatically. They also apparently thought that

---

[66] The forms of the "letters of credit" in the *People's State Bank* case have some vague similarity to certificates of deposit, but they meet the "letter of credit" definition squarely. See U.C.C. § 5-103(1)(a).

[67] For a discussion of the scope provision, see ¶¶ 2.03–2.06.

[68] See U.C.C. § 5-102, comment 1 (2d para.); Wiley, "How to Use Letters of Credit in Financing the Sale of Goods," 20 Bus. Law 495, 516 (1965).

standby credits, not calling for documents, would be covered by Article 5 only if the parties conspicuously designated them as letters of credit. In that case, the standby would fall into Section 5-102(1)(c) and would not benefit from the priority rule in Section 5-117.

[b] Code Rationale

The comment to Section 5-117 justifies the priority treatment of commercial credits in issuer insolvencies on the ground that documents and special deposits taken by an issuer in connection with a commercial letter of credit should be considered separate from the bank's deposit liabilities and general assets. That distinction does not justify different treatment for bank creditors under commercial letter of credit transactions from that accorded other creditors. The comment rationalizes the different treatment on the ground that the preference serves to satisfy everybody's expectations.[69]

Bank insolvencies frustrate expectations in all of the bank's activities, not just those in letter of credit transactions, and it is probably fairer to say that the drafters simply made a policy judgment that bank insolvencies that disrupt a good bit of commerce should not disrupt the commercial letter of credit. Significantly, the drafters did not resort to the failure of consideration rationales that the *Seltzer* and *Greenough* courts invoked. It is also significant that the drafters justified the exception for clean credits (those falling into the permissive scope provision of Section 5-102(1)(c)) in order "to prevent abuse in situations where the commercial purpose of facilitating the movement of goods, securities or the like may be lacking."[70] It may be, however, that the drafters were attempting to codify the law as they read it, giving commercial letters of credit protection under the trust theory and depriving that protection to credits such as that in *Taussig* that are uncommon and commercially unimportant.

[c] Problem Defined

It may be, contrary to the view advanced by this treatise, that the drafters were correct in distinguishing commercial and standby credits by according priority in the former but not in the latter. The language of the section, however, does not achieve that result, because the courts have expanded the automatic scope provisions to the point that they

---

[69] U.C.C. § 5-117, comment (2d para.).
[70] Id. (4th para.).

cover letters of credit that call for "any piece of paper."[71] Standby credits usually call for drafts or some kind of certificate. They therefore fall within the automatic scope provisions and qualify for the priority rule of Section 5-117, contrary to the drafters' assumption.

It is not clear why the drafters thought standby credits that do not facilitate the purchase of goods might create possibilities for abuse. If they do, however, courts should not extend the priority rule to standby credit situations. Applying the priority rule of Section 5-117 to the standby credit would be consistent with the language of the section but would be inconsistent with the section's intent to exclude noncommercial credits.[72] It may be that the abuse the drafters wanted to avoid is illustrated by the case in which a depositor, in order to protect himself from a bank's insolvency, alters what normally would be a straight bank-depositor relationship into a letter of credit transaction.[73]

The *Taussig* case resembles such an arrangement, and it may have been that concern that prompted the result in *Taussig*. Yet all letter of credit transactions resemble such an arrangement. Section 5-117 gives priority to special deposits earmarked for payment under the credit. That arrangement is not far removed from one in which a bank customer makes a significant deposit to cover a check. Yet Section 5-117 grants priority to the former and general creditor status to the latter.

[d] Preemption Question

Section 194 of the National Bank Act[74] requires the liquidator of an insolvent national bank to make ratable distribution of the closed bank's assets. Courts might construe that provision as inconsistent with the priority rule of Section 5-117, which pays some depositors in full while others receive only partial dividends. Even if courts accept the general priority rule of the section, they might reject the exception. Certainly, the *First Empire* case[75] suggests as much, though other authority recognizing in some instances the notion that such a deposit is im-

---

[71] U.C.C. § 5-102, comment 1 (1st para., last sentence); cf. U.C.C. § 5-103(1)(b) (defining documentary requirement broadly). For general discussion of the cases, see ¶¶ 2.03–2.04.

[72] Cf. U.C.C. § 1-102(2) & comment 1 (2d para., last sentence) (suggesting that Code provisions must be applied not literally but in order to serve their underlying purpose).

[73] For two such cases, see American Nat'l Bank v. FDIC, 710 F.2d 1528 (11th Cir. 1983); In re Peoples State Bank, 51 Mich. App. 421, 215 N.W.2d 722 (1974).

[74] 12 U.S.C. § 194 (1988).

[75] For a discussion of *First Empire*, see supra ¶ 12.01[1][a]. Accord Philadelphia Gear Corp. v. FDIC, 751 F.2d 1131 (10th Cir. 1984), rev'd, 476 U.S. 426 (1986).

pressed with a trust and that such a deposit merits preferred treatment.[76]

[5] Protecting Against Issuer Insolvency

For the beneficiary of the credit, the financial integrity of the issuer is of paramount importance, and beneficiaries should not fail to investigate the strength of the credit issuer. Given the complexity of the credit transaction, the many industries to which parties have adapted the standby credit, and the large number of new entrants into the ranks of credit issuers,[77] some beneficiaries may be lulled into a false sense of security by virtue of the credit's issuance. It is not surprising that letters of credit have figured in a number of fraudulent or allegedly fraudulent schemes.[78] Sophisticated beneficiaries insist in the underlying contract on the right to reject credits issued by unsatisfactory issuers or insist on confirmation by a bank or other institution of known financial strength. Some government agencies have established procedures for approving issuers, based on their ratings by independent rating services and on their financial statements.[79]

¶ 12.02   THE ULTRA VIRES QUESTION

Few arguments have provoked as much concern and deserved it less than the argument that standby letters of credit are unauthorized bank promises that the issuer may repudiate. Virtually all considered authority rejects this argument, because the issuance of standby credits is consistent with traditional banking functions and, even if the activity were

---

[76] See discussion and authority supra ¶ 12.01[1][b]. Cf. Philadelphia Gear Corp. v. FDIC, 476 U.S. 426, 429 (Marshall, J., dissenting) (suggesting that certain creditors do have priority under Section 5-117).

[77] For discussion of the growth of the commercial credit and the standby credit and the expanded number of credit issuers, see ¶¶ 3.05, 3.06.

[78] See, e.g., United States v. Tucker, 773 F.2d 136 (7th Cir. 1985), cert. denied, 478 U.S. 1022 (1986); Kranzdorf v. Green, 76 Bankr. 974 (Bankr. E.D. Pa. 1987); Cromwell v. Commerce & Energy Bank, 464 So. 2d 721 (La. 1985).

[79] See Federal National Mortgage Association, Multifamily Guide, Part II, Conventional Selling, Underwriting Guidelines § 307 (Aug. 1, 1988); "NAIC Letters on 'Qualified' Bank Listing," Letters of Credit Update 45 (Oct. 1989) (describing program of National Association of Insurance Commissioners); Austin, Tex. City Council Resolution (Sept. 24, 1987) (city ordinance to similar effect). For discussion of similar efforts by the Saudi Arabian government, see Slimane, "Guarantee Bonds Issued in Favor of Saudi Public Entities," Int'l Fin. L. Rev. 27 (Sept. 1986).

beyond the authority granted in the bank's charter or under governing law, most cases and commentators would hold that neither the bank nor its customer should be able to assert the defense.

[1] The Standby Credit Is Not a Guaranty

[a] Rule Against Guaranties

It has long been the general view that a bank may not guarantee the performance of a third party.[80] There are many clear exceptions to that general rule, and the critical question is to determine what the law finds objectionable in bank guaranties. Banks endorse billions of negotiable instruments every year, and an endorser, in a sense, guarantees payment of the instrument to subsequent holders.[81] Banks issue commercial letters of credit in significant numbers. Commercial letters of credit, in a sense, are also guaranties because they substitute the liability of the issuer for that of the account party. Banks are authorized by law to issue some indemnities,[82] which are a clear form of guaranty.

---

[80] See, e.g., United Bank v. Quadrangle, Ltd., 42 Colo. App. 486, 506 P.2d 408 (1979); Bridge v. Welda State Bank, 222 Mo. App. 586, 292 S.W. 1079 (1927); Republic Nat'l Bank v. Northwest Nat'l Bank, 566 S.W.2d 358 (Tex. Civ. App.), rev'd, 578 S.W.2d 109 (Tex. 1978); cf. 12 C.F.R. § 332.1 (1990) (FDIC rule generally prohibiting banks from issuing guaranties); 12 C.F.R. § 347.3(c)(1) (1990) (FDIC exception from general prohibition against guaranties for letters of credit). For the history of the rule, see Lord, "The No-Guaranty Rule and the Standby Letter of Credit Controversy," 96 Banking L.J. 46 (1979). For a defense of the right of banks to issue commercial letters of credit, see Trimble, "The Implied Power of National Banks to Issue Letters of Credit and Accept Bills," 58 Yale L.J. 713 (1949). For discussion of the authority of a national bank to issue guaranties, see Comptroller of the Currency, Interpretive Letter No. 376, reprinted in [1985–1987 Transfer Binder] Fed. Banking L. Rep. (CCH) ¶ 85,600 (Oct. 25, 1986).

[81] See U.C.C. § 3-414(1).

[82] See, e.g., U.C.C. § 5-113. Some contend that the proper distinction is not one between guaranties and nonguaranties but one between guaranties of a transaction in which the bank has an interest and has done a credit analysis and one in which it is simply a surety. See Comptroller of the Currency, Staff Interpretive Letter No. 218, reprinted in [1981–1982 Transfer Binder] Fed. Banking L. Rep. (CCH) ¶ 85,299 (Sept. 16, 1981); see also 12 C.F.R. § 7.7010(a) (1989) (Comptroller of the Currency Interpretive Ruling permitting a national bank to become a guarantor "if it has a substantial interest in the performance of the transaction involved"); 12 C.F.R. § 7.7016 (1989) (Comptroller of the Currency interpretive ruling setting out authority of a national bank to issue letters of credit and sound banking procedures therefor); 12 C.F.R. § 347.3(c)(1) (1989) (FDIC regulation authorizing foreign branches of insured state nonmember banks to guarantee a customer's debts). The FDIC has explicitly approved issuance of a "letter of guaranty" by a state nonmember bank. See FDIC, Opinion Letter 85-1, reprinted in [1988–1989 Transfer Binder] Fed. Banking L. Rep. (CCH) ¶ 81,172 (Jan. 9, 1985); cf. 12 C.F.R. § 332.1 (1989) (limiting power of an insured state nonmember bank to engage in surety business).

For a considerable period of time, there have been no serious challenges to the authority of banks to endorse negotiable instruments, to issue commercial letters of credit, or to issue various indemnities. The issue has arisen in the standby credit setting. The gravamen of the complaint that a standby credit is a guaranty and is therefore ultra vires lies not in the fact that the standby bears some of the features of a guaranty, but elsewhere. The valid complaint against bank issuance of guaranties rests on the notion that banks are ill equipped to deal with them, that is, that the issuance of guaranties is not the proper business of banking.

[b] Business of Banking

Generally, banks are creatures of the legislature. They have only those powers that the legislatures grant them, and the legislatures have been careful to limit that power. Section 24 of the National Bank Act authorizes national banks "to carry on the business of banking."[83] Endorsement of negotiable instruments and issuance of commercial credits are two practices clearly within the traditional notion of that business. Not all guaranties fit that traditional notion, however. The critical question in determining whether banks should issue standby credits is whether standby credits come within the banking framework. They do.

The trouble with bank issuance of traditional guaranties or surety contracts lies in the fact that they involve secondary liability. The traditional guarantor or surety faces two questions. Before undertaking the guaranty the surety may calculate the chances that the principal will default and, after undertaking the guaranty, must determine whether default has occurred. Neither of these determinations fits traditional concepts of the banking business. The former may involve actuarial judgments; the latter involves factual investigation. Traditionally, these activities have not been a part of the business of banking.

Standby letters of credit almost never involve either kind of activity. In one case where the credit involved factual investigation, the Court of Appeals for the Ninth Circuit held that the bank's undertaking had strayed too far from the nature of a letter of credit to be classified as such. The court refused to apply letter of credit law to the controversy.[84]

In the standby credit, the issuer knows that its liability is primary, and it assumes, as sound banking practices require,[85] that it will pay,

---

[83] 12 U.S.C. § 24 (1988).

[84] See Wichita Eagle & Beacon Publishing Co. v. Pacific Nat'l Bank, 493 F.2d 1285 (9th Cir. 1974). See generally ¶ 2.05.

[85] The Federal Reserve Board, for example, takes the position that state member banks should not issue standby letters of credit without subjecting the customer's creditworthiness to analysis. See 12 C.F.R. § 208.8(d)(2)(ii) (1989). See also infra notes 86, 101.

even though the beneficiary may never draw. The careful bank assumes that, by issuing a standby credit, it has undertaken to advance the amount of the credit for the account of its customer. Given that assumption, the bank does not try to determine whether default will occur in the underlying transaction—a nonbanking function. Instead it investigates the creditworthiness of that customer and decides whether to seek collateral, guaranties, or other protection for the bank's right of reimbursement. The bank has replaced the actuarial judgment process or the judgment concerning the commercial viability of the account party's underlying obligation (both of which involve nonbanking judgments) with an evaluation of the account party's financial ability to repay the bank (a typical financial judgment process similar to the one the bank undertakes in any commercial loan setting). Rather than giving rise to actuarial or commercial questions, which are usually not within a bank's area of expertise, the standby credit gives rise to financial questions that are squarely within its area of expertise.[86]

In a similar way, the standby credit substitutes traditional banking activity for the surety's factual investigation. In the case of a surety contract, because the surety's liability is secondary, the surety must investigate the underlying transaction to determine whether default has occurred. Questions of default depend on performance of the contract between the principal and the beneficiary, and the determination of performance or default of that contract often depends on facts gleaned from field investigation. Under the standby credit, however, the bank issuer is under no duty to engage in such investigation. It can avoid the field, and it can make its decision on the basis of document examination at its banking house.[87]

---

[86] Courts should take solace, moreover, from the fact that federal regulatory agencies insist that commercial banks observe these sound banking practices. See 12 C.F.R. § 7.7016 (covering national banks); 12 C.F.R. § 208.8(d)(2)(ii) (1989) (covering member banks); 12 C.F.R. § 337.2 (1989) (covering state insured nonmember banks); cf. 12 C.F.R. § 545.48 (1989) (rule for thrifts); Comptroller of the Currency, No-Objection Letter 87-5, reprinted in [1988–1989 Transfer Binder] Fed. Banking L. Rep. (CCH) ¶ 84,034 (July 20, 1987) (holding that, because it was proper banking function for bank to issue two standby letters of credit to secure matched obligations of users and producers under commodity price index swaps, it was proper for bank to achieve same result by acting as principal with its commodity user and commodity producer customers in commodity price index swap transactions); Comptroller of the Currency, Staff Interpretive Letter No. 295, reprinted in [1985–1987 Transfer Binder] Fed. Banking L. Rep. (CCH) ¶ 85,465, (July 3, 1984) (opinion that political risk standby credit would be ultra vires and an unsound banking practice under 12 C.F.R. § 7.7016 (1984)).

[87] Cf. Bank of N.C., N.A. v. Rock Island Bank, 570 F.2d 202 (7th Cir. 1978) (holding that this feature of credit—i.e., examination of documents rather than determination of facts—distinguishes letter of credit from guaranty).

The documents the bank examines (e.g., drafts, bills of lading, certificates) are papers with which bankers are familiar. These papers permit the document examination process to be ministerial and short rather than judgmental and lengthy, as decisions of default and performance inevitably become. Finally, the law of credits itself, by insisting that the document examination process be ministerial[88] and that the credit be independent of the underlying transaction,[89] sharpens the distinction between standby credits and surety contracts.[90]

[c] Primary Obligation: The Material Distinction

Many courts recognize, as the Court of Appeals for the Seventh Circuit did in *Bank of North Carolina, N.A. v. Rock Island Bank*,[91] that "every letter of credit serves, in one sense or another, as a guaranty."[92] Most courts, however, accept the distinction between obligations that are primary and those that are secondary.[93] The issuer of the primary

---

[88] See U.C.C. § 5-109(2); U.C.P. art. 15 (1983).

[89] See U.C.C. § 5-109(1); U.C.P. arts. 3, 4 (1983).

[90] For a general discussion of the distinction between surety contracts and standby letters of credit, see ¶ 2.10[1]. To some extent, the Office of the Comptroller of the Currency may have departed from these distinctions in a staff interpretive letter it issued in 1985. Comptroller of the Currency, Staff Interpretive Letter No. 338, reprinted in [1985–1987 Transfer Binder] Fed. Banking L. Rep. (CCH) ¶ 85,508 (May 2, 1985). In that letter, the Comptroller took the position that it was proper for a bank operating subsidiary to issue insurance policies (without designating them as letters of credit) to secure repayment of municipal obligations. The letter attempts to analogize this kind of debt enhancement insurance to standby letters of credit that often have been used for the same purpose. In American Ins. Ass'n v. Clarke, 656 F. Supp. 404 (D.D.C. 1987), aff'd in part, rev'd in part, 865 F.2d 278 (D.C. Cir. 1989), the court upheld the Comptroller's ruling. The court put great store by the fact that letter of credit liability is primary and that the operating subsidiary made credit judgments, not actuarial judgments, in deciding whether to issue the insurance. Given the fact that the insurance was the functional equivalent of a standby credit, the court was not moved by the name the subsidiary gave its product. Cf. Comptroller of the Currency, Interpretive Letter No. 468, reprinted in [1988–1989 Transfer Binder] Fed. Banking L. Rep. (CCH) ¶ 85,692 (Jan. 17, 1989) (opining that bank wholly owned subsidiary may participate in American Loan Guarantee Association's insurance of securitized debt obligations).

[91] 570 F.2d 202 (7th Cir. 1978).

[92] Id. at 206.

[93] See, e.g., Prudential Ins. Co. of Am. v. Marquette Nat'l Bank, 419 F. Supp. 734 (D. Minn. 1976); American Empire Ins. Co. v. Hanover Nat'l Bank, 409 F. Supp. 459 (M.D. Pa. 1976), aff'd mem., 556 F.2d 564 (3d Cir. 1977); United Bank v. Quadrangle, Ltd., 42 Colo. App. 486, 596 P.2d 408 (1979); Western Petroleum Co. v. First Bank Aberdeen, N.A., 367 N.W.2d 773 (S.D. 1985); Republic Nat'l Bank v. Northwest Nat'l Bank, 578 S.W.2d 109 (Tex. 1978); cf. Barclays Bank D.C.O. v. Mercantile Nat'l Bank, 481 F.2d 1221 (5th Cir. 1973), cert. dismissed, 414 U.S. 1139 (1974) (adopting same distinction for confirming bank).

obligation avoids the need to investigate the account party's default.[94]

In *Republic National Bank v. Northwest National Bank*,[95] the primary-secondary distinction troubled the Texas Court of Civil Appeals. That case involved a standby credit securing payment of a promissory note. In the court's view, the credit was payable on the default of the note's maker. The Texas court recognized the distinction between a letter of credit's primary obligation and a surety contract's secondary obligation, but the court viewed this obligation as secondary and held that it was not a letter of credit but an ultra vires bank guaranty.

That view failed to give proper weight to the fact that the issuer's obligation under the credit was independent of the account party's obligation on the note. The credit predicated the liability of the issuer on presentation of documents, not on the maker's default. It is true that the credit referred to the note and to the default, as did the documents that were to be presented under the credit. Proper regard for the independence principle requires the court to disregard these references, however, not only because the nature of the credit as a primary obligation depends on that independence but also because the efficiency of the credit as a commercial device depends on that independence.[96] The court made the fatal error of telescoping the broader transaction into the credit transaction and concluding that the issuer's liability was secondary and therefore ultra vires.

The Supreme Court of Texas reversed,[97] holding that the obligation of the issuer to honor a conforming presentation arises "without reference to the rights and obligations of the parties to the underlying contract."[98] Significantly, the court dismissed the credit's specific references to the underlying note as "surplusage unless they impose some condition to the issuer's liability."[99] The Texas court also emphasized that the issuer in the *Republic National Bank* case would evaluate documents, not the breach or performance of the underlying contract, and the court expressly recognized the *Wichita* requirement[100] that credits not involve complicated factual determinations.[101]

---

[94] For further discussion of the significance of this distinction, see supra ¶ 12.02[1][b].

[95] 566 S.W.2d 358 (Tex. Civ. App.), rev'd, 578 S.W.2d 109 (Tex. 1978).

[96] For a discussion of the independence principle, see ¶¶ 2.08, 2.09.

[97] Republic Nat'l Bank v. Northwest Nat'l Bank, 578 S.W.2d 109 (Tex. 1978).

[98] Id. at 114.

[99] Id. at 116.

[100] The *Wichita* requirement comes from the opinion in Wichita Eagle & Beacon Publishing Co. v. Pacific Nat'l Bank, 493 F.2d 1285 (9th Cir. 1974), and requires engagements that would otherwise meet the Code definition of a letter of credit to meet a general purpose test before the court will apply letter of credit rules. See generally ¶ 2.05.

[101] Accord Bank of N.C., N.A. v. Rock Island Bank, 570 F.2d 202 (7th Cir.

[2] Raising the Ultra Vires Issue

The *Republic National Bank* opinion seems to presuppose that if the issuer's engagement had violated the *Wichita* requirement,[102] thereby becoming a surety contract with secondary liability rather than a letter of credit with primary liability, the issuer could have raised the ultra vires defense. Significantly, in *Wichita Eagle & Beacon Publishing Co. v. Pacific National Bank*,[103] after finding that the undertaking was not a letter of credit, the Court of Appeals for the Ninth Circuit nonetheless enforced the obligation as a matter of surety law. Other courts have taken the position that even if the bank's engagement is ultra vires, the bank may not assert the defense and neither may the account party.

In *First American National Bank v. Alcorn, Inc.*,[104] the issuer's standby credit arguably constituted an extension of credit in excess of the bank's credit limits.[105] The *First American* court held, however, that enforcement of such limits is a matter for bank regulators. There being no evidence that the beneficiary was aware of the violation, the court would not permit the issuer to raise the ultra vires defense. To so hold, in the view of the court, would have had the effect of "frustrating well-intentioned unwary borrowers."[106]

In *Union County Bank v. FDIC*,[107] the personnel of two banks used a letter of credit participation arrangement to augment the earnings of a troubled bank. The lead bank had earned fees on the issuance of standby credits, and its troubled cognate agreed to participate in several of the credits and to accept a prorated portion of the fees. The participations by the cognate had the effect of exceeding its lending limits; and when the lead bank made a claim on a participation agreement, the cog-

---

1978); see also 12 C.F.R. § 7.7016 (1989) (Comptroller of the Currency interpretive ruling to effect that national bank "[a]s a matter of sound banking practice" should not issue credit, unless "bank's obligation to pay [arises] only upon the presentation of a draft or other documents as specified in the letter of credit," and noting further that "the bank must not be called upon to determine questions of fact or law at issue between the account party and the beneficiary"); cf. 12 C.F.R. § 545.48 (1989) (same rule for thrifts); Comptroller of the Currency, Staff Interpretive Letter No. 295, reprinted in [1985–1987 Transfer Binder] Fed. Banking L. Rep. (CCH) ¶ 85,465 (July 3, 1984) (rejecting political risk standby program on ground that it involved issuing bank in political, rather than financial, evaluations).

[102] See supra note 100.

[103] 493 F.2d 1285 (9th Cir. 1974).

[104] 361 So. 2d 481 (Miss. 1978).

[105] For a discussion of the lending-limit rules, see infra ¶ 12.03.

[106] First Am. Nat'l Bank v. Alcorn, Inc., 361 So. 2d 481, 489 (Miss. 1978).

[107] No. 712 (Tenn. Ct. App. Sept. 18, 1987).

nate's receiver argued that it was unenforceable. Given that state of affairs, the *Union County Bank* court appears to have been prepared to leave the two participants to an illegal scheme without any legal remedy. When the lead bank also became insolvent and the FDIC assumed the role of receiver, however, the court invoked federal common law, under which the FDIC takes the failed bank's assets free of equitable claims.[108] Under that rule, the court held, the receiver of the participating bank could not raise the illegality defense against the FDIC.[109]

In *FDIC v. Freudenfeld*,[110] the customer of an issuing bank attempted to avoid reimbursing the issuer's receiver. The account party argued that the standby credit had been a surety contract which the bank had no authority to issue. The *Freudenfeld* court held, however, that any conduct violative of the National Bank Act was a matter for federal authorities and did not give the account party a defense.[111]

Ultimately, the ability of an issuer to raise the ultra vires defense may be a question of state law.[112] If state law permits a corporation to raise the defense of ultra vires, standby credits that violate the traditional prohibitions against guaranties or that violate statutory or regulatory restrictions on bank activity may be unenforceable against the issuer. In one case, the court permitted the issuing bank to defend a claim under a standby, when issuance of the credit allegedly violated the rules on lend-

---

[108] The common-law doctrine the *Union County Bank* invoked arises from D'Oench, Duhme & Co. v. FDIC, 315 U.S. 447 (1942), discussed supra ¶ 12.01[1][a].

[109] For cases recognizing a bank's cause of action against officers and directors that issue a credit in violation of the bank's regulations, see First Nat'l Bank v. Pelican Homestead Sav. & Loan Ass'n, 869 F. 2d 896 (5th Cir. 1989); Fitch v. Midland Bank & Trust Co., 737 S.W.2d 785 (Tenn. Ct. App. 1987). For a case limiting the liability of a bank's officers and directors policy issuer for losses resulting from such officer conduct, see MGIC Indem. Corp. v. Central Bank, 838 F.2d 1382 (5th Cir. 1988). For discussion of efforts by some issuers to avoid liability on the ground that the officer executing the credit instrument was not authorized, see ¶ 5.01[4].

[110] 492 F. Supp. 763 (E.D. Wis. 1980).

[111] Accord Seattle-First Nat'l Bank v. FDIC, 619 F. Supp. 1351 (W.D. Okla. 1985); City Nat'l Bank v. First Nat'l Bank, 22 Ark. App. 5, 732 S.W.2d 489 (1987).

[112] There is one federal statute that gives the issuer a defense in the nature of an ultra vires defense. The Export Administration Act's antiboycott provisions stipulate that no person may be obligated to pay a letter of credit whose terms violate the Act. See 50 U.S.C. § 2407(a)(1)(F) (1982); 15 C.F.R. § 769.2(f)(1) (1989). See generally U.S. Department of Commerce, International Trade Association, Office of Antiboycott Compliance, "Restrictive Trade Practices or Boycotts" 22–26 (1987). For discussion of the effect of illegality in the underlying transaction on enforcement of the credit, see ¶ 9.06[6].

ing limits. *International Dairy Queen, Inc. v. Bank of Wadley*[113] holds that, even though the state abolished the ultra vires defense for corporations, a contract that violates a regulatory statute is void and unenforceable as a matter of public policy. In *Western Petroleum Co. v. First Bank Aberdeen, N.A.*,[114] the court held that the issuer, a nationally chartered bank, had made an engagement that was not a letter of credit but a secondary obligation in the nature of a guaranty. The court held that, under the circumstances, the guaranty was ultra vires and unenforceable.[115]

These cases may reflect judicial concern that parties be required to investigate the authority of their issuers. From a commercial standpoint that policy creates problems. It has the unfortunate effect of permitting banks to renege on their obligations.

[3] Moves Toward Further Regulation

In the past, some commentators called for legislation or regulation that would restrict the authority of banks to issue standby letters of credit.[116] It is important to distinguish these concerns from the notion that all standby credits are beyond the authority of commercial banks. The commentators calling for regulatory reform argued that banks sometimes use standby credits for unlawful purposes or in a way that jeopardizes bank solvency.

At face value, these concerns may have merit[117]; but they are distinct from the ultra vires argument in two ways. First, they do not suggest that all banks have no power to issue standby credits; they suggest that some banks abuse that power. Second, they urge legislative or regu-

---

[113] 407 F. Supp. 1270 (M.D. Ala. 1976).

[114] 367 N.W.2d 773 (S.D. 1985).

[115] For the view that a letter of credit that causes the bank to violate its state lending limits is nonetheless enforceable, see Security Fin. Group, Inc. v. Northern Ky. Bank & Trust Co., 858 F.2d 304 (6th Cir.), clarified, 875 F.2d 529 (6th Cir. 1988).

[116] See Barrett, "Bank Regulatory Aspects and Legislative Proposals," 1981 Practising L. Inst., Letters of Credit 111; Katskee, "The Standby Letter of Credit Debate—The Case for Congressional Resolution," 92 Banking L.J. 697 (1975); Verkuil, "Bank Solvency and Standby Letters of Credit: Lessons From the USNB Failure," 53 Tul. L. Rev. 314 (1979); Verkuil, "Bank Solvency and Guaranty Letters of Credit," 25 Stan. L. Rev. 716 (1973).

[117] Some commentators have suggested that part of the objection to commercial bank standby letters of credit stems from a desire of certain parties to avoid competition. See Arnold & Bransilver, "The Standby Letter of Credit—The Controversy Continues," 10 U.C.C. L.J. 272, 284 (1978); Harfield, "The Standby Letter of Credit Debate," 94 Banking L.J. 293, 302 (1977).

latory reform of bank standby practices; they do not urge ad hoc court decisions invalidating credits that are issued and on which parties have reasonably relied. Nothing in the standby letter of credit debate, moreover, should be taken to support the argument of a banker that he should be excused from the duty to honor standby letters of credit that are already issued.

Bank regulators became concerned in the mid-1980s that bank balance sheets and capital ratios did not reflect significant bank risks. A bank's loans are its most important assets. A letter of credit and especially a standby letter of credit are akin to an unfunded loan to the account party. Because the funding of a standby is contingent (the standby may never be drawn upon), banks traditionally have not carried the standby on their balance sheets but have noted contingent, standby obligations off–balance sheet, rendering them "off–balance sheet" (OBS) items. Under this practice standby credits have become a problem for determining a bank's capital adequacy. By virtue of the standby's nature, no one can know whether the beneficiary of a standby will draw and, in many instances, if there is a draw, what the amount of the draw will be, because both the event of drawing and the amount are contingent.

Commercial credits are much less of a problem. All parties expect a draw under commercial credits, which are most often trade related (so that there are goods in the underlying transaction in which the issuer usually has a security interest). A draw under a commercial credit, rather than signaling trouble, indicates that all is going well.

As the number and aggregate amount of standby credits and other OBS items grew to the hundreds of billions of dollars, regulators began exploring ways to include them in asset ratios.[118] At the same time, regulators of a number of industrialized countries engaged in discussions with a view toward establishing uniform capital adequacy standards for financial institutions that would reduce the anticompetitive effects of nonuniform national regulation.

In July 1988, the Basle Committee on Banking Regulations and Supervisory Practices, a committee with representatives from twelve industrialized countries, including the United States, adopted a regulatory

---

[118] See, e.g., General Accounting Office, Banking: Off-Balance Sheet Activities, Briefing Report to the Chairman, Subcommittee on Financial Institutions Supervision, Regulation and Insurance, Committee on Banking, Finance and Urban Affairs, House of Representatives (Mar. 1988); Benveniste & Berger, "An Empirical Analysis of Standby Letters of Credit," in Federal Reserve Bank of Chicago, Proceedings—A Conference on Bank Structure and Competition (1986); Bennett, Off Balance Sheet Risk in Banking: The Case of Standby Letters of Credit, Fed. Reserve Bank Econ. Rev. 19 (Winter 1986).

framework.[119] In December of that year, the Federal Reserve Board became the first of the federal regulatory agencies to implement the framework. The Board amended its regulations[120] to provide for the inclusion of all letters of credit, including standby letters of credit, in a bank's capital ratios. The Comptroller of the Currency, the chief regulator of national banks, and the FDIC, the chief federal regulator of nonmember insured state banks, followed suit.[121]

The regulations promulgated by the agencies treat letters of credit in a two-step process. First, the regulations call for the conversion of the OBS item to an on–balance sheet item. That conversion process consists of multiplying the OBS item by a conversion factor. The conversion factor for "financial standby credits" is 100 percent; for "performance standby credits," it is 50 percent; and for commercial letters of credit, it is 20 percent. "Financial standby credits" are those credits that secure obligations, such as bonds or commercial paper, for the payment of money. "Performance standby credits" are those that secure the performance of a contract, such as a construction contract.

Application of these conversion factors yields the "credit equivalent amount" for the asset in question. The regulation then weights the credit equivalent amount, as it weights all of the bank's assets, by assigning it to one of four risk-weight categories. Those categories depend on the nature of the party that is the obligor on the issuer's reimbursement agreement, that is, the nature of the account party. Claims secured by the direct obligations of the United States, for example, are assigned a zero risk; claims secured conditionally by Organization for Economic Cooperation and Development (OECD) nonlocal governments are assigned a 20 percent risk; and claims secured by central governments of non-OECD countries are assigned a 100 percent risk.[122]

---

[119] See generally Gossling, "The Capital Adequacy Framework—An Introduction," 6 J. Int'l Banking L. 243 (1988); Board of Governors of the Federal Reserve System, Release and Notice in Full Text (Jan. 18, 1989), reprinted in Fed. Banking L. Rep. (CCH) ¶ 87,555 (1989).

[120] See 12 C.F.R. pt. 225, app. A (1989).

[121] For the Comptroller's regulations, see Risk-Based Capital Guidelines, 12 C.F.R. pt. 3, app. A (1989). For the FDIC regulations, see Capital Maintenance, 12 C.F.R. pt. 325 (1989). For the Office of Thrift Supervision rule, see 12 C.F.R. § 567.6 (1990).

[122] For discussion of the effect of the guidelines on standby credit practices and prices, see Kopenhaver, "Standby Letters of Credit," Economic Perspectives 28 (July/Aug. 1987); Chessen, "Feeling the Heat of Risk-Based Capital: The Case of Off-Balance-Sheet Activity," Regulatory Rev. (Aug. 1987). For an explanation of the guidelines, see Millard & Semkow, "The New Risk-Based Capital Framework and Its Application to Letters of Credit," 106 Banking L.J. 500 (1989). For discussion of the effect of including standby letters of credit in the computation of a bank's capital ratios, see Laplante, "Reexamining an Old Standby: Letters of Credit and Capital Ra-

¶ 12.03 LENDING LIMITS, PARTICIPATIONS, AND AFFILIATES

[1] Section 84 of the National Bank Act

The National Bank Act establishes formulas for computing the maximum amounts that a nationally chartered bank may loan to a single entity.[123] States have adopted similar rules.[124]

It makes sense for banks to include the amounts of outstanding standby letters of credit in determining the loan limit for a borrower. That conclusion follows from the argument that issuance of standby credits is consistent with the business of banking. The argument consists of two parts: (1) that standby credits are different from guaranties and (2) that the bank's standby activity falls within traditional notions of banking business. It would not be consistent with these notions for banks to issue primary obligations on behalf of a customer without evaluating the customer's creditworthiness and making provision for reimbursement. Letter of credit application agreements[125] generally provide this feature, and banks, as a matter of sound banking practice, evaluate the customer's creditworthiness at the time of the application. The application agreement and the procedures attending it are redolent of bank lending practices.[126]

The Comptroller of the Currency, on the other hand, has defined terms in such a way as to exclude commercial letters of credit in determining aggregate loans.[127] That decision reflects a significant difference between commercial and standby credits. Commercial credits are trade

---

tios," Letter of Credit Update 33 (Nov. 1985). For general discussion of the application of the guidelines to standby credits, see Gabriel, "Standby Letters of Credit: Does the Risk Outweigh the Benefits?" 3 Colum. Bus. L. Rev. 705 (1988). For discussion of the application of the guidelines to participations in letters of credit, see infra ¶ 12.03[4].

[123] 12 U.S.C. § 84 (1989).

[124] See, e.g., Ill. Ann. Stat. ch. 17, § 339 (Smith-Hurd Supp. 1989); Mich. Comp. Laws Ann. § 487.496 (1987); N.Y. Banking Law § 103 (McKinney Supp. 1990).

[125] See App. C, Doc. 14, for an example of a letter of credit application agreement.

[126] See 12 C.F.R. § 7.7016 (1989) (Comptroller of the Currency's interpretive ruling on sound practices regarding letters of credit); cf. 12 C.F.R. § 545.48 (1990) (similar Office of Thrift Supervision regulation). The equivalence of loans and letters of credit for lending-limit purposes does not necessarily extend to other inquiries. In First Nat'l Bank v. Pelican Homestead Sav. & Loan Ass'n, 869 F.2d 896 (5th Cir. 1989), an issuer sued one of its officers for issuing a credit without authorization. The court held that written policy authorizing the officer to make loans did not determine his authority to issue letters of credit on behalf of the association.

[127] See 12 C.F.R. § 32.4(d), 32.4(e) (1990).

related; that is, they generally support the sale of goods or commodities, something of value that drives the transaction. In the trade-related transaction, the account party is usually anxious to have the bank issuer honor the credit, so that the account party will have the goods. In the event the account party does not want the goods and does not reimburse the issuer, the goods stand as security for that reimbursement obligation.[128] Standby credits usually are not trade related and therefore do not enjoy these benefits. In fact, often, in the standby case, the account party does not want the issuer to honor the beneficiary's draft and resists reimbursement or is financially incapable of reimbursing.[129]

[2] State Loan Limits

In a manner consistent with the rule of federal regulators that commercial credits issued by national banks are not subject to the loan limits of the National Bank Act,[130] some state statutes have exempted letters of credit from their statutory lending limits or have established separate limits for letters of credit.[131] Clearly, courts should construe the provisions restrictively, so that standby credits do not fall within the exclusion.[132] State rules do not insulate insured banks and state member banks from the rules of the FDIC[133] and the Federal Reserve Board[134] commanding such state banks to include standby credits as loans in applying state lending limits.

[3] Exceptions for Some Standby Credits

There are exceptions to the general rule that standby credits should be considered in applying the loan limit. Under its current regulation, the Comptroller's office adopts a scheme of exceptions by equating standby credits with loans and applying all of the statutory exceptions in the

---

[128] For discussion of the issuer's security interest, see ¶ 8.03.

[129] For further discussion of the differences between commercial and standby credits, see ¶ 1.04.

[130] See supra ¶ 12.03[1].

[131] See, e.g., Ill. Ann. Stat. ch. 17, § 342(5) (Smith-Hurd Supp. 1989); N.Y. Banking Law § 103(f) (McKinney Supp. 1990).

[132] For a state case that recognizes that the issuance of a standby credit may constitute the extension of credit in excess of the issuer's lending limits, see Union County Bank v. FDIC, No. 712 (Tenn. Ct. App. Sept. 18, 1987).

[133] 12 C.F.R. § 337.2(b) (1989).

[134] 12 C.F.R. § 208.8(d)(2) (1989).

lending limits provision of the Act to standby credits.[135] Generally, under the Comptroller's ruling, standby credits are subject to the limit that loans to a single customer cannot exceed 15 percent of the issuer's capital and surplus.[136] That limit increases by 10 percent if that increased part of the credit is secured by "readily marketable collateral"[137] having a value at all times of not less than 100 percent of the increased amount.[138] There are no limits on standby credits fully secured by segregated deposit accounts or by U.S. government securities.[139]

Under interpretations of the Comptroller of the Currency, loans secured by general obligations of a state or political subdivision thereof are not considered obligations of the bank's borrower for loan-limit purposes.[140] In an opinion letter, the Comptroller's office determined that that exception applies, even though the general obligation bonds secure not only the bank as issuer of a standby but the beneficiary of the standby as well. In the transaction in question, the bank, at the request of a municipal authority that held general obligation bonds of other municipalities, issued a letter of credit to secure repayment of the authority's bonds. The authority, in turn, granted a security interest in the municipalities' bonds in favor of both the bank and the holders of the authority's bonds. The arrangement (dual secured parties) stemmed from a bankruptcy court ruling, since largely discredited, that rendered a standby secured by a pledge of bonds to the bank alone a possible preference

---

[135] See 12 C.F.R. §§ 32.2(a), 32.2(d), 32.2(e) (1989); cf. 12 C.F.R. § 563.93(b)(12) (1990) (similar rule for thrifts); see also Glidden, "National Bank Lending Limits and the Comptroller's Regs: A Clarification" (pts. 1 & 2), 101 Banking L.J. 430, 554 (1984) (discussing regulations).

[136] See 12 U.S.C. § 84(a)(1) (1988); cf. 12 C.F.R. §§ 32.2(a), 32.2(d) (1989) (defining "loan and extensions of credit" in 12 U.S.C. § 84(a)(1) as including standby letters of credit).

[137] 12 U.S.C. § 84(a)(2) (1988). For a ruling that a standby letter of credit is not "readily marketable collateral" and does not qualify for any other exception to the loan-limit rule, see Comptroller of the Currency, Staff Interpretive Letter No. 322, reprinted in [1985–1987 Transfer Binder] Fed. Banking L. Rep. (CCH) ¶ 85,492 (Dec. 31, 1984).

[138] References in the text to the credit assume that all extensions of credit of any kind are aggregated for purposes of applying the 15 percent and additional 10 percent rules, as the ruling requires. The additional 10 percent limit for extensions of credit secured by readily marketable collateral is subject to the limits in the Federal Reserve Act on loans secured by securities. See 12 U.S.C. § 248(m) (1988); Barrett, "Bank Regulatory Aspects of Letters of Credit," 1983 Practising L. Inst., Letters of Credit 68.

[139] 12 U.S.C. §§ 84(c)(4), 84(c)(6) (1988); 12 C.F.R. §§ 32.6(d), 32.6(f) (1989).

[140] See 12 C.F.R. § 32.109 (1989).

that could interfere with the security of the authority's bondholders.[141] The Comptroller's office opined that the dual nature of the security interest did not place the arrangement outside the scope of the exception for loans secured by general obligation bonds.[142]

If the lending limits do apply to a credit, the Comptroller's office has ruled[143] that a renewal of the credit is an extension of credit. Significantly, however, in the same opinion, the Comptroller also ruled that failure to give notice of termination under an evergreen clause[144] does not constitute an extension of credit.

Because its loans were secured by the standby credits of another bank, a lender sought to exclude them from the lending limit or to obtain the benefit of the additional 10 percent limit permitted by the Act. The Comptroller's office ruled, however, that there was no exception for loans secured by standby letters of credit under the general rule and that the 10 percent added limit did not apply, because standby credits were not readily marketable collateral.[145] In another interpretive letter, the Comptroller's office refused to treat direct pay standby letters of credit as commercial letters of credit for lending-limit purposes.[146]

State member banks are subject to provisions in Regulation H, which require inclusion of the amount of standby letters of credit in aggregating loans for state lending-limit purposes and for the purposes of loan limits on extensions of credit to affiliates.[147] The FDIC rule for

[141] The bankruptcy case was Twist Cap, Inc. v. Southeast Bank (In re Twist Cap, Inc.), 1 Bankr. 284 (Bankr. D. Fla. 1979). For discussion of it and the cases that discredit it, see ¶ 7.03[3][a].

[142] Comptroller of the Currency, Staff Interpretive Letter No. 412, reprinted in [1988–1989 Transfer Binder] Fed. Banking L. Rep. (CCH) ¶ 85,636 (Jan. 26, 1988).

[143] See Comptroller of the Currency, Interpretive Letter No. 477, reprinted in Fed. Banking L. Rep. (CCH) ¶ 83,027 (Jan. 11, 1989).

[144] For discussion of evergreen clauses and the way notice of termination by the issuer serves to terminate credits containing them, see ¶ 5.03[3][b]. See also Citronelle Unit Operators Comm. v. AmSouth Bank, N.A., 536 So. 2d 1387 (Ala. 1988) (opinion setting forth terms of credit containing evergreen clause). For an example of a credit with an evergreen clause fashioned by insurance regulators for use in the insurance industry, see App. C, Doc. 24.

[145] Comptroller of the Currency, Staff Interpretive Letter No. 322, reprinted in [1985–1987 Transfer Binder] Fed. Banking L. Rep. (CCH) ¶ 85,492 (Dec. 31, 1984).

[146] Comptroller of the Currency, Interpretive Letter No. 361, reprinted in [1985–1987 Transfer Binder] Fed. Banking L. Rep. (CCH) ¶ 85,531 (Apr. 30, 1986).

[147] 12 C.F.R. § 208.8(d)(2) (1989); see also 12 U.S.C. § 371(c) (1988) (imposing limit on loans to affiliates). For discussion of participations in standby letters of credit as loans to affiliates, see infra ¶ 12.03[4]. For discussion of the effect of participations on capital adequacy guidelines, see supra ¶ 12.02[3].

state nonmember banks is virtually the same.[148] The Federal Reserve Board and the FDIC also have similar exceptions to these loan-limit rules, whereby standby letters of credit are not included in aggregating loans if the bank is paid the amount of the credit or has set aside sufficient funds in a segregated deposit account earmarked for the purpose of covering the bank's liability under the credit.[149]

[4] Participations

Banks frequently avoid the impact of the loan limits imposed under the National Bank Act[150] by inviting a correspondent or several correspondents to participate in the loan.[151] In the Comptroller's view, loan participations do not satisfy the policy of the Act's lending limits unless all of the participants, not just the lead bank, analyze the credit risk independently.[152] The Comptroller takes the clear position that the lead bank does not avoid the lending limits unless there is "a pro rata sharing of credit risk proportionate to the respective interests of the originating and participating lenders."[153]

The Comptroller and the FDIC also make it clear that if there is a true participation, the lead bank must add, for the purpose of aggregating loans, only the unparticipated amount of the standby.[154] The language of Regulation H may be ambiguous,[155] but one commentator suggests convincingly that any reading of the regulation's language to render it inconsistent with the positions of the Comptroller and the FDIC is problematic.[156]

Although a participation arrangement may relieve the lead bank of a lending-limit violation, the participating bank must also take care that its participation obligation does not constitute a lending-limit violation. In *Union County Bank v. FDIC*,[157] the court held that the participating bank's obligation exceeded its lending limit.

---

[148] 12 C.F.R. § 337.2(b) (1989).

[149] 12 C.F.R. §§ 208.8(d)(4), 337.2(c) (1989).

[150] For discussion of loan limits, see supra ¶ 12.03[3].

[151] See generally Ryan, "Letters of Credit Supporting Debt for Borrowed Money: The Standby as Backup," 100 Banking L.J. 404 (1983).

[152] See Office of the Comptroller of the Currency, Banking Circular 181, 5 Fed. Banking L. Rep. (CCH) ¶ 60,799 (rev. Aug. 2, 1984).

[153] 12 C.F.R. § 32.107 (1989).

[154] See 12 C.F.R. §§ 32.107(a), 337.2(b) n.2 (1989).

[155] See 12 C.F.R. § 208.8(d)(2)(iii) (1989).

[156] See Ryan, supra note 151, at 417.

[157] No. 712 (Tenn. Ct. App. Sept. 18, 1987).

The Comptroller has ruled that it is permissible for the issuer of a standby to "participate out" portions of the standby obligation indirectly through the use of "backup" letters of credit.[158] Under this arrangement, the issuer asks participating banks to issue backup standby credits in favor of the lead bank in amounts equal to the participating banks' respective shares of the entire obligation. The Comptroller's office concluded that the backup standby credit is sufficient to satisfy the participation rules.

The capital adequacy guidelines established by federal bank regulatory agencies[159] also deal with participations of credits. If the originating or "lead" bank retains liability for the full amount of the credit under the participation agreement, the lead bank must include the entire amount of the credit for purposes of computing its assets under the regulation. Thus, this kind of participation does not change the balance sheet equivalent amount of the lead bank's asset. The fact of the participation may affect the lead bank's credit equivalent amount, however, if the financial standing of the participating bank or banks is better under the broad risk categories than that of the original account party. The regulation permits the lead bank to substitute the participating bank for the account party in weighting the asset under the risk category rules. If the lead bank does not retain any liability under the participation agreement for the amount participated out, the lead bank does not need to include that amount in computing its balance sheet equivalent amount, and the participation will affect the balance sheet of the lead bank.

In either case, that is, whether the lead bank remains liable or is not liable on the participated amount, the participating banks or bank must include in its credit equivalent computations the portion of the credit it undertakes to pay.

[5] Letters of Credit and Affiliates of Issuer

Section 371c[160] of the Federal Reserve Act imposes certain restrictions on a member bank's transactions with its affiliates.[161] Included in the provision's definition of a "covered transaction" is "the issuance of a guarantee, acceptance, or letter of credit, including an endorsement or

---

[158] Comptroller of the Currency, Staff Interpretive Letter No. 412, reprinted in [1988–1989 Transfer Binder] Fed. Banking L. Rep. (CCH) ¶ 85,636 (Jan. 26, 1988).

[159] For general discussion of those guidelines, see supra ¶ 12.02.

[160] 12 U.S.C. § 371c (1988).

[161] Cf. 12 U.S.C. § 371c(b)(1) (1988) (defining "affiliate").

standby letter of credit, on behalf of an affiliate."[162] Thus, both commercial and standby letters of credit may fall within the restriction.

Section 371c(a) of the Act sets forth two limits on transactions with affiliates. Section 371c(c) of the Act stipulates collateral requirements for a covered transaction. Section 371c(d) of the Act provides significant exemptions from the limits and collateral requirements. Those exemptions[163] include transactions between sister banks that are 80 percent owned and include letters of credit that are "fully secured" by obligations of, or guaranteed by, the United States or its agencies or by a segregated, earmarked deposit account.[164]

Bank regulators have questioned whether a letter of credit issued on behalf of a foreign bank affiliate is exempt from the collateralization requirements.[165] Because a bank chartered under foreign law is not a "bank" for purposes of the statute,[166] the affiliate exemptions do not apply.[167] If a foreign bank asks its domestic subsidiary to issue a credit on behalf of itself, that view makes sense; but if the foreign bank asks its domestic affiliate to issue a credit on behalf of the foreign bank's customer, it may not. The issue here is one of defining the role of the foreign bank. If it is the customer of the domestic issuer, then the affiliate rules arguably apply; but if the domestic bank evaluates the creditworthiness of the foreign bank's customer, that customer is the true account party of the domestic bank, and the affiliate rules should not apply.

At present, the Federal Reserve Board has not addressed the issue. Some bankers and regulators feel that in the event the United States and foreign governments standardize bank regulation sufficiently, there will be no reason for the rule against treating banks chartered by those foreign governments as banks.

---

[162] 12 U.S.C. § 371c(b)(7)(E) (1988).

[163] The exemptions do not apply to certain low-quality-asset transactions. See 12 U.S.C. § 371c(a)(3) (1988).

[164] For further discussion of transactions with affiliates, see Barrett, "Bank Regulatory Aspects of Letters of Credit," 1983 Practising L. Inst., Letters of Credit and Bankers' Acceptances 63; Rose & Talley, "Bank Transactions With Affiliates: The New Section 23A," 100 Banking L.J. 423 (1983).

[165] See letter of Ford Barrett in C. Mooney & R. Ryan, Letters of Credit and Bankers' Acceptances 1986, at 175–179 (1986).

[166] See 12 U.S.C. § 371c(b)(5) (1988).

[167] See 12 U.S.C. § 371c(d)(1)(A) (1988).

¶ 12.04 MISCELLANEOUS

[1] Other Unsound Practices

Recognizing the potential conflict between an account party and a beneficiary, the Office of the Comptroller of the Currency considers it poor banking practice for the same bank to serve as the issuer of a credit and as the beneficiary acting as trustee for the holders of industrial revenue bonds.[168] That view takes into account the nature of the issuer's obligation to the account party, an obligation that includes the duty to refuse payment when the beneficiary's documents do not comply. It is significant, perhaps, that in a least one case involving a bank issuer that named itself as beneficiary of the credit[169] the issuer failed to exact strict compliance from itself as beneficiary, though the court found that the account party suffered no prejudice thereby. The Comptroller's policy guards against the potential conflict which that case reveals.

The Comptroller's office also has opined that it is unsound and unsafe for a bank to pledge assets to secure letters of credit that the bank issues. The Comptroller takes the position that such pledges reduce the liquidity of the bank's assets to an impermissible extent.[170]

---

[168] Comptroller of the Currency Staff Interpretive Letter No. 293, reprinted in [1985–1987 Transfer Binder] Fed. Banking L. Rep. (CCH) ¶ 85,463 (May 11, 1984); cf. Comptroller of the Currency, Trust Interpretation No. 182, reprinted in [1988–1989 Transfer Binder] Fed. Banking L. Rep. (CCH) ¶ 84,949 (Oct. 24, 1988) (advising that bank should not act as trustee of notes secured by its own letter of credit); Comptroller of the Currency, Trust Interpretation No. 180, reprinted in [1988–1989 Transfer Binder] Fed. Banking L. Rep. (CCH) ¶ 84,947 (Oct. 18, 1988) (advising that bank should not purchase securities secured by affiliate's letter of credit); Comptroller of the Currency, Staff Interpretive Letter No. 304, reprinted in [1985–1987 Transfer Binder] Fed. Banking L. Rep. (CCH) ¶ 85,474 (Aug. 17, 1984) (similar prohibition when trustee is affiliate of issuer).

[169] National Bank of N. Am. v. Alizio, 103 A.D.2d 690, 477 N.Y.S.2d 356 (1984), aff'd mem., 65 N.Y.2d 788, 482 N.E.2d 907, 493 N.Y.S.2d 111 (1985).

[170] Comptroller of the Currency, Staff Interpretive Letter, Mar. 21, 1983, reprinted in F. Barrett, "Bank Regulatory Aspects of Letters of Credit," in Letters of Credit and Bankers' Acceptances 91, 193 (1985). But cf. Comptroller of the Currency, Interpretations, Staff Interpretive Letter No. 445, reprinted in [1988–1989 Transfer Binder] Fed. Banking L. Rep. (CCH) ¶ 85,669 (Aug. 16, 1988) (opining that national banks may purchase letters of credit from another bank to secure private deposits but may not issue their own letters of credit to secure private deposits); 12 C.F.R. § 545.48 (1990) (contrary rule for thrifts). The Comptroller's office also has concluded that the sale of participation certificates in a bank's pool of mortgages is not a deposit and therefore does not violate the rule against pledging assets to secure deposits, even though the sale is partially secured by the bank's own letter of credit. The staff opinion concluded that the sale, when backed by the bank's letter of credit, is a borrowing that could be secured by a pledge of assets. See Comptroller of the Currency, Staff Interpretive Letter No. 417, reprinted in [1988–1989 Transfer Binder] Fed. Banking L. Rep. (CCH) ¶ 85,641 (Feb. 17, 1988).

Banks that pool their loans and sell them often use standby letters of credit to secure a portion of the pool. In *Securities Industry Association v. Clarke*,[171] the court held that it was not an unsound practice for a lender to issue a credit for that purpose. Prior to the sale of the loans, the court noted, the lender was at risk for 100 percent of any defaults. After the sale, it was at risk for only the portion secured by its standby, being 10 percent of the outstanding balance due on the loans in the *Securities Industry Association* case.

[2] Securities Law Considerations

Letters of credit frequently serve to enhance the value of an instrument. Early authority describes the function of credits as one of enhancing the value of the account party's drafts.[172] Increasingly, corporate and municipal borrowers have used the standby to obtain enhanced ratings for their paper.[173]

Under the securities laws, moreover, corporate borrowers whose paper is secured by bank-issued letters of credit enjoy the advantage that such paper is not subject to the registration requirements of the federal securities laws.[174] The Securities and Exchange Commission (SEC) traditionally did not permit paper secured by foreign bank letters of credit to come within the statutory exception. The SEC took the position that the word "bank" in the statute meant a domestic bank subject to federal regulation and that paper secured by branches of foreign banks subject to state or federal regulation were free of registration requirements only after issuance of a no-action letter by the SEC. The SEC revised that rule and now permits paper that is secured by credits issued by foreign bank branches that are established under state or federal law to qualify for that exception.[175]

The use of credit enhancement letters of credit has played a role in the charge that some banks are violating the Glass-Steagall Act.[176] In *Se-*

---

[171] 885 F.2d 1034 (2d Cir. 1989).

[172] For discussion of this function of the credit, see ¶ 3.07[1].

[173] See ¶ 1.06. See generally Federal Reserve Board Division of Research and Statistics, Survey Results, reprinted in Letter of Credit Update 34 (Oct. 1986).

[174] Securities Act of 1933, 15 U.S.C. § 77c(a)(2) (1988).

[175] See Securities and Exchange Commission, Interpretive Release No. 6661 (Sept. 23, 1986); see generally Klegerman, "Tapping US Capital Markets Without Registration," 5 Int'l Fin. L. Rev. 10 (1986).

[176] 12 U.S.C. § 24 (seventh) (1988).

curities Industries Association v. Board of Governors,[177] the securities industry, the Federal Reserve Board, and the bank issuer were in agreement that, in the event a bank places commercial paper that it has guaranteed by its own letters of credit, its conduct violates the Act.

In *Reid v. Walsh*,[178] the court held that a private action under the securities laws was time-barred. The plaintiff argued that the fraud had occurred within the statutory period by virtue of a draw on the letter of credit issued to secure the plaintiff's obligation under the allegedly fraudulent contract. The court held that the draw under the credit was analogous to payment under a note. Because the law is clear that payment on a note is not sufficient to toll the statute, the court ruled, payment under the credit cannot toll the statute.

In *Leslie v. Minson*,[179] the account party alleged that the beneficiary of a four-party credit[180] had engaged in reckless lending practices by lending funds to a partnership in which the account party had an interest. The account party argued that the beneficiary's reckless practices and failure to advise the account party of its practices constituted a violation of federal securities laws.[181] The *Leslie* court held that the account party had not made out a case and dismissed the complaint with prejudice.

Under the Glass-Steagall Act,[182] national banks may not invest in certain securities to an amount greater than 10 percent of the bank's paid-in capital and surplus. For the purpose of applying that 10 percent limit, it is necessary to identify the obligor or maker of the security.[183] In the event a municipal obligation is secured by a letter of credit, the limit arguably could apply to the municipality or to the credit issuer. The Comptroller of the Currency has ruled that an issue of variable rate demand notes by Cobb County, Georgia secured by a direct pay credit issued by Bankers Trust Company is a marketable security available for investment by a national bank because it is secured by the credit. Accordingly, the Comptroller ruled that the 10 percent limit should be applied against the obligation issued by Bankers Trust.[184]

---

[177] 627 F. Supp. 695 (D.D.C. 1986).

[178] 645 F. Supp. 685 (M.D. La. 1986).

[179] 679 F. Supp. 280 (S.D.N.Y. 1988).

[180] For a description of the four-party credit, see ¶ 7.04[4][b].

[181] The complaint alleged violations of the Securities Exchange Act of 1934, 15 U.S.C. § 78(j) (1988), and Rule 10(b)-5 of the SEC.

[182] 12 U.S.C. § 24 (seventh) (1988).

[183] See Investment Securities Regulation, 12 C.F.R. § 1.7 (1989).

[184] Comptroller of the Currency, Investment Securities Letter No. 3, reprinted in [1988–1989 Transfer Binder] Fed. Banking L. Rep. (CCH) ¶ 83,003 (July 17, 1986).

A national bank that proposed to sell securitized loans asked the Comptroller's office for an opinion on whether, in fact, the plan constituted a sale. Under the plan, the bank intended to sell automobile loans secured by a letter of credit issued by a third party. In the event of default on the loans, the buyers would have recourse against a collection account that contained proceeds from the loans collected by the bank; in the event the collection account was insufficient to cover the defaults, the buyers could resort to the letter of credit. The Comptroller's office opined that the transaction was a true sale because there was no recourse against the bank; the collection account was not an asset of the bank, and the credit was issued by a third party.[185] Although the Comptroller's opinion does not include any mention of the fact, one assumes that the arrangement would not be a sale if the issuer of the credit had a right of reimbursement against the bank.

---

[185] Comptroller of the Currency, Investment Securities Letter No. 2, reprinted in [1988–1989 Transfer Binder] Fed. Banking L. Rep. (CCH) ¶ 85,872 (June 16, 1986); cf. Comptroller of the Currency, Staff Interpretive Letter No. 416, reprinted in [1988–1989 Transfer Binder] Fed. Banking L. Rep. (CCH) ¶ 85,640 (Feb. 16, 1988) (approving similar arrangement).

Uniform Customs and Practice for Documentary Credits (1983 Version)*

The Uniform Customs and Practice for Documentary Credits (UCP or the Uniform Customs) and their predecessors are more than sixty years old. It was not until 1963, however, with the adoption of the 1962 revision (ICC Brochure No. 222), that credit issuers throughout the world accepted the Uniform Customs. Most of the litigation in this country has dealt with the 1962 revision or the 1974 revision, though cases under the 1983 revision are beginning to find their way into the reports.

The following text of the 1983 version contains an unofficial annotation assembled by the author of this volume. Similar unofficial annotations appear in Appendix B, which contains the text of the 1974 version of the UCP, on which much of the 1983 version is based. The Table of Parallel Provisions, with the corresponding provisions of the 1962, 1974, and 1983 revisions of the Uniform Customs, appears after the Bibliography.

Bibliographic Notes

For discussion of versions of the Uniform Customs prior to the 1962 revision, see Mentschikoff, "Letters of Credit: The Need for Uniform Legislation," 23 U. Chi. L. Rev. 571 (1956); Penney, "New York Revisits the Code: Some Variations in the New York Enactment of the Uniform Commercial Code," 62 Colum. L. Rev. 992 (1962); Shattuck & Guernsey, "Letters of Credit—A Comparison of Article 5 of the Uniform Commercial Code and the Washington Practice" (pts. 1 & 2), 37 Wash.

---

*ICC Pub. No. 400, Uniform Customs and Practice for Documentary Credits/1983 Revision, copyright © 1983 by ICC Publishing S.A. All rights reserved. Reprinted with the permission of ICC Publishing Corporation, Inc.

L. Rev. 325, 500 (1962); Note, "Revised International Rules for Documentary Credits," 61 Harv. L. Rev. 1420 (1952).

For discussion of the 1962 revision, see Axworthy, "The Revision of the Uniform Customs on Documentary Credits," 1971 J. Bus. L. 38; Funk, "Letters of Credit: U.C.C. Article 5 and the Uniform Customs and Practice," 11 How. L.J. 88 (1965); Gewolb, "The Law Applicable to International Letters of Credit," 11 Vill. L. Rev. 742 (1966).

For discussion of the 1974 revision, see Jhirad, "Uniform Customs and Practice for Documentary Credits, 1974 Revision: The Principal Emendations of the 1962 Text," 9 U.C.C. L.J. 109 (1976); Wheble, "Uniform Customs and Practice for Documentary Credits (1974 Revision)," 1975 J. Bus. L. 281; Note, "Documentary Letters of Credit and the Uniform Customs and Practice for Documentary Credits (1974 Revision): A Selective Analysis," 3 J. Corp. L. 147 (1977).

For discussion of the 1983 revision of the Uniform Customs, see B. Wheble, "UCP 1974/1983 Revision Compared and Explained (Documentary Credit)," ICC Pub. No. 411 (1984); Byrne, "The 1983 Revision of the Uniform Customs and Practice for Documentary Credits," 102 Banking L.J. 151 (1985); Cannon, "The Uniform Customs and Practice for Documentary Credits: The 1983 Revision," 17 U.C.C. L.J. 42 (1984); Chapman, "The 1983 Revisions to the Uniform Customs and Practice for Documentary Credits," 90 Com. L.J. 13 (1985); del Busto, "Operational Rules for Letters of Credit: Effect of New Uniform Customs and Practice Rules," 17 U.C.C. L.J. 298 (1985); Ellinger, "The Uniform Customs—Their Nature and the 1983 Revision," 1984 Lloyd's Mar. & Com. L.Q. 578; Farrar, "Uniform Commercial Code Survey: Letters of Credit," 39 Bus. Law. 1319 (1984); Kozolchyk, "The 1983 UCP Revision, Trade Practices and Court Decisions: A Plea for a Closer Relationship," 9 Can. Bus. L.J. 214 (1984); Schmitthoff, "The New Uniform Customs for Letters of Credit," 1983 J. Bus. L. 193; American Bankers Association, Letters of Credit (2d ed. 1983) (multivolume pamphlets for training bank document examiners).

In addition, for treatment of many technical issues arising out of the Uniform Customs, see American Bankers Association, Letters of Credit (1968); J. Dekker, Case Studies on Documentary Credits, ICC Pub. No. 459 (1989); International Chamber of Commerce, Opinions of the ICC Banking Commission 1987–1988, ICC Pub. No. 469 (1989); International Chamber of Commerce, Opinions of the ICC Banking Commission 1984–1986, ICC Pub. No. 434 (1987); International Chamber of Commerce, Opinions (1980–1981) of the ICC Banking Commission on Queries Relating to Uniform Customs and Practice for Documentary Credits, ICC Pub. No. 399 (1982); International Chamber of Commerce, Decisions (1975–1979) of the ICC Banking Commission on

Queries Relating to Uniform Customs and Practice for Documentary Credits, ICC Pub. No. 371 (1980); International Chamber of Commerce, Standard Forms for Issuing Documentary Credits, ICC Pub. No. 323 (1978); International Chamber of Commerce, Guide to Documentary Credit Operations, ICC Pub. No. 305 (1978).

On questions concerning the scope of the Uniform Customs, see Banco Tornquist, S.A. v. American Bank & Trust Co., 71 Misc. 2d 874, 337 N.Y.S.2d 489 (Sup. Ct. 1972) (Uniform Customs do not govern questions of fraud); Intraworld Indus., Inc. v. Girard Trust Bank, 461 Pa. 343, 336 A.2d 316 (1975) (Uniform Customs do not govern questions concerning issuance of an injunction against issuer). See generally ¶¶ 4.04–4.05.

A. General provisions and definitions

Article 1

These articles apply to all documentary credits, including, to the extent to which they may be applicable, standby letters of credit, and are binding on all parties thereto unless otherwise expressly agreed. They shall be incorporated into each documentary credit by wording in the credit indicating that such credit is issued subject to Uniform Customs and Practice for Documentary Credits, 1983 Revision, ICC Publication No. 400.

Prior Rule: 1974 version, General Provision (a).

Cases: Trans Meridian Trading, Inc. v. Empresa Nacional De Comercializacion De Insumos, 829 F.2d 949 (9th Cir. 1987)
Incorporation of Uniform Customs does not prevent court from applying California version of U.C.C. § 5-114, implicitly forbidding courts from enjoining payment of credit.

Article 2

For the purposes of these articles, the expressions "documentary credit(s)" and "standby letter(s) of credit" used herein (hereinafter referred to as credit(s)) mean any arrangement, however named or described, whereby a bank (the issuing bank), acting at the request and on the instructions of a customer (the applicant for the credit),

i is to make a payment to, or to the order of, a third party (the beneficiary), or is to pay or accept bills of exchange (drafts) drawn by the beneficiary,

or

ii authorizes another bank to effect such payment, or to pay, accept, or negotiate such bills of exchange (drafts), against stipulated documents, provided
that the terms and conditions of the credit are complied with.

Prior Rule: 1974 version, General Provision (b).

Article 3

Credits, by their nature, are transactions separate from the sales or other con-
tract(s) on which they may be based, and banks are in no way concerned with or
bound by such contract(s), even if any reference whatsoever to such contract(s) is
included in the credit.

Prior Rule: 1974 version, General Provision (c).
Cases: For cases applying prior rule, see Appendix B.

Article 4

In credit operations all parties concerned deal in documents, not in goods, services, and/or other performances to which the documents may relate.

Prior Rule: 1974 version, Article 8a.
Cases: For cases applying prior rules, see Appendix B.

Article 5

Instructions for the issuance of credits, the credits themselves, instructions for any
amendments thereto, and the amendments themselves must be complete and precise. In order to guard against confusion and misunderstanding, banks should discourage any attempt to include excessive detail in the credit or in any amendment
thereto.

Prior Rule: 1974 version, General Provision (d).

Article 6

In no case can a beneficiary avail himself of the contractual relationships existing
between the banks or between the applicant for the credit and the issuing bank.

Prior Rule: 1974 version, General Provision (f).

B. Form and notification of credits

Article 7

a. Credits may be either

   i revocable, or

   ii irrevocable.

b. All credits, therefore, should clearly indicate whether they are revocable or irrevocable.

c. In the absence of such indication, the credit shall be deemed to be revocable.

Prior Rule: 1974 version, Article 1.

Cases: For cases applying the prior rule, see Appendix B.

Article 8

A credit may be advised to a beneficiary through another bank (the advising bank) without engagement on the part of the advising bank, but that bank shall take reasonable care to check the apparent authenticity of the credit that it advises.

Prior Rule: 1974 version, Article 3b.

Article 9

a. A revocable credit may be amended or canceled by the issuing bank at any moment and without prior notice to the beneficiary.

b. However, the issuing bank is bound to:

   i reimburse a branch or bank with which a revocable credit has been made available for sight payment, acceptance, or negotiation, for any payment, acceptance, or negotiation made by such branch or bank prior to receipt by it of notice of amendment or cancelation, against documents that appear, on their face, to be in accordance with the terms and conditions of the credit.

   ii reimburse a branch or bank with which a revocable credit has been made available for deferred payment, if such branch or bank has, prior to receipt by it of notice of amendment or cancelation, taken up documents that appear, on their face, to be in accordance with the terms and conditions of the credit.

Prior Rule: 1974 version, Article 2.

Cases: For cases applying prior rule, see Appendix B.

Article 10

a. An irrevocable credit constitutes a definite undertaking of the issuing bank, provided that the stipulated documents are presented and that the terms and conditions of the credit are complied with:

i if the credit provides for sight payment—to pay or that payment will be made;

ii if the credit provides for deferred payment—to pay, or that payment will be made, on the date(s) determinable in accordance with the stipulations of the credit;

iii if the credit provides for acceptance—to accept drafts drawn by the beneficiary if the credit stipulates that they are to be drawn on the issuing bank, or to be responsible for their acceptance and payment at maturity if the credit stipulates that they are to be drawn on the applicant for the credit or any other drawee stipulated in the credit;

iv if the credit provides for negotiation—to pay without recourse to drawers and/or bona fide holders, draft(s) drawn by the beneficiary, at sight or at a tenor, on the applicant for the credit or on any other drawee stipulated in the credit, other than the issuing bank itself, or to provide for negotiation by another bank and to pay, as above, if such negotiation is not effected.

b. When an issuing bank authorizes or requests another bank to confirm its irrevocable credit and the latter has added its confirmation, such confirmation constitutes a definite undertaking of such bank (the confirming bank), in addition to that of the issuing bank, provided that the stipulated documents are presented and that the terms and conditions of the credit are complied with:

i if the credit provides for sight payment—to pay or that payment will be made;

ii if the credit provides for deferred payment—to pay, or that payment will be made, on the date(s) determinable in accordance with the stipulations of the credit;

iii if the credit provides for acceptance—to accept drafts drawn by the beneficiary, if the credit stipulates that they are to be drawn on the confirming bank, or to be responsible for their acceptance and payment at maturity, if the credit stipulates that they are to be drawn on the applicant for the credit or on any other drawee stipulated in the credit;

iv if the credit provides for negotiation—to negotiate, without recourse to drawers and/or bona fide holders, draft(s) drawn by the beneficiary, at sight or at a tenor, on the issuing bank or on the applicant for the credit or on any other drawee stipulated in the credit other than the confirming bank itself.

c. If a bank is authorized or requested by the issuing bank to add its confirmation to a credit but is not prepared to do so, it must so inform the issuing bank, without delay. Unless the issuing bank specifies otherwise in its confirmation authorization or request, the advising bank will advise the credit to the beneficiary, without adding its confirmation.

d. Such undertakings can be neither amended nor canceled without the agreement of the issuing bank, the confirming bank (if any), and the beneficiary. Partial acceptance of amendments contained in one and the same advice of amendment is not effective without the agreement of all of the above-named parties.

Prior Rule: 1974 version, Article 3.

Cases: For cases applying prior rule, see Appendix B.

Citronelle Unit Operators Comm. v. AmSouth Bank, N.A., 536 So. 2d 1387 (Ala. 1988)

Under Article 10(d), account party may not force issuer to cancel letter of credit when beneficiary does not consent.

Banque Worms v. Banque Commerciale Privee, 679 F. Supp. 1173 (S.D.N.Y. 1988), aff'd per curiam, 849 F.2d 787 (2d Cir. 1988)

Article 10(d) makes it clear that, under Article 3(c) of 1974 version of Uniform Customs, it is not necessary to obtain consent of account party to amendment of credit.

Forestal Mimosa Ltd. v. Oriental Credit Ltd., [1986] 1 W.L.R. 631 (C.A.)

Article 10(b)(iii) requires issuer to see that account party honors drafts drawn on him, when account party fails to accept draft, even though credit recited that issuer engaged that "drafts accepted . . . will be duly honored at maturity." Id. at 633.

Despite reference in credit to issuer's obligation as arising only after buyer accepted beneficiary's drafts and provision in credit reciting that it was subject to Uniform Customs "except as otherwise expressly stated," issuer was not relieved of obligation in Article 10(b)(iii) to honor drafts if buyer refused to accept them.

Article 11

a. All credits must indicate clearly whether they are available by sight payment, by deferred payment, by acceptance, or by negotiation.

b. All credits must nominate the bank (nominated bank) that is authorized to pay (paying bank), or to accept drafts (accepting bank), or to negotiate (negotiating bank), unless the credit allows negotiation by any bank (negotiating bank).

c. Unless the nominated bank is the issuing bank or the confirming bank, its nomination by the issuing bank does not constitute any undertaking by the nominated bank to pay, to accept, or to negotiate.

d. By nominating a bank other than itself, or by allowing for negotiation by any bank, or by authorizing or requesting a bank to add its confirmation, the issuing bank authorizes such bank to pay, accept, or negotiate, as the case may be, against documents that appear, on their face, to be in accordance with the terms and conditions of the credit and undertakes to reimburse such bank in accordance with the provisions of these articles.

Prior Rule: 1974 version, none.

Article 12

a. When an issuing bank instructs a bank (advising bank) by any teletransmission to advise a credit or an amendment to a credit and intends the mail confirmation to be the operative credit instrument, or the operative amendment, the teletransmission must state "full details to follow" (or words of similar effect) or that the mail confirmation will be the operative credit instrument or the operative amendment. The issuing bank must forward the operative credit instrument or the operative amendment to such advising bank without delay.

b. The teletransmission will be deemed to be the operative credit instrument or the operative amendment, and no mail confirmation should be sent, unless the teletransmission states "full details to follow" (or words of similar effect) or states that the mail confirmation is to be the operative credit instrument or the operative amendment.

c. A teletransmission intended by the issuing bank to be the operative credit instrument should indicate clearly that the credit is issued subject to Uniform Customs and Practice for Documentary Credits, 1983 revision, ICC Publication No. 400.

d. If a bank uses the services of another bank or banks (the advising bank) to have the credit advised to the beneficiary, it also must use the service of the same bank(s) for advising any amendments.

e. Banks shall be responsible for any consequences arising from their failure to follow the procedures set out in the preceding paragraphs.

Prior Rule: 1974 version, Article 4.

Article 13

When a bank is instructed to issue, confirm, or advise a credit similar in terms to one previously issued, confirmed, or advised (similar credit), and the previous credit has been the subject of amendment(s), it shall be understood that the similar credit will not include any such amendment(s) unless the instructions specify clearly the amendment(s) that is/are to apply to the similar credit. Banks should discourage instructions to issue, confirm, or advise a credit in this manner.

Prior Rule: 1974 version, Article 5.
Cases: For a case construing prior rule, see Appendix B.

Article 14

If incomplete or unclear instructions are received to issue, confirm, advise, or amend a credit, the bank requested to act on such instructions may give preliminary notification to the beneficiary for information only and without responsibility. The credit will be issued, confirmed, advised, or amended only when the necessary information has been received and only if the bank is then prepared to act on the instructions. Banks should provide the necessary information without delay.

Prior Rule: 1974 version, Article 6.

Cases: For a case construing prior rule, see Appendix B.

C. Liabilities and responsibilities

Article 15

Banks must examine all documents with reasonable care to ascertain that they appear, on their face, to be in accordance with the terms and conditions of the credit. Documents that appear, on their face, to be inconsistent with one another will be considered as not appearing, on their face, to be in accordance with the terms and conditions of the credit.

Prior Rule: 1974 version, Article 7.

Cases: For cases construing prior rule, see Appendix B.
   Bank of Cochin Ltd. v. Manufacturers Hanover Trust Co., 612 F. Supp. 1533 (S.D.N.Y. 1985), aff'd, 808 F.2d 209 (2d Cir. 1986) (dictum)
   Article 15 supports position that confirming payor bank owes duty of care to opening bank.

Article 16

a. If a bank so authorized effects payment, or incurs a deferred payment undertaking, or accepts, or negotiates against documents that appear, on their face, to be in accordance with terms and conditions of a credit, the party giving such authority shall be bound to reimburse the bank that has effected payment, or has incurred a deferred payment undertaking, or has accepted, or has negotiated, and to take up the documents.

b. If, upon receipt of the documents, the issuing bank considers that they appear, on their face, not to be in accordance with the terms and conditions of the credit, it must determine, on the basis of the documents alone, whether to take up such documents or to refuse them and claim that they appear, on their face, not to be in accordance with the terms and conditions of the credit.

c. The issuing bank shall have a reasonable time in which to examine the documents and to determine, as above, whether to take up or to refuse the documents.

d. If the issuing bank decides to refuse the documents, it must give notice to that effect, without delay, by telecommunication or, if that is not possible, by other expeditious means, to the bank from which it received the documents (the remitting bank), or to the beneficiary, if it received the documents directly from him. Such notice must state the discrepancies in respect of which the issuing bank refuses the documents and also must state whether it is holding the documents at the disposal of, or is returning them to, the presenter (remitting bank or the beneficiary, as the case may be). The issuing bank then shall be entitled to claim from the remitting bank refund of any reimbursement that may have been made to that bank.

e. If the issuing bank fails to act in accordance with the provisions of paragraphs (c) and (d) of this article and/or fails to hold the documents at the disposal of, or to return them to, the presenter, the issuing bank shall be precluded from claiming that the documents are not in accordance with the terms and conditions of the credit.

f. If the remitting bank draws the attention of the issuing bank to any discrepancies in the documents or advises the issuing bank that it has paid, incurred a deferred payment undertaking, accepted, or negotiated under reserve or against an indemnity in respect of such discrepancies, the issuing bank shall not be relieved thereby from any of its obligations under any provision of this article. Such reserve or indemnity concerns only the relations between the remitting bank and the party toward whom the reserve was made, or from whom or on whose behalf the indemnity was obtained.

Prior Rule: 1974 version, Articles 8b–8g.

Cases: For cases construing the prior rule, see Appendix B.

Kerr-McGee Chem. Corp. v. FDIC, 872 F.2d 971 (11th Cir. 1989)

Issuer that fails to include defect in notice of defects may not thereafter raise defect under rule of Article 16(e).

Bank of Cochin, Ltd. v. Manufacturers Hanover Trust Co., 808 F.2d 209 (2d Cir. 1986)

Citing with approval lower court's dictum to effect that Article 16(e) makes explicit what is implicit in U.C.P. Article 8(e) (1974 version), i.e., that issuer which fails to notify beneficiary or presenting bank of defects promptly loses right to raise those defects as defense in action for wrongful dishonor.

Esso Petroleum Can., a Div. of Imperial Oil Ltd. v. Security Pac. Bank, 710 F. Supp. 275 (D. Or. 1989)

When issuer gave notice of dishonor on Friday at 5:15 P.M. but delayed giving reasons for dishonor until following Monday, issuer violated rule of Article 16(d) and lost its defenses under Article 16(e).

Kuntal, S.A. v. Bank of N.Y., 703 F. Supp. 312 (S.D.N.Y. 1989)

Issuer that delays giving notice of defects for nine banking days after determining that documents do not conform is estopped under rule of Article 16(e) from asserting that documents are defective in beneficiary's action for wrongful dishonor.

Article 16(d) does not authorize issuer to wait to give notice of defects for nine banking days while account party considers whether to waive defects.

Jeri-Jo Knitwear, Inc. v. Gonul Besen Konfeksiyon Sanayii Ve Ticaret Ltd., No. C2535 (E.D.N.Y. Sept. 20, 1988)

When beneficiary supplies defective goods bearing account party's labels and account party justifiably rejects goods but, in order to protect trademark, seeks injunction against bank holding documents from redelivering documents to beneficiary's bank or other agent, bank holding documents will not be relieved from injunction, any damage to its reputation notwithstanding.

North Beach Leather Int'l, Inc. v. Morgan Guar. Trust Co., 687 F. Supp. 127 (S.D.N.Y. 1988)

Summary judgment is not warranted under Article 16(d) when issuer fails to give notice of defects, for factual questions remain concerning compliance of documents.

Crist v. J. Henry Schroder Bank & Trust Co., 693 F. Supp. 1429 (S.D.N.Y. 1988)

Issuer that receives documents on Friday, December 27, 1985, decides on January 2, 1986 to dishonor and gives notice of dishonor on January 3, 1986 has acted in timely fashion under Article 16(c).

Under Articles 16(d) and 16(e), issuer is confined to those defects that it lists in its notice of dishonor. An issuer that failed to list beneficiary's failure to submit certified copy of its appointment order cannot use that omission as ground justifying dishonor.

Offshore Trading Co. v. Citizens Nat'l Bank, 650 F. Supp. 1487 (D. Kan. 1987)

If issuer fails to comply with Article 16(d), it is precluded by Article 16(e) from claiming nonconformities.

The reason for Article 16(e) and its preclusion rule is to give beneficiary notice of defects promptly so that it can cure them.

Bank of Cochin Ltd. v. Manufacturers Hanover Trust Co., 612 F. Supp. 1533 (S.D.N.Y. 1985), aff'd, 808 F.2d 209 (2d Cir. 1986) (dictum)

Article 16(e) estops issuer from asserting that documents are defective if issuer fails to comply with Article 16(d).

Datapoint Corp. v. M&I Bank, 665 F. Supp. 722 (W.D. Wis. 1987)

If issuer decides to dishonor beneficiary's draft on first day it is submitted, issuer does not have reasonable time within which to give notice to beneficiary but must give notice immediately.

When documents are presented on day before credit's expiry and issuer determines that they are not conforming, issuer must give telephonic notice to beneficiary to allow beneficiary opportunity to cure defects, reasonable time rule being one for determining whether documents comply.

Issuer that fails to give telephonic notice of defect in beneficiary's draft when only one day remains before credit's expiry and instead mails documents to beneficiary is estopped to assert that draft is not complying.

Habib Bank Ltd. v. Convermat Corp., 145 Misc. 2d 980, 554 N.Y.S.2d 757 (App. Term. 1990) (per curiam)

A breach of warranty cause of action by an issuer against a beneficiary for presenting documents that are facially nonconforming conflicts with the rule of Article 16(e) that estops an issuer from claiming that documents are defective unless the issuer gives the beneficiary prompt notice of the defects.

Article 17

Banks assume no liability or responsibility for the form, sufficiency, accuracy, genuineness, falsification, or legal effect of any documents, or for the general and/or particular conditions stipulated in the documents or superimposed thereon. Nor do they assume any liability or responsibility for the description, quantity, weight, quality, condition, packing, delivery, value, or existence of the goods represented by any documents, or for the good faith or acts and/or omissions, solvency, performance, or standing of the consignor, the carriers, or the insurers of the goods, or for any other person whomsoever.

Prior Rule: 1974 version, Article 9.

Cases: For cases construing the prior rule, see Appendix B.

Article 18

Banks assume no liability or responsibility for the consequences arising out of delay and/or loss in transit of any messages, letters, or documents, or for delay, mutilation, or other errors arising in the transmission of any telecommunication. Banks assume no liability or responsibility for errors in translation or interpretation of technical terms and reserve the right to transmit credit terms without translating them.

Prior Rule: 1974 version, Article 10.

Cases: For a case construing prior rule, see Appendix B.

Article 19

Banks assume no liability or responsibility for consequences arising out of the interruption of their business by acts of God, riots, civil commotions, insurrections, wars, or any other causes beyond their control, or by any strikes or lockouts.

Unless specifically authorized, banks will not, upon resumption of their business, incur a deferred payment undertaking or effect payment, acceptance, or negotiation under credits that expired during such interruption of their business.

Prior Rule: 1974 version, Article 11.

Cases: For a case construing prior rule, see Appendix B.

Article 20

a. Banks utilizing the services of another bank or other banks for the purpose of giving effect to the instructions of the applicant for the credit do so for the account and at the risk of such applicant.

b. Banks assume no liability or responsibility should the instructions they transmit not be carried out, even if they themselves have taken the initiative in the choice of such other bank(s).

c. The applicant for the credit shall be bound by and liable to indemnify the banks against all obligations and responsibilities imposed by foreign laws and usages.

Prior Rule: 1974 version, Article 12.

Cases: For a case construing prior rule, see Appendix B.
   Bank of Cochin Ltd. v. Manufacturers Hanover Trust Co., 612 F. Supp. 1533 (S.D.N.Y. 1985), aff'd, 808 F.2d 209 (2d Cir. 1986) (dictum)
   Articles 20(a) and 20(c) support position that confirming bank owes duty toward account party.

Article 21

a. If an issuing bank intends that the reimbursement to which a paying, accepting, or negotiating bank is entitled shall be obtained by such bank claiming on another branch or office of the issuing bank or on a third bank (all referred to hereinafter as the reimbursing bank) it shall provide such reimbursing bank in good time with the proper instructions or authorization to honor such reimbursement claims and without making it a condition that the bank entitled to claim reimbursement must certify compliance with the terms and conditions of the credit to the reimbursing bank.

b. An issuing bank will not be relieved from any of its obligations to provide reimbursement itself if and when reimbursement is not effected by the reimbursing bank.

c. The issuing bank will be responsible to the paying, accepting, or negotiating bank for any loss of interest if reimbursement is not provided on first demand made to the reimbursing bank, or as otherwise specified in the credit, or as mutually agreed, as the case may be.

Prior Rule: 1974 version, Article 13.

D. Documents

Article 22

a. All instructions for the issuance of credits and the credits themselves and, where applicable, all instructions for amendments thereto and the amendments themselves, must state precisely the document(s) against which payment, acceptance, or negotiation is to be made.

b. Terms such as "first class," "well known," "qualified," "independent," "official," and the like shall not be used to describe the issuers of any documents to be presented under a credit. If such terms are incorporated in the credit terms, banks will accept the relative documents as presented, provided that they appear, on their face, to be in accordance with the other terms and conditions of the credit.

c. Unless otherwise stipulated in the credit, banks will accept as originals documents produced or appearing to have been produced:

i by reprographic systems;

ii by, or as the result of, automated or computerized systems;

iii as carbon copies,

if marked as originals, always provided that, where necessary, such documents appear to have been authenticated.

Prior Rule: 1974 version, Article 14.

Article 23

When documents other than transport documents, insurance documents, and commercial invoices are called for, the credit should stipulate by whom such documents are to be issued and their wording or data content. If the credit does not so stipulate, banks will accept such documents as presented, provided that their data content makes it possible to relate the goods and/or services referred to therein to those referred to in the commercial invoices(s) presented, or to those referred to in the credit if the credit does not stipulate presentation of a commercial invoice.

Prior Rule: 1974 version, Article 33.

Cases: For cases construing prior rule, see Appendix B.

Article 24

Unless otherwise stipulated in the credit, banks will accept a document bearing a date of issuance prior to that of the credit, subject to such document being presented within the time limits set out in the credit and in these articles.

Prior Rule: 1974 version, none.

D1. Transport documents (documents indicating loading on board or dispatch or taking in charge)

Article 25

Unless a credit calling for a transport document stipulates as such document a marine bill of lading (ocean bill of lading or a bill of lading covering carriage by sea), or a post receipt or certificate of posting:

a. Banks will, unless otherwise stipulated in the credit, accept a transport document that:

i appears, on its face, to have been issued by a named carrier or his agent, and

ii indicates dispatch or taking in charge of the goods, or loading on board, as the case may be, and

iii consists of the full set of originals issued to the consignor if issued in more than one original, and

iv meets all other stipulations of the credit.

b. Subject to the above, and unless otherwise stipulated in the credit, banks will not reject a transport document that:

i bears a title such as "Combined transport bill of lading," "Combined transport document," "Combined transport bill of lading or port-to-port bill of lading," or a title or a combination of titles of similar intent and effect, and/or

ii indicates some or all of the conditions of carriage by reference to a source or document other than the transport document itself (short-form blank-back transport document), and/or

iii indicates a place of taking in charge different from the port of loading and/or a place of final destination different from the port of discharge, and/or

iv relates to cargoes such as those in containers or on pallets, and the like, and/or

v contains the indication "intended," or similar qualification, in relation to the vessel or other means of transport, and/or the port of loading and/or the port of discharge.

c. Unless otherwise stipulated in the credit in the case of carriage by sea or by more than one mode of transport but including carriage by sea, banks will reject a transport document that:

   i indicates that it is subject to a charter party, and/or

   ii indicates that the carrying vessel is propelled by sail only.

d. Unless otherwise stipulated in the credit, banks will reject a transport document issued by a freight forwarder unless it is the FIATA Combined Transport Bill of Lading approved by the International Chamber of Commerce or otherwise indicates that it is issued by a freight forwarder acting as a carrier or agent of a named carrier.

Prior Rule: 1974 version, Articles 19, 23, 24.

Cases: For cases construing prior rules, see Appendix B.

Article 26

If a credit calling for a transport document stipulates as such document a marine bill of lading:

a. Banks will, unless otherwise stipulated in the credit, accept a document which:

   i appears, on its face, to have been issued by a named carrier, or his agent, and

   ii indicates that the goods have been loaded on board or shipped on a named vessel, and

   iii consists of the full set or originals issued to the consignor if issued in more than one original, and

   iv meets all other stipulations of the credit.

b. Subject to the above, and unless otherwise stipulated in the credit, banks will not reject a document that:

   i bears a title such as "Combined transport bill of lading," "Combined transport document," "Combined transport bill of lading or port-to-port bill of lading," or a title or a combination of titles of similar intent and effect, and/or

   ii indicates some or all of the conditions of carriage by reference to a source or document other than the transport document itself (short-form blank-back transport document), and/or

   iii indicates a place of taking in charge different from the port of loading, and/or a place of final destination different from the port of discharge, and/or

   iv relates to cargoes such as those in containers or on pallets, and the like.

c. Unless otherwise stipulated in the credit, banks will reject a document that:

   i indicates that it is subject to a charter party, and/or

   ii indicates that the carrying vessel is propelled by sail only, and/or

iii contains the indication "intended," or similar qualification in relation to— the vessel and/or the port of loading—unless such document bears an on-board notation in accordance with Article 27(b) and also indicates the actual port of loading, and/or—the port of discharge—unless the place of final destination indicated on the document is other than the port of discharge, and/or

iv is issued by a freight forwarder, unless it indicates that it is issued by such freight forwarder acting as a carrier or as the agent of a named carrier.

Prior Rule: 1974 version, Article 19.

Article 27

a. Unless a credit specifically calls for an on-board transport document, or unless inconsistent with other stipulation(s) in the credit, or with Article 26, banks will accept a transport document which indicates that the goods have been taken in charge or received for shipment.

b. Loading on board or shipment on a vessel may be evidenced either by a transport document bearing wording indicating loading on board a named vessel or shipment on a named vessel, or, in the case of a transport document stating "received for shipment," by means of a notation of loading on board on the transport document signed or initialed and dated by the carrier or his agent, and the date of this notation shall be regarded as the date of loading on board the named vessel or shipment on the named vessel.

Prior Rule: 1974 version, Article 20.

Cases: For cases construing prior rule, see Appendix B.
   In re Standard Chartered Bank, Letter of Credit Update 27 (Jan. 1988) (Wheble, arb.)
   Article 27(b) requires received-for-shipment bill of lading to bear signed and dated on-board stamp in order to qualify as on-board bill of lading.
   Received-for-shipment bill of lading bearing notation that goods were "clean on board" did not satisfy credit calling for on-board bill, because stamped language was not signed and dated.
   Whether bill of lading form is on-board bill or received-for-shipment bill is question to be determined from document as whole.
   If bill of lading does not indicate that it is received-for-shipment bill or on-board bill, it is received-for-shipment bill and must contain signed and dated on-board stamp in order to qualify as on-board bill.

Article 28

a. In the case of carriage by sea or by more than one mode of transport, but including carriage by sea, banks will refuse a transport document stating that the goods are, or will be, loaded on deck, unless specifically authorized in the credit.

b. Banks will not refuse a transport document which contains a provision that the goods may be carried on deck, provided it does not state specifically that they are or will be loaded on deck.

Prior Rule: 1974 version, Article 22.

Article 29

a. For the purpose of this article, transshipment means a transfer and reloading during the course of carriage from the port of loading or place of dispatch or taking in charge to the port of discharge or place of destination either from one conveyance or vessel to another conveyance or vessel within the same mode of transport or from one mode of transport to another mode of transport.

b. Unless transshipment is prohibited by the terms of the credit, banks will accept transport documents which indicate that the goods will be transshipped, provided the entire carriage is covered by one and the same transport document.

c. Even if transhipment is prohibited by the terms of the credit, banks will accept transport documents that:

i incorporate printed clauses stating that the carrier has the right to transship, or

ii state or indicate that transshipment will or may take place, when the credit stipulates a combined transport document, or indicates carriage from a place of taking in charge to a place of final destination by different modes of transport, including a carriage by sea, provided that the entire carriage is covered by one and the same transport document, or

iii state or indicate that the goods are in a container(s), trailer(s), "LASH" barge(s), and the like and will be carried from the place of taking in charge to the place of final destination in the same container(s), trailer(s), "LASH" barge(s), and the like under one and the same transport document, or

iv state or indicate the place of receipt and/or of final destination as "C.F.S." (container freight station) or "C.Y." (container yard) at, or associated with, the port of loading and/or the port of destination.

Prior Rule: 1974 version, Article 24.

Article 30

If the credit stipulates dispatch of goods by post and calls for a post receipt or certificate of posting, banks will accept such post receipt or certificate of posting if it appears to have been stamped or otherwise authenticated and dated in the place from which the credit stipulates the goods are to be dispatched.

Prior Rule: 1974 version, Article 24.

Cases: For cases construing prior rule, see Appendix B.

Article 31

a. Unless otherwise stipulated in the credit, or inconsistent with any of the documents presented under the credit, banks will accept transport documents stating that freight or transportation charges (hereinafter referred to as "freight") still have to be paid.

b. If a credit stipulates that the transport document has to indicate that freight has been paid or prepaid, banks will accept a transport document on which words clearly indicating payment or prepayment of freight appear by stamp or otherwise, or on which payment of freight is indicated by other means.

c. The words "freight prepayable," "freight to be prepaid," or words of similar effect, if appearing on transport documents, will not be accepted as constituting evidence of the payment of freight.

d. Banks will accept transport documents bearing reference by stamp or otherwise to costs additional to the freight charges, such as costs of, or disbursements incurred in connection with, loading, unloading, or similar operations, unless the conditions of the credit specifically prohibit such reference.

Prior Rule: 1974 version, Article 16.

Cases: For a case construing prior rule, see Appendix B.

Article 32

Unless otherwise stipulated in the credit, banks will accept transport documents that bear a clause on the face thereof such as "shipper's load and count" or "said by shipper to contain" or words of similar effect.

Prior Rule: 1974 version, Article 17.

Article 33

Unless otherwise stipulated in the credit, banks will accept transport documents indicating as the consignor of the goods a party other than the beneficiary of the credit.

Prior Rule: 1974 version, none.

Article 34

a. A clean transport document is one that bears no superimposed clause or notation which expressly declares a defective condition of the goods and/or the packaging.

b. Banks will refuse transport documents bearing such clauses or notations, unless the credit expressly stipulates the clauses or notations that may be accepted.

c. Banks will regard a requirement in a credit for a transport document to bear the clause "clean on board" as complied with if such transport document meets the requirements of this article and of Article 27(b).

Prior Rule: 1974 version, Article 18.

Cases: For a case construing prior rule, see Appendix B.

D2. Insurance documents

Article 35

a. Insurance documents must be as stipulated in the credit, and must be issued and/or signed by insurance companies or underwriters or by their agents.

b. Cover notes issued by brokers will not be accepted, unless specifically authorized by the credit.

Prior Rule: 1974 version, Article 26.

Article 36

Unless otherwise stipulated in the credit, or unless it appears from the insurance document(s) that the cover is effective at the latest from the date of loading on board or dispatch or taking in charge of the goods, banks will refuse insurance documents presented that bear a date later than the date of loading on board or dispatch or taking in charge of the goods as indicated by the transport document(s).

Prior Rule: 1974 version, Article 27.

Article 37

a. Unless otherwise stipulated in the credit, the insurance document must be expressed in the same currency as the credit.

b. Unless otherwise stipulated in the credit, the minimum amount for which the insurance document must indicate the insurance cover to have been effected is the CIF (cost, insurance, and freight . . . "named port of destination") or CIP (freight/carriage and insurance paid to "named point of destination") value of the goods, as the case may be, plus 10 percent. However, if banks cannot determine the CIF or CIP value, as the case may be, from the documents on their face, they will accept as such minimum amount the amount for which payment, acceptance, or negotiation is requested under the credit, or the amount of the commercial invoice, whichever is the greater.

Prior Rule: 1974 version, Article 28.

Article 38

a. Credits should stipulate the type of insurance required and, if any, the additional risks that are to be covered. Imprecise terms such as "usual risks" or "customary risks" should not be used; if they are used, banks will accept insurance documents as presented, without responsibility for any risks not being covered.

b. Failing specific stipulations in the credit, banks will accept insurance documents as presented, without responsibility for any risks not being covered.

Prior Rule: 1974 version, Article 29.

Article 39

Where a credit stipulates "insurance against all risks," banks will accept an insurance document that contains any "all risks" notation or clause, regardless of whether it bears the heading "all risks," even if indicating that certain risks are excluded, without responsibility for any risk(s) not being covered.

Prior Rule: 1974 version, Article 30.

Article 40

Banks will accept an insurance document which indicates that the cover is subject to a franchise or an excess (deductible), unless it is specifically stipulated in the credit that the insurance must be issued irrespective of percentage.

Prior Rule: 1974 version, Article 31.

D3. Commercial invoice

Article 41

a. Unless otherwise stipulated in the credit, commercial invoices must be made out in the name of the applicant for the credit.

b. Unless otherwise stipulated in the credit, banks may refuse commercial invoices issued for amounts in excess of the amount permitted by the credit. Nevertheless, if a bank authorized to pay, incur a deferred payment undertaking, accept, or negotiate under a credit accepts such invoices, its decision will be binding upon all parties, provided such bank has not paid, incurred a deferred payment undertaking, accepted, or effected negotiation for an amount in excess of that permitted by the credit.

c. The description of the goods in the commercial invoice must correspond with the description in the credit. In all other documents, the goods may be described in general terms not inconsistent with the description of the goods in the credit.

Prior Rule: 1974 version, Article 32, General Provision (e).

Cases: For cases construing the prior rule, see Appendix B.
North Beach Leather Int'l, Inc. v. Morgan Guar. Trust, Co., 687 F. Supp. 127 (S.D.N.Y. 1988)
When beneficiary made single, combined draw under two letters of credit and submitted invoices whose combined amounts totaled amounts of credits, issuer complained that invoices were for amounts in excess of amount permitted under either of credits and gave issuer ground to dishonor under Uniform Customs. (Opinion recites that issuer was relying on "Article 30 of the UCP." Id. at 130. That reference probably results from fact that invoice provision under 1962 version of Uniform Customs was indeed Article 30. See International Chamber of Commerce, Uniform Customs and Practice for Documentary Credits (1962 version) (ICC Brochure No. 222). See also Table of Parallel Provisions at page T-1. Presumably, court meant to refer to Article 41(b), invoice article in 1983 version of Uniform Customs, which court's opinion otherwise suggests applied in *North Beach Leather* case.) Court held that, because amount of invoices did not exceed total amount of credits, there was no justification under Uniform Customs to dishonor.

D4. Other documents

Article 42

If a credit calls for an attestation or certification of weight in the case of transport other than by sea, banks will accept a weight stamp or declaration of weight that appears to have been superimposed on the transport document by the carrier or his agent, unless the credit specifically stipulates that the attestation or certification of weight must be by means of a separate document.

Prior Rule: 1974 version, Article 25.

E. Miscellaneous provisions

Quality and amount

Article 43

a. The words "about," "circa," or similar expressions used in connection with the amount of the credit or the quantity or the unit price stated in the credit are to be construed as allowing a difference not to exceed 10 percent more or 10 percent less than the amount or the quantity or the unit price to which they refer.

b. Unless a credit stipulates that the quantity of the goods specified must not be exceeded or reduced, a tolerance of 5 percent more or 5 percent less will be permissible, even if partial shipments are not permitted, always provided that the amount of the drawings does not exceed the amount of the credit. This tolerance does not apply when the credit stipulates the quantity in terms of a stated number of packing units or individual items.

Prior Rule: 1974 version, Article 34.

Partial drawings and/or shipments

Article 44

a. Partial drawing and/or shipments are allowed, unless the credit stipulates otherwise.

b. Shipments by sea or by more than one mode of transport, but including carriage by sea, made on the same vessel and for the same voyage will not be regarded as partial shipments, even if the transport documents indicating loading on board bear different dates of issuance and/or indicate different ports of loading on board.

c. Shipments made by post will not be regarded as partial shipments if the post receipts or certificates of posting appear to have been stamped or otherwise authenticated in the place from which the credit stipulates the goods are to be dispatched, and on the same date.

d. Shipments made by modes of transport other than those referred to in paragraphs (b) and (c) of this article will not be regarded as partial shipments, provided the transport documents are issued by one and the same carrier or by his agent and indicate the same date of issuance, the same place of dispatch or taking in charge of the goods, and the same destination.

Prior Rule: 1974 version, Article 35.

Cases: For a case construing the prior rule, see Appendix B.

Drawings and/or shipments by installment
Article 45

If drawings and/or shipments by installments within given periods are stipulated in the credit, and if any installment is not drawn and/or shipped within the period allowed for that installment, the credit ceases to be available for that and any subsequent installments, unless otherwise stipulated in the credit.

Prior Rule: 1974 version, Article 36.

Expiry date and presentation
Article 46

a. All credits must stipulate an expiry date for presentation of documents for payment, acceptance or negotiation.

b. Except as provided in Article 48(l), documents must be presented on or before such expiry date.

c. If an issuing bank states that the credit is to be available "for one month," "for six months," or the like, but does not specify the date from which the time is to run, the date of issuance of the credit by the issuing bank will be deemed to be the first day from which such time is to run. Banks should discourage indication of the expiry date of the credit in this manner.

Prior Rule: 1974 version, Articles 37, 45.

Cases: For a case construing the prior rule, see Appendix B.
FDIC v. Bank of Boulder, 865 F.2d 1134 (10th Cir. 1988)
Article 46 does not prevent voluntary transfer of letter of credit by FDIC (receiver) to itself as insurer in connection with purchase-and-assumption agreement of failed bank's assets.

Article 47

a. In addition to stipulating an expiry date for presentation of documents, every credit that calls for a transport document(s) should also stipulate a specified period of time after the date of issuance of the transport document(s) during which presentation of documents for payment, acceptance, or negotiation must be made. If no such period of time is stipulated, banks will refuse documents presented to them later than twenty-one days after the date of issuance of the transport document(s). In every case, however, documents must be presented not later than the expiry date of the credit.

b. For the purpose of these articles, the date of issuance of a transport document(s) will be deemed to be:

i in the case of a transport document evidencing dispatch, or taking in charge, or receipt of goods for shipment by a mode of transport other than by air — the date of issuance indicated on the transport document or the date of the reception stamp thereon, whichever is later.

ii in the case of a transport document evidencing carriage by air — the date of issuance indicated on the transport document or, if the credit stipulates that the transport document shall indicate an actual flight date, the actual flight date, as indicated on the transport document.

iii in the case of a transport document evidencing loading on board a named vessel — the date of issuance of the transport document or, in the case of an on-board notation in accordance with Article 27(b), the date of such notation.

iv in cases to which Article 44(b) applies, the date, determined as above, of the latest transport document issued.

Prior Rule: 1974 version, Articles 15, 41.

Cases: For cases construing the prior rules, see Appendix B.

Article 48

a. If the expiry date of the credit and/or the last day of the period of time after the date of issuance of the transport document(s) for presentation of documents stipulated by the credit or applicable by virtue of Article 47 falls on a day on which the bank to which presentation has to be made is closed for reasons other than those referred to in Article 19, the stipulated expiry date and/or the last day of the period of time after the date of issuance of the transport document(s) for presentation of documents, as the case may be, shall be extended to the first following business day on which such bank is open.

b. The latest date for loading on board, or dispatch, or taking in charge shall not be extended by reason of the extension of the expiry date and/or the period of time after the date of issuance of the transport document(s) for presentation of document(s) in accordance with this article. If no such latest date for shipment is stipulated in the credit or in amendments thereto, banks will reject transport documents indicating a date of issuance later than the expiry date stipulated in the credit or in amendments thereto.

c. The bank to which presentation is made on such first following business day must add to the documents its certificate that the documents were presented within the time limits extended in accordance with Article 48(a) of the Uniform Customs and Practice for Documentary Credit, 1983 revision, ICC Publication No. 400.

Prior Rule: 1974 version, Article 39.

Cases: For a case construing the prior rule, see Appendix B.
    Esso Petroleum Can., a Div. of Imperial Oil Ltd. v. Security Pac. Bank, 710 F. Supp. 275 (D. Or. 1989)
    Credit that expires by its terms on November 15, a Sunday, expires under the UCP on November 16.

Article 49

Banks are under no obligation to accept presentation of documents outside their banking hours.

Prior Rule: 1974 version, Article 42.

Cases: For a case construing the prior rule, see Appendix B.

Loading on board, dispatch and taking in charge (shipment)
Article 50

a. Unless otherwise stipulated in the credit, the expression "shipment" used in stipulating an earliest and/or latest shipment date will be understood to include the expressions "loading on board," "dispatch," and "taking in charge."

b. The date of issuance of the transport document determined in accordance with Article 47(b) will be taken to be the date of shipment.

c. Expressions such as "prompt," "immediately," "as soon as possible," and the like should not be used. If they are used, banks will interpret them as a stipulation that shipment is to be made within thirty days from the date of issuance of the credit by the issuing bank.

d. If the expression "on or about" and similar expressions are used, banks will interpret them as a stipulation that shipment is to be made during the period from five days before to five days after the specified date, both end days included.

Prior Rule: 1974 version, Article 40.

Date terms

Article 51

The words "to," "until," "till," "from," and words of similar import applying to any date term in the credit will be understood to include the date mentioned. The word "after" will be understood to exclude the date mentioned.

Prior Rule: 1974 version, Article 38.

Cases: For a case construing prior rule, see Appendix B.

Article 52

The terms "first half" and "second half" of a month shall be construed, respectively, as from the first to the fifteenth, and the sixteenth to the last day of each month, inclusive.

Prior Rule: 1974 version, Article 43.

Article 53

The terms "beginning," "middle," and "end" of a month shall be construed respectively as from the first to the tenth, the eleventh to the twentieth, and the twenty-first to the last day of each month, inclusive.

Prior Rule: 1974 version, Article 44.

F. Transfer

Article 54

a. A transferable credit is a credit under which the beneficiary has the right to request the bank called upon to effect payment or acceptance or any bank entitled to effect negotiation to make the credit available, in whole or in part, to one or more other parties (second beneficiaries).

b. A credit can be transferred only if it is expressly designated as "transferable" by the issuing bank. Terms such as "divisible," "fractionable," "assignable," and "transmissible" add nothing to the meaning of the term "transferable" and shall not be used.

c. The bank requested to effect the transfer (transferring bank), regardless of whether it has confirmed the credit, shall be under no obligation to effect such transfer except to the extent and in the manner expressly consented to by such bank.

d. Bank charges in respect of transfers are payable by the first beneficiary unless otherwise specified. The transferring bank shall be under no obligation to effect the transfer until such charges are paid.

e. A transferable credit can be transferred only once. Fractions of a transferable credit (not exceeding, in the aggregate, the amount of the credit) can be transferred separately, provided partial shipments are not prohibited, and the aggregate of such transfers will be considered as constituting only one transfer of the credit. The credit can be transferred only on the terms and conditions specified in the original credit, with the exception of the amount of the credit, of any unit prices stated therein, of the period of validity, of the last date for presentation of documents in accordance with Article 47 and the period for shipment, any or all of which may be reduced or curtailed, or the percentage for which insurance cover must be effected, which may be increased in such a way as to provide the amount of cover stipulated in the original credit, or these articles. Additionally, the name of the first beneficiary can be substituted for that of the applicant for the credit, but if the name of the applicant for the credit is specifically required by the original credit to appear in any document other than the invoice, such requirement must be fulfilled.

f. The first beneficiary has the right to substitute his own invoices (and drafts if the credit stipulates that drafts are to be drawn on the applicant for the credit) in exchange for those of the second beneficiary, for amounts not in excess of the original amount stipulated in the credit and for the original unit prices if stipulated in the credit, and, upon such substitution of invoices (and drafts), the first beneficiary can draw under the credit for the difference, if any, between his invoices and the second beneficiary's invoices. When a credit has been transferred and the first beneficiary is to supply his own invoices (and drafts) in exchange for the second beneficiary's invoices (and drafts) but fails to do so on first demand, the paying, accepting, or negotiating bank has the right to deliver to the issuing bank the documents received under the credit, including the second beneficiary's invoices (and drafts), without further responsibility to the first beneficiary.

g. Unless otherwise stipulated in the credit, the first beneficiary of a transferable credit may request that the credit be transferred to a second beneficiary in the same country or in another country. Further, unless otherwise stipulated in the credit, the first beneficiary shall have the right to request that payment or negotiation be effected to the second beneficiary at the place to which the credit has been transferred, up to and including the expiry date of the original credit, and without prejudice to the first beneficiary's right subsequently to substitute his own invoices and drafts (if any) for those of the second beneficiary and to claim any difference due to him.

Prior Rule: 1974 version, Article 46.

Cases: For cases construing prior rule, see Appendix B.

Anchor Centre Partners, Ltd. v. Mercantile Bank, N.A., 783 S.W.2d 108 (Mo. Ct. App. 1989), aff'd on rehearing, id.

Article 54(e) prevents multiple transfers of credit, even though transfers are effected by amendment and by agreement of issuer.

Hongkong & Shanghai Banking Corp. v. Kloeckner & Co., [1989] 2 Lloyd's Rep. 323 (Q.B.)

In certain circumstances, issuer may use setoff against beneficiary. That holding is consistent with Article 46 of 1974 version of UCP, since Article 46(b) permits issuer to refuse transfer of letter of credit and thereby protects its right of setoff. (Judgment refers to 1974 version of UCP, whose Articles 46(a) and 46(b) correspond to Articles 54(a) and 54(c) of the 1983 version of UCP, version that credit in *Hongkong Bank* case incorporated.)

Godwin, *"Transferable Letters of Credit—The Effect of Lariza,"* 1990 J. Bus. L. 48

Bank Negara is correct, but for reasons not set forth in the judgment of the Privy Council.

Goode, *"Reflections on Letters of Credit—V,"* 1981 J. Bus. L. 150

Article 46, predecessor of Article 54 is inconsistent in fashioning right on part of beneficiary but no correlative duty on part of issuer for transfer of credit.

Inconsistency noted above may lie in English translation of predecessor of Article 54. French version of Article 46 indicates that there is correlative duty if beneficiary's request for transfer conforms to issuer's announced procedures for transfers.

Schmitthoff, *"The Transferable Credit,"* J. Bus. L. 49 (Jan. 1988)

Because letter of credit rules permit transfer of credits in parts, such transfer is not assignment in English law.

Because Article 54 permits only one assignment of credit, letter of credit is not negotiable instrument under English law.

Assignment of proceeds

Article 55

The fact that a credit is not stated to be transferable shall not affect the beneficiary's right to assign any proceeds to which he may be, or may become, entitled under such credit, in accordance with the provisions of the applicable law.

Prior Rule: 1974 version, Article 47.

Ellinger, *"Performance Bonds, First-Demand Guarantees and Standby Letters of Credit—A Comparison,"* Letters of Credit Report 1 (May/June 1987)

Because there is no distinction in common law between assignment of right to proceeds and transfer of right to draw, Article 55 may not be effective for credits that are subject to common law but not to Uniform Commercial Code.

APPENDIX **B**

Uniform Customs and Practice for Documentary Credits (1974 Revision)*

The 1974 revision of the Uniform Customs and Practice for Documentary Credits (UCP or the Uniform Customs), frequently referred to as ICC Publication No. 290, effective on October 1, 1975, was superseded on October 1, 1984 by ICC Publication No. 400, which appears in Appendix A. Because the 1983 version of the UCP draws heavily on the 1974 version and because cases decided under the 1974 version are often persuasive authority for construing the 1983 version, this treatise retains the 1974 version with its unofficial annotation. In addition, the Table of Parallel UCP Provisions following the Bibliography provides access to cases decided under predecessor versions.

General provisions and definitions

a. These provisions and definitions and the following articles apply to all documentary credits and are binding upon all parties thereto unless otherwise expressly agreed.

b. For the purposes of such provisions, definitions, and articles, the expressions "documentary credit(s)" and "credit(s)" used therein mean any arrangement, however named or described, whereby a bank (the issuing bank), acting at the request of and in accordance with the instructions of a customer (the applicant for the credit),

i is to make payment to, or to the order of, a third party (the beneficiary), or is to pay, accept, or negotiate bills of exchange (drafts) drawn by the beneficiary, or

---

*ICC Pub. No. 290, Uniform Customs and Practice for Documentary Credits/1974 Revision, copyright © 1975 by the International Chamber of Commerce.

ii authorizes such payments to be made or such drafts to be paid, accepted, or negotiated by another bank, against stipulated documents, provided that the terms and conditions of the credit are complied with.

c. Credits, by their nature, are transactions separate from the sales or other contracts on which they may be based, and banks are in no way concerned with or bound by such contracts.

d. Credit instructions and the credits themselves must be complete and precise. In order to guard against confusion and misunderstanding, issuing banks should discourage any attempt by the applicant for the credit to include excessive detail.

e. The bank first entitled to exercise the option available under Article 32b shall be the bank authorized to pay, accept, or negotiate under a credit. The decision of such bank shall bind all parties concerned. A bank is authorized to pay or accept under a credit by being specifically nominated in the credit. A bank is authorized to negotiate under a credit either

i by being specifically nominated in the credit, or

ii by the credit being freely negotiable by any bank.

f. In no case can a beneficiary avail himself of the contractual relationships existing between banks or between the applicant for the credit and the issuing bank.

Unofficial Annotation: The following authority has construed the general provisions. Sound of Mkt. St., Inc. v. Continental Bank, Int'l, 819 F.2d 384 (3d Cir. 1987) (holding that, under General Provision (f), advising bank owes no duty to beneficiary to give timely advice of credit); Banco Nacional De Desarrollo v. Mellon Bank, N.A., 726 F.2d 87 (3d Cir. 1984) (construing General Provision (c) as support for the independence principle); Harris Corp. v. National Iranian Radio & Television, 691 F.2d 1344 (11th Cir. 1982) (construing independence principle); KMW Int'l v. Chase Manhattan Bank, N.A., 606 F.2d 10 (2d Cir. 1979) (same); Cappaert Enters. v. Citizens & S. Int'l Bank, 486 F. Supp. 819 (E.D. La. 1980) (same); Sabolyk v. Morgan Guar. Trust Co., No. 84 Civ. 3179 (MJL) (S.D.N.Y. Nov. 27, 1984) (holding, under General Provision (c), that acceleration clause in underlying transaction did not give beneficiary right to accelerate payments under credit); Werner Lehara Int'l, Inc. v. Harris Trust & Sav. Bank, 484 F. Supp. 65 (W.D. Mich. 1980) (construing independence principle); Consolidated Aluminum Corp. v. Bank of Va., 544 F. Supp. 386 (D. Md. 1982), aff'd, 704 F.2d 136 (4th Cir. 1983) (Uniform Customs may apply to standby credits); Raiffeisen-Zentralkasse Tirol v. First Nat'l Bank, 671 P.2d 1008 (Colo. Ct. App. 1983) (nondocumentary credit not subject to Uniform Customs); State v. Morganstein, 703 S.W.2d 894 (Mo. 1986) (invoking independence principle); Waidmann v. Mercantile Trust Co., No. 49296 (Mo. Ct. App. May 13, 1986) (relying on General Provision (b) as support for strict compliance rule and General Provision (c) for independence principle); Eljay, Jrs., Inc. v. Rahda Exports, 99 A.D.2d 408, 470 N.Y.S.2d 12 (1984) (holding that Code governed in fraud question in New York case involving credits subject to Uniform Customs);

Hohenberg Co. v. Comitex Knitters Ltd., 104 Misc. 2d 232, 428 N.Y.S.2d 156 (Sup. Ct. 1980) (invoking independence principle); Power Curber Int'l Ltd. v. National Bank of Kuwait S.A.K., [1981] 3 All E.R. 607 (C.A.) (holding that General Provision (c) prevents account party from using set-off from related transactions in letter of credit transaction); cf. Corporacion De Mercadeo Agricola v. Mellon Bank Int'l, 608 F.2d 43 (2d Cir. 1979) (1962 revision applies to standby credits); Verlinden B.V. v. Central Bank of Nig., 488 F. Supp. 1284 (S.D.N.Y. 1980), rev'd, 647 F.2d 320 (2d Cir. 1981), rev'd, 103 S. Ct. 1962 (1983) (construing independence principle under 1962 revision); International Leather Distribs., Inc. v. Chase Manhattan Bank, N.A., 464 F. Supp. 1197 (S.D.N.Y.), aff'd mem., 607 F.2d 996 (2d Cir. 1979) (dictum construing General Provision (b) of the 1962 revision as imposing liability on issuer if it fails to insist on strict compliance by beneficiary); Courtaulds N. Am., Inc. v. North Carolina Nat'l Bank, 387 F. Supp. 92 (M.D.N.C.), rev'd, 528 F.2d 802 (4th Cir. 1975) (construing General Provision (c) of 1962 revision); Ahmed v. National Bank of Pak., 572 F. Supp. 550 (S.D.N.Y. 1983) (same); United Bank Ltd. v. Cambridge Sporting Goods Corp., 41 N.Y.2d 254, 360 N.E.2d 943, 392 N.Y.S.2d 265 (1976) (recognizing independence principle under 1962 revision); Offshore Int'l S.A. v. Banco Central S.A., [1976] 2 Lloyd's Rep. 402 (Q.B.) (construing General Provision (e) of 1962 revision as inapplicable when advising bank communicated extension of credit, because advising bank cannot exercise option provided for).

A. Form and notification of credits

Article 1

a. Credits may be either

  i revocable, or

  ii irrevocable.

b. All credits, therefore, should clearly indicate whether they are revocable or irrevocable.

c. In the absence of such indication, the credit shall be deemed to be revocable.

Unofficial Annotation: Conoco, Inc. v. Norwest Bank Mason City, N.A., 767 F.2d 470 (8th Cir. 1985) (credit reciting that it would remain in force for six months and would be available to beneficiary was clearly irrevocable under Article 1(c)); Beathard v. Chicago Football Club, Inc., 419 F. Supp. 1133 (N.D. Ill. 1976) (construing a credit silent on the issue to be revocable); Hohenberg Co. v. Comitex Knitters Ltd., 104 Misc. 2d 232, 428 N.Y.S.2d 156 (Sup. Ct. 1980).

Article 2

A revocable credit may be amended or canceled at any moment, without prior notice to the beneficiary. However, the issuing bank is bound to reimburse a branch or other bank to which such a credit has been transmitted and made available for payment, acceptance, or negotiation, for any payment, acceptance, or negotiation complying with the terms and conditions of the credit and any amendments received up to the time of payment, acceptance, or negotiation made by such branch or other bank prior to receipt by it of notice of amendment or of cancelation.

Unofficial Annotation: Cf. Beathard v. Chicago Football Club, Inc., 419 F. Supp. 1133 (N.D. Ill. 1976) (construing revocable credit as no binding obligation).

Article 3

a. An irrevocable credit constitutes a definite undertaking of the issuing bank, provided that the terms and conditions of the credit are complied with:

i to pay, or that payment will be made, if the credit provides for payment, regardless of whether against a draft;

ii to accept drafts, if the credit provides for acceptance by the issuing bank, or to be responsible for their acceptance and payment at maturity, if the credit provides for the acceptance of drafts drawn on the applicant for the credit or any other drawee specified in the credit;

iii to purchase or negotiate, without recourse to drawers and/or bona fide holders, drafts drawn by the beneficiary, at sight or at a tenor, on the applicant for the credit or on any other drawee specified in the credit, or to provide for purchase or negotiation by another bank, if the credit provides for purchase or negotiation.

b. An irrevocable credit may be advised to a beneficiary through another bank (the advising bank) without engagement on the part of that bank, but when an issuing bank authorizes or requests another bank to confirm its irrevocable credit, and the latter does so, such confirmation constitutes a definite undertaking of the confirming bank in addition to the undertaking of the issuing bank, provided that the terms and conditions of the credit are complied with:

i to pay, if the credit is payable at its own counters, regardless of whether against a draft, or that payment will be made, if the credit provides for payment elsewhere;

ii to accept drafts, if the credit provides for acceptance by the confirming bank at its own counters, or to be responsible for their acceptance and payment at maturity, if the credit provides for the acceptance of drafts drawn on the applicant for the credit or any other drawee specified in the credit;

iii to purchase or negotiate, without recourse to drawers and/or bona fide holders, drafts drawn by the beneficiary, at sight or at tenor, on the issuing bank, or on the applicant for the credit or on any other drawee specified in the credit, if the credit provides for purchase or negotiation.

c. Such undertakings can be neither amended nor canceled without the agreement of all parties thereto. Partial acceptance of amendments is not effective without the agreement of all parties thereto.

Unofficial Annotation: Northern Trust Co. v. Community Bank, 873 F.2d 227 (9th Cir. 1989) (under Article 3(b), confirmer could not complain that beneficiary presented documents at counters of opening bank, not at counter of confirmer, prior to expiry); Consolidated Aluminum Corp. v. Bank of Va., 704 F.2d 136 (4th Cir. 1983) (construing Article 3 as requiring strict compliance by beneficiary); KMW Int'l v. Chase Manhattan Bank, N.A., 606 F.2d 10 (2d Cir. 1979) (construing Article 3(c) as forbidding unilateral modification of a credit); Occidental Fire & Casualty Co. v. Continental Ill. Nat'l Bank & Trust Co., 718 F. Supp. 1364 (1989) (interpreting Article 3(a) as requiring beneficiary's documents to comply strictly with terms of credit under Illinois law); Five Star Parking v. Philadelphia Parking Auth., 703 F. Supp. 20 (E.D. Pa. 1989) (issuer has no duty to notify account party before paying beneficiary against conforming documents); Banque Worms v. Banque Commerciale Privee, 679 F. Supp. 1173 (S.D.N.Y.), aff'd per curiam, 849 F.2d 787 (2d Cir. 1988) (consent of account party is not necessary to amend credit); Beyene v. Irving Trust Co., 596 F. Supp. 438 (S.D.N.Y. 1984), aff'd, 762 F.2d 4 (2d Cir. 1985) (Article 3(c) requires confirming bank to obtain issuer's waiver of any discrepancy in documents before paying beneficiary); Ahmed v. National Bank of Pak., 572 F. Supp. 550 (S.D.N.Y. 1983) (construing Article 3 to deny standing as plaintiffs to nonbeneficiaries); AMF Head Sports Wear, Inc. v. Ray Scott's All-Am. Sports Club, Inc., 448 F. Supp. 222 (D. Ariz. 1978) (Article 3(c) permits issuer to refuse an amendment to a credit, even though account party and beneficiary agree to it); Bank of the Southeast v. Jackson, 413 So. 2d 1091 (Ala. 1982) (reading Article 3(c) to prohibit issuer from adding to requirements of the credit); Continental Time Corp. v. Merchants Bank, 117 Misc. 2d 907, 459 N.Y.S.2d 396 (Sup. Ct. 1983) (collecting bank that, without authorization, placed drafts drawn under a letter of credit on a collection basis violated Article 3(c)); cf. Verlinden B.V. v. Central Bank of Nig., 647 F.2d 320 (2d Cir. 1981), rev'd, 461 U.S. 480 (1983) (construing 1962 revision to forbid unilateral amendment of irrevocable credit); Texas Trading & Milling Corp. v. Federal Republic of Nig., 647 F.2d 300 (2d Cir. 1981), cert. denied, 454 U.S. 1148 (1982) (same); Decor by Nikkei Int'l, Inc. v. Federal Republic of Nig., 497 F. Supp. 893 (S.D.N.Y. 1980), aff'd, 647 F.2d 300 (2d Cir. 1981), cert. denied, 454 U.S. 1148 (1982) (same); Banco di Roma v. Fidelity Union Trust Co., 464 F. Supp. 817 (D.N.J. 1979) (account party may not unilaterally alter terms of credit); National Am. Corp. v. Federal Republic of Nig., 425 F. Supp. 1365 (S.D.N.Y. 1977) (relying on Article 3 of 1962 revision to determine whether bank had advised or confirmed credit); National Bank & Trust Co. of N. Am., Ltd. v. J.L.M. Int'l, Inc., 421 F. Supp. 1269 (S.D.N.Y. 1976) (citing Article 3 as support for view that credit established with beneficiary may not be amended without beneficiary's consent); Beathard v. Chicago Football Club, Inc., 419 F. Supp. 1133 (N.D. Ill. 1976) (explaining difference between revocable and irrevocable credits); Lantz Int'l Corp. v. Industria Termotecnica Campana, S.p.A., 358 F. Supp. 510 (E.D. Pa. 1973) (construing 1962 revision as creating presumption that holder of draft drawn under, and in compliance with, irrevocable credit is entitled to proceeds of credit).

Article 4

a. When an issuing bank instructs a bank by cable, telegram, or telex to advise a credit, and intends the mail confirmation to be the operative credit instrument, the cable, telegram, or telex must state that the credit will be effective only on receipt of such mail confirmation. In this event, the issuing bank must send the operative credit instrument (mail confirmation) and any subsequent amendments to the credit to the beneficiary through the advising bank.

b. The issuing bank will be responsible for any consequences arising from its failure to follow the procedure set out in the preceding paragraph.

c. Unless a cable, telegram, or telex states "details to follow" (or words of similar effect) or states that the mail confirmation is to be the operative credit instrument, the cable, telegram, or telex will be deemed to be the operative credit instrument, and the issuing bank need not send the mail confirmation to the advising bank.

Article 5

When a bank is instructed by cable, telegram, or telex to issue, confirm, or advise a credit similar in terms to one previously established and that has been the subject of amendments, it shall be understood that the details of the credit being issued, confirmed, or advised will be transmitted to the beneficiary excluding the amendments, unless the instructions specify clearly any amendments that are to apply.

Unofficial Annotation: Cf. Banco di Roma v. Fidelity Union Trust Co., 464 F. Supp. 817 (D.N.J. 1979) (holding that issuer's instructions to advising bank were not ambiguous).

Article 6

If incomplete or unclear instructions are received to issue, confirm, or advise a credit, the bank requested to act on such instructions may give preliminary notification of the credit to the beneficiary for information only and without responsibility; in this event, the credit will be issued, confirmed, or advised only when the necessary information has been received.

Unofficial Annotation: Cf. Savarin Corp. v. National Bank of Pak., 290 F. Supp. 285 (S.D.N.Y. 1968), modified, 447 F.2d 727 (2d Cir. 1971) (applying Article 6 of 1962 revision).

B. Liabilities and responsibilities

Article 7

Banks must examine all documents with reasonable care to ascertain that they appear, on their face, to be in accordance with the terms and conditions of the credit. Documents that appear, on their face, to be inconsistent with one another will be considered as not appearing, on their face, to be in accordance with the terms and conditions of the credit.

Unofficial Annotation: Instituto Nacional De Comercializacion Agricola (Indeca) v. Continental Ill. Nat'l Bank & Trust Co., 858 F.2d 1264 (7th Cir. 1988) (policy of Article 7 is not served by creating duties on confirming bank in addition to those imposed by Code); Voest-Alpine Int'l Corp. v. Chase Manhattan Bank, N.A., 545 F. Supp. 301 (S.D.N.Y. 1982), aff'd in part, rev'd in part, 707 F.2d 680 (2d Cir. 1983) (finding documents to be inconsistent on their face); Five Star Parking v. Philadelphia Parking Auth., 703 F. Supp. 20 (E.D. Pa. 1989) (having satisfied duty of examining documents to determine that they comply on their face with terms of credit, issuer need not fulfill additional duty of notifying account party); Arabian Fiberglass Insulation Co. v. Continental Ill. Nat'l Bank & Trust Co., No. 85 C 1268 (N.D. Ill. Dec. 12, 1986) (credit calling for invoices approved by Arnold H. Montgomery satisfied by invoices without Montgomery's signature, because credit did not say that invoices must be signed by Montgomery); United States v. Foster Wheeler Corp., No. 84 Civ. 2992 (S.D.N.Y. July 17, 1986) (confirming bank owes no duty to account party); Larsen v. Carpenter, 620 F. Supp. 1084 (E.D.N.Y. 1985) (confirming bank and issuer have duty to examine bill of lading for defects); Bank of Cochin Ltd. v. Manufacturers Hanover Trust Co., 612 F. Supp. 1533 (S.D.N.Y. 1985), aff'd, 808 F.2d 209 (2d Cir. 1986) (Article 7 imposes duty on confirming paying bank toward opening bank); Almatrood v. Sallee Int'l, Inc., No. 83 Civ. 1800 (WCC) (S.D.N.Y. May 13, 1985) (as long as the documents appear to be regular on their face, confirming bank has not breached any duty by paying beneficiary); Instituto Nacional De Comercializacion Agricola (Indeca) v. Continental Ill. Nat'l Bank & Trust Co., 530 F. Supp. 279 (N.D. Ill. 1982) (duty of confirming bank under Article 7 runs only to opening bank, not to opening bank's customer); Crocker Commercial Servs., Inc. v. Countryside Bank, 538 F. Supp. 1360 (N.D. Ill. 1981) (alternate holding to effect that rule of Article 7 rendering "inconsistent" documents nonconfirming refers only to documents required by credit, not to inconsistencies in documents gratuitously enclosed); Bank of Canton, Ltd. v. Republic Nat'l Bank, 509 F. Supp. 1310 (S.D.N.Y.), aff'd, 636 F.2d 30 (2d Cir. 1980) (documents were not inconsistent); Armac Indus. Ltd. v. Citytrust, 203 Conn. 394, 525 A.2d 77 (1987) (Article 7 does not command strict compliance, but leaves standard of compliance for courts to decide); Mount Prospect State Bank v. Marine Midland Bank, 121 Ill. App. 3d 295, 459 N.E.2d 979 (1983) (Article 7 requires issuer to examine documents to determine whether they are facially conforming); Waidmann v. Mercantile Trust Co., No. 49296 (Mo. Ct. App. May 13, 1986) (Article 7 requires strict compliance of beneficiary's documents and justifies issuer's refusal to pay against inconsistent documents); Continental Time Corp. v. Merchants Bank, 117 Misc. 2d 907, 459 N.Y.S.2d 396 (Sup. Ct. 1983) (collecting bank did not breach any duty imposed by Article 7); Gian Singh & Co. v. Banque De L'Indochine, [1974] 2 All E.R. 754 (P.C.) (issuer was not negligent in accepting forged certificate); cf. Chase Manhattan Bank v. Equibank, 550 F.2d 882 (3d Cir. 1977) (recognizing independence principle in Article 7 context); Courtaulds N. Am., Inc. v. North Carolina Nat'l Bank, 528 F.2d 802 (4th Cir. 1975) (Article 7 requires strict compliance by beneficiary); Auto Servicio San Ignacio, S.R.L. v. Compania Anonima Venezolana De Navegacion, 586 F. Supp. 259 (E.D. La. 1984) (refusing to extend confirming bank's duties, under Article 7, to issuer's customer and third parties); International Leather Distribs., Inc. v. Chase Manhattan Bank, N.A., 464 F. Supp. 1197 (S.D.N.Y.), aff'd mem., 607 F.2d 996 (2d Cir. 1979) (applying independence principle); Banco di Roma v. Fidelity Union Trust Co., 464 F. Supp. 817 (D.N.J. 1979) (bill of lading and certificate of origin that contained incorrect destination information violated Article 7 under 1962 revision); Corporacion de Mercadeo Agricola v. Mellon Bank Int'l, 464 F. Supp. 88 (S.D.N.Y. 1978), aff'd, 608 F.2d 43 (2d Cir. 1979) (under 1962 revision, documents did not comply on their face); Kydon Compania Naviera S.A. v. National Westminster Bank Ltd., [1981] 1 Lloyd's Rep. 68 (Q.B.) (construing 1962 revision to impose duty toward account party, but not toward beneficiary).

Article 8

a. In documentary credit operations, all parties concerned deal in documents, not in goods.

b. Payment, acceptance, or negotiation against documents that appear, on their face, to be in accordance with the terms and conditions of a credit by a bank authorized to do so binds the party giving the authorization to take up the documents and reimburse the bank which has effected the payment, acceptance, or negotiation.

c. If, upon receipt of the documents, the issuing bank considers that they appear on their face not to be in accordance with the terms and conditions of the credit, that bank must determine, on the basis of the documents alone, whether to claim that payment, acceptance, or negotiation was not effected in accordance with the terms and conditions of the credit.

d. The issuing bank shall have a reasonable time to examine the documents and to determine, as above, whether to make such a claim.

e. If such claim is to be made, notice to that effect, stating the reasons therefor, must be given by cable or by other expeditious means, without delay, to the bank from which the documents have been received (the remitting bank), and such notice must state that the documents are being held at the disposal of such bank or are being returned thereto.

f. If the issuing bank fails to hold the documents at the disposal of the remitting bank or fails to return the documents to such bank, the issuing bank shall be

precluded from claiming that the relative payment, acceptance, or negotiation
was not effected in accordance with the terms and conditions of the credit.

g. If the remitting bank draws the attention of the issuing bank to any irregularities
in the documents or advises such bank that it has paid, accepted, or negotiated under reserve or against a guarantee in respect of such irregularities, the issuing bank shall not be relieved thereby from any of its obligations under this
article. Such guarantee or reserve concerns only the relations between the
remitting bank and the beneficiary.

Unofficial Annotation: Bank of Cochin, Ltd. v. Manufacturers Hanover
Trust Co., 808 F.2d 209 (2d Cir. 1986) ((1) twelve- or thirteen-day delay
in giving confirming bank notice of defects estops issuer from raising
those defects as defense to reimbursement of confirming bank, and (2) it is
not necessary for confirming bank to show any reliance or detriment resulting from late notice); Auto Servicio San Ignacio, S.R.L. v. Compania
Anonima Venezola De Navigacion (Venezuelan Line), 765 F.2d 1306 (5th
Cir. 1985) (it was not proper for issuer or account party to complain of defects in documents over which paying bank had paid beneficiary at least
one year before claim was first raised); Pubali Bank v. City Nat'l Bank,
769 F.2d 605 (9th Cir. 1985) (bank that has arranged for issuance of credit
on behalf of its customer and that has indemnified issuer's right of reimbursement against customer is not prevented by Uniform Customs from
suing beneficiary and its assignee of credit proceeds for drawing improperly on credit); Banco Nacional De Desarrollo v. Mellon Bank, N.A., 726
F.2d 87 (3d Cir. 1984) (Article 8(a) supports independence principle);
Philadelphia Gear Corp. v. Central Bank, 717 F.2d 230 (5th Cir. 1983)
((1) issuer that fails to specify defects, as Article 8(e) requires, is not precluded from raising those defects as defense against presenter that should
have known about them; (2) issuer is under no duty to advise beneficiary
of defects of which it has knowledge; and (3) several days is reasonable
time under Article 8(d)); Marino Indus. Corp. v. Chase Manhattan Bank,
N.A., 686 F.2d 112 (2d Cir. 1982) (by not returning certificates for one
and one-half months after credit expired, issuer raised question whether
Article 8(d) precluded it from relying on defects in certificates); KMW
Int'l v. Chase Manhattan Bank, N.A., 606 F.2d 10 (2d Cir. 1979) (Article
8(a) embodies independence principle; Article 8(c) negates illegality and
impossibility as defenses; and Article 8(d) supports an order requiring issuer to give account party three days' notice before honoring beneficiary's
request for payment); Flagship Cruises, Ltd. v. New England Merchants
Nat'l Bank, 569 F.2d 699 (1st Cir. 1978) (failure to comply fully with Article 8 of 1962 revision (1) does not create estoppel against issuer unless
beneficiary can show it could have cured unspecified defects, but (2) does
create obligation to reimburse accepting or negotiating bank); Courtaulds
N. Am., Inc. v. North Carolina Nat'l Bank, 528 F.2d 802 (4th Cir. 1975)
(accepting independence principle); Chase Manhattan Bank v. Equibank,
550 F.2d 882 (3d Cir. 1977) (acknowledging independence principle);
Banque Worms v. Banque Commerciale Privee, 679 F. Supp. 1173
(S.D.N.Y. 1988), aff'd per curiam, 849 F.2d 787 (2d Cir. 1988) (general
statement of purpose clause in credit does not create additional documentary requirement); Newvector Communications, Inc. v. Union Bank, 663

F. Supp. 252 (D. Utah 1987) (denying summary judgment pending resolution of factual issues in case where issuer failed to dishonor beneficiary's presentation for seven weeks and gave notice of dishonor on expiry date); Breathless Assocs. v. First Sav. & Loan Ass'n, 654 F. Supp. 832 (N.D. Tex. 1986) (issuer that fails to give notice of defects is not estopped, absent evidence of damage to beneficiary as consequence of failure); Bank of Cochin Ltd. v. Manufacturers Hanover Trust Co., 612 F. Supp. 1533 (S.D.N.Y. 1985), aff'd, 808 F.2d 209 (2d Cir. 1986) (applying estoppel rule of Article 8(f)); Sabolyk v. Morgan Guar. Trust Co., No. 84 Civ. 3179 (MJL) (S.D.N.Y. Nov. 27, 1984) (account party's attachment in foreign jurisdiction of credit did not offend Article 8(c) and would qualify for doctrine of comity); Auto Servicio San Ignacio, S.R.L. v. Compania Anonima Venezolana De Navegacion, 586 F. Supp. 259 (E.D. La. 1984), aff'd, 765 F.2d 1306 (5th Cir. 1985) (Article 8(c) requires issuer not to look beyond face of documents); Voest-Alpine Int'l Corp. v. Chase Manhattan Bank, N.A., 545 F. Supp. 301 (S.D.N.Y. 1982), aff'd in part, rev'd in part, 707 F.2d 680 (2d Cir. 1983) (Article 8 adopts independence principle and sanctions issuer's practice of taking three to five days (excluding weekends) to examine documents); Consolidated Aluminum Corp. v. Bank of Va., 544 F. Supp. 386 (D. Md. 1982), aff'd, 704 F.2d 136 (4th Cir. 1983) (Article 8 requires strict compliance by beneficiary); Banco De Vizcaya, S.A. v. First Nat'l Bank, 514 F. Supp. 1280 (N.D. Ill. 1981), vacated, id. (Article 8(b) supports summary judgment against bank that dishonored acceptances under letter of credit); Prutscher v. Fidelity Int'l Bank, 502 F. Supp. 535 (S.D.N.Y. 1980) (dictum to effect that Article 8 does not control questions of false or fraudulent documents); Werner Lehara Int'l, Inc. v. Harris Trust & Sav. Bank, 484 F. Supp. 65 (W.D. Mich. 1980) (Article 8 incorporates independence principle); International Leather Distribs., Inc. v. Chase Manhattan Bank, N.A., 464 F. Supp. 1197 (S.D.N.Y.), aff'd mem., 607 F.2d 996 (2d Cir. 1979) (applying independence principle); Paramount Export Co. v. Asia Trust Bank, Ltd., 193 Cal. App. 3d 1474, 238 Cal. Rptr. 920 (1987) (issuer that fails to comply with Articles 8(e) and 8(f) is strictly precluded from asserting defects in action by beneficiary for wrongful dishonor); Raiffeisen-Zentralkasse Tirol v. First Nat'l Bank, 36 U.C.C. Rep. Serv. (Callaghan) 254 (Colo. Ct. App. 1983) (refusing to apply Uniform Customs to conditions of credit that court viewed as nondocumentary conditions); Armac Indus. Ltd. v. Citytrust, 203 Conn. 394, 525 A.2d 77 (1987) (Article 8 does not command courts to apply strict compliance rule, but leaves question for courts to decide); Mount Prospect State Bank v. Marine Midland Bank, 121 Ill. App. 3d 295, 459 N.E.2d 979 (1983) (Article 8(c) requires issuer to look only to face of documents); Waidmann v. Mercantile Trust Co., 711 S.W.2d 907 (Mo. Ct. App. 1986) (Article 8 requires strict compliance of beneficiary's documents and Articles 8(c) and 8(d) require documents to be consistent on their face); Morgan Guar. Trust Co. v. Vend Technologies, Inc., 100 A.D.2d 782, 474 N.Y.S.2d 67 (1984) (Article 8 permits issuer to pay beneficiary after expiry so long as issuer receives documents before expiry or before expiry as extended by Article 39(a)); Fertico Belg., S.A. v. Phosphate Chems. Export Ass'n, 100 A.D.2d 165, 473 N.Y.S.2d 403, appeal dismissed, 62 N.Y.2d 802 (1984) (in absence of fraud, issuer may honor beneficiary's draft when draft is accompanied by conforming documents); Dorf Overseas, Inc. v. Chemical Bank, 91 A.D.2d 895, 457 N.Y.S.2d 513

(1983) (under Article 8, issuer was authorized to pay letter of credit); Foreign Venture Ltd. Partnership v. Chemical Bank, 59 A.D.2d 352, 399 N.Y.S.2d 114 (1977) (applying independence principle); Price & Pierce Int'l, Inc. v. Cimex U.S.A., Inc. (N.Y. Sup. Ct. 1987), reprinted in Letter of Credit Update 35 (July 1987), aff'd without op. sub nom. Price & Pierce Int'l, Inc. v. Hanil Bank Ltd., 136 A.D.2d 977, 523 N.Y.S.2d 333, appeal denied, 72 N.Y.2d 803, 528 N.E.2d 521, 532 N.Y.S.2d 369 (1988) (issuer that fails to dishonor within three days after receipt of documents and that fails to give notice that it is holding documents is precluded from asserting defects in action for wrongful dishonor); Exchange Mut. Ins. Co. v. Commerce Union Bank, 686 S.W.2d 913 (Tenn. Ct. App. 1984) (issuer that fails to specify defects is estopped from asserting them as defense to nonpayment); cf. Wing On Bank Ltd. v. American Nat'l Bank & Trust Co., 457 F.2d 328 (5th Cir. 1972) (issuer's breach of duty to notify presenter of incurable defects in the documents did not estop issuer under 1962 revision); Banco Espanol de Credito v. State St. Bank & Trust Co., 385 F.2d 230 (1st Cir. 1967), cert. denied, 390 U.S. 1013 (1968) (Article 8 of 1962 revision, in substance, embodies same rule as that of Code); Banco di Roma v. Fidelity Union Trust Co., 464 F. Supp. 817 (D.N.J. 1979) (recognizing independence principle and construing issuer's obligation under Article 8 to notify beneficiary of defects in documents under 1962 revision); Corporacion De Mercadeo Agricola v. Mellon Bank Int'l, 464 F. Supp. 88 (S.D.N.Y. 1978), aff'd, 608 F.2d 43 (2d Cir. 1979) (under 1962 revision, Article 8 is not violated when, under circumstances, issuer investigated authority of signatory to statement); Investitions-Und Handels-Bank A.G. v. United Cal. Bank Int'l, 277 F. Supp. 1005 (S.D.N.Y. 1968) (Article 8 of 1962 revision does not excuse advising bank's failure to report certain information concerning beneficiary to opening bank); Schweibish v. Pontchartrain State Bank, 389 So. 2d 731 (La. Ct. App. 1980) (construing 1962 revision and 1974 revision, along with U.C.C. § 5-102(3), to preclude issuer from asserting defects in documents when it did not notify beneficiary of defects promptly); Kydon Compania Naviera S.A. v. National Westminster Bank Ltd., [1981] 1 Lloyd's Rep. 68 (Q.B.) (construing Article 8 of 1962 revision as not protecting bank assignee of credit).

Article 9

Banks assume no liability or responsibility for the form, sufficiency, accuracy, genuineness, falsification, or legal effect of any documents, or for the general and/or particular conditions stipulated in the documents or superimposed thereon, nor do they assume any liability or responsibility for the description, quantity, weight, quality, condition, packing, delivery, value, or existence of the goods represented thereby, or for the good faith or acts and/or omissions, solvency, performance, or standing of the consignor, the carriers, or the insurers of the goods or any other person whomsoever.

Unofficial Annotation: Continental Time Corp. v. Merchants Bank, 117 Misc. 2d 907, 459 N.Y.S.2d 396 (Sup. Ct. 1983) (collecting bank did not breach any duty imposed by Article 9); cf. Courtaulds N. Am., Inc. v.

North Carolina Nat'l Bank, 528 F.2d 802 (4th Cir. 1975) (language in Article 30 of 1962 revision requires beneficiary to present invoice describing goods as credit describes them); Corporacion De Mercadeo Agricola v. Mellon Bank Int'l, 464 F. Supp. 88 (S.D.N.Y. 1978), aff'd, 608 F.2d 43 (2d Cir. 1979) (under the 1962 revision, Article 9 supports independence principle); Investitions-Und Handels-Bank A.G. v. United Cal. Bank Int'l, 277 F. Supp. 1005 (S.D.N.Y. 1968) (Article 9 of 1962 revision does not excuse advising bank from duty to inform opening bank of information concerning beneficiary).

Article 10

Banks assume no liability or responsibility for the consequences arising out of delay and/or loss in transit of any messages, letters, or documents, or for delay, mutilation, or other errors arising in the transmission of cables, telegrams, or telex. Banks assume no liability or responsibility for errors in translation or interpretation of technical terms and reserve the right to transmit credit terms without translating them.

Unofficial Annotation: Consolidated Aluminum Corp. v. Bank of Va., 704 F.2d 136 (4th Cir. 1983) (Article 10 requires strict enforcement of credit's expiry).

Article 11

Banks assume no liability or responsibility for consequences arising out of the interruption of their business by acts of God, riots, civil commotions, insurrections, wars, or any other causes beyond their control, or by any strikes or lockouts. Unless specifically authorized, banks will not effect payment, acceptance, or negotiation after expiration under credits expiring during such interruption of business.

Unofficial Annotation: Consolidated Aluminum Corp. v. Bank of Va., 704 F.2d 136 (4th Cir. 1983) (Article 11 requires strict enforcement of credit's expiry).

Article 12

a. Banks utilizing the services of another bank for the purpose of giving effect to the instructions of the applicant for the credit do so for the account and at the risk of the latter.

b. Banks assume no liability or responsibility should the instructions they transmit not be carried out, even if they themselves have taken the initiative in the choice of such other bank.

c. The applicant for the credit shall be bound by and liable to indemnify the banks against all obligations and responsibilities imposed by foreign laws and usages.

Unofficial Annotation: Bank of Cochin Ltd. v. Manufacturers Hanover Trust Co., 612 F. Supp. 1533 (S.D.N.Y. 1985), aff'd, 808 F.2d 209 (2d Cir. 1986) (dictum to effect that Articles 12(a) and 12(c) are authority for proposition that confirming bank owes duty to account party); National Am. Corp. v. Federal Republic of Nig., 425 F. Supp. 1365 (S.D.N.Y. 1977) (defining duty of advising bank).

Article 13

A paying or negotiating bank that has been authorized to claim reimbursement from a third bank nominated by the issuing bank and that has effected such payment or negotiation shall not be required to confirm to the third bank that it has done so in accordance with the terms and conditions of the credit.

C. Documents

Article 14

a. All instructions to issue, confirm or advise a credit must state precisely the documents against which payment, acceptance or negotiation is to be made.

b. Terms such as "first class," "well known," "qualified" and the like shall not be used to describe the issuers of any documents called for under credits and if they are incorporated in the credit terms banks will accept documents as tendered.

C1. Documents evidencing shipment or dispatch or taking in charge (shipping documents)

Article 15

Except as stated in Article 20, the date of the bill of lading, or the date of any other document evidencing shipment or dispatch or taking in charge, or the date indicated in the reception stamp or by notation on any such document will be taken in each case to be the date of shipment or dispatch or taking in charge of the goods.

Unofficial Annotation: Fertico Belg., S.A. v. Phosphate Chems. Export Ass'n, 100 A.D.2d 165, 473 N.Y.S.2d 403, appeal dismissed, 62 N.Y.2d 802 (1984) (under Article 15, date of shipment is date of delivery of goods to carrier); Westpac Banking Corp. v. South Carolina Nat'l Bank, [1986] 1 Lloyd's Rep. 311 (P.C.) (date rule under Article 15 is for applying timing rules and is not to be taken as actual date of shipment for purpose of rendering bill of lading internally inconsistent); cf. Corporacion De Mercadeo Agricola v. Mellon Bank Int'l, 464 F. Supp. 88 (S.D.N.Y. 1978), aff'd, 608 F.2d 43 (2d Cir. 1979) (Article 14 of 1962 Revision supports independence principle).

Article 16

a. If words clearly indicating payment or prepayment of freight, however named or described, appear by stamp or otherwise on documents evidencing shipment or dispatch or taking in charge, they will be accepted as constituting evidence of payment of freight.

b. If the words "freight prepayable" or "freight to be prepaid" or words of similar effect appear by stamp or otherwise on such documents, they will not be accepted as constituting evidence of the payment of freight.

c. Unless otherwise specified in the credit or inconsistent with any of the documents presented under the credit, banks will accept documents stating that freight or transportation charges are payable on delivery.

d. Banks will accept shipping documents bearing reference by stamp or otherwise to costs additional to the freight charges, such as costs of, or disbursements incurred in connection with, loading, unloading, or similar operations, unless the conditions of the credit specifically prohibit such reference.

Unofficial Annotation: Banque De L'Indochine Et De Suez S.A. v. J.H. Rayner (Mincing Lane) Ltd., [1983] 1 Lloyd's Rep. 228 (C.A.) (under Article 16(d), credit may stipulate that account party assumes certain shipping charges, while beneficiary assumes others); cf. Corporacion De Mercadeo Agricola v. Mellon Bank Int'l, 464 F. Supp. 88 (S.D.N.Y. 1978), aff'd, 608 F.2d 43 (2d Cir. 1979) (Article 15 of 1962 revision does not support view that issuer should not question authority of party signing statement).

Article 17

Shipping documents that bear a clause on the face thereof such as "shipper's load and count" or "said by shipper to contain" or words of similar effect will be accepted unless otherwise specified in the credit.

Unofficial Annotation: Austracan (USA) Inc. v. Neptune Orient Lines, Ltd., 612 F. Supp. 578 (S.D.N.Y. 1985) (unless credit provides otherwise, issuer may accept bill of lading with exculpatory language).

Article 18

a. A clean shipping document is one that bears no superimposed clause or notation that expressly declares a defective condition of the goods and/or the packaging.

b. Banks will refuse shipping documents bearing such clauses or notations unless the credit expressly states the clauses or notations that may be accepted.

Unofficial Annotation: Cf. Talbot v. Bank of Hendersonville, 495 S.W.2d 548 (Tenn. Ct. App. 1972) (Article 16 of 1962 revision does not permit issuer to reject invoice with superimposed clause or notation); see generally International Chamber of Commerce, "The Problem of Clean Bills of Lading," ICC Pub. No. 283 (1963).

C1.1 Marine bills of lading

Article 19

a. Unless specifically authorized in the credit, bills of lading of the following nature will be rejected:

i bills of lading issued by forwarding agents,

ii bills of lading that are issued under and are subject to the conditions of a charter-party, and

iii bills of lading covering shipment by sailing vessels.

b. However, subject to the above and unless otherwise specified in the credit, bills of lading of the following nature will be accepted:

i "through" bills of lading issued by shipping companies or their agents, even though they cover several modes of transport,

ii short-form bills of lading (i.e. bills of lading issued by shipping companies or their agents that indicate some or all of the conditions of carriage by reference to a source or document other than the bill of lading), and

iii bills of lading issued by shipping companies or their agents covering unitized cargoes, such as those on pallets or in containers.

Unofficial Annotation: Larsen v. Carpenter, 620 F. Supp. 1084 (E.D.N.Y. 1985) (bill of lading subject to charter party is defective under Article 19(a)(ii)).

Article 20

a. Unless otherwise specified in the credit, bills of lading must show that the goods are loaded on board a named vessel or are shipped on a named vessel.

b. Loading on board a named vessel or shipment on a named vessel may be evidenced either by a bill of lading bearing wording indicating loading on board a named vessel or shipment on a named vessel, or by means of a notation to that effect on the bill of lading signed or initialed and dated by the carrier or by his agent, and the date of this notation shall be regarded as the date of loading on board the named vessel or shipment on the named vessel.

Unofficial Annotation: Cf. Marine Midland Grace Trust Co. v. Banco Del Pais, S.A., 261 F. Supp. 884 (S.D.N.Y. 1966) (under 1962 revision, credit calling for on-board truck bill of lading was not satisfied by truck bill without on-board stamp and inspection certificate indicating that goods were loaded); Siderius, Inc. v. Wallace Co., 583 S.W.2d 852 (Tex. Civ. App. 1979) (applying requirement of Article 18 of 1962 revision relating to on-board bills of lading); Van Elkins & Stoett, Inc. v. S.S. Rio Para., 573 F. Supp. 1475 (S.D.N.Y. 1983) (reciting banker's testimony that a bill with a printed "received on board" notation is good, despite carrier's failure to sign and date stamped notation to same effect); Westpac Banking Corp. v. South Carolina Nat'l Bank, [1986] 1 Lloyd's Rep. 311 (P.C.) ((1) presence of undated and unsigned "loaded on board" stamp on "received for shipment" bill of lading that had been modified to indicate loading on board did not render bill internally inconsistent, and, by way of dictum, (2) "received for shipment" bill of lading prepared to indicate that issuer intended it to be on-board bill did not need separate signature and date for "on board" stamp).

Article 21

a. Unless transshipment is prohibited by the terms of the credit, bills of lading will be accepted which indicate that the goods will be transshipped en route, provided the entire voyage is covered by one and the same bill of lading.

b. Bills of lading incorporating printed clauses stating that the carriers have the right to transship will be accepted, notwithstanding the fact that the credit prohibits transshipment.

Article 22

a. Banks will refuse a bill of lading stating that the goods are loaded on deck unless specifically authorized in the credit.

b. Banks will not refuse a bill of lading which contains a provision that the goods may be carried on deck, provided it does not specifically state that they are loaded on deck.

C1.2 Combined transport documents

Article 23

a. If the credit calls for a combined transport document, that is, one that provides for a combined transport by at least two different modes of transport from a place at which the goods are taken in charge to a place designated for delivery, or if the credit provides for a combined transport, but in either case does not specify the form of document required and/or the issuer of such document, banks will accept such documents as tendered.

b. If the combined transport includes transport by sea, the document will be accepted, although it does not indicate that the goods are on board a named vessel, and although it contains a provision that the goods, if packed in a container, may be carried on deck, provided it does not specifically state that they are loaded on deck.

> *Unofficial Annotation:*   See generally International Chamber of Commerce, "Uniform Rules for a Combined Transport Document," ICC Pub. No. 298 (1975).

C1.3 Other shipping documents, etc.

Article 24

Banks will consider a railway or inland waterway bill of lading or consignment note, counterfoil waybill, postal receipt, certificate of mailing, air mail receipt, air waybill, air consignment note, or air receipt, trucking company bill of lading, or any other similar document as regular when such document bears the reception stamp of the carrier or his agent, or when it bears a signature purporting to be that of the carrier or his agent.

> *Unofficial Annotation:*   Corporacion De Mercadeo Agricola v. Mellon Bank Int'l, 464 F. Supp. 88 (S.D.N.Y. 1978), aff'd, 608 F.2d 43 (2d Cir. 1979) (Article 22 of 1962 revision does not support argument that issuer should not question authority of one who signs statement); Marine Midland Grace Trust Co. v. Banco Del Pais, S.A., 261 F. Supp. 884 (S.D.N.Y. 1966) (under Article 22 of 1962 revision, credit calling for on-board truck bill of lading is not satisfied by bill of lading that does not indicate whether goods are loaded on board); Cooper's Finer Foods, Inc. v. Pan Am. World Airways, Inc., 178 So. 2d 62 (Fla. Dist. Ct. App. 1965) (construing 1962 revision of Article 22 concerning air waybill of lading).

Article 25

Where a credit calls for an attestation or certification of weight in the case of transport other than by sea, banks will accept a weight stamp or declaration of weight superimposed by the carrier on the shipping document, unless the credit calls for a separate or independent certificate of weight.

C2. Insurance documents

Article 26

a. Insurance documents must be as specified in the credit and must be issued and/or signed by insurance companies or their agents or by underwriters.

b. Cover notes issued by brokers will not be accepted unless specifically authorized in the credit.

Article 27

Unless otherwise specified in the credit, or unless the insurance documents presented establish that the cover is effective, at the latest, from the date of shipment or dispatch or, in the case of combined transport, the date of taking the goods in charge, banks will refuse insurance documents presented that bear a date later than the date of shipment or dispatch or, in the case of combined transport, the date of taking the goods in charge, as evidenced by the shipping documents.

Article 28

a. Unless otherwise specified in the credit, the insurance document must be expressed in the same currency as the credit.

b. The minimum amount for which insurance must be effected is the CIF value of the goods concerned. However, when the CIF value of the goods cannot be determined from the documents on their face, banks will accept as such minimum amount the amount of the drawing under the credit or the amount of the relative commercial invoice, whichever is the greater.

Article 29

a. Credits should expressly state the type of insurance required and, if any, the additional risks that are to be covered. Imprecise terms such as "usual risks" or "customary risks" should not be used; however, if such imprecise terms are used, banks will accept insurance documents as tendered.

b. Failing specific instructions, banks will accept insurance cover as tendered.

Article 30

Where a credit stipulates "insurance against all risks," banks will accept an insurance document that contains any "all risks" notation or clause and will assume no responsibility if any particular risk is not covered.

Article 31

Banks will accept an insurance document which indicates that the cover is subject to a franchise or an excess (deductible), unless it is specifically stated in the credit that the insurance must be issued irrespective of percentage.

C3. Commercial invoices

Article 32

a. Unless otherwise specified in the credit, commercial invoices must be made out in the name of the applicant for the credit.

b. Unless otherwise specified in the credit, banks may refuse commercial invoices issued for amounts in excess of the amount permitted by the credit.

c. The description of the goods in the commercial invoice must correspond with the description in the credit. In all other documents, the goods may be described in general terms that are not inconsistent with the description of the goods in the credit.

Unofficial Annotation: Bank of Canton, Ltd. v. Republic Nat'l Bank, 509 F. Supp. 1310 (S.D.N.Y.), aff'd, 636 F.2d 30 (2d Cir. 1980) (using Article 32(a) to construe Article 7); Davidcraft Corp. v. First Nat'l Bank, No. 83 C 5481 (N.D. Ill. Jan. 6, 1986) (invoice describing goods as "52+m2 ceiling fan" when credit described goods as "52+mh ceiling fan" is defective); Atari, Inc. v. Harris Trust & Sav. Bank, 599 F. Supp. 592 (N.D. Ill. 1984) ((1) Article 32(b) applies only to commercial credits, not to standby credits, and (2) Article 32(c) supports view that description of goods in bill of lading need not correspond to that in invoice); Banque De L'Indochine Et De Suez S.A. v. J.H. Rayner (Mincing Lane) Ltd., [1983] 1 Lloyd's Rep. 228 (C.A.) (holding that vague references in documents to goods as "bags of sugar" are insufficient under Article 32(c)); cf. Oriental Pac. (USA), Inc. v. Toronto Dominion Bank, 78 Misc. 2d 819, 357 N.Y.S.2d 957 (Sup. Ct. 1974) (construing Article 30 of 1962 revision as rendering defective invoice that is in amount greater than balance available on credit and that misdescribes goods); Kydon Compania Naviera S.A. v. National Westminster Bank Ltd., [1981] 1 Lloyd's Rep. 68 (Q.B.) (rejecting as defective under Article 30 of 1962 revision invoice whose description of goods varied that in credit).

C4. Other documents

Article 33

When other documents are required, such as warehouse receipts, delivery orders, consular invoices, certificates of origin, of weight, of quality, or of analysis, etc., and when no further definition is given, banks will accept such documents as tendered.

Unofficial Annotation: Bank of Canton, Ltd. v. Republic Nat'l Bank, 509 F. Supp. 1310 (S.D.N.Y.), aff'd, 636 F.2d 30 (2d Cir. 1980) (Article 33 permits beneficiary to supply copy of certificate without having it legalized); Lustrelon, Inc. v. Prutscher, 178 N.J. Super. 128, 428 A.2d 518 (App. Div. 1981) (under Article 33, credit calling for "signed, certified statement" is satisfied by statement reciting that it was "duly signed and confirmed" and certified to be true and correct by beneficiary); Banque De L'Indochine Et De Suez S.A. v. J.H. Rayner (Mincing Lane) Ltd., [1983] 1 Lloyd's Rep. 228 (C.A.) (under Article 33, issuer may accept document for what it purports to be, but still must insist on compliance with Article 32(c)); cf. Corporacion De Mercadeo Agricola v. Mellon Bank Int'l, 464 F. Supp. 88 (S.D.N.Y. 1978), aff'd, 608 F.2d 43 (2d Cir. 1979) (Article 31 of 1962 revision does not support argument that issuer should not question authority of one who signs statement); Fertico Belg. S.A. v. Phosphate Chems. Export Ass'n, 100 A.D.2d 165, 473 N.Y.S.2d 403, appeal dismissed, 62 N.Y.2d 802 (1984) (issuer need give only cursory glance at copy of telex advising that ship had sailed, that copy not being shipping or insurance document or invoice).

D. Miscellaneous provisions

Quantity and amount

Article 34

a. The words "about," "circa," or similar expressions used in connection with the amount of the credit or the quantity or the unit price or the goods are to be construed as allowing a difference not to exceed 10 percent more or 10 percent less.

b. Unless a credit stipulates that the quantity of the goods specified must not be exceeded or reduced, a tolerance of 3 percent more or 3 percent less will be permissible, always provided that the total amount of the drawings does not exceed the amount of the credit. This tolerance does not apply when the credit specifies quantity in terms of a stated number of packing units or individual items.

Unofficial Annotation: Kydon Compania Naviera S.A. v. National Westminster Bank Ltd., [1981] 1 Lloyd's Rep. 68 (Q.B.) (holding that 1962 predecessor to Article 34 does not apply to tonnage of ship that is subject of underlying sales contract).

Partial shipments

Article 35

a. Partial shipments are allowed, unless the credit specifically states otherwise.

b. Shipments made on the same ship and for the same voyage, even if the bills of lading evidencing shipment "on board" bear different dates and/or indicate different ports of shipment, will not be regarded as partial shipments.

Unofficial Annotation: Bank of Canton, Ltd. v. Republic Nat'l Bank, 509 F. Supp. 1310 (S.D.N.Y.), aff'd, 636 F.2d 30 (2d Cir. 1980) (applying rule of Article 35(a) to permit beneficiary to ship merchandise without spare parts called for, such parts being subject to inclusion in later shipments).

Article 36

If shipment by installments within given periods is stipulated, and if any installment is not shipped within the period allowed for that installment, the credit ceases to be available for that or for any subsequent installments unless otherwise specified in the credit.

> *Unofficial Annotation:* Trans-Global Alloy, Ltd. v. First Nat'l Bank, 490 So. 2d 769 (La. Ct. App. 1986) (credit that called for ten shipments over ten consecutive months expired when beneficiary made first shipment but failed to make shipment during next two months).

Expiry date

Article 37

All credits, whether revocable or irrevocable, must stipulate an expiry date for presentation of documents for payment, acceptance, or negotiation, notwithstanding the stipulation of a latest date for shipment.

> *Unofficial Annotation:* Consolidated Aluminum Corp. v. Bank of Va., 544 F. Supp. 386 (D. Md. 1982), aff'd, 704 F.2d 136 (4th Cir. 1983) (construing Article 37 as implying that credit's expiry must be enforced strictly); Tuthill v. Union Sav. Bank, 141 Misc. 2d 88, 534 N.Y.S.2d 88 (1988) (dictum) (issuer that drafts credit without expiry violates Article 37 and will not be permitted to terminate credit more than one year after occurrence of event of default against which credit served as security).

Article 38

The words "to," "until," "till," and words of similar import applying to the stipulated expiry date for presentation of documents for payment, acceptance, or negotiation, or to the stipulated latest date for shipment, will be understood to include the date mentioned.

> *Unofficial Annotation:* Consolidated Aluminum Corp. v. Bank of Va., 544 F. Supp. 386 (D. Md. 1982), aff'd, 704 F.2d 136 (4th Cir. 1983) (construing Article 38 as implying that credit's expiry must be enforced strictly); Almatrood v. Sallee Int'l, Inc., 83 Civ. 1800 (WCC) (S.D.N.Y. May 13, 1985) (construing Article 38 as permitting payment if nonconforming documents are corrected before credit's expiry).

Article 39

a. When the stipulated expiry date falls on a day on which banks are closed for reasons other than those mentioned in Article 11, the expiry date will be extended until the first following business day.

b. The latest date for shipment shall not be extended by reason of the extension of the expiry date in accordance with this Article. Where the credit stipulates a latest date for shipment, shipping documents dated later than such stipulated date will not be accepted. If no latest date for shipment is stipulated in the credit, shipping documents dated later than the expiry date stipulated in the credit or in amendments thereto will not be accepted. Documents other than the shipping documents may, however, be dated up to and including the extended expiry date.

c. Banks paying, accepting, or negotiating on such extended expiry date must add to the documents their certification in the following wording:

> Presented for payment (or acceptance or negotiation as the case may be) within the expiry date extended in accordance with Article 39 of the Uniform Customs.

Unofficial Annotation: Consolidated Aluminum Corp. v. Bank of Va., 544 F. Supp. 386 (D. Md. 1982), aff'd, 704 F.2d 136 (4th Cir. 1983) (construing Article 39 as implying that credit's expiry must be enforced strictly); Almatrood v. Sallee Int'l, Inc., No. 83 Civ. 1800 (WCC) (S.D.N.Y. May 13, 1985) (confirming bank may pay beneficiary under Article 39 as long as defects in documents are cured prior to expiry); Morgan Guar. Trust Co. v. Vend Technologies, Inc., 100 A.D.2d 782, 474 N.Y.S.2d 67 (1984) ((1) it is no violation of Article 39 for issuer to receive documents on December 30, 1982 or on January 1, 1983, a Saturday, and to pay on January 4, 1983 under credit whose expiry was January 1, 1983, and (2) failure of issuer to certify documents as required in Article 39(c) does not affect issuer's right of reimbursement).

Shipment, loading, or dispatch

Article 40

a. Unless the terms of the credit indicate otherwise, the words "departure," "dispatch," "loading," or "sailing" used in stipulating the latest date for shipment of the goods will be understood to be synonymous with "shipment."

b. Expressions such as "prompt," "immediately," "as soon as possible," and the like should not be used. If they are used, banks will interpret them as a request for shipment within thirty days from the date on the advice of the credit to the beneficiary by the issuing bank or by an advising bank, as the case may be.

c. The expression "on or about" and similar expressions will be interpreted as a request for shipment during the period from five days before to five days after the specified date, both end days included.

Presentation

Article 41

Notwithstanding the requirement of Article 37 that every credit must stipulate an expiry date for presentation of documents, credits also must stipulate a specified period of time after the date of issuance of the bills of lading or other shipping documents during which presentation of documents for payment, acceptance, or negotiation must be made. If no such period of time is stipulated in the credit, banks will refuse documents presented to them later than twenty-one days after the date of issuance of the bills of lading or other shipping documents.

Unofficial Annotation: Philadelphia Gear Corp. v. Central Bank, 717 F.2d 230 (5th Cir. 1983) (applying twenty-one-day rule of Article 41); Bank of Canton, Ltd. v. Republic Nat'l Bank, 509 F. Supp. 1310 (S.D.N.Y.), aff'd, 636 F.2d 30 (2d Cir. 1980) (same); Beckman Cotton Co. v. First Nat'l Bank, 34 U.C.C. Rep. Serv. (Callaghan) 966 (N.D. Ga. 1982) (twenty-one-day rule of Article 41 applied to ocean bills, not to earlier-dated inland bills); Peoples State Bank v. Gulf Oil Corp., 446 N.E.2d 1358 (Ind. Ct. App. 1983) (Article 41 (1) does not require bills of lading if letter of credit does not require them and (2) requires invoices to be presented within twenty-one days of their date); cf. Flagship Cruises, Ltd. v. New England Merchants Nat'l Bank, 569 F.2d 699 (1st Cir. 1978) (appearing to confuse rule of Article 41 under 1962 revision with rules on expiry); Tuthill v. Union Sav. Bank, 141 Misc. 2d 88, 534 N.Y.S.2d 88 (1988) (by analogy to Article 41, credit with no expiry may be terminated by issuer twenty-one days after event of default in underlying contract that credit secured against).

Article 42

Banks are under no obligation to accept presentation of documents outside their banking hours.

Unofficial Annotation: Cf. Chase Manhattan Bank v. Equibank, 550 F.2d 882 (3d Cir. 1977) (noting rule of Article 42 of 1962 revision).

Date terms
Article 43

The terms "first half" and "second half" of a month shall be construed, respectively, as from the first to the fifteenth and as the sixteenth to the last day of each month, inclusive.

Article 44

The terms "beginning," "middle," and "end" of a month shall be construed respectively as from the first to the tenth, the eleventh to the twentieth, and the twenty-first to the last day of each month, inclusive.

Article 45

When a bank issuing a credit instructs that the credit be confirmed or advised as available "for one month," "for six months," or the like but does not specify the date from which the time is to run, the confirming or advising bank will confirm or advise the credit as expiring at the end of such indicated period from the date of its confirmation or advice.

E. Transfer

Article 46

a. A transferable credit is a credit under which the beneficiary has the right to give instructions to the bank called upon to effect payment or acceptance or to any bank entitled to effect negotiation to make the credit available in whole or in part to one or more third parties (second beneficiaries).

b. The bank requested to effect the transfer, regardless of whether it has confirmed the credit, shall be under no obligation to effect such transfer, except to the extent and in the manner expressly consented to by such bank and until such bank's charges in respect of transfer are paid.

c. Bank charges in respect of transfers are payable by the first beneficiary unless otherwise specified.

d. A credit can be transferred only if it is expressly designated as "transferable" by the issuing bank. Terms such as "divisible," "fractionable," "assignable," and "transmissible" add nothing to the meaning of the term "transferable" and shall not be used.

e. A transferable credit can be transferred only once. Fractions of a transferable credit (not exceeding, in the aggregate, the amount of the credit) can be transferred separately, provided partial shipments are not prohibited, and the aggregate of such transfers will be considered as constituting only one transfer of the credit. The credit can be transferred only on the terms and conditions specified in the original credit, with the exception of the amount of the credit, of any unit prices stated therein, and of the period of validity or period for shipment, any or all of which may be reduced or curtailed. Additionally, the name of the first beneficiary can be substituted for that of the applicant for the credit, but if the name of the applicant for the credit is specifically required by the original credit to appear in any document other than the invoice, such requirement must be fulfilled.

f. The first beneficiary has the right to substitute his own invoices for those of the second beneficiary, for amounts not in excess of the original amount stipulated in the credit, and for the original unit prices if stipulated in the credit, and, upon such substitution of invoices, the first beneficiary can draw under the credit for the difference, if any, between his invoices and the second beneficiary's invoices. When a credit has been transferred and the first beneficiary is to supply his own invoices in exchange for the second beneficiary's invoices but fails to do so on first demand, the paying, accepting, or negotiating bank has the right to deliver to the issuing bank the documents received under the credit, including the second beneficiary's invoices, without further responsibility to the first beneficiary.

g. The first beneficiary of a transferable credit can transfer the credit to a second beneficiary in the same country or in another country, unless the credit specifically states otherwise. The first beneficiary shall have the right to request that payment or negotiation be effected to the second beneficiary at the place to which the credit has been transferred, up to and including the expiry date of the original credit, and without prejudice to the first beneficiary's right subsequently to substitute his own invoices for those of the second beneficiary and to claim any difference due to him.

Unofficial Annotation: FDIC v. Bank of Boulder, 865 F.2d 1134 (10th Cir. 1988) (federal common law overrides state statutory and contract law rules against transfer of credit when FDIC acquires credit in purchase and assumption transaction); FDIC v. Bank of Boulder, 622 F. Supp. 288 (D. Colo. 1985), rev'd, 865 F.2d 1134 (10th Cir. 1988) (credit that is not designated transferable cannot be conveyed by FDIC as receiver of failed bank to itself in its corporate capacity but may be conveyed by operation of law from failed bank to state banking commissioner and from him by operation of law to FDIC as receiver); Verlinden B.V. v. Central Bank of Nig., 488 F. Supp. 1284 (S.D.N.Y. 1980), aff'd, 647 F.2d 320 (2d Cir. 1981), rev'd, 461 U.S. 480 (1983) (noting that term "divisible" under 1962 revision is meaningless); European Asian Bank A.G. v. Punjab & Sind Bank, [1983] 2 All E.R. 508 (C.A.) (holding that use of term "divisionable" in credit subject to Uniform Customs renders credit transferable, provisions of Article 46 notwithstanding); Goodsons & Co. v. Federal Republic of Nig., 558 F. Supp. 1204 (S.D.N.Y. 1983) (construing Article 46 of the 1962 revision to permit original beneficiary of credit to shorten time within which second beneficiary may draw under a transferred credit); Kingdom of Swed. v. New York Trust Co., 197 Misc. 431, 96 N.Y.S.2d 779 (Sup. Ct. 1949) (construing transfer provision of Uniform Customs adopted by Seventh Congress of the ICC); Eriksson v. Refiners Export Co., 264 A.D. 525, 35 N.Y.S.2d 829 (1942) (same); cf. AOV Indus. Inc. v. Lambert Coal Co., 64 Bankr. 933 (Bankr. D.D.C. 1986) (theoretical right of first beneficiary to draw for balance of credit not drawn by transferee is not sufficient interest to render payments under transferred credit preferences under Bankruptcy Code).

Article 47

The fact that a credit is not stated to be transferable shall not affect the beneficiary's rights to assign the proceeds of such credit in accordance with the provisions of the applicable law.

APPENDIX C

Sample Letter of Credit Documents

The following documents are illustrative. They serve (1) to provide samples of certain papers that arise frequently in letter-of-credit transactions and (2) to clarify terms and concepts that have been the source of confusion. There is no attempt here to provide a comprehensive list of the plethora of forms that might arise in letter-of-credit transactions.

DOCUMENT 1 **Letter of Credit (General)**

FIRST BANK, N.A.
Kuala Lumpur Branch

Irrevocable Commercial Letter of Credit

P.O. Box 1000, Kuala Lumpur,
Cable Address: Firstbank

KUALA LUMPUR, _____ 19__

DRAFTS DRAWN HEREUNDER MUST BE MARKED:
"DRAWN UNDER THE FIRST BANK, N.A.,
KUALA LUMPUR CREDIT NO. _____ " AND
INDICATE THE DATE HEREOF.

SELLER, B.V.,

AIR MAIL TO

GENTLEMEN:

WE HEREBY AUTHORIZE YOU TO DRAW ON   First Bank, New York, U.S.A.

BY ORDER OF

AND FOR ACCOUNT OF

UP TO AN AGGREGATE AMOUNT OF

AVAILABLE BY YOUR DRAFTS AT sight for 100% of the invoice value.

ACCOMPANIED BY:

6/6   Signed Commercial invoice stating the Import License Number.

3/3   Insurance policy or certificate, endorsed in blank; covering
Institute Marine Cargo clauses (W.A.) Institute War, S.R.C.C.
clauses including all risks for 110% of the invoice value up
to Buyer's warehouse.

6/6   Certificate of Origin.

3/3   Full set clean "On Board" ocean bills of lading, made out to
order and endorsed to First Bank N.A., mentioning "freight
prepaid" and dated not later than   , covering
shipment of   from
                       to CIF Port

Part shipments prohibited.   Transshipments prohibited.

SPECIAL INSTRUCTIONS:

2/2   Beneficiary's certificate indicating that 2 (two) copies of
invoice have been mailed directly to buyer on receipt of the
Letter of Credit.

DRAFTS MUST BE DRAWN AND NEGOTIATED NOT LATER THAN

THE AMOUNTS THEREOF MUST BE ENDORSED ON THIS LETTER OF CREDIT.

THE NEGOTIATING BANK IS TO FORWARD THE DRAFT(S) NEGOTIATED IN COMPLIANCE WITH THE TERMS ABOVE-
MENTIONED TO THE DRAWEE BANK FOR REIMBURSEMENT AND THE REMAINING DOCUMENTS BY AIRMAIL DIRECT
TO US.

WE HEREBY AGREE WITH THE DRAWERS, ENDORSERS, AND BONA FIDE HOLDERS OF ALL DRAFTS DRAWN UNDER
AND IN COMPLIANCE WITH THE TERMS OF THIS CREDIT, THAT SUCH DRAFTS WILL BE DULY HONORED UPON PRE-
SENTATION TO THE DRAWEE.

THIS CREDIT IS SUBJECT TO THE UNIFORM CUSTOMS AND PRACTICE FOR DOCUMENTARY CREDITS (1974 REVISION).
INTERNATIONAL CHAMBER OF COMMERCE PUB. NO. 290.

YOURS VERY TRULY,

_____
Authorized Signature

DOCUMENT 2 **Advice of Credit**

Except so far as otherwise expressly stated, this documentary credit is subject to the Uniform Customs and Practice for Documentary Credits (1974 Revision), International Chamber of Commerce (Brochure No. 290).

FIRST BANK LIMITED

Cable address	Telex number	Place and date of issue	19/9/78

IRREVOCABLE DOCUMENTARY CREDIT	Credit number of issuing bank: 37/2295	Credit number of advising bank: HB 675 321

Advising bank: SECOND BANK	Applicant: BUYER & CO.

Beneficiary: SELLER LTD.	Amount: $50,000.00
	Expiry date: 15 January 1979 at the counters of: SECOND BANK

Further to our cable dated September 19, 1978

We hereby issue this documentary letter of credit

which is available ☐ against presentations of the following documents: ☐ against beneficiary's draft at

drawn on

bearing the clause: "Drawn under documentary letter of credit No. 37/2295 ."

1. Full set of clean on board bill of lading in one original and 3 copies.

Marked freight prepaid   Issued or endorsed to our order. Indicating our L/C number.

2. Invoice in 4 copies 1 certified by the local chamber of commerce and the   Consulate.

3. Certificate of origin in 4 copies issued by the local chamber of commerce confirming goods

originated in

(One copy certified by the Consulate in ....)

4. Surveillance Certificate evidencing goods shipped corresponds with the detail of the pro forma invoice mentioned below. (Cost of this certificate at buyer's A/C.)

5. Detailed Packing List showing the number of bales as per specifications of the pro forma invoice indicated below.

purporting to cover   C & F   value of the following: About 500,000 to 500,100 Bags (1667 Bales) Ltwill Gunny Bags of .... Origin, Overhead Dry Safetsewn, 3 Blue Stripes, Size 44" x 28.5", Port and Shot 8x8 each Bale of 300 Bags, Weight per Bag 2.625 LBS (1190 Grams) as per Pro Forma Invoice dated September 11, 1978, Customs Tariff No. 57/10.

Shipment from BRISTOL to HARTFORD	Partial shipments PERMITTED	Transshipments PROHIBITED

Special conditions:
1. Shipment not to be effected later than December 31, 1978.
2. The L/C is Transferable and Divisible.

We hereby engage that payment will be duly made against documents presented in conformity with the terms of this credit.	This advice is sent to you without engagement on our part.
Yours faithfully,	Yours faithfully,
.... FIRST BANK LIMITED	.... SECOND BANK

DOCUMENT 3 **Confirmation**

FIRST BANK, N.A.
123 Main Street
New York, NY

Confirmed Irrevocable Credit

_____, 19__

Gentlemen:

We are pleased to advise that _____
has opened its irrevocable credit No. _____
in your favor in the amount of _____
against your drafts drawn at _____
on us to be accompanied by the following documents:

The said issuer engages that each draft drawn under and in compliance with the terms of this advice will be duly honored if presented
at our counters on or before _____. Each draft must recite
that it is "Drawn under Confirmed Irrevocable Credit No. _____."
This advice is subject to the Uniform Customs and Practice for
Documentary Credits (1974 revision), ICC publication No. 290.

We hereby confirm said credit and engage to honor all drafts drawn
under and in compliance with the terms hereof.

Yours truly,

FIRST BANK, N.A.

By: _____
Its

DOCUMENT 4 **Negotiable Draft Drawn Under a Credit**

"Drawn under Second Bank Credit No. 10001-5."

$ 80,000.00 (U.S.)   1 May **19**83

At sight   **Pay to the order of**

Seller, Inc.

Eighty thousand and No/100 -------------------- **Dollars**

To: Second Bank, N.A. Seller, Inc.
New York, N.Y.

DOCUMENT 5 **Commercial Invoice**

GENERAL ELECTRONICS, LTD
1776 Liberty Street, Andover, Mass. 01810

COMMERCIAL INVOICE

SOLD TO: Adams Supply Co.
123 Jefferson Avenue
Peoria, Illinois 61602

DATE: December 8, 1983

QUANTITY	DESCRIPTION	UNIT PRICE	AMOUNT
12 Cartons of Computer Accessories			$36,212.00
	Transportation		452.17
	Amount Due		$36,664.17

DOCUMENT 6 **Negotiable Bill of Lading**

UNIFORM THROUGH BILL OF LADING **B. R. BAILEY & CO., INC.** (N.V.O.C.C. BILL OF LADING)

SHIPPER (Principal or Seller-licensee and address)	BOOKING NUMBER B/L No.
	EXPORT REFERENCES
CONSIGNEE (Non-Negotiable unless consigned to order)	FORWARDING AGENT (References)
	POINT AND COUNTRY OF ORIGIN
NOTIFY PARTY/INTERMEDIATE CONSIGNEE (Name and address)	ROUTING INSTRUCTIONS
PIER	

EXPORT CARRIER (Vessel, voyage & flag)	PORT OF LOADING	TO OBTAIN DELIVERY, CONTACT:
PORT OF DISCHARGE	FOR TRANS-SHIPMENT TO	

MARKS AND NUMBERS	NO. OF PKGS.	DESCRIPTION OF PACKAGES AND GOODS PARTICULARS FURNISHED BY SHIPPER	GROSS WEIGHT	MEASUREMENT

Container No.   Intended Vessel   Sailing Date

These Commodities Licensed by U.S. for Ultimate Destination

* If weight shown by shipper is incorrect the figure should be circled, correct weight entered and the words "Carrier's Weight" written opposite the figures.

MARINE INSURANCE Shipper Requests Insurance ☐ YES	**Amount Requested** ☐ NO (If neither of these is checked, shipment is not insured)	If shipper has requested insurance as provided for at the left hereof, shipment is insured in the amount specified (recovery is limited to actual loss) insurance is payable to shipper unless another payee is designated in writing by the shipper.

FREIGHT RATES, CHARGES, WEIGHTS AND/OR MEASUREMENTS			IN WITNESS WHEREOF, the undersigned, signing on behalf of B. R. Bailey & Co., Inc., has on the date indicated above affirmed to this bill of lading. IN WITNESS WHEREOF three (3) original bills of lading all of this tenor and date have been signed one of which being accomplished, the others to stand void. **B. R. BAILEY & CO., INC.**
SUBJECT TO CORRECTION	PREPAID	COLLECT	
			For the Company
			ATTENTION OF SHIPPER. The terms and conditions of the Order Bill of Lading under which this shipment is accepted are printed on the back hereof. **NOTE:** Unless otherwise specified, the charges listed above DO NOT INCLUDE customs duties, taxes, customs clearance charges and similar non-transportation charges which are for the account of the consignee.
TOTAL PREPAID			
TOTAL COLLECT			B/L No.

[Reverse side]

UNIFORM THROUGH BILL OF LADING

RECEIVED by **B. R. Bailey & Co., Inc.,** hereinafter (BAILEY), from the shipper named on the reverse side hereof, the goods, or packages, said to contain goods herein mentioned in apparent good order and condition unless otherwise indicated in this bill of lading, to be transported to the BAILEY distributing depot at the point of destination in accordance with the terms and conditions set forth herein.

1. In this bill of lading the word "carrier" shall include BAILEY and any person, individual, corporation, partnership or other entity, providing or assuming responsibility for any part of the transportation of the goods shipped pursuant to this bill of lading; the word "underlying carrier" shall include any water, air, rail, or motor carrier used by BAILEY for any part of the transportation of the goods or for any part of the transportation of the container into which the goods are loaded; the word "water carrier" shall include the ship, her owner, master, operator or demise or time charterer; the word "container" shall include any van, trailer or enclosed cargo box utilized by BAILEY in connection with the transportation of the goods; the word "shipper" shall include the person named as such in this bill of lading and the person for whose account the goods are shipped; the word "consignee" shall include the holder of this bill of lading, properly endorsed, or the person who owns or is entitled to receive delivery of the goods; the word "charges" shall include freight and all other expenses, losses, special charges, amounts and money obligations whatsoever, payable by or chargeable to or for the account of the goods, shipper or consignee, or any of them.

2. To the extent that the goods covered herein are carried by water, this shipment shall have effect subject to the provisions of the Carriage of Goods by Sea Act of the United States, approved April 16, 1936, which shall be deemed to be incorporated herein and nothing herein contained shall be deemed a surrender by BAILEY, or any underlying carrier, of any of their rights or immunities or an increase of any of their responsibilities er liabilities under said Act.

3. The rights and obligations, whatsover they may be, of each and every person having any interest or duty whatsoever in respect of the receipt, care, custody, carriage, delivery or trans-shipment of the goods whether as shipper, consignee, holder or endorsee of the bill of lading, receiver or owner of the goods, carrier, master of the ship, shipowner, demise charterer, operator, agent, bailee, warehouseman, forwarder or otherwise howsoever, shall be subject to and governed by the terms of the bill of lading, receipt, freight note, contract or other shipping document issued by the underlying water, air, rail or motor carrier participating in the transportation hereunder and accepted by BAILEY for the shipment of the goods or for the shipment of the container in which the goods are loaded, and which bill of lading, receipt, freight note, contract or other shipping document shall be deemed to be incorporated herein, including any amendment thereto or special provisions thereof which may be in effect at the time the goods are received for shipment and applicable to the intended transportation. The liability of BAILEY herein shall in no event be greater than that of the underlying carrier under its bill of lading, receipt, freight, note, contract or other shipping document, and BAILEY shall be entitled to all of the exemptions from liabilty therein contained. Copies of such underlying carriers' bill of lading(s), receipt(s), freight note(s), contract(s) or other shipping document(s) may be obtained on application to the office of BAILEY, or its agent, at the point of shipment or at the point of destination.

4. BAILEY shall not be obligated to transport the goods by any particular water, air, rail, or motor carrier, on any particular vessel, train or other means of conveyance, in any particular container, or in time for any particular market or otherwise than with reasonable dispatch. Selection of the underlying carriers shall be within the sole discretion of BAILEY.

5. In any situation whatsover which in the judgment of BAILEY is likely to give rise to risk of capture, seizure, detention, damage, delay or disadvantage to or loss of the goods of a container in which the goods are loaded, to make it unsafe, imprudent or unlawful for any reason to commence or proceed on or continue the transportation or to enter or discharge the goods at the port of discharge or agreed destination, BAILEY may, before the commencement of the transportation hereunder, require the shipper or other person entitled thereto to take delivery of the goods at the point of shipment and upon failure to do so, may warehouse the goods at the risk and expense of the goods; or the goods may be discharged at any port or place as BAILEY may consider safe or advisable under the circumstances, or the goods may be discharged and forwarded by any means at the risk and expense of the goods. BAILEY is not required to give notice of discharge of the goods or the forwarding thereof as herein provided. BAILEY shall have the right to withhold delivery of, reship to, dispose or discharge the goods at any place whatsoever, surrender or dispose of the goods in accordance with any direction, condition or agreement imposed upon or exacted from BAILEY by any government or department thereof, or any person purporting to act with the authority of either of them. In any of the above circumstances the goods shall be solely at their risk and expenses and charges so incurred shall be payable by the shipper or consignee thereof and shall be a lien on the goods.

6. The shipper and consignee shall be liable for, and BAILEY shall have a lien on the goods, for all expenses of mending cooperage, baling or reconditioning of the goods or packages, or for the expenses of gathering of loose contents of packages; also for any payment, expense, fine, dues, duty, tax, impost, loss, damage or detention sustained or incurred by or levied upon BAILEY in connection with the goods, howsoever caused, including any action or requirement of any government or governmental authority or person purporting to act under the authority thereof, seizure under legal process or attempted seizure, incorrect or insufficient markings, numbering or addressing of packages or description of the contents, failure of the shipper to procure Consular, Board of Health or other certificates to accompany the goods, or to comply with laws or regulations of any kind imposed with respect to the goods by the authorities at any port or place, or for any other act or omission of the shipper or consignee. The shipper or the consignee shall be obligated to pay all customs duties and clearance charges upon arrival of the goods. Goods not cleared through customs for any reason may be cleared by BAILEY at the expense of the goods, and may be warehoused at the risk and expense of the goods, or may be turned over to the port authorities without any further responsibility on the part of BAILEY.

7. Unless otherwise stated in the bill of lading, the description of the goods and the particulars of the packages are those furnished by the shipper and BAILEY shall not be responsible for the correctness of marks, number, quantity, weight, gauge, measurement, contents nature, quality or value. All measurements must be based upon dimensions taken at the points of greatest length, width and breadth of the package regardless of shape. In case shipper's particulars are found to be erroneous and additional freight is payable, the shipper shall be liable for any expense incurred for examining, weighing, measuring and valuing the goods.

8. *In the event of loss and/or damage, BAILEY's liability shall not exceed $500.00 per package or other customary freight unit, unless such valuation is shown on the bills of lading and extra freight paid thereon in accordance with the tariff of BAILEY. In no event shall BAILEY's liability exceed actual value. BAILEY shall not be liable for any consequential or special damage and shall have the option of replacing any lost or replacing or repairing any damaged goods. The shipper expressly authorizes the lowest valuation of the goods or limitation of liability contained in the bills of lading or shipping document of any underlying carrier, which valuation or limitation shall apply even though lower than the valuation or limitation herein.*

9. Unless notice of loss or damage and the general nature of such loss or damage be given in writing to BAILEY, or its agent at the point of destination before or at the time of the removal of the goods into the custody of the person entitled to delivery thereof under this bill of lading, such removal shall be prima facie evidence of the delivery of the goods as described in the bill of lading. If the loss or damage is not apparent, notice must be given within three (3) days of delivery. Any claim against BAILEY for any adjustment, refund of, or with respect to charges or for delay or any claim other than for loss or damages to goods, must be given to BAILEY or its agent, in writing within twenty (20) days from the date when the goods are or should have been delivered. In any event BAILEY shall be discharged from all liability in respect of loss or damage unless suit is brought within one (1) year of the delivery of the goods or the date when the goods should have been delivered. Suit should not be deemed brought until jurisdiction shall have been obtained over BAILEY by service of process or by an agreement to appear.

10. BAILEY charges will be calculated in accordance with its tariff rate in effect at the time of shipment. All charges shall be due and payable in full on the date the goods are delivered to BAILEY and without any offset, counterclaim or deduction in United States currency. All BAILEY charges shall be deemed completely earned on receipt of the goods and are to be absolutely payable, ship or other conveyance and/or cargo lost or not lost. The shipper and the consignee shall remain jointly and severally liable to BAILEY for all charges due. BAILEY shall have a lien on the goods which shall survive delivery, for all charges due hereunder and may enforce this lien by public or private sale and without notice.

11. All agreements or freight engagements for the shipment of the goods are superseded by this bill of lading. If required by BAILEY, a signed original bill of lading, duly endorsed, must be surrendered to BAILEY upon delivery of the goods. The terms of this bill of lading shall be separable, and if any part or term thereof is invalid or unenforceable, such circumstances should not affect the validity of enforceability of any other part or term thereof.

12. Nothing herein contained, whether by express statement, reference, implication or otherwise, shall be deemed a surrender of any rights or immunities or an increase of responsibilities or liabilities which BAILEY, any carrier, the ship, her owner, charterer, operator, agent or master or bailee, warehouseman, or forwarder of the goods or the agent of any of them, would have in the absence of this bill of lading. None of the terms of this bill of lading shall be deemed to have been waived except by express waiver signed by a duly authorized agent of BAILEY.

DOCUMENT 7 Insurance Certificate

$ _____   CERTIFICATE OF MARINE INSURANCE   NO. _____

OLD NATIONAL INSURANCE COMPANY
Pittsburgh, Pennsylvania

This is to Certify, that on the   day of   19

this Company insured under Policy No.   made for

for the sum of   Dollars, on

Valued at sum insured. Shipped on board the S/S or M/S
and/or following steamer or steamers

at and from
                    (Initial Point of Shipment).

via
                         (Port of Shipment)

to   and
                         (Port of Places of Destination)

it is understood and agreed, that in case of loss, the same is payable to the
order of   on
surrender of the Certificate which conveys the right of collecting any such loss as fully as if the property were covered by a special policy direct to the holder hereof, and free from any liability for unpaid
premiums. This certificate is subject to all the terms of the open policy, provided, however, that the
rights of a bona fide holder of this certificate for value shall not be prejudiced by any terms of the
open policy that are in conflict with the terms of this certificate.

SPECIAL CONDITIONS	MARKS & NUMBERS	

ON DECK SHIPMENTS (subject to an ON DECK bill of lading)
insured—
     Warranted free of particular average unless caused by the
vessel being stranded, sunk, burnt, on fire or in collision, but
including risk of jettison and/or washing overboard, irrespective
of percentage.

SCHEDULE B CODE (commodity)	SCHEDULE C-E CODE (country)

Foreign Currency		AMOUNT INSURED	MARINE RATE	MARINE PREMIUM	WAR RATE	WAR PREMIUM	DISC.	MARINE COMM.	WAR COMM.
U.S. $	(On Deck) (Under Deck)								
	S/S Penalty								

by _____
                                                Authorized Agent

DOCUMENT 8 **Visaed Invoice**

GENERAL ELECTRONICS, LTD.
1776 Liberty Street, Andover, Mass. 01810

COMMERCIAL INVOICE

SOLD TO: Salaam Supply Co.
3512 LT Alexandria

DATE: December 8, 1983

QUANTITY	DESCRIPTION	UNIT PRICE	AMOUNT
12 Cartons of Computer Accessories			$36,212.00
	Transportation		452.17
	Amount Due		$36,664.17

DOCUMENT 9 **Consular Invoice**

REPUBLICA DE COLOMBIA

FACTURA CONSULAR NO.   NO. ....
                                 Pagina No. ....

2. *Pais de venta:*

3. *Pais de origen:*

4. *Lugar de embarque:*

5. *Nombre del barco o Compania Aerea:*

6. *Consignatario: Nombre y direccion:*

7. *Destinatario: Nombre y direccion:*

8. *Remitente: Nombre y direccion:*

9. *Numero de paginas:*

10. *Numero de conocimiento o guia:*

11. *Aduana de destino:*

Cantidad y clase de bultos	Marca y numeros	Peso en Kilos		No. de unidades	Denominacion comercial de la mercancia	Precio de la mercancia
		Bruto	Neto			

Total en pesos colombianos: $

Registre de importacion No.

Oficina expedidora:

Cantidad autorizada: US $

Cantidad despachada:

Cantidad por despachar:

....
                Lugar y fecha   *Firma y sello del Consul*

DOCUMENT 10 **Certificate of Origin**

CERTIFICATE OF ORIGIN

(for general use)

The undersigned ....
                                                                    (Owner or Agent, or &c.)

for .... *declares*
                                              (Name and Address of Shipper)

that the following mentioned goods shipped on S/S ....
                                                                                                        (Name of Ship)

on the date of .... consigned to ....

.... are the product of the United States of America.

Marks and Numbers	No. of Pkgs., Boxes or Cases	Weight in Kilos		Description
		Gross	**Net**	

Dated at .... on the .... day of .... 19.......

  Sworn to before me
this .... day of .... 19.......

....
                                                                                  (Signature of Owner or Agent)

The ...., a recognized Chamber of Commerce under the laws of the State of ...., has examined the manufacturer's invoice or shipper's affidavit concerning the origin of the merchandise, and, according to the best of its knowledge and belief, finds that the products named originated in the United States of North America.

        Secretary ....

DOCUMENT 11   Inspection Certificate

TENNYSON ASSOCIATES
123 Main Street
St. Louis, MO

Buyer Co.
14 May Street
Portland, OR

RE: Order No. 7360421-8A/5·1·83

Gentlemen:

We certify that we have examined brass fittings comprising the above
order and find them to be manufactured of quality brass in dimensions, quantity, and quality as specified in said order.

                          Yours truly,

                          TENNYSON ASSOCIATES

                          By: _____

DOCUMENT 12 **Time Draft**

$3,000.00

May 1 , 19 83

At 60 days sight pay to the order of
ourselves Three Thousand and no/100   ($3,000.00   ) Dollars.

TO: Buyer, Ltd.   Seller Corp.
     100 Oak Street
     Los Angeles, CA   by Conrad Cooper

DOCUMENT 13 **Trade Acceptance**

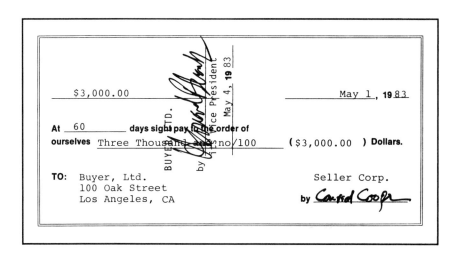

$3,000.00   May 1 , 19 83

At 60 days sight pay to the order of
ourselves Three Thousand and no/100   ($3,000.00) Dollars.

TO: Buyer, Ltd.   Seller Corp.
     100 Oak Street
     Los Angeles, CA   by Conrad Cooper

DOCUMENT 14 **Application Agreement**

<table>
<tr><td colspan="2">COMMERCIAL LETTER OF CREDIT
APPLICATION</td><td>NO.

DO NOT FILL IN</td></tr>
</table>

Gentlemen: Date: _____

Please issue an Irrevocable Letter of Credit and either
a) Notify through correspondent by ☐ Mail/Airmail: ☐ Airmail with brief advice by cable; or
b) ☐ Return to us for mailing to beneficiary; or
c) ☐ Mail directly to beneficiary; as follows:

You are hereby authorized to instruct the negotiation bank to forward to you all documents relating to this letter of credit in one mailing only, *unless the box shown below has been checked by us.* ☐ Please instruct the negotiation bank to forward the relative documents to you in two mailings.	For Account of (Applicant) (Name) (Complete Address)
In Favor of (Beneficiary) (Name) (Complete Address)	Amount Drafts must be presented for negotiation or presented to drawee on or before (Expiry Date)

Available by drafts at _____ drawn, at your option,
                                      Indicate Tenor
on you or your correspondent for _____ % of the Invoice value.

DRAFTS MUST BE ACCOMPANIED BY THE FOLLOWING DOCUMENTS AS CHECKED:

(Invoices must include substantially the below commodity description, but only general description of the commodity on the remaining documents is required.)

1 ☐ Commercial Invoices in original and _____ copies
2 ☐ Special Customs Invoice in original and _____ copies
3 ☐ Weight list in _____ copies
4 ☐ Packing list in _____ copies
5 ☐ Other documents _____

6 ☐ Marine/War Insurance Policy or Certificate _____

(If Other Insurance Is Required, Please State Risks)
Full set Clean "On Board" Ocean Bills of Lading consigned
7 ☐ to order, endorsed in blank, or consigned to order of _____
_____

Marked Notify: _____

COVERING: Merchandise described in the invoice as: (Mention commodity only in generic terms omitting details as to grade, quality, etc.)
_____
_____
_____

CHECK ONE: ☐ FAS ☐ FOB ☐ C & F ☐ CIF ☐ C & I _____
                                                           (Indicate Place or Port)

SHIPMENT FROM TO	Partial shipments are permitted/prohibited Transshipment is permitted/prohibited.

☐ Drafts(s) and documents must be presented to negotiating or paying bank within _____ days after the date of issuance of the Bill(s) of Lading or other shipping documents but within expiry date.
☐ Insurance effected by ourselves. **We agree to keep Insurance coverage In force until this transaction is completed.**
The credit will be subject to the Uniform Customs and Practice for Documentary Credits of the International Chamber of Commerce presently in effect.
SPECIAL INSTRUCTIONS _____
_____
_____

This Application is made subject to the Continuing Letter of Credit Agreement (Security Agreement) heretofore most recently executed by us and delivered to you, the provisions of which are hereby made applicable to this Application and the Credit.	_____ (Applicant)
	_____ (Address)
We warrant that no shipment involved in this Application is in violation of U.S. Treasury Foreign Assets Control or Cuban Assets Control Regulations.	(Authorized Signature) (Title)
	(Authorized Signature) (Title)

CONTINUING LETTER OF CREDIT AGREEMENT
(Security Agreement)

Date: _____

TO:

Gentlemen:

In consideration of your issuance of letters of credit at your option from time to time substantially in accordance with our applications therefor, as the same may be amended with our agreement or consent, we hereby agree that, except as you and we shall otherwise specifically agree in writing in each instance, the Terms and Conditions hereinafter set forth shall apply to each such application and to each letter of credit issued pursuant to such application.

_____   _____
(Applicant)   (Applicant)

_____   _____
(Address)   (Address)

_____   _____
(Authorized Signature)   (Title)   (Authorized Signature)   (Title)

PLEASE SIGN OFFICIALLY

TERMS AND CONDITIONS

In these provisions:

(1) The "Bank" means

(2) The "Applicant" means the undersigned.

(3) An "instrument" means any draft, receipt, acceptance or cable or written demand for payment.

(4) "Property" means goods and merchandise and any and all documents relative thereto, securities, funds, choses in action, and any and all other forms of property, whether real, personal or mixed and any right or interest therein.

(5) "Uniform Customs and Practice" means the Uniform Customs and Practice for Documentary Credits (1974 Revision), International Chamber of Commerce Publication No. 290, and any subsequent revisions thereof approved by a Congress of the International Chamber of Commerce and adhered to by the Bank.

(6) "Security Agreement" means an agreement which creates or provides for a security interest, including, where applicable law provides therefor, a trust receipt as defined in and complying with such law.

(7) "Financing Statement" means a Financing Statement or a Statement of Trust Receipt Financing in the form specified in applicable law.

(8) "Application" means each application by the Applicant for a letter of credit as such application may be amended or modified from time to time with the written or oral agreement or consent of the Applicant.

In consideration of the issuance by the Bank, upon application by the Applicant from time to time, at the Bank's option, of one or more letters of credit (each such letter of credit as from time to time amended or modified with the consent of the Applicant being hereinafter referred to as the "Credit"), the Applicant hereby agrees with the Bank as follows with respect to each Credit:

1. As to instruments drawn under or purporting to be drawn under the Credit, which are payable in United States currency: (a) in the case of each sight draft, demand or receipt, to reimburse the Bank, at its main office, on demand, in United States currency, the amount paid thereon, or, if so demanded by the Bank, to pay to the Bank, at its main office, in advance in such currency, the amount required to pay the same; and (b) in the case of each acceptance, to pay to the Bank, at its main office, in United States currency, the amount thereof, on demand but in any event not later than one business day prior to maturity or, in case the acceptance is not payable at the Bank, then on demand but in any event in time to reach the place of payment in the course of ordinary mail not later than one business day prior to maturity.

2. As to instruments drawn under or purporting to be drawn under the Credit, which are payable in currency other than United States currency: (a) in the case of each sight draft, demand or receipt, to reimburse the Bank, at its main office, on demand, in United States currency, the equivalent of the amount paid at the Bank's then current selling rate of exchange in Detroit for cable transfers to the place of payment in the currency in which such draft, demand or receipt is payable, with interest from the date of payment of the instrument, or if so demanded by the Bank, to pay to the Bank, at its main office, in advance, in United States currency, the equivalent of the amount required to pay the same; and (b) in the case of each acceptance, to pay to the Bank, at its main office, on demand but in any event sufficiently in advance of maturity to enable the Bank to arrange for cover to reach the place of payment not later than one business day prior to maturity, the equivalent of the acceptance in United States currency at the Bank's then current selling rate of exchange in Detroit for cable transfers to the place of payment in the currency of the acceptance. If for any cause whatsoever there exists at the time in question no rate of exchange generally current in Detroit for effecting cable transfers of the sort above mentioned, the Applicant agrees to pay the Bank on demand an amount in United States currency equivalent to the actual cost to the Bank of settlement of the Bank's obligation to the holder of the instrument or other person, however and whenever such settlement shall be made by the Bank, including interest on the amount payable by the Applicant from the date of such settlement to the date of the Applicant's payment to the Bank. The Applicant will comply with any and all governmental exchange regulations now or hereafter applicable to the Credit or instruments or payments relative thereto, and will pay the Bank, on demand, in United States currency, such amount as the Bank may be required to expend on account of such regulations.

3. To pay the Bank, on demand, the Bank's commission at such rate as the Bank may determine to be proper, and all charges and expenses paid or incurred by the Bank in connection with the Credit, and interest where chargeable. Interest payable hereunder shall be at the rate customarily charged by the Bank at the time in like circumstances.

4. If the Bank delivers to or upon the order of the Applicant any of the property and/or documents covered by the Credit, or which may be held by the Bank or for its account as security hereunder, prior to the Bank's having received reimbursement in full with respect to the relative instrument(s), to sign and deliver to the Bank a Security Agreement or Security Agreements and Financing Statement(s), each duly signed by the Applicant, and to pay all filing and recording fees, it being understood that any such delivery of property and/or documents will be made by the Bank in reliance upon these Terms and Conditions, and that the Bank's rights as specified herein shall be in addition to and not in limitation of its rights under applicable law. Upon any transfer, sale, delivery, surrender or endorsement of any bill of lading, warehouse receipt or other document at any time(s) held by the Bank, or held for its account by any of its correspondents, relative to the Credit, the Applicant will indemnify and hold the Bank, and any such correspondent(s), harmless from and against each and every claim, demand, action or suit which may arise against the Bank, or any such correspondent(s), by reason thereof.

5. These Terms and Conditions and the Credit shall be subject to the Uniform Customs and Practice (receipt of a copy of which is hereby acknowledged by Applicant), and, in the event any provision of the Uniform Customs

and Practice is or is construed to vary from or be in conflict with any provision of the Michigan Uniform Commercial Code, as from time to time amended and in force, (hereinafter called the Commercial Code), the Uniform Customs and Practice shall prevail. In addition to other rights of the Bank hereunder or under application for the Credit, any action, inaction or omission taken or suffered by the Bank, or by any of its correspondents, under or in connection with the Credit or the relative instruments, documents, or property, if in good faith and in conformity with such foreign or domestic laws, regulations, or customs as the Bank or any of its correspondents may deem to be applicable thereto, shall be binding upon the Applicant and shall not place the Bank or any of its correspondents under any liability to the Applicant. The Applicant agrees to hold the Bank and its correspondents indemnified and harmless against any and all loss, liability or damage, including reasonable counsel fees, howsoever arising from or in connection with the Credit.

6. That the Bank may accept or pay any draft presented to it, regardless of when drawn and whether or not negotiated, if such draft, the other required documents and any transmittal advice are dated on or before the expiration date of the Credit, and that except in so far as instructions may be given by the Applicant in writing expressly to the contrary with regard to, and prior to, the Bank's issuance of the Credit: (a) although shipment(s) in excess of the quantity called for under the Credit are made, the Bank may honor the relative instrument(s) in an amount or amounts not exceeding the amount of the Credit; (b) documents of insurance under the Credit need not be for an amount of insurance greater than the amount paid by the Bank under the Credit; and (c) the Bank may honor, as complying with the terms of the Credit and of the application therefor, any instruments or other documents otherwise in order signed or issued by an administrator, executor, trustee in bankruptcy, debtor in possession, assignee for the benefit of creditors, liquidator, receiver or other legal representative of the party authorized under the Credit to draw or issue such instruments or other documents.

7. That in the event of any change or modification, with the consent of the Applicant, relative to the Credit or any instrument or documents called for thereunder, including waiver of noncompliance of any such instruments or documents with the terms of the Credit, these Terms and Conditions shall be binding upon the Applicant with regard to the Credit as so changed or modified, and to any action taken by the Bank or any of its correspondents relative thereto.

8. That the user(s) of the Credit shall be deemed agents of the Applicant and neither the Bank nor its correspondents shall be responsible for: (a) the use which may be made of the Credit or for any acts or omissions of the user(s) of the Credit; (b) the existence, character, quality, quantity, condition, packing or value of the property purporting to be represented by the documents; (c) the time, place, manner or order in which shipment is made; (d) the validity, sufficiency, or genuineness of documents, or of any endorsements thereon, even if such documents should in fact prove to be in any or all respects invalid, insufficient, fraudulent, or forged; (e) partial or incomplete shipment, or failure or omission to ship any or all of the property referred to in the Credit; (f) the character, adequacy, validity or genuineness of any insurance or the solvency or responsibility of any insurer or any other risk connected with insurance; (g) any deviation from instructions, delay, default or fraud by the shipper or anyone else in connection with the property or the shipping thereof; (h) the solvency, responsibility or relationship to the property of any party issuing any documents in connection with the property; (i) delay in arrival or failure to arrive of either the property or any of the documents relating thereto; (j) delay in giving or failure to give notice of arrival or any other notice; (k) any breach of contract between the shipper(s) or vendor(s) and the consignee(s) or buyer(s); (l) failure of any instrument to bear any reference or adequate reference to the Credit, or failure of documents to accompany any instrument at negotiation, or failure of any person to note the amount of any instrument on the reverse of the Credit, or to surrender or take up the Credit or to send forward documents apart from instruments as required by the terms of the Credit, each of which provisions, if contained in the Credit itself, it is agreed may be waived by the Bank; or (m) errors, omissions, interruptions or delays in transmission or delivery of any messages, by mail, cable, telegraph, wireless or otherwise, whether or not they may be in cipher; that the Bank shall not be responsible for any act, error, neglect or default, omission, insolvency or failure in business of any of its correspondents; that the occurrence of any one or more of the contingencies referred to in the preceding clauses of this paragraph shall not affect, impair or prevent the vesting of any of the Bank's rights or powers hereunder or the Applicant's obligation to make reimbursement; and that the Applicant will promptly examine (i) the copy of the Credit (and of any amendments thereof) sent to it by the Bank and (ii) all documents and instruments delivered to it from time to time by the Bank, and, in the event of any claim of noncompliance with Applicant's instructions or other irregularity, will immediately notify the Bank thereof in writing, the Applicant being conclusively deemed to have waived any such claim against the Bank and its correspondents unless such notice is given as aforesaid.

9. To procure promptly any necessary import, export or other licenses for the import, export or shipping of the property shipped under or pursuant to or in connection with the Credit, and to comply with all foreign and domestic governmental regulations in regard to the shipment of such property or the financing thereof, and to furnish such certificates in that respect as the Bank may at any time(s) require, and to keep such property adequately covered by insurance in amounts, against risks and in companies satisfactory to the Bank, and to assign the policies or certificates of insurance to the Bank, or to make the loss or adjustment, if any, payable to the Bank, at its option, and to furnish the Bank, on its demand, with evidence of acceptance by the insurers of such assignment. Should the insurance upon such property for any reason be unsatisfactory to the Bank, the Bank may, at the Applicant's expense, obtain insurance satisfactory to the Bank.

10. That, as security for the payment or performance of any and all of the Applicant's obligations and/or liabilities hereunder, absolute or contingent, and also for the payment or performance of any and all other obligations and/or liabilities, absolute or contingent, due or to become due, which are now, or may at any time(s) hereafter be owing by the Applicant to the Bank, or which are now or hereafter existing, the Applicant hereby: (a) recognizes and admits the Bank's ownership in and unqualified right to the possession

and disposal of any and all shipping documents, warehouse receipts, policies or certificates of insurance and other documents accompanying or relative to instruments drawn under the Credit and in and to any and all property shipped under or pursuant to or in connection with the Credit, or in any way relative thereto or to any of the instruments drawn thereunder (whether or not such documents, goods or other property be released to or upon the order of the Applicant under a Security Agreement or bailee receipt), and in and to the proceeds of each and all of the foregoing; (b) pledges to the Bank and/or gives the Bank a general lien upon and/or right of set-off against, all right, title and interest of the Applicant in and to the balance of every deposit account now or at any time hereafter existing, of the Applicant with the Bank, and any other claims of the Applicant against the Bank, and in and to all property, claims and demands and rights and interests therein of the Applicant, and in and to all evidences thereof, which have been or at any time shall be delivered to or otherwise come into the Bank's possession, custody or control, or into the possession, custody or control of any of its agents or correspondents for any purpose, whether or not for the express purpose of being used by the Bank as collateral security or for safekeeping or for any other or different purpose, the Bank being deemed to have possession, custody or control of all such property actually in transit to or set apart for the Bank or any of its agents, correspondents or others acting in its behalf, it being understood that the receipt at any time by the Bank, or any of its correspondents, of other security, of whatever nature, including cash, shall not be deemed a waiver of any of the Bank's rights or powers hereunder; (c) if any party shall have joined in the application for the Credit, assigns and transfers to the Bank all right, title and interest of the Applicant in and to all property and interests which the Applicant may now or hereafter obtain from such party as security for the obligations of such party arising in connection with the transaction to which the Credit relates; and (d) agrees at any time and from time to time, on demand, to deliver, convey, transfer or assign to the Bank additional security of a value and character satisfactory to the Bank, or to make such payment as the Bank may require.

11. That upon the failure of the Applicant at any time to keep a margin of security with the Bank satisfactory to the Bank; or upon the death of any Applicant; or if any of the obligations and/or liabilities of the Applicant to the Bank shall not be paid or performed when due; or if there is a breach in any warranty or representation herein; or if the Applicant shall become insolvent (however such insolvency may be evidenced) or commit any act of bankruptcy or insolvency, or make a general assignment for the benefit of creditors; or if the Applicant shall suspend the transaction of its usual business or be expelled or suspended from any exchange; or if an application is made by any judgment creditor of the Applicant for an order directing the Bank to pay over money or to deliver other property; or if a petition in bankruptcy shall be filed by or against the Applicant; or if a petition shall be filed by or against the Applicant or any proceeding shall be instituted by or against the Applicant for any relief under any bankruptcy or insolvency laws or any law relating to the relief of debtors, readjustment of indebtedness, reorganization, composition or extensions; or if any governmental authority, or any court at the instance of any governmental authority, shall take possession of any substantial part of the property of the Applicant or shall assume control over the affairs or operations of the Applicant; or if a receiver shall be appointed of, or a writ or order of attachment or garnishment shall be issued or made against, any of the property or assets of the Applicant; thereupon, unless the Bank shall otherwise elect, any and all obligations and liabilities of the Applicant to the Bank, whether now existing or hereafter incurred, shall become and be due and payable forthwith without presentation, demand or notice, all of which are waived, and the Bank is hereby authorized (itself or by agent) without previous demand or notice to sell at public or private sale the whole or any part of (a) any goods or merchandise, shipped or to be shipped under the Credit, or sell the same "to arrive" and (b) any and all securities or other collateral deposited with Bank or subject to Bank's security interest, applying the proceeds, less the costs and expenses of such sale and any other expenses paid or incurred in respect of said collateral, in and towards any indebtedness of the Applicant to Bank, paying the surplus to the Applicant or the latter's legal representative. If any deficiency shall arise, the Applicant will pay the same to Bank on demand. At any such sale Bank may become the purchaser and hold the goods or security free of any right of redemption. If any applicable provision of the Commercial Code or other law requires Bank to give the Applicant or any other person reasonable notice of any sale or disposition or other action with respect to any collateral, five days' prior written notice thereof shall constitute reasonable notice. Bank may require the Applicant to assemble the collateral and make it available to Bank at a place to be designated by Bank. Attorneys' fees and legal expenses incurred by Bank in enforcement of Bank's rights and remedies hereunder shall be paid by the Applicant and shall become part of the indebtedness secured hereby. The Applicant represents, warrants and agrees that, except for the security interest in Bank, no security interest or lien has been created or exists with respect to any of the collateral covered hereby and the proceeds thereof and no Financing Statement or other Security Agreement is on file in any jurisdiction covering such collateral or proceeds; the Applicant will not create or suffer to exist any such security interest or lien and will not permit any such Financing Statement or other Security Agreement to be on file; the Applicant will execute, deliver and file such Financing Statements and other documents as may be requested by Bank from time to time to create, perfect and preserve the security .interest created hereby; and the right is granted Bank, to be exercised at its option, to file from time to time Financing Statements signed by Bank alone and naming Bank as the secured party and the Applicant as the debtor, and indicating the types, or describing the items, of collateral covered hereby, all at the expense of the Applicant. Without limitation of its rights, powers and remedies hereunder and regardless of whether or not the Commercial Code is in effect in the jurisdiction where such rights, powers and remedies are asserted, Bank shall have the rights, powers and remedies under the Commercial Code,

12. That the Bank's rights and liens hereunder shall continue unimpaired, and the Applicant shall be and remain obligated in accordance with the terms and provisions hereof, notwithstanding the release and/or substitution of any property which may be held as security hereunder at any time(s), or of any rights or interests therein. No delay, extension of time, renewal, compromise or other indulgence which may occur or be granted by the Bank, shall impair the Bank's rights or powers hereunder. The Bank shall not be deemed to have waived any of its rights hereunder, unless the Bank or its authorized agent shall have signed such waiver in writing. No such waiver, unless expressly as stated

therein, shall be effective as to any transaction which occurs subsequent to the date of such waiver, nor as to any continuance of a breach, after such waiver.

13. That if the Applicant is a banking institution, the Applicant hereby appoints the Bank its agent to issue the Credit in acccordance with, and subject to, these Terms and Conditions and the application for the Credit.

14. That if the Applicant is a partnership, the obligations hereof shall continue in force, and apply, notwithstanding any change in the membership of such partnership, whether arising from the death or retirement of one or more partners or the accession of one or more new partners.

15. That the obligations hereof shall bind the heirs, executors, administrators, successors and assigns of the Applicant, and all rights, benefits and privileges hereby conferred on the Bank shall be and hereby are extended to and conferred upon and may be enforced by its successors and assigns.

16. Any notice from Bank to Applicant, if mailed, shall be deemed given when mailed, postage paid, addressed to Applicant at the last business address furnished by Applicant to Bank. Whenever possible each provision of this Agreement shall be interpreted in such manner as to be effective and valid under applicable law but if any provision of this Agreement shall be prohibited by or invalid under applicable law, such provision shall be ineffective only to the extent of such prohibition or invalidity, without invalidating the remainder of such provision or the remaining provisions of this Agreement.

17. If this Agreement is signed by two or more Applicants, it shall be the joint and several agreement of each Applicant.

18. That, subject to the provision of 5 above, this Agreement and all rights, obligations and liabilities arising hereunder shall be governed by, and construed in accordance with, the law of the State of Michigan.

DOCUMENT 15 **Straight Credit (Commercial)**

TELEGRAM aan (naam en plaatsnaam voluit)

BANQUE VERNES ET COMMERCIALE DE PARIS
PARIS

Date: 24-11-1981/vgp

(telegramadres en plaatsnaam onder de streep-tekst binnen de lijnen houden) | Afd. Accreditieven

TELEX TESTKEY

notify beneficiaries that we herewith issue our irrevocable credit
no. 51056.
date and place of expiry: 30th december 1981 in paris applicant:
Buyer Corp.

beneficiary: Seller, Ltd.

amount: usdlrs 48.500,--cost and freight value credit available
with banque vernes et commerciale de paris, paris by acceptance of
beneficiary's draft at 90 days date after b/lading date drawn on
banque vernes et commerciale de paris, paris.
partial shipments and transshipment prohibited.
shipment from antwerp/belgium per conference vessel to guayaquil/
ecuador not later than december 15, 1981.
shipment of 100.00 kilos caustic soda flakes packed in 500 iron
drums of 200 kilos net each, marked "Buyer Corp./guayaquil/ecuador"
at the price of usdlr 485,00 per 1.000 kilos net, packing included,
cost and freight guayaquil/ecuador.

documents required:

1- signed commercial invoice in 5-fold in the name of the
   applicant.
2- 3/3 original clean "on board" ocean bills of lading plus 5 n.n.
   copies, made out to order of Seller, Ltd. guayaquil/ecuador
   and notify "same" marked "freight prepaid" and showing full
   freight amount, particulars on the bladings "a bordo" "flete
   pagado" apartida aranceleria no. 28.
   17.01.99 "permiso de imporacionno: 02-1-28115", evidencing
   shipment by conference vessel.
3- weight and packing list in duplicate.
4- quality certificate in duplicate.
5- certificate of origin issued by the chambre of commerce.

period after issuance of shipping documents for presentation:
15 days.
without adding your confirmation please advise beneficiaries
reimbursement: for your acceptance we authorize you to reimburse
yourselves upon continental bank international, new york on due
date.
documents to be sent to us in two successive registered airmails.
subject to u.c.p. 1974, icc publication no. 290

first bank n.v.
amsterdam

DOCUMENT 16 Negotiation Credit (Commercial)

FIRST BANK, N.A.

Irrevocable Negotiation Letter of Credit No.　　　　Date:

<u>BENEFICIARY</u>:　　　　　　　　<u>APPLICANT</u>:

Gentlemen:

We hereby establish our irrevocable negotiation letter of credit in your favor available by your drafts drawn at sight on us marked Drawn under First Bank Credit No. indicated above.

Accompanied by the following documents covering full invoice value of merchandise described as:

All documents must be forwarded to us by airmail in one cover.

In reimbursement, the negotiating bank may forward sight drafts to us.

This credit is subject to the UCP (1974 Revision), ICC Pub. No. 290.

We hereby agree with bona fide holders that all drafts drawn under and in compliance with the terms of this credit shall meet with due honor.

　　　　　　　　　　　　Sincerely yours,

　　　　　　　　　　　　FIRST BANK, N.A.

　　　　　　　　　By: _____

DOCUMENT 17 **Standby Credit**

FIRST BANK, N.A.
Detroit, MI

Irrevocable Letter of Credit No.   Date:

BENEFICIARY: ACCOUNT PARTY:
Seller Co.   Buyer Co.
123 Main Street   101 Elm Street
Lawrence, Massachusetts   Grand Rapids, Michigan

Gentlemen:

We hereby open our irrevocable credit in your favor for the sum or
sums not exceeding a total of   Dollars ($)
available by your requests for payment to be made not later than 240
days after presentation of the following documents:

This Letter of Credit is valid until   , provided,
however, that this Letter of Credit will be automatically extended
without amendment for one (1) year from the present or any future
expiration date hereof, unless thirty (30) days prior to any such
expiration date the Issuing Bank elects not to renew this Letter of
Credit for such additional one (1) year period. The notice required
hereunder will be deemed to have been given when received by you.

This Letter of Credit is transferable and assignable in its entirety.

Except as otherwise herein provided, this Letter of Credit shall be
governed by the Michigan Uniform Commercial Code.

FIRST BANK, N.A.

By: _____

DOCUMENT 18 Invoice Credit

TELEGRAM aan (naam en plaatsnaam voluit)

NAAM BANK
WOONSTEDE   S.1982

Date:

(telegramadres en plaatsnaam onder de streep-tekst binnen de lijnen houden)

notify beneficiary that we issue herewith our irrevocable 'standby' credit nr. 60.S
date and place of expiry: S 1982 at our counters
applicant: Buyer Co. b.v., amsterdam
beneficiary: Seller Co.

amount: S +/- 5 o/o
credit available with us, by payment at sight
neither partshipment nor transshipment allowed
documents required:
1. commercial invoice covering the delivery of mton
    five pet moless at mton,
    for rotterdam, quality as per applicant's contract
    nr. p.
2. a signed statement by an officer of Seller Co. certifying,
    that invoice as in (1) above was presented for payment to
    Buyer Co. and that payment was not made against receipt of
    invoice, at the latest   days from date of invoice.

special instructions:
a. this standby credit will become null and void against payment
    by
    product delivered as described above in case that such a
    payment is to be made through you we shall cover you in
    accordance with your wishes but anticipating any claim under
    this standby please give us the name of your main usdollrs-
    correspondent in your acknowledgement of receipt of this
    credit
b. all banking charges and commissions in connection with this
    credit outside the netherlands are for beneficiary's account
c. documents are to be forwarded to us in one lot
d. documents presented more than 21 days after bill of lading
    date are acceptable
e. charter-party bills of lading are acceptable
in reimbursement we shall cover the remitting party in accordance
with their wishes upon receipt by us of credit-complying documents
please advise beneficiary u r g e n t l y without adding your
confirmation

subject to ucp 1974 revision, i.c.c. publication nr. 290

amsterdam, 1983
first bank

DOCUMENT 19 **Indemnity**

GUARANTY FOR DELIVERY OF CARGO OR ISSUANCE OF CARRIER'S CERTIFICATE WITHOUT SURRENDER OF PROPERLY ENDORSED NEGOTIABLE BILL OF LADING

Guaranty No.

Amount:

Gentlemen:

S/S or M/S:

Voy. No.

Vessel Line:

B/L No. & Date:

Port of Shipment:

Port of Discharge:

Description of Goods:

We are advised that the above-described shipment has been discharged at port of and is available for delivery upon presentation of an original bill of lading properly endorsed. While we are otherwise entitled to the delivery of this shipment, we are unable to obtain such delivery because of our present inability to produce and surrender the bill or bills of lading issued for the goods due to the nonarrival, or loss, of all of the original bills of lading.

Accordingly, we desire, and request, that you issue Carrier's Certificate in the name of and release the shipment to   without the prior surrender of an original bill of lading, properly endorsed; and in consideration of your releasing the goods to us or to the person named previously, we jointly and severally undertake, agree, represent, and warrant, as follows:

1. To pay on demand all freights, and other charges that may be due or may appear to be due and chargeable to the said goods.

2. To indemnify and save you, the vessel, her owners, charterers, operators, the master and agents, their successors in interest, heirs, and assigns, harmless from all claims, liabilities, demands, actions, expenses, and consequences of whatever nature that may arise out of or be made against you or any of you, including losses, damages, interest, legal costs, or any other expenses that you or any of you may sustain or incur by reason of making such delivery prior to the receipt of an original order bill.

3. To make every reasonable effort to procure and to subsequently surrender to you an original bill properly endorsed.

4. We are otherwise entitled to the delivery of such merchandise, and no other person than those joining herein have any claim to such delivery.

5. In order to induce you and others to whom these undertakings are made to accept this guaranty and release the cargo, we hereby warrant and represent that all of the financial interests or other facts necessary to justify making of this guarantee by us exist to the full extent required for this purpose; and that the persons executing for and on behalf of each of the undersigned has full authority to do so. This representation of fact is made with the full knowledge that you will rely thereon in releasing the cargo.

6. It is understood that as and when you shall have been provided with the aforesaid bills of lading, this undertaking will thereupon terminate.

_____

(Person claiming right of delivery)

By _____

_____

Dated: _____   By _____

DOCUMENT 20   Deferred Payment Credit

FIRST BANK, N.A.
Detroit, MI

Irrevocable Letter of Credit No.   Date:

BENEFICIARY: ACCOUNT PARTY:
Seller Co.   Buyer Co.
123 Main Street   101 Elm Street
Lawrence, Massachusetts   Grand Rapids, Michigan

Gentlemen:

We hereby open our irrevocable credit in your favor for the sum or
sums not exceeding a total of
                  Dollars ($) available by
your requests for payment to be made not later than 240 days after
presentation of the following documents:

All documents must be submitted to us on or before

We engage that we will honor your requests for payment made under
and in compliance with the terms of this advice. Requests must
recite that they are made under First Bank, N.A. Irrevocable Letter
of Credit No.

                    Yours truly,

                    FIRST BANK, N.A.

                    By: _____
                          Authorized Signature

DOCUMENT 21 **Negotiation Credit Designating Negotiating Bank**

FIRST BANK, N.A.
123 Main Street
New York, NY

TO: Seller Corp.   Irrevocable Letter of   January 2, 19
                       Credit No.

We issue our irrevocable credit in your favor for   by
your drafts to be drawn on
at sight for full C & F invoice value of merchandise purporting to
be
from Any European Port to Chittagong. Drafts bearing clause "Drawn
under First Bank, N.A. Letter of Credit No.   " are to be
accompanied by the following shipping documents unless otherwise
specified:

1. Your signed invoices in octuplicate certifying merchandise to be
   of   origin. Six copies of the invoices must accompany original documents and the remaining copies to accompany
   duplicate documents. Goods are being imported by the openers
   under Registration No.   against L/C Application
   Form No.   , both of which numbers should appear in
   the invoices along with the Bangladesh Bank Registration Number.

2. On board negotiable clean Ocean Bills of Lading marked Freight
   prepaid evidencing Shipment by Steamer made out to the order of
   Opening Bank or 'To Order' and endorsed to the Opening Bank.
   All negotiable copies are required. Through Railway Bills of
   Lading are unacceptable. Bill of Lading must be marked notify
   the Bank and openers of credit.

3. Insurance covered in Bangladesh. Declaration of shipment to be
   made to Bogra, Bangladesh, quoting their cover note No.
   dated   , and also direct to the importer quoting
   this Letter of Credit number. A copy of such declaration to
   accompany the shipping documents at the time of negotiation.

ADDITIONAL CONDITIONS:

1. All negotiation charges are on buyer's account.

2. Six additional copies of Invoice and nonnegotiable copy of
   shipping order to be sent to the importer immediately after
   shipment.

Bills of Lading must be dated not later than

Drafts must be dated and negotiated not later than within 15 days
from the date of the Bill of Lading. Transmitted through
NEGOTIATING BANK, LTD., who are authorized to negotiate your drafts.

                    FIRST BANK, N.A.

                    By: _____

DOCUMENT 22 **Agent's Credit***

Dear Sir
                     Washington. U.S. of America. July 4. 1803

In the journey which you are about to undertake for the discovery of the course and source of the Missisipi, and of the most convenient water communication from thence to the Pacific ocean, your party being small, it is to be expected that you will encounter considerable dangers from the Indian inhabitants. should you escape those dangers and reach the Pacific ocean, you may find it imprudent to hazard a return the same way, and be forced to seek a passage round by sea in such vessels as you may find on the Western coast. but you will be without money, without clothes, & other necessaries; as a sufficient supply cannot be carried with you from hence. your resource in that case can only be in the credit of the US. for which purpose I hereby authorise you to draw on the Secretaries of State, of the Treasury, of War & of the Navy of the US. according as you may find your draughts will be most negociable, for the purpose of obtaining money or necessaries for yourself & your men: and I solemnly pledge the faith of the United States that these draughts shall be paid punctually at the date they are made payable. I also ask of the Consuls, agents, merchants & citizens of any nation with which we have intercourse or amity, to furnish you with those sup-plies which your necessities may call for, assuring them of honorable and prompt retribution. and our own Consuls in foreign parts where you may happen to be, are hereby instructed & required to be aiding & assisting to you in whatsoever may be necessary for procuring your return back to the United States. And to give more entire satisfaction & confidence to those who may be disposed to aid you I Thomas Jefferson, President of the United States of America, have written this letter of general credit for you with my own hand, and signed it with my name.

                                     Th: Jefferson

To
   Capt. Meriwether Lewis.

* The existence of this letter was brought to the attention of the author by Prof. Gerald T. Dunne of the Saint Louis University School of Law and is reproduced with the permission of the Missouri Historical Society.

DOCUMENT 23 Letter of Credit in Lieu of Developer's Bond

FIRST BANK, N.A.
Detroit, MI

IRREVOCABLE LETTER OF CREDIT

City of East Bay
P.O. Box 1234
East Bay, MI 10000-0001

GENTLEMEN:

You are hereby authorized to draw on us for the account of _____ up to an aggregate amount of $_____ available by your drafts at sight to be accompanied by the original of this Letter of Credit and the following documents:

1. Written statement signed by the Director of Financial Services or designee of the City of East Bay and stating "[*developer*] has failed to construct [*infrastructure type*] in [*subdivision name*] in accordance with the terms of the [*subdivision name*] Construction Agreement dated _____, 19__"; or

2. Written statement signed by the Director of Financial Services or designee of the City of East Bay stating "payment is due to the City for construction of [*infrastructure type*] within [*subdivision name*] in accordance with the terms of the [*subdivision name*] Construction Agreement dated _____, 19__, in the amount shown on the draft that accompanies this written statement"; or

3. Written statement signed by the Director of Financial Services or designee of the City of East Bay stating "[*developer*] has failed to renew or replace this letter of credit at least forty-five (45) days prior to its expiration date"; or

4. Written statement signed by the Director of Financial Services or designee of the City of East Bay stating "[*financial institution*] has failed to maintain a minimum rating acceptable to the City of East Bay under the financial institution rating system in effect at the time [*financial institution*] issued its Irrevocable Letter of Credit No. _____ to the City of East Bay"; or

5. Written statement signed by the Director of Financial Services or designee of the City of East Bay stating "[*financial institution*] has acquired an interest in [*subdivision name*].

The conditions of draw detailed above are governed by the following:

1. Evidence of cure of the circumstance(s) occasioning the draw satisfactory to the City may be provided within fourteen (14) days of date of the drawing document. If a letter from the City of East Bay acknowledging cure is not received by the fourteenth day, the draft will be honored on the fifteenth day after date of the drawing document.

2. Reductions in the face amount of this credit shall occur for work secured by this credit that is completed and accepted by the City of East Bay.

3. Draws under this credit for failure to construct work secured by this credit may, in the sole discretion of the City, be utilized to complete the construction or may be placed in an interest-bearing account and held in escrow. Upon completion of the work by a party other than the City, the moneys held in escrow, including interest, shall be returned to [*developer*]. Any funds remaining after completion of the work by the City shall likewise be returned to [*developer*].

4. Draws under condition 5 above shall be discretionary, but such draws shall be within the sole discretion of the City of East Bay.

Multiple drafts may be presented.

Drafts must be presented to drawee bank not later than _____, 19__, all drafts must state on their face "DRAWN UNDER [*financial institution*] IRREVOCABLE LETTER OF CREDIT NO. _____.

We hereby engage with you, that all drafts drawn under and in compliance with the terms of this credit will be duly honored, if drawn and presented for payment at our office in _____, on or before the expiration date of this credit.

We further state and agree that this letter of credit is irrevocable prior to the expiration date unless all parties, including for all purposes the City of East Bay, consent to such a revocation in writing. In the event of wrongful dishonor, we will reimburse the City for all court costs, investigative costs and reasonable attorney fees incurred by the City in enforcing this letter of credit according to its terms.

Except so far as otherwise expressly stated, this Letter of Credit is subject to the Uniform Customs and Practice for Documentary Credits (1983 Revision), International Chamber of Commerce Publication No. 400.

                    Very truly yours,

                    [*authorized signature*]

DOCUMENT 24   **Letter of Credit With Evergreen Clause**

IRREVOCABLE LETTER OF CREDIT NO. _____

_____, 19__

TO:

We hereby establish this irrevocable Letter of Credit in favor of the aforesaid
addressee ("Beneficiary") for drawings up to United States $_____ effective
immediately. This Letter of Credit is issued, presentable, and payable at our
office at [issuing bank's address] and expires with our close of business on
_____, 19__.

We hereby undertake to promptly honor your sight draft(s) drawn on us, indicating
our Credit No. _____, for all or any part of this Credit if presented at our
office, specified in paragraph one, on or before the expiry date or any extended
expiry date.

Except as expressly stated herein, this undertaking is not subject to any
agreement, condition, or qualification. The obligation of [issuing bank] under
this Letter of Credit is the individual obligation of [issuing bank] and is in no
way contingent upon reimbursement with respect thereto.

It is a condition of this Letter of Credit that it is deemed to be automatically
extended without amendment for one year from the expiry date hereof, or any future
expiration date, unless 30 days prior to any expiration date we notify you by
registered mail that we elect not to consider this Letter of Credit renewed for any
such additional period.

This Letter of Credit is subject to and governed by the laws of the State of New
York and the 1983 revision of the Uniform Customs and Practice for Documentary
Credits of the International Chamber of Commerce (Publication 400), and, in the
event of any conflict, the laws of the State of New York will control. If this
Credit expires during an interruption of business as described in Article 19 of
said Publication 400, the bank hereby specifically agrees to effect payment if this
Credit is drawn against within 30 days after the resumption of business.

Very truly yours,

[issuing bank]

DOCUMENT 25 **Amendment to Letter of Credit**

FIRST BANK, N.A.
123 Main Street
East Bay, MI   10000

Amendment to Documentary Credit No. _____   Dated _____, 19__

Advising Bank	Amendment Number _____
Beneficiary	[ ] This refers to our cable of today through the Advising Bank. [ ] This Amendment is forwarded to the Advising Bank by Air Mail.
Applicant	This Amendment is to be considered part of the Letter of Credit described above and must be attached thereto.

Dear Sirs:

The above described Credit is amended as follows:

All Other Terms and Conditions remain unchanged.

The advising Bank is requested to inform the beneficiary of this amendment.	Advising Bank's Notification
Sincerely, _____ Issuing Bank's Authorized Signature	Place, Date, Name and Signature of Advising Bank

DOCUMENT 26 Assignment of Letter of Credit Proceeds

FIRST BANK, N.A.
123 Main Street
East Bay, MI   10000

_____, 19__   Re: Credit _____
                             Issued by: _____

                             First Bank, N.A. Advice No. _____

Gentlemen:

We hereby authorize you to pay the proceeds of each draft, drawn by us, payable to our order, under and in compliance with the above described Letter of Credit (herein called the "Credit"), if and when such draft is honored by you, as follows:

(1) _____%, not exceeding $_____ or

(2) At the rate of $_____ per _____ , not exeeding $ _____ or

(3) $_____ to: _____, whose address is _____ (herein called the "Designated Payee"), and to pay the balance, if any, of such proceeds to us.

This instrument and your acceptance thereof is not a transfer of the Credit, does not give the Designated Payee any interest therein and does not affect our or your right to agree to amendments thereto, the cancelation thereof, or any substitution therefor .

We warrant to you that we have not, and will not, by negotiation of drafts or otherwise, assign the right to receive the whole or any part of such proceeds or give any other authorization or direction to make any payment thereof to any third party.

Please advise the Designated Payee of your acceptance of this instrument, and, in consideration thereof, we agree that this instrument is irrevocable.

In the event of any refusal by you to make any payment upon any draft drawn under the Credit, the Designated Payee will not have any rights as against you and shall be bound by your determination.

We agree to indemnify you and hold you harmless for any cost, liability, or expense to which you may become subject in connection with this instrument.

We transmit to you herewith the Credit (including all amendments, if any) and request you to note thereon the foregoing authorization and direction, and also enclose our check for $_____, to cover your charges.

Very truly yours,   GUARANTEE OF SIGNATURE

                                     Name of Bank: _____

                                     By: _____
_____   [authorized signature]
[authorized signature and
title of beneficiary]

_____, 19__ .   FIRST BANK, N.A.

We accept the foregoing instrument.   By: _____
                                          [authorized signature]

DOCUMENT 27 **Transfer of Letter of Credit in Its Entirety**

Transfer of Letter of Credit in Its Entirety
(no substitution of invoices)

To: FIRST BANK, N.A.   From: [*beneficiary's name and address*]
  123 Main Street
  East Bay, MI 10000

Re: Credit No. _____   issued by _____
  Advice No. _____

We, the undersigned beneficiary, hereby request you to transfer the referenced Letter of Credit in its entirety to _____, whose address is _____ (herein called the "Transferee"), with no changes in the terms and conditions of the Letter of Credit.

We are returning the original instrument to you in order that you may deliver it to the Transferee, together with your customary letter of transfer.

Any amendments to the Letter of Credit that you may issue or receive are to be advised by you directly to the Transferee, and the documents (including drafts if required under the Credit) of the Transferee are to be processed by you (or any intermediary), without our intervention and without any further responsibility on your part to us.

We also

( ) enclose our certified check or cashier's check
( ) authorize you to debit our account no. _____ with you

for $_____ to cover your fee.

In addition, we agree to pay to you, on demand, any expenses that may be incurred by you in connection with this transfer.

_____
[*name of beneficiary*]

_____   By: _____
[*name of bank*]   [*authorized signature*]

By: _____   _____
  [*authorized signature*]   [*title*]

_____
[*title*]

                                              Date _____, 19__

DOCUMENT 28   Partial Transfer of Letter of Credit

Partial Transfer of Letter of Credit
(with substitution of invoices)

To: FIRST BANK, N.A.   From: [*beneficiary's name and address*]
    123 Main Street
    East Bay, MI 10000

Re: Credit No. _____   issued by: _____
    Advice No. _____

We, the undersigned beneficiary, hereby request you to transfer the referenced Letter of Credit and issue a Transfer Advice of Letter of Credit to: _____, whose address is _____ (herein called the "Transferee"), with no changes in the terms and conditions of the Letter of Credit other than the following changes that are permissible in accordance with Article 54 of the Uniform Customs and Practice for Documentary Credits, 1983 Revision, International Chamber of Commerce Publication No. 400:

1. Amount $_____
2. Expiry Date _____ 19 __
3. Quantity of Merchandise/Unit Price _____
4. Other Changes _____

We will deliver to you, on or before the date on which the Transferee's documents are presented to you for payment or negotiation or acceptance, our own invoices (and drafts, if required under the credit), which you are authorized to substitute for those presented by or on behalf of the Transferee. Upon such substitution of our invoices (and drafts), you will remit to us in settlement of our drawing under the credit for the difference, if any, between our invoices and the Transferee's invoices, provided, of course, that the Transferee's documents and our invoices (and drafts) conform with the conditions of the credit and are honored by the issuing bank (or the confirming bank, if any).

If, for any reason, you should not receive proper invoices (and drafts) from us within the period of time specified above, you shall process the Transferee's documents under the Credit and forward them to the party for whose account the credit was issued (or any intermediary), without our intervention and without any responsibility on your part to us.

Any amendments to the Letter of Credit that you may receive are to be advised to us, and we promptly shall notify you if any such amendments are acceptable, and if they are to be advised to the Transferee. Any amendment to the Letter of Credit that effects the Transfer Advice of Letter of Credit will be subject to Transferee's acceptance.

Kindly notify the Transferee of the Terms and Conditions of the credit as transferred, and, after noting the transfer of the original instrument, which we are forwarding to you herewith, please retain it and send us a copy of the instrument, together with a copy of your notification to the Transferee.

We also

( ) enclose our certified check or cashier's check
( ) authorize you to debit our account no. _____ with you

for $_____ to cover your fee.

In addition, we agree to pay to you, on demand, any expenses that may be incurred by you in connection with this transfer.

_____
[name of beneficiary]

By: _____
_____   [authorized signature]
[name of bank]

By: _____   _____
     [authorized signature]   [title]

_____   _____
[title]   [telephone number]

_____   Date _____
[telephone number]

DOCUMENT 29 **Advice of Transfer of Letter of Credit**

FIRST BANK, N.A.

Transfer of Credit

Credit No. _____

_____
Place   Date

Drafts drawn under this transfer must be
marked "Drawn Under"

Gentlemen:

First National Bank, N.A., has established its Irrevocable Transferable Letter of
Credit No. _____ in favor of _____ for account of _____.
Against this credit the beneficiaries have transferred to you the sum of $_____
available by your drafts drawn at _____ on _____, 19__, and
accompanied by the following documents:_____
_____
_____
_____.

The above-mentioned correspondent engages with you that drafts drawn under and in
compliance with the terms of this transfer will be duly honored on due presentation
and delivery of documents as specified if presented at this office on or before
_____, 19__.

The amount and date of each negotiation must be endorsed by the negotiating bank.

This letter is solely an advice of transfer and conveys no engagement by us.

Yours truly,

Provisions Applicable to This Transfer

"This credit is subject to the Uniform
Customs and Practice for Documentary
Credits (1983 Revision), International
Chamber of Commerce, Document No. 400."

DOCUMENT 30 Advice of Partial Transfer of Letter of Credit

FIRST BANK, N.A.

Advice of Partial Transfer of Letter of Credit

No. _____

_____, 19__

Second Bank, N.A.
123 Main Street
New York, NY 10000

Re: Credit No.   Dated: _____, 19__
Our Ref. No.
In favor of

_____
[original beneficiary]

Gentlemen:

This is to advise you that the above-mentioned original beneficiary has irrevocably transferred to you under date of _____, 19__ a part of their rights in the captioned credit as follows:

1. Amount: _____

2. Quantity of merchandise: _____

3. Latest shipping date: _____

4. Expiration date: _____, 19__

Other terms and conditions of the credit as transferred are as per the attached sheet signed by us.

The amount and date of each negotiation must be endorsed on the reverse hereof by the negotiating bank.

This letter is solely an advice of transfer and conveys no engagement by us.

Yours truly,

[authorized signature]

"This advice is subject to the Uniform Customs
and Practice for Documentary Credits (1983
Revision), International Chamber of Commerce
Document No. 400."

DOCUMENT 31 **Clean Letter of Credit**

FIRST BANK, N.A.
East Bay, MI

IRREVOCABLE LETTER OF CREDIT

Beneficiary: _____   Letter of Credit No. _____
                                       Date _____

Gentlemen:

For the account of _____, we hereby authorize you to draw on us at sight up to an aggregate amount of _____ dollars ($_____).

This Letter of Credit is irrevocable, unconditional, and nontransferable.

Drafts drawn under this Letter of Credit must specify the letter of credit number and must be presented at the office identified below not later than _____, 19__.

This Letter of Credit sets forth in full the terms of our obligations to you, and such undertaking shall not in any way be modified or amplified by any agreement in which this Letter of Credit relates, and any such reference shall not be deemed to incorporate herein by reference any agreement.

We engage with you that sight drafts drawn under, and in compliance with, the terms of this Letter of Credit will be duly honored at _____.

                              Yours very truly,

                              FIRST BANK, N.A.

                              By: _____

Glossary of
Letter of Credit Terms

The following terms appear with some frequency in letter of credit transactions. The citations are mostly representative rather than definitive; that is, they refer the reader to a case or a journal article that uses the term but may not define it.

abstraction principle   Used to define the idea that the credit is independent of the underlying contract and other incidents of the broad credit transaction.

> See B. Kozolchyk, "Letters of Credit," in IX International Encyclopedia of Comparative Law ch. 5, at 113 (1980); Note, "The Trade Embargo and the Irrevocable Letter of Credit," 1 Ariz. J. Int'l & Comp. L. 213, 217 (1982).

accept   To engage to honor a time draft according to its terms.

> See U.C.C. § 3-410; cf. *pay.*

acceptance credit   Credit entailing the engagement to accept and pay time drafts drawn on the issuer or on someone else.

accountee   Term sometimes used to designate the account party, the customer.

> See Corporacion De Mercadeo Agricola v. Mellon Bank Int'l, 608 F.2d 43, 45 (2d Cir. 1979).

account party   Party that applies to the issuing or opening bank for the issuance of the letter of credit. The Uniform Commercial Code uses the term "customer."

> See U.C.C. § 5-103(1)(g).

accredited party   Beneficiary of a commercial letter of credit.

See McCurdy, "Commercial Letters of Credit" (pt. 1), 35 Harv. L. Rev. 539, 544 (1922).

accrediting party   Sometimes said of the negotiating bank.

See McCurdy, "Commercial Letters of Credit" (pt. 1), 35 Harv. L. Rev. 539, 544 (1922).

advice   In letter of credit settings, this term refers to a communication that relates to the terms of a credit. It may refer to the credit itself, to a preliminary advice, to a confirmation, or to a notice from an advising bank that the credit has been issued.

See U.C.C. §§ 5-103(1)(e), 5-103(1)(f); U.C.P. arts. 13, 14; Samuel Kronman & Co. v. Public Nat'l Bank, 218 A.D. 624, 218 N.Y.S. 616 (1926); cf. *advice of credit; advice for advising bank; advice for beneficiary.* In Titanium Metals Corp. of Am. v. Space Metals, Inc., 529 P.2d 431 (Utah 1974), a bank used an "advice" to notify the beneficiary that the bank was dishonoring the beneficiary's demands for payment.

advice for advising bank   Term used to describe the communication from the issuing bank to the advising bank.

See International Chamber of Commerce, "Standard Forms for Issuing Documentary Credits," ICC Pub. No. 323, at 5 (1978).

advice for beneficiary   Name the International Chamber of Commerce gives to the credit issued by the issuing bank.

See International Chamber of Commerce, "Standard Forms for Issuing Documentary Credits," ICC Pub. No. 323, at 5 (1978).

advice of credit   Communication from a party, usually a bank, advising a beneficiary that a second bank, usually a correspondent of the advising bank, has opened a credit in favor of the beneficiary.

See App. C, Doc. 2.

advising bank   Bank that is usually a correspondent of the issuing bank and that notifies the beneficiary that the credit has issued. An advising bank may, but does not always, confirm the credit.

See U.C.C. § 5-103(1)(e); U.C.P. art. 8.

agented credit   When a number of issuers participate in a credit engagement by issuing a master credit, they may designate one of their number to deal with the beneficiary. Such a credit is "agented."

See Ryan, "Letters of Credit Supporting Debt for Borrowed Money: The Standby as Backup," 100 Banking L.J. 404, 421 (1983).

all-risk insurance   Term describing the coverage of an insurance policy insuring goods during transport. All-risk insurance does not cover every risk and excludes war, civil disturbance, and spoilage.

A. Watson, Finance of International Trade 49 (2d ed. 1981); cf. *free of capture and seizure; strikes, riots, and civil commotions; inherent vice.*

anticipatory credit   "Red clause" or "green clause" credit that permits the beneficiary to borrow on the credit before he complies with its terms.

See H. Gutteridge & M. Megrah, The Law of Bankers' Commercial Credits 12 (4th ed. 1968).

applicant   Account party or customer.

See FDIC v. Freudenfeld, 492 F. Supp. 763, 767 (E.D. Wis. 1980).

application   Agreement between the account party and the issuer. This document usually describes the terms that the issuer should incorporate in the credit and covers the arrangements for the issuer's reimbursement by the account party.

See Transamerica Delaval, Inc. v. Citibank, N.A., 545 F. Supp. 200 (S.D.N.Y. 1982); App. C, Doc. 14.

assignable credit   Traditionally, credit whose proceeds the beneficiary has the right to assign. Sometimes a credit under which the beneficiary may assign his right to draw.

See U.C.C. § 5-116; U.C.P. arts. 54, 55; Axworthy, "The Revisions of the Uniform Customs on Documentary Credits," 1971 J. Bus. L. 38, 47; cf. *transferable credit.*

assured person   Person designated in a policy or certificate of insurance as the insured party.

See A. Watson, Finance of International Trade 142 (2d ed. 1981).

autonomy principle   Principle that the credit is independent of the underlying transaction and other related transactions.

See Graham & Geva, "Standby Credits in Canada," 9 Can. Bus. L.J. 180, 181 (1984). Cf. *abstraction principle.*

available at   A credit is often payable at the counters of a correspondent of the issuer. In that case, the credit may recite that it is "available at" the correspondent.

See Funk, "Letters of Credit: UCC Article 5 and the Uniform Customs and Practice," 11 How. L.J. 88, 97 (1965).

back-to-back credit   Sometimes the beneficiary of a credit (a seller) will use the credit (by pledge or otherwise) to induce a second bank to issue a second credit (the back-to-back credit) in favor of the first beneficiary's supplier.

See Decker Steel Co. v. Exchange Nat'l Bank, 330 F.2d 82, 86 (7th Cir. 1964); Asociacion De Azucareros De Guat. v. United States Nat'l Bank, 423 F.2d 638 (9th Cir. 1970); Kingdom of Swed. v. New York Trust Co., 197 Misc. 431, 96 N.Y.S.2d 779 (Sup. Ct. 1949).

backup credit   Second credit used to secure the issuer of the original credit for a portion of its liability. The backup credit is in the nature of a participation agreement between the two issuers.

See Ryan, "Letters of Credit Supporting Debt for Borrowed Money: The Standby as Backup," 100 Banking L.J. 404, 418 (1983).

backup standby   A standby credit from an issuer in favor of the issuer of another credit in order to secure the first issuer for a portion of its standby undertaking. Banks sometimes use the backup standby credits as participations.

See Comptroller of the Currency, Staff Interpretive Letter No. 412, reprinted in [1988–1989 Transfer Binder] Fed. Banking L. Rep. (CCH) ¶ 85,636 (Jan. 26, 1988).

banker's acceptance   Time or usance draft that the drawee bank has honored by acceptance. An acceptance is noted on the face of the draft by a stamp designating the name of the accepting bank and the date, and it bears the signature of an authorized bank employee.

See U.C.C. § 3-410; H. Harfield, Bank Credits and Acceptances (5th ed. 1974).

beneficiary of a credit   Person who can draw or demand payment under the credit.

U.C.C. § 5-103(1)(d); Housing Sec., Inc. v. Maine Nat'l Bank, 391 A.2d 311, 315 (Me. 1978).

bill of exchange   Draft, that is, a negotiable order to pay money.

See Pillans v. Van Mierop, 97 Eng. Rep. 1035 (K.B. 1765) (report speaks of instrument as "bill," "bill of exchange," and "draught"); U.C.C. § 3-104(2)(a).

breach of warranty   In letter of credit law, the failure of a party to fulfill the warranties on transfer and presentment.

See U.C.C. § 5-111.

buyer's credit   Credit given by the issuer to an agent to induce sellers to give the agent credit. The credit was often "open"; that is, it did not specify any particular beneficiary.

See H. Finkelstein, Legal Aspects of Commercial Letters of Credit 18 (1930); Bank of Seneca v. First Nat'l Bank, 105 Mo. App. 722, 78 S.W. 1092 (Kansas City Ct. App. 1904); cf. *general credit.*

cashing   Said of the process whereby the beneficiary presents a draft or demand for payment and the issuer honors such a draft or demand.

See Edgewater Constr. Co. v. Percy Wilson Mortgage & Fin. Corp., 44 Ill. App. 3d 220, 220, 357 N.E.2d 1307, 1309 (1976).

certificate of insurance   Evidence of insurance prepared by a shipper or his agent and countersigned by an authorized agent of the insurance company.

See App. C, Doc. 7.

certificate of origin   Certificate signed by an authorized agent of the seller or other designated person, such as the secretary of the local chamber of commerce, specifying the country of origin of the goods. Sometimes the certificate of origin is visaed by the consul of the country of importation.

See App. C, Doc. 10.

charterer   In maritime law, party who "leases" the vessel from the owner for the transportation of goods.

See Pubali Bank v. City Nat'l Bank, 676 F.2d 1326, 1327 (9th Cir. 1982).

charter party   Admiralty term for a contract with the owner of a vessel for the use of the entire vessel for one or more voyages.

See Pubali Bank v. City Nat'l Bank, 676 F.2d 1326, 1327 (9th Cir. 1982); Venizelos, S.A. v. Chase Manhattan Bank, N.A., 425 F.2d 461, 463 (2d Cir. 1970).

charter party bill of lading   Bill of lading that indicates that the shipper has chartered the entire vessel for the shipment.

See U.C.P. art. 25(c).

circular credit   Credit permitting the drawer to obtain honor of his drafts at more than one designated payor.

Sec Ufitec, S.A. v. Trade Bank & Trust Co., 21 A.D.2d 187, 189, 249 N.Y.S.2d 557, 559 (1964), aff'd, 16 N.Y.2d 698, 209 N.E.2d 551, 261 N.Y.S.2d 893 (1965); Hershey, "Letters of Credit," 32 Harv. L. Rev. 1, 5 (1918).

claused bill   Bill of lading that is "dirty" or "unclean," that is, a bill that contains a notation to the effect that the merchandise or the packages are damaged or in disrepair.

See U.C.P. art. 34(a); cf. *clean bill of lading.*

clean bill of lading   Bill of lading that bears no notation indicating that the goods or packages may be damaged or in disrepair.

See U.C.P. art. 34(a); Bank of Am. Nat'l Trust & Sav. Ass'n v. Liberty Nat'l Bank & Trust Co., 116 F. Supp. 233, 238 (W.D. Okla. 1953), aff'd, 218 F.2d 831 (10th Cir. 1955); International Chamber of Commerce, "The Problem of Clean Bills of Lading," ICC Pub. No. 283 (1963); Axworthy, "The Revisions of the Uniform Customs on Documentary Credits," J. Bus. L. 38, 43 (1971); cf. *dirty bill of lading; claused bill.*

clean credit   Credit that requires no documents other than a draft or other simple demand for payment, or perhaps a demand and a certificate.

See American Coleman Co. v. Intrawest Bank, 887 F.2d 1382 (10th Cir. 1989) (parties' designating as "clean" credit that called for certificate of default); GATX Leasing Corp. v. Capital Bank & Trust Co., 717 F. Supp. 1160 (M.D. La. 1988) (same); Baker v. National Boulevard Bank, 399 F. Supp. 1021, 1024 (N.D. Ill. 1975); American Nat'l Bank & Trust Co. v. Banco Nacional De Nicaragua, 231 Ala. 614, 620, 166 So. 8, 13 (Ala. 1936); Fair Pavilions, Inc. v. First Nat'l City Bank, 24 A.D.2d 109, 110, 264 N.Y.S.2d 255, 256 (1965), rev'd, 19 N.Y.2d 512, 227 N.E.2d 839, 281 N.Y.S.2d 23 (1967). In East Girard Sav. Ass'n v. Citizens Nat'l Bank & Trust Co., 593 F.2d 598, 601 (5th Cir. 1979), the court took the view that a credit calling for a certificate was a documentary credit. See also Housing Sec., Inc. v. Maine Nat'l Bank, 391 A.2d 311, 319 (Me. 1978) (written notice accompanied by letter of credit is not documentary demand); Scarsdale Nat'l Bank & Trust Co. v. Toronto-Dominion Bank, 533 F. Supp. 378, 380 (S.D.N.Y. 1982) ("clean" means no accompanying documents).

collection basis   When documents do not conform to the credit's requirements, the beneficiary may ask that his draft be presented on a "collection basis," that is, that it be presented as any other draft, not as one drawn under a letter of credit.

See Merchants Bank v. Credit Suisse Bank, 585 F. Supp. 304 (S.D.N.Y. 1984).

combined transport   Shipment of goods by more than one mode (e.g., truck and steamship, truck and railroad). Also called multimodal transport.

See International Chamber of Commerce, "Uniform Rules for a Combined Transport Document," ICC Pub. No. 298 (1975); Jhirad, "Uniform Customs and Practice for Documentary Credits, 1974 Revision: The Principal Emendations of the 1962 Text," 9 U.C.C. L.J. 109, 111 (1976).

combined transport document   Document of title issued to a shipper when the goods will be transported by more than one mode of transportation (e.g., by railroad and steamship).

See International Chamber of Commerce, "Uniform Rules for a Combined Transport Document," ICC Pub. No. 298 (1975).

commercial contract   The underlying contract, when it is one for the sale of goods.

See B. Wheble, "UCP 1974/1983 Revisions Compared and Explained (Documentary Credits)," ICC Pub. No. 411, at 13 (1984).

commercial credit   Sometimes applied to a credit issued in connection with the purchase and sale of goods. It was used originally to distinguish this type of credit from the precommercial buyer's and traveler's letters of credit.

See Republic Nat'l Bank v. Northwest Nat'l Bank, 578 S.W.2d 109, 113 (Tex. 1978); Kingdom of Swed. v. New York Trust Co., 197 Misc. 431, 441, 96 N.Y.S.2d 779, 787 (Sup. Ct. 1949); cf. *standby credit.*

commercial invoice   Statement of charges and description of goods, all under the name of the seller.

See App. C, Doc. 5.

commercial parties   In the commercial credit transaction, the buyer (account party) and the seller (beneficiary) are the commercial parties.

> See Wheble, "Uniform Customs and Practice for Documentary Credits (1974 Revision)," 1975 J. Bus. L. 281, 282.

commercials   Credits, not standby credits, that secure payment under a contract for the sale of goods. Cf. *commercial credit*; *standby credit*.

commission agent   Purchasing agent, the analogue to the factor. Until the beginning of this century, commission brokers would travel to distant markets or ports and acquire merchandise for their principals. Often these brokers carried letters of credit with them addressed to the world in general and engaging to honor the drafts of persons who sold the brokers on credit.

> See Union Bank v. Executors of John G. Coster, 3 N.Y. 203 (1850); cf. *buyer's credit*.

complete shipment   Shipment of goods by a beneficiary that, as the documents submitted under the letter of credit indicate, complies with the quantity term in the conditions of the letter of credit or meets either the 5 percent or 10 percent leeway rule.

> See U.C.P. art. 43.

confirmed credit   (1) Credit to which a party, usually a bank that does business in the market of the beneficiary, has added its own primary obligation by engaging to pay, accept, or negotiate pursuant to the terms of the credit.

> See U.C.C. § 2-325(3); U.C.P. art. 10(b); Venizelos, S.A. v. Chase Manhattan Bank, N.A., 425 F.2d 461, 463 (2d Cir. 1970).

(2) Formerly—and to some extent it is still true—English bankers and lawyers used the term "confirmed credit" to mean "irrevocable credit."

> See Mentschikoff, "Letters of Credit: The Need for Uniform Legislation," 23 U. Chi. L. Rev. 571, 589 n.72 (1956); Thayer, "Irrevocable Credits in International Commerce: Their Legal Nature," 36 Colum. L. Rev. 1031, 1034 (1936).

confirming bank   Advising bank that not only advises the beneficiary of the issuance of the letter but also adds its own obligation or that of a third party to honor drafts under the credit.

> See U.C.C. §§ 5-103(1)(f), 5-107(2); Venizelos, S.A. v. Chase Manhattan Bank, N.A., 425 F.2d 461, 463 (2d Cir. 1970); Barclays Bank D.C.O. v. Mercantile Nat'l Bank, 339 F. Supp. 457 (N.D. Ga. 1972), aff'd, 481 F.2d 1221 (5th Cir. 1973), cert. dismissed, 414 U.S. 1139 (1974).

consignee   Person designated in a shipping document as the person entitled to delivery of shipped goods at the destination point.

> See U.C.C. § 7-102(1)(b).

consular invoice   Invoice form, different from the commercial invoice, provided by the country of importation and signed by an official of that country, authorizing the importation of merchandise.

> See App. C, Doc. 9.

correspondent bank   Used in letter of credit circumstances to describe a bank in which the issuing bank usually maintains an account and at which the beneficiary of a letter of credit may present drafts under the credit.

cost and freight (C&F)   Shipment term wherein the seller of goods is required to bear the cost of transporting and delivering the goods to the destination. The term is used with a named destination (e.g., "C&F Rotterdam").

> See International Chamber of Commerce, "Incoterms," ICC Pub. No. 350, at 40 (1980).

cost, insurance, freight (CIF)   Shipment term wherein the seller of goods is required to bear the cost of not only transporting the goods for delivery to a named destination but also insuring the goods during that transport. The term is used in connection with a named destination (e.g., "CIF Bremen").

> See International Chamber of Commerce, "Incoterms," ICC Pub. No. 350, at 48 (1980).

countersigned   The necessity that a document be "countersigned" is a requirement that someone other than the issuer of the document sign it.

> In Eximetals Corp. v. Pinheiro Guimares, S.A., 73 A.D.2d 526, 422 N.Y.S.2d 684 (1979), aff'd, 51 N.Y.2d 865, 414 N.E.2d 399, 433 N.Y.S.2d 1019 (1980), the court held that the requirement of a countersignature by the plaintiff on an inspection certificate did not excuse the signature of the inspector on the certificate.

covered credit   Infrequently used to describe a credit payable against documents.

> See E. Ellinger, Documentary Letters of Credit 29 (1970); cf. *documentary credit.*

credit application agreement   See *application.*

credit available by acceptance   Referring to a time credit or acceptance credit, that is, a credit that stipulates that the beneficiary present a time draft for acceptance rather than a sight draft for payment.

> See App. C, Doc. 15.

credit available by negotiation   Referring to a credit that runs to drawers, endorsers, and bona fide holders of drafts drawn under the credit and that therefore includes a direct engagement to the negotiating bank to honor the credit.

> See International Chamber of Commerce, "Standard Forms for Issuing Documentary Credits," ICC Pub. No. 323, at 10 (1978).

credit available by payment   Referring to a sight credit that specifies the name and place of a drawee bank as a place of payment.

> See International Chamber of Commerce, "Standard Forms for Issuing Documentary Credits," ICC Pub. No. 323, at 9 (1978).

credit line   Aggregate amount to which a bank has committed itself to make loans to a designated borrower. A line of credit may be "clean"—that is, requiring no collateral from the borrower—or "secured"—that is, requiring collateral from the borrower. A line of credit is not a letter of credit, even though banks sometimes commit themselves to a line of credit in writing.

cumulative revolving credit A revolving credit under which the amount, by which draws and payments during the "revolution" period are less than the face amount of the credit, accumulate and are available during subsequent periods.

> Maullela, "Nature of Revolving and Installment L/Cs," Letter of Credit Update 13 (Dec. 1988). Cf. *revolving credit*.

customer Used in the Uniform Commercial Code to describe the party that applies for the credit.

> See U.C.C. § 5-103(1)(g); Edgewater Constr. Co. v. Percy Wilson Mortgage & Fin. Corp., 44 Ill. App. 3d 220, 227, 357 N.E.2d 1307, 1312 (1976); cf. *account party*.

customs invoice Invoice prepared by the seller on a form provided by the government of the importing country and used in clearing the merchandise through customs.

> See J. Harrington, Opening Financial Doors to International Trade—A Guide to Effective Use of Letters of Credit and Bankers Acceptances 18 (1980).

days date Used in a letter of credit, it is preceded by a number (e.g., "thirty days date") and requires the drawee or payor bank to place the presenter in funds a certain number of days after some date specified elsewhere in the letter of credit. For example, an issuing bank may undertake to honor drafts at ninety days date and stipulate that drafts are payable ninety days after the date of the bill of lading to be submitted with the draft.

> See American Bankers Association, Letters of Credit (Book 3—Payment and Reimbursement) 3 (1968); cf. *days sight*.

days sight Used in letters of credit, it is preceded by a number (e.g., "thirty days sight") and requires the drawee or payor bank to put the presenter of the draft in funds a certain number of days after the drawee or payor bank has honored the draft by accepting it.

> American Bankers Association, Letters of Credit (Book 3—Payment and Reimbursement) 3 (1968); cf. *banker's acceptance; days date*.

deferred payment credit   Credit that calls for payment a period of time after the beneficiary presents his documents. A deferred payment credit, then, differs from a "time" or "usance" credit in that, under a deferred payment credit, the beneficiary does not receive an acceptance when he presents his documents.

See J. Harrington, Opening Financial Doors to International Trade—A Guide to Effective Use of Letters of Credit and Bankers Acceptances 30 (1980); App. C, Doc. 20.

demurrage   Costs incurred when a vessel is detained in port for a period longer than anticipated in the charter party.

See Decor by Nikkei Int'l, Inc. v. Federal Republic of Nig., 497 F. Supp. 893 (S.D.N.Y. 1980), aff'd, 647 F.2d 300 (2d Cir. 1981), cert. denied, 454 U.S. 1148 (1982); Venizelos, S.A. v. Chase Manhattan Bank, N.A., 425 F.2d 461 (2d Cir. 1970).

direct-pay letter of credit   A standby letter of credit, usually one securing the payment of commercial paper or other securities, under which the holders of the securities looks to the issuer for payment in the first instance, that is, a standby under which the parties expect the issuer to pay.

Saunders, "Preference Avoidance and Letter of Credit Supported Debt: The Bank's Reimbursement Risk in Its Customer's Bankruptcy," 102 Banking L.J. 240, 244 (1985).

dirty bill of lading   Bill of lading bearing a notation indicating that the goods themselves or the packages containing them are damaged or in disrepair. Cf. *claused bill*; *clean bill of lading*.

discrepancy   Used to describe the failure of a document presented to conform to the terms of the credit.

See American Bankers Association, Letters of Credit (Book 4–Document Examination) 4, 5 (1968).

dishonor   Failure of the issuer or the designated payor to honor the credit engagement.

documentary credit   Credit payable against presentation of documents.

See U.C.P. art. 2.

documentary demand   (1) Demand accompanied by a document or other paper.

See U.C.C. § 5-103(1)(b).

(2) There is some authority that a demand that is itself in writing is a documentary demand.

U.C.C. § 5-102, comment 1 (1st para., last sentence); cf. *clean credit*.

documentary draft   Draft accompanied by a document or other paper.

See U.C.C. § 5-103(1)(b).

domestic credit   Sometimes said of a credit, whether commercial or standby, that does not involve the international shipment of goods.

See Beathard v. Chicago Football Club, Inc., 419 F. Supp. 1133, 1135 (N.D. Ill. 1976); Doelger v. Battery Park Nat'l Bank, 201 A.D. 515, 517, 194 N.Y.S. 582, 584 (1922); cf. *export credit*; *import credit*.

domiciled credit   Credit that stipulates that payment will be made only at a designated bank, usually a correspondent of the issuer.

See U.C.C. § 5-108, comment 1 (2d para., last sentence).

draft   Negotiable instrument that orders the payment of money; sometimes called a bill of exchange.

See Pillans v. Van Mierop, 97 Eng. Rep. 1035 (K.B. 1765); U.C.C. § 3-104(2)(a).

draft authorization agreement   Agreement between a manufacturer and a dealer's bank whereby the bank agrees to honor the manufacturer's drafts covering goods shipped to the dealer. The Comptroller of the Currency, in a letter opinion, concluded that the arrangement is a letter of credit and, under 12 C.F.R. § 7.7016, should be so designated if the bank is a national association.

See Comptroller of the Currency, Staff Interpretive Letter No. 214, reprinted in [1981–1982 Transfer Binder] Fed. Banking L. Rep. (CCH) ¶ 85,295 (July 23, 1981).

drawee bank   Bank designated on a draft drawn under a letter of credit as the payor. Cf. *paying bank.*

drawer   Party that draws the draft under a letter of credit; the beneficiary of the credit.

elcee   Term meaning "letter of credit."

See East Eur. D.I.S.C. v. Terra, 467 F. Supp. 383, 386 (S.D.N.Y. 1979).

eligibility certificate   Stamp placed on a banker's acceptance indicating that the acceptance qualifies for discount by the Federal Reserve bank under provisions of Section 13 of the Federal Reserve Act (1913) and under Regulation A.

See 12 U.S.C. § 372 (1988); 12 C.F.R. §§ 201.1–201.110 (1989).

endorsers   Persons, usually banks, that take up the draft from the beneficiary and endorse it before presenting it to the opening bank for payment.

evergreen clause   Term in a letter of credit providing for automatic renewal of the credit.

See National Sur. Corp. v. Midland Bank, 551 F.2d 21 (3d Cir. 1977); Comptroller of the Currency, Staff Interpretive Letter No. 239, reprinted in [1983–1984 Transfer Binder] Fed. Banking L. Rep. (CCH) ¶ 85,403 (Mar. 10, 1982).

executory letter of credit   A credit that has not expired and whose conditions the beneficiary has yet to satisfy.

See Supreme Merchandise Co. v. Chemical Bank, 117 A.D.2d 424, 425, 503 N.Y.S.2d 9 (1986). Cf. *open credit.*

ex factory Contract term requiring the seller of goods to make the goods available to the buyer at the seller's facility.

See American Bankers Association, Letters of Credit (Book 1 — Shipping Documents) 59 (1968); cf. *ex works.*

expiry date Last date, unless it is a bank holiday, on which drafts may be presented for payment under a letter of credit. If the expiry date is a bank holiday, the last date on which the draft may be presented is the first banking day following the holiday.

See U.C.P. art. 46.

exploding letter of credit A letter of credit that automatically terminates in the event of the issuer's insolvency, it is intended by the drafters to prevent the beneficiary from having a claim as an insured depositor of the issuing bank.

export credit Said by a domestic bank of a credit covering goods to be exported (i.e., a credit issued by a bank in the seller's country).

See M. Golodetz Export Corp. v. Credit Lyonnais, 493 F. Supp. 480, 481 (C.D. Cal. 1980).

ex quay Contract term describing the responsibility of the seller of goods requiring that the seller make the goods available to the buyer on the wharf at a named destination, said destination customarily following the term "ex quay." Usually, the party stipulates explicitly whether the goods are to be delivered "ex quay" with "duty paid" or with, in the alternative, "duties on buyer's account."

See International Chamber of Commerce, "Incoterms," ICC Pub. No. 350, at 64 (1980).

external reserve A negotiating or collecting bank's imposition of a reserve against the proceeds of a credit, which reserve is communicated to the opening bank.

See F. de Rooy, Documentary Credits 153 (1984). Cf. *internal reserve.*

ex works Describes the responsibility of the seller of goods requiring the seller to make the goods available at his premises, without responsibility for loading or transportation.

See International Chamber of Commerce, "Incoterms," ICC Pub. No. 350, at 16 (1980).

financial obligation standby A standby letter of credit that secures repayment of financial obligations, such as municipal bonds or commercial paper.

See Chessen, Feeling the Heat of Risk-Based Capital: The Case of Off-Balance-Sheet Activity, Regulatory Rev. 1, 3 (Aug. 1987). Cf. *performance standby*.

fine trade bill A banker's acceptance from an acceptance issuer of good repute.

See Eberth & Ellinger, "Deferred Payment Credits: A Comparative Analysis of Their Special Problems," 14 J. Mar. L. & Com. 387, 390 (1983).

first beneficiary Under a transferable credit, first party who has the right to draw. The first beneficiary may transfer that right to a second beneficiary.

See U.C.P. art. 54.

foreign currency credit Letter of credit that calls for drafts drawn in a currency other than that of the beneficiary's country.

See Wiley, "How to Use Letters of Credit in Financing the Sale of Goods," 20 Bus. Law. 495, 500 (1965).

franchise Used in marine insurance policies in clauses designating that portion of the loss that is not covered by the insurance. A policy that describes the coverage as "5 percent franchise" does not cover losses below 5 percent, losses of 5 percent or more being completely covered. The franchise provision applies only to particular average losses resulting from sea perils or from additional named perils.

See U.C.P. art. 40; American Bankers Association, Letters of Credit (Book 1 — Shipping Documents) 128 (1968).

free alongside (FAS)   Shipment term that requires the seller of merchandise to bear the cost of transporting the merchandise to the loading dock.

See International Chamber of Commerce, "Incoterms," ICC Pub. No. 350, at 28 (1980).

free carrier   Describes the responsibility of the seller of goods, requiring that he deliver the goods into the charge of the carrier. This term finds use in connection with shipments by combined transport.

See International Chamber of Commerce, "Incoterms," ICC Pub. No. 350, at 100 (1980).

freely negotiable credit   Credit that permits any bank, not just a designated correspondent of the issuer, to negotiate the credit (and to be paid by the issuing bank).

See International Chamber of Commerce, "Standard Forms for Issuing Documentary Credits," ICC Pub. No. 323, at 10 (1978).

free of capture and seizure (FC&S)   A marine insurance term that excludes war risk from most marine insurance policies.

See American Bankers Association, Letters of Credit (Book 1 — Shipping Documents) 97 (1968).

free of value   If a deferred payment or time credit is unconfirmed, the advising bank sends the documents to the opening bank, without giving any value to the beneficiary or receiving any value from the opening bank. The advising bank then asks the beneficiary to authorize it to transfer these documents "free of value."

free on board (FOB)   Shipment term that requires the seller of goods to transport them to the dock and to load them onto the vessel.

See International Chamber of Commerce, "Incoterms," ICC Pub. No. 350, at 34 (1980).

free on board airport (FOB Airport)   Shipment term describing the responsibility of a seller under a contract calling for carriage of the goods by air. Contrary to the conventional meaning of "FOB," this term does not require the seller to load the goods on the aircraft, but only to deliver them into the charge of the carrier. Customarily, the term "FOB Airport" is followed by the designation of an airport.

See International Chamber of Commerce, "Incoterms," ICC Pub. No. 350, at 92 (1980).

free on rail (FOR)   Shipment term describing the responsibility of the seller of goods, requiring that he load carload quantities on the carrier. The term is normally followed by the designation of a departure point (e.g., "free on rail, Columbus").

See International Chamber of Commerce, "Incoterms," ICC Pub. No. 350, at 22 (1980).

full invoice value   It is implicit in all commercial letters of credit that the beneficiary may draw for the full amount of the invoice. Some credits, however, limit the right to draw to a percentage of invoice value, such as "90 percent of invoice value." The phrase "full invoice value" makes the implication explicit.

full set bills of lading   Bills of lading in international transactions are usually issued in sets (i.e., in a number of originals). The bill of lading recites that the agent has "signed for *x* bills of lading, all of this tenor and date, and if one is accomplished, the others shall be void."

See Honnold, "Letters of Credit, Custom, Missing Documents and the Dixon Case: A Reply to Backus and Harfield," 53 Colum. L. Rev. 504 (1953); Backus & Harfield, "Custom and Letters of Credit: The Dixon, Irmaos Case," 52 Colum. L. Rev. 589 (1952).

general credit   Credit that is addressed to all persons and that does not designate a specific beneficiary. Until the first part of the twentieth century, such credits were common. They are now relatively rare.

See Adams v. Jones, 37 U.S. 207, 213 (1838); Bank of Seneca v. First Nat'l Bank, 105 Mo. App. 722, 723, 78 S.W. 1092, 1093 (Kansas City Ct. App. 1904), Birckhead v. Carlisle, 5 Hill (N.Y.) 634, 642 (Sup. Ct. 1843); cf. *special credit.*

green clause credit   Credit that stipulates that the opening or confirming bank may make advances to the beneficiary prior to the time he satisfies the documentary terms of the credit, such advances to be made for the purpose of purchasing or shipping the merchandise called for under the credit. The green clause credit differs from the red clause credit in that the former provides for the pledging by the beneficiary of negotiable warehouse receipts to the bank to secure the advances. Once the beneficiary has assembled the merchandise and is prepared to ship it, the bank surrenders the receipts to the beneficiary so that he can deliver the goods to the carrier. The beneficiary repays the advances plus interest out of the proceeds of the drafts he presents under the credit. Formerly, the language authorizing these advances was printed in green.

See A. Watson, Finance of International Trade 185 (2d ed. 1981); cf. *red clause credit*.

guaranty credit   Standby credit.

See O'Grady v. First Union Nat'l Bank, 296 N.C. 212, 230, 250 S.E.2d 587, 599 (1978); Note, "Guaranty Letters of Credit: Problems and Possibilities," 16 Ariz. L. Rev. 822 (1974).

guillotine letter of credit   A credit, usually a standby, that calls for little or no documentation.

Jones, "Letters of Credit in the United States Construction Industry," 14 Int'l Bus. Law. 17, 17 (1986). Cf. *suicide credit*.

holder   (1) In some of the older literature, the beneficiary of a credit is referred to as the "holder."

See McCurdy, "Commercial Letters of Credit" (pt. 1), 35 Harv. L. Rev. 539, 544 (1922); Hershey, "Letters of Credit," 32 Harv. L. Rev. 1, 9 (1918).

(2) The term is used more often now to refer to the holder of a draft drawn under the credit or a document of title negotiated in connection with a credit.

See U.C.C. § 1-201(20).

honor   Act of fulfilling the credit engagement by paying, accepting, or negotiating.

> See U.C.C. § 1-201(21).

import credit   Credit covering goods to be imported (i.e., a credit issued by a bank in the buyer's country).

> See McCurdy, "Commercial Letters of Credit" (pt. 1), 35 Harv. L. Rev. 539, 551 (1922).

indemnity   In letter of credit law, the promise of a presenter or another to hold the issuer harmless from loss arising from a missing or defective document.

> See U.C.C. § 5-113; Dixon, Irmaos & CIA v. Chase Nat'l Bank, 144 F.2d 759, 761 n.2 (2d Cir.), cert. denied, 324 U.S. 850 (1944).

inherent vice   Insurance term normally used to exclude losses resulting from spoilage as a consequence of the inherent nature of the goods.

> See Missouri Pac. R.R. v. Elmore & Stahl, 377 U.S. 134, 136 (1964).

internal reserve   A negotiating or collecting bank's imposition of a reserve against the proceeds of a credit without notice to the opening bank.

> See F. de Rooy, Documentary Credits 153 (1984). Cf. *external reserve.*

international credit   Sometimes said of a credit involving an underlying international transaction. The credit may secure the price of goods or may be standby in nature.

> See KMW Int'l v. Chase Manhattan Bank, N.A., 606 F.2d 10, 16 (2d Cir. 1979).

issue   Act of establishing or opening a credit.

> See U.C.C. § 5-106.

issuer   Party that opens the credit. Cf. *opening bank.*

latest negotiation date   The latest day on which a draft may be negotiated under a negotiation credit.

American Bankers Association, 2 Letters of Credit 140 (2d ed. 1983).

leeway rules   When the quantity in the credit is expressed as a measurement, Article 43 of the Uniform Customs stipulates that a leeway of 5 percent more or 5 percent less than that specified is permissible. The words "about," "circa," or similar terms used in connection with the amount of the credit or the quantity permit a leeway of 10 percent more or 10 percent less than such a quantity or amount under Article 43(a).

See U.C.P. art. 43.

legalized   A document is legalized when it is authenticated by a public official, usually a consular officer.

See Instituto Nacional De Comercializacion Agricola (Indeca) v. Continental Ill. Nat'l Bank & Trust Co., 530 F. Supp. 279, 281 (N.D. Ill. 1982); Bank of Canton, Ltd. v. Republic Nat'l Bank, 509 F. Supp. 1310, 1316 (S.D.N.Y.), aff'd, 636 F.2d 30 (2d Cir. 1980).

local currency credit   Letter of credit that calls for drafts drawn in the currency of the beneficiary's country.

mail confirmation   Written letter incorporating the terms of a letter of credit sent by the opening bank to a confirming bank or advising bank after the opening bank has sent a cable or telegram containing the same terms.

marks and numbers   Information identifying the packages in which merchandise is being shipped.

See A. Watson, Finance of International Trade 61 (2d ed. 1981).

multibank credits   Arrangements whereby a number of banks participate in the issuance of separate credits or in a master credit signed by all participants.

See Ryan, "Letters of Credit Supporting Debt for Borrowed Money: The Standby as Backup," 100 Banking L.J. 404, 420–421 (1983).

multimodal transport   See *combined transport.*

municipal credit   A standby credit securing municipal bonds.

American Banker, Apr. 19, 1984, at 14.

negotiable credit   Sometimes courts refer to the "negotiability" of credits in describing that feature of the credit that permits the negotiation of drafts drawn under the credit. Credits, however, are not negotiable instruments, and the term "negotiable credit" is a misnomer.

U.C.C. § 3-104; Consolidated Aluminum Corp. v. Bank of Va., 704 F.2d 136 (4th Cir. 1983); Shaffer v. Brooklyn Park Garden Apartments, 311 Minn. 452, 250 N.W.2d 172 (1977); Samuel Kronman & Co. v. Public Nat'l Bank, 218 A.D. 624, 626, 218 N.Y.S. 616, 618 (1926); cf. *negotiation credit.*

negotiating bank   Bank, other than the issuing bank, that has discounted or purchased a draft drawn under a letter of credit.

See International Chamber of Commerce, "Standard Forms for Issuing Documentary Credits," ICC Pub. No. 323, at 10 (1978); McCurdy, "Commercial Letters of Credit" (pt. 1), 35 Harv. L. Rev. 539, 543–544 (1922).

negotiation   In letter of credit settings, it is usually a draft or a negotiable instrument that is negotiated. A bill of lading or other negotiable documents of title also might be negotiated. Courts, however, sometimes speak of "negotiating" credits. Presumably, the courts mean that the draft was negotiated.

See, e.g., Bank of Canton, Ltd. v. Republic Nat'l Bank, 509 F. Supp. 1310, 1312 (S.D.N.Y.), aff'd, 636 F.2d 30 (2d Cir. 1980); Eximetals Corp. v. Pinheiro Guimares, S.A., 73 A.D.2d 526, 526, 422 N.Y.S.2d 684, 686 (1979), aff'd, 51 N.Y.2d 865, 414 N.E.2d 399, 433 N.Y.S.2d 1019 (1980); see generally U.C.C. §§ 3-202, 7-501; cf. *negotiation credit; negotiable credit.*

negotiation credit   Credit under which the issuer's engagement runs to drawers, endorsers, and bona fide holders of drafts drawn under the credit or under which the issuer indicates expressly that the credit is available by negotiation.

> See International Chamber of Commerce, "Standard Forms for Issuing Documentary Credits," ICC Pub. No. 323, at 10 (1978).

net landed weights   Weights of goods after unloading and after customs officials have computed the duty.

> See Old Colony Trust Co. v. Lawyers' Title & Trust Co., 297 F. 152, 156 (2d Cir.), cert. denied, 265 U.S. 585 (1924).

nominated bank   The bank designated in the credit as the bank that will pay, accept, incur a deferred payment obligation, or negotiate the beneficiary's drafts.

> See U.C.P. art. 11.

notation credit   Credit that stipulates that the person honoring drafts drawn under the credit must note the amount of the draft on the credit.

> See U.C.C. § 5-108(1); Anglo-S. Am. Trust Co. v. Uhe, 261 N.Y. 150, 184 N.E. 741 (1933); Harfield, "Code Treatment of Letters of Credit," 48 Cornell L.Q. 92, 99–100 (1962).

notified without engagement   Referring to a credit that the correspondent will advise but will not confirm.

> See International Chamber of Commerce, "Standard Forms for Issuing Documentary Credits," ICC Pub. No. 323, at 4 (1978).

notifying bank   Confirming or advising bank.

on-board bill of lading   Bill of lading containing a notation, dated and signed by an agent of the carrier, to the effect that the goods are loaded on board the vessel, truck, or car.

> See A. Watson, Finance of International Trade 54 (2d ed. 1981).

on deck   Notation that appears on an ocean bill of lading indicating that the goods have been stored on the deck of the vessel.

See Swiss Bank Corp., Documentary Operations 84 (1979).

open credit   (1) Sometimes said of a credit that runs to an undesignated beneficiary such as "any holder in due course" of a described note.

See Bank of N.C., N.A. v. Rock Island Bank, 630 F.2d 1243, 1249 (7th Cir. 1980); Russell v. Wiggin, 21 F. Cas. 68, 71 (C.C.D. Mass. 1842); cf. *negotiation credit; straight credit; circular credit; general credit.*

(2) Also said of a credit that has not expired and whose conditions the beneficiary has yet to satisfy.

See Ferrostaal Metals Corp. v. S.S. Lash Pacifico, Nos. 82 Civ. 2825 (CBM), 83 Civ. 1524 (CBM) (S.D.N.Y. Jan. 23, 1987); cf. *executory letter of credit.*

opening bank   Bank that issues the letter of credit.

operative credit instrument   Document, telex, or telegram that constitutes the credit.

See U.C.P. art. 12; cf. *advice of credit; preadvice.*

packing credit   Green clause or red clause credit.

See Swiss Bank Corp., Documentary Operations 84 (1979).

packing list   Description of the contents of cartons, boxes, or other containers.

See A. Watson, Finance of International Trade 46, 66 (2d ed. 1981).

partial shipment   Describes a seller's shipment, as indicated by documents submitted under a letter of credit, that is not a complete shipment and does not qualify as a complete shipment under the 10 percent or 3 percent leeway rule. Many credits do not permit partial shipments.

pay   To honor the credit by putting the beneficiary in funds.

paying bank   Bank designated in the credit as the party that will honor drafts drawn under the credit.

performance credit   Standby credit payable against certificates, reciting in effect that the beneficiary has performed the underlying contract.

> See Scarsdale Nat'l Bank & Trust Co. v. Toronto-Dominion Bank, 533 F. Supp. 378, 380 (S.D.N.Y. 1982). Compare *performance standby.*

performance standby   Standby credit that secures the performance of a contract, such as a construction contract or a contract for the sale of goods or provision of services, rather than a standby credit that secures uniquely monetary obligations, such as commercial paper or municipal bonds.

> See Chessen, Feeling the Heat of Risk-Based Capital: The Case of Off-Balance-Sheet Activity, Regulatory Rev. 1, 3 (Aug. 1987). Compare *performance credit.*

point of origin   Generally, the location of the seller's facility. In a "point of origin" contract, the buyer takes delivery of the goods at the seller's place of business and bears all costs of loading and transporting the goods.

political risk standby   A standby letter of credit that secures the beneficiary against the risk of political upheaval in, or currency restrictions of, the account party's country.

> See Comptroller of the Currency, Staff Interpretive Letter No. 295, reprinted in [1985–1987 Transfer Binder] Fed. Banking L. Rep. (CCH) ¶ 84,465 (July 3, 1984).

preadvice   Telex sent to an advising bank by an issuing bank that wants a mailed copy of the credit terms to be the "operative credit instrument." A preadvice contains such language as "details to follow" or "credit to be effective upon receipt of mail confirmation."

> See U.C.P. art. 12; cf. *operative credit instrument.*

preliminary advice   When time is short, an opening bank may notify an advising bank that it has opened a credit in a given amount for a named beneficiary and that "the credit will follow." The advising bank, not having the terms of the credit, does not issue an advice of credit but notifies the beneficiary by giving him a "preliminary advice" to the effect that the credit has been issued and that the advice will issue shortly. Some beneficiaries, on the basis of such preliminary advice, may be willing to initiate performance, although a preliminary advice is not an advice of credit and does not impose the same obligations on the advising bank that an advice does.

See U.C.P. art. 14.

presentation credit   Credit requiring the beneficiary to present the credit document at the time of payment.

presentation date   The date by which transport documents must be presented under the rule of UCP Article 47.

See American Bankers Association, 2 Letters of Credit 29 (2d ed. 1983).

presenter   Person that delivers the draft and accompanying documents to the payor. The Uniform Commercial Code defines "presenter" to include the advising or confirming bank.

See U.C.C. § 5-112(3).

principal   Formerly used to refer to the account party or customer who caused the credit to issue.

See Evansville Nat'l Bank v. Kaufmann, 93 N.Y. 273, 280 (1883).

purchaser   Sometimes the account party is called the "purchaser" of the credit.

See Anglo-S. Am. Trust Co. v. Uhe, 261 N.Y. 150, 155, 184 N.E. 741, 742 (1933).

received-for-shipment bill of lading Bill issued before the goods are loaded on board the vessel. This bill does not satisfy the requirement for an on-board bill.

> See U.C.P. art. 27(b); Pan-Am. Bank & Trust Co. v. National City Bank, 6 F.2d 762, 768 (2d Cir.), cert. denied, 269 U.S. 554 (1925).

reciprocal credit Standby credit usually issued to secure a seller's performance at the same time that a commercial credit is issued to secure the buyer's payment.

> See, e.g., Werner Lehara Int'l, Inc. v. Harris Trust & Sav. Bank, 484 F. Supp. 65, 67 (W.D. Mich. 1980).

reciprocal draft Sometimes an issuer inserts in a credit a term calling for the beneficiary's reciprocal draft, that is, a second draft (in addition to the draft to be drawn on the issuer and in the same amount), this second draft to be drawn on the account party. The provision raises serious concerns for the beneficiary, for if the account party dishonors the reciprocal draft, the beneficiary will be liable on the instrument to the holder.

> See U.C.C. § 3-413(2).

red clause credit Credit that permits the beneficiary to receive temporary advances from the opening or confirming bank to enable him to make purchases and shipment of the goods described in the credit, said advances to be repaid with interest out of the proceeds of the beneficiary's drafts ultimately drawn under the credit. The clause permitting such advances, being such an extraordinary provision in a letter of credit, formerly was printed in red to call attention to it.

> See Oelbermann v. National City Bank, 79 F.2d 534, 535 (2d Cir.), modified per curiam, 298 U.S. 638 (1935); E. Ellinger, Documentary Letters of Credit 7–9 (1970).

reimbursement Repayment to the payor of a credit of sums paid under the credit. Traditionally, the issuer has a right of reimbursement against the account party. Sometimes, banks use the term to describe the right of a payor or negotiating bank to collect from the issuer.

See U.C.C. § 5-114(3); J. Zeevi & Sons v. Grindlays Bank (Uganda) Ltd., 37 N.Y.2d 220, 333 N.E.2d 168, 371 N.Y.S.2d 892, cert. denied, 432 U.S. 866 (1975).

reimbursing bank   An opening bank sometimes directs paying, accepting, or negotiating banks to seek reimbursement from a branch of the issuer or from a third bank, which is then the reimbursing bank.

See U.C.P. art. 21(a); Banco De Vizcaya, S.A. v. First Nat'l Bank, 514 F. Supp. 1280, 1283 (N.D. Ill. 1981).

remitting bank   Bank that forwards or presents the documents to the issuing bank.

See U.C.P. art. 16(d).

request   Contract between the account party and the issuing bank, now usually called the application.

See Pan-Am. Bank & Trust Co. v. National City Bank, 6 F.2d 762, 765 (2d Cir.), cert. denied, 269 U.S. 554 (1925).

requester   Used to describe the party seeking payment; the presenter.

See FDIC v. Freudenfeld, 492 F. Supp. 763, 766 (E.D. Wis. 1980).

revolving credit   Letter of credit pursuant to which the bank undertakes to continue to honor drafts so long as the account party has reimbursed the bank and has not exceeded the "line of credit" that the bank has granted to the account party.

See A. Davis, The Law Relating to Commercial Letters of Credit 28 (3d ed. 1963); Venizelos, S.A. v. Chase Manhattan Bank, N.A., 425 F.2d 461, 463 (2d Cir. 1970); Banco Nacional De Credito Ejidal, S.A., v. Bank of Am., 118 F. Supp. 308, 309 (N.D. Cal. 1954); Trans-Global Alloy, Ltd. v. First Nat'l Bank, 490 So. 2d 769 (La. Ct. App. 1986).

secondary credit   Credit issued on the strength of another credit.

See Kingdom of Swed. v. New York Trust Co., 197 Misc. 431, 443, 96 N.Y.S.2d 779, 789 (Sup. Ct. 1949); cf. *back-to-back credit*.

second beneficiary   Under a transferable credit, the first party that has the right to draw (the first beneficiary) may transfer that right to a second beneficiary.

See U.C.P. art. 54.

separate entity doctrine   Rule of banking law which holds that a bank's branches are entities separate from each other and from the bank's home office. The doctrine has limited application.

See Banco De Vizcaya, S.A. v. First Nat'l Bank, 514 F. Supp. 1280, 1284–1285 (N.D. Ill. 1981), vacated, id.; cf. U.C.C. § 4-106 (treatment of branches in computing time within which and places at which actions may be taken or notices or orders given).

shipped bill of lading   Bill issued by the carrier after the goods are loaded on board.

See Carriage of Goods by Sea Act, § 3(7), 46 U.S.C. app. § 1303(7) (Supp. V 1987); cf. *received-for-shipment bill of lading*; U.C.P. art. 27; Siderius, Inc. v. Wallace Co., 583 S.W.2d 852, 858 (Tex. Civ. App. 1979).

shipper's load and count   Stamp noted on a bill of lading indicating that the carrier has not verified the weight or number of packages.

See U.C.C. § 7-301(1); U.C.P. art. 32.

sight credit   Letter of credit whose terms require the issuer to honor sight drafts. Cf. *time credit*.

sight draft   Draft that calls for payment upon presentation. Cf. *usance draft*; *time draft*.

single-mode transport   Transportation of goods by one method of transport only (e.g., ship, rail, or truck). Cf. *combined transport*.

special credit   Credit addressed to a single beneficiary, not to the world in general. Formerly, merchants issued such credits as accommodations for their suppliers or for related persons. Such credits were not assignable.

See Regis v. Hebert, 16 La. Ann. 224, 225 (1861); Lyon v. Van Raden, 126 Mich. 259, 261–262, 85 N.W. 727, 727 (1901); Eriksson v. Refiners Export Co., 264 A.D. 525, 526, 35 N.Y.S.2d 829, 831 (1942); Robbins v. Bingham, 4 Johns. 476 (N.Y. Sup. Ct. 1809); cf. *general credit.*

specially advised credit Credit that specifies only one place of payment and, hence, not a circular credit.

See Wiley, "How to Use Letters of Credit in Financing the Sale of Goods," 20 Bus. Law. 495, 500 (1965).

special purpose credit Standby credit.

stale bills Under Article 41 of the Uniform Customs, unless the credit stipulates a different period of time, banks will reject bills of lading presented later than twenty-one days after the date of issuance.

See Bank of Canton, Ltd. v. Republic Nat'l Bank, 509 F. Supp. 1310, 1317 (S.D.N.Y.), aff'd, 636 F.2d 30 (2d Cir. 1980).

standby credit A credit, not a commercial credit, that is designed to be payable in the event of default or other nonperformance by a party obliged to the beneficiary, said event to be satisfied by the presentation of documents.

See Republic Nat'l Bank v. Northwest Nat'l Bank, 578 S.W.2d 109, 113 (Tex. 1978); see also 12 C.F.R. § 7.1160(a) (1988); cf. *commercial credit.*

steamship guaranty Written undertaking, usually given by an issuing bank, addressed to a carrier indemnifying the carrier against losses that might be incurred by virtue of the carrier's delivery of the goods without receipt of a document of title. This guaranty arises when the goods arrive prior to the arrival of the bill of lading or if the bill of lading is lost.

See App. C, Doc. 19.

straight credit Credit that requires that drafts be presented to a designated party, usually the issuer or another bank. This credit usually contains language such as the following: "Drafts must clearly specify the number of this advice and be presented at this company not later than . . . " or "We undertake that all drafts drawn and presented to us as above specified will be duly honored."

See Mid-States Mortgage Corp. v. National Bank, 77 Mich. App. 651, 653, 259 N.W.2d 175, 176 (1977); Dixon, Irmaos & CIA v. Chase Nat'l Bank, 144 F.2d 759, 760 n.1 (2d Cir.), cert. denied, 324 U.S. 850 (1944); Edgewater Constr. Co. v. Percy Wilson Mortgage & Fin. Corp., 44 Ill. App. 3d 220, 357 N.E.2d 1307 (1976); cf. *negotiation credit.*

strict compliance rule   Letter of credit rule that (1) requires the beneficiary to comply strictly with the terms of the credit so that the function of the issuer becomes ministerial and nonjudgmental, and (2) prevents the issuer from adding any requirements to the credit. This principle is the first corollary of the independence principle.

See Corporacion De Mercadeo Agricola v. Mellon Bank Int'l, 608 F.2d 43 (2d Cir. 1979); Bank of Canton, Ltd. v. Republic Nat'l Bank, 509 F. Supp. 1310 (S.D.N.Y.), aff'd, 636 F.2d 30 (2d Cir. 1980).

strict construction principle   Broad rule encompassing the unique features of a letter of credit, including the ideas that the credit is independent of related agreements and that the beneficiary must comply strictly with its terms.

See Banco Espanol de Credito v. State St. Bank & Trust Co., 385 F.2d 230, 234 (1st Cir. 1967), cert. denied, 390 U.S. 1013 (1968); Harfield, "Identity Crises in Letter of Credit Law," 24 Ariz. L. Rev. 239, 240 (1982).

strikes, riots, and civil commotions (SR&CC)   Marine insurance term that excludes loss from civil disturbances from most marine insurance policies.

See A. Watson, Finance of International Trade 49 (2d ed. 1981).

suicide credit   Term sometimes used to describe a clean standby letter of credit, that is, a standby credit payable against a draft and without any further supporting documents.

See Comment, "Enjoining the 'Suicide' Letter of Credit: KMW International v. Chase Manhattan Bank," 17 Willamette L. Rev. 253 (1980).

SWIFT   Society for Worldwide Interbank Financial Telecommunications.

tenor   Letters of credit derive their tenor from the tenor of the drafts to be drawn under them. Tenor refers to the nature of the draft as either one payable "at sight" or one payable at some other time. Cf. *sight draft*; *time draft*; *usance draft*.

tested telex   In order to guard against counterfeit instructions by telex, banks have developed a simple code for identifying the sender. Such communication is "tested" or "keyed."

> See American Bell Int'l, Inc. v. Islamic Republic of Iran, 474 F. Supp. 420, 421 (S.D.N.Y. 1979).

third-party transport document   A transport document indicating that someone other than the beneficiary is the shipper.

> See B. Wheble, "UCP 1974/1983 Revisions Compared and Explained (Documentary Credits)," ICC Pub. No. 411, at 57 (1984).

time credit   Letter of credit in which the issuer undertakes to honor time drafts. Cf. *time draft*; *sight credit*.

time draft   Draft that calls for payment at a time other than at sight. A usance draft is the same as a time draft. Cf. *sight draft*.

trade acceptance   Undertaking by a merchant, as opposed to a bank, to pay a draft according to its tenor when it becomes due. The acceptance of a draft by a bank is a "banker's acceptance."

> See U.C.C. § 3-410; J. Harrington, Opening Financial Doors to International Trade—A Guide to Effective Use of Letters of Credit and Bankers Acceptances 72 (1980).

transferable credit   Credit under which the beneficiary may assign the right to draw drafts under the credit.

> See U.C.C. § 5-116; U.C.P. art. 54; Axworthy, "The Revisions of the Uniform Customs on Documentary Credits," 1971 J. Bus. L. 38, 47; cf. *assignable credit*.

transship (*also* tranship)   To transport merchandise from one method of transport or vessel to another.

See U.C.P. art. 29.

traveler's credit   (1) Credit now largely in disuse whereby the account party itself or its agent was the beneficiary and could draw on the credit, often at foreign correspondents of the opening bank.

See W. Spaulding, Bankers' Credits 12 (3d ed. 1930); Ufitec, S.A. v. Trade Bank & Trust Co., 21 A.D.2d 187, 188, 249 N.Y.S.2d 557, 559 (1964), aff'd, 16 N.Y.2d 698, 209 N.E.2d 551, 261 N.Y.S.2d 893 (1965).

(2) The old buyer's credit predating the commercial letter of credit was in the nature of a traveler's credit.

See Russell v. Wiggin, 21 F. Cas. 68 (C.C.D. Mass. 1842).

trust receipt   Security agreement. "Trust receipt" is a vestige of the Uniform Trust Receipts Act, now repealed in American jurisdictions, under which a borrower issued a receipt acknowledging that he held goods in trust for the lender.

Cf. U.C.C.. §§ 1-201(37), 9-102(2).

underlying transaction   Transaction between the account party and the beneficiary. It is this transaction of which the credit is so often said to be independent.

See U.C.C. §§ 5-109(1), 5-114(1); U.C.P. art. 3.

under reserve   Frequently, a collecting bank takes a draft drawn under a credit and credits its customer's account provisionally. Such a bank takes the draft "under reserve."

See Banque De L'Indochine Et De Suez S.A. v. J.H. Rayner (Mincing Lane) Ltd., [1983] 1 Lloyd's Rep. 228 (C.A.); U.C.P. art. 16(f); Wheble, "Uniform Customs and Practice for Documentary Credits (1974 Revision)," 1975 J. Bus. L. 281, 284.

Uniform Customs   The Uniform Customs and Practice for Documentary Credits (Uniform Customs or the UCP), published by the International Chamber of Commerce. The 1974 revision, in force as of October 1, 1975, appears in ICC Publication No. 290. The 1983 revision, effective October 1, 1984, appears in ICC Publication No. 400.

usance draft   Draft that calls for payment at a time other than at sight. A usance draft is the same as a time draft. Cf. *sight draft.*

value   To draw a draft upon, such as in "value on us up to $x."

See Clarke v. Cock, 102 Eng. Rep. 751, 752 (K.B. 1803); Anglo-S. Am. Trust Co. v. Uhe, 261 N.Y. 150, 153, 184 N.E. 741, 741 (1933).

visaed   Describing a document, such as a bill of lading or commercial invoice, bearing the stamp of an official of the country of importation authorizing the importation of the goods and signed by an authorized agent of the importing country.

See App. C, Doc. 8.

without recourse   By drawing or endorsing a draft, a party undertakes certain obligations by virtue of negotiable instruments law. By drawing or endorsing "without recourse," the party disclaims such obligations. The Uniform Customs stipulate that an issuing bank's duty to negotiate drafts drawn on the account party must be "without recourse to drawers and/or bona fide holders."

See U.C.C. §§ 3-413, 3-414, 3-417(3); U.C.P. art. 10(a)(iv).

Bibliography

BOOKS AND MONOGRAPHS

Alderman, R., and R. Dole, *A Transactional Guide to the Uniform Commercial Code* (2d ed. 1983).

American Bankers Association, *Letters of Credit* (2d ed. 1983).

American Bar Association, *Letters of Credit and Financial Institution Insolvencies* (1989).

Barrett, "Bank Regulatory Aspects and Legislative Proposals," in *Letters of Credit* (1981).

———, "Bank Regulatory Aspects of Letters of Credit," in *Letters of Credit and Bankers' Acceptances* (1985).

Bewes, W., *The Romance of the Law Merchant* (1923).

Byrne, *An Examination of U.C.C. Article 5 (Letters of Credit, a Report of the Task Force on the Study of U.C.C. Article 5* (American Bar Association 1989).

Clark, B., *The Law of Bank Deposits, Collections and Credit Cards* (rev. ed. 1981).

Davis, A., *The Law Relating to Commercial Letters of Credit* (3d ed. 1963).

Dekker, J., *Case Studies on Documentary Credits*, ICC Pub. No. 459 (1988).

———, *Standard Documentary Credit Forms*, ICC Pub. No. 416 (1986).

———, *Standard Form and Guidance Notes for Credit Applicants*, ICC Pub. No. 416A (1986).

Ellinger, E., *Documentary Letters of Credit* (1970).

Federal Reserve Bank of Chicago, *Proceedings, A Conference on Bank Structure and Competition* (1986).

Finklestein, H., *Legal Aspects of Commercial Letters of Credit* (1930).

Gilmore, G., *The Death of Contract* (1974).

———, *The Ages of American Law* (1977).

Goode, R., *Commercial Law* (1985).

Gutteridge, H., and M. Megrah, *The Law of Bankers' Commercial Credits* (7th ed. 1984).

Harfield, H., *Bank Credits and Acceptances* (5th ed. 1974).

Harrington, J., *Opening Financial Doors to International Trade—A Guide to Effective Use of Letters of Credit and Bankers Acceptances* (1980).

Henson, R., *Handbook on Secured Transactions Under the Uniform Commercial Code* (2d ed. 1979).

———, *Documents of Title Under the Uniform Commercial Code* (2d ed. 1990).

Hillman, W., *Letters of Credit: Current Thinking in America* (1987).

Holden, J., *The History of Negotiable Instruments in English Law* (1955).

Holdsworth, W., *A History of English Law* (2d ed. 1937).

Horwitz, M., *The Transformation of American Law* (1977).

International Chamber of Commerce, *The Problem of Clean Bills of Lading*, ICC Pub. No. 283 (1963).

———, *Uniform Customs and Practice for Documentary Credits*, ICC Pub. No. 290 (1975).

———, *Uniform Rules for a Combined Transport Document*, ICC Pub. No. 298 (1975).

———, *Guide to Documentary Credit Operations*, ICC Pub. No. 305 (1978).

———, *Standard Forms for Issuing Documentary Credits*, ICC Pub. No. 323 (1978).

———, *Decisions (1975–1979) of the ICC Banking Commission on Queries Relating to Uniform Customs and Practice for Documentary Credits*, ICC Pub. No. 371 (1980).

———, *Incoterms*, ICC Pub. No. 460 (1990).

———, *Opinions (1980–1981) of the ICC Banking Commission on Queries Relating to Uniform Customs and Practice for Documentary Credits*, ICC Pub. No. 399 (1982).

———, *Guide to Documentary Credit Operations*, ICC Pub. No. 415 (rev. ed. 1985).

———, *Opinions of the ICC Banking Commission 1984–1986*, ICC Pub. No. 434 (1987).

———, *UNCID, Uniform Rules of Conduct for Interchange of Trade Data by Teletransmission*, ICC Pub. No. 452 (1988).

Kozolchyk, B., *Commercial Letters of Credit in the Americas* (1966).

———, "Letters of Credit," in IX *International Encyclopedia of Comparative Law* ch. 5 (1979).

Kurkela, M., *Letters of Credit Under International Trade Law* (1985).

Lowenfeld, A., *International Private Trade* (2d ed. 1981).

Malynes, G., *The Ancient Law Merchant* (1969).

McCullough, B., *Letters of Credit* (1987).

McDonnell, J., "Traditional and Standby Letters of Credit: Fitting the Form to the Function," in 1B *Bender's Uniform Commercial Code Service* (1982).

McGuinness, K., *The Law of Contract Guarantee* (1986).

McLaughlin, G., *Letters of Credit* (1985).

Michie on Banks and Banking (1980).

Prosser, W., *Handbook of the Law of Torts* (4th ed. 1971).

Rowe, M., *Letters of Credit* (1985).

Sanborn, F., *Origins of the Early English Maritime and Commercial Law* (1930).

Sarna, L., *Letters of Credit: The Law and Current Practice* (3d ed. 1989).

Schlesinger, R., "Article 5 — Documentary Letters of Credit," in New York Law Revision Commission, *Study of Uniform Commercial Code* (1955).

Schmitthoff, C., *Schmitthoff's Export Trade* (8th ed. 1986).

Spalding, W., *Bankers' Credits* (1930).

Story, J., *Commentaries on the Law of Bills of Exchange Foreign and Inland, as Administered in England and America* (1943).

Streng, W., and F. Pedersen, "Letters of Credit," 418 *Tax Manual* (1980).

Swiss Bank Corp., *Documentary Operations* (1979).

Ventris, F., *Bankers' Documentary Credits* (2d ed. 1983).

Watson, A., *Finance of International Trade* (2d ed. 1981).

Wheble, B., *UCP 1974/1983 Revisions Compared and Explained (Documentary Credits)*, ICC Pub. No. 411 (1984).

White, J., and R. Summers, *Uniform Commercial Code* (3d ed. (practitioner's ed.) 1980).

Williston, S., and G. Thompson, *A Treatise on the Law of Contracts* (rev. ed. 1936).

Wunnicke, B., and D. Wunnicke, *Standby Letters of Credit* (1989).

Zimmett, M., "Letters of Credit," 2 *New York Practice Guide* ch. 16 (1990).

ARTICLES

Armstrong, "The Letter of Credit as a Lending Device in a Tight Money Market," 22 Bus. Law. 1105 (1967).

Arnold & Bransilver, "The Standby Letter of Credit — The Controversy Continues," 10 U.C.C. L.J. 272 (1978).

Artz, "Selected Letter of Credit Issues in Bank Insolvencies," in American Bar Association, *Letters of Credit and Financial Institution Insolvencies* (1989).

Auerbach, "Letters of Credit—A Concise Codification," 23 Ohio St. L.J. 246 (1962).

Axworthy, "The Revision of the Uniform Customs on Documentary Credits," 1971 J. Bus. L. 38.

Backus & Harfield, "Custom and Letters of Credit: The Dixon, Irmaos Case," 52 Colum. L. Rev. 589 (1959).

Baggett & Lettellier, "Beneficiary Courses of Action Following Issuer Insolvency," Letters of Credit Report 7 (Jan./Feb. 1990).

Baird, "Standby Letters of Credit in Bankruptcy," 49 U. Chi. L. Rev. 130 (1982).

Barclay, "Court Orders Against Payment Under First Demand Guarantees Used in International Trade," 3 J. Int'l Banking L. 110 (1989).

Becker, "Standby Letters of Credit and the Iranian Cases: Will the Independence of the Credit Survive?" 13 U.C.C. L.J. 335 (1981).

Berger, "The Effects of Issuing Bank Insolvency on Letters of Credit," 21 Harv. Int'l L.J. 161 (1980).

Blau & Jedzig, "Bank Guarantees to Pay Upon First Written Demand in German Courts," 23 Int'l Law. 725 (1989).

Bulger, "Letters of Credit: A Question of Honor," 16 N.Y.U. J. Int'l L. & Pol. 799 (1984).

Byrne, "The 1983 Revision of the Uniform Customs and Practice for Documentary Credits," 102 Banking L.J. 151 (1985).

———, "UCC Survey: Letters of Credit," 43 Bus. Law. 1353 (1988).

———, "L/C Transfer by Operation of Law—It Ought to Be Against the Law" (pt. 1), Letter of Credit Update 8 (July 1989).

Campbell, "Guaranties and the Suretyship Phases of Letters of Credit" (pts. 1, 2), 85 U. Pa. L. Rev. 175, 261 (1936–1937).

Cannon, "The Uniform Customs and Practice for Documentary Credits: The 1983 Revision," 17 U.C.C. L.J. 42 (1984).

Casner, "Letters of Credit: Iranian Cases and the Need to Adapt Letters of Credit to Their Proposed Uses," 4 B.C. Third World L.J. 221 (1984).

Chadsey, "Practical Effect of the Uniform Commercial Code on Documentary Letter of Credit Transactions," 102 U. Pa. L. Rev. 618 (1954).

Chaitman & Sovern, "Enjoining Payment on a Letter of Credit in Bankruptcy: A Tempest in a Twist Cap," 38 Bus. Law. 21 (1982).

Chapman, "The 1983 Revisions to the Uniform Customs and Practice for Documentary Credits," 90 Com. L.J. 13 (1985).

Chessen, "Standby Letters of Credit," 2 Letter of Credit Update 25 (1986).

————, "Feeling the Heat of Risk-Based Capital: The Case of Off-Balance-Sheet Activity," Regulatory Rev. 1 (Aug. 1987).

Chiaw, "Reflections on Payment Under Reserve: Waiver, Estoppel, and Implied Terms," 2 J. Int'l Banking L. 81 (1988).

Clark, "Suretyship in the Uniform Commercial Code," 46 Tex. L. Rev. 453 (1968).

Colon, "Letters of Credit in Times of Business and Bank Failures," 107 Banking L.J. 6 (1990).

Comment, "'Unless Otherwise Agreed' and Article 5: An Exercise in Freedom of Contract," 11 St. Louis U.L.J. 416 (1967).

Comment, "Act of State Negated: *J. Zeevi & Sons, Ltd. v. Grindlays Bank (Uganda) Ltd.* (N.Y. Ct. App. 1975)," 15 Colum. J. Transnat'l L. 497 (1976).

Comment, "United States Banks and the Arab Boycott of Israel," 17 Colum. J. Transnat'l L. 119 (1978).

Comment, "Letters of Credit: Current Theories and Usage," 39 La. L. Rev. 581 (1979).

Comment, "Enjoining the 'Suicide' Letter of Credit: *KMW Int'l v. Chase Manhattan Bank*," 17 Willamette L. Rev. 253 (1980).

Comment, "'Fraud in the Transaction': Enjoining Letters of Credit During the Iranian Revolution," 93 Harv. L. Rev. 992 (1980).

Comment, "Judicial Development of Letters of Credit Law: A Reappraisal," 66 Cornell L. Rev. 144 (1980).

Comment, "Injunctions of Letters of Credit: Judicial Insurance Against Fraud," 3 J.L. & Com. 305 (1983).

Comment, "Bank Insolvencies and Depositor Setoff," 51 U. Chi. L. Rev. 188 (1984).

Comment, "The Independence Rule in Standby Letters of Credit," 52 U. Chi. L. Rev. 218 (1985).

Comment, "Performance Bonds, Bankers' Guarantees, and the Mareva Injunction," 7 Nw. J. Int'l L. & Bus. 380 (1985).

David, "Rise and Fall of Strict Compliance Doctrine—A Banker's Thoughts," Letter of Credit Update 13 (Mar. 1988).

Davis, "The Relationship Between Banker and Seller Under a Confirmed Credit," 52 L.Q. Rev. 225 (1936).

del Busto, "Operational Rules for Letters of Credit: Effect of New Uniform Customs and Practice Rules," 17 U.C.C. L.J. 298 (1985).

del Duca, "Pitfalls of 'Boiler Plating' Letters of Credit," 13 U.C.C. L.J. 3 (1980).

de May, "Bills of Lading Problems in the Oil Trade: Documentary Credit Aspects," 2 J. Energy & Nat. Resources L. 197 (1984).

De Rosa, "Know Your UCP: Be Careful in Using Term 'Revolving L/C,'" Letter of Credit Update 10 (Dec. 1986).

Dolan, "Good Faith Purchase and Warehouse Receipts: Thoughts on the Interplay of Articles 2, 7, and 9 of the U.C.C.," 30 Hastings L.J. 1 (1978).

————, "The Uniform Commercial Code and the Concept of Possession in the Marketing and Financing of Goods," 56 Tex. L. Rev. 1147 (1978).

————, "The U.C.C. Framework: Conveyancing Principles and Property Interests," 59 B.U.L. Rev. 811 (1979).

————, "Standby Letters of Credit and Fraud (Is the Standby Only Another Invention of the Goldsmiths in Lombard Street?)," 7 Cardozo L. Rev. 1 (1985).

————, "Strict Compliance With Letters of Credit: Striking a Fair Balance," 102 Banking L.J. 18 (1985).

————, "Letters of Credit, Article 5 Warranties, and the Beneficiary's Certificate," 41 Bus. Law. 347 (1986).

————, "Documentary Credit Fundamentals—Comparative Aspects," 3 Banking & Fin. L. Rev. 121 (1988).

————, "Letter of Credit Disputes Between the Issuer and Its Customer: The Issuer's Rights Under the Misnamed 'Bifurcated Standard,'" 105 Banking L.J. 380 (1988).

————, "Efforts at International Standardization of Bank Guarantees," 4 Banking & Fin. L. Rev. 237 (1990).

Downey, "The Letter of Credit as Security for Completion of Streets, Sidewalks, and Other Bonded Municipal Improvements," 23 U. Rich. L. Rev. 161 (1988).

Eberth & Ellinger, "Assignment and Presentation of Documents in Commercial Credit Transactions," 24 Ariz. L. Rev. 277 (1982).

————, "Deferred Payment Credits: A Comparative Analysis of Their Special Problems," 14 J. Mar. L. & Com. 387 (1983).

Effros, "Current Legal Matters Affecting Central Banks," 13 Ga. J. Int'l & Comp. L. 621 (1983).

Ellinger, "The Relationship Between Banker and Buyer Under Documentary Letters of Credit," 7 U.W. Austl. L. Rev. 40 (1965).

————, "Fraud in Documentary Credit Transactions," 1981 J. Bus. L. 258.

————, "Discount of Letters of Credit," 1984 J. Bus. L. 379.

————, "The Uniform Customs—Their Nature and the 1983 Revision," 1984 Lloyd's Mar. & Com. L.Q. 578.

————, "Performance Bonds, First-Demand Guarantees and Standby Letters of Credit—A Comparison," Letters of Credit Rep. 1 (May/June 1987).

Farnsworth, "Documentary Drafts Under the Uniform Commercial Code," 22 Bus. Law. 479 (1967).

Farrar, "UCC Survey: Letters of Credit," 38 Bus. Law. 1169 (1983).

————, "UCC Survey: Letters of Credit," 39 Bus. Law. 1319 (1984).

Farrar & Landau, "UCC Survey: Letters of Credit," 40 Bus. Law. 1177 (1985).

————, "UCC Survey: Letters of Credit," 41 Bus. Law. 1435 (1986).

Flax-Davidson, "The ALADI Treaty and Letter of Credit Transactions in Latin America," 19 Int'l Law. 1303 (1985).

Funk, "Letters of Credit: U.C.C. Article 5 and the Uniform Customs and Practice," 11 How. L.J. 88 (1965).

Gable, "Standby Letters of Credit: Nomenclature Has Confounded Analysis," 12 Law & Pol'y in Int'l Bus. 903 (1980).

Geva, "Contractual Defenses As Claims to the Instrument: The Right to Block Payment of a Banker's Instrument," 58 Or. L. Rev. 283 (1979).

Gewolb, "The Law Applicable to International Letters of Credit," 11 Vill. L. Rev. 742 (1966).

Giger, "Problems of Bank Guarantee Abuse in Swiss Law," 2 Ariz. J. Int'l & Comp. L. 38 (1987).

Gilmore, "The Commercial Doctrine of Good Faith Purchase," 63 Yale L.J. 1057 (1954).

Givray, "UCC Survey: Letters of Credit," 44 Bus. Law. 1567 (1989).

Glidden, "National Bank Lending Limits and the Comptroller's Regs: A Clarification" (pts. 1, 2), 101 Banking L.J. 430, 554 (1984).

Godwin, "Transferable Letters of Credit—The Effect of Lariza," 1990 J. Bus. L. 48.

Goldberg & Lloyd-Davies, "Standby Letters of Credit: Are Banks Overextending Themselves?" 16 J. Bank Research 28 (1985).

Goode, "Reflections on Letters of Credit" (pts. 1–4), 1980 J. Bus. L. 291, 378, 443; 1981 J. Bus. L. 73.

Gossling, "The Capital Adequacy Framework—An Introduction," 6 J. Int'l Banking L. 243 (1988).

Graham & Geva, "Standby Credits in Canada," 9 Can. Bus. L.J. 180 (1984).

Green, "Letters of Credit and the Computerization of Maritime Trade," 3 Fla. Int'l L.J. 221 (1988).

Gross & Borowitz, "A New Twist on *Twist Cap*: Invalidating a Preferential Letter of Credit in *In re Air Conditioning*," 103 Banking L.J. 368 (1986).

Hahn & Schwartz, "Letters of Credit Under the Bankruptcy Code," 16 U.C.C. L.J. 91 (1983).

Harfield, "Secondary Uses of Commercial Credits," 44 Colum. L. Rev. 899 (1944).

———, "Code Treatment of Letters of Credit," 48 Cornell L.Q. 92 (1962).

———, "Code, Customs and Conscience in Letter-of-Credit Law," 4 U.C.C. L.J. 7 (1971).

———, "Article 5—Trade Without Tears, or Around Letters of Credit in 17 Sections, " 1972 Wis. L. Rev. 298.

———, "The Increasing Domestic Use of the Letter of Credit," 4 U.C.C. L.J. 251 (1972).

———, "International Transactions in a Cold Climate: Or Whatever Became of the Law Merchant," 6 Vand. J. Transnat'l L. 5 (1972).

———, "The Standby Letter of Credit Debate," 94 Banking L.J. 293 (1977).

———, "Enjoining Letter of Credit Transactions," 95 Banking L.J. 596 (1978).

———, "Identity Crises in Letter of Credit Law," 24 Ariz. L. Rev. 239 (1982).

———, "In Defense of Present Letter of Credit Law: A Plea in Confession and Avoidance," 2 Geo. Mason U.L. Rev. 211 (1987).

———, "Operating Within the Law: Harfield Views Difficulties for International Bankers" (pts. 1 & 2), Letter of Credit Update 11 (Dec. 1989), 6 (Jan. 1990).

Hershey, "Letters of Credit," 32 Harv. L. Rev. 1 (1918).

Holdsworth, "The Origins and Early History of Negotiable Instruments" (pts. II, IV), 31 L.Q. Rev. 173 (1915), 32 L.Q. Rev. 20 (1916).

Honnold, "Footnote to the Controversy Over the Dixon Case, Custom and Letter of Credit: The Position of the Uniform Commercial Code," 53 Colum. L. Rev. 973 (1953).

———, "Letters of Credit, Custom, Missing Documents and the Dixon Case: A Reply to Backus and Harfield," 53 Colum. L. Rev. 504 (1953).

Huff & Griffen, "How Banks Can Cut the Risks of Setoff in Participations," Banking L. Rev. 40 (Summer 1989).

Jarvis, "Standby Letters of Credit—Issuer's Subrogation and Assignment Rights" (pts. 1, 2), 9 U.C.C. L.J. 356 (1977), 10 U.C.C. L.J. 38 (1977).

Jhirad, "Uniform Customs and Practice for Documentary Credits, 1974 Revision: The Principal Emendations of the 1962 Text," 9 U.C.C. L.J. 109 (1976).

Jones, "Letters of Credit in the United States Construction Industry," 14 Int'l Bus. Law. 17 (1986).

Joseph, "Letters of Credit: The Developing Concepts and Financing Functions," 94 Banking L.J. 816 (1977).

Justice, "Letters of Credit: Expectations and Frustrations" (pts. 1, 2), 94 Banking L.J. 424, 493 (1977).

Katskee, "The Standby Letter of Credit Debate—The Case for Congressional Resolution," 92 Banking L.J. 697 (1975).

Kelley & Shultz, "'. . . Or Other Adequate Security': Using, Structuring, and Managing the Standby Letter of Credit to Ensure the Completion of Subdivision Improvements," 19 Urb. Law. 39 (1987).

Kimball & Sanders, "Preventing Wrongful Payment of Guaranty Letters of Credit—Lessons From Iran," 39 Bus. Law. 417 (1984).

Klegerman, "Tapping US Capital Markets Without Registration," 5 Int'l Fin. L. Rev. 10 (1986).

Koppenhaver, "Standby Letters of Credit," Economic Perspectives 28 (July/Aug. 1987).

Kozolchyk, "The Legal Nature of the Irrevocable Commercial Letter of Credit," Am. J. Comp. L. 395 (1965).

———, "The Emerging Law of Standby Letters of Credit and Bank Guarantees," 24 Ariz. L. Rev. 319 (1982).

———, "The Letter of Credit in Court: An Expert Testifies," 99 Banking L.J. 340 (1982).

———, "Preface (to Symposium)," 24 Ariz. L. Rev. 235 (1982).

———, "The 1983 Revision, Trade Practices and Court Decisions: A Plea for a Closer Relationship," 9 Can. Bus. L.J. 214 (1984).

———, "Is Present Letter of Credit Law Up to Its Task?" 8 Geo. Mason U.L. Rev. 285 (1986).

———, "Bank Guarantees and Letters of Credit: Time for a Return to the Fold," 11 U. Pa. J. Bus. L. 1 (1989).

Laplante, "Re-examining an Old Standby: Letters of Credit and Capital Ratios," Letter of Credit Update 33 (Nov. 1985).

Lawson, "Performance Bonds—Irrevocable Obligations," 1987 J. Bus. L. 259.

Leacock, "Fraud in the International Transaction: Enjoining Payment of Letters of Credit in International Transactions," 17 Vand. J. Transnat'l L. 885 (1984).

Leary & Ippoliti, "Letters of Credit: Have We Fully Recovered From Three Insolvency Shocks?" U. Pa. J. Int'l Bus. L. 595 (1987).

Ledlie, "Letters of Credit or Escrow Accounts Used as Security in Installment Sale Transactions," 60 Taxes 130 (1982).

Llewellyn, "Some Advantages of Letters of Credit," 2 J. Bus. U. Chi. 1 (1929).

Lloyd, "The Development of Setoff," 64 U. Pa. L. Rev. 541 (1916).

Lloyd-Davies, "Survey of Standby Letters of Credit," 65 Fed. Res. Bull. 716 (1979).

Lord, "The No-Guaranty Rule and the Standby Letter of Credit Controversy," 96 Banking L.J. 46 (1979).

Macintosh, "Letters of Credit: Dishonor When a Required Document Fails to Conform to the Section 7-507(b) Warranty," 6 J.L. & Com. 1 (1986).

Maulella, "Uncorking the Letter of Credit for Quicker Export Collections," Corporate Cashflow (Feb. 1989), reprinted in Letter of Credit Update 42 (Oct. 1989).

McCurdy, "Commercial Letters of Credit" (pts. 1, 2), 35 Harv. L. Rev., 539, 715 (1922).

———, "The Right of the Beneficiary Under a Commercial Letter of Credit," 37 Harv. L. Rev. 323 (1924).

McGivern, "International Letters of Credit and Their Use in Agricultural Export Situations," 37 Ark. L. Rev. 217 (1983).

McGowan, "Assignability of Documentary Credits," 13 Law & Contemp. Probs. 666 (1948).

C. McLaughlin, "The Letter of Credit Provisions of the Proposed Uniform Commercial Code," 63 Harv. L. Rev. 1373 (1950).

G. McLaughlin, "Letters of Credit as Preferential Transfers in Bankruptcy," 50 Fordham L. Rev. 1033 (1982).

———, "Standby Letters of Credit and Penalty Clauses: An Unexpected Synergy," 43 Ohio St. L.J. 1 (1982).

———, "Letters of Credit and Illegal Contracts: The Limits of the Independence Principle," 49 Ohio St. L.J. 1197 (1989).

———, "On the Periphery of Letter-of-Credit Law: Softening the Rigors of Strict Compliance," 106 Banking L.J. 4 (1989).

———, "Structuring Commercial Letter-of-Credit Transactions to Safeguard the Interests of the Buyer," 21 U.C.C. L.J. 318 (1989).

McLaughlin & Cohen, "Scope of Bankruptcy Trustee's Avoidance Powers," 200 N.Y.L.J. 6 (Dec. 14, 1988).

Mead, "Documentary Letters of Credit," 22 Colum. L. Rev. 297 (1922).

Megrah, "Risk Aspects of the Irrevocable Documentary Credit," 24 Ariz. L. Rev. 255 (1982).

Mentschikoff, "Letters of Credit: The Need for Uniform Legislation," 23 U. Chi. L. Rev. 571 (1956).

Merchant, "New Developments in Transport Documents," Letters of Credit Report 8 (Mar./Apr. 1988).

Merges & Reynolds, "Toward a Computerized System for Negotiating Ocean Bills of Lading," 6 J.L. & Com. 23 (1986).

Millard & Semkow, "The New Risk-Based Capital Framework and Its Application to Letters of Credit," 106 Banking L.J. 500 (1989).

Miller, "Problems and Patterns of the Letter of Credit," 1959 U. Ill. L.F. 162.

Murphy, "A Banker's View of Electronic Documents," Letters of Credit Report 12 (Sept./Oct. 1988).

Murray, "Letters of Credit in Nonsale of Goods Transactions," 30 Bus. Law. 1103 (1975).

————, "History and Development of the Bill of Lading," 37 Miami L. Rev. 689 (1983).

Neidle & Bishop, "Commercial Letters of Credit: Effect of Suspension of Issuing Bank," 32 Colum. L. Rev. 1 (1932).

Note, "Revised International Rules for Documentary Credits," 65 Harv. L. Rev. 1420 (1952).

Note, "Letter of Credit Under the Proposed Uniform Commercial Code: An Opportunity Missed," 62 Yale L.J. 227 (1953).

Note, "Recent Extensions in the Use of Commercial Letters of Credit," 66 Yale L.J. 902 (1957).

Note, "Guaranty Letters of Credit: Problems and Possibilities," 16 Ariz. L. Rev. 822 (1974).

Note, "Documentary Letters of Credit and the Uniform Customs and Practice for Documentary Credits (1974 Revision): A Selective Analysis," 3 J. Corp. L. 147 (1977).

Note, "Letters of Credit: Injunction as a Remedy for Fraud in U.C.C. Section 5-114," 63 Minn. L. Rev. 487 (1979).

Note, "Enjoining the International Standby Letter of Credit: The Iranian Letter of Credit Cases," 21 Harv. Int'l L.J. 189 (1980).

Note, "The Role of Standby Letters of Credit in International Commerce: Reflections After Iran," 20 Va. J. Int'l L. 459 (1980).

Note, "A Reconsideration of American Bell International v. Islamic Republic of Iran, 474 F. Supp. 420 (S.D.N.Y. 1979)," 19 Colum J. Transnat'l L. 301 (1981).

Note, "The Trade Embargo and the Irrevocable Letter of Credit," 1 Ariz J. Int'l & Comp. L. 213 (1982).

Note, "Letters of Credit: A Solution to the Problem of Documentary Compliance," 50 Fordham L. Rev. 848 (1982).

Note, "Confirming Bank Liability in Letter of Credit Transactions: Whose Bank Is It Anyway?" 51 Fordham L. Rev. 1219 (1983).

Note, "The International Monetary Fund Agreement and Letters of Credit: A Balancing of Purposes," 44 U. Pitt. L. Rev. 1061 (1983).

Note, "Irrevocable Letters of Credit in Bankruptcy: Obligations in Full Force and Effect Despite Debtor Relief?" 1983 Ann. Survey Bankr. L. 299 (1983).

Note, "The Application of Compulsory Joinder Intervention, Impleader and Attachment to Letter of Credit Litigation," 52 Fordham L. Rev. 957 (1984).

Note, "Letters of Credit: A Question of Honor," 16 N.Y.U. J. Int'l L. & Pol. 799 (1984).

Note, "Letters of Credit: The Role of Issuer Discretion in Determining Documentary Compliance," 53 Fordham L. Rev. 1519 (1985).

Note, "Letter of Credit Litigation—Bank Liability for Punitive Damages," 54 Fordham L. Rev. 905 (1986).

Note, "Standby Letters of Credit: Are They Insured Deposits?" 32 Wayne L. Rev. 1165 (1986).

Note, "Standby Letters of Credit: Recent Limitations on the Fraud in the Transaction Defense," 35 Wayne L. Rev. 119 (1988).

Penn, "On-Demand Bonds—Primary or Secondary Obligations?" 4 J. Int'l Banking L. 224 (1986).

Penney, "New York Revisits the Code: Some Variations in the New York Enactment of the Uniform Commercial Code," 62 Colum. L. Rev. 992 (1962).

Petkovic, "Set-Off and Letters of Credit," Int'l Fin. L. Rev. 29 (Aug. 1989).

Rapson, "Problems in Perspectives: The Lure and Snare of Standby Letters of Credit," N.J.L.J., Feb. 24, 1983, at 8, col. 1.

Rojc, "National Bank Lending Limits—A New Framework," 40 Bus. Law. 903 (1985).

Rose & Talley, "Bank Transactions With Affiliates: The New Section 23A," 100 Banking L.J. 423 (1983).

Rosenblith, "What Happens When Operations Go Wrong: Enjoining the Letter of Credit Transaction and Other Legal Stratagems," 17 U.C.C. L.J. 307 (1985).

———, "Modifying Letters of Credit: The Rules and the Reality," 19 U.C.C. L.J. 245 (1987).

Rowe, "Automating International Trade Payments—Legal and Regulatory Issues," 4 J. Int'l Bus. L. 234 (1987).

———, "Bank Guarantees: Rules Changes Proposed," 7 Int'l Fin. L. Rev. 36 (1988).

Rowland, "Letters of Credit—Article 5 of the Uniform Commercial Code," 30 Mo. L. Rev. 288 (1965).

Ryan, "Letters of Credit Supporting Debt for Borrowed Money: The Standby as Backup," 100 Banking L.J. 404 (1983).

Sarna, "Letters of Credit: Bankruptcy, Fraud and Identity of Parties," 65 Can. B. Rev. 303 (1986).

Saunders, "Preference Avoidance and Letter of Credit Supported Debt: The Bank's Reimbursement Risk in Its Customer's Bankruptcy," 102 Banking L.J. 240 (1985).

Schmitthoff, "The Transferable Credit," 1988 J. Bus. L. 49.

———, "Discrepancy of Documents in Letter of Credit Transactions," 1987 J. Bus. L. 94.

———, "The New Uniform Customs for Letters of Credit," 1983 J. Bus. L. 193.

Schwank & Mitchell, "Data and the Documentary Credit," Int'l Fin. L. Rev. 33 (Aug. 1988).

Shattuck & Guernsey, "Letter of Credit—A Comparison of Article 5 of the Uniform Commercial Code and the Washington Practice" (pts. 1, 2), 37 Wash. L. Rev. 325, 500 (1962).

Skilton, "Buyer in Ordinary Course of Business Under Article 9 of the Uniform Commercial Code (and Related Matters)," 1974 Wis. L. Rev. 1.

Slimane, "Guarantee Bonds Issued in Favor of Saudi Public Entities," Int'l Fin. L. Rev. 27 (Sept. 1986).

Smith, "Irrevocable Letters of Credit and Third Party Fraud: The America Accord," 24 Va. J. Int'l L. 55 (1983).

Spencer, Alesci, & MacMillen, "Letter of Credit Issues in the Thrift Industry," in American Bar Association, *Letters of Credit and Financial Institution Insolvencies* (1989).

Stack, "The Conflicts of Law in International Letters of Credit," 24 Va. J. Int'l L. 171 (1983).

Stoufflet, "Payment and Transfer in Documentary Letters of Credit: Interaction Between the French General Law of Obligations and the Uniform Customs and Practice," 24 Ariz. L. Rev. 267 (1982).

———, "Recent Developments in the Law of International Bank Guarantees in France and Belgium," 2 Ariz. J. Int'l & Comp. L. 48 (1987).

Symons, "Letters of Credit: Fraud, Good Faith and the Basis for Injunctive Relief," 54 Tul. L. Rev. 338 (1980).

———, "The 'Business of Banking' in Historical Perspective," 51 Geo. Wash. L. Rev. 676 (1983).

Thorup, "Injunctions Against Payment of Standby Letters of Credit: How Can Banks Best Protect Themselves?" 101 Banking L.J. 6 (1984).

Todd, "Sellers and Documentary Credits," 1983 J. Bus. L. 468.

Trimble, "The Law Merchant and the Letter of Credit," 61 Harv. L. Rev. 981 (1948).

————, "The Implied Power of National Banks to Issue Letters of Credit and Accept Bills," 58 Yale L.J. 713 (1949).

Ufford, "Transfer and Assignment of Letters of Credit Under the Uniform Commercial Code," 7 Wayne L. Rev. 263 (1960).

UNCITRAL, "Report of the Secretary General, Standby Letters of Credit and Guarantees," A/CN.9/301 (Mar. 21, 1988).

Uzzelle, "Letters of Credit," 10 Mar. L. Rev. 47 (1985).

Van Houten, "Letters of Credit and Fraud: A Revisionist View," 62 Can. B. Rev. 371 (1984).

Verkuil, "Bank Solvency and Guaranty Letters of Credit," 25 Stan. L. Rev. 716 (1973).

————, "Bank Solvency and Standby Letters of Credit: Lessons From the USNB Failure," 53 Tul. L. Rev. 314 (1979).

Verner, "'Fraud in the Transaction': *Intraworld* Comes of Age in *Itek*," 14 Mem. St. U.L. Rev. 153 (1984).

Weintraub, "*In re Air Conditioning*—A Blessing in Disguise," 104 Banking L.J. 187 (1987).

Weintraub & Resnick, "Enforceability of Letters of Credit When the Customer Is in Bankruptcy: From *Twist Cap* to *Air Conditioning*," 20 U.C.C. L.J. 96 (1987).

Weisz & Blackman, "Standby Letters of Credit After Iran: Remedies of the Account Party," 1982 U. Ill. L. Rev. 355.

Wheble, "Uniform Customs and Practice for Documentary Credits (1974 Revision)," 1975 J. Bus. L. 281.

————, "'Problem Children': Stand-By Letters of Credit and Simple First Demand Guarantees," 24 Ariz. L. Rev. 301 (1982).

White, "Bankers Guarantees and the Problem of Unfair Calling," 11 J. Mar. L. 121 (1979).

Wiley, "How to Use Letters of Credit in Financing the Sale of Goods," 20 Bus. Law. 495 (1965).

Zimmett, "Standby Letters of Credit in the Iran Litigation: Two Hundred Problems in Search of a Solution," 16 Law & Pol'y in Int'l Bus. 927 (1984).

Table of Parallel UCP Provisions

The table below shows the corresponding provisions of the 1962, 1974, and 1983 revisions of the Uniform Customs.

Subject	1962 (Brochure No. 222)	1974 (Pub. No. 290)	1983 (Pub. No. 400)
GENERAL			
Scope	GPD(a)	GPD(a)	Art. 1
Definitions	GPD(b)	GPD(b)	Art. 2
Indepenence	GPD(c), Art. 8	GPD(c), Art 8(a)	Arts. 3, 4
Instructions	GPD(d)	GPD(d)	Art. 5
Options	GPD(e)	GPD(e)	Art. 41
Application agreement	GPD(f)	GPD(f)	Art. 6
FORM AND NOTIFICATION			
Revocability	Arts. 1, 2	Arts. 1, 2	Arts. 7, 9
Irrevocability	Art. 3	Art. 3	Art. 10
Advising bank	Art. 3	Art. 3	Art. 10
Confirming bank	Art. 3	Art. 3	Art. 10
Nature	—	—	Art. 11
Operative credit instrument	Art. 4	Art. 4	Art. 12
Amendments	Art. 5	Art. 5	Art. 13
Preliminary notification	Art. 6	Art. 6	Art. 14
LIABILITIES AND RESPONSIBILITIES			
Duty of banks	Arts. 7, 8	Arts. 7, 8	Arts. 15, 16
Form of documents	Art. 9	Art. 9	Art. 17
Communications	Art. 10	Art. 10	Art. 18
Interruptions	Art. 11	Art. 11	Art. 19
Agent banks	Art. 12	Art. 12	Art. 20
Paying bank's reimbursement	—	Art. 13	Art. 21
DOCUMENTS			
Description	Art. 13	Art. 14	Art. 22
Date	—	—	Art. 24

Subject	*1962* *(Brochure No. 222)*	*1974* *(Pub. No. 290)*	*1983* *(Pub. No. 400)*
Shipping Documents:			
Bill of lading date	Art. 14	Art. 15	Art. 47
Freight charges	Art. 15	Art. 16	Art. 31
Carrier disclaimer	—	Art. 17	Art. 32
Clean bill	Art. 16	Art. 18	Art. 34
Marine Bills:			
Defective	Arts. 17, 18, 20, 21	Art. 19	Arts. 25, 26
"On board"	Art. 18	Art. 20	Art. 27
Acceptable	Arts. 17, 19	Arts. 21, 22	Arts. 25, 29
Combined Transport Documents:	—	Art. 23	Art. 25
Other Shipping Documents:			
In general	Art. 22	Art. 24	Art. 42
Certificate of weight	Art. 23	Art. 25	Art. 42
By post	Art. 22	Art. 24	Art. 30
Consignor	—	—	Art. 33
Insurance Documents:			
In general	Art. 24	Art. 26	Art. 35
Date	Art. 25	Art. 27	Art. 36
Currency and value	Art. 26	Art. 28	Art. 37
Risks	Arts. 27, 28	Arts. 29, 30	Arts. 38, 39
Franchise	Art. 29	Art. 31	Art. 40
Commercial Invoices:			
In general	Art. 30	Art. 32	Art. 41
Other Documents:	Art. 31	Art. 33	Art. 23

MISCELLANEOUS PROVISIONS

Quantity and amount	Art. 32	Art. 34	Art. 43
Partial shipment	Arts. 33, 34	Arts. 35, 36	Arts. 44, 45
Expiry date	Arts. 35–39	Arts. 37–39	Arts. 46, 48, 51
Shipment, loading, or dispatch	Art. 40	Art. 40	Art. 50
Presentation	Arts. 41, 42	Arts. 41, 42	Arts. 47, 49
Date terms	Arts. 43–45	Arts. 43–45	Arts. 46, 52, 53

TRANSFER

Right to draw	Art. 46	Art. 46	Art. 54
Right to proceeds	—	Art. 47	Art. 55

Table of Uniform Commercial Code Citations

[References are to paragraphs (¶).]

[References are to paragraphs (¶).]

[References are to paragraphs (¶).]

[References are to paragraphs (¶).]

Table of Statutes, Rules, and Regulations

[References are to paragraphs (¶).]

[References are to paragraphs (¶).]

[References are to paragraphs (¶).]

[References are to paragraphs (¶).]

Table of Cases

[References are to paragraphs (¶).]

[*References are to paragraphs (¶).*]

[References are to paragraphs (¶).]

[References are to paragraphs (¶).]

[References are to paragraphs (¶).]

[References are to paragraphs (¶).]

[*References are to paragraphs (¶).*]

[References are to paragraphs (¶).]

[References are to paragraphs (¶).]

[References are to paragraphs (¶).]

[References are to paragraphs (¶).]

Muir v. Transportation Mut. Ins. Co.
    . . . . 5.02[1], 7.03[3][f], 11.06
Munroe, Greenough v. . . . . . 2.09[1],
            12.01[1][b], 12.01[2]
Munzenrieder, In re . . . . . . 2.08[1],
            7.05[2][b]
Murray v. Eisenberg 1.06

N

Nadler v. Mei Loong Corp. . . . .
            7.04[4][e][ii]
Nagase, D., & Co., Imbrie v. 9.04
Nateman, Southern Marine Research,
    Inc. v. . . . . 11.05[1]
National Am. Corp. v. Federal Republic
    of Nig. . . . . . . 9.06[4][c], App. B
National Bank, Mid-States Mortgage
    Corp. v. . . . . 1.06, 7.04[4][b],
            9.02[5][b][ii]
National Bank & Trust Co. of N. Am.
    Ltd. v. J.L.M. Int'l, Inc. . . . 5.02[1],
    6.06[3], 9.02[3], 9.05, 10.02[4],
    10.06[3][a], 11.02[1][b], 11.06,
            App. B
National Bank of Aus., North Valley
    Bank v. . . . 4.02, 6.04[3], 6.06[1][a]
National Bank of N. Am. v. Alizio . . . .
            7.05[1], 12.05[1]
National Bank of Pak., Ahmed v.. . . . .
            9.02[3], App. B
National Bank of Pak., Savarin Corp. v.
    . . . . 5.01[3], 5.02[1], 9.02[2],
            9.02[5][d], App. B
National Boulevard Bank, Baker v.. . . . .
    1.07[2], 2.06, 2.07, 7.04[3][b],
    7.04[4][b], 9.01, 11.01[3]
National City Bank, Asbury Park &
    Ocean Grove Bank v. . . . . 7.04[2],
            7.04[4][g]
National City Bank, Continental Nat'l
    Bank v. . . . . . . 6.06[1][a], 9.02[3]
National City Bank, Linden v. . . . . . .
            9.03[2], 9.03[5]
National City Bank, North Woods Paper
    Mills, Ltd. v. . . . . . . 6.03, 11.05[1]
National City Bank, Pan-Am. Bank &
    Trust Co. v. . . . . 5.03[2][a]
National City Bank v. Seattle Nat'l Bank
    . . . . 6.04[1]

National Iranian Radio & Television,
    Harris Corp. v. . . . . 7.04[1],
    7.04[3][b], 7.04[4][e][ii],
    7.04[4][f], 9.06[4][c], App. B
National Park Bank, Maurice O'Meara
    Co. v. . . . . 3.07[7], 4.08, 6.01,
    6.04[1], 6.05[1][a], 6.05[1][c],
    6.06[1][a], 7.04[1]
National Republic Bank, Pastor v. . . . .
    1.06, 6.04[5][b], 10.02[3]
National Serv. Lines, Inc., In re . . . . .
            7.05[2][b], 11.01[5]
National Sur. Corp. v. Midland Bank
    . . . . 5.03[3][b], 9.06[2]
National Union Fire Ins. Co. v. Walton
    Ins. Ltd. 1.06
Native Alaskan Reclamation & Pest
    Control, Inc. v. United Bank Alaska
    . . . . . 2.10[2][b], 9.02[3][c],
            9.03[3]
NCF Fin. Corp., Northwestern Bank v.
    . . . . 5.01[4], 6.04[5][b],
    7.04[3][b], 7.04[4][b]
Nelson v. First Nat'l Bank 3.02,
            3.03[3], 4.02[2]
Neptune Orient Lines, Ltd., Austracan
    (USA) Inc. v. . . . 1.07[1][c], 6.04[4],
            App. B
New Braunfels Nat'l Bank v. Odiorne
    . . . . 6.03, 6.04[3], 7.05[1],
            11.05[3]
New England Merchants Nat'l Bank,
    Flagship Cruises, Ltd. v. 1.06,
    4.08[2], 5.03[2][b], 6.04[3],
    6.05[1], 6.05[1][b], 6.06[1][b],
    10.03[3], App. B
New Jersey Bank v. Palladino . . . 2.04
New Tech Devs., Div. of San Diego
    Carleton Lewis Corp. v. Bank of N.S.
    . . . 2.09[1], 7.04[4][f], 8.02[6],
    11.04[3][b][iii], 11.04[5]
Newvector Communications, Inc. v.
    Union Bank . . . . . 2.05[2], 2.05[4],
    4.08[3], 6.03, 6.04[7], 6.06[1][b],
    6.07, 7.06, 9.04, App. B
New York City Hous. Dev. Corp.,
    Lombard-Wall, Inc. v. (In re
    Lombard-Wall, Inc.) 1.06,
            11.01[5]

[References are to paragraphs (¶).]

[References are to paragraphs (¶).]

[References are to paragraphs (¶).]

[References are to paragraphs (¶).]

[*References are to paragraphs (¶).*]

[*References are to paragraphs (¶).*]

[References are to paragraphs (¶).]

[References are to paragraphs (¶).]

Index

[References are to paragraphs (¶).]

A

Acceptance
See also Extrinsic acceptance; Virtual
   acceptance
   breach, 9.02[3]
   credit, versus, 2.01, 2.09[1], 3.03[5],
     5.03[2]
   generally, 1.01[2]
   governing law, 2.09[1]
   injunction, 2.09[1]
   negotiable instrument, 2.08[4]
   proof, 2.09[1]

Acceptance credit
   advantages, 1.02[5]
   vs. deferred payment credit, 1.02[6]
   generally, 1.01[2]
   honor, 5.03[2]
     time of, 5.03[3][a]
   negotiating drafts under, 1.02[4]
   presentment under, 1.02[4]
   reimbursement, 7.05[1]

Account financing, 3.07[1]

Account party
See also Customer
   advising bank, 4.03[5][b]
   breach of credit engagement, 9.02[4]
   claims against beneficiary, 1.05
     setoff, 2.09[6]
   confirming bank, 4.03[5][b], 9.03[3]
   correspondent bank, 4.03[5][b]
   creditor attachment, 9.05, 10.06[3]
   definition, 1.01[3]
   dishonor, 9.01, 9.02[4]
   documents, signed by, 2.05[3]
   duties under credit, 2.08[2]
   injunction against, 6.04[5][a]
   issuer as, 2.06
   and issuer, relationship, 4.03[5][a],
     7.06, 9.03
   litigation burden, 1.05
   mandatory injunction, 6.04[5][a]

   rights under credit, 9.03[1]
   substantial compliance rule,
     9.03[1][a]
   underlying contract liability, 9.02[4]

Act of state. *See* Defenses

Advice of credit
   confirmation, 5.01[3]
   general, 5.01[3]
   late, 1.03
   perfection of security interest,
     10.04[2][b]
   preadvice, 5.01[3]
   telex, 5.01[3]
   transfer, 10.04[2][b]

Advising bank
   account party, 4.03[5][b]
   attachment, 9.04
   bad faith, 9.03[3]
   beneficiary, 9.02[4]
   collecting bank as, 9.02[3]
   definition, 1.03
   duty to account party, 9.03[3]
   issuer, relation to, 8.01[7][a], 9.02[3]
   liability, 1.03
   negligence, 9.03[3]
   setoff, 9.06[3]
   subrogation, 9.02[3]
   warranty, 4.03[5][b], 8.01[7][b]

Affirmative defenses. *See* Defenses

Agent credit. *See* Buyer's credit

Amendment
   anticipatory breach, 5.02[1], 6.06[3],
     9.02[2]
   back-to-back, 1.08, 6.06[3]
   breach of application, 9.03[1][b]
   consent
     beneficiary, 5.02[1]
     confirming bank, 1.08
     customer, 5.02[1]
     issuer, 5.02[1]
   expiry, 5.03[3][d]

[References are to paragraphs (¶).]

[*References are to paragraphs (¶).*]

documents, 5.03[1]
instructions, 5.03[1]
knowledge, 8.01[2]
negligence, 9.02[4]
under-the-credit rule, 8.01[6]

Collection
contractual arrangements, 2.08[3]
correspondent bank, 2.08[3]

Comity, 9.06[4][f], 11.01[7]

Commercial credit
See also Commercial credit transaction
vs. buyer's credit, 5.01[1]
cost, 1.05
damages, 9.02[5][b][i]
documents, 1.07[1]
domestic, 3.05
history, 3.04, 3.05
international, 3.05
sales transaction, 1.01[3]
vs. standby credit, 1.04

Commercial credit transaction, 1.01,
1.03[3]
See also Commercial credit

Commercial invoice
benchmark, 1.07[1][b]
description of goods, 1.07[1][b],
6.04[1]
generally, 1.07[1][b]

Commercial paper
general, 1.06
preference, 7.03[3][e]

Comptroller of the Currency
capital adequacy, 12.02[3]
guidelines, 5.03[3][e], 12.02[1][a],
12.02[1][c]
rulings, 5.02[1], 5.03[3][b], 5.03[3][e],
12.02[1][a], 12.02[1][b],
12.02[1][c], 12.03[1], 12.03[3],
12.04[1], 12.04[2]

Conditions
bifurcated standard, 9.03[1][a]
drafting, 2.05[4], 7.06
nondocumentary, 2.05[2], 4.04,
6.04[7]
strict compliance, 6.02, 6.03, 6.04
substantial compliance, 6.02, 6.03,
6.05

Confirmation
Article 5, 5.01[5]
establishment, 5.01[5]
opening bank, 5.01[5]

Confirming bank
account party, 4.03[5][b], 5.01[5],
6.07, 9.03[3]
attachment, 9.05
back-to-back credit, 1.08
beneficiary, vs., 2.09[5]
bifurcated standard, 9.03[1][a]
choice of law, 4.02
credit functions, 3.07[2]
definition, 1.03
duties, 9.02[4], 9.03[1][a]
fraud, 9.04
good faith, 9.04
issuer, relation to, 8.01[7][a]
negligence, 9.04
obligations, 1.03
opening bank, 5.01[5]
presentment, 5.03[3][a]
reimbursement right, 6.04[5][b],
8.01[5], 8.01[7][a]
strict compliance, 9.03[1][a]
subrogation, 5.01[5], 7.05[2], 9.03[3]
tort liability, 9.03[3]
Uniform Customs, 4.04
warranty, 4.03[5][b], 8.01[7][b],
9.03[3], 9.04

Conflicts of law. *See* Choice of law

Consideration
Article 5, 3.03[1], 4.03[3]
guaranty, 2.10[1]
requirement, 2.02
role, 3.03[1]
virtual acceptance, 3.03[5]

Consolidation. *See* Joinder

Conspicuously designated rule
Article 5's scope, 2.05
capital letters, 2.07
intent, 2.07
meaning, 2.06, 2.07
reason, 2.06
title, 2.07
Wichita requirement, 2.05[2]

Construction of credit
See also Strict compliance rule; Substantial compliance rule

[References are to paragraphs (¶).]

[*References are to paragraphs (¶).*]

Holder in due course (*cont'd*)
  notice, 8.01[2]
  transferee of credit, 8.01[2], 10.03[4]
  value, 8.01[2]
Honor
  See also Dishonor
  acceptance credit, 1.02[2], 5.03[2]
  general, 5.03[2]
  good faith, 7.04[4][g]
  injunction, 9.03[4]
  · negotiation credit, 1.02[4], 5.03[2][b]
  payment credit, 1.02[1], 5.03[2]
  revocable credit, 5.02[2]
  time, 4.06[2][b], 5.03[2]
  wrongful, 9.01
Hostages, 1.06

I

ICC. *See* International Chamber of
  Commerce
Illegality
  ground for injunction, 7.03[2]
  issuer defense, 9.06[6]
  lending limits, 12.02[2]
Incidental damages
  attorney fees, 9.02[5][c]
  general, 9.02[5][c]
  interest, 9.02[5][c]
  litigation expense, 9.02[5][c]
  lost profits, 9.02[5][c]
Indemnity
  banks, 6.06[1][b]
  bill of lading, 4.07[1]
Independence principle
  acceleration clause, 2.09[1]
  application, 2.09[5]
  Article 5, 4.03[6][a]
  attachment, 7.03[5]
  beneficiary's certificate, 1.07[2]
  breach of warranty, assignment,
    9.06[3]
  codified, 4.03[6][a]
  confirming bank, 4.03[6][a]
  conflicting policies, 7.03[3][d],
    7.03[4]
  damages, 9.02[1]
  expiry, 5.03[3][b]
  fraud, 7.04[3][d], 7.04[4][d]

  illegality of underlying contract,
    7.03[2]
  injunction against beneficiary,
    7.04[4][f]
  insolvency of account party,
    7.03[3][c]
  joinder, 11.02[2]
  nature of credit, 3.03[6]
  release, 9.06[2]
  setoff, 2.09[6], 7.04[4], 9.06[3]
  side agreement, 2.09[5]
  strict compliance, relation, 7.01
  summary judgment, 11.05[2]
  violated
    arbitration, 2.09[3]
    Iranian cases, 7.04[4][e][ii]
    mitigation, 9.02[5][b][i]
    setoff, 2.09[6]
    underlying contract, 2.09[3],
      7.04[4][c], 10.03[3]
  Wichita requirement, 2.05[1]

Injunctions
  account party, 6.04[5][a]
  assets control, 9.06[4][b]
  against beneficiary, 7.04[4][f]
  breach of warranty, 11.04[2][c]
  credit functions, 3.07[7]
  damages, 11.04[2][c]
    to reputation, 7.04[1], 11.04[2][c]
  expiry, 3.07[7]
  financial loss, 7.04[1], 7.04[4][e][i],
    11.04[2][b]
  foreign sovereign, 7.04[1][a]
  fraud, 7.04, 11.04[3]
  Iranian Assets Control Regulations,
    9.06[4][b]
  irreparable harm
    account party insolvency,
      11.04[2][b]
    general, 7.04[1], 7.04[1][e],
      11.04[2]
  likelihood of success, 11.04[4]
  mandatory, 6.04[5][a]
  nonconforming documents,
    11.04[2][c]
  notice, 7.04[4][e][ii]
  plaintiff's burden of proof, 7.04[4][d]
  prerequisites, 7.04[1], 7.04[4][e][i],
    11.04[1]
  relief, 11.04[2][a]

[References are to paragraphs (¶).]

[References are to paragraphs (¶).]

[References are to paragraphs (¶).]

history, 3.05, 4.06
incorporation, 4.04
installment
    drawings, 4.06[2][e], 4.06[2][f]
    shipments, 4.06[2][e], 4.06[2][f]
invoice
    absence, 6.04[2]
    amount, 6.04[2]
    general, 4.08, 6.04[1], 6.04[2],
        6.04[5][a]
    issuer's discretion, 6.04[2]
nature
    contract term, 4.06[1][a]
    descriptive, 4.06[1][b]
    industry custom, 4.04, 4.06[1][c]
    prescriptive, 4.06[1][c], 4.06[2][f]
nondocumentary conditions, 4.04
operative credit instrument, 5.01[3]
other documents, 4.08
preclusion, 6.06[1][b]
reimbursement right, 7.05[3]
revocability, 5.02[2]
scope, 4.04
signed writing requirement, 5.01[4]
standby credits, 4.03[7]
tolerances, 6.04[6]
transmissions, 5.02[1]
underlying contract, 4.06[2][d],
    6.04[5][a]
usage, 4.06[1][b]–4.06[1][d]
Uniform Customs and Practice for Doc-
    umentary Credits. *See* Uniform
    Customs
United States Council on International
    Business, 4.06[1]
Unjust enrichment, 2.08[1]

V

Value
    collecting bank, 8.01[5]
    holder in due course, 8.01[2]
    issuer, 8.02
    negotiable document of title, 8.01[5]
Venue, 11.01[4][b], 11.01[6]
    See also Jurisdiction
Virtual acceptance
    abolition, 3.03[5]
    vs. credit, 3.03[1]

general, 3.03[1], 3.03[5]
Visaed document. *See* Consularized doc-
    ument

W

Waiver
    vs. amendment, 5.02[1], 6.06[2]
    course of performance, 4.07
    document nonconformity, 4.07[1]
    vs. estoppel, 6.06[1]
    foreign sovereign immunity,
        9.06[4][c]
    general, 6.06[2]
    knowledge, 6.06[2]
    oral, 5.02[1], 6.06[2]
    strict compliance, 5.03[3][d], 6.02
    substantial compliance, 6.05[2]
    summary judgment, 11.05[4][c]
Warehouse receipt, 8.03[2][b]
Warranty
    account party, 4.03[5][b], 9.04
    advising bank, 4.03[5][b]
    assignee of credit, 9.03[3], 9.04
    beneficiary, 4.03[5][b], 6.07
    bill of lading, 7.04[3]
    breach, 9.04
    certificate, false, 6.07
    confirming bank, 4.03[5][b], 6.07,
        9.03[3], 9.04
    document
        facially conforming, 9.04
        facially defective, 6.07
        fraudulent, 9.04
    estoppel, 6.07
    general, 6.07
    injunction, 11.04[2][c]
    independence principle, 2.09[5], 6.07
    interested parties, 6.07
    intermediary parties, 6.07, 9.04
    negotiating bank, 4.03[5][b]
    securities, 7.04[3]
    standby credit, 6.07, 9.04
    underlying agreement, 9.04
Wholesale finance commitment,
    2.10[2][b]
Wichita requirement
    Article 5 scope, 2.05
    documents, 2.05[1]